Oxford Primary Dictionary

Chief Editor: Susan Rennie

OXFORD

UNIVERSITY PRESS

OXFORD
UNIVERSITY PRESS

First edition 2006
Second edition 2011
Third edition 2018
Based on *Oxford Primary Dictionary* 2024 edition

British Library Cataloguing in Publication Data

Data available

ISBN: 978-0-19-279488-8

10 9 8 7 6

Printed in India by Multivista Global Pvt. Ltd

FSC
www.fsc.org

MIX
Paper | Supporting
responsible forestry
FSC® C199630

Picture credits:
All images: OUP except human body girl: Gelpi / Shutterstock; running: Flashon
Studio / Shutterstock; chopsticks: Kongsak / Shutterstock; volcano: corbac40 /
Shutterstock; ship: tsuneomp / Shutterstock; laptop: ifong / Shutterstock.com;
aeroplane ifont / Shutterstock.com; taxi: Nerthuz / Shutterstock

The manufacturer's authorised representative in the EU for product safety is
Oxford University Press España S.A. of El Parque Empresarial San Fernando de
Henares, Avenida de Castilla, 2 – 28830 Madrid (www.oup.es/en or product.
safety@oup.com). OUP España S.A. also acts as importer into Spain of
products made by the manufacturer.

Oxford Corpus

You can trust this dictionary
to be up to date, relevant
and engaging because
it is powered by the
Oxford Corpus, a unique
living database of children's
and adults' language.

For school: Discover eBooks,
inspirational resources,
advice and support.

For home: Helping your
child's learning with free eBooks,
essential tips and fun activities.

www.oxfordowl.co.uk

Contents

Preface	iii
How to use your dictionary	iv–v
Introduction	vi
Oxford Primary Dictionary	1–586

Colour Illustrated Section
– Writing letters and emails	587
– The human body	588–589
– Healthy living, food and cooking	590–591
– Volcanoes	592
– Pirates	592
– Transport	593
– Computing	594
– Word origins	595
– Useful idioms and phrases	596
– Grammar—word classes	597–598
– Spelling	599–600
– Punctuation	601–602

Preface

The Oxford Primary Dictionary has been specially written for primary school children aged 8+. It is designed to address school and curriculum needs and has been compiled in consultation with teachers, and with reference to the Oxford Children's Corpus, a large language database consisting of millions of words of texts written for, and by, children.

The words in this dictionary are defined in simple language and are supported by example sentences or phrases showing the words in use, including a selection of literary quotations by well-known children's authors. There is a vocabulary boosting colour illustrated section on topics such as writing letters and emails, the human body, healthy living, food and cooking, volcanoes, pirates, transport and computing. It also features word origins, idioms and phrases, key grammar such as word classes, spelling and punctuation help.

How to use your dictionary

headword
in alphabetical order, in blue

guide words
show the first and last word on a page

definition
tells you what the word means; if there is more than one meaning, the definitions are numbered

DID YOU KNOW?
tells you interesting facts about words, take a look and see if you can find any

SPELLING ALERT!
points out tricky spellings of similar sounding words

cross-reference
points you to another entry in the dictionary where you will find more information

example
shows you how you might use a word; each meaning of a word has a separate example sentence or phrase

butt to byte

butt *NOUN* butts
❶ the thicker end of a weapon or tool ❷ (*North American, informal*) your bottom or buttocks ❸ a large barrel ❹ someone people often make fun of • *He was always the butt of their jokes.*

butt *VERB* butts, butting, butted
to butt someone is to hit them hard with your head
➤ **to butt in** is to interrupt suddenly or rudely

butter *NOUN*
butter is a fatty yellow food made from cream

buttercup *NOUN* buttercups
a yellow wild flower

butterfingers *NOUN* (*informal*)
someone who is clumsy and keeps dropping things

butterfly *NOUN* butterflies
❶ an insect with a thin body and large white or brightly coloured wings ❷ a stroke you use when swimming on your front, by raising both arms together over your head

butterscotch *NOUN* butterscotches
butterscotch is a kind of hard toffee

buttocks *PLURAL NOUN*
your buttocks are the part of the body on which you sit, your bottom

button *NOUN* buttons
❶ a flat plastic or metal disc sewn on clothes and passed through a buttonhole to fasten them ❷ a small knob you press to work an electric device

button *VERB* buttons, buttoning, buttoned
to button clothes or to button up clothes is to fasten them with buttons

buttonhole *NOUN* buttonholes
❶ a slit for a button to pass through ❷ a flower worn on a lapel

buttress *NOUN* buttresses
a support built against a wall

buy *VERB* buys, buying, bought
to buy something is to get it by paying for it • *I bought new jeans yesterday.*
➤ buyer *NOUN*

buy *NOUN* buys
something you buy • *Those boots were a good buy.*

buzz *NOUN* buzzes
a sharp humming sound, like bees make

buzz *VERB* buzzes, buzzing, buzzed
to buzz is to make a buzzing sound

buzzard *NOUN* buzzards
a bird of prey like a large hawk

buzzer *NOUN* buzzers
an alarm or signalling device that makes a buzzing noise

by *PREPOSITION, ADVERB*
❶ near, close • *Sit here by me.* ❷ using; by means of • *I fixed the tyre by sticking on a patch.* ❸ before • *I need to finish my homework by tomorrow.* ❹ past • *A crowd of people went by.* • *I can't get by all these boxes.*
➤ **by and large** mostly; on the whole
➤ **by the way** a phrase you use to add something else to what you have said • *When is your birthday, by the way?*

bye-bye *EXCLAMATION* (*informal*)
goodbye

by-election *NOUN* by-elections
an election in one district only, when a Member of Parliament has died or resigned

bypass *NOUN* bypasses
a road that takes traffic round the edge of a town or city rather than going through the centre

by-product *NOUN* by-products
something useful that is made while something else is being made

bystander *NOUN* bystanders
someone who sees something happening but takes no part in it

byte *NOUN* bytes (*computing*)
a unit that measures data or memory

66

derivative
an additional word from the same family as the headword

label
tells you that a word or meaning is used in a special context, or is only for *informal* or *formal* use

alphabetical opener
shows you the start
of the next letter

PLURAL ALERT!
tells you the
unusual plural
spelling of some
tricky words

literary quotation
shows you how
an author has
used a word in a
story or poem

alphabet
on every page to
help you find your
way around the
dictionary easily

C to caked

Cc

over it, snapping and biting and sending up a
cacophony of noise.—HOW TO TRAIN YOUR DRAGON,
Cressida Cowell
➤ **cacophonous** ADJECTIVE

cactus NOUN cacti
a fleshy plant with prickly spines that grows in
hot dry places
PLURAL ALERT! The word **cactus** has a Latin plural:
some potted cacti (not *cactuses*).

caddie NOUN caddies
someone whose job is to help a golfer by
carrying the clubs and giving advice

highlighted letter
shows you which
letter you are on

C ABBREVIATION
① short for Celsius ② 100 in Roman numerals

cab NOUN cabs
① a taxi ② the place for the driver in a lorry,
bus, train or crane

cabbage NOUN cabbages
a large round green vegetable with layers of
closely packed leaves

cabin NOUN cabins
① a hut or shelter ② one of the small rooms on
a ship for sleeping in ③ the part of an aircraft
where the passengers sit

cabinet NOUN cabinets
① a cupboard with shelves and doors, used for
storing things ② the group of chief ministers
who run the government

cable NOUN cables
① a thick rope, wire or chain used for lifting
heavy loads or tying up ships ② a bundle of
wires inside a tube, used for transmitting
electricity or electrical signals ③ a telegram
sent overseas

cable car NOUN cable cars
a small cabin that hangs from a moving cable,
used for carrying people up and down the side
of a mountain

cable television NOUN
a television system in which programmes are
transmitted along underground cables into
people's houses

cackle VERB cackles, cackling, cackled
to give a loud harsh laugh • *The witch cackled*
as she stirred the pot.
cackle NOUN cackles
① a cackle is a loud harsh laugh ② a cackle is
also the clucking of a hen or goose

cacophony (say ka-kof-o-nee) NOUN
a chorus of loud clashing noises
In summer you could barely even see the cliff
as dragons of all shapes and sizes swarmed

cadet NOUN cadets
a young person who is being trained for the
armed forces or the police

cadge VERB cadges, cadging, cadged
(*informal*)
to cadge something is to get it by asking for it
in a blunt or direct way

cafe (say kaf-ay) NOUN cafes
a place that sells hot and cold drinks and
light meals

cafeteria (say kaf-e-teer-i-a) NOUN
cafeterias
a cafe where customers serve themselves from
a counter

caffeine NOUN
caffeine is a substance in tea and coffee and
some other drinks, that keeps you awake and
makes you feel active

cage NOUN cages
an enclosure made of bars or wires, for
keeping birds or animals so that they can't
get away

cagoule NOUN cagoules
a lightweight waterproof jacket

cake NOUN cakes
① a sweet food made from a baked mixture of
flour, eggs, fat and sugar ② something made
into a lump rather like a cake, such as soap
➤ **a piece of cake** (*informal*) something very
easy to do

caked ADJECTIVE
covered with something that has dried hard,
like mud

a b c d e f g h i j k l m n o p q r s t u v w x y z

other forms
show you how
to spell different
forms of the word,
such as plurals or
past tenses

pronunciation
helps you to say the
word (not how to
spell it)

word class
tells you what type
of word it is, for
example NOUN, VERB,
ADJECTIVE or ADVERB

SPOT THE DIFFERENCE!
tells you the
difference between
words that can
be confused with
each other—try and
spot them in your
dictionary

67

phrase
shows you how the word is used
in everyday phrases and idioms

related adjective
tells you the adjective that is linked to the
headword, these are indicated by an arrow (➤)

v

Introduction

What is a dictionary for?

Here are some good reasons to use your dictionary:

- to find the meaning of a word you have read or heard
  What is a **manatee**? What colour is **magenta**? What does the abbreviation **NASA** stand for?
- to find out how to spell a word you want to use
  How many **a**'s are there in **aardvark**? Is the correct spelling *chocolate moose* or *mousse*?
- to find out how to form a plural or comparative
  What is the plural of **hippopotamus**? Do you say something is **more silly** or **sillier**?
- to find out how to say a word
  How do you pronounce **cyclops**? Do you stress the first or second syllable of **porpoise**?
- to build your vocabulary
  Is there a word that means 'cat-like' or 'to do with cats'?
- to learn about the history of words
  Where does the word **pyjamas** come from?

Pronunciation

This dictionary will help you to pronounce difficult words. The pronunciation is given in brackets, introduced by *rhymes with* or *say*. Words are divided into syllables, and the main stress is shown in bold type **like this**.

brooch (*rhymes with* **coach**) NOUN brooches

bronchitis (*say* brong-**ky**-tiss) NOUN

. . . .

Note the following:
- th shows the sound as in **thin**

breath (*say* breth) NOUN breaths

- *th* shows the sound as in **this**
- *zh* shows the sound as in vision

breathe (*say* breeth) VERB breathes, breathing, breathed

Related adjectives

Some entries may include adjectives that come from a different root, but are related in meaning to the headword.

cat *NOUN* cats
❶ a small furry animal, often kept as a pet and known for catching mice
❷ a larger member of the same family, for example a lion, tiger or leopard
➤ **to let the cat out of the bag** is to give away a secret
➤ A related adjective is feline.

Language notes

Special notes at the end of some entries highlight points about language.

DID YOU KNOW? notes point out interesting word histories.

SPELLING ALERT! and **PLURAL ALERT!** notes highlight tricky spellings or plurals, or confusable pairs of words.

SPOT THE DIFFERENCE! notes explain the difference between words that describe similar things.

a DETERMINER (called the **indefinite article**)
❶ one; any • *I've bought you a present.*
❷ each; every • *I go swimming twice
a week.*

aardvark (say ard-vark) NOUN **aardvarks**
an African animal with a long snout that eats
ants and termites

aback ADVERB
➤ **to be taken aback** is to be surprised and
slightly shocked by something • *We were taken
aback by this silly idea.*

abacus NOUN **abacuses**
a frame with rows of sliding beads, used for
counting and doing sums

abandon VERB **abandons, abandoning,
abandoned**
to abandon something or someone is to go
away and leave them, without intending to
go back • *The lioness had abandoned her
two cubs.*
➤ **abandonment** NOUN

abashed ADJECTIVE
slightly embarrassed or ashamed
*The two little country girls were rather abashed
by the splendour of the parlour.*—ANNE OF GREEN
GABLES, L. M. Montgomery

abbey NOUN **abbeys**
❶ a group of buildings where monks or nuns
live and work ❷ a church which is or was
part of an abbey, such as Westminster Abbey
in London

abbot NOUN **abbots**
the head of an abbey of monks

abbreviate VERB **abbreviates,
abbreviating, abbreviated**
to abbreviate a word or phrase is to write it
with fewer letters so that it is shorter

abbreviation NOUN **abbreviations**
a word or group of letters that is a shorter form

of a word or phrase • *BBC is an abbreviation of
'British Broadcasting Corporation'.*

ABC NOUN
a name for the alphabet
'Of course you know your ABC?' said the Red Queen.
—ALICE THROUGH THE LOOKING-GLASS, Lewis Carroll

abdomen NOUN **abdomens**
❶ the part of your body below your chest,
which contains your stomach and intestines
❷ the back part of the body of an insect
or spider

abdominal ADJECTIVE
in your stomach or intestines • *an abdominal
pain*

abduct (say ab-**dukt**) VERB **abducts,
abducting, abducted**
to abduct someone is to kidnap them

abide VERB **abides, abiding, abode** or
abided
❶ you cannot abide something or someone
when you don't like them at all • *Some people
can't abide spiders.* ❷ to abide by a rule or
promise is to keep to it

ability NOUN **abilities**
❶ ability is the skill or talent to do something
• *the ability to see in the dark* ❷ an ability
is a special skill or talent • *a player with
many abilities*

ablaze ADJECTIVE
a building is ablaze when it is on fire and
burning strongly

able ADJECTIVE **abler, ablest**
❶ having the power or skill or opportunity
to do something • *No one was able to crack
the code.* ❷ having a special talent or skill
• *You must be an able swimmer to join the team.*

abnormal ADJECTIVE
unusual or peculiar, not normal
➤ **abnormality** NOUN ➤ **abnormally** ADVERB

aboard ADVERB, PREPOSITION
someone is aboard when they have got on a
train, ship or aircraft • *The passengers were all
aboard.* • *It's time to get aboard the train.*

abode NOUN **abodes**
a formal word for the place where someone
lives

abolish VERB abolishes, abolishing, abolished
to abolish a rule or custom is to get rid of it
• *The class voted to abolish homework.*

abolition (*say* ab-o-**lish**-on) NOUN
getting rid of something • *the abolition of slavery*

abominable ADJECTIVE
very shocking, dreadful • *a series of abominable crimes*

Abominable Snowman NOUN
Abominable Snowmen
another name for yeti

Aboriginal Australian NOUN
Aboriginal Australians
one of, or a descendant of, the people who were living in Australia before European settlers arrived

abort VERB aborts, aborting, aborted
to abort a plan or mission is to cancel it after it has begun

abound VERB abounds, abounding, abounded
things abound when there are a lot of them
• *Fish abound in the river.*

about PREPOSITION
❶ to do with, connected with • *The film is about a family of superheroes.* ❷ approximately, roughly • *The castle wall is about 10 metres high.*

about ADVERB
❶ in various directions or places • *People were running about madly.* ❷ somewhere near by
• *There may be bears and wolves about.*
➤ **to be about to do something** is to be just going to do it • *They are about to announce the winner.*

above PREPOSITION
❶ higher than, over • *on the shelf above the fireplace* ❷ more than • *The temperature was just above freezing.*

above ADVERB
at a higher point, overhead • *Fireworks lit up the sky above.*

abracadabra EXCLAMATION
a word that people say when they are doing magic tricks

abroad ADVERB
in a foreign country • *They live abroad now.*

abrupt ADJECTIVE
❶ sudden and unexpected • *an abrupt change in the weather* ❷ rude and unfriendly • *He gave an abrupt reply.*
➤ **abruptly** ADVERB

abscess NOUN abscesses
a painful swelling on the body containing pus

abseil VERB abseils, abseiling, abseiled
to abseil is to lower yourself down a steep cliff or rock by sliding down a rope

absence NOUN absences
not being in a place where you are expected, for example school or work

absent ADJECTIVE
not present; away

absentee NOUN absentees
someone who is away, for example not at school or work

absent-minded ADJECTIVE
forgetting things easily
➤ **absent-mindedly** ADVERB to do something absent-mindedly is to do it without thinking about it much • *Lydia absent-mindedly put too much sugar in her tea.*

absolute ADJECTIVE
total, complete, not restricted • *I have absolute confidence in you.*

absolutely ADVERB
❶ completely ❷ (*informal*) definitely • *'Are you going to Beth's party?' 'Absolutely!'*

absorb VERB absorbs, absorbing, absorbed
❶ to absorb something like liquid is to soak it up ❷ to be absorbed in something is to be interested in it and give it all your attention
• *He was very absorbed in his book.*

absorbent ADJECTIVE
an absorbent material soaks up liquid easily

abstract (*say* **ab**-strakt) ADJECTIVE
to do with ideas and not with physical things
• *abstract patterns*

absurd ADJECTIVE
silly or ridiculous • *What an absurd idea!*

abundance *NOUN*
a large amount, plenty • *an abundance of fresh air*

abundant *ADJECTIVE*
large in amount, plentiful • *an abundant supply of food*

abuse (*say* a-**bewz**) *VERB* **abuses, abusing, abused**
❶ to abuse something is to treat it badly and harm it ❷ to abuse someone is to say unpleasant things about them ❸ to abuse someone also means to hurt them or treat them cruelly

abuse (*say* a-**bewss**) *NOUN* **abuses**
❶ treating something badly ❷ unpleasant words said about someone • *She got a lot of abuse from her so-called friends.* ❸ physical harm or cruelty done to someone

abusive *ADJECTIVE*
saying unpleasant things about someone

abysmal *ADJECTIVE* (*informal*)
very bad • *The weather was abysmal.*

abyss *NOUN* **abysses**
a deep dark hole that seems to go on forever

academic *ADJECTIVE*
to do with learning in a school or university • *an academic subject*

academy *NOUN* **academies**
❶ a college or school ❷ a society of scholars or scientists who meet to discuss their work

accelerate *VERB* **accelerates, accelerating, accelerated**
to accelerate is to go faster

acceleration *NOUN*
an increase of speed, going faster

accelerator *NOUN* **accelerators**
a pedal that you press down to make a motor vehicle go faster

accent (*say* **ak**-sent) *NOUN* **accents**
❶ an accent is the way that people from a particular area pronounce words • *He has a Yorkshire accent.* ❷ the accent in a word is the part you speak more strongly than the rest of it • *The accent in 'dinner' is on the first syllable.* ❸ an accent is a special mark put over a letter in a foreign word, to show its pronunciation • *The word 'cliché' has an accent on the 'e'.*

accent (*say* ak-**sent**) *VERB* **accents, accenting, accented**
to accent part of a word is to speak it more strongly than the rest of it

accept *VERB* **accepts, accepting, accepted**
❶ to accept something is to take it when someone offers it to you ❷ to accept an invitation is to say 'yes' to it ❸ to accept an idea or suggestion is to agree that it is true or worth thinking about

acceptable *ADJECTIVE*
❶ good enough to accept • *We think it is an acceptable offer.* ❷ all right, satisfactory • *Their behaviour was not acceptable.*

acceptance *NOUN*
taking something that someone offers you

access *NOUN* **accesses**
a way to reach a place • *This road is the only access to the house.*

access *VERB* **accesses, accessing, accessed**
to access a computer file is to find and be able to use it

accessible *ADJECTIVE*
easy to reach or approach

accessory *NOUN* **accessories**
❶ an extra or spare part that goes with something bigger ❷ an item like a piece of jewellery or a handbag that goes with clothes

accident *NOUN* **accidents**
something unexpected that happens, especially when something is broken, or someone is hurt or killed
➤ **by accident** by chance, not intentionally

accidental *ADJECTIVE*
something is accidental when it happens by chance and not because someone wants it to happen • *accidental damage*
➤ **accidentally** *ADVERB*

accommodate *VERB* **accommodates, accommodating, accommodated**
❶ to accommodate someone or something is to provide them with a place to stay ❷ to accommodate someone also means to do what you can to please them

a
b
c
d
e
f
g
h
i
j
k
l
m
n
o
p
q
r
s
t
u
v
w
x
y
z

accommodation *NOUN*
accommodation is a place to live or stay
• *We need accommodation for two nights.*

accompaniment *NOUN* **accompaniments**
the music played on a piano or another
instrument while a singer sings

accompany *VERB* **accompanies**,
accompanying, **accompanied**
❶ to accompany someone is to go somewhere
with them ❷ to accompany a singer is to play
the piano or another instrument while they sing

accomplish *VERB* **accomplishes**,
accomplishing, **accomplished**
to accomplish something is to do it successfully

accomplished *ADJECTIVE*
good at doing something; skilful

accomplishment *NOUN* **accomplishments**
something you do well

accord *NOUN* **accords**
➤ **to do something of your own accord** is to
do it willingly and without being told to

according to *PREPOSITION*
❶ you say **according to someone** to show
where a piece of information comes from
• *According to Katie, there is a party tomorrow.*
❷ you say **according to something** when
you are comparing two things • *Nothing went
according to our plan.*

accordion *NOUN* **accordions**
a portable musical instrument which you play
by squeezing the sides and pressing on the keys

account *NOUN* **accounts**
❶ a description or story about something
that happened • *a thrilling account of their
adventures* ❷ an amount of money someone
has in a bank or building society ❸ a statement
showing how much money someone owes;
a bill
➤ **on account of something** because of it
➤ **on no account** certainly not
➤ **to take something into account** is to
consider it along with other things

account *VERB* **accounts, accounting,
accounted**
to account for something is to be an
explanation of it • *What could account for
his odd behaviour?*

accountant *NOUN* **accountants**
a person whose job is to write and organize
the money accounts of a person or
organization

accumulate *VERB* **accumulates,
accumulating, accumulated**
❶ to accumulate things is to collect them or
pile them up ❷ things accumulate when they
form a heap or pile

accumulation *NOUN*
❶ accumulating things ❷ a heap or pile,
a collection • *an accumulation of junk*

accuracy *NOUN*
accuracy is being exactly right or correct

accurate *ADJECTIVE*
correct, done exactly and carefully
• *an accurate drawing of a skeleton*
➤ **accurately** *ADVERB*

accusation *NOUN* **accusations**
a statement accusing someone of something

accuse *VERB* **accuses, accusing, accused**
to accuse someone is to say that they did
something wrong • *He accused them of
stealing.*

accustomed *ADJECTIVE*
➤ **to be accustomed to something** is to
be used to it • *I'm not accustomed to staying
up late.*

ace *NOUN* **aces**
❶ a playing card with an A in the corner and a
large emblem of the suit in the centre ❷ a very
clever or skilful person • *She is an ace at sudoku.*
❸ in tennis, an ace is a serve that the other
player cannot return

ache *NOUN* **aches**
a dull steady pain
ache *VERB* **aches, aching, ached**
to ache is to feel a dull steady pain

achieve *VERB* **achieves, achieving, achieved**
to achieve something is to succeed in doing it
or getting it

achievement *NOUN* **achievements**
something someone has succeeded in doing
• *Winning the gold medal was a great
achievement.*

achoo EXCLAMATION
the sound someone makes when they sneeze
• *I heard a loud sneeze, 'Achoo!'.*

acid NOUN acids
a substance that contains hydrogen and causes chemical change. Acids are the opposite of alkalis.

acid ADJECTIVE
sour or bitter to taste
➤ **acidity** NOUN

acidic (*say* a-**sid**-ik) ADJECTIVE
containing a lot of acid

acid rain NOUN
rain that contains harmful acids because it has mixed with waste gases from the air

acknowledge VERB acknowledges, acknowledging, acknowledged
❶ to acknowledge something is to admit that it is true ❷ to acknowledge a letter or email is to say that you have received it ❸ to acknowledge a debt or favour is to say you are grateful for it

acknowledgement NOUN acknowledgements
❶ something that you admit or confess ❷ a note to say that you have received a letter or message • *This is an acknowledgement of your email.*

acne (*say* **ak**-nee) NOUN
a skin disease which causes red pimples on the face and neck and is common among teenagers

acorn NOUN acorns
an oval nut which grows on an oak tree and has a cup on its stem

acoustic (*say* a-**koo**-stik) ADJECTIVE
❶ to do with sound or hearing ❷ an acoustic guitar or other musical instrument uses its own shape to make the sound, and does not have an electrical amplifier

acoustics (*say* a-**koo**-stiks) PLURAL NOUN
❶ the acoustics of a place are the qualities that make it good or bad for sound ❷ (*singular noun*) the science of sound

acquaint VERB acquaints, acquainting, acquainted
❶ to acquaint someone with something is to

tell them about it ❷ to be acquainted with someone is to know them slightly

acquaintance NOUN acquaintances
someone you know slightly
➤ **to make someone's acquaintance** is to get to know them

acquire VERB acquires, acquiring, acquired
to acquire something is to obtain it, usually with some effort or difficulty

acquit VERB acquits, acquitting, acquitted
to acquit someone is to decide that they are not guilty of a crime, especially in a law trial

acre (*say* **ay**-ker) NOUN acres
an area of land measuring 4,840 square yards (about 4,047 square metres)

acrid ADJECTIVE
an acrid smell is sharp and bitter • *a cloud of acrid smoke*

acrobat (*say* **ak**-ro-bat) NOUN acrobats
an entertainer who gives displays of jumping and balancing
DID YOU KNOW? The word **acrobat** comes from Greek words meaning 'to walk on tiptoe'.

acrobatic ADJECTIVE
to do with an acrobat; like an acrobat
• *the acrobatic skills of a chimpanzee*

acrobatics PLURAL NOUN
exercises of jumping and balancing that an acrobat does

acronym (*say* **ak**-ro-nim) NOUN acronyms
a word or name that is formed from the first letters of other words, for example *UFO* is an acronym of *unidentified flying object*

across ADVERB, PREPOSITION
❶ from one side of something to the other
• *The table measures 1.5 metres across.*
❷ to the other side of something • *How can we get across the busy road?*

act NOUN acts
❶ something that someone does ❷ an individual performance in a programme of entertainment, for example a juggling act or a comic act ❸ one of the main sections of a play or opera ❹ a new law that a government makes

A
B
C
D
E
F
G
H
I
J
K
L
M
N
O
P
Q
R
S
T
U
V
W
X
Y
Z

act VERB **acts, acting, acted**
❶ to act is to do something useful or necessary • *We need to act straightaway.*
❷ to act stupid or act clever is to behave stupidly or cleverly ❸ to act in a play or film is to take part in it

action NOUN **actions**
❶ an action is something that someone does ❷ action is moving or doing things • *The film is full of fast-paced action.* ❸ action is also fighting in a battle • *He was killed in action.*
➤ **out of action** not working properly

activate VERB **activates, activating, activated**
to activate a machine or device is to start it working

active ADJECTIVE
❶ busy, taking part in lots of activities
❷ doing things, working • *an active volcano*
❸ (*grammar*) an active verb is one where the subject does the action, for example in *We made a cake*, the subject is *We*, and *made* is an active verb

activism NOUN
when a person takes action to try to bring about political or social change

activist NOUN **activists**
a person who takes action to try to bring about political or social change

activity NOUN **activities**
❶ activity is doing things ❷ an activity is something special that someone does
• *They enjoy outdoor activities.*

actor NOUN **actors**
someone who acts in a play or film

actress NOUN **actresses**
a girl or woman who acts in a play or film

actual ADJECTIVE
really there or really happening • *Is that an actual dinosaur bone?*

actually ADVERB
really; in fact • *Actually, I think you are wrong.*

acute ADJECTIVE
❶ sharp or intense • *an acute stomach pain*
❷ severe • *an acute shortage of food* ❸ clever;

quick to understand something ❹ an acute accent is the mark (´) put over a letter, as in *cliché* ❺ an acute angle is an angle of less than 90°

AD ABBREVIATION
short for Latin *Anno Domini*, used with dates that come after the birth of Jesus Christ
• AD *1492 is the year Columbus reached America.*

Adam's apple NOUN **Adam's apples**
the lump at the front of a man's neck

adapt VERB **adapts, adapting, adapted**
❶ to adapt something is to change it so you can use it for something different ❷ to adapt to something is to make yourself cope with it
• *They adapted to life in the country very quickly.*
➤ **adaptation** NOUN

adaptable ADJECTIVE
able to adapt to or become suitable for different things

adaptor NOUN **adaptors**
a device for connecting different pieces of equipment

add VERB **adds, adding, added**
❶ to add one number to another is to put them together to get a bigger number ❷ to add one thing to another is to mix them together, for example the different things in a recipe
➤ **to add up** is what numbers do to make a bigger number, called a total

adder NOUN **adders**
a small poisonous snake

addict NOUN **addicts**
someone with a habit they can't give up
➤ **addicted** ADJECTIVE

addiction NOUN **addictions**
a habit that someone can't give up

addition NOUN **additions**
❶ addition is the process of adding numbers together ❷ an addition is something or someone that has been added • *Matt was a late addition to the team.*
➤ **in addition** also, as well

additional ADJECTIVE
extra, added on

additive NOUN **additives**
something that is added to food or to something else in small amounts

address NOUN **addresses**
❶ the details of the place where someone lives • *My address is 29 High Street, Newtown.* ❷ (*computing*) a set of letters and symbols that you use to find a website or to send an email • *What's your email address?* ❸ a speech
address VERB **addresses, addressing, addressed**
❶ to address a letter or parcel is to write the address on it before sending it ❷ to address a group of people is to make a speech to them • *A man stepped forward and addressed the crowd.*

adenoids PLURAL NOUN
your adenoids are the spongy flesh at the back of your nose, which can become swollen, making it difficult to breathe

adequate ADJECTIVE
enough; sufficient
➤ **adequately** ADVERB

adhere VERB **adheres, adhering, adhered**
❶ something adheres to a surface when it sticks to it ❷ you adhere to a promise or rule when you keep it

adhesive NOUN **adhesives**
something such as glue that you use to stick things together
adhesive ADJECTIVE
causing things to stick together

Adi Granth (*say* ah-di **grunt**) NOUN
the holy book of the Sikhs

adjacent ADJECTIVE
near or next to something • *Her house is adjacent to the shop.*

adjective NOUN **adjectives**
an adjective is a word that describes a noun or adds to its meaning, for example *big, blue, friendly, hairy*

adjourn VERB **adjourns, adjourning, adjourned**
to adjourn, or to adjourn a meeting, is to take a break before continuing later

'In that case,' said the Dodo solemnly, rising to its feet, 'I move that the meeting adjourn.'
—ALICE'S ADVENTURES IN WONDERLAND, Lewis Carroll

adjust VERB **adjusts, adjusting, adjusted**
❶ to adjust something is to change it slightly or change its position ❷ to adjust to something is to try to get used to it • *They found it hard to adjust to life in the city.*

adjustment NOUN **adjustments**
a small change you make to something • *She made a quick adjustment to her hair.*

administer VERB **administers, administering, administered**
❶ to administer a country is to govern it ❷ to administer a medicine is to give it to someone

administrate VERB **administrates, administrating, administrated**
to administrate a country or business is to govern it or run it
➤ **administrative** ADJECTIVE

administration NOUN **administrations**
❶ administration is running a business or governing a country ❷ in the USA, an administration is a government that is holding office • *the Obama administration*

admirable ADJECTIVE
worth admiring; excellent • *an admirable piece of work*
➤ **admirably** ADVERB

admiral NOUN **admirals**
an officer of the highest rank in the navy

admiration NOUN
you feel admiration for someone or something when you think they are very good or very beautiful • *I'm full of admiration for her courage.*

admire VERB **admires, admiring, admired**
❶ to admire someone or something is to think they are very good or very beautiful ❷ to admire something is also to look at it and enjoy it • *They went to the top of the hill to admire the view.*

admirer NOUN **admirers**
a person who likes someone or something very much • *Cleopatra had many admirers.*

a
b
c
d
e
f
g
h
i
j
k
l
m
n
o
p
q
r
s
t
u
v
w
x
y
z

admission NOUN admissions
❶ admission is being allowed to go into a place
• *Admission to the show is by ticket only.*
❷ an admission is something that someone admits or confesses • *They are guilty by their own admission.*

admit VERB admits, admitting, admitted
❶ to admit someone is to let them come into a place ❷ to admit something is to say that it has happened or that you have done it

admittance NOUN
admittance is being allowed to go into a private place

admittedly ADVERB
as an agreed fact; without denying it
• *Admittedly, it was a silly thing to do.*

ado NOUN
➤ **without more ado** without wasting any more time

adolescent NOUN adolescents
a young person who is older than a child and not yet an adult, from about 15 to 18
➤ **adolescence** NOUN

adopt VERB adopts, adopting, adopted
❶ to adopt a child is to take them into your family and bring them up as your own ❷ to adopt a system or method is to start using it
➤ **adopted** ADJECTIVE ➤ **adoption** NOUN

adorable ADJECTIVE
lovely, worth adoring • *an adorable new puppy*

adore VERB adores, adoring, adored
to adore someone or something is to love them or admire them very much
➤ **adoration** NOUN

adorn VERB adorns, adorning, adorned
to adorn something is to decorate it or make it pretty

adrenalin NOUN
a hormone that stimulates your nervous system and makes you feel ready to do something

adrift ADVERB, ADJECTIVE
something such as a boat is adrift when it is loose and drifting about

adult NOUN adults
a fully grown person or animal

advance NOUN advances
❶ an advance is a forward movement
❷ advance is improvement or progress
❸ an advance of money is a loan

advance ADJECTIVE
given or arranged beforehand • *They gave us an advance warning.*
➤ **in advance** beforehand

advance VERB advances, advancing, advanced
❶ to advance is to move forward ❷ to advance is also to make progress

advanced ADJECTIVE
an advanced course or exam is one at a higher level

advantage NOUN advantages
something useful or helpful
➤ **to take advantage of someone** is to treat them unfairly when they are not likely to complain
➤ **to take advantage of something** is to make good use of it

Advent NOUN
in the Christian Church, the period before Christmas
DID YOU KNOW? The word **Advent** comes from a Latin word meaning 'arrival', and refers to the arrival of Christ.

Advent calendar NOUN Advent calendars
a decorative card with numbered windows to open on each of the days of Advent

adventure NOUN adventures
❶ an adventure is something exciting or interesting that someone does
Not long ago there lived in Suffolk a hundred and one Dalmatians whose adventures had once thrilled all the dogs of England.—THE STARLIGHT BARKING, Dodie Smith
❷ adventure is doing bold and exciting things • *Who doesn't enjoy a bit of adventure now and then?*

adventurous ADJECTIVE
an adventurous person likes to do interesting or exciting things

adverb NOUN adverbs
an adverb is a word that tells you how or when or where or why something happens. In these

sentences, the words in italics are adverbs: *The detective listened carefully. Please reply immediately. I could hear voices upstairs.*

adverbial *NOUN* adverbials
an adverbial is a group of words that acts as an adverb. In these sentences, the phrases in italics are adverbials: *The queue moved as slowly as a glacier. You must leave before the clock strikes twelve.*

adversary (*say* ad-ver-sa-ree) *NOUN* adversaries
an opponent or enemy

adverse *ADJECTIVE*
not good; harmful • *The magic potion had an adverse effect.*

adversity *NOUN* adversities
adversity is bad things that happen to someone

advert *NOUN* adverts (*informal*)
an advertisement

advertise *VERB* advertises, advertising, advertised
❶ to advertise something is to praise it in a newspaper or on television so that people will want it ❷ to advertise an event is to tell people when it will take place • *Have you advertised the concert?*

advertisement *NOUN* advertisements
a public notice or short television film that tries to persuade people to buy something

advice *NOUN*
advice is something you say to someone to help them decide what to do

advisable *ADJECTIVE*
sensible; worth doing

advise *VERB* advises, advising, advised
to advise someone is to tell them what you think they should do • *I advised her to ignore the email.*

advocate (*say* ad-vo-kat) *NOUN* advocates
❶ a person who speaks in favour of someone or something ❷ in Scotland, an advocate is a lawyer who presents a case in court

advocate (*say* ad-vo-kayt) *VERB* advocates, advocating, advocated
to advocate something is to speak in favour of it

aerial *NOUN* aerials
a wire or metal rod for receiving or sending radio or television signals

aerial *ADJECTIVE*
from or in the air, or from aircraft • *an aerial view of the island*

aerobatics *PLURAL NOUN*
an exciting display by flying aircraft
➤ aerobatic *ADJECTIVE*

aerobics *PLURAL NOUN*
aerobics are energetic exercises that strengthen your heart and lungs

aeronautics *PLURAL NOUN*
the study of aircraft and flying

aeroplane *NOUN* aeroplanes
a flying vehicle with fixed wings and powerful engines

aerosol *NOUN* aerosols
a device that holds a liquid under pressure and lets it out in a fine spray

affair *NOUN* affairs
❶ something interesting that happens, an event • *The party was a very strange affair.* ❷ someone's affairs are their private business • *Why are you so interested in my affairs?*

affect *VERB* affects, affecting, affected
to affect someone or something is to cause them to change or to harm them • *The dampness might affect his health.*
SPELLING ALERT! Affect is different from effect, which is a noun: *the effects of climate change.*

affected *ADJECTIVE*
not real; pretended
'Really, Daisy!' said Chloe, clutching her ears in an affected way. 'You practically deafened me.' —SLEEPOVERS, Jacqueline Wilson

affection *NOUN* affections
affection or an affection is love or fondness • *She has a great affection for her cat.*
➤ affectionate *ADJECTIVE*

afflict to aghast

afflict VERB **afflicts, afflicting, afflicted**
to be afflicted by something is to suffer
because of it
➤ **affliction** NOUN

affluent (say af-loo-ent) ADJECTIVE
having a lot of money or wealth • *This is an affluent part of the city.*
➤ **affluence** NOUN

afford VERB **affords, affording, afforded**
❶ to be able to afford something is to have
enough money to pay for it ❷ to be unable to
afford the time to do something is not to have
enough time for it

afloat ADVERB
floating • *We managed to keep the raft afloat.*

afraid ADJECTIVE
frightened • *Please don't be afraid.*
➤ **I'm afraid** I am sorry; I regret • *I'm afraid I can't help you.*

afresh ADVERB
again; in a new way • *Let's start the day afresh.*

African ADJECTIVE
to do with Africa or its people

African NOUN **Africans**
a person from Africa

after PREPOSITION, ADVERB
❶ later or later than, following • *They set off after breakfast.* • *We saw them again the week after.* ❷ following or coming behind
• *They were after us in the queue.* ❸ to be named after someone is to be given their name
• *She was named after her grandmother.*

afternoon NOUN **afternoons**
the time from midday until evening

afterwards ADVERB
at a later time

again ADVERB
❶ once more; another time • *Can you say that again, slowly?* ❷ as before • *You'll soon be well again.*
➤ **again and again** lots of times

against PREPOSITION
❶ touching or hitting • *He was leaning against*

the wall. ❷ opposed to, not liking • *Are you against animal testing?*

age NOUN **ages**
❶ your age is how old you are • *at the age of twelve* ❷ an age is a period of history
• *the Victorian age* ❸ age is the last part of someone's life • *the wisdom that comes with age*
➤ **ages** (informal) a long time • *We've been waiting ages.*

age VERB **ages, ageing, aged**
to age is to become old

aged ADJECTIVE
❶ (say ayjd) having the age of • *The girl was aged 9.* ❷ (say ay-jid) very old • *We saw an aged man.*

agency NOUN **agencies**
the office or business of someone who organizes things

agenda (say a-jen-da) NOUN **agendas**
a list of things that people have to do or talk about, for example at a business meeting

agent NOUN **agents**
❶ someone whose job is to organize things for other people • *We booked our holiday with a travel agent.* ❷ a spy • *He is a secret agent.*

aggravate VERB **aggravates, aggravating, aggravated**
❶ to aggravate something is to make it worse
❷ (informal) to aggravate someone is to annoy them
➤ **aggravation** NOUN

aggression NOUN
starting a war or attack; being aggressive

aggressive ADJECTIVE
❶ an aggressive person or group is one that is likely to attack or use violence ❷ an aggressive activity is done with energy and has a strong effect • *They began an aggressive sales campaign.*

aghast ADJECTIVE
horrified or shocked
'Travel in a balloon!' exclaimed the Duchess, aghast. 'William! Are you out of your mind?'–BLACK HEARTS IN BATTERSEA, Joan Aiken

10

agile *ADJECTIVE*
able to move quickly and easily • *Mountain goats are amazingly agile.*
➤ **agility** *NOUN*

agitated *ADJECTIVE*
feeling worried and anxious • *Frank was starting to look agitated.*
➤ **agitation** *NOUN*

agnostic (*say* ag-**nos**-tik) *NOUN* **agnostics**
someone who believes that we cannot know if there is a God

ago *ADVERB*
in the past • *Dinosaurs lived on earth long ago.*

agonizing (*also* **agonising**) *ADJECTIVE*
❶ an agonizing pain is one that hurts terribly ❷ an agonizing choice or decision is one that you find very difficult to make

agony *NOUN* **agonies**
severe pain or suffering

agree *VERB* **agrees, agreeing, agreed**
❶ to agree with someone is to think the same as them ❷ to agree to do something is to say that you are willing to do it • *She agreed to show us the way.* ❸ food does not agree with you when it upsets your stomach • *Spicy food doesn't agree with me.*

agreeable *ADJECTIVE*
❶ willing to do something that someone suggests • *Both sides were agreeable to the idea.* ❷ pleasant • *an agreeable place for a holiday*

agreement *NOUN* **agreements**
❶ agreement is thinking the same • *Are we in agreement?* ❷ an agreement is an arrangement that people have agreed on

agriculture *NOUN*
agriculture is farming, or growing food on the land
➤ **agricultural** *ADJECTIVE*

aground *ADVERB*
a ship runs aground when it gets stuck in shallow water

ah *EXCLAMATION*
a word you shout out when you are surprised or pleased • *Ah! There you are!*

ahead *ADVERB*
forwards, in front • *Rohan went ahead to show us the way.*

ahoy *EXCLAMATION*
a shout used by sailors to attract attention

AI *ABBREVIATION*
short for *artificial intelligence*, the use of computers to do things that humans do, for example thinking and making decisions

aid *NOUN* **aids**
❶ aid is help you give someone ❷ aid is also money or food or other help that a country sends to a poorer country ❸ an aid is something that helps someone to do something better • *Thomas wears a hearing aid.*

aid *VERB* **aids, aiding, aided**
to aid someone is to help them

ailing *ADJECTIVE*
suffering, in a bad way

ailment *NOUN* **ailments**
a minor illness

aim *VERB* **aims, aiming, aimed**
❶ to aim a gun at someone or something is to point it at them so as to shoot them ❷ to aim something like a ball is to throw it or kick it in a particular direction ❸ to aim to do something is to try to do it

aim *NOUN* **aims**
❶ a person's aim is what they intend to do ❷ aim is also pointing a weapon in a particular direction

aimless *ADJECTIVE*
not having any definite aim or purpose • *He led an aimless life.*
➤ **aimlessly** *ADVERB*

air *NOUN* **airs**
❶ air is the mixture of gases which surrounds the earth and which everyone breathes ❷ an air is a tune ❸ an air of mystery or secrecy is a feeling that things are mysterious or secret
➤ **to be in the air** is to be just an idea, and not something certain • *Our plans are still in the air.*
➤ **to be on the air** is to be on the radio or television

a
b
c
d
e
f
g
h
i
j
k
l
m
n
o
p
q
r
s
t
u
v
w
x
y
z

A

➤ **to put on airs** is to behave grandly, as if you are important

air VERB **airs**, **airing**, **aired**
❶ to air clothes or washing is to put them in a warm place to finish drying ❷ to air a room is to let fresh air into it ❸ to air views or opinions is to say them so that people know them

air conditioning NOUN
a system for controlling the temperature and freshness of the air in a building, so that it is kept cool in hot weather and warm in cold weather

aircraft NOUN **aircraft**
an aeroplane or a helicopter • *The sound of enemy aircraft was getting closer.*

aircraft carrier NOUN **aircraft carriers**
a large ship with a flat deck on which aircraft can take off and land

airfield NOUN **airfields**
a place where aircraft can take off and land

air force NOUN **air forces**
the part of a country's fighting force that uses aircraft

airline NOUN **airlines**
a company that takes people to places by aircraft

airmail NOUN
airmail is mail that is sent by air

airport NOUN **airports**
a place where aircraft land and take off, with passenger terminals and other buildings

air raid NOUN **air raids**
an attack by bombs dropped from aircraft

airship NOUN **airships**
a large balloon with engines, designed to carry passengers or cargo

airstrip NOUN **airstrips**
a strip of land prepared for aircraft to take off and land

airtight ADJECTIVE
not letting air get in or out

airy ADJECTIVE **airier**, **airiest**
❶ with plenty of fresh air ❷ vague and insincere • *They were just airy promises.*

aisle (*rhymes with* **mile**) NOUN **aisles**
❶ a part at the side of a church ❷ a passage between or beside rows of seats or pews

ajar ADJECTIVE
slightly open • *Please leave the door ajar.*

akimbo ADVERB
➤ **arms akimbo** with your hands on your hips and your elbows out

alarm VERB **alarms**, **alarming**, **alarmed**
to alarm someone is to make them frightened or anxious

alarm NOUN **alarms**
❶ a warning sound or signal ❷ a feeling of fear or anxiety • *He cried out in alarm.*

alarm clock NOUN **alarm clocks**
a clock with a loud ring or bleep, which can be set to wake someone who is asleep

alas EXCLAMATION (*old use*)
a word people say when they are sad
'Aren't you also much loved in the world?'
'Alas, no,' Miss Spider answered, sighing long and loud.—JAMES AND THE GIANT PEACH, Roald Dahl

albatross NOUN **albatrosses**
a large seabird with long wings

album NOUN **albums**
❶ a book in which you keep things like photographs or stamps or autographs ❷ a collection of songs on a CD, record or digital platform

alcohol NOUN
❶ a colourless liquid made by fermenting sugar or starch ❷ drinks containing this liquid (for example beer, wine, gin), which affects people's behaviour and can make them drunk if they have too much
➤ **alcoholic** ADJECTIVE containing alcohol

alcove NOUN **alcoves**
a part of a room where the wall is set back from the main part

alert ADJECTIVE
watching for something; ready to act

alert VERB **alerts**, **alerting**, **alerted**
to alert someone to a danger or problem is to warn them about it

alert *NOUN* **alerts**
an alarm
➤ **on the alert** on the lookout for danger
or attack

A level *NOUN* **A levels**
a higher standard of examination that is taken
after GCSEs in England and Wales

algae (*say* al-gee *or* al-jee) *PLURAL NOUN*
a group of plants that grow in water without
roots or stems

algebra (*say* al-ji-bra) *NOUN*
mathematics in which letters and symbols are
used to represent numbers
DID YOU KNOW? The word **algebra** comes from
an Arabic word meaning 'putting broken parts
together'.

alias (*say* ay-li-as) *NOUN* **aliases**
a false or different name that someone uses
instead of their real name

alias *ADVERB*
also named • *Clark Kent, alias Superman*

alibi (*say* al-i-by) *NOUN* **alibis**
evidence that someone accused of a crime was
not there when the crime was committed
DID YOU KNOW? Alibi is a Latin word meaning
'elsewhere'.

alien (*say* ay-li-en) *NOUN* **aliens**
❶ someone who is not a citizen of the country
where they are living ❷ in science fiction,
a being from another world

alien *ADJECTIVE*
❶ foreign ❷ not in keeping; quite unlike • *Lying
was alien to his nature.*

alienate *VERB* **alienates**, **alienating**, **alienated**
to alienate someone is to make them unfriendly
to you
➤ **alienation** *NOUN*

alight *VERB* **alights**, **alighting**, **alighted**
❶ to alight from a bus or train is to step down
from it ❷ when a bird alights on a branch, it
lands on it

alight *ADJECTIVE*
❶ on fire, burning ❷ lit up, illuminated
*The house was all alight within, and the joyous
hubbub of its activity contrasted with the sombre
sighing of the wind.*—THE WOLVES OF WILLOUGHBY
CHASE, Joan Aiken

alike *ADJECTIVE*
similar; like each other

alike *ADVERB*
in the same way • *He treats everybody alike.*

alive *ADJECTIVE*
living; existing • *Is he alive?*

alkali (*say* al-ka-ly) *NOUN* **alkalis**
a substance that neutralizes acids or that
combines with acids to form salts
➤ **alkaline** *ADJECTIVE* ➤ **alkalinity** *NOUN*

all *DETERMINER, ADVERB, PRONOUN*
meaning 'everything' or 'everyone' • *That is all
I know.* • *She was dressed all in white.* • *All my
books are in the desk.*
➤ **to do something all out** (*informal*) is to
use all your ability to do it • *Go all out
to win.*
➤ **all the same** nevertheless; making no
difference • *It was raining but I went out all
the same.*

Allah *NOUN*
God, in Islam

all-clear *NOUN*
a signal that a danger has passed

allegation (*say* a-li-**gay**-shun) *NOUN*
allegations
you make an allegation when you accuse
someone of doing something wrong

allege (*say* a-**lej**) *VERB* **alleges**, **alleging**,
alleged
to allege that someone has done something
is to accuse them of it, usually without proof
• *He alleged that I stole his watch.*

allegiance (*say* a-**lee**-jans) *NOUN*
allegiances
loyalty shown to a person or organization

allegory *NOUN* **allegories**
a story or poem with made-up people and
places that are meant to stand for real people
and places
➤ **allegorical** *ADJECTIVE*

allergic (*say* a-**ler**-jik) *ADJECTIVE*
someone is allergic to something if they
become ill or uncomfortable when they
eat it or touch it • *My sister is allergic to
peanuts.*

a
b
c
d
e
f
g
h
i
j
k
l
m
n
o
p
q
r
s
t
u
v
w
x
y
z

allergy (*say* a-ler-jee) NOUN **allergies**
a condition that some people have that makes their body react badly to things they eat or drink or touch or breathe in, for example dust, milk or some kinds of food

alley NOUN **alleys**
❶ a narrow street or passage ❷ a place where you can play at skittles or tenpin bowling

alliance NOUN **alliances**
an agreement between countries or political parties to support each other

alligator NOUN **alligators**
a large reptile like a crocodile but with a rounded snout, found in North America and China
DID YOU KNOW? The word **alligator** comes from the Spanish words *el lagarto* meaning 'the lizard'. In English the two words became merged into one.

alliteration NOUN
alliteration is when the same letter or sound occurs several times in a group of words, for special effect, as in *slugs slowly slithering* or *Vladimir the Vampire*
➤ **alliterative** ADJECTIVE

allocate VERB **allocates**, **allocating**, **allocated**
to allocate something is to give it to someone for a particular purpose • *We've been allocated this room.*
➤ **allocation** NOUN

allot VERB **allots**, **allotting**, **allotted**
to allot jobs is to give them to various people

allotment NOUN **allotments**
a small rented piece of ground used for growing vegetables

allow VERB **allows**, **allowing**, **allowed**
❶ to allow someone to do something is to let them do it • *Will you allow me to take a photograph?* • *Skateboarding is not allowed.*
❷ to allow an amount of money is to provide it for some reason • *We were each allowed five pounds for lunch.*

allowance NOUN **allowances**
a sum of money given regularly to someone
➤ **to make allowances** is to be considerate
• *We must make allowances for his age.*

alloy NOUN **alloys**
a metal formed from a mixture of other metals

all right ADJECTIVE
❶ satisfactory; reasonably good • *The book was all right, but the film was better.* ❷ acceptable; allowed • *Is it all right to take photographs?* ❸ safe and well; not harmed • *Are you sure you're all right?*

all right EXCLAMATION
you can also say **all right** when you agree to something • *'Would you like to come with us?' 'All right.'*

all-round ADJECTIVE
having many skills • *She's a good all-round athlete.*

ally (*say* al-eye) NOUN **allies**
❶ a country in alliance with another country
❷ a person who helps or cooperates with you

ally VERB **allies**, **allying**, **allied**
to ally oneself with someone else is to form an alliance with them

almighty ADJECTIVE
❶ having a lot of power ❷ (*informal*) very great
• *They were making an almighty din.*

almond (*say* ah-mond) NOUN **almonds**
an oval nut that you can eat

almost ADVERB
very close to but not quite • *I am almost ready.*

aloft ADVERB
high up
When the wind blows and the rain comes down, it's jolly sitting up aloft in the snug tree-house.
—THE MAGIC PUDDING, Norman Lindsay

alone ADJECTIVE, ADVERB
without any other people or other things
• *She lived alone on the island for a whole year.*
• *The drinks alone cost £10.*

along PREPOSITION, ADVERB
❶ from one end of something to the other
❷ on; onwards • *Move along, please!*
❸ accompanying someone • *I have brought my brother along.*

alongside PREPOSITION, ADVERB
next to something

aloud *ADVERB*
in a voice that can be heard
SPELLING ALERT! You can read something **aloud**, but you are **allowed** to borrow a book.

alphabet *NOUN* **alphabets**
the letters used in a language, usually arranged in a set order
➤ **alphabetical** *ADJECTIVE*
DID YOU KNOW? The word **alphabet** comes from *alpha* and *beta*, the first two letters of the Greek alphabet.

alpine *ADJECTIVE*
to do with high mountains

already *ADVERB*
by or before now • *I've already told you once.*

Alsatian (*say* al-**say**-shan) *NOUN* **Alsatians**
a large strong dog, also sometimes called a German shepherd

also *ADVERB*
as an extra, besides • *We also need some bread.*

altar *NOUN* **altars**
a table or raised surface used in religious ceremonies

alter *VERB* **alters**, **altering**, **altered**
to alter something is to change it
➤ **alteration** *NOUN*

alternate (*say* ol-**ter**-nat) *ADJECTIVE*
❶ happening on every other one
In the Doldrums, laughter is frowned upon and smiling is permitted only on alternate Thursdays.
—THE PHANTOM TOLLBOOTH, Norton Juster
❷ coming in turns, one after the other • *alternate laughter and tears*

alternate (*say* **ol**-ter-nayt) *VERB* **alternates**, **alternating**, **alternated**
to alternate is to happen in turns

alternately *ADVERB*
one after the other in turn • *The weather was alternately fine and wet.*

alternative (*say* ol-**ter**-na-tiv) *NOUN* **alternatives**
something you can choose instead of something else • *If you don't like this book, there is an alternative.*

alternative *ADJECTIVE*
for you to choose instead of something else
• *There is an alternative dish for vegans.*

although *CONJUNCTION*
in spite of the fact that • *Although it was morning, the sky was still dark.*

altitude *NOUN* **altitudes**
the height of something, especially above sea level

alto *NOUN* **altos**
❶ a singer with a low female voice, also called a contralto ❷ a singer with a male voice higher than a tenor's

altogether *ADVERB*
❶ completely • *I've stopped playing football altogether now.* ❷ on the whole • *Altogether, it was an enjoyable match.*

aluminium *NOUN*
a silver-coloured metal that is light in weight

always *ADVERB*
❶ all the time, at all times ❷ often, constantly • *You are always giggling.* ❸ whatever happens • *You can always sleep on the floor.*

AM *NOUN* **AMs**
Assembly Member, a Member of the Welsh Assembly

am *VERB* (*1st person singular present tense of* **be**)

a.m. *ABBREVIATION*
short for Latin *ante meridiem*, which means 'before midday'

amalgamate *VERB* **amalgamates**, **amalgamating**, **amalgamated**
❶ to amalgamate things is to mix them or join them together ❷ to amalgamate is to join together to form one thing

amalgamation *NOUN* **amalgamations**
❶ amalgamation is mixing or joining things together ❷ an amalgamation is a mixture of things put together

amateur (*say* **am**-a-ter) *NOUN* **amateurs**
someone who does something because they like it, without being paid for it

amaze VERB amazes, amazing, amazed
to amaze someone is to surprise them greatly
➤ **amazement** NOUN

amazing ADJECTIVE
very surprising or remarkable; extraordinary
• *The spacecraft took amazing pictures of the surface of Mars.*
➤ **amazingly** ADVERB

ambassador NOUN ambassadors
someone sent to a foreign country to represent their own government

amber NOUN
❶ a hard, clear, yellow substance used for making ornaments ❷ a yellowish colour, the one used in traffic lights as a signal for caution

ambiguity NOUN ambiguities
❶ ambiguity is uncertainty about what something means ❷ an ambiguity is something that has more than one possible meaning

ambiguous ADJECTIVE
having more than one possible meaning; uncertain • *His reply was ambiguous.*

ambition NOUN ambitions
❶ ambition is a strong desire to be successful in life ❷ an ambition is something you want to do very much • *His ambition is to play for his country.*

ambitious ADJECTIVE
❶ an ambitious person wants very much to be successful in life ❷ an ambitious idea or plan is difficult or challenging

amble VERB ambles, ambling, ambled
to amble along is to walk slowly

ambulance NOUN ambulances
a vehicle for carrying sick or injured people

ambush NOUN ambushes
a surprise attack from a hidden place
ambush VERB ambushes, ambushing, ambushed
to ambush someone is to attack them suddenly from a hidden place

amend VERB amends, amending, amended
to amend something like a piece of writing is to change or improve it
➤ **amendment** NOUN

American ADJECTIVE
to do with the USA or the continent of America
American NOUN Americans
a person from the USA or the continent of America

amiable ADJECTIVE
friendly, good-tempered
➤ **amiably** ADVERB

amicable ADJECTIVE
friendly
➤ **amicably** ADVERB

amid, amidst PREPOSITION
in the middle of, among • *Something was moving amid the wreckage.*

ammonite (*say* am-o-nyt) NOUN ammonites
a type of fossil with a ribbed spiral shell

ammunition NOUN
bullets, bombs and other explosive objects used in fighting

amoeba (*say* a-mee-ba) NOUN amoebas
an amoeba is a tiny creature made of one cell; it can change shape and split itself in two

amok ADVERB
➤ **to run amok** is to run about wildly

among, amongst PREPOSITION
❶ surrounded by, in the middle of • *The bandits were hiding among the bushes.* ❷ between • *We divided the chocolate amongst ourselves.*

amount NOUN amounts
a quantity or total
amount VERB amounts, amounting, amounted
to amount to something is to reach it as a total • *The bill amounted to £55.*

ampere (*say* am-pair) NOUN amperes
a unit for measuring the rate of flow of an electric current

ampersand NOUN ampersands
the sign &, which means 'and'

amphibian *NOUN* **amphibians**
❶ an animal that can live on land and in water
❷ a vehicle that can travel on land and in water

amphibious *ADJECTIVE*
an amphibious animal or vehicle is able to live or travel on land and in water

amphitheatre *NOUN* **amphitheatres**
a circular or oval building without a roof, which has rows of seats arranged round a central area

amphora (*say* **am**-fo-ra) *NOUN* **amphoras**
an ancient Greek or Roman vase with two handles

ample *ADJECTIVE* **ampler, amplest**
❶ large, having plenty of space • *an ample inside pocket* ❷ more than enough
All of us had an ample share of the treasure, and used it wisely or foolishly, according to our natures.—TREASURE ISLAND, Robert Louis Stevenson
➤ **amply** *ADVERB*

amplifier *NOUN* **amplifiers**
an electronic device for making music or other sounds louder

amplify *VERB* **amplifies, amplifying, amplified**
❶ to amplify sounds is to make them louder or stronger ❷ to amplify something you say is to give more details about it

amputate *VERB* **amputates, amputating, amputated**
to amputate an arm or a leg is to cut it off in an operation
➤ **amputation** *NOUN*

amulet (*say* **am**-yoo-let) *NOUN* **amulets**
an ornament or piece of jewellery believed to protect its owner from harm
'The part of the Amulet which is lost,' said the beautiful voice, 'was broken and ground into the dust of the shrine that held it.'—THE STORY OF THE AMULET, Edith Nesbit

amuse *VERB* **amuses, amusing, amused**
❶ to amuse someone is to make them laugh or smile ❷ to amuse yourself is to find pleasant things to do

amusement *NOUN* **amusements**
❶ an amusement is something that amuses you
❷ amusement is being amused; laughing or smiling

amusing *ADJECTIVE*
making you laugh or smile • *It was an amusing story.*

an *DETERMINER* (*called the* **indefinite article**)
a word used instead of **a** when the next word begins with a vowel sound or a silent *h* • *Would you like an apple?* • *The film lasts an hour and a half.*

anaemia (*say* a-**nee**-mi-a) *NOUN*
a poor condition of the blood that makes someone look pale
➤ **anaemic** *ADJECTIVE*

anaesthetic (*say* an-iss-**thet**-ik) *NOUN* **anaesthetics**
a drug or gas that makes you unable to feel pain

anaesthetist *NOUN* **anaesthetists**
a doctor who gives patients an anaesthetic to stop them feeling pain

anaesthetize (*also* **anaesthetise**)
(*say* a-**nees**-the-tyz) *VERB* **anaesthetizes, anaesthetizing, anaesthetized**
to anaesthetize a person or an animal is to give them an anaesthetic

anagram *NOUN* **anagrams**
an anagram is a word or phrase made by rearranging the letters of another word or phrase, for example *carthorse* is an anagram of *orchestra*

analogue *ADJECTIVE*
an analogue clock or watch has hands and a dial to indicate numbers (*compare* **digital**)

analogy *NOUN* **analogies**
a comparison or similarity between two things that are fairly like each other • *There is an analogy between the human heart and a pump.*

analyse *VERB* **analyses, analysing, analysed**
❶ to analyse something is to examine it carefully ❷ to analyse a substance is to divide it into its parts

a
b
c
d
e
f
g
h
i
j
k
l
m
n
o
p
q
r
s
t
u
v
w
x
y
z

A

analysis NOUN **analyses**
a detailed study or examination of something

anarchy NOUN
❶ anarchy is having no government or controls, leading to a breakdown in law and order
❷ complete disorder or confusion

anatomy NOUN
the study of the parts of the body
➤ **anatomical** ADJECTIVE

ancestor NOUN **ancestors**
a person who lived in the past and was in the same family as someone alive now
➤ **ancestry** NOUN a person's ancestry is the list of all their ancestors

anchor NOUN **anchors**
a heavy object joined to a ship by a chain or rope and dropped to the bottom of the sea to stop the ship from moving

ancient ADJECTIVE
❶ belonging to times that were long ago
❷ very old • *They came from an ancient family.*

and CONJUNCTION
you use **and** to link words and phrases together • *We had cakes and lemonade.* • *Go upstairs and have a rest.*

anecdote NOUN **anecdotes**
a short amusing or interesting story about a real person or thing

anemone (*say* a-**nem**-on-ee) NOUN **anemones**
a small flower with the shape of a cup

angel NOUN **angels**
❶ a human-like being with wings that some people believe is a messenger from God
❷ someone who is perfectly behaved or very kind to others
DID YOU KNOW? The word **angel** comes from a Greek word meaning 'messenger'.

angelic ADJECTIVE
kind and beautiful, like an angel

anger NOUN
a strong feeling that you do not like what someone has said or done, making you want to quarrel or fight with them

angle NOUN **angles**
❶ the space between two lines or surfaces that meet ❷ a point of view • *What is your angle on this?*

angle VERB **angles**, **angling**, **angled**
❶ to angle something is to put it in a slanting position ❷ to angle news or a story is to tell it in a special way • *The report was angled so that the robbers looked like heroes.*

angler NOUN **anglers**
someone who fishes with a fishing rod

Anglican ADJECTIVE
belonging to the Church of England
Anglican NOUN **Anglicans**
a member of the Church of England

Anglo-Saxon NOUN
❶ (**Anglo-Saxons**) an English person, especially of the time before the Norman Conquest in 1066 ❷ the old form of English spoken before 1066

angry ADJECTIVE **angrier**, **angriest**
feeling or showing anger
➤ **angrily** ADVERB

anguish NOUN
great suffering or unhappiness

angular ADJECTIVE
❶ having sharp corners ❷ bony • *She has a thin, angular face.*

animal NOUN **animals**
an animal is a living thing that can move and feel. The word **animal** is normally used to mean creatures that are not humans.

animated ADJECTIVE
❶ lively and excited ❷ an animated film is one made by photographing a series of still pictures and showing them rapidly one after another so they appear to move

animation NOUN
❶ being lively or excited ❷ a way of making films from still pictures so they appear to move

animosity NOUN **animosities**
a feeling of being an enemy towards someone • *There was a lot of animosity in his voice.*

aniseed NOUN
a seed with a strong sweet taste like liquorice

ankle *NOUN* **ankles**
the part of your leg where it is joined to your foot

annex (*say* a-**neks**) *VERB* **annexes, annexing, annexed**
to annex something, like a piece of land, is to add it to something larger

annexe (*say* **an**-eks) *NOUN* **annexes**
a building added to a larger building

annihilate (*say* a-**ny**-il-ayt) *VERB* **annihilates, annihilating, annihilated**
to annihilate something is to destroy it completely
➤ **annihilation** *NOUN*

anniversary *NOUN* **anniversaries**
a day when you remember something special that happened on the same date in an earlier year

announce *VERB* **announces, announcing, announced**
to announce something is to say it publicly
➤ **announcer** *NOUN*

announcement *NOUN* **announcements**
something that is made known publicly, especially in a newspaper or on radio or television

annoy *VERB* **annoys, annoying, annoyed**
to annoy someone is to give them a feeling of not being pleased

annoyance *NOUN* **annoyances**
❶ annoyance is the feeling of being annoyed ❷ an annoyance is something that annoys you • *Wasps are a great annoyance at a picnic.*

annual *ADJECTIVE*
happening or coming every year • *the annual school book sale*
➤ **annually** *ADVERB*

annual *NOUN* **annuals**
❶ a children's book of stories or comic strips that comes out once a year ❷ a plant that dies when winter comes

anonymous *ADJECTIVE*
an anonymous book or letter is written by someone who does not give their name

➤ **anonymity** *NOUN* anonymity is keeping your name secret
➤ **anonymously** *ADVERB*

anorak *NOUN* **anoraks**
a thick warm jacket with a hood
DID YOU KNOW? The word **anorak** comes from an Inuit word meaning 'waterproof coat'.

anorexia (*say* an-er-**eks**-ee-a) *NOUN*
a mental illness that makes someone limit the amount they eat and drink to keep their weight as low as possible
➤ **anorexic** *ADJECTIVE*

another *DETERMINER, PRONOUN*
a different person or thing • *Have another look.* • *May I have another?*

answer *NOUN* **answers**
❶ an answer is what you say when someone asks you a question ❷ the answer to a problem is something that solves it

answer *VERB* **answers, answering, answered**
❶ to answer someone is to give them an answer ❷ to answer a telephone is to pick it up when it rings
➤ **to answer back** is to say something rude or cheeky as an answer

ant *NOUN* **ants**
a tiny insect that lives with others in a colony

antagonism *NOUN*
antagonism is a feeling of being someone's enemy

antagonize (*also* **antagonise**) *VERB* **antagonizes, antagonizing, antagonized**
to antagonize someone is to make them feel hostile or angry

Antarctic, Antarctica *NOUN*
the area round the South Pole
Antarctic *ADJECTIVE*
in the Antarctic or to do with the Antarctic • *an Antarctic expedition*

anteater *NOUN* **anteaters**
an animal with a long tongue that lives by eating ants

antelope *NOUN* **antelope** *or* **antelopes**
an animal like a deer that lives in Africa and parts of Asia

a
b
c
d
e
f
g
h
i
j
k
l
m
n
o
p
q
r
s
t
u
v
w
x
y
z

A B C D E F G H I J K L M N O P Q R S T U V W X Y Z

antenna *NOUN* **antennae** *or* **antennas**
❶ a long thin feeler on the head of an insect or shellfish ❷ an aerial
PLURAL ALERT! Each sense of **antenna** has a different plural. You say *an insect's antennae* but *radio antennas.*

anthem *NOUN* **anthems**
a religious or patriotic song, usually sung by a choir or group of people

anther *NOUN* **anthers**
the part of a flower's stamen that contains pollen

anthill *NOUN* **anthills**
a mound of earth over an ants' nest

anthology *NOUN* **anthologies**
a collection of poems, stories or songs in one book

anthropology *NOUN*
the study of human beings and the way they live
➤ **anthropologist** *NOUN*

anti– *PREFIX*
meaning 'against something', as in *antibiotic* and *anti-nuclear* (the opposite is **pro–**)

antibiotic *NOUN* **antibiotics**
a drug that kills bacteria, for example penicillin

anticipate *VERB* **anticipates, anticipating, anticipated**
❶ to anticipate something is to expect it and be ready for it • *The police were anticipating trouble.* ❷ to anticipate someone is to act before they do • *They anticipated us in getting the early train.*

anticipation *NOUN*
looking forward to doing something

anticlimax *NOUN* **anticlimaxes**
a disappointing ending or result after something exciting

anticlockwise *ADVERB, ADJECTIVE*
moving in the opposite direction to the hands of a clock

antidote *NOUN* **antidotes**
something which stops the effects of a poison

antiquated *ADJECTIVE*
old-fashioned

antique (*say* an-**teek**) *NOUN* **antiques**
something that is valuable because it is very old

antiseptic *NOUN* **antiseptics**
a chemical that kills germs

antler *NOUN* **antlers**
the horn of a deer, which divides into several branches

antonym (*say* **ant**-o-nim) *NOUN* **antonyms**
a word that is opposite in meaning to another
• *'Soft' is an antonym of 'hard'.*

anvil *NOUN* **anvils**
a large block of iron on which a blacksmith hammers metal into shape

anxiety *NOUN* **anxieties**
❶ anxiety is a feeling of being worried ❷ an anxiety is something that worries you

anxious *ADJECTIVE*
❶ worried and nervous ❷ eager to do something • *They were anxious to help us.*

any *DETERMINER*
❶ one or some • *Have you any spare paper?*
❷ no matter which • *Come any day you like.*
❸ every • *Any fool knows that!*

any *PRONOUN*
one or some • *I don't have any left.*

any *ADVERB*
at all; in some degree • *Is the cake any good?*

anybody *PRONOUN*
anyone

anyhow *ADVERB*
❶ anyway ❷ (*informal*) carelessly, without much thought • *He does his work anyhow.*

anyone *PRONOUN*
any person

anything *PRONOUN*
any thing

anyway *ADVERB*
whatever happens; whatever the situation may be • *If it rains, we'll go anyway.*

anywhere *ADVERB*
in any place or to any place

apart *ADVERB*
❶ away from each other; separately • *The male lion and cubs are kept apart.* ❷ into pieces • *The book was beginning to fall apart.* ❸ excluded • *Joking apart, what do you think?*

apartment *NOUN* **apartments**
❶ a set of rooms ❷ (*North American*) a flat

apathy *NOUN*
not having much interest in something
➤ **apathetic** *ADJECTIVE*

ape *NOUN* **apes**
a monkey without a tail, such as a gorilla or a chimpanzee

aphid *NOUN* **aphids**
a tiny insect that sucks sap from plants

apologetic *ADJECTIVE*
saying you are sorry for something
➤ **apologetically** *ADVERB*

apologize (*also* **apologise**) *VERB*
apologizes, apologizing, apologized
to apologize to someone is to tell them you are sorry

apology *NOUN* **apologies**
a statement that you are sorry for doing something wrong

apostle *NOUN* **apostles**
in Christianity, one of the twelve men sent out by Christ to tell people about God

apostrophe (*say* a-**poss**-tro-fee) *NOUN* **apostrophes**
an apostrophe is a punctuation mark (') used to show that letters have been left out, as in *can't* and *we'll*. It is also used with *s* to show who owns something, as in *the cat's paws* (one cat), or *the cats' paws* (more than one cat).

apothecary *NOUN* **apothecaries**
(*historical*)
a person who prepared and sold medicines

app *NOUN* **apps**
an app is a computer program with a single function, especially one that you download to a mobile phone

appal *VERB* **appals, appalling, appalled**
to appal someone is to shock them a lot
• *The violence appalled everyone.*

appalling *ADJECTIVE*
dreadful, shocking • *The room was in an appalling mess.*

apparatus *NOUN* **apparatuses**
an apparatus is a set of equipment for a special use

apparent *ADJECTIVE*
❶ clear, obvious • *He burst out laughing for no apparent reason.* ❷ appearing to be true • *Police are investigating an apparent theft.*

apparently *ADVERB*
as it seems; so it appears • *The door had apparently been locked.*

appeal *VERB* **appeals, appealing, appealed**
❶ to appeal to someone for something is to ask for it when you need it badly
'Is there nothing we can do?' asked the Ladybird, appealing to James.—JAMES AND THE GIANT PEACH, Roald Dahl
❷ if something appeals to someone, it interests or attracts them • *Rock-climbing has never appealed to me.* ❸ to appeal against a decision is to ask for it to be changed

appeal *NOUN* **appeals**
❶ an appeal is asking for something you need ❷ appeal is what makes something interesting • *The book has a lot of appeal for both kids and adults.* ❸ an appeal is asking for a decision to be changed

appear *VERB* **appears, appearing, appeared**
❶ to appear is to become visible ❷ to appear is also to seem • *They appeared very anxious.* ❸ to appear in a film or play is to take part in it

appearance *NOUN* **appearances**
❶ coming into sight ❷ taking part in a play, film, show, etc. ❸ what someone looks like ❹ what something seems to be

appease *VERB* **appeases, appeasing, appeased**
to appease someone is to make them peaceful or calm, often by giving them what they want

a b c d e f g h i j k l m n o p q r s t u v w x y z

appendicitis *NOUN*
an inflammation or disease of the appendix

appendix *NOUN* **appendixes** *or* **appendices**
❶ a small tube leading off from the intestines in the body ❷ an extra section at the end of a book

PLURAL ALERT! Each sense of **appendix** has a different plural. People have *appendixes* but books have *appendices*.

appetite *NOUN* **appetites**
a desire for something, especially for food

appetizer (*also* **appetiser**) *NOUN* **appetizers**
something you eat or drink before a meal, to give you an appetite

appetizing (*also* **appetising**) *ADJECTIVE*
looking or smelling good to eat

applaud *VERB* **applauds**, **applauding**, **applauded**
to applaud someone or something is to show that you like them, especially by clapping

applause *NOUN*
clapping or cheering after someone has given a speech or given a performance

apple *NOUN* **apples**
a round fruit with skin that is red, green or yellow

appliance *NOUN* **appliances**
a device or gadget

applicable *ADJECTIVE*
❶ that applies to someone • *This rule is now applicable to everyone.* ❷ relevant • *Ignore any questions which are not applicable.*

applicant *NOUN* **applicants**
someone who applies for something, for example a job

application *NOUN* **applications**
❶ an application is a letter or form you use to ask for something important, such as a job ❷ an application is a program for a computer or mobile phone that allows you to perform a particular activity on it ❸ application is when you make a lot of effort to do something

apply *VERB* **applies**, **applying**, **applied**
❶ to apply something is to put it on something else • *Apply a generous amount of sun cream.* ❷ to apply for a job is to write formally and ask for it ❸ to apply to someone is to concern them • *These rules apply to everybody.* ❹ to apply yourself to something is to give it all your attention

appoint *VERB* **appoints**, **appointing**, **appointed**
❶ to appoint someone is to choose them for a job ❷ to appoint a time and place for a meeting is to decide when and where to have it

appointment *NOUN* **appointments**
❶ an arrangement to meet or visit someone • *an appointment with the dentist* ❷ choosing someone for a job • *the appointment of a new teacher*

appreciate *VERB* **appreciates**, **appreciating**, **appreciated**
❶ to appreciate something is to enjoy or value it ❷ to appreciate a fact is to understand it • *We didn't appreciate how much danger we were in.*
➤ **appreciation** *NOUN*

appreciative *ADJECTIVE*
an appreciative person or group shows how much they enjoy or value something • *I enjoy playing to an appreciative audience.*

apprehension *NOUN* **apprehensions**
nervous fear or worry
➤ **apprehensive** *ADJECTIVE*

apprentice *NOUN* **apprentices**
someone who is learning a trade or craft
It was the custom that when a clockmaker's apprentice finished his period of service, he made a new figure for the great clock of Glockenheim.
—CLOCKWORK, Philip Pullman
➤ **apprenticeship** *NOUN* the time when someone is an apprentice

approach *VERB* **approaches**, **approaching**, **approached**
❶ to approach a place is to come near to it ❷ to approach someone is to go to them with a request or offer ❸ to approach a problem or difficulty is to start solving it

approach *NOUN* **approaches**
❶ coming near to a place ❷ a way of tackling

a problem • *Let's try a different approach.*
❸ a way or road leading up to a building
• *The approach to the house had trees on each side.*

approachable *ADJECTIVE*
friendly and easy to talk to

appropriate *ADJECTIVE*
suitable

approval *NOUN*
thinking well of someone or something

approve *VERB* **approves**, **approving**, **approved**
to approve of someone or something is to think they are good or suitable

approximate *ADJECTIVE*
roughly correct but not exact • *What is your approximate height?*
➤ **approximately** *ADVERB*

approximation *NOUN* **approximations**
something that is a rough estimate and not exact

apricot *NOUN* **apricots**
a juicy orange-coloured fruit like a small peach, with a stone in it

April *NOUN*
the fourth month of the year
DID YOU KNOW? April is named after *Aphrodite*, the Greek goddess of love and beauty.

April fool *NOUN*
someone who is fooled on April Fool's Day (1 April)

apron *NOUN* **aprons**
a piece of clothing worn over the front of your body to protect your clothes

apt *ADJECTIVE*
❶ likely to do something • *He is apt to be careless.* ❷ suitable • *I need to find an apt quotation.*

aptitude *NOUN* **aptitudes**
a talent in something • *You have a real aptitude for music.*

aquarium *NOUN* **aquariums**
a tank or building for keeping live fish

aquatic *ADJECTIVE*
to do with water and swimming • *water polo and other aquatic sports*

aqueduct *NOUN* **aqueducts**
a bridge that carries water across a valley

Arab *NOUN* **Arabs**
a member of a people living in parts of the Middle East and North Africa
➤ **Arabian** *ADJECTIVE*

Arabic *NOUN*
the language of the Arab people
DID YOU KNOW? The words **algebra**, **monsoon** and **zero** come from Arabic.

Arabic numerals *PLURAL NOUN*
the figures 1, 2, 3, 4 and so on (compare **Roman numerals**)

arable *ADJECTIVE*
to do with the growing of crops

arbitrary (*say* ar-bi-trer-ee) *ADJECTIVE*
done or chosen at random or without a proper reason • *It was an arbitrary decision.*

arc *NOUN* **arcs**
part of the circumference of a circle, a curve

arcade *NOUN* **arcades**
a covered place to walk, with shops down each side

arch *NOUN* **arches**
a curved structure that helps to support a bridge or building

arch *VERB* **arches**, **arching**, **arched**
to curve
The wind itself had ceased and a brilliant, deep blue sky arched high over the moorland.—THE SECRET GARDEN, Frances Hodgson Burnett

archaeology (*say* ar-kee-ol-o-jee) *NOUN*
the study of ancient people from the remains of their buildings
➤ **archaeologist** *NOUN*

archbishop *NOUN* **archbishops**
the chief bishop of a region

archer *NOUN* **archers**
someone who shoots with a bow and arrows

archery *NOUN*
the sport of shooting with a bow and arrows

a
b
c
d
e
f
g
h
i
j
k
l
m
n
o
p
q
r
s
t
u
v
w
x
y
z

architect (*say* ar-ki-tekt) NOUN **architects**
someone whose work is to design buildings

architecture NOUN
❶ the work of designing buildings ❷ a style of building • *ancient Roman architecture*

Arctic NOUN
the area round the North Pole

Arctic ADJECTIVE
in the Arctic or to do with the Arctic • *a famous Arctic explorer*

are VERB (*plural and 2nd person singular present tense of* **be**)

area NOUN **areas**
❶ part of a country, place, etc. ❷ the space occupied by something • *The area of this room is 20 square metres.*

arena (*say* a-ree-na) NOUN **arenas**
❶ the level space in the middle of a stadium or sports ground ❷ the place where a sports event takes place

aren't
short for *are not* • *Aren't you ready yet?*

argue VERB **argues, arguing, argued**
❶ to argue with someone is to quarrel with them ❷ to argue is also to give reasons for something • *She argued that it was wrong to eat meat.*

argument NOUN **arguments**
❶ a quarrel ❷ a reason someone gives to try to convince someone about something

arid ADJECTIVE
dry and barren

arise VERB **arises, arising, arose, arisen**
❶ to arise is to appear or to come into existence ❷ (*old use*) to rise; to stand up • *'Arise, Sir Lancelot.'*

aristocrat (*say* a-ris-to-krat) NOUN **aristocrats**
a nobleman or noblewoman
➤ **aristocratic** ADJECTIVE

arithmetic NOUN
the study of using numbers and working things out with them

ark NOUN **arks**
in the Bible, the ship in which Noah and his family escaped the Flood

arm NOUN **arms**
❶ the part of your body between your shoulder and your hand ❷ the sleeve of a coat or dress ❸ the side part of a chair, on which you can rest your arm

arm VERB **arms, arming, armed**
❶ to arm people is to give them weapons ❷ to arm is to prepare for war

armada (*say* ar-mah-da) NOUN **armadas**
a fleet of warships, especially the Spanish Armada which attacked England in 1588

armadillo NOUN **armadillos**
a South American animal whose body is covered with a shell of bony plates

armchair NOUN **armchairs**
a chair with parts on either side to rest your arms on

armed forces PLURAL NOUN
the army, navy and air force of a country

armful NOUN **armfuls**
as much of something as you can hold in your arms • *Mel was carrying an armful of books.*

armistice NOUN **armistices**
an agreement to stop fighting in a war or battle

armour NOUN
armour is a metal covering to protect people or things in battle
➤ **armoured** ADJECTIVE

armpit NOUN **armpits**
the hollow part under your arm at your shoulder

arms PLURAL NOUN
❶ weapons • *Lay down your arms.* ❷ a coat of arms

army NOUN **armies**
❶ a large number of soldiers ready to fight ❷ a large group • *They had an army of supporters.*

aroma (*say* a-roh-ma) NOUN **aromas**
a pleasant smell, for example of food
➤ **aromatic** ADJECTIVE

arose *VERB* (*past tense of* **arise**)

around *ADVERB, PREPOSITION*
❶ round • *A group of people stood around the platform.* ❷ about • *Please stop running around.*

arouse *VERB* **arouses**, **arousing**, **aroused**
❶ to arouse someone is to make them wake up ❷ to arouse feelings in someone is to cause them to have those feelings

arrange *VERB* **arranges**, **arranging**, **arranged**
❶ to arrange things is to put them all in the position you want ❷ to arrange a meeting or event is to organize it ❸ to arrange to do something is to make sure that it happens

arrangement *NOUN* **arrangements**
❶ arrangement is how you arrange or display something, for example flowers or a table setting ❷ an arrangement is something you agree with someone else • *We made an arrangement to meet outside the cinema.*

array *NOUN* **arrays**
a display of things for people to see • *There was a huge array of pots and pans.*

arrears *PLURAL NOUN*
➤ **in arrears** owing money • *He's in arrears with his rent.*

arrest *VERB* **arrests**, **arresting**, **arrested**
❶ to arrest someone is to take hold of them by the power of the law ❷ to arrest something is to stop it • *The doctors were trying to arrest the spread of disease.*

arrest *NOUN* **arrests**
taking hold of someone by the power of the law
➤ **under arrest** taken in and held by the police

arrival *NOUN* **arrivals**
❶ an arrival is when someone or something arrives at a place ❷ an arrival is also someone who is new or has just arrived • *Have you met the new arrivals?*

arrive *VERB* **arrives**, **arriving**, **arrived**
❶ to arrive at a place is to get there at the end of a journey ❷ to arrive is also to happen • *The great day finally arrived.*

arrogance *NOUN*
arrogance is a feeling someone has that they are more important than anyone else

arrogant *ADJECTIVE*
an arrogant person is unpleasantly proud and thinks they are more important than anyone else

arrow *NOUN* **arrows**
❶ a pointed stick shot from a bow ❷ a sign used to show direction or position

arsenal *NOUN* **arsenals**
a place where bullets, shells and weapons are made or stored

arsenic *NOUN*
a strong poison made from a metallic element

arson *NOUN*
the crime of deliberately setting fire to a building

art *NOUN* **arts**
❶ art is producing something by drawing or painting or sculpture ❷ the arts are subjects such as history and languages, as distinct from the sciences ❸ an art is also a skill in something • *the art of public speaking*

artefact *NOUN* **artefacts**
an object made by humans, especially one from the past that is studied by archaeologists

artery *NOUN* **arteries**
a tube that carries blood from your heart to other parts of your body

artful *ADJECTIVE*
clever at getting what you want by fooling people
➤ **artfully** *ADVERB*

arthritis (*say* arth-ry-tiss) *NOUN*
a medical condition that makes joints in the body painful and stiff

article *NOUN* **articles**
❶ an object or thing that you can touch or pick up ❷ a piece of writing published in a newspaper or magazine ❸ (*grammar*) the word *a* or *an* (called the **indefinite article**) or the word *the* (called the **definite article**)

a b c d e f g h i j k l m n o p q r s t u v w x y z

articulate (*say* ar-**tik**-yoo-lat) *ADJECTIVE*
an articulate person is able to speak clearly and fluently

articulate (*say* ar-**tik**-yoo-layt) *VERB*
articulates, articulating, articulated
to articulate a word or phrase is to pronounce it clearly
➤ **articulation** *NOUN*

artificial *ADJECTIVE*
made by human beings and not by nature
➤ **artificially** *ADVERB*

artillery *NOUN* **artilleries**
❶ artillery is a collection of large guns
❷ the artillery is the part of the army that uses large guns

artist *NOUN* **artists**
❶ someone who produces art, especially a painter ❷ an entertainer

artistic *ADJECTIVE*
❶ to do with art and artists ❷ showing skill and beauty • *an artistic flower arrangement*
➤ **artistically** *ADVERB*

artistry *NOUN*
the skill of an artist • *The carving showed great artistry.*

as *CONJUNCTION, ADVERB, PREPOSITION*
❶ you use **as** to link words and phrases together • *As it was late, everyone had gone home.* • *She slipped as she got off the bus.* • *It is not as easy as you think.* • *Peter was dressed as a pirate.* ❷ you can also use **as** to make similes • *as flat as a pancake* • *as cold as ice*

asbestos *NOUN*
a fireproof material that is made up of fine soft fibres

ascend *VERB* **ascends, ascending, ascended**
to ascend something like a hill or staircase is to go up it

ascent *NOUN* **ascents**
an ascent is a climb, usually a hard or long one

ash *NOUN* **ashes**
❶ ash is the powder that is left after something has been burned ❷ an ash or ash tree is a tree with silvery bark and winged seeds

ashamed *ADJECTIVE*
feeling shame

ashen *ADJECTIVE*
grey and pale • *Her face was ashen.*

ashore *ADVERB*
on the shore

Asian *ADJECTIVE*
to do with Asia or its people

Asian *NOUN* **Asians**
a person from Asia

aside *ADVERB*
to or at one side; away • *Step aside and let them pass.*

aside *NOUN* **asides**
something said so that only some people will hear

ask *VERB* **asks, asking, asked**
❶ to ask someone something is to speak to them so as to find out or get something • *I asked the stranger her name.* • *Can I ask you to keep a secret?* ❷ to ask someone to a party or event is to invite them to it
➤ **to ask for it** *or* **to ask for trouble** (*informal*) is to do something that will bring trouble

askew (*say* as-**kew**) *ADJECTIVE*
not straight or level as it should be • *His tie was all askew.*

asleep *ADVERB, ADJECTIVE*
sleeping

aspect *NOUN* **aspects**
❶ one part of a problem or situation • *Perhaps the worst aspect of winter is the dark mornings.* ❷ the direction something such as a building or a room faces • *This room has a southern aspect.*

asphalt (*say* **ass**-falt) *NOUN*
a sticky black substance which is mixed with gravel to make a surface for roads and playgrounds

aspirin *NOUN* **aspirins**
a drug used to relieve pain or reduce fever

ass *NOUN* **asses**
❶ a donkey ❷ (*informal*) a fool • *You are an ass!*

assassinate VERB assassinates, assassinating, assassinated
to assassinate a ruler or leader is to murder them to stop them having power
➤ **assassination** NOUN

assault NOUN assaults
a violent attack on someone

assault VERB assaults, assaulting, assaulted
to assault someone is to attack them violently

assemble VERB assembles, assembling, assembled
❶ to assemble people or things is to bring them together in one place ❷ to assemble is to come together in one place • *Please assemble in the playground.*

assembly NOUN assemblies
❶ an assembly is when people come together and someone speaks to them, for example in a school ❷ an assembly is also a group of people who meet together, such as a parliament ❸ assembly of a machine or piece of furniture is putting the parts together to make it

assent NOUN
assent is agreement or permission to do something • *Have your parents given their assent?*

assert VERB asserts, asserting, asserted
to assert something is to say it strongly and clearly
➤ **assertion** NOUN

assertive ADJECTIVE
speaking or behaving strongly and firmly

assess VERB assesses, assessing, assessed
to assess someone or something is to decide how good or useful they are

assessment NOUN assessments
an opinion about something after thinking about it carefully

asset NOUN assets
something useful or valuable to someone • *Katie is a real asset to the team.*

assets PLURAL NOUN
the property of a person or company that they could sell to raise money if they wanted to

assign VERB assigns, assigning, assigned
to assign a job or task to someone is to give it to them to do • *A guard was assigned to watch the prisoner.*

assignment NOUN assignments
a piece of work that someone is given to do

assist VERB assists, assisting, assisted
to assist someone is to help them, usually in a practical way

assistance NOUN
help someone gets when they need information or support

assistant NOUN assistants
❶ someone whose job is to help another person in their work ❷ someone who serves in a shop

associate (*say* a-soh-shi-ayt) VERB associates, associating, associated
❶ to associate one thing with another is to connect them in your mind • *People associate the number 13 with bad luck.* ❷ to associate with someone is to spend time with them • *He likes to associate with famous people.*

association NOUN associations
❶ an organization for people sharing an interest or doing the same work • *the local athletics association* ❷ a connection between things

assonance (*say* ass-on-ans) NOUN
assonance is when the same vowel sound is repeated, for special effect, as in *The bright kite flies high in the sky.*

assorted ADJECTIVE
of various kinds; mixed and different
A large wooden trunk stood open at the foot of his bed, revealing a cauldron, broomstick, black robes and assorted spellbooks.—HARRY POTTER AND THE GOBLET OF FIRE, J. K. Rowling

assortment NOUN assortments
a mixture of different things or people

assume VERB assumes, assuming, assumed
to assume something is to think it is true or likely without being sure of it • *I assume you will be coming tomorrow.*
➤ **assumed** ADJECTIVE an assumed name is one that is not the person's real name

a
b
c
d
e
f
g
h
i
j
k
l
m
n
o
p
q
r
s
t
u
v
w
x
y
z

assumption *NOUN* **assumptions**
something you assume or take for granted

assurance *NOUN* **assurances**
❶ assurance is a feeling of certainty about something ❷ an assurance is a promise or guarantee

assure *VERB* **assures**, **assuring**, **assured**
to assure someone is to tell someone something definite • *I assure you that you will be quite safe.*

asterisk *NOUN* **asterisks**
a star-shaped sign (*) used in printing and writing to draw attention to something

asteroid *NOUN* **asteroids**
a small rocky body that orbits the sun, found mainly between the orbits of Mars and Jupiter
SPOT THE DIFFERENCE! Asteroids orbit the sun, but **meteors** enter the earth's atmosphere.

asthma (*say* **ass**-ma) *NOUN*
a lung condition that makes breathing difficult

asthmatic *ADJECTIVE*
suffering from asthma

asthmatic *NOUN* **asthmatics**
someone who is suffering from asthma

astonish *VERB* **astonishes**, **astonishing**, **astonished**
to astonish someone is to surprise them very much
➤ **astonishment** *NOUN*

astound *VERB* **astounds**, **astounding**, **astounded**
to astound someone is to amaze or shock them very much

astrology *NOUN*
astrology is studying how the planets and stars may affect people's lives
➤ **astrologer** *NOUN*

astronaut *NOUN* **astronauts**
someone who travels in a spacecraft
DID YOU KNOW? The word **astronaut** comes from Greek words meaning 'star sailor'.

astronomical *ADJECTIVE*
❶ to do with astronomy ❷ (*informal*) extremely large • *The cost of the party was astronomical.*

astronomy *NOUN*
astronomy is studying the sun, moon, planets and stars
➤ **astronomer** *NOUN*

at *PREPOSITION*
showing where someone or something is, or when something happens • *I was at the hospital all morning.* • *The postbox is at the end of the road.* • *The match starts at 3 o'clock.*

ate *VERB* (past tense of **eat**)
• *We ate the rest of the sandwiches.*

atheist *NOUN* **atheists**
someone who does not believe in a God
➤ **atheism** *NOUN*

athlete *NOUN* **athletes**
someone who is good at athletics or other sports

athletic *ADJECTIVE*
❶ to do with athletics • *an athletic competition* ❷ good at sports; strong

athletics *PLURAL NOUN*
physical exercises and sports such as running and jumping

atlas *NOUN* **atlases**
a book of maps
DID YOU KNOW? Atlases are named after *Atlas*, a character in Greek mythology who was made to carry the universe on his shoulders, and who was often pictured in old books of maps.

atmosphere *NOUN* **atmospheres**
❶ the earth's atmosphere is the air around it ❷ an atmosphere is a feeling you get in a room or at a place • *There was a happy atmosphere at the fairground.*

atmospheric *ADJECTIVE*
❶ to do with the earth's atmosphere ❷ having a strong atmosphere

atoll *NOUN* **atolls**
a ring-shaped island of coral in the sea

atom *NOUN* **atoms**
the smallest possible part of a chemical element
➤ **atomic** *ADJECTIVE*

at once *ADVERB*
immediately • *Come here at once!*

atrocious (*say* a-**troh**-shus) *ADJECTIVE*
awful; terrible

atrocity *NOUN* **atrocities**
a terrible and cruel act, such as the killing of a large number of people

attach *VERB* **attaches**, **attaching**, **attached**
❶ to attach one thing to another is to fix or fasten it ❷ (*computing*) to attach a document is to send it with an email message

attached *ADJECTIVE*
to be attached to someone is to be fond of them

attachment *NOUN* **attachments**
❶ an extra part you fix to a device so that it can do a special kind of work • *The garden hose has an attachment for washing cars.* ❷ a fondness or friendship • *The boys felt a real attachment to their pet hamster.* ❸ (*computing*) a document that you send to someone with an email message

attack *NOUN* **attacks**
❶ an attempt to hurt someone with violence ❷ an attempt to harm someone or something by using unfriendly words ❸ a sudden illness or pain

attack *VERB* **attacks**, **attacking**, **attacked**
to attack someone is to try to hurt them with violence, or to harm them with unfriendly words

attain *VERB* **attains**, **attaining**, **attained**
to attain something is to reach or achieve it • *I have attained Grade 3 on the violin.*
➤ **attainment** *NOUN*

attempt *VERB* **attempts**, **attempting**, **attempted**
to attempt to do something is to make an effort to do it

attempt *NOUN* **attempts**
an attempt at something is making an effort to do it

attend *VERB* **attends**, **attending**, **attended**
❶ to attend something like a meeting or a wedding is to be there ❷ to attend school or college is to be a pupil or student there ❸ to attend to someone is to look after them, especially when they are ill ❹ to attend to something is to spend time dealing with it • *She had some business to attend to.*

attendance *NOUN* **attendances**
❶ attendance is being somewhere where you are supposed to be ❷ the attendance at an event is the number of people who are there to see it

attendant *NOUN* **attendants**
someone who helps or goes with another person

attention *NOUN*
giving care or thought to someone or something
➤ **to stand to attention** is to stand with your feet together and your arms straight down, like soldiers on parade

attentive *ADJECTIVE*
listening closely
➤ **attentively** *ADVERB*

attic *NOUN* **attics**
a room or space under the roof of a house
DID YOU KNOW? The word **attic** comes from *Attica*, an area in ancient Greece which was famous for the special design of its upper buildings.

attitude *NOUN* **attitudes**
your attitude is the way you think or feel about something, and the way you behave

attract *VERB* **attracts**, **attracting**, **attracted**
❶ to attract someone is to seem pleasant to them and get their attention or interest ❷ to attract something unwelcome is to make it come • *Empty bottles of drink attract wasps.* ❸ to attract something is also to pull it by a physical force like magnetism • *Magnets attract metal pins.*

attraction *NOUN* **attractions**
❶ attraction is the power to attract someone ❷ an attraction is something pleasant that people like to see, such as a fair or a rock concert

attractive *ADJECTIVE*
❶ interesting or welcome • *They made us an attractive offer of a free holiday.* ❷ pleasant, good-looking

a b c d e f g h i j k l m n o p q r s t u v w x y z

auburn ADJECTIVE
auburn hair is a reddish-brown colour

auction NOUN **auctions**
a sale at which things are sold to the person who offers the most money for them
➤ **auctioneer** NOUN an official in charge of an auction

audible ADJECTIVE
loud enough to be heard • *an audible whisper*

audience NOUN **audiences**
❶ the people who have come to see or hear an event like a concert or film ❷ a formal interview with an important person
• *an audience with the King*

audiobook NOUN **audiobooks**
a spoken, recorded version of a printed book

audition NOUN **auditions**
a test to see if an actor or musician is suitable for a part

auditorium (*say* aw-dit-**or**-i-um) NOUN **auditoriums**
the part of a building where the audience sits

August NOUN
the eighth month of the year
DID YOU KNOW? **August** is named after the Roman emperor *Augustus*, who reformed the Roman calendar.

auk (*say* awk) NOUN **auks**
a northern seabird with a black head and short wings

aunt NOUN **aunts**
❶ the sister of your mother or father
❷ the wife or female partner of your uncle or aunt

auntie, aunty NOUN **aunties** (*informal*)
an aunt

aural ADJECTIVE
using the sense of hearing • *an aural comprehension test*

austere ADJECTIVE
❶ not having much comfort or luxury
❷ an austere person is severe and strict

Australian ADJECTIVE
to do with Australia or its people

Australian NOUN **Australians**
a person from Australia

authentic ADJECTIVE
real; genuine
➤ **authenticity** NOUN

author NOUN **authors**
the writer of a book or other work such as a poem or magazine article

authority NOUN **authorities**
❶ authority is the power to give orders to other people ❷ an authority on a subject is an expert on it or a book that gives you reliable information about it

authorize (*also* **authorise**) VERB
authorizes, authorizing, authorized
❶ to authorize something is to give official permission for it ❷ to authorize someone to do something is to give them permission to do it

autism NOUN
someone who has autism experiences the world differently from other people, and may understand things and communicate with others differently from other people
➤ **autistic** ADJECTIVE

autobiography NOUN **autobiographies**
the story of someone's life that they have written themselves
➤ **autobiographical** ADJECTIVE

autograph NOUN **autographs**
the signature of a famous person
autograph VERB **autographs, autographing, autographed**
when a famous person autographs something, they sign it with their name

automatic ADJECTIVE
❶ an automatic process is one that works on its own, without needing attention or control by humans ❷ an automatic action is one that you do without specially thinking about it
➤ **automatically** ADVERB

automation (*say* aw-tom-**ay**-shun) NOUN
making processes automatic, and using machines instead of people to do work

automobile NOUN **automobiles**
(*North American*)
a motor car

autumn (*say* aw-tum) *NOUN* **autumns**
the season when leaves fall off the trees, between summer and winter

SPELLING ALERT! There is a silent letter at the end of **autumn**. Think of the sentence *It's nice at the end of autumn* to help you remember!

autumnal (*say* aw-**tum**-nal) *ADJECTIVE*
in autumn; to do with autumn

auxiliary verb *NOUN* **auxiliary verbs**
a type of verb that is used in forming parts of other verbs • *In 'I have finished', the auxiliary is 'have'.*

available *ADJECTIVE*
able to be found or used • *Fresh strawberries are available in June.*
➤ **availability** *NOUN*

avalanche (*say* av-a-lahnsh) *NOUN* **avalanches**
a sudden heavy fall of rocks or snow down the side of a mountain

avenue *NOUN* **avenues**
a wide street, usually with trees along each side

average *NOUN* **averages**
❶ an average is the number you get by adding several amounts together and dividing the total by the number of amounts • *The average of 2, 4, 6 and 8 is 5.* ❷ the average is the usual or ordinary standard • *Their work is well above the average.*

average *ADJECTIVE*
of the usual or ordinary standard
Hiccup was just absolutely average, the kind of unremarkable, skinny, freckled boy who was easy to overlook in a crowd.—HOW TO BE A PIRATE, Cressida Cowell

avert *VERB* **averts, averting, averted**
❶ to avert something is to turn it away • *People averted their eyes from the accident.* ❷ to avert something is also to stop it happening • *The train driver's quick reaction had averted a disaster.*

aviary *NOUN* **aviaries**
a place where birds are kept

aviation *NOUN*
aviation is flying in aircraft

avid *ADJECTIVE*
keen; eager • *Matilda has always been an avid reader.*

avocado *NOUN* **avocados**
a pear-shaped fruit with a creamy green flesh

avoid *VERB* **avoids, avoiding, avoided**
❶ to avoid something or someone is to keep yourself away from them • *They try to avoid their relations at Christmas.* ❷ to avoid something is also to find a way of not doing it • *We wanted to avoid extra homework.*

await *VERB* **awaits, awaiting, awaited**
to await someone or something is to wait for them

awake *ADJECTIVE*
not sleeping

awake *VERB* **awakes, awaking, awoke, awoken**
to awake is to wake up

awaken *VERB* **awakens, awakening, awakened**
❶ to awaken is to wake up ❷ to awaken someone is to wake them up

award *NOUN* **awards**
something such as a prize given to a person who has done something successful

award *VERB* **awards, awarding, awarded**
to award something to someone is to give it to them as an award

aware *ADJECTIVE*
to be aware of something is to know about it or realize it is there • *They soon became aware of the danger.*
➤ **awareness** *NOUN*

away *ADVERB*
❶ at a distance or somewhere else • *I wish those people would go away.* • *The ice cream melted so I threw it away.* ❷ you can also use **away** with special meanings • *They are working away at their exams.* • *The noise gradually died away.*

away *ADJECTIVE*
an away match is one that is played at the opponents' ground

awe *NOUN*
fear and wonder • *The mountains filled him with awe.*

A
B
C
D
E
F
G
H
I
J
K
L
M
N
O
P
Q
R
S
T
U
V
W
X
Y
Z

awesome *ADJECTIVE*
❶ very impressive and powerful
For a brief moment, the terrible Red-Hot Smoke-Belching Gruncher made the lake boil and smoke like a volcano, then the fire went out and the awesome beast disappeared under the waves. —BILLY AND THE MINPINS, Roald Dahl
❷ (*informal*) very good; excellent • *That new video game is awesome!*

awful *ADJECTIVE*
❶ very bad; terrible • *The phone reception here is awful.* ❷ (*informal*) very big or great • *There's still an awful lot to do!*
➤ **awfulness** *NOUN*

awfully *ADVERB* (*informal*)
very, extremely • *It's getting awfully hot in here.*

awkward *ADJECTIVE*
❶ difficult to use or cope with • *The box was an awkward shape.* ❷ embarrassed and uncomfortable • *He always felt awkward among strangers.*

awoke *VERB* (*past tense of* awake)

awoken *VERB* (*past participle of* awake)

axe *NOUN* axes
a tool for chopping

axe *VERB* axes, axing, axed (*informal*)
to axe something is to cancel or abolish it

axis *NOUN* axes
❶ a line through the centre of a spinning object • *The earth spins on its axis.* ❷ a line dividing something in half

axle *NOUN* axles
the rod through the centre of a wheel, on which it turns

azalea (*say* a-**zay**-li-a) *NOUN* azaleas
a flowering shrub like a rhododendron

Aztec *NOUN* Aztecs
one of a native Indian people who lived in Mexico before the Spanish conquest of 1521

Aztec *ADJECTIVE*
to do with the Aztecs

azure *ADJECTIVE*
sky-blue

Bb

babble *VERB* babbles, babbling, babbled
❶ to babble is to talk quickly, without making much sense ❷ to babble is also to make a murmuring or bubbling sound • *They came across a babbling brook.*

baboon *NOUN* baboons
a large kind of monkey with a long muzzle

baby *NOUN* babies
❶ a very young child ❷ a baby animal is a very young animal • *a baby elephant*

babyish *ADJECTIVE*
silly and childish

babysit *VERB* babysits, babysitting, babysat
to babysit is to look after a child while its parents are out

babysitter *NOUN* babysitters
someone who babysits

bachelor *NOUN* bachelors
a man who has not married

back *NOUN* backs
❶ the part of your body between your shoulders and your bottom ❷ the upper part of a four-legged animal's body ❸ the part of a thing that is furthest away from the front • *The back of the house faces a river.*

back *ADJECTIVE*
placed at or near the back • *Let's sit in the back row.*

back *ADVERB*
❶ backwards or towards the back • *Go back!*
❷ to where someone or something was before • *When will you be coming back?* ❸ to an earlier time • *Think back to when you were little.*

back *VERB* backs, backing, backed
❶ to back a vehicle is to move it backwards
❷ to back someone is to support them or give them help
➤ **to back down** is to admit you were wrong about something
➤ **to back out** is to decide not to get involved in something

➤ **to back someone up** is to give them support or help

➤ **to back something up** (*computing*) is to make a spare copy of a file for safety

backache NOUN **backaches**
a pain in your back, usually lasting for a long time

backbone NOUN **backbones**
your backbone is your spine

background NOUN **backgrounds**
❶ the background of a picture or view is the part that is farthest away from you, behind the main subject ❷ the background to an event or situation is all the things that help to explain why it happened ❸ a person's background is their family and education, and what they have done in their life

➤ **in the background** not noticeable or obvious

backing NOUN
❶ backing is support or help ❷ backing is also the material that forms a support or back for something ❸ the backing on a pop song is the music that is played or sung to support the main singer or tune

backlash NOUN **backlashes**
a strong and often angry reaction to something

backlog NOUN **backlogs**
a backlog is work that should have been finished but still has to be done

backpack NOUN **backpacks**
a bag you carry on your back; a rucksack

backside NOUN **backsides** (*informal*)
your backside is your bottom

backstroke NOUN
a stroke you use when swimming on your back

back-up NOUN **back-ups** (*computing*)
a spare copy of a file stored for safety in case the original is lost or damaged

backward ADJECTIVE
❶ facing or aimed towards the back • *She walked past him without a backward glance.* ❷ slow in learning or developing

backward ADVERB
backwards

backwards ADVERB
❶ towards the back ❷ with the back end going first ❸ in the opposite order to the usual one • *Can you say the alphabet backwards?*

backyard NOUN **backyards**
an open area at the back of a building

bacon NOUN
smoked or salted meat from the back or sides of a pig

bacteria PLURAL NOUN
tiny organisms that can cause diseases

bad ADJECTIVE **worse, worst**
❶ not good or well done • *I had a bad dream last night.* • *The acting in the film is really bad.* ❷ someone who is bad is wicked or naughty ❸ someone is bad at something when they can't do it very well • *I've always been bad at maths.* ❹ serious or unpleasant • *The skier had a bad fall.* ❺ harmful to your health • *Eating junk food is bad for you.*

➤ **not bad** fairly good, all right

baddy NOUN **baddies** (*informal*)
a bad person, especially in a story or a film • *Captain Hook is the baddy in Peter Pan.*

badge NOUN **badges**
a small piece of metal, plastic or cloth that you pin or sew on your clothes to tell people something about you, such as what club or school you belong to or what kind of thing you like

badger NOUN **badgers**
a grey animal with a black and white head, which lives underground and comes out at night to feed

badger VERB **badgers, badgering, badgered**
to badger someone is to keep asking them to do something • *He kept badgering his mother for his pocket money.*

badly ADVERB
❶ not well • *They did the work badly.* ❷ seriously • *He was badly wounded.* ❸ very much • *They needed sleep badly.*

➤ **badly off** poor or unfortunate

badminton NOUN
a game in which players use rackets to hit a light object called a *shuttlecock* backwards and forwards across a high net

bad-tempered ADJECTIVE
a bad-tempered person is one who often becomes angry

baffle VERB baffles, baffling, baffled
to baffle someone is to puzzle or confuse them completely

bag NOUN bags
a container made of soft material, for holding or carrying things
➤ **bags of something** (informal) plenty
• There's bags of room.

bag VERB bags, bagging, bagged
to bag something is to get hold of it or take it
• I bagged the best seat.

bagel NOUN bagels
a ring-shaped bread roll

baggage NOUN
baggage is the suitcases and bags you take on a journey

baggy ADJECTIVE baggier, baggiest
baggy clothes hang loosely from your body
➤ **bagginess** NOUN

bagpipes PLURAL NOUN
bagpipes are a musical instrument you play by squeezing air out of a bag into a set of pipes

bail NOUN bails
❶ bail is money that has to be paid or promised so that a person accused of a crime will not be kept in prison before their trial ❷ bails are the two small pieces of wood placed on top of the stumps in cricket

bail VERB bails, bailing, bailed
to bail water out of a boat is to scoop it over the side

Bairam (say by-ram) NOUN Bairams
either of two Muslim festivals, one in the tenth month and one in the twelfth month of the Islamic year

Baisakhi (say by-sa-kee) NOUN
a Sikh festival held in April

bait NOUN
bait is a small amount of food put on a hook or in a trap to catch fish or animals

bait VERB baits, baiting, baited
to bait a hook or trap is to put the bait on it or in it, to catch fish or animals

bake VERB bakes, baking, baked
❶ to bake food is to cook it in an oven, especially bread or cakes ❷ to bake something like clay is to make it hard by heating it in an oven ❸ to bake is to become very hot, especially in the sun

baker NOUN bakers
someone who makes or sells bread and cakes

bakery NOUN bakeries
a place where bread is made or sold

baking powder NOUN
a special powder used in baking to make cakes rise

balance NOUN balances
❶ a person's balance is their feeling of being steady • He lost his balance and fell over. ❷ a balance is a device for weighing things, with two trays hanging from the ends of a horizontal bar ❸ the balance of a bank account is the difference between the money paid into it and the money taken out of it ❹ a balance is also an amount of money that someone owes • I will transfer you the balance on Saturday.

balance VERB balances, balancing, balanced
❶ to balance something is to keep it steady • He was balancing a tray on one hand. ❷ a balanced diet is one that has all the right kinds of food for being healthy

balcony NOUN balconies
❶ a platform built out from the wall of a building, with railings round it ❷ the upstairs part of a cinema or theatre

bald ADJECTIVE balder, baldest
a bald person does not have much hair or any hair on their head

bale NOUN bales
a large bundle of something like hay or straw, usually tied up tightly

bale VERB bales, baling, baled
➤ **to bale out** is to jump out of an aircraft with a parachute

ball NOUN balls
❶ a round object used in many games ❷ anything that is made into a round shape • a ball of string ❸ a grand or formal party where people dance

ballad *NOUN* **ballads**
a simple song or poem that tells a story

ballerina (*say* bal-e-**ree**-na) *NOUN*
ballerinas
a female ballet dancer

ballet (*say* **bal**-ay) *NOUN* **ballets**
a form of dancing in which a group of dancers perform special steps and movements to tell a story to music

ballet dancer *NOUN* **ballet dancers**
someone who performs ballet

balloon *NOUN* **balloons**
❶ a small rubber pouch that you fill up with air or gas, especially for parties or celebrations • *a big balloon saying 'Happy Birthday!'* ❷ a large bag filled with a light gas or hot air, often with a basket to carry passengers • *a daring flight in a hot-air balloon* ❸ a round shape in a strip cartoon containing the words the characters are saying

ballot (*say* **bal**-ot) *NOUN* **ballots**
a method of voting in secret by making a mark on a piece of paper and putting it into a box

ballroom *NOUN* **ballrooms**
a large room where dances are held

bamboo *NOUN* **bamboos**
a tall tropical plant with hard hollow stems, used for making furniture

ban *VERB* **bans, banning, banned**
to ban something is to forbid people to do it

banana *NOUN* **bananas**
a long curved fruit with a yellow skin that you peel before eating the flesh inside

band *NOUN* **bands**
❶ a group of people playing music together ❷ an organized group of people doing something together ❸ a circular strip of something

band *VERB* **bands, banding, banded**
to band together is to join together to form an organized group

bandage (*say* **ban**-dij) *NOUN* **bandages**
a strip of material that you wrap round a wound to protect it

bandit *NOUN* **bandits**
a member of a gang of robbers who attack travellers

bandstand *NOUN* **bandstands**
a platform for a band playing music outdoors, usually in a park

bandwagon *NOUN* **bandwagons**
➤ **to jump** *or* **climb on the bandwagon** (*informal*) is to join in something that looks like being successful

bandy *ADJECTIVE* **bandier, bandiest**
bandy legs curve outwards at the knees

bang *NOUN* **bangs**
❶ a sudden loud noise ❷ a heavy blow or knock

bang *VERB* **bangs, banging, banged**
❶ to bang something is to hit or shut it noisily • *Don't bang the door when you go out.* ❷ to bang something is to knock it hard against something else • *She banged her knee on the desk.*

banger *NOUN* **bangers** (*informal*)
❶ a firework that explodes noisily ❷ a sausage ❸ a noisy old car

banish *VERB* **banishes, banishing, banished**
to banish someone is to punish them by sending them away and ordering them not to return
The wicked witch Duchess shall be banished for seven years to the tiny Isle of Stones where nothing grows and the sea-current is strong.—THE BRAVE WHALE, Alan Temperley
➤ **banishment** *NOUN*

banister *NOUN* **banisters**
a handrail beside a staircase

banjo *NOUN* **banjos**
a musical instrument like a small guitar with a round body

bank *NOUN* **banks**
❶ a business which looks after people's money ❷ the ground beside a river or lake ❸ a piece of raised or sloping ground ❹ a place where something is stored and collected • *a blood bank* ❺ a bank of clouds is a mass of them ❻ a bank of lights or switches is a row of them

bank *VERB* **banks, banking, banked**
❶ to bank money is to put it in a bank ❷ to bank is to lean over while changing

a
b
c
d
e
f
g
h
i
j
k
l
m
n
o
p
q
r
s
t
u
v
w
x
y
z

direction • *The plane banked as it turned to land.*

➤ **to bank on something** is to rely on it • *We're banking on the weather being good.*

bank holiday *NOUN* **bank holidays**
a public holiday

banknote *NOUN* **banknotes**
a piece of paper money

bankrupt *ADJECTIVE*
not able to pay all the money you owe
➤ **bankruptcy** *NOUN*

banner *NOUN* **banners**
❶ a large sign with a written message or symbol carried in a procession or demonstration ❷ a main title or image at the top of a newspaper or website

banquet (*say* bank-wit) *NOUN* **banquets**
a large formal dinner, often with speeches

banshee (*say* ban-shee) *NOUN* **banshees**
in Celtic mythology, a banshee is a female spirit who wails to warn of someone's death

Bantu *NOUN* **Bantu, Bantus**
❶ a member of a group of Central and Southern African peoples ❷ the group of languages spoken by these peoples
DID YOU KNOW? The words **banjo** and **chimpanzee** come from Bantu.

banyan *NOUN* **banyans**
an Indian fig tree with roots which hang down from its branches
Many of the banyan tree's branches had gone deep into the earth and come up again to form a deliciously cool grove.—SEASONS OF SPLENDOUR, Madhur Jaffrey

baobab (*say* bay-o-bab) *NOUN* **baobabs**
a tropical tree with a thick trunk and edible fruit
Now there were some terrible seeds on the planet that was the home of the little prince; and these were the seeds of the baobab.—THE LITTLE PRINCE, Antoine de Saint-Exupéry

baptism *NOUN* **baptisms**
baptism is the ceremony of baptizing someone

baptize (*also* **baptise**) *VERB* **baptizes, baptizing, baptized**
to baptize someone is to sprinkle them with water, or dip them in water, in a ceremony welcoming them into the Christian Church

bar *NOUN* **bars**
❶ a long piece of something hard • *a bar of solid iron* ❷ a counter or room where drinks and refreshments are served ❸ one of the small equal sections into which music is divided • *A waltz has three beats in a bar.*

bar *VERB* **bars, barring, barred**
❶ to bar something is to fasten it with a bar ❷ to bar someone from something is to prevent them from taking part in it ❸ to bar someone's way is to stop them getting past

barb *NOUN* **barbs**
a backward-curving point on a fish hook or spear, which makes it stick in more firmly

barbarian *NOUN* **barbarians**
(*historical*) an uncivilized or brutal person

barbaric *ADJECTIVE*
brutal and cruel • *the barbaric spectacle of gladiators fighting to the death*
➤ **barbarity** *NOUN*

barbecue *NOUN* **barbecues**
❶ a metal frame used for grilling food over a charcoal fire outdoors ❷ a party at which food is cooked outdoors on a barbecue

barbed wire *NOUN*
wire with sharp twisted spikes on it, used to make fences

barber *NOUN* **barbers**
someone whose job is to cut men's hair

bar chart *NOUN* **bar charts**
a diagram showing amounts as bars of equal width but different heights

barcode *NOUN* **barcodes**
a set of black lines that are printed on goods, library books, etc. so that they can be identified by a computer

bard *NOUN* **bards** (*old use*)
a poet or minstrel

bare *ADJECTIVE* **barer, barest**
❶ not covered with anything • *The trees were bare.* ❷ empty or almost empty • *The cupboard was bare.* ❸ only just enough • *They just had the bare necessities of life.*

bareback *ADJECTIVE, ADVERB*
riding on a horse without a saddle

barely *ADVERB*
only just; with difficulty • *They were barely able to see in the fog.*

bargain *NOUN* **bargains**
❶ something that you buy cheaply
❷ an agreement between two people to do something for each other • *I expect you to keep your side of the bargain.*
➤ **into the bargain** as well • *He spent all his money and got lost into the bargain.*

bargain *VERB* **bargains, bargaining, bargained**
to bargain over something is to argue over its price
➤ **to get more than you bargained for** is to get an unwelcome surprise

barge *NOUN* **barges**
a long flat-bottomed boat used especially on canals

barge *VERB* **barges, barging, barged**
to barge into someone is to bump clumsily into them or push them out of the way

baritone *NOUN* **baritones**
a singer with a male voice between a tenor and a bass

bark *NOUN* **barks**
❶ a bark is the sound made by a dog or a fox
❷ bark is the outer covering of a tree's branches or trunk

bark *VERB* **barks, barking, barked**
❶ a dog or fox barks when it makes its special sound ❷ you can say a person barks when they speak loudly or sharply
'Attention!' he barked in his fearsome monkey-trainer's voice.–THE TWITS, Roald Dahl

barley *NOUN*
a kind of grain which is used for food and to make beer

bar mitzvah *NOUN* **bar mitzvahs**
a religious ceremony for Jewish boys who have reached the age of 13, when they accept some of the responsibilities of an adult

barn *NOUN* **barns**
a building on a farm used to store things such as grain or hay

barnacle *NOUN* **barnacles**
a shellfish that attaches itself to rocks and the bottoms of ships

barometer (*say* ba-**rom**-it-er) *NOUN* **barometers**
an instrument that measures air pressure, used in forecasting the weather

baron *NOUN* **barons**
a member of the lowest rank of noblemen

baroness *NOUN* **baronesses**
a female baron or a baron's wife

barracks *NOUN* **barracks**
the buildings where soldiers live

barrage (*say* ba-**razh**) *NOUN* **barrages**
❶ heavy gunfire ❷ a large amount of something • *We received a barrage of complaints.* ❸ a dam or barrier built across a river to make the water deeper

barrel *NOUN* **barrels**
❶ a large container for liquids, with curved sides and flat ends ❷ the metal tube of a gun, through which the shot is fired

barren *ADJECTIVE*
barren land or plants cannot produce any crops or fruit

barricade *NOUN* **barricades**
a barrier, especially one put up quickly to block a street

barricade *VERB* **barricades, barricading, barricaded**
to barricade a place is to block or defend it with a barrier

barrier *NOUN* **barriers**
❶ a fence or wall put up to stop people getting past ❷ something that stops you doing something • *Lack of confidence can be a barrier to success.*

barrister *NOUN* **barristers**
a lawyer who presents legal cases in the higher courts

barrow *NOUN* **barrows**
❶ a small cart ❷ an ancient mound of earth over a grave

barter *VERB* **barters, bartering, bartered**
to barter is to exchange goods for other goods, without using money

base *NOUN* **bases**
❶ the lowest part of something, or the part on which something stands ❷ a place from which

a b c d e f g h i j k l m n o p q r s t u v w x y z

an organization like an army or business is controlled

base VERB **bases**, **basing**, **based**
to base one thing on another thing is to use the second thing as the starting point for the first • *She based the story on an event in her own childhood.*

baseball NOUN **baseballs**
❶ baseball is an American team game in which the players hit a ball and run round a series of four 'bases' to score points ❷ a baseball is the ball used in this game

baseball cap NOUN **baseball caps**
a close-fitting cap with a large peak, originally worn by baseball players

basement NOUN **basements**
a room or part of a building below ground level

bash VERB **bashes**, **bashing**, **bashed** (*informal*)
to bash someone or something is to hit them hard

bash NOUN **bashes** (*informal*)
a hard hit
➤ **to have a bash at something** (*informal*) is to try it even though it is difficult and you think you might not succeed

bashful ADJECTIVE
shy
➤ **bashfulness** NOUN

basic ADJECTIVE
forming the first or most important part • *He has a basic knowledge of French.* • *Food is a basic human need.*

basically ADVERB
in the most important ways; essentially • *Trolls are basically lazy.*

basil NOUN
a Mediterranean herb used in cooking

basilisk NOUN **basilisks**
a mythological creature like a snake which could kill people just by looking at them

basin NOUN **basins**
❶ a deep bowl for mixing food in ❷ a large container to hold water for washing your face and hands in ❸ a river basin is the area of land where the river's water comes from

basis NOUN **bases**
❶ the basis of something is what you start from or add to • *These players will be the basis of a new team.* ❷ a basis is the way in which something is arranged or organized • *The competition is organized on a knockout basis.*

bask VERB **basks**, **basking**, **basked**
to bask is to lie or sit comfortably warming yourself in the sun

basket NOUN **baskets**
a container made of strips of wood, cane or wire woven together

basketball NOUN **basketballs**
❶ basketball is a team game in which players try to throw a large ball through a high net hanging from a hoop ❷ a basketball is the ball used in this game

bass (*say* bayss) ADJECTIVE
forming the lowest sounds in music
bass (*say* bayss) NOUN **basses**
a singer or an instrument with a very deep sound

bassoon NOUN **bassoons**
a woodwind instrument that plays low notes

bat NOUN **bats**
❶ a shaped piece of wood used to hit the ball in cricket, baseball and other games ❷ a bat is also a flying mammal that looks like a mouse with wings. Bats come out at night to feed.
➤ **to do something off your own bat** (*informal*) is to do it without any help from other people
bat VERB **bats**, **batting**, **batted**
to bat is to take a turn at using a bat in cricket, baseball and other games

batch NOUN **batches**
a set of things made at one time or dealt with together

bated ADJECTIVE
➤ **with bated breath** waiting nervously

bath NOUN **baths**
❶ a bath is a large container you fill with water and get into to wash yourself ❷ a bath sometimes means the water in a bath • *Your bath is getting cold.* ❸ the baths are also a public swimming pool

bathe (*say* bay*th*) *VERB* **bathes**, **bathing**, **bathed**
❶ to bathe is to go swimming in the sea or a river ❷ to bathe a sore part of your body is to wash it gently ❸ to bathe something in light is to cover or fill it with light
The evening light streamed in through the stained-glass windows, bathing everything in a mysterious glow.—THE LETTER FOR THE KING, Tonke Dragt

bathe *NOUN* **bathes**
a bathe is a swim

bathroom *NOUN* **bathrooms**
a room for having a bath or wash in

bat mitzvah *NOUN* **bat mitzvahs**
a religious ceremony for Jewish girls who have reached the age of 12, when they accept some of the responsibilities of an adult

baton *NOUN* **batons**
a short stick, especially one you use to conduct an orchestra or in a relay race

batsman, **batswoman** *NOUN* **batsmen**, **batswomen**
a player who uses a bat in cricket

battalion *NOUN* **battalions**
an army unit consisting of two or more companies

batten *NOUN* **battens**
a flat strip of wood used to hold something in place

batten *VERB* **battens**, **battening**, **battened**
➤ **to batten something down** is to fix it securely

batter *VERB* **batters**, **battering**, **battered**
to batter something is to hit it hard and often • *The huge waves battered the rocks.*

batter *NOUN*
❶ batter is a mixture of flour, eggs and milk, beaten together and used to make pancakes or to coat food before you fry it ❷ (**batters**) a player who is batting in cricket or baseball

battering ram *NOUN* **battering rams**
(*historical*)
a heavy pole used to break through the walls and gates of a city or fort

battery *NOUN* **batteries**
❶ a portable device for storing and supplying electricity ❷ a series of cages in which animals are kept close together on a farm • *Free-range hens are not kept in batteries.* ❸ a set of devices that are used together, especially a group of large guns

battle *NOUN* **battles**
❶ a fight between two armies ❷ a struggle

battlefield *NOUN* **battlefields**
a place where a battle is or was fought

battlements *PLURAL NOUN*
the top of a castle wall, usually with gaps through which people defending the castle could fire arrows at the enemy

battleship *NOUN* **battleships**
a large warship armed with powerful guns

bauble *NOUN* **baubles**
a bright and showy ornament, especially one hung on a Christmas tree

bawl *VERB* **bawls**, **bawling**, **bawled**
to bawl is to shout or cry loudly

bay *NOUN* **bays**
❶ a place by the sea or a lake where the shore curves inwards ❷ an area that is marked out to be used for parking vehicles, storing things, etc.
➤ **to keep someone at bay** is to prevent them from coming near you

bayonet *NOUN* **bayonets**
a steel blade that can be fixed to the end of a rifle and used for stabbing

bay window *NOUN* **bay windows**
a window that sticks out from the wall of a house

bazaar *NOUN* **bazaars**
❶ a market in a Middle Eastern country ❷ a sale held to raise money for charity

BC *ABBREVIATION*
short for *before Christ*, used with dates that come before the birth of Jesus Christ • *Julius Caesar came to Britain in 55 BC.*

be *VERB* **am**, **are**, **is**; **was**, **were**; **being**, **been**
❶ to be is to live or exist • *Three boys were in the classroom.* • *There is a bus stop at the corner.* ❷ to be someone or something is to have that position or quality • *She is my teacher.* • *You are very tall.* ❸ the verb **be** can also be used to help make other verbs • *They*

a
b
c
d
e
f
g
h
i
j
k
l
m
n
o
p
q
r
s
t
u
v
w
x
y
z

are having a good time. • *A man was injured in the accident.* ❹ the verb **be** can also be used instead of **go** in questions and in statements with **not** • *Have you been to Paris?* • *No, I've never been there.*

beach *NOUN* beaches
the strip of pebbles or sand close to the sea

beacon *NOUN* beacons
a light or fire used as a warning signal

bead *NOUN* beads
❶ a small piece of glass, wood or plastic with a hole through it, threaded on a string or wire to make a necklace or bracelet ❷ a small drop of liquid • *She had beads of sweat on her face.*

beady *ADJECTIVE* beadier, beadiest
beady eyes are small and bright

beagle *NOUN* beagles
a type of dog with long ears, used for hunting hares

beak *NOUN* beaks
the hard pointed part of a bird's mouth

beaker *NOUN* beakers
❶ a tall drinking mug, usually without a handle ❷ (*science*) a glass container used for pouring liquids in a laboratory

beam *NOUN* beams
❶ a long thick bar of wood or metal ❷ a ray of light

beam *VERB* beams, beaming, beamed
❶ to beam is to send out a beam of light or radio waves ❷ you can say a person beams when they smile very happily

bean *NOUN* beans
❶ a kind of plant with seeds growing in pods ❷ the seed or pod of this kind of plant, eaten as food

bear *VERB* bears, bearing, bore, born *or* borne
❶ to bear something is to carry or support it ❷ to bear something such as a signature or mark is to have or show it • *The letter bore her signature.* ❸ to bear something is to put up with it or suffer it • *I can't bear all this noise.* ❹ a woman bears children when she gives birth to them • *She was born in 1950.* • *She has borne three sons.*

bear *NOUN* bears
a large heavy animal with thick fur and sharp hooked claws

bearable *ADJECTIVE*
something that is bearable is something you are able to put up with • *His toothache was hardly bearable.*

beard *NOUN* beards
hair on the lower part of a person's face

bearing *NOUN* bearings
❶ your bearing is the way you stand, walk or behave ❷ the direction or position of something in relation to something else
➤ **to get your bearings** is to work out where you are in relation to other things
➤ **to lose your bearings** is to forget where you are in relation to other things

beast *NOUN* beasts
❶ any large four-footed animal ❷ (*informal*) a person you think is cruel or unkind

beastly *ADJECTIVE* beastlier, beastliest
(*informal*)
cruel or unkind
Mrs Twit may have been beastly, but she was not stupid.—THE TWITS, Roald Dahl
➤ **beastliness** *NOUN*

beat *VERB* beats, beating, beat, beaten
❶ to beat someone or something is to hit them repeatedly, especially with a stick ❷ to beat someone in a game or match is to do better than them and win it ❸ to beat a cooking mixture is to stir it quickly so that it becomes thicker ❹ to beat something is to shape or flatten it by hitting it many times ❺ to beat is also to make regular movements like your heart does
➤ **to beat someone up** is to attack them very violently

beat *NOUN* beats
❶ a regular rhythm or stroke, like your heart makes ❷ a strong rhythm in pop music ❸ the regular route of a police officer

beautiful *ADJECTIVE*
very pleasing to look at or listen to • *Mermaids are said to have beautiful voices.*
SPELLING ALERT! The word **beautiful** has three vowels in the middle. Think of the phrase **e**very **a**ncient **u**nicorn is beautiful to help you remember!

beautifully ADVERB
when you do something beautifully, you do it in a beautiful or pleasing way • *You sang that beautifully!*

beauty NOUN **beauties**
❶ beauty is a quality that gives delight or pleasure, especially to your senses • *They enjoyed the beauty of the sunset.*
❷ a beauty is a particularly beautiful person or thing

beaver NOUN **beavers**
a brown furry animal with strong teeth and a long flat tail, which builds dams in rivers

became VERB (*past tense of* **become**)
• *The dark passageway became completely black.*

because CONJUNCTION
for the reason that • *We were excited because we were going on holiday.*
➤ **because of someone** *or* **something**
for that reason; on account of them • *The horse was limping because of its wounded leg.*

beckon VERB **beckons**, **beckoning**, **beckoned**
to beckon to someone is to make a sign asking them to come to you

become VERB **becomes**, **becoming**, **became**, **become**
❶ to become is to start being something described • *It was gradually becoming darker.*
❷ to become a type of person is to grow to be that type • *I had always wanted to become an explorer.* ❸ a style or clothing becomes someone if it makes them look attractive
➤ **to ask what became of someone** *or* **something** is to wonder what happened to them in the end • *What do you think became of Peter Pan?*

bed NOUN **beds**
❶ a bed is a piece of furniture for sleeping on ❷ bed is the place where you sleep • *I'm going to bed now.* ❸ a bed is also a part of a garden where plants are grown ❹ the bed of the sea or of a river is the bottom of it

bedclothes PLURAL NOUN
sheets, blankets and duvets for using on a bed

bedding NOUN
things for making a bed, such as sheets, blankets and duvets

bedlam NOUN
a loud noise or disturbance • *There was bedlam at the playgroup.*

bedraggled (*say* bi-**drag**-uld) ADJECTIVE
wet and dirty

bedridden (*say* **bed**-rid-en) ADJECTIVE
too ill or injured to get out of bed

bedroom NOUN **bedrooms**
a room where you sleep

bedside NOUN
the space beside a bed, especially the bed of someone who is ill • *He sat by his son's bedside all night.*

bedspread NOUN **bedspreads**
a covering put over the top of a bed

bedstead NOUN **bedsteads**
the framework of a bed

bedtime NOUN
the time when you are supposed to go to bed

bee NOUN **bees**
a stinging insect that makes honey

beech NOUN **beeches**
a tree with smooth bark and glossy leaves

beef NOUN
the meat of an ox, bull or cow

beefy ADJECTIVE **beefier**, **beefiest** (*informal*)
a beefy person is big, with strong muscles

beehive NOUN **beehives**
a container that bees are kept in so that their honey can be collected

beekeeper NOUN **beekeepers**
someone who owns bees and collects their honey
➤ **beekeeping** NOUN

beeline NOUN
➤ **to make a beeline for something** is to go quickly and directly towards it

been VERB (*past participle of* **be**)
• *I have been feeling poorly for a while.*

beer NOUN **beers**
beer is an alcoholic drink made from malt and hops

a
b
c
d
e
f
g
h
i
j
k
l
m
n
o
p
q
r
s
t
u
v
w
x
y
z

beet *NOUN* beet *or* beets
beet is a plant used as a vegetable or for making sugar

beetle *NOUN* beetles
an insect with hard shiny covers over its wings

beetroot *NOUN* beetroot
the dark red root of beet used as a vegetable

before *ADVERB, PREPOSITION*
❶ earlier, or earlier than • *Have you been here before?* • *They came the day before yesterday.* ❷ in front of • *He stood up before the whole school.*

beforehand *ADVERB*
earlier, or before something else happens
• *She had tried to phone me beforehand.*
• *Let me know beforehand if you want to come on the picnic.*

beg *VERB* begs, begging, begged
❶ to beg is to ask people to give you money or food ❷ to beg someone is to ask them seriously or desperately • *He begged me not to tell the teacher.*
➤ **I beg your pardon** I didn't hear or understand what you said; I apologize

began (*past tense of* begin)
• *The ground beneath them began to shake.*

beggar *NOUN* beggars
someone who lives by begging in the street

begin *VERB* begins, beginning, began, begun
❶ to begin something is to start doing it
❷ to begin is to start doing something
• *I really don't know where to begin.*

beginner *NOUN* beginners
someone who is just starting to learn or is still learning a subject

beginning *NOUN* beginnings
the start of something

begun *VERB* (*past participle of* begin)
• *Tears had begun to run down Emily's face.*

behalf *NOUN*
➤ **on behalf of something** to help a cause
• *They were collecting money on behalf of cancer research.*
➤ **on someone's behalf** for them or in their name • *Will you accept the prize on my behalf?*

behave *VERB* behaves, behaving, behaved
❶ to behave well or badly is to act in a good or bad way • *They behaved very badly at the party.* ❷ to show good manners • *Why can't you behave?*

behaviour *NOUN*
❶ your behaviour is the way you behave
❷ animal behaviour is the way animals normally behave and treat one another

behead *VERB* beheads, beheading, beheaded
to behead someone is to cut off their head, as a form of execution

behind *ADVERB, PREPOSITION*
❶ at or to the back • *The others are a long way behind.* • *She hid behind a tree.* ❷ not making good progress • *He's behind the rest of the class in maths.* ❸ supporting or encouraging • *We're all behind you.*
➤ **behind someone's back** without them knowing about it

behold *VERB* beholds, beholding, beheld
(*old use*)
to behold something is to see it in front of you
Scrooge ... beheld a solemn Phantom, draped and hooded, coming, like a mist along the ground, towards him.—A CHRISTMAS CAROL, Charles Dickens

beige (*say* bayzh) *NOUN, ADJECTIVE*
a light yellow-brown colour

being *NOUN* beings
a being is a person or creature of any kind
• *Could there be living beings on Mars?*

belch *VERB* belches, belching, belched
❶ to belch is to make a noise by letting air come up from your stomach through your mouth ❷ a chimney or factory belches smoke or fumes when it sends out thick smoke or fumes into the air

belch *NOUN* belches
the act or sound of belching

belfry *NOUN* belfries
the top part of a tower or steeple, in which bells hang

belief NOUN **beliefs**
❶ a belief is something you believe • *They have very few beliefs.* ❷ belief is when you believe something

believe VERB **believes**, **believing**, **believed**
❶ to believe something is to think that it is true ❷ to believe someone is to think that they are telling the truth ❸ to believe in something is to think it is real or important • *Do you believe in ghosts?*
➤ **believable** ADJECTIVE if something is believable, you are able to believe it could happen

bell NOUN **bells**
a device that makes a ringing sound, especially a cup-shaped metal object with a clapper

bellow VERB **bellows**, **bellowing**, **bellowed**
to bellow is to roar or shout loudly and deeply

bellows PLURAL NOUN
bellows are a device for blowing out air, especially into a fire to make it burn more strongly

belly NOUN **bellies**
❶ the abdomen or the stomach of a human ❷ the under part of a four-legged animal

belong VERB **belongs**, **belonging**, **belonged**
❶ to belong to someone is to be their property • *The pencil belongs to me.* ❷ to belong to a club or group is to be a member of it • *We both belong to the tennis club.* ❸ to belong somewhere is to have a special place where it goes • *The butter belongs in the fridge.*

belongings PLURAL NOUN
your belongings are the things that you own

beloved (*say* bi-**luvd** *or* bi-**luv**-id) ADJECTIVE
greatly loved

below PREPOSITION
lower than, under • *We have nice neighbours in the flat below us.*

below ADVERB
at a lower point, or to a lower point • *I'll have the top bunk, and you can sleep below.*

belt NOUN **belts**
❶ a strip of material, often leather or cloth, that you wear round your waist ❷ a long narrow area • *As we went further north we met a belt of rain.*

belt VERB **belts**, **belting**, **belted** (*informal*)
❶ to belt someone is to hit them hard ❷ to belt along is to move very fast

bench NOUN **benches**
❶ a long seat ❷ a long table for working at

bend VERB **bends**, **bending**, **bent**
❶ to bend something is to make it curved or crooked ❷ to bend is to become curved or crooked • *The trees were bending in the wind.* ❸ to bend is also to move the top of your body downwards • *She bent down to pick up the cat.*

bend NOUN **bends**
a part where something curves or turns

beneath PREPOSITION, ADVERB
under or underneath • *What lies beneath the surface of Mars?* • *They cut through the ice to reach the water beneath.*

benefactor NOUN **benefactors**
someone who gives money or other help to a person or organization that needs it

beneficial ADJECTIVE
something is beneficial when it is useful or helpful

benefit NOUN **benefits**
❶ a benefit is something that is useful or helpful • *A big benefit of exercise is that it makes you feel good.* ❷ benefit is money that the government pays to help people who are poor, unemployed or ill, or have a disability ❸ a benefit concert or match is one organized to raise money for a good cause

benefit VERB **benefits**, **benefiting**, **benefited**
you benefit from something, or it benefits you, when it helps you

benevolent ADJECTIVE
kind and helpful
➤ **benevolence** NOUN

bent ADJECTIVE
curved or crooked
➤ **to be bent on something** is to be determined to do it

bequeath (*rhymes with* **breathe**) VERB
bequeaths, **bequeathing**, **bequeathed**
to bequeath something to someone is to leave it to them in a will

a
b
c
d
e
f
g
h
i
j
k
l
m
n
o
p
q
r
s
t
u
v
w
x
y
z

A
B
C
D
E
F
G
H
I
J
K
L
M
N
O
P
Q
R
S
T
U
V
W
X
Y
Z

bereaved *ADJECTIVE*
a bereaved person is someone with a close relative who has recently died
➤ **bereavement** *NOUN*

bereft *ADJECTIVE*
to be bereft of something is to be deprived of it • *He was bereft of hope.*

beret (*say* bair-ay) *NOUN* berets
a soft, round, flat cap

berry *NOUN* berries
a small juicy fruit

berserk *ADJECTIVE*
to go berserk is to become extremely angry or lose control • *My dad will go berserk when he finds out.*
DID YOU KNOW? The word **berserk** comes from the *Berserkers*, Viking warriors who wore bear skins and went into a frenzy during battle.

berth *NOUN* berths
❶ a sleeping place on a ship or train ❷ a place where a ship is tied up

beside *PREPOSITION*
next to; close to • *A house beside the sea.*
➤ **to be beside yourself** is to be very excited or upset • *He was beside himself with anger.*

besides *PREPOSITION*
in addition to • *Who is on the team besides you?*

besides *ADVERB*
also; in addition to this • *The shoes are expensive. Besides, they're the wrong colour.*

besiege (*say* bi-seej) *VERB* besieges, besieging, besieged
❶ to besiege a place is to surround it until the people inside surrender ❷ to besiege someone famous is to crowd round them • *The rock group was besieged by hundreds of fans.*

best *ADJECTIVE*
most excellent; most able to do something • *She is the best swimmer in the class.*

best *ADVERB*
❶ in the best way; most • *We'll do what suits you best.* ❷ most usefully; most wisely • *He is best ignored.*

best *NOUN*
the best person or thing, or the best people or things • *She was the best at tennis.* • *These boots are the best you can buy.*
➤ **to make the best of something** is to accept it and enjoy it as much as you can, even though it is not very good

best man *NOUN*
someone who helps the bridegroom at his wedding

bestseller *NOUN* bestsellers
a book or other product that has sold in very large numbers

bet *NOUN* bets
❶ an agreement that you will receive money if you are correct in choosing the winner of a race or in saying something will happen, and will lose money if you are not correct ❷ the money you risk losing in a bet

bet *VERB* bets, betting, bet *or* betted
❶ to bet, or to bet money, is to make a bet ❷ (*informal*) to bet something is to say you are sure about it • *I bet I'm right.*

betray *VERB* betrays, betraying, betrayed
❶ to betray someone is to do them harm when they are expecting your support ❷ to betray something like a secret is to give it away
➤ **betrayal** *NOUN*

better *ADJECTIVE*
❶ more excellent; more able to do something • *This bike is better than my last one.* ❷ well again after an illness • *I'm feeling much better now.*
➤ **to get the better of someone** is to defeat or outwit them

better *ADVERB*
❶ in a better way • *I'll try to play better next time.* ❷ if you had better do something, you should do it or ought to do it • *We had better go before it gets dark.*
➤ **to be better off** is to be more fortunate, for example by having more money

better *VERB* betters, bettering, bettered
to better something is to improve on it • *She hopes to better her own record time.*

between *PREPOSITION, ADVERB*
within two or more points; among • *Call me between Tuesday and Friday.* • *The train runs between London and Glasgow.* • *What is the difference between butter and margarine?* • *Divide the sweets between the children.* • *The two houses are side by side with a fence between.*

beware *VERB*
a warning to be careful • *Beware of pickpockets.*
SPELLING ALERT! Beware has no other forms; it is only ever used as a command.

bewilder *VERB* bewilders, bewildering, bewildered
to bewilder someone is to puzzle them completely
➤ **bewilderment** *NOUN*

bewitch *VERB* bewitches, bewitching, bewitched
❶ to bewitch someone is to put a spell on them ❷ to bewitch someone is also to delight them very much • *We were completely bewitched by the fireworks.*

beyond *PREPOSITION, ADVERB*
farther on • *Don't go beyond the end of the street.* • *You can see the next valley and the mountains beyond.*

bias *NOUN* biases
❶ bias is a strong feeling in favour of one person or side and against another • *The referee was accused of bias.* ❷ bias is also a tendency for a ball to swerve, especially in a game of bowls
➤ **biased** *ADJECTIVE* someone is biased when they show that they prefer one person or side over another

bib *NOUN* bibs
a piece of cloth or plastic you put under a baby's chin during meals to protect its clothes from stains

Bible *NOUN* Bibles
the holy book of Christianity and Judaism
➤ **biblical** *ADJECTIVE*

bibliography (*say* bib-lee-**og**-ra-fee) *NOUN* bibliographies
a list of books about a subject or by a particular author

bicycle *NOUN* bicycles
a two-wheeled vehicle that you ride by pushing down on pedals with your feet

bid *NOUN* bids
❶ offering an amount you will pay for something, especially at an auction
❷ an attempt • *He will make a bid for the world record tomorrow.*

bid *VERB* bids, bidding, bid
to bid an amount of money is to offer it for something at an auction

bide *VERB* bides, biding, bided
➤ **to bide your time** is to wait, expecting something to happen that will help you

big *ADJECTIVE* bigger, biggest
❶ more than the normal size; large • *We bought a big tub of popcorn to share.* ❷ important • *This is a big decision.* ❸ elder • *Have you met my big sister?*

bike *NOUN* bikes (*informal*)
a bicycle or motorcycle

bikini *NOUN* bikinis
a two-piece swimsuit

bilingual *ADJECTIVE*
speaking two languages well

bill *NOUN* bills
❶ a piece of paper that tells you how much money you owe for something
❷ a plan for a new law in parliament
❸ a poster giving information about something ❹ a programme of entertainment • *There's a magician on the bill.* ❺ a bill is also a bird's beak

billiards *NOUN*
a game played with long sticks (called *cues*) and three balls on a cloth-covered table

billion *NOUN* billions
a thousand million (1,000,000,000)
➤ **billionth** *ADJECTIVE, NOUN*

billionaire *NOUN* billionaires
an extremely rich person who has at least a billion pounds or dollars

billow *VERB* billows, billowing, billowed
to billow is to rise up or move like waves on the sea
As she floated gently down, Mrs Twit's

a
b
c
d
e
f
g
h
i
j
k
l
m
n
o
p
q
r
s
t
u
v
w
x
y
z

billy goat NOUN **billy goats**
a male goat

bin NOUN **bins**
a large or deep container, especially one that you put rubbish or litter in

binary number NOUN **binary numbers**
a number that uses only the digits 0 and 1. Binary numbers are used in computer programming.

bind VERB **binds, binding, bound**
❶ to bind things is to tie them up or tie them together ❷ to bind something is to wrap a piece of material round it ❸ to bind a book is to fasten the pages inside a cover ❹ to bind someone is to make them do something or promise something

bingo NOUN
a game played with cards with numbered squares. These are covered or crossed out as the numbers are called, and the first person to complete the card wins the game.

binoculars PLURAL NOUN
a device with lenses for both eyes, for making distant objects seem nearer

biodegradable ADJECTIVE
able to be broken down by bacteria in the environment • *All our packaging is biodegradable.*

biography NOUN **biographies**
the story of a person's life
➤ **biographical** ADJECTIVE

biology NOUN
the science or study of living things
➤ **biological** ADJECTIVE ➤ **biologist** NOUN

birch NOUN **birches**
a thin tree with shiny bark and slender branches

bird NOUN **birds**
a feathered animal with two wings, two legs and a beak

bird of prey NOUN **birds of prey**
a bird that feeds on animal flesh, such as an eagle or hawk

birdseed NOUN
seeds for birds to eat

bird's-eye view NOUN
a general view of something, seen from above

birth NOUN **births**
birth is the beginning of a person's or animal's life, when they come out of their mother's body

birthday NOUN **birthdays**
the anniversary of the day on which you were born

birthmark NOUN **birthmarks**
a coloured mark which has been on someone's skin since they were born

birthplace NOUN **birthplaces**
the place where someone was born

biscuit NOUN **biscuits**
a small flat kind of cake that has been baked until it is hard

bishop NOUN **bishops**
❶ a senior priest in the Christian Church who is in charge of all the churches in a city or district ❷ a chess piece shaped like a bishop's mitre

bison NOUN **bison**
a wild ox with shaggy hair

bit VERB (*past tense of* **bite**)
• *I bit my lip, thinking hard.*

bit NOUN **bits**
❶ a small piece or amount of something ❷ the part of a horse's bridle that is put into its mouth ❸ the part of a tool that cuts or grips ❹ (*computing*) the smallest unit of data or memory
➤ **bits and pieces** small things of various kinds

bitch NOUN **bitches**
a female dog, fox or wolf

bite VERB **bites, biting, bit, bitten**
❶ to bite something is to cut it or hold it with your teeth ❷ to bite into something is to penetrate it • *The tyres bit into the mud.* ❸ to accept bait • *The fish are biting.* ❹ to sting or hurt • *a biting wind*

bite *NOUN* bites
❶ to give a person or animal a bite is to bite them ❷ a mark or spot made by biting • *You've had an insect bite.* ❸ a snack • *Would you like a bite?*

bitter *ADJECTIVE*
❶ tasting sour and unpleasant ❷ feeling angry and resentful because you are disappointed about something • *She is still bitter about losing.* ❸ extremely cold
Much rain fell in the night; and the next morning there blew a bitter wintry wind out of the northwest, driving scattered clouds.—KIDNAPPED, Robert Louis Stevenson
➤ **bitterly** *ADVERB*

bizarre *ADJECTIVE*
very strange or unusual • *There is a bizarre twist in the plot.*
➤ **bizarrely** *ADVERB*

black *ADJECTIVE* blacker, blackest
❶ of the darkest colour, the opposite of white ❷ having dark skin; to do with people with dark skin, especially people of African ancestry ❸ dismal; not hopeful • *The outlook is black.* ❹ very dirty

black *NOUN* blacks
a black colour

blackberry *NOUN* blackberries
a sweet dark-purple berry

blackbird *NOUN* blackbirds
a dark European songbird

blackboard *NOUN* blackboards
a dark board for writing on with chalk

blacken *VERB* blackens, blackening, blackened
❶ to blacken something is to make it black ❷ to blacken someone's name is to say bad things about them

black eye *NOUN* black eyes
an eye with heavy bruises round it

black hole *NOUN* black holes
a region in space with such strong gravity that no light escapes

black ice *NOUN*
thin transparent ice on roads

blackmail *VERB* blackmails, blackmailing, blackmailed
to blackmail someone is to get money from them by threatening to tell people something that they want to keep secret

black market *NOUN*
a black market in goods is illegal trading in them

blackout *NOUN* blackouts
❶ when a person becomes unconscious for a short time ❷ a time when lights are kept hidden or turned off

blacksmith *NOUN* blacksmiths
someone who makes and repairs things made of iron, and fits shoes on horses

bladder *NOUN* bladders
❶ the bladder is the bag-like part of your body where urine collects ❷ a bladder is also an inflatable bag inside a football

blade *NOUN* blades
❶ the sharp part of a device for cutting, such as a knife or sword ❷ the flat, wide part of an oar or propeller ❸ a long narrow leaf of grass

blame *VERB* blames, blaming, blamed
to blame someone is to say that they have done something wrong • *My brother broke the window, but they blamed me.*

blame *NOUN*
to get the blame for something is to be blamed for it
➤ **to be to blame** is to be the person who has done something wrong

blancmange (*say* bla-**monj**) *NOUN* blancmanges
blancmange is a pudding like a jelly made with milk
The Trunchbull, this mighty female giant, stood there in her green breeches, quivering like a blancmange. —MATILDA, Roald Dahl

bland *ADJECTIVE*
not strong or noticeable • *The soup had a bland flavour.*
➤ **blandness** *NOUN*

blank *ADJECTIVE*
❶ not written, drawn or printed on • *The piece of paper was blank.* ❷ showing no expression or interest • *His face looked blank.*

a b c d e f g h i j k l m n o p q r s t u v w x y z

blank NOUN **blanks**
❶ an empty space ❷ a cartridge for a gun which makes a noise but does not fire a bullet

blanket NOUN **blankets**
❶ a large piece of thick cloth, used as a warm covering for a bed ❷ a thick layer covering the ground or a surface • *a blanket of powdery snow*

blare VERB **blares, blaring, blared**
to blare is to make a harsh loud sound

blast NOUN **blasts**
❶ a strong rush of wind or air ❷ a sharp or loud noise • *The referee gave a long blast of their whistle.*

blast VERB **blasts, blasting, blasted**
to blast something is to blow it up with explosives

blast-off NOUN
the launch of a spacecraft

blatant (*say* blay-tant) ADJECTIVE
clear and obvious; making no attempt to hide • *a blatant lie*
➤ **blatantly** ADVERB

blaze NOUN **blazes**
❶ a very bright fire ❷ a very bright colour or light

blaze VERB **blazes, blazing, blazed**
❶ to blaze is to burn or shine brightly ❷ to blaze with a feeling is to feel it very strongly • *He was blazing with anger.*
➤ **to blaze a trail** is to show the way for others to follow

blazer NOUN **blazers**
a kind of jacket, often with a badge on the front

bleach NOUN **bleaches**
a substance used to clean things or make clothes white

bleach VERB **bleaches, bleaching, bleached**
to bleach something is to make it white

bleak ADJECTIVE **bleaker, bleakest**
❶ bare and cold • *a bleak and barren landscape* ❷ dreary and miserable • *In those days, the future looked bleak.*

bleary ADJECTIVE **blearier, bleariest**
bleary eyes are tired and do not see clearly

bleat NOUN **bleats**
the cry of a sheep or goat

bleat VERB **bleats, bleating, bleated**
a sheep or goat bleats when it makes a bleat

bleed VERB **bleeds, bleeding, bled**
❶ to bleed is to lose blood from your body, for example if you are injured ❷ to bleed a person or animal is to take blood from them

bleep NOUN **bleeps**
a short high sound made by an electronic device

bleep VERB **bleeps, bleeping, bleeped**
to make a short high sound • *The robot bleeped and swivelled its head.*

blemish NOUN **blemishes**
❶ a mark or stain on something ❷ a fault or weakness

blend VERB **blends, blending, blended**
to blend things is to mix them together smoothly or easily

blend NOUN **blends**
❶ a smooth mixture ❷ a word made by combining parts of two other words, for example *brunch* from *breakfast* and *lunch*

blender NOUN **blenders**
a kitchen device to mix food or turn it into liquid

bless VERB **blesses, blessing, blessed**
❶ to bless someone is to wish or bring them happiness ❷ to bless someone is also to ask God to look after them

blessing NOUN **blessings**
❶ a prayer or act of blessing someone ❷ something you are glad of or happy about • *It's a blessing that they are safe.*

blew (*past tense of* **blow**)
• *A gusty wind blew rain into his face.*

blight NOUN **blights**
❶ blight is a plant disease ❷ a blight is a thing that spoils or damages something

blind ADJECTIVE **blinder, blindest**
❶ not able to see ❷ without thought or understanding

blind VERB **blinds, blinding, blinded**
❶ to blind someone is to make them blind

2 a bright light blinds you when it makes you unable to see for a time

blind *NOUN* **blinds**
a screen for a window

blindfold *NOUN* **blindfolds**
a piece of cloth used to cover someone's eyes so that they cannot see where they are or what is happening

blindfold *VERB* **blindfolds**, **blindfolding**, **blindfolded**
to blindfold someone is to cover their eyes with a blindfold

blindfold *ADJECTIVE*
with a blindfold over the eyes

blink *VERB* **blinks**, **blinking**, **blinked**
to blink is to shut and open your eyes quickly

bliss *NOUN*
bliss is great happiness

blister *NOUN* **blisters**
a swelling like a bubble on your skin

blitz *NOUN* **blitzes**
a sudden violent attack, especially from aircraft

blitz *VERB* **blitzes**, **blitzing**, **blitzed**
to blitz something is to attack it fiercely and suddenly

blizzard *NOUN* **blizzards**
a severe snowstorm

bloated *ADJECTIVE*
swollen or puffed out

blob *NOUN* **blobs**
a small round lump of something like paint or ice cream

block *NOUN* **blocks**
1 a solid piece of something hard such as wood **2** a large building or group of buildings with streets all around it **3** something that stops people getting through • *They came to a road block and had to turn back.*

block *VERB* **blocks**, **blocking**, **blocked**
1 to block something is to get in the way of it • *Tall buildings blocked our view.* **2** to block something like a pipe or drain is to prevent water flowing through it

blockade *NOUN* **blockades**
a blockade is when a city or port is surrounded to stop people or goods from getting in or out

blockage *NOUN* **blockages**
1 something that stops up a pipe or drain **2** a blocked state • *Roadworks are causing blockages in the traffic.*

block capitals, **block letters**
PLURAL NOUN
large capital letters

blog *NOUN* **blogs**
a website on which someone writes regularly about their own life or opinions

blog *VERB* **blogs**, **blogging**, **blogged**
to write or update a blog
➤ **blogging** *NOUN*

blogger *NOUN* **bloggers**
someone who writes regularly for a blog

blond, **blonde** *ADJECTIVE* **blonder**, **blondest**
fair-haired

blood *NOUN*
1 blood is the red liquid that flows through your veins and arteries **2** someone who is of noble or royal blood has ancestors who were noble or royal
➤ **to do something in cold blood** is to do it deliberately and cruelly

blood-curdling *ADJECTIVE*
horrific and terrifying • *There was a blood-curdling scream in the night.*

bloodhound *NOUN* **bloodhounds**
a large breed of dog which can track people over long distances by following their scent

bloodshed *NOUN*
bloodshed is the killing and injuring of people

bloodshot *ADJECTIVE*
eyes are bloodshot when they are streaked with red from being strained or tired

bloodstream *NOUN*
your bloodstream is the blood flowing round your body

bloodthirsty *ADJECTIVE* **bloodthirstier**, **bloodthirstiest**
enjoying killing and violence

a
b
c
d
e
f
g
h
i
j
k
l
m
n
o
p
q
r
s
t
u
v
w
x
y
z

A
B
C
D
E
F
G
H
I
J
K
L
M
N
O
P
Q
R
S
T
U
V
W
X
Y
Z

bloody ADJECTIVE **bloodier**, **bloodiest**
❶ bleeding ❷ covered in blood ❸ a bloody fight or battle is one in which a lot of people are killed or badly hurt

bloom VERB **blooms**, **blooming**, **bloomed**
to bloom is to produce flowers • *Look! The roses have bloomed!*

bloom NOUN **blooms**
a bloom is a flower
➤ **in bloom** trees and plants are in bloom when they are producing flowers

blossom NOUN **blossoms**
❶ a blossom is a flower, especially on a fruit tree ❷ blossom is a mass of flowers on a tree

blossom VERB **blossoms**, **blossoming**, **blossomed**
❶ a tree or bush blossoms when it produces flowers ❷ to blossom is also to develop into something very fine or good • *She has blossomed into a confident singer.*

blot NOUN **blots**
❶ a spot or blob of ink ❷ a flaw or fault

blot VERB **blots**, **blotting**, **blotted**
to blot something is to make a blot on it
➤ **to blot something out** is to cover it over so that it cannot be seen • *A large dark cloud blotted out the sun.*

blotch NOUN **blotches**
an untidy patch of colour
➤ **blotchy** ADJECTIVE

blouse NOUN **blouses**
a loose piece of clothing like a shirt

blow NOUN **blows**
❶ a hard knock or hit ❷ a shock or disappointment • *Losing the cup final was a terrible blow.* ❸ the action of blowing

blow VERB **blows**, **blowing**, **blew**, **blown**
❶ to blow is to force out air from your mouth or nose • *He blew on his cold hands to warm them up.* ❷ to move in the wind • *Her hat blew off.* ❸ to blow something is to form it by blowing • *Let's blow bubbles.* ❹ to blow something such as a whistle is to make a sound with it ❺ a fuse or light bulb blows when it melts or breaks

➤ **to blow something up** is to destroy it with an explosion
➤ **to blow up** is to be destroyed in an explosion

blowhole NOUN **blowholes**
the hole on the head of a whale or dolphin through which it breathes

blue ADJECTIVE **bluer**, **bluest**
❶ of the colour of a bright cloudless sky ❷ sad and miserable • *I often feel blue on Monday mornings.*

blue NOUN **blues**
a blue colour
➤ **out of the blue** with no warning • *An old friend turned up out of the blue.*

bluebell NOUN **bluebells**
a blue wild flower

blueberry NOUN **blueberries**
a round bluish-purple berry originally from North America

bluebottle NOUN **bluebottles**
a large blue fly that makes a loud buzz

blueprint NOUN **blueprints**
a detailed plan of something that is going to be built

blues PLURAL NOUN
blues is a type of music that is often sad
➤ **to get the blues** is to feel sad and miserable

bluff VERB **bluffs**, **bluffing**, **bluffed**
to bluff someone is to make them think that you will do something that you don't intend to do or that you know something that you don't really know

bluff NOUN **bluffs**
a bluff is something that someone says or does to bluff someone else, for example an empty promise or threat • *He said he'd report us, but that was just a bluff.*

blunder NOUN **blunders**
a careless mistake

blunt ADJECTIVE **blunter**, **bluntest**
❶ having an edge that is not good for cutting ❷ saying what you mean without trying to be polite or tactful

blur VERB **blurs**, **blurring**, **blurred**
to blur something is to make it unclear or smeared

blur *NOUN* **blurs**
an unclear shape with no definite outline
• *Without her glasses on, everything was a blur.*

blurb *NOUN* **blurbs**
a short description of a book that is printed on the back and meant to attract your attention and make you want to buy it

blurry *ADJECTIVE* **blurrier, blurriest**
not able to be seen clearly • *The photographs came out all blurry.*
➤ **blurriness** *NOUN*

blurt *VERB* **blurt, blurting, blurted**
to blurt something out is to say it suddenly, without thinking

blush *VERB* **blushes, blushing, blushed**
to blush is to have a strong pink colour in your face because you are embarrassed or ashamed

bluster *VERB* **blusters, blustering, blustered**
to bluster is to boast or make threats that don't mean very much

blustery *ADJECTIVE*
blustery weather is when the wind is blowing in gusts

boa, boa constrictor *NOUN* **boas, boa constrictors**
a large South American snake that coils round its prey and crushes it

boar *NOUN* **boars**
❶ a wild pig ❷ a male pig

board *NOUN* **boards**
❶ a board is a flat piece of wood, used in building ❷ a board is also a flat piece of wood or cardboard used to play games with, for example a dartboard or a chess board ❸ a board is also a group of people who run a company or organization ❹ board is daily meals supplied in return for money or work • *The price of the holiday includes full board.*
➤ **on board** aboard a ship

board *VERB* **boards, boarding, boarded**
❶ to board a ship or train or aircraft is to get on it for a journey ❷ to board is to get meals and accommodation

➤ **to board something up** is to cover it with boards

boarder *NOUN* **boarders**
❶ a child who lives at a boarding school during the term ❷ a lodger

board game *NOUN* **board games**
a game played on a board, such as chess or draughts

boarding school *NOUN* **boarding schools**
a school in which the pupils live during the term

boast *VERB* **boasts, boasting, boasted**
to boast about something that you own or that you have done is to talk proudly about it, often in order to impress people

boastful *ADJECTIVE*
a boastful person likes to boast about what they own or what they have done
➤ **boastfulness** *NOUN*

boat *NOUN* **boats**
a vehicle designed to float and travel on water
➤ **to be in the same boat** is to share the same problems or difficulties

bob *VERB* **bobs, bobbing, bobbed**
to bob is to move gently up and down, like something floating on water

bobble *NOUN* **bobbles**
a small round ball of something soft such as wool, used as a decoration on a hat or clothing

bobsleigh, bobsled *NOUN* **bobsleighs, bobsleds**
a large sledge with two sets of runners

bodice *NOUN* **bodices**
the upper part of a woman's dress

bodily *ADJECTIVE*
to do with your body

bodily *ADVERB*
by taking hold of someone's body • *He was picked up bodily and bundled into the car.*

body *NOUN* **bodies**
❶ the body is the flesh and bones and other parts of a person or animal ❷ the body is also the main part of a person or animal, not including the head, arms or legs ❸ a body

a b c d e f g h i j k l m n o p q r s t u v w x y z

is a dead person or corpse ❹ the body of something is the main part of it • *They entered the huge body of the castle.* ❺ a body of people is a group of them in one place ❻ a body is a distinct object or piece of matter • *Stars and planets are heavenly bodies.*

bodyguard NOUN **bodyguards**
a guard who protects someone from being attacked

bog NOUN **bogs**
a bog is an area of wet spongy ground
➤ **boggy** ADJECTIVE

bogus ADJECTIVE
false; not real or genuine • *He gave a name that turned out to be bogus.*

boil VERB **boils, boiling, boiled**
❶ to boil a liquid is to heat it until it starts to bubble and give off vapour ❷ to boil is to start bubbling, like water ❸ to boil food is to cook it in boiling water
➤ **to be boiling** (*informal*) is to be very hot • *It's boiling outside.*

boil NOUN **boils**
a painful red swelling on the skin

boiler NOUN **boilers**
a container for heating water or making steam

boisterous ADJECTIVE
noisy and lively

bold ADJECTIVE **bolder, boldest**
❶ brave and adventurous ❷ clear and easy to see • *bold colours* ❸ printed in thick black type

bollard NOUN **bollards**
❶ a short thick post put up on a road, used to keep out traffic ❷ a short thick post on a ship or quay for tying ropes to

bolster VERB **bolsters, bolstering, bolstered**
to bolster something such as a feeling is to increase it • *Her win last week has really bolstered her confidence.*
➤ **to bolster something up** is to support it when it is weak

bolt NOUN **bolts**
❶ a sliding bar for fastening a door or window ❷ a thick metal pin for fastening things together ❸ a flash of lightning
➤ **a bolt from the blue** an unwelcome surprise

bolt VERB **bolts, bolting, bolted**
❶ to bolt a door or window is to fasten it with a bolt ❷ to bolt is to run away in panic, as a horse does ❸ to bolt food is to swallow it too quickly

bomb NOUN **bombs**
a container with explosives, which blows up when it is detonated

bomb VERB **bombs, bombing, bombed**
to bomb a place is to attack it with bombs

bombard VERB **bombards, bombarding, bombarded**
❶ to bombard a place is to attack it with heavy gunfire ❷ to bombard someone with questions or complaints is to direct a large number of questions or complaints at them
➤ **bombardment** NOUN

bomber NOUN **bombers**
❶ an aircraft built to drop bombs ❷ a person who plants or sets off a bomb

bond NOUN **bonds**
❶ a shared experience or feeling that brings people close together ❷ bonds are ropes or chains used to tie people up

bondage NOUN
bondage is being a slave

bone NOUN **bones**
a bone is one of the hard pieces of a skeleton
➤ **to have a bone to pick with someone** is to have a reason to argue with them about something

bonfire NOUN **bonfires**
a large fire lit out of doors

bonnet NOUN **bonnets**
❶ the hinged cover over the front part of a car ❷ a hat with strings that tie under the chin

bonus NOUN **bonuses**
❶ an extra payment that someone gets for their work ❷ an extra advantage or reward

bony ADJECTIVE **bonier, boniest**
❶ bony people or animals have bones without much flesh on them ❷ full of bones ❸ thin and hard, like a bone

boo VERB **boos, booing, booed**
to boo is to shout out that you don't like what someone has said or done, like an angry audience in a theatre

booby prize NOUN **booby prizes**
a prize given as a joke to someone who comes last in a contest

booby trap NOUN **booby traps**
something designed to hit or injure someone when they do not expect it

book NOUN **books**
a set of sheets of paper, usually with printing or writing on, fastened together inside a cover

book VERB **books, booking, booked**
❶ to book something such as a seat in a theatre or on a train, or a room in a hotel, is to arrange for it to be kept for you ❷ to book someone is to record their name in a book or list

bookcase NOUN **bookcases**
a piece of furniture with shelves for holding books

bookkeeping NOUN
bookkeeping is recording details of all the money that a business receives and spends

booklet NOUN **booklets**
a small book with paper covers

bookmark NOUN **bookmarks**
❶ something you use to mark a place in a book ❷ a link you make on a computer to one of your favourite websites

bookmark VERB **bookmarks, bookmarking, bookmarked**
to bookmark a page or website is to put a bookmark on it

boom NOUN **booms**
❶ a deep hollow sound • *There was a loud boom from below deck.* ❷ a time when people are well off ❸ a long pole at the bottom of a sail to keep it stretched

boom VERB **booms, booming, boomed**
❶ to boom is to make a deep hollow sound, like a heavy gun ❷ to boom is also to speak in a loud deep voice

'Hello hello hello!' a loud voice boomed out, and from behind the door stepped a short, chubby man with a round red face.—THE REPTILE ROOM, Lemony Snicket

❸ to boom is also to grow quickly or be prosperous • *Business is booming.*

boomerang NOUN **boomerangs**
a curved stick which moves in a curve and comes back to you when you throw it

boost VERB **boosts, boosting, boosted**
to boost something is to increase its size or value or power • *Being in the drama group has really boosted their confidence.*

booster NOUN **boosters**
❶ something that increases the power of a system, especially a radio or television transmitter ❷ an additional engine or rocket for a spacecraft ❸ an additional dose of a vaccine

boot NOUN **boots**
❶ a heavy shoe that covers the ankle and sometimes part of your leg ❷ the space for luggage at the back of a car

boot VERB **boots, booting, booted**
❶ to boot someone is to kick them hard ❷ to boot up a computer is to switch it on and start it

booth NOUN **booths**
a small compartment for a special purpose, such as having your photo taken

booty NOUN
booty is the valuable things that invading soldiers or pirates take from others by force

border NOUN **borders**
❶ the border between two countries is the line where they meet • *We're about to cross the Scottish border.* ❷ an edge • *There is a black border around the poster.* ❸ a flower bed

borderline ADJECTIVE
only just acceptable or valid

bore VERB (*past tense of* **bear**)
• *Their faces bore the scars of battle.*

bore VERB **bores, boring, bored**
❶ to bore someone is to make them feel tired and uninterested ❷ to bore a hole is to drill it through something

bore NOUN **bores**
a dull or uninteresting person or thing

boredom NOUN
a feeling of tiredness and lack of interest

boring ADJECTIVE
dull and uninteresting • *The book was really boring.*

born *ADJECTIVE*
to be born is to have come into existence
by birth • *The puppies were born in*
December.

borne *VERB* (*past participle of* **bear**)
• *She has borne three children.*

borough (*say* bu-ro) *NOUN* **boroughs**
an important town or district with its own local
council

borrow *VERB* **borrows**, **borrowing**,
borrowed
to borrow something is to have it for a time
and then return it to its owner

bosom *NOUN* **bosoms**
a woman's breasts

boss *NOUN* **bosses** (*informal*)
a person who is in charge of a business or
group of workers

boss *VERB* **bosses**, **bossing**, **bossed** (*informal*)
to boss someone is to order them around

bossy *ADJECTIVE* **bossier**, **bossiest** (*informal*)
a bossy person is fond of ordering people
about
➤ **bossiness** *NOUN*

botanical *ADJECTIVE*
a botanical garden is one that has a lot of
interesting plants that the public can go
and see

botany *NOUN*
botany is the study of plants
➤ **botanist** *NOUN*

both *DETERMINER, PRONOUN*
the two of them, not just one • *I want them*
both in the team.

both *ADVERB*
you use **both** with **and** to say two things
about someone or something • *He is both*
friendly and helpful. • *The cake was both hard*
and dry.

bother *VERB* **bothers**, **bothering**,
bothered
❶ to bother someone is to cause them trouble
or worry ❷ to be bothered to do something is
to take trouble over it

bother *NOUN*
bother is trouble or worry

bottle *NOUN* **bottles**
a glass or plastic container with a narrow neck
for holding liquids

bottle *VERB* **bottles**, **bottling**, **bottled**
to bottle something is to put it in a bottle
➤ **to bottle something up** is to keep
something you are worried about to yourself

bottle bank *NOUN* **bottle banks**
a large tank or drum for putting glass bottles
and jars in for recycling

bottleneck *NOUN* **bottlenecks**
a place where traffic is slowed down or stuck by
a blockage or hazard

bottom *NOUN* **bottoms**
❶ the bottom of something is its lowest point
❷ the bottom of a garden is the farther end
of it, away from the house ❸ your bottom is
the part of you that you sit on, also called your
buttocks

bottomless *ADJECTIVE*
❶ very deep ❷ not seeming to have any limit
• *I don't have a bottomless purse.*

bough (*rhymes with* **cow**) *NOUN* **boughs**
a large branch of a tree that reaches out from
the trunk

bought *VERB* (*past tense and past participle*
of **buy**)
• *I bought the baby some lovely toys to*
play with. • *She looked at the map she had*
bought.

boulder *NOUN* **boulders**
a very large smooth stone

bounce *VERB* **bounces**, **bouncing**,
bounced
❶ to bounce is to spring back when thrown
against something, like a rubber ball
❷ to bounce something like a ball is to
throw it so that it bounces

bounce *NOUN* **bounces**
❶ a bounce is the action of bouncing
❷ bounce is liveliness, such as a young child or
puppy has

bouncy *ADJECTIVE* **bouncier**, **bounciest**
❶ a bouncy person is lively and full of
energy ❷ a bouncy ball is able to bounce
well
➤ **bounciness** *NOUN*

bound *VERB* (*past tense and past participle of* **bind**)
• *She bound his arm firmly with the bandage.*
• *The prisoners had been bound and gagged.*

bound *ADJECTIVE*
➤ **to be bound for a place** is to be travelling towards it • *The Titanic was bound for New York.*
➤ **to be bound to do something** is to have to do it or be likely to do it • *The team is bound to win a medal.*

bound *VERB* **bounds, bounding, bounded**
to bound is to leap or to run with leaping steps

bound *NOUN* **bounds**
a leaping movement

boundary *NOUN* **boundaries**
a line that marks a limit • *the boundary between north and south*

bounds *PLURAL NOUN*
➤ a place that is **out of bounds** is somewhere you are not allowed to go • *The teachers' common room is out of bounds to pupils.*

bouquet (*say* boo-**kay** *or* boh-**kay**) *NOUN* **bouquets**
a bunch of flowers

bout (*say* bowt) *NOUN* **bouts**
❶ a period of illness • *I've just had a bout of flu.*
❷ a boxing or wrestling fight

boutique (*say* boo-**teek**) *NOUN* **boutiques**
a small shop, especially one that sells fashionable clothes

bovine *ADJECTIVE*
to do with cows, or like a cow

bow (*rhymes with* go) *NOUN* **bows**
❶ a knot made with loops ❷ the stick used for playing a stringed musical instrument such as a violin or cello ❸ a long curved piece of wood with a tight string joining its ends, used for shooting arrows

bow (*rhymes with* cow) *VERB* **bows, bowing, bowed**
to bow is to bend your body forwards to show respect or as a greeting

bow (*rhymes with* cow) *NOUN* **bows**
❶ a movement of bowing your body
• *The pianist stood up to take a bow.* ❷ a bow is also the front part of a ship

bowels *PLURAL NOUN*
the bowels are the intestines

bowl *NOUN* **bowls**
❶ a deep round dish for eating from ❷ the rounded part of a spoon ❸ a heavy ball used in the game of bowls or tenpin bowling

bowl *VERB* **bowls, bowling, bowled**
❶ to bowl in cricket is to send the ball towards the batsman or batswoman ❷ to bowl someone is to get them out by hitting the wicket with the ball

bow-legged *ADJECTIVE*
a bow-legged person has legs that curve outwards at the knees

bowler *NOUN* **bowlers**
❶ someone who bowls in cricket ❷ a hat with a rounded top and a narrow brim

bowling *NOUN*
❶ a game in which you have to knock down skittles with a ball you roll down an alley ❷ the game of bowls ❸ the action of throwing a cricket ball

bowls *PLURAL NOUN*
a game played on a smooth piece of grass, in which you roll heavy balls towards a small target ball

bow tie *NOUN* **bow ties**
a tie in the form of a bow, worn by men as part of formal dress

box *NOUN* **boxes**
❶ a container made of wood or cardboard, often with a lid ❷ a small rectangle that you fill in on a form or computer screen ❸ a special compartment or booth, such as a phone box or a witness box in a law court

box *VERB* **boxes, boxing, boxed**
❶ to box is to fight with the fists ❷ to box something is to put it into a box

boxer *NOUN* **boxers**
❶ someone who boxes ❷ a breed of dog that looks like a bulldog

Boxing Day *NOUN* **Boxing Days**
the first weekday after Christmas Day

box office *NOUN* **box offices**
a place where you can buy seats for the theatre or cinema

a b c d e f g h i j k l m n o p q r s t u v w x y z

boy *NOUN* **boys**
a male child
► **boyish** *ADJECTIVE*

boycott *VERB* **boycotts, boycotting, boycotted**
to boycott something is to refuse to buy it or have anything to do with it
• *They boycotted the buses when the fares went up.*

boyfriend *NOUN* **boyfriends**
a male romantic partner

bra *NOUN* **bras** (*informal*)
a piece of underwear women wear to support their breasts

brace *NOUN* **braces**
❶ a device for holding something in place
❷ a wire device for straightening the teeth

bracelet *NOUN* **bracelets**
a small band or chain you wear round your wrist

braces *PLURAL NOUN*
braces are a pair of stretching straps worn over the shoulders to hold trousers up

bracken *NOUN*
bracken is a kind of large fern that grows in open country

bracket *NOUN* **brackets**
❶ a kind of punctuation mark used in pairs round words or figures to separate them from what comes before and after. Brackets are round ( ) or square [ ]. ❷ a support attached to a wall to hold up a shelf or light fitting

brae (*say* bray) *NOUN* **braes** (*Scottish*)
a hillside or slope

brag *VERB* **brags, bragging, bragged**
to brag is to boast

braid *NOUN* **braids**
❶ a plait ❷ a decorative ribbon or band

Braille *NOUN*
Braille is a system of writing or printing using raised dots, which blind people can read by touch
DID YOU KNOW? **Braille** is named after its inventor, a blind French teacher called Louis Braille (1809–1852).

brain *NOUN* **brains**
❶ your brain is the part inside the top of your head that controls your body ❷ brain also means a person's mind or intelligence • *He's got a good brain.*

brainy *ADJECTIVE* **brainier, brainiest** (*informal*)
clever, intelligent • *She's the brainiest child in the school.*

brake *NOUN* **brakes**
a device for making a vehicle stop or slow down

brake *VERB* **brakes, braking, braked**
to use a brake to stop or slow down
SPELLING ALERT! There is a **brake** on a bicycle, but you take a **break** from school.

bramble *NOUN* **brambles**
a bramble is a blackberry bush or a prickly bush like it

bran *NOUN*
the outer parts of the seeds of grain which is usually left when the grain is made into flour

branch *NOUN* **branches**
❶ a part that sticks out from the trunk of a tree ❷ a part of a railway or river or road that leads off from the main part ❸ a part of a large organization

branch *VERB* **branches, branching, branched**
to branch is to form a branch
► **to branch out** is to start doing something new

brand *NOUN* **brands**
a particular make or kind of goods • *Just get a cheap brand of tea.*

brand *VERB* **brands, branding, branded**
to brand sheep or cattle is to mark them with a hot iron to identify them as yours

brandish *VERB* **brandishes, brandishing, brandished**
to brandish something is to wave it about
Before Eddie knew what was happening, Mad Uncle Jack had leapt to his feet and was brandishing a small ceremonial sword.
—TERRIBLE TIMES, Philip Ardagh

brand new *ADJECTIVE*
completely new

brandy *NOUN* **brandies**
brandy is a kind of strong alcoholic drink

brass *NOUN*
❶ brass is an alloy made from copper and zinc ❷ brass also means the wind instruments made of brass, such as trumpets and trombones

brass band *NOUN* **brass bands**
a musical band made up of brass instruments

brassy *ADJECTIVE* **brassier, brassiest**
❶ having the colour of brass ❷ loud and harsh • *We heard a brassy laugh.* ❸ cheeky and showy

brave *ADJECTIVE* **braver, bravest**
ready to face danger or suffering
➤ **bravely** *ADVERB* ➤ **bravery** *NOUN*

brawl *NOUN* **brawls**
a noisy fight or quarrel

brawny *ADJECTIVE* **brawnier, brawniest**
a brawny person has a strong body and muscles

bray *VERB* **brays, braying, brayed**
to bray is to make a noise like a donkey

brazen *ADJECTIVE*
❶ shameless or cheeky ❷ made of brass

brazier (*say* **bray-zi-er**) *NOUN* **braziers**
a metal container holding hot coal

breach *NOUN* **breaches**
❶ the breaking of an agreement or rule ❷ a gap or broken place in something like a wall

bread *NOUN*
bread is food made by baking flour and water, usually with yeast

breadth *NOUN* **breadths**
a thing's breadth is its width from side to side

breadwinner *NOUN* **breadwinners**
the member of a family who earns most of the money

break *VERB* **breaks, breaking, broke, broken**
❶ to break something is to make it go into two or more pieces by hitting it or dropping it ❷ to break is to stop working properly • *The printer broke again yesterday.*
❸ to break a law or rule or promise is to fail to keep it or observe it ❹ the weather breaks when it changes after being hot ❺ waves break over rocks when they fall and froth over them ❻ a boy's voice breaks when it starts to go deeper at about the age of 14 ❼ to break a record is to do better than the previous holder, for example in athletics
➤ **to break down** a machine or vehicle breaks down when it stops working properly
➤ **to break off** is to stop doing something for a time • *We broke off for lunch.*
➤ **to break out** if something such as a disease or fighting breaks out, it suddenly starts
➤ **to break the news** is to make it known
➤ **to break up** ❶ people break up when they leave one another after a long time together ❷ school breaks up when it closes at the end of term

break *NOUN* **breaks**
❶ a broken place; a gap ❷ a sudden dash or attempt to escape ❸ a short rest from work ❹ (*informal*) a piece of luck; a fair chance • *That was a lucky break!*

breakable *ADJECTIVE*
easy to break • *Be careful with that box—there are breakable things in it.*

breakage *NOUN* **breakages**
something that is broken • *All breakages must be paid for.*

breakdown *NOUN* **breakdowns**
❶ a sudden failure to work, especially by a car • *We had a breakdown on the motorway.* ❷ a failure or collapse of something • *There has been a breakdown of communications.* ❸ (*old use*) a sudden or severe period of mental illness ❹ a detailed look at the parts of something to make it easier to understand • *Here's a breakdown of last season's football results.*

breaker *NOUN* **breakers**
a wave breaking on the shore

breakfast *NOUN* **breakfasts**
breakfast is the first meal of the day

break-in *NOUN* **break-ins**
a break-in is when someone forces their way into a building, usually in order to steal something

a b c d e f g h i j k l m n o p q r s t u v w x y z

breakneck *ADJECTIVE*
dangerously fast • *He drove at breakneck speed.*

breakthrough *NOUN* **breakthroughs**
an important piece of progress, for example in medical research

breakwater *NOUN* **breakwaters**
a wall built out into the sea to protect a harbour or coast against heavy waves

breast *NOUN* **breasts**
❶ one of the two parts on the front of a woman's body where milk is produced after she has had a baby ❷ a person's or animal's chest

breaststroke *NOUN*
a stroke you use when swimming on your front, by pushing your arms forward and bringing them round and back

breath (*say* breth) *NOUN* **breaths**
the air that you take into your lungs and send out again
➤ **to be out of breath** is to gasp for air after exercise
➤ **to take someone's breath away** is to surprise or delight them
SPELLING ALERT! **Breath** is a noun whereas **breathe** is a verb: *Take a deep breath. Don't breathe a word!*

breathe (*say* bree*th*) *VERB* **breathes**, **breathing**, **breathed**
to breathe is to take air into your lungs through your nose or mouth and send it out again

breather *NOUN* **breathers** (*informal*)
a pause for a rest • *We all need a breather.*

breathless *ADJECTIVE*
short of breath

breathtaking *ADJECTIVE*
extremely beautiful or delightful

bred *VERB* (*past tense and past participle of* **breed**)
• *My uncle bred pigeons for racing.* • *Humans have bred dogs for all sorts of jobs.*

breech *NOUN* **breeches**
the part of a gun barrel where the bullets are put in

breeches (*say* brich-iz) *PLURAL NOUN*
short trousers that fit tightly at the knee

breed *VERB* **breeds**, **breeding**, **bred**
❶ to breed is to produce offspring ❷ to breed animals is to keep them in order to get young ones from them ❸ to breed something like illness or poverty is to cause it

breed *NOUN* **breeds**
a variety of similar animals

breeder *NOUN* **breeders**
someone who breeds animals

breeze *NOUN* **breezes**
a gentle wind

breezy *ADJECTIVE* **breezier**, **breeziest**
❶ slightly windy ❷ bright and cheerful

brethren *PLURAL NOUN* (*old use*)
brothers

brew *VERB* **brews**, **brewing**, **brewed**
❶ to brew beer or tea is to make it ❷ to be brewing is to start or develop • *Trouble is brewing.*

brewer *NOUN* **brewers**
someone whose work is to make beer

brewery *NOUN* **breweries**
a place where beer is made

Brexit *NOUN*
the departure of the United Kingdom from the European Union

briar *NOUN* **briars**
a thorny bush, especially a wild rose bush

bribe *NOUN* **bribes**
a bribe is money or a gift offered to someone to make them do something

bribe *VERB* **bribes**, **bribing**, **bribed**
to bribe someone is to give them a bribe
➤ **bribery** *NOUN*

brick *NOUN* **bricks**
❶ a small hard block of baked clay used in building ❷ a rectangular block of something

bricklayer *NOUN* **bricklayers**
a worker who builds with bricks

bridal *ADJECTIVE*
to do with brides

bride *NOUN* **brides**
a woman on her wedding day

bridegroom *NOUN* **bridegrooms**
a man on his wedding day

bridesmaid *NOUN* **bridesmaids**
someone who helps the bride at her wedding

bridge *NOUN* **bridges**
❶ a bridge is a structure built over a river, railway or road, to allow people to cross it
❷ the bridge of a ship is the high platform above the deck, from where the ship is controlled ❸ the bridge of your nose is the bony upper part of your nose ❹ bridge is a card game rather like whist

bridle *NOUN* **bridles**
the part of a horse's harness that fits over its head

brief *ADJECTIVE* **briefer, briefest**
lasting a short time or using only a few words
➤ **in brief** in a few words
➤ **briefly** *ADVERB*

brief *NOUN* **briefs**
a brief is a set of instructions about a job to be done, especially one given to a lawyer about a case

brief *VERB* **briefs, briefing, briefed**
to brief someone is to give them instructions about a job to be done

briefcase *NOUN* **briefcases**
a flat case for keeping documents and papers in

briefs *PLURAL NOUN*
short underpants

brigade *NOUN* **brigades**
❶ an army unit usually consisting of three battalions ❷ a group of people in uniform, for example the fire brigade

brigadier *NOUN* **brigadiers**
an army officer who commands a brigade and is higher in rank than a colonel

brigand *NOUN* **brigands**
an old word for a robber or outlaw
The chief brigand was a ferocious-looking man, with two belts full of bullets criss-cross over his shoulders.—THE SCARECROW AND HIS SERVANT, Philip Pullman

bright *ADJECTIVE* **brighter, brightest**
❶ giving out a strong light; shining ❷ a bright colour is strong and vivid ❸ clever • *He's a bright lad.* ❹ cheerful
➤ **brightly** *ADVERB* ➤ **brightness** *NOUN*

brighten *VERB* **brightens, brightening, brightened**
❶ to brighten something is to make it brighter
❷ to brighten is to become brighter, like the sky when the weather improves

brilliance *NOUN*
❶ brilliance is bright light • *the brilliance of the summer sky* ❷ brilliance is also being very intelligent or clever

brilliant *ADJECTIVE*
❶ a brilliant person is very intelligent or clever
❷ (*informal*) really good or enjoyable • *That was a brilliant film!* ❸ very bright and sparkling
➤ **brilliantly** *ADVERB*

brim *NOUN* **brims**
❶ the edge round the top of a container
❷ the bottom edge of a hat that sticks out

brimming *ADJECTIVE*
completely full

brine *NOUN*
brine is salty water

bring *VERB* **brings, bringing, brought**
to bring someone or something is to make them come with you to a place
➤ **to bring someone round** is to make them conscious again after they have fainted
➤ **to bring someone up** is to look after them and educate them as a child
➤ **to bring something about** is to make it happen
➤ **to bring something off** is to achieve something difficult or unexpected
➤ **to bring something up** is to mention it in a conversation

brink *NOUN*
the edge of a steep or dangerous place

brisk *ADJECTIVE* **brisker, briskest**
quick and lively
➤ **briskly** *ADVERB*

bristle *NOUN* **bristles**
a short, stiff hair

a
b
c
d
e
f
g
h
i
j
k
l
m
n
o
p
q
r
s
t
u
v
w
x
y
z

A
B
C
D
E
F
G
H
I
J
K
L
M
N
O
P
Q
R
S
T
U
V
W
X
Y
Z

British *ADJECTIVE*
to do with Great Britain

Briton *NOUN* **Britons**
❶ someone born in Great Britain
❷ a member of the Celtic peoples who lived in southern Britain at the time of the Romans

brittle *ADJECTIVE* **brittler**, **brittlest**
hard but likely to break or snap

broad *ADJECTIVE* **broader**, **broadest**
❶ wide and open • *They walked down a broad avenue.* ❷ broad daylight is clear and full daylight ❸ general, not detailed • *a broad outline*

broadband *NOUN*
a system for connecting computers to the internet and sending information very quickly

broad bean *NOUN* **broad beans**
a type of large flat bean

broadcast *NOUN* **broadcasts**
a radio or television programme

broadcast *VERB* **broadcasts**, **broadcasting**, **broadcast**
to broadcast a radio or television programme is to transmit it or take part in it

broaden *VERB* **broadens**, **broadening**, **broadened**
to broaden something is to make it broader

broadly *ADVERB*
in general terms • *They were broadly right.*

broad-minded *ADJECTIVE*
tolerant of other people's views and opinions and not easily shocked

broccoli *NOUN*
a vegetable with green or purple heads on green stalks

brochure *NOUN* **brochures**
a booklet containing information, especially about a place

brogue *NOUN* **brogues**
❶ a strong kind of shoe ❷ a strong accent • *He spoke with an Irish brogue.*

broke (*past tense of* **break**)
• *He never broke a promise.*

broke *ADJECTIVE* (*informal*)
not having any money • *By the end of the week I was completely broke.*

broken (*past participle of* **break**)
• *He was sure he had broken his leg.*

broken *ADJECTIVE*
❶ broken English is English spoken with a strong foreign accent and lots of mistakes
❷ a broken home is a home in which the parents have separated

bronchitis (*say* brong-**ky**-tiss) *NOUN*
bronchitis is an infection of the lungs

bronze *NOUN*
❶ bronze is an alloy of copper and tin ❷ bronze is also a yellow-brown colour

bronze medal *NOUN* **bronze medals**
a medal made of bronze, usually awarded as the third prize

brooch (*rhymes with* **coach**) *NOUN* **brooches**
a piece of jewellery that can be pinned on to clothes

brood *NOUN* **broods**
a brood is a number of young birds hatched together

brood *VERB* **broods**, **brooding**, **brooded**
❶ birds such as chickens brood when they sit on eggs to hatch them ❷ to brood over something is to keep on thinking and worrying about it
Brom Bones, sorely smitten with love and jealousy, sat brooding by himself in one corner.—THE LEGEND OF SLEEPY HOLLOW, Washington Irving

broody *ADJECTIVE* **broodier**, **broodiest**
❶ a broody hen is one that wants to hatch its eggs ❷ a broody person is eager to have children

brook *NOUN* **brooks**
a small stream

broom *NOUN* **brooms**
❶ a broom is a brush with a long handle, for sweeping ❷ broom is a shrub with yellow, white or pink flowers

broomstick *NOUN* **broomsticks**
the handle of a broom

broth *NOUN* **broths**
broth is a thin kind of soup

brother *NOUN* **brothers**
your brother is a man or boy who has the same parents as you

brother-in-law *NOUN* **brothers-in-law**
a person's brother-in-law is the brother of their husband or wife, or the husband of their sibling

brotherly *ADJECTIVE*
like a brother

brought *VERB* (*past tense and past participle of* **bring**)
• *She brought out a bowl of trifle.* • *Have you brought presents?*

brow *NOUN* **brows**
❶ your brow is your forehead ❷ your brows are your eyebrows ❸ the brow of a hill is the top of it

brown *ADJECTIVE* **browner, brownest**
❶ of the colour of earth, wood or toast ❷ suntanned

brown *NOUN*
a brown colour

brownie *NOUN* **brownies**
a small chocolate cake with nuts

browse *VERB* **browses, browsing, browsed**
❶ to browse is to read or look at something casually ❷ to look for information on the internet ❸ animals browse when they feed on grass or leaves

browser *NOUN* **browsers**
a computer program that allows you to look at websites on the internet

bruise *NOUN* **bruises**
a dark mark that appears on your skin when it is hit or hurt

bruise *VERB* **bruises, bruising, bruised**
to bruise your skin or a part of your body is to get a bruise on it

brunch *NOUN* **brunches**
a meal that you have in the late morning instead of breakfast and lunch

brush *NOUN* **brushes**
❶ a device with hairs or bristles for sweeping, painting or arranging the hair ❷ a fox's bushy tail

brush *VERB* **brushes, brushing, brushed**
❶ to brush something is to use a brush on it • *Have you brushed your hair yet?* ❷ to brush against someone is to touch them gently as you pass them
➤ **to brush something aside** is to ignore it
➤ **to brush something up** is to improve your knowledge of it • *You need to brush up on your maths.*

Brussels sprout *NOUN* **Brussels sprouts**
a green vegetable like a tiny cabbage

brutal *ADJECTIVE*
savage and cruel
➤ **brutality** *NOUN* ➤ **brutally** *ADVERB*

brute *NOUN* **brutes**
❶ a cruel or violent person • *The pirate captain was an ugly brute of a man.* ❷ an animal

bubble *NOUN* **bubbles**
❶ a thin transparent ball of liquid filled with air or gas ❷ a small ball of air in a liquid or a solid ❸ a small group of people who you are allowed to have close contact with at a time when you have to keep your distance from most people

bubble *VERB* **bubbles, bubbling, bubbled**
a liquid bubbles when it produces bubbles, as it does when it boils

bubblegum *NOUN*
bubblegum is a kind of chewing gum that you can blow into a bubble out of the front of your mouth

bubbly *ADJECTIVE* **bubblier, bubbliest**
❶ full of bubbles, like fizzy water ❷ a bubbly person is cheerful and lively

buccaneer *NOUN* **buccaneers**
an old word for a pirate

buck *NOUN* **bucks**
a male deer, rabbit or hare

buck *VERB* **bucks, bucking, bucked**
a horse bucks when it jumps with its back arched

bucket *NOUN* **buckets**
a container with a handle, for carrying liquids or something such as sand

a b c d e f g h i j k l m n o p q r s t u v w x y z

bucketful *NOUN* **bucketfuls**
as much of something as you can carry in a bucket

buckle *NOUN* **buckles**
a clip at the end of a belt or strap for fastening it

buckle *VERB* **buckles, buckling, buckled**
❶ to buckle something is to fasten it with a buckle ❷ to buckle is to bend or give way under a strain • *The bars on the cage were beginning to buckle.*
➤ **to buckle down** is to start work on something with determination

bud *NOUN* **buds**
a flower or leaf before it has opened

Buddhism (*say* **bood**-izm) *NOUN*
Buddhism is a religion that started in Asia and follows the teachings of Buddha
➤ **Buddhist** *NOUN*

budding *ADJECTIVE*
showing great promise • *The class has several budding musicians.*

budge *VERB* **budges, budging, budged**
to budge is to move slightly • *The door was stuck and wouldn't budge.*

budgerigar (*say* **bud**-jer-i-gar) *NOUN* **budgerigars**
a small, brightly coloured Australian bird often kept as a pet in a cage

budget *NOUN* **budgets**
❶ the money someone plans to spend on something ❷ a plan for earning and spending money

budget *VERB* **budgets, budgeting, budgeted**
to budget is to plan how much you are going to spend

budgie *NOUN* **budgies** (*informal*)
a budgerigar

buff *ADJECTIVE*
of a dull yellow colour

buffalo *NOUN* **buffalo** *or* **buffaloes**
a wild ox with long curved horns

buffer *NOUN* **buffers**
❶ something that softens a blow or collision, especially a device on a railway engine or wagon or at the end of a railway line

❷ (*computing*) a memory in which data can be stored for a time, especially while being sent from one device to another

buffet (*say* **boo**-fay) *NOUN* **buffets**
❶ a cafe or place for buying drinks and snacks ❷ a meal where guests serve themselves

buffoon (*say* bu-**foon**) *NOUN* **buffoons**
a stupid or silly person

bug *NOUN* **bugs**
❶ a tiny insect ❷ (*informal*) a germ that causes illness • *I may have a tummy bug.*
❸ a hidden microphone ❹ a fault or problem in a computer program that stops it working properly

bug *VERB* **bugs, bugging, bugged**
❶ to bug a place is to put a hidden microphone into it ❷ (*informal*) to bug someone is to annoy them • *This loud music is really beginning to bug me.*

buggy *NOUN* **buggies**
❶ a folding pram for small children ❷ a small vehicle with an open top • *The moon buggy can carry two astronauts.*

bugle (*say* **byoo**-gul) *NOUN* **bugles**
a brass instrument like a small trumpet

build *VERB* **builds, building, built**
to build something is to make it by putting the parts together
➤ **to build something up** is to make it larger or stronger • *Regular exercise will build up your health.*
➤ **to build up** is to become larger or stronger • *The work was starting to build up.*

build *NOUN* **builds**
your build is the shape of your body

builder *NOUN* **builders**
someone who puts up buildings

building *NOUN* **buildings**
❶ a building is a structure that someone has built, such as a house or a block of flats
❷ building is the business of making houses and other structures

build-up *NOUN*
❶ a gradual increase in the amount of something ❷ the part of a story or series of events which is before the most important part and leads up to it

built-in *ADJECTIVE*
made into a permanent part of something
• *The house had built-in kitchen units.*

built-up *ADJECTIVE*
a built-up area is one with lots of houses and other buildings

bulb *NOUN* **bulbs**
❶ an onion-shaped root which grows into a plant or flower when it is put in the ground
❷ a light bulb

bulge *NOUN* **bulges**
a part that sticks out; a swelling

bulge *VERB* **bulges**, **bulging**, **bulged**
to bulge is to stick out or swell

bulk *NOUN*
❶ a thing's bulk is its size, especially when it is large ❷ the bulk of something is most of it • *He spends the bulk of his time on the computer.*
➤ **in bulk** in large quantities

bulky *ADJECTIVE* **bulkier**, **bulkiest**
taking up a lot of space

bull *NOUN* **bulls**
❶ the male of the cattle family ❷ a male seal, whale or elephant

bulldog *NOUN* **bulldogs**
a breed of dog with a short thick neck

bulldozer *NOUN* **bulldozers**
a heavy vehicle with a wide metal blade in front, used to clear or flatten land
➤ **bulldoze** *VERB*

bullet *NOUN* **bullets**
a piece of shaped metal shot from a rifle or pistol

bulletin *NOUN* **bulletins**
a short announcement of news on radio or television

bullet point *NOUN* **bullet points**
an important item in a list, printed with a black dot in front of it

bulletproof *ADJECTIVE*
able to stop bullets getting through

bullfight *NOUN* **bullfights**
in Spain, a public entertainment in which people challenge bulls, and sometimes kill them

➤ **bullfighter** *NOUN*

bullion *NOUN*
gold or silver in the form of bars

bullock *NOUN* **bullocks**
a young bull

bullseye *NOUN* **bullseyes**
the centre of a target

bully *VERB* **bullies**, **bullying**, **bullied**
to bully someone is to hurt or frighten them when they are weaker

bully *NOUN* **bullies**
someone who bullies people

bulrush *NOUN* **bulrushes**
a tall reed that grows in water or on boggy land

bulwarks *PLURAL NOUN*
a ship's side above the level of the deck

bum *NOUN* **bums** (*informal*)
your bottom or buttocks

bumblebee *NOUN* **bumblebees**
a large kind of bee with a loud buzz

bump *VERB* **bumps**, **bumping**, **bumped**
❶ to bump something is to knock against it accidentally ❷ to bump along is to move along unsteadily, like an old car
➤ **to bump into someone** (*informal*) is to meet them unexpectedly

bump *NOUN* **bumps**
❶ an accidental knock ❷ a swelling or lump

bumper *NOUN* **bumpers**
a bar along the front or back of a motor vehicle to protect it in collisions

bumper *ADJECTIVE*
unusually large or fine • *We had a bumper crop of apples this year.*

bumpy *ADJECTIVE* **bumpier**, **bumpiest**
having lots of bumps

bun *NOUN* **buns**
❶ a small, round sweet cake ❷ a soft sandwich roll ❸ a round bunch of hair that some women make at the back of their head

bunch *NOUN* **bunches**
a number of things joined or tied together, such as fruit or flowers or keys • *He was eating a bunch of grapes.*

a
b
c
d
e
f
g
h
i
j
k
l
m
n
o
p
q
r
s
t
u
v
w
x
y
z

bundle *NOUN* **bundles**
a number of things tied or wrapped loosely together, such as clothes or papers

bundle *VERB* **bundles, bundling, bundled**
❶ to bundle things together is to tie or wrap them loosely ❷ to bundle someone into a room or car is to push them there hurriedly • *They bundled him into the back of a taxi.*

bung *VERB* **bungs, bunging, bunged**
➤ **to bung something up** (*informal*) is to block it

bungalow *NOUN* **bungalows**
a house with all the rooms on one floor

bungee jumping (*say* **bun**-jee jump-ing) *NOUN*
bungee jumping is jumping from a height with your legs tied to an elastic rope (called a **bungee**) to stop you hitting the ground

bungle *VERB* **bungles, bungling, bungled**
to bungle something is to do it badly and clumsily

bunk *NOUN* **bunks**
a narrow bed fixed to a wall, as on a ship

bunk bed *NOUN* **bunk beds**
a single bed with another bed above it or below it

bunker *NOUN* **bunkers**
❶ a container for storing fuel such as coal ❷ a hollow filled with sand, made as an obstacle on a golf course ❸ an underground shelter

bunny *NOUN* **bunnies** (*informal*)
a rabbit

buoy (*say* boi) *NOUN* **buoys**
a floating object fixed to the bottom of the sea and used to mark a channel or a stretch of shallow water

buoyant *ADJECTIVE*
❶ able to float ❷ lively and cheerful • *He was in a buoyant mood.*
➤ **buoyancy** *NOUN*

burble *VERB* **burbles, burbling, burbled**
❶ to burble is to make a light bubbling sound, like water in a stream ❷ to burble is also to talk in a rambling way • *Miss Chisholm burbled on endlessly.*

DID YOU KNOW? **Burble** is an old word that was made popular by Lewis Carroll.

burden *NOUN* **burdens**
❶ a heavy load ❷ something troublesome that you have to put up with

burger *NOUN* **burgers**
❶ a hamburger ❷ a flat round cake made from another type of meat or vegetables • *a spicy chicken burger*

burglar *NOUN* **burglars**
someone who breaks into a building to steal things
➤ **burglary** *NOUN* burglary is the crime of stealing things from a building

burgle *VERB* **burgles, burgling, burgled**
to burgle someone is to steal from their house

burial *NOUN* **burials**
putting a dead body in a grave

burly *ADJECTIVE* **burlier, burliest**
a burly person is big and strong

burn *VERB* **burns, burning, burnt** *or* **burned**
❶ to burn something is to damage or destroy it by fire or strong heat ❷ to burn is to be damaged or destroyed by fire or heat ❸ to be burning is to be on fire ❹ to be burning is also to feel very hot

burn *NOUN* **burns**
❶ an injury or mark caused by fire or strong heat ❷ the firing of a spacecraft's rocket ❸ (*Scottish*) a small stream

burner *NOUN* **burners**
the part of a lamp or cooker that forms the flame

burning *ADJECTIVE*
a burning wish or desire is one that is very strong

burp *VERB* **burps, burping, burped**
to burp is to make a noise through your mouth by letting air come up from your stomach

burp *NOUN* **burps**
the act or sound of burping

burr *NOUN* **burrs**
part of a plant that clings to your clothes or hair

burrow *NOUN* **burrows**
a hole dug by an animal such as a rabbit or fox

burrow *VERB* **burrows**, **burrowing**, **burrowed**
❶ an animal burrows when it digs a burrow
❷ to burrow is also to dig or search deeply
• *He burrowed in his pockets to find a pound coin.*

burst *VERB* **bursts**, **bursting**, **burst**
❶ to burst is to break apart suddenly
❷ to burst something is to make it break apart
❸ to be bursting with energy or excitement is to have a lot of energy or to be very excited
➤ **to burst in** is to rush in noisily or clumsily
➤ **to burst into tears** is to suddenly start crying
➤ **to burst out laughing** is to start laughing noisily

burst *NOUN* **bursts**
❶ a split caused by something bursting
• *There's a burst in one of the pipes.*
❷ something short and quick • *a burst of gunfire*

bury *VERB* **buries**, **burying**, **buried**
❶ to bury something is to put it under the ground ❷ to bury someone is to put them in a grave when they are dead
➤ **to bury the hatchet** is to agree to stop quarrelling or fighting

bus *NOUN* **buses**
a large road vehicle for carrying passengers
DID YOU KNOW? A **bus** used to be called an *omnibus*, which comes from a Latin word meaning 'for everyone'.

bush *NOUN* **bushes**
❶ a bush is a plant like a small tree with a lot of stems or branches ❷ the bush is wild land, especially in Australia or Africa

bushy *ADJECTIVE* **bushier**, **bushiest**
thick and hairy • *His dad has bushy eyebrows.*

busily *ADVERB*
in a busy way

business (*say* biz-niss) *NOUN* **businesses**
❶ a business is an organization that makes money by selling goods or services
• *His uncle worked in a garage business.*
❷ business is what an organization does to make money • *She has made a career in the banking business.* ❸ a person's business is what concerns them and no one else
• *Mind your own business.* ❹ a business is also an affair or subject • *I am tired of the whole business.*
➤ **to go out of business** is to stop trading because you are not making enough money

businesslike *ADJECTIVE*
efficient and practical

busker *NOUN* **buskers**
someone who plays music in the street, hoping for money from people passing by

bus stop *NOUN* **bus stops**
a place where a bus regularly stops

bust *NOUN* **busts**
❶ a sculpture of a person's head and shoulders
❷ a woman's breasts

bust *ADJECTIVE* (*informal*)
❶ broken • *My watch is bust.* ❷ bankrupt

bustle *VERB* **bustles**, **bustling**, **bustled**
to bustle is to be in a hurry or rushing about busily
Mum bustled into the kitchen, stuffing papers into her briefcase.—GRANNY NOTHING, Catherine MacPhail

busy *ADJECTIVE* **busier**, **busiest**
❶ a busy person is one with a lot to do
❷ a busy place is one with a lot going on
❸ a busy telephone line is one that someone is already using

busybody *NOUN* **busybodies**
someone who interferes in things that have nothing to do with them

but *CONJUNCTION*
you use **but** to join two words or statements that say different or opposite things • *I wanted to go but I couldn't.*

but *PREPOSITION*
except • *There's no one here but me.*

butcher *NOUN* **butchers**
❶ someone who runs a shop that cuts and sells meat ❷ a person who kills people cruelly

butler *NOUN* **butlers**
a male servant in charge of other servants in a large private house

A
B
C
D
E
F
G
H
I
J
K
L
M
N
O
P
Q
R
S
T
U
V
W
X
Y
Z

butt *NOUN* **butts**
❶ the thicker end of a weapon or tool
❷ (*North American, informal*) your bottom or buttocks ❸ a large barrel ❹ someone people often make fun of • *He was always the butt of their jokes.*

butt *VERB* **butts**, **butting**, **butted**
to butt someone is to hit them hard with your head
➤ **to butt in** is to interrupt suddenly or rudely

butter *NOUN*
butter is a fatty yellow food made from cream

buttercup *NOUN* **buttercups**
a yellow wild flower

butterfingers *NOUN* (*informal*)
someone who is clumsy and keeps dropping things

butterfly *NOUN* **butterflies**
❶ an insect with a thin body and large white or brightly coloured wings ❷ a stroke you use when swimming on your front, by raising both arms together over your head

butterscotch *NOUN* **butterscotches**
butterscotch is a kind of hard toffee

buttocks *PLURAL NOUN*
your buttocks are the part of the body on which you sit, your bottom

button *NOUN* **buttons**
❶ a flat plastic or metal disc sewn on clothes and passed through a buttonhole to fasten them ❷ a small knob you press to work an electric device

button *VERB* **buttons**, **buttoning**, **buttoned**
to button clothes or to button up clothes is to fasten them with buttons

buttonhole *NOUN* **buttonholes**
❶ a slit for a button to pass through ❷ a flower worn on a lapel

buttress *NOUN* **buttresses**
a support built against a wall

buy *VERB* **buys**, **buying**, **bought**
to buy something is to get it by paying for it
• *I bought new jeans yesterday.*
➤ **buyer** *NOUN*

buy *NOUN* **buys**
something you buy • *Those boots were a good buy.*

buzz *NOUN* **buzzes**
a sharp humming sound, like bees make

buzz *VERB* **buzzes**, **buzzing**, **buzzed**
to buzz is to make a buzzing sound

buzzard *NOUN* **buzzards**
a bird of prey like a large hawk

buzzer *NOUN* **buzzers**
an alarm or signalling device that makes a buzzing noise

by *PREPOSITION, ADVERB*
❶ near, close • *Sit here by me.* ❷ using; by means of • *I fixed the tyre by sticking on a patch.* ❸ before • *I need to finish my homework by tomorrow.* ❹ past • *A crowd of people went by.* • *I can't get by all these boxes.*
➤ **by and large** mostly; on the whole
➤ **by the way** a phrase you use to add something else to what you have said
• *When is your birthday, by the way?*

bye-bye *EXCLAMATION* (*informal*)
goodbye

by-election *NOUN* **by-elections**
an election in one district only, when a Member of Parliament has died or resigned

bypass *NOUN* **bypasses**
a road that takes traffic round the edge of a town or city rather than going through the centre

by-product *NOUN* **by-products**
something useful that is made while something else is being made

bystander *NOUN* **bystanders**
someone who sees something happening but takes no part in it

byte *NOUN* **bytes** (*computing*)
a unit that measures data or memory

Cc

C *ABBREVIATION*
❶ short for **Celsius** ❷ 100 in Roman numerals

cab *NOUN* **cabs**
❶ a taxi ❷ the place for the driver in a lorry, bus, train or crane

cabbage *NOUN* **cabbages**
a large round green vegetable with layers of closely packed leaves

cabin *NOUN* **cabins**
❶ a hut or shelter ❷ one of the small rooms on a ship for sleeping in ❸ the part of an aircraft where the passengers sit

cabinet *NOUN* **cabinets**
❶ a cupboard with shelves and doors, used for storing things ❷ the group of chief ministers who run the government

cable *NOUN* **cables**
❶ a thick rope, wire or chain used for lifting heavy loads or tying up ships ❷ a bundle of wires inside a tube, used for transmitting electricity or electrical signals ❸ a telegram sent overseas

cable car *NOUN* **cable cars**
a small cabin that hangs from a moving cable, used for carrying people up and down the side of a mountain

cable television *NOUN*
a television system in which programmes are transmitted along underground cables into people's houses

cackle *VERB* **cackles**, **cackling**, **cackled**
to give a loud harsh laugh • *The witch cackled as she stirred the pot.*

cackle *NOUN* **cackles**
❶ a cackle is a loud harsh laugh ❷ a cackle is also the clucking of a hen or goose

cacophony (*say* ka-**kof**-o-nee) *NOUN*
a chorus of loud clashing noises
In summer you could barely even see the cliff as dragons of all shapes and sizes swarmed

over it, snapping and biting and sending up a cacophony of noise.—HOW TO TRAIN YOUR DRAGON, Cressida Cowell
➤ **cacophonous** *ADJECTIVE*

cactus *NOUN* **cacti**
a fleshy plant with prickly spines that grows in hot dry places
PLURAL ALERT! The word **cactus** has a Latin plural: *some potted cacti* (not *cactuses*).

caddie *NOUN* **caddies**
someone whose job is to help a golfer by carrying the clubs and giving advice

cadet *NOUN* **cadets**
a young person who is being trained for the armed forces or the police

cadge *VERB* **cadges**, **cadging**, **cadged** (*informal*)
to cadge something is to get it by asking for it in a blunt or direct way

cafe (*say* **kaf**-ay) *NOUN* **cafes**
a place that sells hot and cold drinks and light meals

cafeteria (*say* kaf-e-**teer**-i-a) *NOUN* **cafeterias**
a cafe where customers serve themselves from a counter

caffeine *NOUN*
caffeine is a substance in tea and coffee and some other drinks, that keeps you awake and makes you feel active

cage *NOUN* **cages**
an enclosure made of bars or wires, for keeping birds or animals so that they can't get away

cagoule *NOUN* **cagoules**
a lightweight waterproof jacket

cake *NOUN* **cakes**
❶ a sweet food made from a baked mixture of flour, eggs, fat and sugar ❷ something made into a lump rather like a cake, such as soap
➤ **a piece of cake** (*informal*) something very easy to do

caked *ADJECTIVE*
covered with something that has dried hard, like mud

calamity *NOUN* **calamities**
a disaster
➤ **calamitous** *ADJECTIVE*

calcium *NOUN*
a grey-white element contained in teeth, bones and lime

calculate *VERB* **calculates, calculating, calculated**
❶ to calculate something is to work it out by arithmetic or with a calculator
❷ to calculate on something is to plan round it • *They were calculating on a fine day for the picnic.*

calculation *NOUN* **calculations**
something you work out by using numbers or other information

calculator *NOUN* **calculators**
a machine or app for adding up figures and doing other calculations with numbers

calendar *NOUN* **calendars**
a chart or display that shows the days of the year

calf *NOUN* **calves**
❶ a young cow or ox ❷ a young seal, whale or elephant ❸ your calf is the back part of your leg below your knee

call *NOUN* **calls**
❶ a shout or cry • *They heard a call for help.*
❷ a short visit • *She decided to pay her father a call.* ❸ a telephone conversation with someone

call *VERB* **calls, calling, called**
❶ to call is to shout out ❷ to call someone is to telephone them • *I'll call you at the weekend.* ❸ to call someone near you is to ask them to come to you ❹ to call on someone is to visit them ❺ to be called something is to have it as your name • *His friend was called Damon.* ❻ to call something a certain thing is to describe it that way • *I call that a swindle.*
➤ **to call someone names** is to be rude to them or insult them
➤ **to call something off** is to cancel it

calligraphy *NOUN*
decorative handwriting or lettering
➤ **calligrapher** *NOUN*

callous *ADJECTIVE*
a callous person is very unkind and doesn't care about other people's feelings

calm *ADJECTIVE* **calmer, calmest**
❶ the sea or the weather is calm when it is quiet and still ❷ someone is calm when they are not excited or agitated • *Please try to keep calm.*
➤ **calmly** *ADVERB* ➤ **calmness** *NOUN*

calorie *NOUN* **calories**
a unit for measuring the amount of heat or the energy produced by food

calves (*plural of* **calf**)

calypso *NOUN* **calypsos**
a Caribbean song about current happenings, made up as the singer goes along

came *VERB* (*past tense of* **come**)
• *The truck came to a stop.*

camel *NOUN* **camels**
a large animal with a long neck and one or two humps on its back • *Arabian camels have one hump, and Bactrian camels have two.*

camera *NOUN* **cameras**
a device for taking photographs, films or television pictures
DID YOU KNOW? The word **camera** comes from a Latin word meaning 'chamber' or 'room'.

camouflage (*say* **kam**-o-flah*zh*) *NOUN*
❶ clothes or coverings that make people or things look like part of their surroundings
❷ the natural markings on an animal that allow it to blend in with its surroundings
• *Some animals use camouflage to hide from predators.*
➤ **camouflaged** *ADJECTIVE*

camp *NOUN* **camps**
a place where people live in tents or huts or caravans for a short time
camp *VERB* **camps, camping, camped**
❶ to camp or go camping is to have a holiday in a tent ❷ to camp is also to put up a tent or tents • *Let's camp here for the night.*
➤ **camper** *NOUN* ➤ **camping** *NOUN*

campaign *NOUN* **campaigns**
❶ a planned series of actions, especially

to get people to support you or become interested in something • *a campaign for human rights* ❷ a series of battles in one area or with one aim

campaign *VERB* **campaigns, campaigning, campaigned**
to campaign is to carry out a plan of action to raise people's interest in something such as a good cause • *They are campaigning to stop the destruction of the rainforests.*

campsite *NOUN* **campsites**
a place for camping

can *VERB* (*past tense* **could**)
❶ to be able to do something or to know how to do it • *Can you lift that box?* • *Her mother can speak Russian.* ❷ to be allowed to do something • *Can I go home now?*

can *NOUN* **cans**
a sealed metal container holding food or drink

Canadian *ADJECTIVE*
to do with Canada or its people

Canadian *NOUN* **Canadians**
a person from Canada

canal *NOUN* **canals**
❶ a long channel specially dug and filled with water for boats to travel along ❷ a tube in the body of a human being or animal • *The canals in your ears help you balance.*

canary *NOUN* **canaries**
a small yellow bird that sings, often kept in a cage as a pet

cancel *VERB* **cancels, cancelling, cancelled**
❶ to cancel something planned is to say that it will not be done or not take place after all ❷ to cancel an order or instruction is to stop it ❸ to cancel a stamp or ticket is to mark it so that it cannot be used again
➤ **cancellation** *NOUN*

cancer *NOUN* **cancers**
a serious illness in which a harmful growth forms in the body
➤ **cancerous** *ADJECTIVE*

candidate *NOUN* **candidates**
❶ someone who has applied for a job or position ❷ someone who is taking an exam

candle *NOUN* **candles**
a stick of wax with a wick through it, which gives out light when it is burning

candlelight *NOUN*
candlelight is the light given out by a candle

candlestick *NOUN* **candlesticks**
a holder for a candle or candles

candy *NOUN* **candies**
❶ candy is crystallized sugar ❷ (*North American*) a sweet or chocolate

candyfloss *NOUN*
candyfloss is a fluffy mass of sugar that has been spun into fine threads

cane *NOUN* **canes**
a cane is the hollow stem of a reed or tall grass

cane *VERB* **canes, caning, caned**
to cane someone is to beat them with a cane

canine *ADJECTIVE*
to do with dogs, or like a dog

canine tooth *NOUN* **canine teeth**
a canine tooth is a pointed tooth at the front of the mouth. Human beings have four of these.

cannibal *NOUN* **cannibals**
❶ a person who eats human flesh ❷ an animal that eats animals of its own kind
➤ **cannibalism** *NOUN*

cannon *NOUN* **cannon** *or* **cannons**
a large gun that fires heavy balls made of metal or stone

cannonball *NOUN* **cannonballs**
a heavy metal or stone ball fired from a cannon

cannot
can not • *I cannot believe it.*

canoe *NOUN* **canoes**
a light narrow boat driven with paddles

canoe *VERB* **canoes, canoeing, canoed**
to canoe is to travel in a canoe
➤ **canoeist** *NOUN*

canopy *NOUN* **canopies**
❶ a covering that hangs over something ❷ the topmost branches of trees in a rainforest

can't
short for *cannot* • *I'm sorry I can't help you.*

cantankerous ADJECTIVE
bad-tempered

canteen NOUN canteens
a restaurant in a factory or office or school, where the people working there can get a meal or snack

canter VERB canters, cantering, cantered
to canter is to go at a gentle gallop on a horse

canvas NOUN canvases
❶ canvas is strong coarse cloth ❷ a canvas is a piece of this kind of cloth used for painting on

canvass VERB canvasses, canvassing, canvassed
to canvass people is to visit them to ask them for their support, especially in an election

canyon NOUN canyons
a deep valley with a river running through it

cap NOUN caps
❶ a soft hat without a brim but often with a peak ❷ a cover or top

cap VERB caps, capping, capped
❶ to cap something is to cover it ❷ to cap a story or joke is to tell one that is better

capable ADJECTIVE
able to do something • *Bats are the only mammals capable of flight.*
➤ capability NOUN

capacity NOUN capacities
❶ ability to do something • *He has a great capacity for work.* ❷ the amount that something can hold ❸ the position someone occupies • *He was there in his capacity as our leader.*

cape NOUN capes
❶ a piece of high land sticking out into the sea • *the Cape of Good Hope* ❷ a cape is also a cloak • *Superheroes often wear capes.*

caper VERB capers, capering, capered
to caper is to jump about playfully

caper NOUN capers
❶ a leap or jump ❷ (*informal*) an activity or adventure

capital NOUN capitals
❶ the capital of a country is the main city in it, where the government is based ❷ capital is money or property that can be used to make more money

capitalism (*say* kap-i-ta-lizm) NOUN
capitalism is a system in which the wealth of a country is owned by private individuals and not by the state
➤ capitalist NOUN

capital letter NOUN capital letters
a large letter of the kind used at the start of a name or a sentence, such as A, B, C

capital punishment NOUN
capital punishment is when someone is killed as a punishment for a crime, such as murder or treason

capsize VERB capsizes, capsizing, capsized
to capsize is to overturn in a boat in the water

capsule NOUN capsules
❶ a hollow pill containing medicine ❷ a small spacecraft or pressurized cabin

captain NOUN captains
❶ an officer in charge of a ship or aircraft ❷ an officer in the army or navy ❸ the leader in a sports team

caption NOUN captions
❶ the words printed beside a picture to describe it ❷ a heading in a newspaper or magazine

captivate VERB captivates, captivating, captivated
to captivate someone is to charm them or make them interested
➤ captivating ADJECTIVE

captive NOUN captives
a prisoner

captive ADJECTIVE
imprisoned; unable to escape

captivity NOUN
❶ captivity is being held prisoner ❷ an animal in captivity is one kept in a zoo or wildlife park rather than living in the wild

captor NOUN captors
someone who has captured a person or animal

capture *VERB* **captures**, **capturing**, **captured**
❶ to capture an animal or person is to catch or imprison them ❷ (*computing*) to capture data is to put it into a form that a computer can accept

capture *NOUN*
catching or imprisoning an animal or person

car *NOUN* **cars**
❶ a private motor vehicle ❷ a railway carriage • *The train has a dining car.*

caramel *NOUN* **caramels**
❶ caramel is burnt sugar used to give a sweet taste to food ❷ a caramel is a sweet made from butter, milk and sugar

carat *NOUN* **carats**
❶ a measure of weight for precious stones
❷ a measure of the purity of gold

caravan *NOUN* **caravans**
❶ a vehicle towed by a car and used for living in, especially by people on holiday ❷ a large number of people travelling together, especially across a desert

carbohydrate *NOUN* **carbohydrates**
a compound of carbon, oxygen and hydrogen • *Sugar and starch are carbohydrates.*

carbon *NOUN*
carbon is an element found in charcoal, graphite, diamonds and other substances

carbon cycle *NOUN*
the process by which carbon moves from the atmosphere, through living and then dead organisms, and then back into the atmosphere again

carbon dioxide *NOUN*
a colourless gas made by humans and animals breathing

carbon footprint *NOUN*
carbon footprints
a measure of the amount of carbon dioxide produced by the activities of a person, organization or country

carbon monoxide *NOUN*
a colourless poisonous gas found especially in the exhaust fumes of motor vehicles

car boot sale *NOUN* **car boot sales**
an outdoor sale where people sell things which they have brought by car

carcass *NOUN* **carcasses**
the dead body of an animal or bird

card *NOUN* **cards**
❶ card is thick stiff paper ❷ a card is a piece of thick paper that you use to put information on or to send greetings to someone, for example a business card or a birthday card ❸ a card is also a playing card ❹ a card is also a small piece of plastic that a bank or building society issues to a customer, with an electronic strip recording details of their account
➤ **cards** is a game with playing cards
➤ **something is on the cards** when it is likely to happen

cardboard *NOUN*
cardboard is thick stiff paper

cardigan *NOUN* **cardigans**
a knitted jumper fastened with buttons down the front
DID YOU KNOW? The word **cardigan** is named after the Earl of *Cardigan*, a commander in the Crimean War whose soldiers wore a kind of woollen jacket.

cardinal *NOUN* **cardinals**
one of the most senior priests in the Roman Catholic Church

cardinal number *NOUN*
cardinal numbers
a number for counting things, for example 1, 2, 3 (*compare* **ordinal number**)

care *NOUN* **cares**
❶ care is worry or trouble • *He was weighed down by care and responsibility.* ❷ care is also serious thought or attention • *Take extra care crossing the road at night.* ❸ care is also protection or supervision • *You can leave your dog in my care.*
➤ **to take care of someone** or **something** is to look after them • *Please take care of my cactus while I'm away.*

care *VERB* **cares**, **caring**, **cared**
to care about something or someone is to feel interested or concerned about them
➤ **to care for someone** is to look after them • *She cared for her mother when she was ill.*
➤ **to care for something** is to like it or want it • *I don't much care for fast food.*

career *NOUN* careers
a person's career is what they have been trained to do to earn a living and make progress during their lives

career *VERB* careers, careering, careered
to career along or down somewhere is to rush along wildly
The beast was careering through the tunnels, crashing, bellowing, thundering through the maze. —SHADOW OF MINOTAUR, Alan Gibbons

carefree *ADJECTIVE*
not having any worries or responsibilities

careful *ADJECTIVE*
making sure that you do something well without any mistakes and without causing any danger • *She is a careful driver.* • *He was careful to speak slowly.*
➤ **carefully** *ADVERB*

careless *ADJECTIVE*
not taking care; clumsy
➤ **carelessly** *ADVERB* ➤ **carelessness** *NOUN*

carer *NOUN* carers
a carer is someone who looks after a person when they are ill or elderly

caress (*say* ka-**ress**) *NOUN* caresses
a gentle and loving touch

caress *VERB* caresses, caressing, caressed
to caress someone is to touch them gently and fondly

caretaker *NOUN* caretakers
someone who looks after a large building

cargo *NOUN* cargoes
cargo or a cargo is the goods carried in a ship or aircraft

Caribbean (*say* ka-ri-**bee**-an) *ADJECTIVE*
to do with the Caribbean Sea or the islands of the West Indies

caricature *NOUN* caricatures
a drawing or description of someone that exaggerates their features and makes them look funny or absurd

carnation *NOUN* carnations
a garden flower with a sweet smell

carnival *NOUN* carnivals
a festival or celebration with a procession of people in fancy dress

carnivore *NOUN* carnivores
an animal that eats meat
➤ **carnivorous** *ADJECTIVE*

carol *NOUN* carols
a hymn or song that you sing at Christmas time

carp *NOUN* carp
a freshwater fish

carpenter *NOUN* carpenters
someone who makes things, especially parts of buildings, out of wood
➤ **carpentry** *NOUN*

carpet *NOUN* carpets
a thick soft covering for a floor

carpet *VERB* carpets, carpeting, carpeted
to carpet a floor is to cover it with a carpet or other thick layer
The floor of the sitting-room was carpeted with deep red blotting-paper, which was warm and cosy, and soaked up the spills.—THE BORROWERS, Mary Norton

carriage *NOUN* carriages
❶ a carriage is one of the separate sections of a train where passengers sit ❷ a carriage is also a passenger vehicle pulled by horses ❸ carriage is taking goods from one place to another • *You will have to pay extra for carriage.*

carriageway *NOUN* carriageways
the part of a road that vehicles travel on

carrier bag *NOUN* carrier bags
a large bag for holding shopping

carrot *NOUN* carrots
a long thin orange-coloured vegetable

carry *VERB* carries, carrying, carried
❶ to carry something is to lift it and take it somewhere ❷ to carry something is also to have it with you • *I always carry my mobile in my pocket.* ❸ a sound carries when it can be heard a long way away
➤ **to be carried away** is to become very excited
➤ **to carry on** is to continue doing something • *They carried on chatting.*
➤ **to carry something out** is to put it into practice • *Will you please carry out my orders?*

cart *NOUN* **carts**
a small vehicle for carrying loads
➤ **to put the cart before the horse** is to do things in the wrong order

cart *VERB* **carts, carting, carted** (*informal*)
to cart something somewhere is to carry or transport it, especially when it is heavy or tiring • *I've been carting these books around all afternoon.*

carthorse *NOUN* **carthorses**
a large heavy horse

cartilage (*say* **kar-ti-lij**) *NOUN*
cartilage is tough and flexible tissue attached to a bone

carton *NOUN* **cartons**
a lightweight cardboard box

cartoon *NOUN* **cartoons**
❶ a drawing that is funny or tells a joke
❷ a series of drawings that tell a story
❸ an animated film
➤ **cartoonist** *NOUN*

cartridge *NOUN* **cartridges**
❶ a container holding film to be put into a camera or ink to be put into a pen or printer
❷ the case containing the explosive for a bullet or shell

cartwheel *NOUN* **cartwheels**
a somersault done sideways, with your arms and legs spread wide

carve *VERB* **carves, carving, carved**
❶ to carve wood or stone is to make something artistic by cutting it carefully ❷ to carve meat is to cut it into slices

cascade *NOUN* **cascades**
a waterfall or a series of waterfalls

cascade *VERB* **cascades, cascading, cascaded**
to cascade is to tumble down like the water in a waterfall • *Pieces of rubble cascaded down on us.*

case *NOUN* **cases**
❶ a container ❷ a suitcase ❸ an example of something existing or happening • *We've had four cases of chickenpox.* • *It's just a case of being patient.* ❹ a crime or incident that the police or a law court are investigating • *The next case was a murder.*
➤ **in case** because something may happen • *Take an umbrella in case it rains.*

cash *NOUN*
cash is coins and banknotes that you use to pay for something

cash *VERB* **cashes, cashing, cashed**
to cash a cheque is to exchange it for coins and banknotes
➤ **to cash in on something** (*informal*) is to take advantage of it

cashew *NOUN* **cashews**
a small edible nut, shaped like a kidney

cashier *NOUN* **cashiers**
someone in charge of the money in a bank, office or shop

cash register *NOUN* **cash registers**
a machine that records and stores money received in a shop

cask *NOUN* **casks**
a barrel

casket *NOUN* **caskets**
a small box for jewellery or other small objects

casserole *NOUN* **casseroles**
❶ a covered dish in which food is cooked ❷ the food cooked in a dish of this kind

cast *VERB* **casts, casting, cast**
❶ to cast something is to throw it ❷ to cast a vote is to make your vote in an election ❸ to cast something made of metal or plaster is to make it in a mould ❹ to cast a play or film is to choose the performers for it
➤ **to cast off** is to untie a boat and start sailing in it

cast *NOUN* **casts**
❶ a shape you make by pouring liquid metal or plaster into a mould ❷ the performers in a play or film

castanets *PLURAL NOUN*
two pieces of wood held in one hand and clapped together to make a clicking sound, as in Spanish dancing

castaway *NOUN* **castaways**
someone who has been left in a deserted place, especially after a shipwreck

caster sugar *NOUN*
finely ground white sugar

castle *NOUN* **castles**
❶ a large old building with heavy stone walls and battlements, made to protect people in it from attack
*Toad was a helpless prisoner in the remotest dungeon ... of the stoutest castle in all the length and breadth of Merry England.—*THE WIND IN THE WILLOWS, Kenneth Grahame
❷ a piece in chess, also called a *rook*

castor (*say* **kah**-ster) *NOUN* **castors**
a small wheel on the leg of a piece of furniture

castor oil *NOUN*
a yellow oil made from the seeds of a tropical plant, used as medicine

casual *ADJECTIVE*
❶ not deliberate or planned • *It was just a casual remark.* ❷ casual clothes are informal clothes that you wear for leisure time ❸ not regular or permanent • *His dad was doing casual work.*
➤ **casually** *ADVERB*

casualty *NOUN* **casualties**
someone killed or injured in war or in an accident

cat *NOUN* **cats**
❶ a small furry animal, often kept as a pet and known for catching mice ❷ a larger member of the same family, for example a lion, tiger or leopard
➤ **to let the cat out of the bag** is to give away a secret
➤ A related adjective is **feline**.

catalogue *NOUN* **catalogues**
a list of goods for sale or of books in a library

catalyst (*say* **kat**-a-list) *NOUN* **catalysts**
❶ something that starts or speeds up a chemical reaction ❷ something important that results in a change

catamaran *NOUN* **catamarans**
a sailing boat with two hulls fixed side by side

catapult *NOUN* **catapults**
❶ a small weapon made from a forked stick with an elastic band attached, used for shooting pellets or small stones ❷ (*historical*) a machine used to hurl large stones or missiles in war

catastrophe (*say* ka-**tass**-tro-fee) *NOUN* **catastrophes**
a great or sudden disaster
➤ **catastrophic** *ADJECTIVE*

catch *VERB* **catches**, **catching**, **caught**
❶ to catch something is to get hold of it, for example a ball that is coming towards you ❷ to catch an animal is to capture it and not let it escape ❸ to catch someone is to discover them doing something wrong • *He was caught going home early.* ❹ to catch an illness is to get it from someone else ❺ to catch a bus or train is to get on it before it leaves ❻ to catch something someone says is to manage to hear it • *I'm afraid I didn't catch your question.*
❼ to catch your clothes is to get them entangled in something • *I've caught my sleeve on a bramble.*
➤ **to catch fire** is to start burning
➤ **to catch on** (*informal*) is to become popular, as a craze or fashion does
➤ **to catch someone out** is to show that they are wrong or mistaken
➤ **to catch up with someone** is to reach them when they have been ahead of you

catch *NOUN* **catches**
❶ something caught or worth catching • *They had a large catch of fish.* ❷ a hidden difficulty or snag • *The car was so cheap there had to be a catch.* ❸ a device for fastening a door or window

catching *ADJECTIVE*
if an illness is catching, it is infectious

catchphrase *NOUN* **catchphrases**
a phrase that someone famous has used and a lot of people now use

catchy *ADJECTIVE* **catchier**, **catchiest**
pleasant and easy to remember, like a tune

category *NOUN* **categories**
a group or division of similar people or things • *I'm going to enter the competition in the under-twelves category.*

cater *VERB* **caters**, **catering**, **catered**
to cater for someone or something is to give them what they need

caterer *NOUN* **caterers**
someone whose job is to provide food for people, especially at an important function

caterpillar *NOUN* **caterpillars**
a long creeping creature that turns into a butterfly or moth
DID YOU KNOW? The word **caterpillar** is thought to come from an Old French word meaning 'hairy cat'.

cathedral *NOUN* **cathedrals**
a large and important church in a major city, with a bishop in charge of it

Catholic *ADJECTIVE*
belonging to the Roman Catholic Church
Catholic *NOUN* **Catholics**
a member of the Roman Catholic Church

catkin *NOUN* **catkins**
a tiny flower hanging down from a willow or hazel

Catseye *NOUN* **Catseyes** (*trademark*)
a stud containing small pieces of glass or plastic that reflect the lights of vehicles, set in a row in the road to help drivers see their way at night

cattle *PLURAL NOUN*
cattle are cows and bulls and other large grass-eating animals

caught *VERB* (*past tense and past participle of* **catch**)
• *I caught Hannah looking at me.* • *I think you've caught a cold.*

cauldron *NOUN* **cauldrons**
a large round iron cooking pot, used especially by witches in stories

cauliflower *NOUN* **cauliflowers**
a kind of cabbage with a large head of white flowers

cause *NOUN* **causes**
❶ what makes something happen; a reason • *You have no cause for complaint.* ❷ the aim or purpose that a group of people are working for • *They were raising money for a good cause.*

cause *VERB* **causes, causing, caused**
to cause something is to make it happen

caution *NOUN* **cautions**
❶ caution is being careful to avoid danger or mistakes ❷ a caution is a warning
➤ **cautionary** *ADJECTIVE* a cautionary story is one that gives a warning about a danger or difficulty

cautious *ADJECTIVE*
careful to avoid a risk or difficulty
➤ **cautiously** *ADVERB*

cavalry *NOUN*
soldiers who fight on horseback or in armoured vehicles

cave *NOUN* **caves**
a large hole in the side of a hill or cliff, or under the ground
cave *VERB* **caves, caving, caved**
to cave or go caving is to explore caves
➤ **to cave in** is to collapse

caveman, **cavewoman** *NOUN* **cavemen**, **cavewomen**
a person who lived in a cave in prehistoric times

cavern *NOUN* **caverns**
a cave, especially a deep or dark one
The farmer ... turned with the wizard into a further cavern, and here mounds of gold and silver and precious stones lay strewn along the ground.—THE WEIRDSTONE OF BRISINGAMEN, Alan Garner

cavity *NOUN* **cavities**
a hollow or hole

cc *ABBREVIATION*
❶ short for *cubic centimetres* ❷ used to show a copy of an email is being sent to another person

CD *NOUN* **CDs**
short for *compact disc*, a small plastic disc on which music or data is stored and read by a laser beam

cease *VERB* **ceases, ceasing, ceased**
to cease doing something is to stop doing it

ceasefire *NOUN* **ceasefires**
an agreement to stop using weapons, made by people who are fighting a war

ceaseless *ADJECTIVE*
going on all the time, not stopping

cedar *NOUN* **cedars**
an evergreen tree with hard sweet-smelling wood

ceilidh (*say* **kay**-lee) *NOUN* **ceilidhs**
a party with Scottish or Irish traditional music and dancing

a b c d e f g h i j k l m n o p q r s t u v w x y z

ceiling (say see-ling) NOUN **ceilings**
❶ the flat surface along the top of a room
❷ the highest limit that something can reach
• *They agreed to put a ceiling on pay.*

celebrate VERB **celebrates**, **celebrating**, **celebrated**
to celebrate a day or event is to do something special to show that it is important

celebrated ADJECTIVE
famous, well known • *He won a prize to meet a celebrated film star.*

celebration NOUN **celebrations**
a celebration is a party or other special event to celebrate something

celebrity NOUN **celebrities**
a famous person, especially in show business or on television

celery NOUN
a vegetable with crisp white or green stems

cell NOUN **cells**
❶ a small room, especially in a prison
❷ a tiny part of a living creature or plant
❸ a device for producing electric current using chemicals

cellar NOUN **cellars**
an underground room for storing things

cello (say chel-oh) NOUN **cellos**
a large stringed musical instrument, which you play by placing it upright between the knees and using a bow
➤ **cellist** NOUN

cellular ADJECTIVE
made of cells, or having cells • *the cellular structure of a leaf*

Celsius ADJECTIVE
using a scale for measuring temperature in which water freezes at 0 degrees and boils at 100 degrees • *Set the oven to 180 degrees Celsius.*

Celt (say kelt) NOUN **Celts**
a member of the peoples who lived in Britain and parts of Europe before the Romans came, or their descendants

Celtic (say kel-tik) ADJECTIVE
to do with the Celts

cement NOUN
❶ cement is a mixture of lime and clay, used in building to make floors and join bricks together ❷ cement is also a strong glue

cemetery (say sem-e-tree) NOUN **cemeteries**
a place where dead people are buried

censor VERB **censors**, **censoring**, **censored**
to censor films, plays or books is to look at them to make sure that they do not have any parts which are unsuitable for people to see or read
➤ **censorship** NOUN

census NOUN **censuses**
an official count or survey of the number of people or the volume of traffic in a place

cent NOUN **cents**
a coin worth one-hundredth of a dollar or euro, used in the USA and some other countries

centaur (say sen-tor) NOUN **centaurs**
a mythological creature with the head and upper body of a man and the lower body and legs of a horse

centenary NOUN **centenaries**
the hundredth anniversary of something special or important

centigrade ADJECTIVE
a non-technical word for **Celsius**

centimetre NOUN **centimetres**
one-hundredth of a metre, about four-tenths of an inch

centipede NOUN **centipedes**
a small long creature with many pairs of legs
DID YOU KNOW? The word **centipede** means 'hundred feet', but most centipedes have fewer than a hundred legs.

central ADJECTIVE
❶ at or near the centre of something
❷ most important • *She will have the central role in the play.*
➤ **centrally** ADVERB in a central position

central heating NOUN
central heating is a system of heating a building by sending hot water, hot air or steam round it in pipes

centre *NOUN* **centres**
❶ the middle of something ❷ an important place • *Vienna is one of the great music centres of Europe.* ❸ a building or place for a special purpose, such as a sports centre or a shopping centre

centre *VERB* **centres**, **centring**, **centred**
when you centre a word or picture on a computer you move it to the middle of the screen

centre forward *NOUN* **centre forwards**
the middle player in the front line of a team in football or hockey

centurion *NOUN* **centurions**
an officer in the ancient Roman army, originally commanding a hundred men

century *NOUN* **centuries**
❶ a period of a hundred years ❷ a hundred runs scored by one batsman or batswoman in an innings at cricket
DID YOU KNOW? The word **century** comes from the Latin word for 'a hundred'.

ceramics (*say* ser-**am**-iks) *PLURAL NOUN*
ceramics is the art of making pottery

cereal *NOUN* **cereals**
❶ a grass that produces seeds which are used as food ❷ a breakfast food made from seeds of this kind
DID YOU KNOW? The word **cereal** comes from *Ceres*, the Roman goddess of farming and agriculture.

ceremonial *ADJECTIVE*
to do with a ceremony, or used in a ceremony • *ceremonial robes*

ceremonious *ADJECTIVE*
ceremonious behaviour is formal and dignified • *He made a ceremonious bow.*
➤ **ceremoniously** *ADVERB*

ceremony (*say* se-ri-mo-nee) *NOUN* **ceremonies**
❶ ceremony is the formal actions carried out at a wedding, funeral or other important occasion ❷ a ceremony is a formal event such as a wedding or funeral

certain *ADJECTIVE*
❶ something is certain when it is definitely true or is going to happen • *They look certain to win the championship.* ❷ you are certain about

something when you know it is definitely true
• *Are you certain that is a dinosaur bone?*
➤ **for certain** definitely, for sure
➤ **to make certain** is to make sure

certainly *ADVERB*
as a fact, without any doubt • *They were certainly here last night.*

certainty *NOUN* **certainties**
❶ a certainty is something that is sure to happen ❷ certainty is being sure

certificate *NOUN* **certificates**
an official document that records an important event or achievement, such as someone's birth or passing an exam

certify *VERB* **certifies**, **certifying**, **certified**
to certify something is to say in writing that it is true

CGI *ABBREVIATION*
short for *computer generated imagery*, used to create special effects in films

chaffinch *NOUN* **chaffinches**
a small bird

chain *NOUN* **chains**
❶ a row of metal rings fastened together ❷ a line of people ❸ a connected series of things • *The story told of a strange chain of events.*

chain letter *NOUN* **chain letters**
a letter someone sends you asking you to copy it and send it to several other people, who are supposed to do the same

chain reaction *NOUN* **chain reactions**
a series of happenings, each causing the next

chainsaw *NOUN* **chainsaws**
a saw with teeth on a chain that is moved round very fast by a motor

chair *NOUN* **chairs**
❶ a seat with a back for one person ❷ the person who is in charge of a meeting

chairlift *NOUN* **chairlifts**
a set of seats hanging from a moving cable, carrying people up the side of a mountain

a
b
c
d
e
f
g
h
i
j
k
l
m
n
o
p
q
r
s
t
u
v
w
x
y
z

A
B
C
D
E
F
G
H
I
J
K
L
M
N
O
P
Q
R
S
T
U
V
W
X
Y
Z

chairman, **chairperson** *NOUN*
chairmen, chairpersons
the person who is in charge of a meeting

chalet (*say* **shal**-ay) *NOUN* **chalets**
a small house, usually built of wood

chalk *NOUN* **chalks**
❶ a kind of soft white rock ❷ a soft white or coloured stick of a similar rock, used for writing on blackboards
➤ **chalky** *ADJECTIVE*

challenge *VERB* **challenges, challenging, challenged**
to challenge someone is to demand that they perform some feat or take part in a fight
➤ **challenger** *NOUN*

challenge *NOUN* **challenges**
something difficult that someone has to do

chamber *NOUN* **chambers**
❶ (*old use*) a room ❷ a hall used for meetings of a parliament or council

chameleon (*say* ka-**mee**-li-on) *NOUN* **chameleons**
a small lizard that can change the colour of its skin to match its surroundings and appear almost invisible

champagne (*say* sham-**payn**) *NOUN*
a bubbly white French wine

champion *NOUN* **champions**
❶ the best person in a sport or competition ❷ someone who supports a cause by fighting or speaking for it • *Martin Luther King was a champion of human rights.*

championship *NOUN* **championships**
a contest to decide who is the best player or competitor in a game or sport

chance *NOUN* **chances**
❶ a chance is a possibility or opportunity • *This is your only chance to see them.* ❷ chance is the way things happen accidentally • *It was pure chance that we met.*
➤ **by chance** accidentally, without any planning • *We found the place by chance.*
➤ **to take a chance** is to take a risk

chancellor *NOUN* **chancellors**
❶ an important government or legal official ❷ the chief minister of the government in some European countries

Chancellor of the Exchequer *NOUN*
the government minister in charge of a country's finances and taxes

chandelier (*say* shan-de-**leer**) *NOUN* **chandeliers**
a light fitting that hangs from the ceiling and has a lot of bright bulbs

change *VERB* **changes, changing, changed**
❶ to change something or someone is to make them different ❷ to change is to become different • *My granny said I'd changed since she last saw me.* ❸ to change one thing for another is to exchange them • *I'm going to change my bike for a new one.* ❹ to change money is to give coins or notes of small values in exchange for higher value money • *Can you change a £5 note?* ❺ to change trains or buses is to get off one and get on another • *Change at York for the train to Durham.*

change *NOUN* **changes**
❶ change is the process of changing ❷ your change is the money you get back when you give more money than the price of something you are buying, for example if you don't have the right money ❸ a change of clothes is a set of fresh clothes
➤ **to do something for a change** is to do it because it is different or unusual • *Let's walk home for a change.*

changeable *ADJECTIVE*
likely to change; often changing • *The weather has been very changeable.*

channel *NOUN* **channels**
❶ a stretch of water joining two seas, like the English Channel between England and France ❷ a television or radio station that transmits on a particular frequency ❸ a way for water to flow along ❹ the part of a river or sea that is deep enough for ships to sail on

chant *NOUN* **chants**
a tune, especially one that is often repeated

chant *VERB* **chants, chanting, chanted**
to chant words is to say them or call them out in a special rhythm

chaos (*say* **kay**-oss) *NOUN*
chaos is complete disorder or confusion • *The room was in chaos.*

chaotic (*say* kay-**ot**-ik) *ADJECTIVE*
completely confused or in a mess

chap *NOUN* **chaps** (*informal*)
a man or boy • *What a funny chap he is.*

chapatti *NOUN* **chapattis**
an Indian flat round bread made without yeast

chapel *NOUN* **chapels**
❶ a small church or part of a large church
❷ a room in a large house, used for worship

chapped *ADJECTIVE*
having rough cracked skin

chapter *NOUN* **chapters**
a section of a book

char *VERB* **chars**, **charring**, **charred**
to char something is to scorch it or blacken it with fire

character *NOUN* **characters**
❶ the special nature and qualities of a person or thing ❷ a person in a story or play

characteristic *NOUN* **characteristics**
something that makes a person or thing noticeable or different from others

characteristic *ADJECTIVE*
typical; what you would expect of someone

characterize (*also* **characterise**) *VERB*
characterizes, **characterizing**, **characterized**
❶ to characterize something is to give it special character or qualities • *Hot spices characterize Mexican cooking.* ❷ to characterize someone is to describe their character in a certain way • *How would you characterize Scrooge?*

charades (*say* sha-**rahdz**) *NOUN*
charades is a game in which people have to guess a word or the title of a book or film when other people act it out

charcoal *NOUN*
charcoal is a black substance made by burning wood slowly

charge *NOUN* **charges**
❶ the price asked for something • *Their charges have gone up since last year.* ❷ an accusation that someone committed a crime • *The gang is facing three charges of burglary.* ❸ an attack in a battle ❹ the amount of explosive needed to fire a weapon ❺ the amount of an electric current

➤ **to be in charge of something** *or* **someone** is to be the one who decides what will happen to them

charge *VERB* **charges**, **charging**, **charged**
❶ to charge a price for something is to ask people to pay it ❷ to charge a mobile phone, laptop or camera is to top up the electricity in its battery ❸ to charge someone is to accuse them of committing a crime ❹ to charge in a battle is to rush to attack the enemy

charger *NOUN* **chargers**
a device used to top up the electricity in the battery of a mobile phone, laptop or camera

chariot *NOUN* **chariots**
a horse-drawn vehicle with two wheels, used in ancient times for fighting and racing

charitable *ADJECTIVE*
❶ a charitable person or act is one that is kind and generous ❷ a charitable organization is one that gives money or other kinds of help to those who need it

charity *NOUN* **charities**
❶ charity is giving money and help to other people ❷ a charity is an organization that offers help and support to people

charlatan (*say* **shar**-la-tan) *NOUN* **charlatans**
someone who pretends to be something they are not; an impostor
A cunning charlatan with no magical power saw a chance of enriching himself, and arrived at the palace, claiming to be a wizard of enormous skill.—THE TALES OF BEEDLE THE BARD, J. K. Rowling

charm *NOUN* **charms**
❶ charm is being pleasant and attractive ❷ a charm is a magic spell ❸ a charm is also something small worn or carried to bring good luck

charm *VERB* **charms**, **charming**, **charmed**
❶ to charm someone is to give them pleasure or delight ❷ to charm someone is also to put a spell on them

charming ADJECTIVE
pleasant and attractive

chart NOUN **charts**
❶ a large plan or map ❷ a diagram or list with information set out in columns or rows ❸ a list of the most popular CDs and recordings that are sold or downloaded

charter NOUN **charters**
❶ an official document explaining people's rights or privileges ❷ the hire of an aircraft or vehicle for a special purpose

charter VERB **charters, chartering, chartered**
to charter an aircraft or vehicle is to hire it for a special journey

chase VERB **chases, chasing, chased**
to chase someone is to go quickly after them to try to catch them up

chase NOUN **chases**
a chase is when you chase someone

chasm (say ka-zum) NOUN **chasms**
a deep opening in the ground
The ice bridge ... was a mighty structure stretching the entire length between two sides of a deep, yawning chasm.—THE POLAR BEAR EXPLORERS' CLUB, Alex Bell

chassis (say shass-ee) NOUN **chassis**
the frame and wheels of a vehicle, which support the body

chat NOUN **chats**
❶ a friendly or informal talk with someone ❷ an exchange of messages between people on the internet

chat VERB **chats, chatting, chatted**
❶ to chat to someone is to talk to them in a friendly or informal way ❷ to chat is also to exchange messages with other people on the internet
➤ **chatty** ADJECTIVE

chatter VERB **chatters, chattering, chattered**
❶ to talk quickly or stupidly; to talk too much ❷ to make a rattling noise

chauffeur (say shoh-fer) NOUN **chauffeurs**
someone who is paid to drive a large smart car for someone important

cheap ADJECTIVE **cheaper, cheapest**
❶ something cheap does not cost much ❷ you call something cheap when it is shoddy or inferior
➤ **cheaply** ADVERB

cheat VERB **cheats, cheating, cheated**
❶ to cheat someone is to trick them so they lose something ❷ to cheat is to try to do well in an exam or game by breaking the rules

cheat NOUN **cheats**
someone who cheats

check VERB **checks, checking, checked**
❶ to check something is to make sure that it is correct or all right ❷ to check someone or something is to make them stop or slow down
➤ **to check in** is to sign your name to show you have arrived at a hotel or to show your ticket at an airport
➤ **to check out** is to pay your bill and leave a hotel

check NOUN **checks**
❶ a check is when you check something ❷ in chess, check is when the king is threatened by another piece ❸ a check is a pattern of squares

checkmate NOUN **checkmates**
checkmate in chess is when one side wins by trapping the other side's king
DID YOU KNOW? The word **checkmate** comes from Persian words which mean 'the king is dead'.

checkout NOUN **checkouts**
the place where you pay for your shopping

check-up NOUN **check-ups**
a careful check or examination

Cheddar NOUN
a hard cheese with a strong flavour, originally made in Cheddar in the English county Somerset

cheek NOUN **cheeks**
❶ your cheek is the side of your face below your eye ❷ cheek, or a cheek, is being rude or impolite

cheek VERB **cheeks, cheeking, cheeked**
to cheek someone is to be rude to them

cheeky *ADJECTIVE* **cheekier, cheekiest**
rude or impolite, without being unpleasant
or nasty
➤ **cheekily** *ADVERB*

cheer *NOUN* **cheers**
a shout praising or supporting someone

cheer *VERB* **cheers, cheering, cheered**
❶ to cheer someone is to support them by
cheering ❷ to cheer someone is to comfort or
encourage them
➤ **to cheer someone up** is to make them
more cheerful
➤ **to cheer up** is to become more cheerful

cheerful *ADJECTIVE*
happy and bright
Dr Mead ... was a tall, broad-shouldered man
with kind grey eyes, and a cheerful smile.
Pollyanna liked him at once.—POLLYANNA,
Eleanor Porter
➤ **cheerfulness** *NOUN*

cheerio *EXCLAMATION* (*informal*)
goodbye

cheese *NOUN* **cheeses**
cheese is a white or yellow food made from
milk, which can be either hard like Cheddar or
soft like mozzarella

cheeseburger *NOUN* **cheeseburgers**
a beefburger served in a roll with a slice of
melted cheese

cheesy *ADJECTIVE* **cheesier, cheesiest**
❶ tasting or smelling like cheese • *a cheesy*
toasted sandwich ❷ a cheesy smile or grin is
very wide
➤ **cheesiness** *NOUN*

cheetah *NOUN* **cheetahs**
a large spotted animal of the cat family, which
can run very fast

chef (*say* shef) *NOUN* **chefs**
the chief cook in a hotel or restaurant

chemical *NOUN* **chemicals**
a substance used in or made by chemistry

chemical *ADJECTIVE*
to do with chemistry or made by chemistry

chemist *NOUN* **chemists**
❶ someone who makes or sells medicines
❷ an expert in chemistry

chemistry *NOUN*
chemistry is the study of the way
substances combine and react with one
another

cheque *NOUN* **cheques**
a written form instructing a bank to pay money
out of an account

chequered *ADJECTIVE*
marked with a pattern of squares

cherish *VERB* **cherishes, cherishing,
cherished**
to cherish something is to look after
it lovingly

cherry *NOUN* **cherries**
a small bright red fruit with a large stone

chess *NOUN*
a game for two players played with
sixteen pieces (called **chessmen**) each
on a board (called a **chessboard**) of
64 squares

chest *NOUN* **chests**
❶ a chest is a large strong box ❷ your chest is
the front part of your body between your neck
and your waist
➤ **to get something off your chest** (*informal*)
is to admit something you are worried about or
feel bad about

chestnut *NOUN* **chestnuts**
❶ a hard brown nut ❷ the tree that produces
this kind of nut

chest of drawers *NOUN* **chests of
drawers**
a piece of furniture with drawers for
holding clothes

chew *VERB* **chews, chewing, chewed**
to chew food is to grind it into pieces between
your teeth
➤ **chewy** *ADJECTIVE* chewy food is tough and
needs a lot of chewing

chewing gum *NOUN*
a sticky flavoured gum for chewing

chick *NOUN* **chicks**
a young bird

chicken *NOUN* **chickens**
❶ a chicken is a young hen ❷ chicken is the
meat of a hen used as food

a b c d e f g h i j k l m n o p q r s t u v w x y z

chicken *ADJECTIVE* (*informal*)
cowardly

chicken *VERB* **chickens, chickening, chickened**
➤ **to chicken out of something** (*informal*)
is to avoid it because you are afraid

chickenpox *NOUN*
an illness that produces red itchy spots on your skin

chickpea *NOUN* **chickpeas**
a yellowish seed like a pea, which is eaten as a vegetable

chief *NOUN* **chiefs**
❶ a leader or ruler ❷ the most important person, the boss
chief *ADJECTIVE*
❶ having the highest rank or power ❷ most important

chiefly *ADVERB*
mainly, mostly • *Peter is the one who is chiefly to blame.*

chieftain *NOUN* **chieftains**
the chief of a tribe or clan

child *NOUN* **children**
❶ a young person ❷ someone's son or daughter • *Whose child is that?*

childhood *NOUN* **childhoods**
the time when you are a child

childish *ADJECTIVE*
silly and immature • *Don't be childish!*

childminder *NOUN* **childminders**
a person who is paid to look after children while their parents are out at work

chill *NOUN* **chills**
❶ chill is an unpleasant feeling of being cold ❷ a chill is a cold that makes you shiver
chill *VERB* **chills, chilling, chilled**
❶ to chill something is to make it cold ❷ (*informal*) to relax completely

chilli *NOUN* **chillies**
❶ a hot-tasting pod of a type of pepper, used in cooking ❷ a spicy stew made with meat, beans and chillies

chilly *ADJECTIVE* **chillier, chilliest**
❶ slightly cold ❷ unfriendly • *They went to see the head and got a chilly reception.*

chime *NOUN* **chimes**
a ringing sound made by a bell
chime *VERB* **chimes, chiming, chimed**
to chime is to ring • *The clock chimes every quarter-hour.*

chimney *NOUN* **chimneys**
a tall pipe or passage that carries away smoke from a fire

chimney sweep *NOUN* **chimney sweeps**
someone who cleans the soot out of chimneys

chimpanzee *NOUN* **chimpanzees**
a small African ape with black fur and large eyes

chin *NOUN* **chins**
your chin is the part of your face under your mouth

china *NOUN*
china is thin and delicate pottery
DID YOU KNOW? The word **china** originally meant 'from China', because the pottery was first made there.

Chinese *ADJECTIVE*
to do with China or its people
Chinese *NOUN*
one of the languages spoken in China, especially its main language, also called *Mandarin*
DID YOU KNOW? The words **tea** and **typhoon** come from Chinese.

chink *NOUN* **chinks**
❶ a narrow opening • *He looked through a chink in the curtains.* ❷ a clinking sound • *They heard the chink of coins.*

chip *NOUN* **chips**
❶ a small piece of something ❷ a place where a small piece has been knocked off something ❸ a small piece of fried potato ❹ a small counter used in gambling games ❺ a silicon chip
chip *VERB* **chips, chipping, chipped**
to chip something is to knock a small piece off it by accident
➤ **to chip in** is to make a suggestion or comment during a conversation that other people are having

chipmunk *NOUN* **chipmunks**
a North American animal like a squirrel, with cheek pouches and stripes along its body

chirp VERB chirps, chirping, chirped
to chirp is to make short sharp sounds like a small bird

chirpy ADJECTIVE chirpier, chirpiest
(informal)
lively and cheerful

chisel NOUN chisels
a tool with a sharp end for shaping wood or stone

chisel VERB chisels, chiselling, chiselled
to chisel wood or stone is to shape or cut it with a chisel

chivalry NOUN
being ready to help people who are less strong than you are
➤ **chivalrous** ADJECTIVE

chlorine NOUN
a chemical used to disinfect water

chlorophyll NOUN
the substance found in plants that makes their leaves and stems green

chock-a-block, **chock-full**
ADJECTIVE, ADVERB
a place that is chock-a-block is completely full so there is hardly any room to move

chocolate NOUN chocolates
❶ chocolate is a sweet food made from roasted cocoa beans, usually shaped into bars for eating
'Wouldn't it be something, Charlie, to open a bar of chocolate and see a Golden Ticket glistening inside!'–CHARLIE AND THE CHOCOLATE FACTORY, Roald Dahl
❷ a chocolate is a sweet made of, or covered with, chocolate ❸ chocolate is also a hot drink made from melted or powdered chocolate
➤ **chocolatey** ADJECTIVE
DID YOU KNOW? The word **chocolate** comes from the Nahuatl (Mexican) word *chocolatl*.

choice NOUN choices
❶ choice is the process of choosing or the power to choose • *I'm afraid we have no choice.* ❷ a choice is what someone chooses • *Let me know your choice of book.*

choir NOUN choirs
a group of singers, especially in a church

choke VERB chokes, choking, choked
❶ to choke on something is to be unable to breathe properly because it is stuck in your throat ❷ to choke someone is to stop them breathing properly ❸ to choke something is to block it up

choke NOUN chokes
a valve in a motor vehicle that controls the mixture of air and petrol

cholera (say kol-er-a) NOUN
cholera is a severe infectious illness that affects the intestines

cholesterol (say ko-less-te-rol) NOUN
cholesterol is a substance found in the cells of your body which helps to carry fat in the bloodstream

chomp VERB chomps, chomping, chomped
if you chomp on something, you chew it

choose VERB chooses, choosing, chose, chosen
to choose something or someone is to decide that you want them rather than any of the others

choosy ADJECTIVE choosier, choosiest
(informal)
a choosy person is fussy and difficult to please

chop VERB chops, chopping, chopped
❶ to chop something up is to cut it into small pieces ❷ to chop something is to cut or hit it with a heavy blow

chop NOUN chops
❶ a chopping blow ❷ a small thick slice of meat

chopper NOUN choppers
❶ a small axe ❷ (informal) a helicopter

choppy ADJECTIVE choppier, choppiest
a choppy sea is fairly rough with lots of small waves

chopsticks PLURAL NOUN
a pair of thin sticks used for eating East Asian or Southeast Asian food

choral (say kor-al) ADJECTIVE
for a choir or chorus

chord (say kord) NOUN chords
a number of musical notes sounded together
SPELLING ALERT! You play a musical **chord**, but you tie a knot in a **cord**.

a b c d e f g h i j k l m n o p q r s t u v w x y z

chore (*say* chor) *NOUN* **chores**
a tedious or difficult task

chorus (*say* **kor**-us) *NOUN* **choruses**
❶ a group of people singing or speaking together ❷ a piece of music sung by a group of people ❸ the words repeated after every verse of a song or poem

chose *VERB* (*past tense of* **choose**)
• He chose carefully from the library.

chosen *VERB* (*past participle of* **choose**)
• I have chosen a name for my dog.

christen *VERB* **christens, christening, christened**
to christen a child is to baptize it and give it a name
➤ **christening** *NOUN* the ceremony at which a child is baptized

Christian *NOUN* **Christians**
someone who believes in Christ
Christian *ADJECTIVE*
to do with Christ or Christians

Christianity *NOUN*
the religion of Christians

Christian name *NOUN* **Christian names**
a person's first name, for example *John* or *Mary*

Christmas *NOUN* **Christmases**
the time of celebrating the birth of Christ on 25 December

chrome, chromium *NOUN*
a shiny silvery metal

chronic *ADJECTIVE*
a chronic illness or problem is one that lasts for a long time

chronicle *NOUN* **chronicles**
a list of events with their dates

chronology *NOUN*
the arrangement of events in the order in which they happened, especially in history or geology
➤ **chronological** *ADJECTIVE*

chrysalis (*say* **kris**-a-lis) *NOUN* **chrysalises**
the hard cover a caterpillar makes round itself before it turns into a butterfly or moth

chrysanthemum *NOUN* **chrysanthemums**
a garden flower that blooms in autumn

chubby *ADJECTIVE* **chubbier, chubbiest**
plump and rounded • *a chipmunk with chubby cheeks*
➤ **chubbiness** *NOUN*

chuck *VERB* **chucks, chucking, chucked** (*informal*)
to chuck something is to throw it roughly
• *He chucked a brick through the window.*

chuckle *VERB* **chuckles, chuckling, chuckled**
to chuckle is to laugh quietly

chuckle *NOUN* **chuckles**
a quiet laugh

chug *VERB* **chugs, chugging, chugged**
to chug is to move with the sound of a slow-running engine

chum *NOUN* **chums** (*informal*)
a friend

chunk *NOUN* **chunks**
a thick lump of something
➤ **chunky** *ADJECTIVE* big and thick

church *NOUN* **churches**
❶ a church is a building where Christians worship ❷ a church is also a particular Christian religion, for example the Church of England

churchyard *NOUN* **churchyards**
the ground round a church, used as a graveyard

churn *NOUN* **churns**
❶ a large container for milk ❷ a machine for making butter

churn *VERB* **churns, churning, churned**
❶ to churn butter is to make it in a churn
❷ to churn something is to stir it vigorously
➤ **to churn something out** (*informal*) is to produce lots of it very quickly

chute (*say* shoot) *NOUN* **chutes**
a steep channel for people or things to slide down • *Put the bag in the rubbish chute.*

chutney *NOUN*
chutney is a spicy mixture of fruit and peppers in a sauce, eaten with meat or cheese

cider *NOUN* **ciders**
cider is an alcoholic drink made from apples
Bean ... never ate any food at all. Instead, he drank gallons of strong cider which he made from the apples in his orchard.—FANTASTIC MR FOX, Roald Dahl

cigar *NOUN* **cigars**
a roll of compressed tobacco leaves for smoking

cigarette *NOUN* **cigarettes**
a small thin roll of shredded tobacco in thin paper for smoking

cinder *NOUN* **cinders**
a small piece of coal or wood that is partly burned

cinema *NOUN* **cinemas**
❶ a cinema is a place where people go to see films ❷ cinema is the art or business of making films • *recent trends in British cinema*

cinnamon *NOUN*
a yellow-brown spice

circle *NOUN* **circles**
❶ a round flat shape, the shape of a coin or wheel ❷ a balcony in a cinema or theatre

circle *VERB* **circles, circling, circled**
❶ to circle is to move in a circle • *Vultures circled overhead.* ❷ to circle a place is to go round it • *The space probe circled Mars.*

circuit (*say* ser-kit) *NOUN* **circuits**
❶ a circular line or journey ❷ a racecourse ❸ the path of an electric current

circular *ADJECTIVE*
round like a circle

circular *NOUN* **circulars**
a letter or advertisement sent to a lot of people

circulate *VERB* **circulates, circulating, circulated**
❶ to circulate is to move around and come back to the beginning • *Blood circulates in the body.* ❷ to circulate something like a letter or notice is to send it to a lot of people

circulation *NOUN* **circulations**
❶ the movement of blood around your body ❷ the number of copies of each issue of a newspaper or magazine that are sold

circumference *NOUN* **circumferences**
the line or distance round something, especially round a circle

circumstance *NOUN* **circumstances**
❶ a circumstance is a fact or event that makes a difference to something • *He won under difficult circumstances.* ❷ a person's circumstances are how much money they have, where they live and the sort of life they lead

circus *NOUN* **circuses**
an entertainment with clowns and acrobats, usually performed in a large tent

cistern *NOUN* **cisterns**
a water tank

citizen *NOUN* **citizens**
a citizen of a place is someone who was born there or who lives there

citizenship *NOUN*
❶ the citizenship of a country is the right to live there and be a citizen of it • *She has applied for American citizenship.* ❷ citizenship is also the duties a person has when they are the citizen of a country • *The school has lessons in citizenship.*

citrus fruit *NOUN* **citrus fruits**
citrus fruits are juicy fruits with a tough skin, such as oranges, lemons, limes and grapefruit

city *NOUN* **cities**
a large and important town, often having a cathedral

civic *ADJECTIVE*
to do with a city or its citizens • *the civic authorities*

civil *ADJECTIVE*
❶ to do with the citizens of a place ❷ to do with the ordinary people and not those who are in the armed forces ❸ a civil person is polite and courteous to other people

civilian *NOUN* **civilians**
someone who is an ordinary citizen and not in the armed forces

civilization (*also* **civilisation**) *NOUN* **civilizations**
❶ a civilization is a society or culture at a particular time in history • *They were learning*

a
b
c
d
e
f
g
h
i
j
k
l
m
n
o
p
q
r
s
t
u
v
w
x
y
z

about the Ancient Egyptian civilization.
❷ civilization is a developed or organized way of life • *We are studying a primitive society with little civilization.*

civilize (*also* **civilise**) *VERB* **civilizes, civilizing, civilized**
to civilize someone is to improve their education and manners

civil war *NOUN* **civil wars**
a war fought between people of the same country, such as the English Civil War (1642–51) or the American Civil War (1861–65)

clad *ADJECTIVE*
clothed or covered • *The story was about a knight clad in shining armour.*

claim *VERB* **claims, claiming, claimed**
❶ to claim something is to ask for it when you think it belongs to you • *I'd like to claim the three weeks' money you owe me.*
❷ to claim something is to state or assert it • *They claimed they had been at home all evening.*

claim *NOUN* **claims**
❶ an act of claiming ❷ something claimed

claimant *NOUN* **claimants**
someone who makes a claim, especially for a right or benefit

clam *NOUN* **clams**
a shellfish

clamber *VERB* **clambers, clambering, clambered**
to clamber is to climb up or over something difficult using your hands and feet
• *We clambered over the slippery rocks.*

clammy *ADJECTIVE* **clammier, clammiest**
damp and slimy • *The Count extended a clammy hand.*
➤ **clamminess** *NOUN*

clamp *NOUN* **clamps**
a device for holding things together

clamp *VERB* **clamps, clamping, clamped**
to clamp something is to fit a clamp on it
➤ **to clamp down on something** is to be strict about it • *The teachers decided to clamp down on homework.*

clan *NOUN* **clans**
a number of families with the same ancestor
• *The Scottish clans include the Campbells and the MacDonalds.*

clang *VERB* **clangs, clanging, clanged**
to make a loud ringing sound

clank *VERB* **clanks, clanking, clanked**
to make a loud sound like heavy pieces of metal banging together

clank *NOUN* **clanks**
a clanking sound
Mr Otis was awakened by a curious noise in the corridor, outside his room. It sounded like the clank of metal, and seemed to be coming nearer every moment.—THE CANTERVILLE GHOST, Oscar Wilde

clap *VERB* **claps, clapping, clapped**
to clap is to make a noise by hitting the palms of your hands together, especially to show you like something

clap *NOUN* **claps**
❶ a round of clapping, especially to show you like something • *They gave the winners a loud clap.* ❷ a clap of thunder is a sudden sound of loud thunder

clarify *VERB* **clarifies, clarifying, clarified**
to clarify something is to explain it and make it easier to understand
➤ **clarification** *NOUN*

clarinet *NOUN* **clarinets**
a woodwind instrument with a low tone
➤ **clarinettist** *NOUN*

clarity *NOUN*
clarity is a clear quality • *They spoke with clarity.*

clash *VERB* **clashes, clashing, clashed**
❶ to clash is to make a loud sound like cymbals banging together ❷ two events clash when they happen at the same time
• *My favourite TV programmes clash at 8 o'clock tonight.* ❸ two or more people clash when they have a fight or argument
• *Groups of rival fans clashed outside the stadium.*

clash *NOUN* **clashes**
❶ a clashing sound ❷ a fight or argument

clasp *VERB* **clasps, clasping, clasped**
to clasp someone or something is to hold them tightly

clasp *NOUN* **clasps**
❶ a device for fastening things ❷ a tight grasp

class *NOUN* **classes**
❶ a class is a group of similar people, animals or things ❷ a class is also a division according to how good or important something is • *Send the letter by first-class post.* ❸ a class is also a group of children or students who are taught together ❹ class is a system of different ranks in society

class *VERB* **classes, classing, classed**
to class things is to put them in classes or groups

classic *NOUN* **classics**
a book, film or story that is well known and thought to be very good and important
➤ **classics** the study of the ancient Greek and Latin languages and writers

classic *ADJECTIVE*
❶ a classic story is one that most people think is very good and important ❷ very typical or common • *They made the classic mistake of leaving things to the last moment.*

classical *ADJECTIVE*
❶ to do with ancient Greek or Roman art or culture • *a classical marble statue* ❷ classical music is music written in a long-established European musical tradition, of the type often played by orchestras

classified *ADJECTIVE*
❶ classified advertisements in newspapers are organized into types or subjects ❷ classified information is officially secret and not told to the public

classify *VERB* **classifies, classifying, classified**
to classify things is to put them in classes or groups
➤ **classification** *NOUN*

classmate *NOUN* **classmates**
your classmates are the people in the same class as you at school

classroom *NOUN* **classrooms**
a room where lessons are given at a school

clatter *NOUN*
a loud noise of things being rattled or banged

clatter *VERB* **clatters, clattering, clattered**
to clatter is to make a clatter

clause *NOUN* **clauses**
❶ (*grammar*) a part of a sentence that has its own verb ❷ a part of a contract, treaty or law

claustrophobia *NOUN*
claustrophobia is feeling afraid of being inside an enclosed space
➤ **claustrophobic** *ADJECTIVE*

claw *NOUN* **claws**
one of the hard sharp nails that some birds and animals have on their feet

claw *VERB* **claws, clawing, clawed**
to claw something is to grasp or scratch it with a claw or hand

clay *NOUN*
clay is a sticky kind of earth, and is used for making bricks and pottery

clean *ADJECTIVE* **cleaner, cleanest**
❶ something is clean when it does not have any dirt or stains on it ❷ fresh, not yet used • *Start on a clean page.* ❸ not rude or offensive • *I hope your jokes are clean ones.* ❹ fair and honest • *They wanted a clean fight.*

clean *VERB* **cleans, cleaning, cleaned**
to clean something is to make it clean

cleaner *NOUN* **cleaners**
❶ someone who cleans rooms or offices ❷ something used for cleaning
➤ **the cleaners** a firm which cleans clothes

cleanliness (*say* klen-li-nes) *NOUN*
the practice of keeping things clean

cleanly *ADVERB*
neatly, exactly • *He cut the brick cleanly in two.*

cleanse (*say* klenz) *VERB* **cleanses, cleansing, cleansed**
to cleanse something is to clean it and make it pure
➤ **cleanser** *NOUN*

clear *ADJECTIVE* **clearer, clearest**
❶ easy to see or hear or understand • *He spoke with a clear voice.* ❷ free from things that get in the way or are not wanted • *Make sure the table's clear for dinner.*

clear ADVERB
❶ clearly • *Speak loud and clear.* ❷ completely • *He got clear away.* ❸ at a distance from something • *You'd better stand clear of the gates.*

clear VERB clears, clearing, cleared
❶ to clear something is to make it free of unwanted things • *Will you clear the table for dinner?* ❷ to clear is to become clearer • *After the storm, the sky slowly cleared.* ❸ to clear someone is to find out that they are not to blame for something people thought they had done ❹ to clear something is to jump over it without touching it
➤ **to clear off** or **clear out** (*informal*) is to go away
➤ **to clear something out** is to empty or tidy it
➤ **to clear up** is to make things tidy

clearance NOUN clearances
❶ clearance between two things is how close together they are when one passes the other or comes near it • *There was not much clearance between the bridge and the top of the bus.* ❷ clearance to do something is official permission for it to happen • *The pilot wanted clearance for take-off.* ❸ clearance is moving away things that are in the way or not wanted

clearing NOUN clearings
an open space in a wood or forest

clearly ADVERB
❶ in a clear way • *We could see the house clearly.* ❷ obviously • *They were clearly going to win.*

clef NOUN clefs
a sign that shows the pitch of a stave in music

clench VERB clenches, clenching, clenched
to clench your teeth or fingers is to close them tightly

clergy PLURAL NOUN
the clergy are the priests or ministers of the Christian Church

clergyman, **clergywoman** NOUN clergymen, clergywomen
a man or woman who is a member of the clergy

clerical ADJECTIVE
❶ to do with the routine work in an office, such as filing and writing letters ❷ to do with the clergy

clerk (*say* klark) NOUN clerks
someone who works in an office to keep records and accounts and file papers

clever ADJECTIVE cleverer, cleverest
quick to learn and understand things; skilful
➤ **cleverly** ADVERB

cliché (*say* **klee**-shay) NOUN clichés
a phrase that people use a lot, so that it does not mean very much, for example *in this day and age* and *have a nice day*

click NOUN clicks
❶ a short sharp sound • *She heard a click as someone turned on the light.* ❷ an act of pressing a button on a computer mouse

click VERB clicks, clicking, clicked
❶ to make a short sharp sound ❷ to press a button on a mouse to select something on a computer screen • *Click here to move to the next section.*

client NOUN clients
someone who gets help or advice from a professional person such as a lawyer or architect; a customer

cliff NOUN cliffs
a steep rock face, especially on the coast

cliffhanger NOUN cliffhangers
a story or situation that is exciting because you do not know what will happen next

climate NOUN climates
the usual sort of weather in a particular area • *the warm humid climate of the rainforest*

climate change NOUN
climate change is a change in the world's climate, especially rising temperatures, caused by increased levels of carbon dioxide and other gases

climax NOUN climaxes
the most important or exciting part of a story or series of events

climb VERB climbs, climbing, climbed
❶ to climb or climb up something is to go up it ❷ to climb down something is to go

down it ❸ to climb is to grow or rise upwards, like a tall plant or a building

➤ **to climb down** is to admit that you have been wrong about something or have had to change your mind

climb *NOUN* climbs
an act of climbing • *It's a long climb to the top of the hill.*

climber *NOUN* climbers
someone who climbs hills and mountains for sport

cling *VERB* clings, clinging, clung
to cling to someone or something is to hold on tightly • *The child was clinging to its mother.*

clingfilm *NOUN*
clingfilm is a thin clear sheet of plastic that sticks to itself easily and is used for wrapping food

clinic *NOUN* clinics
a place where people see doctors for treatment or advice

clink *VERB* clinks, clinking, clinked
to make a short ringing sound, like a coin being dropped

clip *NOUN* clips
a fastener for keeping things together

clip *VERB* clips, clipping, clipped
❶ to clip things together is to fasten them with a clip ❷ to clip something is to cut it with shears or scissors

clipboard *NOUN* clipboards
a board that you can carry around, with a clip at the top to hold papers

clipper *NOUN* clippers
an old type of fast sailing ship

clippers *PLURAL NOUN*
clippers are large scissors for clipping

clipping *NOUN* clippings
a piece cut from a newspaper or magazine

cloak *NOUN* cloaks
a piece of outdoor clothing, usually without sleeves, that hangs loosely from your shoulders

cloakroom *NOUN* cloakrooms
❶ a place where you can leave coats and

bags while you are visiting a building ❷ a toilet

clobber *VERB* clobbers, clobbering, clobbered (*informal*)
to clobber someone is to hit them very hard

clock *NOUN* clocks
an instrument that shows what the time is

clockwise *ADVERB, ADJECTIVE*
moving round a circle in the same direction as the hands of a clock

clockwork *ADJECTIVE*
worked by a spring which you wind up

clog *VERB* clogs, clogging, clogged
to clog something is to block it up accidentally

clog *NOUN* clogs
a shoe with a wooden sole

cloister *NOUN* cloisters
a covered path that is open on one side and goes round a courtyard or along the side of a cathedral or monastery

clone *NOUN* clones
an animal or plant made from the cells of another animal or plant

clone *VERB* clones, cloning, cloned
to clone something is to copy it

close (*say* klohss) *ADJECTIVE* closer, closest
❶ near, either in time or place • *They were close to finding the answer.* • *The shops were quite close to their new house.* ❷ careful and detailed • *Please pay close attention.* ❸ tight; with little empty space • *They got the wardrobe in, but it was a close fit.* ❹ a close race or finish is one in which competitors are nearly equal at the end ❺ stuffy; without fresh air • *It's very close in this room.*

close (*say* klohss) *ADVERB* closer, closest
at a close distance • *The children were following close behind.*

close (*say* klohss) *NOUN* closes
❶ a street that is closed at one end
❷ an enclosed area, especially round a cathedral

close (*say* klohz) *VERB* closes, closing, closed
❶ to close something is to shut it ❷ to close an event or meeting is to finish it ❸ to close a

a
b
c
d
e
f
g
h
i
j
k
l
m
n
o
p
q
r
s
t
u
v
w
x
y
z

A B **C** D E F G H I J K L M N O P Q R S T U V W X Y Z

computer file or program is to stop using it and put it away

➤ **to close down** is to stop doing business
• *Several shops in the High Street have closed down recently.*

➤ **to close in** is to get nearer • *The police closed in around the house.*

closely (*say* **klohss**-lee) ADVERB
❶ carefully, with attention • *His friends were watching closely.* ❷ tightly • *The box was closely packed with toys.*

close–up (*say* **klohss**-up) NOUN **close-ups**
a photograph or film taken at short range

clot NOUN **clots**
❶ a mass of thick liquid like blood or cream that has become nearly solid ❷ (*informal*) a stupid person

clot VERB **clots**, **clotting**, **clotted**
to clot is to form into clots, like blood or cream

cloth NOUN **cloths**
❶ cloth is material woven from wool, cotton or some other fabric ❷ a cloth is a piece of this material

clothe (*say* kloh*th*) VERB **clothes**, **clothing**, **clothed**
to clothe someone is to put clothes on them

clothes (*say* kloh*thz*) PLURAL NOUN
clothes are the things you wear to cover your body • *Please bring a spare change of clothes.*

clothing NOUN
clothing is the clothes you wear

cloud NOUN **clouds**
❶ a mass of water vapour floating in the air ❷ a mass of smoke or something else dense in the air ❸ (computing) a remote network to store and process computer data

cloud VERB **clouds**, **clouding**, **clouded**
to cloud or cloud over is to become full of clouds • *In the afternoon the sky clouded over.*

➤ **cloudless** ADJECTIVE a cloudless sky does not have any clouds

cloudburst NOUN **cloudbursts**
a sudden heavy downpour of rain

cloudy ADJECTIVE **cloudier**, **cloudiest**
❶ full of clouds ❷ hard to see through
• *The glass contained a cloudy liquid.*

clout VERB **clouts**, **clouting**, **clouted**
to clout someone is to give them a hard blow

clove NOUN **cloves**
the dried bud of a tropical tree used as a spice

clover NOUN
a small wild plant, usually with leaves in three parts

clown NOUN **clowns**
❶ a circus performer who dresses up and wears bright face paint and does silly things to make people laugh ❷ an amusing or silly person

clown VERB **clowns**, **clowning**, **clowned**
to clown is to behave like a clown

club NOUN **clubs**
❶ a heavy stick ❷ a stick for playing golf ❸ a group of people who meet together because they are interested in the same thing ❹ a playing card with a black clover leaf printed on it

club VERB **clubs**, **clubbing**, **clubbed**
to club someone is to hit them hard with a heavy stick

➤ **to club together** is to join with other people in doing something, especially raising money

cluck VERB **clucks**, **clucking**, **clucked**
to make a noise like a hen

clue NOUN **clues**
something that helps you to solve a puzzle or a mystery

clueless ADJECTIVE (*informal*)
stupid, having no idea how to do something

clump NOUN **clumps**
a cluster of trees or plants

clumsy ADJECTIVE **clumsier**, **clumsiest**
a clumsy person is careless and awkward, and likely to knock things over or drop things
➤ **clumsily** ADVERB ➤ **clumsiness** NOUN

clung VERB (*past tense and past participle of* **cling**)
• *She clung to the side of the boat.* • *The child had clung to her hand.*

cluster NOUN **clusters**
a group of people or things close together
Miss Octavia Scrimshaw's Finishing Academy for Young Ladies was a cluster of wind-blown red-brick buildings that stood in a wild corner of England.—COGHEART, Peter Bunzl

clutch VERB **clutches, clutching, clutched**
to clutch something or clutch at something is to grab hold of it

clutch NOUN **clutches**
❶ a tight grasp ❷ a device for disconnecting the engine of a motor vehicle from its gears and wheels ❸ a clutch is also a set of eggs in a nest

clutter VERB **clutters, cluttering, cluttered**
to clutter a place up is to make it untidy or messy

clutter NOUN
clutter is a lot of things left around untidily

cm ABBREVIATION
short for *centimetres*

Co. ABBREVIATION
short for *company*

coach NOUN **coaches**
❶ a comfortable single-deck bus used for long journeys ❷ a carriage of a railway train ❸ a carriage pulled by horses ❹ a person who trains or instructs people in a sport or skill

coach VERB **coaches, coaching, coached**
to coach someone is to instruct or train them in a sport or skill

coal NOUN
coal is a hard black mineral used as fuel

coarse ADJECTIVE **coarser, coarsest**
❶ rough, not delicate or smooth ❷ rude or offensive • *You have a very coarse sense of humour.*

coast NOUN **coasts**
the seashore and the land close to it
➤ **the coast is clear** when there is no one about to catch you or stop you doing something

coast VERB **coasts, coasting, coasted**
to coast is to ride downhill without using power • *They stopped pedalling and coasted down the slope.*

coastal ADJECTIVE
by the coast or near the coast

coastguard NOUN **coastguards**
someone whose job is to keep watch on coasts to prevent smuggling

coastline NOUN
the edge of the land by the sea

coat NOUN **coats**
❶ a piece of clothing with sleeves, that covers most of the body and is worn outdoors over other clothes ❷ a layer of paint

coat VERB **coats, coating, coated**
to coat something is to cover it with a coating

coating NOUN **coatings**
a covering or layer, especially of paint

coat of arms NOUN **coats of arms**
a design on a shield or building that represents an old family or town

coax VERB **coaxes, coaxing, coaxed**
to coax someone is to persuade them gently or patiently

cobbler NOUN **cobblers**
someone whose job is to mend shoes

cobbles PLURAL NOUN
cobbles are a surface of cobblestones on a road
➤ **cobbled** ADJECTIVE

cobblestone NOUN **cobblestones**
a small smooth and rounded stone sometimes used in large numbers to pave roads in towns

cobra (*say* koh-bra) NOUN **cobras**
a poisonous snake

cobweb NOUN **cobwebs**
a net of thin sticky threads that spiders spin to catch insects
DID YOU KNOW? The first part of **cobweb** comes from an old word *coppe* meaning 'spider'.

cock NOUN **cocks**
a male bird, especially a male fowl

cock VERB **cocks, cocking, cocked**
❶ to cock your eye or ear is to turn it in a particular direction ❷ to cock a gun is to make it ready to fire

cockerel NOUN **cockerels**
a young male fowl

a b c d e f g h i j k l m n o p q r s t u v w x y z

cocker spaniel *NOUN* **cocker spaniels**
a kind of small spaniel with long hanging ears

cockle *NOUN* **cockles**
an edible shellfish

cockney *NOUN* **cockneys**
❶ a cockney is someone born in the East End of London ❷ cockney is also a kind of English spoken by people from this part of London

cockpit *NOUN* **cockpits**
the place in an aircraft where the pilot sits

cockroach *NOUN* **cockroaches**
a dark brown insect

cocky *ADJECTIVE* **cockier, cockiest** (*informal*)
conceited and cheeky

cocoa *NOUN* **cocoas**
❶ a hot drink made from chocolate, milk and sugar ❷ a powdered form of chocolate used in baking or to make hot drinks

coconut *NOUN* **coconuts**
a large round nut containing a milky juice, that grows on palm trees

cocoon *NOUN* **cocoons**
the covering round a pupa

cod *NOUN* **cod**
a large edible sea fish

code *NOUN* **codes**
❶ a set of signs and letters for sending messages secretly • *No one has yet managed to decipher the code.* ❷ a set of rules • *The club has a strict dress code.* ❸ (*computing*) the name for the instructions that make up a computer program

code *VERB* **codes, coding, coded**
❶ to code a message is to use special signs and letters, so that other people cannot understand it ❷ (*computing*) to code is to write code for a computer program

co-education *NOUN*
the teaching of boys and girls together
➤ **co-educational** *ADJECTIVE*

coffee *NOUN* **coffees**
❶ a hot drink made from the roasted and crushed beans of a tropical plant ❷ the powder from which you make this drink

coffin *NOUN* **coffins**
a long box in which a dead body is buried or cremated

cog *NOUN* **cogs**
one of a number of pieces sticking out from the edge of a wheel and allowing it to drive another wheel

cohesive *ADJECTIVE*
if something is cohesive, it is united and works as a whole
➤ **cohesion** *NOUN*

coil *NOUN* **coils**
a circle or spiral of rope or wire

coil *VERB* **coils, coiling, coiled**
to coil something is to wind it into circles or spirals

coin *NOUN* **coins**
a piece of metal money

coin *VERB* **coins, coining, coined**
❶ to coin money is to manufacture it ❷ to coin a new word is to invent it

coinage *NOUN* **coinages**
❶ a country's coinage is the system of money that it uses ❷ a coinage is also a new word or phrase that someone has invented

coincide *VERB* **coincides, coinciding, coincided**
to coincide is to happen at the same time as something else • *The end of term coincides with my birthday.*

coincidence *NOUN* **coincidences**
coincidence, or a coincidence, is when two things can happen by chance at the same time

coke *NOUN*
coke is a solid fuel made out of coal

cola *NOUN* **colas**
cola is a sweet brown fizzy drink

colander (*say* **kul**-an-der) *NOUN* **colanders**
a bowl with holes, for draining water from vegetables

cold *ADJECTIVE* **colder, coldest**
❶ low in temperature, not hot or warm
❷ a cold person is unfriendly and distant
➤ **coldly** *ADVERB* ➤ **coldness** *NOUN*

cold *NOUN* **colds**
❶ cold weather or temperature ❷ a cold is an illness that makes your nose run and gives you a sore throat

cold-blooded *ADJECTIVE*
❶ a cold-blooded animal has blood that changes temperature according to the surroundings • *Lizards are cold-blooded animals.* ❷ cruel, ruthless

coleslaw *NOUN*
a salad made of chopped cabbage covered in mayonnaise

collaborate *VERB* **collaborates, collaborating, collaborated**
❶ people collaborate when they work together or share their information ❷ to collaborate with an enemy is to work secretly on their side
➤ **collaboration** *NOUN*

collaborator *NOUN*
❶ someone who works with someone else or shares ideas with them ❷ someone who betrays their country during a war by sharing information with the enemy

collage (*say* **kol**-ah*zh*) *NOUN* **collages**
a picture made by arranging scraps of paper and other things on a card

collapse *VERB* **collapses, collapsing, collapsed**
❶ to collapse is to fall or break into pieces because of too much weight ❷ someone collapses when they fall from being very weak or ill

collapse *NOUN* **collapses**
an act of collapsing

collapsible *ADJECTIVE*
a collapsible piece of furniture or equipment can be folded up into a smaller space

collar *NOUN* **collars**
❶ the part of a piece of clothing that goes round your neck ❷ a band that goes round an animal's neck

collate *VERB* **collates, collating, collated**
to collate pieces of information is to collect and arrange them in an organized way • *They had to collate the results in the form of a graph.*

colleague *NOUN* **colleagues**
someone's colleague is a person they work with

collect *VERB* **collects, collecting, collected**
❶ to collect things is to get them together from various places, especially as a hobby • *She collects stamps, and I collect coins.* ❷ to collect someone or something is to go and get them
➤ **collector** *NOUN*

collection *NOUN* **collections**
❶ things you have collected as a hobby ❷ money given by people at a meeting or concert or church service

collective *ADJECTIVE*
involving several people or things • *It was a collective decision.*

collective noun *NOUN* **collective nouns**
a singular noun that is a name for a group of things or people or animals, for example *a **flock** of birds, a **fleet** of ships* or *a **gang** of thieves*

college *NOUN* **colleges**
a place where people continue to study after they have left school

collide *VERB* **collides, colliding, collided**
to collide with something is to hit it while moving • *The bicycle collided with the car.*

collie *NOUN* **collies**
a breed of dog with a long pointed muzzle and long hair

collision *NOUN* **collisions**
a crash between moving vehicles • *There has been a collision on the motorway.*

colloquial *ADJECTIVE*
colloquial language is used for conversation but not for formal speech or writing • *'Chuck' is a colloquial word for 'throw'.*

colon *NOUN* **colons**
a punctuation mark (:) used to separate parts of a sentence or before items in a list • *There are two things I love about my room: the walls are bright yellow and you can see the sea out of the window.*

colonel (*say* **ker**-nel) *NOUN* **colonels**
a senior army officer

a b c d e f g h i j k l m n o p q r s t u v w x y z

colonial *ADJECTIVE*
from or to do with a country's colonies abroad

colonist *NOUN* **colonists**
a person who goes to live in a colony abroad

colony *NOUN* **colonies**
❶ a country that another country governs and sends people out to live there ❷ a group of people or animals living together

colossal *ADJECTIVE*
huge, enormous
The monster did not laugh. He set off, up from the earth, beating his colossal wings.—THE IRON MAN, Ted Hughes

colour *NOUN* **colours**
❶ the quality of being red, green, blue and so on, produced by rays of light of different wavelengths ❷ the use of all colours, not just black and white • *Is this film in colour?* ❸ the colour of someone's skin ❹ a substance used to give colour to things ❺ the special flag of a ship or regiment

colour *VERB* **colours, colouring, coloured**
to colour something is to give it a colour or colours with paints or crayons

colour-blind *ADJECTIVE*
not able to see or distinguish between some colours, usually red and green

coloured *ADJECTIVE*
having a particular colour

colourful *ADJECTIVE*
❶ having a lot of bright colours ❷ lively
• *a colourful account of life at sea*
➤ **colourfully** *ADVERB*

colouring *NOUN*
❶ colouring is a substance you add to something to give it a special colour
❷ a person's colouring is the colour and appearance of their skin and hair

colourless *ADJECTIVE*
not having any colour • *Many gases are colourless.*

colt *NOUN* **colts**
a young male horse

column *NOUN* **columns**
❶ a pillar ❷ something long and narrow
• *a column of smoke in the distance* ❸ a strip of

printing in a book, newspaper or website
❹ a regular feature in a newspaper, magazine or website • *the weekly sports column*

coma (*say* koh-ma) *NOUN* **comas**
someone is in a coma when they are unconscious for a long time

comb *NOUN* **combs**
❶ a tool with teeth for making the hair tidy
❷ the red fleshy crest on the head of some birds, such as cockerels

comb *VERB* **combs, combing, combed**
❶ to comb the hair is to tidy it with a comb
❷ to comb an area is to search it carefully for something lost • *We combed the woods all day but couldn't find our dog.*

combat *NOUN* **combats**
a fight or contest

combat *VERB* **combats, combating, combated**
to combat something bad or unpleasant is to fight it and try to get rid of it • *The police force combats crime.*

combination *NOUN* **combinations**
❶ combination is joining or mixing things
❷ a combination is a group of things that have been joined or mixed together

combine (*say* kom-byn) *VERB* **combines, combining, combined**
to combine things is to join them or mix them together

combustion *NOUN*
combustion is what happens when something burns

come *VERB* **comes, coming, came, come**
❶ to come is to move towards the person or place that is here (the opposite of **go**)
• *Do you want to come to my house?* • *Has that email come yet?* ❷ to come is also to occur or be present • *The scene comes near the end of the film.*
➤ **to come about** is to happen
➤ **to come across someone** is to meet them by chance
➤ **to come by something** is to get it • *How did you come by the tickets?*
➤ **to come round** *or* **come to** is to revive after being unconscious

➤ **to come to something** is to add up to it
• *Altogether that comes to £12.50.*
➤ **to come true** is to actually happen • *The trip will be a dream come true.*

comeback *NOUN* comebacks
someone makes a comeback when they start doing something again that they have been famous for in the past

comedian *NOUN* comedians
someone who entertains people with humour and jokes

comedy *NOUN* comedies
❶ a comedy is a play or film that makes people laugh ❷ comedy is using humour to make people laugh

comet *NOUN* comets
a bright moving object in space with a core of ice and a tail of dust particles pointing away from the sun
The comet roared with its flaming tail right through the valley ... and then disappeared again over the edge of the world.—COMET IN MOOMINLAND, Tove Jansson
DID YOU KNOW? The word **comet** comes from a Greek word meaning 'long-haired star'.

comfort *NOUN*
❶ comfort is a feeling of relief from worry or pain ❷ your comforts are the things you have around you that you enjoy and that make life pleasant

comfort *VERB* comforts, comforting, comforted
to comfort someone is to make them feel happier when they are feeling sad or worried

comfortable *ADJECTIVE*
❶ pleasant to use or wear • *a comfortable chair* ❷ free from worry or pain • *The nurse made the patient comfortable.*
➤ **comfortably** *ADVERB*

comic *NOUN* comics
❶ a children's magazine that has stories with pictures ❷ a comedian

comic, comical *ADJECTIVE*
funny, making people laugh
➤ **comically** *ADVERB*

comic strip *NOUN* comic strips
a series of drawings that tell a story

comma *NOUN* commas
a punctuation mark (,) used to mark a pause in a sentence or between items in a list

command *NOUN* commands
❶ a command is an instruction telling someone to do something ❷ command is authority or control • *Who has command of these soldiers?* ❸ a command of a subject is the skill or ability to understand it • *She has a good command of Spanish.*

command *VERB* commands, commanding, commanded
❶ to command someone is to tell them to do something ❷ to command a group of people is to be in charge of them • *A centurion commanded a hundred soldiers.*

commander *NOUN* commanders
someone who commands, especially a senior naval officer

commandment *NOUN* commandments
a sacred command, especially one of the Ten Commandments of Moses

commando *NOUN* commandos
a soldier trained for making dangerous raids

commemorate *VERB* commemorates, commemorating, commemorated
to commemorate a past event is to do something special so that people remember it
➤ **commemoration** *NOUN*

commence *VERB* commences, commencing, commenced
to commence something is to begin it
➤ **commencement** *NOUN*

commend *VERB* commends, commending, commended
to commend someone is to praise them
• *He was commended for bravery.*
➤ **commendable** *ADJECTIVE*
➤ **commendation** *NOUN*

comment *NOUN* comments
a remark or opinion

commentary *NOUN* commentaries
a description of an event by someone who is watching it, especially for radio or television

commentator to company

commentator *NOUN* **commentators**
a person who gives a commentary, especially of a sports event
➤ **commentate** *VERB*

commerce *NOUN*
commerce is trade, or buying and selling goods

commercial *ADJECTIVE*
❶ connected with trade and making money ❷ paid for by advertising
• *a commercial radio station*

commercial *NOUN* **commercials**
an advertisement, especially on television or radio

commit *VERB* **commits, committing, committed**
to commit a crime is to do something against the law
➤ **to commit yourself to something** is to decide to do it or to promise that you will do it

commitment *NOUN* **commitments**
❶ commitment is being determined to do something ❷ a commitment is something you have promised to do

committee *NOUN* **committees**
a group of people who meet to organize or discuss something

commodity *NOUN* **commodities**
something that can be bought and sold
• *commodities like coffee, cocoa and sugar*

common *ADJECTIVE* **commoner, commonest**
❶ ordinary or usual • *The dandelion is a common plant.* ❷ happening or used often
• *Traffic jams are common where we live.*
❸ shared by many people • *The story was common knowledge.* • *Music was their common interest.*

common *NOUN* **commons**
a piece of open land that anyone can use

commonplace *ADJECTIVE*
ordinary, familiar

common room *NOUN* **common rooms**
a room for teachers or pupils to relax in at a school or college

commotion *NOUN* **commotions**
a noisy uproar
At that moment there was a commotion from downstairs, and Bonnie turned, her face alight with expectancy.—THE WOLVES OF WILLOUGHBY CHASE, Joan Aiken

communal *ADJECTIVE*
shared by several people

commune *NOUN* **communes**
a group of people who live in the same house and share the money and work

communicate *VERB* **communicates, communicating, communicated**
to communicate news or information is to pass it on to other people
➤ **communicative** *ADJECTIVE* a communicative person is willing to talk to people and give them information

communication *NOUN* **communications**
❶ communication is giving people useful information and telling them about things that have happened ❷ a communication is a message or piece of information that someone gives you ❸ communication is also a form of technology for passing on information, for example television and text messages

Communion *NOUN*
Communion is the Christian ceremony in which holy bread and wine are given to worshippers

community *NOUN* **communities**
the people living in one area

commute *NOUN* **commutes, commuting, commuted**
to travel from home to work every morning and back again in the evening
➤ **commuter** *NOUN*

compact *ADJECTIVE*
small and neat

companion *NOUN* **companions**
a companion is someone who spends a lot of time with you
➤ **companionship** *NOUN* companionship is being with someone and enjoying their friendship

company *NOUN* **companies**
❶ a company is a group of people, especially

a business firm ❷ company is having people with you • *Jill was lonely and longed for some company.* ❸ a company is an army unit consisting of two or more platoons

comparable (*say* kom-per-a-bul)
ADJECTIVE
able to be compared, similar

comparative *ADJECTIVE*
compared with something else • *After the noise of her own house she enjoyed the comparative peace of her friend's place.*

comparative *NOUN* comparatives
the form of an adjective or adverb that expresses 'more' • *The comparative of 'big' is 'bigger', and the comparative of 'bad' is 'worse'.*

comparatively *ADVERB*
compared to something else or what is usual • *They all went to bed comparatively late.*

compare *VERB* compares, comparing, compared
❶ to compare things is to see how they are similar • *Compare your answers.* ❷ to compare with something is to be as good as it • *Our football pitch cannot compare with Wembley Stadium.*

comparison *NOUN* comparisons
comparison, or a comparison, is thinking about several things and seeing how they are similar or different

compartment *NOUN* compartments
a special place or section where you can put something • *The coach had a luggage compartment under the floor.*

compass *NOUN* compasses
❶ an instrument with a magnetized needle that shows which direction you are facing ❷ a compass, or pair of compasses, is a device for drawing circles

compassion *NOUN*
compassion is pity or mercy you show to people who are suffering
➤ compassionate *ADJECTIVE*

compatible *ADJECTIVE*
❶ people are compatible when they are able to live or exist together without trouble

❷ machines and devices are compatible when they can be used together

compel *VERB* compels, compelling, compelled
to compel someone to do something is to force them to do it

compensate *VERB* compensates, compensating, compensated
to compensate someone is to give them something to make up for something they have lost or suffered
➤ compensation *NOUN*

compete *VERB* competes, competing, competed
to compete in a competition is to try to win it by being better than other people

competent *ADJECTIVE*
having the skill or knowledge to do something well • *She is a competent football player.*
➤ competence *NOUN*

competition *NOUN* competitions
a game or race in which you try to do better than other people

competitive *ADJECTIVE*
a competitive person enjoys competing with other people and likes to win

competitor *NOUN* competitors
❶ someone who competes in a game or race ❷ if two companies are competitors, they sell the same type of product or service

compile *VERB* compiles, compiling, compiled
to compile information is to collect and arrange it, especially in a book • *She compiled a collection of children's poems.*
➤ compilation *NOUN* a collection of information, stories or poems, that someone has put together

complacent *ADJECTIVE*
smugly satisfied with the way things are, without wanting to improve them

complain *VERB* complains, complaining, complained
to complain about something is to say that you are not pleased about it

a
b
c
d
e
f
g
h
i
j
k
l
m
n
o
p
q
r
s
t
u
v
w
x
y
z

A
B
C
D
E
F
G
H
I
J
K
L
M
N
O
P
Q
R
S
T
U
V
W
X
Y
Z

complaint *NOUN* **complaints**
❶ you make a complaint when you are not pleased about something ❷ you suffer from a complaint when you are slightly ill

complement *NOUN* **complements**
the amount needed to fill or complete something • *This ship has a full complement of sailors.*

complementary *ADJECTIVE*
❶ complementary colours and designs go well together ❷ complementary parts together make up a whole

complete *ADJECTIVE*
❶ having all its parts, with nothing missing • *I hope the tool kit is complete.* ❷ finished, achieved • *By evening the jigsaw puzzle was complete.* ❸ utter, total • *It came as a complete surprise.*

complete *VERB* **completes**, **completing**, **completed**
to complete something is to finish it or make it complete
➤ **completion** *NOUN*

completely *ADVERB*
totally, utterly • *You are completely wrong.*

complex *ADJECTIVE*
difficult and complicated
➤ **complexity** *NOUN*

complex *NOUN* **complexes**
❶ a group of buildings, such as a sports centre ❷ something that someone has a strange attitude or obsession about • *He has a complex about winning.*

complexion *NOUN* **complexions**
the colour or appearance of your skin

complicate *VERB* **complicates**, **complicating**, **complicated**
to complicate something is to make it difficult or awkward

complicated *ADJECTIVE*
difficult to understand or cope with because it has so many parts or details

complication *NOUN* **complications**
❶ a difficult or awkward situation ❷ a difficulty that makes something worse

compliment *NOUN* **compliments**
words or actions that show you approve of a person or thing

complimentary *ADJECTIVE*
❶ praising someone or saying good things about them • *She liked Neil and was very complimentary about him.* ❷ given to someone free of charge • *We were given complimentary tickets for the match.*

comply (*say* kom-**ply**) *VERB* **complies**, **complying**, **complied**
to comply with a law or rule is to obey it
➤ **compliance** *NOUN*

component *NOUN* **components**
one of the parts that a machine is made of

compose *VERB* **composes**, **composing**, **composed**
❶ to compose music or poetry is to write it ❷ to be composed of several people or things is to be made up of them • *The class is composed of children up to the age of 8.*
➤ **composer** *NOUN*

composition *NOUN* **compositions**
❶ composition is composing or writing something ❷ a composition is a piece of music or an essay

compost *NOUN*
compost is a mixture of decayed leaves, grass and other natural refuse, and is used as manure

compound *NOUN* **compounds**
❶ a substance that is made of two or more parts or ingredients ❷ a word that is made from two or more other words, such as *bathroom* and *website* ❸ a compound is also a fenced area containing buildings

comprehend *VERB* **comprehends**, **comprehending**, **comprehended**
to comprehend something is to understand it

comprehension *NOUN* **comprehensions**
❶ comprehension is understanding ❷ a comprehension is an exercise that tests or helps your understanding of a language

comprehensive *ADJECTIVE*
including everything or everyone
• *a comprehensive list*

comprehensive school NOUN
comprehensive schools
a secondary school for children of all abilities

compress VERB **compresses, compressing, compressed**
❶ to compress something is to press it or squeeze it together ❷ to be compressed is to be forced into a small space
➤ **compression** NOUN

comprise VERB **comprises, comprising, comprised**
to comprise several people or things is to include them • *A football team comprises eleven players.*

compromise (*say* kom-pro-myz) VERB **compromises, compromising, compromised**
to compromise is to accept less than you really wanted, especially so as to settle a disagreement • *We both wanted to sit beside Mum, so we compromised by swapping seats every half-hour.*

compromise (*say* kom-pro-myz) NOUN **compromises**
accepting less than you really wanted

compulsive ADJECTIVE
not able to stop doing something • *He was a compulsive liar.*
➤ **compulsively** ADVERB

compulsory ADJECTIVE
something is compulsory when you have to do it • *Wearing seat belts is compulsory.*

compute VERB **computes, computing, computed**
to compute something is to calculate it

computer NOUN **computers**
an electronic machine that does word processing, sorts data and does rapid calculations

comrade NOUN **comrades**
a friend or companion

con VERB **cons, conning, conned** (*informal*)
to con someone is to swindle them

concave ADJECTIVE
a concave surface is curved like the inside of a circle or ball (the opposite of **convex**)

conceal VERB **conceals, concealing, concealed**
to conceal something is to hide it carefully or cleverly
➤ **concealment** NOUN

conceit NOUN
conceit is thinking a lot about how clever or attractive you are
➤ **conceited** ADJECTIVE

conceive VERB **conceives, conceiving, conceived**
❶ to conceive an idea or plan is to form it in your mind ❷ a woman conceives when she becomes pregnant

concentrate VERB **concentrates, concentrating, concentrated**
❶ to concentrate on something is to think hard about it ❷ to concentrate people or things is to bring them together in one place

concentrated ADJECTIVE
a liquid is concentrated when it is made stronger by having water removed from it

concentration NOUN
concentration is thinking hard about something

concentric ADJECTIVE
circles that are concentric are placed one inside another and have the same centre

concept NOUN **concepts**
an idea • *the concept of right and wrong*

conception NOUN **conceptions**
❶ conception is forming an idea in your mind ❷ conception is also when a woman becomes pregnant

concern VERB **concerns, concerning, concerned**
❶ to concern someone is to be important or interesting to them ❷ to concern something is to be about a particular subject • *This story concerns a shipwreck.* ❸ to worry someone

concern NOUN **concerns**
❶ something that matters to someone • *I think that is my concern.* ❷ a business

concerning PREPOSITION
on the subject of; in connection with • *The head teacher wrote to all parents concerning the school report.*

concert *NOUN* **concerts**
a performance of music

concertina *NOUN* **concertinas**
a portable musical instrument that you squeeze to push air past reeds

concerto (*say* kon-**cher**-toh) *NOUN* **concertos**
a piece of music for a solo instrument and an orchestra • *a violin concerto*

concession *NOUN* **concessions**
something that someone allows you to have or do, to be helpful or to reach an agreement • *As a special concession, parents may park in the teachers' car park on Sports Day.*

concise *ADJECTIVE*
giving a lot of information in a few words

conclude *VERB* **concludes**, **concluding**, **concluded**
❶ to conclude something is to end it
❷ to conclude something is also to decide about it • *The jury concluded that they were not guilty.*

conclusion *NOUN* **conclusions**
❶ the ending of something ❷ a decision that you reach after a lot of thought

concoct (*say* kon-**kokt**) *VERB* **concocts**, **concocting**, **concocted**
to concoct something is to create or devise it
➤ **concoction** *NOUN*

concrete *NOUN*
cement mixed with water and gravel or sand and used in building

concrete *ADJECTIVE*
real, definite • *We need concrete evidence.*

concussion *NOUN*
a temporary injury to the brain that is caused by a hard knock and leaves you feeling dizzy or unconscious

condemn *VERB* **condemns**, **condemning**, **condemned**
❶ to condemn someone or something is to say that you strongly disapprove of them
❷ to condemn criminals is to sentence them to a punishment • *He was condemned to*

death. ❸ to condemn a building is to declare that it is not fit to be used
➤ **condemnation** *NOUN*

condensation *NOUN*
drops of liquid formed from vapour that has condensed

condense *VERB* **condenses**, **condensing**, **condensed**
❶ to condense a piece of writing is to make it shorter ❷ to condense is to change into water or other liquid • *Steam condenses on cold windows.*

condensed *ADJECTIVE*
a condensed liquid, such as milk, is one that is made stronger or thicker

condition *NOUN* **conditions**
❶ the state in which a person or thing is • *This bike is in good condition.* ❷ something that must happen if something else is to happen • *Learning to swim is a condition of going sailing.* • *You can come on condition that you bring your sister too.*

conduct (*say* kon-**dukt**) *VERB* **conducts**, **conducting**, **conducted**
❶ to conduct someone is to lead or guide them ❷ to conduct something is to organize or manage it ❸ to conduct an orchestra or band is to direct it in a piece of music
❹ to conduct electricity or heat is to allow it to pass along • *Copper conducts electricity well.*

conduct (*say* **kon**-dukt) *NOUN*
a person's conduct is their behaviour

conductor *NOUN* **conductors**
❶ someone who conducts an orchestra or band ❷ something that conducts electricity or heat ❸ someone who collects the fares on a bus or coach

cone *NOUN* **cones**
❶ an object which is circular at one end and pointed at the other end ❷ an ice cream cornet ❸ the fruit of a pine, fir or cedar

confectioner *NOUN* **confectioners**
someone who makes or sells sweets
➤ **confectionery** *NOUN* confectionery is sweets and cakes that a shop sells

confer VERB confers, conferring, conferred
❶ to confer a title or honour on someone is to give it to them ❷ to confer is to have a discussion

conference NOUN conferences
a meeting for discussion

confess VERB confesses, confessing, confessed
to confess to something wrong is to admit that you have done it

confession NOUN confessions
an act of admitting that you have committed a crime or done wrong • *The burglar made a full confession.*

confetti PLURAL NOUN
tiny bits of coloured paper thrown at the bride and bridegroom after a wedding

confide VERB confides, confiding, confided
to confide in someone is to tell them a secret

confidence NOUN
❶ you have confidence when you are sure that you are right or can do something ❷ confidence in someone is trusting or believing them
➤ **in confidence** as a secret • *He told me all this in confidence.*

confidence trick NOUN confidence tricks
a trick to get money out of someone by deceiving them into giving their trust

confident ADJECTIVE
❶ being sure that you are right or can do something ❷ certain that something will happen • *We are confident it will be an enjoyable day.*
➤ **confidently** ADVERB

confidential ADJECTIVE
information is confidential when it has to be kept secret
➤ **confidentially** ADVERB

confine VERB confines, confining, confined
❶ to confine something is to restrict or limit it • *Please confine your comments to points of fact.* ❷ to confine someone is to lock them up or shut them in a place
➤ **confinement** NOUN

confirm VERB confirms, confirming, confirmed
❶ to confirm something is to say that it is true or to show that it is true ❷ to confirm an arrangement is to make it definite • *Please write to confirm your order.* ❸ to confirm someone is to make them a full member of a Christian Church

confirmation NOUN
❶ a fact or piece of information that shows something is true or has happened • *You will receive confirmation of your booking by email.* ❷ confirmation is a ceremony that makes someone a full member of a Christian Church

confiscate VERB confiscates, confiscating, confiscated
to confiscate something is to take it away from someone as a punishment
➤ **confiscation** NOUN

conflict (*say* kon-flikt) NOUN conflicts
a fight or disagreement • *Jack was trying to resolve a conflict between his parents.*

conflict (*say* kon-flikt) VERB conflicts, conflicting, conflicted
two things conflict when they contradict or disagree with one another • *The two reports of the incident conflict.*

conform VERB conforms, conforming, conformed
to conform is to follow other people's rules or ideas about something

confront VERB confronts, confronting, confronted
❶ to confront someone is to challenge them face to face for a fight or argument • *The police decided to confront the criminals there and then.* ❷ to confront a problem or difficulty is to deal with it firmly and positively
➤ **confrontation** NOUN

confuse VERB confuses, confusing, confused
❶ to confuse someone is to make them puzzled or muddled ❷ to confuse things is to mistake one thing for another
➤ **confusing** ADJECTIVE ➤ **confusion** NOUN

congested *ADJECTIVE*
crowded, especially with people or traffic
➤ **congestion** *NOUN*

conglomeration *NOUN*
conglomerations
a mixture of things put together
Most motor-cars are conglomerations ... of steel and wire and rubber and plastic, and electricity and oil and petrol and water.—CHITTY CHITTY BANG BANG, Ian Fleming

congratulate *VERB* **congratulates, congratulating, congratulated**
to congratulate someone is to tell them how pleased you are about something they have done
➤ **congratulations** *PLURAL NOUN*

congregate *VERB* **congregates, congregating, congregated**
to congregate is to come together in a group

congregation *NOUN* **congregations**
the people who take part in a church service

congress *NOUN* **congresses**
a large meeting or conference
➤ **Congress** the parliament or government of the USA

conical *ADJECTIVE*
shaped like a cone

conifer (*say* **kon-i-fer**) *NOUN* **conifers**
an evergreen tree with cones
➤ **coniferous** *ADJECTIVE*

conjunction *NOUN* **conjunctions**
a conjunction is a word that joins other words and parts of a sentence, for example *and*, *but* and *whether*

conjure *VERB* **conjures, conjuring, conjured**
to conjure is to perform tricks that look like magic
➤ **conjurer** *NOUN*

conker *NOUN* **conkers**
a hard and shiny brown nut that grows on a horse chestnut tree
➤ **conkers** a game played with conkers threaded on pieces of string
SPELLING ALERT! When you play **conkers**, you try to **conquer** your opponent.

DID YOU KNOW? Conker comes from an English dialect word meaning 'snail shell', because the game was first played with snail shells.

connect *VERB* **connects, connecting, connected**
❶ to connect things is to join them together
❷ to connect a computer or device is to join it to the internet or a computer network

connection *NOUN* **connections**
❶ a link between things ❷ joining together

connective *NOUN* **connectives**
a connective is a word or phrase that links clauses or sentences, for example *because*, *however* or *on the other hand*

conquer *VERB* **conquers, conquering, conquered**
to conquer a people or country is to defeat them and take them over • *William I conquered England.* • *He managed to conquer all his fears.*
➤ **conqueror** *NOUN*

conquest *NOUN* **conquests**
a victory over another country or people

conscience (*say* **kon**-shens) *NOUN*
a feeling people have about what is right or wrong

conscientious (*say* kon-shee-**en**-shus) *ADJECTIVE*
careful and hard-working
➤ **conscientiously** *ADVERB*

conscious (*say* **kon**-shus) *ADJECTIVE*
❶ awake and knowing what is happening
❷ aware of something • *Were you conscious you were being watched?* ❸ deliberate • *He's making a conscious effort to get fit.*
➤ **consciously** *ADVERB*
➤ **consciousness** *NOUN*

consecutive *ADJECTIVE*
things are consecutive when they come one after another in a list or sequence

consensus *NOUN*
an agreement between most people about something • *There was a consensus that the law should be changed.*

consent *NOUN*
consent is agreement or permission

consent VERB consents, consenting, consented
to consent to something is to agree to it or permit it

consequence NOUN consequences
❶ a consequence is something which happens because of an event or action • *His injury was the consequence of an accident.* ❷ consequence is the importance that something has • *My feelings were of no consequence to her.*
➤ **consequently** ADVERB as a result

conservation NOUN
conservation is keeping buildings and natural surroundings in a good state
➤ **conservationist** NOUN

Conservative NOUN Conservatives
someone who supports the Conservative Party, a British political party

conservative ADJECTIVE
❶ a conservative person doesn't like change and wants things to stay the same ❷ a conservative estimate or guess is a careful or cautious one

conservatory NOUN conservatories
a room built on the back or side of a house, with glass walls and a glass roof

conserve VERB conserves, conserving, conserved
to conserve something is to keep it from being changed or spoilt

consider VERB considers, considering, considered
❶ to consider something is to think carefully about it ❷ to consider something is also to believe it • *We consider that people should be allowed to follow their own religion.*

considerable ADJECTIVE
large or important • *The journey takes a considerable time.*
➤ **considerably** ADVERB very much • *Her new house is considerably larger.*

considerate ADJECTIVE
kind and thoughtful towards other people

consideration NOUN considerations
❶ consideration is careful thought or attention ❷ a consideration is a serious thought or reason • *Money is a major consideration in this plan.*

considering PREPOSITION
in view of • *The car goes well, considering its age.*

consist VERB consists, consisting, consisted
to consist of something is to be made from it • *The meal consisted of pasta and cheese.*

consistency NOUN consistencies
❶ consistency is being the same ❷ the consistency of a liquid is how thick it is

consistent ADJECTIVE
❶ always the same, regular ❷ always acting in the same way
➤ **consistently** ADVERB

consolation NOUN consolations
consolation is comfort or sympathy given to someone

consolation prize NOUN consolation prizes
a prize given to someone who does not win a main prize

console (*say* kon-**sohl**) VERB consoles, consoling, consoled
to console someone is to give them comfort or sympathy

console (*say* kon-**sohl**) NOUN consoles
a games console

consonant NOUN consonants
a letter that is not a vowel

conspicuous ADJECTIVE
something conspicuous stands out and is easy to see or notice

conspiracy NOUN conspiracies
a plot to do something bad or illegal
➤ **conspirator** NOUN

conspire VERB conspires, conspiring, conspired
if people conspire, they plot together

constable NOUN constables
an ordinary member of the police

constant ADJECTIVE
❶ not changing; continual ❷ a constant person is loyal and faithful
➤ **constancy** NOUN constancy is being loyal and faithful

a b c d e f g h i j k l m n o p q r s t u v w x y z

➤ **constantly** ADVERB continually, all the time • *They are constantly complaining.*

constellation NOUN constellations
a group of stars that you can see in the sky at night • *The Pole Star is in the constellation Ursa Minor.*

constipated ADJECTIVE
someone is constipated when they cannot empty their bowels easily to get rid of the waste in their body
➤ **constipation** NOUN

constituency NOUN constituencies
a district of the country that chooses its own Member of Parliament

constituent NOUN constituents
❶ a part of something ❷ someone who lives in the district of a particular Member of Parliament

constitute VERB constitutes, constituting, constituted
to constitute something is to form it or make it up • *Fifty states constitute the USA.*

constitution NOUN constitutions
❶ the set of principles or laws by which a country is governed ❷ a person's condition or state of health
➤ **constitutional** ADJECTIVE

construct VERB constructs, constructing, constructed
to construct something is to build it

construction NOUN constructions
❶ construction is the process of building ❷ a construction is something that someone has built

constructive ADJECTIVE
helpful and positive • *Their criticism was very constructive.*

consul NOUN consuls
an official representative of one country, living in another country

consult VERB consults, consulting, consulted
to consult a person or book is to look for information or advice
➤ **consultation** NOUN

consultant NOUN consultants
❶ a person who provides professional advice ❷ a senior hospital doctor

consume VERB consumes, consuming, consumed
❶ to consume food or drink is to eat or drink it ❷ to consume something is to use it up or destroy it • *The building was consumed by fire.*

consumer NOUN consumers
someone who buys goods or services

consumption NOUN
the using up of food or fuel • *The consumption of oil has increased.*

contact NOUN contacts
❶ contact is touching someone or something ❷ contact is also communication • *I've lost contact with my uncle.* ❸ a contact is a person you communicate with

contact VERB contacts, contacting, contacted
to contact someone is to get in touch with them

contact lens NOUN contact lenses
a small plastic lens worn against the eyeball instead of glasses

contagious (say kon-**tay**-jus) ADJECTIVE
a contagious illness is one that spreads from one person or animal to another

contain VERB contains, containing, contained
to contain something is to have it inside • *This site contains a great deal of information.*

container NOUN containers
❶ something that is designed to contain things ❷ a large box-shaped container for taking goods abroad by sea

contaminate VERB contaminates, contaminating, contaminated
to contaminate something is to make it dirty or impure
➤ **contamination** NOUN

contemplate VERB contemplates, contemplating, contemplated
❶ to contemplate something is to look hard

contemporary to contract

at it or think about it ❷ to contemplate doing something is to plan or intend to do it
➤ **contemplation** *NOUN*

contemporary *ADJECTIVE*
❶ people or things are contemporary when they belong to the same time
• *Florence Nightingale was contemporary with Queen Victoria.* ❷ modern or up to date
• *We like contemporary music.*

contempt *NOUN*
a feeling of strong disapproval when you despise someone or something
➤ **contemptible** *ADJECTIVE* someone or something is contemptible when people strongly disapprove of them or despise them

contemptuous *ADJECTIVE*
to be contemptuous of someone or something is to strongly disapprove of them
➤ **contemptuously** *ADVERB*

contend *VERB* **contends, contending, contended**
❶ to contend is to struggle or compete
❷ to contend something is to state or claim it • *I contend that we've been treated unfairly.*
➤ **contender** *NOUN* someone who takes part in a competition

content (*say* kon-tent) *NOUN*
❶ the amount of a substance that there is in something • *Drink milk with a low fat content.* ❷ the content of a book, magazine or piece of writing is what you read in it

content (*say* kon-tent) *ADJECTIVE*
happy and willing • *Are you content to stay behind?*
➤ **contentment** *NOUN*

contented (*say* kon-tent-id) *ADJECTIVE*
happy and satisfied • *After his big dinner, he looked very contented.*
➤ **contentedly** *ADVERB*

contents (*say* kon-tents) *PLURAL NOUN*
❶ the contents of a box or other container are what is inside it ❷ the contents of a book or magazine are the things you read in it

contest (*say* kon-test) *NOUN* **contests**
a competition

contest (*say* kon-test) *VERB* **contests, contesting, contested**
to contest something is to argue about it
• *After her death, relatives contested her will.*

contestant (*say* kon-test-ant) *NOUN* **contestants**
someone who takes part in a contest or competition

context *NOUN* **contexts**
the context of a word or phrase is the words that come before or after it and help to tell you what it means

continent *NOUN* **continents**
❶ the continents are the main masses of land in the world, which are Africa, Antarctica, Asia, Oceania, Europe, North America and South America ❷ (**the Continent**) the Continent is the mainland of Europe, not including the British Isles
➤ **continental** *ADJECTIVE*

continual *ADJECTIVE*
happening repeatedly • *I get fed up with his continual shouting.*
➤ **continually** *ADVERB*

continue *VERB* **continues, continuing, continued**
to continue something, or to continue to do something, is to go on doing it
➤ **continuation** *NOUN*

continuity *NOUN*
the process of going on without any breaks or changes

continuous *ADJECTIVE*
going on all the time; without a break
• *There was the continuous drone of traffic outside.*
➤ **continuously** *ADVERB*

contour *NOUN* **contours**
❶ the contour of something is its shape or outline ❷ a line on a map joining points that are the same height above sea level

contract (*say* kon-trakt) *NOUN* **contracts**
a legal agreement

contract (*say* kon-trakt) *VERB* **contracts, contracting, contracted**
❶ to contract is to become smaller • *Heated*

a b c d e f g h i j k l m n o p q r s t u v w x y z

contraction to converge

metal *contracts* as it cools. **2** to contract to
do something is to make a contract about it
3 to contract an illness is to catch it • *She
contracted pneumonia.*

contraction NOUN (*grammar*)
a shortened form of a word or words. *Can't* is a
contraction of *cannot.*

contradict VERB **contradicts,**
contradicting, contradicted
to contradict someone or something is to say
they are wrong or untrue
➤ **contradiction** NOUN

contraption NOUN **contraptions**
a clumsy or strange-looking device or machine

contrary ADJECTIVE
1 (*say* **kon-**tra-ree) one thing is contrary to
another when they are opposites or contradict
one another • *The two sisters had contrary views
about computer games.* **2** (*say* kon-**trair**-ee)
someone who is contrary is obstinate and
difficult to deal with • *Mary, Mary, quite contrary.*
➤ **on the contrary** the opposite is true
• *'Are you pleased?' 'On the contrary, I'm
very annoyed.'*

contrast (*say* kon-**trahst**) VERB **contrasts,**
contrasting, contrasted
1 to contrast two things is to show they are
different **2** one thing contrasts with another
when it is clearly different

contrast (*say* **kon-**trahst) NOUN **contrasts**
1 the action of contrasting **2** a clear
difference **3** the amount of difference
between colours or tones

contribute VERB **contributes,**
contributing, contributed
1 to contribute to something is to give money
to help it **2** to contribute to a result is to
help cause it • *His tiredness contributed to the
accident.*
➤ **contributor** NOUN

contribution NOUN **contributions**
a contribution is money or help that someone
gives towards something

contrive VERB **contrives, contriving,**
contrived
1 to contrive something is to plan or
invent it in a clever way **2** to contrive
to do something is to manage to do it

though it is probably foolish or dangerous
• *He contrived to get stuck in the lift near the
fifth floor.*
➤ **contrivance** NOUN

control NOUN **controls**
1 control is the power to make someone or
something do what you want **2** the controls
of a machine are the switches and levers that
make it work

control VERB **controls, controlling,**
controlled
to control something or someone is to have
power over what they do
➤ **controller** NOUN

controversial ADJECTIVE
a controversial action or statement is one that
is likely to cause people to have strong opinions
and disagree about it

controversy (*say* **kon-**tro-ver-see *or*
kon-**trov-**er-see) NOUN **controversies**
a long argument or disagreement

conundrum NOUN **conundrums**
a riddle

convalescent ADJECTIVE
recovering from an illness
➤ **convalescence** NOUN

convenience NOUN **conveniences**
1 convenience is usefulness and comfort
2 a convenience is something that is useful
3 a convenience is also a public toilet

convenient ADJECTIVE
easy to use or reach
➤ **conveniently** ADVERB

convent NOUN **convents**
a group of buildings where nuns live
and work

convention NOUN **conventions**
an accepted way of doing things

conventional ADJECTIVE
done in the accepted way; usual, traditional
➤ **conventionally** ADVERB

converge VERB **converges, converging,**
converged
to converge is to come together • *The two
roads converge at the pub.* • *Thousands of fans
converged on the football ground.*

conversation NOUN **conversations**
conversation, or a conversation, is when you talk to someone for a while
➤ **conversational** ADJECTIVE

converse (say kon-**verss**) VERB **converses, conversing, conversed**
to converse is to talk together • *They conversed in low voices.*

converse (say kon-**verss**) NOUN
the converse of something is the opposite of it

conversion NOUN **conversions**
the process of changing something from one form, system or use to another

convert (say kon-**vert**) VERB **converts, converting, converted**
❶ to convert something is to change it for a new purpose ❷ to convert someone is to persuade them to change their religion or beliefs ❸ (*rugby*) to convert a try is to kick a goal after scoring

convert (say kon-**vert**) NOUN **converts**
a person who has changed their religion
➤ **convertible** ADJECTIVE something is convertible when it can be changed from one form or shape to another

convex ADJECTIVE
a convex surface is curved like the outside of a circle or ball (the opposite of **concave**)

convey VERB **conveys, conveying, conveyed**
❶ to convey someone or something is to take them somewhere ❷ to convey a message or idea is to get someone to understand it

conveyor belt NOUN **conveyor belts**
a long belt or chain for carrying goods in a factory

convict (say kon-vikt) NOUN **convicts**
a criminal in a prison

convict (say kon-vikt) VERB **convicts, convicting, convicted**
to convict someone of a crime is to decide at their trial that they are guilty of it and punish them

conviction NOUN **convictions**
❶ being convicted of a crime ❷ being convinced of something; a strong opinion

convince VERB **convinces, convincing, convinced**
to convince someone is to persuade them about something

convoy NOUN **convoys**
a group of ships or vehicles travelling together

cook VERB **cooks, cooking, cooked**
to cook food is to make it ready to eat by heating it

cook NOUN **cooks**
someone who cooks, especially as their job

cooker NOUN **cookers**
a device with an oven and hot surfaces for cooking food

cookery NOUN
the art or skill of cooking food

cookie NOUN **cookies** (*North American*)
a sweet biscuit

cool ADJECTIVE **cooler, coolest**
❶ not very warm; fairly cold ❷ a cool person is calm and not easily excited ❸ (*informal*) good or fashionable • *He looks cool in those glasses.*
➤ **coolly** ADVERB calmly
➤ **coolness** NOUN

cool VERB **cools, cooling, cooled**
❶ to cool something is to make it cool ❷ to cool is to become cool

coop NOUN **coops**
a cage for poultry

cooperate VERB **cooperates, cooperating, cooperated**
to cooperate with people is to work helpfully with them
➤ **cooperative** ADJECTIVE

cooperation NOUN
❶ cooperation is working together to achieve something ❷ you give someone your cooperation when you do what they ask and help them

coordinate (say koh-**or**-din-ayt) VERB **coordinates, coordinating, coordinated**
to coordinate people or things is to get them to work well together

coordinate (*say* koh-**or**-din-at) *NOUN* **coordinates**
two numbers or letters used to show the position of something on a graph or map
• *The coordinates of point P are (4,2).*

coordination *NOUN*
❶ coordination is organizing people or things so that they work well together
❷ the coordination of parts of your body, for example your hands and your eyes, is making them help each other and work well together

coot *NOUN* **coots**
a water bird with a hard white plate on its forehead

cop *NOUN* **cops** (*informal*)
a police officer

cope *VERB* **copes**, **coping**, **coped**
to cope with something awkward or difficult is to deal with it successfully

copper *NOUN* **coppers**
❶ copper is a reddish-brown metal used for making wire and pipes ❷ copper is also a reddish-brown colour ❸ a copper is a coin made of copper or bronze ❹ (*informal*) a copper is a police officer

copy *NOUN* **copies**
❶ something made to look exactly like something else ❷ something written out a second time ❸ one newspaper, magazine or book • *We each have a copy of 'Alice in Wonderland'.*

copy *VERB* **copies**, **copying**, **copied**
❶ to copy something is to make a copy of it ❷ to copy someone is to do the same as them ❸ to copy a computer file or program or piece of text is to make another one that is exactly the same, usually one that you store somewhere else
➤ **copier** *NOUN* a machine for copying pages

coral *NOUN*
coral is a hard substance made of the skeletons of tiny sea creatures

cord *NOUN* **cords**
a cord is a piece of thin rope

cordial *ADJECTIVE*
warm and friendly • *We got a cordial welcome.*
➤ **cordially** *ADVERB*

cordial *NOUN* **cordials**
a sweet drink

corduroy (*say* **kor**-der-oi) *NOUN*
thick cotton cloth with ridges along it

core *NOUN* **cores**
the part in the middle of something

corgi *NOUN* **corgis**
a small breed of dog with short legs and large upright ears

cork *NOUN* **corks**
❶ cork is the lightweight bark of a kind of oak tree ❷ a cork is a piece of this bark used to close a bottle

corkscrew *NOUN* **corkscrews**
❶ a device for removing corks from bottles ❷ a spiral

cormorant *NOUN* **cormorants**
a large black seabird

corn *NOUN* **corns**
❶ corn is grain • *a field of corn* ❷ a corn is a small hard lump on your toe or foot

corned beef *NOUN*
tinned beef preserved with salt

corner *NOUN* **corners**
❶ the point where two lines, roads or walls meet ❷ a kick from the corner of a football field; a hit from the corner of a hockey field

corner *VERB* **corners**, **cornering**, **cornered**
❶ to corner someone is to trap them • *The police cornered the escaped prisoner.* ❷ to corner is to go round a corner • *The car cornered slowly and accelerated up the road.*

cornet *NOUN* **cornets**
❶ a long cone-shaped biscuit open at the top for ice cream ❷ a musical instrument like a trumpet

cornfield *NOUN* **cornfields**
a field where corn grows

cornflakes *PLURAL NOUN*
toasted maize flakes eaten for breakfast

cornflour *NOUN*
fine flour used for making puddings

cornflower *NOUN* **cornflowers**
a blue wild flower

corny *ADJECTIVE* **cornier, corniest** (*informal*)
a corny joke is one that is feeble and often repeated

coronation *NOUN* **coronations**
the ceremony of crowning a king or queen

coronavirus *NOUN*
a type of virus that causes the common cold and can also cause some more serious illnesses, such as Covid-19

coroner *NOUN* **coroners**
an official who holds an inquiry into the cause of an unnatural death

corporal *NOUN* **corporals**
a soldier just below sergeant in rank

corporal *ADJECTIVE*
to do with the human body

corporal punishment *NOUN*
punishment by hitting or beating someone

corporation *NOUN* **corporations**
a group of people elected to govern a town

corps (*say* kor) *NOUN* **corps**
❶ a large unit of soldiers ❷ a special army unit • *He is in the Medical Corps.*

corpse *NOUN* **corpses**
a dead body

corral (*say* ko-**rahl**) *NOUN* **corrals**
an enclosure for horses or cattle

correct *ADJECTIVE*
❶ true or accurate; without any mistakes • *Your answers are all correct.* ❷ proper, suitable • *Is that the correct way to talk to your parents?*
➤ **correctly** *ADVERB*

correct *VERB* **corrects, correcting, corrected**
to correct a piece of work is to mark the mistakes in it, or to put them right

correction *NOUN* **corrections**
❶ correction is correcting something ❷ a correction is a change made to something in order to correct it

correspond *VERB* **corresponds, corresponding, corresponded**
❶ to correspond with something is to agree with it or match it • *Your story corresponds with what I heard.* ❷ to correspond with someone is to exchange letters or emails with them

correspondence *NOUN*
❶ similarity or agreement ❷ letters or writing letters

correspondent *NOUN* **correspondents**
❶ someone who writes letters ❷ someone employed to send news or articles to a newspaper or television channel

corridor *NOUN* **corridors**
❶ a long narrow passage from which doors open into rooms or compartments ❷ a route an aircraft follows

corrode *VERB* **corrodes, corroding, corroded**
to corrode is to wear away by rust or be eaten away by a chemical
➤ **corrosion** *NOUN*

corrugated *ADJECTIVE*
shaped into folds or ridges • *The roof was made of corrugated iron.*

corrupt *ADJECTIVE*
a corrupt person is dishonest in carrying out their responsibilities or duties, for example by taking bribes

corrupt *VERB* **corrupts, corrupting, corrupted**
❶ to corrupt someone is to make them dishonest, especially when they have important responsibilities ❷ in a computer, a bug or other problem corrupts a file when it makes it impossible to read or use

corruption *NOUN*
corruption is dishonest behaviour by people who are in authority or have important responsibilities

corset *NOUN* **corsets**
a tight piece of underwear worn round the hips and waist

cosmetics *PLURAL NOUN*
substances like lipstick and face powder, for making the skin or hair look beautiful or different

cosmic (*say* **koz**-mik) *ADJECTIVE*
to do with the universe

a
b
c
d
e
f
g
h
i
j
k
l
m
n
o
p
q
r
s
t
u
v
w
x
y
z

cosmonaut NOUN **cosmonauts**
a Russian astronaut

cost VERB **costs, costing, cost**
to cost a certain amount is to have that amount as its price • *The book only cost £5 last year.*

cost NOUN **costs**
what you have to spend to do or get something • *the cost of admission to the zoo*
➤ **at all costs** or **at any cost** no matter what the cost or difficulty may be

costly ADJECTIVE **costlier, costliest**
expensive

costume NOUN **costumes**
clothes, especially for a particular purpose or of a particular period

cosy ADJECTIVE **cosier, cosiest**
warm and comfortable • *a pair of cosy pyjamas*

cot NOUN **cots**
a baby's bed with high sides

cottage NOUN **cottages**
a small house, especially in the country

cotton NOUN
❶ a soft white substance covering the seeds of a tropical plant ❷ thread made from this substance ❸ cloth made from cotton thread

couch NOUN **couches**
a long soft seat or sofa

couch potato NOUN **couch potatoes**
(*informal*)
a person who spends a lot of time watching television

cough (*say* kof) VERB **coughs, coughing, coughed**
to cough is to push air suddenly out of your lungs with a harsh noise

cough NOUN **coughs**
❶ the action or sound of coughing ❷ an illness which makes you cough a lot

could VERB (*past tense of* **can**)
• *I could feel my heart pounding.*

couldn't
short for *could not* • *I couldn't open the door.*

council NOUN **councils**
a group of people chosen to organize or discuss something, especially to plan the affairs of a town

councillor NOUN **councillors**
a member of a council

counsel NOUN **counsels**
❶ advice ❷ the barrister or barristers involved in a case in a law court

counsel VERB **counsels, counselling, counselled**
to counsel someone is to give them advice

counsellor NOUN **counsellors**
someone who gives advice, especially as their job

count VERB **counts, counting, counted**
❶ to count is to use numbers to find out how many people or things there are in a place ❷ to count or count out is to say numbers in their proper order ❸ to count someone or something is to include them in a total • *There are 30 in the class, counting the teacher.* ❹ to count is to have a particular value or importance • *Playing well counts a lot even if you lose.*
➤ **to count on someone** or **something** is to rely on them

count NOUN **counts**
❶ the total reached by counting ❷ one of the things that someone is accused of • *They were found guilty on all counts.* ❸ a count is also a foreign nobleman • *the Count of Monte Cristo*

countable ADJECTIVE
able to be counted

countdown NOUN **countdowns**
a counting down to 0, especially before launching a rocket

countenance NOUN **countenances**
someone's face or the expression on their face

counter NOUN **counters**
❶ a long table where customers are served in a shop or cafe ❷ a small plastic disc used in board games

counterfeit (*say* kown-ter-fit) ADJECTIVE
faked to deceive or swindle people • *They were using counterfeit money.*

countess *NOUN* **countesses**
the wife or widow of a count or earl;
a female earl

countless *ADJECTIVE*
too many to count; very many

country *NOUN* **countries**
❶ a country is a part of the world where a
particular nation of people lives ❷ the country
is the countryside

countryman, **countrywoman** *NOUN*
countrymen, **countrywomen**
❶ a person who lives in the countryside
❷ a fellow countryman is someone who lives
in the same country

countryside *NOUN*
an area with fields, woods and villages away
from towns

county *NOUN* **counties**
one of the areas that a country is divided into,
for example Kent in England, Fife in Scotland
and Powys in Wales

couple *NOUN* **couples**
a couple is two people or things

couple *VERB* **couples**, **coupling**, **coupled**
to couple things is to join them together

coupon *NOUN* **coupons**
a piece of paper that gives you the right to
receive or do something

courage *NOUN*
being courageous

courageous *ADJECTIVE*
ready to face danger or pain

courgette *NOUN* **courgettes**
a kind of vegetable like a small marrow

courier (*say* koor-i-er) *NOUN* **couriers**
❶ someone who carries a message ❷ someone
employed to guide and help people on holiday,
especially abroad

course *NOUN* **courses**
❶ the direction in which something moves
along • *The ship's course was to the west.*
❷ a series of lessons or exercises in learning
something • *My friend's starting a cookery
course.* ❸ a part of a meal, such as the meat
course or the pudding course ❹ a racecourse or
golf course

➤ **in due course** eventually; at the right time
➤ **in the course of something** while it is
happening
➤ **of course** naturally; certainly • *Of course
they will help us.* • *'Will you help us?' 'Of course!'*

court *NOUN* **courts**
❶ a law court ❷ an enclosed place for
games like tennis or netball ❸ a courtyard
❹ the place where a king or queen lives
❺ the people who are usually at a king's or
queen's court

court *VERB* **courts**, **courting**, **courted**
(*old use*) to court someone is to try to win their
love or support

courteous (*say* ker-ti-us) *ADJECTIVE*
friendly and polite towards other people
➤ **courteously** *ADVERB* ➤ **courtesy** *NOUN*

court martial *NOUN* **courts martial**
❶ a court for trying offenders against
military law ❷ a trial in this court

courtship *NOUN*
(*old use*) courting someone, especially a
boyfriend or girlfriend

courtyard *NOUN* **courtyards**
a paved area surrounded by walls or
buildings

couscous (*say* koos-koos) *NOUN*
a North African grain cooked by steaming or
soaking in water

cousin *NOUN* **cousins**
your cousin is a child of your uncle or aunt

cove *NOUN* **coves**
a small bay

cover *VERB* **covers**, **covering**, **covered**
❶ to cover something is to put something
else over it to hide or protect it ❷ to cover
a distance is to travel over it • *We managed
to cover ten miles a day.* ❸ to cover a subject
is to deal with it or include it • *This book
covers everything you need to know about
football.* ❹ to cover something is to be enough
money for it • *I expect £2 will cover my fare.*
❺ to cover someone is to aim a gun at or near
them • *I've got you covered.*
➤ **to cover something up** is to make sure
no one knows about something wrong
or illegal

a
b
c
d
e
f
g
h
i
j
k
l
m
n
o
p
q
r
s
t
u
v
w
x
y
z

A
B
C
D
E
F
G
H
I
J
K
L
M
N
O
P
Q
R
S
T
U
V
W
X
Y
Z

cover *NOUN* covers
❶ a cover is something used for covering something else; a lid or wrapper ❷ cover is a place where someone can hide or take shelter

coverage *NOUN*
the amount of time or space given to reporting an event on radio, on television or in a newspaper

cover-up *NOUN* cover-ups
a cover-up is when people in power prevent other people knowing about something wrong or illegal • *The government were accused of a cover-up of their mistakes.*

Covid-19 *NOUN*
an infectious disease that causes fever, tiredness and a cough, and in some people can cause serious breathing difficulties and death

cow *NOUN* cows
a large female animal kept by farmers for its milk and beef
➤ A related adjective is **bovine**.

coward *NOUN* cowards
someone who has no courage and runs away from danger and difficulties
➤ **cowardice** *NOUN* ➤ **cowardly** *ADJECTIVE*

cowboy *NOUN* cowboys
❶ a person who looks after the cattle on a large farm in North America, usually while riding a horse ❷ (*informal*) a person who uses dishonest methods in business

cower *VERB* cowers, cowering, cowered
to cower is to crouch because you are afraid
Anne cowered deeper into her pillows as if desirous of hiding herself for ever from mortal eyes.—ANNE OF GREEN GABLES, L. M. Montgomery

cowslip *NOUN* cowslips
a wild plant that has yellow flowers in spring

cox *NOUN* coxes
someone who steers a racing boat

coy *ADJECTIVE*
shy; pretending to be shy or modest
➤ **coyly** *ADVERB*

crab *NOUN* crabs
a shellfish with ten legs

crab apple *NOUN* crab apples
a small sour apple

crack *NOUN* cracks
❶ a line on the surface of something where it has broken but not come completely apart; a narrow gap • *There's a crack in this cup.* ❷ a sudden sharp noise • *They heard the crack of a pistol shot.* ❸ a sudden sharp blow • *He got a crack on the head.*

crack *VERB* cracks, cracking, cracked
❶ to crack something is to make a crack in it ❷ something cracks when it splits without breaking • *The plate has cracked.* ❸ to crack is to make a sudden sharp noise ❹ to crack a joke is to tell it

cracker *NOUN* crackers
❶ a pretty paper tube with a small gift inside it, which bangs when two people pull it apart ❷ a thin biscuit

crackle *VERB* crackles, crackling, crackled
to make small cracking sounds, like a fire

crackling *NOUN*
the hard skin of roast pork

crackpot *ADJECTIVE* (*informal*)
mad or eccentric • *Is this another of your crackpot ideas?*

cradle *NOUN* cradles
❶ a cot for a baby ❷ a supporting frame for something

craft *NOUN* crafts
❶ a craft is an activity which needs skill with the hands ❷ a boat ❸ craft is cunning or trickery

craftsman, craftswoman *NOUN* craftsmen, craftswomen
someone who is skilled at making things with their hands
➤ **craftsmanship** *NOUN* the skill of a craftsman or craftswoman

crafty *ADJECTIVE* craftier, craftiest
cunning and clever
➤ **craftily** *ADVERB* ➤ **craftiness** *NOUN*

crag *NOUN* crags
a steep piece of rough rock
➤ **craggy** *ADJECTIVE*

cram VERB **crams**, **cramming**, **crammed**
❶ to cram things is to force them into a small space ❷ to cram is to study very hard for an examination

cramp NOUN **cramps**
pain caused by a muscle tightening suddenly

cramp VERB **cramps**, **cramping**, **cramped**
to cramp someone is to restrict their freedom or growth

cramped ADJECTIVE
in a space that is too small or tight • *We felt cramped sleeping three in the same room.*

cranberry NOUN **cranberries**
a sour red berry originally from North America, used to make juice and sauces

crane NOUN **cranes**
❶ a large machine for lifting and moving heavy objects ❷ a large bird with long legs and neck

crane VERB **cranes**, **craning**, **craned**
to crane your neck is to stretch it so that you can see something

cranefly NOUN **craneflies**
an insect with long thin legs

crank NOUN **cranks**
❶ an L-shaped rod used to turn or control something ❷ a person with weird or unusual ideas

cranky ADJECTIVE **crankier**, **crankiest**
weird or unusual

cranny NOUN **crannies**
a crevice; a narrow hole or space

crash NOUN **crashes**
❶ the loud noise of something falling or breaking ❷ a collision between road vehicles, causing damage

crash VERB **crashes**, **crashing**, **crashed**
❶ to crash is to collide or fall violently
❷ to crash a vehicle is to have a crash while driving it ❸ to crash along or through something is to move violently and loudly

crash helmet NOUN **crash helmets**
a padded helmet worn by cyclists and motorcyclists

crate NOUN **crates**
a container in which goods are transported

crater NOUN **craters**
❶ the mouth of a volcano ❷ a hole in the ground made by a bomb

crave VERB **craves**, **craving**, **craved**
to crave something is to want it very badly

crawl VERB **crawls**, **crawling**, **crawled**
❶ to crawl is to move along on your hands and knees ❷ to crawl is also to move slowly in a vehicle ❸ to be crawling with something unpleasant is to be full of it or covered in it
• *This room's crawling with cockroaches.*

crawl NOUN
❶ a crawling movement ❷ a powerful swimming stroke with the arms hitting the water alternately

crayon NOUN **crayons**
a coloured pencil for drawing or writing

craze NOUN **crazes**
a brief enthusiasm for something

crazy ADJECTIVE **crazier**, **craziest**
❶ strange or foolish ❷ (*informal*) mentally ill
➤ **crazily** ADVERB ➤ **craziness** NOUN

creak NOUN **creaks**
a sound like the noise made by a stiff door opening

creak VERB **creaks**, **creaking**, **creaked**
to make a creak
The door creaked open slowly, and the Baudelaire orphans held their breath as they peered into the dark entryway.—THE REPTILE ROOM, Lemony Snicket

creaky ADJECTIVE **creakier**, **creakiest**
old and creaking • *the sound of creaky floorboards*

cream NOUN **creams**
❶ the rich fatty part of milk ❷ a yellow-white colour ❸ a food containing or looking like cream ❹ something that looks like cream, for example face cream
➤ **creamy** ADJECTIVE

crease NOUN **creases**
a line made in something by folding or pressing it

crease VERB **creases**, **creasing**, **creased**
to crease something is to make a crease in it

create VERB **creates**, **creating**, **created**
to create something is to make it exist
➤ **creation** NOUN

a
b
c
d
e
f
g
h
i
j
k
l
m
n
o
p
q
r
s
t
u
v
w
x
y
z

creative *ADJECTIVE*
showing imagination and thought as well
as skill • *The older children have started some
creative writing.*
➤ **creativity** *NOUN*

creator *NOUN* **creators**
someone who creates something • *Tove Jansson
was the creator of the Moomins.*

creature *NOUN* **creatures**
a living animal or person

crèche (*say* kresh) *NOUN* **crèches**
a place where babies or small children are
looked after while their parents are busy

credible *ADJECTIVE*
able to be believed; trustworthy • *Their story
was not very credible.*
➤ **credibility** *NOUN* ➤ **credibly** *ADVERB*

credit *NOUN*
❶ honour or approval • *Give her credit for
her honesty.* ❷ a system of allowing someone
to pay for something later on • *Do you want
cash now or can I have it on credit?* ❸ an
amount of money in an account
➤ **credits** the list of people who have helped to
produce a film, television programme, etc.

credit *VERB* **credits, crediting, credited**
❶ to credit something is to believe it • *Can
you credit that?* ❷ to credit someone with
something is to enter it as a credit in their
bank account • *We will credit you with a
£50 refund.*

creditable *ADJECTIVE*
deserving praise
➤ **creditably** *ADVERB*

credit card *NOUN* **credit cards**
a card allowing someone to buy goods
on credit

creed *NOUN* **creeds**
a set or statement of beliefs

creek *NOUN* **creeks**
❶ a narrow inlet ❷ (*Australian, North American*)
a small stream

creep *VERB* **creeps, creeping, crept**
❶ to creep is to move along with the body
close to the ground ❷ to creep about is to
move quietly or secretly

➤ **to creep up on someone** is to go up to
them quietly from behind

creep *NOUN* **creeps**
❶ a creeping movement ❷ (*informal*)
a nasty or unpleasant person
➤ **the creeps** (*informal*) a feeling of fear
or disgust

creeper *NOUN* **creepers**
a plant that grows close to the ground or
up walls

creepy *ADJECTIVE* **creepier, creepiest**
(*informal*)
weird and slightly frightening

creepy–crawly *NOUN* **creepy-crawlies**
(*informal*)
an insect or minibeast

cremate *VERB* **cremates, cremating,
cremated**
to cremate a dead body is to burn it into fine
ashes instead of burying it
➤ **cremation** *NOUN*

crematorium *NOUN* **crematoria**
a place where dead bodies are cremated

crêpe (*say* krayp) *NOUN* **crêpes**
❶ cloth or paper with a wrinkled surface
❷ a kind of thin French pancake

crept *VERB* (*past tense and past participle of
creep*)
• *He got up and crept down the stairs.*
• *An angry look had crept into his face.*

crescendo (*say* kri-**shen**-doh) *NOUN*
crescendos
music that gets gradually louder

crescent *NOUN* **crescents**
❶ a narrow curved shape, pointed at both ends,
like a new moon ❷ a curved street

cress *NOUN*
a green plant used in salads and sandwiches

crest *NOUN* **crests**
❶ a tuft of hair, feathers or skin on an animal's
head ❷ the top of a hill or wave

crevice *NOUN* **crevices**
a crack in rock or in a wall

crew *NOUN* **crews**
❶ the people who work on a ship or aircraft

❷ a team of people who work together
• *an ambulance crew*

crib NOUN **cribs**
❶ a baby's cot ❷ a framework containing fodder for animals

crib VERB **cribs, cribbing, cribbed**
to crib someone else's work is to copy it

cricket NOUN **crickets**
❶ cricket is a game played outdoors by two teams with a ball, two bats and two wickets ❷ a cricket is a brown insect like a grasshopper
➤ **cricketer** NOUN someone who plays cricket

cried VERB (*past tense and past participle of* **cry**)
• *'Look out!' cried Tom.* • *After he had cried a long time, he wiped his eyes.*

crime NOUN **crimes**
an act that breaks the law

criminal NOUN **criminals**
someone who has committed one or more crimes

criminal ADJECTIVE
to do with crime or criminals

crimson NOUN, ADJECTIVE
a dark red colour

cringe VERB **cringes, cringing, cringed**
to cringe is to shrink or cower because you are afraid or embarrassed • *It makes me cringe to remember how silly I was.*

crinkle VERB **crinkles, crinkling, crinkled**
to crinkle something is to crease or wrinkle it
➤ **crinkly** ADJECTIVE

cripple VERB **cripples, crippling, crippled**
to cripple something is to damage it so it will not work properly

crisis (*say* **kry**-sis) NOUN **crises**
an important or difficult time or situation

crisp ADJECTIVE **crisper, crispest**
❶ very dry so that it breaks easily ❷ firm and fresh • *I'd like a nice crisp apple.* ❸ cold and frosty • *We woke up to a crisp winter morning.*

crisp NOUN **crisps**
a thin fried slice of potato, sold in packets

crispy ADJECTIVE **crispier, crispiest**
crispy food is pleasantly crisp
➤ **crispiness** NOUN

criss-cross ADJECTIVE, ADVERB
with crossing lines

critic NOUN **critics**
❶ a person who criticizes someone or something ❷ someone who gives opinions on books, plays, films, music or other performances

critical ADJECTIVE
❶ criticizing ❷ to do with critics or criticism ❸ serious, amounting to a crisis
➤ **critically** ADVERB ❶ in a critical way ❷ seriously

criticism (*say* **krit**-i-si-zum) NOUN **criticisms**
an opinion or judgement about something or someone, usually pointing out its or their faults

criticize (*also* **criticise**) VERB **criticizes, criticizing, criticized**
to criticize something or someone is to give an opinion pointing out their faults

croak NOUN **croaks**
a deep sound, like a frog makes

croak VERB **croaks, croaking, croaked**
to make a croak

crochet (*say* **kroh**-shay) NOUN
a kind of needlework done with a hooked needle

crock NOUN **crocks**
a large pot made out of clay

crockery NOUN
dishes, plates and cups and saucers used for eating

crocodile NOUN **crocodiles**
a large reptile that lives near rivers in tropical countries, with a thick skin, long tail and huge jaws
DID YOU KNOW? The word **crocodile** comes from a Greek word meaning 'worm of the stones'.

a
b
c
d
e
f
g
h
i
j
k
l
m
n
o
p
q
r
s
t
u
v
w
x
y
z

crocodile tears *PLURAL NOUN*
sorrow that is not genuine

crocus *NOUN* **crocuses**
a small spring flower that is yellow, purple
or white

croft *NOUN* **crofts**
a small farm in Scotland
➤ **crofter** *NOUN*

croissant (*say* **krwa**-sahn) *NOUN*
croissants
a crescent-shaped roll of rich pastry, first
made in France and usually eaten for
breakfast

crook *NOUN* **crooks**
❶ (*informal*) someone who cheats or robs
people; a criminal ❷ a shepherd's or bishop's
stick with a curved end

crooked (*say* **krook**-id) *ADJECTIVE*
❶ bent or twisted ❷ (*informal*) dishonest or
criminal

croon *VERB* **croons**, **crooning**, **crooned**
to croon is to sing softly or sentimentally

crop *NOUN* **crops**
❶ something grown for food, especially in
a field • *They had a good crop of wheat last
year.* ❷ a riding whip with a loop instead of
a lash

crop *VERB* **crops**, **cropping**, **cropped**
to crop something is to cut or bite the top
off it • *They could see sheep in a field, cropping
the grass.*
➤ **to crop up** is to happen or appear
unexpectedly

cross *NOUN* **crosses**
❶ a mark or shape like + or x ❷ an upright
post with another post across it ❸ an animal
produced by mixing one breed with another
• *A mule is a cross between a donkey and
a horse.*

cross *VERB* **crosses**, **crossing**, **crossed**
❶ to cross something is to go across it
• *She crossed the room to meet him.*
❷ to cross your fingers or legs is to put
one over the other
➤ **to cross something out** is to draw a line
across something because it is unwanted or
wrong

cross *ADJECTIVE*
❶ angry or bad-tempered ❷ going from one
side to another • *There were cross winds on
the bridge.*
➤ **crossly** *ADVERB* ➤ **crossness** *NOUN*

crossbar *NOUN* **crossbars**
a horizontal bar between two upright bars

crossbow *NOUN* **crossbows**
a kind of bow used for shooting arrows, held
like a gun and fired by pulling a trigger

cross-country *NOUN*
a running race through fields and country

cross-examine *VERB* **cross-examines**,
cross-examining, **cross-examined**
to cross-examine someone is to question them
about information they have given, usually in a
law court
➤ **cross-examination** *NOUN*

cross-eyed *ADJECTIVE*
having eyes that appear to look in different
directions

crossing *NOUN* **crossings**
a place where people can cross a road
or railway

cross-legged *ADVERB*, *ADJECTIVE*
having crossed legs

crossroads *NOUN* **crossroads**
a place where two or more roads cross one
another

cross-section *NOUN* **cross-sections**
❶ a drawing of something as if it has been cut
through ❷ a sample that includes all the
different types of something • *A cross-section
of parents said they wanted an
after-school club.*

crosswise *ADVERB*, *ADJECTIVE*
with one thing crossing another

crossword *NOUN* **crosswords**
a puzzle with blank squares in which you put
the letters of words worked out from clues

crotchet (*say* **kroch**-it) *NOUN* **crotchets**
a musical note equal to half a minim,
written (♩)

crouch VERB **crouches, crouching, crouched**
to crouch is to lower your body, with your arms and legs bent

crow NOUN **crows**
a large black bird
➤ **as the crow flies** in a straight line
crow VERB **crows, crowing, crowed**
❶ to make a noise like a cock ❷ to boast; to be proudly triumphant

crowbar NOUN **crowbars**
an iron bar used as a lever

crowd NOUN **crowds**
a large number of people in one place
crowd VERB **crowds, crowding, crowded**
❶ to crowd or crowd round is to form a crowd ❷ to crowd a place is to make it uncomfortably full of people • *The town is crowded with tourists in summer.*

crown NOUN **crowns**
❶ a crown is an ornamental headdress worn by a king or queen ❷ the crown is the king or queen of a country • *This land belongs to the crown.* ❸ the top of the head ❹ the middle part of a road, which is higher than the sides
crown VERB **crowns, crowning, crowned**
❶ to crown someone is to make them king or queen ❷ to crown something is to form the top of it ❸ to crown an achievement is to finish it happily • *Their efforts were crowned with success.*

crow's nest NOUN **crow's nests**
a lookout position at the top of a ship's mast

crucial (*say* **kroo-**shal) ADJECTIVE
extremely important

crucifix NOUN **crucifixes**
in Christianity, a crucifix is a model of the cross or of Christ on the cross

crucify VERB **crucifies, crucifying, crucified**
to crucify someone is to execute them by fixing their hands and feet to a cross and leaving them to die. The ancient Romans used this method of executing criminals.
➤ **crucifixion** NOUN

crude ADJECTIVE **cruder, crudest**
❶ natural; not purified • *The country exported crude oil.* ❷ rough and simple • *They stayed in a crude hut in the mountains.* ❸ rude or dirty • *They were telling each other crude jokes.*

cruel ADJECTIVE **crueller, cruellest**
causing pain and suffering to others • *They were ruled by a cruel tyrant.* • *War is cruel.*
➤ **cruelly** ADVERB ➤ **cruelty** NOUN

cruise NOUN **cruises**
a holiday on a ship, usually visiting different places
cruise VERB **cruises, cruising, cruised**
❶ to cruise is to sail or travel at a gentle speed ❷ to cruise is also to have a cruise on a ship

cruiser NOUN **cruisers**
❶ a fast warship ❷ a large motor boat

crumb NOUN **crumbs**
a tiny piece of bread or cake

crumble VERB **crumbles, crumbling, crumbled**
❶ to crumble something is to break it into small pieces ❷ to crumble is to be broken into small pieces
➤ **crumbly** ADJECTIVE

crumpet NOUN **crumpets**
a soft flat cake made with yeast, toasted and eaten with butter

crumple VERB **crumples, crumpling, crumpled**
❶ to crumple something is to make it creased ❷ to crumple is to become creased

crunch NOUN **crunches**
the noise made by chewing hard food or walking on gravel or snow
Crunch, crunch. Crunch, crunch. The sound of heavy footsteps, trudging through knee-deep snow, echoes through the night's silence.—THE LEGEND OF PODKIN ONE-EAR, Kieran Larwood
crunch VERB **crunches, crunching, crunched**
to crunch something is to chew or crush it with a crunch

crunchy ADJECTIVE **crunchier, crunchiest**
something crunchy makes a crunching sound

a
b
c
d
e
f
g
h
i
j
k
l
m
n
o
p
q
r
s
t
u
v
w
x
y
z

when you chew it or crush it • *a bowl of crunchy cornflakes*
➤ **crunchiness** NOUN

crusade NOUN **crusades**
❶ a military expedition to Palestine made by Christians in the Middle Ages ❷ a campaign against something that you think is bad
➤ **crusader** NOUN

crush VERB **crushes, crushing, crushed**
❶ to crush something is to press it so that it gets broken or damaged ❷ to crush an enemy is to defeat them

crush NOUN **crushes**
❶ a crowd; a crowded place ❷ a fruit-flavoured drink ❸ (*informal*) a sudden liking you have for someone

crust NOUN **crusts**
❶ the hard outside part of something, especially of a loaf ❷ the rocky outer part of a planet

crustacean (*say* krus-**tay**-shan) NOUN **crustaceans**
a shellfish

crutch NOUN **crutches**
a stick that fits under the arm, used as a support in walking

cry VERB **cries, crying, cried**
❶ to cry is to shout ❷ to cry is also to let tears fall from your eyes

cry NOUN **cries**
❶ a loud shout ❷ a period of weeping

crypt NOUN **crypts**
a large room underneath a church

cryptic (*say* **krip**-tik) ADJECTIVE
puzzling and hard to solve or decipher • *a series of cryptic clues*

cryptography NOUN
cryptography is the study of how to make and break codes
➤ **cryptographer** NOUN

crystal NOUN **crystals**
❶ a clear mineral rather like glass ❷ a small solid piece of a substance with a symmetrical shape, such as snow and ice
➤ **crystalline** ADJECTIVE

crystallize (*also* **crystallise**) VERB
crystallizes, crystallizing, crystallized
to form into crystals

cub NOUN **cubs**
❶ a young animal, especially a lion, tiger, fox or bear ❷ a junior Scout

cubbyhole NOUN **cubbyholes**
a small compartment or snug place

cube NOUN **cubes**
❶ an object that has six square sides, like a box or dice ❷ the result of multiplying something by itself twice • *The cube of 3 is 3 x 3 x 3 = 27.*

cube VERB **cubes, cubing, cubed**
❶ to cube a number is to multiply it by itself twice • *4 cubed is 4 x 4 x 4 = 64.* ❷ to cube something is to cut it into small cubes

cube root NOUN **cube roots**
a number that gives another number if it is multiplied by itself twice • *2 is the cube root of 8.*

cubic, cubical ADJECTIVE
❶ shaped like a cube ❷ a cubic metre or foot is the volume of a cube with sides that are one metre or foot long

cubicle NOUN **cubicles**
a small division of a room

cuboid NOUN **cuboids**
an object with six rectangular sides

cuckoo NOUN **cuckoos**
a bird that makes a sound like 'cuck-oo', and lays its eggs in other birds' nests

cucumber NOUN **cucumbers**
a long green vegetable, eaten raw

cud NOUN
half-digested food that a cow brings back from its first stomach to chew again

cuddle VERB **cuddles, cuddling, cuddled**
to cuddle someone is to put your arms closely round them and squeeze them in a loving way
➤ **cuddly** ADJECTIVE a cuddly person or thing is nice to cuddle

cue *NOUN* **cues**
❶ something that tells an actor when to start speaking or come on the stage ❷ a cue is also a long stick used to strike the ball in billiards or snooker

cuff *NOUN* **cuffs**
❶ the end of a sleeve that fits round your wrist ❷ a blow given to someone with your hand

cuff *VERB* **cuffs, cuffing, cuffed**
to cuff someone is to hit them with the hand

cul-de-sac (*say* **kul**-de-sak) *NOUN* **cul-de-sacs**
a street that is closed at one end
DID YOU KNOW? The word **cul-de-sac** is French, and literally means 'bottom of a sack'.

culminate *VERB* **culminates, culminating, culminated**
to reach the end or the most important part • *Their long struggle for freedom culminated in victory.*
➤ **culmination** *NOUN*

culprit *NOUN* **culprits**
someone who is to blame for something

cult *NOUN* **cults**
❶ a religion ❷ being extremely keen on someone or something • *The TV series is a bit of a cult now.*

cultivate *VERB* **cultivates, cultivating, cultivated**
❶ to cultivate land is to grow crops on it ❷ to cultivate something is to try to make it grow or develop
➤ **cultivation** *NOUN*

cultivated *ADJECTIVE*
having good manners and education

cultural *ADJECTIVE*
a cultural activity is one to do with education and learning

culture *NOUN* **cultures**
❶ culture is the development of the mind by education and learning ❷ a culture is the customs and traditions of a people • *They were studying Greek culture.*

cunning *ADJECTIVE*
clever at deceiving people

Said the cunning Spider to the Fly, 'Dear Friend, what can I do, To prove the warm affection I've always felt for you?'—THE SPIDER AND THE FLY, Mary Howitt

cup *NOUN* **cups**
❶ a small container with a handle, from which you drink liquid ❷ a prize in the form of a silver cup, usually with two handles

cup *VERB* **cups, cupping, cupped**
to cup your hands is to form them into the shape of a cup
John lifted up one of the eggs, cupping it carefully in his hands.—AKIMBO AND THE CROCODILE MAN, Alexander McCall Smith

cupboard (*say* **kub**-erd) *NOUN* **cupboards**
a compartment or piece of furniture with a door, for storing things

cupcake *NOUN* **cupcakes**
a small sponge cake, often topped with icing or buttercream

cupful *NOUN* **cupfuls**
as much as a cup will hold • *Add two cupfuls of milk to the mixture.*

curator (*say* kewr-ay-ter) *NOUN* **curators**
someone in charge of a museum or art gallery

curb *VERB* **curbs, curbing, curbed**
to curb a feeling is to hold it back or hide it • *I tried hard to curb my anger.*

curd *NOUN* **curds**
a thick substance formed when milk turns sour

curdle *VERB* **curdles, curdling, curdled**
to curdle is to form into curds

cure *VERB* **cures, curing, cured**
❶ to cure someone who is ill is to make them better ❷ to cure something bad is to stop it ❸ to cure food is to treat it so as to preserve it • *Fish can be cured in smoke.*

cure *NOUN* **cures**
something that cures a person or thing • *They are still trying to find a cure for cancer.*

curfew *NOUN* **curfews**
a time or signal after which people must stay indoors until the next day

a
b
c
d
e
f
g
h
i
j
k
l
m
n
o
p
q
r
s
t
u
v
w
x
y
z

A B C D E F G H I J K L M N O P Q R S T U V W X Y Z

curiosity *NOUN* **curiosities**
❶ curiosity is being curious ❷ a curiosity is something strange or interesting

curious *ADJECTIVE*
❶ wanting to find out about things
❷ strange or unusual • *a curious kind of handwriting*
➤ **curiously** *ADVERB*

curl *NOUN* **curls**
a curve or coil, especially of hair

curl *VERB* **curls, curling, curled**
to curl is to form into curls
➤ **to curl up** is to sit or lie with your knees drawn up

curling *NOUN*
a sport played on ice, in which large round flat stones are slid towards a target mark
➤ **curler** *NOUN*

curly *ADJECTIVE* **curlier, curliest**
full of curls

currant *NOUN* **currants**
❶ a small black fruit made from dried grapes
❷ a small juicy berry, or the bush that produces it

currency *NOUN* **currencies**
money that is in use in a place • *The euro is the currency in Ireland.*

current *NOUN* **currents**
a flow of water, air or electricity

current *ADJECTIVE*
happening or used now • *the current fashion for trainers*
➤ **currently** *ADVERB* now; at the moment
• *The admission charge is currently £10.*

curriculum *NOUN* **curriculums** *or* **curricula**
a course of study

curry *NOUN* **curries**
curry is a dish of meat or vegetables cooked with hot spices
➤ **curried** *ADJECTIVE*
DID YOU KNOW? The word **curry** comes from a Tamil (Indian language) word *kari* meaning 'hot sauce'.

curse *NOUN* **curses**
❶ a call or prayer for someone to be harmed or killed ❷ something very unpleasant
❸ an angry word or words

curse *VERB* **curses, cursing, cursed**
to curse someone is to use a curse against them

cursor *NOUN* **cursors**
a movable flashing signal on a computer screen, showing where new data will go

curtain *NOUN* **curtains**
a piece of material hung at a window or door, or at the front of a stage

curtsy *NOUN* **curtsies**
a greeting made by bending the knees, as a mark of respect

curtsy *VERB* **curtsies, curtsying, curtsied**
to curtsy is to make a curtsy

curvature *NOUN* **curvatures**
a curving or bending, especially of the earth's horizon

curve *NOUN* **curves**
a line that bends smoothly

curve *VERB* **curves, curving, curved**
to curve is to bend smoothly

cushion *NOUN* **cushions**
a fabric cover filled with soft material so that it is comfortable to sit on or rest against

cushion *VERB* **cushions, cushioning, cushioned**
to cushion someone is to protect them from harm • *If you slip, the rubber mat will cushion your fall.*

custard *NOUN*
a sweet yellow sauce eaten with puddings

custom *NOUN* **customs**
❶ the usual way of doing things • *It is the custom in Japan to bow when you meet someone.* ❷ regular business from customers
• *That shop won't get my custom any more.*
➤ **customs** are the group of officials at a port or airport to whom people coming into a country declare what goods they have with them

customary *ADJECTIVE*
something that is customary is usually done • *It is customary to knock before you enter.*
➤ **customarily** *ADVERB*

customer *NOUN* **customers**
someone who uses a shop, bank or business

customize (*also* **customise**) *NOUN* **customizes, customizing, customized**
to customize something is to alter it for a special use

cut *VERB* **cuts, cutting, cut**
❶ to cut something is to divide it or make a slit in it with a knife or scissors ❷ to cut something like prices or taxes is to reduce them ❸ to cut a pack of playing cards is to divide it ❹ to cut a corner is to go across it rather than round it ❺ to cut a meeting or lesson is to stay away from it ❻ a baby cuts a tooth when it has a new tooth coming
➤ **to cut and paste** is to remove text on a computer screen from one place and put it in another place
➤ **to cut someone off** is to interrupt them • *He cut me off before I could finish my sentence.*
➤ **to cut something out** (*informal*) is to stop doing it • *Cut out the talking!*

cut *NOUN* **cuts**
❶ an act of cutting; the result of cutting • *My hair could do with a cut.* ❷ a small wound caused by something sharp ❸ (*informal*) a share • *They each got a cut of the prize money.*

cute *ADJECTIVE* **cuter, cutest** (*informal*)
attractive in a quaint or simple way

cutlass *NOUN* **cutlasses**
a short sword with a wide curved blade
The captain had risen earlier than usual, and set out down the beach, his cutlass swinging under the broad skirts of the old blue coat.–TREASURE ISLAND, Robert Louis Stevenson

cutlery *NOUN*
knives, forks and spoons used for eating

cutlet *NOUN* **cutlets**
a thick slice of meat still on the bone

cut-out *NOUN* **cut-outs**
something cut out of paper or cardboard

cut-price *ADJECTIVE*
sold at a reduced price

cutting *NOUN* **cuttings**
❶ something cut from a newspaper or magazine ❷ a piece cut off a plant to grow as a new plant ❸ a deep passage cut through high ground for a railway or road

cyberman *NOUN* **cybermen**
in science fiction, a cyberman is a creature that is part-human and part-robot

cycle *NOUN* **cycles**
❶ a bicycle ❷ a series of events that are regularly repeated • *Rainfall is part of the water cycle.*

cycle *VERB* **cycles, cycling, cycled**
to cycle is to ride a bicycle
➤ **cyclist** *NOUN*

cyclone *NOUN* **cyclones**
a strong wind rotating round a calm central area

cyclops (*say* sy-klops) *NOUN* **cyclops**
in Greek mythology, a cyclops is a terrifying monster with one eye

cygnet (*say* sig-nit) *NOUN* **cygnets**
a young swan

cylinder *NOUN* **cylinders**
❶ an object with straight sides and circular ends ❷ part of an engine in which a piston moves

cylindrical *ADJECTIVE*
shaped like a cylinder

cymbal *NOUN* **cymbals**
a cymbal is a round, slightly hollowed metal plate that you hit to make a ringing sound in music

cynic (*say* sin-ik) *NOUN* **cynics**
someone who doubts that anything is good or worthwhile
➤ **cynical** *ADJECTIVE*

cypress *NOUN* **cypresses**
an evergreen tree with dark leaves

a b **c** d e f g h i j k l m n o p q r s t u v w x y z

Dd

dab NOUN **dabs**
a gentle touch with something soft

dab VERB **dabs**, **dabbing**, **dabbed**
to dab something is to touch it gently with
something soft • *I dabbed my eyes with a
handkerchief.*

dabble VERB **dabbles**, **dabbling**, **dabbled**
❶ to dabble something is to splash it about
in water ❷ to dabble in something is to do it
as a hobby or not very seriously • *She likes to
dabble in photography.*

dachshund (*say* **daks**-hund) NOUN
dachshunds
a small dog with a long body and short legs

dad NOUN **dads** (*informal*)
father

daddy NOUN **daddies** (*informal*)
father

daddy-long-legs NOUN **daddy-long-legs**
a crane-fly

daffodil NOUN **daffodils**
a yellow flower that grows from a bulb

daft ADJECTIVE **dafter**, **daftest**
silly or stupid

dagger NOUN **daggers**
a short pointed knife, used as a weapon

dahlia (*say* **day**-li-a) NOUN **dahlias**
a garden plant with brightly coloured flowers

daily ADJECTIVE, ADVERB
something that happens daily happens
every day

dainty ADJECTIVE **daintier**, **daintiest**
small and delicate
➤ **daintily** ADVERB ➤ **daintiness** NOUN

dairy NOUN **dairies**
a place where milk, butter, cream and cheese
are made or sold

dairy ADJECTIVE
dairy foods are made from milk

daisy NOUN **daisies**
a small flower with white petals and a
yellow centre
DID YOU KNOW? The word **daisy** comes from
Old English words meaning 'day's eye', because
the petals open in the morning and close
at night.

daisy chain NOUN **daisy chains**
a string of daisies linked together by
their stems

dale NOUN **dales**
a valley

Dalmatian NOUN **Dalmatians**
a large dog that is white with black or
brown spots

dam NOUN **dams**
a wall built across a river to hold the
water back

dam VERB **dams**, **damming**, **dammed**
to dam a river is to build a dam across it

damage VERB **damages**, **damaging**,
damaged
to damage something is to injure or harm it

damage NOUN
damage is injury or harm • *The storm caused
a lot of damage.*

damages PLURAL NOUN
damages are money paid to someone to make
up for an injury or loss

Dame NOUN **Dames**
a woman who has been given an honorary title
that allows her to put 'Dame' before her name

damn VERB **damns**, **damning**, **damned**
to damn something is to say it is bad
or wrong

damp ADJECTIVE **damper**, **dampest**
slightly wet; not quite dry

damp NOUN
damp or the damp is wetness in the air or on
something
➤ **dampness** NOUN

dampen VERB **dampens**, **dampening**,
dampened
❶ to dampen something is to make it damp
❷ to dampen sound or noise is to make it
softer

damson *NOUN* **damsons**
a small purple plum

dance *VERB* **dances**, **dancing**, **danced**
to dance is to move about in time to music

dance *NOUN* **dances**
❶ a piece of music or set of movements for dancing ❷ a party or gathering where people dance

dancer *NOUN* **dancers**
someone who dances

dandelion *NOUN* **dandelions**
a wild plant like a daisy with bright yellow flowers and jagged leaves
DID YOU KNOW? The word **dandelion** comes from French words meaning 'lion's tooth', because of its jagged leaves.

dandelion clock *NOUN* **dandelion clocks**
the round fluffy seed head of a dandelion

dandruff *NOUN*
dandruff is small white flakes of dead skin in a person's hair

danger *NOUN* **dangers**
❶ a dangerous situation • *Don't worry. You won't be in any danger.* ❷ something that is dangerous • *There may be terrible dangers ahead.*

dangerous *ADJECTIVE*
something dangerous is likely to harm you
• *It is dangerous to look directly at the sun.*
➤ **dangerously** *ADVERB*

dangle *VERB* **dangles**, **dangling**, **dangled**
to swing or hang down loosely

dank *ADJECTIVE* **danker**, **dankest**
a dank place is damp and cold
What a place to sleep! Fog Row was the dirtiest, dankest, miserablest spot in the whole of the East End.—SPRING-HEELED JACK, Philip Pullman

dappled *ADJECTIVE*
marked with patches of different colours
She was a strong, well-made animal, of a bright dun colour, beautifully dappled, and with a dark-brown mane and tail.—BLACK BEAUTY, Anna Sewell

dare *VERB* **dares**, **daring**, **dared**
❶ to dare to do something is to be brave or bold enough to do it

Only that very morning, Xar's father ... King of Wizards, had reminded everyone that it was forbidden for any Wizard to dare set one toe in the Badwoods.—THE WIZARDS OF ONCE, Cressida Cowell
❷ to dare someone to do something is to challenge them to do it • *I dare you to ring the doorbell.*

dare *NOUN* **dares** (*informal*)
a challenge to do something risky

daredevil *NOUN* **daredevils**
a person who enjoys doing dangerous things

daren't
short for *dare not* • *I daren't ask her to leave.*

daring *ADJECTIVE*
bold or brave

dark *ADJECTIVE* **darker**, **darkest**
❶ with little or no light ❷ deep and rich in colour • *She wore a dark green coat.*

dark *NOUN*
❶ dark or the dark is when there is no light • *Cats can see in the dark.* ❷ dark is also the time when it becomes dark just after sunset • *Be home before dark.*
➤ **darkness** *NOUN*

darken *VERB* **darkens**, **darkening**, **darkened**
❶ to darken something is to make it dark ❷ to darken is to become dark • *The sky suddenly darkened.*

darkroom *NOUN* **darkrooms**
a room kept dark for developing and printing photographs

darling *NOUN* **darlings**
someone who is loved very much

darn *VERB* **darns**, **darning**, **darned**
to darn a hole is to mend it by sewing across it

dart *NOUN* **darts**
an object with a sharp point that you throw at a dartboard in the game of **darts**

dart *VERB* **darts**, **darting**, **darted**
to dart is to run very quickly and lightly
Daniel Holmes darted through the Saturday shopping crowds in Glasgow, pushing and twisting and weaving.—THE NOWHERE EMPORIUM, Ross MacKenzie

a
b
c
d
e
f
g
h
i
j
k
l
m
n
o
p
q
r
s
t
u
v
w
x
y
z

dartboard *NOUN* **dartboards**
a round target at which you throw darts

dash *NOUN* **dashes**
❶ a quick rush or a hurry • *They made a dash for the door.* ❷ a dash of something is a small amount of it • *Add a dash of lemon juice.*
❸ a short line (–) used in writing or printing

dash *VERB* **dashes**, **dashing**, **dashed**
❶ to dash somewhere is to rush there
❷ to dash something is to hurl it and smash it • *In her anger she dashed the cup against the wall.*

dashboard *NOUN* **dashboards**
a panel with dials and controls in front of the driver of a car

data (*say* **day**-ta) *NOUN*
data is pieces of information

database *NOUN* **databases**
a store of information held in a computer

date *NOUN* **dates**
❶ the day of the month, or the year, when something happens or happened
❷ an appointment to go out with someone
❸ a date is also a sweet brown fruit that grows on a palm tree

date *VERB* **dates**, **dating**, **dated**
❶ to date something is to work out how old it is • *Trees can be dated by the number of rings in their wood.* ❷ to date something such as a letter is to put the date on it • *a letter dated 1950* ❸ to date from a time is to have existed from then • *The church dates from the 15th century.* ❹ to date is also to seem old-fashioned • *Some fashions date very quickly.*

daughter *NOUN* **daughters**
a person's female child

dawdle *VERB* **dawdles**, **dawdling**, **dawdled**
to walk or do something too slowly

dawn *NOUN* **dawns**
the time of the day when the sun rises

dawn *VERB* **dawns**, **dawning**, **dawned**
❶ to dawn is to begin to become light in the morning ❷ something dawns on you when you begin to realize it

day *NOUN* **days**
❶ the 24 hours between midnight and the next

midnight ❷ the light part of the day ❸ a period in time • *Write about what it was like in Queen Victoria's day.*

daybreak *NOUN*
the first light of day; dawn

daydream *VERB* **daydreams**, **daydreaming**, **daydreamed**
to have pleasant thoughts about things you would like to happen

daylight *NOUN*
❶ the light of day ❷ dawn • *They left before daylight.*

daytime *NOUN*
the time between sunrise and sunset

daze *NOUN*
➤ **to be in a daze** is to be unable to think or see clearly

dazed *ADJECTIVE*
someone is dazed when they can't think or see clearly

dazzle *VERB* **dazzles**, **dazzling**, **dazzled**
a light dazzles you when it shines so brightly in your eyes that you are blinded for a moment

dead *ADJECTIVE*
❶ no longer alive ❷ no longer working or active • *The phone went dead.* ❸ a dead place is not at all lively • *This town is dead at the weekend.* ❹ complete or total • *There was dead silence in the room.*

deaden *VERB* **deadens**, **deadening**, **deadened**
to deaden pain or noise is to make it weaker

dead end *NOUN* **dead ends**
a road or passage that is closed at one end

dead heat *NOUN* **dead heats**
a race in which two or more winners finish exactly together

deadline *NOUN* **deadlines**
the time by which you must finish doing something

deadlock *NOUN*
a situation in which people cannot agree or settle an argument

deadly ADJECTIVE **deadlier**, **deadliest**
likely to kill • *The bottle contained a deadly poison.*
➤ **deadliness** NOUN

deaf ADJECTIVE **deafer**, **deafest**
unable to hear
➤ **deafness** NOUN

deafen VERB **deafens**, **deafening**, **deafened**
a noise deafens you when it is very loud
• *The noise from the party upstairs was deafening me.*

deal VERB **deals**, **dealing**, **dealt**
❶ to deal something is to hand it out
❷ to deal in something is to buy and sell it
• *He deals in scrap metal.* ❸ to deal playing cards is to give them to players in a card game
➤ **to deal with someone** or **something** is to spend time sorting them out • *I'll deal with you later.*
➤ **to deal with something** is to be concerned with it • *This book deals with cacti.*

deal NOUN **deals**
❶ an agreement or bargain ❷ someone's turn to give out playing cards • *Whose deal is it?*
➤ **a good deal** or **a great deal** a large amount

dealer NOUN **dealers**
❶ someone who buys and sells things
❷ the person dealing at cards

dean NOUN **deans**
❶ an important member of the clergy in a cathedral or large church ❷ the head of part of a college or university

dear ADJECTIVE **dearer**, **dearest**
❶ loved very much • *He was a dear close friend.* ❷ you use dear as the usual way of beginning a letter • *Dear Auntie Fran*
❸ expensive • *The tickets are far too dear.*

dearly ADVERB
very much • *I would dearly like to know the answer.*

death NOUN **deaths**
dying; the end of life

deathly ADJECTIVE
❶ like death; very quiet or spooky • *Suddenly there was a deathly hush.* ❷ (old use) to do

with death • *Harry Potter and the Deathly Hallows*

debate NOUN **debates**
a formal discussion about a subject

debate VERB **debates**, **debating**, **debated**
to debate is to discuss or argue about something

debris (say deb-ree) NOUN
debris is scattered pieces that are left after something has been destroyed

debt (say det) NOUN **debts**
something that someone owes
➤ **to be in debt** is to owe money

debut (say day-bew or day-boo) NOUN **debuts**
someone's first public appearance as a performer

decade NOUN **decades**
a period of ten years

decathlon (say dek-ath-lon) NOUN **decathlons**
a sports competition in which athletes take part in ten different events
➤ **decathlete** NOUN

decay VERB **decays**, **decaying**, **decayed**
to rot or go bad

decay NOUN
decay is going bad or rotting

deceased (say di-seest) ADJECTIVE
a formal word for dead

deceit (say di-seet) NOUN
deceit is telling lies or doing something dishonest

deceitful ADJECTIVE
someone who is deceitful tells lies or does something dishonest
➤ **deceitfully** ADVERB

deceive (say di-seev) VERB **deceives**, **deceiving**, **deceived**
to deceive someone is to make them believe something that is not true

December NOUN
the last month of the year
DID YOU KNOW? December is based on the Latin word *decem* meaning 'ten', because it was the tenth month in the Roman calendar.

decency *NOUN*
decency is respectable and honest behaviour

decent *ADJECTIVE*
❶ respectable and honest ❷ of good enough quality • *Was it a decent film?*
➤ **decently** *ADVERB*

deception *NOUN* **deceptions**
❶ deception is making someone believe something that is not true ❷ a deception is a trick or a lie

deceptive *ADJECTIVE*
not what it seems to be • *The depth of the river is deceptive here.*

decibel *NOUN* **decibels**
a unit for measuring how loud a sound is

decide *VERB* **decides, deciding, decided**
❶ to decide something is to make up your mind about it or make a choice ❷ to decide a contest or argument is to settle it

decided *ADJECTIVE*
very definite and clear • *She spoke in a decided voice.* • *He walked with a decided limp.*

decidedly *ADVERB*
very much • *She was looking decidedly worried.*

deciduous *ADJECTIVE*
a deciduous tree loses its leaves in autumn

decimal *ADJECTIVE*
a decimal system uses tens or tenths to count things

decimal *NOUN* **decimals**
a decimal fraction

decimal fraction *NOUN*
decimal fractions
a fraction with tenths shown as numbers after a dot, for example ½ is 0.5, and 1¼ is 1.25 (*compare* **vulgar fraction**)

decimal point *NOUN* **decimal points**
the dot in a decimal fraction

decipher (*say* di-sy-fer) *VERB* **deciphers, deciphering, deciphered**
to decipher writing is to work out what it means when it is in code or difficult to read

decision *NOUN* **decisions**
a decision is what someone has decided

decisive *ADJECTIVE*
❶ ending or deciding something important
• *The decisive battle of the war was fought here.*
❷ a decisive person decides things quickly and firmly
➤ **decisively** *ADVERB*

deck *NOUN* **decks**
a floor on a ship or bus • *The crew slept on the lower deck.*

deckchair *NOUN* **deckchairs**
a folding chair with a seat of canvas or plastic material

declaration *NOUN* **declarations**
an official or public statement

declare *VERB* **declares, declaring, declared**
to declare something is to say it clearly and openly

decline *VERB* **declines, declining, declined**
❶ to decline is to become weaker or smaller
❷ to decline an offer is to refuse it politely

decode *VERB* **decodes, decoding, decoded**
to decode something written in code is to work out its meaning

decompose *VERB* **decomposes, decomposing, decomposed**
to decay or rot
➤ **decomposition** *NOUN*

decorate *VERB* **decorates, decorating, decorated**
❶ to decorate something is to make it look more beautiful or colourful
❷ to decorate a room or building is to put fresh paint or paper on the walls
❸ to decorate someone is to give them a medal for bravery

decoration *NOUN* **decorations**
❶ decorations are the paint, wallpaper and ornaments that make a place look more attractive ❷ decoration is making something look more attractive or colourful
❸ a decoration is a medal

decorative *ADJECTIVE*
used to make something look colourful and pretty • *The parcel was tied with a decorative ribbon.*

decoy (*say* dee-koi *or* di-**koi**) *NOUN* **decoys**
something used to tempt a person or animal into a trap

decrease (*say* di-**kreess**) *VERB* **decreases, decreasing, decreased**
❶ to decrease something is to make it smaller or less ❷ to decrease is to become smaller or less

decrease (*say* dee-**kreess**) *NOUN* **decreases**
the amount by which something decreases

decree *NOUN* **decrees**
an official order or decision

decree *VERB* **decrees, decreeing, decreed**
to decree something is to give an official order that it must happen

decrepit (*say* dik-**rep**-it) *ADJECTIVE*
old and weak
➤ **decrepitude** *NOUN*

dedicate *VERB* **dedicates, dedicating, dedicated**
❶ to dedicate yourself or your life to something is to spend all your time doing it • *They dedicated their working life to nursing.* ❷ to dedicate a book to someone is to name them at the beginning, as a sign of friendship or thanks

dedication *NOUN* **dedications**
❶ dedication is hard work and effort ❷ a dedication is a message at the beginning of a book in which the author names or thanks someone

deduce *VERB* **deduces, deducing, deduced**
to deduce a fact or answer is to work it out from what you already know is true • *We can deduce from this letter that he was lying.*

deduct *VERB* **deducts, deducting, deducted**
to deduct an amount is to subtract it from a total • *They deducted ten points from the other team for cheating.*

deduction *NOUN* **deductions**
❶ something that you work out by reasoning ❷ an amount taken away from a bigger amount

deed *NOUN* **deeds**
❶ something that someone has done ❷ a legal document that shows who owns something

deep *ADJECTIVE* **deeper, deepest**
❶ going down or back a long way from the top or front ❷ measured from top to bottom or from front to back • *The hole was two metres deep.* ❸ intense or strong • *The room was painted a deep blue.* ❹ a deep voice is very low in pitch
➤ **deeply** *ADVERB* very, extremely • *She was deeply upset.*

deepen *VERB* **deepens, deepening, deepened**
to deepen is to become deeper • *The pool deepened to 2 metres half way along.*

deep-freeze *NOUN* **deep-freezes**
a freezer for food

deer *NOUN* **deer**
a fast-running graceful animal with hoofs and (in the male) antlers
PLURAL ALERT! The word **deer** does not change in the plural: *a herd of wild deer.*

deface *VERB* **defaces, defacing, defaced**
to deface something is to spoil its appearance by writing or drawing on it

defeat *VERB* **defeats, defeating, defeated**
to defeat someone is to beat them in a game or battle

defeat *NOUN* **defeats**
❶ defeat is losing a game or battle ❷ a defeat is a lost game or battle

defect (*say* dee-fekt) *NOUN* **defects**
a flaw or weakness
The Chief Defect of Henry King Was chewing little bits of String. At last he swallowed some which tied Itself in ugly knots inside.—CAUTIONARY VERSES, Hilaire Belloc

defect (*say* di-fekt) *VERB* **defects, defecting, defected**
to defect is to desert a country or cause and join the other side

a
b
c
d
e
f
g
h
i
j
k
l
m
n
o
p
q
r
s
t
u
v
w
x
y
z

defective *ADJECTIVE*
something is defective when it has flaws or faults or doesn't work properly

defence *NOUN* **defences**
❶ something that protects you • *High walls were built around the city as a defence against enemy attacks.* ❷ protecting yourself or a place from an attack or from criticism • *In her defence, she thought she was acting for the best.* ❸ the players whose job is to stop the other team scoring in football and other games
➤ **defenceless** *ADJECTIVE* someone who is defenceless cannot protect themselves

defend *VERB* **defends**, **defending**, **defended**
❶ to defend someone or something is to protect them from an attack ❷ to defend an idea, belief or person is to argue in support of them ❸ to defend an accused person is to try to prove that they are innocent
➤ **defender** *NOUN*

defendant *NOUN* **defendants**
a person accused of something in a law court

defensive *ADJECTIVE*
❶ used to defend something • *We need to take defensive measures.* ❷ a defensive person is anxious about being criticized

defer *VERB* **defers**, **deferring**, **deferred**
to defer something is to put it off until later • *She deferred her departure until Saturday.*

defiant *ADJECTIVE*
openly showing that you refuse to obey someone
➤ **defiance** *NOUN* ➤ **defiantly** *ADVERB*

deficiency *NOUN* **deficiencies**
a lack or shortage
➤ **deficient** *ADJECTIVE*

defile *VERB* **defiles**, **defiling**, **defiled**
to defile something is to make it dirty or impure

define *VERB* **defines**, **defining**, **defined**
❶ to define a word is to explain what it means ❷ to define an idea or problem is to show exactly what it is

definite *ADJECTIVE*
fixed or certain • *Is there a definite date for the party yet?*

SPELLING ALERT! There is an **e** at the end of **definite**. Think of the sentence *The road comes to a definite end* to help you remember!

definite article *NOUN* **definite articles**
the word *the*

definitely *ADVERB*
certainly; without doubt • *I'll definitely be there!*

definition *NOUN* **definitions**
an explanation of what a word means

deflate *VERB* **deflates**, **deflating**, **deflated**
❶ to deflate a tyre or balloon is to let air out of it ❷ to deflate someone is to make them feel less confident or proud

deflect *VERB* **deflects**, **deflecting**, **deflected**
to deflect something that is moving is to make it go in a different direction
➤ **deflection** *NOUN*

deforestation *NOUN*
the cutting down of a large number of trees in an area

deformed *ADJECTIVE*
not properly shaped
➤ **deformity** *NOUN*

defrost *VERB* **defrosts**, **defrosting**, **defrosted**
❶ to defrost a refrigerator or freezer is to remove the ice from it ❷ to defrost frozen food is to thaw it out

deft *ADJECTIVE* **defter**, **deftest**
skilful and quick • *a few deft strokes with a paintbrush*
➤ **deftly** *ADVERB*

defuse *VERB* **defuses**, **defusing**, **defused**
❶ to defuse a bomb is to remove its fuse so that it will not blow up ❷ to defuse a situation is to make it less dangerous or tense

defy *VERB* **defies**, **defying**, **defied**
❶ to defy someone is to refuse to obey them ❷ to defy something is to prevent it happening • *The door defied all attempts to open it.* ❸ to defy someone to do something is to challenge them • *I defy you to say it is not true.*

degenerate VERB **degenerates, degenerating, degenerated**
to degenerate is to become worse • *The game degenerated into a succession of fouls.*

degrade VERB **degrades, degrading, degraded**
to degrade someone is to humiliate them

degree NOUN **degrees**
❶ a unit for measuring temperature • *Water boils at 100 degrees centigrade, or 100°C.*
❷ a unit for measuring angles • *There are 90 degrees (90°) in a right angle.* ❸ the level or amount of something • *I agree with you to a large degree.* ❹ an award to someone at a university or college who has successfully finished a course • *She has a degree in English.*

dehydrated ADJECTIVE
dried up, with all the water removed
➤ **dehydration** NOUN someone suffers from dehydration when they lose too much water from their body

deity (*say* dee-i-tee *or* day-i-tee) NOUN **deities**
a god or goddess

dejected ADJECTIVE
sad or depressed
➤ **dejection** NOUN

delay VERB **delays, delaying, delayed**
❶ to delay someone is to make them late
❷ to delay something is to put it off until later
❸ to delay is to wait before doing something

delay NOUN **delays**
❶ delaying or waiting • *Do it without delay.*
❷ the period you have to wait when something happens late • *There will be a delay of 20 minutes.*

delegate (*say* del-i-gayt) VERB **delegates, delegating, delegated**
to delegate someone is to choose them to do a job that you are responsible for

delegate (*say* del-i-gat) NOUN **delegates**
a person who represents other people at a meeting or conference
➤ **delegation** NOUN a delegation is a group of delegates

delete VERB **deletes, deleting, deleted**
to delete something is to cross it out or remove it
➤ **deletion** NOUN

deliberate (*say* di-lib-er-at) ADJECTIVE
❶ done on purpose • *It was a deliberate lie.*
❷ slow and careful • *He has a deliberate way of talking.*
➤ **deliberately** ADVERB

deliberate (*say* di-lib-er-ayt) VERB **deliberates, deliberating, deliberated**
to deliberate is to think carefully about something
➤ **deliberation** NOUN

delicacy NOUN **delicacies**
❶ delicacy is being delicate ❷ a delicacy is something small and tasty to eat

delicate ADJECTIVE
❶ fine and graceful • *The cloth had delicate embroidery.* ❷ fragile and easily damaged
❸ a delicate person becomes ill easily
❹ a delicate situation needs great care
➤ **delicately** ADVERB

delicatessen NOUN **delicatessens**
a shop that sells cooked meats, cheeses, salads, etc.

delicious ADJECTIVE
tasting or smelling very pleasant

delight VERB **delights, delighting, delighted**
to delight someone is to please them a lot

delight NOUN **delights**
great pleasure

delightful ADJECTIVE
giving great pleasure • *What a delightful surprise!*
➤ **delightfully** ADVERB

delirious ADJECTIVE
❶ in a confused state of mind caused by illness with a high fever ❷ extremely excited or enthusiastic
➤ **deliriously** ADVERB

delirium NOUN **deliriums**
❶ a confused state of mind caused by illness with a high fever ❷ wild excitement

deliver VERB **delivers, delivering, delivered**
❶ to deliver something is to take it to a house or office ❷ to deliver a speech or lecture is to give it to an audience ❸ to deliver a baby is to help with its birth

delivery *NOUN* **deliveries**
❶ delivery is when letters or goods are taken to a house or office ❷ a person's delivery is the way they give a speech or lecture ❸ giving birth to a baby

delta *NOUN* **deltas**
a triangular area at the mouth of a river where it spreads into branches

delude *VERB* **deludes**, **deluding**, **deluded**
to be deluded is to believe something that is not true

deluge *NOUN* **deluges**
❶ a large flood ❷ a heavy fall of rain ❸ something coming in great numbers
• *After the speech there was a deluge of questions.*

deluge *VERB* **deluges**, **deluging**, **deluged**
to be deluged with something is to get a huge amount of it • *We have been deluged with replies.*

delusion *NOUN* **delusions**
a false belief

deluxe *ADJECTIVE*
of very high quality • *a deluxe five-star hotel*

demand *VERB* **demands**, **demanding**, **demanded**
to demand something is to ask for it forcefully

demand *NOUN* **demands**
❶ a demand is a very firm request for something ❷ demand is a desire to have something • *There's not much demand for ice cream at this time of year.*

demanding *ADJECTIVE*
❶ asking for many things • *Toddlers can be very demanding.* ❷ needing a lot of time or effort • *She has a demanding job.*

demented *ADJECTIVE*
behaving in an uncontrolled way because you are upset or angry • *This computer is driving me demented!*

dementia (*say* di-**men**-sha) *NOUN*
a serious brain disease that causes memory loss and confusion

demo *NOUN* **demos** (*informal*)
a demonstration

democracy *NOUN* **democracies**
❶ democracy is government by leaders elected by the people ❷ a democracy is a country governed in this way

democrat *NOUN* **democrats**
a person who believes in or supports democracy

democratic *ADJECTIVE*
a democratic idea or process is one that involves all the people and takes account of their views

demolish *VERB* **demolishes**, **demolishing**, **demolished**
to demolish a building is to knock it down and break it up
➤ **demolition** *NOUN*

demon *NOUN* **demons**
❶ a devil or evil spirit ❷ a fierce or forceful person • *The professor was a demon for work.*

demonic *ADJECTIVE*
like a demon; evil • *a demonic laugh*

demonstrate *VERB* **demonstrates**, **demonstrating**, **demonstrated**
❶ to demonstrate something is to show or prove it ❷ to demonstrate is to take part in a demonstration

demonstration *NOUN* **demonstrations**
❶ showing how to do or work something ❷ a march or meeting to show everyone what you think about something • *There will be a demonstration against the new motorway.*

demonstrator *NOUN* **demonstrators**
❶ someone who takes part in a demonstration or meeting ❷ someone who demonstrates something

demote *VERB* **demotes**, **demoting**, **demoted**
to demote someone is to reduce them to a lower position or rank

den *NOUN* **dens**
❶ the home of a wild animal • *a lion's den* ❷ a hiding place, especially for children

denial *NOUN* **denials**
saying that something is not true

denim *NOUN*
strong cotton cloth, used to make jeans

denominator *NOUN* **denominators**
the number below the line in a fraction (*compare* **numerator**). In ¼ the denominator is the number 4.

denote *VERB* **denotes, denoting, denoted**
to denote something is to indicate or mean it • *On the menu, the letter V denotes 'vegetarian'.*

denounce *VERB* **denounces, denouncing, denounced**
to denounce someone or something is to speak strongly against them, or accuse them of something • *They denounced him as a spy.*

dense *ADJECTIVE* **denser, densest**
❶ thick • *The fog was getting very dense.*
❷ packed close together • *They walked through a dense forest.*
➤ **densely** *ADVERB* thickly; close together • *a densely populated area*

density *NOUN* **densities**
how thick or tightly packed something is

dent *NOUN* **dents**
a hollow made in a surface by hitting it or pressing it

dent *VERB* **dents, denting, dented**
to dent something is to make a dent in it

dental *ADJECTIVE*
to do with the teeth or dentistry

dentist *NOUN* **dentists**
a person who is trained to treat teeth, fill them or take them out, and fit false ones

deny *VERB* **denies, denying, denied**
❶ to deny something is to say that it is not true ❷ to deny a request is to refuse it

deodorant *NOUN* **deodorants**
a powder or liquid that removes unpleasant smells

depart *VERB* **departs, departing, departed**
to depart is to go away or leave
➤ **departure** *NOUN*

department *NOUN* **departments**
one part of a large organization or shop

department store *NOUN* **department stores**
a large shop that sells many different kinds of goods

depend *VERB* **depends, depending, depended**
➤ **to depend on someone** *or* **something** is to rely on them • *We depend on you for help.*
➤ **to depend on something** is to be decided or controlled by it • *Whether we can have a picnic depends on the weather.*

dependable *ADJECTIVE*
if someone or something is dependable, they are reliable and you can depend on them

dependant *NOUN* **dependants**
a person who depends on someone else, especially for money • *She has two dependants, a son and a daughter.*

dependent *ADJECTIVE*
depending or relying on someone • *He was dependent on his father.* • *She has two dependent children.*
➤ **dependence** *NOUN*

depict *VERB* **depicts, depicting, depicted**
❶ to depict something is to show it in a painting or drawing ❷ to depict a scene is to describe it • *The story depicted a small village in Austria.*

deplorable *ADJECTIVE*
extremely bad; shocking • *The giants had deplorable table manners.*

deplore *VERB* **deplores, deploring, deplored**
to deplore something is to dislike it very much because it upsets or annoys you

deport *VERB* **deports, deporting, deported**
to deport someone is to send them out of a country
➤ **deportation** *NOUN*

deposit *NOUN* **deposits**
❶ an amount of money you pay into a bank or building society ❷ a sum of money paid as the first instalment of a bigger sum ❸ a layer of matter in or on

A B C D E F G H I J K L M N O P Q R S T U V W X Y Z

the earth • *deposits of oil and gas under the ground*

deposit VERB **deposits**, **depositing**, **deposited**
❶ to deposit something is to put it down somewhere ❷ to deposit money is to pay it into a bank or building society

depot (*say* **dep**-oh) NOUN **depots**
❶ a place where things are stored ❷ a place where buses or trains are kept and repaired

depress VERB **depresses**, **depressing**, **depressed**
to depress someone is to make them very sad

depressed ADJECTIVE
someone who is depressed feels very sad and without hope

depression NOUN **depressions**
❶ a feeling of great sadness and lack of hope ❷ a long period when there is less trade and business than usual and many people have no work ❸ a shallow hollow or dip in the ground

deprive VERB **deprives**, **depriving**, **deprived**
to deprive someone of something is to take it away from them • *Prisoners are deprived of their freedom.*

deprived ADJECTIVE
without all the things you need to live a happy and comfortable life, like enough food and good housing

depth NOUN **depths**
the depth of something is how deep it is • *What is the depth of the river here?*
➤ **in depth** thoroughly
➤ **out of your depth** ❶ in water that is too deep to stand in ❷ trying to do something that is too difficult for you
➤ **the depths** the deepest or innermost part of something • *the darkest depths of the cave*

deputy NOUN **deputies**
a person who acts as a substitute or chief assistant for someone and does that person's job when they are away

derail VERB **derails**, **derailing**, **derailed**
a train is derailed when something causes it to leave the track

derby (*say* **dar**-bee) NOUN **derbies**
a sports match between two teams from the same city or area

derelict (*say* **de**-re-likt) ADJECTIVE
abandoned and left to fall into ruin
• *The factory is now completely derelict.*

deride VERB **derides**, **deriding**, **derided**
to deride someone or something is to treat them with scorn • *He was derided for his beliefs.*

derision NOUN
scorn or ridicule • *They treated him with derision.*

derivation NOUN **derivations**
the derivation of a word is where it comes from

derive VERB **derives**, **deriving**, **derived**
to get something from another person or thing • *She derived a lot of pleasure from music.* • *Many English words are derived from Latin.*

derrick NOUN **derricks**
❶ a kind of large crane for lifting things ❷ a tall framework that holds the machinery used for drilling an oil well
DID YOU KNOW? The word **derrick** originally meant 'gallows' and was named after a famous London hangman called *Derrick*.

descant NOUN **descants**
a tune sung or played above another tune

descend VERB **descends**, **descending**, **descended**
to descend something like a hill or staircase is to go down it
➤ **to be descended from someone** is to be in the same family as them but living at a later time

descendant NOUN **descendants**
a person's descendants are the people who are descended from them

descent NOUN **descents**
a descent is a climb down, usually a hard or long one

describe VERB **describes**, **describing**, **described**
to describe something or someone is to say what they are like

description *NOUN* **descriptions**
❶ description is saying what someone or something is like • *She's a writer who's very good at description.* ❷ a description is something you write or say that describes what someone or something is like • *He gave the police a description of the robbers.*
➤ **descriptive** *ADJECTIVE* a descriptive word or piece of writing describes someone or something • *a descriptive poem*

desert (*say* dez-ert) *NOUN* **deserts**
a large area of very dry, often sandy, land

desert (*say* di-zert) *VERB* **deserts, deserting, deserted**
to desert someone or something is to leave them without intending to return
➤ **desertion** *NOUN*

deserted *ADJECTIVE*
a place is deserted when there is nobody there

deserter *NOUN* **deserters**
a soldier who runs away from the army

desert island *NOUN* **desert islands**
a tropical island where nobody lives

deserts (*say* di-zerts) *PLURAL NOUN*
someone's deserts are what they deserve • *He got his deserts.*

deserve *VERB* **deserves, deserving, deserved**
to deserve something is to be worthy of it or to have a right to it
➤ **deservedly** *ADVERB* rightly, because it is deserved • *She is friendly and deservedly popular.*

design *NOUN* **designs**
❶ the way that something is made or arranged • *the design of the Space Shuttle* ❷ a drawing that shows how something is to be made ❸ lines and shapes forming a pattern • *a pretty floral design*

design *VERB* **designs, designing, designed**
to design something is to make a design or plan for it

designate *VERB* **designates, designating, designated**
to designate something is to choose it for a special purpose • *The meadow was designated a picnic area.*

designer *NOUN* **designers**
someone who designs things, especially clothes

desirable *ADJECTIVE*
worth having or doing • *It would be desirable to repeat the experiment if possible.*

desire *VERB* **desires, desiring, desired**
to desire something is to want it very much

desire *NOUN* **desires**
a feeling of wanting something very much

desk *NOUN* **desks**
❶ a piece of furniture with a flat top and drawers, used for writing, reading or working at ❷ a counter at which a cashier or receptionist sits

desktop *ADJECTIVE*
small enough to use on a desk • *I've bought a desktop computer.*

desolate *ADJECTIVE*
❶ lonely and sad ❷ a desolate place is empty, with no people living there
They had come to the edge of a clearing in the wood, a desolate place like a quarry strewn with boulders.—THE LITTLE WHITE HORSE, Elizabeth Goudge
➤ **desolation** *NOUN*

despair *NOUN*
despair is a complete loss of hope

despair *VERB* **despairs, despairing, despaired**
to despair is to lose hope completely

despatch *NOUN, VERB*
another spelling of **dispatch**

desperate *ADJECTIVE*
❶ extremely serious or hopeless • *The crew were in a desperate situation.* ❷ ready to do anything to get out of a difficulty • *a desperate gang of criminals* ❸ needing or wanting something very much • *I was desperate to go home.*
➤ **desperation** *NOUN*

desperately *ADVERB*
❶ extremely; seriously • *She was desperately worried about what she had seen.* ❷ if you do something desperately, you do it in a despairing or reckless way • *'Please don't call the police,' she said desperately.*

a b c d e f g h i j k l m n o p q r s t u v w x y z

despicable *ADJECTIVE*
very unpleasant or evil
➤ **despicably** *ADVERB*

despise *VERB* **despises**, **despising**, **despised**
to despise someone is to hate them and have no respect at all for them

despite *PREPOSITION*
in spite of • *They went out despite the rain.*

dessert (say di-**zert**) *NOUN* **desserts**
fruit or a sweet food eaten at the end of a meal

SPELLING ALERT! There is sand in a **desert**, but sugar in a **dessert**.

dessertspoon *NOUN* **dessertspoons**
a medium-sized spoon used for eating puddings

destination *NOUN* **destinations**
the place you are travelling to

destined *ADJECTIVE*
intended by fate; meant to happen • *They felt they were destined to win.*

destiny *NOUN* **destinies**
your destiny is what is intended for you in the future; your fate • *His destiny was to travel the world.*

destroy *VERB* **destroys**, **destroying**, **destroyed**
to destroy something is to ruin it or put an end to it

destroyer *NOUN* **destroyers**
a fast warship

destruction *NOUN*
destruction is completely destroying something • *the destruction of the rainforests*

destructive *ADJECTIVE*
something that is destructive causes a lot of damage

detach *VERB* **detaches**, **detaching**, **detached**
to detach something is to remove it or separate it • *Detach the coupon from the bottom of the page.*
➤ **detachable** *ADJECTIVE*

detached *ADJECTIVE*
❶ able to stand back from a situation and not get emotionally involved in it • *She was watching with a detached expression, as though the argument had nothing to do with her.* ❷ a detached house is one that is not joined to another house

detachment *NOUN* **detachments**
a detachment is a special group of people, especially soldiers

detail *NOUN* **details**
❶ a small piece of information ❷ a small part of a design or picture or piece of decoration
➤ **detailed** *ADJECTIVE*
➤ **in detail** describing or dealing with everything fully

detain *VERB* **detains**, **detaining**, **detained**
❶ to detain someone is to keep them in a place ❷ to detain someone is also to keep them waiting • *I'll try not to detain you for long.*

detect *VERB* **detects**, **detecting**, **detected**
to detect something is to discover or notice it
➤ **detection** *NOUN* ➤ **detector** *NOUN*

detective *NOUN* **detectives**
a person, especially a police officer, who investigates crimes

detention *NOUN* **detentions**
detention is when someone is made to stay in a place, especially made to stay late in school as a punishment

deter *VERB* **deters**, **deterring**, **deterred**
to deter someone is to put them off doing something

detergent *NOUN* **detergents**
a kind of washing powder or liquid

deteriorate *VERB* **deteriorates**, **deteriorating**, **deteriorated**
to deteriorate is to become worse • *The weather was starting to deteriorate.*
➤ **deterioration** *NOUN*

determination *NOUN*
a strong intention to achieve something, even though it is difficult

determine *VERB* **determines**, **determining**, **determined**
to determine something is to decide it or work it out • *The task was to determine the height of the mountain.*

determined *ADJECTIVE*
having your mind firmly made up

determiner *NOUN* **determiners**
a determiner is a word that introduces a noun, for example *a*, *the* and *many*

deterrent *NOUN* **deterrents**
something that is meant to put people off doing something, such as a powerful weapon

detest *VERB* **detests**, **detesting**, **detested**
to detest something or someone is to dislike them very much
I truly detested that Jamie. He was just the most annoying person in the whole world to have to sit next to.—THE LOTTIE PROJECT, Jacqueline Wilson
► **detestable** *ADJECTIVE*

detonate *VERB* **detonates**, **detonating**, **detonated**
to detonate a bomb is to make it explode
► **detonation** *NOUN* ► **detonator** *NOUN*

detour *NOUN* **detours**
a roundabout route you use instead of the normal route

detrimental *ADJECTIVE*
harmful or damaging • *Litter has a detrimental effect on wildlife.*
► **detrimentally** *ADVERB*

deuce *NOUN*
a tennis score when each player has 40 points and needs two more points in a row to win the game

devastate *VERB* **devastates**, **devastating**, **devastated**
to devastate a place is to ruin or destroy it, making it impossible to live in
► **devastation** *NOUN*

devastated *ADJECTIVE*
someone is devastated when they are extremely shocked and upset

develop *VERB* **develops**, **developing**, **developed**
❶ to develop something is to make it bigger or better ❷ to develop is to become bigger

or better ❸ to develop land is to put up new buildings on it ❹ to develop photographic film is to treat it with chemicals so that pictures appear on it

development *NOUN* **developments**
❶ a development is something interesting that has happened • *Have there been any developments since I last saw you?*
❷ development is putting up new buildings

deviate *VERB* **deviates**, **deviating**, **deviated**
to deviate is to turn aside from a particular path or way of doing something
► **deviation** *NOUN*

device *NOUN* **devices**
❶ a piece of equipment used for a particular purpose • *We need a device for opening tins.*
❷ any piece of digital equipment, such as a smartphone or laptop
► **to leave someone to their own devices** is to leave them alone to do as they wish and not tell them what to do

devil *NOUN* **devils**
an evil spirit or person
► **devilry** *NOUN* wickedness or evil

devilish *ADJECTIVE*
cruel or wicked, like a devil
► **devilishness** *NOUN*

devious *ADJECTIVE*
❶ using unfair and dishonest methods • *He got rich by devious means.* ❷ not straight or direct
• *The coach took us by a devious route to avoid the traffic jams.*

devise *VERB* **devises**, **devising**, **devised**
to devise a plan or idea is to think it up

devote *VERB* **devotes**, **devoting**, **devoted**
to devote yourself or your time to something is to spend all your time doing it • *They devote all their free time to sport.*

devoted *ADJECTIVE*
loving and loyal • *They are devoted parents.*

devotion *NOUN*
great love or loyalty

devour *VERB* **devours**, **devouring**, **devoured**
to devour something is to eat or swallow it greedily
Latch and the beasts sat round the kitchen table

a
b
c
d
e
f
g
h
i
j
k
l
m
n
o
p
q
r
s
t
u
v
w
x
y
z

drinking tea and devouring an overlooked packet of digestive biscuits.—PURE DEAD WICKED, Debi Gliori

devout *ADJECTIVE*
deeply religious

dew *NOUN*
tiny drops of water that form during the night on the ground and other surfaces out of doors
➤ **dewy** *ADJECTIVE*

diabetes (*say* dy-a-**bee**-teez) *NOUN*
a medical condition in which there is too much sugar in a person's blood

diabetic (*say* dy-a-**bet**-ik) *NOUN* **diabetics**
a person who has diabetes

diabetic *ADJECTIVE*
having diabetes

diabolical *ADJECTIVE*
like a devil; very wicked

diagnose *VERB* **diagnoses**, **diagnosing**, **diagnosed**
to find out and say what illness or condition a person has

diagnosis *NOUN* **diagnoses**
a doctor makes a diagnosis when they decide what disease someone has

diagonal *NOUN* **diagonals**
a straight line joining opposite corners
➤ **diagonally** *ADVERB*

diagram *NOUN* **diagrams**
a drawing or picture that shows the parts of something or how it works

dial *NOUN* **dials**
a circular piece of plastic or card with numbers or letters round it

dial *VERB* **dials**, **dialling**, **dialled**
to dial a telephone number is to choose it by tapping numbers on a screen or pressing numbered buttons

dialect *NOUN* **dialects**
the form of a language used by people in one area of the country but not in the rest of the country

dialogue *NOUN* **dialogues**
talk between people, especially in a play, film or book

diameter *NOUN* **diameters**
❶ a line drawn from one side of a circle to the other, passing through the centre ❷ the length of this line

diamond *NOUN* **diamonds**
❶ a very hard jewel that looks like clear glass ❷ a shape which has four equal sides but which is not a square ❸ a playing card with red diamond shapes on it

diaphragm (*say* dy-a-fram) *NOUN* **diaphragms**
the muscular layer inside your body between your chest and your abdomen, used when you breathe

diarrhoea (*say* dy-a-**ree**-a) *NOUN*
an illness that makes the waste matter you empty from your bowels very watery

diary *NOUN* **diaries**
a book with a separate space to write in for each day of the year, in which you write down what happens each day or to plan what you need to do in the future

dice *NOUN* **dice**
a small cube marked with one to six dots on each side, thrown to give a number in some games

dictate *VERB* **dictates**, **dictating**, **dictated**
❶ to dictate something is to speak or read it aloud for someone else to write down ❷ to dictate to someone is to give them orders in a bossy way
➤ **dictation** *NOUN* dictation, or a dictation, is an exercise in writing down what someone reads out

dictator *NOUN* **dictators**
a ruler who has complete power over the people of a country

dictionary *NOUN* **dictionaries**
a book with words listed in alphabetical order, so that you can find out what a word means and how to spell it

did *VERB* (*past tense of* **do**)
• *Where did you go to school before?*

didn't
short for *did not* • *I didn't want to wake you.*

die *VERB* **dies, dying, died**
to die is to stop living
➤ **to die down** is to gradually become less strong • *The wind died down at last.*
➤ **to die out** is to gradually disappear • *The tiger is beginning to die out.*

diesel *NOUN* **diesels**
① a diesel is an engine that works by burning oil in compressed air ② diesel is fuel for this kind of engine

diet *NOUN* **diets**
① a diet is special meals that someone eats to be healthy or to lose weight • *Dad's on a diet.* ② someone's diet is the food they normally eat

diet *VERB* **diets, dieting, dieted**
to diet is to keep to a special diet, especially in order to lose weight

differ *VERB* **differs, differing, differed**
① to differ from something is to be not the same as it ② to differ is to disagree • *The two writers differ on this point.*

difference *NOUN* **differences**
① the way in which something is different from something else ② the amount between two numbers • *The difference between 8 and 3 is 5.*

different *ADJECTIVE*
one person or thing is different from another when they are not the same
➤ **differently** *ADVERB*

difficult *ADJECTIVE*
needing a lot of effort or skill; not easy

difficulty *NOUN* **difficulties**
① difficulty is not being easy; trouble • *I had difficulty answering most of the questions.* ② a difficulty is something that causes a problem

diffuse *VERB* **diffuses, diffusing, diffused**
to diffuse something is to spread it widely or thinly • *A rosy light seemed to diffuse itself through the room.*
➤ **diffusion** *NOUN*

dig *VERB* **digs, digging, dug**
① to dig soil or the ground is to break it up and move it ② to dig a hole is to make it

③ to dig someone is to poke them • *He dug me in the ribs.*
➤ **digger** *NOUN*

dig *NOUN* **digs**
① a place where archaeologists dig to look for ancient remains ② a sharp thrust or poke • *She gave me a dig in the ribs with her elbow.* ③ an unpleasant remark • *What he said was clearly a dig at me.*

digest *VERB* **digests, digesting, digested**
to digest food is to soften and change it in the stomach and intestine so that the body can absorb it
➤ **digestion** *NOUN*

digestive *ADJECTIVE*
to do with digesting food

digit (*say* dij-it) *NOUN* **digits**
① any of the numbers from 0 to 9 ② a finger or toe

digital *ADJECTIVE*
① to do with or using digits ② a digital computer or recording stores the data or sound as a series of binary digits ③ a digital clock or watch has a row of digits to indicate numbers (*compare* **analogue**)
➤ **digitally** *ADVERB*

dignified *ADJECTIVE*
having dignity

dignity *NOUN*
a calm and serious manner

dike *NOUN* **dikes**
another spelling of **dyke**

dilapidated *ADJECTIVE*
looking run down and in need of repair • *an old dilapidated caravan*

dilemma *NOUN* **dilemmas**
an awkward choice between two possible actions, either of which would cause difficulties

dilute *VERB* **dilutes, diluting, diluted**
to dilute a liquid is to make it weaker by mixing it with water

dim *ADJECTIVE* **dimmer, dimmest**
only faintly lit and difficult to see
➤ **dimly** *ADVERB* to see something dimly is to find it hard to see clearly

a b c d e f g h i j k l m n o p q r s t u v w x y z

A B C D E F G H I J K L M N O P Q R S T U V W X Y Z

dim VERB dims, dimming, dimmed
a light dims when it becomes less bright
• *As the curtain rose, the lights dimmed.*

dimension NOUN dimensions
❶ a measurement such as length, width, area or volume • *What are the dimensions of the box?* ❷ a feature of something • *The day trips added another dimension to our holiday.*

diminish VERB diminishes, diminishing, diminished
❶ to diminish something is to make it smaller ❷ to diminish is to become smaller

diminutive (say dim-in-yoo-tiv) ADJECTIVE
very small

diminutive NOUN diminutives
a word, name or ending of a word that shows that something is small, for example the name *Tiny Tim* or the word *piglet*

dimple NOUN dimples
a small hollow on a person's cheek or chin

din NOUN
a loud noise

dine VERB dines, dining, dined
to dine is to have dinner
➤ **diner** NOUN

dinghy (say ding-ee) NOUN dinghies
a kind of small boat

dingy (say din-jee) ADJECTIVE dingier, dingiest
shabby and dirty-looking
➤ **dinginess** NOUN

dinner NOUN dinners
the main meal of the day, eaten either in the middle of the day or in the evening

dinosaur NOUN dinosaurs
a prehistoric reptile, often of enormous size
DID YOU KNOW? The word **dinosaur** comes from Greek words meaning 'terrible lizard'.

dip VERB dips, dipping, dipped
❶ to dip something is to put it into a liquid and then take it out again • *Dip the marshmallows in melted chocolate.* ❷ to dip is to go or slope downwards • *The road dips steeply on the other side.*

dip NOUN dips
❶ dipping ❷ a downward slope ❸ a quick swim • *I'm going for a dip in the pool.* ❹ a mixture into which things are dipped • *a spicy yoghurt-based dip*

diplodocus (say di-plod-okus) NOUN
a large plant-eating dinosaur with a long slender neck and tail

diploma NOUN diplomas
a certificate awarded for skill in a particular subject

diplomacy NOUN
❶ the business of keeping friendly with other nations ❷ dealing with other people without upsetting or offending them

diplomatic ADJECTIVE
❶ to do with diplomacy ❷ tactful and courteous
➤ **diplomat** NOUN someone who works in diplomacy

dire ADJECTIVE direr, direst
dreadful or serious • *The refugees are in dire need of food and shelter.*

direct ADJECTIVE
❶ as straight or quick as possible ❷ frank and honest
➤ **directness** NOUN

direct VERB directs, directing, directed
❶ to direct someone is to show them the way ❷ to direct a film or play is to decide how it should be made or performed

direction NOUN directions
❶ a direction is the way you go to get somewhere ❷ the job of managing or controlling someone or something
➤ **directions** information on how to use or do something or how to get somewhere

directly ADVERB
❶ by a direct route • *Go directly to the shop.* ❷ immediately • *I want you to come directly.*

director NOUN directors
❶ a person who is in charge of something, especially one of a group of people managing a company ❷ a person who decides how a film or play should be made or performed

directory NOUN directories
❶ a book or website which lists names, addresses and telephone numbers

2 a computer file which contains a number of other files

direct speech NOUN

someone's words written down exactly in the way they were said, for example, *'I want to go home,' said Josh.*

dirt NOUN

earth or soil; anything that is not clean

dirty ADJECTIVE dirtier, dirtiest

1 covered with dirt; not clean **2** rude or offensive • *Someone has written dirty words on the wall.* **3** unfair or mean • *That was a dirty trick.*
➤ **dirtily** ADVERB ➤ **dirtiness** NOUN

dis– PREFIX

1 showing the opposite of something, as in *dishonest* **2** showing that something has been taken away or apart, as in *disarm* or *dismantle*

disability NOUN disabilities

a physical or mental condition that restricts someone's movements, senses or activities

disabled ADJECTIVE

having a physical or mental condition that limits your movements, senses or activities

disadvantage NOUN disadvantages

something that hinders you or makes things difficult

disagree VERB disagrees, disagreeing, disagreed

1 to disagree with someone is to have or express a different opinion from them **2** to disagree with someone is also to have a bad effect on them • *Rich food disagrees with me.*
➤ **disagreement** NOUN

disagreeable ADJECTIVE

unpleasant

disappear VERB disappears, disappearing, disappeared

1 to disappear is to become impossible to see; to vanish • *The footprints had mysteriously disappeared.* **2** to disappear is also to stop happening or existing • *My worries soon disappeared.*
➤ **disappearance** NOUN

disappoint VERB disappoints, disappointing, disappointed

to disappoint someone is to fail to do what they want
➤ **disappointing** ADJECTIVE
➤ **disappointment** NOUN

disapprove VERB disapproves, disapproving, disapproved

to disapprove of someone or something is to have a bad opinion of them
➤ **disapproval** NOUN

disarm VERB disarms, disarming, disarmed

1 to disarm is to reduce the size of armed forces **2** to disarm someone is to take away their weapons
➤ **disarmament** NOUN

disaster NOUN disasters

1 a very bad accident or misfortune, often one where many people are killed or injured **2** a complete failure • *The first performance of our play was a disaster.*

disastrous ADJECTIVE

causing great misfortune; going completely wrong • *It was a disastrous end to the day.*
➤ **disastrously** ADVERB

disc NOUN discs

1 a round flat object **2** a round, flat piece of plastic on which sound, pictures or other data is recorded

discard VERB discards, discarding, discarded

to discard something is to throw it away

discharge VERB discharges, discharging, discharged

1 to release someone • *She was discharged from hospital yesterday.* **2** to send something out • *Vehicles must not discharge smoke.*

disciple NOUN disciples

a follower of a political or religious leader, especially one of Christ's first followers

discipline NOUN

1 training people to obey rules and punishing them if they don't **2** the control you have over how you behave • *You need lots of discipline to learn the piano.*

a
b
c
d
e
f
g
h
i
j
k
l
m
n
o
p
q
r
s
t
u
v
w
x
y
z

disclose VERB discloses, disclosing, disclosed
to disclose information or a secret is to tell someone about it

disco NOUN discos
a place or party where records are played for dancing

discolour VERB discolours, discolouring, discoloured
to discolour something is to spoil its colour

discomfort NOUN
being uncomfortable

disconnect VERB disconnects, disconnecting, disconnected
to disconnect something is to break its connection or detach it
➤ **disconnection** NOUN

discontented ADJECTIVE
unhappy and not satisfied
➤ **discontent** NOUN

discontinue VERB discontinues, discontinuing, discontinued
to discontinue doing something is to stop doing it
➤ **discontinuity** NOUN

discord NOUN discords
❶ disagreement or quarrelling ❷ musical notes sounded together that make a harsh or unpleasant sound

discount NOUN discounts
an amount by which a price is reduced

discourage VERB discourages, discouraging, discouraged
❶ to discourage someone is to take away their enthusiasm or confidence ❷ to discourage someone from doing something is to try to persuade them not to do it
➤ **discouragement** NOUN

discover VERB discovers, discovering, discovered
to discover something is to find it or learn about it, especially by chance or for the first time

discovery NOUN discoveries
❶ discovery is finding or learning about something by chance or for the first time

• the discovery of a hoard of Viking treasure
❷ a discovery is something that is found or learned about for the first time • This drug was an important discovery for medicine.

discreet ADJECTIVE
being careful in what you say and do, especially when you have a secret to keep
➤ **discreetly** ADVERB

discriminate VERB discriminates, discriminating, discriminated
❶ to discriminate between things is to notice the differences between them, or to prefer one thing to another ❷ to discriminate between people is to treat them differently or unfairly because of their race, sex or religion

discrimination NOUN
❶ discrimination is treating people differently or unfairly because of their race, sex or religion ❷ discrimination is also the ability to notice the differences between things

discus (say dis-kuss) NOUN discuses
a thick heavy disc thrown in an athletic contest

discuss (say dis-kuss) VERB discusses, discussing, discussed
to discuss a subject is to talk with other people about it or to write about it in detail

discussion NOUN discussions
❶ a conversation about a subject ❷ a piece of writing in which you look at a subject from different points of view

disease NOUN diseases
a disease is an illness or an unhealthy condition
➤ **diseased** ADJECTIVE

disembark VERB disembarks, disembarking, disembarked
to disembark is to get out of a boat or aircraft

disgrace NOUN
❶ disgrace is shame • You have brought disgrace to your family. ❷ a disgrace is a person or thing that is so bad that people should feel ashamed • This room is an absolute disgrace.
➤ **disgraceful** ADJECTIVE
➤ **disgracefully** ADVERB

disgrace VERB disgraces, disgracing, disgraced
to disgrace someone or something is to bring them shame

disguise VERB disguises, disguising, disguised
to disguise someone is to make them look different so that other people will not recognize them

disguise NOUN disguises
clothes or make-up you put on to change the way you look so that people will not recognize you

disgust NOUN
a strong feeling of dislike or contempt

disgust VERB disgusts, disgusting, disgusted
to disgust someone is to make them feel disgust
➤ **disgusted** ADJECTIVE
➤ **disgusting** ADJECTIVE

dish NOUN dishes
❶ a plate or bowl for food ❷ food that has been prepared for eating

dish VERB dishes, dishing, dished
➤ **to dish something out** (informal) is to give it to people

dishcloth NOUN dishcloths
a cloth you use for washing or drying dishes

dishevelled ADJECTIVE
untidy in appearance

dishonest ADJECTIVE
not honest or truthful
➤ **dishonesty** NOUN ➤ **dishonestly** ADVERB

dishwasher NOUN dishwashers
a machine for washing dishes automatically

disinfect VERB disinfects, disinfecting, disinfected
to disinfect something is to treat it to kill all the germs in it

disinfectant NOUN disinfectants
a liquid used to disinfect things

disintegrate VERB disintegrates, disintegrating, disintegrated
to disintegrate is to break up into small pieces
➤ **disintegration** NOUN

disinterested ADJECTIVE
not favouring one side more than the other; impartial

disk NOUN disks
a disc, especially one used to store computer data

dislike VERB dislikes, disliking, disliked
to dislike someone or something is not to like them

dislike NOUN dislikes
a feeling of not liking someone or something

dislocate VERB dislocates, dislocating, dislocated
to dislocate a bone or joint in your body is to make it come out of its proper place by accident
➤ **dislocation** NOUN

dislodge VERB dislodges, dislodging, dislodged
to dislodge something is to move it from its place

disloyal ADJECTIVE
not loyal

dismal ADJECTIVE
gloomy and sad
➤ **dismally** ADVERB

dismantle VERB dismantles, dismantling, dismantled
to dismantle something is to take it to pieces

dismay NOUN
a feeling of strong disappointment and surprise
➤ **dismayed** ADJECTIVE

dismiss VERB dismisses, dismissing, dismissed
❶ to dismiss someone is to tell them that they have to leave, especially to leave their job ❷ to dismiss an idea or suggestion is to reject it
➤ **dismissal** NOUN

dismount VERB dismounts, dismounting, dismounted
to dismount is to get off a horse or bicycle

disobedience NOUN
disobedience is refusing to do what someone tells you to do

A
B
C
D
E
F
G
H
I
J
K
L
M
N
O
P
Q
R
S
T
U
V
W
X
Y
Z

disobedient *ADJECTIVE*
a disobedient person refuses to do what they are told to do
Xar was the most disobedient boy in the Wizard kingdom in about four generations, and forbidding things only encouraged him.—THE WIZARDS OF ONCE, Cressida Cowell
➤ **disobediently** *ADVERB*

disobey *VERB* **disobeys**, **disobeying**, **disobeyed**
to disobey someone is to refuse to do what they tell you to do

disorder *NOUN* **disorders**
❶ disorder is confusion or disturbance
❷ a disorder is an illness, or a physical or mental condition that causes difficulties
➤ **disorderly** *ADJECTIVE* behaving in a wild and noisy way

dispatch *NOUN* **dispatches**
a report or message

dispatch *VERB* **dispatches**, **dispatching**, **dispatched**
to dispatch something or someone is to send them somewhere

dispense *VERB* **dispenses**, **dispensing**, **dispensed**
❶ to dispense something is to give it out to people • *The machine dispenses drinks and snacks.* ❷ to dispense medicine is to prepare it for patients
➤ **to dispense with something** is to do without it

dispenser *NOUN* **dispensers**
a device that gives you things, especially in special amounts • *There is a soap dispenser above each washbasin.*

disperse *VERB* **disperses**, **dispersing**, **dispersed**
❶ to disperse people is to send them away in various directions • *The police dispersed the crowd.* ❷ to disperse is to go off in various directions
➤ **dispersal** *NOUN*

displace *VERB* **displaces**, **displacing**, **displaced**
❶ to displace something is to move it from its place • *Some roof tiles had been displaced by the wind.* ❷ to displace someone is to take

their place • *Last year she displaced him as captain.*

display *VERB* **displays**, **displaying**, **displayed**
to display something is to arrange it so that it can be clearly seen

display *NOUN* **displays**
❶ a show or exhibition ❷ the showing of information on a computer screen

displease *VERB* **displeases**, **displeasing**, **displeased**
to displease someone is to annoy them

disposable *ADJECTIVE*
something that is disposable is made to be thrown away after it has been used

disposal *NOUN*
getting rid of something
➤ **at your disposal** ready for you to use

dispose *VERB* **disposes**, **disposing**, **disposed**
to be disposed to do something is to be ready and willing to do it • *They were not disposed to help us.*
➤ **to dispose of something** is to get rid of it

disposition *NOUN* **dispositions**
a person's nature or qualities • *He has a cheerful disposition.*

disprove *VERB* **disproves**, **disproving**, **disproved**
to disprove something is to prove that it is not true

dispute *NOUN* **disputes**
a quarrel or disagreement

disqualify *VERB* **disqualifies**, **disqualifying**, **disqualified**
to disqualify someone is to remove them from a race or competition because they have broken the rules
➤ **disqualification** *NOUN*

disregard *VERB* **disregards**, **disregarding**, **disregarded**
to disregard someone or something is to take no notice of them

disrespect *NOUN*
lack of respect; rudeness
➤ **disrespectful** *ADJECTIVE*
➤ **disrespectfully** *ADVERB*

disrupt *VERB* **disrupts**, **disrupting**, **disrupted**
to disrupt something is to stop it running smoothly or throw it into confusion • *Floods have disrupted local traffic.*
➤ **disruption** *NOUN* ➤ **disruptive** *ADJECTIVE*

dissatisfied *ADJECTIVE*
not satisfied or pleased
➤ **dissatisfaction** *NOUN*

dissect *VERB* **dissects**, **dissecting**, **dissected**
to dissect something is to cut it up so that you can examine it
➤ **dissection** *NOUN*

dissolve *VERB* **dissolves**, **dissolving**, **dissolved**
❶ to dissolve something is to mix it with a liquid so that it becomes part of the liquid ❷ to dissolve is to melt or become liquid
As the book sank into the green sea the ink dissolved from its pages. And as each page washed blank, the spell written upon it was broken.—THE BRAVE WHALE, Alan Temperley

dissuade *VERB* **dissuades**, **dissuading**, **dissuaded**
to dissuade someone is to persuade them not to do something

distance *NOUN* **distances**
the amount of space between two places or things
➤ **in the distance** a long way off but able to be seen

distant *ADJECTIVE*
❶ far away ❷ a person who is distant is not friendly or sociable

distil *VERB* **distils**, **distilling**, **distilled**
to distil a liquid is to purify it by boiling it and condensing the vapour

distillery *NOUN* **distilleries**
a place where spirits such as whisky are produced

distinct *ADJECTIVE*
❶ easily heard or seen; clear or definite • *You have made a distinct improvement.* ❷ clearly separate or different • *A rabbit is quite distinct from a hare.*
➤ **distinctly** *ADVERB*

distinction *NOUN* **distinctions**
❶ a distinction is a clear difference between two things ❷ distinction is excellence or

honour • *She is a writer of distinction.*
❸ a distinction is also a high mark in an examination

distinctive *ADJECTIVE*
clearly different from all the others and easy to recognize or notice • *The school has a distinctive blue football strip.*

distinguish *VERB* **distinguishes**, **distinguishing**, **distinguished**
❶ to distinguish things is to notice the differences between them ❷ to distinguish something is to see or hear it clearly

distinguished *ADJECTIVE*
famous, successful and much admired by other people • *There was a distinguished scientist visiting the school.*

distort *VERB* **distorts**, **distorting**, **distorted**
❶ to distort something is to change it into a strange shape • *His face was distorted with anger.* ❷ to distort facts is to change them so that they are untrue or misleading
➤ **distortion** *NOUN*

distract *VERB* **distracts**, **distracting**, **distracted**
to distract someone is to take their attention away from what they are doing • *Don't distract the bus driver.*
➤ **distraction** *NOUN*

distress *NOUN*
great sorrow, suffering or trouble
➤ **in distress** a ship or plane is in distress when it is in difficulty and needs help

distress *VERB* **distresses**, **distressing**, **distressed**
to distress someone is to make them feel very upset or worried

distribute *VERB* **distributes**, **distributing**, **distributed**
❶ to distribute things is to give them out or deliver them • *She distributed copies of the exam paper.* ❷ to distribute something is to share it among a number of people • *The money was distributed among all the local schools.* ❸ to distribute something is also to spread or scatter it around • *Make sure your weight is evenly distributed.*
➤ **distribution** *NOUN*

a
b
c
d
e
f
g
h
i
j
k
l
m
n
o
p
q
r
s
t
u
v
w
x
y
z

district *NOUN* **districts**
part of a town or country

distrust *NOUN*
lack of trust; suspicion
➤ **distrustful** *ADJECTIVE* not trusting people
distrust *VERB* **distrusts, distrusting, distrusted**
to think that someone or something cannot be trusted

disturb *VERB* **disturbs, disturbing, disturbed**
❶ to disturb someone is to interrupt them or spoil their peace ❷ to disturb someone is also to worry or upset them ❸ to disturb something is to move it from its right position
➤ **disturbance** *NOUN*

disused *ADJECTIVE*
no longer used • *The house was next to a disused warehouse.*

ditch *NOUN* **ditches**
a narrow trench to hold or carry away water

dither *VERB* **dithers, dithering, dithered**
to dither is to hesitate nervously

ditto *NOUN*
the same again

divan *NOUN* **divans**
a bed or couch without a raised back or sides

dive *VERB* **dives, diving, dived**
❶ to dive is to go into water head first ❷ to dive is also to move downwards quickly • *The aeroplane then dived.*

diver *NOUN* **divers**
❶ a swimmer who dives ❷ someone who works under water using special breathing equipment ❸ a bird that dives for its food

diverse *ADJECTIVE*
very different from each other and of several different kinds • *He has a diverse collection of comics.*
➤ **diversity** *NOUN*

diversion *NOUN* **diversions**
❶ a different way for traffic to go when the usual road is closed ❷ something amusing or entertaining

divert *VERB* **diverts, diverting, diverted**
❶ to divert something is to change the

direction it is moving in ❷ to divert someone is to amuse or entertain them

divide *VERB* **divides, dividing, divided**
❶ to divide something is to separate it into smaller parts or shares ❷ (*mathematics*) to divide a number by another number is to find out how many times the second number is contained in the first • *Divide six by two and you get three (6 ÷ 2 = 3).*

dividend *NOUN* **dividends**
a share in the profit a business makes

divine *ADJECTIVE*
❶ belonging to God or coming from God ❷ like a god ❸ (*informal*) excellent; extremely beautiful
➤ **divinity** *NOUN*
divine *VERB* **divines, divining, divined**
to divine something is to discover it by guessing or instinct

division *NOUN* **divisions**
❶ the process of dividing numbers or things ❷ a dividing line or partition ❸ one of the parts into which something is divided

divorce *NOUN* **divorces**
the legal ending of a marriage
divorce *VERB* **divorces, divorcing, divorced**
two people divorce when they end their marriage by law

Diwali (*say* di-**wah**-lee) *NOUN*
a Hindu festival at which lamps are lit, held in October or November

DIY *ABBREVIATION*
short for *do-it-yourself*

dizzy *ADJECTIVE* **dizzier, dizziest**
giddy and feeling confused
➤ **dizzily** *ADVERB* ➤ **dizziness** *NOUN*

DNA *NOUN*
the chemical substance which makes up your genes

do *VERB* **does, doing, did, done**
❶ to do something is to perform it or deal with it • *Are you doing your work?* • *I can't do this sum.* ❷ to do well is to manage; to do badly is not to manage very well ❸ you say that something will do

when it is all right or suitable • *I'd really like some football boots but trainers will do.*
❹ you also use **do** with other verbs in special ways • *Do you want this? • He does not want it. • I do like crisps. • We work as hard as they do.*
➤ **to do away with something** (*informal*) is to get rid of it
➤ **to do something up** is to fasten it • *Do up your coat.*
➤ **to do without something** is to manage without having it

docile *ADJECTIVE*
gentle and obedient

dock *NOUN* **docks**
❶ a part of a harbour where ships are loaded, unloaded or repaired ❷ a place for the prisoner on trial in a law court ❸ dock is also a weed with broad leaves

dock *VERB* **docks**, **docking**, **docked**
❶ a ship docks when it comes into a dock
❷ spacecraft dock when they join together in orbit ❸ to dock an animal's tail is to cut it short ❹ to dock someone's pay is to take something off it as a penalty

docker *NOUN* **dockers**
a person whose job is loading and unloading ships

dockyard *NOUN* **dockyards**
an open area with docks and equipment for building or repairing ships

doctor *NOUN* **doctors**
a person trained to heal sick or injured people

doctrine (*say* dok-trin) *NOUN* **doctrines**
a religious or political belief

document *NOUN* **documents**
❶ an important written or printed piece of paper ❷ something stored in a computer or on a disk, such as a piece of text or a picture
➤ **documentation** *NOUN* a collection of documents

documentary *NOUN* **documentaries**
a film or a television programme that tells you about real events or situations

doddery *ADJECTIVE*
someone who is doddery is shaking or unsteady because they are old

doddle *NOUN* (*informal*)
you say that something is a doddle when it is very easy to do • *My piano test was a doddle.*

dodge *VERB* **dodges**, **dodging**, **dodged**
to dodge something is to move quickly to avoid it

dodge *NOUN* **dodges**
❶ a dodging movement ❷ a trick; a clever way of doing something

dodgem *NOUN* **dodgems**
a small, electrically driven car at a fair, in which you drive round an enclosure, dodging and bumping other cars

dodgy *ADJECTIVE* **dodgier**, **dodgiest** (*informal*)
❶ awkward or tricky ❷ dishonest or not reliable

dodo *NOUN* **dodos**
an extinct bird with a large hooked beak that was unable to fly

doe *NOUN* **does**
a female deer, rabbit or hare

does (*3rd singular present tense of* **do**)
• *She does what she likes.*

doesn't
short for *does not* • *It doesn't matter.*

dog *NOUN* **dogs**
a four-legged animal that barks, often kept as a pet
➤ A related adjective is **canine**.

dog-eared *ADJECTIVE*
a dog-eared book has the corners of its pages bent or worn because it has been read so much

dogged (*say* dog-id) *ADJECTIVE*
not giving up in spite of difficulties; obstinate
➤ **doggedly** *ADVERB*

do-it-yourself *ADJECTIVE*
suitable for anyone to make or use at home, rather than paying for someone else to do it

doldrums *PLURAL NOUN*
the ocean regions near the equator, where there is little or no wind
➤ **in the doldrums** bored and unhappy

a b c d e f g h i j k l m n o p q r s t u v w x y z

A
B
C
D
E
F
G
H
I
J
K
L
M
N
O
P
Q
R
S
T
U
V
W
X
Y
Z

dole *NOUN (informal)*
the dole is money paid by the government to unemployed people

doll *NOUN* **dolls**
a toy model of a person, especially a baby or child

dollar *NOUN* **dollars**
the main unit of money in the USA, Canada, Australia and several other countries

dollop *NOUN* **dollops**
a soft pile or scoop of something • *a dollop of ice cream*

dolly *NOUN* **dollies** *(informal)*
a doll

dolphin *NOUN* **dolphins**
a sea mammal like a small whale with a snout like a beak

domain *NOUN* **domains**
an area that is ruled or controlled by someone

dome *NOUN* **domes**
a roof shaped like the top half of a ball

domestic *ADJECTIVE*
❶ to do with the home ❷ a domestic animal is tame and kept at home

domesticated *ADJECTIVE*
❶ a domesticated animal is trained to live with people ❷ a domesticated person enjoys household work and home life

dominant *ADJECTIVE*
most powerful or important
➤ **dominance** *NOUN*

dominate *VERB* **dominates**, **dominating**, **dominated**
to dominate people is to control them by being the most powerful
➤ **domination** *NOUN*

dominion *NOUN* **dominions**
❶ rule or authority ❷ an area ruled by one ruler

domino *NOUN* **dominoes**
a small oblong piece of wood or plastic with dots (1 to 6) or a blank space at each end, used in the game of **dominoes**

donate *VERB* **donates**, **donating**, **donated**
to donate something, especially money, is to give it to a charity or organization
➤ **donation** *NOUN*

done *VERB (past participle of* **do***)*
• *I have done nothing wrong.*

donkey *NOUN* **donkeys**
an animal that looks like a small horse with long ears

donor *NOUN* **donors**
someone who gives something • *New blood donors are needed.*

don't
short for *do not* • *Don't ask me again.*

doodle *NOUN* **doodles**
a quick drawing or scribble

doodle *VERB* **doodles**, **doodling**, **doodled**
to doodle is to draw a doodle
I get my felt tips and doodle all around my name, drawing a little sun on one side and a cloud with raindrops on the other.—LITTLE DARLINGS, Jacqueline Wilson

doom *NOUN*
a grim fate like ruin or death

doom *VERB* **dooms**, **dooming**, **doomed**
to be doomed to something is to have a grim fate you cannot avoid

door *NOUN* **doors**
a movable panel that opens and closes the entrance to a room, building or cupboard

doorbell *NOUN* **doorbells**
a bell outside a house that visitors ring to gain entry • *No one answered the doorbell.*

doorstep *NOUN* **doorsteps**
the step or piece of ground outside a door

doorway *NOUN* **doorways**
the opening into which a door fits

dopey *ADJECTIVE* **dopier**, **dopiest** *(informal)*
❶ half asleep ❷ stupid

dormant *ADJECTIVE*
sleeping or inactive • *a dormant volcano*

dormitory *NOUN* **dormitories**
a room for several people to sleep in, especially in a school

dormouse *NOUN* **dormice**
an animal like a large mouse that hibernates in winter

dorsal *ADJECTIVE*
a dorsal fin or spine is on the back of an animal

dose *NOUN* **doses**
the amount of a medicine that you are meant to take at one time

dossier (*say* **doss**-i-er *or* **doss**-i-ay) *NOUN* **dossiers**
a set of documents with information about a person or event

dot *NOUN* **dots**
a tiny spot

dot *VERB* **dots**, **dotting**, **dotted**
to dot something is to mark it with dots

dotty *ADJECTIVE* **dottier**, **dottiest** (*informal*)
crazy or silly

double *ADJECTIVE*
❶ twice as much or twice as many ❷ having two of something • *double doors* ❸ suitable for two people • *a double bed*

double *NOUN* **doubles**
❶ double is twice the amount or cost ❷ a double is someone who looks like someone else ❸ you play doubles in tennis when you play with someone else against another pair of players

double *VERB* **doubles**, **doubling**, **doubled**
❶ to double something is to make it twice as big ❷ to double is to become twice as big
➤ **to double up** is to bend over because you are in pain or laughing so much

double bass *NOUN* **double basses**
a musical instrument with strings, like a large cello

double-cross *VERB* **double-crosses**, **double-crossing**, **double-crossed**
to double-cross someone is to cheat or betray them when you are supposed to be supporting them

double-decker *NOUN* **double-deckers**
a bus with two floors, one above the other

doubloon (*say* du-**bloon**) *NOUN* **doubloons**
an old Spanish gold coin

doubly *ADVERB*
twice as much • *It's doubly important that you should go.*

doubt *NOUN* **doubts**
not feeling sure about something
doubt *VERB* **doubts**, **doubting**, **doubted**
to doubt something is to feel unsure about it • *I doubt whether he is telling the truth.*

doubtful *ADJECTIVE*
❶ having doubts • *She looked doubtful.*
❷ making you feel doubt • *Their story was very doubtful.*
➤ **doubtfully** *ADVERB*

doubtless *ADVERB*
certainly; without any doubt

dough *NOUN*
a thick mixture of flour and water used for making bread or pastry

doughnut *NOUN* **doughnuts**
a round or ring-shaped bun that has been fried and covered with sugar

doughy *ADJECTIVE* **doughier**, **doughiest**
thick and sticky like dough

dove *NOUN* **doves**
a kind of pigeon, often used as a symbol of peace

dowel *NOUN* **dowels**
a wooden or metal pin for holding together two pieces of wood or stone

down *ADVERB*, *PREPOSITION*
❶ to or in a lower place • *One of the shelves fell down.* • *The sledge sped down the hill.* ❷ along • *We're going down to the shops.*
down *NOUN*
very soft feathers or hair • *Ducks are covered with down.*
➤ **downy** *ADJECTIVE* soft like down

downcast *ADJECTIVE*
❶ looking downward • *Her eyes were downcast.* ❷ sad or dejected

downfall *NOUN* **downfalls**
❶ a person's downfall is their ruin or fall from power ❷ a heavy fall of rain or snow

a
b
c
d
e
f
g
h
i
j
k
l
m
n
o
p
q
r
s
t
u
v
w
x
y
z

downhill *ADVERB*
down a slope

download *VERB* **downloads, downloading, downloaded**
to download data is to transfer it from the internet to a computer or phone

download *NOUN* **downloads**
data that has been downloaded

downpour *NOUN* **downpours**
a heavy fall of rain

downright *ADJECTIVE*
complete, total • *a downright lie*

downright *ADVERB*
thoroughly, extremely • *I felt downright angry about it.*

downs *PLURAL NOUN*
grass-covered hills • *Let's have a picnic on the downs.*

downstairs *ADVERB, ADJECTIVE*
to or on a lower floor

downstream *ADVERB*
in the direction that a river or stream flows

downward, downwards *ADJECTIVE, ADVERB*
going towards what is lower

doze *VERB* **dozes, dozing, dozed**
to doze is to sleep lightly • *My cat likes dozing on top of my bed.*

dozen *NOUN* **dozens**
a set of twelve

dozy *ADJECTIVE* **dozier, doziest**
when you are dozy you are feeling sleepy
➤ **doziness** *NOUN*

Dr *ABBREVIATION*
short for *Doctor* in titles, for example *Dr Doolittle*

drab *ADJECTIVE* **drabber, drabbest**
❶ dull and without colour • *His clothes were drab.* ❷ dreary and uninteresting

draft *NOUN* **drafts**
a rough plan for something you are going to write

draft *VERB* **drafts, drafting, drafted**
to draft something you are going to write is to make a rough plan of it

drag *VERB* **drags, dragging, dragged**
❶ to drag something heavy is to pull it along ❷ to drag a river or lake is to search it with nets and hooks ❸ to drag a computer file or image is to move it by clicking on it with the mouse and moving the mouse while holding the button down

drag *NOUN* (*informal*)
something annoying or tedious

dragon *NOUN* **dragons** (*in stories*)
a winged lizard-like monster that breathes fire

dragonfly *NOUN* **dragonflies**
an insect with a long body and two pairs of transparent wings

drain *NOUN* **drains**
❶ a pipe or ditch for taking away water or sewage ❷ something that uses up your strength or money

drain *VERB* **drains, draining, drained**
❶ to drain water is to take it away with drains ❷ to drain is to flow or trickle away ❸ to drain a glass or bottle is to empty liquid out of it ❹ to drain someone is to exhaust them
➤ **drainage** *NOUN*

drake *NOUN* **drakes**
a male duck

drama *NOUN* **dramas**
❶ drama is writing or performing plays ❷ a drama is a play ❸ a drama is also a series of exciting events

dramatic *ADJECTIVE*
❶ to do with drama ❷ exciting and impressive • *A dramatic change has taken place.*
➤ **dramatically** *ADVERB*

dramatics *PLURAL NOUN*
performing plays

dramatist *NOUN* **dramatists**
someone who writes plays

dramatize (*also* **dramatise**) *VERB* **dramatizes, dramatizing, dramatized**
❶ to dramatize a story is to make it into a play ❷ to dramatize an event is to exaggerate it • *Why do you always dramatize everything?*
➤ **dramatization** *NOUN*

drank VERB (*past tense of* **drink**)
• *Grandad drank his tea.*

drape VERB **drapes**, **draping**, **draped**
to drape something like cloth is to hang it loosely over something

drastic ADJECTIVE
having a strong or violent effect
➤ **drastically** ADVERB

draught (*rhymes with* **craft**) NOUN **draughts**
a current of cold air indoors
➤ **draughty** ADJECTIVE

draughts NOUN
a game played with 24 round pieces on a chessboard

draughtsman, **draughtswoman** NOUN **draughtsmen**, **draughtswomen**
a person whose job is to draw plans

draw VERB **draws**, **drawing**, **drew**, **drawn**
❶ to draw a picture or outline is to form it with a pencil or pen ❷ to draw something is to pull it • *She drew her chair up to the table.* ❸ to draw people is to attract them • *The fair drew large crowds.* ❹ to draw is to end a game or contest with the same score on both sides • *They drew 2-2 last Saturday.* ❺ to draw the curtains is to open or close them ❻ to draw near is to come nearer • *The ship was drawing nearer.*

draw NOUN **draws**
❶ a raffle or similar competition in which the winner is chosen by picking tickets or numbers at random ❷ a game that ends with the same score on both sides ❸ an attraction

drawback NOUN **drawbacks**
a disadvantage

drawbridge NOUN **drawbridges**
a bridge over a moat, hinged at one end so that it can be raised or lowered

drawer NOUN **drawers**
a sliding box-like container in a piece of furniture

drawing NOUN **drawings**
something drawn with a pencil or pen

drawing pin NOUN **drawing pins**
a short pin with a large flat top that you use for fixing paper to a surface

drawl VERB **drawls**, **drawling**, **drawled**
to speak very slowly or lazily

dread VERB **dreads**, **dreading**, **dreaded**
to dread something is to fear it very much
dread NOUN
great fear

dreadful ADJECTIVE
very bad • *We've had dreadful weather.*
➤ **dreadfully** ADVERB

dreadlocks PLURAL NOUN
hair in long, tightly curled ringlets, originally worn by Rastafarians

dream NOUN **dreams**
❶ things you seem to see while you are sleeping ❷ something you imagine; an ambition or ideal • *His dream is to be famous.*
➤ **dreamy** ADJECTIVE like a dream; not real
dream VERB **dreams**, **dreaming**, **dreamt** or **dreamed**
❶ to dream is to have a dream ❷ to dream is also to want something badly • *She dreams of being a ballet dancer.* ❸ to dream something is to think it may happen • *I never dreamt she would leave.*

dreary ADJECTIVE **drearier**, **dreariest**
❶ dull or boring ❷ gloomy
➤ **dreariness** NOUN

dredge VERB **dredges**, **dredging**, **dredged**
to dredge something is to drag it up, especially mud from the bottom of water
➤ **dredger** NOUN

drench VERB **drenches**, **drenching**, **drenched**
to drench someone or something is to soak them • *They got drenched in the rain.*

dress NOUN **dresses**
❶ a dress is a piece of clothing with a top and skirt in one piece ❷ dress is clothes or costume • *We have to wear fancy dress.*
dress VERB **dresses**, **dressing**, **dressed**
❶ to dress is to put clothes on ❷ to dress a wound is to put a bandage or plaster on it

❸ to dress food is to prepare it for cooking or eating

dresser *NOUN* **dressers**
a sideboard with shelves at the top

dressing *NOUN* **dressings**
❶ a sauce of oil, vinegar and spices for a salad **❷** a bandage or plaster used to cover a wound

dressing gown *NOUN* **dressing gowns**
a loose light indoor coat you wear over pyjamas or a nightdress

dressmaker *NOUN* **dressmakers**
a person whose job is to make clothes

drew *VERB* (*past tense of* **draw**)
• *Toby drew in a deep breath.*

dribble *VERB* **dribbles, dribbling, dribbled**
❶ to dribble is to let saliva trickle out of your mouth **❷** to dribble is also to kick a ball gently in front of you as you run forward

dried *VERB* (*past tense and past participle of* **dry**)
• *He dried himself with a towel.* • *The mud had dried on his shoes.*

drier *NOUN* **driers**
a device for drying hair or washing

drift *VERB* **drifts, drifting, drifted**
❶ to drift is to be carried gently along by water or air **❷** to drift is also to live casually or wander about without any real plan or purpose

drift *NOUN* **drifts**
❶ a drifting movement **❷** a mass of snow or sand piled up by the wind **❸** the general meaning of what someone says • *Do you get my drift?*

driftwood *NOUN*
wood floating on the sea or washed ashore

drill *NOUN* **drills**
❶ a tool for making holes **❷** repeated exercises in military training, gymnastics or sport **❸** a set way of doing something • *Do you know the drill?*

drill *VERB* **drills, drilling, drilled**
❶ to drill a hole is to make a hole with a drill **❷** to drill is to do repeated exercises

drink *VERB* **drinks, drinking, drank, drunk**
❶ to drink is to swallow liquid **❷** to drink can also mean to have a lot of alcohol • *Don't drink and drive.*

drink *NOUN* **drinks**
❶ a liquid for drinking **❷** an alcoholic drink

drip *VERB* **drips, dripping, dripped**
❶ to drip is to fall in drops **❷** to drip is also to let liquid fall in drops • *The tap was dripping.*

drip *NOUN* **drips**
a falling drop of liquid

dripping *NOUN*
fat that melts from roasted meat and is allowed to set

drive *VERB* **drives, driving, drove, driven**
❶ to drive a vehicle is to operate it **❷** to drive someone or something is to make them move **❸** to drive someone into a state or feeling is to force them into it • *That music is driving me mad!*
➤ **driver** *NOUN*

drive *NOUN* **drives**
❶ a drive is a journey in a vehicle **❷** drive is energy and enthusiasm **❸** a drive is a road leading to a house **❹** a drive is a powerful stroke of the ball in cricket, golf and other games

drizzle *NOUN*
gentle rain

drizzle *VERB* **drizzles, drizzling, drizzled**
to rain gently

drone *VERB* **drones, droning, droned**
❶ to drone is to make a low humming sound **❷** you can also say that someone drones when they talk in a boring voice

drone *NOUN* **drones**
❶ a droning sound **❷** a male bee **❸** a small flying robot that a person controls from the ground

drool *VERB* **drools, drooling, drooled**
to drool is to dribble continuously

droop *VERB* **droops, drooping, drooped**
to hang down weakly

drop *NOUN* **drops**
❶ a tiny amount of liquid **❷** a fall or decrease • *There has been a sharp drop in attendance.*

drop *VERB* **drops, dropping, dropped**
❶ to drop is to fall **❷** to drop something is to

let it fall ❸ to drop is also to become less or lower • *The temperature suddenly dropped.*
➤ **to drop in** is to visit someone casually
➤ **to drop out** is to stop taking part in something

droplet *NOUN* **droplets**
a small drop

drought (*rhymes with* **out**) *NOUN* **droughts**
a long period of dry weather

drove *VERB* (*past tense of* **drive**)
• *Uncle Gareth drove them all the way home.*

drown *VERB* **drowns**, **drowning**, **drowned**
❶ to drown is to die from being under water and unable to breathe ❷ to drown a person or animal is to kill them by forcing them to stay under water ❸ to drown sounds is to make so much noise that they cannot be heard

drowsy *ADJECTIVE* **drowsier**, **drowsiest**
sleepy
➤ **drowsily** *ADVERB* ➤ **drowsiness** *NOUN*

drug *NOUN* **drugs**
❶ a substance that kills pain or cures a disease ❷ a substance that people take because it affects their senses or their mind. Some drugs cause addiction or are illegal.

drug *VERB* **drugs**, **drugging**, **drugged**
to drug someone is to make them unconscious with drugs

Druid *NOUN* **Druids**
a priest of an ancient religion in Britain and France

drum *NOUN* **drums**
❶ a musical instrument made of a cylinder with a thin skin stretched over one end or both ends ❷ a cylindrical container • *There was a row of oil drums along the side of the road.*

drum *VERB* **drums**, **drumming**, **drummed**
❶ to drum is to play a drum or drums ❷ to drum on something is to tap it repeatedly • *He drummed his fingers on the table.*
➤ **drummer** *NOUN*

drumstick *NOUN* **drumsticks**
❶ a stick used for hitting a drum ❷ the lower part of a cooked bird's leg

drunk *VERB* (*past participle of* **drink**)
• *Somebody has drunk all the juice.*

drunk *ADJECTIVE*
not able to control your behaviour through drinking too much alcohol

drunk *NOUN* **drunks**
someone who is drunk

dry *ADJECTIVE* **drier**, **driest**
❶ not wet or damp ❷ boring and dull • *The book I'm reading is rather dry.* ❸ funny in a clever and sarcastic way • *He has a very dry sense of humour.*
➤ **drily** *ADVERB* ➤ **dryness** *NOUN*

dry *VERB* **dries**, **drying**, **dried**
❶ to dry is to become dry ❷ to dry something is to make it dry

dry-cleaning *NOUN*
a method of cleaning clothes using chemicals rather than water

dual *ADJECTIVE*
having two parts or aspects; double • *This building has a dual purpose.*

dual carriageway *NOUN* **dual carriageways**
a road with several lanes in each direction

dub *VERB* **dubs**, **dubbing**, **dubbed**
❶ to change or add new sound to the sound on a film • *It's a Japanese film but has been dubbed into English.* ❷ to give someone a name or title

dubious *ADJECTIVE*
❶ feeling doubtful or uncertain • *I'm dubious about our chances of winning.* ❷ probably not honest or not good

duchess *NOUN* **duchesses**
❶ a duke's wife or widow ❷ a woman whose rank is equal to that of a duke

duck *NOUN* **ducks**
a web-footed water bird with a flat beak

duck *VERB* **ducks**, **ducking**, **ducked**
❶ to duck is to bend down quickly to avoid something ❷ to duck someone is to push them under water quickly

duckling *NOUN* **ducklings**
a young duck

duct *NOUN* **ducts**
a tube or pipe

a b c d e f g h i j k l m n o p q r s t u v w x y z

due *ADJECTIVE*
❶ expected to arrive • *The train is due in five minutes.* ❷ needing to be paid • *Payment for the trip is due next week.*
➤ **due to something** *or* **someone** because of something or someone • *The traffic jam was due to an accident.*
➤ **in due course** eventually; at the expected time

due *ADVERB*
directly • *The camp is due north.*

duel *NOUN* **duels**
a fight between two people, especially with pistols or swords

duet *NOUN* **duets**
a piece of music for two players or two singers

duffel coat *NOUN* **duffel coats**
a thick overcoat with a hood

dug *VERB* (*past tense and past participle of* **dig**)
• *He dug in his pocket for some change.*
• *The dog has dug a hole in the lawn.*

dugout *NOUN* **dugouts**
❶ an underground shelter ❷ a canoe made by hollowing out a tree trunk

duke *NOUN* **dukes**
a member of the highest rank of noblemen

dull *ADJECTIVE* **duller**, **dullest**
❶ not bright or clear; gloomy • *It was a dull day.* ❷ boring • *What a dull programme.*
❸ not sharp • *I had a dull pain.* ❹ stupid
• *You are a dull boy.*
➤ **dully** *ADVERB* ➤ **dullness** *NOUN*

duly *ADVERB*
rightly; as expected • *They promised to come, and later they duly arrived.*

dumb *ADJECTIVE* **dumber**, **dumbest**
❶ unable to speak; silent ❷ (*informal*) stupid

dumbfounded *ADJECTIVE*
unable to say anything because you are so astonished

dummy *NOUN* **dummies**
❶ something made to look like a person or thing; an imitation ❷ an imitation teat for a baby to suck

dump *NOUN* **dumps**
❶ a place where something, especially rubbish, is left or stored ❷ (*informal*) if you call a place a dump, you do not like it

dump *VERB* **dumps**, **dumping**, **dumped**
❶ to dump something is to get rid of it when you do not want it ❷ to dump something somewhere is to put it down carelessly

dumpling *NOUN* **dumplings**
a lump of boiled or baked dough

dumpy *ADJECTIVE* **dumpier**, **dumpiest**
short and fat

dune *NOUN* **dunes**
a hill of loose sand formed by the wind

dung *NOUN*
solid waste matter from an animal

dungarees *PLURAL NOUN*
trousers with a piece in front covering your chest, held up by straps over your shoulders

dungeon (*say* **dun**-jon) *NOUN* **dungeons**
an underground prison cell

dunk *VERB* **dunks**, **dunking**, **dunked**
to dunk something is to dip it into a liquid

duo *NOUN* **duos**
a pair of people, especially playing music

duplicate (*say* **dew**-pli-kat) *NOUN* **duplicates**
something that is exactly the same as something else; an exact copy

duplicate (*say* **dew**-pli-kayt) *VERB* **duplicates**, **duplicating**, **duplicated**
to duplicate something is to make an exact copy of it
➤ **duplication** *NOUN*

durable *ADJECTIVE*
lasting and strong

duration *NOUN*
the time something lasts

during *PREPOSITION*
while something else is going on • *Let's see each other during the holidays.*

dusk *NOUN*
the time of the day just after sunset when it is starting to get dark

dust *NOUN*
a fine powder made up of tiny pieces of dry earth or other material

dust *VERB* **dusts**, **dusting**, **dusted**
1 to dust things is to clear the dust off them
2 to dust something is to sprinkle it with dust or powder • *You can dust the cake with sugar.*

dustbin *NOUN* **dustbins**
a bin for household rubbish

duster *NOUN* **dusters**
a cloth for dusting things

dustpan *NOUN* **dustpans**
a pan into which you brush dust

dusty *ADJECTIVE* **dustier**, **dustiest**
covered with or full of dust

Dutch *ADJECTIVE*
to do with the Netherlands or its people

Dutch *NOUN*
the main language of the Netherlands
DID YOU KNOW? The words **easel**, **wagon** and **yacht** come from Dutch.

dutiful *ADJECTIVE*
doing your duty; obedient
➤ **dutifully** *ADVERB*

duty *NOUN* **duties**
1 your duty is what you have to do, perhaps as part of your job **2** a duty is a kind of tax

duvet (*say* **doo**-vay) *NOUN* **duvets**
a thick quilt used instead of other bedclothes

DVD *NOUN* **DVDs**
short for *digital versatile disc*, a disc on which large amounts of sound and pictures can be stored, especially films

DVD player *NOUN* **DVD players**
a machine for playing DVDs

dwarf *NOUN* **dwarfs** *or* **dwarves**
(may be considered offensive) a very small person or thing

dwarf *VERB* **dwarfs**, **dwarfing**, **dwarfed**
to dwarf something is to make it seem very small • *The skyscraper dwarfs all the buildings round it.*

dwell *VERB* **dwells**, **dwelling**, **dwelt**
to dwell in a place is to live there
➤ **to dwell on something** is to think or talk about it constantly

dwelling *NOUN* **dwellings**
a house or other place to live in

dwindle *VERB* **dwindles**, **dwindling**, **dwindled**
to get smaller gradually
A trickle of woodsmoke from the Schloss chimneys slowly dwindled to a thin line, etching a message of embers and ash across the night sky.—PURE DEAD MAGIC, Debi Gliori

dye *VERB* **dyes**, **dyeing**, **dyed**
to dye something is to change its colour by putting it in a special liquid

dye *NOUN* **dyes**
a liquid used to dye things

dying *VERB* (*present participle of* **die**)
• *The wind is dying down.*
➤ **to be dying to do something** is to be very eager to do it • *I'm dying to see the film.*

dyke *NOUN* **dykes**
1 a long wall or embankment to hold back water and prevent flooding **2** a ditch for draining water from land

dynamic *ADJECTIVE*
energetic and active
➤ **dynamically** *ADVERB*

dynamite *NOUN*
a powerful explosive

dynamo *NOUN* **dynamos**
a machine that makes electricity

dynasty (*say* **din**-a-stee) *NOUN* **dynasties**
a series of kings and queens from the same family

dyslexia (*say* dis-**lek**-si-a) *NOUN*
a specific learning difficulty that can cause problems with reading and writing but does not affect general intelligence

dyslexic (*say* dis-**lek**-sik) *ADJECTIVE*
to do with or having dyslexia

a
b
c
d
e
f
g
h
i
j
k
l
m
n
o
p
q
r
s
t
u
v
w
x
y
z

Ee

each *DETERMINER, PRONOUN*
each person or thing in a group is every one of them when you think of them separately • *Each film lasts an hour.* • *You get ten marks for each of these questions.* • *We all knew each other.*

eager *ADJECTIVE*
badly wanting to do something or to have something; enthusiastic • *I'm eager to read the sequel.*
➤ **eagerly** *ADVERB* ➤ **eagerness** *NOUN*

eagle *NOUN* **eagles**
a large bird of prey with strong eyesight

eagle-eyed *ADJECTIVE*
an eagle-eyed person has strong eyesight

ear *NOUN* **ears**
❶ the part of your body that you hear with ❷ someone with an ear, or a good ear, for something is able to hear it clearly and understand it well • *She has a very good ear for music.* ❸ an ear is also the spike of seeds at the top of a stalk of corn

earache *NOUN*
a pain inside your ear

eardrum *NOUN* **eardrums**
a membrane in the ear that vibrates when sound reaches it

earl *NOUN* **earls**
a British nobleman

earlobe *NOUN* **earlobes**
the rounded part that hangs down at the bottom of your ear

early *ADVERB, ADJECTIVE* **earlier, earliest**
❶ arriving or happening before the usual or expected time • *I'm getting picked up early from school today.* ❷ happening near the beginning • *The team was helped by an early goal.* • *They became friends early in their lives.*

earmark *VERB* **earmarks, earmarking, earmarked**
to earmark something, especially money, is to put it aside for a special purpose

earn *VERB* **earns, earning, earned**
❶ to earn money is to get it by working for it ❷ to earn a reward or praise is to do something good so that you deserve it

earnest *ADJECTIVE*
serious about something you want to do or about something important
➤ **earnestly** *ADVERB*

earnings *PLURAL NOUN*
earnings are money that someone earns

earphones *PLURAL NOUN*
earphones are a set of two small speakers that fit over your ears so that you can listen to music without other people hearing it

earplugs *PLURAL NOUN*
earplugs are a pair of small plugs that fit into your ears to cut out loud sounds

earring *NOUN* **earrings**
an ornament worn on the ear

earshot *NOUN*
a sound is in earshot when it is close enough for you to be able to hear it

earth *NOUN* **earths**
❶ the earth is the planet that we live on ❷ earth is soil or the ground ❸ an earth is a hole or burrow where a fox or badger lives ❹ an earth is also a connection to the ground to complete an electric circuit
➤ you use **on earth** with words like *what, who* and *where* to make the point stronger • *What on earth are you doing?*

earthly *ADJECTIVE*
to do with life on earth

earthquake *NOUN* **earthquakes**
a violent movement of part of the earth's surface caused by pressure that has built up underneath

earthworm *NOUN* **earthworms**
a common worm that is found in the soil

earthy *ADJECTIVE* **earthier, earthiest**
like earth or soil • *The cave had a damp, earthy smell.*
➤ **earthiness** *NOUN*

earwig NOUN **earwigs**
a crawling garden insect with pincers at the end of its body
DID YOU KNOW? The word **earwig** means 'ear insect', because people used to believe that earwigs crawled into their ears.

ease NOUN
to do something with ease is to do it without any difficulty or trouble
➤ **to be at ease** is to be comfortable and relaxed • *They liked each other and felt at ease together.*

ease VERB **eases**, **easing**, **eased**
❶ to ease something unpleasant is to make it easier or less troublesome ❷ a pain or problem eases when it becomes less severe or troublesome ❸ to ease something is to move it gently into position

easel NOUN **easels**
a stand or frame for holding a painting so an artist can work on it

easily ADVERB
❶ without difficulty; with ease • *Pencil marks can be easily rubbed out afterwards.* ❷ by far • *This was easily the best victory of his career.* ❸ very likely • *They could easily be wrong.*

east NOUN
❶ the direction in which the sun rises ❷ the part of a country or city that is in this direction

east ADJECTIVE, ADVERB
❶ towards the east or in the east ❷ coming from the east • *An east wind made the day very cold.*

Easter NOUN
a Christian festival in spring, commemorating Christ's rising from the dead

Easter egg NOUN **Easter eggs**
a painted or chocolate egg given as a gift at Easter

easterly ADJECTIVE
an easterly wind is one that blows from the east

eastern ADJECTIVE
coming from or to do with the east

eastward, **eastwards** ADJECTIVE, ADVERB
towards the east

easy ADJECTIVE **easier**, **easiest**
something easy can be done or understood without trouble • *I'll start with an easy question.* • *The camera is easy to use.*
➤ **to take it easy** is to relax or go carefully

eat VERB **eats**, **eating**, **ate**, **eaten**
❶ to eat food is to chew it and swallow it • *Koala bears eat eucalyptus leaves.* ❷ to eat is to have a meal • *Have you already eaten?*
➤ **to eat something up** is to use it up • *Social media can eat up a lot of time.*

eaves PLURAL NOUN
eaves are the overhanging edges of a roof

eavesdrop VERB **eavesdrops**, **eavesdropping**, **eavesdropped**
to eavesdrop on someone is to listen to their conversation in secret
Kat eavesdrops all the time. She lurks in the hallway when Mum and Dad are talking about serious matters such as school reports.—THE LONDON EYE MYSTERY, Siobhan Dowd

ebb NOUN
the movement of the tide when it is going out

ebb VERB **ebbs**, **ebbing**, **ebbed**
❶ the tide ebbs when it goes away from the land ❷ a good feeling ebbs or ebbs away when it becomes much weaker • *When he saw his opponent, his courage ebbed away.*

ebony NOUN
ebony is a hard black wood

e-book NOUN **e-books**
an electronic version of a printed book, which can be read on a computer, tablet or phone

eccentric (*say* ik-**sen**-trik) ADJECTIVE
behaving strangely
➤ **eccentricity** NOUN

echidna (*say* e-**kid**-nah) NOUN **echidnas**
an Australian animal like an anteater with sharp spines on its back

echo NOUN **echoes**
a second sound that you hear when the original sound is reflected off a hard surface such as walls or high rocks

echo VERB **echoes**, **echoing**, **echoed**
❶ to echo is to make an echo • *Their voices echoed around the cave.* ❷ to echo something said is to repeat it

a
b
c
d
e
f
g
h
i
j
k
l
m
n
o
p
q
r
s
t
u
v
w
x
y
z

eclair (*say* ay-klair) NOUN **eclairs**
a finger-shaped cake of pastry with a cream filling

eclipse NOUN **eclipses**
an eclipse is the blocking of light from the sun or moon, causing a short period of darkness. An **eclipse of the sun** happens when the moon comes between the sun and the earth, and an **eclipse of the moon** happens when the earth comes between the moon and the sun.

eco-friendly ADJECTIVE
not harmful to the natural environment • *We use eco-friendly washing-up liquid.*

ecology (*say* ee-kol-o-jee) NOUN
ecology is the study of living creatures and plants in their surroundings

economic (*say* eek-o-**nom**-ik *or* ek-o-**nom**-ik) ADJECTIVE
to do with economics or the economy

economical ADJECTIVE
using money and resources carefully
➤ **economically** ADVERB

economics (*say* eek-o-**nom**-iks *or* ek-o-**nom**-iks) NOUN
economics is the study of how money is used and how goods and services are provided and used

economist (*say* i-**kon**-o-mist) NOUN **economists**
someone who studies economics

economy (*say* i-**kon**-o-mee) NOUN **economies**
❶ an economy is a country's or family's income and the way it is spent ❷ economy is being careful with money ❸ economies are ways of saving money

ecstasy NOUN **ecstasies**
ecstasy is a feeling of great delight or joy
➤ **ecstatic** ADJECTIVE

eczema (*say* **ek**-si-ma) NOUN
eczema is a skin condition that causes rough itching patches

edge NOUN **edges**
❶ the part along the side or end of something ❷ the sharp part of a knife or other cutting device

➤ **to be on edge** is to feel nervous and irritable

edge VERB **edges**, **edging**, **edged**
❶ to edge is to move gradually and carefully • *He edged carefully round the puddles in the garden.* ❷ to edge something is to form a border to it

edgeways ADVERB
with the edge outwards or forwards

edgy ADJECTIVE **edgier**, **edgiest**
nervous and irritable • *Alex was feeling edgy all evening.*
➤ **edginess** NOUN

edible ADJECTIVE
an edible substance is one that you can eat, and is not poisonous • *Are those mushrooms edible?*

edit VERB **edits**, **editing**, **edited**
❶ to edit a book, newspaper or magazine is to get it ready for publishing ❷ to edit a film or tape recording is to choose parts of it and put them in the right order

edition NOUN **editions**
❶ the form in which something is published • *a new illustrated edition of the Harry Potter book* ❷ all the copies of a newspaper, magazine or book issued at the same time

editor NOUN **editors**
❶ someone who prepares a book, newspaper or magazine for publishing ❷ the person who manages a newspaper or magazine and is in charge of everything that is published in it

educate VERB **educates**, **educating**, **educated**
to educate someone is to teach them and give them knowledge and skills

education NOUN
education, or an education, is the process of teaching people and giving them knowledge and skills
➤ **educational** ADJECTIVE

eel NOUN **eels**
a long thin fish that looks like a snake

eerie ADJECTIVE **eerier**, **eeriest**
weird and frightening • *It was dark outside and there was an eerie silence.*
➤ **eerily** ADVERB ➤ **eeriness** NOUN

effect NOUN effects
❶ something that happens because of something else • *The drink had a strange effect on Alice.* ❷ a general impression • *The fairy lights give a cosy effect.*
SPELLING ALERT! Effect is different from **affect**, which is a verb: *The noise was starting to affect the cats.*

effective ADJECTIVE
producing what you want; successful • *Our fundraising campaign has been very effective this year.*
➤ **effectively** ADVERB ➤ **effectiveness** NOUN

effervescent (*say* ef-er-**vess**-ent) ADJECTIVE
an effervescent liquid is fizzy and gives off bubbles
➤ **effervescence** NOUN

efficient ADJECTIVE
doing work well; effective
➤ **efficiency** NOUN ➤ **efficiently** ADVERB

effort NOUN efforts
❶ effort is using energy or hard work
❷ an effort is an attempt • *That was my best effort so far.*

effortless ADJECTIVE
something that is effortless doesn't need much work or effort

e.g. ABBREVIATION
short for Latin *exempli gratia*, meaning 'for example' • *There are lots of ways to contact us, e.g. by phone, email or text.*

egg NOUN eggs
❶ an oval or round object with a thin shell that birds, fish, reptiles and insects lay, and in which their offspring develop ❷ a hen's or duck's egg used as food

egg VERB eggs, egging, egged
➤ **to egg someone on** is to encourage them with taunts or dares • *He didn't want to dance, but his friends egged him on.*

Egyptian (*say* ee-**jip**-shan) ADJECTIVE
to do with modern or ancient Egypt • *the tomb of an Egyptian pharaoh*

Egyptian NOUN Egyptians
a person from Egypt

Eid (*say* eed) NOUN
a Muslim festival that marks the end of the fast of Ramadan

eight NOUN eights
the number 8

eighteen NOUN eighteens
the number 18
➤ **eighteenth** ADJECTIVE, NOUN

eighth ADJECTIVE, NOUN
the next after the seventh
➤ **eighthly** ADVERB in the eighth place; as the eighth one

eighty NOUN eighties
the number 80
➤ **eightieth** ADJECTIVE, NOUN

either DETERMINER
❶ one or the other of two people or things • *Either road will take us there.* ❷ both of two things • *The houses on either side were all boarded up.*

either PRONOUN
one or the other of two people or things • *Either of them might have been lying.*

either ADVERB
also; similarly • *I didn't rush, but I didn't hang about either.*

either CONJUNCTION
➤ **either ... or ...** one thing or another, but not both • *We can get tickets for either Friday or Saturday.*

eject VERB ejects, ejecting, ejected
❶ to eject something is to send it out with force ❷ to eject someone is to make them leave

elaborate (*say* i-**lab**-er-at) ADJECTIVE
complicated or detailed

elastic NOUN
cord or material with strands of rubber in it so that it can stretch

elastic ADJECTIVE
able to stretch and then return to its original shape or length
➤ **elasticity** NOUN

elated ADJECTIVE
very pleased and excited

a b c d e f g h i j k l m n o p q r s t u v w x y z

elbow NOUN **elbows**
the joint in the middle of your arm, where it bends

elbow VERB **elbows, elbowing, elbowed**
to elbow someone is to push or prod them with your elbow

elder ADJECTIVE
older • *I didn't know you had an elder brother.*

elder NOUN **elders**
❶ an older person or relative ❷ a tree with white flowers and black berries

elderberry NOUN **elderberries**
a small black berry that grows on an elder tree

elderly ADJECTIVE
rather old

eldest ADJECTIVE
oldest • *Their eldest son George was born in 2017.*

elect VERB **elects, electing, elected**
to elect someone is to choose them by voting

election NOUN **elections**
the process of voting for people, especially to form a country's government

electorate NOUN
a country's electorate is all the people who can vote in an election

electric, electrical ADJECTIVE
to do with electricity, or worked by electricity
➤ **electrically** ADVERB

electrician NOUN **electricians**
someone whose job is to fit and repair electrical equipment

electricity NOUN
electricity is a kind of energy used to produce light and heat, and to make machines work

electrify VERB **electrifies, electrifying, electrified**
❶ to electrify something is to make it work by electricity, or to give it an electric charge
❷ to electrify someone is to excite or startle them • *Her singing electrified the audience.*
➤ **electrification** NOUN

electrocute VERB **electrocutes, electrocuting, electrocuted**
to electrocute someone is to kill them when a large charge of electricity passes through them
➤ **electrocution** NOUN

electronic ADJECTIVE
electronic equipment uses transistors and silicon chips
➤ **electronically** ADVERB

electronics NOUN
electronics is the use or study of electronic devices

elegant ADJECTIVE
graceful and stylish
➤ **elegance** NOUN ➤ **elegantly** ADVERB

element NOUN **elements**
❶ (*science*) a substance that cannot be split up into simpler substances, for example copper and oxygen ❷ a part of something ❸ the elements of a subject are the basic facts to do with it • *Next term you will learn the elements of algebra.* ❹ the elements are forces that make the weather, such as rain and wind ❺ a wire or coil that gives out heat in an electric heater or cooker
➤ **to be in your element** is to be doing something you enjoy

elementary ADJECTIVE
dealing with the simplest stages of something; easy

elephant NOUN **elephants**
a very large animal found in Africa and Asia, with a thick grey skin, large ears, a trunk and tusks

elevate VERB **elevates, elevating, elevated**
to elevate something is to lift it or raise it to a higher position

elevator NOUN **elevators** (*North American*)
a lift for carrying people between floors in a building
The Elevator shuddered, and then with a fearful whooshing noise it shot vertically upward like a rocket.—CHARLIE AND THE GREAT GLASS ELEVATOR, Roald Dahl

eleven NOUN **elevens**
❶ the number 11 ❷ a team of eleven people in cricket, football and other sports
➤ **eleventh** ADJECTIVE, NOUN

elf NOUN **elves**
a tiny mischievous fairy in stories

eligible ADJECTIVE
a person is eligible for something when they are qualified or suitable for it

eliminate VERB **eliminates, eliminating, eliminated**
to eliminate someone or something is to get rid of them
➤ **elimination** NOUN

elite NOUN **elites**
a group of people with special privileges

elixir (say i-**lik**-ser) NOUN **elixirs**
a liquid believed to have magic or healing powers
The Stone will transform any metal into pure gold. It also produces the Elixir of Life, which will make the drinker immortal.—HARRY POTTER AND THE PHILOSOPHER'S STONE, J. K. Rowling

elk NOUN **elk** or **elks**
a large kind of deer

ellipse NOUN **ellipses**
an oval shape
➤ **elliptical** ADJECTIVE

elm NOUN **elms**
a tall tree with large rough leaves

elocution NOUN
elocution is the art of speaking clearly and correctly

elongated ADJECTIVE
made longer; lengthened

eloquent ADJECTIVE
speaking well and expressing ideas clearly
➤ **eloquence** NOUN

else ADVERB
besides; instead • *Nobody else knows.*
➤ **or else** otherwise • *Run or else you'll be late.*

elsewhere ADVERB
somewhere else

elude VERB **eludes, eluding, eluded**
❶ to elude someone is to escape from them or avoid being caught by them ❷ something eludes you when you cannot find it or remember it

elusive ADJECTIVE
difficult to find or catch • *Deer are elusive animals.*

elves NOUN (plural of **elf**)

email NOUN **emails**
❶ a system of sending messages from one computer to another using a network. Email is short for *electronic mail.* ❷ a message sent by email

email VERB **emails, emailing, emailed**
you email someone when you send them a message by email

emancipate VERB **emancipates, emancipating, emancipated**
to emancipate someone is to set them free from slavery
➤ **emancipation** NOUN

embankment NOUN **embankments**
a long wall or bank of earth that holds back water or supports a road or railway

embark VERB **embarks, embarking, embarked**
to embark is to go on board a ship
➤ **to embark on something** is to begin something important

embarrass VERB **embarrasses, embarrassing, embarrassed**
to embarrass someone is to make them feel shy or awkward
➤ **embarrassment** NOUN

embassy NOUN **embassies**
a building where an ambassador from another country lives and has an office

embers PLURAL NOUN
the embers of a fire are small pieces of coal or wood that keep glowing when the fire is going out

emblazoned ADJECTIVE
decorated with an emblem or design • *His shield was emblazoned with a golden unicorn.*

emblem NOUN **emblems**
a symbol that stands for something • *The dove is an emblem of peace.*

embrace VERB **embraces, embracing, embraced**
❶ to embrace someone is to hold them closely in your arms ❷ to embrace a cause or belief is to accept it or adopt it ❸ to embrace several things is to include them • *The treaty embraces seventeen countries.*

A
B
C
D
E
F
G
H
I
J
K
L
M
N
O
P
Q
R
S
T
U
V
W
X
Y
Z

embroider VERB **embroiders, embroidering, embroidered**
to embroider cloth is to decorate it by stitching in designs or pictures
➤ **embroidery** NOUN

embryo NOUN **embryos**
a baby or young animal that is growing in the womb

emerald NOUN **emeralds**
❶ a green jewel ❷ a bright green colour

emerge VERB **emerges, emerging, emerged**
to emerge is to come out or appear
➤ **emergence** NOUN

emergency NOUN **emergencies**
a sudden dangerous event that needs to be dealt with very quickly

emigrant NOUN **emigrants**
someone who leaves their own country and goes to live in another country

emigrate VERB **emigrates, emigrating, emigrated**
to emigrate is to leave your own country and go and live in another country
➤ **emigration** NOUN

eminent ADJECTIVE
famous and respected • *Britain's most eminent mountaineer died ten years ago.*
➤ **eminence** NOUN

emission NOUN **emissions**
❶ the action of sending something out ❷ something that is emitted, for example fumes or radiation

emit VERB **emits, emitting, emitted**
to emit something such as smoke or fumes is to send it out

emoji (*say* i-moh-jee) NOUN **emojis**
a small digital image, such as a smiling face, used to express an idea or emotion
DID YOU KNOW? The word **emoji** comes from a Japanese word meaning 'picture letter'.

emotion NOUN **emotions**
❶ an emotion is a strong feeling in your mind, such as love or fear ❷ emotion is being excited or upset • *Tears of emotion flooded his eyes.*

emotional ADJECTIVE
❶ an emotional person expresses their feelings openly ❷ an emotional event or experience is one that excites strong feelings in people • *The film has a very emotional ending.*

emperor NOUN **emperors**
the ruler of an empire

emphasis NOUN **emphases**
special importance given to something or extra attention drawn to something

emphasize (*also* **emphasise**) VERB **emphasizes, emphasizing, emphasized**
to emphasize something is to give it special importance or draw special attention to it
• *Underline the words you want to emphasize.*

emphatic ADJECTIVE
an emphatic statement or expression is one that you make very firmly or strongly • *He agreed, with an emphatic nod of the head.*
➤ **emphatically** ADVERB

empire NOUN **empires**
❶ a group of countries ruled by one person or group of people ❷ a large group of businesses or shops under the control of one person or group of people

employ VERB **employs, employing, employed**
❶ to employ someone is to pay them to work for you ❷ to employ something is to use it

employee (*say* im-**ploi**-ee) NOUN **employees**
someone who works for another person or group of people

employer NOUN **employers**
a person or organization that has people working for them

employment NOUN
❶ employment is having paid work ❷ employment is a paid job

empower VERB **empowers, empowering, empowered**
to empower someone is to give them power to do something or more control over their life
• *Drama classes can help to empower young people and give them more confidence.*

empress *NOUN* **empresses**
a female emperor, or the wife of an emperor

empty *ADJECTIVE* **emptier, emptiest**
an empty place or container has nothing or no one in it • *The shop had an empty flat above it.* • *My water bottle was completely empty.*
➤ **emptiness** *NOUN*

empty *VERB* **empties, emptying, emptied**
❶ to empty something is to make it empty
❷ to empty is to become empty • *After the show the hall quickly emptied.*

emu (*say* ee-mew) *NOUN* **emus**
a large Australian bird that cannot fly, like an ostrich but smaller

emulate *VERB* **emulates, emulating, emulated**
to emulate someone is to do what they do because you respect or admire them

emulsion *NOUN* **emulsions**
❶ emulsion is a creamy or slightly oily liquid
❷ emulsion, or emulsion paint, is a kind of water paint used for decorating buildings

enable *VERB* **enables, enabling, enabled**
to enable someone to do something is to make it possible for them • *The password will enable you to log in easily.*

enamel *NOUN* **enamels**
❶ enamel is a shiny glassy substance that is baked on to metal or pottery to form a hard bright surface ❷ enamel is also the hard shiny surface of teeth ❸ an enamel paint is a hard glossy paint

encampment *NOUN* **encampments**
a military camp

encapsulate *VERB* **encapsulate, encapsulating, encapsulated**
to encapsulate something is to express it in a few words that give the main ideas or facts • *The words of this song encapsulate my feelings very well.*

enchant *VERB* **enchants, enchanting, enchanted**
❶ to enchant someone is to delight or please them ❷ to enchant someone is also to put a magic spell on them
➤ **enchantment** *NOUN*

enchanted *ADJECTIVE*
an enchanted place is one that has come under a magic spell
High on a hill in an enchanted garden, enclosed by tall walls and protected by strong magic, flowed the Fountain of Fair Fortune.—THE TALES OF BEEDLE THE BARD, J. K. Rowling

encircle *VERB* **encircles, encircling, encircled**
to encircle something or someone is to surround them • *The lake was completely encircled by a road.*

enclose *VERB* **encloses, enclosing, enclosed**
❶ to enclose an area is to put a fence or wall round it ❷ to enclose something is to put it in an envelope or packet with a letter

enclosure *NOUN* **enclosures**
❶ a piece of ground with a fence or wall round it ❷ something you put in an envelope or packet together with a letter

encore (*say* on-kor) *NOUN* **encores**
an extra item performed at a concert or show when the audience has clapped or cheered the main items

encounter *VERB* **encounters, encountering, encountered**
❶ to encounter someone is to meet them unexpectedly ❷ to encounter something is to experience it • *Did you encounter any difficulties?*

encourage *VERB* **encourages, encouraging, encouraged**
❶ to encourage someone is to give them confidence or hope • *We were encouraged by all the messages of support.* ❷ to encourage someone to do something is to urge them to do it • *My teacher encouraged me to enter the competition.*
➤ **encouragement** *NOUN*

encrusted *ADJECTIVE*
covered with a hard layer of something • *The roof of the cave was encrusted with ice.*

encyclopedia *NOUN* **encyclopedias**
a book or set of books containing a lot of information on a particular subject, or on all subjects, often with headings arranged in alphabetical order like a dictionary
➤ **encyclopedic** *ADJECTIVE*
DID YOU KNOW? The word **encyclopedia** comes from Greek words meaning 'complete education'.

a
b
c
d
e
f
g
h
i
j
k
l
m
n
o
p
q
r
s
t
u
v
w
x
y
z

end NOUN ends
❶ the end of something is the last part of it or the point where it stops • *Holly stood at the end of the pier.* • *I've nearly reached the end of the book.* ❷ each end of a sports pitch is the part defended by one team or player ❸ an end is an aim or purpose • *They used the money for their own ends.*
➤ **on end** ❶ upright • *The hairs on the back of my neck stood on end.* ❷ continuously • *The storm lasted for days on end.*

end VERB ends, ending, ended
❶ to end something is to finish it ❷ to end is to finish

endanger VERB endangers, endangering, endangered
to endanger someone or something is to cause them danger, especially of being injured

endeavour VERB endeavours, endeavouring, endeavoured
to endeavour to do something is to try hard to do it • *Let me endeavour to explain the problem.*

ending NOUN endings
the last part of something • *I decided to give my story a surprise ending.*

endless ADJECTIVE
never stopping • *Top athletes need endless training.*
➤ **endlessly** ADVERB

endure VERB endures, enduring, endured
❶ to endure pain or suffering is to put up with it ❷ to endure is to continue or last
➤ **endurance** NOUN

enemy NOUN enemies
❶ someone who is opposed to someone else and wants to harm them ❷ a nation or army that is at war with another country

energetic ADJECTIVE
❶ an energetic person has a lot of energy ❷ an energetic activity needs a lot of energy • *Ice hockey is a very energetic sport.*
➤ **energetically** ADVERB

energy NOUN energies
❶ energy is the ability to do work or provide power, for example electrical energy ❷ a person's energy is the strength they have to do things

enforce VERB enforces, enforcing, enforced
to enforce a law or order is to make people obey it
➤ **enforcement** NOUN

engage VERB engages, engaging, engaged
❶ to engage someone is to give them a job ❷ to engage someone in conversation is to talk to them ❸ to engage the enemy is to start a battle

engaged ADJECTIVE
❶ someone is engaged when they have promised to marry someone ❷ a telephone line or toilet is engaged when someone is already using it

engagement NOUN engagements
❶ a promise to marry someone ❷ an appointment to meet someone or do something ❸ a battle

engine NOUN engines
❶ a machine that turns energy into motion ❷ a vehicle that pulls a railway train

engineer NOUN engineers
a person who designs and builds machines, roads and bridges

engineering NOUN
engineering is the designing and building of machines, roads, bridges and other large buildings

English ADJECTIVE
❶ to do with England or its people • *a book about English history* ❷ to do with the language of English • *a new English dictionary*

English NOUN
the main language of the United Kingdom, the USA, Canada, Australia, Ghana, Nigeria and many other countries around the world
DID YOU KNOW? The word **English** comes from *Angles*, a Germanic people who came to England in the 5th century AD.

engrave VERB engraves, engraving, engraved
to engrave a surface is to carve figures or words on it

engrossed ADJECTIVE
to be engrossed in something is to concentrate on it and ignore other things around you • *She*

was so engrossed in her book that she didn't hear me come in.

engulf VERB **engulfs, engulfing, engulfed**
to engulf something is to flow over it and swamp it • *The town was engulfed by smoke from a huge forest fire.*

enhance VERB **enhances, enhancing, enhanced**
to enhance something is to make it more valuable or attractive • *The illustrations definitely enhance the story.*
➤ **enhancement** NOUN

enjoy VERB **enjoys, enjoying, enjoyed**
❶ to enjoy something is to get pleasure from it ❷ to enjoy yourself is to have a good time
➤ **enjoyable** ADJECTIVE ➤ **enjoyment** NOUN

enlarge VERB **enlarges, enlarging, enlarged**
to enlarge something is to make it larger
➤ **enlargement** NOUN

enlist VERB **enlists, enlisting, enlisted**
❶ to enlist is to join the army, navy or air force ❷ to enlist someone's help is to ask them to help you
➤ **enlistment** NOUN

enormity NOUN
something very wicked or harmful • *No one yet realized the full enormity of the crime.*

enormous ADJECTIVE
very large; huge
➤ **enormously** ADVERB hugely; a lot • *I enjoyed the party enormously.*
➤ **enormousness** NOUN

enough DETERMINER, NOUN, ADVERB
as much or as many as you need or can cope with

enquire VERB **enquires, enquiring, enquired**
to enquire about something is to ask for information about it • *I'm enquiring about guitar lessons.*

enquiry NOUN **enquiries**
a question you ask when you want information • *I have an enquiry about bus times.*

enrage VERB **enrages, enraging, enraged**
to enrage a person or animal is to make them very angry

enrich VERB **enriches, enriching, enriched**
to enrich something is to make it richer

enrol VERB **enrols, enrolling, enrolled**
❶ to enrol in a society or class is to become a member of it ❷ to enrol someone is to make them a member
➤ **enrolment** NOUN

ensue VERB **ensues, ensuing, ensued**
to ensue is to happen or come after something else, often as a result of it

ensure VERB **ensures, ensuring, ensured**
to ensure that something happens or has happened is to make sure of it • *Please ensure that you leave the room tidy when you go.*

entangle VERB **entangles, entangling, entangled**
to entangle something is to get it tangled or caught up
➤ **entanglement** NOUN

enter VERB **enters, entering, entered**
❶ to enter a place is to come into it or go into it ❷ to enter something in a list or book is to write or record it there ❸ to enter data in a computer is to key it in ❹ to enter for a competition or examination is to take part in it

enterprise NOUN **enterprises**
❶ enterprise is being bold and adventurous ❷ an enterprise is a difficult or important task or project

enterprising ADJECTIVE
an enterprising person or activity is one that is exciting or adventurous

entertain VERB **entertains, entertaining, entertained**
❶ to entertain someone is to amuse them or give them pleasure, as a singer or comedian does ❷ to entertain people is to have them as guests and give them food and drink
➤ **entertainer** NOUN ➤ **entertainment** NOUN

enthusiasm NOUN **enthusiasms**
❶ enthusiasm is a feeling of excitement and interest you show for something ❷ an enthusiasm is a strong liking or interest
DID YOU KNOW? The word **enthusiasm** comes from a Greek word meaning 'possessed by a god'.

a b c d e f g h i j k l m n o p q r s t u v w x y z

enthusiast NOUN **enthusiasts**
a person who has a strong interest in
something • *My dad is a jazz enthusiast.*

enthusiastic ADJECTIVE
full of enthusiasm • *She has always been
enthusiastic about science.*
➤ **enthusiastically** ADVERB

entire ADJECTIVE
whole or complete • *The entire school gathered
in the field for a photograph.*
➤ **entirely** ADVERB completely; in every way
• *The brothers look entirely different.*
➤ **entirety** NOUN the entirety of something is
all of it

entitle VERB **entitles**, **entitling**, **entitled**
to entitle someone to something is to give them
a right to it • *The voucher entitles you to a free
drink with your pizza.*
➤ **entitlement** NOUN

entrance (*say* en-transs) NOUN **entrances**
❶ the way into a place ❷ coming into a
room or on to a stage or arena • *The crowd
went wild when the band made their
entrance.*

entrance (*say* in-trahnss) VERB **entrances**,
entrancing, **entranced**
to entrance someone is to delight or enchant
them

entrant NOUN **entrants**
someone who goes in for a competition or
examination

entreat VERB **entreats**, **entreating**,
entreated
to entreat someone is to ask them seriously or
earnestly
➤ **entreaty** NOUN

entrust VERB **entrusts**, **entrusting**,
entrusted
to entrust someone with something, or to
entrust something to someone, is to give it to
them to look after

entry NOUN **entries**
❶ an entrance ❷ something written in a list
or diary

envelop (*say* in-**vel**-op) VERB **envelops**,
enveloping, **enveloped**
to envelop something is to cover or wrap it

completely • *The mountain was enveloped
in mist.*

envelope (*say* en-ve-lohp *or* on-ve-lohp) NOUN
envelopes
a wrapper or covering, especially for a letter

envious ADJECTIVE
you are envious of someone when they have
something you would like to have too
➤ **enviously** ADVERB

environment NOUN **environments**
❶ the environment in which someone or
something lives is their everyday surroundings
• *These plants can live in extreme environments.*
❷ the environment is the natural world of the
land and sea and air • *We need to care more
about the environment.*
➤ **environmental** ADJECTIVE

envisage VERB **envisage**, **envisaging**,
envisaged
to envisage something is to imagine or expect it
• *I don't envisage going there again.*

envy NOUN
an unhappy feeling you have when you want
something that someone else has got

envy VERB **envies**, **envying**, **envied**
to envy someone is to feel envy about them

enzyme NOUN **enzymes**
a chemical substance that humans, animals and
plants produce and that sets off processes such
as the digestion of food

epic NOUN **epics**
❶ a story or poem about heroes ❷ an exciting
or spectacular film

epic ADJECTIVE
heroic or grand in scale • *an epic journey to the
South Pole*

epidemic NOUN **epidemics**
an outbreak of an illness that spreads quickly
among the people in an area

epilepsy NOUN
epilepsy is a serious condition of the nervous
system that causes periods of unconsciousness
and uncontrolled body movements

epileptic ADJECTIVE
to do with epilepsy • *an epileptic fit*

epileptic NOUN **epileptics**
someone who has epilepsy

episode NOUN **episodes**
❶ one event that is part of a series of happenings or forms part of a story ❷ one programme in a radio or television serial

epitaph NOUN **epitaphs**
words written on a tomb or describing a person who has died

epoch (say ee-pok) NOUN **epochs**
a long period of time in the past, during which important events happened

eponym NOUN **eponyms**
an eponym is a word that is named after someone, often the inventor, for example *Braille*, *cardigan* and *sandwich*

equal ADJECTIVE
things are equal when they are the same in amount, size or value
➤ **to be equal to something** is to have the strength or ability to do it • *Are you sure he is equal to the task?*

equal NOUN **equals**
a person or thing that is equal to another • *She is her brother's equal at maths.*

equal VERB **equals**, **equalling**, **equalled**
to equal something is to be the same in amount, size or value

equality NOUN
equality is being equal

equalize (also **equalise**) VERB **equalizes**, **equalizing**, **equalized**
to equalize things is to make them equal

equalizer (also **equaliser**) NOUN **equalizers**
a goal or point that makes the scores in a game equal

equally ADVERB
in the same way or to the same extent • *We are all equally to blame.*

equation (say i-kway-zhon) NOUN **equations** (mathematics)
a statement that two amounts are equal, for example 3 + 4 = 2 + 5

equator (say i-kway-ter) NOUN
an imaginary line round the earth at an equal distance from the North and South Poles
➤ **equatorial** ADJECTIVE

equestrian ADJECTIVE
to do with horse-riding

equilateral (say ee-kwi-lat-er-al) ADJECTIVE
an equilateral triangle has all its sides equal

equinox NOUN **equinoxes**
the time of year when day and night are equal in length (about 20 March in spring and about 22 September in autumn)

equip VERB **equips**, **equipping**, **equipped**
to equip someone or something is to supply them with what is needed • *Are you equipped for mountaineering?*

equipment NOUN
equipment is a set of things needed for a special purpose

equivalent ADJECTIVE
things are equivalent when they are equal in value, importance or meaning
➤ **equivalence** NOUN

era (say eer-a) NOUN **eras**
a long period of history • *The museum was built in the Victorian era.*

erase VERB **erases**, **erasing**, **erased**
❶ to erase something written or drawn is to rub it out ❷ to erase a recording on magnetic tape is to wipe it out

eraser NOUN **erasers**
a piece of rubber or plastic for rubbing out writing or drawing

erect ADJECTIVE
standing straight up

erect VERB **erects**, **erecting**, **erected**
to erect something is to set it up or build it
➤ **erection** NOUN

erode VERB **erodes**, **eroding**, **eroded**
to erode something is to wear it away • *Water has eroded the rocks over time.*

erosion NOUN
erosion is the wearing away of the earth's surface by the action of water and wind

a b c d e f g h i j k l m n o p q r s t u v w x y z

errand *NOUN* **errands**
a short journey to take a message or fetch something

erratic (*say* i-**rat**-ik) *ADJECTIVE*
not reliable or regular
➤ **erratically** *ADVERB*

error *NOUN* **errors**
❶ a mistake ❷ a problem with a computer process that stops it from working properly

erupt *VERB* **erupts, erupting, erupted**
❶ a volcano erupts when it shoots out lava ❷ something powerful or violent erupts when it suddenly happens • *An argument erupted over a disputed goal.*
➤ **eruption** *NOUN*

escalate *VERB* **escalates, escalating, escalated**
to escalate is to become gradually greater or more serious • *The riots escalated into a war.*

escalator *NOUN* **escalators**
a staircase with a revolving band of steps moving up or down

escapade (*say* es-ka-**payd**) *NOUN* **escapades**
an escapade is a daring adventure
Cold and hunger drove me to ever more desperate and hazardous escapades.—THE LAST WOLF, Michael Morpurgo

escape *VERB* **escapes, escaping, escaped**
❶ to escape is to get free or get away ❷ to escape something is to avoid it • *I managed to escape the washing-up.*

escape *NOUN* **escapes**
❶ an act of escaping • *the story of a daring escape from a prison camp* ❷ a way to escape • *He suddenly saw his escape and ran for it.*

escort (*say* **ess**-kort) *NOUN* **escorts**
❶ a person or group who accompanies someone, especially to give protection ❷ a group of vehicles, ships or aircraft accompanying someone or something

escort (*say* i-**skort**) *VERB* **escorts, escorting, escorted**
to escort someone or something is to act as an escort to them

especially *ADVERB*
chiefly; more than anything else • *I like writing poems, especially limericks.*

espionage (*say* **ess**-pee-on-ah*zh*) *NOUN*
espionage is spying on other countries or people

esplanade *NOUN* **esplanades**
a flat open area for walking, especially by the sea

essay *NOUN* **essays**
a short piece of writing on one subject

essence *NOUN* **essences**
❶ the most important quality or ingredient of something ❷ a concentrated liquid

essential *ADJECTIVE*
something is essential when it is very important and you must have it or do it • *It is essential to wear a helmet while cycling.*
➤ **essentially** *ADVERB* basically; in many ways • *The two stories are essentially the same.*

essential *NOUN* **essentials**
something you must have or do

establish *VERB* **establishes, establishing, established**
❶ to establish a business, government or relationship is to start it on a firm basis ❷ to establish a fact is to show that it is true • *He managed to establish his innocence.*

establishment *NOUN* **establishments**
❶ a place where people do business ❷ establishing something

estate *NOUN* **estates**
❶ an area of land with a set of houses or factories on it ❷ a large area of land belonging to one person ❸ everything that a person owns when they die

estate agent *NOUN* **estate agents**
someone whose business is selling or letting buildings and land

esteem *VERB* **esteems, esteeming, esteemed**
to esteem someone or something is to think they are excellent

estimate (*say* **ess**-ti-mat) *NOUN* **estimates**
a rough calculation or guess about an amount or value

estimate (*say* **ess**-ti-mayt) *VERB* **estimates, estimating, estimated**
to estimate is to make an estimate

estimation NOUN
❶ estimation is making a rough estimate
❷ a person's estimation is their opinion • *She is the best player, in my estimation.*

estuary (*say* ess-tew-er-ee) NOUN **estuaries**
the mouth of a large river where it flows into the sea

etc. ABBREVIATION
short for Latin *et cetera*, used after a list to mean 'and other similar things' or 'and so on' • *We study maths, English, science, etc.*

etch VERB **etches, etching, etched**
to etch a picture is to make it by engraving on a metal plate with an acid
➤ **etching** NOUN

eternal ADJECTIVE
lasting forever; not ending or changing
➤ **eternally** ADVERB
➤ **eternity** NOUN time that goes on forever

ether (*say* ee-ther) NOUN
❶ ether is a colourless liquid that evaporates easily, and is used as an anaesthetic or a solvent
❷ the ether is the upper air

ethnic ADJECTIVE
belonging to a particular national or racial group within a larger set of people

EU ABBREVIATION
short for *European Union*

eucalyptus (*say* yoo-ka-**lip**-tus) NOUN **eucalyptuses**
an evergreen tree from which an oil is obtained

euphemism NOUN **euphemisms**
a word or phrase that is used instead of an impolite or less tactful one • *'pass away' is a euphemism for 'die'*

euro NOUN **euros** or **euro**
the currency used in many countries in the European Union

European ADJECTIVE
to do with Europe or its people
European NOUN **Europeans**
a person from Europe

evacuate VERB **evacuates, evacuating, evacuated**
to evacuate people is to move them away from a dangerous place

➤ **evacuation** NOUN

evacuee (*say* i-vak-yoo-ee) NOUN **evacuees**
someone who is evacuated, especially during a war
Since September and the continual blitzing of London that followed, the number of evacuees that came flooding into the village grew weekly.—GOODNIGHT MISTER TOM, Michelle Magorian

evade VERB **evades, evading, evaded**
to evade someone or something is to make an effort to avoid them

evaluate VERB **evaluates, evaluating, evaluated**
to evaluate something is to estimate its value
➤ **evaluation** NOUN

evaporate VERB **evaporates, evaporating, evaporated**
to evaporate is to change from liquid into steam or vapour
➤ **evaporation** NOUN

evasion NOUN **evasions**
❶ evasion is evading something ❷ an evasion is an answer that tries to avoid the question being asked

evasive ADJECTIVE
trying to avoid answering something; not honest or straightforward

eve NOUN **eves**
the day or evening before an important day, for example Christmas Eve

even ADJECTIVE
❶ level and smooth ❷ calm and stable • *Labrador dogs have an even temperament.* ❸ equal • *The scores were even at half-time.* ❹ (*mathematics*) able to be divided exactly by two • *6 and 14 are even numbers.*
➤ **to get even with someone** is to take revenge on them
➤ **evenly** ADVERB ➤ **evenness** NOUN
even VERB **evens, evening, evened**
❶ to even something is to make it even ❷ to even or even out is to become even
even ADVERB
used to emphasize another word • *You haven't even started your homework!* • *I ran fast, but she ran even faster.*
➤ **even so** although that is correct

evening *NOUN* **evenings**
the time at the end of the day before night-time

event *NOUN* **events**
❶ something that happens, especially something important ❷ an item in an athletics contest • *The next event will be the long jump.*

eventful *ADJECTIVE*
full of happenings, especially remarkable or exciting ones • *They had an eventful train journey across the USA.*

eventual *ADJECTIVE*
happening at last or as a result • *He had many failures before his eventual success.*

eventually *ADVERB*
finally, in the end • *We eventually managed to get the door open.*

ever *ADVERB*
❶ at any time • *It's the best present I've ever had.* ❷ always • *ever hopeful* ❸ (*informal*) used for emphasis • *Why ever didn't you tell me?*
➤ **ever so** or **ever such** (*informal*) very much • *I'm ever so pleased.* • *She's ever such a nice girl.*

evergreen *ADJECTIVE*
having green leaves all through the year

evergreen *NOUN* **evergreens**
an evergreen tree

everlasting *ADJECTIVE*
lasting forever or for a long time

every *DETERMINER*
all the people or things of a particular kind; each • *Every pupil in the school will receive a letter.*
➤ **every other** each alternate one; every second one • *Every other tile has a pattern on it.*

everybody *PRONOUN*
everyone

everyday *ADJECTIVE*
happening or used every day; ordinary • *Just wear your everyday clothes.*

everyone *PRONOUN*
every person; all people • *Everyone thinks I'm brave but I'm not.*

everything *PRONOUN*
❶ all things; all • *You'll find everything you need in the kitchen.* ❷ the only or most important thing • *They say that money is not everything.*

everywhere *ADVERB*
in all places

evict *VERB* **evicts, evicting, evicted**
to evict someone is to make them move out of their house
➤ **eviction** *NOUN*

evidence *NOUN*
evidence is facts and information that give people reason to believe something

evident *ADJECTIVE*
obvious; clearly seen • *It is evident that they are lying.*
➤ **evidently** *ADVERB*

evil *ADJECTIVE*
an evil person or action is one that is wicked and harmful

evil *NOUN* **evils**
evil, or an evil, is something wicked or harmful

evolution (*say* ee-vo-**loo**-shon) *NOUN*
❶ gradual change into something different ❷ the development of animals and plants from earlier or simpler forms of life

evolve *VERB* **evolves, evolving, evolved**
to develop gradually or naturally

ewe (*say* yoo) *NOUN* **ewes**
a female sheep

ex– *PREFIX*
meaning something or someone that used to be, as in ex-prime minister

exact *ADJECTIVE*
❶ completely correct • *I can't remember the exact date.* ❷ giving all the details • *The police will need an exact description of what happened.*
➤ **exactly** *ADVERB* ➤ **exactness** *NOUN*

exaggerate *VERB* **exaggerates, exaggerating, exaggerated**
to exaggerate something is to make it seem bigger or better or worse than it really is
➤ **exaggeration** *NOUN*

exalt *VERB* **exalts, exalting, exalted**
❶ to exalt someone is to make them higher in rank ❷ to exalt someone is also to praise them highly

exam *NOUN* **exams** (*informal*)
an examination

examination *NOUN* **examinations**
❶ a test of someone's knowledge or skill
❷ a close inspection of something

examine *VERB* **examines, examining, examined**
to examine something is to look at it closely or in detail

examiner *NOUN* **examiners**
a person who sets and marks an examination to test students' knowledge

example *NOUN* **examples**
❶ a single thing or event that shows what others of the same kind are like ❷ a person or thing that you should copy or learn from
➤ **for example** as an example

exasperate *VERB* **exasperates, exasperating, exasperated**
to exasperate someone is to make them very annoyed
➤ **exasperation** *NOUN*

excavate *VERB* **excavates, excavating, excavated**
to excavate a piece of land is to dig in it, especially in building or archaeology
➤ **excavation** *NOUN*

exceed *VERB* **exceeds, exceeding, exceeded**
❶ to exceed an amount or achievement is to be more than it or do better than it ❷ to exceed a rule or limit is to go beyond it when you are not supposed to • *The driver was exceeding the speed limit.*

exceedingly *ADVERB*
extremely; very much

excel *VERB* **excels, excelling, excelled**
to excel at something is to be very good at it, and better than everyone else

excellent *ADJECTIVE*
extremely good; of the best kind
➤ **excellence** *NOUN*

except *PREPOSITION*
not including; apart from • *Everyone got a prize except me.*

exception *NOUN* **exceptions**
❶ something or someone that does not follow the normal rule ❷ something that is left out

exceptional *ADJECTIVE*
unusual • *She has exceptional skill.*
➤ **exceptionally** *ADVERB* • *exceptionally heavy rain*

excerpt *NOUN* **excerpts**
a piece taken from a book or story or film

excess *NOUN* **excesses**
excess, or an excess, is too much of something • *We have an excess of food.*

excessive *ADJECTIVE*
too much or too great
➤ **excessively** *ADVERB*

exchange *VERB* **exchanges, exchanging, exchanged**
to exchange something is to give it and receive something else for it

exchange *NOUN* **exchanges**
❶ a place where telephone lines are connected to each other when a call is made ❷ a place where company shares are bought and sold ❸ a process of exchanging things

excite *VERB* **excites, exciting, excited**
to excite someone is to make them eager and enthusiastic about something • *The thought of seeing a polar bear excited them.*
➤ **excitable** *ADJECTIVE* an excitable person is easily excited

excited *ADJECTIVE*
eager and enthusiastic about something • *We were far too excited to sleep.*
➤ **excitedly** *ADVERB*

excitement *NOUN* **excitements**
❶ excitement is being excited ❷ an excitement is something that excites you

exclaim *VERB* **exclaims, exclaiming, exclaimed**
to exclaim is to shout or cry out • '*My goodness!*' *exclaimed Miss Appleton.*

a b c d e f g h i j k l m n o p q r s t u v w x y z

exclamation NOUN **exclamations**
❶ exclamation is shouting or crying out
❷ an exclamation is a word or phrase you say out loud that expresses a strong feeling such as surprise or pain

exclamation mark NOUN **exclamation marks**
the punctuation mark (!) placed after an exclamation

exclude VERB **excludes**, **excluding**, **excluded**
❶ to exclude someone or something is to keep them out ❷ to exclude something is to leave it out • *Do not exclude the possibility of rain.*
➤ **exclusion** NOUN

exclusive ADJECTIVE
❶ not shared with others • *Today's newspaper has an exclusive report about the match.*
❷ allowing only a few people to be involved • *They joined an exclusive club.*
➤ **exclusively** ADVERB

excursion NOUN **excursions**
a short journey or outing made for pleasure

excuse (*say* iks-kewss) NOUN **excuses**
a reason given to explain why something wrong has been done

excuse (*say* iks-kewz) VERB **excuses**, **excusing**, **excused**
❶ to excuse someone is to forgive them
❷ to excuse someone something is to allow them not to do it • *Please may I be excused swimming?*
➤ **excuse me** a polite apology for interrupting or disagreeing
➤ **excusable** ADJECTIVE

execute VERB **executes**, **executing**, **executed**
❶ to execute someone is to put them to death as a punishment ❷ to execute something is to perform or produce it • *She executed the somersault perfectly.*
➤ **execution** NOUN ➤ **executioner** NOUN

executive NOUN **executives**
a senior person with authority in a business or government organization

exempt ADJECTIVE
not having to do something that others have

to do • *School groups are exempt from paying the entrance fee.*

exercise NOUN **exercises**
❶ exercise is using your body to make it strong and healthy ❷ an exercise is a piece of work done for practice

exercise VERB **exercises**, **exercising**, **exercised**
❶ to exercise is to do exercises ❷ to exercise an animal is to give it exercise ❸ to exercise something is to use it • *You will have to exercise patience.*

exercise book NOUN **exercise books**
a book for writing in

exert VERB **exerts**, **exerting**, **exerted**
to exert oneself or one's ability is to make an effort to get something done • *He exerted all his strength to bend the bar.*
➤ **exertion** NOUN

exhale VERB **exhales**, **exhaling**, **exhaled**
to exhale is to breathe out
➤ **exhalation** NOUN

exhaust NOUN **exhausts**
❶ the waste gases from an engine ❷ the pipe these gases are sent out through

exhaust VERB **exhausts**, **exhausting**, **exhausted**
❶ to exhaust someone is to make them very tired ❷ to exhaust something is to use it up completely
➤ **exhaustion** NOUN

exhibit VERB **exhibits**, **exhibiting**, **exhibited**
to exhibit something is to show it in public, especially in a gallery or museum
➤ **exhibitor** NOUN

exhibit NOUN **exhibits**
something displayed in a gallery or museum

exhibition NOUN **exhibitions**
a collection of things put on display for people to look at

exile VERB **exiles**, **exiling**, **exiled**
to exile someone is to send them away from their country

exile NOUN **exiles**
❶ exile is having to live away from your own country • *He was in exile for ten years.*
❷ an exile is a person who is exiled

exist *VERB* **exists, existing, existed**
❶ to exist is to have life or be real • *Do ghosts exist?* ❷ to exist is also to stay alive • *They existed on biscuits and water.*

existence *NOUN* **existences**
❶ existing or being ❷ staying alive • *It was a real struggle for existence.*

exit *NOUN* **exits**
❶ the way out of a place ❷ going out of a room or going off a stage or arena • *The clowns then made their exit.*

exit *VERB* **exits, exiting, exited**
❶ to exit is to leave a stage or arena ❷ to exit is also to stop a program or app on a computer

exotic *ADJECTIVE*
unusual and colourful, especially because it comes from another part of the world

expand *VERB* **expands, expanding, expanded**
❶ to expand something is to make it larger ❷ to expand is to become larger
➤ **expansion** *NOUN*

expanse *NOUN* **expanses**
a wide area

expect *VERB* **expects, expecting, expected**
❶ to expect something is to think that it will probably happen • *No one expected him to win.* ❷ to be expecting someone is to be waiting for them to arrive ❸ to expect something is to think that it ought to happen • *I expect you to pay attention.*

expectant *ADJECTIVE*
❶ full of expectation or hope ❷ an expectant mother is a woman who is pregnant
➤ **expectancy** *NOUN*

expectation *NOUN* **expectations**
❶ expectation is expecting something or being hopeful ❷ an expectation is something you hope to get

expecting *ADJECTIVE*
a woman is expecting when she is pregnant

expedition *NOUN* **expeditions**
a journey made in order to do something • *They are going on a climbing expedition.*

expel *VERB* **expels, expelling, expelled**
❶ to expel something is to send or force it out • *The fan expels stale air and fumes.* ❷ to expel someone is to make them leave a school or country • *He was expelled for bullying.*

expenditure *NOUN*
expenditure is when you spend money or use effort

expense *NOUN* **expenses**
expense, or an expense, is the cost of doing something

expensive *ADJECTIVE*
costing a lot of money

experience *NOUN* **experiences**
❶ experience is what you learn from doing and seeing things ❷ an experience is something that has happened to you

experience *VERB* **experiences, experiencing, experienced**
to experience something is to have it happen to you

experienced *ADJECTIVE*
having gained skill or knowledge from much experience

experiment *NOUN* **experiments**
a test made in order to study what happens

experiment *VERB* **experiments, experimenting, experimented**
to experiment is to carry out experiments
➤ **experimentation** *NOUN*

experimental *ADJECTIVE*
something is experimental when it is being tried out to see how good or successful it is • *an experimental treatment for cancer*

expert *NOUN* **experts**
someone who has skill or special knowledge in something

expert *ADJECTIVE*
having great knowledge or skill

expertise (*say* eks-per-**teez**) *NOUN*
expertise is expert ability or knowledge

expire *VERB* **expires, expiring, expired**
to expire is to come to an end or to stop being usable • *Your library card has expired.*
➤ **expiry** *NOUN*

a
b
c
d
e
f
g
h
i
j
k
l
m
n
o
p
q
r
s
t
u
v
w
x
y
z

explain *VERB* **explains, explaining, explained**
❶ to explain something is to make it clear to someone else • *Can you please explain the question?* ❷ to explain a fact or event is to show why it happens • *That explains why I haven't heard from her.*

explanation *NOUN* **explanations**
something you say that explains something or gives reasons for it • *He gave an explanation for what had happened.*
➤ **explanatory** *ADJECTIVE* an explanatory statement is one that explains something

explode *VERB* **explodes, exploding, exploded**
❶ to explode is to burst or suddenly release energy with a loud bang ❷ to explode a bomb is to set it off ❸ to explode is to increase suddenly or quickly • *The city's population exploded to 3 million in a year.*

exploit (*say* eks-ploit) *NOUN* **exploits**
a brave or exciting deed

exploit (*say* iks-ploit) *VERB* **exploits, exploiting, exploited**
❶ to exploit resources is to use or develop them ❷ to exploit someone is to use them selfishly
➤ **exploitation** *NOUN*

explore *VERB* **explores, exploring, explored**
❶ to explore a place is to travel through it to find out more about it • *They spent the day exploring the caves.* ❷ to explore a subject is to examine it carefully • *We need to explore all the possibilities.*
➤ **exploration** *NOUN*

explorer *NOUN* **explorers**
someone who explores a remote country to find out more about it

explosion *NOUN* **explosions**
❶ the exploding of a bomb or other weapon ❷ a sudden or quick increase • *There was a population explosion after the war.*

explosive *NOUN* **explosives**
explosive, or an explosive, is a substance that can explode

explosive *ADJECTIVE*
likely to explode; able to cause an explosion

export (*say* iks-**port**) *VERB* **exports, exporting, exported**
❶ when a company exports things, it sends them to another country to sell ❷ (*computing*) when you export information on a computer, you move it from one file or computer to another

export (*say* eks-port) *NOUN* **exports**
something that is sent abroad to be sold

expose *VERB* **exposes, exposing, exposed**
❶ to expose something is to reveal or uncover it ❷ to expose someone is to show that they are to blame for something ❸ to expose a photographic film is to let light reach it in a camera, so as to take a picture

exposure *NOUN* **exposures**
❶ exposure is being harmed by the weather when in the open without enough protection ❷ an exposure is a single photograph or frame on a film

express *ADJECTIVE*
going or sent quickly

express *NOUN* **expresses**
a fast train stopping at only a few stations

express *VERB* **expresses, expressing, expressed**
to express an idea or feeling is to put it into words
The BFG expressed a wish to learn how to speak properly, and Sophie herself … volunteered to give him lessons every day.—THE BFG, Roald Dahl

expression *NOUN* **expressions**
❶ the look on a person's face that shows what they are thinking or feeling ❷ a word or phrase ❸ a way of speaking or performing music that expresses feelings
➤ **expressive** *ADJECTIVE* an expressive look or statement is one that shows your feelings

expressly *ADVERB*
clearly or specifically
The Prices, like all the other children in the village, were expressly forbidden to go tadpoling in the Park.—BOGWOPPIT, Ursula Moray Williams

expulsion *NOUN* **expulsions**
expulsion, or an expulsion, is when someone is driven away or made to leave

exquisite *ADJECTIVE*
very delicate or beautiful
Next came a tall, beautiful woman clothed in a splendid trailing gown, trimmed with exquisite lace as fine as cobweb.—THE ROAD TO OZ, L. Frank Baum
➤ **exquisitely** *ADVERB*

extend *VERB* **extends, extending, extended**
❶ to extend is to stretch out ❷ to extend something is to make it longer or larger ❸ to extend a greeting or welcome is to offer it

extension *NOUN* **extensions**
❶ extension is extending or being extended ❷ an extension is something added on, especially to a building ❸ an extension is also an extra telephone in an office or house

extensive *ADJECTIVE*
covering a large area • *The bomb caused extensive damage.*
➤ **extensively** *ADVERB* over a large area • *She travelled extensively with her children.*

extent *NOUN* **extents**
❶ the area or length of something ❷ an amount or level • *The extent of the damage was enormous.*

exterior *NOUN* **exteriors**
the outside of something

exterminate *VERB* **exterminates, exterminating, exterminated**
to exterminate a people or breed of animal is to kill all the members of it
➤ **extermination** *NOUN*

external *ADJECTIVE*
outside
➤ **externally** *ADVERB*

extinct *ADJECTIVE*
❶ an animal or bird is extinct when there are no more examples of it alive • *Dodos became extinct over 300 years ago.* ❷ a volcano is extinct when it is not burning or active any more
➤ **extinction** *NOUN*

extinguish *VERB* **extinguishes, extinguishing, extinguished**
to extinguish a fire or light is to put it out
➤ **extinguisher** *NOUN*

extra *ADJECTIVE*
more than usual; added • *There is an extra charge for taking a bicycle on the train.*

extra *NOUN* **extras**
❶ an extra person or thing ❷ someone acting as part of the crowd in a film or play

extra– *PREFIX*
❶ more than usual, as in *extra-special* ❷ outside or beyond something, as in *extraterrestrial*

extract (*say* eks-trakt) *NOUN* **extracts**
❶ a piece taken from a book, play or film ❷ something obtained from something else • *a plant extract*

extract (*say* iks-trakt) *VERB* **extracts, extracting, extracted**
to extract something is to remove it or take it out of something else

extraction *NOUN*
❶ a person's extraction is the place or people they come from • *My family is of Italian extraction.* ❷ extraction is the process of taking something out or removing it

extraordinary *ADJECTIVE*
unusual or very strange
➤ **extraordinarily** *ADVERB*

extraterrestrial *ADJECTIVE*
existing in or coming from another planet

extraterrestrial *NOUN* **extraterrestrials**
a living thing from another planet, especially in science fiction

extravagant *ADJECTIVE*
spending or using too much of something
➤ **extravagance** *NOUN*
➤ **extravagantly** *ADVERB*

extreme *ADJECTIVE*
❶ very great or strong • *They were suffering from extreme cold.* ❷ farthest away • *She lives in the extreme north of the country.*

extreme *NOUN* **extremes**
❶ something very great, strong or far away ❷ either end of something

a b c d e f g h i j k l m n o p q r s t u v w x y z

A
B
C
D
E
F
G
H
I
J
K
L
M
N
O
P
Q
R
S
T
U
V
W
X
Y
Z

extremely *ADVERB*
as much or as far as possible; very much • *They are extremely pleased.*

extremity (*say* iks-**trem**-it-ee) *NOUN* **extremities**
an extreme point; the very end of something

exuberant *ADJECTIVE*
very cheerful or lively
➤ **exuberance** *NOUN*

exult *VERB* **exults, exulting, exulted**
to rejoice or be very pleased
➤ **exultant** *ADJECTIVE* ➤ **exultation** *NOUN*

eye *NOUN* **eyes**
❶ the organ that humans and some animals use for seeing ❷ the small hole in a needle ❸ the centre of a storm

eye *VERB* **eyes, eyeing, eyed**
to eye someone or something is to look at them closely • *The cat eyed the mouse with interest.*

eyeball *NOUN* **eyeballs**
the ball-shaped part of your eye, inside your eyelids

eyebrow *NOUN* **eyebrows**
the curved fringe of hair growing above each eye

eyelash *NOUN* **eyelashes**
one of the short hairs that grow on your eyelids

eyelid *NOUN* **eyelids**
the upper or lower fold of skin that can close over your eyeball

eyesight *NOUN*
a person's eyesight is their ability to see

eyesore *NOUN* **eyesores**
something that is ugly to look at

eyewitness *NOUN* **eyewitnesses**
someone who actually saw something happen, especially an accident or crime

F *ABBREVIATION*
short for *Fahrenheit*

fable *NOUN* **fables**
a short story which teaches a lesson about how people should behave, often with animals as characters

fabric *NOUN* **fabrics**
cloth

fabulous *ADJECTIVE*
❶ very great • *The prince had fabulous wealth.*
❷ (*informal*) wonderful; marvellous ❸ described in stories and fables, not existing in real life
• *Dragons are fabulous creatures.*

face *NOUN* **faces**
❶ the front part of your head, where your eyes, nose and mouth are ❷ the look on a person's face • *She had a friendly face.* ❸ the front or upper side of something • *Put the cards face down.* ❹ one of the surfaces of a shape • *A cube has six faces.* ❺ the side of a mountain or cliff
• *They reached the face of the rock.*

face *VERB* **faces, facing, faced**
❶ to face in a certain direction is to look there or have the front in that direction • *Please face the front.* • *The church faces the school.*
❷ to face a problem or danger is to accept that you have to deal with it

facet (*say* **fass**-it) *NOUN* **facets**
one small surface of an object such as a diamond, which reflects light and makes it sparkle

facial *ADJECTIVE*
on or to do with your face • *Smiling is a facial expression.*

facility (*say* fa-**sil**-i-tee) *NOUN* **facilities**
a place where you can take part in an activity, or a piece of equipment that helps you to do things • *The school has facilities for computing and sport.*

fact NOUN **facts**
fact, or a fact, is something that is true or certain
➤ **as a matter of fact** or **in fact** really • *I'm leaving this morning. Now, in fact.*

factor NOUN **factors**
❶ one of the reasons for something • *What has been the most important factor behind your success?* ❷ a number by which a larger number can be divided exactly, without leaving a remainder • *2 and 3 are factors of 6.*

factory NOUN **factories**
a large building where machines are used to make things in large amounts

factual ADJECTIVE
containing facts, not stories • *a factual book about the making of the Harry Potter films*
➤ **factually** ADVERB

fad NOUN **fads**
something that is popular for only a short time • *There used to be a fad for Pokemon.*

fade VERB **fades, fading, faded**
❶ to lose colour, freshness or strength ❷ to fade or fade away is to disappear gradually

faeces (*say* **fee-seez**) PLURAL NOUN
the solid waste that collects in your bowels and is passed out of your body

Fahrenheit (*say* **fa-ren-hyt**) ADJECTIVE
using a scale for measuring temperature that gives 32 degrees for freezing water and 212 degrees for boiling water • *Set the oven to 350 degrees Fahrenheit.*

fail VERB **fails, failing, failed**
❶ to fail is to try to do something but not be able to do it ❷ to fail an exam or test is not to pass it ❸ to fail is also to become weak or useless or to come to an end • *The batteries are failing.* ❹ to fail to do something is not to do it when you should • *My friend failed to show up at the cinema.*

fail NOUN **fails**
not being successful in an examination • *She has five passes and one fail.*
➤ **without fail** definitely or always • *I'll be there without fail.*

failing NOUN **failings**
a fault or weakness

failure NOUN **failures**
❶ failure is not being successful ❷ a failure is something that has failed • *The storm caused a sudden power failure.* ❸ someone who has failed to achieve success • *He had felt like a failure his whole life.*

faint ADJECTIVE **fainter, faintest**
❶ weak; not clear or distinct ❷ nearly unconscious, often because you are exhausted or very hungry
➤ **faintly** ADVERB ➤ **faintness** NOUN

faint VERB **faints, fainting, fainted**
to faint is to become unconscious for a short time

faint-hearted ADJECTIVE
not having much courage or confidence

fair ADJECTIVE **fairer, fairest**
❶ right or just; honest • *It's not fair to cheat in games.* ❷ light in colour • *The sisters both had fair hair.* ❸ quite good • *We've got a fair chance of winning.* ❹ weather is fair when it is fine and not raining
➤ **fairness** NOUN

fair NOUN **fairs**
❶ an outdoor entertainment with rides, amusements and stalls ❷ an exhibition or market • *a craft fair*

fairground NOUN **fairgrounds**
a place where a fair is held

fairly ADVERB
❶ quite or rather • *This recipe is fairly easy to follow.* ❷ honestly; justly • *He promised to treat everyone fairly.*

fairy NOUN **fairies**
an imaginary small creature with wings and magic powers

fairyland NOUN
a place where fairies live; an imaginary place

fairy story, fairy tale NOUN
fairy stories, fairy tales
a story about fairies or magic

faith NOUN **faiths**
❶ faith is strong belief or trust • *We have a lot of faith in her.* ❷ a faith is a religion

a
b
c
d
e
f
g
h
i
j
k
l
m
n
o
p
q
r
s
t
u
v
w
x
y
z

faithful *ADJECTIVE*
loyal and trustworthy
➤ **faithfully** *ADVERB* ➤ **faithfulness** *NOUN*

fake *NOUN* **fakes**
a copy of something made to deceive people
into thinking it is real

fake *ADJECTIVE*
not real or genuine • *fake diamonds*

fake *VERB* **fakes, faking, faked**
❶ to fake something is to make it look real in
order to deceive people ❷ to fake something
is also to pretend to have it • *He was always
faking illness so he could miss PE.*

falafel (*say* fa-la-fal) *NOUN* **falafels**
a small ball of mashed chickpeas and spices,
fried as a Middle Eastern dish

falcon *NOUN* **falcons**
a small kind of hawk

fall *VERB* **falls, falling, fell, fallen**
❶ to come down quickly towards the ground
• *Meteors regularly fall to earth from space.*
❷ numbers or prices fall when they get lower
or smaller ❸ a city or castle falls when it is
captured ❹ soldiers fall when they die in
battle ❺ when silence falls it becomes quiet
❻ to fall sick or ill is to become ill ❼ a look or
glance falls on someone when it is directed
at them
➤ **to fall back on something** *or* **someone**
is to rely on them in a difficulty
➤ **to fall for someone** is to start loving them
➤ **to fall for something** is to be tricked into
believing it
➤ **to fall out** is to quarrel and stop being
friends
➤ **to fall through** is to fail to happen • *Our
plans have fallen through.*

fall *NOUN* **falls**
❶ a time when a person or thing falls
• *My grandma had a bad fall.* ❷ (*North
American*) autumn

fallow *ADJECTIVE*
land that is fallow has been ploughed but not
planted with crops • *The field was left fallow
every three years.*

falls *PLURAL NOUN*
a waterfall • *Niagara Falls*

false *ADJECTIVE* **falser, falsest**
❶ untrue or incorrect ❷ faked; not genuine
• *He was travelling under a false passport.*
➤ **falsely** *ADVERB* ➤ **falseness** *NOUN*

falsehood *NOUN* **falsehoods**
❶ falsehood is telling lies ❷ a falsehood is
a lie

falter *VERB* **falters, faltering, faltered**
❶ to falter is to keep stopping when you move
or speak ❷ to falter is also to become weaker
• *His courage began to falter.*

fame *NOUN*
fame is being famous
➤ **famed** *ADJECTIVE*

familiar *ADJECTIVE*
❶ well known; often seen or experienced
• *Pigeons are a familiar sight in the city.*
❷ knowing something well • *Are you familiar
with the legend of Robin Hood?* ❸ very friendly
➤ **familiarity** *NOUN*

familiarize (*also* **familiarise**) *VERB*
familiarize, familiarizing, familiarized
to familiarize yourself with something is to
learn about it so that you understand it • *You
will need to familiarize yourself with the rules
first.*

family *NOUN* **families**
❶ parents and their children, sometimes
including grandchildren and other relations
❷ a group of animals, plants or things that are
alike in some way • *The tiger is a member of the
cat family.*

family tree *NOUN* **family trees**
a diagram showing how people in a family are
related and who their ancestors are

famine *NOUN* **famines**
famine, or a famine, is a severe shortage of
food that causes many people to die

famished *ADJECTIVE*
extremely hungry

famous *ADJECTIVE*
known to a lot of people • *Her aunt is a famous
scientist.*

fan *NOUN* **fans**
❶ a device for making the air move about,
in order to cool people or things ❷ a fan is

also an enthusiastic follower or supporter of someone or something

fan VERB **fans, fanning, fanned**
to fan something is to send a draught of air at it • *She fanned her face with a newspaper.*
➤ **to fan out** is to spread out in the shape of a fan
Lloyd could see the men in brown overalls fanning out across the Dome, like hounds searching for a scent.—THE REVENGE OF THE DEMON HEADMASTER, Gillian Cross

fanatic (*say* fa-**nat**-ik) NOUN **fanatics**
someone who is too enthusiastic about something
➤ **fanatical** ADJECTIVE

fanciful ADJECTIVE
imagined rather than based on the way things really are • *a fanciful painting of an enchanted forest*

fancy NOUN **fancies**
❶ fancy is imagination ❷ a fancy is a liking or desire for something

fancy ADJECTIVE **fancier, fanciest**
decorated; not plain

fancy VERB **fancies, fancying, fancied**
❶ to fancy something is to want it • *Does anyone fancy an ice cream?* ❷ to fancy something unusual is to imagine or think of it • *Just fancy him riding a horse!*

fancy dress NOUN
unusual costume that you wear to a party or dance, often to make you look like someone else

fanfare NOUN **fanfares**
a short burst of music, often with trumpets and to announce something

fang NOUN **fangs**
a long sharp tooth
DID YOU KNOW? The word **fang** comes from an Old Norse word meaning 'catch' or 'grasp', because fangs can catch hold of things.

fantabulous ADJECTIVE (*informal*)
fantastic and wonderful • *That's a fantabulous idea!*

fantastic ADJECTIVE
❶ strange or unusual

Some of my companions pass the time by carving sea monsters' teeth into fantastic shapes, or by engraving pictures on them.—PIRATE DIARY, Richard Platt
❷ (*informal*) excellent
➤ **fantastically** ADVERB

fantasy NOUN **fantasies**
❶ something pleasant that you imagine but is not likely to happen • *Her fantasy is to be an Olympic champion.* ❷ a very imaginative story

far ADVERB **farther, farthest**
❶ a long way • *We didn't go far.* ❷ much; by a great amount • *She's a far better singer than I am.*
➤ **so far** up to now

far ADJECTIVE **farther, farthest**
distant; opposite • *Their house is on the far side of the river.*

faraway ADJECTIVE
distant or remote • *It is my dream to travel to faraway countries.*

farce NOUN **farces**
❶ a farce is a far-fetched or absurd kind of comedy ❷ farce, or a farce, is a series of ridiculous events • *The match ended up in farce.*
➤ **farcical** ADJECTIVE

fare NOUN **fares**
the money you pay to travel on a bus, train, ship or aircraft

fare VERB **fares, faring, fared**
to fare is to get on or make progress • *How did you fare in your exam?*

farewell EXCLAMATION
goodbye

far-fetched ADJECTIVE
unlikely to be true; difficult to believe

farm NOUN **farms**
❶ an area of land where someone grows crops and keeps animals for food ❷ the buildings on land of this kind ❸ a farmhouse

farm VERB **farms, farming, farmed**
❶ to farm is to grow crops and raise animals for food ❷ to farm land is to use it for growing crops

farmer *NOUN* **farmers**
someone who owns or looks after a farm

farmhouse *NOUN* **farmhouses**
the house where a farmer lives

farmyard *NOUN* **farmyards**
the open area surrounded by farm buildings

farther *ADVERB, ADJECTIVE*
at or to a greater distance; more distant • *The town lies farther west.*

farthest *ADVERB, ADJECTIVE*
at or to the greatest distance; most distant • *Which planet is the farthest from the sun?*

farthing *NOUN* **farthings**
an old British coin that was worth a quarter of an old penny

fascinate *VERB* **fascinates, fascinating, fascinated**
to fascinate someone is to attract or interest them very much • *I've always been fascinated by the Antarctic.*
➤ **fascination** *NOUN*

fashion *NOUN* **fashions**
❶ fashion, or a fashion, is the style of clothes or other things that most people like at a particular time • *a blog about the latest high-street fashions* ❷ a way of doing something • *The man spoke in a friendly fashion.*

fashion *VERB* **fashions, fashioning, fashioned**
to fashion something is to make it in a particular shape or style

fashionable *ADJECTIVE*
something is fashionable when it follows a style that is popular at a particular time

fast *ADJECTIVE* **faster, fastest**
❶ moving or done quickly • *Cheetahs are fast runners.* ❷ allowing fast movement • *This is the fast lane of the pool.* ❸ a watch or clock is fast when it shows a time later than the correct time ❹ secure; firmly held in place • *Make sure the rope is fast.* ❺ a fast colour is one that is not likely to fade

fast *ADVERB*
❶ quickly ❷ firmly
➤ **fast asleep** deeply asleep

fast *VERB* **fasts, fasting, fasted**
to fast is to go without food • *He's fasting for Ramadan.*

fast *NOUN* **fasts**
a period of fasting

fasten *VERB* **fastens, fastening, fastened**
to fasten something is to join it firmly to something else
➤ **fastener** *NOUN* a device used to fasten something

fat *NOUN* **fats**
❶ the white greasy part of meat ❷ an oily or greasy substance used in cooking

fat *ADJECTIVE* **fatter, fattest**
❶ having a very thick round body ❷ thick • *What a fat book!*

fatal *ADJECTIVE*
❶ causing someone's death • *There has been a fatal accident on the motorway.* ❷ likely to have bad results • *He then made a fatal mistake.*
➤ **fatally** *ADVERB*

fatality *NOUN* **fatalities**
a death caused by war or an accident

fate *NOUN* **fates**
❶ a power that is thought to make things happen ❷ someone's fate is what has happened or will happen to them

father *NOUN* **fathers**
a male parent
➤ A related word is **paternal**.

father-in-law *NOUN* **fathers-in-law**
the father of your husband or wife

Father's Day *NOUN*
a day of the year on which fathers are celebrated by their children

fathom *VERB* **fathoms, fathoming, fathomed**
to fathom something difficult or tricky is to work it out • *I can't fathom how you did it.*

fathom *NOUN* **fathoms**
a unit used in measuring the depth of water, equal to 1.83 metres or 6 feet

fatigue (*say* fa-**teeg**) *NOUN*
❶ extreme tiredness ❷ weakness in metals, caused by stress
➤ **fatigued** *ADJECTIVE*

fatten *VERB* **fattens, fattening, fattened**
❶ to fatten something is to make it fat
❷ to fatten is to become fat

fattening *ADJECTIVE*
fattening food is food that is likely to make you fat

fatty *ADJECTIVE* **fattier, fattiest**
fatty food contains a lot of fat

fault *NOUN* **faults**
❶ something wrong that spoils a person or thing; a flaw or mistake ❷ the responsibility or blame for something • *It's my fault we are late.*

fault *VERB* **faults, faulting, faulted**
to fault something is to find faults in it

faultless *ADJECTIVE*
something is faultless when it is perfect and has nothing wrong with it

faulty *ADJECTIVE* **faultier, faultiest**
having a fault or faults; not working properly

fauna (*say* **faw**-na) *NOUN*
the animals that live in an area or during a period of time

favour *NOUN* **favours**
❶ a favour is something kind that you do for someone • *Will you do me a favour?* ❷ favour is approval or goodwill • *The idea found favour with most people.*
➤ **to be in favour of something** is to like or support it

favour *VERB* **favours, favouring, favoured**
to favour someone or something is to like or support them, or prefer them to others

favourable *ADJECTIVE*
❶ helpful or suitable • *favourable weather for sailing* ❷ showing approval
➤ **favourably** *ADVERB*

favourite *ADJECTIVE*
liked more than others • *Purple is my favourite colour.*

favourite *NOUN* **favourites**
the person or thing that you like best • *This song is my favourite.*

favouritism *NOUN*
favouritism is when someone is unfairly kinder to one person than to others

fawn *NOUN* **fawns**
❶ a young deer ❷ a light brown colour

fear *NOUN* **fears**
fear, or a fear, is a feeling that something unpleasant may happen

fear *VERB* **fears, fearing, feared**
❶ to fear someone or something is to be afraid of them ❷ to fear something is also to be anxious or sad about it • *I feared we would be too late.*

fearful *ADJECTIVE*
❶ frightened
I came upon what I perceived to be a wolf pup. I was not fearful for I could see that he was too weak to do me harm.–THE LAST WOLF, Michael Morpurgo
❷ (*informal*) very bad, awful • *They had a fearful quarrel.*
➤ **fearfully** *ADVERB*

fearless *ADJECTIVE*
having no fear • *Sir Graysteel the knight was fearless in battle.*
➤ **fearlessly** *ADVERB*

fearsome *ADJECTIVE*
frightening
'As I was saying,' the Scarecrow went on, 'the brigands were a fearsome crew. Armed to the teeth, every single one.'–THE SCARECROW AND HIS SERVANT, Philip Pullman

feasible *ADJECTIVE*
able to be done; possible or likely

feast *NOUN* **feasts**
a large and splendid meal for a lot of people

feast *VERB* **feasts, feasting, feasted**
to feast is to have a feast

feat *NOUN* **feats**
a brave or clever deed

feather *NOUN* **feathers**
a bird's feathers are the very light pieces that grow from its skin and cover its body

a
b
c
d
e
f
g
h
i
j
k
l
m
n
o
p
q
r
s
t
u
v
w
x
y
z

feature NOUN **features**
❶ your features are the different parts of your face • *He has handsome features.*
❷ an important or noticeable part of something; a characteristic ❸ a newspaper article or television programme on a particular subject

feature VERB **features, featuring, featured**
❶ to feature something is to make it an important part of something • *Ghost stories often feature haunted houses.* ❷ to feature in something is to be an important part of it

February NOUN
the second month of the year
DID YOU KNOW? February is based on *Februa*, an ancient Roman festival that was held around this time.

fed VERB (*past tense and past participle* of **feed**)
• *He fed us hearty meals of soup.* • *Have you fed the dog?*

federal ADJECTIVE
to do with a system in which different states of a country are ruled by a central government, but each state still makes some of its own laws

federation NOUN
a group of different states that have joined together under a central government

fed up ADJECTIVE (*informal*)
bored or unhappy

fee NOUN **fees**
a payment or charge

feeble ADJECTIVE **feebler, feeblest**
weak; not having much strength or force • *The elderly knight had grown weak and feeble.*
➤ **feebly** ADVERB

feed VERB **feeds, feeding, fed**
❶ to feed a person or animal is to give them food ❷ to feed on something is to eat it • *Sheep feed on grass.* ❸ to feed a machine is to put paper, coins or other things into it

feed NOUN **feeds**
❶ a feed is a meal ❷ feed is food for animals

feedback NOUN
someone gives you feedback when they speak to you about something you have done

for them • *Your teacher will give you feedback on your homework.*

feel VERB **feels, feeling, felt**
❶ to feel something is to touch it to find out what it is like ❷ to feel a feeling or emotion is to experience it • *I felt annoyed at being left out.*
➤ **to feel like something** is to want it

feel NOUN
what something is like when you touch it • *This wool has a lovely feel to it.*

feeler NOUN **feelers**
an insect's feelers are the two long thin parts that extend from the front of its body and are used for feeling

feeling NOUN **feelings**
❶ feeling is the ability to feel or touch things • *She lost the feeling in her right hand.*
❷ feeling is also what a person feels in the mind, such as love or fear • *I have hurt her feelings.* ❸ a feeling is what you think about something • *My feeling is that he's right.*

feet NOUN (*plural of* **foot**)

feline ADJECTIVE
to do with cats, or like a cat

fell VERB (*past tense of* **fall**)
• *He was so tired he fell asleep instantly.*

fell VERB **fells, felling, felled**
❶ to fell a tree is to cut it down ❷ to fell someone is to knock them down

fell NOUN **fells**
a hill or stretch of high moorland

fellow NOUN **fellows**
❶ a friend or companion; someone who belongs to the same group ❷ (*informal*) a man or boy • *He's a clever fellow.*

fellow ADJECTIVE
of the same group or kind • *a group of fellow football fans*

fellowship NOUN **fellowships**
❶ fellowship is friendship ❷ a fellowship is a group of friends; a society

felt VERB (*past tense and past participle of* **feel**)
• *He felt a sharp pain in his leg.* • *I had felt sorry for her.*

felt *NOUN*
felt is a type of thick woollen material

felt-tip pen *NOUN* **felt-tip pens**
a pen with a tip made of felt or fibre

female *ADJECTIVE*
belonging to the sex that can produce young by giving birth or laying eggs

female *NOUN* **females**
a female person or animal

feminine *ADJECTIVE*
to do with women or like women; suitable for women
➤ **femininity** *NOUN*

fen *NOUN* **fens**
an area of low-lying marshy or flooded land

fence *NOUN* **fences**
a wooden or metal barrier round an area of land

fence *VERB* **fences, fencing, fenced**
❶ to fence something or to fence it in is to put a fence round it ❷ to fence is to fight with long narrow swords called *foils*, as a sport

fencing *NOUN*
a sport that involves fighting with swords

fend *VERB* **fends, fending, fended**
➤ **to fend for yourself** is to take care of yourself
➤ **to fend someone** or **something off** is to keep them away from yourself when they are attacking you

fender *NOUN* **fenders**
❶ a low guard placed round a fireplace to stop coal from falling out
❷ (*North American*) a bumper on a car

fern *NOUN* **ferns**
a plant with feathery leaves and no flowers

ferocious *ADJECTIVE*
fierce or savage • *a ferocious fire-breathing dragon*
➤ **ferociously** *ADVERB*

ferocity *NOUN*
fierceness

ferret *NOUN* **ferrets**
a small fierce animal with a long thin body, used for catching rabbits and rats

ferret *VERB* **ferrets, ferreting, ferreted**
to ferret, or ferret about, is to search busily for something

ferry *NOUN* **ferries**
a boat that takes people or things across a river or other stretch of water

ferry *VERB* **ferries, ferrying, ferried**
to ferry people or things is to take them from one place to another, especially by boat or car

fertile *ADJECTIVE*
❶ land that is fertile is good for growing crops and plants ❷ people or animals that are fertile can produce babies or young animals
➤ **fertility** *NOUN*

fertilize (*also* **fertilise**) *VERB* **fertilizes, fertilizing, fertilized**
❶ to fertilize the soil is to add chemicals or manure to it so that crops and plants grow better ❷ to fertilize an egg or plant is to put male cells into it so that it develops its young or seeds
➤ **fertilization** *NOUN*

fertilizer (*also* **fertiliser**) *NOUN* **fertilizers**
chemicals or manure added to the soil to make crops and plants grow better

fervent *ADJECTIVE*
very enthusiastic about something • *He is a fervent supporter of the team.*
➤ **fervently** *ADVERB*

fervour *NOUN*
strong feeling or great enthusiasm

festival *NOUN* **festivals**
❶ a time of celebration, especially for religious reasons ❷ an organized set of concerts, shows or other events, especially one that is arranged every year

festive *ADJECTIVE*
to do with joyful celebrating

festivities *PLURAL NOUN*
parties and other events that are held to celebrate something

festoon *VERB* **festoons, festooning, festooned**
to festoon a place is to decorate it with chains of flowers or ribbons

a b c d e f g h i j k l m n o p q r s t u v w x y z

fetch VERB **fetches, fetching, fetched**
❶ to fetch something or someone is to go and get them ❷ something fetches a particular price when it is sold for that price • *My old bike fetched £10.*

fete (*say* fayt) NOUN **fetes**
an outdoor event with stalls, games and things for sale, often held to raise money

fetters PLURAL NOUN
fetters are chains put round a prisoner's ankles

feud (*say* fewd) NOUN **feuds**
a bitter quarrel between two people or families that lasts a long time

feud VERB **feuds, feuding, feuded**
people feud when they keep up a quarrel for a long time

fever NOUN **fevers**
❶ a person has a fever when their body temperature is higher than usual because they are ill ❷ fever is excitement or agitation

feverish ADJECTIVE
❶ someone is feverish when they have a slight fever ❷ excited or frantic • *There was feverish activity getting the hall ready for the show.*
➤ **feverishly** ADVERB

few DETERMINER **fewer, fewest**
not many

few PRONOUN
a small number of people or things
➤ **a good few** *or* **quite a few** a fairly large number

fiancé (*say* fee-ahn-say) NOUN **fiancés**
someone's fiancé is the man who they are engaged to be married to

fiancée (*say* fee-ahn-say) NOUN **fiancées**
someone's fiancée is the woman who they are engaged to be married to

fiasco (*say* fi-ass-koh) NOUN **fiascos**
a complete failure • *The party turned into a fiasco.*

fib NOUN **fibs**
a lie about something unimportant

fib VERB **fibs, fibbing, fibbed**
to fib is to tell a lie about something unimportant
➤ **fibber** NOUN someone who tells fibs

fibre (*say* fy-ber) NOUN **fibres**
❶ a fibre is a very thin thread ❷ fibre is a substance made up of thin threads ❸ fibre is also a substance in food that your body cannot digest but that moves the rest of the food quickly through your body and helps you to digest it

fickle ADJECTIVE
someone is fickle when they often change their mind or do not stay loyal to one person or group

fiction NOUN **fictions**
❶ fiction is writing, such as stories and novels, about events that have not really happened ❷ a fiction is something untrue or made up

fictional ADJECTIVE
a fictional character or event exists only in a story, not in real life

fictitious ADJECTIVE
made up by someone and untrue

fiddle NOUN **fiddles** (*informal*)
a violin

fiddle VERB **fiddles, fiddling, fiddled**
❶ to fiddle is to play the violin ❷ to fiddle with something is to keep touching or playing with it with your fingers • *Please stop fiddling with your phone!*
➤ **fiddler** NOUN

fiddly ADJECTIVE **fiddlier, fiddliest** (*informal*)
awkward to use or do because it involves handling small objects • *Replacing the battery is a fiddly job.*

fidelity (*say* fi-del-i-tee) NOUN
fidelity is being faithful or loyal

fidget VERB **fidgets, fidgeting, fidgeted**
to make small restless movements because you are bored or nervous
➤ **fidgety** ADJECTIVE

field NOUN **fields**
❶ a piece of land with crops or grass growing on it ❷ an area of interest or study • *She wants to work in the field of science.*

field VERB **fields, fielding, fielded**
to field a ball in cricket or other games is to stop it or catch it
➤ **fielder** NOUN

field trip NOUN field trips
a visit to a place with your school to study something in its natural environment

fiend (say feend) NOUN fiends
❶ a devil or evil spirit ❷ a wicked or cruel person

fiendish ADJECTIVE
❶ wicked or cruel ❷ very difficult or complicated • *That was a fiendish puzzle.*
➤ fiendishly ADVERB

fierce ADJECTIVE fiercer, fiercest
❶ angry and violent and likely to attack you ❷ strong or intense • *The heat from the fire was fierce.*
➤ fiercely ADVERB ➤ fierceness NOUN

fiery ADJECTIVE fierier, fieriest
❶ full of flames or heat
The building looked like a fiery ghost, with great bursts of flame coming from the windows.—THE HOSTILE HOSPITAL, Lemony Snicket
❷ easily made angry • *Olaf the Viking had a fiery temper.*

fifteen NOUN fifteens
the number 15
➤ fifteenth ADJECTIVE, NOUN

fifth ADJECTIVE, NOUN
the next after the fourth
➤ fifthly ADVERB in the fifth place; as the fifth one

fifty NOUN fifties
the number 50
➤ fiftieth ADJECTIVE, NOUN

fig NOUN figs
a soft fruit full of small seeds

fight NOUN fights
❶ a struggle against someone, using hands or weapons ❷ an attempt to achieve or overcome something • *Recycling is part of the fight against waste.*

fight VERB fights, fighting, fought
❶ to fight someone is to have a fight with them ❷ to fight something is to try to stop it • *Firefighters fought the blaze all night.*
❸ to fight for something, or fight to do something, is to try hard to make it happen • *Women fought for the right to vote.*

fighter NOUN fighters
❶ someone who fights ❷ a fast military plane that attacks other aircraft

figurative ADJECTIVE
figurative language uses words for special effect and not in their usual way, often in order to describe what something is like. For example *flood* in *a flood of emails* is a figurative use of the word.

figure NOUN figures
❶ one of the symbols that stand for numbers, such as 1, 2 and 3 ❷ the shape of someone's body ❸ a diagram or illustration in a book or magazine ❹ a pattern or shape • *He drew a figure of eight.*

figure VERB figures, figuring, figured
❶ to appear or take part in something • *His name does not figure in the list of entrants.*
❷ to think that something is probably true • *I figure the best thing to do is to wait.*
➤ to figure something out is to work it out • *Can you figure out the answer?*

figure of speech NOUN figures of speech
a special way of using words that makes what you say or write interesting, such as a metaphor or a simile

filament NOUN filaments
a thread or thin wire

file NOUN files
❶ a box or folder for keeping papers in ❷ a set of information that has been stored under one name in a computer ❸ a file is also a tool with a rough surface that you rub on things to make them smooth or shape them
➤ to walk in single file is to walk one behind the other

file VERB files, filing, filed
❶ to file a paper or document is to put it in a box or folder ❷ to file is to walk one behind the other ❸ to file something is also to make it smooth or shape it with a file

filings PLURAL NOUN
tiny pieces of metal that have been rubbed from a larger piece

fill VERB fills, filling, filled
❶ to fill something is to make it full ❷ to fill is to become full • *The room was filling quickly.*
❸ to fill a tooth is to put a filling in it

A B C D E F G H I J K L M N O P Q R S T U V W X Y Z

➤ **to fill in a form** is to write answers to all the questions on it

➤ **to fill something up** is to fill it completely

fill NOUN **fills**
enough to make you full • *Eat your fill.*

fillet NOUN **fillets**
a piece of fish or meat without bones

filling NOUN **fillings**
❶ a piece of metal put in your tooth by a dentist to replace a decayed part ❷ food you put inside a pie, sandwich or cake

filly NOUN **fillies**
a young female horse

film NOUN **films**
❶ a series of moving pictures that tells a story, such as those shown in a cinema or on television ❷ a roll or piece of thin plastic that you put in some types of camera to take photographs ❸ a very thin layer of something • *The table was covered in a film of grease.*

film VERB **films**, **filming**, **filmed**
to film something is to make a film of it

filter NOUN **filters**
❶ a device for removing dirt or other unwanted things from a liquid or gas that passes through it ❷ a system allowing a line of traffic to move in one direction while other lines are held up

filter VERB **filters**, **filtering**, **filtered**
❶ to filter a liquid or gas is to pass it through a filter ❷ to move gradually • *People started to filter into the hall.*

filth NOUN
disgusting dirt

filthy ADJECTIVE **filthier**, **filthiest**
very dirty

fin NOUN **fins**
❶ a thin flat part that sticks out from a fish's body and helps it to swim ❷ a small part that sticks out from an aircraft or rocket and helps it to balance

final ADJECTIVE
❶ coming at the end; last ❷ a decision is final when it puts an end to argument or doubt • *You must not go, and that's final!*

final NOUN **finals**
the last of a series of contests that decides the overall winner

finale (*say* fin-ah-lee) NOUN **finales**
the last part of a show or piece of music

finalist NOUN **finalists**
a person or team taking part in a final

finally ADVERB
❶ after a long time, at last • *We finally got there around midnight.* ❷ as the last thing • *Finally, I would like to thank my parents.*

finance NOUN
❶ finance is the use and control of money ❷ someone's finances are the amount of money or funds they have

finance VERB **finances**, **financing**, **financed**
to finance something is to provide money for it

financial ADJECTIVE
to do with money

finch NOUN **finches**
a small bird with a short thick beak

find VERB **finds**, **finding**, **found**
❶ to find something is to see or get it by chance or by looking for it ❷ to find something is also to learn it by experience • *He found that digging is hard work.*

➤ **to find someone out** is to discover that they have done something wrong

➤ **to find something out** is to get information about it

findings PLURAL NOUN
things someone has found out

fine ADJECTIVE **finer**, **finest**
❶ of high quality; excellent • *They cooked a fine meal.* ❷ the weather is fine when it is sunny and not raining ❸ very thin or delicate • *The curtains were made of a fine material.* ❹ made of small particles • *The sand on the beach was very fine.*

➤ **finely** ADVERB into fine or small parts • *Slice the tomato finely.*

fine NOUN **fines**
a fine is money that someone must pay as a punishment

fine *VERB* **fines, fining, fined**
to fine someone is to make them pay money as a punishment

finger *NOUN* **fingers**
1 one of the long thin parts that stick out on your hand **2** something that is shaped like a finger

finger *VERB* **fingers, fingering, fingered**
to finger something is to touch it with your fingers

fingernail *NOUN* **fingernails**
the hard covering at the end of your finger

fingerprint *NOUN* **fingerprints**
a mark made by the pattern of curved lines on the tip of your finger

finicky *ADJECTIVE*
fussy or hard to please

finish *VERB* **finishes, finishing, finished**
1 to finish something is to bring it to an end **2** to finish is to come to an end

finish *NOUN* **finishes**
the end of something

fir *NOUN* **firs**
an evergreen tree with leaves like needles

fire *NOUN* **fires**
1 fire, or a fire, is the flames, heat and light that come from burning things **2** coal or wood burning in a grate or furnace to give heat **3** a device using electricity or gas to heat a room **4** the shooting of guns • *Hold your fire!*
➤ **to set fire to something** is to start it burning

fire *VERB* **fires, firing, fired**
1 to fire a gun is to shoot it **2** (*informal*) to fire someone is to dismiss them from their job **3** to fire pottery or bricks is to bake them in an oven to make them hard

firearm *NOUN* **firearms**
a gun or rifle

fire brigade *NOUN* **fire brigades**
a team of people whose job is to put out fires and rescue people from fires

fire engine *NOUN* **fire engines**
a large vehicle that carries firefighters and equipment to fight fires

fire extinguisher *NOUN*
fire extinguishers
a metal cylinder containing water or foam for spraying over a fire to put it out

firefighter *NOUN* **firefighters**
a person whose job is to put out fires

fireplace *NOUN* **fireplaces**
an open space for a fire in the wall of a room

fireproof *ADJECTIVE*
something is fireproof when it can stand great heat without burning

fireside *NOUN* **firesides**
the part of a room near the fire

fire station *NOUN* **fire stations**
the headquarters of a fire brigade

firewood *NOUN*
wood suitable for burning as fuel

firework *NOUN* **fireworks**
a tube containing chemicals that give off sparks when set alight, used to create displays of coloured lights in the sky

firm *NOUN* **firms**
a business organization • *She works for a clothing firm.*

firm *ADJECTIVE* **firmer, firmest**
1 fixed or solid so that it will not move **2** definite and not likely to change • *She has made a firm decision to go.*
➤ **firmly** *ADVERB* ➤ **firmness** *NOUN*

first *ADJECTIVE*
1 coming before all others • *I'd like to be the first woman on the moon!* **2** the most important • *The team has been moved up to the first division.*

first *ADVERB*
before everything else • *Finish your homework first.*

first *NOUN*
a person or thing that is first
➤ **at first** at the beginning; to start with

first aid *NOUN*
simple medical treatment that is given to an injured person before a doctor comes

a b c d e **f** g h i j k l m n o p q r s t u v w x y z

first-class ADJECTIVE
❶ belonging to the best part of a service • *Send the letter by first-class post.* ❷ excellent

first floor NOUN **first floors**
the next floor above the ground floor

first-hand ADJECTIVE, ADVERB
you get first-hand information directly, rather than from other people or from books

firstly ADVERB
as the first thing • *Firstly, let me tell you about our holiday.*

first minister NOUN **first ministers**
the leader of the government in some countries, especially Scotland and Wales

first-rate ADJECTIVE
excellent

firth NOUN **firths**
an estuary or river mouth on the coast of Scotland • *the Firth of Forth*

fish NOUN **fish** or **fishes**
a cold-blooded animal with gills and fins that lives and breathes in water

fish VERB **fishes, fishing, fished**
to fish is to try to catch fish
➤ **to fish something out** is to pull or take it out of somewhere carefully

fisherman, fisherwoman NOUN
fishermen, fisherwomen
a person who tries to catch fish, either as a job or as a sport

fishmonger NOUN **fishmongers**
a shopkeeper who sells fish

fishy ADJECTIVE **fishier, fishiest**
❶ smelling or tasting of fish ❷ (*informal*) suspicious or a bit strange • *His excuse was rather fishy.*

fissure NOUN **fissures**
a narrow opening or crack • *A fissure opened up in the ice.*

fist NOUN **fists**
your hand when it is tightly closed with your fingers bent into your palm

fit ADJECTIVE **fitter, fittest**
❶ healthy and strong because you get a lot of exercise ❷ suitable or good enough • *It was*

a meal fit for a king. ❸ ready or likely • *They worked till they were fit to collapse.*
➤ **to see fit** or **think fit to do something** is to decide or choose to do it

fit VERB **fits, fitting, fitted**
❶ when something fits someone, it is the right size and shape for them • *This dress doesn't fit me any more.* ❷ to fit something is to be suitable for it • *The music fitted the film perfectly.* ❸ to fit something is to put it into place • *We need to fit a new lock on the door.*

fit NOUN **fits**
❶ the way something fits • *The jeans are a good fit.* ❷ a sudden illness, especially one that makes you move violently or become unconscious ❸ (*informal*) a sudden outburst • *He rushed off in a fit of rage.*

fitness NOUN
being healthy and strong because of doing a lot of exercise

fitted ADJECTIVE
made to fit something exactly • *The room has a fitted carpet.*

fitter NOUN **fitters**
someone who fits clothes or machinery

fitting ADJECTIVE
suitable or proper

fitting NOUN **fittings**
fittings are pieces of furniture or equipment in a room or building

five NOUN **fives**
the number 5

fiver NOUN **fivers** (*informal*)
a five-pound note; £5

fix VERB **fixes, fixing, fixed**
❶ to fix something is to join it firmly to something else or to put it where it will not move ❷ to fix something is also to decide or settle it • *We have fixed a date for the party.* ❸ to fix something that is broken is to mend it • *He's fixing my bike.*
➤ **to fix something up** is to arrange or organize something

fix NOUN **fixes** (*informal*)
an awkward situation • *I'm in a fix.*

fixture NOUN **fixtures**
❶ a sports event planned for a particular day

❷ something fixed in its place, like a cupboard or a washbasin

fizz VERB fizzes, fizzing, fizzed
❶ to fizz is to make a hissing or spluttering sound **❷** liquid fizzes when it produces a lot of small bubbles

fizzle VERB fizzles, fizzling, fizzled
to fizzle is to make a slight hissing sound
➤ **to fizzle out** is to end in a disappointing or unsuccessful way

fizzy ADJECTIVE fizzier, fizziest
a fizzy drink has a lot of bubbles

fjord (say fyord or fee-ord) NOUN fjords
a narrow strip of water coming in from the sea between high cliffs, found especially in Norway
Odd's mother, who was as dark as Odd's father had been fair, had been brought to the fjord on a longship from Scotland.—ODD AND THE FROST GIANTS, Neil Gaiman

flabbergasted ADJECTIVE (informal)
completely astonished

flabby ADJECTIVE flabbier, flabbiest
fat and soft; not firm

flag NOUN flags
❶ a piece of material with a coloured pattern or shape on it, often used as the symbol of a country or organization **❷** a flag is also a flat slab of paving stone
flag VERB flags, flagging, flagged
to flag is to become weak or droop
➤ **to flag a vehicle down** is to make the driver stop by waving your hand

flagpole NOUN flagpoles
a pole that a flag is attached to

flagship NOUN flagships
the main ship in a navy's fleet, which has the commander of the fleet on board

flagstone NOUN flagstones
a flat slab of paving stone

flake NOUN flakes
❶ a very light thin piece of something • *Flakes of old paint came off the wall.* **❷** a piece of falling snow
flake VERB flakes, flaking, flaked
to flake is to come off in light thin pieces

flaky ADJECTIVE flakier, flakiest
something that is flaky is likely to break into light thin pieces • *flaky pastry*

flame NOUN flames
a bright strip of fire that flickers and leaps
flame VERB flames, flaming, flamed
to flame is to produce flames or become bright red

flamingo NOUN flamingos
a large wading bird with long legs, a long neck and pale pink feathers

flammable ADJECTIVE
something that is flammable can be set alight easily

flan NOUN flans
a pie without any pastry on top

flank NOUN flanks
the side of something, especially an animal's body or an army

flannel NOUN flannels
❶ a flannel is a piece of soft cloth you use to wash yourself **❷** flannel is a soft woollen material

flap NOUN flaps
❶ a part that hangs down from one edge of something, usually to cover an opening **❷** the action or sound of flapping **❸** (informal) a panic or fuss • *Don't get in a flap.*
flap VERB flaps, flapping, flapped
❶ to flap something is to move it up and down or from side to side • *The bird flapped its wings.* **❷** to flap is to wave about • *The sails were flapping in the breeze.*

flapjack NOUN flapjacks
a cake made from oats and syrup

flare VERB flares, flaring, flared
❶ to flare is to burn with a sudden bright flame **❷** to flare is also to become suddenly angry **❸** things flare or flare out when they get gradually wider
flare NOUN flares
❶ a bright light fired into the sky as a signal **❷** a gradual widening, especially in skirts or trousers

a b c d e f g h i j k l m n o p q r s t u v w x y z

flash NOUN **flashes**
❶ a sudden bright burst of light ❷ a device for making a brief bright light when you take a photograph ❸ a sudden display of anger or humour
➤ **to happen in a flash** is to happen immediately or very quickly

flash VERB **flashes, flashing, flashed**
❶ to make a sudden bright burst of light
❷ to flash past or across is to approach and go past very fast • *We stopped as an express train flashed past.*

flashback NOUN **flashbacks**
going back in a film or story to something that happened earlier • *The hero's childhood was shown in flashbacks.*

flashy ADJECTIVE **flashier, flashiest**
showy and expensive • *He wore a flashy suit with a garish tie.*

flask NOUN **flasks**
❶ a bottle with a narrow neck ❷ a vacuum flask

flat ADJECTIVE **flatter, flattest**
❶ having no curves or bumps; smooth and level ❷ spread out; lying at full length
• *Lie flat on the ground.* ❸ dull or uninteresting
• *He spoke in a flat voice.* ❹ complete; not changing • *We got a flat refusal.* ❺ a liquid is flat when it is no longer fizzy ❻ a tyre is flat when it is punctured and has lost its air ❼ feet are flat when they do not have the normal shape underneath ❽ below the proper musical pitch • *Can you hear which note is flat?*
➤ **flatness** NOUN

flat ADVERB
exactly and no more • *He won the race in ten seconds flat.*
➤ **flat out** as fast as possible • *They worked flat out to get their homework finished in time.*

flat NOUN **flats**
❶ a set of rooms for living in, usually on one floor of a building ❷ (*music*) the note that is a semitone lower than the natural note; the sign (♭) that indicates this

flatly ADVERB
in a definite way, leaving no room for doubt
• *They flatly refused to go.*

flatten VERB **flattens, flattening, flattened**
❶ to flatten something is to make it flat
❷ to flatten is to become flat

flatter VERB **flatters, flattering, flattered**
to flatter someone is to praise them more than they deserve, often because you want to please them
➤ **flattery** NOUN

flaunt VERB **flaunts, flaunting, flaunted**
to flaunt something is to show it off too proudly • *He is always flaunting his new phone.*

flautist NOUN **flautists**
someone who plays the flute

flavour NOUN **flavours**
flavour, or a flavour, is the taste and smell of a food or drink

flavour VERB **flavours, flavouring, flavoured**
to flavour food or drink is to give it a particular taste and smell

flavouring NOUN **flavourings**
something added to food or drink to give it a particular flavour

flaw NOUN **flaws**
a fault that stops a person or thing from being perfect • *There was a major flaw in their escape plan.*

flawless ADJECTIVE
perfect, with no faults

flax NOUN
a plant that produces fibres that are used to make cloth, and seeds that are used to make oil

flea NOUN **fleas**
a small jumping insect that sucks blood

fleck NOUN **flecks**
a small piece or speck • *There were flecks of dirt on the table.*

fled VERB (*past tense and past participle of flee*)
• *People fled in panic as the fire started.*
• *He had fled from England, never to return.*

flee VERB **flees, fleeing, fled**
to flee is to run away from something

fleece *NOUN* fleeces
❶ a sheep's fleece is the wool that covers its body ❷ a type of jacket or top made from a soft warm material

fleece *VERB* fleeces, fleecing, fleeced
to fleece a sheep is to shear it

fleet *NOUN* fleets
a number of ships, aircraft or vehicles owned by one country or company

fleeting *ADJECTIVE*
very brief; passing quickly • *I caught a fleeting glimpse of a deer.*

flesh *NOUN*
the soft substance of the bodies of people and animals, made of muscle and fat

flew *VERB* (*past tense of* fly)
• *The door flew open.*

flex *NOUN* flexes
flexible wire for carrying an electric current

flex *VERB* flexes, flexing, flexed
to flex something is to move or bend it • *Try flexing your ankle.*

flexible *ADJECTIVE*
❶ easy to bend or stretch ❷ able to be changed • *Our plans are flexible.*
➤ **flexibility** *NOUN*

flick *NOUN* flicks
a quick light hit or movement

flick *VERB* flicks, flicking, flicked
to flick something is to hit or move it with a flick
Harry flicked his wand at the oil lamps as he entered and they illuminated the shabby but cosy room.—HARRY POTTER AND THE DEATHLY HALLOWS, J. K. Rowling

flicker *VERB* flickers, flickering, flickered
to burn or shine unsteadily
The sky was quite black and the big stars flickered as if they were alive, and far in the distance shone something red, like a wicked eye.—COMET IN MOOMINLAND, Tove Jansson

flight *NOUN* flights
❶ flight is the action of flying • *a film about the history of space flight* ❷ flight is also running away or escape • *The enemy were in full flight.* ❸ a flight is a journey in an aircraft or rocket ❹ a flight is also a group of flying birds or aircraft ❺ a flight of stairs is one set of stairs

flight attendant *NOUN* flight attendants
someone whose job is to look after the passengers on an aircraft

flightless *ADJECTIVE*
a flightless bird or insect is unable to fly

flimsy *ADJECTIVE* flimsier, flimsiest
light and thin; fragile • *flimsy tissue paper* • *a flimsy wooden hut*

flinch *VERB* flinches, flinching, flinched
to make a sudden movement because you are frightened or in pain

fling *VERB* flings, flinging, flung
to fling something is to throw it violently or carelessly • *He flung his shoes under the bed.*

flint *NOUN* flints
❶ flint is a very hard kind of stone ❷ a flint is a piece of this stone or hard metal used to produce sparks

flip *VERB* flips, flipping, flipped
to flip something is to turn it over quickly • *Flip the pancake over to cook the other side.*

flip chart *NOUN* flip charts
a large pad of paper on a stand with pages which you turn over at the top

flippant *ADJECTIVE*
not being serious when you should be • *Don't be flippant about his illness.*

flipper *NOUN* flippers
❶ one of the limbs that water animals such as seals and turtles have to help them swim ❷ a flat rubber shoe shaped like a duck's foot, that you wear on your feet to help you swim

flirt *VERB* flirts, flirting, flirted
to flirt with someone is to talk to them as if you wanted to get them to love you, not seriously but just for fun

flit *VERB* flits, flitting, flitted
to flit is to fly or move lightly and quickly • *A moth flitted across the room.*

float *VERB* floats, floating, floated
❶ to float is to stay or move on the surface of a liquid or in the air ❷ to float something is to make it stay on the surface of a liquid

a
b
c
d
e
f
g
h
i
j
k
l
m
n
o
p
q
r
s
t
u
v
w
x
y
z

A
B
C
D
E
F
G
H
I
J
K
L
M
N
O
P
Q
R
S
T
U
V
W
X
Y
Z

float *NOUN* **floats**
❶ a device designed to float • *Use the floats if you are just learning to swim.* ❷ a vehicle with a platform used for a display in a parade

flock *NOUN* **flocks**
a group of sheep, goats or birds

flock *VERB* **flocks**, **flocking**, **flocked**
to flock is to gather or move in a crowd • *People flocked to see the fireworks.*

flog *VERB* **flogs**, **flogging**, **flogged**
❶ to flog someone is to beat them severely with a whip or stick ❷ (*informal*) to flog something is to sell it

flood *NOUN* **floods**
❶ a large amount of water spreading over a place that is usually dry ❷ a great amount of something • *The TV station received a flood of complaints.*

flood *VERB* **floods**, **flooding**, **flooded**
❶ to flood something is to cover it with a large amount of water ❷ a river floods when it flows over its banks ❸ to arrive in large amounts • *Offers of help came flooding in from all over the country.*

floodlight *NOUN* **floodlights**
a lamp that gives a broad bright beam, used to light up a public building or a sports ground at night
➤ **floodlit** *ADJECTIVE*

floor *NOUN* **floors**
❶ the part of a room that people walk on ❷ all the rooms on the same level in a building • *The sports department is on the top floor.*

floor *VERB* **floors**, **flooring**, **floored**
to floor someone is to knock them down

floorboard *NOUN* **floorboards**
one of the long flat boards in a wooden floor

flop *VERB* **flops**, **flopping**, **flopped**
❶ to flop, or flop down, is to fall or sit down heavily ❷ to flop is also to fall or hang loosely or heavily • *His hair flopped over his eyes.* ❸ (*informal*) to flop is to be a failure

flop *NOUN* **flops**
❶ the movement or sound of sudden falling or sitting down ❷ (*informal*) a failure or disappointment • *The play was a complete flop.*

floppy *ADJECTIVE* **floppier**, **floppiest**
hanging loosely or heavily • *Our dog has huge floppy ears.*

flora (*say* flor-a) *NOUN*
the plants that live in an area or during a period of time

floral *ADJECTIVE*
made of flowers or to do with flowers

florist *NOUN* **florists**
a shopkeeper who sells flowers

floss *NOUN*
❶ a mass of silky thread or fibres ❷ a kind of thread that you pull between your teeth to clean them

flounder *VERB* **flounders**, **floundering**, **floundered**
to move or struggle clumsily because you are in difficulties
The animals floundered in the shallows at the river's edge, trampling the banks to mud, treading on each other.—HOW THE WHALE BECAME AND OTHER STORIES, Ted Hughes

flour *NOUN*
a fine powder made from corn or wheat and used for making bread, cakes and pastry
➤ **floury** *ADJECTIVE* powdery like flour

flourish *VERB* **flourishes**, **flourishing**, **flourished**
❶ to flourish is to grow or develop strongly; to be successful ❷ to flourish something is to wave it about • *Mrs Brown flourished a big spoon.*

flourish *NOUN* **flourishes**
if you do something with a flourish, you do it in a dramatic way that people will notice • *He signed his name with a flourish.*

flow *VERB* **flows**, **flowing**, **flowed**
❶ to flow is to move along smoothly, like a river does ❷ to flow is also to hang loosely • *She had golden flowing hair.*

flow *NOUN* **flows**
a continuous steady movement of something

flower *NOUN* **flowers**
❶ the part of a plant from which the seed or fruit develops ❷ a plant with a flower • *The poppy is a wild flower.*
➤ **to be in flower** is to be producing flowers

flower *VERB* flowers, flowering, flowered
a plant flowers when it produces flowers

flowerpot *NOUN* flowerpots
a pot in which plants are grown

flowery *ADJECTIVE*
❶ decorated with flowers or pictures of them
• *a room with flowery wallpaper* ❷ using fancy words • *a flowery style of writing*

flown *VERB* (*past participle of* **fly**)
• *A gorgeous butterfly had flown into the room.*

flu *NOUN*
an infectious disease that causes pain in your muscles and fever

fluctuate *VERB* fluctuates, fluctuating, fluctuated
to keep changing
➤ **fluctuation** *NOUN*

flue *NOUN* flues
a pipe that takes smoke and fumes away from a stove or boiler

fluent *ADJECTIVE*
skilful at speaking, especially a foreign language

fluff *NOUN*
fluff is the small soft bits that come off wool and cloth

fluffy *ADJECTIVE* fluffier, fluffiest
soft like fluff • *a pair of fluffy slippers*
➤ **fluffiness** *NOUN*

fluid *NOUN* fluids
a substance that flows easily, like liquids and gases

fluke *NOUN* flukes
a success that you achieve by unexpected good luck

flung *VERB* (*past tense and past participle of* **fling**)
• *He flung his arms up to protect himself.*
• *He was flung backwards by the blast.*

fluorescent *ADJECTIVE*
a fluorescent light or lamp is one that produces a bright light by means of radiation

fluoride *NOUN*
a chemical that is thought to help prevent tooth decay

flurry *NOUN* flurries
a sudden gust of wind or rain or snow

flush *VERB* flushes, flushing, flushed
❶ to flush is to go slightly red in the face
❷ to flush something is to clean or remove it with a fast flow of liquid

flush *NOUN* flushes
❶ a slight blush ❷ a fast flow of water

flustered *ADJECTIVE*
nervous and confused
Aunty Rose looked around her like a flustered hen. 'What are you all talking about?' she asked.—TOM'S SAUSAGE LION, Michael Morpurgo

flute *NOUN* flutes
a flute is a musical instrument consisting of a long pipe with holes that are covered by fingers or keys. You play it by holding it to one side of your mouth and blowing over a hole at one end.

flutter *VERB* flutters, fluttering, fluttered
❶ to move with a quick flapping of wings
• *A butterfly fluttered in through the window.*
❷ to move or flap quickly and lightly • *The flags fluttered in the breeze.*

flutter *NOUN* flutters
a fluttering movement
➤ **to be in a flutter** is to be nervous and excited

fly *VERB* flies, flying, flew, flown
❶ to fly is to move through the air with wings or in an aircraft ❷ to fly is also to wave in the air • *Flags were flying.* ❸ to fly something is to make it move through the air • *They were flying model aircraft.* ❹ to fly is to move or pass quickly • *The door flew open.* • *The weeks just flew by.*

fly *NOUN* flies
❶ a small flying insect with two wings ❷ the front opening of a pair of trousers

flying saucer *NOUN* flying saucers
a saucer-shaped flying object believed to come from outer space, especially in science fiction stories

flyover *NOUN* flyovers
a bridge that carries one road over another

a b c d e f g h i j k l m n o p q r s t u v w x y z

foal to fond

foal NOUN **foals**
a young horse

foam NOUN
❶ a mass of tiny bubbles on top of a liquid ❷ a spongy kind of rubber or plastic, used to fill cushions and mattresses

foam VERB **foams, foaming, foamed**
to foam is to form a mass of tiny bubbles

focus NOUN **focuses** or **foci**
❶ the point at which something appears most clearly to your eye or in a lens ❷ the part of something that people pay most attention to
➤ **to be in focus** is to appear clearly and not blurred
➤ **to be out of focus** is to appear blurred

focus VERB **focuses, focusing, focused**
❶ to focus your eye or a camera lens is to adjust it so that objects appear clearly ❷ to focus your attention on something is to concentrate on it

fodder NOUN
fodder is food for horses and farm animals

foe NOUN **foes** (old use)
an enemy

foetus (say fee-tus) NOUN **foetuses**
a developing embryo, especially an unborn human baby

fog NOUN **fogs**
thick mist which makes it difficult to see

foggy ADJECTIVE **foggier, foggiest**
the weather is foggy when there is a lot of fog
➤ **fogginess** NOUN

foghorn NOUN **foghorns**
a loud horn used to warn ships of the danger of fog
➤ **to have a voice like a foghorn** is to speak in a very loud voice

foil NOUN **foils**
❶ foil is very thin sheets of metal, sometimes used to wrap food ❷ a foil is also a long narrow sword used in the sport of fencing

foil VERB **foils, foiling, foiled**
to foil someone or something is to stop them from succeeding • Police foiled the robbers' plan.

fold VERB **folds, folding, folded**
❶ to fold something is to bend it so that one part lies over another part ❷ to fold is to bend or move in this way • The table folds up when you are not using it. ❸ to fold your arms is to put one of your arms over the other one and hold them against your chest

fold NOUN **folds**
❶ a line where something has been folded ❷ a fold is also an enclosure for sheep

folder NOUN **folders**
❶ a folding cardboard or plastic cover to keep loose papers in ❷ a place where a set of files are grouped together in a computer

foliage NOUN
the leaves of a tree or plant

folk PLURAL NOUN
people

folk dance NOUN **folk dances**
a dance in the traditional style of a country

folklore NOUN
old beliefs and legends

folk song NOUN **folk songs**
a song in the traditional style of a country

follow VERB **follows, following, followed**
❶ to follow someone or something is to go or come after them, or to do something after they have ❷ to follow someone's instructions or advice is to obey them ❸ to follow a road or path is to go along it ❹ to follow something is to understand it • I couldn't follow the plot of the film. ❺ to follow a sport or team is to take an interest in them or support them • Which football team do you follow? ❻ to follow someone on social media is to sign up to receive their news or updates

follower NOUN **followers**
a person who follows or supports someone or something

following PREPOSITION
after or as a result of • Following the break-in, my parents had new locks fitted.

fond ADJECTIVE **fonder, fondest**
kind and loving • She wished me a fond farewell.

➤ **to be fond of someone** *or* **something** is to like them very much
➤ **fondly** *ADVERB* ➤ **fondness** *NOUN*

font *NOUN* **fonts**
❶ a stone or wooden basin in a church, to hold water for baptism ❷ a font is also a design of type used in printing or word processing • *The poster uses a variety of fonts.*

food *NOUN* **foods**
anything that a plant or animal can take into its body to make it grow or give it energy

food chain *NOUN* **food chains**
a series of plants and animals, each of which is eaten as food by the one above in the series

fool *NOUN* **fools**
❶ a silly or stupid person ❷ a jester or clown • *Stop playing the fool.* ❸ a pudding made of fruit mixed with custard or cream
fool *VERB* **fools, fooling, fooled**
to fool someone is to trick or deceive them
➤ **to fool about** *or* **fool around** is to behave in a silly or stupid way

foolhardy *ADJECTIVE*
bold but foolish; reckless
A sugar coating of white snow covered the dirty grey ice, hiding the huge cracks that threatened to swallow foolhardy travellers.—PETER PAN IN SCARLET, Geraldine McCaughrean
➤ **foolhardiness** *NOUN*

foolish *ADJECTIVE*
stupid
➤ **foolishly** *ADVERB* ➤ **foolishness** *NOUN*

foolproof *ADJECTIVE*
a plan or method is foolproof when it is easy to follow and cannot easily go wrong

foot *NOUN* **feet**
❶ the lower part of your leg below your ankle ❷ the lowest part of something • *They met up at the foot of the hill.* ❸ a measure of length, 12 inches or about 30 centimetres
➤ **on foot** walking

football *NOUN* **footballs**
❶ a game played by two teams which try to kick an inflated ball into their opponents' goal ❷ the ball used in this game

footballer *NOUN* **footballers**
someone who plays football

foothill *NOUN* **foothills**
a low hill near the bottom of a mountain or range of mountains

foothold *NOUN* **footholds**
a place where you can put your foot when you are climbing

footing *NOUN*
your footing is the position of your feet when you are standing firmly on something • *He lost his footing and slipped.*

footpath *NOUN* **footpaths**
a path for people to walk along, especially one in the countryside

footprint *NOUN* **footprints**
a mark made by a foot or shoe

footstep *NOUN* **footsteps**
the sound made each time your foot touches the ground • *We heard creaky footsteps coming up the stairs.*

for *PREPOSITION*
This word is used to show ❶ purpose or direction • *This letter is for you.* • *We set out for home.* • *Let's go for a walk.* ❷ length of time or distance • *We've been waiting for hours.* • *They walked for three miles.* ❸ price or cost • *He bought it for £2.* ❹ a replacement • *I swapped my broken pencil for a new one.* ❺ cause or reason • *She was rewarded for bravery.* • *I only did it for fun.* ❻ a particular person or thing • *I feel sorry for you.* • *She has a good ear for music.* ❼ support • *Are you for us or against us?*
➤ **forever** always

for *CONJUNCTION*
because • *They paused, for they heard a noise.*

forbid *VERB* **forbids, forbidding, forbade, forbidden**
❶ to forbid someone to do something is to tell them that they must not do it ❷ to forbid something is not to allow it • *Running is forbidden in the school corridor.*

forbidding *ADJECTIVE*
looking stern or threatening • *The sky was dark and forbidding.*

a
b
c
d
e
f
g
h
i
j
k
l
m
n
o
p
q
r
s
t
u
v
w
x
y
z

force *NOUN* **forces**
❶ strength or power ❷ an organized team of soldiers or police
➤ **in force** a law or rule is in force if it exists and has to be obeyed • *Is the rule still in force?*

force *VERB* **forces, forcing, forced**
❶ to force someone to do something is to use your power or strength to make them do it
❷ to force something is to break it open using your strength

forceful *ADJECTIVE*
strong and effective
➤ **forcefully** *ADVERB*

forceps (*say* **for**-seps) *PLURAL NOUN*
a pair of pincers or tongs that a dentist or surgeon uses

forcibly *ADVERB*
if you do something forcibly, you use a lot of force

ford *NOUN* **fords**
a shallow place where you can wade or drive across a river

fore *ADJECTIVE*
at or towards the front

forecast *NOUN* **forecasts**
a statement about what is likely to happen, especially what the weather is likely to be

forecast *VERB* **forecasts, forecasting, forecast** *or* **forecasted**
to forecast something is to say what is likely to happen • *The weather report forecasts snow for tomorrow.*

forecourt *NOUN* **forecourts**
an area in front of a petrol station or large building

forefathers *PLURAL NOUN*
your forefathers are your ancestors

forefinger *NOUN* **forefingers**
the finger next to your thumb

foreground *NOUN* **foregrounds**
the part of a scene or view that is nearest to you

forehead (*say* **for**-hed *or* **fo**-rid) *NOUN* **foreheads**
the part of your face above your eyes

foreign *ADJECTIVE*
❶ belonging to or coming from another country ❷ strange or unnatural • *Lying is foreign to her nature.*

foreigner *NOUN* **foreigners**
a person from another country

foreman *NOUN* **foremen**
a worker who is in charge of other workers in a group

foremost *ADJECTIVE*
most important, chief • *the foremost dragon-slayer in the land*

forename *NOUN* **forenames**
a person's first name

foresee *VERB* **foresees, foreseeing, foresaw, foreseen**
to foresee something is to realize that it is likely to happen

foresight *NOUN*
the ability to realize that something is likely to happen in the future and prepare for it

forest *NOUN* **forests**
a large area of trees growing close together

forester *NOUN* **foresters**
someone whose job is to look after a forest

forestry *NOUN*
forestry is planting forests and looking after them

foretell *VERB* **foretells, foretelling, foretold**
to foretell something is to say it will happen • *This magic mirror can foretell the future.*

forever *ADVERB*
continually or always • *He is forever complaining.*

forfeit *NOUN* **forfeits**
something that is taken away from you as a penalty for doing something wrong

forfeit *VERB* **forfeits, forfeiting, forfeited**
to forfeit something is to lose it as a penalty

forgave *VERB* (*past tense of* **forgive**)
• *He had done his best, so she forgave him.*

forge NOUN **forges**
a place where metal is heated and shaped;
a blacksmith's workshop

forge VERB **forges, forging, forged**
❶ to forge metal is to shape it by heating and
hammering ❷ to forge money or a signature is
to copy it in order to deceive people
➤ **to forge ahead** is to make progress with
a strong effort

forgery NOUN **forgeries**
❶ forgery is copying something in order
to deceive people ❷ a forgery is a copy of
something made to deceive people

forget VERB **forgets, forgetting, forgot,
forgotten**
❶ to forget something is to fail to remember it
❷ to forget something is also to stop thinking
about it • *Try to forget your worries.*

forgetful ADJECTIVE
tending to forget things
➤ **forgetfulness** NOUN

forget-me-not NOUN **forget-me-nots**
a plant with small blue flowers

forgive VERB **forgives, forgiving, forgave,
forgiven**
to forgive someone is to stop being angry with
them for something they have done
➤ **forgiveness** NOUN

fork NOUN **forks**
❶ a small device with prongs for lifting food
to your mouth ❷ a large device with prongs
used for digging or lifting things ❸ a place
where a road or river divides into two or more
parts

fork VERB **forks, forking, forked**
❶ to fork something is to dig or lift it with
a fork ❷ to fork is to divide into two or more
branches • *The path ahead forked into two.*

fork-lift truck NOUN **fork-lift trucks**
a truck with two metal bars at the front for
lifting and moving heavy loads

forlorn ADJECTIVE
looking sad and lonely

form NOUN **forms**
❶ a form is a kind or type of thing • *planes
and other forms of transport* ❷ the form of
something is its shape and general

appearance • *They could see a shadowy form
in front of them.* ❸ a form is also a class
in a school ❹ a form is also a piece of paper
with printed questions and spaces for the
answers

form VERB **forms, forming, formed**
❶ to form something is to shape or make it
❷ to form is to come into being or develop
• *Icicles formed on the window.*

formal ADJECTIVE
❶ something that is formal strictly follows
certain rules or customs • *She is very formal
and never calls me by my first name.* ❷ a formal
event is official or has a ceremony • *The formal
opening of the bridge takes place tomorrow.*
❸ formal language strictly follows the rules of
grammar, has longer words, and does not have
friendly or slang words
➤ **formally** ADVERB

formality NOUN
formality is behaviour that follows certain
rules and customs

format NOUN **formats**
❶ the way something is arranged or
organized • *What will the format of the lesson
be?* ❷ the way the information is arranged in
a computer file or disk • *The files are in MP3
format.* ❸ the shape and size of a book or
magazine

formation NOUN **formations**
❶ the action of forming something • *This
chapter is about the formation of ice crystals.*
❷ something that is formed • *We were
studying formations of rock.* ❸ a special
pattern or arrangement • *The aircraft were
flying in formation.*

former ADJECTIVE
earlier; in the past • *In former times the house
had been an inn.* • *He is a former president of
the USA.*
➤ **the former** the first of two people or
things just mentioned • *If it's a choice between
a picnic or a swim, I prefer the former.*

formerly ADVERB
once; previously

formidable (*say* for-mid-a-bul) ADJECTIVE
❶ deserving respect because of being so
powerful or impressive

The Sheepdog was a formidable Twilight Barker. Tonight, with the most important news in Dogdom to send out, he surpassed himself.—THE HUNDRED AND ONE DALMATIANS, Dodie Smith
❷ very difficult to deal with or do • *Repairing the engine was a formidable job.*

formula *NOUN* formulas *or* formulae
❶ a set of chemical symbols showing what a substance consists of • H_2O *is the formula for water.* ❷ a rule or problem in maths shown as a sequence of symbols and numbers • $2a + 4b = 4c.$ ❸ a list of what you need to make something ❹ one of the groups into which racing cars are placed according to their engine size, for example Formula 1

formulate *VERB* formulates, formulating, formulated
to formulate an idea or plan is to work it out and express it clearly and exactly

forsake *VERB* forsakes, forsaking, forsook, forsaken
to forsake someone is to abandon them

fort *NOUN* forts
a building that has been strongly built against attack

forth *ADVERB*
forwards or onwards

fortification *NOUN* fortifications
a tower or wall that is built to help defend a place against attack

fortify *VERB* fortifies, fortifying, fortified
❶ to fortify a place is to make it strong against attack ❷ to fortify someone is to make them feel stronger • *A bowl of hot soup will fortify you.*

fortnight *NOUN* fortnights
a period of two weeks
➤ **fortnightly** *ADVERB* something that happens fortnightly happens every two weeks

fortress *NOUN* fortresses
a castle or town that has been strongly built against attack

fortunate *ADJECTIVE*
lucky
➤ **fortunately** *ADVERB*

fortune *NOUN* fortunes
❶ fortune is luck or chance ❷ a fortune is a large amount of money

fortune-teller *NOUN* fortune-tellers
someone who tells you what will happen to you in the future
➤ **fortune-telling** *NOUN*

forty *NOUN* forties
the number 40
➤ **fortieth** *ADJECTIVE, NOUN*

forward *ADJECTIVE*
❶ going towards the front ❷ placed in the front ❸ too eager or bold

forward *ADVERB*
forwards

forward *NOUN* forwards
a player in an attacking position in a team at football, hockey and other games

forwards *ADVERB*
to or towards the front; in the direction you are facing

fossil *NOUN* fossils
the remains of a prehistoric animal or plant that has been in the ground for a very long time and become hardened in rock
➤ **fossilized** *ADJECTIVE* a fossilized animal or plant has been formed into a fossil

foster *VERB* fosters, fostering, fostered
to foster someone is to look after someone else's child as if they were your own, but without adopting them

foster child *NOUN* foster children
a child brought up by foster parents

foster parent *NOUN* foster parents
a parent who is fostering a child

fought *VERB* (*past tense and past participle of* fight)
• *I fought my way towards the front.* • *He had just fought with his best friend.*

foul *ADJECTIVE* fouler, foulest
❶ disgusting; tasting or smelling unpleasant ❷ breaking the rules of a game • *That was a foul shot.*
➤ **foulness** *NOUN*

foul *NOUN* fouls
an action that breaks the rules of a game

foul *VERB* **fouls, fouling, fouled**
to foul a player in a game is to commit a foul against them

found *VERB* (*past tense and past participle of* **find**)
• *They suddenly found themselves surrounded by tigers.* • *I have found the book I had lost.*

found *VERB* **founds, founding, founded**
to found an organization or society is to start it or set it up • *When was the hospital founded?*

foundation *NOUN* **foundations**
❶ a building's foundations are the solid base under the ground on which it is built ❷ the basis for something • *His story had no foundation in truth.* ❸ the founding of something

founder *NOUN* **founders**
someone who founds something • *Guru Nanak was the founder of the Sikh religion.*

founder *VERB* **founders, foundering, foundered**
❶ to founder is to fill with water and sink • *The ship foundered on the rocks.* ❷ to founder is to fail completely • *Their plans have foundered.*

foundry *NOUN* **foundries**
a factory or workshop where metal or glass is made

fountain *NOUN* **fountains**
a structure in which jets of water shoot up into the air, used to decorate a park or garden

fountain pen *NOUN* **fountain pens**
a pen that can be filled with a cartridge or a supply of ink that flows through its sharp nib

four *NOUN* **fours**
the number 4
➤ **to be on all fours** is to be on your hands and knees

fourteen *NOUN* **fourteens**
the number 14
➤ **fourteenth** *ADJECTIVE, NOUN*

fourth *ADJECTIVE, NOUN*
the next after the third
➤ **fourthly** *ADVERB* in the fourth place; as the fourth one

fowl *NOUN* **fowl** *or* **fowls**
a bird, such as a chicken or duck, that is kept for its eggs or meat

fox *NOUN* **foxes**
a wild animal that looks like a dog with a long furry tail
➤ A related adjective is **vulpine**.

fox *VERB* **foxes, foxing, foxed**
to fox someone is to puzzle them

foxglove *NOUN* **foxgloves**
a tall plant with flowers like the fingers of gloves

foyer (*say* foi-ay) *NOUN* **foyers**
the entrance hall of a cinema, theatre or hotel

fraction *NOUN* **fractions**
❶ a number that is not a whole number, for example ½ or 0.5 ❷ a tiny part or amount of something

fractionally *ADVERB*
by a small amount; very slightly • *The ball was fractionally over the line.*

fracture *VERB* **fractures, fracturing, fractured**
to fracture something, especially a bone, is to break it

fracture *NOUN* **fractures**
the breaking of something, especially a bone

fragile (*say* fra-jyl) *ADJECTIVE*
easy to break or damage
➤ **fragility** *NOUN*

fragment *NOUN* **fragments**
❶ a small piece broken off something
❷ a small part • *She overheard fragments of conversation.*

fragrance (*say* fray-granss) *NOUN* **fragrances**
a thing's fragrance is the sweet or pleasant smell it has

fragrant (*say* fray-grant) *ADJECTIVE*
having a sweet or pleasant smell

frail *ADJECTIVE* **frailer, frailest**
weak or fragile
➤ **frailty** *NOUN*

a
b
c
d
e
f
g
h
i
j
k
l
m
n
o
p
q
r
s
t
u
v
w
x
y
z

frame NOUN **frames**
❶ a set of wooden or metal strips that fit round the outside of a picture or mirror to hold it ❷ a rigid structure that supports something • *I've broken the frame of my glasses.* ❸ a human body • *He has a small frame.*

frame VERB **frames, framing, framed**
❶ to frame a picture is to put a frame round it ❷ to frame laws or questions is to put them together ❸ (*informal*) to frame someone is to make them seem guilty of a crime by giving false evidence against them

framework NOUN **frameworks**
❶ a structure that supports something ❷ a basic plan or system

franchise NOUN **franchises**
❶ the franchise is the right to vote in elections ❷ a franchise is a licence to sell a firm's goods or services in a certain area

frank ADJECTIVE **franker, frankest**
honest and saying exactly what you think • *I'll be frank with you.*
➤ **frankly** ADVERB

frank VERB **franks, franking, franked**
to frank a letter or parcel is to mark it with a postmark

frankincense NOUN
a resin that produces a strong perfume when it is burned

frantic ADJECTIVE
wildly anxious or excited
➤ **frantically** ADVERB

fraud NOUN **frauds**
❶ fraud is the crime of getting money by tricking people ❷ a fraud is a dishonest trick ❸ a fraud is also someone who is not what they pretend to be

fraudulent ADJECTIVE
taking part in fraud; dishonest

fraught ADJECTIVE
❶ someone is fraught when they are tense and upset ❷ a situation is fraught when it is full of problems and makes you worried

frayed ADJECTIVE
❶ frayed material is worn and ragged at the edge • *Your shirt collar is frayed.* ❷ tempers or

nerves are frayed when people feel strained or upset • *Tempers were becoming frayed.*

freak NOUN **freaks**
❶ a very strange or abnormal person, animal or thing ❷ (*informal*) someone who is a keen fan of something • *She is a fitness freak.*

freckle NOUN **freckles**
a small brown spot on someone's skin
'It isn't sunny enough for my freckles to thrive here,' said Pippi. 'And I do think it's nice having freckles.'—PIPPI LONGSTOCKING, Astrid Lindgren
➤ **freckled** ADJECTIVE covered in freckles

free ADJECTIVE **freer, freest**
❶ able to do what you want to do, or to go where you want to go ❷ not costing any money • *Entrance to the museum is free.* ❸ available; not being used or occupied • *Is this seat free?* ❹ not busy doing something • *Are you free tomorrow morning?* ❺ generous • *She is very free with her money.*
➤ **to be free of something** is not to have it or be affected by it • *The roads are free of ice.*

free VERB **frees, freeing, freed**
to free someone or something is to make them free
➤ **freely** ADVERB to do something freely is to do it as you want, without anyone or anything stopping you

freedom NOUN
the right to go where you like or do what you like

freehand ADJECTIVE, ADVERB
to draw something freehand is to do it without using a ruler or compasses

free-range ADJECTIVE
❶ free-range hens are allowed to move about freely in the open instead of being caged ❷ free-range eggs are those laid by free-range hens

freewheel VERB **freewheels, freewheeling, freewheeled**
to freewheel is to ride a bicycle without pedalling

freeze VERB **freezes, freezing, froze, frozen**
❶ to freeze is to turn into ice, or to become covered with ice • *The pond froze last night.*

❷ to be freezing or to be frozen is to be very cold • *My hands are frozen.* ❸ to freeze food is to store it at a low temperature to preserve it ❹ a person or animal freezes when they suddenly stand still with fright ❺ to freeze pay or prices is to keep them at a fixed level and not change them

freezer NOUN **freezers**
a large refrigerator for keeping food frozen

freight (*say* frayt) NOUN
goods carried by road or in a ship or aircraft

freighter NOUN **freighters**
a ship or aircraft for carrying goods

French ADJECTIVE
to do with France or its people

French NOUN
the main language of France and some other countries

DID YOU KNOW? The words **ambulance**, **ballad**, **restaurant** and **tennis** come from French.

French fries PLURAL NOUN (*North American*)
fried potato chips

frenzy NOUN **frenzies**
➤ to be in a frenzy is to be wildly excited or angry about something
➤ **frenzied** ADJECTIVE

frequency NOUN **frequencies**
❶ how often something happens ❷ being frequent ❸ the number of vibrations made each second by a wave of sound or light

frequent (*say* free-kwent) ADJECTIVE
happening often
➤ **frequently** ADVERB

frequent (*say* fri-kwent) VERB **frequents**, **frequenting**, **frequented**
to frequent a place is to visit it often

fresh ADJECTIVE **fresher**, **freshest**
❶ newly made or produced; not old or used • *We need fresh bread.* ❷ not tinned or preserved • *Would you like some fresh fruit?* ❸ cool and clean • *It's nice to be in the fresh air.* ❹ fresh water is water that is not salty
➤ **freshly** ADVERB newly or recently done • *Here are some freshly made biscuits.*
➤ **freshness** NOUN

freshen VERB **freshens**, **freshening**, **freshened**
❶ to freshen something is to make it fresh
❷ to freshen is to become fresh

freshwater ADJECTIVE
freshwater fish live in rivers or lakes and not the sea

fret VERB **frets**, **fretting**, **fretted**
to fret is to worry or be upset about something

fret NOUN
frets are the bars on the neck of a guitar where you press the strings

fretful ADJECTIVE
worried and upset

friar NOUN **friars**
a man who is a member of a Roman Catholic order and has vowed to live a life of poverty

friction NOUN
❶ the rubbing of one thing against another
❷ disagreement and quarrelling

Friday NOUN **Fridays**
the sixth day of the week
DID YOU KNOW? Friday is named after the Norse goddess *Frigga*, the wife of Odin.

fridge NOUN **fridges** (*informal*)
a refrigerator

friend NOUN **friends**
❶ your friend is someone you like and who likes you ❷ a friend is also a person you send messages to on a social media website

friendless ADJECTIVE
someone who is friendless has no friends
A friendless, bitter old man, Roxanne's grandfather was interested in nothing unless there was some money in it.—THE DANCING BEAR, Michael Morpurgo

friendly ADJECTIVE **friendlier**, **friendliest**
kind and pleasant
➤ **friendliness** NOUN

friendship NOUN **friendships**
friendship, or a friendship, is being friends with someone

frieze (*say* freez) NOUN **friezes**
a strip of designs or pictures along the top of a wall

a
b
c
d
e
f
g
h
i
j
k
l
m
n
o
p
q
r
s
t
u
v
w
x
y
z

frigate *NOUN* **frigates**
a small fast warship

fright *NOUN* **frights**
a sudden feeling of fear

frighten *VERB* **frightens**, **frightening**, **frightened**
to frighten someone is to make them afraid

frightful *ADJECTIVE*
awful; very great or bad • *It's a frightful shame.*
➤ **frightfully** *ADVERB* awfully • *I'm frightfully sorry.*

frill *NOUN* **frills**
❶ a strip of pleated material used to decorate the edge of a dress or curtain
❷ an unnecessary extra • *We lead a simple life with no frills.*
➤ **frilly** *ADJECTIVE*

fringe *NOUN* **fringes**
❶ a straight line of short hair that hangs down over your forehead ❷ a decorative edge of hanging threads on something like a piece of clothing or a curtain ❸ the edge of something • *We walked around on the fringe of the crowd.*

frisbee *NOUN* **frisbees**
a plastic disc which you skim through the air as an outdoor game

frisk *VERB* **frisks**, **frisking**, **frisked**
❶ to frisk is to skip or leap playfully
❷ (*informal*) to frisk someone is to search them by moving your hands over their body

frisky *ADJECTIVE* **friskier**, **friskiest**
playful or lively

fritter *NOUN* **fritters**
a slice of meat, potato or fruit that is covered in batter and fried

fritter *VERB* **fritters**, **frittering**, **frittered**
to fritter something, or fritter it away, is to waste it gradually • *She frittered away the money on clothes.*

frivolity *NOUN*
playfulness

frivolous *ADJECTIVE*
light-hearted and playful; not serious

frizzy *ADJECTIVE* **frizzier**, **frizziest**
frizzy hair has tight short curls

fro *ADVERB*
➤ **to and fro** backwards and forwards

frock *NOUN* **frocks**
a dress
My smocked dress was my best frock—tiny red and white checks with red gathers across the chest and a proper sash at the back.—WAVE ME GOODBYE, Jacqueline Wilson

frog *NOUN* **frogs**
a small jumping animal that can live both in water and on land

frolic *VERB* **frolics**, **frolicking**, **frolicked**
to frolic is to spend time playing in a lively and cheerful way

frolic *NOUN* **frolics**
a lively cheerful game or entertainment

from *PREPOSITION*
This word is used to show ❶ a beginning or starting point • *She comes from London.* • *Buses run from 8 o'clock.* ❷ distance • *We are a mile from home.* ❸ separation • *Get the sweets from him.* ❹ origin or source • *Get water from the tap.* ❺ cause • *I was shivering from cold.* ❻ difference • *Can you tell one twin from the other?*

frond *NOUN* **fronds**
a leaf-like part of a fern or similar plant • *swirling fronds of seaweed*

front *NOUN* **fronts**
❶ the part of a person or thing that faces forwards • *The front of the house is blue.*
❷ the part of a thing or place that is furthest forward • *Go to the front of the class.* ❸ a road or promenade that runs alongside the seashore
❹ the place where fighting is happening in a war • *More troops were moved to the front.*
❺ in weather systems, the forward edge of an approaching mass of air • *There is a warm front out in the Atlantic.*
➤ **in front** at or near the front

front *ADJECTIVE*
placed at or near the front • *We sat in the front row.*

frontier *NOUN* **frontiers**
the boundary between two countries or regions

frost *NOUN* **frosts**
❶ powdery ice that forms on things in freezing weather ❷ weather with a temperature below freezing point

frostbite *NOUN*
harm done to a person's body by very cold weather
➤ **frostbitten** *ADJECTIVE*

frosting *NOUN*
sugar icing you put on cakes

frosty *ADJECTIVE* **frostier, frostiest**
❶ so cold that there is frost • *It was a frosty morning.* ❷ unfriendly • *She gave us a frosty look.*
➤ **frostiness** *NOUN*

froth *NOUN*
a white mass of tiny bubbles on or in a liquid
➤ **frothy** *ADJECTIVE*

froth *VERB* **froths, frothing, frothed**
to froth is to form a froth

frown *VERB* **frowns, frowning, frowned**
to frown is to wrinkle your forehead because you are angry or worried

frown *NOUN* **frowns**
the wrinkling of your forehead when you frown

froze *VERB* (*past tense of* **freeze**)
• *The boy froze on the spot.*

frozen *VERB* (*past participle of* **freeze**)
• *The entire river had frozen solid.*

frugal (*say* **froo**-gal) *ADJECTIVE*
❶ spending very little money • *The girls tried to be frugal with their pocket money.* ❷ costing little money • *They ate a frugal meal.*

fruit *NOUN* **fruit** or **fruits**
❶ the seed container that grows on a tree or plant and is often used as food, such as apples, oranges and bananas ❷ the result of doing something • *He lived to see the fruits of his efforts.*

fruitful *ADJECTIVE*
something is fruitful when it is successful or has good results • *Their work was fruitful.*

fruitless *ADJECTIVE*
something is fruitless when it is unsuccessful or has no results • *It was a fruitless search.*

fruity *ADJECTIVE* **fruitier, fruitiest**
tasting like fruit

frustrate *VERB* **frustrates, frustrating, frustrated**
to frustrate someone is to prevent them from doing something or from succeeding in something, in a way that annoys them

frustration *NOUN*
the feeling of annoyance you have when you cannot do what you want to do

fry *VERB* **fries, frying, fried**
to fry food is to cook it in hot fat

frying pan *NOUN* **frying pans**
a shallow pan in which things are fried

fuchsia (*say* **fyoo**-sha) *NOUN* **fuchsias**
a plant with bright red, pink or purple hanging flowers

fudge *NOUN*
a soft sweet made with milk, sugar and butter

fuel *NOUN* **fuels**
something that is burnt to make heat or power, such as coal and oil

fuel *VERB* **fuels, fuelling, fuelled**
to fuel something is to provide it with material to burn to make heat or power

fugitive (*say* **few**-ji-tiv) *NOUN* **fugitives**
a person who is running away from something, especially from the police

fulfil *VERB* **fulfils, fulfilling, fulfilled**
❶ to fulfil something is to achieve it or carry it out • *She fulfilled her dream of appearing on television.* ❷ to fulfil a prophecy is to make it come true

fulfilment *NOUN*
the feeling that you have achieved something important

full *ADJECTIVE* **fuller, fullest**
❶ if a building or container is full, it contains as much or as many as it possibly can • *The cinema was full.* ❷ having many people or things • *You are full of ideas.* ❸ complete

• *Tell me the full story.* ❹ the greatest possible • *They drove at full speed.* ❺ fitting loosely; having many folds • *She's wearing a full skirt.*
➤ **fullness** NOUN
➤ **in full** not leaving anything out

full ADVERB
completely; very • *You knew full well what I wanted.*
➤ **fully** ADVERB completely

full moon NOUN **full moons**
the moon when you can see the whole of it as a bright disc

full stop NOUN **full stops**
the dot used as a punctuation mark at the end of a sentence or an abbreviation

full-time ADJECTIVE, ADVERB
you do something full-time when you do it for all the normal working hours of the day • *She has a full-time job.* • *She works full-time.*

fumble VERB **fumbles, fumbling, fumbled**
to fumble is to handle or feel for something clumsily • *He fumbled in the dark for the light switch.*

fume VERB **fumes, fuming, fumed**
❶ to fume is to give off strong-smelling smoke or gas ❷ to be fuming is to be very angry

fumes PLURAL NOUN
strong-smelling smoke or gas

fun NOUN
amusement or enjoyment
➤ **to make fun of someone** *or* **something** is to make them look silly or make people laugh at them

function NOUN **functions**
❶ what someone or something does or ought to do • *The function of a doctor is to cure sick people.* ❷ an important event or party ❸ a basic operation of a computer or calculator

function VERB **functions, functioning, functioned**
to function is to work properly or perform a function • *The chair also functions as a small table.*

functional ADJECTIVE
practical and useful • *The furniture was basic but functional.*

fund NOUN **funds**
a fund is an amount of money collected or kept for a special purpose • *They started a fund for refugees.*

fundamental ADJECTIVE
basic and necessary • *Let me explain the fundamental rules of the game.*
➤ **fundamentally** ADVERB basically

funeral NOUN **funerals**
the ceremony where a person who has died is buried or cremated

fungus NOUN **fungi**
an organism without leaves or flowers, such as a mushroom or toadstool, that grows on plants or on decayed material
PLURAL ALERT! The word **fungus** has a Latin plural: *some poisonous fungi* (not *funguses*).

funnel NOUN **funnels**
❶ a tube that is wide at the top and narrow at the bottom, to help you pour things into bottles or other containers ❷ a chimney on a ship or steam engine

funny ADJECTIVE **funnier, funniest**
❶ something that is funny makes you laugh or smile • *We heard a funny joke.* ❷ strange or odd • *There's a funny smell in here.*
➤ **funnily** ADVERB

funny bone NOUN **funny bones**
part of your elbow which gives you a strange tingling feeling if you knock it

fur NOUN **furs**
❶ the soft hair that covers some animals ❷ animal skin with the hair on it, used for clothing; fabric that looks like animal skin with hair on it • *She was wearing a fur hat.*

furious ADJECTIVE
❶ very angry ❷ violent or extreme • *They were travelling at a furious speed.*

furiously ADVERB
❶ to say something furiously is to say it very angrily ❷ to do something furiously is to put a lot of effort into doing it • *We worked furiously to get the poster finished in time.*

furl VERB furls, furling, furled
to furl a sail or flag or umbrella is to roll it up and fasten it

furlong NOUN furlongs
one-eighth of a mile, 220 yards or about 201 metres

furnace NOUN furnaces
an oven in which great heat can be produced for making glass or heating metals

furnish VERB furnishes, furnishing, furnished
to furnish a room or building is to put furniture in it

furniture NOUN
tables, chairs, beds, cupboards and other movable things that you need inside a building

furrow NOUN furrows
❶ a long cut in the ground made by a plough ❷ a deep wrinkle on the skin

furry ADJECTIVE furrier, furriest
❶ soft and hairy like fur ❷ covered with fur
➤ **furriness** NOUN

further ADVERB, ADJECTIVE
❶ at or to a greater distance; more distant • I can't walk any further. ❷ more • There are further details on our website.

further VERB furthers, furthering, furthered
to further something is to help it make progress • The experiment aims to further scientific knowledge.

furthermore ADVERB
also; moreover

furthest ADVERB, ADJECTIVE
at or to the greatest distance; most distant • an expedition to the furthest corners of the earth

furtive ADJECTIVE
cautious, trying not to be seen • He gave a furtive glance and helped himself to the biscuits.

fury NOUN furies
violent or extreme anger

fuse NOUN fuses
❶ a safety device containing a short piece of wire that melts if too much electricity passes through it ❷ a fuse is also a device for setting off an explosive

fuse VERB fuses, fusing, fused
❶ a piece of electrical equipment fuses when it stops working because a fuse has melted • The lights have fused. ❷ to fuse things is to blend them together, especially through melting

fuselage (say few-ze-lahzh) NOUN fuselages
the main body of an aircraft

fusion (say few-zhon) NOUN
the action of blending or joining together

fuss NOUN fusses
fuss, or a fuss, is unnecessary excitement or worry about something that is not important
➤ **to make a fuss of someone** is to pay a lot of attention to them in a kind way

fuss VERB fusses, fussing, fussed
to fuss is to be excited or worried about something that is not important

fussy ADJECTIVE fussier, fussiest
❶ worrying too much about something that is not important ❷ full of unnecessary details or decorations
➤ **fussily** ADVERB ➤ **fussiness** NOUN

futile (say few-tyl) ADJECTIVE
useless or having no purpose
➤ **futility** NOUN

future NOUN
❶ the time that will come ❷ what is going to happen in the time that will come
➤ **in future** from now onwards

future tense NOUN
the future tense is the form of a verb that shows that something is going to happen in the time that will come. In English, the future tense uses will and shall in front of the verb, for example I shall reply soon. They will arrive tomorrow.

fuzzy ADJECTIVE fuzzier, fuzziest
❶ blurred or not clear ❷ soft and fluffy
➤ **fuzziness** NOUN

Gg

g *ABBREVIATION*
short for *grams*

gabble *VERB* **gabbles, gabbling, gabbled**
to gabble is to talk so quickly that it is difficult to hear the words

gable *NOUN* **gables**
the three-sided part of a wall between two sloping roofs

gadget (*say* gaj-it) *NOUN* **gadgets**
a small device or tool that helps you with a particular task

Gaelic *NOUN*
❶ (*say* ga-lik) a language spoken in the Highlands and western islands of Scotland ❷ (*say* gay-lik) another name for the Irish language
DID YOU KNOW? The words **galore** and **slogan** come from Gaelic.

gag *NOUN* **gags**
❶ something put over someone's mouth to stop them from speaking ❷ (*informal*) a joke

gag *VERB* **gags, gagging, gagged**
to gag someone is to put a gag over their mouth

gain *VERB* **gains, gaining, gained**
❶ to gain something is to get it when you did not have it before ❷ a clock or watch gains when it goes ahead of the correct time
➤ **to gain on someone** is to come closer to them when you are following them

gain *NOUN* **gains**
something you have got that you did not have before; profit

gala (*say* gah-la) *NOUN* **galas**
❶ a festival ❷ a series of sports contests, especially in swimming

galaxy (*say* gal-ak-see) *NOUN* **galaxies**
a very large group of stars
➤ **galactic** *ADJECTIVE*

DID YOU KNOW? The word **galaxy** comes from a Greek word meaning 'milky'.

gale *NOUN* **gales**
a very strong wind

gallant *ADJECTIVE*
brave or courteous
➤ **gallantly** *ADVERB* ➤ **gallantry** *NOUN*

galleon *NOUN* **galleons**
a large Spanish sailing ship used in the 16th and 17th centuries
The moon was a ghostly galleon tossed upon cloudy seas.—THE HIGHWAYMAN, Alfred Noyes

gallery *NOUN* **galleries**
❶ a platform sticking out from the inside wall of a building ❷ the highest set of seats in a cinema or theatre ❸ a long room or passage ❹ a building or room for showing works of art

galley *NOUN* **galleys**
the kitchen in a ship

gallon *NOUN* **gallons**
a measure of liquid, 8 pints or about 4.5 litres

gallop *NOUN* **gallops**
❶ the fastest pace that a horse can go ❷ a fast ride on a horse

gallop *VERB* **gallops, galloping, galloped**
❶ a horse gallops when it runs very fast ❷ to gallop is to ride fast on a horse

gallows *PLURAL NOUN*
gallows are a framework with a noose for hanging criminals

galore *ADJECTIVE*
in large amounts • *The team were scoring goals galore.*

gamble *VERB* **gambles, gambling, gambled**
❶ to gamble is to play a betting game for money ❷ to gamble with something is to take great risks with it
➤ **gambler** *NOUN*

gamble *NOUN* **gambles**
❶ a bet or chance ❷ a risk • *We were taking a bit of a gamble on the weather being good.*

game *NOUN* **games**
❶ something that you can play, usually with rules • *My favourite board game is snakes and*

ladders. • *They sell all the latest video games.*
❷ wild animals or birds hunted for sport
or food
➤ **to give the game away** is to reveal
a secret

game ADJECTIVE
able and willing to do something • *Are you
game for a swim?*

gamekeeper NOUN **gamekeepers**
someone whose job is to protect game birds
and animals, especially from poachers

gamer NOUN **gamers**
a person who likes playing computer or video
games

games console NOUN **games consoles**
a small machine for playing computer games

gaming NOUN
gaming is playing computer or video games

gammon NOUN
gammon is a kind of ham or thick bacon

gander NOUN **ganders**
a male goose

gang NOUN **gangs**
❶ a group of people who do things together
❷ a group of criminals

gang VERB **gangs, ganging, ganged**
➤ **to gang up on someone** is to form a group
to oppose them or frighten them

gangplank NOUN **gangplanks**
a plank for walking on to or off a ship

gangster NOUN **gangsters**
a member of a gang of violent criminals

gangway NOUN **gangways**
❶ a gap left for people to move along between
rows of seats or through a crowd ❷ a movable
bridge for getting on or off a ship

gannet NOUN **gannets**
a large seabird which catches fish by diving into
the sea

gaol, gaoler
another spelling of **jail, jailer**

gap NOUN **gaps**
❶ an opening or break in something
❷ an interval

gape VERB **gapes, gaping, gaped**
❶ to gape is to open your mouth wide
❷ to gape is also to stare in amazement

garage (*say* ga-rah*zh* *or* ga-rij) NOUN
garages
❶ a building for keeping motor vehicles in
❷ a place where motor vehicles are
serviced and repaired and where petrol
is sold

garbage NOUN
garbage is household refuse or rubbish

garden NOUN **gardens**
a piece of ground where flowers, fruit or
vegetables are grown • *There is a small garden
at the back of the house.*

gardener NOUN **gardeners**
someone who looks after gardens, especially
as a job

gardening NOUN
gardening is looking after a garden

gargle VERB **gargles, gargling, gargled**
to wash your throat by holding liquid at the
back of your mouth and washing it out

gargoyle NOUN **gargoyles**
an ugly or comical carving of a face on a
building, especially one that sticks out from
a gutter and sends out rainwater through
its mouth

garish ADJECTIVE
a garish colour is bright and harsh

garland NOUN **garlands**
a wreath of flowers worn as a decoration

garlic NOUN
a plant with a bulb divided into sections (called
cloves), which have a strong smell and taste and
are used in cooking

garment NOUN **garments**
a piece of clothing

garnish VERB **garnishes, garnishing,
garnished**
to garnish a dish of food is to decorate it with
extra items such as salad

garrison NOUN **garrisons**
troops who stay in a town or fort to defend it

a
b
c
d
e
f
g
h
i
j
k
l
m
n
o
p
q
r
s
t
u
v
w
x
y
z

garter *NOUN* **garters**
a band of elastic to hold up a sock or stocking

gas *NOUN* **gases**
❶ gas, or a gas, is a substance, such as oxygen, that can move freely and is not liquid or solid ❷ a gas that burns and is used for heating or cooking
➤ **gaseous** *ADJECTIVE* in the form of a gas

gas *VERB* **gasses**, **gassing**, **gassed**
to gas someone is to kill or injure them with a poisonous gas

gas giant *NOUN* **gas giants**
a planet, such as Jupiter or Saturn, that is made up of gases rather than solid matter

gash *NOUN* **gashes**
a long deep cut or wound

gasoline *NOUN* (*North American*)
petrol

gasometer (*say* gas-om-it-er) *NOUN* **gasometers**
a large round tank in which gas is stored

gasp *VERB* **gasps**, **gasping**, **gasped**
❶ to gasp is to breathe in suddenly when you are shocked or surprised ❷ to gasp is also to struggle to breathe when you are ill or tired ❸ to gasp something is to say it in a breathless way

gastric *ADJECTIVE*
to do with the stomach

gate *NOUN* **gates**
❶ a movable barrier, usually on hinges, used as a door in a wall or fence ❷ a barrier used to control the flow of water in a dam or lock ❸ a place where you wait before you board an aircraft ❹ the number of people attending a football match

gateau (*say* gat-oh) *NOUN* **gateaux**
a rich cream cake
PLURAL ALERT! The word **gateau** is French and has a French plural: *two chocolate gateaux* (not *gateaus*).

gateway *NOUN* **gateways**
an opening containing a gate

gather *VERB* **gathers**, **gathering**, **gathered**
❶ to gather is to come together ❷ to gather people or things is to bring them together

❸ to gather flowers or fruit is to pick them ❹ to gather a piece of information is to hear or read about it • *I gather our parents know each other.*

gathering *NOUN* **gatherings**
an assembly or meeting of people; a party

gaudy *ADJECTIVE* **gaudier**, **gaudiest**
very showy and bright

gauge (*say* gayj) *NOUN* **gauges**
❶ a measuring instrument, such as a fuel gauge ❷ one of the standard sizes of something ❸ the distance between a pair of railway lines

gauge *VERB* **gauges**, **gauging**, **gauged**
to gauge something is to measure it or estimate it • *We can gauge the size of the cave from the time it takes for an echo to reach us.*

gaunt *ADJECTIVE*
a gaunt person is thin and tired-looking

gauntlet *NOUN* **gauntlets**
a glove with a wide covering for the wrist
➤ **to run the gauntlet** is to face a lot of criticism or risks
➤ **to throw down the gauntlet** is to offer a challenge
DID YOU KNOW? The word **gauntlet** comes from a French word meaning 'glove'.

gauze *NOUN*
gauze is thin transparent material

gave *VERB* (*past tense of* **give**)
• *He gave me a sympathetic look.*

gaze *VERB* **gazes**, **gazing**, **gazed**
to gaze at something or someone is to look at them hard for a long time

gaze *NOUN* **gazes**
a long steady look

GCSE *ABBREVIATION*
short for *General Certificate of Secondary Education*

gear *NOUN* **gears**
❶ a gear is a set of toothed wheels working together in a machine, especially those connecting the engine to the wheels of a vehicle ❷ gear is equipment or clothes

• *He had left all his fishing gear behind by the river.*

gecko NOUN **geckos**
a small lizard found in tropical countries, which has sticky pads on its feet for climbing

geek NOUN **geeks** (*informal*)
an obsessive expert • *a computer geek*

geese NOUN (*plural of* **goose**)

gel NOUN **gels**
gel is a substance like jelly, especially one used to give a style to hair

gelatine NOUN
gelatine is a clear tasteless substance used to make jellies

gem NOUN **gems**
❶ a precious stone or jewel ❷ an excellent person or thing • *Her auntie's a real gem.*

gender (*say* jen-der) NOUN **genders**
❶ your gender is whether you are male or female ❷ a person's sense of identity which may or may not be the same as the sex registered for them at birth

gene (*say* jeen) NOUN **genes**
the part of a living cell that controls which characteristics (such as the colour of your hair or eyes) you inherit from your parents

genealogy (*say* jeen-ee-al-o-jee) NOUN **genealogies**
❶ genealogy is the study of the history of families ❷ a genealogy is a list or diagram of the members of a family

general ADJECTIVE
❶ to do with most people or things • *The general opinion is that there needs to be a new school building.* ❷ not detailed or specialized • *That is the general idea.*
➤ **in general** usually; to do with most people

general NOUN **generals**
an army officer of high rank

general election NOUN **general elections**
an election of politicians to represent the people for the whole country

generalize (*also* **generalise**) VERB **generalizes, generalizing, generalized**
to generalize is to say about people or things generally
➤ **generalization** NOUN

generally ADVERB
usually; to do with most people

generate VERB **generates, generating, generated**
to generate something is to produce or create it

generation NOUN **generations**
❶ a single stage in a family • *Three generations were included: children, parents and grandparents.* ❷ all the people born about the same time • *His generation grew up during the war.*

generator NOUN **generators**
a machine for producing electricity

generosity NOUN
being generous and ready to give a lot • *Thanks to the public's generosity, the appeal has raised a lot of money.*

generous ADJECTIVE
ready to give or share what you have
➤ **generously** ADVERB

genetic (*say* ji-net-ik) ADJECTIVE
to do with genes or with characteristics inherited from parents
➤ **genetically** ADVERB

genetics NOUN
genetics is the study of genes and genetic behaviour

genial ADJECTIVE
kind and pleasant

genie (*say* jee-nee) NOUN **genies**
in Arabic folklore, a genie is a magical being imprisoned in a bottle or lamp who grants wishes when someone summons it
'Child,' the genie said to me, 'you have released me from my prison. Tell me how I may reward you.'
—MIO'S KINGDOM, Astrid Lindgren

genius NOUN **geniuses**
❶ an unusually clever person ❷ an unusually great ability

genre *NOUN* **genres**
a genre is one type of writing. Poetry, adventure stories and fairy tales are examples of different genres.

gent *NOUN* **gents** (*informal*)
a gentleman; a man

gentle *ADJECTIVE* **gentler, gentlest**
kind and quiet; not rough or severe
➤ **gentleness** *NOUN* ➤ **gently** *ADVERB*

gentleman *NOUN* **gentlemen**
❶ a man ❷ a well-mannered or honest man
• *He's a real gentleman.*
➤ **gentlemanly** *ADJECTIVE* polite and courteous

genuine *ADJECTIVE*
❶ something is genuine when it is real and not fake ❷ a person is genuine when they are honest and sincere
➤ **genuinely** *ADVERB*

geography *NOUN*
geography is the science or study of the world and its climate, peoples and products
➤ **geographical** *ADJECTIVE*
DID YOU KNOW? The word **geography** comes from Greek words meaning 'earth writing'.

geology (*say* ji-ol-o-jee) *NOUN*
geology is the study of the earth's crust and its layers
➤ **geologist** *NOUN* ➤ **geological** *ADJECTIVE*

geometry *NOUN*
geometry is the study of lines, angles, surfaces and solids in mathematics

geranium (*say* je-ray-ni-um) *NOUN* **geraniums**
a plant with red, pink or white flowers

gerbil (*say* jer-bil) *NOUN* **gerbils**
a small brown animal with long back legs

germ *NOUN* **germs**
❶ a micro-organism, especially one that can cause illness ❷ part of the seed of a cereal plant ❸ the first stage of a plan or idea • *It was the germ of a brilliant idea.*

German *ADJECTIVE*
to do with Germany or its people

German *NOUN*
❶ the main language of Germany
❷ (**Germans**) a person from Germany
DID YOU KNOW? The words **delicatessen** and **waltz** come from German.

germinate *VERB* **germinates, germinating, germinated**
a seed germinates when it starts growing and developing
➤ **germination** *NOUN*

gesticulate *VERB* **gesticulates, gesticulating, gesticulated**
to make movements with your hands and arms while you are talking

gesture (*say* jes-cher) *NOUN* **gestures**
a movement or action which expresses what you feel

get *VERB* **gets, getting, got**
This word has many meanings, depending on the words that go with it. ❶ to get something is to obtain or receive it • *I got a new bike yesterday.* ❷ to get (for example) angry or upset is to become angry or upset ❸ to get to a place is to reach it • *We had to borrow money to get home.* ❹ to get something (for example) on or off is take it on or off • *I can't get my shoe on.* ❺ to get (for example) a meal is to prepare it ❻ to get an illness is to catch it • *I think she's got measles.* ❼ to get someone to do something is to persuade or order them to do it • *Lara might get him to say yes.* ❽ (*informal*) to get something is to understand it • *Do you get what I mean?*
➤ **to get by** is to manage with what you have
➤ **to get on** ❶ is to make progress ❷ is to be friendly with someone
➤ **to get out of something** is to avoid having to do it
➤ **to get over something** is to recover from an illness or shock
➤ **to get your own back** is to have your revenge
➤ **to have got to do something** is to have no choice about it

getaway *NOUN* **getaways**
an escape

geyser (*say* gee-zer *or* gy-zer) *NOUN* **geysers**
a natural spring that shoots up columns of hot water

ghastly ADJECTIVE **ghastlier, ghastliest**
horrible; awful

ghee (*say* gee) NOUN
clarified butter, used in South Asian cooking

ghetto (*say* get-oh) NOUN **ghettos**
a deprived area of a city, where people are
treated unfairly compared with those in
other areas

ghost NOUN **ghosts**
the spirit of a dead person seen by a living
person
➤ **ghostly** ADJECTIVE unreal or frightening
• *The moon gave a ghostly light to the
scene.*

ghoul (*say* gool) NOUN **ghouls**
an evil spirit believed to eat dead bodies

ghoulish (*say* gool-ish) ADJECTIVE
enjoying looking at things to do with death and
suffering

giant NOUN **giants**
❶ a creature in stories, like a huge human being
❷ something that is much larger than the
usual size
giant ADJECTIVE
huge

giddy ADJECTIVE **giddier, giddiest**
feeling unsteady or dizzy
➤ **giddily** ADVERB ➤ **giddiness** NOUN

gift NOUN **gifts**
❶ a present ❷ a talent • *She has a special gift
for drawing.*

gifted ADJECTIVE
a gifted person has a special talent or ability

gigabyte NOUN **gigabytes**
a unit that measures computer data or
memory, roughly equal to one thousand
million bytes

gigantic ADJECTIVE
extremely large; huge
*Suddenly the boy let out a gigantic belch which
rolled around the Assembly Hall like thunder.*
—MATILDA, Roald Dahl

giggle VERB **giggles, giggling, giggled**
to giggle is to laugh in a silly way

giggle NOUN **giggles**
❶ a silly laugh ❷ (*informal*) something
amusing; a joke • *We did it for a giggle.*

gild VERB **gilds, gilding, gilded**
to gild something is to cover it with a thin layer
of gold paint or gold

gills PLURAL NOUN
the gills are the part of a fish's body that it
breathes through

gimmick NOUN **gimmicks**
something unusual done or used to attract
people's attention

gin NOUN
gin is a strong alcoholic drink

ginger NOUN
❶ ginger is a hot-tasting tropical root, used as
a flavouring for food ❷ ginger is also a reddish-
yellow colour

gingerbread NOUN
a cake or biscuit flavoured with ginger

gingerly ADVERB
you do something gingerly when you do it
carefully and cautiously because you are not
sure about it

ginormous ADJECTIVE (*informal*)
extremely large; enormous

gipsy
another spelling of **gypsy**

giraffe (*say* ji-**raf**) NOUN **giraffes**
a tall African mammal with a very long neck
and a coat patterned with brown patches
DID YOU KNOW? An old word for a **giraffe** is
camelopard, which means 'camel leopard'.

girder NOUN **girders**
a metal beam supporting part of a building
or bridge

girdle NOUN **girdles** (*old use*)
a belt or cord worn around your waist

girl NOUN **girls**
❶ a female child ❷ a young woman
➤ **girlish** ADJECTIVE

girlfriend NOUN **girlfriends**
❶ a female romantic partner ❷ a female
friend

girth NOUN **girths**
❶ the measurement round something ❷ a band fastened round a horse's belly to keep its saddle in place

gist (say jist) NOUN
the main points or general meaning of a speech or conversation

give VERB **gives**, **giving**, **gave**, **given**
❶ to give someone something is to let them have it • *She gave me a sweet.* ❷ to give (for example) a laugh or shout is to laugh or shout out ❸ to give a performance is to present or perform something • *They gave a concert to raise money.* ❹ something gives if it bends or goes down under a strain • *Will this branch give if I sit on it?*
➤ **to give in** is to surrender
➤ **to give up** is to stop doing or trying something
➤ **to give way** is to break or collapse
➤ **giver** NOUN

given ADJECTIVE
stated or agreed in advance • *Work out how much you can do in a given time.*

glacial (say glay-shal) ADJECTIVE
❶ made of ice or formed by glaciers ❷ to move at a glacial pace is to move very slowly

glacier (say glass-i-er) NOUN **glaciers**
a mass of ice moving slowly along a valley

glad ADJECTIVE **gladder**, **gladdest**
happy and pleased
➤ **gladly** ADVERB ➤ **gladness** NOUN

gladden VERB **gladdens**, **gladdening**, **gladdened**
to gladden someone is to make them glad

gladiator NOUN **gladiators**
a man who fought with a sword or other weapons at public shows in ancient Rome

glamorous ADJECTIVE
attractive and exciting

glamour NOUN
the glamour of something is what makes it attractive or exciting
The Basic Brown was the most common type of dragon, a serviceable beast but without much glamour.—HOW TO TRAIN YOUR DRAGON, Cressida Cowell

DID YOU KNOW? The word **glamour** originally meant 'magic' or enchantment'.

glance VERB **glances**, **glancing**, **glanced**
❶ to glance at something is to look at it quickly
Little Billy glanced back quickly over his shoulder, and now, in the distance, he saw a sight that froze his blood and made icicles in his veins.—BILLY AND THE MINPINS, Roald Dahl
❷ to glance off something is to hit it and slide off • *The ball glanced off his bat.*

glance NOUN **glances**
a quick look

gland NOUN **glands**
an organ of the body that separates substances from your blood, so that they can be used or passed out of your body
➤ **glandular** ADJECTIVE glandular fever is a disease that affects glands in the body

glare VERB **glares**, **glaring**, **glared**
❶ to glare is to shine with a bright or dazzling light ❷ to glare at someone is to look angrily at them
The bald man glared down at the children and spoke to them in a frightening whisper.—THE HOSTILE HOSPITAL, Lemony Snicket

glare NOUN **glares**
❶ a strong light ❷ an angry stare • *The librarian gave us a withering glare.*

glaring ADJECTIVE
❶ very bright ❷ very obvious and embarrassing • *Fortunately there were no glaring mistakes in their work.*

glass NOUN **glasses**
❶ glass is a hard brittle substance that lets light through ❷ a glass is a container made of glass, for drinking out of ❸ a glass is also a mirror or a lens

glasses PLURAL NOUN
spectacles or binoculars

glassful NOUN **glassfuls**
as much as a glass will hold

glassy ADJECTIVE **glassier**, **glassiest**
❶ like glass ❷ dull; without liveliness or expression • *He gave a glassy stare.*

glaze VERB **glazes**, **glazing**, **glazed**
❶ to glaze something is to cover or fit it with glass ❷ to glaze pottery is to give it a shiny

surface ❸ to glaze, or glaze over, is to become glassy or dull • *Her eyes glazed over with boredom.*

glaze NOUN **glazes**
a shiny surface

glazier NOUN **glaziers**
someone whose job is to fit glass into windows and doors

gleam NOUN **gleams**
❶ a beam of soft light, especially one that comes and goes ❷ a clear sign of something • *She could see the gleam of excitement in his eyes.*

gleam VERB **gleams**, **gleaming**, **gleamed**
to gleam is to shine with beams of soft light

glee NOUN
glee is when you feel happy and excited about something

glen NOUN **glens**
a narrow valley, especially in Scotland

glide VERB **glides**, **gliding**, **glided**
❶ to glide is to fly or move smoothly ❷ to glide is also to fly without using an engine

glider NOUN **gliders**
an aircraft that does not use an engine and floats on air currents

glimmer NOUN **glimmers**
a faint light

glimmer VERB **glimmers**, **glimmering**, **glimmered**
to glimmer is to shine with a faint light

glimpse VERB **glimpses**, **glimpsing**, **glimpsed**
to glimpse something is to see it briefly

glimpse NOUN **glimpses**
a brief view of something

glint VERB **glints**, **glinting**, **glinted**
to glint is to shine with a flash of light
High upon the slope to our right, in among the trees, a little frozen waterfall glinted brilliantly. —COUNT KARLSTEIN, Philip Pullman

glint NOUN **glints**
a brief flash of light

glisten VERB **glistens**, **glistening**, **glistened**
to shine like something wet or oily

glitter VERB **glitters**, **glittering**, **glittered**
to glitter is to shine with tiny flashes of light
There was the dragon she had longed for and dreamed of. His green scales glittered, his eyes were bright and black. —DRAGON RIDE, Helen Cresswell

gloat VERB **gloats**, **gloating**, **gloated**
to gloat is to be pleased in an unkind way that you have succeeded or that someone else has been hurt or upset

global ADJECTIVE
to do with the whole world • *the global effects of climate change*
➤ **globally** ADVERB

global warming NOUN
global warming is the gradual increase in the average temperature of the earth's climate, caused by the greenhouse effect

globe NOUN **globes**
❶ a globe is something shaped like a ball, especially one with a map of the world on it ❷ the globe is the world

globule NOUN **globules**
a small round drop • *a globule of saliva*

gloom NOUN
gloom is a feeling or condition of being sad or depressed

gloomy ADJECTIVE **gloomier**, **gloomiest**
❶ almost dark; not well lit ❷ sad or depressed
➤ **gloomily** ADVERB ➤ **gloominess** NOUN

glorify VERB **glorifies**, **glorifying**, **glorified**
❶ to glorify someone is to praise them highly ❷ to glorify something is to make it seem splendid
➤ **glorification** NOUN

glorious ADJECTIVE
splendid or magnificent
➤ **gloriously** ADVERB

glory NOUN **glories**
❶ glory is fame and honour ❷ a thing's glory is its splendour or beauty

gloss NOUN **glosses**
the shine on a smooth surface

glossary NOUN **glossaries**
a list of words with their meanings explained

a
b
c
d
e
f
g
h
i
j
k
l
m
n
o
p
q
r
s
t
u
v
w
x
y
z

glossy *ADJECTIVE* **glossier**, **glossiest**
smooth and shiny

glove *NOUN* **gloves**
a covering for the hand, with a separate division for each finger

glow *NOUN*
❶ a brightness and warmth without flames • *They sat and finished their drinks in the glow from the fire.* ❷ a warm or cheerful feeling • *Sarah felt a deep glow of satisfaction at her win.*

glow *VERB* **glows**, **glowing**, **glowed**
to glow is to shine with a soft light

glower (*rhymes with* **flower**) *VERB* **glowers**, **glowering**, **glowered**
to glower is to stare with an angry look

glow–worm *NOUN* **glow–worms**
an insect with a tail that gives out a green light

glucose *NOUN*
glucose is a type of sugar found in fruits and honey

glue *NOUN* **glues**
glue is a thick liquid for sticking things together

glue *VERB* **glues**, **gluing**, **glued**
to glue something is to stick it with glue

glum *ADJECTIVE* **glummer**, **glummest**
sad or depressed
➤ **glumly** *ADVERB*

glutton *NOUN* **gluttons**
someone who is greedy and enjoys eating too much
➤ **gluttony** *NOUN*

gnarled (*say* narld) *ADJECTIVE*
twisted and knobbly, like an old tree

gnash (*say* nash) *VERB* **gnashes**, **gnashing**, **gnashed**
to gnash your teeth is to grind them together
SPELLING ALERT! The **g** is silent in words that start with **gn–**, like **gnash**, **gnaw** and **gnome**.

gnat (*say* nat) *NOUN* **gnats**
a tiny fly that bites

gnaw (*say* naw) *VERB* **gnaws**, **gnawing**, **gnawed**
to gnaw something hard is to keep biting it

gnome (*say* nohm) *NOUN* **gnomes**
a kind of dwarf in fairy tales that usually lives underground

gnu (*say* noo *or* ge-**noo**) *NOUN* **gnus**
a large African antelope with a long head, a beard and a sloping back

go *VERB* **goes**, **going**, **went**, **gone**
❶ to go is to move or lead from one place to another • *Let's go in and see Mrs Cooper.* • *We'll have to go soon.* • *This road goes to Bristol.* ❷ a machine or device goes when it is working • *My watch isn't going.* • *A car that doesn't go is not much use.* ❸ you say that someone or something has gone when they are no longer there and you cannot find them • *All her money had gone.* ❹ the word **go** also has many special uses, as in these examples • *The milk went sour.* • *The plates go on that shelf.* • *The party went well.* • *The firework went bang.*
➤ **to be going to do something** is to be ready to do it
➤ **to go in for something** is to take part in it
➤ **to go off** is to explode
➤ **to go off someone** *or* **something** is to stop liking them
➤ **to go on** is to happen or continue • *What's going on?*

go *NOUN* **goes**
❶ a go is a turn or try • *May I have a go?*
❷ (*informal*) a go is also a successful try • *They made a go of it.*
➤ **on the go** always working or moving

go-ahead *NOUN*
permission to do something • *The council has given the go-ahead for a recycling scheme in the area.*

go-ahead *ADJECTIVE*
adventurous and keen to try out new methods

goal *NOUN* **goals**
❶ the two posts that the ball must go between to score a point in football, hockey and other games ❷ a point scored in football, hockey, netball and other games ❸ something that you

try to do or to achieve • *Her goal is to become a pilot.*

goalie *NOUN* **goalies** (*informal*)
a goalkeeper

goalkeeper *NOUN* **goalkeepers**
the player who guards the goal in football and hockey

goalpost *NOUN* **goalposts**
each of the upright posts of a goal in sports

goat *NOUN* **goats**
an animal with horns, belonging to the same family as sheep

gobble *VERB* **gobbles**, **gobbling**, **gobbled**
to gobble something is to eat it quickly and greedily

gobbledegook (*also* **gobbledygook**) *NOUN*
the pompous technical language used by officials, that is difficult to understand

goblet *NOUN* **goblets**
a drinking glass with a long stem and a base

goblin *NOUN* **goblins**
an evil or mischievous fairy in stories
Goblins do not usually venture very far from their mountains, unless they are driven out and are looking for new homes.—THE HOBBIT, J. R. R. Tolkien

God *NOUN*
the supreme being worshipped in many religions

god *NOUN* **gods**
a male being that is worshipped • *Thor was the Norse god of thunder.*

godchild *NOUN* **godchildren**
a child that a godparent promises to see brought up as a Christian. A boy is a **godson** and a girl is a **god-daughter**.

goddess *NOUN* **goddesses**
a female being that is worshipped • *Freya was the Norse goddess of love and beauty.*

godparent *NOUN* **godparents**
a person at a child's christening who promises to see that it is brought up as a Christian. A man is a **godfather** and a woman is a **godmother**.

goggles *PLURAL NOUN*
goggles are large glasses that you wear to protect your eyes from wind, water or dust

gold *NOUN*
❶ gold is a precious yellow metal ❷ gold is also a bright yellow colour

golden *ADJECTIVE*
❶ made of gold ❷ coloured like gold ❸ precious or excellent • *It was a golden opportunity.*

golden wedding *NOUN* **golden weddings**
the 50th anniversary of a wedding

goldfinch *NOUN* **goldfinches**
a small, brightly coloured bird with yellow feathers in its wings

goldfish *NOUN* **goldfish**
a small red or orange fish, often kept as a pet

golf *NOUN*
golf is an outdoor game played on a prepared course by hitting a small ball into a series of small holes, using a club
➤ **golfer** *NOUN* ➤ **golfing** *NOUN*

gone *VERB* (*past participle of* **go**)
• *I don't know where Jack has gone.*

gong *NOUN* **gongs**
a large metal disc that makes a deep hollow sound when it is hit

goo *NOUN* (*informal*)
a sticky or slimy substance • *The cave walls were covered in a slippery goo.*

good *ADJECTIVE* **better**, **best**
❶ of the kind that people like, want or praise • *They wanted to have a good time.* ❷ kind • *It was good of you to come.* ❸ well-behaved • *What a good dog!* ❹ healthy; giving benefit • *Exercise is good for you.* ❺ thorough; large enough • *Let's give it a good clean.* ❻ quite large or long • *It's a good walk to the station.*

good *NOUN*
❶ something good or right • *Do good to others.* ❷ benefit or advantage • *I'm telling you for your own good.*
➤ **for good** forever
➤ **no good** useless

a b c d e f g h i j k l m n o p q r s t u v w x y z

goodbye *EXCLAMATION*
a word you say when you leave someone or at the end of a telephone call

Good Friday *NOUN*
the Friday before Easter, when Christians remember Christ's death on the Cross

good-looking *ADJECTIVE*
attractive or handsome

good-natured *ADJECTIVE*
kind

goodness *NOUN*
❶ goodness is being good ❷ a thing's goodness is the good it does

goods *PLURAL NOUN*
goods are things that people buy and sell

goodwill *NOUN*
goodwill is a kindly and helpful feeling towards people

gooey *ADJECTIVE* **gooier**, **gooiest** (*informal*)
soft and sticky • *a puddle of gooey melted fudge*
➤ **gooeyness** *NOUN*

goose *NOUN* **geese**
a water bird with webbed feet, larger than a duck

gooseberry *NOUN* **gooseberries**
a small green fruit that grows on a prickly bush

goose pimples, **goosebumps** *PLURAL NOUN*
goose pimples are lots of tiny bumps you get on your skin when you are cold or afraid

gore *VERB* **gores**, **goring**, **gored**
to gore a person or animal is to wound them savagely with a horn or tusk • *Several dogs had been gored by a wild boar.*

gorge *NOUN* **gorges**
a narrow valley with steep sides

gorgeous *ADJECTIVE*
magnificent; beautiful

gorilla *NOUN* **gorillas**
a large strong African ape

gorse *NOUN*
gorse is a prickly bush with small yellow flowers

gory *ADJECTIVE* **gorier**, **goriest**
❶ covered in blood ❷ involving a lot of killing

gosh *EXCLAMATION*
a word you say when you are surprised
• *Gosh! I completely forgot!*

gosling *NOUN* **goslings**
a young goose

gospel *NOUN* **gospels**
❶ the gospel is the teachings of Jesus Christ ❷ gospel is something you can safely believe
• *You can take what she says as gospel.*
➤ **the Gospels** the first four books of the New Testament

gossip *VERB* **gossips**, **gossiping**, **gossiped**
to gossip is to talk a lot about other people

gossip *NOUN* **gossips**
❶ gossip is talk or rumours about other people ❷ a gossip is someone who likes talking about other people

got *VERB* (*past tense and past participle of* **get**)
• *I got a bike for my birthday.* • *I've got homework to do.*

gouge (*say* gowj) *VERB* **gouges**, **gouging**, **gouged**
to gouge something is to press or scoop it out

govern *VERB* **governs**, **governing**, **governed**
to govern a country or organization is to be in charge of it

government *NOUN* **governments**
the group of people who are in charge of a country

governor *NOUN* **governors**
someone who governs or runs a place

gown *NOUN* **gowns**
a dress, especially a long formal dress

GP *NOUN* **GPs**
short for *general practitioner*, a doctor who treats people with all kinds of illnesses and is usually the first doctor that people see when they are ill

grab VERB **grabs**, **grabbing**, **grabbed**
to grab something is to take hold of it firmly or suddenly

grace NOUN **graces**
❶ grace is beauty, especially in movement
❷ someone behaves with grace when they are kind and friendly to people

graceful ADJECTIVE
beautiful and elegant in movement or shape
➤ **gracefully** ADVERB

gracious ADJECTIVE
❶ kind and pleasant to other people
❷ merciful
➤ **graciously** ADVERB

grade NOUN **grades**
a step in a scale of quality, value or rank

grade VERB **grades**, **grading**, **graded**
to grade things is to sort or divide them into grades

gradient (say **gray**-di-ent) NOUN
gradients
❶ a slope ❷ the amount that a road or railway slopes

gradual ADJECTIVE
happening slowly but steadily
➤ **gradually** ADVERB

graduate (say **grad**-yoo-at) NOUN
graduates
someone who has a degree from a university or college

graduate (say **grad**-yoo-ayt) VERB
graduates, **graduating**, **graduated**
❶ to graduate is to get a university degree
❷ to graduate something is to divide it into graded sections, or to mark it so that it can be used for measuring • *The ruler was graduated in millimetres.*
➤ **graduation** NOUN

graffiti (say gra-**fee**-tee) NOUN
graffiti is words or drawings scribbled, sprayed or painted on a wall
DID YOU KNOW? The word **graffiti** comes from an Italian word meaning 'scratches'.

grain NOUN **grains**
❶ grain is cereals when they are growing or after they have been harvested ❷ a grain is the hard seed of a cereal ❸ a grain of

something is a small amount of it • *The story had a grain of truth in it.* ❹ the grain on a piece of wood is the pattern of lines going through it

gram NOUN **grams**
a unit of weight in the metric system, a thousandth of a kilogram

grammar NOUN **grammars**
❶ grammar is the rules for using words
❷ a grammar is a book that gives the rules for using words
DID YOU KNOW? The word **grammar** comes from a Latin word *grammatica* which could mean 'witchcraft' as well as 'learning'.

grammar school NOUN
grammar schools
a kind of secondary school

grammatical ADJECTIVE
something you say or write is grammatical when it follows the rules of grammar

grand ADJECTIVE **grander**, **grandest**
❶ great or splendid ❷ a grand total is one that includes everything
➤ **grandly** ADVERB

grandad NOUN **grandads** (*informal*)
grandfather

grandchild NOUN **grandchildren**
a child of a person's son or daughter. A girl is a **grand-daughter** and a boy is a **grandson**.

grandeur NOUN
grandeur is greatness and splendour

grandfather NOUN **grandfathers**
the father of a person's mother or father

grandfather clock NOUN
grandfather clocks
a clock in a tall wooden case

grandma NOUN **grandmas** (*informal*)
grandmother

grandmother NOUN **grandmothers**
the mother of a person's mother or father

grandpa NOUN **grandpas** (*informal*)
grandfather

grandparent NOUN **grandparents**
a grandmother or grandfather

a
b
c
d
e
f
g
h
i
j
k
l
m
n
o
p
q
r
s
t
u
v
w
x
y
z

grandstand NOUN **grandstands**
a building at a racecourse or sports ground, that is open at the front with rows of seats for spectators

granite NOUN
granite is a very hard kind of rock

granny NOUN **grannies** (*informal*)
grandmother

granny knot NOUN **granny knots**
a reef knot with the strings crossed the wrong way

grant VERB **grants, granting, granted**
to grant someone something is to give or allow them what they have asked for
➤ **to take something for granted** is to assume that it is true or will happen

grant NOUN **grants**
something given, especially a sum of money

grape NOUN **grapes**
a small green or purple fruit that grows in bunches on a vine

grapefruit NOUN **grapefruit**
a large, round, yellow citrus fruit with soft juicy flesh

grapevine NOUN **grapevines**
❶ a climbing plant on which grapes grow
❷ **to hear something on the grapevine** is to be told it by friends and people you know • *We heard the rumour on the grapevine.*

graph NOUN **graphs**
a diagram that shows how two amounts are related

graphic ADJECTIVE
❶ to do with drawing or painting • *a course in graphic design* ❷ very detailed and lively • *a graphic eyewitness account of the battle*
➤ **graphically** ADVERB

graphics PLURAL NOUN
graphics are diagrams, lettering and drawings, especially pictures that are produced by a computer

graphite NOUN
graphite is a soft kind of carbon used for the lead in pencils

grapple VERB **grapples, grappling, grappled**
❶ to grapple someone or grapple with someone is to fight them ❷ to grapple something is to hold it tightly ❸ to grapple with a problem is to try to deal with it

grasp VERB **grasps, grasping, grasped**
❶ to grasp someone or something is to hold them tightly ❷ to grasp something is to understand it

grasp NOUN
❶ a firm hold ❷ a person's grasp of something is how well they understand it • *His grasp of English was limited.*

grasping ADJECTIVE
greedy for money or possessions

grass NOUN **grasses**
❶ grass is a green plant with thin stalks ❷ a piece of grass is an area of ground covered with grass
➤ **grassy** ADJECTIVE

grasshopper NOUN **grasshoppers**
a jumping insect that makes a shrill noise

grate NOUN **grates**
❶ a metal framework that keeps fuel in the fireplace ❷ a fireplace

grate VERB **grates, grating, grated**
❶ to grate something is to shred it into small pieces ❷ to grate is to make an unpleasant noise by rubbing something • *The chalk grated on the blackboard.*

grateful ADJECTIVE
feeling glad that someone has done something for you • *I was grateful for their kindness in giving me food and drink.*
➤ **gratefully** ADVERB

grating NOUN **gratings**
a framework of metal bars placed across an opening

gratitude NOUN
you show gratitude when you are grateful or thankful for something

grave NOUN **graves**
the place where a dead body is buried

grave ADJECTIVE **graver, gravest**
serious or solemn • *We've had grave news.*
➤ **gravely** ADVERB

gravel *NOUN*
gravel is small stones mixed with coarse sand, used to make paths

gravestone *NOUN* **gravestones**
a stone monument over a grave

graveyard *NOUN* **graveyards**
a place where dead bodies are buried

gravity *NOUN*
❶ gravity is the force that pulls all objects in the universe towards each other ❷ the earth's gravity is the force that pulls everything towards itself ❸ the importance or seriousness of a situation

gravy *NOUN*
a hot brown sauce made from meat juices

graze *VERB* **grazes**, **grazing**, **grazed**
❶ to graze is to feed on growing grass
❷ to graze your skin is to scrape it slightly against something rough

graze *NOUN* **grazes**
a sore place where skin has been scraped

grease *NOUN*
grease is thick fat or oil
➤ **greasy** *ADJECTIVE*

great *ADJECTIVE* **greater**, **greatest**
❶ very large ❷ very important or distinguished • *She was a great writer.*
❸ (*informal*) very good or enjoyable
• *It's great to see you again.* ❹ older or younger by one generation, as in *great-grandmother* and *great-grandson*
➤ **greatly** *ADVERB* ➤ **greatness** *NOUN*

greed *NOUN*
greed is being greedy and wanting too much

greedy *ADJECTIVE* **greedier**, **greediest**
wanting more food or money than you need
➤ **greedily** *ADVERB*

Greek *ADJECTIVE*
to do with modern or ancient Greece • *tales of the Greek gods and heroes*

Greek *NOUN*
❶ the language of modern or ancient Greece
❷ (**Greeks**) a person from Greece
DID YOU KNOW? Many English words are based wholly or partly on Greek, including **geography**, **myth**, **orchestra** and **skeleton**.

green *ADJECTIVE* **greener**, **greenest**
❶ of the colour of grass and leaves
❷ concerned with protecting the natural environment

green *NOUN* **greens**
❶ green is a green colour ❷ a green is an area of grass

greenery *NOUN*
green leaves or plants

greengage *NOUN* **greengages**
a kind of green plum

greengrocer *NOUN* **greengrocers**
someone who keeps a shop that sells fruit and vegetables
➤ **greengrocery** *NOUN* a greengrocer's shop

greenhouse *NOUN* **greenhouses**
a glass building that is kept warm inside for growing plants

greenhouse effect *NOUN*
the warming of the earth's surface by gases (called **greenhouse gases**) such as methane and carbon dioxide, which trap heat in the earth's atmosphere

greens *PLURAL NOUN*
greens are green vegetables, such as cabbage and spinach

greet *VERB* **greets**, **greeting**, **greeted**
❶ to greet someone is to welcome them when they arrive • *His cat Moxie greeted him with a soft miaow.* ❷ to greet something is to respond to it in a certain way • *They greeted the news with loud cheering.*

greeting *NOUN* **greetings**
a greeting is the words or actions used to greet someone
➤ **greetings** are good wishes when you meet someone or talk to them

grenade *NOUN* **grenades**
a small bomb, usually thrown by hand

grew *VERB* (*past tense of* **grow**)
• *The road grew busier as we neared the town.*

grey *ADJECTIVE* **greyer**, **greyest**
of the colour between black and white, like ashes or dark clouds

a b c d e f g h i j k l m n o p q r s t u v w x y z

grey *NOUN*
a grey colour

greyhound *NOUN* **greyhounds**
a slim dog with smooth hair, used in racing

grid *NOUN* **grids**
a framework or pattern of bars or lines crossing each other

grief *NOUN*
grief is deep sadness or sorrow people feel when someone has died
➤ **to come to grief** is to have an accident or misfortune

grievance *NOUN* **grievances**
something that people are unhappy or angry about

grieve *VERB* **grieves**, **grieving**, **grieved**
❶ to grieve is to feel sad or sorrowful
❷ to grieve someone is to make them feel very sad • *It grieves me to have to tell you this.*

grievous *ADJECTIVE*
❶ causing great sadness ❷ serious • *We have suffered a grievous loss.*
➤ **grievously** *ADVERB*

griffin *NOUN* **griffins**
a mythological creature with the body of a lion and the head and wings of an eagle

grill *NOUN* **grills**
❶ an element or burner on a cooker, that sends heat downwards ❷ grilled food
❸ a grating

grill *VERB* **grills**, **grilling**, **grilled**
❶ to grill food is to cook it under a grill
❷ to grill someone is to question them closely and severely • *The police grilled him for hours.*

grim *ADJECTIVE* **grimmer**, **grimmest**
❶ stern or severe ❷ frightening or unpleasant
• *They had a grim experience.*
➤ **grimly** *ADVERB*

grimace *NOUN* **grimaces**
a strange or twisted expression on your face

grime *NOUN*
grime is a layer of dirt on a surface

grimy *ADJECTIVE* **grimier**, **grimiest**
very dirty • *a grimy unwashed floor*
➤ **griminess** *NOUN*

grin *NOUN* **grins**
a smile showing your teeth

grin *VERB* **grins**, **grinning**, **grinned**
to grin is to smile showing your teeth

grind *VERB* **grinds**, **grinding**, **ground**
❶ to grind something is to crush it into a powder ❷ to grind something hard is to sharpen or polish it by rubbing it on a rough surface
➤ **grinder** *NOUN*

grindstone *NOUN* **grindstones**
a rough round revolving stone used for grinding things
➤ **to keep your nose to the grindstone** is to keep working hard

grip *VERB* **grips**, **gripping**, **gripped**
❶ to grip something is to hold it tightly
❷ a story, film, game or other activity grips you when you find it very interesting or exciting

grip *NOUN* **grips**
❶ a firm hold on something ❷ a handle

grisly *ADJECTIVE* **grislier**, **grisliest**
disgusting or horrible • *Please spare me the grisly details!*
SPELLING ALERT! Do not confuse **grisly** details with **grizzly** bears: *He met a grisly end by being eaten by a grizzly bear.*

gristle *NOUN*
gristle is the tough rubbery part of meat
➤ **gristly** *ADJECTIVE*

grit *NOUN*
❶ grit is tiny pieces of stone or sand
❷ a person's grit is their courage and determination to do something difficult
➤ **gritty** *ADJECTIVE*

grit *VERB* **grits**, **gritting**, **gritted**
❶ to grit your teeth is to clench them tightly when in pain or trouble ❷ to grit a road or path is to put grit on it

grizzly bear *NOUN* **grizzly bears**
a large brown bear found in North America

groan *VERB* **groans**, **groaning**, **groaned**
to groan is to make a long deep sound when in pain or distress

groan *NOUN* **groans**
a long deep sound of pain or distress

grocer *NOUN* **grocers**
someone who keeps a shop that sells food, drink and other goods for the house

grocery *NOUN* **groceries**
a grocer's shop
➤ **groceries** goods sold by a grocer

groggy *ADJECTIVE* **groggier**, **groggiest**
dizzy or unsteady, especially from illness or injury
➤ **grogginess** *NOUN*

groin *NOUN* **groins**
the flat part between your thighs and your trunk

groom *NOUN* **grooms**
❶ someone whose job is to look after horses
❷ a bridegroom
groom *VERB* **grooms**, **grooming**, **groomed**
❶ to groom a horse or other animal is to clean and brush it ❷ to groom the hair or a beard is to make it neat and trim

groove *NOUN* **grooves**
a long narrow channel cut in the surface of something

grope *VERB* **gropes**, **groping**, **groped**
to grope for something is to feel about for it when you cannot see it

gross *ADJECTIVE* **grosser**, **grossest**
❶ unattractively large and bloated
❷ having bad manners; crude or vulgar
❸ very bad or shocking • *an example of gross stupidity* ❹ a person's gross income is the total amount they earn before taxes have been taken off
➤ **grossly** *ADVERB* by a very large amount

grotesque (*say* groh-**tesk**) *ADJECTIVE*
strange and ugly
➤ **grotesquely** *ADVERB*

grotty *ADJECTIVE* **grottier**, **grottiest**
(*informal*)
unpleasant or dirty

ground *VERB* (*past tense and past participle of* **grind**)
• *The witch scowled and ground her teeth.*
• *The traffic had ground to a halt.*

ground *NOUN* **grounds**
❶ the ground is the surface of the earth
❷ a ground is a sports field

grounded *ADJECTIVE*
❶ aircraft are grounded when they are prevented from flying, for example because of the weather ❷ (*informal*) someone is grounded when they are not allowed to go out

ground floor *NOUN* **ground floors**
in a building, the floor that is level with the ground

grounds *PLURAL NOUN*
❶ the grounds for something are the reasons that explain it or justify it
• *There are grounds for suspecting that a crime has been committed.* ❷ the gardens of a large house ❸ bits of coffee at the bottom of a cup

groundsheet *NOUN* **groundsheets**
a piece of waterproof material for spreading on the ground, especially in a tent

groundsman, **groundswoman** *NOUN*
groundsmen, **groundswomen**
a person whose job is to look after a sports ground

group *NOUN* **groups**
a number of people, animals or things that belong together in some way
group *VERB* **groups**, **grouping**, **grouped**
to group people or things is to make them into a group

grouse *VERB* **grouses**, **grousing**, **groused**
to grumble or complain
grouse *NOUN* **grouse**
a large game bird with feathered legs

grove *NOUN* **groves**
a group of trees; a small wood

grovel *VERB* **grovels**, **grovelling**, **grovelled**
❶ to grovel is to crawl on the ground
❷ to grovel is to be extremely humble and obedient towards someone, usually because you want something from them

a b c d e f **g** h i j k l m n o p q r s t u v w x y z

A B C D E F G H I J K L M N O P Q R S T U V W X Y Z

grow *VERB* **grows**, **growing**, **grew**, **grown**
❶ a person grows when they become bigger with age ❷ a plant or seed grows when it develops in the ground ❸ to grow something is to plant it in the ground and look after it • *He grows lovely roses.* ❹ to grow is also to become • *By now it was growing dark on the moor.* • *She grew richer and richer.*
➤ **to grow on someone** is to become more attractive to them • *This music grows on you.*
➤ **to grow out of something** is to become too big or too old for it
➤ **to grow up** is to become an adult
➤ **grower** *NOUN*

growl *VERB* **growls**, **growling**, **growled**
to growl is to make a deep rough sound, like an angry dog
growl *NOUN* **growls**
a deep rough sound

grown-up *NOUN* **grown-ups**
an adult

growth *NOUN* **growths**
❶ growth is growing or development
❷ a growth is something that has grown, especially something unwanted in the body such as a tumour

grub *NOUN* **grubs**
❶ a grub is a tiny creature that will become an insect; a larva ❷ (*informal*) grub is food

grubby *ADJECTIVE* **grubbier**, **grubbiest**
rather dirty

grudge *NOUN* **grudges**
a dislike of someone because you think they have harmed you, or because you are jealous
grudge *VERB* **grudges**, **grudging**, **grudged**
to grudge someone something is to feel unwilling to let them have it
➤ **grudgingly** *ADVERB* you do something grudgingly when you don't really want to do it, and only do it because you have to

gruelling *ADJECTIVE*
a gruelling test or journey or other experience is one that is very hard and tiring

gruesome *ADJECTIVE*
horrible or disgusting to look at or think about • *the tale of a gruesome and ghastly murder*
➤ **gruesomeness** *NOUN*

gruff *ADJECTIVE* **gruffer**, **gruffest**
a gruff voice or manner is rough and unfriendly
➤ **gruffly** *ADVERB*

grumble *VERB* **grumbles**, **grumbling**, **grumbled**
to complain in a bad-tempered way

grumpy *ADJECTIVE* **grumpier**, **grumpiest**
bad-tempered
➤ **grumpily** *ADVERB* ➤ **grumpiness** *NOUN*

grunt *VERB* **grunts**, **grunting**, **grunted**
to grunt is to make a snorting sound like a pig
grunt *NOUN* **grunts**
a snort like that of a pig

guarantee *NOUN* **guarantees**
a formal promise to do something, especially to repair something you have sold someone if it goes wrong
guarantee *VERB* **guarantees**, **guaranteeing**, **guaranteed**
to guarantee something is to make a promise to do it

guard *VERB* **guards**, **guarding**, **guarded**
❶ to guard something or someone is to keep them safe ❷ to guard a prisoner is to prevent them from escaping
➤ **to guard against something** is to be careful to prevent it happening
guard *NOUN* **guards**
❶ a guard is someone who protects a person or place, or a group of people guarding a prisoner ❷ a guard is also an official in charge of a railway train
➤ **on guard** protecting; acting as a guard

guardian *NOUN* **guardians**
❶ someone who protects something
❷ someone who is legally in charge of a child instead of the child's parents

guerrilla (*say* ge-ril-a) *NOUN* **guerrillas**
a member of a small army or band that fights by means of surprise attacks

guess *NOUN* **guesses**
an opinion or answer that you give without working it out in detail or being sure of it

guess *VERB* **guesses**, **guessing**, **guessed**
to guess is to make a guess

guest (*say* gest) *NOUN* **guests**
❶ a person who is invited to visit or stay at someone's house ❷ someone staying at a hotel ❸ a performer in a show in which someone else is the main performer

guest house *NOUN* **guest houses**
a kind of small hotel

guidance *NOUN*
guidance is giving help or information to someone, or telling them how to do something

guide *NOUN* **guides**
❶ someone who shows people the way, helps them or points out interesting sights ❷ a book that tells you about a place

guide *VERB* **guides**, **guiding**, **guided**
to guide someone is to show them the way or help them do something • *He guided her into the sitting room where the piano was.*

guide dog *NOUN* **guide dogs**
a dog specially trained to lead a person who is blind

guidelines *PLURAL NOUN*
guidelines are rules and information about how to do something

guild (*say* gild) *NOUN* **guilds**
a society of people with similar skills or interests

guillotine (*say* gil-o-teen) *NOUN* **guillotines**
❶ (*historical*) a machine once used in France for beheading people ❷ a device with a sharp blade for cutting paper
DID YOU KNOW? The **guillotine** is named after Joseph *Guillotin*, a French doctor who suggested using it for executions, although he did not invent it.

guilt *NOUN*
❶ guilt is an unpleasant feeling you have when you have done something wrong ❷ a person's guilt is the fact that they have

done something wrong • *Everyone was convinced of their guilt.*

guilty *ADJECTIVE* **guiltier**, **guiltiest**
❶ someone is guilty when they have done wrong ❷ someone feels guilty when they know they have done wrong

guinea *NOUN* **guineas**
a British gold coin worth 21 shillings or £1.05, no longer in use
'Let us now talk about the fees. That will be fifty guineas, please.'—REVOLTING RHYMES, Roald Dahl

guinea pig *NOUN* **guinea pigs**
❶ a small furry animal without a tail, kept as a pet ❷ a person who is used in an experiment

guitar *NOUN* **guitars**
a musical instrument played by plucking its strings
➤ **guitarist** *NOUN*

gulf *NOUN* **gulfs**
a large area of sea partly surrounded by land

gull *NOUN* **gulls**
a seagull

gullet *NOUN* **gullets**
the tube from the throat to the stomach

gullible *ADJECTIVE*
someone is gullible when they can be easily fooled about something

gully *NOUN* **gullies**
a narrow channel that carries water

gulp *VERB* **gulps**, **gulping**, **gulped**
❶ to gulp something is to swallow it quickly or greedily ❷ to gulp is to make a loud swallowing noise, especially out of fear

gulp *NOUN* **gulps**
a loud swallowing noise

gum *NOUN* **gums**
❶ the firm fleshy part of your mouth that holds your teeth ❷ a sticky substance used as glue ❸ chewing gum

gun *NOUN* **guns**
❶ a weapon that fires shells or bullets from a metal tube ❷ a pistol fired to signal the start

a
b
c
d
e
f
g
h
i
j
k
l
m
n
o
p
q
r
s
t
u
v
w
x
y
z

of a race ❸ a device that forces a substance such as grease out of a tube

gunboat *NOUN* **gunboats**
a small warship

gunfire *NOUN*
gunfire is the firing of guns, or the noise they make

gunman *NOUN* **gunmen**
a person armed with a gun

gunner *NOUN* **gunners**
someone who works with guns, especially in the army

gunpowder *NOUN*
gunpowder is a type of explosive

gunshot *NOUN* **gunshots**
gunshot is the shot that some guns fire

gurdwara *NOUN* **gurdwaras**
a building where Sikhs worship

gurgle *VERB* **gurgles**, **gurgling**, **gurgled**
to make a bubbling sound • *Water gurgled down the waste pipe.* • *Anna's clear voice gurgled with laughter.*

guru *NOUN* **gurus**
❶ a Hindu religious teacher ❷ a wise and respected teacher

Guru Granth Sahib *NOUN*
the most important book of the Sikh religion

gush *VERB* **gushes**, **gushing**, **gushed**
❶ to gush is to flow quickly ❷ to gush is also to talk quickly and with excitement

gust *NOUN* **gusts**
a sudden rush of wind or rain
➤ **gusty** *ADJECTIVE*

gusto (*say* **gus**-toh) *NOUN*
if you do something with gusto, you do it with energy and enthusiasm
There was macaroni cheese with ham in it—Emil's favourite dish—and he tucked into it with gusto.
—EMIL AND THE DETECTIVES, Erich Kästner

gut *NOUN* **guts**
the lower part of the digestive system; the intestine

gut *VERB* **guts**, **gutting**, **gutted**
❶ to gut a dead fish or animal is to remove its insides before cooking it ❷ to gut a place is to remove or destroy the inside of it • *Flames gutted the bedroom of the flat.*

guts *PLURAL NOUN*
❶ your guts are your insides, especially your stomach and intestines ❷ (*informal*) a person has guts when they show courage and determination to do something difficult

gutter *NOUN* **gutters**
a long narrow channel at the side of a street or along the edge of a roof, to carry away rainwater

guy *NOUN* **guys**
❶ a figure in the form of Guy Fawkes, burnt on or near 5 November in memory of the Gunpowder Plot to blow up Parliament in 1605 ❷ (*informal*) a man

guy rope *NOUN* **guy ropes**
a rope used to hold something in place, especially a tent

guzzle *VERB* **guzzles**, **guzzling**, **guzzled**
to guzzle food or drink is to eat or drink it greedily

gym (*say* jim) *NOUN* **gyms** (*informal*)
❶ a gym is a gymnasium ❷ gym is the exercises and games you do in PE

gymkhana (*say* jim-**kah**-na) *NOUN* **gymkhanas**
a show of horse-riding contests and other events

gymnasium *NOUN* **gymnasiums**
a large room equipped for gymnastics and other exercises

gymnast *NOUN* **gymnasts**
an expert in gymnastics

gymnastics *PLURAL NOUN*
gymnastics are exercises and movements that show the body's agility and strength

gypsy *NOUN* **gypsies**
a member of a community of people (also called *travellers*) who traditionally live in caravans or similar vehicles and travel from place to place. This word is sometimes considered offensive.

Hh

habit NOUN **habits**
something that you do often and almost without thinking

habitat NOUN **habitats**
an animal's or plant's habitat is the place where it naturally lives or grows

habitual ADJECTIVE
something is habitual when you do it regularly • *her brother's face with its habitual smile*

hack VERB **hacks, hacking, hacked**
to hack something is to chop or cut it roughly

hacker NOUN **hackers**
someone who uses a computer to get access to a company's or government's computer system without permission

hacksaw NOUN **hacksaws**
a saw with a thin blade for cutting metal

had VERB (*past tense and past participle of* **have**)
• *I had to bite my tongue to stop myself answering back.* • *He had had a brilliant day.*

haddock NOUN **haddock**
a sea fish used for food

hadn't
short for *had not* • *She hadn't heard us.*

hag NOUN **hags**
an offensive word for a woman thought to be ugly and old

haggard ADJECTIVE
looking ill or very tired

haggis NOUN **haggises**
a Scottish food made from some of the inner parts of a sheep mixed with oatmeal and spices

haggle VERB **haggles, haggling, haggled**
to argue about a price or agreement

haiku (*say* **hy**-koo) NOUN **haiku**
a Japanese short poem, with three lines and seventeen syllables in the pattern 5, 7, 5

hail NOUN
hail is frozen drops of rain

hail VERB **hails, hailing, hailed**
❶ it hails or it is hailing when hail falls
❷ to hail someone is to call out or wave to them to get their attention

hailstone NOUN **hailstones**
a piece of hail

hair NOUN **hairs**
❶ hair is the soft covering that grows on the heads and bodies of people and animals
❷ a hair is one of the fine threads that makes up this soft covering

hairbrush NOUN **hairbrushes**
a brush for tidying your hair

haircut NOUN **haircuts**
cutting a person's hair when it gets too long; the style into which it is cut

hairdresser NOUN **hairdressers**
someone whose job is to cut and arrange people's hair

hairpin NOUN **hairpins**
a pin for keeping your hair in place

hair-raising ADJECTIVE
terrifying or dangerous

hairstyle NOUN **hairstyles**
a way or style of arranging your hair

hairy ADJECTIVE **hairier, hairiest**
❶ having a lot of hair ❷ (*informal*) dangerous or risky

Hajj NOUN
the Hajj is the journey to Mecca that all Muslims try to make at least once in their lives

hake NOUN **hake**
a sea fish used for food

halal ADJECTIVE
acceptable, according to Muslim religious law, especially laws concerning the preparation of meat

a
b
c
d
e
f
g
h
i
j
k
l
m
n
o
p
q
r
s
t
u
v
w
x
y
z

half *NOUN* **halves**
each of the two equal parts that something is or can be divided into

half *ADVERB*
partly; not completely • *This meat is only half cooked.*

half-baked *ADJECTIVE* (*informal*)
a half-baked plan or idea has not been properly worked out

half-hearted *ADJECTIVE*
not very enthusiastic
➤ **half-heartedly** *ADVERB*

half-mast *NOUN*
a flag is at half-mast when it is lowered to halfway down its flagpole, as a sign that someone important has died

halfpenny (*say* **hayp**-nee) *NOUN* **halfpennies** *or* **halfpence**
an old British coin that was worth half a penny

half-term *NOUN* **half-terms**
a short holiday from school in the middle of a school term

half-time *NOUN* **half-times**
a short break in the middle of a game

halfway *ADVERB, ADJECTIVE*
at a point half the distance or amount between two places or times

halibut *NOUN* **halibut**
a large flat sea fish used for food

hall *NOUN* **halls**
❶ a space or passage inside the front door of a house ❷ a very large room for meetings, concerts or other large gatherings of people ❸ a large important building or house, such as a town hall

hallo
another spelling of **hello**

hallow *NOUN* **hallows** (*old use*)
a sacred object or relic • *Harry Potter and the Deathly Hallows*

Halloween *NOUN*
the night of 31 October, when people used to think that ghosts and witches might appear

DID YOU KNOW? The word **Halloween** is a shortened form of *All Hallow Even*, meaning the evening before All Saints' Day.

hallucination *NOUN* **hallucinations**
something you think you can see or hear when it is not really there

halo *NOUN* **haloes**
a circle of light, especially one shown round the head of a saint or angel in a painting

halt *VERB* **halts**, **halting**, **halted**
to halt is to stop
halt *NOUN*
➤ **to call a halt** is to stop something
➤ **to come to a halt** is to stop

halter *NOUN* **halters**
a rope or strap put round a horse's head so that it can be controlled

halting *ADJECTIVE*
slow and uncertain • *He has a halting walk.*

halve *VERB* **halves**, **halving**, **halved**
❶ to halve something is to divide it into halves ❷ to halve something is to reduce to half its size or amount • *If the shop had another checkout, it would halve the queues.*

halves *NOUN* (*plural of* **half**)

ham *NOUN* **hams**
❶ ham is meat from a pig's leg ❷ (*informal*) a ham is an actor who is not very good and acts in a very exaggerated way

hamburger *NOUN* **hamburgers**
a flat round cake of minced beef, often grilled and served in a soft roll

hammer *NOUN* **hammers**
a tool with a heavy metal head at the end of a handle, used for hitting nails in or beating out things
hammer *VERB* **hammers**, **hammering**, **hammered**
❶ to hammer something is to hit it with a hammer ❷ to hammer is to knock loudly • *We heard someone hammering on the door.* ❸ (*informal*) to hammer someone in a game or contest is to defeat them completely

hammock *NOUN* **hammocks**
a bed made of a strong net or piece of cloth hung up above the ground or floor

hamper *NOUN* **hampers**
a large box-shaped basket with a lid

hamper *VERB* **hampers, hampering, hampered**
to hamper someone or something is to get in their way or make it difficult for them to work

hamster *NOUN* **hamsters**
a small furry animal with cheek pouches, often kept as a pet

hand *NOUN* **hands**
❶ the part of your body at the end of your arm ❷ a pointer on a clock or watch ❸ the cards held by one player in a card game ❹ a worker, especially a member of a ship's crew ❺ side or direction • *the right-hand side* • *on the other hand*
➤ **at hand** near or close by
➤ **to do or make something by hand** is to do or make it using your hands
➤ **to give someone a hand** is to help them
➤ **hands down** winning easily or completely
➤ **on hand** ready and available
➤ **to get out of hand** is to get out of control

hand *VERB* **hands, handing, handed**
to hand something to someone is to give or pass it to them

handbag *NOUN* **handbags**
a small bag for holding money, keys and other personal items

handbook *NOUN* **handbooks**
a book that gives useful facts about something

handcuffs *PLURAL NOUN*
a pair of metal rings joined by a chain, used for locking a prisoner's wrists together
➤ **handcuffed** *ADJECTIVE*

handful *NOUN* **handfuls**
❶ as much as you can carry in one hand ❷ a small number of people or things • *There were only a handful of people in the audience.* ❸ (*informal*) a troublesome person

handicap *NOUN* **handicaps**
a disadvantage
➤ **handicapped** *ADJECTIVE*

handicraft *NOUN* **handicrafts**
artistic work done with your hands, such as woodwork and pottery

handiwork *NOUN*
something you have done or made using your artistic skill

handkerchief (*say* **hang-ker-cheef**) *NOUN* **handkerchiefs**
a square piece of material for wiping your nose

handle *NOUN* **handles**
the part of a thing by which you can hold or control it or pick it up

handle *VERB* **handles, handling, handled**
❶ to handle something is to touch or feel it with your hands ❷ to handle a task or problem is to deal with it • *I thought you handled the situation very well.*

handlebars *PLURAL NOUN*
a bar with a handle at each end, used to steer a bicycle or motorcycle

handrail *NOUN* **handrails**
a rail for holding on to for support

handshake *NOUN* **handshakes**
a handshake is when you shake someone's hand as a greeting

handsome *ADJECTIVE* **handsomer, handsomest**
❶ attractive or good-looking
'I have no children of my own, and as you are the cleverest and handsomest young man I've ever met, I think I would like to make you the Prince of Narnia.'—THE LION, THE WITCH AND THE WARDROBE, C. S. Lewis
❷ large or generous • *They are offering a very handsome reward.*

handstand *NOUN* **handstands**
an exercise in which you balance on your hands with your feet in the air

handwriting *NOUN*
writing done by hand; a person's style of writing
➤ **handwritten** *ADJECTIVE* written by hand, not typed or printed

handy *ADJECTIVE* **handier, handiest**
useful or convenient

a b c d e f g h i j k l m n o p q r s t u v w x y z

hang VERB **hangs, hanging, hung**
❶ to hang something is to fix the top part of it to a hook or nail • *Hang your coat on one of the pegs.* ❷ something hangs when it is supported from the top and does not touch the ground • *The bat was hanging by its feet.* ❸ to hang wallpaper is to paste it in strips on to a wall ❹ to hang is to float in the air ❺ (in this meaning, the past tense and past participle are **hanged**) to hang someone is to execute them by hanging them from a rope that tightens around their neck • *Guy Fawkes was sentenced to be hanged for treason.*
➤ **to hang about** or **hang around** is to wait around doing nothing
➤ **to hang on** (*informal*) is to wait • *Hang on! I'm not ready yet.*
➤ **to hang on to something** is to hold it tightly
➤ **to hang up** is to end a telephone conversation by putting back the receiver or by pressing a button

hangar NOUN **hangars**
a large shed where aircraft are kept

hanger NOUN **hangers**
a curved piece of wood, plastic or wire with a hook at the top, that you use to hang clothes up on

hang-glider NOUN **hang-gliders**
a frame like a large kite on which a person can glide through the air
➤ **hang-gliding** NOUN

hangman NOUN **hangmen** (*historical*)
a person whose job was to execute people by hanging them

hank NOUN **hanks**
a coil or piece of wool or thread

hanker VERB **hankers, hankering, hankered**
to hanker after something is to want it badly • *My friend Pete had always hankered after the good life.*

hanky NOUN **hankies** (*informal*)
a handkerchief

Hanukkah NOUN
the eight-day Jewish festival of lights held in December

haphazard (*say* hap-**haz**-erd) ADJECTIVE
done or chosen at random, with no particular order or plan • *The books were arranged on the shelf in a haphazard way.*

haphazardly ADVERB
at random, with no particular method or order
Mrs Weasley was clattering around, cooking breakfast a little haphazardly, throwing dirty looks at her sons as she threw sausages into the frying pan.—HARRY POTTER AND THE CHAMBER OF SECRETS, J. K. Rowling

happen VERB **happens, happening, happened**
to happen is to take place or occur
➤ **to happen to do something** is to do it by chance without planning it • *I happened to see him in the street.*

happening NOUN **happenings**
something that happens; an unusual event

happily ADVERB
❶ to do something happily is to do it in a happy way • *She was singing happily to herself.* ❷ in a contended or willing way • *I will happily wait until tomorrow.*

happiness NOUN
being happy • *Her eyes were shining with happiness.*

happy ADJECTIVE **happier, happiest**
❶ pleased or contented ❷ satisfied that something is good • *My teacher is happy with my work this term.* ❸ lucky or fortunate • *By a happy coincidence, we met Jenny in town.*

happy-go-lucky ADJECTIVE
being cheerful and not worrying about the future

harass (*say* ha-ras) VERB **harasses, harassing, harassed**
to harass someone is to annoy or trouble them a lot
➤ **harassed** ADJECTIVE ➤ **harassment** NOUN

harbour NOUN **harbours**
a place where ships can shelter or unload
harbour VERB **harbours, harbouring, harboured**
to harbour a criminal is to give them shelter

hard ADJECTIVE **harder**, **hardest**
❶ firm or solid; not soft • *The ground was hard.*
❷ difficult • *These sums are quite hard.*
❸ severe or harsh • *There has been a hard frost.*
❹ energetic; using great effort • *She is a hard worker.*
➤ **hard up** short of money
➤ **hardness** NOUN

hard ADVERB **harder**, **hardest**
❶ with great effort • *We'll try to work harder.*
❷ with a lot of force • *It was raining hard.*

hardboard NOUN
stiff board made of compressed wood pulp

hard-boiled ADJECTIVE
a hard-boiled egg is one that has been boiled until it is hard

hard disk NOUN **hard disks**
a disk fitted inside a computer, able to store large amounts of data

harden VERB **hardens**, **hardening**, **hardened**
❶ to harden is to become hard • *Wait for the varnish to harden.* ❷ to harden something is to make it hard • *What's the best way to harden a conker?*

hardly ADVERB
only just; only with difficulty • *She was hardly able to walk.*

hardship NOUN **hardships**
❶ hardship is suffering or difficulty
❷ a hardship is something that causes suffering

hardware NOUN
❶ tools and other pieces of equipment you use in the house and garden ❷ the machinery and electronic parts of a computer, not the software

hard-wearing ADJECTIVE
able to stand a lot of wear

hardwood NOUN **hardwoods**
hard heavy wood from deciduous trees, such as oak and teak

hardy ADJECTIVE **hardier**, **hardiest**
able to endure cold or difficult conditions

hare NOUN **hares**
a fast-running animal like a large rabbit

hare-brained ADJECTIVE
a hare-brained idea is rash and not well thought through
Toad set forth cautiously on what seemed to be a most hare-brained and hazardous undertaking.
—THE WIND IN THE WILLOWS, Kenneth Grahame

hark VERB **harks**, **harking**, **harked** (*old use*)
to hark is to listen
➤ **to hark back** is to return to an earlier subject

harm VERB **harms**, **harming**, **harmed**
to harm someone or something is to hurt or damage them

harm NOUN
injury or damage
➤ **harmful** ADJECTIVE causing injury or damage
➤ **harmless** ADJECTIVE not at all dangerous

harmonica NOUN **harmonicas**
a mouth organ

harmonious ADJECTIVE
❶ music is harmonious when it is pleasant to listen to ❷ peaceful and friendly
➤ **harmoniously** ADVERB

harmonize (*also* **harmonise**) VERB **harmonizes**, **harmonizing**, **harmonized**
❶ musicians or singers harmonize when they play or sing together with notes that combine well with the main tune
❷ to harmonize is to combine together in a way that works well
➤ **harmonization** NOUN

harmony NOUN **harmonies**
❶ a pleasant combination of musical notes played or sung at the same time ❷ agreement or friendship • *They live in perfect harmony.*
➤ **harmonic** ADJECTIVE to do with musical harmony

harness NOUN **harnesses**
the straps put over a horse's head and round its neck to control it

harness VERB **harnesses**, **harnessing**, **harnessed**
❶ to harness a horse is to put a harness on it
❷ to harness something is to control it and make use of it • *They tried to harness the power of the wind to make electricity.*

a
b
c
d
e
f
g
h
i
j
k
l
m
n
o
p
q
r
s
t
u
v
w
x
y
z

harp *NOUN* **harps**
a musical instrument made of a frame with strings stretched across it that you pluck with your fingers
➤ **harpist** *NOUN*

harp *VERB* **harps, harping, harped**
to harp on about something is to keep on talking about it in an annoying way • *He keeps harping on about all the work he has to do.*

harpoon *NOUN* **harpoons**
a spear attached to a rope, fired from a gun to catch whales and large fish

harpsichord *NOUN* **harpsichords**
a musical instrument like a piano but with the strings plucked and not struck

harrow *NOUN* **harrows**
a heavy device pulled over the ground to break up the soil

harsh *ADJECTIVE* **harsher, harshest**
❶ rough and unpleasant to your senses • *the harsh glare of a spotlight* ❷ cruel or severe • *Those are harsh words.*
➤ **harshly** *ADVERB* ➤ **harshness** *NOUN*

harvest *NOUN* **harvests**
❶ the time when farmers gather in the corn, fruit or vegetables they have grown ❷ the crop that is gathered in
harvest *VERB* **harvests, harvesting, harvested**
to harvest crops is to gather them in

has *VERB* (*3rd person singular of* **have**) • *He has a very nice nature.*

hash *NOUN* **hashes**
a mixture of small pieces of meat and vegetables, usually fried

hashtag *NOUN* **hashtags**
the symbol #; used in messages on social media

hasn't
short for *has not* • *It hasn't been all bad.*

hassle *NOUN* **hassles** (*informal*)
hassle, or a hassle, is something that is difficult or causes problems
hassle *VERB* **hassles, hassling, hassled**
to hassle someone is to annoy them or cause them problems

haste *NOUN*
hurry or speed
➤ **to make haste** is to hurry

hasten *VERB* **hastens, hastening, hastened**
❶ to hasten is to hurry ❷ to hasten something is to speed it up

hasty *ADJECTIVE* **hastier, hastiest**
hurried; done too quickly • *a hasty decision*
➤ **hastily** *ADVERB* ➤ **hastiness** *NOUN*

hat *NOUN* **hats**
a covering for the head

hatch *NOUN* **hatches**
an opening in a floor, wall or door, usually with a covering

hatch *VERB* **hatches, hatching, hatched**
❶ to hatch is to break out of an egg • *The chicks hatched this morning.*
❷ to hatch an egg is to keep it warm until a young bird hatches from it ❸ to hatch a plan is to form it

hatchet *NOUN* **hatchets**
a small axe

hate *VERB* **hates, hating, hated**
to hate someone or something is to dislike them very much
hate *NOUN* **hates**
❶ hate is a feeling of great dislike ❷ (*informal*) a hate is someone or something that you dislike very much • *Sweetcorn is one of my pet hates.*

hateful *ADJECTIVE*
hated; very nasty
➤ **hatefully** *ADVERB*

hatred (*say* **hay**-trid) *NOUN*
a strong feeling of great dislike

hat trick *NOUN* **hat tricks**
getting three goals, wickets or victories one after another

haughty (*say* **haw**-tee) *ADJECTIVE* **haughtier, haughtiest**
proud of yourself and looking down on other people
➤ **haughtily** *ADVERB* ➤ **haughtiness** *NOUN*

haul VERB **hauls, hauling, hauled**
to haul something is to pull it using a lot of power or strength • *It took three of us to haul the suitcase up the stairs.*

haul NOUN **hauls**
an amount that someone has gained; a catch or booty • *They made off with a haul of stolen jewels.*

haunt VERB **haunts, haunting, haunted**
❶ a ghost haunts a place or person when it appears often ❷ to haunt a place is to visit it often ❸ an idea or memory haunts someone when they are always thinking of it
➤ **haunted** ADJECTIVE a haunted place is one that people think is visited by ghosts

have VERB **has, having, had**
This word has many meanings, depending on the words that go with it. ❶ to have something is to own or possess it • *We haven't any money.* ❷ to contain something • *I thought this tin had biscuits in it.* ❸ to have (for example) a party is to organize it ❹ to have (for example) a shock or accident is to experience it • *I'm afraid she has had an accident.* ❺ to have to do something is to be obliged or forced to do it • *We really have to go now.* ❻ to have something (for example) mended or built is to get someone to mend or build it • *I'm having my watch mended.* ❼ to have (for example) a letter is to receive it • *I had an email from my cousin.* ❽ the verb **have** can also be used to help make other verbs • *They have gone away now.* • *Has he replied yet?* • *We had already eaten.*
➤ **to have someone on** (*informal*) is to fool them

haven (*say* **hay-ven**) NOUN **havens**
❶ a safe place ❷ a harbour

haven't
short for *have not* • *I haven't a clue.*

havoc NOUN
great destruction or disorder • *The storm wreaked havoc along the coast.*

hawk NOUN **hawks**
a bird of prey with very strong eyesight and a hooked beak

hawk VERB **hawks, hawking, hawked**
to hawk things is to go from place to place selling them

hawthorn NOUN **hawthorns**
a thorny tree with small red berries

hay NOUN
cut grass that is dried and used to feed animals

hay fever NOUN
an allergy to pollen that makes you sneeze and makes your eyes water or itch

haystack NOUN **haystacks**
a large neat pile of stored hay

hazard NOUN **hazards**
a risk or danger

hazardous ADJECTIVE
something is hazardous when it is dangerous or risky • *The sea crossing is hazardous at this time of year.*

haze NOUN **hazes**
thin mist

hazel NOUN **hazels**
❶ a type of small nut tree ❷ a nut from this tree ❸ a light brown colour

hazy ADJECTIVE **hazier, haziest**
❶ misty • *hazy sunshine* ❷ vague and unclear • *I have a hazy memory of that day.*
➤ **hazily** ADVERB ➤ **haziness** NOUN

he PRONOUN, NOUN
a male person or animal: used as the subject of a verb

head NOUN **heads**
❶ the part of your body containing your brains, eyes and mouth ❷ brains or intelligence • *Use your head!* ❸ a talent or ability • *He has a good head for sums.* ❹ the side of a coin on which someone's head is shown ❺ a person • *It costs £3 per head.* ❻ the top or front of something, such as a pin or nail ❼ the person in charge • *She's the head of this school.*
➤ **to keep your head** is to stay calm
➤ **off the top of your head** (*informal*) without preparation or thinking carefully • *He gave an answer off the top of his head.*

head VERB **heads, heading, headed**
❶ to head a group or organization is to lead it or be the person in charge ❷ to head a ball is to hit it with your head ❸ to head in a particular direction is to start going there • *They headed for home.*

➤ to head someone off is to get in front of them in order to turn them aside

headache *NOUN* **headaches**
❶ a pain in your head that goes on hurting ❷ (*informal*) a problem or difficulty

headdress *NOUN* **headdresses**
a decorative covering for the head

header *NOUN* **headers**
the act of hitting the ball with your head in football

head first *ADVERB*
with your head at the front • *I dived in head first.*

heading *NOUN* **headings**
a word or words at the top of a piece of printing or writing

headland *NOUN* **headlands**
a piece of high land sticking out into the sea

headlight *NOUN* **headlights**
a strong light at the front of a vehicle

headline *NOUN* **headlines**
a heading in a newspaper, printed in large type

headlong *ADVERB, ADJECTIVE*
❶ falling head first • *He missed the step and fell headlong into the snow.* ❷ in a hasty or reckless way • *They were rushing headlong into danger.*

headmaster *NOUN* **headmasters**
a male head teacher

headmistress *NOUN* **headmistresses**
a female head teacher

head-on *ADVERB, ADJECTIVE*
with the front parts hitting each other • *a head-on collision between a bus and a lorry*

headphones *PLURAL NOUN*
a set of earphones joined by a band that fits over the top of your head

headquarters *NOUN* **headquarters**
the place from which an organization is controlled

head teacher *NOUN* **head teachers**
the person in charge of a school

heal *VERB* **heals, healing, healed**
❶ to heal someone is to make them healthy ❷ a wound or injury heals when it gets better • *The cut soon healed.* ❸ to heal a disease is to cure it
➤ healer *NOUN*

health *NOUN*
❶ the condition of a person's body or mind • *His health is bad.* ❷ being healthy • *We wished the couple health and happiness.*

healthy *ADJECTIVE* **healthier, healthiest**
❶ not ill or unwell ❷ producing good health • *Fresh air is healthy.*
➤ healthily *ADVERB* **➤ healthiness** *NOUN*

heap *NOUN* **heaps**
a pile, especially an untidy pile
➤ heaps (*informal*) a large amount • *We've got heaps of time.*

heap *VERB* **heaps, heaping, heaped**
❶ to heap things is to pile them up ❷ to heap something is to put large amounts on it • *She heaped his plate with food.*

hear *VERB* **hears, hearing, heard**
❶ to hear is to take in sounds through the ears ❷ to hear a sound is to take it in through the ear ❸ to hear news or information is to receive it ❹ you hear from someone when they write to you or phone you

hearing *NOUN* **hearings**
❶ the ability to hear ❷ a chance to be heard • *Please give me a fair hearing.* ❸ a trial in court

hearing aid *NOUN* **hearing aids**
a device to help a person who is deaf to hear

hearse (*say* herss) *NOUN* **hearses**
a vehicle for taking a coffin to a funeral

heart *NOUN* **hearts**
❶ the part of the body inside your chest that pumps blood around your body ❷ a person's feelings or emotions
'I will honour Christmas in my heart, and try to keep it all the year.'—A CHRISTMAS CAROL, Charles Dickens
❸ courage or enthusiasm • *We mustn't lose heart now.* ❹ the middle or most important part of something • *This is the real heart of the city.* ❺ a curved shape representing a heart, or a playing card with this shape on it

➤ **to break someone's heart** is to make them very unhappy

➤ **by heart** by using your memory

heart attack *NOUN* **heart attacks**
a sudden failure of the heart to work properly, causing pain and sometimes death

hearth (*say* harth) *NOUN* **hearths**
the floor of a fireplace or the area near it

heartless *ADJECTIVE*
cruel or without pity • *a cold-blooded and heartless pirate*

hearty *ADJECTIVE* **heartier, heartiest**
❶ strong and healthy ❷ enthusiastic or sincere • *Hearty congratulations!* ❸ a hearty meal is large and filling
➤ **heartily** *ADVERB* ➤ **heartiness** *NOUN*

heat *NOUN* **heats**
❶ being hot; great warmth ❷ a race or contest to decide who will take part in the final

heat *VERB* **heats, heating, heated**
❶ to heat something, or heat something up, is to make it hot ❷ to heat, or heat up, is to become hot

heater *NOUN* **heaters**
a device for heating a place, especially a room or a car

heath *NOUN* **heaths**
wild flat land, often covered with heather or bushes

heathen *NOUN* **heathens** (*old use*)
someone who does not believe in any of the main world religions

heather *NOUN*
a low bush with small purple, pink or white flowers

heatwave *NOUN* **heatwaves**
a long period of hot weather

heave *VERB* **heaves, heaving, heaved**
❶ to heave something is to lift or move it with great effort ❷ (*informal*) to heave something is to throw it
➤ **to heave a sigh** is to sigh deeply

heave *NOUN* **heaves**
a strong pull or shove

heaven *NOUN*
❶ the place where, in some religions, good people are thought to go when they die and where God and the angels are thought to live ❷ a very pleasant place or condition
➤ **the heavens** the sky

heavenly *ADJECTIVE*
❶ to do with the sky or in the sky ❷ (*informal*) pleasing or delicious
Pauline sipped her drink. It was very hot, but simply heavenly—the sort of drink certain to make a cold feel better.—BALLET SHOES, Noel Streatfeild

heavy *ADJECTIVE* **heavier, heaviest**
❶ weighing a lot; hard to lift or carry ❷ you talk about how heavy something is when you are talking about how much it weighs ❸ strong or severe • *Heavy rain was falling.* • *He brought his fist down upon the table with a heavy blow.* ❹ hard or difficult • *The climb up the hill was heavy going.*
➤ **heavily** *ADVERB* with a lot of weight or force
➤ **heaviness** *NOUN*

heavyweight *NOUN* **heavyweights**
❶ a heavy person ❷ a boxer or wrestler of the heaviest weight

Hebrew *NOUN*
the language of the ancient Jewish people, or a modern form of the language used in Israel

hectare (*say* hek-tar) *NOUN* **hectares**
a unit of area equal to 10,000 square metres or just over 2 acres

hectic *ADJECTIVE*
very active or busy • *It's been a hectic morning.*

he'd
short for *he had* or *he should* or *he would*

hedge *NOUN* **hedges**
a row of bushes forming a barrier or boundary

hedge *VERB* **hedges, hedging, hedged**
❶ to hedge a field or other area is to surround it with a hedge ❷ to hedge is also to avoid giving a definite answer • *I could tell he was hedging.*

hedgehog *NOUN* **hedgehogs**
a small animal covered with prickles

a b c d e f g h i j k l m n o p q r s t u v w x y z

hedgerow NOUN **hedgerows**
a row of bushes forming a hedge
The rising sun glimmered through the hedgerows and turned the dust in the roadway to pale gold.
—BEDKNOBS AND BROOMSTICKS, Mary Norton

heed VERB **heeds**, **heeding**, **heeded**
to heed something is to pay attention to it
heed NOUN
attention given to something
➤ **heedless** ADJECTIVE to be heedless of something is to take no notice of it

heel NOUN **heels**
❶ the back part of your foot ❷ the part of a sock or shoe round or under the back part of your foot
➤ **to take to your heels** is to run away
heel VERB **heels**, **heeling**, **heeled**
to heel a shoe is to mend its heel

hefty ADJECTIVE **heftier**, **heftiest**
large and heavy • *The ogre was carrying a hefty club.*

heifer (*say* hef-er) NOUN **heifers**
a young female cow

height NOUN **heights**
❶ how high someone or something is • *Let me measure your height.* ❷ a high place • *My dog is afraid of heights.* ❸ the highest or most important part of something • *the height of the holiday season*

heighten VERB **heightens**, **heightening**, **heightened**
❶ to heighten something is to make it higher or more intense ❷ to heighten is to become higher or more intense • *Their excitement heightened as the kick-off approached.*

heir (*say* air) NOUN **heirs**
someone who inherits money or a title

heiress (*say* air-ess) NOUN **heiresses**
a girl or woman who inherits great wealth

held VERB (*past tense and past participle of* hold) • *He held out his hand.* • *She should have held her tongue.*

helicopter NOUN **helicopters**
a kind of aircraft without wings, lifted by a large horizontal propeller on top
DID YOU KNOW? The word **helicopter** comes from Greek words meaning 'spiral wing'.

helium (*say* hee-li-um) NOUN
a colourless gas that is lighter than air and is sometimes used in balloons

helix NOUN **helices**
a three-dimensional spiral, shaped like a screw

hell NOUN
❶ a place where, in some religions, wicked people are thought to be punished after they die and where the Devil is thought to live ❷ a very unpleasant place or situation

he'll
short for *he will* • *He'll be here soon.*

hellish ADJECTIVE
very unpleasant or difficult

hello EXCLAMATION
a word you say to greet someone or to attract their attention

helm NOUN **helms**
the handle or wheel used to steer a ship

helmet NOUN **helmets**
a strong covering that you wear to protect your head

help VERB **helps**, **helping**, **helped**
❶ to help someone is to do something useful for them or make things easier for them ❷ when you cannot help doing something, you cannot avoid doing it • *I can't help coughing.* ❸ to help yourself to food is to take some
help NOUN **helps**
❶ doing something useful for someone ❷ someone who does something, especially housework, for someone

helper NOUN **helpers**
someone who helps another person

helpful ADJECTIVE
giving help; useful • *a very helpful suggestion*
➤ **helpfully** ADVERB

helping NOUN **helpings**
a portion of food at a meal

helpless ADJECTIVE
not able to do things or look after yourself
➤ **helplessly** ADVERB

helter-skelter NOUN **helter-skelters**
a spiral slide at a fair

hem NOUN **hems**
the edge of a piece of cloth that has been folded over and sewn down

hem VERB **hems, hemming, hemmed**
to hem material is to fold it over and sew down its edge
➤ **to hem someone in** is to surround them or restrict their movements

hemisphere NOUN **hemispheres**
❶ half a sphere ❷ half the earth • *Australia is in the southern hemisphere.*

hemp NOUN
a plant that produces coarse fibres from which cloth and ropes are made

hen NOUN **hens**
a female bird, especially a chicken

hence ADVERB
❶ from this time on ❷ therefore

heptagon NOUN **heptagons**
a shape with seven straight sides
➤ **heptagonal** (*say* hep-**ta**-go-nal) ADJECTIVE

heptathlon (*say* hept-**ath**-lon) NOUN **heptathlons**
a sports competition in which athletes take part in seven different events
➤ **heptathlete** NOUN

her PRONOUN
a word used for *she* when it is the object of a verb, or when it comes after a preposition
• *Can you see her?* • *I got a present from her.*

her DETERMINER
belonging to her • *I think that is her book.*

herald NOUN **heralds**
❶ an official who in the past used to make announcements or carry messages for a king or queen ❷ someone or something that is a sign of things to come

herald VERB **heralds, heralding, heralded**
to herald something or someone is to say or show that they are coming

heraldry NOUN
the study of coats of arms

herb NOUN **herbs**
a plant used for flavouring or for making medicines
➤ **herbal** ADJECTIVE

herbivore NOUN **herbivores**
an animal that only eats plants

herd NOUN **herds**
a large group of animals, especially cattle

herd VERB **herds, herding, herded**
to herd animals or people is to gather them together or move them in a large group

here ADVERB
in or to this place
➤ **here and there** in various places or directions

hereditary ADJECTIVE
a hereditary physical or mental characteristic is passed down to a child from a parent

heredity (*say* hir-**ed**-it-ee) NOUN
the process of inheriting physical or mental characteristics from parents or ancestors

heritage NOUN **heritages**
things that have been passed from one generation to another; a country's history and traditions • *Music is part of our cultural heritage.*

hermit NOUN **hermits**
someone who lives alone and keeps away from people, often for religious reasons

hero NOUN **heroes**
❶ a person who is admired for doing something very brave or impressive ❷ the most important character in a story, film or play • *Bilbo Baggins is the hero of 'The Hobbit'.*
SPELLING ALERT! Remember to put an e in the plural: *tales of ancient heroes and heroines.*

heroic (*say* hi-**roh**-ik) ADJECTIVE
like a hero; very brave • *a heroic soldier* • *heroic deeds*
➤ **heroically** ADVERB

heroine NOUN **heroines**
❶ a woman or girl who has done something very brave ❷ the most important female character in a story, film or play • *Sophie is the heroine of 'The BFG'.*

heroism (*say* **her**-oh-izm) NOUN
being a hero; great bravery

heron NOUN **herons**
a wading bird with long legs and a long neck

a b c d e f g h i j k l m n o p q r s t u v w x y z

herring *NOUN* **herring** *or* **herrings**
a sea fish that swims in large groups and is used for food

hers *PRONOUN*
belonging to her • *Those books are hers.*

herself *PRONOUN*
she or her and nobody else, used to refer back to the subject of a verb • *She has hurt herself.*
➤ **by herself** on her own; alone • *She did the work all by herself.*

he's
short for *he is* or *he has* • *He's my friend.*
• *He's been ill.*

hesitant *ADJECTIVE*
being slow or uncertain when you speak or move
➤ **hesitantly** *ADVERB*

hesitate *VERB* **hesitates**, **hesitating**, **hesitated**
to hesitate is to be slow or uncertain when you speak or move

hesitation *NOUN*
❶ hesitation is when you hesitate • *She answered without hesitation.* ❷ a hesitation is a pause

hewn *ADJECTIVE*
cut or carved from a hard material like wood or stone • *The temple had been hewn out of solid rock.*

hex *NOUN* **hexes**
a magical charm or curse

hexagon *NOUN* **hexagons**
a flat shape with six sides
➤ **hexagonal** (*say* hek-**sa**-go-nal) *ADJECTIVE*

hey *EXCLAMATION*
a word you say to show you are surprised, or to call someone's attention • *Hey! Where are you going?*

hi *EXCLAMATION*
a word you say to greet someone or to call their attention

hibernate (*say* **hy**-ber-nayt) *VERB* **hibernates**, **hibernating**, **hibernated**
animals hibernate when they sleep for a long time during cold weather
➤ **hibernation** *NOUN*

hiccup *NOUN* **hiccups**
a high gulping sound you make when your breath is briefly interrupted

hiccup *VERB* **hiccups**, **hiccupping**, **hiccupped**
to make a high gulping sound

hide *VERB* **hides**, **hiding**, **hid**, **hidden**
❶ to hide is to get into a place where you cannot be seen or found • *I hid behind a tree.* ❷ to hide someone or something is to keep them from being seen • *The gold was hidden in a cave.* ❸ to hide information is to keep it secret • *Are you hiding the truth from me?*

hide-and-seek *NOUN*
a game in which one person looks for others who are hiding

hideous *ADJECTIVE*
very ugly or unpleasant
Aunt Sponge had a long-handled mirror on her lap and she kept picking it up and gazing at her own hideous face.–JAMES AND THE GIANT PEACH, Roald Dahl
➤ **hideously** *ADVERB*

hideout *NOUN* **hideouts**
a place where someone hides

hiding *NOUN* **hidings**
❶ to be in hiding is to keep yourself hidden • *The outlaws were in hiding somewhere.* ❷ a hiding is also a thrashing or beating

hieroglyphics (*say* hyr-o-**glif**-iks) *PLURAL NOUN*
pictures or symbols used in ancient Egypt to represent words

higgledy-piggledy *ADVERB, ADJECTIVE*
in disorder; completely mixed up

high *ADJECTIVE* **higher**, **highest**
❶ reaching a long way up • *They could see a high building.* ❷ far above the ground or sea • *The clouds were high in the sky.* ❸ measuring from top to bottom • *The post is two metres high.* ❹ above average in amount or importance • *They are people of a high rank.* • *Prices are high.* ❺ lively; happy • *They are in high spirits.* ❻ a high note is one at the top end of a musical scale

Higher *NOUN* **Highers**
an examination that is taken by secondary school pupils in Scotland

high jump *NOUN*
an athletic contest in which competitors jump over a high bar

highland *ADJECTIVE*
in the highlands; to do with the highlands

highlands *PLURAL NOUN*
mountainous country, especially in Scotland

highlight *NOUN* **highlights**
the most interesting part of something
• *We watched the highlights of the match on the TV.*

highlight *VERB* **highlights, highlighting, highlighted**
to highlight something is to draw attention to it

highlighter *NOUN* **highlighters**
a pen with bright coloured ink that you spread over words on paper to draw attention to them

highly *ADVERB*
extremely • *It is highly unlikely that anyone survived.*
➤ **to think highly of someone** is to admire them very much

highly strung *ADJECTIVE*
very sensitive or nervous

Highness *NOUN* **Highnesses**
a title of a prince or princess • *His Royal Highness, the Prince of Wales*

high-pitched *ADJECTIVE*
high in sound

high-rise *ADJECTIVE*
a high-rise building is a tall one with many storeys

high school *NOUN* **high schools**
a secondary school

highwayman *NOUN* **highwaymen**
a man who in earlier times robbed travellers on highways
The road was a ribbon of moonlight over the purple moor, And the highwayman came riding— Riding— riding— The highwayman came riding, up to the old inn-door.—THE HIGHWAYMAN, Alfred Noyes

hijab *NOUN* **hijabs**
a head covering worn in public by some Muslim women

hijack *VERB* **hijacks, hijacking, hijacked**
to hijack an aircraft or vehicle is to take control of it by force during a journey
➤ **hijacker** *NOUN*

hike *NOUN* **hikes**
a long walk in the countryside

hike *VERB* **hikes, hiking, hiked**
to hike is to go for a long walk in the countryside
➤ **hiker** *NOUN*

hilarious *ADJECTIVE*
very funny
➤ **hilariously** *ADVERB*
➤ **hilarity** *NOUN* loud laughter

hill *NOUN* **hills**
a piece of ground that is higher than the ground around it
➤ **hilly** *ADJECTIVE*

hillside *NOUN* **hillsides**
the side of a hill

hilt *NOUN* **hilts**
the handle of a sword or dagger

him *PRONOUN*
a word used for *he* when it is the object of a verb, or when it comes after a preposition • *Do you like him?* • *I gave the money to him.*

himself *PRONOUN*
he or him and nobody else, used to refer back to the subject of a verb • *He has hurt himself.*
➤ **by himself** on his own; alone • *He did the work all by himself.*

hind (*say* hynd) *ADJECTIVE*
at the back • *The donkey had hurt one of its hind legs.*

hind (*say* hynd) *NOUN* **hinds**
a female deer

hinder (*say* hin-der) *VERB* **hinders, hindering, hindered**
to hinder someone is to get in their way, or to make it difficult for them to do something
➤ **hindrance** *NOUN*

a b c d e f g h i j k l m n o p q r s t u v w x y z

Hindi *NOUN*
the main language of northern India
DID YOU KNOW? The words **bungalow** and **shampoo** come from Hindi.

Hindu *NOUN* **Hindus**
someone who believes in **Hinduism**, one of the religions of South Asia

hinge *NOUN* **hinges**
a joining device on which a door, gate or lid swings when it opens

hinge *VERB* **hinges**, **hinging**, **hinged**
to hinge on something is to depend on it • *It all hinges on the weather.*

hinged *ADJECTIVE*
a hinged door, window or lid is fixed on a hinge

hint *NOUN* **hints**
❶ a slight indication or suggestion • *Give me a hint of what you want for your birthday.* ❷ a useful piece of advice • *The blog gives hints on how to write a great story.*

hint *VERB* **hints**, **hinting**, **hinted**
to hint is to suggest something without actually saying it • *She hinted that she'd like to have a puppy.*

hip *NOUN* **hips**
your hips are the bony parts at the side of your body between your waist and your thighs

hip *EXCLAMATION*
a word that you say when you give a cheer • *Hip, hip, hooray!*

hippo *NOUN* **hippos** (*informal*)
a hippopotamus

hippogriff *NOUN* **hippogriffs**
a mythological creature with the body of a horse and the wings and head of an eagle

hippopotamus *NOUN* **hippopotamuses**
a large African mammal with a thick skin and huge jaws that lives near lakes and rivers
DID YOU KNOW? The word **hippopotamus** comes from Greek words meaning 'river horse'.

hire *VERB* **hires**, **hiring**, **hired**
to hire something is to pay to use it for a time

hire *NOUN*
➤ **something is for hire** when you can hire it

his *DETERMINER, PRONOUN*
belonging to him • *Those books are his.*

hiss *VERB* **hisses**, **hissing**, **hissed**
to make a sound like a continuous *s*, as some snakes do

historian *NOUN* **historians**
someone who writes or studies history

historic *ADJECTIVE*
famous or important in history

historical *ADJECTIVE*
❶ to do with history ❷ that really happened in the past • *The story is based on historical events.*

history *NOUN* **histories**
❶ history is what happened in the past ❷ history is also the study of past events and people ❸ a description of important events • *a history of the First World War*

hit *VERB* **hits**, **hitting**, **hit**
❶ to hit someone or something is to come up against them with force, or to give them a blow ❷ something hits you when you suddenly realise or feel it • *The answer suddenly hit me.* ❸ to hit a place or people is to have a bad effect on them • *Storms hit the coastal region.* ❹ to hit a note is to reach it when you are singing
➤ **to hit it off with someone** is to get on well with them when you meet them
➤ **to hit on something** is to think of an idea suddenly

hit *NOUN* **hits**
❶ a knock or stroke ❷ a shot that hits the target ❸ a successful song or show

hitch *VERB* **hitches**, **hitching**, **hitched**
❶ to hitch something is to tie it up with a loop ❷ (*informal*) to hitch a lift is to hitch-hike
➤ **to hitch something up** is to pull it up quickly or with a jerk • *He hitched up his trousers.*

hitch *NOUN* **hitches**
❶ a slight difficulty or delay ❷ a knot

hitch-hike *VERB* **hitch-hikes, hitch-hiking, hitch-hiked**
to hitch-hike is to travel by getting lifts in other people's vehicles
➤ **hitch-hiker** *NOUN*

hither *ADVERB* (*old use*)
to or towards this place

hive *NOUN* **hives**
❶ a beehive ❷ a very busy place
• *The classroom was a hive of activity.*

HMS *ABBREVIATION*
short for *His* or *Her Majesty's Ship*
• *Darwin sailed to the Galapagos Islands on HMS Beagle.*

hoard *NOUN* **hoards**
a hidden store of something valuable • *a hoard of pirate treasure*

hoard *VERB* **hoards, hoarding, hoarded**
to hoard things is to collect them and store them away
➤ **hoarder** *NOUN*

hoarding *NOUN* **hoardings**
a tall fence covered with advertisements

hoar frost *NOUN*
white frost

hoarse *ADJECTIVE* **hoarser, hoarsest**
having a rough or croaking voice • *He was hoarse from shouting.*

hoax *NOUN* **hoaxes**
a trick played on someone in which they are told about something but it is not true • *The bomb scare was a hoax.*

hoax *VERB* **hoaxes, hoaxing, hoaxed**
to hoax someone is to trick them by telling them about something that is not true

hobble *VERB* **hobbles, hobbling, hobbled**
to hobble is to walk with unsteady steps, especially because your feet are sore

hobby *NOUN* **hobbies**
something that you enjoy doing in your spare time

hobgoblin *NOUN* **hobgoblins**
a hobgoblin is a mischievous imp or sprite

hockey *NOUN*
an outdoor game played by two teams with long curved sticks and a small hard ball

hoe *NOUN* **hoes**
a gardening tool with a long handle and a metal blade, used for scraping up weeds and making soil loose

hoe *VERB* **hoes, hoeing, hoed**
to hoe ground is to scrape it or dig it with a hoe

hog *NOUN* **hogs**
a male pig
➤ **to go the whole hog** (*informal*) is to do something completely or thoroughly

hog *VERB* **hogs, hogging, hogged** (*informal*)
to hog something is to take more than your fair share of it

Hogmanay *NOUN*
New Year's Eve in Scotland

hoist *VERB* **hoists, hoisting, hoisted**
to hoist something is to lift it up using ropes or pulleys

hold *VERB* **holds, holding, held**
❶ to hold something is to have it in your hands ❷ to hold something is to possess it or be the owner of it • *She holds the world high jump record.* ❸ to hold a party, meeting or event is to organize it • *The 2016 Olympic Games were held in Brazil.* ❹ a container holds an amount when that is what you can put in it • *This jug holds a litre.* ❺ to hold someone or something is to support them • *This plank won't hold my weight.* ❻ to hold someone is to keep them and stop them getting away • *They held the thief until help arrived.* ❼ something like the weather holds when it stays the same • *Will this good weather hold?* ❽ to hold an opinion is to believe it
➤ **hold it** (*informal*) stop; wait a minute
➤ **to hold on** (*informal*) is to wait • *Hold on! I'm not ready yet.*
➤ **to hold on to something** is to keep holding it
➤ **to hold out** is to last or continue
➤ **to hold someone up** is to rob them with threats of force
➤ **to hold someone** *or* **something up** is to hinder or delay them • *We were held up by the traffic.*

hold *NOUN* **holds**
❶ holding something • *Don't lose hold of the rope.* ❷ the part of a ship or aeroplane where cargo is stored

► **to get hold of someone** is to make contact with them • *I want to invite Jane to the party, but I can't get hold of her.*

holdall *NOUN* **holdalls**
a large portable bag or case

holder *NOUN* **holders**
a person or thing that holds something

hold-up *NOUN* **hold-ups**
❶ a delay ❷ a robbery with threats or force

hole *NOUN* **holes**
❶ a gap or opening made in something • *a tiny hole in the pocket* ❷ an animal's burrow • *a rabbit hole*
► **holey** *ADJECTIVE*
full of holes
SPELLING ALERT! You can fill in a **hole**, but you eat a **whole** pizza.

Holi *NOUN*
the Hindu festival of colours held in the spring in honour of the god Krishna

holiday *NOUN* **holidays**
❶ a day when you do not go to work or school • *Next Monday is a holiday.* ❷ a time when you go away to enjoy yourself • *some photos from our summer holiday*
► **to be on holiday** is to be away from work or school

hollow *ADJECTIVE*
having an empty space inside; not solid
hollow *VERB* **hollows, hollowing, hollowed**
to hollow something is to make it hollow • *We always hollow out a pumpkin at Halloween.*
hollow *NOUN* **hollows**
❶ a hollow place ❷ a small valley

holly *NOUN*
an evergreen bush with shiny prickly leaves and red berries

hologram *NOUN* **holograms**
a type of photograph where the image appears to be three-dimensional

holster *NOUN* **holsters**
a leather case for a pistol, usually attached to a belt

holt *NOUN* **holts**
the den of an otter

holy *ADJECTIVE* **holier, holiest**
❶ to do with God and treated with religious respect ❷ a holy person is devoted to God or a religion
► **holiness** *NOUN*

home *NOUN* **homes**
❶ the place where you live ❷ the place where you were born or where you feel you belong ❸ a place where people are looked after • *She went to a care home when she was 90.* ❹ the place that you try to reach in a game • *The far end of the gym is home.*
► **to feel at home** is to feel comfortable and happy
home *ADVERB*
❶ to or at the place where you live • *Go home!* • *Is she home yet?* ❷ to the place aimed at • *Push the bolt home.*
home *VERB* **homes, homing, homed**
► **to home in on something** is to aim for it

homeless *ADJECTIVE*
not having a place to live

homely *ADJECTIVE*
simple or ordinary
► **homeliness** *NOUN*

home-made *ADJECTIVE*
made at home and not bought from a shop

homesick *ADJECTIVE*
sad or upset because you are away from home
► **homesickness** *NOUN*

homestead *NOUN* **homesteads**
a farmhouse and the land around it

homeward, homewards *ADVERB, ADJECTIVE*
going or leading towards home

homework *NOUN*
school work that you have to do at home

homograph *NOUN* **homographs**
a word spelt the same as another word but with a different meaning or origin, such as *bat* (a flying animal) and *bat* (for hitting a ball)

homonym *NOUN* **homonyms**
a **homograph** or **homophone**

homophone *NOUN* **homophones**
a word with the same sound as another word but with a different spelling and meaning, such as *son* and *sun*

honest *ADJECTIVE*
truthful and able to be trusted; not stealing, cheating or telling lies
➤ **honesty** *NOUN*

honestly *ADVERB*
❶ to say something honestly is to say it truthfully ❷ to do something honestly is to do it without stealing or cheating ❸ you say honestly when you want to show you are really telling the truth • *It was an accident, honestly.* ❹ you can also say honestly when you are annoyed by something • *Honestly, I'm tired of being told what to do!*

honey *NOUN*
a sweet sticky food made by bees

honeycomb *NOUN* **honeycombs**
a wax framework made by bees to hold their honey and eggs

honeymoon *NOUN* **honeymoons**
a holiday that a newly married couple spend together

honeysuckle *NOUN*
a climbing plant with sweet-smelling yellow or pink flowers

honk *NOUN* **honks**
a loud sound like the one made by a car horn or a wild goose
honk *VERB* **honks**, **honking**, **honked**
to make a honking sound

honour *NOUN* **honours**
❶ honour is great respect or reputation ❷ an honour is something given to a person who deserves it because of the good work they have done ❸ an honour is also something a person is proud to do • *It is an honour to meet you.*
honour *VERB* **honours**, **honouring**, **honoured**
❶ to honour someone is to show them respect or to give them an honour ❷ to honour a promise or agreement is to keep it

honourable *ADJECTIVE*
someone is honourable when they can be trusted and always try to do the right thing
➤ **honourably** *ADVERB*

hood *NOUN* **hoods**
❶ a covering of soft material for the head and neck, usually part of a coat or sweatshirt ❷ a folding roof or cover
➤ **hooded** *ADJECTIVE* a hooded person is wearing a hood

hoody, **hoodie** *NOUN* **hoodies** (*informal*)
a sweatshirt with a hood

hoof *NOUN* **hoofs** *or* **hooves**
the hard bony part of the foot of horses, cattle or deer

hook *NOUN* **hooks**
a piece of bent or curved metal or plastic for hanging things on or catching hold of something
hook *VERB* **hooks**, **hooking**, **hooked**
❶ to hook something is to fasten it with or on a hook ❷ to hook a fish is to catch it with a hook

hooked *ADJECTIVE*
a hooked nose or beak has a curved shape like a hook

hooligan *NOUN* **hooligans**
a rough or noisy person

hoop *NOUN* **hoops**
a large ring made of metal, wood or plastic

hoopla *NOUN*
a game in which you try to throw hoops round an object, which you then win

hooray
another spelling of **hurray**

hoot *NOUN* **hoots**
❶ a sound like the one made by an owl or a car horn ❷ a jeer
hoot *VERB* **hoots**, **hooting**, **hooted**
to hoot is to make a sound like an owl or a car horn

hooter *NOUN* **hooters**
a horn or other device that makes a hoot

hop *VERB* **hops**, **hopping**, **hopped**
❶ to hop is to jump on one foot ❷ animals hop when they move in jumps ❸ (*informal*) to hop

a b c d e f g h i j k l m n o p q r s t u v w x y z

A B C D E F G **H** I J K L M N O P Q R S T U V W X Y Z

is also to move quickly • *Hop in and I'll give you a lift.*
➤ **hop it** (*informal*) go away

hop *NOUN* **hops**
❶ a hop is a jump you make on one foot ❷ hop is also a climbing plant used to give beer its flavour

hope *NOUN* **hopes**
❶ the feeling of wanting something to happen, and thinking that it will happen ❷ a person or thing that makes you feel like this • *She is our big hope for a gold medal.*

hope *VERB* **hopes**, **hoping**, **hoped**
to hope for something is to want it and expect it to happen

hopeful *ADJECTIVE*
❶ having hope • *We are hopeful that the team will qualify.* ❷ likely to be good or successful • *The future did not seem very hopeful.*
➤ **hopefulness** *NOUN*

hopefully *ADVERB*
❶ in a hopeful way ❷ I hope that... • *Hopefully, the weather will improve tomorrow.*

hopeless *ADJECTIVE*
❶ without hope ❷ very bad at something • *I'm hopeless at singing.*
➤ **hopelessly** *ADVERB*

hopscotch *NOUN*
a game in which you hop into squares drawn on the ground

horde *NOUN* **hordes**
a large group or crowd • *a horde of football fans*
SPELLING ALERT! You can see a **horde** of tourists, but you find a **hoard** of treasure.

horizon (*say* ho-**ry**-zon) *NOUN* **horizons**
the line where the sky appears to meet the land or sea

horizontal (*say* ho-ri-**zon**-tal) *ADJECTIVE*
level or flat; going across from left to right
➤ **horizontally** *ADVERB*

hormone *NOUN* **hormones**
a substance made in your body that controls things like how you develop and grow

horn *NOUN* **horns**
❶ a kind of pointed bone that grows on the head of a bull, cow, ram and other animals ❷ a brass musical instrument that you blow ❸ a device for making a warning sound

hornet *NOUN* **hornets**
a large kind of wasp

horoscope *NOUN* **horoscopes**
your horoscope is an astrologer's forecast about what will happen to you, based on your zodiac sign

horrible *ADJECTIVE*
very unpleasant or nasty
➤ **horribly** *ADVERB*

horrid *ADJECTIVE*
nasty or unpleasant
'How horrid,' cried Mrs Otis; 'I don't at all care for blood-stains in a sitting-room. It must be removed at once.'—THE CANTERVILLE GHOST, Oscar Wilde

horrific *ADJECTIVE*
shocking or terrifying
➤ **horrifically** *ADVERB*

horrify *VERB* **horrifies**, **horrifying**, **horrified**
to horrify someone is to make them feel shocked and disgusted

horror *NOUN* **horrors**
❶ horror is great fear or disgust ❷ a horror is a person or thing you really dislike

horse *NOUN* **horses**
❶ a four-legged animal used for riding on or pulling carts ❷ a tall box that you jump over when you are doing gymnastics

horseback *NOUN*
➤ **to be on horseback** is to be riding a horse

horse chestnut *NOUN* **horse chestnuts**
a large tree that produces dark brown nuts called conkers

horseman, horsewoman *NOUN* **horsemen, horsewomen**
a person who rides a horse, especially a skilful rider
➤ **horsemanship** *NOUN* the art of riding a horse

horsepower *NOUN* **horsepower**
a unit for measuring the power of an engine, equal to 746 watts

horseshoe *NOUN* **horseshoes**
a U-shaped piece of metal nailed as a shoe to a horse's hoof

horticulture *NOUN*
the art of planning and looking after gardens

hose *NOUN* **hoses**
a long flexible tube through which liquids or gases can travel

hospitable *ADJECTIVE*
a hospitable person or place is very welcoming to other people and makes them feel at home
➤ **hospitably** *ADVERB*

hospital *NOUN* **hospitals**
a place where sick or injured people are given medical treatment

hospitality *NOUN*
welcoming people and giving them food and entertainment

host *NOUN* **hosts**
❶ someone who has guests and looks after them ❷ a large number of people or things • *We looked out and saw a host of faces.*

hostage *NOUN* **hostages**
someone who is held prisoner until the people who are holding them get what they want

hostel *NOUN* **hostels**
a building with rooms where students or other people can stay cheaply

hostess *NOUN* **hostesses**
a woman who has guests and looks after them

hostile *ADJECTIVE*
❶ unfriendly and angry
In the bedroom, the children were grouped in two corners of the room, regarding each other in hostile silence.—NANNY MCPHEE AND THE BIG BANG, Emma Thompson
❷ opposed to someone or something
➤ **hostility** *NOUN*

hot *ADJECTIVE* **hotter, hottest**
❶ having a high temperature; very warm
❷ having a burning taste like pepper or mustard
❸ excited or angry • *He has a hot temper.*
➤ **to be in hot water** (*informal*) is to be in trouble or difficulty

hot cross bun *NOUN* **hot cross buns**
a spicy bun with a cross marked on it, eaten at Easter

hot dog *NOUN* **hot dogs**
a hot sausage in a bread roll

hotel *NOUN* **hotels**
a building where people pay to stay for the night and have meals

hothouse *NOUN* **hothouses**
a heated greenhouse

hotly *ADVERB*
strongly or forcefully • *He hotly denied that he'd done it.*

hotpot *NOUN* **hotpots**
a kind of stew

hot-water bottle *NOUN* **hot-water bottles**
a container that you fill with hot water to make a bed warm

hound *NOUN* **hounds**
a dog used for hunting or racing

hound *VERB* **hounds, hounding, hounded**
to hound someone is to keep on chasing and bothering them • *We were hounded by newspaper reporters.*

hour *NOUN* **hours**
❶ one of the twenty-four parts into which a day is divided ❷ a particular time • *Why are you up at this hour?*

hourglass *NOUN* **hourglasses**
an old-fashioned device for telling the time, with sand running from one half of a glass container into the other through a narrow middle part

hourly *ADJECTIVE, ADVERB*
every hour; done once an hour

house (*say* howss) *NOUN* **houses**
❶ a building where people live, usually designed for one family ❷ a building used for a special purpose • *They passed the*

a b c d e f g h i j k l m n o p q r s t u v w x y z

opera house. ❸ a building for a government assembly, or the assembly itself, for example the Houses of Parliament or the House of Commons ❹ one of the divisions in some schools for sports competitions and other events

house (*say* howz) *VERB* **houses, housing, housed**
to house someone or something is to provide a house or room for them

houseboat *NOUN* **houseboats**
a boat for living in

household *NOUN* **households**
all the people who live together in the same house

householder *NOUN* **householders**
someone who owns or rents a house

housekeeper *NOUN* **housekeepers**
a person employed to look after a household

house-trained *ADJECTIVE*
an animal that is house-trained is trained to be clean in the house

house-warming *NOUN* **house-warmings**
a party you have to celebrate moving into a new home

housewife, househusband *NOUN* **housewives, househusbands**
a person who looks after their family's home and children, and does not have a paid job

housework *NOUN*
the work of cooking and cleaning that has to be done in a house

housing *NOUN* **housings**
❶ housing is accommodation or houses ❷ a housing is a cover or guard for a piece of machinery

hover *VERB* **hovers, hovering, hovered**
❶ to hover is to stay in one place in the air ❷ to hover round someone is to wait near them to watch what they do

hovercraft *NOUN* **hovercraft**
a vehicle that travels just above the surface of water or land, supported by a strong current of air sent downwards by its engines

how *ADVERB*
❶ in what way • *How did you do it?*
❷ to what extent • *How much do you want?*
❸ in what condition • *How are you?*
➤ **how about ...** would you like ... ?
• *How about a game of football?*
➤ **how do you do?** a more formal greeting when you meet someone

however *ADVERB*
❶ no matter how; in whatever way • *You will never catch him, however hard you try.*
❷ nevertheless • *It was snowing; however, he went out.*

however *CONJUNCTION*
in any way • *You can do it however you like.*

howl *NOUN* **howls**
a long loud cry like an animal in pain
howl *VERB* **howls, howling, howled**
❶ to howl is to make a long loud cry like an animal in pain ❷ to howl is also to weep loudly

HQ *ABBREVIATION*
short for *headquarters*

hub *NOUN* **hubs**
the centre of a wheel

hubbub *NOUN*
a hubbub is a noisy mixture of voices from a crowd of people

huddle *VERB* **huddles, huddling, huddled**
to crowd together with other people for warmth or comfort
Behind the village was a stony field where a flock of thin sheep huddled together under the shadow of a few spindly apple trees.—UNDER THE MOON, Vivian French

hue *NOUN* **hues**
a colour or tint • *The sky was alight with the reddish hues of sunset.*

huff *NOUN*
➤ **to be in a huff** is to be annoyed or offended

hug *VERB* **hugs, hugging, hugged**
❶ to hug someone is to clasp them tightly in your arms ❷ to hug something is to keep close to it • *The ship hugged the shore.*
hug *NOUN* **hugs**
clasping someone tightly in your arms

huge ADJECTIVE **huger**, **hugest**
extremely large
➤ **hugely** ADVERB greatly; very

hulk NOUN **hulks**
❶ the remains of an old decaying ship
❷ a large clumsy person or thing

hull NOUN **hulls**
the main part or framework of a ship

hullabaloo NOUN **hullabaloos**
a noisy uproar
*Quite a hullabaloo was breaking out upstairs,
and most of the sounds were by no means
pleasant.*—THE WEIRDSTONE OF BRISINGAMEN,
Alan Garner

hullo
another spelling of **hello**

hum VERB **hums**, **humming**, **hummed**
❶ to hum is to sing a tune with your lips closed
❷ to hum is also to make a low continuous
sound like a bee
hum NOUN **hums**
a humming sound

human NOUN **humans**
a person; a human being
human ADJECTIVE
to do with humans

human being NOUN **human beings**
a person; a human

humane (*say* hew-**mayn**) ADJECTIVE
showing kindness and a wish to cause as little
suffering or pain as possible
➤ **humanely** ADVERB

humanitarian ADJECTIVE
concerned with helping humanity and relieving
suffering

humanity NOUN
❶ all the people in the world ❷ the condition
of being human ❸ kindness and sympathy to
other people

humanoid ADJECTIVE
looking like a human being
*Trolls bear a humanoid appearance, walk upright,
may be taught a few simple words and yet are
less intelligent than the dullest unicorn.*
—FANTASTIC BEASTS AND WHERE TO FIND THEM,
J. K. Rowling

humble ADJECTIVE **humbler**, **humblest**
modest and not proud
➤ **humbly** ADVERB

humid (*say* hew-mid) ADJECTIVE
damp and warm in the air
➤ **humidity** NOUN

humiliate VERB **humiliates**, **humiliating**,
humiliated
to humiliate someone is to make them feel
ashamed or foolish in front of other people
➤ **humiliation** NOUN

humility NOUN
being humble

hummingbird NOUN **hummingbirds**
a small tropical bird that makes a humming
sound by beating its wings rapidly

hummus, **houmous** (*say* hoo-mus)
NOUN
a Middle-Eastern spread or dip made from
crushed chickpeas and sesame seeds
SPELLING ALERT! You can eat **hummus**, but not
humus, which is rich soil.

humorous ADJECTIVE
amusing or funny

humour NOUN
❶ being amusing; what makes people
laugh ❷ being able to enjoy things
that are funny • *He has a good sense of
humour.* ❸ a person's mood • *Keep him in
a good humour.*
humour VERB **humours**, **humouring**,
humoured
to humour someone is to keep them happy by
doing what they want

hump NOUN **humps**
❶ a rounded lump or mound ❷ a lump on a
person's back
hump VERB **humps**, **humping**, **humped**
to hump something heavy is to carry it with
difficulty on your back

humus (*say* hew-mus) NOUN
rich soil made by decaying leaves and plants

hunch NOUN **hunches**
a feeling that you can guess what will
happen • *I have a hunch that this is a
lucky ticket.*

a
b
c
d
e
f
g
h
i
j
k
l
m
n
o
p
q
r
s
t
u
v
w
x
y
z

hunch *VERB* **hunches, hunching, hunched**
to hunch your shoulders is to bring them up and forward so that your back is rounded

hunchback *NOUN* **hunchbacks**
someone with a hump on their back

hundred *NOUN* **hundreds**
the number 100
➤ **hundredth** *ADJECTIVE, NOUN*

hung *VERB* (*past tense and past participle of* **hang**)
• *Cobwebs hung from the ceiling.* • *Lanterns were hung around the hall.*

hunger *NOUN*
the feeling you get when you want or need to eat

hungry *ADJECTIVE* **hungrier, hungriest**
you are hungry when you want or need to eat
➤ **hungrily** *ADVERB*

hunk *NOUN* **hunks**
a large piece or chunk of something • *a hunk of cheese*

hunt *VERB* **hunts, hunting, hunted**
❶ to hunt animals is to chase and kill them for food or sport ❷ to hunt for something is to look hard for it

hunt *NOUN* **hunts**
❶ a time when a group of people chase and kill animals for food or sport ❷ a group of people who go hunting

hunter, huntsman *NOUN* **hunters, huntsmen**
someone who hunts for sport

hurdle *NOUN* **hurdles**
❶ an upright frame that runners jump over in hurdling ❷ a problem or difficulty

hurdling *NOUN*
racing in which the runners run and jump over hurdles
➤ **hurdler** *NOUN*

hurl *VERB* **hurls, hurling, hurled**
to hurl something is to throw it as far as you can

hurray, hurrah *EXCLAMATION*
a word you shout out when you are very happy or excited • *We won! Hurray!*

hurricane *NOUN* **hurricanes**
a severe storm with a strong wind

hurry *VERB* **hurries, hurrying, hurried**
❶ to hurry is to move or act quickly ❷ to hurry someone is to try to make them be quick
➤ **hurriedly** *ADVERB*

hurry *NOUN*
moving quickly; doing something quickly
➤ **in a hurry** hurrying or impatient • *They were in a hurry to catch their train.*

hurt *VERB* **hurts, hurting, hurt**
❶ to hurt a person or animal is to harm them or cause them pain ❷ part of your body hurts when you feel pain there ❸ to hurt someone is also to upset them by doing or saying something unkind

hurt *NOUN*
pain or injury

hurtful *ADJECTIVE*
a hurtful remark upsets someone because it is unkind

hurtle *VERB* **hurtles, hurtling, hurtled**
to move quickly or dangerously
The front three rows of students drew backwards as the carriage hurtled ever lower, coming in to land at a tremendous speed.—HARRY POTTER AND THE GOBLET OF FIRE, J. K. Rowling

husband *NOUN* **husbands**
the man that a person is married to

hush *VERB* **hushes, hushing, hushed**
to hush someone is to make them be quiet
➤ **to hush something up** is to prevent people knowing about it

hush *NOUN*
silence or quiet • *Let's have a bit of hush.*

husk *NOUN* **husks**
the dry outer covering of a seed

husky *ADJECTIVE* **huskier, huskiest**
a husky voice sounds deep and rough
➤ **huskiness** *NOUN*

husky *NOUN* **huskies**
a large strong dog used in the Arctic for pulling sledges

hustle *VERB* **hustles, hustling, hustled**
❶ to hustle is to hurry ❷ to hustle someone is to push them rudely

hut *NOUN* **huts**
a small, roughly made house or shelter

hutch *NOUN* **hutches**
a box or cage for a rabbit or other pet animal

hyacinth (*say* **hy**-a-sinth) *NOUN*
hyacinths
a sweet-smelling flower that grows from a bulb

hybrid *NOUN* **hybrids**
❶ an animal or plant that combines two different species • *A mule is a hybrid of a donkey and a mare.* ❷ something that is a mixture of two things

hydrangea (*say* hy-**drayn**-ja) *NOUN*
hydrangeas
a shrub with large pink, blue or white flowers

hydrant *NOUN* **hydrants**
an outdoor water tap connected to the main water supply, for fixing a hose to

hydraulic *ADJECTIVE*
worked by the movement of water or other liquid

hydroelectric *ADJECTIVE*
using water power to make electricity

hydrogen *NOUN*
a very light gas which with oxygen makes water

hyena (*say* hy-**ee**-na) *NOUN* **hyenas**
a wild animal that looks like a wolf and makes a shrieking howl

hygiene (*say* **hy**-jeen) *NOUN*
keeping things clean in order to remain healthy and prevent disease

hygienic *ADJECTIVE*
clean and healthy and free of germs

hymn *NOUN* **hymns**
a Christian religious song, especially one that praises God

hyperactive *ADJECTIVE*
unable to relax and always moving about or doing things

hyphen *NOUN* **hyphens**
a short dash used to join words or parts of words together, for example in *free-range* and *house-trained*
➤ **hyphenated** *ADJECTIVE* spelt with a hyphen

hypnosis (*say* hip-**noh**-sis) *NOUN*
to be under hypnosis is to be in a condition like a deep sleep in which a person follows the instructions of another person
DID YOU KNOW? The word **hypnosis** comes from the Greek word *hypnos* meaning 'sleep'.

hypnotism (*say* **hip**-no-tizm) *NOUN*
hypnotizing people
➤ **hypnotist** *NOUN*

hypnotize (*also* **hypnotise**) *VERB*
hypnotizes, hypnotizing, hypnotized
to hypnotize someone is to put them to sleep by hypnosis

hypocrite (*say* **hip**-o-krit) *NOUN*
hypocrites
someone who pretends to be a better person than they really are
➤ **hypocrisy** *NOUN* ➤ **hypocritical** *ADJECTIVE*

hypothermia *NOUN*
a person suffers from hypothermia when they become so cold that their body temperature falls well below normal

hysteria *NOUN*
wild uncontrollable excitement or emotion

hysterical *ADJECTIVE*
❶ very excited or emotional • *The crowd were hysterical.* ❷ (*informal*) very funny • *Have you seen the film? It's hysterical!*
➤ **hysterically** *ADVERB*

hysterics *PLURAL NOUN*
a fit of hysteria
➤ **to be in hysterics** (*informal*) is to be laughing a lot

a
b
c
d
e
f
g
h
i
j
k
l
m
n
o
p
q
r
s
t
u
v
w
x
y
z

Ii

I *PRONOUN*
a word used by someone to speak about themselves

ice *NOUN* **ices**
❶ ice is frozen water ❷ an ice is an ice cream

ice *VERB* **ices, icing, iced**
❶ to ice or ice up is to become covered in ice
❷ to ice a cake is to put icing on it

ice age *NOUN*
a time in the past when ice covered large areas of the earth's surface

iceberg *NOUN* **icebergs**
a large mass of ice floating in the sea, with most of it under water

ice cap *NOUN* **ice caps**
a thick covering of ice and snow at the North or South Pole

ice cream *NOUN* **ice creams**
❶ ice cream is a sweet creamy frozen food
❷ an ice cream is a portion of this

ice hockey *NOUN*
ice hockey is a game like hockey played on ice

ice lolly *NOUN* **ice lollies**
a piece of flavoured ice on a stick

ice skate *NOUN* **ice skates**
ice skates are boots with a steel blade attached to the sole, so that you can slide smoothly over ice
➤ **ice skater** *NOUN*

ice skating *NOUN*
ice skating is moving on ice wearing ice skates

icicle *NOUN* **icicles**
a thin pointed piece of hanging ice formed from dripping water

icing *NOUN*
icing is a sugary paste for decorating cakes and biscuits

icon *NOUN* **icons**
❶ a small picture or symbol standing for a program on a computer screen ❷ a painting of a holy person

ICT *ABBREVIATION*
short for *information and communication technology*

icy *ADJECTIVE* **icier, iciest**
❶ an icy road has ice on it ❷ an icy wind is very cold ❸ very unfriendly; hostile • *He gave them an icy stare.*
➤ **icily** *ADVERB* ➤ **iciness** *NOUN*

I'd
short for *I had* or *I should* or *I would*

idea *NOUN* **ideas**
something that you have thought of; a plan

ideal *ADJECTIVE*
exactly what you want; perfect

ideal *NOUN* **ideals**
something that is perfect or the best thing to have; a very high standard

ideally *ADVERB*
if things were perfect • *Ideally, I'd like to live by the sea.*

identical *ADJECTIVE*
exactly the same • *Liam and Finn are identical twins.*
➤ **identically** *ADVERB*

identification *NOUN*
❶ identification is any document, such as a passport, that proves who you are
❷ identification is the process of discovering who someone is or what something is

identify *VERB* **identifies, identifying, identified**
to identify someone or something is to discover who or what they are • *The police have identified the car used in the robbery.*
➤ **to identify with someone** is to understand or share their feelings or opinions

identity *NOUN* **identities**
who someone is or what something is
• *Can you guess the identity of our mystery guest?*

idiom (*say* id-i-om) *NOUN* **idioms**
a phrase or group of words that together have a special meaning that is not obvious from the words themselves, for example *to be in hot water* means to be in trouble or difficulty

idiomatic *ADJECTIVE*
a person's language is idiomatic when it is natural and uses a lot of idioms

idiot *NOUN* **idiots** (*informal*)
a stupid or foolish person

idiotic *ADJECTIVE* (*informal*)
stupid or foolish • *That was an idiotic thing to do.*

idle *ADJECTIVE* **idler**, **idlest**
❶ a person is idle when they are lazy or doing nothing ❷ a machine is idle when it is not being used ❸ idle talk or gossip is talk that is silly or pointless
➤ **idly** *ADVERB* ➤ **idleness** *NOUN*

idle *VERB* **idles**, **idling**, **idled**
a machine or engine idles when it is working slowly

idol *NOUN* **idols**
❶ a famous person who is admired by a lot of people ❷ a statue or image that people worship as a god

idolize (*also* **idolise**) *VERB* **idolizes**, **idolizing**, **idolized**
to idolize someone is to admire them very much

i.e. *ABBREVIATION*
short for Latin *id est*, which means 'that is', used to explain something • *The world's highest mountain (i.e. Mount Everest) is in the Himalayas.*

if *CONJUNCTION*
❶ on condition that • *I'll tell you what happened if you promise to keep it secret.* ❷ although; even though • *I'll finish this job if it kills me!* ❸ whether • *Do you know if lunch is ready?*
➤ **if only...** I wish... • *If only I could go with you!*

igloo *NOUN* **igloos**
an Inuit round house made of blocks of hard snow

igneous (*say* ig-ni-us) *ADJECTIVE*
igneous rocks are formed by the action of a volcano

ignite *VERB* **ignites**, **igniting**, **ignited**
❶ to ignite something is to set fire to it ❷ to ignite is to catch fire

ignition *NOUN*
❶ igniting ❷ ignition is the system in a motor engine that starts the fuel burning

ignorance *NOUN*
not knowing about something or knowing very little

ignorant *ADJECTIVE*
not knowing about something; knowing very little

ignore *VERB* **ignores**, **ignoring**, **ignored**
to ignore someone or something is to take no notice of them

ill *ADJECTIVE*
❶ not well; in bad health ❷ bad or harmful • *Fortunately, there were no ill effects.*

ill *ADVERB*
badly • *The animals had been ill-treated.* • *The team was ill prepared for the race.*

I'll
short for *I shall* or *I will*

illegal *ADJECTIVE*
something is illegal when it is against the law
➤ **illegally** *ADVERB*

illegible (*say* i-lej-i-bul) *ADJECTIVE*
illegible writing is not clear enough to read

illiterate (*say* i-lit-er-at) *ADJECTIVE*
unable to read or write

illness *NOUN* **illnesses**
❶ illness is being ill ❷ an illness is something that makes people ill; a disease

illogical *ADJECTIVE*
not logical or having any good reason

illuminate *VERB* **illuminates**, **illuminating**, **illuminated**
❶ to illuminate a place or street is to light it up or decorate it with lights ❷ to illuminate something difficult is to make it clearer

a
b
c
d
e
f
g
h
i
j
k
l
m
n
o
p
q
r
s
t
u
v
w
x
y
z

➤ **illuminations** *PLURAL NOUN* lights put up to decorate a place or street

illusion *NOUN* **illusions**
❶ something that you think is real or happening but is not ❷ an idea or belief you have that is not true

illustrate *VERB* **illustrates, illustrating, illustrated**
❶ to illustrate something is to show it with pictures or examples ❷ to illustrate a book is to put pictures in it

illustration *NOUN* **illustrations**
❶ an illustration is a picture in a book
❷ an illustration is also an example that helps to explain something

illustrator *NOUN* **illustrators**
a person who produces the illustrations in a book

illustrious (*say* i-**lus**-tri-us) *ADJECTIVE*
famous

I'm
short for *I am • I'm not sure.*

image *NOUN* **images**
❶ a picture or statue of a person or thing
❷ what you see in a mirror or through a lens
❸ a person who looks very much like another
• *She is the image of her mother.* ❹ the way that people think of a person or thing

imagery *NOUN*
imagery is the use of words to produce pictures in the mind of the reader

imaginary *ADJECTIVE*
not real; existing only in your mind

imagination *NOUN* **imaginations**
your ability to form pictures and ideas in your mind

imaginative *ADJECTIVE*
showing that you are good at thinking of new and exciting ideas • *Her stories are always very imaginative.*

imagine *VERB* **imagines, imagining, imagined**
to imagine something or someone is to form a picture of them in your mind
➤ **imaginable** *ADJECTIVE*

imam *NOUN* **imams**
a Muslim religious leader

imbecile (*say* im-bi-seel) *NOUN* **imbeciles**
(*informal*)
a very stupid person

imitate *VERB* **imitates, imitating, imitated**
to imitate someone or something is to do the same as them
➤ **imitation** *NOUN* ➤ **imitator** *NOUN*

immaculate *ADJECTIVE*
perfectly neat and clean • *Her clothes always look immaculate.*
➤ **immaculately** *ADVERB*

immature *ADJECTIVE*
❶ not fully grown or developed ❷ behaving in a silly or childish way
➤ **immaturity** *NOUN*

immediate *ADJECTIVE*
❶ happening or coming without any delay
❷ nearest; with nothing or no one between • *The Smiths are our immediate neighbours.*

immediately *ADVERB*
without any delay; at once • *You must come immediately.*

immense *ADJECTIVE*
extremely large; huge
The largest of the trees was immense: its trunk was as thick and tall as the column in Trafalgar Square.—THE EXPLORER, Katherine Rundell
➤ **immensity** *NOUN*

immensely *ADVERB*
very much; extremely • *The film was immensely enjoyable.*

immerse *VERB* **immerses, immersing, immersed**
❶ to immerse something is to put it completely into a liquid ❷ to be immersed in something is to be very interested or involved in it
➤ **immersion** *NOUN*

immigrant *NOUN* **immigrants**
someone who has come into a country to live there

immigrate *VERB* **immigrates, immigrating, immigrated**
to immigrate is to come into a country to live there
➤ **immigration** *NOUN*

immobile *ADJECTIVE*
not moving
After a few minutes, the crocodiles became quite immobile, their giant heads resting in the warm sand, their tails stretched out behind them. —AKIMBO AND THE CROCODILE MAN, Alexander McCall Smith

immobilize (*also* **immobilise**) *VERB* **immobilizes, immobilizing, immobilized**
to immobilize something is to stop it moving or working
➤ **immobilization** *NOUN*

immoral *ADJECTIVE*
not following the usual standards of right and wrong
➤ **immorality** *NOUN*

immortal *ADJECTIVE*
someone who is immortal lives forever and never dies
➤ **immortality** *NOUN*

immune *ADJECTIVE*
if someone is immune to a disease, they cannot catch it
➤ **immunity** *NOUN*

immunize (*also* **immunise**) *VERB* **immunizes, immunizing, immunized**
to immunize someone is to make them safe from a disease, usually by giving them an injection
➤ **immunization** *NOUN*

imp *NOUN* **imps**
❶ a small devil or sprite ❷ a mischievous child
➤ **impish** *ADJECTIVE*

impact *NOUN* **impacts**
❶ the force of one thing hitting another ❷ a strong influence or effect • *The internet has a big impact on our lives.*

impair *VERB* **impairs, impairing, impaired**
to impair something is to harm or weaken it • *The accident has impaired his health.*

impale *VERB* **impales, impaling, impaled**
to impale something is to push a sharp pointed object through it
They had the perfect view of the mammoths below, their shaggy coats crusted in old snow, their great tusks curving upwards, ready to impale anyone who fell on them. —THE POLAR BEAR EXPLORERS' CLUB, Alex Bell

impartial *ADJECTIVE*
fair and not supporting one side more than the other • *A referee must be impartial.*

impatient *ADJECTIVE*
annoyed because you cannot wait for something to happen
➤ **impatience** *NOUN* ➤ **impatiently** *ADVERB*

impede *VERB* **impedes, impeding, impeded**
to impede someone or something is to hinder them or get in their way

imperative *ADJECTIVE*
❶ essential • *Speed is imperative.* ❷ (*grammar*) an imperative word expresses a command, for example *come* in *Come here!*

imperceptible *ADJECTIVE*
too small or gradual to be noticed • *The change in the weather was imperceptible.*

imperfect *ADJECTIVE*
not perfect or complete
➤ **imperfection** *NOUN* ➤ **imperfectly** *ADVERB*

imperial *ADJECTIVE*
❶ belonging to an empire or its rulers
❷ an imperial unit or measure is a non-metric one such as a gallon, ounce or yard

impersonal *ADJECTIVE*
❶ not showing friendly human feelings • *The email was a bit impersonal.* ❷ not referring to a particular person

impersonate *VERB* **impersonates, impersonating, impersonated**
to impersonate someone is to pretend to be them
➤ **impersonation** *NOUN*
➤ **impersonator** *NOUN*

impertinent *ADJECTIVE*
rude to someone and not showing them respect
➤ **impertinence** *NOUN*

a
b
c
d
e
f
g
h
i
j
k
l
m
n
o
p
q
r
s
t
u
v
w
x
y
z

implement (*say* **im**-pli-ment) *NOUN* **implements**
a tool or device you use to do something

implement (*say* **im**-pli-ment) *VERB* **implements**, **implementing**, **implemented**
to implement a plan or idea is to put it into action

implication *NOUN* **implications**
❶ an implication is something that someone suggests without actually saying it ❷ an implication is also a possible effect or result • *She began to realize the implications of her actions.*

implore *VERB* **implores**, **imploring**, **implored**
to implore someone to do something is to beg them to do it

imply *VERB* **implies**, **implying**, **implied**
to imply something is to suggest it without actually saying it • *Are you implying that I'm lazy?*

impolite *ADJECTIVE*
not having good manners; not respectful and thoughtful towards other people

import (*say* im-**port**) *VERB* **imports**, **importing**, **imported**
to import goods is to bring them in from another country to sell them

import (*say* im-**port**) *NOUN* **imports**
something brought in from another country to be sold

important *ADJECTIVE*
❶ needing to be taken seriously; having a great effect • *This is an important decision.* ❷ an important person is powerful or influential
➤ **importance** *NOUN*
➤ **importantly** *ADVERB* seriously • *Try to win the match but, more importantly, don't lose.*

impose *VERB* **imposes**, **imposing**, **imposed**
❶ to impose something on someone is to make them have to put up with it • *The new school rules were imposed against all our wishes.* ❷ to impose a charge or tax is to make people pay it

imposing *ADJECTIVE*
looking important and impressive

imposition *NOUN* **impositions**
something that someone is made to suffer, especially as a punishment

impossible *ADJECTIVE*
❶ not possible ❷ (*informal*) very annoying • *He is impossible!*
➤ **impossibility** *NOUN* ➤ **impossibly** *ADVERB*

impostor *NOUN* **impostors**
someone who is not what he or she pretends to be

impractical *ADJECTIVE*
❶ impractical people are not good at making or doing things ❷ not likely to work or be useful • *Their ideas are impractical.*

impress *VERB* **impresses**, **impressing**, **impressed**
❶ to impress someone is to make them admire you ❷ to impress something on someone is to make them realize or remember it

impression *NOUN* **impressions**
❶ a vague idea that you have about something ❷ the effect that something has on your mind or feelings ❸ an imitation of a person or a sound

impressive *ADJECTIVE*
something is impressive when it makes you admire it
➤ **impressively** *ADVERB*

imprison *VERB* **imprisons**, **imprisoning**, **imprisoned**
to imprison someone is to put them in prison
➤ **imprisonment** *NOUN*

improbable *ADJECTIVE*
unlikely
➤ **improbability** *NOUN*

impromptu (*say* im-**promp**-tew) *ADJECTIVE, ADVERB*
done without any rehearsal or preparation

improper *ADJECTIVE*
❶ not proper; wrong ❷ rude or indecent

improve *VERB* **improves**, **improving**, **improved**
to make something better, or to become better
➤ **improvement** *NOUN*

improvise *VERB* improvises, improvising, improvised
❶ to improvise is to do something without any rehearsal or preparation, especially to play music without rehearsing ❷ to improvise something is to make it quickly with what is to hand
➤ **improvisation** *NOUN*

impudent *ADJECTIVE*
not respectful; rude
➤ **impudence** *NOUN*

impulse *NOUN* impulses
❶ a sudden desire to do something ❷ a push; a driving force

impulsive *ADJECTIVE*
doing things suddenly without much thought
➤ **impulsively** *ADVERB*

impure *ADJECTIVE*
not pure
➤ **impurity** *NOUN*

in *PREPOSITION, ADVERB*
❶ showing position at or inside something
• *They live in Toronto.* • *Please come in.* • *She fell in the water.* • *Then the others fell in.* ❷ the word **in** also has some special uses, as in these examples • *His birthday is in April.* • *I paid in cash.* • *The book is in three parts.* • *She is in the football team.* • *We knocked on the door but no one was in.*
➤ **to be in for something** is to be likely to get it • *You're in for a shock.*
➤ **to be in on something** is to take part in or know about something secret • *They let me in on their plan.*

in– *PREFIX*
meaning 'not', as in *inefficient*

inability *NOUN*
inability is being unable to do something

inaccessible *ADJECTIVE*
an inaccessible place is impossible to reach

inaccurate *ADJECTIVE*
not accurate
➤ **inaccuracy** *NOUN* ➤ **inaccurately** *ADVERB*

inaction *NOUN*
inaction is lack of action

inactive *ADJECTIVE*
not working or doing anything
➤ **inactivity** *NOUN*

inadequate *ADJECTIVE*
not enough
➤ **inadequacy** *NOUN* ➤ **inadequately** *ADVERB*

inanimate (*say* in-**an**-im-at) *ADJECTIVE*
not living or moving

inappropriate *ADJECTIVE*
not appropriate or suitable
➤ **inappropriately** *ADVERB*

inattentive *ADJECTIVE*
not listening or paying attention

inaudible *ADJECTIVE*
not able to be heard

incapable *ADJECTIVE*
unable to do something • *They are incapable of understanding the problem.*

incapacity *NOUN*
incapacity is inability or disability

incendiary *ADJECTIVE*
an incendiary bomb or device is one that starts a fire

incense (*say* in-**senss**) *NOUN*
incense is a substance that makes a spicy smell when it is burnt

incense (*say* in-**senss**) *VERB* incenses, incensing, incensed
to incense someone is to make them very angry

incentive *NOUN* incentives
something that encourages a person to do something or to work harder

incessant *ADJECTIVE*
going on without stopping, usually in an annoying way • *They were bothered by the incessant noise.*
➤ **incessantly** *ADVERB*

inch *NOUN* inches
a measure of length, one twelfth of a foot or about 2½ centimetres

incident *NOUN* incidents
an event, usually a strange or unusual one

a
b
c
d
e
f
g
h
i
j
k
l
m
n
o
p
q
r
s
t
u
v
w
x
y
z

incidental *ADJECTIVE*
happening along with something else; not so important
➤ **incidentally** *ADVERB*

incinerator *NOUN* **incinerators**
a device for burning rubbish

inclination *NOUN* **inclinations**
a feeling that makes you want to do something • *He had a sudden inclination to sneeze.*

incline (*say* in-**klyn**) *VERB* **inclines, inclining, inclined**
to incline is to lean or bend
➤ **to be inclined to do something** is to feel like doing it • *I'm inclined to wait until later.*

incline (*say* in-klyn) *NOUN* **inclines**
a slope

include *VERB* **includes, including, included**
to include something or someone is to make or consider them as part of a group of things • *Should we include Gavin in the team?* • *The menu includes a vegetarian option.*
➤ **inclusion** *NOUN*

inclusive *ADJECTIVE*
including everything; including all the things mentioned • *We want to stay from Monday to Thursday inclusive.*

income *NOUN* **incomes**
the money that a person earns regularly

incompatible *ADJECTIVE*
❶ not able to live or exist together without trouble ❷ machines and devices are incompatible when they cannot be used together

incompetent *ADJECTIVE*
unable to do something properly
➤ **incompetence** *NOUN*

incomplete *ADJECTIVE*
not complete
➤ **incompletely** *ADVERB*

incomprehensible *ADJECTIVE*
not able to be understood

incongruous (*say* in-**kong**-roo-us) *ADJECTIVE*
not suitable and out of place

inconsiderate *ADJECTIVE*
not thinking of other people

inconsistent *ADJECTIVE*
not consistent
➤ **inconsistency** *NOUN*
➤ **inconsistently** *ADVERB*

inconspicuous *ADJECTIVE*
not noticeable or remarkable

inconvenient *ADJECTIVE*
not convenient; awkward
➤ **inconvenience** *NOUN*

incorporate *VERB* **incorporates, incorporating, incorporated**
to incorporate something is to include it as a part of something else
➤ **incorporation** *NOUN*

incorrect *ADJECTIVE*
not correct; wrong
➤ **incorrectly** *ADVERB*

increase (*say* in-**kreess**) *VERB* **increases, increasing, increased**.
❶ to increase something is to make it bigger
❷ to increase is to become bigger
➤ **increasingly** *ADVERB* more and more • *They were becoming increasingly angry.*

increase (*say* in-kreess) *NOUN* **increases**
❶ increasing ❷ the amount by which something increases

incredible *ADJECTIVE*
unbelievable
➤ **incredibly** *ADVERB*

incredulous *ADJECTIVE*
finding it difficult to believe someone
➤ **incredulity** *NOUN*

incubate *VERB* **incubates, incubating, incubated**
to incubate eggs is to hatch them by keeping them warm
➤ **incubation** *NOUN*

incubator *NOUN* **incubators**
a specially heated container for keeping newly born babies warm and well supplied with oxygen

indebted *ADJECTIVE*
owing something to someone

indecent *ADJECTIVE*
relating to sex or the body in a way that might offend or shock people
➤ **indecency** *NOUN* ➤ **indecently** *ADVERB*

indeed *ADVERB*
used for emphasis • *The dog was very wet indeed.*

indefinite *ADJECTIVE*
not definite; vague and unclear

indefinite article *NOUN*
indefinite articles
the word *a* or *an*

indefinitely *ADVERB*
for an indefinite or unlimited time

indent *VERB* **indents, indenting, indented**
to indent a line of print or writing is to begin it further to the right than usual

indentation *NOUN* **indentations**
a dent or hollow made in something

independent *ADJECTIVE*
❶ free from the control of another person or country ❷ not needing help from other people
➤ **independence** *NOUN*

index *NOUN* **indexes**
a list of names or topics, usually in alphabetical order at the end of a book

index finger *NOUN* **index fingers**
the finger next to the thumb

Indian *ADJECTIVE*
❶ to do with India or its people ❷ to do with Native Americans. This word is now considered to be offensive.

Indian *NOUN* **Indians**
❶ a person from India ❷ a Native American. This word is now considered to be offensive.

indicate *VERB* **indicates, indicating, indicated**
to indicate something is to point it out or show that it is there
➤ **indication** *NOUN* a sign of something

indicative *ADJECTIVE*
being a sign of something

indicator *NOUN* **indicators**
❶ something that tells you what is happening ❷ a flashing light on a vehicle, to show that it is turning left or right

indifferent *ADJECTIVE*
❶ you are indifferent to something when you have no interest in it at all ❷ not very good; ordinary • *He is an indifferent cricketer.*
➤ **indifference** *NOUN*

indigestion *NOUN*
indigestion is pain caused by difficulty in digesting food

indignant *ADJECTIVE*
angry at something that seems wrong or unjust
'Stupid things!' Alice began in a loud, indignant voice.—ALICE'S ADVENTURES IN WONDERLAND, Lewis Carroll
➤ **indignantly** *ADVERB* ➤ **indignation** *NOUN*

indigo *NOUN*
a deep blue colour

indirect *ADJECTIVE*
not direct or straight
➤ **indirectly** *ADVERB*

indirect speech *NOUN*
indirect speech is when someone's words are given in a changed form reported by someone else, as in *He said that he would come* (reporting the words 'I will come')

indispensable *ADJECTIVE*
essential

indistinct *ADJECTIVE*
not clear
➤ **indistinctly** *ADVERB*

indistinguishable *ADJECTIVE*
impossible to see or hear, or to tell apart from something else

individual *ADJECTIVE*
❶ of or for one person ❷ single or separate
➤ **individually** *ADVERB* separately; one by one

individual *NOUN* **individuals**
an individual is one person

individuality *NOUN*
individuality is the things that make one person or thing different from another

indoor ADJECTIVE
placed or done inside a building • *We like indoor sports.*

indoors ADVERB
inside a building

induce VERB induces, inducing, induced
❶ to induce someone to do something is to persuade them to do it ❷ to bring on the birth of a baby artificially through the use of drugs

indulge VERB indulges, indulging, indulged
to indulge someone is to let them have or do what they want
➤ **to indulge in something** is to have or do something that you really like

indulgent ADJECTIVE
kind and allowing people to do what they want
➤ **indulgence** NOUN

industrial ADJECTIVE
to do with industry

industrious ADJECTIVE
hard-working
➤ **industriously** ADVERB

industry NOUN industries
❶ industry is making or producing goods to sell, especially in factories ❷ an industry is a branch of this, such as the motor industry ❸ industry is also working hard

ineffective ADJECTIVE
not effective; not working well
➤ **ineffectively** ADVERB

ineffectual ADJECTIVE
not achieving anything
➤ **ineffectually** ADVERB

inefficient ADJECTIVE
not working well and wasting time or energy
➤ **inefficiency** NOUN

inequality NOUN inequalities
inequality is not being equal

inert ADJECTIVE
not moving or reacting

inertia (*say* in-er-sha) NOUN
inertia is being inert or slow to take action

inevitable ADJECTIVE
something is inevitable when it cannot be avoided
➤ **inevitability** NOUN ➤ **inevitably** ADVERB

inexhaustible ADJECTIVE
that you cannot use up completely; never-ending

inexpensive ADJECTIVE
not expensive; cheap

inexperience NOUN
inexperience is lack of experience
➤ **inexperienced** ADJECTIVE

inexplicable ADJECTIVE
impossible to explain
➤ **inexplicably** ADVERB

infamous (*say* in-fa-mus) ADJECTIVE
well known for being bad or wicked

infant NOUN infants
a baby or young child
➤ **infancy** NOUN the time when someone is a baby or young child
DID YOU KNOW? The word **infant** comes from a Latin word meaning 'unable to speak'.

infantile ADJECTIVE
❶ childish and silly ❷ to do with babies or young children

infantry NOUN
infantry are soldiers trained to fight on foot

infect VERB infects, infecting, infected
to infect someone is to pass on a disease to them

infection NOUN infections
❶ infection is infecting someone ❷ an infection is an infectious disease

infectious ADJECTIVE
❶ an infectious disease is one that can spread from one person to another ❷ something like laughter or fear is infectious when it spreads between people

infer VERB infers, inferring, inferred
to infer something is to work it out from what someone says or does • *I infer from your accent that you are Australian.*

inferior *ADJECTIVE*
not as good or important as something else;
lower in position or quality
➤ **inferiority** *NOUN*

inferior *NOUN* **inferiors**
a person who is lower in position or rank than
someone else

infernal *ADJECTIVE*
like hell or to do with hell

inferno (*say* in-**fer**-noh) *NOUN* **infernos**
a fierce fire

infested *ADJECTIVE*
a place is infested with (for example) insects
or rats when it is full of them

infiltrate *VERB* **infiltrates**, **infiltrating**,
infiltrated
to infiltrate a place or organization is to get
into it without being noticed
➤ **infiltration** *NOUN*

infinite (*say* **in**-fi-nit) *ADJECTIVE*
endless; too large to be measured or imagined
➤ **infinitely** *ADVERB*

infinitive (*say* in-**fin**-i-tiv) *NOUN* **infinitives**
the form of a verb that does not change
to indicate a particular person or tense. In
English it often comes after *to*, as in *to go* and
to think.

infinity (*say* in-**fin**-i-tee) *NOUN*
infinity is an infinite number or distance

infirm *ADJECTIVE*
weak, especially from old age or illness
➤ **infirmity** *NOUN*

infirmary *NOUN* **infirmaries**
a place for sick people; a hospital

inflame *VERB* **inflames**, **inflaming**, **inflamed**
❶ a part of the body is inflamed when it has
become red and sore ❷ to inflame someone is
to make them angry

inflammable *ADJECTIVE*
an inflammable material can be set alight

inflammation *NOUN* **inflammations**
a painful swelling or sore place on the body

inflammatory *ADJECTIVE*
likely to make people angry

inflatable *ADJECTIVE*
something is inflatable when it can be filled
with air to make it swell up

inflate *VERB* **inflates**, **inflating**, **inflated**
❶ to inflate something is to fill it with air or
gas so that it swells up ❷ to inflate a claim or
statement is to exaggerate it

inflation *NOUN*
inflation is a general rise in prices

inflect *VERB* **inflects**, **inflecting**, **inflected**
to inflect your voice is to change the sound of
it when you speak

inflexible *ADJECTIVE*
that you cannot bend or change • *There are
a lot of inflexible rules.*
➤ **inflexibility** *NOUN*

inflict *VERB* **inflicts**, **inflicting**, **inflicted**
to inflict something on someone is to make
them suffer it • *The Red Knight inflicted a
mortal wound on his enemy.*

influence *NOUN* **influences**
the power to affect someone or something

influence *VERB* **influences**, **influencing**,
influenced
to influence someone or something is to have
an effect on what they are or do • *The tides are
influenced by the moon.*

influencer *NOUN* **influencers**
a person who recommends products on social
media and encourages other people to buy or
use them

influential *ADJECTIVE*
having a big influence; important

influenza (*say* in-floo-**en**-za) *NOUN*
influenza is flu

inform *VERB* **informs**, **informing**, **informed**
to inform someone of something is to tell
them about it
➤ **to inform against** *or* **on someone** is to
give information about them, especially to the
police

informal *ADJECTIVE*
not formal; casual and relaxed
➤ **informality** *NOUN* ➤ **informally** *ADVERB*

informant NOUN **informants**
a person who gives information

information NOUN
information is facts or what someone tells you

information technology NOUN
information technology is ways of storing, arranging and giving out information, especially the use of computers and telecommunications

informative (say in-form-a-tiv) ADJECTIVE
containing a lot of helpful information

informed ADJECTIVE
you are informed about something when you know about it

informer NOUN **informers**
a person who tells the police about someone else

infrequent ADJECTIVE
not frequent
➤ **infrequently** ADVERB

infuriate VERB **infuriates**, **infuriating**, **infuriated**
to infuriate someone is to make them very angry

ingenious ADJECTIVE
❶ clever at doing things ❷ cleverly made or done
➤ **ingeniously** ADVERB ➤ **ingenuity** NOUN

ingot NOUN **ingots**
a lump of gold or silver that has been cast in the form of a brick

ingrained ADJECTIVE
deeply fixed • *The picture was ingrained in her memory.*

ingratitude NOUN
ingratitude is not showing that you are grateful for something that someone has done for you

ingredient (say in-greed-i-ent) NOUN **ingredients**
❶ one of the parts of a mixture ❷ one of the items used in a recipe

inhabit VERB **inhabits**, **inhabiting**, **inhabited**
to inhabit a place is to live in it

inhabitant NOUN **inhabitants**
an inhabitant of a place is someone who lives there

inhale VERB **inhales**, **inhaling**, **inhaled**
❶ to inhale is to breathe in ❷ to inhale something is to breathe it in

inhaler NOUN **inhalers**
a device for taking medicine by inhaling it

inherent (say in-heer-ent) ADJECTIVE
naturally or permanently part of something
➤ **inherently** ADVERB

inherit VERB **inherits**, **inheriting**, **inherited**
❶ to inherit money, property or a title is to receive it when its previous owner dies ❷ to inherit qualities or characteristics is to get them from your parents or ancestors
➤ **inheritance** NOUN

inhibited ADJECTIVE
not relaxed enough to show or talk about your feelings

inhospitable (say in-hos-pit-a-bul or in-hos-pit-a-bul) ADJECTIVE
❶ unfriendly to visitors ❷ an inhospitable place is difficult to live in because it gives no shelter • *They reached an inhospitable rocky island.*

inhuman ADJECTIVE
cruel; without pity or kindness
➤ **inhumanity** NOUN

initial NOUN **initials**
the first letter of a word or name, especially of someone's forename
initial ADJECTIVE
first; of the beginning • *This is the initial round of the competition.*
➤ **initially** ADVERB at the beginning

initiate (say in-ish-i-ayt) VERB **initiates**, **initiating**, **initiated**
❶ to initiate something is to start it ❷ to initiate someone is to admit them as a member

of a society or group, often with special ceremonies
➤ **initiation** *NOUN*

initiative (say in-ish-a-tiv) *NOUN* initiatives
❶ the action that starts something • *She took the initiative in planning the party.* ❷ initiative is the ability or power to start things or to get them done on your own

inject *VERB* injects, injecting, injected
❶ to inject someone is to put a medicine or drug through their skin using a hollow needle ❷ to inject something is to add it • *Try to inject some humour into the story.*
➤ **injection** *NOUN*

injure *VERB* injures, injuring, injured
to injure someone is to harm or hurt them

injury *NOUN* injuries
injury, or an injury, is harm or damage done to someone

injustice *NOUN* injustices
injustice, or an injustice, is unjust action or treatment

ink *NOUN* inks
ink is a black or coloured liquid used for writing and printing

inkling *NOUN*
a slight idea or suspicion • *I had an inkling that we'd find them in here.*

inky *ADJECTIVE* inkier, inkiest
❶ inky fingers are covered in ink ❷ very dark or black • *the inky darkness of night*

inland *ADVERB*
in or towards a place on land and away from the coast

in-laws *PLURAL NOUN*
a person's in-laws are the relatives of their husband or wife • *We're going to visit the in-laws at Easter.*

inlet *NOUN* inlets
a strip of water reaching into the land from a sea or lake

inn *NOUN* inns
a hotel or pub, especially in the country

inner *ADJECTIVE*
inside; nearer the centre • *a small inner room*

innermost *ADJECTIVE*
furthest inside
'Ask for the High Priest,' said the Phoenix. 'Say that you have a secret to unfold ... and he will lead you to the innermost sanctuary.'—THE PHOENIX AND THE CARPET, Edith Nesbit

innings *NOUN* innings
the time when a cricket team or player is batting

innocence *NOUN*
❶ innocence is when someone is not guilty of doing something wrong ❷ innocence is also lack of experience of the world and the evil things in it

innocent *ADJECTIVE*
❶ not guilty of doing something wrong ❷ not knowing much about the world and the evil things in it
➤ **innocently** *ADVERB*

innocuous *ADJECTIVE*
harmless

innovation *NOUN* innovations
❶ innovation is inventing or using new things ❷ an innovation is something new that you have just invented or started using

innumerable *ADJECTIVE*
too many to be counted
Innumerable candles were hovering in mid-air over four long, crowded tables, making the golden plates and goblets sparkle.—HARRY POTTER AND THE CHAMBER OF SECRETS, J. K. Rowling

inoculate *VERB* inoculates, inoculating, inoculated
to inoculate someone is to inject them or treat them to protect them against a disease
➤ **inoculation** *NOUN*

in-patient *NOUN* in-patients
someone who stays at a hospital for treatment

input *NOUN* inputs
what you put into something, especially data put into a computer

input *VERB* **inputs, inputting, input**
to input data or programs is to put them into a computer

inquest *NOUN* **inquests**
an official investigation to decide why someone died

inquire *VERB* **inquires, inquiring, inquired**
to inquire into something is to make an official investigation of it • *The police are inquiring into the robbery.*

inquiry *NOUN* **inquiries**
an official investigation

inquisitive *ADJECTIVE*
an inquisitive person is always trying to find out things, especially about other people
➤ **inquisitively** *ADVERB*

insane *ADJECTIVE*
not sane; mentally ill
➤ **insanely** *ADVERB* ➤ **insanity** *NOUN*

inscribe *VERB* **inscribes, inscribing, inscribed**
to inscribe something is to write or carve it on a surface

inscription *NOUN* **inscriptions**
words written or carved on a monument, stone or coin, or written in the front of a book

insect *NOUN* **insects**
a small animal, such as an ant or beetle, with six legs and a body divided into three parts (head, thorax and abdomen)
DID YOU KNOW? The word **insect** comes from a Latin word meaning 'cut up', because of its divided body.

insecticide *NOUN* **insecticides**
a poisonous chemical used for killing insects

insecure *ADJECTIVE*
❶ not safe or protected properly ❷ not feeling safe or confident
➤ **insecurely** *ADVERB* ➤ **insecurity** *NOUN*

insensitive *ADJECTIVE*
not sensitive or thinking about the feelings of other people
➤ **insensitively** *ADVERB* ➤ **insensitivity** *NOUN*

inseparable *ADJECTIVE*
❶ unable to be separated ❷ people are inseparable when they are very good friends and always together • *The two girls were inseparable during the summer.*

insert *VERB* **inserts, inserting, inserted**
to insert something is to put it into something else
➤ **insertion** *NOUN*

inshore *ADJECTIVE, ADVERB*
on the sea near or nearer to the shore

inside *NOUN* **insides**
❶ the inner side, surface or part; the part nearest to the middle ❷ (*informal*) your insides are your stomach or abdomen
➤ **inside out** with the inside turned so that it faces outwards

inside *ADJECTIVE*
on the inside of something • *Check the inside pocket.*

inside *ADVERB, PREPOSITION*
in or to the inside of something • *Please come inside.* • *What's inside that box?*

insight *NOUN* **insights**
❶ insight is being able to see the truth about things ❷ an insight is an understanding of something

insignificant *ADJECTIVE*
not important or influential
➤ **insignificance** *NOUN*

insincere *ADJECTIVE*
not sincere
➤ **insincerely** *ADVERB* ➤ **insincerity** *NOUN*

insist *VERB* **insists, insisting, insisted**
to insist something is to be very firm in saying it • *They insisted that they were innocent.*
➤ **to insist on something** is to demand it • *We insist on seeing the head teacher.*

insistent *ADJECTIVE*
insisting on doing or having something
➤ **insistence** *NOUN*

insolent *ADJECTIVE*
very rude and insulting
Malfoy gave Professor Lupin an insolent stare.—HARRY POTTER AND THE PRISONER OF AZKABAN, J. K. Rowling
➤ **insolence** *NOUN*

insoluble *ADJECTIVE*
❶ impossible to dissolve • *Some chemicals are insoluble.* ❷ impossible to solve • *It is an insoluble problem.*

insomnia *NOUN*
insomnia is being unable to sleep

inspect *VERB* **inspects**, **inspecting**, **inspected**
to inspect something or someone is to look carefully at them, especially to check them

inspection *NOUN* **inspections**
an inspection is a close or careful look at something to check it

inspector *NOUN* **inspectors**
❶ someone employed to inspect things or people ❷ a police officer next in rank above a sergeant

inspiration *NOUN* **inspirations**
an inspiration is a person or thing that encourages you and fills you with ideas

inspire *VERB* **inspires**, **inspiring**, **inspired**
to inspire someone is to fill them with ideas or enthusiasm

install *VERB* **installs**, **installing**, **installed**
❶ to install something is to put it in position ready for use • *We want to install central heating.* ❷ to install a new piece of software is to put it onto a computer or device so that you can use it • *She has installed a brilliant music app on her phone.* ❸ to install someone is to put them into an important position with a ceremony • *He was installed as pope.*
➤ **installation** *NOUN*

instalment *NOUN* **instalments**
one of the parts into which something is divided so that it is spread over a period of time • *He is paying for his bike in monthly instalments.* • *The story was in three instalments.*

instance *NOUN* **instances**
an example
➤ **for instance** for example

instant *ADJECTIVE*
❶ happening immediately • *It has been an instant success.* ❷ an instant food or drink can be made very quickly • *Do you like instant coffee?*

instant *NOUN* **instants**
a moment • *I don't believe it for an instant.*

instantaneous *ADJECTIVE*
happening or done in an instant, or without any delay
Mrs. Cobb had taken an instantaneous and illogical dislike to the Rev. Mr. Burch in the afternoon.—REBECCA OF SUNNYBROOK FARM, Kate Douglas Wiggin
➤ **instantaneously** *ADVERB*

instantly *ADVERB*
to do something instantly is to do it without any delay

instead *ADVERB*
in place of something else; as a substitute • *There were no potatoes, so we had rice instead.*

instep *NOUN* **insteps**
the top of your foot between the toes and the ankle

instinct *NOUN* **instincts**
a natural tendency to do or feel something without being taught • *Spiders spin webs by instinct.*
➤ **instinctive** *ADJECTIVE* instinctive behaviour follows instinct, not thought
➤ **instinctively** *ADVERB*

institute *NOUN* **institutes**
an organization set up to study something or for some other purpose, or the building used by it

institute *VERB* **institutes**, **instituting**, **instituted**
to institute something is to establish it or start it

institution *NOUN* **institutions**
❶ a large organization ❷ something that is an established habit or custom • *Going for a swim on Sunday was a family institution.*

instruct *VERB* **instructs**, **instructing**, **instructed**
❶ to instruct someone is to teach them a subject or skill ❷ to instruct someone is also to give them information or orders
➤ **instructor** *NOUN*

a
b
c
d
e
f
g
h
i
j
k
l
m
n
o
p
q
r
s
t
u
v
w
x
y
z

A
B
C
D
E
F
G
H
I
J
K
L
M
N
O
P
Q
R
S
T
U
V
W
X
Y
Z

instruction *NOUN* **instructions**
❶ instruction is teaching a subject or skill ❷ an instruction is a order or piece of information • *Follow the instructions carefully.*

instrument *NOUN* **instruments**
❶ a device for making musical sounds
❷ a device for delicate or scientific work

instrumental *ADJECTIVE*
❶ instrumental music uses musical instruments without any singing ❷ to be instrumental in something is to be helpful in making it happen • *She was instrumental in getting him a job.*

insufficient *ADJECTIVE*
not enough

insulate *VERB* **insulates**, **insulating**, **insulated**
to insulate something is to cover it to stop heat, cold or electricity from passing in or out
➤ **insulation** *NOUN*

insulin *NOUN*
insulin is a chemical that controls how much sugar there is in the blood

insult (*say* in-**sult**) *VERB* **insults**, **insulting**, **insulted**
to insult someone is to speak or behave in a rude way that offends them

insult (*say* **in**-sult) *NOUN* **insults**
a rude remark or action that offends someone

insurance *NOUN*
insurance is a business agreement to receive money or compensation if you suffer a loss or injury, in return for a regular payment

insure *VERB* **insures**, **insuring**, **insured**
to insure yourself or your goods is to protect them with insurance

intact *ADJECTIVE*
complete and not damaged • *Despite the storm, our tent was still intact.*

intake *NOUN* **intakes**
❶ taking something in ❷ the number of people or things taken in • *The school had a high intake of pupils this year.*

integral (*say* in-ti-gral) *ADJECTIVE*
❶ that is an essential part of something • *Your heart is an integral part of your body.* ❷ whole or complete

integrate (*say* in-ti-grayt) *VERB* **integrates**, **integrating**, **integrated**
❶ to integrate different things or parts is to make them into a whole ❷ to integrate people, especially of different origins, is to bring them together into a single community
➤ **integration** *NOUN*

integrity (*say* in-**teg**-ri-tee) *NOUN*
integrity is being honest and behaving well

intellect *NOUN* **intellects**
the ability to think and work things out with your mind

intellectual *ADJECTIVE*
❶ involving the intellect ❷ able to think effectively; keen to study and learn
➤ **intellectually** *ADVERB*

intellectual *NOUN* **intellectuals**
an intellectual person

intelligence *NOUN*
❶ your intelligence is your ability to think and learn ❷ intelligence is also secret information, especially about the military operations of a country

intelligent *ADJECTIVE*
able to learn and understand things
➤ **intelligently** *ADVERB*

intelligible *ADJECTIVE*
able to be understood • *The message was barely intelligible.*

intend *VERB* **intends**, **intending**, **intended**
❶ to intend to do something is to have it in mind as a plan • *She was intending to go swimming.* ❷ to intend someone to do something is to want them to do it

intense *ADJECTIVE*
❶ very strong or great • *The heat was intense.*
❷ having or showing strong feelings
➤ **intensely** *ADVERB*

intensify *VERB* **intensifies**, **intensifying**, **intensified**
❶ to intensify something is to make it more intense ❷ to intensify is to become more intense

intensity *NOUN* **intensities**
the intensity of something is how strong or great it is

intensive *ADJECTIVE*
using a lot of effort; thorough • *We have made an intensive search.*
➤ **intensively** *ADVERB*

intent *ADJECTIVE*
showing a lot of attention and interest
➤ **to be intent on something** is to be eager or determined to do it

intent *NOUN* **intents**
a person's intent is what they intend to do

intention *NOUN* **intentions**
what you intend to do; a plan

intentional *ADJECTIVE*
done on purpose; deliberate
➤ **intentionally** *ADVERB*

intently *ADVERB*
to listen or look intently is to do so with a lot of attention and interest • *We all looked intently at the door, wondering who, or what, was behind it.*

inter– *PREFIX*
meaning between two or more people or things, as in *interchangeable* and *inter-school*

interact *VERB* **interacts**, **interacting**, **interacted**
two people or things interact when they have an effect on one another • *How will robots interact with humans?*
➤ **interaction** *NOUN*

interactive *ADJECTIVE* (*computing*)
allowing information to be sent in either direction between a computer system and its user

intercept *VERB* **intercepts**, **intercepting**, **intercepted**
to intercept someone or something is to stop them going from one place to another
➤ **interception** *NOUN*

interchange *NOUN* **interchanges**
a place where you can move from one main road or motorway to another

interchangeable *ADJECTIVE*
things are interchangeable when they can be changed or swapped round

interest *VERB* **interests**, **interesting**, **interested**
to interest someone is to make them want to look or listen or take part in something • *Can I interest you in a game of Monopoly?*

interest *NOUN* **interests**
❶ interest is being interested ❷ an interest is a thing that interests you • *My main interests are music and football.*

interfere *VERB* **interferes**, **interfering**, **interfered**
❶ to interfere in something is to become involved in it when it has nothing to do with you ❷ to interfere is to get in the way

interference *NOUN*
❶ interference is interfering in something ❷ interference is also a crackling or distorting of a radio or television signal

interior *NOUN* **interiors**
the inside of something

interjection *NOUN* **interjections**
an exclamation, such as *oh!* or *goodness me!*

interlock *VERB* **interlocks**, **interlocking**, **interlocked**
to interlock is to fit into one another • *The gearwheels interlocked.*

interlude *NOUN* **interludes**
❶ an interval ❷ music played during an interval

intermediate *ADJECTIVE*
coming between two things in place, order or time

intermission *NOUN* **intermissions**
an interval in a play or film

intermittent *ADJECTIVE*
happening at intervals
➤ **intermittently** *ADVERB*

intern *VERB* **interns**, **interning**, **interned**
to intern someone is to imprison them in a special camp or building, usually during a war
➤ **internment** *NOUN*

internal *ADJECTIVE*
of or in the inside of something
➤ **internally** *ADVERB*

international *ADJECTIVE*
to do with more than one country • *Interpol is an international police organization.*
➤ **internationally** *ADVERB*

internet *NOUN*
the internet is the computer network that allows people all over the world to share information and send messages

interplanetary *ADJECTIVE*
between planets • *a spacecraft for interplanetary travel*

interpret *VERB* **interprets, interpreting, interpreted**
❶ to interpret something is to explain what it means ❷ to interpret a foreign language is to translate it into another language
➤ **interpretation** *NOUN*

interpreter *NOUN* **interpreters**
a person who translates what someone says into another language

interrogate *VERB* **interrogates, interrogating, interrogated**
to interrogate someone is to question them closely in order to get information
➤ **interrogation** *NOUN*
➤ **interrogator** *NOUN*

interrupt *VERB* **interrupts, interrupting, interrupted**
❶ to interrupt someone is to stop them talking ❷ to interrupt something is to stop it continuing
➤ **interruption** *NOUN*

intersect *VERB* **intersects, intersecting, intersected**
to intersect something is to cross or divide it • *The paths intersect at this point on the map.*

intersection *NOUN* **intersections**
a place where lines or roads cross each other

interval *NOUN* **intervals**
a time between two events or between two parts of a play or film
➤ **at intervals** with some time or distance between each one; not continuously

intervene *VERB* **intervenes, intervening, intervened**
❶ to intervene is to come between two events • *During the intervening years, they went abroad.* ❷ to intervene in an argument or fight is to interrupt it in order to stop it or affect the result
➤ **intervention** *NOUN*

interview *NOUN* **interviews**
a meeting with someone to ask them questions or discuss something

interview *VERB* **interviews, interviewing, interviewed**
to interview someone is to have an interview with them

interviewer *NOUN* **interviewers**
a person who interviews someone, especially on radio or television

intestine *NOUN* **intestines**
the long tube along which food passes from your stomach
➤ **intestinal** *ADJECTIVE*

intimate (*say* in-ti-mat) *ADJECTIVE*
❶ very friendly with someone ❷ intimate thoughts are thoughts that are private or personal ❸ detailed • *They have an intimate knowledge of the town.*
➤ **intimately** *ADVERB*

intimate (*say* in-ti-mayt) *VERB* **intimates, intimating, intimated**
to intimate something is to hint at it or suggest it • *He has not yet intimated what his plans are.*

intimidate *VERB* **intimidates, intimidating, intimidated**
to frighten a person with threats into doing something
➤ **intimidation** *NOUN*

into *PREPOSITION*
❶ expressing movement to the inside of something • *He led us deeper into the cave.* ❷ the word **into** also has some special uses, as in these examples • *We got into trouble.* • *She went into acting.* • *3 into 12 goes 4 times.*

intolerable *ADJECTIVE*
unbearable • *The noise outside was intolerable.*
➤ **intolerably** *ADVERB*

intolerant *ADJECTIVE*
not tolerant; not willing to put up with people
➤ **intolerance** *NOUN* ➤ **intolerantly** *ADVERB*

intonation *NOUN* **intonations**
❶ the pitch or tone of a voice or musical instrument ❷ when you speak, your intonation is the way you use the pitch of your voice to alter the meaning of what you are saying, for example when asking a question

intransitive *ADJECTIVE*
a verb is intransitive when it is used without a direct object, for example *ate* in *they ate early* (but not in *they ate breakfast*)

intrepid *ADJECTIVE*
brave or fearless
'Perhaps most of the brave defenders were killed quite early in the siege … and now there are only a few intrepid survivors.'–FIVE CHILDREN AND IT, Edith Nesbit
➤ **intrepidly** *ADVERB*

intricate *ADJECTIVE*
an intricate pattern or design is detailed and complicated
➤ **intricacy** *NOUN* ➤ **intricately** *ADVERB*

intrigue (*say* in-**treeg**) *VERB* **intrigues**, **intriguing**, **intrigued**
to intrigue someone is to interest them very much and make them curious
➤ **intriguing** *ADJECTIVE*

intrigue (*say* in-**treeg**) *NOUN* **intrigues**
a secret plot

introduce *VERB* **introduces**, **introducing**, **introduced**
❶ to introduce someone is to make them known to other people ❷ to introduce something is to get it into general use

introduction *NOUN* **introductions**
❶ introducing someone or something ❷ a piece at the beginning of a book, explaining what it is about
➤ **introductory** *ADJECTIVE* coming at the beginning of something

intrude *VERB* **intrudes**, **intruding**, **intruded**
to intrude is to come in or join in without being wanted

intruder *NOUN* **intruders**
someone who forces their way into a place where they are not supposed to be

intrusion *NOUN* **intrusions**
an intrusion is coming in where you are not wanted

intrusive *ADJECTIVE*
something is intrusive when it is not wanted and gets in the way

intuition (*say* in-**tew-ish**-on) *NOUN*
intuition is the power to know or understand things without having to think hard
➤ **intuitive** *ADJECTIVE*

Inuit *NOUN* **Inuit** *or* **Inuits**
❶ one of, or a descendant of, the people who live in northern Canada and Greenland, living there before European settlers arrived ❷ the language of the Inuit people
DID YOU KNOW? The words **igloo** and **kayak** come from Inuit.

inundate *VERB* **inundates**, **inundating**, **inundated**
to inundate someone is to overwhelm them with a large number of things • *We've been inundated with complaints.*
➤ **inundation** *NOUN*

invade *VERB* **invades**, **invading**, **invaded**
to invade a country or place is to attack and enter it

invader *NOUN* **invaders**
an invader is someone who invades a place

invalid (*say* in-va-lid) *NOUN* **invalids**
someone who is ill or weakened by illness
invalid (*say* in-**val**-id) *ADJECTIVE*
not valid • *This passport is invalid.*

invaluable *ADJECTIVE*
very valuable

invariable *ADJECTIVE*
never changing; always the same

invariably *ADVERB*
always

invasion *NOUN* **invasions**
when an army or a large number of people attack and enter a place

a b c d e f g h i j k l m n o p q r s t u v w x y z

invent VERB **invents, inventing, invented**
❶ to invent something is to be the first person to make it or think of it • *Who invented the telescope?* ❷ to invent a story or excuse is to make it up

invention NOUN **inventions**
something that has been invented
Commander Pott's inventions were sometimes dull things like collapsible coat-hangers ... and sometimes clever things that just, only just, wouldn't work, like cubical potatoes.—CHITTY CHITTY BANG BANG, Ian Fleming

inventive ADJECTIVE
someone is being inventive when they cleverly think of new ideas
➤ **inventiveness** NOUN

inventor NOUN **inventors**
a person who invents things

inverse ADJECTIVE
reversed or opposite
➤ **inversely** ADVERB

inverse NOUN
the opposite of something

invert VERB **inverts, inverting, inverted**
to invert something is to turn it upside down
➤ **inversion** NOUN

invertebrate (*say* in-**vert**-i-brat) NOUN
invertebrates
an animal without a backbone, such as a worm or an amoeba

inverted commas PLURAL NOUN
punctuation marks (" ") or (' ') that you put around spoken words and quotations

invest VERB **invests, investing, invested**
❶ to invest money is to use it to earn interest or make a profit ❷ to invest someone is to give them an honour or medal or special title • *He was invested as Prince of Wales.*

investigate VERB **investigates, investigating, investigated**
to investigate something or someone is to find out as much as you can about them • *Police are investigating the robbery.*
➤ **investigation** NOUN ➤ **investigator** NOUN

investment NOUN **investments**
❶ money someone invests ❷ something

someone invests money in • *Houses are a safe investment.*

invigorate VERB **invigorates, invigorating, invigorated**
to fill someone with energy
➤ **invigorating** ADJECTIVE

invincible ADJECTIVE
not able to be defeated

invisible ADJECTIVE
not visible; not able to be seen
➤ **invisibility** NOUN

invitation NOUN **invitations**
a request for someone to do something, such as come to a party

invite VERB **invites, inviting, invited**
❶ to invite someone is to ask them to come to a party or do something special ❷ to invite something unwelcome is to make it likely to happen by your actions • *You are inviting trouble by doing that.*

inviting ADJECTIVE
attractive or tempting

invoice NOUN **invoices**
a list of goods sent or of work done, with the prices charged

involuntary ADJECTIVE
not deliberate; done without thinking

involve VERB **involves, involving, involved**
❶ to involve something is to need it or result in it • *The job involved a lot of effort.* ❷ to be involved in something is to take part in it • *We are involved in charity work.*
➤ **involvement** NOUN

involved ADJECTIVE
long and complicated

inward ADJECTIVE
on the inside, or facing the inside

inward ADVERB
inwards

inwardly ADVERB
in your thoughts; privately
Titus shut his eyes like a clam and inwardly vowed never to grow old.—PURE DEAD MAGIC, Debi Gliori

inwards ADVERB
towards the inside

ion *NOUN* **ions**
an electrically charged particle

IQ *NOUN* **IQs**
a measure of someone's intelligence, calculated from the results of a test
DID YOU KNOW? The letters **IQ** stand for *intelligence quotient.*

irate (*say* eye-**rayt**) *ADJECTIVE*
angry
➤ **irately** *ADVERB*

ire *NOUN*
anger

iridescent *ADJECTIVE*
with bright colours like a rainbow • *a beetle with iridescent wings*
➤ **iridescence** *NOUN*

iris *NOUN* **irises**
❶ the coloured part of your eyeball ❷ a flower with long pointed leaves

Irish *ADJECTIVE*
to do with Ireland or its people
Irish *NOUN*
a language spoken in Ireland

iron *NOUN* **irons**
❶ iron is a strong heavy metal ❷ an iron is a device that you heat up and press on clothes to make them smooth ❸ an iron is also a tool made of iron
iron *VERB* **irons, ironing, ironed**
to iron clothes is to smooth them with an iron
➤ **to iron something out** is to solve a difficulty gradually and carefully

ironic (*say* eye-**ron**-ik) *ADJECTIVE*
❶ an ironic situation is strange because the opposite happens to what you might expect ❷ you are being ironic when you say the opposite of what you mean
➤ **ironical** *ADJECTIVE* ➤ **ironically** *ADVERB*

ironmonger *NOUN* **ironmongers**
someone who keeps a shop that sells tools, nails and other metal things

irony (*say* **eye**-ro-nee) *NOUN* **ironies**
❶ irony is saying the opposite of what you mean in order to emphasize it or be funny, for example *What a lovely day* when it is

pouring with rain ❷ a situation that is the opposite of what you might have expected • *The irony is that global warming leads to wetter weather.*

irrational *ADJECTIVE*
not reasonable or sensible
➤ **irrationally** *ADVERB*

irregular *ADJECTIVE*
❶ not regular; not usual ❷ against the rules
➤ **irregularity** *NOUN* ➤ **irregularly** *ADVERB*

irrelevant (*say* i-**rel**-i-vant) *ADJECTIVE*
not relevant; not having anything to do with what is being discussed
➤ **irrelevance** *NOUN*

irresistible *ADJECTIVE*
too strong or attractive or tempting to resist

irresponsible *ADJECTIVE*
not thinking enough about the effects of your actions
➤ **irresponsibility** *NOUN*
➤ **irresponsibly** *ADVERB*

irrigate *VERB* **irrigates, irrigating, irrigated**
to irrigate land is to supply it with water so that crops can grow
➤ **irrigation** *NOUN*

irritable *ADJECTIVE*
easily annoyed; bad-tempered
➤ **irritability** *NOUN* ➤ **irritably** *ADVERB*

irritate *VERB* **irritates, irritating, irritated**
❶ to irritate someone is to annoy them ❷ to irritate a part of your body is to make it itch or feel sore
➤ **irritant** *NOUN* an irritant is something that makes you sore

irritation *NOUN* **irritations**
❶ irritation is being annoyed ❷ an irritation is something that annoys you

is *VERB* (3rd person singular present tense of **be**)
• *Everything is back to normal.*

Islam (*say* **iz**-lahm) *NOUN*
Islam is the religion of Muslims
➤ **Islamic** *ADJECTIVE* to do with Islam

island *NOUN* **islands**
a piece of land surrounded by water

a
b
c
d
e
f
g
h
i
j
k
l
m
n
o
p
q
r
s
t
u
v
w
x
y
z

islander *NOUN* **islanders**
someone who lives on an island

isle *NOUN* **isles**
an island

isn't
short for *is not* • *That isn't true!*

isolate *VERB* **isolates, isolating, isolated**
to isolate someone or something is to keep them apart from others • *Patients with the disease need to be isolated.*
➤ **isolation** *NOUN*

isosceles triangle (*say* eye-**sos**-i-leez) *NOUN* **isosceles triangles**
a triangle with two sides the same length

issue *VERB* **issues, issuing, issued**
❶ to issue something is to send it or give it out to people • *They issued blankets to the refugees.* ❷ to issue a book or piece of information is to publish it ❸ to issue is to come out of something • *Smoke was issuing from the chimney.*

issue *NOUN* **issues**
❶ an issue is a subject that people are discussing • *What are the most important issues?* ❷ an issue of a magazine or newspaper is the edition sold on a particular day • *There's a good poster in this week's issue of my football magazine.* ❸ the issue of documents is making them available to people

it *PRONOUN*
❶ the thing being talked about, used as the subject or object of a verb ❷ the word **it** also has some special uses, as in these examples • *It is raining.* • *We must go it alone.*

Italian *ADJECTIVE*
to do with Italy or its people

Italian *NOUN*
❶ the main language of Italy ❷ (**Italians**) a person from Italy
DID YOU KNOW? The words **cartoon, piano** and **umbrella** come from Italian.

italics (*say* it-**al**-iks) *PLURAL NOUN*
italics are letters printed with a slant, *like this*

itch *NOUN* **itches**
❶ a tickling feeling in your skin that makes you want to scratch it ❷ a longing

to do something • *He has an itch to go to America.*

itch *VERB* **itches, itching, itched**
a part of your body itches when it makes you want to scratch it

itchy *ADJECTIVE* **itchier, itchiest**
part of your body is itchy when it makes you want to scratch it

item *NOUN* **items**
one thing in a list or group of things

itinerary (*say* eye-**tin**-er-er-ee) *NOUN* **itineraries**
a list of places to be visited on a journey

it'll
short for *it will* • *It'll be dark soon.*

its *DETERMINER, PRONOUN*
of it; belonging to it • *The robot slowly turned its head.*
SPELLING ALERT! **Its** is different from **it's**, which means 'it is' or 'it has': *It's not fair! It's been a while.*

it's
short for *it is* or *it has* • *It's raining.* • *It's been raining all day.*

itself *PRONOUN*
it and nothing else, used to refer back to the subject of a verb • *I think the cat has hurt itself.*
➤ **by itself** on its own; alone • *The house stands by itself in a wood.*

I've
short for *I have* • *I've read that book.*

ivory *NOUN*
❶ ivory is the hard creamy-white substance that forms elephants' tusks ❷ a creamy-white colour

ivy *NOUN*
ivy is a climbing evergreen plant with shiny leaves

Jj

jab *VERB* **jabs, jabbing, jabbed**
❶ to jab someone or something is to poke them roughly
Eddie felt something jab him in the back. He turned to find that it was Malcolm the stuffed stoat's nose.—TERRIBLE TIMES, Philip Ardagh
❷ to jab something is to push it roughly into something else

jab *NOUN* **jabs**
❶ a quick hit with something pointed or a fist ❷ (*informal*) an injection

jabber *VERB* **jabbers, jabbering, jabbered**
to chatter a lot or to speak quickly and not clearly

jack *NOUN* **jacks**
❶ a piece of equipment for lifting something heavy off the ground, especially a car ❷ a playing card with a picture of a young man ❸ a small white ball that you aim at in the game of bowls

jack *VERB* **jacks, jacking, jacked**
to jack something is to lift it with a jack

jackal *NOUN* **jackals**
a wild animal rather like a dog

jackdaw *NOUN* **jackdaws**
a bird like a small crow

jacket *NOUN* **jackets**
❶ a short coat covering the top half of the body ❷ a paper cover for a book ❸ a wrapping round a boiler to insulate it

jacket potato *NOUN* **jacket potatoes**
a potato that is baked without being peeled

jack-in-the-box *NOUN* **jack-in-the-boxes**
a toy figure that springs out of a box when you lift the lid

jackknife *VERB* **jackknifes, jackknifing, jackknifed**
an articulated lorry jackknifes when it goes out of control, with the trailer skidding round towards the cab

jackpot *NOUN* **jackpots**
an amount of prize money that increases until someone wins it

jade *NOUN*
jade is a hard green stone which is carved to make ornaments

jaded *ADJECTIVE*
tired and bored because you have had too much of something

jag *NOUN* **jags** (*Scottish*)
an injection; a jab

jagged (*say* jag-id) *ADJECTIVE*
having an uneven edge with sharp points

jaggy *ADJECTIVE* **jaggier, jaggiest**
❶ jagged ❷ prickly
➤ **jagginess** *NOUN*

jaguar *NOUN* **jaguars**
a large fierce South American animal of the cat family, rather like a leopard

jail *NOUN* **jails**
a prison
jail *VERB* **jails, jailing, jailed**
to jail someone is to put them in prison

jailer *NOUN* **jailers**
a person in charge of a jail

Jain (*rhymes with* **main**) *NOUN* **Jains**
someone who believes in **Jainism**, an Indian religion

jam *NOUN* **jams**
❶ a sweet food made of fruit boiled with sugar until it is thick ❷ a lot of people or cars or other things crowded together so that it is difficult to move
➤ **to be in a jam** (*informal*) is to be in a difficult situation

jam *VERB* **jams, jamming, jammed**
❶ to jam something is to make it stuck and difficult to move ❷ to jam is to become stuck • *The door has jammed.* ❸ to jam something is to push or squeeze it with force • *I jammed on the brakes.*

jamboree *NOUN* **jamborees**
a large party or celebration

a
b
c
d
e
f
g
h
i
j
k
l
m
n
o
p
q
r
s
t
u
v
w
x
y
z

jammy *ADJECTIVE* **jammier**, **jammiest**
❶ covered with jam ❷ (*informal*) very lucky

jangle *VERB* **jangles**, **jangling**, **jangled**
to make a harsh ringing sound

janitor *NOUN* **janitors** (*Scottish, North American*)
a school caretaker

January *NOUN*
the first month of the year
DID YOU KNOW? **January** is named after *Janus*, the Roman god of doors and beginnings.

Japanese *ADJECTIVE*
to do with Japan or its people

Japanese *NOUN*
the main language of Japan
DID YOU KNOW? The words **karaoke** and **emoji** come from Japanese.

jar *NOUN* **jars**
a container made of glass or pottery

jar *VERB* **jars**, **jarring**, **jarred**
❶ to jar a part of your body is to give it a painful jolt • *I jarred my knee when I jumped down.* ❷ when something jars, or jars on you, it makes you feel uncomfortable • *That drilling noise jars on my ears.*

jargon *NOUN*
jargon is words used by people in a particular profession, that are difficult for other people to understand • *The guide is full of computer jargon.*

jaundice *NOUN*
jaundice is an illness that makes a person's skin turn yellow

jaunt *NOUN* **jaunts**
a short trip for fun

jaunty *ADJECTIVE* **jauntier**, **jauntiest**
lively and cheerful

javelin *NOUN* **javelins**
a light spear used for throwing in athletic contests

jaw *NOUN* **jaws**
❶ one of the two bones that hold the teeth ❷ the lower part of the face; the mouth and teeth of a person or animal ❸ the part of a tool that grips something

jawbone *NOUN* **jawbones**
the lower bone of the jaw • *the giant jawbone of a mammoth*

jay *NOUN* **jays**
a noisy, brightly coloured bird

jazz *NOUN*
jazz is a kind of music with a strong rhythm

jazzy *ADJECTIVE* **jazzier**, **jazziest**
bright and colourful

jealous (*say* jel-us) *ADJECTIVE*
❶ unhappy or resentful because you feel that someone is better or luckier than you ❷ upset because you think that someone you love is in love with someone else
➤ **jealously** *ADVERB* ➤ **jealousy** *NOUN*

jeans *PLURAL NOUN*
casual trousers made of denim
DID YOU KNOW? **Jeans** get their name from the Italian city of *Genoa*, which was once famous for producing a type of heavy cotton cloth.

Jeep *NOUN* **Jeeps** (*trademark*)
a small sturdy motor car that can be driven over rough ground

jeer *VERB* **jeers**, **jeering**, **jeered**
to laugh rudely at someone and shout insults at them

jelly *NOUN* **jellies**
❶ a soft sweet food with a fruit flavour ❷ any soft slippery substance

jellyfish *NOUN* **jellyfish**
a sea animal with a body like jelly and tentacles that can sting

jerk *VERB* **jerks**, **jerking**, **jerked**
❶ to jerk is to make a sudden sharp movement ❷ to jerk something is to pull it suddenly

jerk *NOUN* **jerks**
a sudden sharp movement

jerky *ADJECTIVE* **jerkier**, **jerkiest**
moving with sudden sharp movements
➤ **jerkily** *ADVERB*

jersey *NOUN* **jerseys**
a pullover with sleeves

jest *NOUN* **jests**
a joke
➤ to say something **in jest** is to be joking

jest *VERB* jests, jesting, jested
to jest is to make jokes

jester *NOUN* jesters
a professional entertainer at a royal court in the Middle Ages

jet *NOUN* jets
❶ a stream of liquid, gas or flame forced out of a narrow opening ❷ a narrow opening from which a jet comes out ❸ an aircraft driven by jet engines ❹ jet is a hard black mineral ❺ jet is also a deep glossy black colour

jet *VERB* jets, jetting, jetted
❶ to jet is to come out in a strong stream ❷ (*informal*) to travel in a jet aircraft

jet engine *NOUN* jet engines
an engine that drives an aircraft forward by sending out a powerful jet of hot gas at the back

jet lag *NOUN*
jet lag is extreme tiredness that someone feels after a long plane journey because they have not got used to the different time zones

jet-propelled *ADJECTIVE*
driven by jet engines

jetty *NOUN* jetties
a small landing stage for boats
Below the farm at Holly Howe the field sloped steeply to a little bay where there was a boathouse and a jetty.—SWALLOWS AND AMAZONS, Arthur Ransome

Jew *NOUN* Jews
❶ a member of the race of people descended from the ancient Hebrews ❷ someone who believes in Judaism

jewel *NOUN* jewels
❶ a precious stone ❷ an ornament containing precious stones

jeweller *NOUN* jewellers
someone who sells or makes jewellery

jewellery *NOUN*
jewellery is jewels or ornaments that people wear

Jewish *ADJECTIVE*
❶ a Jewish person practises Judaism ❷ to do with Jewish people and their beliefs

jib *NOUN* jibs
❶ a triangular sail of a ship, stretching forward from the mast ❷ the arm of a crane that lifts things

jiffy *NOUN* (*informal*)
a moment • *I won't be a jiffy.*

jig *NOUN* jigs
a lively jumping dance

jig *VERB* jigs, jigging, jigged
to jig is to move up and down with quick jerks

jigsaw *NOUN* jigsaws
❶ a saw that can cut curved shapes ❷ a jigsaw puzzle

jigsaw puzzle *NOUN* jigsaw puzzles
a puzzle made of differently shaped pieces that you fit together to make a picture

jingle *VERB* jingles, jingling, jingled
to jingle is to make a tinkling or clinking sound

jingle *NOUN* jingles
❶ a tinkling or clinking sound
Just as I was getting ready to go to sleep I heard a jingle of harness and a grunt, and a mule passed me shaking his wet ears.—THE JUNGLE BOOK, Rudyard Kipling
❷ a simple tune or song that is used in an advertisement

job *NOUN* jobs
❶ work that someone does regularly to earn a living • *She got a job as a florist.* ❷ a piece of work that needs to be done • *I have a few jobs to do around the house.*

jockey *NOUN* jockeys
someone who rides horses in races

jodhpurs (*say* jod-perz) *PLURAL NOUN*
jodhpurs are trousers for riding a horse, fitting closely from the knee to the ankle
DID YOU KNOW? The word **jodhpurs** comes from *Jodhpur*, a city in India where similar trousers are worn.

jog *VERB* jogs, jogging, jogged
❶ to jog is to run slowly, especially for

a
b
c
d
e
f
g
h
i
j
k
l
m
n
o
p
q
r
s
t
u
v
w
x
y
z

exercise ❷ to jog someone is to give them a slight knock or push
➤ **to jog someone's memory** is to help them remember something
➤ **jogger** NOUN

join VERB **joins**, **joining**, **joined**
❶ to join things together, or join one thing to another, is to put or fix them together ❷ two or more things join when they come together ❸ to join a society or group is to become a member of it
➤ **to join in** is to take part in something

join NOUN **joins**
a place where things join

joiner NOUN **joiners**
someone whose job is to make furniture and other things out of wood

joint NOUN **joints**
❶ a place where things are fixed together ❷ the place where two bones fit together ❸ a large piece of meat

joint ADJECTIVE
shared or done by two or more people or groups • *The new website is a joint effort.*

jointly ADVERB
two or more people jointly do something when they do it together

joist NOUN **joists**
a long beam supporting a floor or ceiling

joke NOUN **jokes**
something that you say or do to make people laugh

joke VERB **jokes**, **joking**, **joked**
to joke is to make jokes, or to talk in a way that is not serious

joker NOUN **jokers**
❶ someone who makes jokes ❷ an extra playing card with a picture of a jester on it

jolly ADJECTIVE **jollier**, **jolliest**
happy and cheerful

jolly ADVERB (*informal*)
very • *That film was jolly good!*

jolly VERB **jollies**, **jollying**, **jollied**
to jolly someone along is to make them more cheerful

Jolly Roger NOUN
a pirate's flag with a white skull and crossbones on a black background

jolt VERB **jolts**, **jolting**, **jolted**
❶ to jolt something or someone is to hit them or move them suddenly and sharply ❷ to jolt is to make a sudden sharp movement • *The bus jolted to a halt.*

jolt NOUN **jolts**
❶ a sudden sharp movement • *The plane landed with a jolt.* ❷ a surprise or shock

jostle VERB **jostles**, **jostling**, **jostled**
to jostle someone is to push them roughly

jot NOUN
a tiny amount • *I don't care a jot.*

jot VERB **jots**, **jotting**, **jotted**
➤ **to jot something down** is to write it quickly

jotter NOUN **jotters**
a notebook or exercise book • *a maths jotter*

joule NOUN **joules** (*science*)
a unit of work or energy

journal NOUN **journals**
❶ a newspaper or magazine ❷ a diary

journalist NOUN **journalists**
someone whose job is to write news stories for a newspaper, magazine or in television or radio or for a news website
➤ **journalism** NOUN

journey NOUN **journeys**
❶ going from one place to another ❷ the distance or time you take to travel somewhere • *The town is a day's journey away.*

journey VERB **journeys**, **journeying**, **journeyed**
to journey is to go from one place to another

joust VERB **jousts**, **jousting**, **jousted**
to joust is to fight on horseback with lances, as knights did in medieval times

jovial ADJECTIVE
cheerful and jolly • *We began the day in a jovial mood.*
➤ **jovially** ADVERB

joy *NOUN* **joys**
❶ joy is great happiness or pleasure ❷ a joy is something that gives happiness

joyful *ADJECTIVE*
very happy
➤ **joyfully** *ADVERB*

joyous *ADJECTIVE*
full of joy; causing joy
The following days were some of the most joyous that Clara had spent on the mountain.—HEIDI, Johanna Spyri
➤ **joyously** *ADVERB*

joyride *NOUN* **joyrides** (*informal*)
a ride in a stolen car for amusement

joystick *NOUN* **joysticks**
❶ (*informal*) the lever that controls the movement of an aircraft ❷ a lever for controlling the cursor on a screen, especially in computer games

jubilant (*say* joo-bi-lant) *ADJECTIVE*
very happy because you have won or succeeded

jubilation *NOUN*
jubilation is rejoicing because you have won or succeeded

jubilee *NOUN* **jubilees**
a special anniversary of an important event

Judaism (*say* joo-day-izm) *NOUN*
Judaism is the religion of the Jewish people

judge *NOUN* **judges**
❶ someone who hears cases in a law court and decides what should be done ❷ someone who decides who has won a contest or competition ❸ someone who is good at forming opinions or making decisions about things • *She's a good judge of musical ability.*

judge *VERB* **judges, judging, judged**
❶ to judge something is to act as judge in a law case or a competition ❷ to judge an amount is to estimate or guess what it is ❸ to judge something is to form an opinion about it

judgement *NOUN* **judgements**
❶ judgement is acting as judge for a law case or a contest ❷ a judgement is the decision made by a law court ❸ judgement is also the

ability to make decisions wisely ❹ someone's judgement is their opinion • *In my judgement, you're making a big mistake.*

judo (*say* joo-doh) *NOUN*
judo is a Japanese form of unarmed combat for sport
DID YOU KNOW? The word **judo** comes from Japanese words meaning 'gentle way'.

jug *NOUN* **jugs**
a container for pouring liquids, with a handle and lip

juggernaut *NOUN* **juggernauts**
a very large articulated lorry
DID YOU KNOW? The word **juggernaut** comes from the name of a Hindu god whose image was carried in a procession on a huge vehicle.

juggle *VERB* **juggles, juggling, juggled**
❶ to juggle is to toss and catch a number of objects in turn, keeping one or more always in the air ❷ to juggle a number of tasks is to try to do them all at the same time
➤ **juggler** *NOUN* a performer who juggles at a fair or circus

juice *NOUN* **juices**
❶ the liquid from fruit, vegetables or other food ❷ a liquid produced by the body, such as the digestive juices
➤ **juicy** *ADJECTIVE*

July *NOUN*
the seventh month of the year
DID YOU KNOW? **July** is named after the Roman general *Julius Caesar*, who reformed the Roman calendar.

jumble *VERB* **jumbles, jumbling, jumbled**
to jumble things is to mix them up in a confused way
jumble *NOUN*
a confused mixture of things; a muddle

jumble sale *NOUN* **jumble sales**
a sale of second-hand goods to raise money

jumbo *NOUN* **jumbos**
a jumbo jet
jumbo *ADJECTIVE*
larger than usual • *a jumbo packet of cornflakes*
DID YOU KNOW? The word **jumbo** comes from *Jumbo*, the name of a very large elephant in

a
b
c
d
e
f
g
h
i
j
k
l
m
n
o
p
q
r
s
t
u
v
w
x
y
z

London Zoo in the 1800s. The name may be based on a Swahili word meaning 'chief'.

jumbo jet *NOUN* **jumbo jets**
a large jet aircraft for carrying a lot of passengers

jump *VERB* **jumps, jumping, jumped**
❶ to jump is to move suddenly from the ground into the air ❷ to jump a fence or other obstacle is to go over it by jumping ❸ to jump up or out is to move quickly or suddenly • *He jumped out of his seat.* ❹ to jump in or out of a vehicle is to get in or out quickly
➤ **to jump the queue** is to go in front of people before it is your turn

jump *NOUN* **jumps**
❶ a sudden movement into the air ❷ an obstacle to jump over

jumper *NOUN* **jumpers**
a pullover with sleeves

jumpsuit *NOUN* **jumpsuits**
a piece of clothing made in one piece and covering the whole body

jumpy *ADJECTIVE* **jumpier, jumpiest**
nervous and anxious

junction *NOUN* **junctions**
a place where roads or railway lines join

June *NOUN*
the sixth month of the year
DID YOU KNOW? **June** is named after *Juno*, the chief Roman goddess.

jungle *NOUN* **jungles**
a thick tangled forest, especially in tropical countries

junior *ADJECTIVE*
❶ younger ❷ for young children • *She goes to a junior school.* ❸ lower in rank or importance

junior *NOUN* **juniors**
❶ a younger person • *Peter is my junior.* ❷ a person of lower rank or importance

junk *NOUN* **junks**
❶ junk is old worthless things that should be thrown away • *The garage is full of old junk.* ❷ a junk is a Chinese sailing boat

junk food *NOUN*
junk food is food that is not nourishing, usually containing a lot of sugar and starch

Jupiter *NOUN*
the fifth planet from the sun in our solar system
DID YOU KNOW? The planet **Jupiter** is named after the king of the Roman gods.

juror *NOUN* **jurors**
a member of a jury

jury *NOUN* **juries**
a group of people (usually twelve) chosen to make a decision about a case in a law court, especially whether a person accused of a crime is innocent or guilty

just *ADJECTIVE*
❶ fair and right; giving proper thought to everybody ❷ deserved • *He got his just reward.*
➤ **justly** *ADVERB*

just *ADVERB*
❶ exactly • *It's just what I wanted.* ❷ only; simply • *I just wanted another cake.* ❸ barely; by only a short amount • *The ball hit her just below the knee.* ❹ a short time ago • *They had just gone.*

justice *NOUN* **justices**
❶ justice is being just or having fair treatment ❷ justice is also the actions of the law • *They were tried in a court of justice.* ❸ a justice is a judge or magistrate

justify *VERB* **justifies, justifying, justified**
to justify something is to show that it is reasonable or necessary • *Do you think that you were justified in taking such a risk?*
➤ **justifiable** *ADJECTIVE* able to be justified
➤ **justification** *NOUN* a justification for something is a good reason for doing it

jut *VERB* **juts, jutting, jutted**
to jut, or to jut out, is to stick out

juvenile (*say* joo-vi-nyl) *ADJECTIVE*
to do with young people
juvenile *NOUN* **juveniles**
a young person who is not yet an adult

Kk

kaboom *EXCLAMATION*
the sound made by a loud explosion • *There was a loud blast behind us. Kaboom!*

kaleidoscope (*say* kal-l-dos-kohp) *NOUN* **kaleidoscopes**
a tube you look through to see coloured patterns which change as you turn the end of the tube
➤ **kaleidoscopic** *ADJECTIVE*

kangaroo *NOUN* **kangaroos**
an Australian animal that moves by jumping on its strong back legs

karaoke (*say* ka-ri-oh-kee) *NOUN*
karaoke is a party entertainment in which people sing songs with a recorded background played from a special machine
DID YOU KNOW? The word **karaoke** is Japanese and means 'empty orchestra'.

karate (*say* ka-rah-tee) *NOUN*
karate is a Japanese method of self-defence using the hands, arms and feet
DID YOU KNOW? The word **karate** comes from Japanese words meaning 'empty hand'.

kayak (*say* ky-ak) *NOUN* **kayaks**
a small canoe with a covering that fits round the canoeist's waist

kebab *NOUN* **kebabs**
small pieces of meat or vegetables grilled on a skewer

keel *NOUN* **keels**
the long piece of wood or metal along the bottom of a boat
➤ **to be on an even keel** is to be steady

keel *VERB* **keels**, **keeling**, **keeled**
➤ **to keel over** is to fall sideways or overturn

keen *ADJECTIVE* **keener**, **keenest**
❶ enthusiastic or eager • *She is keen on swimming.* • *We are keen to go.* ❷ strong or sharp • *The knife had a keen edge.* • *There was a keen wind.*
➤ **keenly** *ADVERB* a keenly fought contest is one in which people are competing very hard
➤ **keenness** *NOUN*

keep *VERB* **keeps**, **keeping**, **kept**
❶ to keep something is to have it and not get rid of it • *She had kept the letter all these years.* ❷ to keep something in a place is to put it there when you are not using it • *He kept the key in a secret drawer.* ❸ to keep (for example) well or still is to continue to be well or still ❹ to keep someone (for example) warm or happy is to cause them to continue to be warm or happy ❺ something keeps when it lasts without going bad • *Will the milk keep until tomorrow?* ❻ to keep doing something is to continue to do it • *They kept staring at me!* ❼ to keep your word or promise is to honour it and not break it ❽ to keep animals or pets is to have them and look after them
➤ **to keep something up** is to continue doing it • *Keep up the good work!*
➤ **to keep up with someone** is to go as fast as them

keep *NOUN* **keeps**
❶ someone's keep is the food or money they need to live • *They have to earn their keep.* ❷ a keep is a strong tower in a castle
➤ **for keeps** (*informal*) to have forever • *Is this football mine for keeps?*

keeper *NOUN* **keepers**
❶ someone who looks after the animals in a zoo ❷ a goalkeeper

keeping *NOUN*
something is in your keeping when you are looking after it • *The diaries are in safe keeping.*
➤ **to be in keeping with something** is to fit in with it or be suitable

keg *NOUN* **kegs**
a small barrel

kelp *NOUN*
a large brown type of seaweed

kelpie *NOUN* **kelpies**
a mythological water horse found in lochs and lakes

a
b
c
d
e
f
g
h
i
j
k
l
m
n
o
p
q
r
s
t
u
v
w
x
y
z

kennel *NOUN* **kennels**
a shelter for a dog

kept *VERB* (*past tense and past participle of keep*)
• *Tom kept out of sight.* • *I have kept the letter.*

kerb *NOUN* **kerbs**
the edge of a pavement

kerbstone *NOUN* **kerbstones**
a long square stone used to make a kerb

kernel *NOUN* **kernels**
the part inside the shell of a nut

kestrel *NOUN* **kestrels**
a kind of small falcon

ketchup *NOUN*
a thick spicy sauce made from tomatoes and vinegar

kettle *NOUN* **kettles**
a container with a spout and handle, used for boiling water in

kettledrum *NOUN* **kettledrums**
a drum made of skin stretched over a large metal bowl

key *NOUN* **keys**
❶ a piece of metal shaped so that it opens a lock ❷ a lever that you press with your finger to play a note on a piano ❸ a small button that you press or tap to send information to a computer ❹ a device for winding up a clock or clockwork toy ❺ a scale of musical notes • *The piece is played in the key of C major.* ❻ something that solves a problem or mystery • *This document is the key to cracking the code.*

keyboard *NOUN* **keyboards**
❶ a set of keys that you press to play a piano ❷ a set of keys attached to a computer or displayed on a touchscreen

keyhole *NOUN* **keyholes**
the hole through which you put a key into a lock

keynote *NOUN* **keynotes**
❶ the note on which a key in music is based • *The keynote of C major is C.* ❷ the main idea in something that is said, written or done

keypad *NOUN* **keypads**
a set of keys on a computer or touchscreen

key word, **key phrase** *NOUN*
key words, **key phrases**
❶ one of the most important words or phrases in a text, that helps you to understand what the text is about ❷ a word or phrase that you type into a computer when you are searching for information

kg *ABBREVIATION*
short for *kilograms*

khaki (*say* kah-kee) *NOUN*
a dull yellow-brown colour, often used for army uniforms

kick *VERB* **kicks**, **kicking**, **kicked**
❶ to kick someone or something is to hit them with your foot ❷ to kick is to move your legs about vigorously ❸ a gun kicks when it moves back sharply as it is fired

kick *NOUN* **kicks**
❶ a kicking movement ❷ the sudden backwards movement a gun makes when it is fired

kick-off *NOUN* **kick-offs**
the start of a football match

kid *NOUN* **kids**
❶ a young goat ❷ (*informal*) a child

kid *VERB* **kids**, **kidding**, **kidded** (*informal*)
to kid someone is to deceive or tease them

kidnap *VERB* **kidnaps**, **kidnapping**, **kidnapped**
to kidnap someone is to capture them by force, usually to get a ransom
➤ **kidnapper** *NOUN*

kidney *NOUN* **kidneys**
each of two organs in your body that remove waste products from your blood and send them as urine to your bladder

kill *VERB* **kills**, **killing**, **killed**
❶ to kill a person or animal is to make them die ❷ to kill something like an idea or plan is to make sure it does not happen

killer *NOUN* **killers**
a person who kills someone

killer whale NOUN killer whales
a whale with black and white markings, which hunts in groups

kiln NOUN kilns
an oven for hardening or drying pottery or bricks

kilo NOUN kilos
a kilogram

DID YOU KNOW? Words beginning with **kilo-** are based on the Greek word *chilioi* meaning 'thousand'.

kilobyte NOUN kilobytes (*computing*)
a unit that measures data or memory, equal to 1,024 bytes

kilogram NOUN kilograms
a unit of weight equal to 1,000 grams or about 2.2 pounds

kilometre (*say* kil-**om**-i-ter *or* kil-o-mee-ter) NOUN kilometres
a unit of length equal to 1,000 metres or about ⅝ of a mile

kilowatt NOUN kilowatts
a unit of electrical power equal to 1,000 watts

kilt NOUN kilts
a kind of pleated skirt worn by men as part of traditional Scottish dress

kimono NOUN kimonos
a traditional Japanese robe, worn by both men and women

kin NOUN
a person's family or relatives
➤ **your next of kin** is your closest relative

kind NOUN kinds
a type or sort of something • *What kind of food do you like?*
➤ **kind of** (*informal*) in a way, to some extent • *We kind of hoped you would come.*

kind ADJECTIVE kinder, kindest
helpful and friendly • *It was kind of you to call.*
➤ **kindness** NOUN

kindergarten NOUN kindergartens
a school or class for very young children

kind-hearted ADJECTIVE
kind and generous

kindle VERB kindles, kindling, kindled
❶ to kindle something is to get it to burn ❷ to kindle is to start burning

kindling NOUN
kindling is small pieces of wood for lighting fires

kindly ADVERB
❶ in a kind way ❷ please • *Kindly close the door.*

kindly ADJECTIVE kindlier, kindliest
kind • *She gave a kindly smile.*
➤ **kindliness** NOUN

kinetic (*say* kin-**et**-ik) ADJECTIVE
to do with movement, or produced by movement, as in *kinetic energy*

king NOUN kings
❶ a man who has been crowned as the ruler of a country ❷ a piece in chess that has to be captured to win the game ❸ a playing card with a picture of a king
➤ **kingly** ADJECTIVE

kingdom NOUN kingdoms
a country that is ruled by a king or queen

kingfisher NOUN kingfishers
a brightly coloured bird that lives near water and catches fish

kink NOUN kinks
a short twist in a rope, wire or piece of hair

kiosk (*say* kee-osk) NOUN kiosks
a small hut or stall where you can buy newspapers, sweets and drinks

kipper NOUN kippers
a smoked herring

kiss NOUN kisses
touching someone with your lips as a sign of affection or greeting

kiss VERB kisses, kissing, kissed
to kiss someone is to give them a kiss

kiss of life NOUN
blowing air from your mouth into someone else's to help them to start breathing again, especially after an accident

a b c d e f g h i j **k** l m n o p q r s t u v w x y z

kit *NOUN* **kits**
❶ equipment or clothes that you need to do a sport, a job or some other activity • *I forgot to bring my gym kit.* ❷ a set of parts sold to be fitted together to make something • *a model aircraft kit*

kitchen *NOUN* **kitchens**
a room where food is prepared and cooked

kite *NOUN* **kites**
a light frame covered with cloth or paper that you fly in the wind at the end of a long piece of string

kitten *NOUN* **kittens**
a very young cat

kitty *NOUN* **kitties**
❶ an amount of money that you can win in a card game ❷ an amount of money that you put aside for a special purpose ❸ (*informal*) a kitten

kiwi (*say* kee-wee) *NOUN* **kiwis**
a New Zealand bird that cannot fly

kiwi fruit *NOUN* **kiwi fruits**
a fruit with thin hairy skin, soft green flesh and black seeds

km *ABBREVIATION*
short for *kilometres*

knack *NOUN*
a special skill or talent • *There's a knack to putting up a deckchair.*

knave *NOUN* **knaves**
❶ (*old use*) a dishonest man ❷ a jack in a pack of playing cards

knead *VERB* **kneads**, **kneading**, **kneaded**
to knead dough or something else soft is to press and stretch it with your hands

knee *NOUN* **knees**
the joint in the middle of your leg

kneecap *NOUN* **kneecaps**
the bony part at the front of your knee

kneel *VERB* **kneels**, **kneeling**, **knelt**
to bend your legs so you are resting on your knees

knew *VERB* (*past tense of* **know**)
• *I knew we would be friends.*

knickers *PLURAL NOUN*
underpants

knife *NOUN* **knives**
a cutting instrument made of a short blade set in a handle

knife *VERB* **knifes**, **knifing**, **knifed**
to knife someone is to stab them with a knife

knight *NOUN* **knights**
❶ a man who has been given an honorary title that allows him to put 'Sir' before his name ❷ a warrior who had been given the rank of a nobleman, in the Middle Ages
The young knight had a helmet on his head and a sword hanging at his side, and the tunic over his armour was blue and gold, the colours of Tehuri.—THE SECRETS OF THE WILD WOOD, Tonke Dragt
❸ a piece in chess, with a horse's head

knight *VERB* **knights**, **knighting**, **knighted**
to knight someone is to make them a knight

DID YOU KNOW? The letter K in **knight** is silent now, but it was once pronounced.

knighthood *NOUN* **knighthoods**
a man receives a knighthood when he is made a knight

knit *VERB* **knits**, **knitting**, **knitted**
to knit something is to make it by looping together threads of wool or other material, using long needles or a machine

knitting *NOUN*
❶ knitting is the activity of making things by knitting ❷ knitting is also something that is being made this way

knives *NOUN* (*plural of* **knife**)

knob *NOUN* **knobs**
❶ the round handle of a door or drawer ❷ a control to adjust a radio or television set ❸ a lump of something

knobbly *ADJECTIVE* **knobblier**, **knobbliest**
something that is knobbly has many lumps and bumps
His head was made of a great knobbly turnip, with a broad crack for a mouth and a long thin

sprout for a nose.—THE SCARECROW AND HIS SERVANT, Philip Pullman

knock *VERB* **knocks, knocking, knocked**
❶ to knock something is to hit it hard or bump into it • *Oops, I knocked the vase over.*
❷ to knock is to hit something with your hand or fist • *Who's knocking at the door?*
❸ (*informal*) to knock someone or something is to criticize them
➤ **to knock someone out** is to hit them so that they become unconscious

knock *NOUN* **knocks**
the act or sound of hitting something

knocker *NOUN* **knockers**
a device for knocking on a door

knockout *NOUN* **knockouts**
❶ knocking someone out ❷ a game or contest in which the loser in each round has to drop out

knot *NOUN* **knots**
❶ a fastening made by tying or looping two ends of string, rope or ribbon together ❷ a round spot on a piece of wood where a branch once joined it ❸ a unit for measuring the speed of ships and aircraft, 2,025 yards (or 1,852 metres) per hour ❹ a knot of people is a small group of them standing close together

knot *VERB* **knots, knotting, knotted**
to knot something is to tie or fasten it with a knot

knotty *ADJECTIVE* **knottier, knottiest**
❶ full of knots ❷ difficult or puzzling • *It's a knotty problem.*

know *VERB* **knows, knowing, knew, known**
❶ to have something in your mind that you have learned or discovered ❷ to know a person or place is to recognize them or it, or be familiar with them or it • *I've known him for years.*

know-all *NOUN* **know-alls**
someone who behaves as if they know everything

know-how *NOUN*
know-how is the skill or knowledge you need for a particular job

knowing *ADJECTIVE*
a knowing look is one that shows that you know something

knowingly *ADVERB*
❶ in a knowing way • *He winked at me knowingly.* ❷ deliberately • *She would never have done such a thing knowingly.*

knowledge (*say* nol-ij) *NOUN*
knowledge is what someone or everybody knows • *a quiz to test our general knowledge*

knowledgeable (*say* nol-ij-a-bul) *ADJECTIVE*
knowing a lot about something
➤ **knowledgeably** *ADVERB*

knuckle *NOUN* **knuckles**
a joint in your finger

koala (*say* koh-ah-la) *NOUN* **koalas**
a furry Australian animal that looks like a small bear

kookaburra (*say* kook-a-bu-ra) *NOUN* **kookaburras**
a large Australian kingfisher that makes a sound like a loud echoing laugh

Koran (*say* kor-ahn) *NOUN*
the holy book of Islam

kosher (*say* koh-sher) *ADJECTIVE*
kosher food is food prepared according to Jewish religious law

kraken *NOUN* **krakens**
a mythological Norse sea monster

kung fu (*say* kung-foo) *NOUN*
kung fu is a Chinese method of self-defence using the hands, arms and feet

a b c d e f g h i j **k** l m n o p q r s t u v w x y z

Ll

l *ABBREVIATION*
short for *litres*

label *NOUN* **labels**
a piece of paper, cloth or metal fixed on or beside something to show what it is or to give other information about it such as its price

label *VERB* **labels, labelling, labelled**
to label something is to put a label on it

laboratory (*say* la-**bo**-ra-ter-ee) *NOUN* **laboratories**
a room or building equipped for scientific work

laborious *ADJECTIVE*
needing a lot of effort; very hard

labour *NOUN*
❶ labour is hard work ❷ labour is also the process of giving birth
➤ **Labour** the Labour Party, a socialist political party

labourer *NOUN* **labourers**
someone who does hard work with their hands, especially outdoors

Labrador *NOUN* **Labradors**
a large black or light-brown dog

laburnum *NOUN* **laburnums**
a tree with hanging yellow flowers

labyrinth *NOUN* **labyrinths**
a complicated set of passages or paths; a maze
McDougal's cave was but a vast labyrinth of crooked aisles that ran into each other and out again and led nowhere.—THE ADVENTURES OF TOM SAWYER, Mark Twain
DID YOU KNOW? The **Labyrinth** was the name of the maze in Greek mythology where the Minotaur lived.

lace *NOUN* **laces**
❶ lace is thin material with decorative patterns of holes in it ❷ a lace is a piece of thin cord used to tie up a shoe or boot
➤ **lacy** *ADJECTIVE*

lace *VERB* **laces, lacing, laced**
❶ to lace up a shoe or boot is to fasten it with a lace ❷ to lace a drink is to add strong spirits to it

lack *NOUN*
there is a lack of something when there is not any of it or there is not enough of it • *The trip was cancelled because of lack of interest.*

lack *VERB* **lacks, lacking, lacked**
to lack something is to be without it • *He lacks courage.*

lacquer *NOUN*
lacquer is a kind of varnish

lacrosse *NOUN*
a game using a stick with a net on it (called a *crosse*) to catch and throw a ball

lad *NOUN* **lads**
a boy or young man

ladder *NOUN* **ladders**
❶ a device to help you climb up or down something, made of upright pieces of wood, metal or rope with steps called rungs across them ❷ a run of damaged stitches in tights or a stocking

laden *ADJECTIVE*
carrying a heavy load

ladle *NOUN* **ladles**
a large deep spoon with a long handle, which you use for serving soup or other liquids

lady *NOUN* **ladies**
❶ a polite name for a woman ❷ a well-mannered woman, or a woman of high social standing
➤ **Lady** the title of a noblewoman

ladybird *NOUN* **ladybirds**
a small flying beetle, usually red with black spots

ladylike *ADJECTIVE*
being polite and quiet, in a way that was traditionally thought to be suitable for a woman
'No, thank you,' said Sylvia, in as ladylike a tone as she could muster. 'I never touch chocolate.'
—THE WOLVES OF WILLOUGHBY CHASE, Joan Aiken

ladyship *NOUN*
a title for a woman of high social standing

lag *VERB* **lags, lagging, lagged**
❶ to lag is to go too slowly and not keep up with others • *My little brother was lagging behind.* ❷ to lag pipes is to wrap them with insulating material to keep in the heat

lager (*say* lah-ger) *NOUN* **lagers**
a light beer

lagoon *NOUN* **lagoons**
a lake separated from the sea by banks of sand or reefs

laid *VERB* (*past tense and past participle of* lay)
• *He laid a hand on the boy's shoulder.*
• *My brother had laid the table.*

lain *VERB* (*past participle of* lie)
• *She had lain awake all night.*

lair *NOUN* **lairs**
the place where a wild animal lives

lake *NOUN* **lakes**
a large area of water completely surrounded by land

lama *NOUN* **lamas**
a Buddhist priest or monk in Tibet and Mongolia

lamb *NOUN* **lambs**
❶ a lamb is a young sheep ❷ lamb is the meat from young sheep

lame *ADJECTIVE* **lamer, lamest**
❶ not able to walk normally ❷ weak and not very convincing • *What a lame excuse.*
➤ **lamely** *ADVERB*

lament *VERB* **laments, lamenting, lamented**
to lament something is to express grief or disappointment about it
➤ **lamentation** *NOUN*

lament *NOUN* **laments**
a song or poem that expresses grief or regret

lamp *NOUN* **lamps**
a device for producing light from electricity, gas or oil

lamp post *NOUN* **lamp posts**
a tall post in a street or public place, with a lamp at the top

lampshade *NOUN* **lampshades**
a cover for the bulb of an electric lamp, to soften the light

lance *NOUN* **lances**
a long spear with a wooden shaft, used by medieval knights when charging

land *NOUN* **lands**
❶ land, or the land, is all the dry parts of the world's surface ❷ land is an area of ground ❸ a land is a country or nation

land *VERB* **lands, landing, landed**
❶ to land is to come down to the ground from the air • *Where did the arrow land?*
❷ to land is also to arrive in a ship or aircraft ❸ to land someone or something is to bring them to a place by means of a ship or aircraft ❹ (*informal*) to land someone in difficulty or trouble is to cause them difficulty or trouble
➤ **to land up** (*informal*) is to get to a particular place or situation • *They landed up in France.*

landing *NOUN* **landings**
the floor at the top of a flight of stairs

landlady *NOUN* **landladies**
❶ a woman who owns a house, room or land that she rents to a tenant ❷ a woman whose job is to manage a pub

landline *NOUN* **landlines**
a telephone line that uses cables, as opposed to a mobile network

landlord *NOUN* **landlords**
❶ a person who rents a house or land to someone else, or lets rooms to lodgers
❷ a person who looks after a pub

landmark *NOUN* **landmarks**
an object on land that you can easily see from a distance

landowner *NOUN* **landowners**
a person who owns a large amount of land

landscape *NOUN* **landscapes**
❶ a view of a particular area of town or countryside ❷ a picture of the countryside
❸ a way of printing a page of text so that it is wider than it is tall

landslide *NOUN* **landslides**
❶ a landslide is when earth or rocks slide down the side of a hill ❷ a landslide is also an overwhelming victory in an election

a
b
c
d
e
f
g
h
i
j
k
l
m
n
o
p
q
r
s
t
u
v
w
x
y
z

lane *NOUN* **lanes**
❶ a narrow road, especially in the country
❷ a strip of road for a single line of traffic
❸ a strip of track or water for one runner or swimmer in a race

language *NOUN* **languages**
❶ language is the use of words in speech and writing ❷ a language is the words used in a particular country or by a particular group of people • *the Welsh language*
❸ a language is also a system of letters, numbers and symbols in which computer programs are written

lanky *ADJECTIVE* **lankier, lankiest**
tall and thin

lantern *NOUN* **lanterns**
a transparent case for holding a light and shielding it from the wind

lap *NOUN* **laps**
❶ your lap is the flat area from your waist to your knees, formed when you are sitting down
❷ a lap is also going once round a racecourse or track

lap *VERB* **laps, lapping, lapped**
❶ to lap someone in a race is to be more than one lap ahead of them ❷ to lap liquid is to drink it with the tongue, as a cat or dog does
❸ waves lap when they make a gentle splash on rocks or the shore

lapel (*say* la-**pel**) *NOUN* **lapels**
the flap folded back at each front edge of a coat or jacket

lapse *NOUN* **lapses**
❶ a slight mistake or fault ❷ the passing of time • *She wrote after a lapse of three months.*

lapse *VERB* **lapses, lapsing, lapsed**
❶ to lapse into a state is to pass gradually into it • *He lapsed into unconsciousness.*
❷ a contract or document lapses when it is no longer valid • *My passport has lapsed.*

laptop *NOUN* **laptops**
a computer small enough to be held and used on your lap

lapwing *NOUN* **lapwings**
a black and white bird with a crest on its head and a shrill cry

larch *NOUN* **larches**
a tall deciduous tree that produces small cones

lard *NOUN*
lard is white greasy fat from pigs, used in cooking

larder *NOUN* **larders**
a cupboard or small room for storing food
In Aunt Gwen's larder there were two cold pork chops, half a trifle, some bananas and some buns and cakes.—TOM'S MIDNIGHT GARDEN, Philippa Pearce

large *ADJECTIVE* **larger, largest**
more than the ordinary or average size; big
➤ **to be at large** is to be free and dangerous • *The escaped prisoners were still at large.*
➤ **largeness** *NOUN*

largely *ADVERB*
mainly; mostly • *His name has been largely forgotten.*

lark *NOUN* **larks**
❶ a small sandy-brown bird, especially a skylark
❷ (*informal*) something amusing; a bit of fun
• *They just did it for a lark.*

lark *VERB* **larks, larking, larked**
➤ **to lark about** is to have fun or play tricks

larva *NOUN* **larvae**
an insect in the first stage of its life, after it comes out of the egg
DID YOU KNOW? The word **larva** comes from a Latin word meaning 'ghost' or 'mask'.

larynx (*say* la-rinks) *NOUN* **larynxes**
the part of your throat that contains your vocal chords

lasagne (*say* la-**zan**-ya) *NOUN*
lasagne is pasta in the form of flat sheets, cooked with minced meat or vegetables and a white sauce

laser (*say* lay-zer) *NOUN* **lasers**
a device that makes a very strong narrow beam of light

lash *NOUN* **lashes**
❶ an eyelash ❷ a stroke with a whip
lash *VERB* **lashes, lashing, lashed**
❶ to lash someone or something is to hit them with a whip or like a whip • *Rain lashed the window.* ❷ to lash something is to tie it tightly

• *During the storm they lashed the boxes to the mast.*
➤ **to lash out** is to speak or hit out angrily

lass NOUN lasses
a girl or young woman

lasso (*say* la-**soo**) NOUN lassos
a rope with a loop at the end which tightens when you pull the rope, used for catching cattle

last ADJECTIVE
❶ coming after all the others; final • *Try not to miss the last bus.* ❷ most recent or latest • *Where were you last night?*
➤ **the last straw** a final or added thing that makes a problem unbearable

last ADVERB
at the end; after everything or everyone else • *He came last in the race.*

last NOUN
a person or thing that is last • *I think I was the last to arrive.*
➤ **at last** finally; at the end

last VERB lasts, lasting, lasted
❶ to continue for an amount of time • *The journey lasts for two hours.* ❷ to go on without being used up • *How long will our supplies last?*

lastly ADVERB
in the last place; finally

latch NOUN latches
a small bar fastening a gate or door

late ADJECTIVE, ADVERB
❶ after the proper or expected time • *I was ten minutes late for my lesson.* • *We stayed up late to watch the film.* ❷ near the end of a period of time • *It was already late in the afternoon.* ❸ no longer alive • *They saw the tomb of the late king.*
➤ **lateness** NOUN

lately ADVERB
recently • *I've been reading a lot lately.*

latent (*say* lay-tent) ADJECTIVE
existing but not yet active, developed or visible • *Some superheroes have latent superpowers.*

later ADVERB
❶ after in time; afterwards • *Ten minutes later, my phone rang.* ❷ at a time in the near future • *I'll tell you the whole story later.*

lateral ADJECTIVE
to do with the sides of something

latest ADJECTIVE
most recent or up to date • *Check our website for the latest news.*

latest NOUN
the most recent or newest thing or piece of news • *the very latest in sportswear design*

lather NOUN lathers
the thick foam you get when you mix soap with water

Latin NOUN
Latin is the language of the ancient Romans
DID YOU KNOW? Many English words are based wholly or partly on Latin, including **beneficial**, **binoculars**, **malevolent** and **submarine**.

latitude NOUN latitudes
❶ the distance of a place north or south of the equator, measured in degrees ❷ freedom to do what you want or make decisions

latter ADJECTIVE
later • *We'd like a holiday in the latter part of the year.*
➤ **the latter** the second of two people or things just mentioned • *If it's a choice between a picnic or a swim, I prefer the latter.*

latterly ADVERB
recently

lattice NOUN lattices
a framework of crossed strips with spaces between

laugh VERB laughs, laughing, laughed
to laugh is to make sounds that show you are happy or that you think something is funny

laugh NOUN laughs
❶ the sound you make when you laugh ❷ (*informal*) something that is fun or amusing • *Yesterday's party was quite a laugh.*

laughable ADJECTIVE
silly and deserving to be laughed at

laughter NOUN
laughter is laughing or the sound of laughing

launch VERB launches, launching, launched
❶ to launch a ship is to send it into the water for the first time ❷ to launch a rocket is to

a
b
c
d
e
f
g
h
i
j
k
l
m
n
o
p
q
r
s
t
u
v
w
x
y
z

send it into space ❸ to launch a new idea or product is to make it available for the first time

launch *NOUN* **launches**
❶ the launching of a ship or spacecraft
❷ a launch is also a large motor boat

launch pad *NOUN* **launch pads**
a platform from which rockets are sent into space

launder *VERB* **launders, laundering, laundered**
to launder clothes is to wash and iron them

launderette *NOUN* **launderettes**
a shop with washing machines that people pay to use

laundry *NOUN* **laundries**
❶ laundry is clothes to be washed ❷ a laundry is a place where clothes are sent or taken to be washed and ironed

laurel *NOUN* **laurels**
an evergreen bush with smooth shiny leaves

lava *NOUN*
lava is the molten rock that flows from a volcano, or the solid rock formed when it cools

lavatory *NOUN* **lavatories**
a toilet

lavender *NOUN*
❶ lavender is a shrub with pale purple flowers that smell very sweet ❷ a pale purple colour

lavish *ADJECTIVE*
❶ rich and plentiful; luxurious • *The table was spread with a lavish banquet.* ❷ very generous • *She is always lavish with her praise.*
➤ **lavishly** *ADVERB*

law *NOUN* **laws**
❶ a rule or set of rules that everyone must keep ❷ something that always happens, for example the law of gravity

law court *NOUN* **law courts**
a room or building where a judge and jury or magistrates decide whether someone has broken the law

lawful *ADJECTIVE*
allowed or accepted by the law
➤ **lawfully** *ADVERB*

lawless *ADJECTIVE*
a lawless place does not have any proper laws • *The Wild West was once a lawless place.*

lawn *NOUN* **lawns**
an area of mown grass in a garden

lawnmower *NOUN* **lawnmowers**
a machine with revolving blades for cutting grass

lawyer *NOUN* **lawyers**
a person whose job is to help people with the law

lax *ADJECTIVE*
not strict; tolerant • *Discipline was very lax.*

lay *VERB* (*past tense of* **lie**)
• *Tom lay in his sleeping bag.*

lay *VERB* **lays, laying, laid**
❶ to lay something somewhere is to put it down in a particular place or in a particular way ❷ to lay a table is to arrange things on it for a meal ❸ to lay an egg is to produce it ❹ to lay plans is to form or prepare them
➤ **to lay something on** is to supply or provide it
➤ **to lay something out** is to arrange or prepare it

layer *NOUN* **layers**
something flat that lies on or under something else • *The cake had a layer of icing on top and a layer of jam inside.*

layout *NOUN* **layouts**
the arrangement or design of something

laze *VERB* **lazes, lazing, lazed**
to laze is to spend time in a lazy way

lazy *ADJECTIVE* **lazier, laziest**
not wanting to work; doing as little as possible
➤ **lazily** *ADVERB* ➤ **laziness** *NOUN*

lb *ABBREVIATION*
short for *pounds* (in weight)

lead (*say* leed) *VERB* **leads, leading, led**
❶ to lead a person or animal is to guide them, especially by going in front ❷ to lead an

activity is to be in charge of it ❸ to lead in a race or contest is to be winning it ❹ a road or path leads somewhere when it goes in that direction • *This road leads to the beach.*
➤ **to lead to something** is to cause it • *Their carelessness led to the accident.*

lead (*say* leed) *NOUN* **leads**
❶ the first or front place or position • *Who's in the lead now?* ❷ help or guidance • *Just follow my lead.* ❸ a strap or cord for leading a dog ❹ an electric wire • *Don't trip over that lead.*

lead (*say* led) *NOUN* **leads**
❶ lead is a soft heavy grey metal ❷ a lead is the writing substance (graphite) in the middle of a pencil

leader *NOUN* **leaders**
❶ someone who leads or is in charge ❷ an article in a newspaper, giving the editor's opinion
➤ **leadership** *NOUN*

leaf *NOUN* **leaves**
❶ a flat and usually green growth on a tree or plant, growing from its stem ❷ a page of a book
➤ **to turn over a new leaf** is to make a fresh start and improve your behaviour
➤ **leafy** *ADJECTIVE*

leaflet *NOUN* **leaflets**
a piece of paper printed with information

league (*say* leeg) *NOUN* **leagues**
❶ a group of teams that play matches against each other ❷ a group of countries that have agreed to work together for a particular reason
➤ **to be in league with someone** is to work or plot together

leak *NOUN* **leaks**
❶ a hole or crack through which liquid or gas escapes ❷ the revealing of some secret information

leak *VERB* **leaks**, **leaking**, **leaked**
❶ something leaks when it lets something out through a hole or crack • *The sink is leaking.* ❷ liquid or gas leaks out when it escapes from a container ❸ to leak secret information is to reveal it
➤ **leakage** *NOUN*

lean *VERB* **leans**, **leaning**, **leaned** *or* **leant**
❶ to lean is to bend your body towards something or over it ❷ to lean something is to put it into a sloping position • *Do not lean bicycles against the window.* ❸ to lean against something is to rest against it

lean *ADJECTIVE* **leaner**, **leanest**
❶ lean meat has little fat ❷ a lean person is thin

leap *NOUN* **leaps**
❶ a high or long jump ❷ a sudden increase or advance

leap *VERB* **leaps**, **leaping**, **leapt** *or* **leaped**
❶ to leap is to jump high or a long way ❷ to leap is also to increase or advance suddenly

leapfrog *NOUN*
a game in which each player jumps with legs apart over another player who is bending down

leap year *NOUN* **leap years**
a year with an extra day in it, on 29 February
DID YOU KNOW? A year is a **leap year** when you can divide it by four, as you can with 2000 and 2024.

learn *VERB* **learns**, **learning**, **learnt** *or* **learned**
❶ to learn something is to find out about it and gain knowledge or skill in it • *She's learning to play the guitar.* ❷ to learn something is to discover some news • *I was sorry to learn that he was ill.*

learned (*say* ler-nid) *ADJECTIVE*
clever and knowledgeable

learner *NOUN* **learners**
someone who is learning something, for example how to drive a car

learning *NOUN*
learning is knowledge you get by studying

lease *NOUN* **leases**
an agreement to let someone use a building or land for a fixed period in return for a payment
➤ **a new lease of life** is a chance to go on being active or useful

leash *NOUN* **leashes**
a strap or cord for leading a dog

a b c d e f g h i j k l m n o p q r s t u v w x y z

least DETERMINER, ADVERB
less than all the others • *I get the least pocket money.* • *I like this one least.*

least PRONOUN
the smallest amount • *I got the least.*
➤ **at least** ❶ not less than what is mentioned • *It will cost at least £50.* ❷ anyway • *He's at home; at least I think he is.*

leather NOUN **leathers**
leather is a strong material made from animals' skins

leave VERB **leaves, leaving, left**
❶ to leave a person, place or group is to go away from them ❷ to leave something is to let it stay where it is or remain as it is • *You can leave your bags by the door.*
❸ to leave something to someone is to give it to them in a will
➤ **to leave something** or **someone out** is not to include them
➤ **to be left over** is to remain when other things have been used

leave NOUN
permission, especially to be away from work

leaves NOUN (*plural of* **leaf**)

lectern NOUN **lecterns**
a stand to hold a large book or notes from which you read

lecture NOUN **lectures**
❶ a talk about a subject to an audience or a class ❷ a long or serious warning given to someone • *We got a lecture about closing the windows.*

lecture VERB **lectures, lecturing, lectured**
to lecture is to give a lecture
➤ **lecturer** NOUN

led VERB (*past tense and past participle of* **lead**)
• *She led the way in to the cave.* • *One thing had led to another.*

ledge NOUN **ledges**
a narrow shelf

lee NOUN
the sheltered side of something, away from the wind

leek NOUN **leeks**
a long green and white vegetable like an onion with broad leaves

leer VERB **leers, leering, leered**
to leer at someone is to look at them in an unpleasant or evil way

leeward ADJECTIVE
facing away from the wind

left VERB (*past tense and past participle of* **leave**)
• *The train left at 2 o'clock.* • *Mum had left the door open for us.*

left ADJECTIVE, ADVERB
❶ on or towards the west if you think of yourself as facing north ❷ in favour of political and social change

left NOUN
the left side

left–hand ADJECTIVE
on the left side of something

left–handed ADJECTIVE
using the left hand more than the right hand

leftovers PLURAL NOUN
food that has not been eaten by the end of a meal

leg NOUN **legs**
❶ one of the parts of a human's or animal's body on which they stand or move ❷ one of the parts of a pair of trousers that cover your legs ❸ each of the supports of a chair or other piece of furniture ❹ one part of a journey ❺ each of a pair of matches between the same teams in a competition

legacy NOUN **legacies**
something given to someone in a will

legal ADJECTIVE
❶ allowed by the law ❷ to do with the law or lawyers
➤ **legally** ADVERB

legend (*say* lej-end) NOUN **legends**
an old story handed down from the past

legendary ADJECTIVE
❶ mentioned in legends • *Maui is a legendary figure in Polynesian culture.* ❷ very famous • *His football ability is legendary.*

leggings *PLURAL NOUN*
leggings are stretchy, very close-fitting trousers

legible *ADJECTIVE*
clear enough to read • *Make sure your writing is legible.*

legion *NOUN* **legions**
❶ a division of the ancient Roman army ❷ a group of soldiers, or men who used to be soldiers

legislate *VERB* **legislates, legislating, legislated**
to legislate is to make laws
➤ **legislation** *NOUN*

legitimate (*say* li-**jit**-i-mat) *ADJECTIVE*
❶ allowed by a law or rule ❷ (*old use*) born of parents who were married to each other

leisure *NOUN*
leisure is free time, when you can do what you like
➤ **to do something at leisure** is to do it without hurrying

leisurely *ADJECTIVE*
done with plenty of time, without hurrying • *They took a leisurely stroll down to the river.*

lemon *NOUN* **lemons**
❶ a yellow citrus fruit with a sour taste ❷ a pale yellow colour

lemonade *NOUN* **lemonades**
a drink with a lemon flavour

lend *VERB* **lends, lending, lent**
❶ to lend something to someone is to let them have it for a short time ❷ when a bank lends someone money it gives them money which they must pay back plus an extra amount called interest
➤ **to lend a hand** is to help someone

length *NOUN* **lengths**
❶ how long something is • *We measured the length of the footprint.* ❷ a piece of something cut from a longer piece • *a length of sewing thread* ❸ the distance of a swimming pool from one end to the other
➤ **at length** after a while; eventually
SPELLING ALERT! The word **length** has a letter **g** in it, just like the adjective **long**.

lengthen *VERB* **lengthens, lengthening, lengthened**
❶ to lengthen something is to make it longer ❷ to lengthen is to become longer

lengthways, lengthwise *ADVERB*
from end to end; along the longest part of something • *Slice the carrots lengthways.*

lengthy *ADJECTIVE* **lengthier, lengthiest**
going on for a long time • *He gave a lengthy speech.*

lenient (*say* lee-ni-ent) *ADJECTIVE*
not as strict as expected, especially when punishing someone

lens *NOUN* **lenses**
❶ a curved piece of glass or plastic used to focus images of things, or to concentrate light ❷ the transparent part of the eye, behind the pupil
DID YOU KNOW? The word **lens** comes from a Latin word meaning 'lentil', because of its round shape, like a lentil or small bean.

Lent *NOUN*
Lent is a period of forty days before Easter when some Christians give up something they enjoy.

lent *VERB* (*past tense and past participle of* **lend**)
• *My sister lent me her dress for the party.*
• *Dad had lent him £5 yesterday.*

lentil *NOUN* **lentils**
a kind of small bean

leopard (*say* **lep**-erd) *NOUN* **leopards**
a large spotted wild animal of the cat family

leotard (*say* lee-o-tard) *NOUN* **leotards**
a close-fitting piece of clothing worn by acrobats and dancers
DID YOU KNOW? A **leotard** is named after a French trapeze artist called *Leotard*, who invented it.

leprechaun *NOUN* **leprechauns**
in Irish mythology, a leprechaun is a mischievous creature that looks like a little old man

a
b
c
d
e
f
g
h
i
j
k
l
m
n
o
p
q
r
s
t
u
v
w
x
y
z

less *DETERMINER, ADVERB*
smaller; not so much • *Please make less noise.*
• *My foot is less painful now.*

less *PRONOUN*
a smaller amount • *I have less than you.*

less *PREPOSITION*
minus; deducting • *I have three pounds, less the pound I owe my brother.*

lessen *VERB* **lessens, lessening, lessened**
❶ to lessen something is to make it smaller or not so much ❷ to lessen is to become smaller or not so much

lesser *ADJECTIVE*
smaller or less great • *The high king ruled over the lesser kings.*

lesson *NOUN* **lessons**
❶ the time when someone is teaching you ❷ something that you have to learn ❸ a passage from the Bible read aloud as part of a church service

lest *CONJUNCTION* (*old use*)
so that something should not happen • *He ran away lest he should be seen.*

let *VERB* **lets, letting, let**
❶ to let someone do something is to allow them to do it ❷ to let something happen is to cause it or not prevent it • *Don't let your bike slide into the ditch.* ❸ to let a house or room or building is to allow someone to use it in return for payment ❹ to let someone in or out is to allow them to go in or out
➤ **to let on** (*informal*) is to reveal a secret • *If I tell you, don't let on.*
➤ **to let someone down** is to disappoint them
➤ **to let someone off** is to excuse them from a punishment or duty
➤ **to let something off** is to make it explode
➤ **to let up** is to relax or do less work

lethal *ADJECTIVE*
something that is lethal can kill you

let's *VERB* (*informal*)
shall we? • *Let's go to the park.*

letter *NOUN* **letters**
❶ one of the symbols used for writing words, such as *a*, *b* or *c*. There are 26 letters in the English alphabet. ❷ a written message sent to another person

letter box *NOUN* **letter boxes**
a box or slot into which letters are delivered or posted

lettering *NOUN*
lettering is letters drawn or painted

lettuce *NOUN* **lettuces**
a green vegetable with crisp leaves used in salads

leukaemia (*say* lew-**kee**-mi-a) *NOUN*
a serious illness in which there are too many white cells in a person's blood

level *ADJECTIVE*
❶ flat or horizontal • *The ground is level near the house.* ❷ at the same height or position • *Are these pictures level?*

level *VERB* **levels, levelling, levelled**
❶ to level something is to make it flat or horizontal ❷ to level, or to level out, is to become horizontal ❸ to level a gun at a target is to aim it

level *NOUN* **levels**
❶ height or position • *Fix the shelf at eye level.* ❷ a standard or grade of achievement • *She has reached level 3 in gymnastics.* ❸ a device that shows if something is horizontal ❹ a flat or horizontal surface

level crossing *NOUN* **level crossings**
a place where a road crosses a railway at the same level

lever *NOUN* **levers**
a bar that is pushed or pulled to lift something heavy, force something open or make a machine work

liability *NOUN* **liabilities**
❶ liability is being responsible for something ❷ a liability is also a disadvantage or handicap

liable *ADJECTIVE*
❶ likely to do or get something • *Loud noises are liable to upset her.* • *Parking on the yellow lines makes you liable to a fine.* ❷ responsible for something • *The company is not liable for damage during delivery.*

liar *NOUN* **liars**
someone who tells lies

liberal *ADJECTIVE*
❶ tolerant of other people's point of view
❷ generous • *She is liberal with her money.*
➤ **Liberal** a supporter of the Liberal Party, now part of the Liberal Democrats
➤ **liberally** *ADVERB* in large amounts or generously • *Apply the suncream liberally.*

liberate *VERB* **liberates, liberating, liberated**
to liberate someone is to set them free
➤ **liberation** *NOUN*

liberty *NOUN* **liberties**
liberty is freedom
➤ **to take liberties** is to behave too casually or informally

librarian *NOUN* **librarians**
someone who looks after a library or works in one

library *NOUN* **libraries**
a place where books are kept for people to use or borrow

lice *NOUN* (*plural of* **louse**)

licence *NOUN* **licences**
an official document allowing someone to do or use or own something • *a valid TV licence*

SPELLING ALERT! Licence is a noun whereas license is a verb: *Is this software licensed?*

license *VERB* **licenses, licensing, licensed**
to license someone to do something is to give them a licence to do it • *The ship was not licensed to carry passengers.*

lichen (*say* **ly**-ken) *NOUN* **lichens**
a dry-looking plant that grows on rocks, walls, trees and other surfaces

lick *VERB* **licks, licking, licked**
❶ to lick something is to move your tongue over it ❷ (*informal*) to lick someone is to defeat them

lick *NOUN* **licks**
the act of moving your tongue over something

lid *NOUN* **lids**
❶ a cover for a box or jar ❷ an eyelid

lido (*say* **lee**-doh) *NOUN* **lidos**
a public open-air swimming pool

lie *VERB* **lies, lying, lay, lain**
❶ to lie is to be in or get into a flat position, especially to rest with your body flat as it is in bed • *She lay on the grass.* • *The cat had lain there all night.* ❷ to lie is to be or remain a certain way • *The castle was lying in ruins.* • *The valley lay before us.*
➤ **to lie low** is to keep yourself hidden

lie *VERB* **lies, lying, lied**
to lie is to say something that you know is not true • *I could tell he was lying.*

lie *NOUN* **lies**
something you say that you know is not true • *That's a lie!*

lieutenant (*say* lef-**ten**-ant) *NOUN* **lieutenants**
an officer in the army or navy

life *NOUN* **lives**
❶ a person's or animal's life is the time between their birth and death ❷ life is being alive and able to grow ❸ life is also all living things • *Is there life on Mars?* ❹ life is also liveliness • *She is full of life.* ❺ the life of a famous person is the story of what they have done

lifebelt *NOUN* **lifebelts**
a large ring that will float, used to support someone's body in water

lifeboat *NOUN* **lifeboats**
a boat for rescuing people at sea

life cycle *NOUN* **life cycles**
the series of changes in the life of a living thing • *The diagram shows the life cycle of a frog.*

lifeguard *NOUN* **lifeguards**
someone whose job is to rescue swimmers who are in difficulty

life jacket *NOUN* **life jackets**
a jacket of material that will float, used to support a person in water

lifeless *ADJECTIVE*
❶ without life ❷ unconscious

lifelike *ADJECTIVE*
looking exactly like a real person or thing

lifelong *ADJECTIVE*
lasting throughout someone's life

lifespan *NOUN* lifespans
how long a person or animal or plant lives

lifestyle *NOUN* lifestyles
the way of life of a person or a group of people

lifetime *NOUN* lifetimes
the period of time during which someone is alive

lift *VERB* lifts, lifting, lifted
❶ to lift something is to pick it up or move it to a higher position ❷ to lift is to rise or go upwards

lift *NOUN* lifts
❶ a movement upwards ❷ a device for taking people or goods from one floor to another in a building ❸ a ride in someone else's car or other vehicle

lift-off *NOUN* lift-offs
when a rocket or spacecraft takes off

light *NOUN* lights
❶ light is the form of energy that makes things visible, the opposite of darkness • *We set off in the early light of dawn.* ❷ a light is something that provides light or a flame, especially an electric lamp • *Switch on the light.*

light *ADJECTIVE* lighter, lightest
❶ full of light; not dark • *a light and airy room* ❷ pale • *a light shade of blue* ❸ not heavy; weighing little • *My suitcase is lighter than yours.* ❹ not large or strong • *We ate a light meal.* • *There is a light wind.* ❺ not needing much effort • *a bit of light housework* ❻ pleasant and entertaining rather than serious • *some light holiday reading*
➤ **lightness** *NOUN*

light *VERB* lights, lighting, lit *or* lighted
❶ to light something is to start it burning • *We lit the candles on the cake.* ❷ to light is to begin to burn • *The fire won't light.* ❸ to light a place is to give it light • *The streets were brightly lit.*
➤ **to light up** is to become bright with lights
➤ **to light something up** is to make it bright with lights

light bulb *NOUN* light bulbs
the glass part of an electric light, with a wire inside that glows when you switch it on

lighten *VERB* lightens, lightening, lightened
❶ to lighten something is to make it lighter or brighter ❷ to lighten is to become lighter

lighter *NOUN* lighters
a device for lighting something like a cigarette or a fire

light-hearted *ADJECTIVE*
❶ cheerful; free from worry ❷ not serious
➤ **light-heartedly** *ADVERB*
➤ **light-heartedness** *NOUN*

lighthouse *NOUN* lighthouses
a tower with a bright light at the top to guide ships and warn them of danger

lighting *NOUN*
lighting is lamps or the light they provide

lightly *ADVERB*
gently or only a little • *It began to snow lightly.*

lightning *NOUN*
lightning is a flash of bright light in the sky during a thunderstorm

lightning conductor *NOUN*
lightning conductors
a metal wire or rod fixed on a building to divert lightning into the earth

lightweight *ADJECTIVE*
less than average weight

light year *NOUN* light years
the distance that light travels in one year (about 9.5 million million kilometres or 6 million million miles)

like *VERB* likes, liking, liked
to like someone or something is to think they are pleasant or satisfactory
➤ **should like** *or* **would like** to want • *I should like to see him.*

like *PREPOSITION*
❶ resembling or similar to; in the manner of • *He cried like a baby.* ❷ such as • *We need things like knives and forks.* ❸ typical of • *It was like her to forgive him.*

likeable *ADJECTIVE*
pleasant and easy to like

A B C D E F G H I J K L M N O P Q R S T U V W X Y Z

likelihood *NOUN*
the chance of something happening • *There's a strong likelihood that we will lose.*

likely *ADJECTIVE* likelier, likeliest
probable; expected to happen or to be true or suitable • *It's likely that it will rain this afternoon.*

liken *VERB* likens, likening, likened
to liken one thing to another is to compare them or show that they are similar

likeness *NOUN* likenesses
a resemblance

likewise *ADVERB*
similarly; in the same way

liking *NOUN* likings
a feeling that you like something or someone • *She has a great liking for chocolate.*

lilac *NOUN* lilacs
❶ lilac is a bush with sweet-smelling purple or white flowers ❷ a pale purple colour

lily *NOUN* lilies
a trumpet-shaped flower grown from a bulb

limb *NOUN* limbs
a leg, arm or wing

limber *VERB* limbers, limbering, limbered
➤ **to limber up** is to do exercises to be ready for a sport or athletic activity

limbo *NOUN*
❶ to be in limbo is to be waiting uncertainly for something to happen ❷ a Caribbean dance in which people bend backwards to pass under a low bar

lime *NOUN* limes
❶ a lime is a green fruit like a small round lemon ❷ a lime is also a tree with yellow blossom ❸ lime is a white chalky powder (calcium oxide) used in making cement or as a fertilizer

limelight *NOUN*
➤ **to be in the limelight** is to get a lot of publicity and attention

limerick *(say* lim-er-ik) *NOUN* limericks
an amusing poem with five lines and a strong rhythm

limestone *NOUN*
limestone is rock from which lime (calcium oxide) is made, used in building and in making cement

limit *NOUN* limits
❶ a line or point that you cannot or should not pass • *You must obey the speed limit.* ❷ a line or edge where something ends • *The white line marks the limit of the road.*

limit *VERB* limits, limiting, limited
to limit something or someone is to keep them within a limit • *You are limited to one choice each.*
➤ **limitation** *NOUN* a thing that stops something or someone from going beyond a certain point

limited *ADJECTIVE*
kept within limits; not great • *The choice of colours was limited.*

limp *VERB* limps, limping, limped
to limp is to walk with difficulty because something is wrong with your leg or foot

limp *NOUN* limps
a limping movement

limp *ADJECTIVE* limper, limpest
not stiff or firm; without much strength • *He gave me a limp handshake.*
➤ **limply** *ADVERB*

limpet *NOUN* limpets
a small shellfish that attaches itself firmly to rocks

line *NOUN* lines
❶ a long thin mark made on a surface ❷ a row or series of people or things ❸ a length of something long and thin like rope, string or wire ❹ a number of words together in a play, film, poem or song ❺ a railway or a length of railway track ❻ a way of working or behaving; a type of business • *What line are you in?*
➤ **in line** ❶ forming a straight line ❷ obeying or behaving well

line *VERB* lines, lining, lined
❶ to line something is to mark it with lines ❷ to line a place is to form an edge or border along it • *People lined the streets to watch the race.* ❸ to line material or a piece of clothing is to put a lining on it

➤ to line up is to form lines or rows
• *Each class lined up in the playground.*
➤ to line things up is to set them up in a line or row

line graph NOUN **line graphs**
a simple graph, using a line to show how two amounts are related

linen NOUN
❶ linen is cloth made from flax, used to make shirts, sheets, tablecloths and so on ❷ linen is also things made of this cloth

liner NOUN **liners**
a large ship or aircraft, usually carrying passengers

linesman, **lineswoman** NOUN **linesmen**, **lineswomen**
an official in football, tennis and other games who decides whether the ball has crossed a line; a referee's assistant

linger VERB **lingers**, **lingering**, **lingered**
to linger is to stay for a long time or be slow to leave • *The smell of her perfume lingered in the room.*

linguist NOUN **linguists**
an expert in languages, or someone who can speak several languages well
➤ linguistic ADJECTIVE to do with languages

lining NOUN **linings**
a layer of material covering the inside of something

link NOUN **links**
❶ one of the rings in a chain ❷ a connection between two things
link VERB **links**, **linking**, **linked**
to link things is to join them together

lino NOUN
lino is linoleum

lint NOUN
lint is a soft material for covering wounds

lion NOUN **lions**
a large strong flesh-eating animal found in Africa and India

lioness NOUN **lionesses**
a female lion

lip NOUN **lips**
❶ each of the two fleshy edges of the mouth ❷ the edge of something hollow such as a cup or a crater ❸ the pointed part at the top of a jug or saucepan, for pouring from

lip-read VERB **lip-reads**, **lip-reading**, **lip-read**
to lip-read is to understand what someone is saying by watching the movements of their lips, not by hearing their voice

lipstick NOUN **lipsticks**
a stick of a waxy substance for colouring the lips

liquid NOUN **liquids**
a substance (such as water or oil) that can flow but is not a gas
liquid ADJECTIVE
in the form of a liquid; flowing freely

liquidizer (*also* **liquidiser**) NOUN **liquidizers**
a device for making food into a pulp or a liquid

liquorice (*say* lik-er-iss) NOUN
liquorice is a soft black sweet with a strong taste, which comes from the root of a plant

lisp NOUN **lisps**
a difficulty in pronouncing some sounds, in which *s* and *z* are pronounced like *th*
lisp VERB **lisps**, **lisping**, **lisped**
to lisp is to speak with a lisp

list NOUN **lists**
a number of names or figures or items written or printed one after another
list VERB **lists**, **listing**, **listed**
❶ to list things is to write or say them one after another ❷ a ship lists when it leans over to one side in the water

listen VERB **listens**, **listening**, **listened**
to listen to someone or something is to pay attention so that you can hear them
• *Listen to me.* • *I like listening to music.*
➤ listener NOUN

listless ADJECTIVE
too tired to be active or enthusiastic
➤ listlessly ADVERB

lit *VERB* (*past tense and past participle of* **light**)
• *Her face lit up.* • *They had lit a bonfire.*

literacy (*say* lit-er-a-see) *NOUN*
literacy is the ability to read and write

literal *ADJECTIVE*
❶ meaning exactly what it says ❷ word for word • *Is that a literal translation?*

literally *ADVERB*
really; exactly as stated • *The noise made me literally jump out of my seat.*

literary (*say* lit-er-er-ee) *ADJECTIVE*
to do with literature; interested in literature

literate (*say* lit-er-at) *ADJECTIVE*
able to read and write

literature *NOUN*
literature is books or writing, especially the best or most famous

litre (*say* lee-ter) *NOUN* **litres**
a measure of liquid, 1,000 cubic centimetres or about 1¾ pints

litter *NOUN* **litters**
❶ litter is rubbish or untidy things left lying about ❷ a litter is a number of young animals born to one mother at one time
litter *VERB* **litters, littering, littered**
to litter a place is to make it untidy with litter

little *ADJECTIVE*
❶ small in size; not great or big • *The box was filled with little scraps of paper.* ❷ short in time or length • *She rang a little while later.* ❸ younger • *I have a little brother and a big sister.*
little *DETERMINER, PRONOUN* **less, least**
❶ not much • *We have very little time.* • *I have little to say.* ❷ a small amount of something • *Would you like a little milk?*
➤ **little by little** gradually
little *ADVERB* **less, least**
hardly or not at all • *Her books are little known these days.*

live (*rhymes with* **give**) *VERB* **lives, living, lived**
❶ to live is to be alive ❷ to live in a particular place is to have your home there • *She is living*

in Sweden now. ❸ to live in a certain way is to pass your life in that way • *He lived for many years as a hermit.*
➤ **to live on something** is to have it as food or income • *The islanders lived mainly on fish.* • *No one can live on £20 a week.*

live (*rhymes with* **hive**) *ADJECTIVE*
❶ alive ❷ carrying electricity ❸ broadcast while it is actually happening, not from a recording

livelihood *NOUN* **livelihoods**
a person's livelihood is the way in which they earn a living

lively *ADJECTIVE* **livelier, liveliest**
cheerful and full of life and energy
➤ **liveliness** *NOUN*
DID YOU KNOW? There is no adverb *livelily*, because it would be too difficult to say!

liver *NOUN* **livers**
❶ a large organ in the body that produces bile and helps keep the blood clean ❷ an animal's liver used as food

lives *NOUN* (*plural of* **life**)

livestock *NOUN*
livestock is farm animals

livid *ADJECTIVE*
❶ very angry ❷ of a dark blue-grey colour, like bruised skin

living *NOUN* **livings**
❶ the way that a person lives • *They have a good standard of living.* ❷ a means of earning money • *What do your parents do for a living?*

living room *NOUN* **living rooms**
a room for sitting and relaxing in

lizard *NOUN* **lizards**
a reptile with a scaly skin, four legs and a long tail

llama (*say* lah-ma) *NOUN* **llamas**
a South American animal with woolly fur

load *NOUN* **loads**
❶ something that is being carried
❷ an amount that can be carried
❸ (*informal*) a large amount • *It's a load of nonsense.*

a
b
c
d
e
f
g
h
i
j
k
l
m
n
o
p
q
r
s
t
u
v
w
x
y
z

load *VERB* **loads, loading, loaded**
❶ to load something is to put things into it so they can be carried • *I'll go and load the back of the car.* ❷ to load someone with something is to give them large amounts of it • *They loaded him with gifts.* ❸ to load a gun is to put a bullet or shell into it ❹ to load a machine is to put something into it, such as dishes in a dishwasher ❺ to load a computer is to enter programs or data on it ❻ to load dice is to put a weight into them to make them fall in a special way

loaf *NOUN* **loaves**
a shaped mass of bread baked in one piece
loaf *VERB* **loafs, loafing, loafed**
to loaf, or loaf about, is to loiter or waste time

loam *NOUN*
loam is rich fertile soil

loan *NOUN* **loans**
something that has been lent to someone, especially money
➤ **on loan** being lent • *The books are on loan from the library.*
loan *VERB* **loans, loaning, loaned**
to loan something is to lend it

loath (*rhymes with* **both**) *ADJECTIVE*
unwilling • *I was loath to go.*

loathe (*rhymes with* **clothe**) *VERB* **loathes, loathing, loathed**
to loathe something or someone is to dislike them very much

loathsome *ADJECTIVE*
something loathsome is horrible and makes you feel disgusted
'Now you've done it, you loathsome pest!' whispered the Earthworm to the Centipede.—JAMES AND THE GIANT PEACH, Roald Dahl

loaves *NOUN* (*plural of* **loaf**)

lob *VERB* **lobs, lobbing, lobbed**
to lob something is to throw or hit it high into the air

lobby *NOUN* **lobbies**
an entrance hall
lobby *VERB* **lobbies, lobbying, lobbied**
to lobby politicians is to try to influence their thinking on a particular issue

lobe *NOUN* **lobes**
the rounded part at the bottom of the ear

lobster *NOUN* **lobsters**
a large shellfish with eight legs and two claws

local *ADJECTIVE*
❶ belonging to a particular place or area • *Where is your local library?* ❷ affecting a certain part of the body • *You'll need a local anaesthetic.*
➤ **locally** *ADVERB* to live or shop locally is to do so nearby, in the area where you are
local *NOUN* **locals** (*informal*)
❶ a local is someone who lives in a particular district ❷ someone's local is the pub nearest their home

locality *NOUN* **localities**
a place and the area that surrounds it

locate *VERB* **locates, locating, located**
❶ to locate something is to discover where it is • *I have located the fault.* ❷ to be located in a place is to be situated there • *The cinema is located in the High Street.*

location *NOUN* **locations**
the place where something is • *What is the exact location of the submarine?*
➤ When a film is filmed **on location**, it is filmed in natural surroundings, not in a studio.

loch *NOUN* **lochs**
a lake in Scotland • *a boat trip on the loch*

lock *NOUN* **locks**
❶ a fastening that you open with a key or other device ❷ a section of a canal or river with gates at each end, so that the level of water can be raised or lowered to allow boats to pass through ❸ a lock is also a few strands of hair formed into a loop
➤ **lock, stock and barrel** completely
lock *VERB* **locks, locking, locked**
❶ to lock a door or window or lid is to fasten or secure it with a lock ❷ to lock something somewhere is to put it in a safe place that can be fastened with a lock ❸ to lock is to become fixed in one place, or to jam

lockdown *NOUN* **lockdowns**
❶ an order forbidding people from entering

or leaving a building because of a dangerous situation ❷ a time when large numbers of people are ordered to stay at home

locker *NOUN* **lockers**
a small cupboard for keeping things safe, often in a changing room

locket *NOUN* **lockets**
a small case holding a photograph or lock of hair, worn on a chain round the neck

locomotive *NOUN* **locomotives**
a railway engine

locust *NOUN* **locusts**
an insect like a large grasshopper, which flies in swarms that eat all the plants in an area

lodge *NOUN* **lodges**
❶ a small house ❷ a room or small house at the entrance to a large house or building ❸ the den of a beaver

lodge *VERB* **lodges, lodging, lodged**
❶ to lodge is to become fixed or get stuck somewhere • *The ball lodged in the branches.* ❷ to lodge somewhere is to stay there as a lodger ❸ to lodge someone is to give them a place to sleep
➤ **to lodge a complaint** is to make an official complaint

lodger *NOUN* **lodgers**
someone who pays to live in someone else's house

lodgings *PLURAL NOUN*
a room or set of rooms that a person rents in someone else's house

loft *NOUN* **lofts**
the room or space under the roof of a house

lofty *ADJECTIVE* **loftier, loftiest**
❶ high or tall ❷ noble and proud • *They have lofty ideas.*
➤ **loftily** *ADVERB* in a proud haughty way

log *NOUN* **logs**
❶ a large piece of a tree that has fallen or been cut down ❷ a detailed record of what happens each day, especially on a journey or voyage

log *VERB* **logs, logging, logged**
to log information is to put it in a log
➤ **to log in** is to gain access to a computer

➤ **to log out** is to finish using a computer

logbook *NOUN* **logbooks**
a book in which a log of a voyage is kept

logic *NOUN*
logic is a system of thinking and working out ideas

logical *ADJECTIVE*
using logic or worked out by logic
➤ **logically** *ADVERB*

logo *NOUN* **logos**
a printed symbol used by a business or other organization as its emblem

loiter *VERB* **loiters, loitering, loitered**
to stand about not doing anything

loll *VERB* **lolls, lolling, lolled**
to sit or lie in an untidy and lazy way

lollipop *NOUN* **lollipops**
a hard sticky sweet on the end of a stick

lollipop man, **lollipop woman** *NOUN* **lollipop men, lollipop women**
an official who uses a circular sign on a stick to signal traffic to stop so that children can cross the road

lolly *NOUN* **lollies** (*informal*)
a lolly is a lollipop or an ice lolly

lone *ADJECTIVE*
on its own; solitary • *a lone rider*

lonely *ADJECTIVE* **lonelier, loneliest**
❶ unhappy because you are on your own ❷ far from other inhabited places; not often used or visited • *They passed through a lonely village.*
➤ **loneliness** *NOUN*

long *ADJECTIVE* **longer, longest**
❶ big when measured from one end to the other • *The cottage was at the end of a long path.* ❷ taking a lot of time • *I'd like to go on a long holiday.* ❸ measuring from one end to the other • *An Olympic swimming pool is 50 metres long.*

long *ADVERB* **longer, longest**
❶ for a long time • *Have you been waiting long?* ❷ a long time before or after • *They left long ago.*
➤ **as long as** *or* **so long as** provided that;

A B C D E F G H I J K L M N O P Q R S T U V W X Y Z

on condition that • *I'll come as long as I can bring a friend.*

long VERB longs, longing, longed
➤ **to long for something** is to want it very much

long division NOUN
long division is dividing one number by another and writing down all the calculations

longitude (say **long**-i-tewd or **lon**-ji-tewd) NOUN longitudes
longitude is the distance of a place east or west, measured in degrees from an imaginary line that passes through Greenwich in London

long jump NOUN
an athletics contest of jumping as far as possible along the ground with one leap

long–range ADJECTIVE
covering a long distance or period of time

longship NOUN longships
a long, narrow Viking warship, powered by oars and sail
Of clean and fresh-smelling oak, the longship was almost eighty feet long, from stern to stern, and sixteen feet broad at her middle.—VIKING'S DAWN, Henry Treece

long–sighted ADJECTIVE
able to see things clearly when they are at a distance but not when they are close

long–term ADJECTIVE
to do with a long period of time

loo NOUN loos (*informal*)
a toilet

look VERB looks, looking, looked
❶ to look is to use your eyes to see something, or to turn your eyes towards something ❷ to look in a particular direction is to face it • *Look right and left before you cross.* ❸ to look (for example) happy or sad is to appear that way
➤ **to look after something** or **someone** is to protect them or take care of them
➤ **to look down on someone** is to despise them
➤ **to look for something** or **someone** is to try to find them

➤ **to look forward to something** is to be waiting eagerly for it to happen
➤ **to look out** is to be careful
➤ **to look up to someone** is to admire or respect them

look NOUN looks
❶ a look is the act of looking • *Take a look at this.* ❷ the expression on someone's face • *She gave me a surprised look.* ❸ the look of someone or something is their appearance • *I don't like the look of that dog.*

look-alike NOUN look-alikes
someone who looks very like a famous person

looking glass NOUN looking glasses (*old use*)
a glass mirror

lookout NOUN lookouts
❶ a place from which you watch for something ❷ someone whose job is to keep watch ❸ watching or being watchful • *Keep a lookout for snakes.* ❹ (*informal*) something that is your lookout is your concern or problem • *It's your lookout if you get hurt.*

loom NOUN looms
a machine for weaving cloth

loom VERB looms, looming, loomed
to loom or loom up is to appear large and threatening • *All of a sudden, a ghostly pirate ship loomed into view.*

loop NOUN loops
the shape made by a curve crossing itself; a piece of string, ribbon or wire made into this shape

loop VERB loops, looping, looped
to loop something is to make it into a loop

loophole NOUN loopholes
❶ a narrow opening ❷ a way of getting round a law or rule without quite breaking it

loose ADJECTIVE looser, loosest
❶ not tight or firmly fixed • *a loose tooth* ❷ not tied up or shut in • *The dog got loose.*
➤ **to be on the loose** is to be free after escaping
➤ **loosely** ADVERB ➤ **looseness** NOUN
SPELLING ALERT! Loose is different from lose, which is a verb: *There is no time to lose!*

loosen *VERB* **loosens, loosening, loosened**
① to loosen something is to make it loose
② to loosen is to become loose

loot *NOUN*
loot is stolen things

loot *VERB* **loots, looting, looted**
to loot a place is to rob it violently, especially during a war or riot
➤ **looter** *NOUN*

lopsided *ADJECTIVE*
uneven, with one side lower than the other
• *She had a lopsided smile.*

lord *NOUN* **lords**
① a nobleman, especially one who is allowed to use the title 'Lord' in front of his name
② (*old use*) a master or ruler
➤ **Our Lord** a name used by Christians for Jesus Christ
➤ **the Lord** a name for God

Lord Mayor *NOUN*
the mayor of a large city

lordship *NOUN*
a title for a lord or a man of high social standing

lorry *NOUN* **lorries**
a large motor vehicle for carrying goods

lose *VERB* **loses, losing, lost**
① to lose something is to no longer have it, especially because you cannot find it
• *I've lost my hat.* ② to lose a contest or game is to be beaten in it • *We lost last Friday's match.* ③ a clock or watch loses when it gives a time that is earlier than the correct time
➤ **to lose your way** is not to know where you are
➤ **loser** *NOUN*

loss *NOUN* **losses**
① losing something ② something you have lost
➤ **to be at a loss** is to be puzzled or unable to do something

lost *VERB* (*past tense and past participle of* **lose**)
• *She lost her balance and fell backwards.*
• *He realized he had lost his phone.*

lost *ADJECTIVE*
① not knowing where you are or not able to find your way • *I think we're lost.* ② missing or strayed • *a lost dog*

lot *NOUN, PRONOUN, ADVERB*
① **a lot** is a large number of people or things
• *A lot of people visited the exhibition.*
• *We have lots of time.* ② **a lot** can also mean very much • *It's a lot warmer today.*
• *Thanks a lot!* ③ a lot is a piece of land
④ at an auction, a lot is one item or group of items for sale
➤ **to draw lots** is to choose one person or thing from a group by a method that depends on chance
➤ **the lot** *or* **the whole lot** everything

loth (*rhymes with* **both**) *ADJECTIVE*
if you are loth to do something, you are very unwilling to do it

lotion *NOUN* **lotions**
a liquid that you put on your skin

lottery *NOUN* **lotteries**
a way of raising money by selling numbered tickets and giving prizes to people who have the winning tickets

loud *ADJECTIVE* **louder, loudest**
① noisy; easily heard ② bright or gaudy
• *The room was painted in loud colours.*
➤ **loudly** *ADVERB* ➤ **loudness** *NOUN*

loudspeaker *NOUN* **loudspeakers**
a device that changes electrical impulses into sound, for reproducing music or voices

lounge *NOUN* **lounges**
a room in a house, hotel or airport for sitting in and relaxing

lounge *VERB* **lounges, lounging, lounged**
to lounge is to sit or stand in a relaxed or lazy way
Sirius was lounging in his chair at his ease, tilting it back on two legs.—HARRY POTTER AND THE ORDER OF THE PHOENIX, J. K. Rowling

louse *NOUN* **lice**
a small insect that sucks the blood of animals or the juices of plants

lout *NOUN* **louts**
a bad-mannered man

a
b
c
d
e
f
g
h
i
j
k
l
m
n
o
p
q
r
s
t
u
v
w
x
y
z

lovable *ADJECTIVE*
someone is lovable when they are easy to love

love *NOUN* **loves**
❶ love is a feeling of liking someone or something very much; great affection or kindness ❷ someone's love is a person or thing that they love ❸ in a game such as tennis, love is a score of nothing
➤ **to be in love** is to love another person very deeply

love *VERB* **loves**, **loving**, **loved**
to love someone or something is to like them very much

lovely *ADJECTIVE* **lovelier**, **loveliest**
❶ beautiful • *That dress is a lovely colour.* ❷ very pleasant or enjoyable • *We had a lovely time.*
➤ **loveliness** *NOUN*

lover *NOUN* **lovers**
someone who loves something • *a music lover*

loving *ADJECTIVE*
feeling or showing love • *a loving son* • *a loving look*
➤ **lovingly** *ADVERB*

low *ADJECTIVE* **lower**, **lowest**
❶ only reaching a short way up; not high • *The garden was enclosed by a low wall.* ❷ below average in amount or importance • *Temperatures have been low for this time of year.* ❸ unhappy • *I've been feeling a bit low recently.* ❹ a low note is one at the bottom end of a musical scale
➤ **lowness** *NOUN*

low *VERB* **lows**, **lowing**, **lowed**
to low is to make a sound like a cow

lower *VERB* **lowers**, **lowering**, **lowered**
to lower something is move it down

lower case *NOUN*
lower case is small letters; not capitals

lowland *ADJECTIVE*
to do with the lowlands

lowlands *PLURAL NOUN*
low-lying country, especially in the south of Scotland

lowly *ADJECTIVE* **lowlier**, **lowliest**
humble
➤ **lowliness** *NOUN*

loyal *ADJECTIVE*
always true to your friends; faithful
➤ **loyally** *ADVERB* ➤ **loyalty** *NOUN*

lozenge *NOUN* **lozenges**
❶ a small sweet tablet, especially one that contains medicine ❷ a diamond-shaped design

lubricant *NOUN* **lubricants**
oil or grease for lubricating machinery

lubricate *VERB* **lubricates**, **lubricating**, **lubricated**
to lubricate part of a machine is to put oil or grease on it so that it moves smoothly
➤ **lubrication** *NOUN*

lucid (*say* loo-sid) *ADJECTIVE*
❶ something is lucid when it is clear and easy to understand ❷ someone is lucid when they are able to think clearly again after being ill

luck *NOUN*
❶ luck is the way things happen by chance, without being planned ❷ luck is also good fortune

luckily *ADVERB*
by a lucky chance; fortunately • *Luckily, it stayed warm all day.*

lucky *ADJECTIVE* **luckier**, **luckiest**
having or bringing good luck

ludicrous (*say* loo-di-krus) *ADJECTIVE*
extremely silly or absurd
➤ **ludicrously** *ADVERB*

ludo *NOUN*
ludo is a game played with dice and counters on a board

lug *VERB* **lugs**, **lugging**, **lugged**
to lug something heavy is to carry it or drag it with difficulty

luge (*say* loozh) *NOUN* **luges**
a light toboggan for one or two people

luggage *NOUN*
luggage is the suitcases and bags you take on a journey

lukewarm *ADJECTIVE*
❶ slightly warm
The fish fingers were lukewarm to start with and so undercooked that I couldn't help imagining the cold slimy little things still had tails and fins. —HOW TO SURVIVE SUMMER CAMP, Jacqueline Wilson
❷ not very keen or enthusiastic • *They got a lukewarm response.*

lull *VERB* **lulls**, **lulling**, **lulled**
to lull someone is to soothe or calm them

lull *NOUN* **lulls**
a short period of quiet or rest • *There was a lull in the fighting.*

lullaby *NOUN* **lullabies**
a song that you sing to send a baby to sleep

lumber *NOUN*
lumber is unwanted furniture or other things

lumber *VERB* **lumbers**, **lumbering**, **lumbered**
❶ to lumber is to move along clumsily and heavily
A shadow under the trees moved and came lumbering out into the sunlight towards us. A monkey, a giant monkey.—KENSUKE'S KINGDOM, Michael Morpurgo
❷ (*informal*) to lumber someone is to leave them with something unpleasant or difficult to do

lumberjack *NOUN* **lumberjacks**
someone whose job is to cut down trees or transport them

luminous (*say* loo-mi-nus) *ADJECTIVE*
shining or glowing in the dark • *a jellyfish with luminous tentacles*
➤ **luminosity** *NOUN*

lump *NOUN* **lumps**
❶ a solid piece of something • *a lump of ice*
❷ a swelling or bump

lump *VERB* **lumps**, **lumping**, **lumped**
to lump different things together is to put them together in the same group
➤ **to lump it** (*informal*) is to put up with something you don't like • *You'll have to like it or lump it.*

lumpy *ADJECTIVE* **lumpier**, **lumpiest**
having lots of lumps • *a bowl of lumpy porridge*
➤ **lumpiness** *NOUN*

lunacy (*say* loo-na-see) *NOUN* **lunacies**
lunacy is madness

lunar *ADJECTIVE*
to do with the moon

lunatic (*say* loo-na-tik) *NOUN* **lunatics**
(considered offensive) a person who is mentally ill

lunch *NOUN* **lunches**
a meal eaten in the middle of the day

lung *NOUN* **lungs**
each of the two organs in your chest, used for breathing

lunge *VERB* **lunges**, **lunging**, **lunged**
to make a sudden movement forwards
Just as the creature lunged forwards to kill him, Hiccup was grabbed around the ankle ... and pulled back through the hole he had climbed in.—HOW TO BE A PIRATE, Cressida Cowell

lupin *NOUN* **lupins**
a garden plant with tall spikes of flowers

lurch *VERB* **lurches**, **lurching**, **lurched**
to lurch is to stagger or lean suddenly

lurch *NOUN* **lurches**
a sudden staggering or leaning movement
➤ **to leave someone in the lurch** is to desert them when they are in difficulty

lure *VERB* **lures**, **luring**, **lured**
to lure a person or animal is to tempt them into a trap or difficulty

lurid *ADJECTIVE*
a lurid colour is very bright and harsh

lurk *VERB* **lurks**, **lurking**, **lurked**
to lurk is to wait quietly where you cannot be seen

luscious (*say* lush-us) *ADJECTIVE*
tasting or smelling delicious
He would buy one luscious bar of chocolate and eat it all up, every bit of it, right then and there.—CHARLIE AND THE CHOCOLATE FACTORY, Roald Dahl

lush *ADJECTIVE* **lusher**, **lushest**
growing thickly and healthily
Below the garden a green field lush with clover sloped down to the hollow where the brook ran and where scores of white birches grew.—ANNE OF GREEN GABLES, L. M. Montgomery

a b c d e f g h i j k l m n o p q r s t u v w x y z

lustre (*say* lus-ter) *NOUN* **lustres**
the lustre of something is its brightness or brilliance

lustrous *ADJECTIVE*
shiny or bright

lute *NOUN* **lutes**
a musical instrument rather like a guitar but with a deeper and rounder body, which was popular in the Middle Ages
➤ **lutenist** *NOUN*

luxurious *ADJECTIVE*
something, like a hotel, that is luxurious is very comfortable and expensive

luxury *NOUN* **luxuries**
❶ a luxury is something expensive that you enjoy but do not really need ❷ luxury is having a very comfortable and expensive lifestyle • *They led a life of luxury.*

Lycra *NOUN* (*trademark*)
Lycra is a thin stretchy material used especially for sports clothing.

lying *VERB* (*present participle of* **lie**)
• *Her clothes were lying in a heap.*
• *I know you're lying to me.*

lynch *VERB* **lynches**, **lynching**, **lynched**
to lynch someone is to execute them without a proper trial

lynx (*say* links) *NOUN* **lynxes**
a wild animal like a very large cat

lyre *NOUN* **lyres**
an ancient musical instrument like a small harp

lyrical *ADJECTIVE*
sounding like a song or a poem

lyrics *PLURAL NOUN*
the words of a popular song

Mm

m *ABBREVIATION*
short for *metres, miles* or *millions*

ma *NOUN* **mas** (*informal*)
mother

macabre (*say* mak-ahbr) *ADJECTIVE*
strange and horrible • *a macabre tale about zombies*

macaroni *NOUN*
macaroni is pasta in the shape of short tubes

macaw *NOUN* **macaws**
a large parrot with brightly coloured feathers and a long tail

machine *NOUN* **machines**
a piece of equipment made of moving parts that work together to make or do something
The Professor ... took out a toothpick, a marmalade spoon and a pair of scissors, and soon had the machine wound up and adjusted ready to start.
—PROFESSOR BRANESTAWM STORIES, Norman Hunter

machine gun *NOUN* **machine guns**
a gun that can keep firing bullets quickly one after another

machinery *NOUN*
❶ the working parts of a machine ❷ machines in general

mackerel *NOUN* **mackerel**
an edible sea fish with greenish-blue skin

mad *ADJECTIVE* **madder**, **maddest**
❶ (may cause offence) mentally ill; not sane ❷ very foolish • *That's a mad idea!* ❸ (*informal*) very keen or enthusiastic • *Rhona is mad about fossils.* ❹ (*informal*) very angry • *Are you still mad at me?*
➤ **like mad** (*informal*) with great speed, energy or enthusiasm
➤ **madly** *ADVERB* ➤ **madness** *NOUN*

madam *NOUN*
a word sometimes used when speaking or writing politely to a woman, instead of her name • *Can I help you, madam?*

madden VERB maddens, maddening, maddened
to madden someone is to make them mad or angry

made VERB (past tense and past participle of make)
• We made a giant sandcastle. • I think you've made a mistake.

madly ADVERB
with energy or enthusiasm • Someone was waving madly from the window.

magazine NOUN magazines
❶ a publication with articles or stories, which comes out regularly ❷ the part of a gun that holds the cartridges

magenta (say ma-jen-ta) NOUN
a reddish-purple colour

maggot NOUN maggots
the larva of some kinds of fly
➤ maggoty ADJECTIVE full of maggots

magic NOUN
❶ magic is the power to make impossible things happen
A witch never gets caught. Don't forget that she has magic in her fingers and devilry dancing in her blood.—THE WITCHES, Roald Dahl
❷ magic is also performing clever tricks

magic VERB magicks, magicking, magicked
to make something happen by using magic
• She magicked the mouse away with a flick of her wand.

magical ADJECTIVE
❶ done by magic or using magic • a book of magical charms and potions ❷ wonderful; marvellous • It was a magical evening.
➤ magically ADVERB

magician NOUN magicians
❶ someone who does magic tricks ❷ a person with magic powers; a wizard
There were magicians in the forest also in those days, as well as strange animals not known to modern works of natural history.—THE SWORD IN THE STONE, T. H. White

magisterial ADJECTIVE
showing power or authority • a magisterial tone of voice

magistrate NOUN magistrates
a judge in a local court who deals with some less serious cases

magma NOUN
magma is the molten substance beneath the earth's crust
SPOT THE DIFFERENCE! Magma is found under the ground, but **lava** is found above ground.

magnesium NOUN
magnesium is a silver-white metal that burns with a very bright flame

magnet NOUN magnets
a piece of metal that can attract iron or steel and that points north and south when it is hung in the air
➤ magnetism NOUN the attraction of a magnet

magnetic ADJECTIVE
❶ having or using the powers of a magnet
❷ strongly attractive, like a magnet
• a magnetic personality

magnetize (also **magnetise**) VERB magnetizes, magnetizing, magnetized
to magnetize something is to make it into a magnet

magnificent ADJECTIVE
❶ looking splendid or impressive
• a magnificent head of hair ❷ excellent
• a magnificent performance
➤ magnificence NOUN
➤ magnificently ADVERB

magnify VERB magnifies, magnifying, magnified
to magnify something is to make it look bigger than it really is
➤ magnification NOUN

magnifying glass NOUN magnifying glasses
a lens that magnifies things

magnitude NOUN magnitudes
magnitude is how large or important something is

magnolia NOUN magnolias
a tree with large white or pale pink flowers

magpie NOUN magpies
a black and white bird, related to the crow

a b c d e f g h i j k l m n o p q r s t u v w x y z

mahogany (*say* ma-**hog**-a-nee) *NOUN*
mahogany is a hard brown wood used for making furniture

maid *NOUN* **maids**
❶ a female servant ❷ (*old use*) a girl

maiden *NOUN* **maidens** (*old use*)
a girl

maiden name *NOUN* **maiden names**
the original family name of a woman who changed her family name after getting married

mail *NOUN*
❶ mail is letters and parcels sent by post, or messages sent by email ❷ mail is also armour made of metal rings joined together
mail *VERB* **mails, mailing, mailed**
to mail something is to send it by post or by email

mailbox *NOUN* **mailboxes**
a postbox

maim *VERB* **maims, maiming, maimed**
to maim someone is to injure them so badly that part of their body is damaged for life

main *ADJECTIVE*
largest or most important
main (*also* **the mains**) *NOUN*
the main pipe or cable in a system carrying water, gas or electricity to a building

main clause *NOUN* **main clauses**
a clause which can be used as a complete sentence

mainland *NOUN*
the main part of a country or continent, not the islands around it • *a tour of the Canadian mainland*

mainly *ADVERB*
chiefly or usually; almost completely

maintain *VERB* **maintains, maintaining, maintained**
❶ to maintain something is to keep it in good condition ❷ to maintain a belief is to have it or state it • *I maintain that animals should not be hunted.*
➤ **maintenance** *NOUN*

maize *NOUN*
maize is a tall kind of corn with large seeds

majestic *ADJECTIVE*
stately and dignified • *She welcomed us with a majestic nod of her head.*
➤ **majestically** *ADVERB*

majesty *NOUN* **majesties**
❶ the title of a king or queen
The White Rabbit put on his spectacles. 'Where shall I begin, please your Majesty?' he asked.—ALICE'S ADVENTURES IN WONDERLAND, Lewis Carroll
❷ majesty is the quality of being stately and dignified

major *ADJECTIVE*
❶ very large or important; main • *This is a major emergency!* ❷ of the musical scale that has a semitone between the 3rd and 4th notes and between the 7th and 8th notes
major *NOUN* **majors**
an army officer above captain in rank

majority (*say* ma-**jo**-ri-tee) *NOUN* **majorities**
❶ the greatest part of a group of people or things; more than half • *The majority of the class wanted a quiz.* ❷ the amount by which the winner in an election beats the loser • *She won with a majority of only ten votes.* ❸ the age at which a person becomes legally an adult, now usually 18

make *VERB* **makes, making, made**
❶ to make something is to build or produce it • *They are making a raft out of logs.* ❷ to make someone or something do something is to cause it to happen • *The bang made him jump.* ❸ to make money is to get it or earn it • *She makes £30,000 a year.* ❹ in a game, to make a score is to achieve it • *He has made 20 runs so far.* ❺ to make a certain point is to reach it • *The swimmer just made the shore.* ❻ to make something is to estimate it or reckon it • *What do you make the time?* ❼ several numbers make a total when they add up to it • *4 and 6 make 10.* ❽ to make (for example) a suggestion or promise is to give it to someone ❾ to make a bed is to tidy it or arrange it for use
➤ **to make someone's day** is to cause them to be happy or successful
➤ **to make do** is to manage with something that is not what you really want
➤ **to make for a place** is to go towards it
➤ **to make off** is to leave quickly

make to manageable

➤ **to make something** *or* **someone out** is to manage to see or hear or understand them
➤ **to make something up** is to invent a false story or excuse
➤ **to make up** is to be friendly again after a disagreement
➤ **to make up for something** is to give or do something in return for a loss or difficulty
➤ **to make up your mind** is to decide

make *NOUN* **makes**
❶ how something is made ❷ a brand of goods; something made by a particular firm • *What make of car is that?*

make–believe *NOUN*
make-believe is pretending or imagining things

makeover *NOUN* **makeover**
a complete change in the way that someone or something looks • *The school canteen has been given a makeover.*

maker *NOUN* **makers**
the person or firm that has made something

makeshift *ADJECTIVE*
used because you have nothing better • *We'll use the bed as a makeshift table.*

make–up *NOUN*
❶ make-up is creams and powders for making your skin look beautiful or different ❷ a person's make-up is their character

malaria (*say* ma-**lair**-i-a) *NOUN*
malaria is a tropical disease spread by mosquito bites, that causes fever

Malay *NOUN*
a language spoken in Malaysia and Indonesia
DID YOU KNOW? The words **amok**, **bamboo** and **orangutan** come from Malay.

male *ADJECTIVE*
belonging to the sex that produces young by fertilizing the female's egg cells
male *NOUN* **males**
a male person or animal

malevolent (*say* ma-**lev**-o-lent) *ADJECTIVE*
wanting to harm other people
'A bad idea, Professor Lockhart,' said Snape, gliding over like a large and malevolent bat.
—HARRY POTTER AND THE CHAMBER OF SECRETS, J. K. Rowling
➤ **malevolently** *ADVERB* ➤ **malevolence** *NOUN*

malice (*say* **mal**-iss) *NOUN*
malice is a desire to harm other people

malicious (*say* ma-**lish**-us) *ADJECTIVE*
intending to do harm
➤ **maliciously** *ADVERB*

mall *NOUN* **malls**
a large covered shopping centre

mallet *NOUN* **mallets**
a large wooden hammer

malnutrition *NOUN*
malnutrition is bad health caused by not having enough food
➤ **malnourished** *ADJECTIVE*

malt *NOUN*
malt is dried barley used in brewing and making vinegar

mamba *NOUN* **mambas**
a large poisonous African snake

mammal *NOUN* **mammals**
any animal of which the female gives birth to live young and can feed them with her own milk

mammoth *NOUN* **mammoths**
an extinct kind of hairy elephant with long curved tusks
mammoth *ADJECTIVE*
huge • *It was a mammoth task to dig the tunnel.*

man *NOUN* **men**
❶ a man is a grown-up male human being ❷ man is mankind, or all the people in the world
man *VERB* **mans**, **manning**, **manned**
to man something is to supply people to work at it • *There was no one there to man the kiosk.*

manage *VERB* **manages**, **managing**, **managed**
❶ to manage something is to be able to do it although it is difficult • *I managed to find my way home in the dark.* ❷ to manage a shop or other business is to be in charge of it

manageable *ADJECTIVE*
able to be managed or done

a b c d e f g h i j k l **m** n o p q r s t u v w x y z

management NOUN
❶ management is the process of managing something ❷ the management of a business is the people in charge of it

manager NOUN managers
a person who manages a business or team of people

manatee NOUN manatees
a large greyish sea mammal with flippers and a flat tail

Mandarin NOUN
the main language of China

mandarin NOUN mandarins
a kind of small sweet orange

mandrake NOUN mandrakes
a plant with a thick forked root that sometimes looks like a human shape
'Mandrake, or Mandragora, is a powerful restorative,' said Hermione.—HARRY POTTER AND THE CHAMBER OF SECRETS, J. K. Rowling

DID YOU KNOW? The word **mandrake** comes from a Latin word meaning 'man dragon'.

mane NOUN manes
the long hair along the back of the neck of a horse or lion

man-eating ADJECTIVE
a man-eating animal or creature eats humans • *a monstrous man-eating dragon*

manger (*say* mayn-jer) NOUN mangers
a trough in a stable for animals to feed from

mangle VERB mangles, mangling, mangled
to mangle something is to crush or twist it so it is badly damaged

mango NOUN mangoes
a juicy tropical fruit with yellow or orange pulp

manhandle VERB manhandles, manhandling, manhandled
to manhandle someone or something is to handle them or move them roughly

manhole NOUN manholes
a hole, usually with a cover, through which a person can get into a sewer or boiler to inspect or repair it

mania NOUN manias
❶ mania is a mental illness that involves periods of excitement and over-activity ❷ a mania is a strong enthusiasm • *They have a mania for sport.*

maniac NOUN maniacs
a person who acts in a violent and wild way

manic ADJECTIVE
❶ caused by a mental illness that involves periods of excitement and over-activity ❷ manic behaviour is busy and excited

manipulate VERB manipulates, manipulating, manipulated
❶ to manipulate something is to handle it skilfully ❷ to manipulate someone is to get them to do what you want in a dishonest or skilful way
➤ manipulation NOUN

mankind NOUN
mankind is all the people in the world • *This is a discovery for the good of all mankind.*

manly ADJECTIVE manlier, manliest
❶ strong or brave ❷ thought suitable for a man, or like a man
➤ manliness NOUN

man-made ADJECTIVE
something man-made has been made by humans and not by nature • *a man-made crater*

manner NOUN manners
the way that something happens or is done

manners PLURAL NOUN
a person's manners are how they behave with other people; behaving politely

manoeuvre (*say* ma-noo-ver) NOUN manoeuvres
a skilful or clever action

manoeuvre VERB manoeuvres, manoeuvring, manoeuvred
❶ to manoeuvre something is to move it skilfully into position ❷ to manoeuvre is to move skilfully or cleverly

man-of-war NOUN men-of-war
in earlier times, a warship

manor NOUN manors
a large important house in the country

mansion NOUN mansions
a large stately house

manslaughter (*say* **man**-slaw-ter) *NOUN*
manslaughter is the crime of killing someone without meaning to

mantelpiece *NOUN* **mantelpieces**
a shelf above a fireplace

mantle *NOUN* **mantles**
❶ (*old use*) a cloak ❷ a covering • *There was a mantle of snow on the hills.*

manual *ADJECTIVE*
manual work is work you do with your hands; manual equipment is equipment used with your hands
➤ **manually** *ADVERB*

manual *NOUN* **manuals**
a handbook or book of instructions

manufacture *VERB* **manufactures, manufacturing, manufactured**
to manufacture things is to make them with machines, usually in a factory

manufacture *NOUN*
manufacture is the process of making things with machines, especially in large quantities for sale
➤ **manufacturer** *NOUN*

manure *NOUN*
manure is animal dung added to the soil to make it more fertile

manuscript *NOUN* **manuscripts**
something written or typed before it has been printed

Manx *ADJECTIVE*
to do with the Isle of Man

Manx cat *NOUN* **Manx cats**
a breed of cat without a tail

many *DETERMINER* **more, most**
large in number • *There were many people at the party.* • *How many potatoes do you want?*

many *PRONOUN*
a large number of people or things • *Many were found.*

Māori (*say* **mow**-ree) *NOUN*
❶ (**Māori**) one of, or a descendant of, the people who were living in New Zealand before European settlers arrived ❷ the language of the Māori

Māori *ADJECTIVE*
to do with the Māori
DID YOU KNOW? The word **kiwi** comes from Māori.

map *NOUN* **maps**
a diagram of part or all of the earth's surface, showing features such as towns, mountains and rivers
➤ **to put a place on the map** is to do something that makes it famous

map *VERB* **maps, mapping, mapped**
to map an area is to make a map of it
➤ **to map something out** is to arrange it or organize it

maple *NOUN* **maples**
a tree with broad leaves

mar *VERB* **mars, marring, marred**
to mar something is to spoil it

marathon *NOUN* **marathons**
a long-distance running race on roads, usually 26 miles long
DID YOU KNOW? Marathon is a place near Athens where the Greeks defeated the Persians in 490 BC. A runner is said to have run from Marathon to Athens with news of the victory.

marauder *NOUN* **marauders**
marauders are people who attack a place and steal things from it

marble *NOUN* **marbles**
❶ a small coloured glass ball used in games ❷ a hard type of limestone that is often polished and used for building or sculpture

March *NOUN*
the third month of the year
DID YOU KNOW? March is named after *Mars*, the Roman god of war.

march *VERB* **marches, marching, marched**
❶ to march is to walk with regular steps ❷ to march someone is to make them walk somewhere • *He marched them up the hill.*

march *NOUN* **marches**
❶ a march is a large group of people marching, sometimes to protest about something ❷ a march is also a piece of music suitable for marching to

mare *NOUN* **mares**
a female horse or donkey

a
b
c
d
e
f
g
h
i
j
k
l
m
n
o
p
q
r
s
t
u
v
w
x
y
z

margarine (*say* mar-ja-**reen**) *NOUN*
margarine is a soft creamy substance used like butter, made from animal or vegetable fats

margin *NOUN* **margins**
❶ the empty space between the edge of a page and the writing or pictures ❷ the small difference between two scores or prices • *She won by a narrow margin.*

marginal *ADJECTIVE*
a marginal difference is a very small or slight one • *The difference in price is marginal.*

marigold *NOUN* **marigolds**
a yellow or orange garden flower

marine (*say* ma-**reen**) *ADJECTIVE*
to do with the sea

marine *NOUN* **marines**
a soldier trained to serve on land and sea

mariner *NOUN* **mariners** (*old use*)
a sailor

marionette *NOUN* **marionettes**
a puppet that you work by strings or wires

mark *NOUN* **marks**
❶ a spot, dot, line or stain on something ❷ a number or letter put on a piece of work to show how good it is ❸ a distinguishing feature or sign of something • *They kept a minute's silence as a mark of respect.* ❹ the place from which you start a race • *On your marks, get set, go!*

mark *VERB* **marks, marking, marked**
❶ to mark something is to put a mark on it ❷ to mark a piece of work is to give it a number or letter to show how good it is ❸ in football or hockey, to mark a player on the other team is to keep close to them to stop them getting the ball ❹ to mark something said is to take note of it • *Mark my words!*

marker *NOUN* **markers**
❶ something you use to mark a place or special spot ❷ a player who marks someone on the opposite team ❸ a felt-tip pen with a thick nib

market *NOUN* **markets**
❶ a place where things are bought and sold, usually from stalls in the open air ❷ a demand for goods • *There is hardly any market for typewriters now.*

market *VERB* **markets, marketing, marketed**
to market a product is to put it on sale

marmalade *NOUN*
marmalade is jam made from oranges or lemons

maroon *VERB* **maroons, marooning, marooned**
to maroon someone is to abandon them in a place far away from other people • *Robinson Crusoe was marooned on a desert island.*

maroon *NOUN*
maroon is a dark red colour

marquee (*say* mar-**kee**) *NOUN* **marquees**
a large tent used for a party or exhibition

marriage *NOUN* **marriages**
❶ marriage is the state of being married ❷ a marriage is a wedding

marrow *NOUN* **marrows**
❶ a marrow is a large green or yellow vegetable with a hard skin ❷ marrow is the soft substance inside your bones

marry *VERB* **marries, marrying, married**
❶ to marry someone is to become their husband or wife ❷ to marry two people is to perform a marriage ceremony

Mars *NOUN*
the fourth planet from the sun in our solar system
DID YOU KNOW? The planet **Mars** is named after the Roman god of war.

marsh *NOUN* **marshes**
a low-lying area of very wet ground
➤ **marshy** *ADJECTIVE*

marshal *NOUN* **marshals**
❶ an official who supervises a contest or ceremony ❷ a high-ranking officer in the armed forces ❸ a police official in the USA

marshmallow *NOUN* **marshmallows**
a marshmallow is a soft spongy sweet
'Mr Willy Wonka can make marshmallows that taste of violets, and rich caramels that change colour every ten seconds as you suck them.'—CHARLIE AND THE CHOCOLATE FACTORY, Roald Dahl

marsupial (*say* mar-**soo**-pi-al) *NOUN* **marsupials**
an animal such as a kangaroo, wallaby or koala. The female has a pouch for carrying her young.

martial arts *PLURAL NOUN*
martial arts are fighting sports such as karate and judo

Martian *NOUN* **Martians**
in stories, a creature from the planet Mars

Martian *ADJECTIVE*
from or found on the planet Mars • *a sample of Martian rock*

martin *NOUN* **martins**
a bird rather like a swallow

martyr (*say* **mar**-ter) *NOUN* **martyrs**
someone who is killed or suffers because of their beliefs
➤ **martyrdom** *NOUN*

marvel *NOUN* **marvels**
a wonderful thing

marvel *VERB* **marvels**, **marvelling**, **marvelled**
to marvel at something is to be filled with wonder or astonishment by it

marvellous *ADJECTIVE*
wonderful
➤ **marvellously** *ADVERB*

marzipan *NOUN*
marzipan is a soft sweet food made from almonds and sugar, sometimes put on the top of cakes

mascot *NOUN* **mascots**
a person, animal or object that is believed to bring good luck

masculine *ADJECTIVE*
to do with men or like men; suitable for men
➤ **masculinity** *NOUN*

mash *VERB* **mashes**, **mashing**, **mashed**
to mash something is to crush it into a soft mass

mash *NOUN* (*informal*)
mashed potatoes

mask *NOUN* **masks**
a covering that you wear over your face to disguise or protect it

mask *VERB* **masks**, **masking**, **masked**
❶ to mask your face is to cover it with a mask ❷ to mask something is to hide it

mason *NOUN* **masons**
someone who builds or works with stone

masonry *NOUN*
masonry is the stone parts of a building

Mass *NOUN* **Masses**
the Communion service in a Roman Catholic church

mass *NOUN* **masses**
❶ a large amount of something ❷ a lump or heap ❸ the amount of matter in an object, measured in grams
➤ **the masses** the ordinary people

mass *VERB* **masses**, **massing**, **massed**
to mass is to collect into a mass • *People were massing in the square.*

massacre (*say* mas-a-ker) *VERB* **massacres**, **massacring**, **massacred**
to massacre people is to kill a large number of them

massacre *NOUN* **massacres**
the killing of a large number of people

massage (*say* mas-ah*zh*) *VERB* **massages**, **massaging**, **massaged**
to massage the body is to rub and press it to make it less stiff or less painful

massage *NOUN*
massaging someone's body

massive *ADJECTIVE*
very big; large and heavy
➤ **massively** *ADVERB* hugely

mast *NOUN* **masts**
a tall pole that holds up a ship's sails or a flag or aerial

master *NOUN* **masters**
❶ a man who is in charge of something ❷ a male teacher ❸ someone who is very good at what they do, such as a great artist or composer ❹ something from which copies are made

master *VERB* **masters**, **mastering**, **mastered**
❶ to master a subject or skill is to learn it completely ❷ to master a fear or difficulty is to control it • *She succeeded in mastering her fear of heights.*

a
b
c
d
e
f
g
h
i
j
k
l
m
n
o
p
q
r
s
t
u
v
w
x
y
z

masterly *ADJECTIVE*
very clever or skilful

mastermind *NOUN* **masterminds**
❶ a very clever person ❷ someone who organizes a scheme or crime

masterpiece *NOUN* **masterpieces**
❶ an excellent piece of work ❷ someone's best piece of work

mastery *NOUN*
mastery is complete control or knowledge of something • *He has a complete mastery of the art of fencing.*

mat *NOUN* **mats**
❶ a small piece of material that partly covers a floor ❷ a small piece of material put on a table to protect the surface

matador *NOUN* **matadors**
someone who fights and kills the bull in a bullfight

match *NOUN* **matches**
❶ a small thin stick with a chemical tip that gives a flame when struck against a rough surface ❷ a game or contest between two teams or players ❸ one person or thing that is equal or similar to another • *Can you find a match for this sock?* ❹ a marriage

match *VERB* **matches**, **matching**, **matched**
❶ to match another person or thing is to be equal to them ❷ one thing matches another when it goes well with it • *Your jacket matches your shoes.* ❸ to match one person with another is to put them in competition

matchstick *NOUN* **matchsticks**
the stem of a match • *as thin as a matchstick*

mate *NOUN* **mates**
❶ a friend or companion ❷ one of a pair of animals that produce young together ❸ one of the officers on a ship

mate *VERB* **mates**, **mating**, **mated**
❶ to mate is to come together in order to have offspring ❷ to mate animals is to put them together so that they will have offspring

material *NOUN* **materials**
❶ anything used for making something else • *Iron and steel are the best materials for magnets.* ❷ cloth or fabric

materialistic *ADJECTIVE*
liking possessions and money more than anything else

maternal *ADJECTIVE*
to do with a mother, or like a mother

maternity *NOUN*
maternity is having a baby; motherhood

math *NOUN* (*North American, informal*)
mathematics

mathematical *ADJECTIVE*
❶ a mathematical problem or calculation is one you need mathematics to work out ❷ mathematical ability is being able to do mathematics

mathematician (*say* math-em-a-**tish**-an) *NOUN* **mathematicians**
an expert in mathematics

mathematics *NOUN*
mathematics is the study of numbers, measurements and shapes

maths *NOUN* (*informal*)
mathematics

matinee (*say* **mat**-i-nay) *NOUN* **matinees**
an afternoon performance at a theatre or cinema

matrimony (*say* **mat**-ri-mo-nee) *NOUN*
matrimony is marriage
➤ **matrimonial** *ADJECTIVE*

matt *ADJECTIVE*
not shiny • *The wall was decorated with matt paint.*

matted *ADJECTIVE*
tangled

matter *NOUN* **matters**
❶ something you need to think about or do • *It is a serious matter.* ❷ a substance • *Peat consists mainly of vegetable matter.*
➤ **a matter of fact** something true
➤ **no matter** it is not important
➤ **what's the matter?** what is wrong?

matter *VERB* **matters, mattering, mattered**
to matter is to be important

mattress *NOUN* **mattresses**
a thick layer of soft or springy material covered in cloth and used on a bed

mature *ADJECTIVE*
❶ fully grown or developed ❷ behaving in a sensible adult manner

mature *VERB* **matures, maturing, matured**
to become fully grown or developed

maturity *NOUN*
❶ maturity is being fully grown ❷ maturity is also sensible adult behaviour

mauve (*say* mohv) *ADJECTIVE*
pale purple in colour
'Rats!' cried Mr Stringer, going mauve in the face. 'There are no rats in this hotel!'–THE WITCHES, Roald Dahl

maximum *NOUN* **maxima**
the greatest number or amount possible
• *The maximum is ten people.*

maximum *ADJECTIVE*
the greatest possible • *The maximum speed is 60 miles per hour.*

May *NOUN*
the fifth month of the year
DID YOU KNOW? **May** is named after *Maia*, a Roman goddess of springtime.

may *VERB* (*past tense*) **might**
❶ may means to be allowed to • *May I have another slice?* ❷ may also means that something is possible or has possibly happened • *He may not know the answer.* • *She might have missed the train.*

maybe *ADVERB*
perhaps

mayday *NOUN* **maydays**
an international radio signal calling for help

May Day *NOUN*
the first day of May, often celebrated with sport and dancing

mayhem *NOUN*
extreme disorder and chaos • *There was mayhem in the streets.*

mayo (*say* **may**-oh) *NOUN* (*informal*)
mayonnaise

mayonnaise (*say* may-on-**ayz**) *NOUN*
a creamy sauce made from eggs, oil and vinegar, used in salads and sandwiches

mayor *NOUN* **mayors**
the person in charge of the council in a town or city

maze *NOUN* **mazes**
a complicated arrangement of paths or lines to follow your way through as a game or puzzle
• *a maze of underground tunnels*

me *PRONOUN*
a word used for *I*, usually when it is the object of a sentence, or when it comes after a preposition • *I think she likes me.* • *She gave that book to me.*

meadow *NOUN* **meadows**
a field of grass

meagre (*say* **meeg**-er) *ADJECTIVE*
very little; barely enough
The Rev. John Whittier was the pastor of this small mission church, and had a very meagre salary. –POLLYANNA, Eleanor H. Porter

meal *NOUN* **meals**
❶ a meal is the food that you eat at one time, such as breakfast, lunch or dinner ❷ meal is grain ground to a coarse powder

mean *VERB* **means, meaning, meant**
❶ to mean something is to have that as its explanation or equivalent, or to have that as its sense • *What does this word mean?*
❷ to mean to do something is to intend to do it • *I meant to tell him, but I forgot.*

mean *ADJECTIVE* **meaner, meanest**
❶ not generous; selfish • *Scrooge was a mean old skinflint!* ❷ unkind or spiteful
They were rich men. They were also nasty men. All three of them were about as nasty and mean as any men you could meet.–FANTASTIC MR FOX, Roald Dahl
➤ **meanly** *ADVERB* ➤ **meanness** *NOUN*

meander (*say* mee-an-der) *VERB* **meanders, meandering, meandered**
a river or road meanders when it takes a winding course, with a lot of bends
DID YOU KNOW? The word **meander** comes from the ancient river *Meander* in Asia Minor (now Turkey), which took a winding course.

a b c d e f g h i j k l **m** n o p q r s t u v w x y z

A B C D E F G H I J K L M N O P Q R S T U V W X Y Z

meaning *NOUN* **meanings**
what something means

meaningful *ADJECTIVE*
a meaningful look is one that expresses
a meaning • *A meaningful glance passed
between my parents.*
➤ **meaningfully** *ADVERB*

meaningless *ADJECTIVE*
something is meaningless when it has no
meaning or purpose

means *NOUN*
a means of doing something is a way or method
of doing it
➤ **by all means** certainly
➤ **by no means** not at all

means *PLURAL NOUN*
money or other resources for doing things

meantime *NOUN*
➤ **in the meantime** meanwhile

meanwhile *ADVERB*
while something else is happening • *I'll cut the
cake up; meanwhile, you get the plates out.*

measles *NOUN*
measles is an infectious disease that causes
small red spots on the skin

measly *ADJECTIVE* **measlier, measliest**
(*informal*)
very small or poor • *All I got was a measly
50 pence.*

measure *VERB* **measures, measuring,
measured**
❶ to measure something is to find out how big
it is ❷ to measure (for example) six feet is to be
six feet long

measure *NOUN* **measures**
❶ a unit used for measuring something
❷ a device used for measuring ❸ the size
of something ❹ something done for a
particular purpose; a law or rule

measurement *NOUN* **measurements**
❶ a measurement is the size or length of
something ❷ measurement is when you
measure something

meat *NOUN* **meats**
meat is animal flesh that is cooked as food

meatball *NOUN* **meatballs**
a ball of minced meat for cooking

meaty *ADJECTIVE* **meatier, meatiest**
meaty food is full of meat • *a meaty
sandwich*

mechanic *NOUN* **mechanics**
someone who maintains and repairs
machinery

mechanical *ADJECTIVE*
❶ to do with machines ❷ done without
thinking about it
➤ **mechanically** *ADVERB*

mechanics *NOUN*
❶ mechanics is the study of movement
and force ❷ mechanics is also the study or
use of machines

mechanism *NOUN* **mechanisms**
❶ the moving parts of a machine ❷ the way
a machine works

medal *NOUN* **medals**
a piece of metal shaped like a coin, star or
cross, given to someone for bravery or for
achieving something • *She won two Olympic
gold medals.*

medallion *NOUN* **medallions**
a large medal worn as a piece of jewellery

medallist *NOUN* **medallists**
a winner of a medal

meddle *VERB* **meddles, meddling, meddled**
to meddle in something is to interfere in it
➤ **meddlesome** *ADJECTIVE* a meddlesome
person likes to interfere

media (*say* mee-di-a) *PLURAL NOUN* (*a plural
of* **medium**)
➤ **the media** newspapers, radio, television and
the internet, which provide information about
current events to the public

medical *ADJECTIVE*
to do with the treatment of disease
➤ **medically** *ADVERB*

medicine *NOUN* **medicines**
❶ a medicine is a substance, usually swallowed,
used to try to cure an illness ❷ medicine is the
treatment of disease and injuries
➤ **medicinal** *ADJECTIVE*

medieval (*say* med-i-ee-val) *ADJECTIVE*
to do with the Middle Ages

mediocre (*say* meed-i-**oh**-ker) *ADJECTIVE*
not very good, only fairly good
➤ **mediocrity** *NOUN*

meditate *VERB* **meditates, meditating, meditated**
to meditate is to think deeply and seriously, usually in silence
➤ **meditation** *NOUN*

Mediterranean (*say* med-i-ter-**ay**-ni-an) *ADJECTIVE*
to do with the Mediterranean Sea, which is between Europe and Africa, or the countries round it

medium *ADJECTIVE*
average; of middle size

medium *NOUN*
❶ (**media**) a thing in which something exists, moves or is expressed • *Air is the medium in which sound travels.* ❷ (**mediums**) someone who claims to communicate with the dead

meek *ADJECTIVE* **meeker, meekest**
quiet and obedient
➤ **meekly** *ADVERB* ➤ **meekness** *NOUN*

meerkat *NOUN* **meerkats**
a small type of mongoose from southern Africa

meet *VERB* **meets, meeting, met**
❶ to meet is to come together from different places • *We all met in London.* ❷ to meet someone is to come face to face with them, especially for the first time or by arrangement • *I met her at a party.* • *I'll meet you at the station.* ❸ to meet a bill or cost is to be able to pay it

meeting *NOUN* **meetings**
a time when people come together for a special purpose, often to discuss something

megabyte *NOUN* **megabytes**
a unit that measures computer data or memory, roughly equal to one million bytes

megaphone *NOUN* **megaphones**
a funnel-shaped device for making someone's voice sound louder

melancholy *ADJECTIVE*
sad and gloomy
By and by there was to be heard a sound at once the most musical and the most melancholy in the world: the mermaids calling to the moon.—THE ADVENTURES OF PETER PAN, J. M. Barrie

mellow *ADJECTIVE* **mellower, mellowest**
having a soft rich sound or colour

melodic *ADJECTIVE*
a melodic piece of music has a tune that is pleasant to listen to

melodious *ADJECTIVE*
sounding sweet; pleasant to listen to

melodrama *NOUN* **melodramas**
a play full of excitement and emotion
➤ **melodramatic** *ADJECTIVE*

melody *NOUN* **melodies**
a tune, especially one that is pleasant to listen to

melon *NOUN* **melons**
a large juicy fruit with yellow or green skin

melt *VERB* **melts, melting, melted**
❶ to melt something solid is to make it liquid by heating it ❷ to melt is to become liquid by heating ❸ to melt, or to melt away, is to go away or disappear slowly • *The crowd gradually melted away.*

member *NOUN* **members**
someone who belongs to a society or group
➤ **membership** *NOUN*

Member of Parliament *NOUN* **Members of Parliament**
someone who has been elected by the people of an area to speak for them in Parliament

membrane *NOUN* **membranes**
a thin skin or covering

meme (*say* meem) *NOUN* **memes**
an image or short video with a caption that is copied and spread on social media

memoirs *PLURAL NOUN*
a famous person's account of their own life and experiences

memorable *ADJECTIVE*
❶ worth remembering • *It was a memorable holiday.* ❷ easy to remember • *He has a memorable name.*
➤ **memorably** *ADVERB*

a
b
c
d
e
f
g
h
i
j
k
l
m
n
o
p
q
r
s
t
u
v
w
x
y
z

memorial *NOUN* **memorials**
something set up to remind people of a person or an event • *They passed a war memorial in the High Street.*

memorize (*also* **memorise**) *VERB* **memorizes**, **memorizing**, **memorized**
to memorize something is to learn it and remember it exactly • *I've memorized the words to 'Auld Lang Syne'.*

memory *NOUN* **memories**
❶ memory is the ability to remember things
❷ a memory is something that you remember, usually something interesting or special • *I have happy memories of that holiday.*
❸ a computer's memory is the part where information is stored

memory stick *NOUN* **memory sticks**
a small portable device that can be plugged into a computer and used for storing and transferring data

men *NOUN* (*plural of* **man**)

menace *VERB* **menaces**, **menacing**, **menaced**
to menace someone is to threaten them with harm or danger • *Captain Bones gave the crew a menacing stare.*

menace *NOUN* **menaces**
❶ something that threatens people with harm or danger ❷ an annoying person or thing • *Midges can be a real menace!*

menagerie (*say* min-aj-er-ee) *NOUN* **menageries**
a small zoo

mend *VERB* **mends**, **mending**, **mended**
to mend something that is broken or damaged is to make it as good as it was before

mend *NOUN*
➤ **to be on the mend** is to be getting better after an illness

menstruation *NOUN*
menstruation is the natural flow of blood from a woman's womb, normally happening every 28 days
➤ **menstrual** *ADJECTIVE*

mental *ADJECTIVE*
❶ to do with the mind • *mental arithmetic*
❷ (*informal*) (may cause offence) mad or crazy
• *Your mum will go mental when she sees the mess!*

mentally *ADVERB*
❶ you do something mentally when you do it in your head • *Edward mentally crossed his fingers.* ❷ someone who is mentally ill is ill in their mind

mention *VERB* **mentions**, **mentioning**, **mentioned**
to mention someone or something is to speak about them briefly

mention *NOUN* **mentions**
when someone or something is mentioned • *Our school got a mention in the local paper.*

menu (*say* men-yoo) *NOUN* **menus**
❶ a list of the food that is available in a restaurant or served at a meal ❷ (*computing*) a list of possible actions, displayed on a screen, from which you choose what you want a computer to do

meow
another spelling of **miaow**

MEP (*say* em-ee-pee) *NOUN* **MEPs**
a Member of the European Parliament

mercenary *ADJECTIVE*
interested only in the money you can get for the work you do

mercenary *NOUN* **mercenaries**
a soldier hired to fight for a foreign country

merchandise *NOUN*
merchandise is goods for buying or selling

merchant *NOUN* **merchants**
someone involved in trade

merciful *ADJECTIVE*
showing mercy
➤ **mercifully** *ADVERB*

merciless *ADJECTIVE*
showing no mercy; cruel
➤ **mercilessly** *ADVERB*

Mercury *NOUN*
the closest planet to the sun in our solar system
DID YOU KNOW? The planet **Mercury** is named after the Roman messenger of the gods.

mercury *NOUN*
mercury is a heavy silvery metal that is usually liquid, used in thermometers

mercy NOUN **mercies**
❶ mercy is kindness or pity shown towards someone instead of harming them or punishing them ❷ a mercy is something to be thankful for • *Thank goodness for small mercies.*

mere ADJECTIVE
not more than • *It's a mere 10 metres away.*

merely ADVERB
only; simply • *She was merely joking.*

merge VERB **merges, merging, merged**
❶ to merge things is to combine or blend them ❷ to merge is to be combined

merger NOUN **mergers**
a merger is when two businesses or companies join together into one

meridian (*say* mer-**rid**-i-an) NOUN **meridians**
a line on a map or globe from the North Pole to the South Pole

meringue (*say* mer-**rang**) NOUN **meringues**
a crisp cake made from the whites of eggs mixed with sugar and baked

merit NOUN **merits**
❶ to have merit is to be good or excellent ❷ a merit is something that deserves praise • *I can see the merits of this plan.*

merit VERB **merits, meriting, merited**
to merit something is to deserve something good

mermaid NOUN **mermaids**
a mythical sea creature with a woman's body and a fish's tail instead of legs

merman NOUN **mermen**
a mythical sea creature with a man's body and a fish's tail instead of legs

merry ADJECTIVE **merrier, merriest**
happy and cheerful
➤ **merrily** ADVERB

merry-go-round NOUN **merry-go-rounds**
a large roundabout with horses and other things to ride on

mesh NOUN **meshes**
mesh is material made like a net, with open spaces between the wire or threads

mesmerize (*also* **mesmerise**) VERB **mesmerizes, mesmerizing, mesmerized**
to mesmerize someone is to fascinate them and hold their attention

mess NOUN **messes**
❶ something untidy or dirty ❷ a difficult or confused situation ❸ a place where soldiers or sailors eat their meals
➤ **to make a mess of something** is to do it very badly

mess VERB **messes, messing, messed**
➤ **to mess about** is to waste time behaving stupidly or doing things slowly • *Stop messing about and give me a hand.*
➤ **to mess something up** is to do it very badly

message NOUN **messages**
a question or piece of information that one person sends to another

messenger NOUN **messengers**
someone who carries a message

messy ADJECTIVE **messier, messiest**
❶ untidy or dirty ❷ difficult or complicated • *I'm afraid it's a messy situation.*
➤ **messily** ADVERB

met VERB (*past tense and past participle of* **meet**)
• *I met my friends after school.* • *Most people I've met have been nice.*

metal NOUN **metals**
a hard substance that melts when it is heated, such as gold, silver, copper and iron

metallic ADJECTIVE
made of metal or like metal • *an odd metallic taste*

metamorphose VERB **metamorphoses, metamorphosing, metamorphosed**
to change through metamorphosis • *The larva will metamorphose into a moth.*

metamorphosis NOUN **metamorphoses**
a complete change made by some living things, such as a caterpillar changing into a butterfly

metaphor (*say* met-a-for) NOUN **metaphors**
a metaphor is used to describe one thing as if it were something else, for example
The moon was a ghostly galleon tossed upon cloudy seas.—THE HIGHWAYMAN, Alfred Noyes
➤ **metaphorical** ADJECTIVE

a b c d e f g h i j k l m n o p q r s t u v w x y z

meteor (*say* **meet**-i-er) *NOUN* **meteors**
a piece of rock or metal from outer space that burns up as it enters the earth's atmosphere, leaving a streak of light in the sky
DID YOU KNOW? The word **meteor** comes from a Greek word meaning 'high in the air'.

meteoric *ADJECTIVE*
very fast and sudden, like a meteor • *They've had a meteoric rise to fame.*

meteorite (*say* **meet**-i-er-ryt) *NOUN* **meteorites**
the remains of a meteor that has landed on the earth

meteorology (*say* mee-tee-er-**ol**-o-jee) *NOUN*
meteorology is the study of the weather
➤ **meteorological** *ADJECTIVE*
➤ **meteorologist** *NOUN*

meter *NOUN* **meters**
a device for measuring something, such as how much gas or electricity has been used

methane *NOUN*
methane is an inflammable gas produced when plants rot away, found mainly in mines and marshes

method *NOUN* **methods**
❶ a method is a way of doing something ❷ method is good organization or orderly behaviour • *There is method in everything she does.*

methodical (*say* mi-**thod**-i-kal) *ADJECTIVE*
done carefully and in a logical way
➤ **methodically** *ADVERB*

meticulous *ADJECTIVE*
very careful and precise
➤ **meticulously** *ADVERB*

metre (*say* **meet**-er) *NOUN* **metres**
❶ the main unit of length in the metric system, equal to about 39½ inches ❷ a particular type of rhythm in poetry
SPELLING ALERT! You measure things in **metres**, but you put money in a parking **meter**.

metric *ADJECTIVE*
❶ to do with the metric system ❷ to do with metre in poetry

metric system *NOUN*
a measuring system based on decimal units (the metre, litre and gram)

metronome (*say* **met**-ro-nohm) *NOUN* **metronomes**
a device that makes a regular clicking noise to help you keep in time when practising music

metropolis *NOUN* **metropolises**
a very large and busy city

mettle *NOUN*
➤ **to be on your mettle** is to be ready to do your best

mew *VERB* **mews**, **mewing**, **mewed**
to make a sound like a cat

miaow *NOUN* **miaows**
the crying sound made by a cat
miaow *VERB* **miaows**, **miaowing**, **miaowed**
a cat miaows when it makes a crying sound

mice *NOUN* (*plural of* **mouse**)

microbe (*say* **my**-krohb) *NOUN* **microbes**
a tiny organism that can only be seen with a microscope

microchip *NOUN* **microchips**
a very small piece of silicon working as an electric circuit, used in computers

microphone *NOUN* **microphones**
an electrical device that picks up sound waves for recording them or making them louder

microscope (*say* **my**-kro-skohp) *NOUN* **microscopes**
a device with lenses that make tiny objects appear larger so you can study them

microscopic (*say* my-kro-**skop**-ik) *ADJECTIVE*
too small to be seen without a microscope; tiny

microwave *NOUN* **microwaves**
❶ energy moving in very short waves ❷ a kind of oven which heats things quickly by using energy in very short waves
microwave *VERB* **microwaves**, **microwaving**, **microwaved**
to microwave food is to cook it in a microwave oven

mid *ADJECTIVE*
in the middle of • *The holiday is from mid-July to mid-August.*

midday *NOUN*
the middle of the day; noon

middle *NOUN* **middles**
❶ the middle of something is the place or part that is at the same distance from all its sides or edges or from both its ends ❷ someone's waist

middle *ADJECTIVE*
placed in the middle

middle-aged *ADJECTIVE*
aged between about 40 and 60

Middle Ages *NOUN*
the period in history from about AD 1100 to 1500

middle class *NOUN* **middle classes**
the class of people between the upper class and the working class, including business and professional people such as teachers, doctors and lawyers
➤ **middle-class** *ADJECTIVE*

Middle East *NOUN*
the countries to the east of the Mediterranean Sea, from Egypt to Iran
➤ **Middle-Eastern** *ADJECTIVE*

midge *NOUN* **midges**
a small insect like a gnat

midget *NOUN* **midgets** (often *offensive*)
an unusually short person

Midlands *PLURAL NOUN*
the central part of England

midnight *NOUN*
twelve o'clock at night

midst *NOUN*
➤ **to be in the midst of something** is to be in the middle of it

midsummer *NOUN*
the middle of summer, about 21 June in the northern hemisphere

midway *ADVERB*
halfway

midwife *NOUN* **midwives**
a person trained to look after someone who is giving birth to a baby

might *VERB* (*past tense of* **may**)
• *I asked if I might go.* • *The parcel might arrive tomorrow.*

might *NOUN*
great power or strength • *the might of the Roman army*

mighty *ADJECTIVE* **mightier, mightiest**
very strong or powerful • *They gave the door a mighty heave.*
➤ **mightily** *ADVERB*

migraine (*say* **mee**-grayn) *NOUN* **migraines**
a severe kind of headache

migrant (*say* **my**-grant) *NOUN* **migrants**
❶ a person who moves from one place to another, usually to find work ❷ a bird or animal that moves from one region to another

migrate (*say* my-**grayt**) *VERB* **migrates, migrating, migrated**
❶ to migrate is to move from one place to another, usually to find work ❷ birds migrate when they fly to a warmer region for the winter
In the sky over Kensington Gardens, a flock of flying children gathered, like birds in autumn getting ready to migrate.—PETER PAN IN SCARLET, Geraldine McCaughrean
➤ **migration** *NOUN*

migratory *ADJECTIVE*
migratory birds migrate every year

mike *NOUN* **mikes** (*informal*)
a microphone

mild *ADJECTIVE* **milder, mildest**
gentle; not harsh or severe
Miss Jennifer Honey was a mild and quiet person who never raised her voice and was seldom seen to smile.—MATILDA, Roald Dahl
➤ **mildly** *ADVERB* ➤ **mildness** *NOUN*

mildly *ADVERB*
to be mildly surprised or interested is to be slightly surprised or interested

mile *NOUN* **miles**
a measure of distance, equal to 1,760 yards or about 1.6 kilometres

mileage *NOUN* **mileages**
the number of miles you have travelled

milestone *NOUN* **milestones**
❶ a stone of a kind that used to be placed beside a road to mark the distance between

towns **2** an important event in history or in a person's life

militant *ADJECTIVE*
aggressive; eager to fight

military *ADJECTIVE*
to do with soldiers or the armed forces

milk *NOUN*
milk is a white liquid that female mammals produce in their bodies to feed to their young

milk *VERB* **milks**, **milking**, **milked**
to milk a cow or other animal is to get milk from it

milkshake *NOUN* **milkshakes**
a frothy drink of milk mixed with a sweet flavouring

milk tooth *NOUN* **milk teeth**
one of the first set of teeth a child or animal has, which are later replaced by adult teeth

milky *ADJECTIVE* **milkier**, **milkiest**
1 like milk; white **2** made with a lot of milk

Milky Way *NOUN*
a faintly shining band of light from the stars in our galaxy

mill *NOUN* **mills**
1 a building with machinery for grinding corn to make flour **2** a factory for making materials, such as a paper mill or a steel mill **3** a machine for grinding something such as coffee or pepper

mill *VERB* **mills**, **milling**, **milled**
1 to mill something is to grind or crush it in a mill **2** people mill or mill about when they move in a confused crowd

millennium *NOUN* **millenniums**
a period of a thousand years
➤ **millennial** *ADJECTIVE*

miller *NOUN* **millers**
someone who runs a flour mill

millet *NOUN*
a kind of cereal with tiny seeds

milligram *NOUN* **milligrams**
one thousandth of a gram

millilitre *NOUN* **millilitres**
one thousandth of a litre

millimetre *NOUN* **millimetres**
one thousandth of a metre

million *NOUN* **millions**
a thousand thousands (1,000,000)
➤ **millionth** *ADJECTIVE, NOUN*

millionaire *NOUN* **millionaires**
an extremely rich person who has at least a million pounds or dollars

millipede *NOUN* **millipedes**
a small crawling creature with many pairs of legs

millstone *NOUN* **millstones**
a large heavy stone used in grinding corn
➤ **a millstone round someone's neck**
a heavy burden or responsibility

mime *VERB* **mimes**, **miming**, **mimed**
to mime is to tell a story by using movements of the body without speaking

mime *NOUN* **mimes**
mime is the art of telling a story by using movements of the body without speaking

mimic *VERB* **mimics**, **mimicking**, **mimicked**
to mimic someone is to imitate them, especially to make people laugh
➤ **mimicry** *NOUN*

mimic *NOUN* **mimics**
a person who is good at imitating other people

minaret *NOUN* **minarets**
a tall tower on a mosque

mince *NOUN*
mince is meat that has been cut up into very small pieces

mince *VERB* **minces**, **mincing**, **minced**
to mince food is to cut it up into very small pieces
➤ **not to mince words** is to speak frankly

mincemeat *NOUN*
mincemeat is a sweet mixture of currants, raisins and chopped fruit, used in pies

mince pie *NOUN* **mince pies**
a pie containing mincemeat

mind *NOUN* **minds**
the function of the brain to think, feel, understand and remember; your thoughts and feelings

➤ **to change your mind** is to have a new opinion or intention about something
➤ **to have a good mind to do something** is to intend to do it

mind *VERB* **minds, minding, minded**
❶ to mind something is to be sad or upset about it • *I don't mind missing the party.*
❷ to mind someone or something is to look after them for a time • *He was minding the baby.* ❸ to mind, or to mind out, is to be careful or watch out for something • *Mind the doors!*

mindless *ADJECTIVE*
done without thinking; stupid or pointless

mine *PRONOUN*
belonging to me • *She is a friend of mine.*

mine *NOUN* **mines**
❶ a place where coal, metal or precious stones are dug out of the ground ❷ a type of bomb hidden under the ground or in the sea that explodes when anything touches it

mine *VERB* **mines, mining, mined**
❶ to mine something is to dig it from a mine
❷ to mine a place is to lay explosives in it

minefield *NOUN* **minefields**
❶ an area where explosive mines have been laid ❷ you can say that an activity is a minefield when it has many dangers

miner *NOUN* **miners**
someone who works in a mine

mineral *NOUN* **minerals**
a hard substance that can be dug out of the ground, such as coal and iron ore

mineral water *NOUN*
mineral water is water that comes from a natural spring. It can be fizzy or still.

mingle *VERB* **mingles, mingling, mingled**
❶ things mingle when they become mixed together ❷ to mingle things is to mix or blend them

mini *ADJECTIVE*
very small or compact • *a mini dictionary*

miniature (*say* **min**-i-cher) *ADJECTIVE*
very small, especially copying something larger
• *a miniature tea-set*
SPELLING ALERT! The word **miniature** starts with **mini**.

minibeast *NOUN* **minibeasts**
a very small creature such as an insect or spider

minibus *NOUN* **minibuses**
a small bus with seats for about ten people

minim *NOUN* **minims**
a musical note equal to two crotchets or half a semibreve, written (♩)

minimal *ADJECTIVE*
very little; as little as possible

minimize (*also* **minimise**) *VERB* **minimizes, minimizing, minimized**
to minimize something is to make it as small as possible

minimum *NOUN* **minima**
the smallest number or amount possible
• *We want the minimum of fuss.*

minimum *ADJECTIVE*
least or smallest • *The minimum number is three.*

minion *NOUN* **minions**
a low-ranking assistant or helper

minister *NOUN* **ministers**
❶ a member of the government who is in charge of a department ❷ a member of the clergy

ministry *NOUN* **ministries**
❶ a government department • *the Ministry of Defence* ❷ the work of a minister in the church

mink *NOUN* **minks**
❶ a mink is a small animal rather like a stoat ❷ mink is this animal's valuable brown fur

minnow *NOUN* **minnows**
a tiny freshwater fish

minor *ADJECTIVE*
❶ not very important, especially when compared to something else ❷ of the musical scale that has a semitone between the 2nd and 3rd notes

minority (*say* myn-o-ri-tee) *NOUN* **minorities**
❶ the smaller part of a group of people or things • *There was a minority who wanted to leave.* ❷ a small group that is different from others

a
b
c
d
e
f
g
h
i
j
k
l
m
n
o
p
q
r
s
t
u
v
w
x
y
z

Minotaur *NOUN*
a mythological creature that is part bull and part man
The labyrinth. Where the Minotaur awaits, hideous, bloody, brooding.—SHADOW OF THE MINOTAUR, Alan Gibbons

minstrel *NOUN* **minstrels**
a travelling singer and musician in the Middle Ages

mint *NOUN* **mints**
❶ mint is a green plant with sweet-smelling leaves used for flavouring ❷ a mint is a sweet flavoured with peppermint ❸ a mint is also a place where a country's coins are made

mint *ADJECTIVE*
➤ **to be in mint condition** is to be as new, as if it had just been made

mint *VERB* **mints, minting, minted**
to mint coins is to make them

minus *PREPOSITION*
❶ less; with the next number taken away
• *Eight minus two equals six (8 - 2 = 6).*
❷ less than zero • *The temperature is minus five degrees.*

minuscule *ADJECTIVE*
extremely tiny • *a minuscule speck of dirt*
SPELLING ALERT! The word **minuscule** starts with **minus** not **mini**.

minute (*say* **min**-it) *NOUN* **minutes**
❶ one-sixtieth of an hour ❷ (*informal*) a short time • *I'll be ready in a minute!*

minute (*say* my-**newt**) *ADJECTIVE*
❶ tiny • *The ladybird was minute.* ❷ very detailed • *She gave the handwriting a minute examination.*

miracle *NOUN* **miracles**
a wonderful or magical happening that is unexpected

miraculous *ADJECTIVE*
something miraculous is wonderful or magical
By lunchtime, the whole place was a seething mass of men, women, and children all pushing and shoving to get a glimpse of this miraculous fruit.—JAMES AND THE GIANT PEACH, Roald Dahl

miraculously *ADVERB*
something happens miraculously when it seems to be a miracle • *The spacecraft had miraculously disappeared.*

mirage (*say* mi-**rahz**h) *NOUN* **mirages**
something that seems to be visible but is not really there, like a lake in a desert

mirror *NOUN* **mirrors**
a glass or metal surface that reflects things clearly

mirth *NOUN*
mirth is laughter or fun

mis- *PREFIX*
meaning 'wrong' or 'wrongly', as in *misbehave* and *misunderstanding*

misbehave *VERB* **misbehaves, misbehaving, misbehaved**
to misbehave is to behave badly
➤ **misbehaviour** *NOUN*

miscarriage *NOUN* **miscarriages**
when a baby is born before it is old enough to survive

miscellaneous (*say* mis-el-**ay**-ni-us) *ADJECTIVE*
a miscellaneous group is one that is made up of different kinds of things

miscellany (*say* mis-**el**-an-ee) *NOUN* **miscellanies**
a mixture of different things

mischief *NOUN*
mischief is naughty or troublesome behaviour

mischievous *ADJECTIVE*
naughty or troublesome
➤ **mischievously** *ADVERB*

miser *NOUN* **misers**
someone who stores money away and spends as little as they can
➤ **miserly** *ADJECTIVE*

miserable *ADJECTIVE*
❶ very unhappy • *He felt miserable.*
❷ unpleasant • *What miserable weather!*
➤ **miserably** *ADVERB*

misery *NOUN* **miseries**
❶ misery is great unhappiness or suffering
❷ (*informal*) a misery is someone who is always unhappy or complaining

misfire *VERB* **misfires, misfiring, misfired**
❶ a gun misfires when it fails to fire ❷ a plan or idea or joke misfires when it goes wrong

A B C D E F G H I J K L M N O P Q R S T U V W X Y Z

misfit *NOUN* **misfits**
someone who does not fit in well with other people

misfortune *NOUN* **misfortunes**
❶ a misfortune is an unlucky event or an accident ❷ misfortune is bad luck

mishap (*say* mis-hap) *NOUN* **mishaps**
an unfortunate accident

misjudge *VERB* **misjudges, misjudging, misjudged**
to misjudge someone or something is to form a wrong idea or opinion about them

mislay *VERB* **mislays, mislaying, mislaid**
to mislay something is to lose it for a short time

mislead *VERB* **misleads, misleading, misled**
to mislead someone is to give them a wrong idea or impression deliberately

misprint *NOUN* **misprints**
a mistake in printing, such as a spelling mistake

Miss *NOUN* **Misses**
a title you put before the name of a girl or unmarried woman

miss *VERB* **misses, missing, missed**
❶ to miss something is to fail to hit, reach, catch, see, hear or find it ❷ to miss someone or something is to be sad because they are not with you • *I missed my sister when she was in hospital.* ❸ to miss a train, bus or plane is to arrive too late to catch it ❹ to miss a lesson or other activity is to fail to attend it • *How many classes have you missed?* ❺ to miss something is also to notice that it is not where it should be • *When did you first miss your wallet?*

miss *NOUN* **misses**
not hitting, reaching or catching something • *Was that shot a hit or a miss?*

missile *NOUN* **missiles**
❶ a weapon that is fired a long distance and explodes when it lands ❷ an object thrown at someone

missing *ADJECTIVE*
something is missing when it is lost or not in the proper place

mission *NOUN* **missions**
❶ an important job that someone is sent to do or that someone feels they must do ❷ a place or building where missionaries work

missionary *NOUN* **missionaries**
someone who goes to another country to spread a religious faith

misspell *VERB* **misspells, misspelling, misspelt** *or* **misspelled**
to misspell a word is to spell it wrongly

mist *NOUN* **mists**
❶ damp cloudy air like a thin fog ❷ condensed water vapour on a window or mirror

mistake *NOUN* **mistakes**
something done or said wrongly

mistake *VERB* **mistakes, mistaking, mistook, mistaken**
to mistake one person or thing for another is to confuse them

mistaken *ADJECTIVE*
to be mistaken is to be incorrect or wrong • *You are mistaken if you believe that.*
➤ **mistakenly** *ADVERB*

mister *NOUN*
❶ Mr ❷ (*informal*) sir • *Can you tell me the time, mister?*

mistletoe *NOUN*
mistletoe is a plant with green leaves and white berries in winter

mistreat *VERB* **mistreats, mistreating, mistreated**
to mistreat someone is to treat them badly or unfairly
➤ **mistreatment** *NOUN*

mistress *NOUN* **mistresses**
❶ a woman who is in charge of something ❷ the woman owner of a dog or other animal

mistrust *VERB* **mistrusts, mistrusting, mistrusted**
to mistrust someone or something is not to trust them

misty *ADJECTIVE* **mistier, mistiest**
❶ if it is misty outside, there is a lot of mist in the air • *It all started on a misty*

morning in April. ❷ misty eyes are full
of tears

misunderstand *VERB* misunderstands, misunderstanding, misunderstood
to misunderstand something is to get
a wrong idea or impression about it
• *Jeff misunderstood the point of the question.*
➤ misunderstanding *NOUN*

misuse *(say mis-yooz) VERB* misuses, misusing, misused
to misuse something is to use it in the wrong
way or treat it badly

misuse *(say mis-yooss) NOUN*
misuse is using something in the wrong way

mite *NOUN* mites
❶ a tiny insect found in food ❷ a small child

mitre *(say my-ter) NOUN* mitres
❶ the tall tapering hat that a bishop wears
❷ a joint of two tapering pieces of wood or
cloth, forming a right angle

mitten *NOUN* mittens
a kind of glove without separate parts for
the fingers

mix *VERB* mixes, mixing, mixed
❶ to mix different things is to stir or shake
them together to make one thing ❷ to mix
is to get on well with other people • *She
mixes well.*
➤ to mix up people *or* things is to
confuse them
➤ mixer *NOUN*

mixed *ADJECTIVE*
containing two or more kinds of things or
people • *a bag of mixed nuts*

mixture *NOUN* mixtures
something made of different things
mixed together • *Sleet is a mixture of
rain and snow.*

mix-up *NOUN* mix-ups
a muddle or confused situation, especially one
that ruins a plan • *a mix-up with the dates for
the party*

ml *ABBREVIATION*
short for *millilitres*

MLA *NOUN* MLAs
a Member of the Legislative Assembly in
Northern Ireland

mm *ABBREVIATION*
short for *millimetres*

mnemonic *(say nim-on-ik) NOUN* mnemonics
a mnemonic is a short rhyme or sentence
that helps you to remember something, for
example the initial letters of *Richard Of York
Gave Battle In Vain* to remember the order of
colours in a rainbow

moan *NOUN* moans
❶ a long low sound, usually of suffering
❷ a complaint or grumble

moan *VERB* moans, moaning, moaned
❶ to moan is to make a long low sound
❷ to moan is also to complain or grumble
• *Megan was always moaning about
something or other.*

moat *NOUN* moats
a deep ditch round a castle, usually filled
with water
*So Gawain mounted, and rode across the great
plain towards the castle, which stood surrounded
by a wide moat and a palisade of pointed
stakes.—SIR GAWAIN AND THE GREEN KNIGHT,
Michael Morpurgo*

mob *NOUN* mobs
❶ a large disorderly crowd of people
❷ a gang

mob *VERB* mobs, mobbing, mobbed
people mob someone when they crowd
round them • *The band was mobbed by fans
wanting autographs.*

mobile *ADJECTIVE*
able to be moved or carried about easily
➤ mobility *NOUN*

mobile *NOUN* mobiles
❶ a mobile phone ❷ a hanging decoration
which moves about in the air

mobile phone *NOUN* mobile phones
a telephone you can carry around with you

moccasin *(say mok-a-sin) NOUN* moccasins
a soft leather shoe like those traditionally worn
by Native Americans

mock *VERB* **mocks, mocking, mocked**
to mock someone is to make fun of them
➤ **mockery** *NOUN*

mock *ADJECTIVE*
not real or genuine; pretended • *Our school held a mock election.*

modal verb *NOUN* **modal verbs**
a verb such as *can, may* or *will* that you use with another verb to say that something is possible or going to happen, or to ask permission to do something, for example *I might go home early,* or *Can I phone you later?*

mode *NOUN* **modes**
❶ the way that something is done • *Flying is the fastest mode of transport.* ❷ a way of behaving • *My mum went into panic mode!*

model *NOUN* **models**
❶ a small copy of an object • *a model of the space shuttle* ❷ a particular version or design of something • *the latest models of road bikes* ❸ someone who displays clothes by wearing them or who poses for an artist or photographer ❹ someone or something worth copying or imitating • *a model of good handwriting*

model *ADJECTIVE*
❶ being a small copy of something • *a collector of model cars* ❷ being a good example for people to follow • *I was never a model pupil.*

model *VERB* **models, modelling, modelled**
❶ to model something is to make a small copy of it ❷ to model one thing on another is to use the second thing as a pattern for the first • *The tent is modelled on the shape of an igloo.* ❸ to model, or to model clothes, is to work as an artist's model or a fashion model

moderate (*say* **mod-er-at**) *ADJECTIVE*
❶ a moderate amount or level is not too little and not too much ❷ moderate opinions are not extreme
➤ **moderately** *ADVERB* ➤ **moderation** *NOUN*

moderate (*say* **mod-er-ayt**) *VERB*
moderates, moderating, moderated
to moderate something is to make it less strong or severe

modern *ADJECTIVE*
belonging to the present day or recent times • *a gallery of modern art*

modernize (*also* **modernise**) *VERB*
modernizes, modernizing, modernized
to modernize something is to make it modern, or suitable for modern tastes
➤ **modernization** *NOUN*

modest *ADJECTIVE*
❶ not thinking or talking too much about how good you are ❷ not large or grand • *They lived in a modest house on the edge of town.*
➤ **modestly** *ADVERB* ➤ **modesty** *NOUN*

modify *VERB* **modifies, modifying, modified**
to modify something is to change it slightly
➤ **modification** *NOUN*

module (*say* **mod**-yool) *NOUN* **modules**
❶ a separate section or part of something larger, such as a spacecraft or building ❷ one of the parts that make up a course of study • *a module in art and design*

moist *ADJECTIVE*
slightly wet

moisten (*say* **moi-sen**) *VERB* **moistens, moistening, moistened**
to moisten something is to make it slightly wet

moisture *NOUN*
moisture is tiny drops of water in the air or on a surface

moisturize (*also* **moisturise**) *VERB*
moisturizes, moisturizing, moisturized
to moisturize skin is to use cream to make it less dry
➤ **moisturizer** *NOUN*

molar (*say* **moh-ler**) *NOUN* **molars**
one of the wide teeth at the back of your mouth

mole *NOUN* **moles**
❶ a small furry animal that digs holes under the ground ❷ a small dark spot on the skin

molecule (*say* **mol-i-kewl**) *NOUN* **molecules**
the smallest part into which a substance can be divided without changing its chemical nature; a group of atoms
➤ **molecular** (*say* **mo-lek-yew-ler**) *ADJECTIVE*

molehill *NOUN* **molehills**
a small pile of earth thrown up by a mole
➤ **to make a mountain out of a molehill** is to give something too much importance

a
b
c
d
e
f
g
h
i
j
k
l
m
n
o
p
q
r
s
t
u
v
w
x
y
z

mollusc *NOUN* **molluscs**
an animal with a soft body and usually a hard shell, such as a snail or an oyster

molten *ADJECTIVE*
molten rock or metal has been made into liquid by great heat

mom *NOUN* **moms** (*North American, informal*)
mother

moment *NOUN* **moments**
❶ a very short period of time • *Please wait a moment.* ❷ a particular time • *At that moment, all the lights went out.*
➤ **at the moment** now

momentary (*say* **moh**-men-ter-ee)
ADJECTIVE
lasting for only a moment
➤ **momentarily** (*say* moh-men-**tar**-i-lee)
ADVERB

momentous (*say* moh-**ment**-us) *ADJECTIVE*
very important • *We are on the verge of a momentous discovery.*

momentum (*say* moh-**ment**-um) *NOUN*
momentum is the amount or force of movement • *The sledge gained momentum as it sped down the hill.*

monarch *NOUN* **monarchs**
a king, queen, emperor or empress ruling a country

monarchy *NOUN* **monarchies**
❶ monarchy is rule by a monarch ❷ a monarchy is a country ruled by a monarch

monastery (*say* **mon**-a-ster-ee) *NOUN*
monasteries
a building where monks live and work
➤ **monastic** *ADJECTIVE* to do with a monastery or monks

Monday *NOUN* **Mondays**
the second day of the week
DID YOU KNOW? **Monday** is an Old English name meaning 'day of the moon'.

money *NOUN*
money is coins and notes used by people to buy things

mongoose *NOUN* **mongooses**
a small animal like a large weasel, that can kill snakes

Rikki-tikki did the real fighting. He was a mongoose, rather like a little cat in his fur and his tail, but quite like a weasel in his head and his habits.—THE JUNGLE BOOK, Rudyard Kipling

mongrel (*say* **mung**-rel) *NOUN* **mongrels**
a dog of mixed breeds

monitor *NOUN* **monitors**
❶ a device used for checking how something is working ❷ a computer or television screen ❸ a pupil who is given a special job to do at school

monitor *VERB* **monitors, monitoring, monitored**
to monitor something or someone is to watch or test them to see how they are working

monk *NOUN* **monks**
a member of a religious community of men

monkey *NOUN* **monkeys**
❶ an animal mainly found in tropical countries, which has a long tail and can climb trees ❷ a mischievous young child
SPOT THE DIFFERENCE! Monkeys have tails, but apes do not.

mono– *PREFIX*
meaning 'having one of something', as in *monocle*

monocle *NOUN* **monocles**
a lens that you wear over one eye, like half of a pair of glasses

monogram *NOUN* **monograms**
a design made up of a letter or a group of letters

monologue (*say* **mon**-o-log) *NOUN*
monologues
a long speech by one person or performer

monotonous (*say* mon-**ot**-on-us)
ADJECTIVE
something monotonous is dull and boring because it does not change • *Miss Plimsoll droned on in a monotonous voice.*
➤ **monotonously** *ADVERB*
➤ **monotony** *NOUN*

monsoon *NOUN* **monsoons**
a strong wind in and around the Indian Ocean, bringing heavy rain in summer

monster *NOUN* **monsters**
a huge frightening creature • *In the story, Perseus fights a terrifying sea monster.*

monster *ADJECTIVE* (*informal*)
huge • *A monster wave destroyed the ship.*

monstrosity *NOUN* **monstrosities**
a monstrosity is a dreadful or shocking thing

monstrous *ADJECTIVE*
❶ like a monster; huge ❷ very shocking or cruel • *This was the scene of a monstrous crime.*

month *NOUN* **months**
one of the twelve parts into which a year is divided
◗ DID YOU KNOW? The word **month** is an Old English word related to **moon**, because time was measured by the phases of the moon.

monthly *ADJECTIVE, ADVERB*
happening every month • *the monthly meeting of the club*

monument *NOUN* **monuments**
a statue, building or column put up to remind people of some person or event

monumental *ADJECTIVE*
❶ built as a monument ❷ great or huge • *The mission was a monumental success.*

moo *VERB* **moos, mooing, mooed**
to make the sound of a cow

mood *NOUN* **moods**
the way someone feels at a particular time • *I could tell Uncle Ted was in a grumpy mood.*

moody *ADJECTIVE* **moodier, moodiest**
❶ gloomy or sulking • *The twins sat in moody silence.* ❷ likely to have sudden changes of mood
➤ **moodily** *ADVERB* ➤ **moodiness** *NOUN*

moon *NOUN* **moons**
❶ the natural satellite which orbits the earth and shines in the sky at night ❷ a similar object which orbits another planet • *Titan is the largest of Saturn's moons.*
➤ A related adjective is **lunar**.

moonbeam *NOUN* **moonbeams**
a beam of light from the moon
The moonbeam was brighter than ever on Sophie's pillow. She decided to get out of bed and close the gap in the curtains.—THE BFG, Roald Dahl

moonless *ADJECTIVE*
without a moon or moonlight • *a moonless night*

moonlight *NOUN*
moonlight is the light reflected from the moon
➤ **moonlit** *ADJECTIVE* lit by the moon

moonstone *NOUN* **moonstones**
a type of gem stone with a pale milky colour

moonwalk *NOUN* **moonwalks**
a walk that an astronaut takes on the surface of the moon

moor *NOUN* **moors**
an area of rough land covered with bracken and bushes
➤ **moorland** *NOUN* land that consists of moors

moor *VERB* **moors, mooring, moored**
to moor a boat is to tie it up to the land

moorhen *NOUN* **moorhens**
a small water bird

mooring *NOUN* **moorings**
a place where a boat can be moored

moose *NOUN* **moose**
a North American elk

mop *NOUN* **mops**
a piece of soft material on the end of a stick, used for cleaning floors or dishes

mop *VERB* **mops, mopping, mopped**
to mop something is to clean it with a mop
➤ **to mop something up** is to clear away spilt liquid

mope *VERB* **mopes, moping, moped**
to mope is to be miserable and not interested in doing anything • *My big sister was still in her room, moping as usual.*

moral *ADJECTIVE*
❶ to do with people's behaviour and what is right and wrong ❷ being or doing good and what is right
➤ **morality** *NOUN* ➤ **morally** *ADVERB*

moral *NOUN* **morals**
a lesson taught by a story or event • *The moral of the story is to be careful what you wish for.*

morale (*say* mo-**rahl**) *NOUN*
morale is confidence or courage

a
b
c
d
e
f
g
h
i
j
k
l
m
n
o
p
q
r
s
t
u
v
w
x
y
z

morals *PLURAL NOUN*
standards of behaviour

morbid *ADJECTIVE*
thinking about gloomy or unpleasant things
such as death
➤ **morbidly** *ADVERB*

more *DETERMINER*
greater in number or amount • *The plants need
more water in summer.*

more *PRONOUN*
a larger number or amount • *Would you like
some more?*

more *ADVERB*
❶ to a greater extent • *You must try to rest
more.* ❷ again • *Please read the letter once
more.*
➤ **more or less** almost; approximately
• *The show will last ninety minutes, more
or less.*

moreover *ADVERB*
also; in addition to what has been said

Mormon *NOUN* **Mormons**
a member of a religious group founded in
the USA

morning *NOUN* **mornings**
the early part of the day before noon

moron *NOUN* **morons** (*informal*)
a very stupid person
➤ **moronic** *ADJECTIVE*

morose (*say* mo-rohss) *ADJECTIVE*
bad-tempered and miserable

morris dance *NOUN* **morris dances**
a traditional English dance performed by people
in costume with ribbons and bells
[DID YOU KNOW?] It was originally called
Moorish dance, because people thought it
came from the *Moors*, a Muslim people of
North Africa.

Morse code *NOUN*
a code for sending radio signals, using dots and
dashes to represent letters and numbers
[DID YOU KNOW?] **Morse code** is named after its
inventor, the American S. F. B. *Morse*.

morsel *NOUN* **morsels**
a small piece of food

mortal *ADJECTIVE*
❶ certain to die • *All humans are mortal.*
❷ causing death; fatal • *The knight received a
mortal wound.* ❸ mortal enemies will try to kill
each other
➤ **mortality** *NOUN*

mortal *NOUN* **mortals**
a human being or other mortal creature

mortally *ADVERB*
someone who is mortally wounded is certain to
die from their wounds

mortar *NOUN* **mortars**
❶ mortar is a mixture of sand, cement and
water, used in building to stick bricks together
❷ a mortar is a small thick bowl for pounding
food with a tool called a pestle ❸ a mortar is
also a small cannon

mortuary *NOUN* **mortuaries**
a place where dead bodies are kept before they
are buried or cremated

mosaic (*say* moh-**zay**-ik) *NOUN* **mosaics**
a picture or design made from small coloured
pieces of glass or stone

mosque (*say* mosk) *NOUN* **mosques**
a building where Muslims worship

mosquito (*say* mos-**kee**-toh) *NOUN*
mosquitoes
an insect that sucks blood and carries disease

moss *NOUN* **mosses**
a plant that grows in damp places and has
no flowers

mossy *ADJECTIVE* **mossier, mossiest**
covered in moss

most *DETERMINER*
greatest in number or amount • *Most people
said they liked the show.*

most *PRONOUN*
the greatest number or amount • *We had
already eaten most of the food.*

most *ADVERB*
❶ more than any other • *I like this flavour most.*
❷ very; extremely • *It was all most peculiar.*

mostly *ADVERB*
mainly

motel (*say* moh-**tel**) *NOUN* **motels**
a hotel near a main road, with parking and
rooms for motorists

moth *NOUN* **moths**
an insect rather like a butterfly, that usually flies around at night

mother *NOUN* **mothers**
your female parent
➤ A related adjective is **maternal**.

motherhood *NOUN*
motherhood is being a mother and looking after children

mother-in-law *NOUN* **mothers-in-law**
someone's mother-in-law is the mother of their husband or wife

motherly *ADJECTIVE*
kind or caring like a mother

mother-of-pearl *NOUN*
a pearly lining in some types of shell, used to make buttons and jewellery

Mother's Day *NOUN*
a day of the year on which mothers are celebrated by their children

motif *NOUN* **motifs**
a decorative design or symbol • *a wall painted with ancient Egyptian motifs*

motion *NOUN* **motions**
a way of moving; movement
➤ **to go through the motions** is to do or say something because you have to, without much interest

motionless *ADJECTIVE*
not moving; still

motivate *VERB* **motivates, motivating, motivated**
to motivate someone is to make them keen to achieve something

motive *NOUN* **motives**
a person's motive is what makes them do something • *The police could find no motive for the murder.*

motor *NOUN* **motors**
a machine that provides power to drive machinery

motorbike *NOUN* **motorbikes**
a motorcycle

motorcycle *NOUN* **motorcycles**
a motor vehicle with two wheels and a saddle for the riders
➤ **motorcyclist** *NOUN*

motorist *NOUN* **motorists**
someone who drives a motor car

motorway *NOUN* **motorways**
a wide road for fast long-distance traffic

mottled *ADJECTIVE*
marked with spots or patches of colour
• *a tortoise with a mottled shell*

motto *NOUN* **mottoes**
❶ a short saying used as a guide for behaviour • *My motto was always 'Keep Calm and Carry On'.* ❷ a short verse or riddle found inside a cracker

mould *NOUN* **moulds**
❶ a mould is a container for making things like jelly or plaster set in a special shape ❷ mould is also a furry growth that appears on moist surfaces, especially on something decaying

mould *VERB* **moulds, moulding, moulded**
to mould something is to make it have a particular shape or character

mouldy *ADJECTIVE* **mouldier, mouldiest**
covered in mould or smelling like mould
• *a mouldy half-eaten sandwich*

moult (*say* mohlt) *VERB* **moults, moulting, moulted**
animals or birds moult when they lose hair or feathers

mound *NOUN* **mounds**
a pile of earth or stones; a small hill

mount *VERB* **mounts, mounting, mounted**
❶ to mount a horse or bicycle is to get on it so that you can ride it ❷ to mount is to increase in amount • *The number of casualties was mounting.* ❸ to mount a picture or photograph is to put it in a frame or album to display it

mount *NOUN* **mounts**
❶ a mountain, especially in names such as *Mount Everest* ❷ something on which a picture or photograph is mounted ❸ an animal for someone to ride on

a b c d e f g h i j k l **m** n o p q r s t u v w x y z

mountain NOUN **mountains**
❶ a very high hill ❷ a large amount • *There is a mountain of washing-up to do.*

mountaineer NOUN **mountaineers**
someone who climbs mountains

mountaineering NOUN
mountaineering is the sport of climbing mountains

mountainous ADJECTIVE
a mountainous place has a lot of mountains • *a mountainous part of Wales*

mourn VERB **mourns, mourning, mourned**
to mourn is to be sad, especially because someone has died
➤ **mourner** NOUN mourners are the people who go to a funeral

mournful ADJECTIVE
sad and sorrowful • *It was the mournful cry of a wounded animal.*
➤ **mournfully** ADVERB

mouse NOUN **mice**
❶ a small animal with a long tail and a pointed nose ❷ (*computing*) a small device that you move around on a mat to control the movements of the cursor on the computer screen

mousetrap NOUN **mousetraps**
a trap for catching and killing mice

mousse (*say* mooss) NOUN **mousses**
❶ a creamy pudding flavoured with chocolate or fruit ❷ a frothy creamy substance used for holding hair while styling it
SPELLING ALERT! You can eat a chocolate **mousse**, but a **moose** is an animal with antlers.

moustache (*say* mus-tahsh) NOUN **moustaches**
a strip of hair that grows above a person's top lip
Captain Hardcastle sported a moustache that was the same colour as his hair, and oh what a moustache it was!—BOY, Roald Dahl

mousy ADJECTIVE **mousier, mousiest**
❶ mousy hair is light brown in colour ❷ a mousy person is timid and feeble

mouth NOUN **mouths**
❶ the part of your face that opens for eating and speaking ❷ the place where

a river flows into the sea ❸ an opening or outlet • *The mouth of the cave was hidden from view.*

mouthful NOUN **mouthfuls**
an amount of food you put in your mouth

mouth organ NOUN **mouth organs**
a small musical instrument you play by blowing and sucking while passing it along your lips

mouthpiece NOUN **mouthpieces**
the part of a musical instrument or other device that you put to your mouth

mouthwatering ADJECTIVE
looking or smelling delicious • *a book of mouthwatering recipes*

movable ADJECTIVE
able to be moved

move VERB **moves, moving, moved**
❶ to move something is to take it from one place to another ❷ to move is to go from one place to another ❸ to move someone is to affect their feelings • *Their story moved us deeply.*

move NOUN **moves**
❶ a movement ❷ a player's turn in a game
➤ **to get a move on** (*informal*) is to hurry up
➤ **to be on the move** is to be moving or making progress

movement NOUN **movements**
❶ movement is moving or being moved ❷ a movement is a group of people working together to achieve something ❸ in music, a movement is one of the main parts of a long piece such as a symphony

movie NOUN **movies** (*North American, informal*)
a cinema film
DID YOU KNOW? The word **movie** is short for *moving picture.*

moving ADJECTIVE
causing someone to feel strong emotion, especially sadness or pity

mow VERB **mows, mowing, mowed, mown**
to mow grass is to cut it with a machine
➤ **to mow people down** is to knock them down and kill them

mozzarella *NOUN*
a soft type of Italian cheese, often used on pizzas

MP (*say* em-**pee**) *NOUN* **MPs**
a Member of Parliament • *There are 650 MPs in the House of Commons.*

Mr (*say* **mis**-ter) *NOUN* **Messrs**
a title you put before a man's name

Mrs (*say* **mis**-iz) *NOUN* **Mrs**
a title you put before a married woman's name

Ms (*say* miz) *NOUN*
a title put before a woman's name

MSP (*say* em-es-**pee**) *NOUN* **MSPs**
a Member of the Scottish Parliament

much *DETERMINER*
existing in a large amount • *There was much excitement that morning.*

much *PRONOUN*
a large amount of something • *Two pounds is not very much for a ticket.*

much *ADVERB*
❶ greatly; considerably • *The parcel arrived, much to my surprise.* ❷ about; approximately • *The two colours are much the same.*

muck *NOUN*
❶ muck is farmyard manure ❷ (*informal*) muck is dirt or filth

muck *VERB* **mucks, mucking, mucked** (*informal*)
➤ **to muck about** *or* **muck around** is to behave stupidly or idly
➤ **to muck something up** is to do it very badly

mucky *ADJECTIVE* **muckier, muckiest**
dirty or messy

mucous (*say* mew-kuss) *ADJECTIVE*
like mucus or covered in mucus
SPELLING ALERT! **Mucous** is an adjective whereas **mucus** is a noun. You say *a mucous coating* but *coated with mucus.*

mucus (*say* mew-kuss) *NOUN*
a thick slimy liquid produced inside your nose and other parts of your body • *The alien ship was covered in a yellowish mucus.*

mud *NOUN*
mud is wet soft earth

muddle *VERB* **muddles, muddling, muddled**
❶ to muddle things is to mix them up
❷ to muddle someone is to confuse them

muddle *NOUN* **muddles**
a confusion or mess • *I've got these papers in a bit of a muddle.*

muddy *ADJECTIVE* **muddier, muddiest**
covered in mud

mudguard *NOUN* **mudguards**
a curved cover fixed over a bicycle wheel to stop mud and water being thrown up on to the rider

muesli (*say* **myooz**-lee) *NOUN*
a breakfast food made of cereals, nuts and dried fruit

muezzin *NOUN* **muezzins**
a man who calls Muslims to prayer from a minaret

muffin *NOUN* **muffins**
a small sponge cake often containing fruit or chocolate chips • *a blueberry muffin*

muffle *VERB* **muffles, muffling, muffled**
❶ to muffle something is to cover or wrap it to protect it or keep it warm ❷ to muffle a sound is to deaden it or reduce it

mug *NOUN* **mugs**
a large cup, usually used without a saucer

mug *VERB* **mugs, mugging, mugged**
to mug someone is to attack and rob them in the street
➤ **mugger** *NOUN* a person who attacks and robs someone in the street

muggy *ADJECTIVE* **muggier, muggiest**
a muggy day is unpleasantly warm and damp

mulberry *NOUN* **mulberries**
a soft purple berry that grows on a tree

mule *NOUN* **mules**
an animal that is the offspring of a donkey and a mare

multi– *PREFIX*
meaning 'having many of something', as in *multicoloured*

a b c d e f g h i j k l m n o p q r s t u v w x y z

multicultural *ADJECTIVE*
a multicultural group or place is made up of many different cultures

multimedia *ADJECTIVE*
a multimedia show or event uses a mixture of sound and images • *a multimedia exhibition about the Vikings*

multiple *ADJECTIVE*
having many parts

multiple *NOUN* **multiples**
a number that can be divided exactly by another number • *30 and 50 are multiples of 10.*

multiplication *NOUN*
multiplication is when you multiply numbers

multiply *VERB* **multiplies, multiplying, multiplied**
❶ to multiply a number is to add it to itself a certain number of times • *Five multiplied by four equals twenty (5 × 4 = 20).* ❷ to multiply is to increase or become many • *His doubts started to multiply.*

multi-storey *ADJECTIVE*
having more than one level or storey • *a multi-storey car park*

multitude *NOUN* **multitudes**
a very large number of people or things

mum *NOUN* **mums** (*informal*)
mother

mumble *VERB* **mumbles, mumbling, mumbled**
to speak softly and unclearly

mummify *VERB* **mummifies, mummifying, mummified**
in ancient Egypt, to mummify a dead body was to prepare it as a mummy
➤ **mummification** *NOUN*

mummy *NOUN* **mummies**
❶ (*informal*) mother ❷ an ancient Egyptian mummy is a dead body that was wrapped in cloth and treated with oils for burial

mumps *NOUN*
mumps is an infectious disease that makes the neck swell painfully

munch *VERB* **munches, munching, munched**
to munch food is to chew it noisily

mundane (*say* **mun**-dayn) *ADJECTIVE*
ordinary or dull

mural *NOUN* **murals**
a picture painted on a wall

murder *VERB* **murders, murdering, murdered**
to murder someone is to kill them deliberately

murder *NOUN* **murders**
❶ murder is the deliberate killing of someone
That stain should have been the final proof that Sir Henry had bumped off his wife in one of the most gruesome murders any detective would have to solve.—MASTER DETECTIVE, Astrid Lindgren
❷ (*informal*) you can say something is murder when it is very difficult or unpleasant • *It was murder cycling uphill in that heat!*

murderer *NOUN* **murderers**
someone who commits murder

murderous *ADJECTIVE*
likely to commit murder; showing you are very angry • *The captain had a murderous leer in his eye.*

murky *ADJECTIVE* **murkier, murkiest**
dark and gloomy • *a cold and murky cave*
➤ **murkiness** *NOUN*

murmur *NOUN* **murmurs**
a low or soft continuous sound, especially of people speaking
The trumpets were sounding, and when the trumpets stopped for breath the children could hear the cling-clang of armour and the murmur of voices.—FIVE CHILDREN AND IT, Edith Nesbit

murmur *VERB* **murmurs, murmuring, murmured**
to murmur is to speak softly with a low continuous sound

muscle *NOUN* **muscles**
a bundle of fibres that can stretch to cause movement of a part of the body

muscle *VERB* **muscles, muscling, muscled**
➤ **to muscle in on something** (*informal*) is to try to take part in something that does not concern you
SPELLING ALERT! You have **muscles** in your body, but you find **mussels** on a beach.

muscular *ADJECTIVE*
having a lot of muscles; powerful
➤ **muscularity** *NOUN*

muse (*say* mewz) *VERB* **muses, musing, mused**
to muse on something is to think about it for a long time • *Ted was still musing on what to do next.*

museum *NOUN* **museums**
a place where interesting old or valuable objects are displayed for people to see

mush *NOUN*
a thick soft pulpy mass • *The rain had turned our picnic into mush.*

mushroom *NOUN* **mushrooms**
a fast-growing edible fungus with a dome-shaped top

mushroom *VERB* **mushrooms, mushrooming, mushroomed**
things mushroom when they grow or appear suddenly like mushrooms • *Blocks of flats mushroomed in the city.*

mushy *ADJECTIVE* **mushier, mushiest**
soft and pulpy like mush
➤ **mushiness** *NOUN*

music *NOUN*
❶ music is pleasant or interesting sounds made by instruments or by the voice ❷ music is also a system of printed or written symbols for making this kind of sound

musical *ADJECTIVE*
❶ to do with music ❷ good at music or interested in it • *She comes from a very musical family.*
➤ **musically** *ADVERB*

musical *NOUN* **musicals**
a play or film with music and songs

musician *NOUN* **musicians**
someone who plays a musical instrument, especially for a living

musket *NOUN* **muskets**
an old type of gun with a long barrel
As we passed the two-pointed hill, we could see the black mouth of Ben Gunn's cave, and a figure standing by it, leaning on a musket.—TREASURE ISLAND, Robert Louis Stevenson

musketeer *NOUN* **musketeers**
a soldier armed with a musket

Muslim *NOUN* **Muslims**
someone who follows the religion of Islam

muslin *NOUN*
a type of fine cotton cloth
DID YOU KNOW? The name of the cloth comes from *Mosel*, a city in Iraq where it was originally made.

mussel *NOUN* **mussels**
a black shellfish, often found sticking to rocks

must *VERB*
This word is used with another verb to show ❶ that someone has to do something • *I must send a reply soon.* ❷ that something is certain • *You must be joking!*

mustang *NOUN* **mustangs**
a wild horse found in North America and Mexico

mustard *NOUN*
a yellow paste or powder used to give food a hot taste

muster *VERB* **musters, mustering, mustered**
to muster something is to assemble it or gather it together • *We couldn't muster the energy to go out.*

mustn't
short for *must not* • *We mustn't make a sound.*

musty *ADJECTIVE* **mustier, mustiest**
smelling or tasting mouldy or stale
➤ **mustiness** *NOUN*

mutant *NOUN* **mutants**
a living creature that is different from others of the same type because of changes in its genes

mutation *NOUN* **mutations**
a change in the form of a living creature because of changes in its genes
➤ **mutate** *VERB*

mute *ADJECTIVE*
not speaking or able to speak
➤ **mutely** *ADVERB*

a
b
c
d
e
f
g
h
i
j
k
l
m
n
o
p
q
r
s
t
u
v
w
x
y
z

mute *NOUN* **mutes**
a device fitted to a musical instrument to soften the sound

mute *VERB* **mutes, muting, muted**
to mute a television or other device is to turn off the sound

muted *ADJECTIVE*
❶ a muted sound is silent or quiet
• *The stranger spoke in a muted voice.*
❷ a muted colour is soft or pale

mutilate *VERB* **mutilates, mutilating, mutilated**
to mutilate something is to damage it by breaking or cutting off part of it
➤ **mutilation** *NOUN*

mutinous *ADJECTIVE*
mutinous people take part in a mutiny or refuse to obey orders

mutiny (*say* **mew**-tin-ee) *NOUN* **mutinies**
a rebellion by sailors or soldiers against their officers

mutiny *VERB* **mutinies, mutinying, mutinied**
to mutiny is to take part in a mutiny
➤ **mutineer** *NOUN*

mutter *VERB* **mutters, muttering, muttered**
to murmur or grumble in a low voice
• *The jailer muttered something under his breath.*

mutton *NOUN*
mutton is meat from an adult sheep

mutual (*say* **mew**-tew-al) *ADJECTIVE*
felt or done equally by two or more people
• *All of us breathed a mutual sigh of relief.*
➤ **mutually** *ADVERB*

muzzle *NOUN* **muzzles**
❶ an animal's nose and mouth
A large hairy pink muzzle broke the surface of the water. 'What is it?' Arthur asked impatiently. 'I believe it is a fresh-water sea-cow!'—HERE BE MONSTERS, Alan Snow
❷ a cover put over an animal's nose and mouth so that it cannot bite

muzzle *VERB* **muzzles, muzzling, muzzled**
to muzzle an animal is to put a muzzle on it

my *DETERMINER*
belonging to me • *That's my bike over there.*

myriad *ADJECTIVE*
very many; countless • *the myriad stars in the night sky*

myrrh (*say* mer) *NOUN*
a type of resin used to make perfumes and incense • *gold, frankincense and myrrh*

myself *PRONOUN*
me and nobody else, used to refer back to the person who is speaking • *I tried not to injure myself.*
➤ **by myself** on my own; alone • *I wrote the story all by myself.*

mysterious *ADJECTIVE*
full of mystery; strange and puzzling
• *Mysterious noises came from inside the trunk.*

mysteriously *ADVERB*
something that happens mysteriously is difficult to explain or understand. • *Next day the door was mysteriously locked.*

mystery *NOUN* **mysteries**
something strange or puzzling • *Exactly why the ship sank is a mystery.*

mystify *VERB* **mystifies, mystifying, mystified**
to mystify someone is to puzzle them very much
➤ **mystification** *NOUN*

myth (*say* mith) *NOUN* **myths**
❶ a traditional story about gods, goddesses and heroes in ancient times ❷ an untrue story or belief • *It is a myth that carrots help you see in the dark.*

mythical *ADJECTIVE*
imaginary; only found in myths • *The Minotaur is a mythical beast.*

mythology *NOUN*
mythology is the study of myths
➤ **mythological** *ADJECTIVE*

Nn

nab VERB **nabs**, **nabbing**, **nabbed** (*informal*)
to nab someone is to catch or grab them

nachos PLURAL NOUN
tortilla chips topped with melted cheese

nag VERB **nags**, **nagging**, **nagged**
to nag someone is to keep criticizing them or
complaining to them
nag NOUN **nags** (*informal*)
a horse

Nahuatl (*say* nah-waht-l) NOUN
a language spoken in southern Mexico and
Central America
DID YOU KNOW? The words **chilli**, **chocolate** and
tomato come from Nahuatl.

nail NOUN **nails**
❶ the hard covering on the end of one of your
fingers or toes ❷ a small sharp piece of metal
used to fix pieces of wood together
nail VERB **nails**, **nailing**, **nailed**
❶ to nail something is to fasten it with a nail
or nails ❷ to nail someone is to catch or trap
them

naive (*say* ny-**eev**) ADJECTIVE
❶ too ready to believe what you are told;
showing a lack of experience ❷ innocent and
trusting
➤ **naively** ADVERB ➤ **naivety** NOUN

naked (*say* nay-kid) ADJECTIVE
without any clothes or coverings on
➤ **to look at something with the naked eye**
is to look at it with your eyes without the help
of a telescope or microscope
➤ **nakedness** NOUN

name NOUN **names**
what you call a person or thing
name VERB **names**, **naming**, **named**
❶ to name someone or something is to
give them a name ❷ to name someone or
something is to say what they are called
• *Can you name these plants?*

nameless ADJECTIVE
❶ not having a name ❷ not named or
identified • *The culprit shall be nameless.*

namely ADVERB
that is to say • *I have two cats, namely Ziggy
and Tom.*

nan NOUN **nans**
❶ an Indian flat bread cooked in a clay oven
❷ (*informal*) grandmother

nanny NOUN **nannies**
❶ a person whose job is to look after small
children ❷ (*informal*) grandmother

nanny goat NOUN **nanny goats**
a female goat

nap NOUN **naps**
a short sleep
nap VERB **naps**, **napping**, **napped**
to have a nap

napkin NOUN **napkins**
a piece of cloth or paper to keep your clothes
clean or to wipe your lips at meals

nappy NOUN **nappies**
a piece of cloth or a paper pad put round
a baby's bottom

narcissus (*say* nar-**sis**-us) NOUN **narcissi**
a garden flower like a daffodil

narrate VERB **narrates**, **narrating**,
narrated
to narrate a story or experience is to tell it
to someone • *Sophie narrated her dream to
the BFG.*
➤ **narration** NOUN

narrative NOUN **narratives**
a story or account that someone tells

narrator NOUN **narrators**
the person who is telling a story

narrow ADJECTIVE **narrower**, **narrowest**
❶ not wide ❷ with only a small margin
of error or safety • *We all had a narrow
escape.*
➤ **narrowly** ADVERB you say that something
narrowly happens when it only just happens
• *She narrowly escaped injury.*

narrow-minded *ADJECTIVE*
not liking or understanding other people's ideas or beliefs

narwhal *NOUN* **narwhals**
a small Arctic whale with a long twisted tusk

nasal *ADJECTIVE*
to do with the nose

nasturtium (*say* na-**ster**-shum) *NOUN* **nasturtiums**
a garden flower with round leaves

nasty *ADJECTIVE* **nastier, nastiest**
not pleasant; unkind
➤ **nastily** *ADVERB* ➤ **nastiness** *NOUN*

nation *NOUN* **nations**
❶ a large number of people who have the same history, language and customs, and live in the same part of the world under one government ❷ a country and the people who live there

national *ADJECTIVE*
to do with a nation or country
➤ **nationally** *ADVERB* something happens nationally when it happens all over the country

nationalism *NOUN*
supporting your country and wanting it to be independent
➤ **nationalist** *NOUN*

nationality *NOUN* **nationalities**
the nation someone belongs to • *'What is your nationality?' 'Canadian.'*

nationwide *ADJECTIVE, ADVERB*
over the whole of a country

native *NOUN* **natives**
a person born in a particular place • *He is a native of Sweden.*

native *ADJECTIVE*
of the country where you were born • *English is my native language.*

Native American *NOUN*
Native Americans
one of, or a descendant of, the people who were living in North, Central or South America before European settlers arrived

nativity (*say* na-**tiv**-i-tee) *NOUN*
nativities (*formal*)
someone's birth
➤ **the Nativity** in Christianity, the Nativity is the birth of Jesus Christ

natural *ADJECTIVE*
❶ made or done by nature, not by people or machines ❷ normal; not surprising ❸ belonging to someone from birth • *a natural talent for music* ❹ in music, not sharp or flat

natural *NOUN* **naturals**
❶ a natural note in music; a sign (♮) that shows a note is natural ❷ someone who is naturally good at something • *She's a natural at juggling.*

natural history *NOUN*
natural history is the study of plants and animals

naturalist *NOUN* **naturalists**
someone who studies natural history

naturally *ADVERB*
❶ in a natural way • *The gas is produced naturally.* ❷ as you would expect • *Naturally we were worried about you.*

nature *NOUN* **natures**
❶ nature is everything in the world that was not made by people, such as plants and animals ❷ a person's or thing's nature is the qualities or characteristics they have • *She has a loving nature.* ❸ a nature is a kind or sort of thing • *He likes insects and things of that nature.*

nature reserve *NOUN* **nature reserves**
an area of land set aside to keep wildlife

nature trail *NOUN* **nature trails**
a path in the country with signs telling you about the plants and wildlife you can see there

naughty *ADJECTIVE* **naughtier, naughtiest**
behaving in a rude or disobedient way
➤ **naughtily** *ADVERB* ➤ **naughtiness** *NOUN*
DID YOU KNOW? The word **naughty** is related to *nought* and used to mean 'very poor'.

nausea *NOUN*
nausea is a feeling of sickness or disgust

nauseating *ADJECTIVE*
something nauseating makes you feel sick or queasy • *the nauseating stench of rotting meat*

nauseous *ADJECTIVE*
if you feel nauseous, you feel as if you are going to be sick

nautical *ADJECTIVE*
connected with ships or sailors

naval *ADJECTIVE*
to do with a navy

nave *NOUN* naves
the main central part of a church

navel *NOUN* navels
the small hollow at the front of your stomach

navigate *VERB* navigates, navigating, navigated
❶ to navigate is to make sure that an aircraft, ship or vehicle is going in the right direction ❷ to navigate a sea or river is to sail a ship on it

navigation *NOUN*
navigation is making sure that an aircraft, ship or vehicle is going in the right direction

navigator *NOUN* navigators
the person who makes sure that an aircraft, ship or vehicle is going in the right direction

navy *NOUN* navies
❶ a fleet of ships and the people trained to use them ❷ navy blue

navy blue *NOUN, ADJECTIVE*
very dark blue

near *ADVERB, ADJECTIVE* nearer, nearest
not far away
➤ **near by** at a place not far away • *They live near by.*

near *PREPOSITION*
not far away from something • *She lives near the town.*

near *VERB* nears, nearing, neared
to near a place is to come close to it • *The ships were nearing the harbour.*

nearby *ADJECTIVE*
near; not far away • *We live in a nearby town.*

nearly *ADVERB*
❶ almost • *It was nearly midnight.* ❷ closely • *They are nearly related.*

neat *ADJECTIVE* neater, neatest
❶ tidy and carefully arranged ❷ skilfully done • *That was a neat goal.* ❸ without water added • *They were drinking neat orange juice.*
➤ **neatly** *ADVERB* ➤ **neatness** *NOUN*

nebula *NOUN* nebulae
a cloud of gas and dust in outer space

necessarily *ADVERB*
for certain; definitely • *It won't necessarily cost you a lot.*

necessary *ADJECTIVE*
needed very much; essential • *It is necessary to wear a bicycle helmet.*

necessity *NOUN* necessities
❶ necessity is need • *There is no necessity for you to come too.* ❷ a necessity is also something needed • *We have brought all the necessities for a picnic.*

neck *NOUN* necks
❶ the part of the body that joins the head to the shoulders ❷ a narrow part of something, especially of a bottle
➤ **to be neck and neck** is to be almost exactly together in a race or contest

necklace *NOUN* necklaces
a piece of jewellery you wear round your neck

nectar *NOUN*
nectar is a sweet liquid collected by bees from flowers

nectarine *NOUN* nectarines
a kind of peach with a smooth skin

need *VERB* needs, needing, needed
❶ to need something is to be without it when you should have it ❷ to need to do something is to have to do it • *I needed to get a haircut.*

need *NOUN* needs
❶ a need is something that you need ❷ need is a situation in which something is necessary • *There's no need to shout.*
➤ **to be in need** is to need money or help

needle *NOUN* needles
❶ a very thin pointed piece of metal used for sewing ❷ something long, thin and sharp,

such as a knitting needle or a pine needle
❸ the pointer of a meter or compass

needless *ADJECTIVE*
not necessary • *That was a needless waste of time.*
➤ **needlessly** *ADVERB*

needlework *NOUN*
needlework is sewing or embroidery

needn't
short for *need not* • *You needn't be so rude!*

needy *ADJECTIVE* **needier, neediest**
needy people are very poor and do not have what they need to live properly

negative *ADJECTIVE*
❶ a negative statement or answer is one that says 'no' ❷ not definite or confident • *Don't be so negative about yourself!* ❸ a negative number is one that is less than nought ❹ a negative electric charge is one that carries electrons
➤ **negatively** *ADVERB*

negative *NOUN* **negatives**
❶ something that means 'no' ❷ a photograph or film with the dark parts light and the light parts dark, from which prints are made

neglect *VERB* **neglects, neglecting, neglected**
❶ to neglect something or someone is to fail to look after them or deal with them ❷ to neglect to do something is to fail to do it

neglect *NOUN*
neglect is failing to look after someone or do something

neglectful *ADJECTIVE*
tending not to do things you should

negligent *ADJECTIVE*
not taking proper care or paying enough attention • *The cleaners had been negligent and left the windows open.*
➤ **negligence** *NOUN*

negligible (*say* neg-li-ji-bul) *ADJECTIVE*
not big enough or important enough to bother about • *Fortunately, the damage was negligible.*

negotiate (*say* nig-**oh**-shi-ayt) *VERB*
negotiates, negotiating, negotiated
❶ to negotiate is to try to reach an agreement about something by discussing it ❷ to negotiate an obstacle or difficulty is to get past it or over it
➤ **negotiation** *NOUN*

neigh *VERB* **neighs, neighing, neighed**
to make a high-pitched cry like a horse
neigh *NOUN* **neighs**
the sound of a horse neighing

neighbour *NOUN* **neighbours**
someone who lives next door or near to you
➤ **neighbouring** *ADJECTIVE*

neighbourhood *NOUN* **neighbourhoods**
the surrounding district

neighbourly *ADJECTIVE*
someone is neighbourly when they are friendly and helpful to people who live near them

neither (*say* **ny**-ther *or* **nee**-ther)
DETERMINER, PRONOUN
not either • *Neither parent was there.* • *Neither of them likes cabbage.*

neither *CONJUNCTION*
➤ **neither ... nor ...** not one thing and not the other • *I neither know nor care.*

nemesis *NOUN* **nemeses**
an arch-rival or arch-enemy • *The Joker is Batman's nemesis.*

neon (*say* **nee**-on) *NOUN*
neon is a gas that glows when electricity passes through it, used in street lighting and signs

nephew *NOUN* **nephews**
the son of a person's brother or sister

Neptune *NOUN*
the eighth planet from the sun in our solar system
DID YOU KNOW? The planet **Neptune** is named after the Roman god of the sea.

nerve *NOUN* **nerves**
❶ a nerve is one of the fibres inside your body that carry messages to and from your brain, so that parts of your body can feel and move ❷ nerve is courage and calmness

in a dangerous situation • *Don't lose your nerve.* ❸ (*informal*) nerve is cheek or impudence • *He had the nerve to ask for more.*
➤ **to get on someone's nerves** is to irritate them
➤ **nerves** nervousness • *I always suffer from nerves before an exam.*

nerve-racking ADJECTIVE
difficult and worrying • *It was a nerve-racking wait for the test results.*

nervous ADJECTIVE
❶ easily upset or agitated; timid ❷ to do with the nerves
➤ **nervously** ADVERB ➤ **nervousness** NOUN

nest NOUN nests
❶ the place where a bird lays its eggs and feeds its young ❷ a warm place where some small animals live

nest VERB nests, nesting, nested
birds or animals nest when they make or have a nest • *Gulls were nesting on the cliffs.*

nestle VERB nestles, nestling, nestled
to curl up comfortably
Moomintroll stood on his doorstep and watched the valley nestle beneath its winter blanket.—FINN FAMILY MOOMINTROLL, Tove Jansson

nestling NOUN nestlings
a young bird before it is old enough to leave the nest

net NOUN nets
❶ net is material made of pieces of thread, cord or wire joined together in a criss-cross pattern with holes between ❷ a net is a piece of this material ❸ the Net is the internet

net ADJECTIVE
a net amount is left over after everything has been taken away • *The net weight, without the box, is 100 grams.*

netball NOUN
netball is a game in which two teams try to throw a ball through a high net hanging from a ring

nettle NOUN nettles
a wild plant with leaves that sting when you touch them

network NOUN networks
❶ a criss-cross arrangement of lines

❷ a system with many connections or parts, such as a railway or broadcasting or computer system

neuter (*say* new-ter) ADJECTIVE
in some languages, belonging to the class of words which are neither masculine nor feminine

neuter (*say* new-ter) VERB neuters, neutering, neutered
to neuter an animal is to remove its sexual organs so that it cannot breed

neutral (*say* new-tral) ADJECTIVE
❶ not supporting either side in a war or quarrel ❷ not distinct or distinctive • *The room was painted in neutral colours.*
➤ **neutrality** NOUN

neutralize (*also* neutralise) VERB neutralizes, neutralizing, neutralized
to neutralize something is to take away its use or effect

never ADVERB
at no time; not ever; not at all

never-ending ADJECTIVE
something never-ending lasts or goes on forever • *I dreamt about a never-ending bar of chocolate.*

nevertheless ADVERB
in spite of this; although that is a fact • *The food was cold, but we ate it nevertheless.*

new ADJECTIVE newer, newest
❶ not existing before; just bought, made or received • *Is that a new top you're wearing?* ❷ different or unfamiliar • *I decided to try a new recipe.*
➤ **newness** NOUN

newcomer NOUN newcomers
someone who has recently arrived in a place

newly ADVERB
recently • *They have newly arrived in this country.*

new moon NOUN new moons
the moon at the beginning of its cycle, when it appears as a thin crescent

news NOUN
❶ news is new information about people or

a b c d e f g h i j k l m **n** o p q r s t u v w x y z

recent events • *I've got some good news.*
❷ news is also a radio or television report about important events

newsagent *NOUN* **newsagents**
a shopkeeper who sells newspapers and magazines

newsletter *NOUN* **newsletters**
a short informal report sent regularly to members of an organization or club

newspaper *NOUN* **newspapers**
❶ a newspaper is a daily or weekly publication of large sheets of printed paper folded together, containing news reports and articles ❷ newspaper is the paper these are printed on • *Wrap it in newspaper.*

newt *NOUN* **newts**
a small animal rather like a lizard, that lives near or in water

New Testament *NOUN*
the second part of the Bible, which describes the life and teachings of Jesus Christ

next *ADJECTIVE*
the nearest; following immediately after

next *ADVERB*
❶ in the nearest place ❷ at the nearest time • *What comes next?*

next door *ADVERB, ADJECTIVE*
in the next house or room

nib *NOUN* **nibs**
the pointed part at the end of a pen or pencil

nibble *VERB* **nibbles, nibbling, nibbled**
to nibble something is to take small or gentle bites at it
It was plain that Miss Angorian was not happy. She refused wine and wandered nervously about, nibbling at a leg of chicken.—HOWL'S MOVING CASTLE, Diana Wynne Jones

nibble *NOUN* **nibbles**
a small or gentle bite at something

nice *ADJECTIVE* **nicer, nicest**
❶ good-natured or kind • *That was a nice thing to do.* ❷ pleasant or enjoyable • *Have a nice time!*
➤ **nicely** *ADVERB* ➤ **niceness** *NOUN*

nicety *NOUN* **niceties**
a small detail or feature

nick *NOUN* **nicks**
a small cut or notch
➤ **in the nick of time** only just in time

nick *VERB* **nicks, nicking, nicked**
❶ to nick something is to make a small cut in it ❷ (*informal*) to nick something is to steal it

nickel *NOUN* **nickels**
❶ a silver-white metal ❷ (*North American*) a five-cent coin

nickname *NOUN* **nicknames**
an informal name given to someone instead of their real name • *The pirate's nickname was 'Billy Two-Scars'.*

niece *NOUN* **nieces**
the daughter of a person's brother or sister

night *NOUN* **nights**
the time when it is dark, between sunset and sunrise
➤ A related adjective is **nocturnal**.
SPELLING ALERT! You sleep at **night**, but a **knight** is a medieval warrior.

nightdress *NOUN* **nightdresses**
a loose dress worn in bed

nightfall *NOUN*
nightfall is the time when it becomes dark just after sunset

nightie *NOUN* **nighties** (*informal*)
a nightdress

nightingale *NOUN* **nightingales**
a small brown bird that sings sweetly

nightly *ADJECTIVE*
happening every night

nightmare *NOUN* **nightmares**
❶ a frightening or unpleasant dream
❷ a terrifying experience
➤ **nightmarish** *ADJECTIVE* terrifying
DID YOU KNOW? The word **nightmare** comes from *night* and *mare*, an evil spirit that was thought to cause bad dreams.

nightshirt *NOUN* **nightshirts**
a long shirt for wearing in bed

night-time *NOUN*
the time between evening and morning

nil *NOUN*
nothing • *We lost three-nil.*

nimble *ADJECTIVE* **nimbler**, **nimblest**
moving quickly or easily
'Grace and charm I do have, at any rate,' she continued, taking a nimble leap over a chair that stood in her way.–PIPPI LONGSTOCKING, Astrid Lindgren
➤ **nimbly** *ADVERB*

nincompoop *NOUN* **nincompoops** (*informal*)
a stupid or silly person

nine *NOUN* **nines**
the number 9

nineteen *NOUN* **nineteens**
the number 19
➤ **nineteenth** *ADJECTIVE, NOUN*

ninety *NOUN* **nineties**
the number 90
➤ **ninetieth** *ADJECTIVE, NOUN*

ninja *NOUN* **ninjas**
an ancient Japanese secret agent who used martial arts

ninth *ADJECTIVE, NOUN*
the next after the eighth
➤ **ninthly** *ADVERB* in the ninth place; as the ninth one

nip *VERB* **nips**, **nipping**, **nipped**
❶ to nip someone is to pinch or bite them sharply ❷ (*informal*) to nip somewhere is to go quickly there • *I'll just nip into the supermarket.*

nip *NOUN* **nips**
❶ a quick pinch or bite ❷ a cold feeling • *There's a nip in the air.*

nipple *NOUN* **nipples**
one of the two small parts that stick out at the front of a person's chest

nippy *ADJECTIVE* **nippier**, **nippiest** (*informal*)
❶ quick or nimble ❷ cold

nit *NOUN* **nits**
a louse or its egg

nit-picking *NOUN*
pointing out small faults or mistakes

nitrogen (*say* ny-tro-jen) *NOUN*
nitrogen is a gas that makes up about four-fifths of the air

nitty-gritty *NOUN* (*informal*)
the important or practical details or facts about something

nitwit *NOUN* **nitwits** (*informal*)
a stupid or silly person

no *EXCLAMATION*
a word you say when you disagree with someone or when you refuse something • *No, I don't want to go.*

no *DETERMINER, ADVERB*
not any • *There is no food in the fridge.*
• *The creature was no bigger than my thumb.*

nobility *NOUN*
❶ the nobility is the nobles or the aristocracy ❷ nobility is being noble

noble *ADJECTIVE* **nobler**, **noblest**
❶ of high social rank; aristocratic ❷ having a good and generous nature • *He is a noble king.* ❸ stately or impressive • *It was a noble building.*

noble *NOUN* **nobles**
a person of high social rank

nobleman, **noblewoman** *NOUN*
noblemen, **noblewomen**
a person of high rank

nobly *ADVERB*
someone does something nobly when they do it in a way that shows their good and generous nature

nobody *PRONOUN*
no person; not anyone • *Nobody knows.*

nobody *NOUN* **nobodies**
an unimportant person • *He's just a nobody.*

nocturnal (*say* nok-ter-nal) *ADJECTIVE*
❶ active at night • *Badgers are nocturnal animals.* ❷ happening at night

nod *VERB* **nods**, **nodding**, **nodded**
to nod, or nod your head, is to move your head up and down as a way of agreeing with someone or as a greeting

a
b
c
d
e
f
g
h
i
j
k
l
m
n
o
p
q
r
s
t
u
v
w
x
y
z

noise *NOUN* noises
a loud sound, especially one that is unpleasant or unwanted

noiseless *ADJECTIVE*
something is noiseless when it does not make any noise
➤ **noiselessly** *ADVERB*

noisy *ADJECTIVE* noisier, noisiest
making a lot of noise
➤ **noisily** *ADVERB*

nominate *VERB* nominates, nominating, nominated
to nominate someone is to suggest that they should be a candidate in an election or should be given a job or award
➤ **nomination** *NOUN*

non– *PREFIX*
meaning 'not', as in *non-existent*

none *PRONOUN*
not any; not one • *None of us went.*

none *ADVERB*
not at all • *He's none too pleased.*

nonetheless *ADVERB*
nevertheless; in spite of this

non–existent *ADJECTIVE*
not existing

non–fiction *NOUN*
non-fiction is writing that is not fiction; books about real things and true events

nonsense *NOUN*
❶ nonsense is words that do not mean anything or make any sense ❷ nonsense is also absurd or silly ideas or behaviour
➤ **nonsensical** *ADJECTIVE*

non–stop *ADVERB, ADJECTIVE*
❶ not stopping • *They talked non-stop all morning.* ❷ not stopping until the end of a journey • *There's a non-stop train to London.*

noodles *PLURAL NOUN*
pasta, traditionally from East and South East Asia, that is made in narrow strips and used in soups

nook *NOUN* nooks
a quiet corner or place • *a hidden nook in the forest*

noon *NOUN*
twelve o'clock; midday

no one *PRONOUN*
no person; not anyone

noose *NOUN* nooses
a loop in a rope that gets smaller when the rope is pulled

nope *NOUN* (*informal*)
no

nor *CONJUNCTION*
and not • *She cannot do it; nor can I.*

normal *ADJECTIVE*
❶ usual or ordinary • *It's normal to want a holiday.* ❷ natural and healthy ❸ not suffering from an illness
➤ **normality** *NOUN*

normally *ADVERB*
❶ usually • *The journey normally takes an hour.* ❷ in the usual way • *Just breathe normally.*

Norse *ADJECTIVE*
relating to ancient Scandinavia or its language • *a book of Norse sagas*

north *NOUN*
❶ north is the direction to the left of a person facing east ❷ north is also the part of a country or city that is in this direction

north *ADJECTIVE, ADVERB*
❶ towards the north or in the north • *The town lies north of the border.* ❷ coming from the north • *A north wind was blowing.*

north–east *NOUN, ADJECTIVE, ADVERB*
midway between north and east

northerly *ADJECTIVE*
a northerly wind is one that blows from the north

northern *ADJECTIVE*
from or to do with the north

northerner *NOUN* northerners
someone who lives in the north of a country

northward, **northwards** *ADJECTIVE*, *ADVERB*
towards the north

north-west *NOUN, ADJECTIVE, ADVERB*
midway between north and west

nose *NOUN* noses
❶ the part of your face that you use for breathing and smelling ❷ the front part of a vehicle or aircraft

nose *VERB* noses, nosing, nosed
to nose forward or through is to make progress cautiously • *The ship nosed through the ice.*
➤ **to nose about** *or* **nose around** is to pry or interfere in someone else's affairs
➤ A related adjective is **nasal**.

nosedive *NOUN* nosedives
a steep dive, especially in an aircraft

nosedive *VERB* nosedives, nosediving, nosedived
to nosedive is to go suddenly downward

nostalgia (*say* nos-**tal**-ja) *NOUN*
you feel nostalgia when you fondly remember something that made you happy in the past
➤ **nostalgic** *ADJECTIVE*

nostril *NOUN* nostrils
each of the two openings in your nose
DID YOU KNOW? The word **nostril** comes from an Old English word meaning 'nose hole'.

nosy, **nosey** *ADJECTIVE* nosier, nosiest
(*informal*)
always wanting to know other people's business
➤ **nosiness** *NOUN*

not *ADVERB*
a word you use to change the meaning of something to its opposite

notable *ADJECTIVE*
remarkable or famous
➤ **notably** *ADVERB* especially or remarkably

notch *NOUN* notches
a small V-shaped cut or mark

note *NOUN* notes
❶ something you write down as a reminder or help ❷ a short letter ❸ a single sound in music ❹ a sound or tone that indicates

something • *There was a note of anger in his voice.* ❺ a banknote • *Have you got a five-pound note?*
➤ **to take note of something** is to listen to it and understand it

note *VERB* notes, noting, noted
to note something is to pay attention to it, or to write it down as a reminder or help

notebook *NOUN* notebooks
❶ a book in which you write things down ❷ a small computer that you can carry around with you

notepad *NOUN* notepads
a pad of blank or ruled pages for writing notes

nothing *NOUN*
nothing is not anything

notice *NOUN* notices
❶ a notice is something written or printed and displayed for people to see ❷ to take notice of something is to pay attention to it • *It escaped my notice.* ❸ a warning that something is going to happen

notice *VERB* notices, noticing, noticed
to notice something is to see it or become aware of it

noticeable *ADJECTIVE*
easy to see or notice
➤ **noticeably** *ADVERB*

noticeboard *NOUN* noticeboards
a board on which notices can be displayed

notion *NOUN* notions
an idea, especially one that is vague or uncertain • *The notion that the earth is flat was disproved long ago.*

notoriety *NOUN*
notoriety is being well known for doing something bad

notorious *ADJECTIVE*
well known for doing something bad • *He was a notorious criminal.*
➤ **notoriously** *ADVERB*

nougat (*say* noo-gah) *NOUN*
nougat is a chewy sweet made from nuts and sugar or honey

a
b
c
d
e
f
g
h
i
j
k
l
m
n
o
p
q
r
s
t
u
v
w
x
y
z

A B C D E F G H I J K L M N O P Q R S T U V W X Y Z

nought (*say* nawt) *NOUN* **noughts**
❶ the figure 0 ❷ nothing

noun *NOUN* **nouns**
a word that stands for a person, place or thing

nourish *VERB* **nourishes**, **nourishing**, **nourished**
to nourish someone is to give them enough good food to keep them alive and well

nourishment *NOUN*
nourishment is the food someone needs to keep them alive and well

novel *NOUN* **novels**
a story that fills a whole book

novel *ADJECTIVE*
unusual • *What a novel idea.*

novelist (*say* nov-el-ist) *NOUN* **novelists**
someone who writes novels

novelty *NOUN* **novelties**
❶ novelty is being new or unusual • *The novelty of living in a tent soon wore off.*
❷ a novelty is something new and unusual
❸ a novelty is also a cheap toy or ornament

November *NOUN*
the eleventh month of the year
DID YOU KNOW? November is based on the Latin word *novem* meaning 'nine', because it was the ninth month in the Roman calendar.

novice *NOUN* **novices**
a beginner

now *ADVERB*
❶ at this time • *I am now living in Glasgow.*
❷ without any delay • *Do it now!*
➤ **for now** until a later time • *Goodbye for now.*
➤ **now and again** *or* **now and then** occasionally; sometimes

now *CONJUNCTION*
since or as • *I do remember, now you mention it.*

now *NOUN*
this moment • *They should be home by now.*

nowadays *ADVERB*
at the present time

nowhere *ADVERB*
not anywhere; in no place or to no place

nozzle *NOUN* **nozzles**
the part at the end of a hose or pipe from which something flows

nuclear (*say* new-kli-er) *ADJECTIVE*
❶ to do with a nucleus, especially of an atom ❷ using the energy that is created by the splitting of atoms • *nuclear weapons*

nucleus (*say* new-kli-us) *NOUN* **nuclei**
❶ the central part of an atom or cell ❷ the part in the centre of something, round which other things are grouped • *The queen bee is the nucleus of the hive.*

nude *ADJECTIVE*
not wearing any clothes

nude *NOUN* **nudes**
a nude person, especially in a work of art
➤ **nudity** *NOUN*

nudge *VERB* **nudges**, **nudging**, **nudged**
to nudge someone is to touch or push them with your elbow

nugget *NOUN* **nuggets**
❶ a rough lump of gold from the ground
❷ a small lump or amount of something
• *a useful nugget of information*

nuisance *NOUN* **nuisances**
an annoying person or thing

numb *ADJECTIVE*
part of your body is numb when you cannot feel anything in it
➤ **numbness** *NOUN*

number *NOUN* **numbers**
❶ a symbol or word that tells you how many of something there are ❷ a quantity of people or things • *Do you know the number of bones in your body?* ❸ a person's number is their telephone number ❹ a song or piece of music

number *VERB* **numbers**, **numbering**, **numbered**
❶ to number things is to count them or mark them with numbers ❷ to number a certain amount is to reach it • *The crowd numbered 10,000.*

numeracy *NOUN*
numeracy is the ability to understand and work with numbers

numeral *NOUN* **numerals**
a symbol or figure that stands for a number

numerator *NOUN* **numerators**
the number above the line in a fraction (*compare* **denominator**). In ¼ the numerator is the number 1.

numerical *ADJECTIVE*
to do with numbers

numerous *ADJECTIVE*
many • *There are numerous kinds of cat.*

nun *NOUN* **nuns**
a member of a religious community of women

nurse *NOUN* **nurses**
a person trained to look after people who are ill or injured

nurse *VERB* **nurses, nursing, nursed**
❶ to nurse someone is to look after them when they are ill or injured ❷ to nurse someone or something is to hold them carefully in your arms • *He was nursing a puppy.*

nursery *NOUN* **nurseries**
❶ a place where young children are looked after or play ❷ a place where young plants are grown and usually offered for sale

nursery rhyme *NOUN* **nursery rhymes**
a simple poem or song for very young children

nursery school *NOUN* **nursery schools**
a school for very young or pre-school children

nursing home *NOUN* **nursing homes**
a small or private hospital

nurture *VERB* **nurtures, nurturing, nurtured**
to nurture children is to look after them and educate them

nut *NOUN* **nuts**
❶ a fruit with a hard shell ❷ the part of this fruit that you can eat • *a bag of mixed nuts*

❸ a small piece of metal for screwing on to a bolt ❹ (*informal*) your head

nutmeg *NOUN* **nutmegs**
a hard seed that is made into a powder and used as a spice

nutrient (*say* new-tri-ent) *NOUN* **nutrients**
a substance that is needed to keep a plant or animal alive and to help it to grow

nutrition (*say* new-trish-on) *NOUN*
nutrition is the food someone needs to keep them alive and well
➤ **nutritional** *ADJECTIVE*

nutritious (*say* new-trish-us) *ADJECTIVE*
nutritious food helps you to grow and keep well • *They ate a nutritious meal.*

nutshell *NOUN* **nutshells**
the shell of a nut
➤ **to put something in a nutshell** is to state it very briefly

nutty *ADJECTIVE* **nuttier, nuttiest**
❶ tasting of nuts or full of nuts • *nutty chocolate spread* ❷ (*informal*) (may cause offence) foolish or mentally ill
➤ **nuttiness** *NOUN*

nuzzle *VERB* **nuzzles, nuzzling, nuzzled**
to nuzzle someone is to rub gently against them with the nose, in the way that some animals do
Bella lowered her head and turned to nuzzle Irina's hair with her warm velvety nose, then she trotted off into the barn.—THE ENCHANTED HORSE, Magdalen Nabb

nylon *NOUN*
nylon is a lightweight synthetic cloth or fibre

nymph *NOUN* **nymphs**
in myths, a young goddess living in trees or rivers or the sea

a
b
c
d
e
f
g
h
i
j
k
l
m
n
o
p
q
r
s
t
u
v
w
x
y
z

Oo

oak NOUN oaks
a large tree that produces seeds called acorns

oar NOUN oars
a pole with a flat blade at one end, used for rowing a boat

oarsman, **oarswoman** NOUN oarsmen, oarswomen
a person who rows a boat

oasis (*say* oh-**ay**-sis) NOUN oases
a fertile place with water and trees in a desert

oath NOUN oaths
❶ a solemn promise to do something or that something is true ❷ a swear word

oatmeal NOUN
oatmeal is ground oats

oats PLURAL NOUN
a cereal used to make food for humans and animals

obedience NOUN
obedience is doing what you are told

obedient ADJECTIVE
an obedient dog is willing to do what someone tells them to do
➤ **obediently** ADVERB

obey VERB obeys, obeying, obeyed
❶ to obey someone is to do what they tell you ❷ to obey a rule or law is to do what it says

obituary (*say* oh-**bi**-tew-er-ee) NOUN obituaries
an announcement in a newspaper that someone has died, often with a short account of their life

object (*say* ob-jikt) NOUN objects
❶ something that can be seen or touched ❷ the purpose of something ❸ (*grammar*) the word naming the person or thing that the action of the verb affects, for example *him* in *I chased him*

object (*say* ob-**jekt**) VERB objects, objecting, objected
to object to something or someone is to say that you do not like them or do not agree with them

objection NOUN objections
❶ objection is objecting to something ❷ an objection is a reason for objecting
• *I have three objections to your plan.*

objectionable ADJECTIVE
unpleasant or nasty

objective NOUN objectives
what you are trying to reach or do; an aim

objective ADJECTIVE
not influenced by your own beliefs or ideas
• *He gave an objective account of the incident.*

obligation NOUN obligations
a duty

obligatory ADJECTIVE
something is obligatory when you must do it because of a rule or law • *Wearing a seat belt is obligatory.*

oblige VERB obliges, obliging, obliged
❶ to oblige someone to do something is to force them to do it ❷ to oblige someone is to help and please them • *Always oblige your customers.*
➤ **to be obliged to someone** is to be grateful to them for helping you

oblique (*say* o-**bleek**) ADJECTIVE
❶ an oblique line slants at an angle ❷ not straightforward or direct • *They gave an oblique reply.*

oblong NOUN oblongs
a rectangle that is longer than it is wide

oblong ADJECTIVE
having the shape of an oblong

obnoxious ADJECTIVE
really horrible

oboe (*say* oh-boh) NOUN oboes
a high-pitched woodwind instrument
➤ **oboist** NOUN

obscure ADJECTIVE obscurer, obscurest
❶ difficult to see or understand; very unclear
❷ not well known
➤ **obscurely** ADVERB ➤ **obscurity** NOUN

observance NOUN observances
obeying a law or keeping a custom

observant ADJECTIVE
an observant person is quick to notice things around them
➤ **observantly** ADVERB

observation NOUN observations
❶ observation is noticing or watching something carefully ❷ an observation is a comment or remark • *He made a few observations about the weather.*

observatory (*say* ob-**zerv**-a-ter-ee) NOUN observatories
a building equipped with telescopes for looking at the stars or weather

observe VERB observes, observing, observed
❶ to observe someone or something is to watch them carefully ❷ to observe something is to notice it ❸ the action of obeying a law, or taking part in a custom or religious festival ❹ to observe a fact is to state it • *She observed that she did not like ice in her drinks.*
➤ **observer** NOUN

obsessed ADJECTIVE
always thinking about something • *He is obsessed with his work.*

obsession NOUN obsessions
an obsession is something that someone thinks about too much

obsolete ADJECTIVE
not used any more; out of date

obstacle NOUN obstacles
something that gets in your way or makes it difficult for you to do something

obstinate ADJECTIVE
not willing to change your ideas or ways, even though they may be wrong
➤ **obstinacy** NOUN ➤ **obstinately** ADVERB

obstruct VERB obstructs, obstructing, obstructed
to obstruct someone or something is to stop them from getting past, or to hinder them
➤ **obstruction** NOUN

obtain VERB obtains, obtaining, obtained
to obtain something is to get it or be given it
➤ **obtainable** ADJECTIVE

obtuse ADJECTIVE obtuser, obtusest
❶ slow to understand; stupid ❷ an obtuse angle is an angle of between 90 and 180 degrees

obvious ADJECTIVE
easy to see or understand

obviously ADVERB
it is obvious that; clearly • *Obviously we don't want to lose.*

occasion NOUN occasions
❶ the time when something happens • *On this occasion, we will not take any action.* ❷ a special event • *The wedding was a marvellous occasion.*

occasional ADJECTIVE
happening from time to time, but not often and not regularly

occasionally ADVERB
something happens occasionally when it happens from time to time

occupant NOUN occupants
someone who occupies a place

occupation NOUN occupations
❶ a person's occupation is their job or profession ❷ the occupation of a country or territory is when an army captures it and stays there

occupy VERB occupies, occupying, occupied
❶ to occupy a place or building is to live in it ❷ to occupy a space or position is to fill it ❸ in a war, to occupy territory is to capture it and keep an army in it ❹ to occupy someone is to keep them busy or interested

occur VERB occurs, occurring, occurred
❶ an event occurs when it happens or takes place • *An earthquake occurred on the island in 1953.* ❷ something occurs when it exists

a b c d e f g h i j k l m n **o** p q r s t u v w x y z

or is found somewhere • *These plants occur in ponds.* ❸ something occurs to you when it suddenly comes into your mind • *Just then an idea occurred to me.*

occurrence NOUN occurrences
something that happens or exists

ocean NOUN oceans
❶ the ocean is the area of salt water surrounding the land of the earth ❷ an ocean is a large part of this water, such as the Pacific Ocean

o'clock ADVERB
by the clock • *Lunch is at one o'clock.*

octagon NOUN octagons
a flat shape with eight sides
➤ **octagonal** (*say* ok-**ta**-go-nal) *ADJECTIVE*

octave NOUN octaves
❶ the interval between one musical note and the next note of the same name above or below it ❷ these two notes played together

October NOUN
the tenth month of the year
DID YOU KNOW? October is based on the Latin word *octo* meaning 'eight', because it was the eighth month in the Roman calendar.

octopus NOUN octopuses
a sea creature with a soft body and eight arms which have rows of suckers
DID YOU KNOW? The word **octopus** comes from Greek words meaning 'eight foot'.

odd ADJECTIVE odder, oddest
❶ strange or unusual ❷ an odd number is one that cannot be divided by 2, such as 5 and 31 ❸ left over or spare • *I've got an odd sock.* ❹ of various kinds; occasional • *He's doing odd jobs.*
➤ **oddness** *NOUN* being odd

oddly ADVERB
to behave oddly is to behave in a strange way

oddments PLURAL NOUN
small things of various kinds

odds PLURAL NOUN
❶ the chances that something will happen ❷ the proportion of money that you will win if a bet is successful • *When the odds are 10 to 1, you will win £10 if you bet £1.*

➤ **odds and ends** small things of various kinds

odour NOUN odours
a smell, usually an unpleasant one
➤ **odorous** *ADJECTIVE*

of PREPOSITION
❶ belonging to • *the mother of the lion cubs* ❷ coming from • *a resident of New York* ❸ away from • *a few miles north of the town* ❹ about; concerning • *Is there any news of your father?* ❺ from; out of • *The house is built of stone.*

off ADVERB
❶ not on; away • *His hat blew off.* ❷ not working or happening • *The heating is off.* • *The match is off because of snow.* ❸ behind or at the side of a stage • *There were noises off.* ❹ beginning to go bad • *I think the milk is off.*

off PREPOSITION
❶ not on; away or down from • *He fell off his chair.* ❷ not taking or wanting • *She is off her food.* ❸ taken away from • *There is £5 off the normal price.*

offence NOUN offences
❶ an offence is a crime or something illegal • *When was the offence committed?* ❷ offence is a feeling of annoyance or hurt

offend VERB offends, offending, offended
❶ to offend someone is to hurt their feelings or be unpleasant to them ❷ to offend is to break a law or do something wrong
➤ **offender** *NOUN*

offensive ADJECTIVE
❶ insulting or causing offence ❷ used for attacking • *He was arrested for carrying an offensive weapon.*
➤ **offensively** *ADVERB*

offer VERB offers, offering, offered
❶ to offer something is to hold it out so that someone can take it if they want it ❷ to offer to do something is to say that you are willing to do it ❸ to offer a sum of money is to say how much you are willing to pay for something

offer NOUN offers
❶ the action of offering something • *Thank you for your offer of help.* ❷ an amount

of money that you are willing to pay for something

offhand ADJECTIVE
❶ said without much thought ❷ rude or abrupt

office NOUN offices
❶ a room or building where people work, often at desks ❷ a place where you can go for tickets, information or some other purpose • *a lost property office* ❸ an important job or position • *He was honoured to hold the office of president.*

officer NOUN officers
❶ someone who is in charge of other people, especially in the armed forces ❷ a policeman or policewoman

official ADJECTIVE
❶ done or said by someone with authority ❷ connected with the job of someone in a position of authority • *The prime minister will make an official visit to Australia next month.*
➤ **officially** ADVERB

official NOUN officials
someone who does a job of authority or trust

officious (say o-**fish**-us) ADJECTIVE
too ready to order people about; bossy and unpleasant
➤ **officiously** ADVERB

offline ADJECTIVE, ADVERB
not using, or disconnected from, the internet • *I'm working offline just now.*

offset VERB offsets, offsetting, offset
one thing offsets another when it balances it out • *The failures were offset by some successes.*

offshore ADJECTIVE, ADVERB
❶ from the land towards the sea • *an offshore breeze* ❷ in the sea some distance from the shore • *an offshore wind farm* • *The island lay a mile offshore.*

offside ADJECTIVE (sport)
in a position which is not allowed by the rules

offspring NOUN offspring
a child or young animal

often ADVERB
many times; in many cases

ogre NOUN ogres
❶ a cruel giant in stories ❷ a frightening person

oh EXCLAMATION
a word you say when you are surprised, annoyed or delighted by something • *Oh, no!* • *Oh, thank goodness!*

oil NOUN oils
❶ an oil is a thick slippery liquid that does not mix with water ❷ oil is a kind of petroleum used as fuel

oil VERB oils, oiling, oiled
to oil something is to put oil on it to make it work smoothly

oilfield NOUN oilfields
an area where oil is found under the ground or under the sea

oil painting NOUN oil paintings
a painting done using paints made with oil

oil rig NOUN oil rigs
a structure set up to support the equipment used for drilling for oil

oilskin NOUN oilskins
a waterproof piece of clothing worn especially by fishermen

oil well NOUN oil wells
a hole drilled in the ground or under the sea to get oil

oily ADJECTIVE
❶ like oil or covered in oil ❷ unpleasantly over-polite • *She didn't like his oily manner.*
➤ **oiliness** NOUN

oink NOUN oinks
the grunting sound made by a pig

ointment NOUN ointments
a cream that you put on sore skin and cuts

OK ADVERB, ADJECTIVE (informal)
all right

old ADJECTIVE older, oldest
❶ not newborn, or made a long time ago ❷ of a particular age • *I'm ten years old.* ❸ former or original • *I liked my old school better than the one I go to now.*

a b c d e f g h i j k l m n **o** p q r s t u v w x y z

old age NOUN
old age is the time when a person is old

old-fashioned ADJECTIVE
of the kind that was usual a long time ago; out of date
His clothes were curiously old-fashioned, mostly brown and black, the sort of thing people wore two or three hundred years ago.—BILLY AND THE MINPINS, Roald Dahl

Old Testament NOUN
the first part of the Christian Bible, corresponding to the Hebrew Bible which is the holy book of the Jewish religion

olive NOUN olives
❶ an evergreen tree with a small bitter fruit
❷ the fruit of this tree, used for eating and to make olive oil

Olympian NOUN Olympians
an athlete who competes in the Olympic Games

Olympic Games, **Olympics** PLURAL NOUN
a series of international sports contests held every four years in different countries

omelette (*say* om-lit) NOUN omelettes
eggs beaten together and fried, often with a filling or flavouring

omen NOUN omens
an event that some people see as a sign that something is going to happen

ominous ADJECTIVE
suggesting that trouble is coming
In winter the dragons were hibernating and the cliff fell silent, except for the ominous, low rumble of their snores.—HOW TO TRAIN YOUR DRAGON, Cressida Cowell
➤ **ominously** ADVERB

omission NOUN omissions
something left out or not done

omit VERB omits, omitting, omitted
❶ to omit something is to leave it out ❷ to omit to do something is to fail to do it

omnivorous ADJECTIVE
an omnivorous animal is one that feeds on plants as well as the flesh of animals

on PREPOSITION
❶ at or over the top or surface of something • *Sit on the floor.* ❷ at the time of • *Come on*

Monday. ❸ about; concerning • *We went to a talk on butterflies.* ❹ towards or near • *They advanced on the town.*

on ADVERB
❶ so as to be on something • *Put your hat on.* ❷ forwards • *Move on.* ❸ working; in action • *Is the heater on?*

once ADVERB
❶ at one time • *I once lived in Leeds.* ❷ one time only • *I've only met him once.*

once CONJUNCTION
as soon as • *We can get out once I open this door.*
➤ **at once** immediately

one NOUN ones
the smallest whole number, 1

one PRONOUN
a person or thing on their own • *One likes to help.* • *One of my friends is ill.*
➤ **one another** each other

one ADJECTIVE
single • *I have one packet left.*

oneself PRONOUN
one's own self; yourself • *One should not always think of oneself.*

one-sided ADJECTIVE
a one-sided contest is one where one side has a big advantage • *It will be a very one-sided game.*

onesie (*say* wun-zee) NOUN onesies
a loose-fitting piece of clothing that covers your whole body including arms and legs
• *We put on our onesies to watch TV.*

one-way ADJECTIVE
a one-way street is one where traffic is only allowed to go in one direction

ongoing ADJECTIVE
continuing to exist or make progress • *It's an ongoing project.*

onion NOUN onions
a round vegetable with a strong flavour

online ADJECTIVE, ADVERB
using or connected to the internet • *an online shopping account* • *Can you get online now?*

onlooker NOUN onlookers
a spectator

only ADJECTIVE
being the one person or thing of a kind • *He's the only person we can trust.*

only ADVERB
no more than • *There are only three cakes.*

only CONJUNCTION
but then; however • *I want to come, only I'm busy that day.*

onomatopoeia (*say* on-om-at-o-**pee**-a) NOUN
onomatopoeia is forming or using words that sound like the thing they describe, such as *crunch*, *hiss* and *splash*
➤ **onomatopoeic** ADJECTIVE

onset NOUN
the onset of (for example) winter or war is the beginning of it

onshore ADJECTIVE
from the sea towards the land • *There is an onshore breeze.*

on to PREPOSITION
to a position; on • *They fell on to the floor.*

onward, onwards ADVERB
forward or forwards

oops EXCLAMATION
a word you say when you have made a mistake or broken something • *'Oops!' said Alice, as she dropped the flask.*

ooze VERB oozes, oozing, oozed
a thick liquid oozes when it flows out slowly, especially through a narrow opening • *Blood oozed from his wound.*

opaque (*say* oh-**payk**) ADJECTIVE
something that is opaque does not allow light through and so cannot be seen through

open ADJECTIVE
❶ allowing people or things to pass through; not shut • *The door is open.* • *The bottles need to be open.* ❷ not enclosed • *There were miles of open land.* ❸ not folded; spread out • *She greeted us with open arms.* ❹ honest; not secret or secretive • *We all want open*

government. ❺ not settled or finished • *That is still an open question.*
➤ **in the open air** outdoors; not inside a house or building

open VERB opens, opening, opened
❶ to open something is to make it open ❷ to open is to become open ❸ to open is also to start • *The jumble sale opens at 2 o'clock.* ❹ a shop opens when it starts business for the day • *What time do you open?* ❺ to open a computer file or app is to start it up so that you are ready to work with it

opener NOUN openers
a device for opening a bottle or can

opening NOUN openings
❶ a space or gap in something ❷ the beginning of something ❸ an opportunity, especially for a job

openly ADVERB
to do something openly is to do it for all to see, not secretly

open-minded ADJECTIVE
ready to listen to other people's ideas and opinions; not having fixed ideas

opera NOUN operas
opera, or an opera, is a form of drama in which the characters sing all or most of the words, with an orchestra
➤ **operatic** ADJECTIVE

operate VERB operates, operating, operated
❶ to operate something is to make it work • *Do you know how to operate the camera?* ❷ to operate is to work or be in action ❸ to operate on someone is to perform a surgical operation on them

operation NOUN operations
❶ something done to a patient's body by a surgeon to remove or repair a part of it ❷ a carefully planned activity
➤ **to be in operation** is to be working • *The new machines are now in operation.*

operator NOUN operators
someone who operates equipment or a machine • *a radio operator*

opinion NOUN opinions
what you think of something; a belief or judgement

opponent NOUN opponents
someone who is against you in a contest, war or argument

opportunity NOUN opportunities
a good time to do something

oppose VERB opposes, opposing, opposed
to oppose someone or something is to be against them or disagree with them
➤ **as opposed to** in contrast with • *fact, as opposed to fiction*

opposite ADJECTIVE, ADVERB
❶ on the other side; facing • *She lives on the opposite side of the road to me.* • *I'll sit opposite.* ❷ completely different • *They went in opposite directions.*

opposite NOUN opposites
something that is completely different from something else • *'Happy' is the opposite of 'sad'.*

opposition NOUN
opposition is opposing something; resistance
➤ **the Opposition** the chief political party opposing the one that has formed the government

oppress VERB oppresses, oppressing, oppressed
❶ to oppress people is to govern them or treat them cruelly or unjustly ❷ to oppress someone is to trouble them with worry or sadness
➤ **oppression** NOUN ➤ **oppressor** NOUN

oppressive ADJECTIVE
❶ harsh and cruel • *They live under an oppressive regime.* ❷ hot and tiring • *The weather can be very oppressive in July.*

opt VERB opts, opting, opted
to opt for something or to do something is to choose it • *I opted for the cash prize.* • *We opted to go abroad.*
➤ **to opt out of something** is to decide not to join in with it

optical ADJECTIVE
to do with sight or the eyes

optical illusion NOUN optical illusions
something you think you see that is not really there

optician (*say* op-**tish**-an) NOUN opticians
someone who tests your eyesight and makes and sells glasses and contact lenses

optimist NOUN optimists
someone who usually expects things to turn out well
➤ **optimism** NOUN the feeling that things will turn out well

optimistic ADJECTIVE
expecting things to turn out well
➤ **optimistically** ADVERB

option NOUN options
❶ one of the things that you can choose • *Your options are to travel by bus or by train.* ❷ the right to choose; choice • *You have the option of staying.*

optional ADJECTIVE
something is optional when you can choose whether to do it or not

opulent (*say* **op**-yoo-lent) ADJECTIVE
❶ made or decorated with expensive things; luxurious ❷ very rich
➤ **opulence** NOUN

or CONJUNCTION
used to show that there is a choice or alternative • *Do you want a cake or a biscuit?*

oral ADJECTIVE
❶ spoken, not written ❷ to do with the mouth or using your mouth
➤ **orally** ADVERB

orange NOUN oranges
❶ a round juicy fruit with thick reddish-yellow peel ❷ a reddish-yellow colour

orange ADJECTIVE
reddish-yellow

orangutan (*say* o-**rang**-u-tan *or* o-rang-u-**tan**) NOUN orangutans
a large kind of ape with long arms and reddish-brown hair
DID YOU KNOW? The word **orangutan** comes from Malay words meaning 'man of the forest'.

oration NOUN **orations**
a long formal speech

orbit NOUN **orbits**
the curved path taken by something moving round a planet or other body in space

orbit VERB **orbits**, **orbiting**, **orbited**
to orbit a planet or other body in space is to move round it • *The satellite orbited the earth.*
➤ **orbital** ADJECTIVE

orca NOUN **orca** or **orcas**
another name for **killer whale**

orchard NOUN **orchards**
a piece of ground with fruit trees

orchestra NOUN **orchestras**
a group of musicians playing various instruments together
➤ **orchestral** ADJECTIVE

orchid (*say* **or**-kid) NOUN **orchids**
a type of brightly coloured flower

ordeal NOUN **ordeals**
a difficult or unpleasant experience

order NOUN **orders**
❶ a command ❷ a request for something to be supplied • *The waiter came to take our order.* ❸ the way things are arranged • *The words are in alphabetical order.* ❹ obedience or good behaviour • *Can we have some order please?* ❺ tidiness or neatness ❻ a kind or sort of thing • *They showed courage of the highest order.* ❼ a group of religious monks, priests or nuns
➤ **in order that** *or* **in order to** for the purpose of
➤ **to be out of order** is to be broken or not working

order VERB **orders**, **ordering**, **ordered**
❶ to order someone to do something is to tell them to do it ❷ to order something is to ask for it to be supplied to you

orderly ADJECTIVE
❶ arranged tidily or well; methodical
❷ well behaved; obedient

ordinal number NOUN **ordinal numbers**
a number that shows where something comes in a series, for example 1st, 2nd, 3rd (*compare* **cardinal number**)

ordinarily ADVERB
usually or normally • *The town was ordinarily quiet on a Sunday.*

ordinary ADJECTIVE
normal or usual; not special • *It began as a very ordinary day.*
➤ **ordinariness** NOUN

ore NOUN **ores**
rock with metal in it, such as iron ore

organ NOUN **organs**
❶ a musical instrument from which sounds are produced by air forced through pipes, played by keys and pedals ❷ a part of your body with a particular function, for example the digestive organs

organic ADJECTIVE
❶ organic food is grown or produced without using artificial chemicals to act as fertilizers or pesticides ❷ made by or found in living things

organism NOUN **organisms**
a living animal or plant

organist NOUN **organists**
someone who plays the organ

organization (*also* **organisation**) NOUN **organizations**
❶ an organization is a group of people who work together to do something ❷ organization is planning or arranging things such as getting people together to do something

organize (*also* **organise**) VERB **organizes**, **organizing**, **organized**
❶ to organize people is to get them together to do something ❷ to organize something is to plan or arrange it • *We're organizing a picnic.* ❸ to organize things is to put them in order
➤ **organizer** NOUN

oriental ADJECTIVE (*old use*)
to do with countries from central to east Asia

orienteering (*say* or-i-en-**teer**-ing) NOUN
orienteering is the sport of finding your way across rough country with a map and compass

a
b
c
d
e
f
g
h
i
j
k
l
m
n
o
p
q
r
s
t
u
v
w
x
y
z

origami (*say* o-ri-**gah**-mee) *NOUN*
a type of Japanese art in which you fold pieces of paper to make decorative shapes

origin *NOUN* origins
the start of something; the point where something began • *a book about the origins of life on earth*

original *ADJECTIVE*
❶ existing from the start; earliest • *They were the original inhabitants.* ❷ new; not a copy or an imitation • *It is an original design.* ❸ producing new ideas; inventive • *He was an original thinker.*
➤ **originally** *ADVERB* what happened originally is what happened in the beginning • *The story was originally published in a magazine.*
➤ **originality** *NOUN*

originate *VERB* originates, originating, originated
❶ to originate something is to create it or develop it ❷ to originate is to start in a certain way • *Pumpkins are believed to have originated in North America.*
➤ **originator** *NOUN*

ornament *NOUN* ornaments
an object you wear or display as a decoration
➤ **ornamental** *ADJECTIVE*

ornate *ADJECTIVE*
highly decorated • *an ornate metal casket*

ornithology (*say* or-ni-**thol**-o-jee) *NOUN*
ornithology is the study of birds
➤ **ornithologist** *NOUN*

orphan *NOUN* orphans
a child whose parents have died

orphanage *NOUN* orphanages
a home for orphans

orthodox *ADJECTIVE*
having beliefs that are correct or generally accepted

Orthodox Church *NOUN*
the Christian Churches of eastern Europe

osprey *NOUN* ospreys
a large fish-eating bird of prey

ostrich *NOUN* ostriches
a large long-legged bird that can run fast but cannot fly

other *DETERMINER*
not the same as this; different • *Play some other tune.* • *Try the other shoe.*
➤ **other than** except • *They have no belongings other than what they are carrying.*
➤ **the other day** *or* **the other week** a few days or weeks ago

other *PRONOUN* others
the other person or thing • *Where are the others?*

otherwise *ADVERB*
❶ if you do not; if things happen differently • *Write it down, otherwise you'll forget it.* ❷ in other ways • *It rained a lot but otherwise the holiday was good.* ❸ differently • *We could not do otherwise.*

otter *NOUN* otters
a mammal with a long body, thick fur and webbed feet that lives near water

ouch *EXCLAMATION*
a word you say when you are in pain • *Ouch! That hurts!*

ought *VERB*
This word is used with other words to show ❶ what you should or must do • *You ought to do your music practice.* ❷ what is likely to happen • *With all these dark clouds it ought to rain.*

ounce *NOUN* ounces
a unit of weight equal to $\frac{1}{16}$ of a pound or about 28 grams

our *DETERMINER*
belonging to us • *This is our house.*

ours *PRONOUN*
belonging to us • *Those seats are ours.*

ourselves *PRONOUN*
us and nobody else, used to refer back to the subject of a verb • *We couldn't hear ourselves speak.*
➤ **by ourselves** on our own; alone • *We did the work all by ourselves.*

out *ADVERB*
❶ away from a place or not in it; not at home ❷ into the open or outdoors • *Are you going out today?* ❸ not burning or working • *The fire has gone out.* ❹ loudly • *He cried out in pain.* ❺ completely • *The tickets have sold out.* ❻ dismissed from a game • *If you don't know the answer, then you're out.*
➤ **to be out for something** is to want it badly
➤ **to be out of something** is to have no more of it left
➤ **out of date** old-fashioned; not used any more
➤ **out of doors** in the open air
➤ **out of the way** remote or distant

out and out *ADJECTIVE*
complete or thorough • *He is an out and out villain.*

outback *NOUN*
the remote inland areas of Australia

outbreak *NOUN* **outbreaks**
the sudden start of a disease, war or show of anger

outburst *NOUN* **outbursts**
the sudden beginning of anger or laughter

outcast *NOUN* **outcasts**
someone who has been rejected by their family, friends or society
By the seventeenth century, any witch or wizard who chose to fraternise with Muggles became suspect, even an outcast in his or her community.—THE TALES OF BEEDLE THE BARD, J. K. Rowling

outcome *NOUN* **outcomes**
the result of what happens or has happened

outcry *NOUN* **outcries**
a strong protest from many people

outdated *ADJECTIVE*
out of date

outdo *VERB* **outdoes, outdoing, outdid, outdone**
to outdo someone else is to do better than them

outdoor *ADJECTIVE*
done or used outside • *You'll need your outdoor clothes.*

outdoors *ADVERB*
in the open air • *It is cold outdoors.*

outer *ADJECTIVE*
nearer the outside; external

outer space *NOUN*
outer space is the universe beyond the earth's atmosphere

outfit *NOUN* **outfits**
❶ a set of clothes you wear together ❷ a set of things you need for doing something

outgrow *VERB* **outgrows, outgrowing, outgrew, outgrown**
❶ to outgrow something such as clothes or a habit is to grow too big or too old for them ❷ to outgrow someone is to grow faster or taller than them

outhouse *NOUN* **outhouses**
a small building attached to a larger building or close to it

outing *NOUN* **outings**
a trip or short journey you make for pleasure

outlast *VERB* **outlasts, outlasting, outlasted**
to outlast something else is to last longer than it

outlaw *NOUN* **outlaws**
a robber or bandit who is hiding to avoid being caught and is not protected by the law

outlaw *VERB* **outlaws, outlawing, outlawed**
to outlaw something is to make it illegal

outlet *NOUN* **outlets**
❶ a way for something to get out • *The tank has an outlet at the bottom.* ❷ a place to sell goods • *We need to find fresh outlets for our products.*

outline *NOUN* **outlines**
❶ a line round the outside of something; a line showing the shape of a thing ❷ a summary

outline *VERB* **outlines, outlining, outlined**
❶ to outline something is to draw a line round it to show its shape ❷ to outline a story or account is to summarize or describe it briefly

a
b
c
d
e
f
g
h
i
j
k
l
m
n
o
p
q
r
s
t
u
v
w
x
y
z

outlook *NOUN* **outlooks**
❶ a view on which people look out ❷ a person's outlook is the way that they look at and think about things • *She has a serious outlook on life.* ❸ what seems likely to happen in the future • *The outlook is bright.*

outlying *ADJECTIVE*
far from a town or city • *We need to visit the outlying districts.*

outnumber *VERB* **outnumbers**, **outnumbering**, **outnumbered**
to outnumber something else is to be greater in number than it • *The girls outnumber the boys in our team.*

outpatient *NOUN* **outpatients**
a patient who visits a hospital for treatment but does not stay there overnight

outpost *NOUN* **outposts**
a distant settlement

output *NOUN* **outputs**
❶ the amount produced, especially by a factory or business ❷ (*computing*) information produced by a computer

output *VERB* **outputs**, **outputting**, **output** (*computing*)
to output information is to get it from a computer

outrage *NOUN* **outrages**
❶ outrage is the anger you feel when something shocking happens ❷ an outrage is something very shocking or cruel

outraged *ADJECTIVE*
very shocked and angry
The Scarecrow was outraged. He waved his road sign, he opened and shut his umbrella, and he stamped with fury.—THE SCARECROW AND HIS SERVANT, Philip Pullman

outrageous *ADJECTIVE*
shocking or dreadful

outright *ADVERB*
❶ completely • *We won outright.*
❷ immediately; instantly • *They were killed outright.*

outset *NOUN*
➤ **at** *or* **from the outset** at or from the beginning of something

outside *NOUN* **outsides**
the outer side or surface of a thing; the part furthest from the middle

outside *ADJECTIVE*
❶ on or coming from the outside ❷ slight or remote • *There is an outside chance that he will come.*

outside *ADVERB, PREPOSITION*
on or to the outside of something • *Go outside.* • *It's outside the house.*

outsider *NOUN* **outsiders**
❶ someone who is not a member of a particular group of people ❷ a horse or person that people think has no chance of winning a race or contest

outskirts *PLURAL NOUN*
the parts on the outside edge of an area, especially of a town or city

outspoken *ADJECTIVE*
speaking frankly even though it might offend people

outstanding *ADJECTIVE*
❶ extremely good or distinguished • *She is an outstanding athlete.* ❷ not yet dealt with • *He has outstanding bills to pay.*

outward *ADJECTIVE*
❶ going outwards ❷ on the outside

outwardly *ADVERB*
on the outside; for people to see • *They were outwardly calm.*

outwards *ADVERB*
towards the outside

outweigh *VERB* **outweighs**, **outweighing**, **outweighed**
to outweigh something is to be more important than it • *The advantages of the plan outweigh the disadvantages.*

outwit *VERB* **outwits**, **outwitting**, **outwitted**
to outwit someone is to deceive or defeat them by being more clever

oval *ADJECTIVE*
shaped like an egg or a number 0

oval *NOUN* **ovals**
an oval shape

ovary *NOUN* **ovaries**
❶ part of a female body where egg cells are produced ❷ the part of a flowering plant that produces seeds

oven *NOUN* **ovens**
a closed space in which things are cooked or heated

over *ADVERB*
❶ down or sideways; out and down from the top or edge • *He fell over.* ❷ across to a place • *We walked over to the house.* ❸ so that a different side shows • *Turn it over.* ❹ finished • *The lesson is over.* ❺ left or remaining • *There are a few apples over.* ❻ through or thoroughly • *Think it over.*
➤ **over and over** repeatedly; many times

over *PREPOSITION*
❶ above or covering • *There's a light over the door.* • *I'll put a cloth over the table.* ❷ across • *They ran over the road.* ❸ more than • *The house is over a mile away.* ❹ concerning; about • *They quarrelled over money.* ❺ during • *We can talk over dinner.* ❻ being better than • *They won a victory over their opponents.*

over *NOUN* **overs**
in cricket, a series of six balls bowled by one person

over– *PREFIX*
meaning 'too much', as in *over-excited*

overall *ADJECTIVE*
including everything; total • *What is the overall cost?*

overall *ADVERB*
as a whole; in all • *The team won three medals overall.*

overalls *PLURAL NOUN*
a piece of clothing that you wear over your other clothes to protect them when you are working

overarm *ADJECTIVE, ADVERB*
with the arm lifted above shoulder level and coming down in front of the body

overboard *ADVERB*
to fall or jump overboard is to go over the side of a boat into the water

overcast *ADJECTIVE*
covered with cloud • *The sky is grey and overcast.*

overcoat *NOUN* **overcoats**
a warm outdoor coat

overcome *VERB* **overcomes, overcoming, overcame, overcome**
❶ to overcome a problem or difficulty is to succeed in dealing with it or controlling it • *He overcame injury to win a gold medal.* ❷ to be overcome by something is to become helpless from it • *She was overcome by the fumes.* ❸ to overcome someone is to beat them

overdo *VERB* **overdoes, overdoing, overdid, overdone**
❶ to overdo something is to do it too much ❷ to overdo food is to cook it for too long

overdose *NOUN* **overdoses**
too large a dose of a drug or medicine

overdue *ADJECTIVE*
something is overdue when it is later than it should be • *The train is overdue.*

overflow *VERB* **overflows, overflowing, overflowed**
to overflow is to flow over the edges or limits of something

overgrown *ADJECTIVE*
❶ a place is overgrown when it is thickly covered with weeds or unwanted plants ❷ something is overgrown when it has grown bigger than its normal size
'But what are you?' said the Queen again. 'Are you a great overgrown dwarf that has cut off its beard?'–THE LION, THE WITCH AND THE WARDROBE, C. S. Lewis

overhang *VERB* **overhangs, overhanging, overhung**
to overhang something is to stick out beyond and above it • *The branches of the tree overhung the pond.*

overhaul *VERB* **overhauls, overhauling, overhauled**
❶ to overhaul a machine or vehicle is to check it thoroughly and repair it if necessary ❷ to overhaul someone or something is to overtake them

overhead *ADJECTIVE, ADVERB*
above your head; in the sky

overhear *VERB* **overhears, overhearing, overheard**
to overhear something is to hear it accidentally or without the speaker knowing

overland *ADJECTIVE, ADVERB*
over the land, not by sea or air • *an overland expedition* • *We travelled overland to Italy.*

overlap *VERB* **overlaps, overlapping, overlapped**
one thing overlaps another when it lies across part of it • *The carpet overlapped the fireplace.*

overlook *VERB* **overlooks, overlooking, overlooked**
❶ to overlook something is not to notice it ❷ to overlook a mistake or offence is not to punish it ❸ to overlook a place is to have a view over it • *The hotel overlooks the city park.*

overnight *ADVERB, ADJECTIVE*
of or during a night • *We stayed overnight in a hotel.* • *There will be an overnight stop in Paris.*

overpower *VERB* **overpowers, overpowering, overpowered**
to overpower someone is to defeat them because you are stronger

overpowering *ADJECTIVE*
very strong • *The smell of the cheese was overpowering.*

overrun *VERB* **overruns, overrunning, overran, overrun**
❶ to overrun an area is to spread quickly over it • *The place is overrun with mice.* ❷ something overruns when it goes on longer than it should • *The programme overran by ten minutes.*

overseas *ADVERB*
abroad • *They travelled overseas.*
overseas *ADJECTIVE*
from abroad; foreign • *We met some overseas students.*

oversight *NOUN* **oversights**
a mistake you make by not noticing something

oversleep *VERB* **oversleeps, oversleeping, overslept**
to sleep longer than you intended to

overtake *VERB* **overtakes, overtaking, overtook, overtaken**
to overtake a moving vehicle or person is to catch them up and pass them in the same direction

overthrow *VERB* **overthrows, overthrowing, overthrew, overthrown**
to overthrow a government is to remove it from power by force
overthrow *NOUN* **overthrows**
the overthrow of a government is when it is forced out of power

overtime *NOUN*
overtime is time someone spends working outside their normal hours

overture *NOUN* **overtures**
a piece of music played at the start of a concert, opera or ballet
➤ **overtures** a friendly attempt to start a discussion with someone

overturn *VERB* **overturns, overturning, overturned**
❶ to overturn something is to make it turn over or fall over ❷ to overturn is to turn over • *The car went out of control and overturned.*

overview *NOUN* **overviews**
a general description or outline of something • *The first chapter gives an overview of the whole subject.*

overweight *ADJECTIVE*
too heavy

overwhelm *VERB* **overwhelms, overwhelming, overwhelmed**
❶ to overwhelm someone is to have a very strong effect on them • *I was overwhelmed by everyone's kindness.* ❷ to overwhelm someone is to defeat them completely

overwork *VERB* **overworks, overworking, overworked**
to overwork is to become exhausted from working too hard
overwork *NOUN*
overwork is too much work, causing exhaustion

owe *VERB* **owes, owing, owed**
❶ to owe something, especially money, is to have a duty to pay or give it to someone • *I owe you a pound.* ❷ to owe something to someone is to have it thanks to them • *They owed their lives to the pilot's skill.*
➤ **owing to something** because of it • *The train was late owing to leaves on the line.*

owl *NOUN* **owls**
a bird of prey with large eyes and a short beak, usually flying at night

own *ADJECTIVE*
belonging to yourself or itself
➤ **to get your own back** (*informal*) is to have your revenge
➤ **on your own** by yourself; alone • *I did it all on my own.* • *I sat on my own in the empty room.*

own *VERB* **owns, owning, owned**
to own something is to have it as your property
➤ **to own up to something** (*informal*) is to admit that you did it

owner *NOUN* **owners**
the person who owns something
➤ **ownership** *NOUN*

ox *NOUN* **oxen**
a bull kept for its meat and for pulling carts

oxygen *NOUN*
oxygen is one of the gases in the air that people need to stay alive

oyster *NOUN* **oysters**
a kind of shellfish whose shell sometimes contains a pearl

oz *ABBREVIATION*
short for *ounces*

ozone *NOUN*
ozone is a strong-smelling gas that is a form of oxygen

ozone layer *NOUN*
a layer of ozone high in the atmosphere, that absorbs harmful radiation from the sun

p *ABBREVIATION*
short for *penny* or *pence*

pa *NOUN* **pas** (*informal*)
father

pace *NOUN* **paces**
❶ one step in walking, marching or running ❷ speed • *He set a fast pace.*

pace *VERB* **paces, pacing, paced**
to pace is to walk up and down with slow or regular steps

The rat, in the dungeon below, was pacing and muttering in the darkness, waiting to take his revenge on the princess.—THE TALE OF DESPEREAUX, Kate DiCamillo
➤ **to pace something out** is to measure a distance in paces

pacemaker *NOUN* **pacemakers**
❶ a person who sets the speed for someone else in a race ❷ an electrical device put into a person by surgery, that keeps the heart beating regularly

pacifist (*say* pas-i-fist) *NOUN* **pacifists**
someone who believes that war is always wrong
➤ **pacifism** *NOUN*

pacify (*say* pas-i-fy) *VERB* **pacifies, pacifying, pacified**
to pacify someone is to calm them down

pack *NOUN* **packs**
❶ a bundle or collection of things wrapped or tied together ❷ a set of playing cards ❸ a strong bag carried on your back ❹ a group of hounds, wolves or other animals

pack *VERB* **packs, packing, packed**
❶ to pack a suitcase, bag or box is to put things in it so that you can store them or take them somewhere ❷ to pack a room or building is to fill it • *The hall was packed.*

a
b
c
d
e
f
g
h
i
j
k
l
m
n
o
p
q
r
s
t
u
v
w
x
y
z

package *NOUN* **packages**
❶ a parcel or packet ❷ a number of things offered or accepted together

packet *NOUN* **packets**
a small parcel

pad *NOUN* **pads**
❶ a number of sheets of paper joined together along one edge ❷ a thick piece of soft material used to protect or shape something ❸ a thick band or strip that you wear to protect a part of your body in cricket and other sports ❹ a flat surface from which helicopters take off or rockets are launched

pad *VERB* **pads**, **padding**, **padded**
❶ to pad something is to put a piece of soft material on it or into it in order to protect or shape it ❷ to pad is also to walk softly • *The cubs padded along behind their mother.*
➤ **to pad something out** is to make a book or story longer than it needs to be

padding *NOUN*
padding is soft material used to protect or shape things

paddle *VERB* **paddles**, **paddling**, **paddled**
❶ to paddle is to walk about with bare feet in shallow water ❷ to paddle a boat is to move it along with a short oar

paddle *NOUN* **paddles**
❶ a time spent paddling in water ❷ a short oar with a broad blade

paddock *NOUN* **paddocks**
a small field for keeping horses

paddy *NOUN* **paddies**
a field where rice is grown

padlock *NOUN* **padlocks**
a lock with a metal loop that you can use to fasten a gate or lock a bicycle

pagan *NOUN* **pagans** (*old use*)
someone who believes in a religion which is not one of the main world religions

page *NOUN* **pages**
❶ a piece of paper that is part of a book or newspaper; one side of this piece of paper ❷ a section of a website designed to be viewed on a screen at one time ❸ (*historical*) a boy who is training to be a knight

pageant (*say* **paj**-ent) *NOUN* **pageants**
❶ a play or entertainment about historical events and people ❷ a procession of people in costume
➤ **pageantry** *NOUN*

pagoda (*say* pa-**goh**-da) *NOUN* **pagodas**
a Buddhist tower or Hindu temple

paid *VERB* (*past tense and past participle of* **pay**)
• *She paid by credit card.* • *Have you paid for the tickets already?*

pail *NOUN* **pails**
a bucket

pain *NOUN* **pains**
❶ pain, or a pain, is an unpleasant feeling caused by injury or disease • *Are you in pain?* ❷ pain is also mental suffering

pain *VERB* **pains**, **paining**, **pained**
to pain someone is to cause them pain, usually mental pain

painful *ADJECTIVE*
causing you pain • *My ankle is too painful to walk on.*

painfully *ADVERB*
❶ in a way that causes you pain • *He grasped my arm in a painfully tight grip.* ❷ to be (for example) painfully thin or painfully slow is to be extremely thin or extremely slow

painkiller *NOUN* **painkillers**
a drug that reduces pain

painless *ADJECTIVE*
not causing any pain

painstaking *ADJECTIVE*
making a careful effort
Rebecca sat down carefully, smoothing her dress under her with painstaking precision.—REBECCA OF SUNNYBROOK FARM, Kate Douglas Wiggin

paint *NOUN* **paints**
a liquid substance put on something to colour or cover it

paint *VERB* **paints**, **painting**, **painted**
❶ to paint something is to put paint on it ❷ to paint a picture is to make it with paints ❸ to paint someone or something is to make a picture of them using paint

paintbox *NOUN* **paintboxes**
a box of coloured paints used in art

paintbrush *NOUN* **paintbrushes**
a brush used in painting

painter *NOUN* **painters**
❶ an artist who paints pictures ❷ a person whose job is painting walls and houses

painting *NOUN* **paintings**
❶ painting is using paints to make a picture • *She likes painting.* ❷ a painting is a painted picture

pair *NOUN* **pairs**
❶ two things or people that go together or are the same kind • *I need a new pair of shoes.* ❷ something made of two parts joined together • *Have you got a pair of scissors?*

Pakistani *ADJECTIVE*
to do with Pakistan or its people

Pakistani *NOUN* **Pakistanis**
a person from Pakistan

pal *NOUN* **pals** (*informal*)
a friend

palace *NOUN* **palaces**
a large and splendid house where a king or queen or other important person lives

palaeontology (*say* pay-lee-on-**tol**-o-jee) *NOUN*
palaeontology is the study of dinosaurs and fossils
➤ **palaeontologist** *NOUN*

palate (*say* **pal**-at) *NOUN* **palates**
❶ the roof of your mouth ❷ a person's sense of taste • *We have food to suit every palate.*

pale *ADJECTIVE* **paler, palest**
❶ almost white • *He had a pale face.* ❷ not bright in colour; faint • *The sky was a pale blue.*
➤ **paleness** *NOUN*

palette (*say* **pal**-it) *NOUN* **palettes**
a board on which an artist mixes colours

palisade *NOUN* **palisades**
a fence made of wooden posts or railings

pall *VERB* **palls, palling, palled**
something palls when it becomes dull or uninteresting after a time • *The novelty of the new computer game soon began to pall.*

pallid *ADJECTIVE*
pale, especially because of illness

pallor *NOUN*
pallor is paleness in a person's face, especially because they are ill

palm *NOUN* **palms**
❶ the inner part of your hand, between your fingers and wrist ❷ a tropical tree with large leaves and no branches

palm *VERB* **palms, palming, palmed**
➤ **to palm something off on someone** is to fool them into taking something they do not want

palmistry *NOUN*
palmistry is fortune-telling by looking for signs in the lines of a person's hand

Palm Sunday *NOUN*
the Sunday before Easter, when Christians celebrate Christ's entry into Jerusalem on a path of palm leaves

paltry *ADJECTIVE*
not very much or not very valuable • *His reward was a paltry 50 pence.*

pampas *PLURAL NOUN*
pampas are wide grassy plains in South America

pamper *VERB* **pampers, pampering, pampered**
to pamper someone is to go to a lot of trouble to make them feel comfortable and let them have whatever they want

pamphlet *NOUN* **pamphlets**
a thin book with a paper cover

pan *NOUN* **pans**
a pot or dish with a flat base, used for cooking

pancake *NOUN* **pancakes**
a flat round cake of batter fried on both sides

panda *NOUN* **pandas**
a large black and white bear-like animal found in China

pandemic *NOUN* **pandemics**
an outbreak of a disease that spreads across all of a country or all of the world

pandemonium *NOUN*
you say there is pandemonium when there is a loud noise or disturbance
At this pandemonium broke loose. All the men leaped to their feet and shouted and waved their cudgels and guns.—THE LITTLE WHITE HORSE, Elizabeth Goudge

a
b
c
d
e
f
g
h
i
j
k
l
m
n
o
p
q
r
s
t
u
v
w
x
y
z

DID YOU KNOW? The word **pandemonium** was invented by the poet John Milton in the 17th century and means 'the place of all demons'.

pander VERB **panders, pandering, pandered**
to pander to someone is to let them have whatever they want

pane NOUN **panes**
a sheet of glass in a window

panel NOUN **panels**
❶ a long flat piece of wood, metal or other material that is part of a door, wall or piece of furniture ❷ a group of people appointed to discuss or decide something • *The winner of the contest will be decided by a panel of judges.*

pang NOUN **pangs**
a sudden feeling of pain or strong emotion

pangolin NOUN **pangolins**
an anteater with a body covered with hard scales

panic NOUN
panic is sudden fear that makes you behave wildly

panic VERB **panics, panicking, panicked**
to panic is to be overcome with fear or anxiety and behave wildly

pannier NOUN **panniers**
a bag or basket hung on one side of a bicycle or horse

panorama NOUN **panoramas**
a view or picture of a wide area
A complete panorama of the town and the surrounding countryside, broken only by the chimney stacks of the factories, was laid out before him.—HERE BE MONSTERS, Alan Snow
➤ **panoramic** ADJECTIVE

pansy NOUN **pansies**
a small, brightly coloured garden flower

pant VERB **pants, panting, panted**
you pant when you take short quick breaths, usually after running or working hard

panther NOUN **panthers**
a leopard

pantomime NOUN **pantomimes**
a Christmas entertainment based on a fairy tale

pantry NOUN **pantries**
a cupboard or small room for storing food

pants PLURAL NOUN
❶ (*informal*) underpants or knickers
❷ (*North American*) trousers

papaya NOUN **papayas**
a juicy tropical fruit with orange pulp and black seeds

paper NOUN **papers**
❶ paper is a thin substance made in sheets and used for writing, printing or drawing on, or for wrapping things ❷ a paper is a newspaper ❸ papers are documents

paper VERB **papers, papering, papered**
to paper a wall or room is to cover it with wallpaper

paperback NOUN **paperbacks**
a book with thin flexible covers

papier mâché (*say* pap-yay-**mash**-ay) NOUN
papier mâché is a mixture of paper pulp and glue you use to make models or ornaments

papyrus (*say* pa-**py**-rus) NOUN **papyri**
❶ papyrus is a kind of paper made from the stems of reeds, used in ancient Egypt
❷ a papyrus is a document written on this paper

parable NOUN **parables**
a story told to teach people something, especially one of the stories told by Jesus Christ

parachute NOUN **parachutes**
an umbrella-shaped device on which people or things can float slowly down to the ground from an aircraft
➤ **parachutist** NOUN

parade NOUN **parades**
❶ a line of people or vehicles moving forward through a place as a celebration ❷ soldiers are on parade when they assemble for inspection or drill ❸ a public square or row of shops

parade VERB **parades, parading, paraded**
❶ to parade is to move forward through a place as a celebration ❷ soldiers parade when they assemble for inspection or drill

paradise NOUN
❶ paradise is heaven or, in the Bible, the Garden of Eden ❷ you can describe a wonderful or perfect place as a paradise
DID YOU KNOW? The word **paradise** comes from an old Persian word meaning 'garden'.

paradox (*say* **pa**-ra-doks) *NOUN* **paradoxes**
a statement which, because it has two opposite ideas in it, does not seem to make sense but may still be true, for example *More haste, less speed*

paradoxical *ADJECTIVE*
a paradoxical statement seems to contradict itself but may still be true
➤ **paradoxically** *ADVERB*

paraffin *NOUN*
paraffin is a kind of oil used as fuel

paragraph *NOUN* **paragraphs**
one of the group of sentences that a piece of writing is divided into, beginning on a new line

parallel *ADJECTIVE*
parallel lines are lines that are the same distance apart for their whole length, like railway lines

parallelogram *NOUN* **parallelograms**
a four-sided figure with its opposite sides parallel to each other and equal in length

Paralympian *NOUN* **Paralympians**
an athlete who competes in the Paralympic Games

Paralympic Games, **Paralympics** *PLURAL NOUN*
an international sports contest for athletes with disabilities

paralyse *VERB* **paralyses**, **paralysing**, **paralysed**
❶ to paralyse someone is to make them unable to move or feel their body • *Some snakes can paralyse you with one bite.* ❷ if you are paralysed with fear or panic, you are so shocked that you cannot move
Just for a second, Measle found himself paralysed with fear. He and Iggy were out in the open, with nowhere to hide!—MEASLE AND THE SLITHERGHOUL, Ian Ogilvy

paralysis (*say* pa-**ral**-i-sis) *NOUN*
paralysis is the loss of the ability to move or feel anything

paramedic *NOUN* **paramedics**
a person trained to give emergency medical treatment, often as part of an ambulance crew

parapet *NOUN* **parapets**
a low wall along the edge of a balcony, bridge or roof

paraphernalia (*say* pa-ra-fer-**nay**-li-a) *NOUN*
paraphernalia is various pieces of equipment or small possessions

paraphrase *VERB* **paraphrases**, **paraphrasing**, **paraphrased**
to paraphrase something that has been said or written is to give its meaning by using different words

parasite *NOUN* **parasites**
an animal or plant that lives in or on another and gets its food from it
➤ **parasitic** *ADJECTIVE*

parasol *NOUN* **parasols**
a lightweight umbrella you use to shade yourself from the sun

paratroops *PLURAL NOUN*
troops trained to be dropped from aircraft by parachute
➤ **paratrooper** *NOUN*

parcel *NOUN* **parcels**
something wrapped up to be posted or carried

parched *ADJECTIVE*
very dry or thirsty

parchment *NOUN*
parchment is a kind of heavy paper originally made from animal skins

pardon *VERB* **pardons**, **pardoning**, **pardoned**
to pardon someone is to forgive or excuse them

pardon *NOUN* **pardons**
forgiveness; an act of pardoning someone

pardon *EXCLAMATION*
a word you say when you want someone to repeat something • *Pardon? What did you say?*

pardonable *ADJECTIVE*
a pardonable mistake is one that can be forgiven

parent *NOUN* **parents**
your parents are your father and mother
➤ **parental** *ADJECTIVE*

parentage *NOUN*
your parentage is who your parents are

parenthesis (*say* pa-**ren**-thi-sis) *NOUN* **parentheses**
❶ something extra put in a sentence between brackets or dashes ❷ one of a pair of brackets (like these) used in the middle of a sentence

parish *NOUN* **parishes**
a district that has its own church
➤ **parishioner** *NOUN* a parishioner of a church is a person who regularly goes to that church

park *NOUN* **parks**
❶ a large area with grass and trees, for public use ❷ a piece of ground belonging to a large country house

park *VERB* **parks**, **parking**, **parked**
to park a vehicle is to leave it somewhere for a time

parka *NOUN* **parkas**
a warm jacket with a hood attached

parliament *NOUN* **parliaments**
the group of people that make a country's laws
➤ **parliamentary** *ADJECTIVE*

parlour *NOUN* **parlours**
an old-fashioned name for a sitting room
DID YOU KNOW? The word **parlour** means literally 'speaking place'.

parmesan *NOUN*
a hard Italian cheese often grated to sprinkle on pasta

parody *NOUN* **parodies**
a play or poem that makes fun of people or things by imitating them

parole (*say* pa-**rohl**) *NOUN*
parole is letting someone out of prison before they have finished their sentence, on condition that they behave well • *He has been released on parole.*

parrot *NOUN* **parrots**
a brightly coloured bird with a curved beak that can learn to repeat words or sounds
DID YOU KNOW? An old word for a **parrot** is *popinjay*, which comes from an Arabic word.

parsley *NOUN*
parsley is a plant with crinkled green leaves used to flavour and decorate food

parsnip *NOUN* **parsnips**
a pale yellow vegetable

part *NOUN* **parts**
❶ some but not all of a thing or a number of things; anything that belongs to something bigger ❷ the character played by an actor or actress; the words spoken by a character in a play • *She has a good part in the school play.*

part *VERB* **parts**, **parting**, **parted**
❶ to part people or things is to separate them or divide them ❷ to part is to separate ❸ to part hair is to divide it so that it goes in two different directions
➤ **to part with something** is to give it away or get rid of it

partial *ADJECTIVE*
❶ not complete or total • *There will be a partial eclipse of the sun.* ❷ unfairly showing more support for one person or side than another
➤ **to be partial to something** is to like it
➤ **partiality** *NOUN* to have a partiality for something is to like it
➤ **partially** *ADVERB*

participant *NOUN* **participants**
someone who participates in something

participate *VERB* **participates**, **participating**, **participated**
to participate in something is to take part in it
➤ **participation** *NOUN*

participle *NOUN* **participles**
a word formed from a verb and used as part of the verb or as an adjective, for example *going, gone, sailed, sailing*

particle *NOUN* **particles**
a very small piece or amount

particular *ADJECTIVE*
❶ only this one and no other; special; individual • *Are you looking for a particular book?* ❷ fussy; hard to please • *He is very particular about his clothes.*
➤ **in particular** especially; chiefly

particular *NOUN* **particulars**
a detail or single fact

particularly *ADVERB*
you can say something is (for example)

particularly good or useful when it is especially good or useful

parting NOUN partings
❶ leaving or separation ❷ the line where hair is combed in different directions

partition NOUN partitions
❶ partition is dividing something into parts ❷ a partition is a thin dividing wall

partly ADVERB
not completely; in some ways

partner NOUN partners
❶ one of a pair of people who do something together, especially dancing, running a business or playing a game ❷ someone's partner is the person they are married to or have a romantic relationship with
➤ **partnership** NOUN

part of speech NOUN parts of speech
each of the groups (also called *word classes*) into which words can be divided in grammar: noun, adjective, verb, pronoun, adverb, preposition, conjunction, determiner, exclamation

partridge NOUN partridges
a game bird with brown feathers

part-time ADJECTIVE, ADVERB
working for only some of the normal hours

party NOUN parties
❶ a time when people get together to enjoy themselves • *Come to my birthday party.* ❷ a group of people working or travelling together • *They organized a search party.* ❸ an organized group of people with similar political beliefs • *The Labour Party* ❹ a person who is involved in an action or legal case • *They are the guilty party.*

pass VERB passes, passing, passed
❶ to pass something or someone is to go past them ❷ to pass in a certain direction is to move or go that way • *They passed over the bridge.* ❸ to pass something to someone is to give it or hand it to them • *Can you pass the butter, please?* ❹ to pass an examination is to be successful in it ❺ to pass time is to use time doing something ❻ to pass is to finish or no longer be there • *His opportunity passed.* ❼ to pass a law or rule is to approve or accept it

pass NOUN passes
❶ when a ball is kicked, hit or thrown from one player to another in a game ❷ a success in an examination ❸ a card or ticket that allows you to go in or out of a place ❹ a narrow way between mountains

passable ADJECTIVE
just about acceptable or all right

passage NOUN passages
❶ a corridor or narrow space between two walls ❷ a section of a piece of writing or music ❸ a journey by sea or air ❹ passing • *the passage of time*

passageway NOUN passageways
a passage or way through, especially between buildings

passenger NOUN passengers
someone who is travelling in a car or other vehicle and is not the driver or a member of the crew

passer-by NOUN passers-by
someone who is going past by chance when something happens
Passers-by stared a lot at Hagrid as they walked through the little town to the station.—HARRY POTTER AND THE PHILOSOPHER'S STONE, J. K. Rowling

passion NOUN passions
❶ passion is strong feeling or emotion ❷ a passion is a great enthusiasm for something

passionate ADJECTIVE
full of passion or strong feeling
➤ **passionately** ADVERB

passive ADJECTIVE
❶ not active; not resisting or fighting against something ❷ (*grammar*) a passive verb is one in which the subject receives the action, for example *was hit* in *She was hit by a car*
➤ **passively** ADVERB ➤ **passivity** NOUN

Passover NOUN
Passover is a Jewish religious festival, celebrating the escape of the ancient Jewish people from slavery in Egypt

passport NOUN passports
an official document that allows you to travel abroad

password *NOUN* **passwords**
a secret word or phrase that you need to know to be allowed to go somewhere or to gain access to a computer system

past *NOUN*
the time gone by • *Try to forget the past.*

past *ADJECTIVE*
of the time gone by • *a list of our past achievements*

past *PREPOSITION*
❶ beyond • *Go past the school and turn right.*
❷ later than • *It is past midnight.*
SPELLING ALERT! **Past** is different from **passed**, which is a form of the verb *to pass: I passed her in the street. She walked right past me.*

pasta *NOUN*
an Italian food made as a dried paste of flour, water and often eggs, formed into various shapes such as spaghetti and lasagne

paste *NOUN* **pastes**
a soft and moist or gluey substance

paste *VERB* **pastes, pasting, pasted**
to paste something is to stick it to a surface with paste

pastel *NOUN* **pastels**
❶ a crayon that is like a slightly greasy chalk
❷ a light delicate colour

pasteurize (*say* pahs-cher-ryz) (*also* **pasteurise**) *VERB* **pasteurizes, pasteurizing, pasteurized**
to pasteurize milk is to purify it by heating and then cooling it
➤ **pasteurization** *NOUN*

pastille *NOUN* **pastilles**
a small flavoured sweet that you suck

pastime *NOUN* **pastimes**
something you do to pass time pleasantly; a hobby or game

pastoral *ADJECTIVE*
to do with the country

past participle *NOUN* **past participles**
a form of a verb used after *has, have, had, was, were,* to describe an action that happened at a time before now, for example *done, overtaken* and *written*

pastry *NOUN* **pastries**
❶ pastry is dough made from flour, fat and water rolled flat and baked ❷ a pastry is a cake made from this dough

past tense *NOUN*
a form of a verb used to describe an action that happened at a time before now, for example *took* is the past tense of *take*

pasture *NOUN* **pastures**
land covered with grass that cattle, sheep or horses can eat

pasty (*say* pas-tee) *NOUN* **pasties**
a pastry filled with meat and vegetables, like a small pie

pasty (*say* pay-stee) *ADJECTIVE* **pastier, pastiest**
looking pale and unhealthy
➤ **pastiness** *NOUN*

pat *VERB* **pats, patting, patted**
to pat something or someone is to tap them gently with your open hand or with something flat

pat *NOUN* **pats**
❶ a patting movement or sound ❷ a small piece of butter

patch *NOUN* **patches**
❶ a piece of material put over a hole or damaged place ❷ an area that is different from its surroundings • *We have a black cat with a white patch on its chest.* ❸ a small area of land ❹ a small piece of something • *There are patches of ice on the road.*

patch *VERB* **patches, patching, patched**
to patch something is to put a piece of material on it to repair it
➤ **to patch something up** is to repair it roughly
➤ **to patch things up** is to be friendly again after a quarrel

patchwork *NOUN*
patchwork is needlework using small pieces of different cloth which are sewn together

patchy *ADJECTIVE* **patchier, patchiest**
occurring in some areas but not others; uneven • *There may be some patchy rain.*

patent (*say* pay-tent *or* pat-ent) *NOUN* **patents**
the official right given to someone to make something they have invented and to stop other people from copying it

patent (*say* **pay**-tent) *ADJECTIVE*
obvious • *What they say is a patent lie.*

patent (*say* **pay**-tent *or* **pat**-ent) *VERB*
patents, patenting, patented
to patent an idea or invention is to get
a patent for it

patent leather *NOUN*
patent leather is leather with a special glossy
surface

patently *ADVERB*
clearly; obviously • *They were patently lying.*

paternal *ADJECTIVE*
to do with a father, or like a father

path *NOUN* **paths**
❶ a narrow way to walk or ride along ❷ the
line along which something moves • *The
diagram shows the path of the meteor.*

pathetic *ADJECTIVE*
❶ sad and pitiful ❷ sadly or comically weak or
useless • *He made a pathetic attempt to climb
the tree.*
➤ **pathetically** *ADVERB*

patience (*say* **pay**-shens) *NOUN*
❶ patience is the ability to stay calm,
especially when you have to wait for a long
time ❷ patience is also a card game for one
person

patient (*say* **pay**-shent) *ADJECTIVE*
❶ able to wait for a long time without getting
anxious or angry ❷ able to bear pain or
trouble

patient (*say* **pay**-shent) *NOUN* **patients**
a person who is getting treatment from
a doctor or dentist

patiently *ADVERB*
you do something patiently when you do
it in a patient way • *He waited patiently for
his turn.*

patio (*say* **pat**-i-oh) *NOUN* **patios**
a paved area beside a house

patriot (*say* **pay**-tri-ot *or* **pat**-ri-ot) *NOUN*
patriots
someone who loves and supports their country
➤ **patriotic** *ADJECTIVE* ➤ **patriotism** *NOUN*

patrol *VERB* **patrols, patrolling, patrolled**
to walk or travel regularly round a place

or a thing to guard it and make sure that all
is well

patrol *NOUN* **patrols**
a group of people or vehicles patrolling a
place
➤ **to be on patrol** is to be patrolling a place

patron (*say* **pay**-tron) *NOUN* **patrons**
❶ someone who supports a person or cause
with money or encouragement ❷ a regular
customer of a shop or business
➤ **patronage** *NOUN*

patron saint *NOUN* **patron saints**
a saint who is thought of as protecting a place
or activity

patter *NOUN* **patters**
❶ a series of light tapping sounds • *the patter
of rain against the window* ❷ patter is also the
quick talk of a performer or salesperson

patter *VERB* **patters, pattering, pattered**
to patter is to make light tapping sounds
• *The rain was pattering on the roof.*

pattern *NOUN* **patterns**
❶ a decorative arrangement of lines or
shapes ❷ a thing that you copy so that you
can make something, such as a piece of
clothing

pause *NOUN* **pauses**
a short stop before continuing with something

pause *VERB* **pauses, pausing, paused**
❶ to pause is to make a short stop before
continuing with something ❷ to pause a
music track or video film is to make it stop
playing for a short time

pave *VERB* **paves, paving, paved**
to pave a road or path is to put a hard surface
on it
➤ **to pave the way** is to prepare for
something

pavement *NOUN* **pavements**
a path with a hard surface, along the side of
a street

pavilion *NOUN* **pavilions**
a building at a sports ground for players and
spectators to use

paw *NOUN* **paws**
an animal's foot

a b c d e f g h i j k l m n o p q r s t u v w x y z

paw *VERB* paws, pawing, pawed
an animal paws something when it touches or scrapes it clumsily with its paw

pawn *NOUN* pawns
❶ one of the sixteen pieces in chess that are at the front on each side and are the least valuable ❷ a person who is controlled by someone else

pawn *VERB* pawns, pawning, pawned
to pawn something is to leave it with a pawnbroker while borrowing money • *He had to pawn his watch.*

pawnbroker *NOUN* pawnbrokers
a shopkeeper who lends money to people in return for objects that they leave and which are sold if the money is not paid back

pay *VERB* pays, paying, paid
❶ to pay for something is to give money in return for it • *Have you paid for your lunch?* ❷ to pay someone is to give them money for something they have done • *Wash my car and I'll pay you £5.* ❸ to pay is to be profitable or worthwhile • *It pays to be honest.* ❹ to pay (for example) attention or a compliment is to give someone your attention or a compliment ❺ to pay for something you have done wrong is to suffer for it • *I'll make you pay for this!*
➤ **to pay someone back** ❶ is to pay money that you owe them ❷ is to get revenge on them

pay *NOUN*
pay is the money you earn when you work

payment *NOUN* payments
❶ payment is when you pay someone or are paid for something ❷ a payment is money you pay

PC *NOUN* PCs
short for *personal computer*, a small computer designed for a single user

PE *ABBREVIATION*
short for *physical education*

pea *NOUN* peas
a small round green seed of a climbing plant, growing inside a pod and used as a vegetable

peace *NOUN*
❶ peace is a time when there is no war or violence • *At last the country was at peace.* ❷ peace is also quiet and calm

peaceful *ADJECTIVE*
❶ quiet and calm ❷ not involving violence
➤ **peacefully** *ADVERB*

peach *NOUN* peaches
a soft round juicy fruit with a slightly furry skin and a large stone

peacock *NOUN* peacocks
a large male bird with a long brightly coloured tail that it can spread out like a fan

peak *NOUN* peaks
❶ the top of a mountain ❷ the highest or best point of something • *Traffic reaches its peak at 5 o'clock.* ❸ the part of a cap that sticks out in front

peak *VERB* peaks, peaking, peaked
to reach the highest point or amount • *Prices peaked in March.*

peal *VERB* peals, pealing, pealed
bells peal when they make a loud ringing sound

peal *NOUN* peals
a loud ringing sound made by bells

peanut *NOUN* peanuts
a small round nut that grows in a pod in the ground

peanut butter *NOUN*
peanut butter is a paste made from crushed roasted peanuts

pear *NOUN* pears
a juicy fruit that gets narrower near the stalk

pearl *NOUN* pearls
a small shiny white ball found in the shells of some oysters and used as a jewel
➤ **pearly** *ADJECTIVE*

peasant *NOUN* peasants
a person who belongs to a farming community, especially in poor areas of the world

peat *NOUN*
peat is rotted plant material that can be dug out of the ground and used as fuel or fertilizer

pebble *NOUN* pebbles
a small round stone found on the beach

peck *VERB* pecks, pecking, pecked
when a bird pecks something, it bites it or eats it with its beak

peck *NOUN* **pecks**
1 a short sharp bite with a bird's beak
2 (*informal*) a quick kiss

peckish *ADJECTIVE* (*informal*)
hungry

peculiar *ADJECTIVE*
strange or unusual
➤ **to be peculiar to someone** *or* **something** is to be restricted to them • *This species of bird is peculiar to Asia.*
➤ **peculiarly** *ADVERB* 1 more than usually 2 strangely • *He is peculiarly fond of brightly coloured socks.*

peculiarity *NOUN* **peculiarities**
something peculiar or special

pedal *NOUN* **pedals**
a lever that you press with your foot to operate a bicycle, car or machine, or to play some musical instruments

pedal *VERB* **pedals, pedalling, pedalled**
to pedal is to push or turn the pedals of a bicycle or other device

peddle *VERB* **peddles, peddling, peddled**
to peddle things is to sell them

pedestal *NOUN* **pedestals**
the base that supports a statue or pillar

pedestrian *NOUN* **pedestrians**
someone who is walking

pedestrian *ADJECTIVE*
a pedestrian area is one where cars or other vehicles are not allowed

pedigree *NOUN* **pedigrees**
a list of an animal's or person's ancestors, especially to show how well an animal has been bred

peel *NOUN* **peels**
the skin of some fruit and vegetables

peel *VERB* **peels, peeling, peeled**
1 to peel a piece of fruit or a vegetable is to remove the peel or covering from it 2 to peel is to lose a covering or skin • *My skin is peeling.*

peep *VERB* **peeps, peeping, peeped**
1 to look quickly or secretly, or through a narrow opening 2 to peep, or peep out, is to come slowly or briefly into view • *The moon peeped out through the clouds.*

peep *NOUN* **peeps**
a quick look

peer *VERB* **peers, peering, peered**
to peer at something or someone is to look at them closely or with difficulty

peer *NOUN* **peers**
1 a noble 2 your peers are the people who are the same age as you

peewit *NOUN* **peewits**
a kind of wading bird

peg *NOUN* **pegs**
a clip or pin for fixing things in place or for hanging things on

peg *VERB* **pegs, pegging, pegged**
to peg something is to fix it with pegs • *We pegged out the tent.*

Pekinese, Pekingese (*say* peek-i-**neez**) *NOUN* **Pekinese, Pekingese**
a small breed of dog with short legs and long silky hair

pelican *NOUN* **pelicans**
a large bird with a pouch in its long beak for storing fish

pelican crossing *NOUN* **pelican crossings**
a place where pedestrians can cross a street by operating lights that signal the traffic to stop

pellet *NOUN* **pellets**
a tiny ball of metal, food, wet paper or other substance

pelt *VERB* **pelts, pelting, pelted**
1 to pelt someone with things is to throw a lot of things at them • *We pelted him with snowballs.* 2 it pelts down when it is raining very hard 3 to pelt is to run fast

pelt *NOUN* **pelts**
an animal skin, especially with the fur or hair still on it

pelvis *NOUN* **pelvises**
your pelvis is the large bowl-shaped bone at your hips, to which the bones of your legs are attached

pen *NOUN* **pens**
1 a device with a metal point for writing with ink 2 a pen is also an enclosure for cattle or other animals

penalize (*also* **penalise**) VERB **penalizes**, **penalizing**, **penalized**
❶ to penalize someone is to punish them
❷ in a game, to penalize someone is to award a penalty against them

penalty NOUN **penalties**
❶ a punishment ❷ a point or advantage given to one side in a game when a member of the other side breaks a rule

pence PLURAL NOUN
pennies • *I need another fifty pence for my bus fare.*

pencil NOUN **pencils**
a device for drawing or writing, made of a thin stick of graphite or coloured chalk inside a cylinder of wood or metal

pencil VERB **pencils**, **pencilling**, **pencilled**
to pencil something is to write it or mark it with a pencil • *I'll pencil that date in my diary.*

pendant NOUN **pendants**
a piece of jewellery hung round the neck on a long chain or string

pendulum NOUN **pendulums**
a weight hung at the end of a rod so that it swings to and fro, especially to keep a clock working

penetrate VERB **penetrates**, **penetrating**, **penetrated**
to penetrate something is to find a way through it or into it
➤ **penetration** NOUN

penguin NOUN **penguins**
an Antarctic seabird that cannot fly but uses its wings as flippers for swimming

penicillin NOUN
penicillin is a drug that kills bacteria, made from mould

peninsula NOUN **peninsulas**
a long piece of land that is almost surrounded by water
➤ **peninsular** ADJECTIVE

penis NOUN **penises**
the part of the body with which a male person or animal passes water from the body

penitent ADJECTIVE
sorry for what you have done
➤ **penitence** NOUN

penknife NOUN **penknives**
a small folding knife

pennant NOUN **pennants**
a long pointed flag

penniless ADJECTIVE
having no money; very poor

penny NOUN **pennies** *or* **pence**
a British coin worth a hundredth of a pound

pension NOUN **pensions**
an income of regular payments made to someone who has retired

pensioner NOUN **pensioners**
someone who receives a pension

pentagon NOUN **pentagons**
a flat shape with five sides
➤ **pentagonal** (*say* pen-**ta**-go-nal) ADJECTIVE

peony (*say* pee-o-nee) NOUN **peonies**
a plant with large round red, pink or white flowers

people PLURAL NOUN
❶ people are human beings ❷ the people of a particular country or area are the ones who live there

people NOUN **peoples**
a people is a community or nation • *They are a peaceful people.*

pepper NOUN **peppers**
❶ pepper is a hot-tasting powder used to flavour food ❷ a pepper is a bright green, red or yellow vegetable
➤ **peppery** ADJECTIVE

peppermint NOUN **peppermints**
❶ peppermint is a kind of mint used for flavouring ❷ a peppermint is a sweet flavoured with this mint

per PREPOSITION
for each • *The charge is £2 per person.*

perceive VERB **perceives**, **perceiving**, **perceived**
to perceive something is to see or notice it or understand it

per cent ADVERB
for every hundred • *Take an extra 10 per cent (10%) off the sale price.*

percentage *NOUN* **percentages**
an amount or rate expressed as a proportion of 100

perceptible *ADJECTIVE*
able to be seen or noticed
➤ **perceptibly** *ADVERB*

perception *NOUN*
perception is the ability to see, notice or understand something

perceptive *ADJECTIVE*
quick to notice or understand things • *It was very perceptive of you to spot that.*

perch *NOUN* **perches**
❶ a perch is a place where a bird sits or rests ❷ a perch is also an edible freshwater fish

perch *VERB* **perches, perching, perched**
to perch is to sit or stand on the edge of something or on something small
Matilda, who was perched on a tall stool at the kitchen table, ate her bread and jam slowly.—MATILDA, Roald Dahl

percussion *NOUN*
percussion is musical instruments that you play by hitting them or shaking them, such as drums and cymbals
➤ **percussionist** *NOUN*

perennial *ADJECTIVE*
lasting or occurring for many years

perennial *NOUN* **perennials**
a plant that lives for many years

perfect (*say* per-fikt) *ADJECTIVE*
❶ so good that it cannot be made any better; without any faults • *She scored a perfect mark on the test.* ❷ complete • *The man is a perfect stranger.* ❸ (*grammar*) the perfect tense of a verb describes a completed action. It is formed with *has* and *have*, for example *I have lost my pen.*
➤ **perfection** *NOUN*

perfect (*say* per-fekt) *VERB* **perfects, perfecting, perfected**
to perfect something is to make it perfect • *I'm trying to perfect my diving.*

perfectly *ADVERB*
❶ completely • *She stood perfectly still.*
❷ without any faults • *The toaster works perfectly now.*

perforate *VERB* **perforates, perforating, perforated**
to perforate something is to make tiny holes in it, especially so that it can be torn off easily
➤ **perforations** *PLURAL NOUN* perforations are the tiny holes made in something so that it can be torn off easily

perform *VERB* **performs, performing, performed**
❶ to perform something is to present it in front of an audience • *They performed a play in the school hall.* ❷ to perform something is also to do something you have to do or ought to do • *The surgeon performed the operation on Tuesday.*

performance *NOUN* **performances**
the showing of something in front of an audience

performer *NOUN* **performers**
someone who performs an entertainment

perfume *NOUN* **perfumes**
❶ a sweet-smelling liquid that people put on their skin ❷ a sweet or pleasant smell

perhaps *ADVERB*
it may be; possibly

peril *NOUN* **perils**
peril is danger • *She was in great peril.*

perilous *ADJECTIVE*
a perilous journey or adventure is a dangerous one • *The family faced a perilous sea crossing.*
➤ **perilously** *ADVERB* dangerously • *We came perilously close to disaster.*

perimeter (*say* per-im-it-er) *NOUN* **perimeters**
❶ a boundary • *A fence marks the perimeter of the park.* ❷ the distance round the edge of something

period *NOUN* **periods**
❶ a length of time ❷ the time every month when a woman or girl bleeds from her womb during menstruation

periodic *ADJECTIVE*
occurring at regular intervals
➤ **periodically** *ADVERB* something happens periodically when it happens from time to time

a
b
c
d
e
f
g
h
i
j
k
l
m
n
o
p
q
r
s
t
u
v
w
x
y
z

periodical *NOUN* **periodicals**
a magazine published regularly, for example once a month

periscope *NOUN* **periscopes**
a device with a tube and mirrors that lets you see things at a higher level, used for example in submarines

perish *VERB* **perishes, perishing, perished**
❶ to perish is to die or be destroyed • *Many sailors perished in the shipwreck.* ❷ to perish is also to rot • *The tyres have perished.* ❸ (*informal*) to be perished is to feel extremely cold • *I was perished after the long walk in the hills.*

perm *NOUN* **perms**
treatment of the hair with chemicals to give it long-lasting waves

perm *VERB* **perms, perming, permed**
to perm hair is to treat it with chemicals to give it long-lasting waves

permanent *ADJECTIVE*
lasting forever or for a long time • *Will there be any permanent damage?*
➤ **permanence** *NOUN*
➤ **permanently** *ADVERB*

permissible *ADJECTIVE*
something is permissible when it is allowed

permission *NOUN*
you have permission to do something when you are allowed to do it

permit (*say* per-mit) *VERB* **permits, permitting, permitted**
❶ to permit someone to do something is to allow them to do it ❷ to permit something is to allow it to be done

permit (*say* per-mit) *NOUN* **permits**
a written or printed statement that says you are allowed to do something

perpendicular *ADJECTIVE*
upright, or at a right angle to a line or surface

perpetual *ADJECTIVE*
lasting forever or for a long time
➤ **perpetually** *ADVERB* continually

perplex *VERB* **perplexes, perplexing, perplexed**
to perplex someone is to puzzle them very much
➤ **perplexity** *NOUN*

persecute *VERB* **persecutes, persecuting, persecuted**
to persecute someone is to be continually cruel to them, especially because you disagree with their beliefs
➤ **persecution** *NOUN* ➤ **persecutor** *NOUN*

persevere *VERB* **perseveres, persevering, persevered**
to persevere is to go on with something even though it is difficult
➤ **perseverance** *NOUN*

persist *VERB* **persists, persisting, persisted**
❶ to persist is to keep on firmly or obstinately doing something • *She persists in breaking the rules.* ❷ to persist is also to last for a long time • *The rain persisted all afternoon.*
➤ **persistence** *NOUN* you show persistence when you keep on doing something without giving up

persistent *ADJECTIVE*
❶ refusing to give up ❷ lasting for a long time • *The rain was persistent.*
➤ **persistently** *ADVERB*

person *NOUN* **persons** *or* **people**
❶ a human being ❷ (*grammar*) each of the parts of a verb and the pronouns that go with the verb. The **first person** (*I, me, we, us*) refers to the person or people speaking; the **second person** (*you*) refers to the person or people spoken to, and the **third person** (*he, him, she, her, it, they, them*) refers to the person or people spoken about.

personal *ADJECTIVE*
❶ belonging to, done by or concerning a particular person • *The stars of the film will be making a personal appearance at the premiere.* ❷ private • *I can't tell you about that because it's personal.*

personality *NOUN* **personalities**
❶ your personality is your nature and character • *She has a cheerful personality.* ❷ a well-known person • *There were several TV personalities at the party.*

personally *ADVERB*
❶ in person; being actually there • *The head thanked me personally.* ❷ as far as I am concerned • *Personally, I'd rather stay here.*

personnel (*say* per-so-**nel**) *NOUN*
the personnel in a business or organization are the people who work there

perspective *NOUN* **perspectives**
❶ perspective is the impression of depth and space in a picture or scene ❷ your perspective on a situation is your point of view
➤ **in perspective** giving a balanced view of things • *Try to see the problem in perspective.*

perspire *VERB* **perspires, perspiring, perspired**
to perspire is to sweat
➤ **perspiration** *NOUN*

persuade *VERB* **persuades, persuading, persuaded**
to persuade someone is to get them to agree about something

persuasion *NOUN*
persuasion is when you persuade someone to do or believe something

persuasive *ADJECTIVE*
a persuasive person is good at persuading people

perverse (*say* per-**verss**) *ADJECTIVE*
obstinate or unreasonable in what you do or say
➤ **perversely** *ADVERB* ➤ **perversity** *NOUN*

Pesach *NOUN*
Pesach is the Hebrew name for Passover.

pesky *ADJECTIVE* **peskier, peskiest** (*informal*)
annoying and troublesome • *a swarm of pesky midges*

pessimist *NOUN* **pessimists**
someone who usually expects things to turn out badly
➤ **pessimism** *NOUN* pessimism is the feeling that things will turn out badly

pessimistic *ADJECTIVE*
expecting things to turn out badly
➤ **pessimistically** *ADVERB*

pest *NOUN* **pests**
❶ a destructive insect or animal, such as a locust or a mouse ❷ a nuisance

pester *VERB* **pesters, pestering, pestered**
to pester someone is to annoy them with frequent questions or interruptions

pesticide *NOUN* **pesticides**
a chemical used to kill insects and grubs

pet *NOUN* **pets**
❶ a tame animal that you keep at home
❷ a person treated as a favourite • *She seems to be teacher's pet.*

petal *NOUN* **petals**
each of the separate coloured outer parts of a flower

petition *NOUN* **petitions**
a written request for something, usually signed by a large number of people

petrify *VERB* **petrifies, petrifying, petrified**
to petrify someone is to make them so terrified that they cannot move
DID YOU KNOW? The word **petrify** comes from a Greek word *petra* meaning 'rock' or 'stone', and originally meant 'to turn into stone'.

petrochemical *NOUN* **petrochemicals**
a chemical substance made from petroleum or natural gas

petrol *NOUN*
petrol is a liquid made from petroleum, used as a fuel for engines

petroleum (*say* pi-**troh**-li-um) *NOUN*
petroleum is an oil found underground that is purified to make petrol, diesel oil and other fuels

petticoat *NOUN* **petticoats**
a piece of clothing worn under a skirt or dress

petty *ADJECTIVE* **pettier, pettiest**
❶ minor and unimportant • *a list of petty regulations* ❷ mean and small-minded
➤ **pettiness** *NOUN*

pew *NOUN* **pews**
one of the long wooden seats in a church

pewter *NOUN*
pewter is a grey alloy of tin and lead

phantom *NOUN* **phantoms**
a ghost

pharaoh (*say* **fay**-roh) *NOUN* **pharaohs**
a ruler in ancient Egypt

pharmacy *NOUN* **pharmacies**
a shop that sells medicines

a b c d e f g h i j k l m n o **p** q r s t u v w x y z

phase *NOUN* **phases**
a stage in the progress or development of something

phase *VERB* **phases**, **phasing**, **phased**
to phase a plan or operation is to carry it out in stages

pheasant (*say* fez-ant) *NOUN* **pheasants**
a game bird with a long tail

phenomenal (*say* fin-**om**-in-al) *ADJECTIVE*
amazing or remarkable
➤ **phenomenally** *ADVERB*

phenomenon *NOUN* **phenomena**
an event or fact, especially one that is remarkable or unusual

phew *EXCLAMATION*
a word you say when you feel relieved • *Phew! That was a lucky escape!*

phial (*say* **fy**-al) *NOUN* **phials**
a small glass flask • *a phial of magic potion*

philosopher *NOUN* **philosophers**
someone who studies philosophy

philosophical *ADJECTIVE*
❶ to do with philosophy ❷ calmly accepting disappointment or suffering • *He was philosophical about losing.*
➤ **philosophically** *ADVERB*

philosophy (*say* fil-**oss**-o-fee) *NOUN* **philosophies**
❶ philosophy is the study of truths about life and human behaviour ❷ a philosophy is a way of thinking or a system of beliefs

phobia (*say* **foh**-bi-a) *NOUN* **phobias**
a great or unusual fear of something

phoenix (*say* **fee**-niks) *NOUN* **phoenixes**
a mythical bird that was said to burn itself to death on a fire and be born again from the ashes

phone *NOUN* **phones**
a telephone

phone *VERB* **phones**, **phoning**, **phoned**
to phone someone is to telephone them

phosphorescent *ADJECTIVE*
shining or glowing in the dark
➤ **phosphorescence** *NOUN*

photo *NOUN* **photos**
a photograph

photocopier *NOUN* **photocopiers**
a machine that makes photocopies

photocopy *NOUN* **photocopies**
a copy of a document or page made by a machine that photographs it on special paper

photocopy *VERB* **photocopies**, **photocopying**, **photocopied**
to photocopy a document is to make a copy of it with a photocopier

photograph *NOUN* **photographs**
a picture made using a camera

photograph *VERB* **photographs**, **photographing**, **photographed**
to photograph someone or something is to take a photograph of them

photographer *NOUN*
someone who takes photographs

photography *NOUN*
photography is taking photographs with a camera
➤ **photographic** *ADJECTIVE*

photosynthesis *NOUN*
photosynthesis is the process by which green plants use sunlight to make their food from carbon dioxide and water

phrase *NOUN* **phrases**
❶ a group of words that form a unit smaller than a clause, for example *on the shelf* in the sentence *The book was on the shelf.* ❷ a short section of a tune

phrase *VERB* **phrases**, **phrasing**, **phrased**
to phrase an idea or thought is to put it into words

physical *ADJECTIVE*
❶ to do with the body rather than the mind or feelings ❷ to do with things you can touch or see
➤ **physically** *ADVERB*

physical education *NOUN*
physical education is gymnastics or other exercises that you do to keep your body healthy

physician *NOUN* **physicians**
a doctor

physics *NOUN*
physics is the study of matter and energy, including movement, heat, light and sound
➤ **physicist** *NOUN*

physiology (*say* fiz-ee-ol-o-jee) *NOUN*
physiology is the study of the body and how it works
➤ **physiological** *ADJECTIVE*

pianist *NOUN* **pianists**
someone who plays the piano

piano *NOUN* **pianos**
a large musical instrument with a row of black and white keys on a keyboard
DID YOU KNOW? The word **piano** is short for *pianoforte*, an Italian word meaning 'quiet (and) loud', because a piano can be played quietly or loudly.

pick *VERB* **picks, picking, picked**
❶ to pick something or someone is to choose them • *Pick a card from this pack.* ❷ to pick flowers or fruit is to cut or pull them off the plant or tree ❸ to pick someone's pocket is to steal from it ❹ to pick a lock is to open it without using a key ❺ to pick bits off or out of something is to pull them away from it
➤ **to pick on someone** is to keep criticizing or bothering them
➤ **to pick someone up** is to give them a lift in a vehicle
➤ **to pick something up** ❶ is to take it from the ground or a surface ❷ is to collect it
• *I'll pick up my bags from the station.*
➤ **to pick up** is to improve or recover

pick *NOUN*
❶ a pick is a choice • *Take your pick.* ❷ the pick of a group of things is the best things in it ❸ a pick is also a pickaxe

pickaxe *NOUN* **pickaxes**
a heavy pointed tool with a long handle, used for breaking up concrete or hard ground

picket *NOUN* **pickets**
a group of strikers who try to persuade other people not to go into a place of work during a strike

picket *VERB* **pickets, picketing, picketed**
a group of people picket a place of work when they stand outside and try to persuade other people not to go in during a strike

pickle *NOUN* **pickles**
❶ a strong-tasting food made of vegetables preserved in vinegar ❷ (*informal*) a difficulty
• *Now we're in a real pickle!*

pickle *VERB* **pickles, pickling, pickled**
to pickle food is to preserve it in vinegar or salt water

pickpocket *NOUN* **pickpockets**
a thief who steals from people's pockets or bags

pick-up *NOUN* **pick-ups**
an open truck for carrying small loads

picnic *NOUN* **picnics**
a meal eaten in the open air away from home

picnic *VERB* **picnics, picnicking, picnicked**
to picnic is to have a picnic
➤ **picnicker** *NOUN*

Pict *NOUN* **Picts**
a member of the ancient people who lived in northern Scotland at the time of the Romans
➤ **Pictish** *ADJECTIVE*

pictogram *NOUN* **pictograms**
a picture or symbol that stands for a word or a phrase

pictorial *ADJECTIVE*
with or using pictures

picture *NOUN* **pictures**
a painting, drawing or photograph

picture *VERB* **pictures, picturing, pictured**
❶ to picture someone or something is to show them in a picture ❷ to picture someone or something in your mind is to imagine them

picturesque (*say* pik-cher-**esk**) *ADJECTIVE*
a picturesque place is attractive or charming
• *We drove through a picturesque village.*

pie *NOUN* **pies**
a baked dish of meat or fruit covered with pastry

piece *NOUN* **pieces**
❶ a part of something; a bit ❷ a work of art or writing or music • *This piece was written by Scott Joplin.* ❸ one of the objects you use on a board to play a game • *a chess piece* ❹ a coin
• *a twenty-pence piece*
➤ **to be in one piece** is to be not broken or injured
➤ **piece by piece** gradually; one bit at a time

a
b
c
d
e
f
g
h
i
j
k
l
m
n
o
p
q
r
s
t
u
v
w
x
y
z

piece VERB pieces, piecing, pieced
to piece things together is to join them to make something

piecemeal ADVERB
you do something piecemeal when you do it gradually, a bit at a time

pie chart NOUN pie charts
a diagram in the form of a circle divided into slices, showing how a quantity or amount is divided up

pier NOUN piers
❶ a long structure built out into the sea for people to walk on ❷ a pillar supporting a bridge or arch

pierce VERB pierces, piercing, pierced
to pierce something is to make a hole through it

piercing ADJECTIVE
❶ a piercing sound is loud and high-pitched • *We heard a piercing shriek.* ❷ something piercing seems to go right through you • *The wind was cold and piercing.*

pig NOUN pigs
a fat animal with short legs and a blunt snout, kept for its meat

pigeon NOUN pigeons
a common grey bird with a small head and large chest

pigeonhole NOUN pigeonholes
a small compartment for holding papers and letters, for someone to collect

piggy NOUN piggies (*informal*)
a little pig

piggyback NOUN piggybacks
a ride on someone's back

pig-headed ADJECTIVE
obstinate; stubborn

piglet NOUN piglets
a young pig

pigment NOUN pigments
a substance that colours something

pigsty NOUN pigsties
❶ a place for keeping pigs ❷ (*informal*) you can describe a very untidy room or place as a pigsty

pigtail NOUN pigtails
a single plait of hair worn hanging at the back of the head

pike NOUN pikes
❶ a large fish that lives in rivers and lakes ❷ a heavy spear

pilchard NOUN pilchards
a small sea fish

pile NOUN piles
❶ a number of things on top of one another • *a pile of laundry* ❷ (*informal*) a large quantity of something • *We've got piles of homework.* ❸ a thick surface on a carpet or piece of fabric

pile VERB piles, piling, piled
to pile things is to put them into a pile
➤ **to pile up** is to become very much or very many • *The work was piling up.*

pilfer VERB pilfers, pilfering, pilfered
to pilfer small or unimportant things is to steal them

pilgrim NOUN pilgrims
someone who goes on a journey to a holy place

pilgrimage NOUN pilgrimages
a journey to a holy place

pill NOUN pills
a small piece of medicine that you swallow

pillage VERB pillages, pillaging, pillaged
to pillage a place is to seize things from it by force and carry them off, especially in a war

pillar NOUN pillars
a tall stone or wooden post

pillar box NOUN pillar boxes
a postbox standing in a street

pillow NOUN pillows
a cushion to rest your head on in bed

pillowcase NOUN pillowcases
a cloth cover for a pillow

pilot NOUN pilots
❶ someone who flies an aircraft ❷ someone who helps to steer a ship in and out of a port or through a difficult stretch of water

pilot *VERB* **pilots, piloting, piloted**
to pilot an aircraft is to be the pilot of it

pimple *NOUN* **pimples**
a small round swelling on your skin

pin *NOUN* **pins**
❶ a short piece of metal with a sharp point and a rounded head, used to fasten pieces of paper or cloth together ❷ a pointed device for fixing or marking something
➤ **pins and needles** a tingling feeling in the skin

pin *VERB* **pins, pinning, pinned**
❶ to pin something is to fasten it with a pin ❷ to pin someone or something in a place is to keep them fixed or trapped there • *He was pinned under the wreckage for hours.*

pinafore *NOUN* **pinafores**
❶ a dress without sleeves, worn over a blouse or jumper ❷ a large apron worn over clothes to keep them clean

pincer *NOUN* **pincers**
the claw of a shellfish such as a lobster

pincers *PLURAL NOUN*
a tool for gripping and pulling things, especially for pulling out nails

pinch *VERB* **pinches, pinching, pinched**
❶ to pinch something is to squeeze it tightly between two things, especially between the finger and thumb ❷ (*informal*) to pinch something is to steal it

pinch *NOUN* **pinches**
❶ a firm squeezing movement ❷ the amount you can pick up between the tips of your finger and thumb • *Add a pinch of salt.*

pincushion *NOUN* **pincushions**
a small pad into which needles and pins are stuck to keep them ready for use

pine *NOUN* **pines**
an evergreen tree with leaves shaped like needles

pine *VERB* **pines, pining, pined**
❶ to pine for someone or something is to feel a strong longing for them ❷ to pine, or pine away, is to become weak or ill through sorrow or yearning

pineapple *NOUN* **pineapples**
a large tropical fruit with yellow flesh and prickly leaves and skin

ping-pong *NOUN*
another word for **table tennis**

pink *ADJECTIVE* **pinker, pinkest**
pale red

pink *NOUN* **pinks**
a pink colour

pinkie *NOUN* **pinkies** (*Scottish, North American*)
your pinkie is your little finger

pint *NOUN* **pints**
a measure of liquid, an eighth of a gallon or about 568 millilitres

pioneer *NOUN* **pioneers**
one of the first people to go to a place or do something new

pious *ADJECTIVE*
very religious or devout
➤ **piously** *ADVERB*

pip *NOUN* **pips**
❶ a small hard seed of a fruit such as an apple, orange or pear ❷ a short high-pitched sound

pipe *NOUN* **pipes**
❶ a tube for carrying water, gas or oil from one place to another ❷ a short tube with a small bowl at one end, used to smoke tobacco ❸ a tubular musical instrument

pipe *VERB* **pipes, piping, piped**
❶ to pipe something is to send it along pipes or wires ❷ to pipe is to play music on a pipe or the bagpipes
➤ **to pipe down** (*informal*) is to be quiet
➤ **to pipe up** (*informal*) is to start saying something

pipeline *NOUN* **pipelines**
a pipe for carrying oil, water or gas over a long distance
➤ **to be in the pipeline** is to be planned and ready to happen soon

piper *NOUN* **pipers**
someone who plays a pipe or the bagpipes

piping *ADJECTIVE*
high-pitched; shrill
➤ **piping hot** very hot, ready to eat

piping *NOUN*
piping is a length of pipes or material used for making pipes

piracy *NOUN*
❶ attacking and robbing ships at sea
❷ making copies of films or music without permission, to sell or pass on

piranha (*say* pi-ran-a) *NOUN* **piranhas**
a South American fish with sharp teeth that tear the flesh of its prey

pirate *NOUN* **pirates**
a sailor who attacks and robs other ships

pistil *NOUN* **pistils**
the part of a flower that produces the seed

pistol *NOUN* **pistols**
a small gun held in the hand

piston *NOUN* **pistons**
a disc that moves up and down inside a cylinder in an engine or pump

pit *NOUN* **pits**
❶ a deep hole or hollow ❷ a coal mine ❸ the part of a race circuit where cars are refuelled and serviced during a race

pit *VERB* **pits**, **pitting**, **pitted**
❶ to pit something is to make deep holes or hollows in it • *The surface of the planet was pitted with craters.* ❷ to pit one person against another is to arrange for them to compete with one another • *In the final she was pitted against the champion.*

pitch *NOUN* **pitches**
❶ a pitch is a piece of ground marked out for cricket, football or another game ❷ pitch is how high or low a voice or musical note is ❸ the pitch of something is also its intensity or strength • *Excitement was at a high pitch.* ❹ pitch is also a black sticky substance like tar

pitch *VERB* **pitches**, **pitching**, **pitched**
❶ to pitch something is to throw or fling it ❷ to pitch a tent is to set it up ❸ to pitch is to fall heavily • *He tripped over the doorstep and pitched headlong.* ❹ a ship pitches when it moves up and down on a rough sea ❺ to pitch something is to set it at a particular level • *We are pitching our hopes high.*
➤ **to pitch in** is to join in and help with something • *Everyone pitched in with ideas.*

pitch-black, **pitch-dark** *ADJECTIVE*
completely black or dark, with no light at all

pitfall *NOUN* **pitfalls**
a hidden danger or difficulty

pitiful *ADJECTIVE*
❶ making you feel pity • *It was a pitiful sight.*
❷ inadequate; feeble • *He made a pitiful attempt to make us laugh.*
➤ **pitifully** *ADVERB*

pitiless *ADJECTIVE*
having or showing no pity
➤ **pitilessly** *ADVERB*

pitta bread *NOUN*
pitta bread is a flat round piece of bread that you can open and fill with food, originally from the Middle East

pity *NOUN*
❶ pity is the feeling of being sorry because someone is in pain or in trouble • *He felt no pity for his victims.* ❷ a pity is something that you regret • *It's a pity we can't meet.*
➤ **to take pity on someone** is to help someone who is in trouble

pity *VERB* **pities**, **pitying**, **pitied**
to pity someone is to feel sorry for them

pivot *NOUN* **pivots**
a point on which something turns or balances

pivot *VERB* **pivots**, **pivoting**, **pivoted**
to pivot is to turn on a pivot or balance

pixel *NOUN* **pixels**
each of the tiny dots on a computer screen from which the image is formed

pixie *NOUN* **pixies**
a small fairy or elf

pizza (*say* peet-sa) *NOUN* **pizzas**
an Italian dish made from a base of dough, topped with cheese, tomatoes and other ingredients and baked
DID YOU KNOW? The word **pizza** is Italian, and originally meant 'pie'.

PJs *PLURAL NOUN* (*informal*)
pyjamas

placard *NOUN* **placards**
a large poster or notice put up on a wall or carried at a demonstration

place NOUN places
❶ a particular part of space, especially where something belongs; an area or position
❷ a position in a race or competition ❸ a seat
• *Save me a place.* ❹ a person's duty or function
• *It's not my place to interfere.*
➤ **in place** in the proper position
➤ **in place of something** or **someone** instead of them
➤ **out of place** ❶ in the wrong position
❷ unsuitable • *Jeans and sandals are out of place in a smart restaurant.*

place VERB places, placing, placed
to place something somewhere is to put it in a particular place

placid ADJECTIVE
calm and gentle; peaceful • *a placid horse.*
➤ **placidly** ADVERB

plague NOUN plagues
❶ a dangerous illness that spreads very quickly ❷ a large number of pests • *The crops were devastated by a plague of locusts.*

plague VERB plagues, plaguing, plagued
to plague someone is to pester or annoy them continuously • *They have been plagued with complaints.*

plaice NOUN plaice
a flat sea fish used for food

plaid (say plad) NOUN plaids
cloth with a tartan or chequered pattern

plain ADJECTIVE plainer, plainest
❶ simple; not decorated ❷ not pretty ❸ easy to understand or see ❹ frank; straightforward
• *I'll be quite plain with you.*
➤ **plainness** NOUN

plain NOUN plains
a large area of flat country without trees

plainly ADVERB
❶ clearly or obviously • *The clock tower was plainly visible in the distance.* ❷ simply
• *She was plainly dressed.*

plaintive ADJECTIVE
sounding sad
The Countess Aurora ... raised her eyes to the ceiling and said in a plaintive voice: 'Is there anyone so unhappy as I?'–PIPPI GOES ABOARD, Astrid Lindgren
➤ **plaintively** ADVERB

plait (say plat) NOUN plaits
a length of hair or rope with several strands twisted together

plait (say plat) VERB plaits, plaiting, plaited
to plait hair or rope is to make it into a plait

plan NOUN plans
❶ a way of doing something that you think out in advance ❷ a drawing showing how the parts of something are arranged ❸ a map of a town or district

plan VERB plans, planning, planned
❶ to plan something is to think out in advance how you are going to do it ❷ to plan to do something is to intend to do it
➤ **planner** NOUN

plane NOUN planes
❶ an aeroplane ❷ a tool for making wood smooth ❸ a flat or level surface ❹ a plane is also a tall tree with broad leaves

plane VERB planes, planing, planed
to plane wood is to smooth it with a plane

planet NOUN planets
one of the bodies that move in an orbit round the sun. The planets of our solar system are Mercury, Venus, Earth, Mars, Jupiter, Saturn, Uranus and Neptune, as well as the dwarf planet Pluto.
➤ **planetary** ADJECTIVE
DID YOU KNOW? The word **planet** comes from a Greek word meaning 'wanderer', because the planets appear to move among the stars.

plank NOUN planks
a long flat piece of wood

plankton NOUN
plankton is made up of tiny creatures that float in the sea and lakes

plant NOUN plants
❶ a living thing that grows out of the ground, including flowers, bushes, trees and vegetables ❷ a factory or its equipment

plant VERB plants, planting, planted
❶ to plant something such as a tree or flower is to put it in the ground to grow ❷ to plant something is also to put it firmly in place
• *He planted his feet on the ground and took hold of the rope.* ❸ to plant something such as a piece of evidence is to put it where it will be

a b c d e f g h i j k l m n o p q r s t u v w x y z

found, usually to mislead people or to cause trouble

plantation *NOUN* plantations
an area of land where a crop such as tobacco, tea or rubber is planted

plaque (*say* plak *or* plahk) *NOUN* plaques
❶ a plaque is a metal or porcelain plate fixed on a wall as a memorial or an ornament ❷ plaque is a substance that forms a thin layer on your teeth, allowing bacteria to develop

plasma (*say* plaz-ma) *NOUN*
❶ plasma is the colourless liquid part of blood, which carries the corpuscles ❷ a plasma television screen uses a special type of gas to show the colours on the screen

plaster *NOUN* plasters
❶ a plaster is a small covering you put over your skin around a cut or wound to protect it ❷ plaster is a mixture of lime, sand and water, used to cover walls and ceilings

plaster *VERB* plasters, plastering, plastered
❶ to plaster a surface is to cover it with plaster ❷ to plaster a surface with something is to cover it thickly • *His clothes were plastered with mud.*

plaster of Paris *NOUN*
plaster of Paris is a white paste used for making moulds and for casts round a broken leg or arm

plastic *NOUN* plastics
a strong light synthetic substance that can be moulded into different shapes

plastic *ADJECTIVE*
made of plastic • *Please reuse this plastic bag.*

plastic surgery *NOUN*
plastic surgery is work done by a surgeon to alter or mend parts of someone's body

plate *NOUN* plates
❶ a dish that is flat or almost flat, used for eating ❷ a thin flat sheet of metal, glass or other hard material ❸ one of the large areas of rock that make up the earth's crust

plate *VERB* plates, plating, plated
to plate metal is to cover it with a thin layer of gold, silver, tin or other soft metal

plateau (*say* plat-oh) *NOUN* plateaux *or* plateaus
a flat area of high land

plateful *NOUN* platefuls
as much as you can put on a plate

platform *NOUN* platforms
❶ a flat raised area along the side of the line at a railway station ❷ a small stage in a hall

platinum *NOUN*
platinum is a silver-coloured metal that does not lose its brightness

platoon *NOUN* platoons
a small unit of soldiers

platypus *NOUN* platypuses
an Australian egg-laying mammal with a beak and feet like those of a duck

play *VERB* plays, playing, played
❶ to play, or play a game, is to take part in a game or other amusement ❷ to play music, or a musical instrument, is to make music or sound with it ❸ to play a part in a film or play is to perform it ❹ to play a CD or DVD is to listen to it or watch it on a computer or other machine

play *NOUN* plays
❶ a play is a story acted on a stage or broadcast on radio or television ❷ play is playing or having fun

player *NOUN* players
someone who plays a game or a musical instrument • *a football player* • *He's an excellent piano player.*

playful *ADJECTIVE*
❶ wanting to play; full of fun • *a playful kitten* ❷ not serious • *She gave him a playful punch.*
➤ playfully *ADVERB* ➤ playfulness *NOUN*

playground *NOUN* playgrounds
a place out of doors where children can play

playgroup *NOUN* playgroups
a group of very young children who play together regularly, with adults to supervise them

playing card *NOUN* playing cards
each of a set of cards (usually 52) used for playing games

playing field *NOUN* **playing fields**
a grassy field for outdoor games

playmate *NOUN* **playmates**
someone that you play games with

play-off *NOUN* **play-offs**
an extra match played to decide a draw or tie

playtime *NOUN* **playtimes**
the time when young schoolchildren go out to play

playwright *NOUN* **playwrights**
someone who writes plays

plea *NOUN* **pleas**
❶ a request or appeal ❷ a statement of 'guilty' or 'not guilty' made in a law court by someone accused of a crime

plead *VERB* **pleads, pleading, pleaded**
to plead with someone is to beg them to do something
➤ **to plead guilty** *or* **not guilty** is to state in a law court that you are guilty or not guilty of a crime

pleasant *ADJECTIVE* **pleasanter, pleasantest**
pleasing or enjoyable or friendly
➤ **pleasantly** *ADVERB*

please *VERB* **pleases, pleasing, pleased**
to please someone is to make them happy or satisfied

please *ADVERB*
used when you want to ask something politely • *Please shut the door.*
➤ **as you please** as you like • *Do as you please.*

pleasurable *ADJECTIVE*
causing pleasure; enjoyable

pleasure *NOUN* **pleasures**
❶ pleasure is being pleased ❷ a pleasure is something that pleases you
➤ **with pleasure** gladly; willingly

pleat *NOUN* **pleats**
a permanent fold made in the cloth of a piece of clothing
➤ **pleated** *ADJECTIVE*

pledge *NOUN* **pledges**
a solemn promise

pledge *VERB* **pledges, pledging, pledged**
to pledge something is to promise it

plentiful *ADJECTIVE*
large in amount • *a plentiful crop of fruit*
➤ **plentifully** *ADVERB*

plenty *PRONOUN*
to have plenty of something is to have a lot of it or more than enough • *We have plenty of chairs.*

pliable *ADJECTIVE*
easy to bend; flexible

pliers *PLURAL NOUN*
pincers with flattened jaws for gripping something or for breaking wire

plight *NOUN* **plights**
a difficult and sad situation • *The programme examines the plight of people who are homeless.*

plinth *NOUN* **plinths**
a thick base that supports a column or statue

plod *VERB* **plods, plodding, plodded**
❶ to plod is to walk slowly and with heavy steps • *We plodded back through the rain.*
❷ to plod, or plod away, is to work slowly but steadily

plonk *VERB* **plonks, plonking, plonked**
(*informal*)
to plonk something down is to set it down without taking care • *Dee plonked her schoolbag on the floor.*

plop *NOUN* **plops**
the sound of something dropping into a liquid

plop *VERB* **plops, plopping, plopped**
to plop is to fall into a liquid with a plop

plot *NOUN* **plots**
❶ a secret plan, especially to do something illegal or bad ❷ what happens in a story, film or play ❸ a piece of land for a house or garden

plot *VERB* **plots, plotting, plotted**
❶ to plot is to make a secret plan to do something ❷ to plot a chart or graph is to make it, marking all the points on it

plotter *NOUN* **plotters**
plotters are people who take part in a plot

plough (*say* plow) *NOUN* **ploughs**
a device used on farms for turning over the soil

a
b
c
d
e
f
g
h
i
j
k
l
m
n
o
p
q
r
s
t
u
v
w
x
y
z

plough VERB **ploughs, ploughing, ploughed**
❶ to plough the soil is to turn it over with a plough ❷ to plough through something is to go through it with effort or difficulty
• *He ploughed through the book.*

plover (*say* pluv-er) NOUN **plovers**
a long-legged wading bird

pluck VERB **plucks, plucking, plucked**
❶ to pluck a bird is to pull the feathers off it to prepare it for cooking ❷ to pluck a flower or fruit is to pick it ❸ to pluck something is to pull it or pull it out • *I'll try and pluck out your splinter.* ❹ in music, to pluck a string is to pull it and let it go again
➤ **to pluck up courage** is to be brave and overcome fear

pluck NOUN
pluck is courage or bravery

plucky ADJECTIVE **pluckier, pluckiest**
brave or courageous
Merrylegs ... was such a cheerful, plucky, good-tempered little fellow, that he was a favourite with everyone.–BLACK BEAUTY, Anna Sewell
➤ **pluckily** ADVERB

plug NOUN **plugs**
❶ something used to stop up a hole, especially in a sink or bath ❷ a device that is used to connect a piece of electric equipment to a socket

plug VERB **plugs, plugging, plugged**
❶ to plug a hole is to stop it up ❷ (*informal*) to plug an event or product is to publicize it
➤ **to plug something in** is to connect it to an electric socket by means of a plug

plum NOUN **plums**
a soft juicy fruit with a stone in the middle

plumage (*say* ploo-mij) NOUN
a bird's plumage is its feathers

plumb VERB **plumbs, plumbing, plumbed**
❶ to plumb a river or the sea is to measure how deep it is ❷ to plumb a mystery or puzzle is to find out what it means

plumber NOUN **plumbers**
someone who fits and mends water pipes in a building

plumbing NOUN
❶ plumbing is the work of a plumber ❷ the

plumbing in a building is all the water pipes and water tanks

plume NOUN **plumes**
❶ a large feather ❷ something shaped like a feather • *We saw a plume of smoke in the distance.*

plump ADJECTIVE **plumper, plumpest**
rounded or slightly fat

plump VERB **plumps, plumping, plumped**
➤ **to plump for something** *or* **someone** is to choose them

plunder VERB **plunders, plundering, plundered**
to plunder a place or person is to rob them violently, especially in a time of war or disorder
The chief brigand counted out the jewels and gold coins they'd plundered and divided them all into twenty heaps.–THE SCARECROW AND HIS SERVANT, Philip Pullman
➤ **plunderer** NOUN

plunder NOUN
❶ plunder is plundering a person or place ❷ plunder is also goods taken by plundering

plunge VERB **plunges, plunging, plunged**
❶ to plunge into water is to jump or dive into it with force ❷ to plunge something into a liquid or something soft is to put it in with force

plunge NOUN **plunges**
a sudden fall or dive

plural NOUN **plurals**
the form of a word meaning more than one person or thing, such as *children* and *mice*

plural ADJECTIVE
in the plural; meaning more than one • *'Mice' is a plural noun.*

plus PREPOSITION
with the next number or thing added
• *2 plus 2 equals 4 (2 + 2 = 4).*

Pluto NOUN
a dwarf planet that lies beyond Neptune in the outermost part of our solar system
DID YOU KNOW? **Pluto** is named after the Roman god of the underworld.

plywood NOUN
plywood is board made from thin sheets of wood glued together

PM *ABBREVIATION*
short for *prime minister*

p.m. *ABBREVIATION*
short for Latin *post meridiem*, which means 'after midday'

pneumatic (*say* new-**mat**-ik) *ADJECTIVE*
filled with air or worked by compressed air
• *a pneumatic tyre* • *a pneumatic drill*

pneumonia (*say* new-**moh**-ni-a) *NOUN*
pneumonia is a serious disease of the lungs

poach *VERB* poaches, poaching, poached
❶ to poach food, especially fish or an egg taken out of its shell, is to cook it in or over boiling water ❷ to poach animals is to hunt them illegally on someone else's land
➤ **poacher** *NOUN*

pocket *NOUN* pockets
❶ part of a piece of clothing shaped like a small bag, for keeping things in ❷ a small area in which something happens • *There will be pockets of rain in the south.* ❸ a person's pocket is their supply of money • *The cost is well beyond my pocket.*
➤ **to be out of pocket** is to have spent more money than you got back

pocket *ADJECTIVE*
small enough to carry in your pocket • *Use a pocket calculator.*

pocket *VERB* pockets, pocketing, pocketed (*informal*)
to pocket something is to steal it

pocketful *NOUN* pocketfuls
an amount you can put in your pocket

pocket money *NOUN*
pocket money is money given to a child to spend

pod *NOUN* pods
❶ a long seed-container on a pea or bean plant ❷ a small vessel attached to a submarine or spacecraft • *The spaceship launched an escape pod.* ❸ a pod is also a group of whales or dolphins

podgy *ADJECTIVE* podgier, podgiest (*informal*)
short and plump

poem *NOUN* poems
a piece of writing arranged in short lines,
often with a particular rhythm and sometimes rhyming

poet *NOUN* poets
someone who writes poetry

poetic, poetical *ADJECTIVE*
like poetry; using the language of poetry
➤ **poetically** *ADVERB*

poetry *NOUN*
poetry is poems as a form of literature • *Do you write poetry?*

point *NOUN* points
❶ the narrow or sharp end of something
• *Use the point of the scissors.* ❷ a written dot
• *Put in a decimal point.* ❸ a single mark in a game or quiz • *How many points did I get?*
❹ a particular place or time • *They gave up at this point.* ❺ something that someone says during a discussion • *That's a very good point.* ❻ a detail or special feature • *He has some good points.* ❼ purpose or advantage
• *There's no point in hurrying.* ❽ the points on a railway line are the movable parts that allow trains to change from one track to another
➤ **to come to the point** is to mention the thing you really want to say

point *VERB* points, pointing, pointed
❶ to point to something is to show where it is, especially by holding out your finger towards it
❷ to point something is to aim it or direct it
• *She pointed her telescope at the moon.*
➤ **to point something out** is to show it or explain it

point-blank *ADJECTIVE, ADVERB*
❶ close to the target • *at point-blank range*
❷ directly and completely • *He refused point-blank to tell us.*

pointed *ADJECTIVE*
❶ a pointed object has a point at the end
❷ a pointed remark is clearly directed at a person, especially to criticize them • *He made a pointed remark about my hair.*

pointer *NOUN* pointers
❶ a stick or device you use to point at something ❷ a dog that points with its muzzle at birds which it scents ❸ a hint or piece of guidance • *She gave us a few pointers on how to write a poem.*

a b c d e f g h i j k l m n o p q r s t u v w x y z

pointless *ADJECTIVE*
something is pointless when it has no purpose or meaning
➤ **pointlessly** *ADVERB*

point of view *NOUN* **points of view**
❶ a way of looking or thinking of something ❷ the way that a writer chooses to tell a story, for example by telling it through the experiences of one of the characters

poise *NOUN*
poise is a dignified and self-confident manner
poise *VERB* **poises, poising, poised**
❶ to poise something is to balance it or keep it steady ❷ to be poised to do something is to be ready to do it

poison *NOUN* **poisons**
a substance that can kill or harm living things
poison *VERB* **poisons, poisoning, poisoned**
❶ to poison someone is to kill or harm them with poison ❷ to poison something is to put poison in it

poisonous *ADJECTIVE*
❶ a poisonous chemical, gas or plant can kill or harm you if you swallow it or breathe it in ❷ poisonous animals or insects can kill or harm you with poison if they bite you
• *a poisonous snake*

poke *VERB* **pokes, poking, poked**
to poke something or someone is to push or jab them hard with your finger or a pointed object
➤ **to poke out** is to stick out
poke *NOUN* **pokes**
a prod or jab

poker *NOUN* **pokers**
❶ a poker is a metal rod for stirring a fire ❷ poker is a card game in which the players bet on who has the best cards

polar *ADJECTIVE*
to do with the North or South Pole, or near one of them

polar bear *NOUN* **polar bears**
a powerful white bear living in Arctic regions

pole *NOUN* **poles**
❶ a long thin piece of wood or metal ❷ each of the two points at the ends of the earth's

axis, the **North Pole** and the **South Pole**
❸ each end of a magnet

Pole Star *NOUN*
the bright star that appears in the sky closest to the North Pole

pole vault *NOUN*
the pole vault is an athletic contest in which you jump over a high bar with the help of a long springy pole

police *NOUN*
the police are the people whose job is to catch criminals and make sure that people obey the law

policeman, policewoman *NOUN*
policemen, policewomen
a male or female police officer

police officer *NOUN* **police officers**
a member of the police

policy *NOUN* **policies**
❶ the aims or plans of a person or group of people ❷ a plan of action • *Honesty is the best policy.*

polio (*say* **poh-li-oh**) *NOUN*
an illness that paralyses a person's body. Polio is short for *poliomyelitis*.

polish (*say* **pol-ish**) *VERB* **polishes, polishing, polished**
to polish something is to make its surface shiny or smooth
➤ **to polish something off** (*informal*) is to finish it quickly
polish (*say* **pol-ish**) *NOUN* **polishes**
❶ polish is a substance used in polishing ❷ a polish is a shine got by polishing • *He gave his shoes a good polish.*

polished *ADJECTIVE*
❶ shiny ❷ well practised or rehearsed • *The choir gave a polished performance.*

polite *ADJECTIVE* **politer, politest**
having good manners; respectful and thoughtful towards other people
➤ **politely** *ADVERB* ➤ **politeness** *NOUN*

political *ADJECTIVE*
to do with the governing of a country
➤ **politically** *ADVERB*

politician *NOUN* **politicians**
someone who is involved in politics

politics *NOUN*
politics is political matters; the business of governing a country

polka *NOUN* **polkas**
a lively dance

poll *NOUN* **polls**
❶ a round of voting at an election ❷ an estimate of what people think, made by questioning a certain number of them

pollen *NOUN*
pollen is yellow powder found inside flowers, containing male seeds for fertilizing other flowers

pollinate *VERB* **pollinates**, **pollinating**, **pollinated**
to pollinate a flower or plant is to put pollen into it so that it becomes fertilized
➤ **pollination** *NOUN*

pollute *VERB* **pollutes**, **polluting**, **polluted**
to pollute a place or thing is to make it dirty or impure

pollution *NOUN*
pollution is the process of making the air, water and soil dirty or impure

polo *NOUN*
polo is a game rather like hockey, with players on horseback using long mallets

polo neck *NOUN* **polo necks**
a high rounded collar that is turned over at the top

poltergeist (*say* **pol**-ter-gyst) *NOUN* **poltergeists**
a noisy mischievous ghost that damages things
Peeves was the school poltergeist, a grinning, airborne menace who lived to cause havoc and distress.—HARRY POTTER AND THE CHAMBER OF SECRETS, J. K. Rowling
DID YOU KNOW? The word **poltergeist** comes from a German word meaning 'to make a disturbance'.

poly– *PREFIX*
meaning 'many', as in *polygon*

polygon *NOUN* **polygons**
a figure or shape with many sides, such as a hexagon or octagon

polystyrene (*say* pol-i-**sty**-reen) *NOUN*
polystyrene is a kind of plastic used for insulating or packing things

polythene (*say* **pol**-i-theen) *NOUN*
polythene is a lightweight plastic used to make bags and wrappings

pomp *NOUN*
pomp is the dignified and solemn way in which an important ceremony is carried out

pompous *ADJECTIVE*
someone is being pompous when they are thinking too much of their own importance
➤ **pompously** *ADVERB*

pond *NOUN* **ponds**
a small lake

ponder *VERB* **ponders**, **pondering**, **pondered**
to ponder something is to think carefully and seriously about it

ponderous *ADJECTIVE*
❶ heavy and awkward ❷ dull and not easy to follow • *He writes in a ponderous style.*
➤ **ponderously** *ADVERB*

pony *NOUN* **ponies**
a small horse

ponytail *NOUN* **ponytails**
a bunch of long hair tied at the back of the head

pony-trekking *NOUN*
pony-trekking is travelling across country on ponies for pleasure

poodle *NOUN* **poodles**
a dog with long curly hair

pool *NOUN* **pools**
❶ a pond • *The waterfall tumbled into a pool of clear water.* ❷ a puddle • *a pool of blood* ❸ a swimming pool ❹ a group of things shared by several people ❺ pool is a game similar to snooker but played on a smaller table

pool *VERB* **pools**, **pooling**, **pooled**
to pool things is to put them all together so that everyone can share them

poor *ADJECTIVE* **poorer**, **poorest**
❶ having very little money • *He came from a poor family.* ❷ not good or adequate • *This is poor work.* ❸ unfortunate • *Poor fellow!*

a b c d e f g h i j k l m n o p q r s t u v w x y z

poorly *ADVERB*
not adequately • *They arrived poorly dressed.*

poorly *ADJECTIVE*
unwell • *I'm feeling poorly today.*

pop *NOUN* **pops**
❶ a pop is a small explosive sound ❷ pop is modern popular music

pop *VERB* **pops**, **popping**, **popped**
❶ to pop is to make a small explosive sound ❷ (*informal*) to pop somewhere is to go there quickly • *I'm just popping out to the shops.* ❸ to pop something somewhere is to put it there quickly • *Will you pop the potatoes in the oven?*

popcorn *NOUN*
popcorn is maize heated till it bursts and forms light fluffy balls for eating

Pope *NOUN* **Popes**
the Pope is the leader of the Roman Catholic Church

poplar *NOUN* **poplars**
a tall straight tree

poppadom *NOUN* **poppadoms**
an Indian thin crisp pancake made from ground lentils and fried in oil

poppy *NOUN* **poppies**
a plant with large red flowers

popular *ADJECTIVE*
liked or enjoyed by a lot of people
➤ **popularly** *ADVERB* something is (for example) popularly believed when it is believed by a large number of people

popularity *NOUN*
popularity is being liked or enjoyed by a lot of people

popularize (*also* **popularise**) *VERB*
popularizes, **popularizing**, **popularized**
to popularize something is to make it known and liked by a lot of people

populated *ADJECTIVE*
a place is populated when it has people living there • *The land is thinly populated.*

population *NOUN* **populations**
the population of a particular place is all the people who live there; the total number of people who live there • *What's the population of London?*

populous *ADJECTIVE*
a populous place is inhabited by a lot of people

porcelain (*say* **por**-se-lin) *NOUN*
porcelain is a fine kind of china

porch *NOUN* **porches**
a small roofed area outside the door of a building

porcupine *NOUN* **porcupines**
a small animal covered with long prickles
DID YOU KNOW? The word **porcupine** comes from old French words meaning 'prickly pig'.

pore *NOUN* **pores**
one of the tiny openings in your skin which sweat can pass through

pore *VERB* **pores**, **poring**, **pored**
➤ **to pore over something** is to study it closely

pork *NOUN*
pork is meat from a pig

porous *ADJECTIVE*
something is porous when it allows liquid or air to pass through • *Sandy soil is porous.*

porpoise (*say* **por**-pus) *NOUN* **porpoises**
a sea animal rather like a small whale

porridge *NOUN*
porridge is a food made by boiling oatmeal to make a thick paste

port *NOUN* **ports**
❶ a port is a harbour ❷ a port is also a city or town with a harbour ❸ port is the left-hand side of a ship or aircraft when you are facing forward

portable *ADJECTIVE*
able to be carried easily • *a portable charger*
➤ **portability** *NOUN*

portcullis *NOUN* **portcullises**
a heavy grating that can be lowered to block the gateway to a castle

portent *NOUN* **portents**
a sign or warning of something likely to happen
Sir Ristridin stopped, wrapped his cloak more closely around him and wondered if the crow had any significance for him. Was it a sign? A portent of danger?—THE SECRETS OF THE WILD WOOD, Tonke Dragt

porter *NOUN* **porters**
❶ someone whose job is to carry luggage or goods ❷ someone whose job is to look after the entrance to a large building

porthole *NOUN* **portholes**
a small round window in the side of a ship or aircraft

portion *NOUN* **portions**
a part or share given to someone

portly *ADJECTIVE* **portlier**, **portliest**
rather fat
They were portly gentlemen, pleasant to behold, and now stood, with their hats off, in Scrooge's office.—A CHRISTMAS CAROL, Charles Dickens

portrait *NOUN* **portraits**
❶ a picture of a person ❷ a way of printing a page of text so that it is taller than it is wide

portray *VERB* **portrays**, **portraying**, **portrayed**
❶ to portray someone is to make a portrait of them ❷ to portray something or someone is to describe or show them in a certain way • *The book portrays the giant as good-natured.*
➤ **portrayal** *NOUN*

pose *NOUN* **poses**
❶ a way of standing or sitting for a portrait or photograph to be made of you • *Just hold that pose for a second.* ❷ a pretence; unnatural behaviour to impress people

pose *VERB* **poses**, **posing**, **posed**
❶ to pose is to put your body into a special position ❷ to pose someone is to put them in a particular position to be painted or photographed ❸ to pose as someone is to pretend to be them • *The man posed as a police officer.* ❹ to pose a question or problem is to present it • *Icy weather poses a problem to motorists.*

posh *ADJECTIVE* **posher**, **poshest** (*informal*)
❶ very smart; high-class • *They stayed at a posh hotel.* ❷ of a high social class • *She spoke with a posh accent.*

position *NOUN* **positions**
❶ the place where something is or should be ❷ the way in which someone or something is placed or arranged • *He was sleeping in an uncomfortable position.* ❸ a person's place

in a race or competition ❹ a situation or condition • *I am in no position to help you.* ❺ a regular job

position *VERB* **positions**, **positioning**, **positioned**
to position something somewhere is to place it there

positive *ADJECTIVE*
❶ sure or definite • *I am positive I saw him.* • *We need positive proof.* ❷ agreeing or saying 'yes' • *We received a positive answer.* ❸ a positive number is one that is greater than nought ❹ a positive electric charge is one that does not carry electrons
➤ **positively** *ADVERB*

posse (*say* **poss-ee**) *NOUN* **posses**
a group of people that helps a sheriff in the USA

possess *VERB* **possesses**, **possessing**, **possessed**
to possess something is to own or have it
➤ **possessor** *NOUN*

possessed *ADJECTIVE*
someone is possessed when they are behaving as if they are controlled by an outside force • *He fought like a man possessed.*

possession *NOUN* **possessions**
❶ a possession is something that you own ❷ possession is owning something • *They gained possession of a piece of land.*

possessive *ADJECTIVE*
❶ you are being possessive when you want to get and keep things for yourself ❷ (*grammar*) showing that someone owns something • *'His' and 'yours' are possessive pronouns.*

possibility *NOUN* **possibilities**
❶ possibility is being possible • *Is there any possibility of changing your mind?* ❷ a possibility is something that is possible • *There are many possibilities.*

possible *ADJECTIVE*
able to exist, happen, be done or be used

possibly *ADVERB*
❶ in any way • *That cannot possibly be right.* ❷ perhaps • *I will arrive at six o'clock, or possibly earlier.*

a
b
c
d
e
f
g
h
i
j
k
l
m
n
o
p
q
r
s
t
u
v
w
x
y
z

post *NOUN* **posts**
❶ an upright piece of wood, concrete or metal fixed in the ground ❷ the post is the collecting and delivering of letters and parcels ❸ post is letters and parcels carried by post ❹ a post is a message or article uploaded to a blog or on social media ❺ a post is also a regular job ❻ the place where a soldier or sentry is on duty

post *VERB* **posts**, **posting**, **posted**
❶ to post a letter or parcel is to send it to someone by post ❷ to post a notice or poster is to put it in a public place ❸ to post a message or article is to upload it to a blog or on social media ❹ to be posted somewhere is to be sent there for a time as part of your job

post- *PREFIX*
meaning 'after', as in *post-war* (the opposite is **pre-**)

postage *NOUN*
postage is the cost of sending a letter or parcel by post

postage stamp *NOUN* **postage stamps**
a stamp for putting on letters and parcels, showing the amount paid

postal *ADJECTIVE*
to do with the post; by post

postbox *NOUN* **postboxes**
a box into which you put letters to be sent by post

postcard *NOUN* **postcards**
a card that you can write a message on and post without an envelope

postcode *NOUN* **postcodes**
a group of letters and numbers included in an address to help in sorting the post

poster *NOUN* **posters**
a large public notice having information or advertising something

postman, **postwoman** *NOUN* **postmen**, **postwomen**
a person who collects and delivers letters and parcels

postmark *NOUN* **postmarks**
an official mark stamped on something sent by post, showing when and where it was posted

post office *NOUN* **post offices**
a place where you can post letters and parcels and buy stamps, postal orders and other official documents

postpone *VERB* **postpones**, **postponing**, **postponed**
to postpone a meeting or event is to arrange for it to take place later than was originally planned
• *The match has been postponed for two weeks.*
➤ **postponement** *NOUN*

postscript *NOUN* **postscripts**
something extra added at the end of a letter or book

posture *NOUN* **postures**
the way that a person stands, sits or walks

posy *NOUN* **posies**
a small bunch of flowers

pot *NOUN* **pots**
❶ a deep container ❷ a flowerpot

pot *VERB* **pots**, **potting**, **potted**
❶ to pot a plant is to put it into a flowerpot ❷ to pot a ball in a game such as snooker or pool is to hit it into a pocket

potato *NOUN* **potatoes**
a vegetable with a brown or red skin that grows underground and is eaten cooked
SPELLING ALERT! Remember to put an *e* in the plural: *a dish of roast potatoes.*

potent *ADJECTIVE*
powerful
Anne got Marilla a glassful of her potent currant wine.—ANNE OF AVONLEA, L. M. Montgomery
➤ **potency** *NOUN* ➤ **potently** *ADVERB*

potential *ADJECTIVE*
capable of happening or becoming important or useful in the future • *She is a potential star.*
➤ **potentially** *ADVERB*

potential *NOUN*
to have potential is to be capable of becoming important or useful in the future

pothole *NOUN* **potholes**
❶ a deep natural hole in the ground ❷ a hole in a road

potholing *NOUN*
potholing is exploring underground caves by climbing down potholes
➤ **potholer** *NOUN*

A B C D E F G H I J K L M N O P Q R S T U V W X Y Z

potion (say **poh**-shon) NOUN **potions**
a drink containing medicine or poison

potter NOUN **potters**
someone who makes pottery

potter VERB **potters, pottering, pottered**
to potter, or potter about, is to spend time
doing little jobs in a relaxed way

pottery NOUN **potteries**
❶ pottery is pots, cups, plates and other
things made of baked clay ❷ pottery is also
the craft of making pottery ❸ a pottery is a
place where a potter works

potty ADJECTIVE **pottier, pottiest** (informal)
(may cause offence) foolish or mentally ill

potty NOUN **potties** (informal)
a small bowl used by young children as a toilet

pouch NOUN **pouches**
❶ a small bag or pocket ❷ a fold of skin in
which a kangaroo keeps its young

poultry NOUN
poultry are birds such as chickens, geese and
turkeys, kept for their eggs and meat

pounce VERB **pounces, pouncing, pounced**
to pounce on someone or something is to
jump on them or attack them suddenly
*The Pelican opened his gigantic beak and
immediately the policemen pounced upon the
burglar who was crouching inside.—THE GIRAFFE AND
THE PELLY AND ME, Roald Dahl*

pound NOUN **pounds**
❶ a unit of money, in Britain equal to 100 pence
❷ a unit of weight equal to 16 ounces or
about 454 grams

pound VERB **pounds, pounding, pounded**
❶ to pound something is to hit it repeatedly
to crush it ❷ to pound, or pound along, is
to walk with heavy steps ❸ your heart is
pounding when it beats heavily, making a dull
thumping sound • *My heart was pounding with
the excitement.*

pour VERB **pours, pouring, poured**
❶ to pour a liquid is to make it flow out of
a container ❷ to pour is to flow in a large
amount • *Blood was pouring from the wound
on her leg.* ❸ it is pouring when it is raining
heavily ❹ to pour in or out is to come or
go in large numbers or amounts • *After the*

programme, letters of complaint poured in. • *The
fans poured out of the stadium.*

pout VERB **pouts, pouting, pouted**
you pout when you stick out your lips because
you are annoyed or sulking

poverty NOUN
poverty is being poor

pow EXCLAMATION
the sound made by a powerful kick, punch or
explosion • *Pow! went the ball into the back of
the net.*

powder NOUN **powders**
❶ a mass of tiny pieces of something dry,
like flour or dust ❷ make-up in the form of
powder
➤ **powdery** ADJECTIVE

powder VERB **powders, powdering,
powdered**
to powder something is to put powder on it
• *She powdered her face.*

power NOUN **powers**
❶ power is strength or great energy ❷ power
is also control over other people ❸ the power
to do something is the ability to do it • *Humans
have the power of speech.* ❹ a power is a
powerful country ❺ power is also electricity
or another form of energy

powerful ADJECTIVE
having a lot of power or strength • *a powerful
magic potion*
➤ **powerfully** ADVERB

powerless ADJECTIVE
someone is powerless if they are unable to act
or control things

power station NOUN **power stations**
a building where electricity is produced

practicable ADJECTIVE
possible or able to be done • *That is not a
practicable plan.*

practical ADJECTIVE
❶ someone is practical when they are able to do
or make useful things • *She is a very practical
person.* ❷ something is practical when it is
likely to be useful • *That is a practical idea.*
❸ concerned with doing or making things
• *He has had practical experience.*

a b c d e f g h i j k l m n o p q r s t u v w x y z

practical *NOUN* **practicals**
a lesson or examination in which you actually do or make something rather than reading or writing about it

practical joke *NOUN* **practical jokes**
a trick played on someone

practically *ADVERB*
❶ in a practical way • *He is practically skilled.*
❷ almost • *It's practically ready now.*

practice *NOUN* **practices**
❶ practice is doing something often and regularly so that you get better at it • *Your playing will get better with practice.* ❷ practice is also actually doing something rather than thinking or talking about it • *I hope my plan works in practice.* ❸ a practice is the business of a doctor or lawyer

SPELLING ALERT! Practice is a noun whereas **practise** is a verb. You say *an hour of piano practice* but *I'm practising my scales.*

practise *VERB* **practises**, **practising**, **practised**
❶ to practise something is to do it often so that you get better at it ❷ to practise an activity or custom is to do it regularly • *She practises yoga.* ❸ to practise (for example) medicine or law is to work as a doctor or lawyer

prairie *NOUN* **prairies**
a large area of flat grass-covered land in North America

praise *VERB* **praises**, **praising**, **praised**
to praise someone or something is to say that they are good or have done well

praise *NOUN* **praises**
praise is words that praise someone or something

pram *NOUN* **prams**
a small open carriage for a baby, pushed by a person walking

prance *VERB* **prances**, **prancing**, **pranced**
to prance, or prance about, is to jump about in a lively or happy way
The Scarecrow leaped all over the room, capering and skipping and prancing like a goat.—THE SCARECROW AND HIS SERVANT, Philip Pullman

prank *NOUN* **pranks**
a trick played on someone for mischief

prawn *NOUN* **prawns**
a shellfish like a large shrimp, used for food

pray *VERB* **prays**, **praying**, **prayed**
❶ to pray is to talk to God ❷ to pray is also to ask earnestly or hope for something • *We are praying for good weather.*

prayer *NOUN* **prayers**
❶ prayer is praying ❷ a prayer is what you say when you pray

pre- *PREFIX*
meaning 'before', as in *pre-war* (the opposite is **post-**)

preach *VERB* **preaches**, **preaching**, **preached**
to preach is to give a talk about religion or about right and wrong
➤ **preacher** *NOUN*

precarious (say pri-**kair**-i-us) *ADJECTIVE*
not at all safe or secure • *Mr Lewis was balanced on top of a precarious ladder.*
➤ **precariously** *ADVERB*

precaution *NOUN* **precautions**
something you do to prevent trouble or danger in the future

precede *VERB* **precedes**, **preceding**, **preceded**
one thing precedes another when it comes or goes in front of the other thing • *The film was preceded by a short cartoon.*

precinct (say **pree**-sinkt) *NOUN* **precincts**
❶ a part of a town where traffic is not allowed • *The town has a large shopping precinct.* ❷ the area round a cathedral

precious (say **pre**-shus) *ADJECTIVE*
very valuable or loved
Remembering her precious cordial, Lucy poured a few drops into her brother's mouth.
—THE LION, THE WITCH AND THE WARDROBE, C. S. Lewis

precipice *NOUN* **precipices**
the steep face of a mountain or cliff

precise *ADJECTIVE*
❶ clear and accurate • *I gave them precise instructions.* ❷ exact • *At that precise moment, the doorbell rang.*
➤ **precisely** *ADVERB* ➤ **precision** *NOUN*

predator (*say* pred-a-ter) *NOUN* **predators**
an animal that hunts other animals
➤ **predatory** *ADJECTIVE*

predecessor (*say* pree-di-ses-er) *NOUN* **predecessors**
an earlier person or thing, such as an ancestor or someone who once did the job you do now

predicament *NOUN* **predicaments**
a predicament is a difficult or unpleasant situation • *There seemed to be no way out of their predicament.*

predict *VERB* **predicts, predicting, predicted**
to predict something is to say that it will happen in the future

predictable *ADJECTIVE*
something is predictable when you are able to say what will happen before it actually happens
➤ **predictably** *ADVERB*

prediction *NOUN* **predictions**
a prediction is something that someone predicts

predominant *ADJECTIVE*
most important or largest in size or number
➤ **predominance** *NOUN*
➤ **predominantly** *ADVERB*

predominate *VERB* **predominates, predominating, predominated**
to predominate is to be the largest in size or number, or the most important • *Girls predominate in our class.*

preen *VERB* **preens, preening, preened**
a bird preens when it smooths and cleans its feathers using its beak

preface (*say* pref-ass) *NOUN* **prefaces**
an introduction at the beginning of a book

prefect *NOUN* **prefects**
❶ a school pupil who is given authority to help to keep order ❷ a local official in some countries

prefer *VERB* **prefers, preferring, preferred**
to prefer one thing to another is to like it better than the other thing

preferable (*say* pref-er-a-bul) *ADJECTIVE*
something is preferable to something else when it is better or you like it more
➤ **preferably** *ADVERB* you use preferably to say what you would prefer • *Meet me tomorrow, preferably before school.*

preference *NOUN* **preferences**
your preference is what you prefer

prefix *NOUN* **prefixes**
a word or syllable joined to the front of a word to change or add to its meaning, as in *dis*order, *out*stretched and *un*happy

pregnant *ADJECTIVE*
a pregnant woman or female animal has a baby developing in her womb
➤ **pregnancy** *NOUN*

prehistoric *ADJECTIVE*
belonging to a very long time ago, before written records were kept

prejudice *NOUN* **prejudices**
a prejudice is when you make up your mind that you do not like someone or something without a good reason or without thinking about it
➤ **prejudiced** *ADJECTIVE*

preliminary *ADJECTIVE*
coming before something or preparing for it

prelude (*say* prel-yood) *NOUN* **preludes**
a short introduction to a play, poem or piece of music

premature *ADJECTIVE*
happening or coming before the expected time • *a premature baby*

premier (*say* prem-i-er) *NOUN* **premiers**
the leader of a government

premiere (*say* prem-yair) *NOUN* **premieres**
the first public performance of a play or showing of a film

premises *PLURAL NOUN*
an organization's or business's premises are the building and land it uses

premium (*say* pree-mi-um) *NOUN* **premiums**
an amount paid regularly to an insurance company

a
b
c
d
e
f
g
h
i
j
k
l
m
n
o
p
q
r
s
t
u
v
w
x
y
z

to be at a premium is to be valued highly and perhaps expensive because of this

premonition NOUN premonitions
a feeling that something bad is going to happen

preoccupied ADJECTIVE
you are preoccupied when you are thinking hard about something and do not notice other things

preoccupation NOUN something you think about most of the time

preparation NOUN preparations
1 preparation is getting something ready **2** preparations are things you do in order to get ready for something • *We were making last-minute preparations.*

preparatory (say pri-**pa**-ra-ter-ee) ADJECTIVE
preparing for something

prepare VERB prepares, preparing, prepared
to prepare something is to get it ready

to be prepared to do something is to be ready or willing to do it

preposition NOUN prepositions
a word you put in front of a noun or pronoun to show how it is connected with another word, for example *on* in *Put the flowers on the table* and *with* in *I'd like some butter with my bread*

prep school NOUN prep schools
a preparatory school; a school that prepares pupils for a higher school

prescribe VERB prescribes, prescribing, prescribed
1 to prescribe a medicine for a patient is to instruct them to take it and give them a prescription for it **2** to prescribe a method or solution is to say what must be done

prescription NOUN prescriptions
a doctor's order for a medicine to be prepared for a patient

presence NOUN
your presence somewhere is the fact that you are there • *Your presence is expected.*

present (say **prez**-ent) ADJECTIVE
1 in a particular place; here • *Nobody else was present.* **2** existing or happening now • *Who is the present king?*

present (say **prez**-ent) NOUN presents
1 the present is the time now • *Our teacher is away at present.* **2** a present is something that you give or receive as a gift

present (say pri-**zent**) VERB presents, presenting, presented
1 to present something to someone is to give it to them, especially with a ceremony • *Who will present the prizes this year?* **2** to present a play or other entertainment is to perform it **3** to present a radio or television programme is to introduce it to the audience **4** to present something you have done or made is to show it formally to people • *We had to present our project to the class.*

presentation NOUN presentations
1 a formal talk showing or demonstrating something **2** a ceremony in which someone is given a gift or prize • *I'd like to make a little presentation.*

presenter NOUN presenters
someone who presents something, especially a radio or television programme

presently ADVERB
soon; in a while

present participle NOUN present participles
a form of a verb used after *am, are* and *is* to describe an action that is happening now, or used after *was, were, has been, have been* and *had been* to describe an action that went on for some time in the past, for example *looking* in *I am looking at the pictures* and *I was looking at the pictures*

present tense NOUN
a form of a verb used to describe something that is happening now, for example *likes* in *He likes swimming*

preservative NOUN preservatives
a substance added to food to preserve it

preserve VERB preserves, preserving, preserved
to preserve something is to keep it safe or in good condition

preservation NOUN

preside to prevent

preside (*say* pri-**zyd**) VERB presides, presiding, presided
to preside over a meeting or other occasion is to be in charge of it

president NOUN presidents
❶ the head of a country that is a republic ❷ the person in charge of a society, business or club
➤ presidency NOUN
➤ presidential ADJECTIVE

press VERB presses, pressing, pressed
❶ to press something is to push it firmly or squeeze it • *Press the red button.* ❷ to press clothes is to make them flat and smooth with an iron ❸ to press someone for something is to urge them to do or give it • *She's pressing me for a decision.*

press NOUN presses
❶ the action of squeezing or pushing on something • *Give the bell another press.* ❷ the press are newspapers and journalists ❸ a machine for printing things ❹ a business that prints or publishes books ❺ a device for flattening and smoothing things • *a trouser press*

press-up NOUN press-ups
an exercise in which you lie face downwards and push down with your hands to lift your body

pressure NOUN pressures
❶ pressure is continuous pushing or squeezing • *Apply pressure to the cut to stop it bleeding.* ❷ pressure is also the force with which a liquid or gas pushes against something ❸ there is pressure on you when someone is trying to persuade or force you to do something

pressurize (*also* pressurise) VERB pressurizes, pressurizing, pressurized
❶ to pressurize a place or compartment is to keep it at the same air pressure all the time • *The cabin of the aeroplane is pressurized.* ❷ to pressurize someone is to try to force them to do something

prestige (*say* pres-**teezh**) NOUN
prestige is the respect something has because it is important or of a high quality
➤ prestigious ADJECTIVE

presumably ADVERB
probably; I suppose

presume VERB presumes, presuming, presumed
to presume something is to suppose it
• *I presumed that he was dead.*

presumption NOUN
❶ presumption is supposing that something is probably true ❷ presumption is also being too bold or confident

presumptuous ADJECTIVE
too bold or confident

pretence NOUN pretences
a pretence is an attempt to pretend something

pretend VERB pretends, pretending, pretended
❶ to pretend is to behave as if something untrue or imaginary is true ❷ to pretend something is to claim it dishonestly • *They pretended they were policemen.*

pretender NOUN pretenders
someone who claims the right to be a king or queen of a country

pretty ADJECTIVE prettier, prettiest
pleasant to look at or hear; attractive
➤ prettily ADVERB ➤ prettiness NOUN
pretty ADVERB (*informal*)
quite; moderately • *It's pretty cold outside.*

prevail VERB prevails, prevailing, prevailed
❶ to prevail is to be most frequent or general • *The prevailing view is that we were wrong.* ❷ to prevail is also to be successful in a battle, contest or game • *In the story, good eventually prevails over evil.*

prevalent ADJECTIVE
most frequent or common; widespread

prevent VERB prevents, preventing, prevented
❶ to prevent something is to stop it from happening or make it impossible ❷ to prevent someone is to stop them from doing something
➤ prevention NOUN
➤ preventive ADJECTIVE something that is preventive is meant to help prevent something • *preventive medicine*

preview *NOUN* previews
a showing of a film or play before it is shown to the public

previous *ADJECTIVE*
coming before this; preceding • *I was in London the previous week.*

previously *ADVERB*
to happen previously is to happen before or earlier • *He looked back over the work he had done previously.*

prey (say pray) *NOUN*
an animal that is hunted or killed by another animal for food

prey (say pray) *VERB* preys, preying, preyed
➤ **to prey on something** is to hunt and kill an animal for food • *Owls prey on mice and other small animals.*

price *NOUN* prices
❶ the amount of money for which something is sold ❷ what you have to give or do to get something • *What is the price of peace?*
➤ **at any price** at any cost

price *VERB* prices, pricing, priced
to price something is to decide its price
➤ **pricey** *ADJECTIVE* expensive

priceless *ADJECTIVE*
❶ very valuable ❷ (*informal*) very amusing

prick *VERB* pricks, pricking, pricked
❶ to prick something is to make a tiny hole in it ❷ to prick someone is to hurt them with something sharp or pointed

prick *NOUN* pricks
a prick is a pricking feeling

prickle *NOUN* prickles
a sharp point on a plant or animal
➤ **prickly** *ADJECTIVE* something prickly is covered in prickles or feels like prickles

prickle *VERB* prickles, prickling, prickled
to prickle is to make your skin feel as though lots of little sharp points are sticking into it • *This jumper is prickling me.*

pride *NOUN* prides
❶ pride is a feeling of being very pleased with yourself or with someone else who has done well • *My heart swelled with pride.* ❷ pride is also being too satisfied because of who you are or what you have done ❸ a pride is something that makes you feel proud • *This fossil is the pride of my collection.* ❹ a pride is also a group of lions

priest *NOUN* priests
❶ a member of the clergy ❷ someone who conducts religious ceremonies; a religious leader

priestess *NOUN* priestesses
a female priest in a non-Christian religion

prig *NOUN* prigs
someone who is smug and self-righteous
➤ **priggish** *ADJECTIVE*

prim *ADJECTIVE* primmer, primmest
someone who is prim likes things to be correct, and disapproves of anything rude or improper
Mary Poppins, neat and prim in her blue skirt and a new hat trimmed with a crimson tulip, looked at them over her knitting.—MARY POPPINS IN THE PARK, P. L. Travers
➤ **primly** *ADVERB* ➤ **primness** *NOUN*

primarily *ADVERB*
mainly or most importantly • *The film is primarily a love story.*

primary *ADJECTIVE*
first; most important

primary colour *NOUN* primary colours
one of the colours from which all other colours can be made by mixing: red, yellow and blue for paint, and red, green and violet for light

primary school *NOUN* primary schools
a school for the first stage of a child's education, between the ages of 5 and 11

primate *NOUN* primates
❶ an animal of the group that includes human beings, apes and monkeys ❷ an archbishop

prime *ADJECTIVE*
❶ chief or most important • *The weather was the prime cause of the accident.* ❷ of the best quality

prime *NOUN* primes
the best part or stage of something • *He was in the prime of life.*

prime *VERB* primes, priming, primed
❶ to prime something is to get it ready for use • *Pour water into the pump to prime it.*

❷ to prime a surface is to put a special liquid on it before painting it

prime minister NOUN prime ministers
the leader of a government

prime number NOUN prime numbers
a number that can only be divided exactly by itself and the number one, for example 2, 3, 5, 7 and 11

primeval (say pry-mee-val) ADJECTIVE
belonging to the earliest times of the world; ancient

primitive ADJECTIVE
❶ at an early stage of development • *Primitive humans learned to make fire.* ❷ basic or simple • *Our accommodation was fairly primitive.*

primrose NOUN primroses
a pale yellow flower that comes out in spring

prince NOUN princes
❶ the son of a king or queen ❷ a man or boy in a royal family

princess NOUN princesses
❶ the daughter of a king or queen ❷ a woman or girl in a royal family ❸ the wife of a prince

principal ADJECTIVE
chief or most important • *Name the principal cities of Britain.*
➤ **principally** ADVERB chiefly or mainly

principal NOUN principals
the head of a college or school

principle NOUN principles
❶ a general rule or truth • *the principles of mathematics* ❷ someone's principles are the basic rules and beliefs they have about how they should behave
➤ **in principle** in general, not in detail • *I agree with your plan in principle.*

print VERB prints, printing, printed
❶ to print words or pictures is to put them on paper with a machine ❷ to print letters is to write them separately and not joined together ❸ to print a photograph is to make it from a negative

print NOUN prints
❶ print is printed words or pictures ❷ a print is a mark made by something pressing on a surface • *Her thumb left a print on the glass.*

❸ a print is also a printed photograph, picture or design

printer NOUN printers
❶ a machine that prints on paper from data in a computer ❷ someone who prints books or newspapers

printout NOUN printouts
the information printed on paper from data in a computer

prior ADJECTIVE
coming before or earlier • *He said he had a prior engagement.*

priority (say pry-o-ri-tee) NOUN priorities
❶ a priority is something that is more urgent or important than other things and needs to be dealt with first • *Repairing the roof is a priority.* ❷ priority is the right to go first or be considered before other things • *People in need of urgent medical help will have priority.*

prise VERB prises, prising, prised
to prise something open is to force or lever it open • *She prised open the lid with a teaspoon.*

prism NOUN prisms
❶ a piece of glass that breaks up light into the colours of the rainbow ❷ (*mathematics*) a solid object with parallel ends that are equal triangles or polygons

prison NOUN prisons
a place where criminals are kept as a punishment

prisoner NOUN prisoners
someone who is kept in a prison or who is a captive

privacy NOUN
❶ privacy is being private or away from other people • *Our new garden fence will give us more privacy.* ❷ privacy is also keeping your personal information from being seen by other people without permission

private ADJECTIVE
❶ belonging to a particular person or group of people • *This is a private road.* ❷ meant to be kept secret • *These letters are private.* ❸ away from other people • *Is there a private place to swim?*

a b c d e f g h i j k l m n o p q r s t u v w x y z

A
B
C
D
E
F
G
H
I
J
K
L
M
N
O
P
Q
R
S
T
U
V
W
X
Y
Z

> **in private** where only particular people can see or hear; not in public

private *NOUN* **privates**
a soldier of the lowest rank

privately *ADVERB*
to do something privately is to do it away from other people • *Can we speak privately?*

privet *NOUN*
privet is an evergreen shrub with small leaves, used to make hedges

privilege *NOUN* **privileges**
a special right or advantage given to one person or group of people
> **privileged** *ADJECTIVE*

prize *NOUN* **prizes**
❶ something you get for winning a game or competition, or for doing well in an examination ❷ something taken from an enemy

prize *VERB* **prizes**, **prizing**, **prized**
to prize something is to value it highly

pro *NOUN* **pros** (*informal*)
a professional

pro– *PREFIX*
meaning 'in favour of' or 'supporting', as in *pro-independence* (the opposite is **anti–**)

probability *NOUN* **probabilities**
the probability of something is how likely it is to happen

probable *ADJECTIVE*
likely to be true or to happen

probably *ADVERB*
you say that something will probably happen or is probably true when you think it is likely to happen or be true

probation *NOUN*
probation is a time when someone is tried out in a new job to make sure they are suitable for the work
> **on probation** if you are on probation, you are being watched to see if you behave properly

probe *NOUN* **probes**
❶ a long thin instrument used to look closely at something such as a wound ❷ an investigation

probe *VERB* **probes**, **probing**, **probed**
❶ to probe something is to look at it with a probe ❷ to probe is to investigate

problem *NOUN* **problems**
something difficult to answer or deal with

procedure *NOUN* **procedures**
a fixed or special way of doing something

proceed (*say* pro-**seed**) *VERB* **proceeds**, **proceeding**, **proceeded**
to proceed is to go on or continue

proceedings *PLURAL NOUN*
❶ things that happen; activities ❷ a dispute that has been brought to a law court

proceeds (*say* **proh**-seedz) *PLURAL NOUN*
the proceeds of a sale or event are the money made from it

process *NOUN* **processes**
a series of actions for making or doing something
> **to be in the process of doing something** is to be in the middle of doing it

process *VERB* **processes**, **processing**, **processed**
to process something is to treat it or deal with it by a process so that it can be used • *Oil can be processed into petrol and diesel.*

procession *NOUN* **processions**
a number of people or vehicles moving steadily forwards

proclaim *VERB* **proclaims**, **proclaiming**, **proclaimed**
to proclaim something is to announce it officially or publicly
> **proclamation** *NOUN*

prod *VERB* **prods**, **prodding**, **prodded**
to prod something or someone is to poke or jab them

prodigal *ADJECTIVE*
wasteful or extravagant

produce (*say* pro-**dewss**) *VERB* **produces**, **producing**, **produced**
❶ to produce something is to make or create it ❷ to produce something that is hidden or put away is to bring it out so that people can see it ❸ to produce a play or film or other entertainment is to organize the performance of it

produce (*say* prod-yewss) *NOUN*
produce is things produced, especially by farmers

producer *NOUN* **producers**
someone who produces a play or film

product *NOUN* **products**
❶ something someone makes or produces for sale ❷ the result of multiplying two numbers • *12 is the product of 4 and 3.*

production *NOUN* **productions**
❶ production is the process of making or creating something • *The factory is engaged in car production.* ❷ production is also the amount someone produces or makes • *Oil production increased last year.* ❸ a production is a version of a play or film

productive *ADJECTIVE*
producing a lot of good or useful things

productivity *NOUN*
productivity is the rate at which someone works or produces something

profession *NOUN* **professions**
a type of work for which you need special knowledge and training, for example medicine, law or teaching

professional *ADJECTIVE*
❶ doing a certain type of work to earn money • *He became a professional tennis player.* ❷ to do with a profession ❸ you can describe something done with great skill and to a high standard as professional
➤ **professionally** *ADVERB*

professional *NOUN* **professionals**
someone doing a certain type of work to earn money

professor *NOUN* **professors**
a teacher of the highest rank in a university

proficient (*say* pro-**fish**-ent) *ADJECTIVE*
to be proficient at something is to be able to do it well
➤ **proficiency** *NOUN* ➤ **proficiently** *ADVERB*

profile *NOUN* **profiles**
❶ a person's profile is a side view of their face ❷ a short description of a person's life or character

profit *NOUN* **profits**
❶ the extra money got by selling something

for more than it cost to buy or make ❷ an advantage or benefit

profit *VERB* **profits**, **profiting**, **profited**
to profit from something is to get an advantage from it

profitable *ADJECTIVE*
making a profit; bringing in money
➤ **profitably** *ADVERB*

profound *ADJECTIVE*
❶ very deep or intense • *The film had a profound effect on us all.* ❷ showing or needing great knowledge or thought • *The poem she wrote was quite profound.*
➤ **profoundly** *ADVERB*

profuse (*say* pro-**fewss**) *ADJECTIVE*
produced in large amounts; plentiful • *He offered his profuse thanks.*
➤ **profusely** *ADVERB*

program *NOUN* **programs**
a series of coded instructions for a computer to carry out

program *VERB* **programs**, **programming**, **programmed**
to program a computer is to prepare or control it by means of a program

programme *NOUN* **programmes**
❶ a show, play or talk on radio or television ❷ a list of a planned series of events ❸ a leaflet or pamphlet that gives details of a play, concert or other event

progress (*say* **proh**-gress) *NOUN*
❶ progress is forward movement • *The march made slow progress.* ❷ progress is also development or improvement • *You have made a lot of progress this term.*

progress (*say* pro-**gress**) *VERB* **progresses**, **progressing**, **progressed**
❶ to progress is to move forward ❷ to progress is also to develop or improve
➤ **progression** *NOUN*
➤ **progressive** *ADJECTIVE* developing steadily

prohibit *VERB* **prohibits**, **prohibiting**, **prohibited**
to prohibit something is to forbid it, especially by law • *Smoking is prohibited.*
➤ **prohibition** *NOUN*

project (*say* **proj**-ekt) *NOUN* **projects**
❶ a planned task in which you find out as

a
b
c
d
e
f
g
h
i
j
k
l
m
n
o
p
q
r
s
t
u
v
w
x
y
z

A
B
C
D
E
F
G
H
I
J
K
L
M
N
O
P
Q
R
S
T
U
V
W
X
Y
Z

much as you can about something and write about it ❷ a plan or scheme

project (*say* pro-**jekt**) *VERB* **projects, projecting, projected**
❶ to project is to stick out ❷ to project your voice is to speak loudly and clearly so that it carries a long way ❸ to project a picture or film is to show it with a projector on a screen

projection *NOUN* **projections**
❶ projection is showing a picture or film on a screen with a projector ❷ a projection is a part of something that sticks out

projector *NOUN* **projectors**
a machine for showing films or photographs on a screen

prologue (*say* **proh**-log) *NOUN* **prologues**
an introduction to a poem or play or long story

prolong *VERB* **prolongs, prolonging, prolonged**
to prolong something is to make it last longer

promenade (*say* prom-en-**ahd**) *NOUN* **promenades**
❶ a place suitable for walking, especially beside the seashore ❷ a leisurely walk

prominent *ADJECTIVE*
❶ easily seen; standing out • *She has prominent teeth.* ❷ important
➤ **prominence** *NOUN*
➤ **prominently** *ADVERB*

promise *NOUN* **promises**
❶ a promise is a statement that you will definitely do or not do something ❷ something shows promise when it shows signs that it will be successful in the future

promise *VERB* **promises, promising, promised**
to promise to do something is to say that you will definitely do it

promising *ADJECTIVE*
likely to be good or successful • *We have several promising pupils.*

promontory (*say* **prom**-on-ter-ee) *NOUN* **promontories**
a piece of high land sticking out into the sea
Beyond the promontory was a wide bay with deep beds of rushes on either side of it.—SWALLOWS AND AMAZONS, Arthur Ransome

promote *VERB* **promotes, promoting, promoted**
❶ to be promoted is to be given a more senior or more important job or rank ❷ a sports team is promoted when it moves to a higher division or league ❸ to promote a product or cause is to make people more aware of it • *He has done much to promote the cause of peace.*
➤ **promoter** *NOUN*

promotion *NOUN* **promotions**
❶ promotion is when someone is given a more senior or more important job or rank ❷ promotion is also when a sports team moves to a higher division or league ❸ a promotion is a piece of publicity or advertising

prompt *ADJECTIVE* **prompter, promptest**
happening soon or without delay • *We need a prompt reply.*
➤ **promptly** *ADVERB* ➤ **promptness** *NOUN*

prompt *VERB* **prompts, prompting, prompted**
❶ to prompt someone to do something is to cause or encourage them to do it ❷ to prompt an actor is to remind them of their words if they forget them during a play

prone *ADJECTIVE*
lying face downwards
➤ **to be prone to something** is to be likely to do it or suffer from it • *He is prone to jealousy.*

prong *NOUN* **prongs**
one of the pointed spikes at the end of a fork

pronoun *NOUN* **pronouns**
a word used instead of a noun, such as *he, her, it, them, those*

pronounce *VERB* **pronounces, pronouncing, pronounced**
❶ to pronounce a word is to say it in a particular way • *'Too' and 'two' are pronounced the same.* ❷ to pronounce something is to declare it formally • *The judge pronounced her verdict.*

pronounced *ADJECTIVE*
noticeable; definite • *This street has a pronounced slope.*

pronouncement *NOUN* **pronouncements**
something said formally; a declaration

pronunciation (*say* pro-nun-si-**ay**-shon)
NOUN **pronunciations**
the way a word is pronounced

proof *NOUN* **proofs**
❶ proof is a fact which shows that something is true or exists
Grown-up people find it very difficult to believe really wonderful things, unless they have what they call 'proof'.—FIVE CHILDREN AND IT, Edith Nesbit
❷ a proof is a printed copy of something, made for checking before other copies are printed

proof *ADJECTIVE*
giving protection against something
• *a weather-proof building*

proofread *VERB* **proofreads, proofreading, proofread**
to proofread something you have written is to read it carefully so that you can mark any mistakes and correct them

prop *NOUN* **props**
❶ a support, especially one made of a long piece of wood or metal ❷ a piece of furniture or other object used on stage in a theatre

prop *VERB* **props, propping, propped**
to prop something somewhere is to lean it there so that it does not fall over • *The ladder was propped up against the wall.*

propaganda *NOUN*
propaganda is information, especially false information, that is spread around to make people believe something

propel *VERB* **propels, propelling, propelled**
to propel something is to move it rapidly forward

propeller *NOUN* **propellers**
a device with blades that spin round to drive an aircraft or ship

proper *ADJECTIVE*
❶ suitable or right • *This is the proper way to hold a bat.* ❷ respectable • *You must behave in a proper fashion.*

proper fraction *NOUN* **proper fractions**
a fraction that is less than 1, such as ½ or ⅗

properly *ADVERB*
to do something properly is to do it in a way that is correct or suitable

proper noun *NOUN* **proper nouns**
the name given to one person or thing, such as *Mary* or *Tokyo*, and written with a capital first letter

property *NOUN* **properties**
❶ a person's property is a thing, or all the things, that belong to them ❷ a property is buildings or land belonging to someone ❸ a property is also a quality or characteristic that something has • *Rubber has elastic properties.*

prophecy (*say* **prof**-i-see) *NOUN* **prophecies**
❶ a prophecy is something that someone has said will happen in the future ❷ prophecy is saying what will happen in the future

prophesy (*say* **prof**-i-sy) *VERB* **prophesies, prophesying, prophesied**
to prophesy something is to say that it will happen in the future

prophet *NOUN* **prophets**
❶ someone who makes prophecies ❷ a religious teacher who is believed to speak the word of God

prophetic *ADJECTIVE*
saying or showing what will happen in the future

proportion *NOUN* **proportions**
❶ a fraction or share of something • *Water covers a large proportion of the earth's surface.* ❷ the proportion of one thing to another is how much there is of one compared to the other ❸ the correct relationship between the size, amount or importance of two things • *You've drawn the head out of proportion with the body.*
➤ **proportions** size or scale • *What are the proportions of the room?*

proportional, proportionate *ADJECTIVE*
in proportion; according to a ratio
➤ **proportionally, proportionately** *ADVERB*
in proportion

proposal *NOUN* **proposals**
❶ a suggestion ❷ when someone asks another person to marry them

propose *VERB* **proposes, proposing, proposed**
❶ to propose an idea or plan is to suggest it

A
B
C
D
E
F
G
H
I
J
K
L
M
N
O
P
Q
R
S
T
U
V
W
X
Y
Z

❷ to propose to someone is to ask them to marry you

proprietor (*say* pro-**pry**-et-er) *NOUN* **proprietors**
the owner of a shop or business

propulsion *NOUN*
propulsion is propelling something or driving it forward

prose *NOUN*
prose is writing that is like ordinary speech, not poetry or verse

prosecute *VERB* **prosecutes**, **prosecuting**, **prosecuted**
to prosecute someone is to make them go to a law court to be tried for a crime
➤ **prosecution** *NOUN*

prospect (*say* **pros**-pekt) *NOUN* **prospects**
❶ a possibility or hope; what may happen in the future • *There's not much prospect of the weather improving.* **❷** a wide view • *We saw a vast prospect from the top of the hill.*

prospect (*say* pro-**spekt**) *VERB* **prospects**, **prospecting**, **prospected**
to prospect is to search for gold or some other mineral

prosper *VERB* **prospers**, **prospering**, **prospered**
to prosper is to be successful or do well

prosperity *NOUN*
prosperity is being successful or rich

prosperous *ADJECTIVE*
successful or rich

protect *VERB* **protects**, **protecting**, **protected**
to protect someone or something is to keep them safe

protection *NOUN*
protection is keeping someone or something safe

protective *ADJECTIVE*
❶ a person is protective when they want to protect someone or something **❷** a thing is protective when it is meant to protect something

protector *NOUN* **protectors**
a protector is a person who protects someone or something

protein (*say* proh-teen) *NOUN* **proteins**
protein is a substance found in some types of food, for example meat, eggs and cheese. Your body needs protein to help you grow and be healthy.

protest (*say* proh-test) *NOUN* **protests**
something you say or do because you disapprove of someone or something

protest (*say* pro-**test**) *VERB* **protests**, **protesting**, **protested**
to protest about something is to say publicly that you think it is wrong
➤ **protester** *NOUN*

Protestant (*say* **prot**-is-tant) *NOUN* **Protestants**
a member of a western Christian Church other than the Roman Catholic Church

prototype (*say* **proh**-to-typ) *NOUN* **prototypes**
the first example of something, used as a model for making others

protractor *NOUN* **protractors**
a device in the shape of a semicircle, used for measuring and drawing angles on paper

protrude *VERB* **protrudes**, **protruding**, **protruded**
to protrude is to stick out • *He had protruding eyes.*
➤ **protrusion** *NOUN*

proud *ADJECTIVE* **prouder**, **proudest**
❶ very pleased with yourself or with someone else who has done well • *I am proud of my sister.* **❷** too satisfied because of who you are or what you have done • *He was too proud to admit that he had made a mistake.*
➤ **proudly** *ADVERB*

prove *VERB* **proves**, **proving**, **proved**
❶ to prove something is to show that it is true **❷** to prove to be something is to turn out to be that way • *The forecast proved to be correct.*

proverb *NOUN* **proverbs**
a short well-known saying that states a truth or gives advice, for example *many hands make light work*

proverbial *ADJECTIVE*
❶ occurring in a proverb ❷ familiar or well known, like a proverb

provide *VERB* **provides**, **providing**, **provided**
❶ to provide something is to supply it
• *A clump of trees provided some welcome shade.*
❷ to provide for someone is to make sure they have enough to live on
'Have you had many brothers, Spirit?' 'More than eighteen hundred', said the Ghost. 'A tremendous family to provide for!' muttered Scrooge.—A CHRISTMAS CAROL, Charles Dickens

provided, providing *CONJUNCTION*
on condition; on condition that
Each Dwarf and Snow-White got a share, And each was soon a millionaire, Which shows that gambling's not a sin Provided that you always win.—REVOLTING RHYMES, Roald Dahl

province *NOUN* **provinces**
❶ a region or division of a country ❷ an area of knowledge or skill
➤ **the provinces** the part of a country outside the capital
➤ **provincial** *ADJECTIVE* in a part of a country away from the capital

provision *NOUN* **provisions**
provision is providing something • *the provision of free meals for schoolchildren*

provisional *ADJECTIVE*
arranged or agreed on for the time being, but not yet definite • *They have set a provisional date for the wedding.*

provisions *PLURAL NOUN*
supplies of food and drink

provocation *NOUN*
provocation is saying or doing something to deliberately make someone angry

provocative *ADJECTIVE*
likely to make someone angry • *That was a provocative remark.*

provoke *VERB* **provokes**, **provoking**, **provoked**
❶ to provoke someone is to deliberately make them angry ❷ to provoke a feeling is to arouse or cause it • *His statement provoked a great deal of criticism.*

prow *NOUN* **prows**
the front end of a ship
The ship … was frozen at an angle in the ice, looking pale and ghostly in the moonlight with the prow rising up into the sky.—THE POLAR BEAR EXPLORERS' CLUB, Alex Bell

prowl *VERB* **prowls**, **prowling**, **prowled**
to prowl is to move about quietly and secretly, as some animals do when they are hunting

proximity *NOUN*
to be in the proximity of something is to be near it

prudent (*say* **proo**-dent) *ADJECTIVE*
wise and careful; not taking risks
➤ **prudence** *NOUN* ➤ **prudently** *ADVERB*

prune *NOUN* **prunes**
a prune is a dried plum

prune *VERB* **prunes**, **pruning**, **pruned**
to prune a tree or bush is to cut off unwanted parts from it

pry *VERB* **pries**, **prying**, **pried**
to pry is to snoop in someone else's business

PS *ABBREVIATION*
short for *postscript* (used when you add something at the end of a letter or message)

psalm (*say* sahm) *NOUN* **psalms**
a religious song, especially one from the Book of Psalms in the Bible

pseudonym (*say* s'**yoo**-do-nim) *NOUN* **pseudonyms**
a false name that an author uses

psychiatrist (*say* sy-**ky**-a-trist) *NOUN* **psychiatrists**
a doctor who treats people who have mental health problems or a mental illness

psychiatry (*say* sy-**ky**-a-tree) *NOUN*
psychiatry is the treatment of people who have mental health problems or a mental illness
➤ **psychiatric** *ADJECTIVE*

psychic (*say* sy-kik) *ADJECTIVE*
someone is psychic when they can tell the future or read other people's minds

psychologist (*say* sy-**kol**-o-jist) *NOUN* **psychologists**
someone who studies how the mind works

a b c d e f g h i j k l m n o **p** q r s t u v w x y z

psychology NOUN
psychology is the study of the mind and the way people behave
➤ **psychological** ADJECTIVE

PTA ABBREVIATION
short for *Parent-Teacher Association*, an organization that arranges meetings between teachers and parents to discuss school matters

pterodactyl (*say* ter-o-**dak**-til) NOUN pterodactyls
an extinct flying reptile with a long head and neck

pub NOUN pubs (*informal*)
a building where people can buy and drink alcoholic drinks

puberty (*say* **pew**-ber-tee) NOUN
puberty is the time when a young person starts to become an adult and their body starts to change

public ADJECTIVE
❶ belonging to everyone or able to be used by everyone • *I often use public transport.*
❷ to do with people in general • *Newspapers can influence public opinion.*
➤ **publicly** ADVERB in public

public NOUN
the public is people in general
➤ **in public** openly; where anyone can see or take part

publication NOUN publications
❶ a publication is a book or magazine that is printed and sold ❷ publication is printing and selling books or magazines

publicity NOUN
publicity is information or advertising that makes people know about someone or something

publicize (*also* **publicise**) VERB publicizes, publicizing, publicized
to publicize something is to make people know about it • *We'll publicize the event on our website.*

public school NOUN public schools
❶ in England and Wales, a secondary school that charges fees ❷ in Scotland and the USA, a school run by the state or by a local authority

publish VERB publishes, publishing, published
❶ to publish books or magazines is to print and sell them ❷ to publish information is to make it known publicly
➤ **publisher** NOUN

puck NOUN pucks
a hard rubber disc used in ice hockey

pucker VERB puckers, puckering, puckered
to pucker is to form into wrinkles

pudding NOUN puddings
❶ a food made in a soft mass, especially with a mixture of flour and other ingredients ❷ the sweet course of a meal

puddle NOUN puddles
a small pool, especially of rainwater

pudgy ADJECTIVE pudgier, pudgiest (*informal*)
short and plump

puff VERB puffs, puffing, puffed
❶ to puff smoke or steam is to blow it out ❷ you puff when you breathe with difficulty • *She was puffing when she got to the top of the hill.* ❸ to puff something, or to puff it out, is to inflate or swell it • *He puffed out his chest.*

puff NOUN puffs
a small amount of breath, wind, smoke or steam • *He vanished in a puff of smoke.*

puffin NOUN puffins
a seabird with a large striped beak

puffy ADJECTIVE puffier, puffiest
puffed out or swollen • *Your eyes are looking a bit puffy.*
➤ **puffiness** NOUN

pull VERB pulls, pulling, pulled
❶ to pull something is to get hold of it and make it come towards you or follow behind you ❷ to pull is to move with an effort • *She tried to grab the boy but he pulled away.*
➤ **to pull a face** is to twist your face into a strange expression
➤ **to pull in** ❶ a car pulls in when it stops at the side of the road ❷ a train pulls in when it comes into a station and stops
➤ **to pull out** is to decide to stop taking part in something • *He had to pull out of the race after he twisted his ankle.*
➤ **to pull someone's leg** is to tease them
➤ **to pull something off** is to achieve it

➤ **to pull through** is to recover from an illness

➤ **to pull up** is to stop • *A car pulled up and two men got out.*

➤ **to pull yourself together** is to become calm or sensible

pull *NOUN* **pulls**
a pull is an action of pulling • *Give the handle a good pull.*

pulley *NOUN* **pulleys**
a wheel with a groove round it to take a rope, used for lifting heavy things

pullover *NOUN* **pullovers**
a knitted piece of clothing for the top half of your body, that you put on over your head

pulp *NOUN* **pulps**
a soft wet mass of something, especially for making paper
➤ **pulpy** *ADJECTIVE*

pulp *VERB* **pulps, pulping, pulped**
to pulp something is to make it into a pulp

pulpit *NOUN* **pulpits**
a raised platform in a church, from which the preacher speaks to the congregation

pulse *NOUN* **pulses**
❶ your pulse is the regular beat you can feel in your wrist or neck as your heart pumps blood through your arteries ❷ a regular vibration or movement • *The music had a throbbing pulse.* ❸ pulses are the edible seeds of certain plants, such as peas, beans and lentils

pulverize (*also* **pulverise**) *VERB*
pulverizes, pulverizing, pulverized
to pulverize something is to crush it into a powder

puma *NOUN* **pumas**
a large wild cat of North and South America

pumice (*say* **pum**-iss) *NOUN*
pumice is a kind of soft sponge-like stone rubbed on hard surfaces to clean or polish them

pummel *VERB* **pummels, pummelling, pummelled**
to pummel someone is to hit them hard over and over

pump *NOUN* **pumps**
❶ a device that forces air or liquid into or out of something, or along pipes ❷ a lightweight shoe • *She took off her pumps.*

pump *VERB* **pumps, pumping, pumped**
to pump air or liquid is to force it into or out of something with a pump
➤ **to pump something up** is to fill something like a balloon or tyre with air or gas

pumpkin *NOUN* **pumpkins**
a large round fruit with a hard skin and orange flesh that is used to make sweet and savoury dishes

pun *NOUN* **puns**
a joke made by using a word with two different meanings, or two words that sound the same, as in *Choosing where to bury him was a grave decision.*

pun *VERB* **puns, punning, punned**
to pun is to make a pun

punch *VERB* **punches, punching, punched**
❶ to punch someone is to hit them with your fist ❷ to punch a hole is to make a hole in something • *The guard checked and punched our tickets.* • *The builder punched a hole in the wall.*

punch *NOUN* **punches**
❶ a punch is a blow or hit with the fist ❷ a punch is also a device for making holes in paper, leather or metal

punchline *NOUN* **punchlines**
the last part of a joke or story, that makes it funny

punctual *ADJECTIVE*
you are punctual when you arrive exactly on time, not late
➤ **punctuality** *NOUN* ➤ **punctually** *ADVERB*

punctuate *VERB* **punctuates, punctuating, punctuated**
to punctuate a piece of writing is to put the commas, full stops and other punctuation in it

punctuation *NOUN*
punctuation is the set of marks such as commas, full stops and brackets put into a piece of writing to make it easier to understand

a
b
c
d
e
f
g
h
i
j
k
l
m
n
o
p
q
r
s
t
u
v
w
x
y
z

puncture *NOUN* **punctures**
a small hole made in a tyre by accident

pungent *ADJECTIVE*
smelling or tasting very strong or sharp

punish *VERB* **punishes, punishing, punished**
to punish someone is to make them suffer in some way because they have done something wrong

punishment *NOUN* **punishments**
a way of punishing someone

punk *NOUN* **punks**
punk is a kind of loud, simple rock music

punt *NOUN* **punts**
a flat-bottomed boat moved by pushing a pole against the bottom of a river while standing in the punt

punt *VERB* **punts, punting, punted**
❶ to punt is to use a pole to push a boat along ❷ to punt a football is to kick it after dropping it from your hands, before it touches the ground

puny (*say* pew-nee) *ADJECTIVE* **punier, puniest**
small and weak • *He looked too puny to be a superhero.*

pup *NOUN* **pups**
a puppy

pupa (*say* pew-pa) *NOUN* **pupae**
an insect at the stage of development between a larva and an adult insect; a chrysalis

pupil *NOUN* **pupils**
❶ someone who is being taught by a teacher ❷ the dark circular opening in the centre of your eye

DID YOU KNOW? Pupil comes from a Latin word meaning 'little girl or doll'. The circles in your eye were called pupils because of the tiny images you can see reflected in them.

puppet *NOUN* **puppets**
a kind of doll that can be made to move by fitting it over your fingers or hand or by pulling strings or wires attached to it
➤ **puppeteer** *NOUN* a person who operates puppets for a show or film

puppy *NOUN* **puppies**
a young dog

purchase *VERB* **purchases, purchasing, purchased**
to purchase something is to buy it

purchase *NOUN* **purchases**
❶ a purchase is something you have bought ❷ purchase is the fact of buying something • *Keep the receipt as proof of purchase.* ❸ a purchase is a firm hold or grip • *It was hard to get a purchase on the slippery rocks.*

pure *ADJECTIVE* **purer, purest**
❶ not mixed with anything else • *Use pure olive oil.* ❷ clean or clear • *They washed in a pure cold mountain stream.*

purely *ADVERB*
only, simply • *They did it purely for the money.*

purge *VERB* **purges, purging, purged**
to purge people or things is to get rid of them when they are not wanted

purge *NOUN* **purges**
an act of purging

purify *VERB* **purifies, purifying, purified**
to purify something is to make it pure
➤ **purification** *NOUN* ➤ **purifier** *NOUN*

puritan *NOUN* **puritans**
someone who believes in leading a strictly moral life

puritanical *ADJECTIVE*
extremely strict in your behaviour and morals

purity *NOUN*
purity is the state of being pure

purple *NOUN, ADJECTIVE*
a deep reddish-blue

purpose *NOUN* **purposes**
the reason why you do something; what something is for
➤ **to do something on purpose** is to do it deliberately

purposeful *ADJECTIVE*
determined to do or say something
Mr Jenkins came striding up to our table with a very purposeful look on his face.—THE WITCHES, Roald Dahl
➤ **purposefully** *ADVERB*

purr VERB **purrs, purring, purred**
a cat purrs when it makes a gentle murmuring sound because it is pleased

purse NOUN **purses**
a small bag for holding money

pursue VERB **pursues, pursuing, pursued**
❶ to pursue someone or something is to chase them ❷ to pursue an activity is to continue to do it or work at it • *She pursued her studies at college.*

pursuit NOUN **pursuits**
❶ pursuit is the action of chasing someone ❷ a pursuit is something you spend a lot of time doing

pus NOUN
pus is a thick yellow substance produced in boils and other sore places on your body

push VERB **pushes, pushing, pushed**
to push something is to move it away from you by pressing against it
➤ **to push off** (*informal*) is to go away

push NOUN **pushes**
a pushing movement

puss, pussy NOUN **pusses, pussies** (*informal*)
a cat

put VERB **puts, putting, put**
❶ to put something in a place is to move it there • *Put it over there.* • *Where shall I put it?* ❷ to put also means to affect someone or something in a particular way • *They've put me in a bad mood.* ❸ to put an idea in a certain way is to express it in words of a special kind • *She put it very tactfully.*
➤ **to put someone off** is to make them less keen on something • *Seeing you eat so much has put me off my food.*
➤ **to put someone up** is to give them a place to sleep • *Can we put them up for the night?*
➤ **to put something off** is to decide to do it later instead of now • *We'll have to put off the party if you're ill.*
➤ **to put something on** ❶ is to switch on an electrical device, for example a light or a television ❷ is to start wearing a piece of clothing • *I'll just put on my coat.*
➤ **to put something out** is to stop something like a fire or light from burning or shining

➤ **to put something up** is to raise it or make it upright • *Let's put up the tent.*
➤ **to put up with something** is to be willing to accept it without complaining

putrid (*say* pew-trid) ADJECTIVE
decaying or rotting • *a piece of putrid meat*

putt VERB **putts, putting, putted**
to putt a golf ball is to tap it gently towards the hole

putt NOUN **putts**
when a golfer taps the ball gently towards the hole

putter NOUN **putters**
a golf club used to putt the ball

putty NOUN
putty is a soft paste that sets hard, used by builders to fit windows in their frames

puzzle NOUN **puzzles**
❶ a tricky game that you have to solve ❷ a difficult question; a problem

puzzle VERB **puzzles, puzzling, puzzled**
❶ to puzzle someone is to give them a problem that is hard to understand ❷ to puzzle over something is to think hard about it

pygmy (*say* pig-mee) NOUN **pygmies**
an unusually small person or animal

pyjamas PLURAL NOUN
a loose lightweight set of jacket and trousers that you wear in bed
DID YOU KNOW? The word **pyjamas** comes from Urdu and Persian words meaning 'leg clothing'.

pylon NOUN **pylons**
a metal tower for supporting electric cables

pyramid NOUN **pyramids**
❶ an object with a square base and four sloping sides coming to a point ❷ an ancient Egyptian monument shaped like this. They were massive and were usually built of huge stone blocks.

python NOUN **pythons**
a large snake that crushes its prey

a
b
c
d
e
f
g
h
i
j
k
l
m
n
o
p
q
r
s
t
u
v
w
x
y
z

Qq

quack *NOUN* **quacks**
the harsh loud sound made by a duck

quack *VERB* **quacks**, **quacking**, **quacked**
a duck quacks when it makes a harsh loud sound

quad *NOUN* **quads** (*informal*)
❶ a quadrangle ❷ a quadruplet

quad bike *NOUN* **quad bikes**
a motorcycle with four large tyres for off-road driving

quadrangle *NOUN* **quadrangles**
a rectangular courtyard with large buildings round it

quadrant *NOUN* **quadrants**
a quarter of a circle

quadrilateral *NOUN* **quadrilaterals**
a flat shape with four straight sides

quadruple *ADJECTIVE*
❶ four times as much or as many ❷ having four parts

quadruple *VERB* **quadruples**, **quadrupling**, **quadrupled**
❶ to quadruple something is to make it four times as much or as many ❷ to quadruple is to become four times as much or as many

quadruplet *NOUN* **quadruplets**
each of four children born to the same mother at one time

quagga *NOUN* **quaggas**
an extinct animal like a zebra but with stripes only on its front half

quagmire (*say* kwog-myr *or* kwag-myr) *NOUN* **quagmires**
an area of boggy or marshy ground
The path squeezed its way through ... In the softer and more level places it was a slithering quagmire.—THE EAGLE OF THE NINTH, Rosemary Sutcliff

quail *NOUN* **quails**
a bird that looks like a small partridge

quail *VERB* **quails**, **quailing**, **quailed**
to quail is to feel or show fear

quaint *ADJECTIVE* **quainter**, **quaintest**
attractive in an unusual or old-fashioned way

quake *VERB* **quakes**, **quaking**, **quaked**
to tremble or shake

Quaker *NOUN* **Quakers**
a member of a religious group called the Society of Friends, founded by George Fox in the 17th century

qualification *NOUN* **qualifications**
❶ a skill or ability to do a job ❷ an examination you have passed or a course you have completed that shows you have a skill or ability

qualify *VERB* **qualifies**, **qualifying**, **qualified**
❶ to qualify for something such as a job is to be suitable for it or show you have gained the abilities you need to do it • *She qualified as a doctor last year.* ❷ to qualify for a competition is to reach a high enough standard to take part in it

quality *NOUN* **qualities**
❶ the quality of something is how good or bad it is ❷ what something is like • *The paper had a shiny quality.*

quantity *NOUN* **quantities**
how much there is of something, or how many things there are of one sort

quarantine (*say* kwo-ran-teen) *NOUN*
quarantine is a period when a person or animal is kept apart from others to prevent a disease from spreading

quarrel *NOUN* **quarrels**
a strong or angry argument

quarrel *VERB* **quarrels**, **quarrelling**, **quarrelled**
to quarrel with someone is to argue fiercely with them

quarrelsome *ADJECTIVE*
fond of quarrelling or often quarrelling

quarry *NOUN* **quarries**
❶ a place where stone or slate is dug out of the ground ❷ an animal that is being hunted

quart (*say* kwort) *NOUN* **quarts**
a measure of liquid, a quarter of a gallon or about 1.136 litres

quarter *NOUN* **quarters**
❶ each of four equal parts into which something is divided or can be divided ❷ three months, one-fourth of a year
➤ **at close quarters** close together • *They fought at close quarters.*

quarters *PLURAL NOUN*
where someone lives for a time; lodgings

quartet (*say* kwor-**tet**) *NOUN* **quartets**
❶ a group of four musicians ❷ a piece of music for four musicians

quartz (*say* kworts) *NOUN*
quartz is a hard mineral, used in making accurate electronic watches and clocks

quaver *VERB* **quavers**, **quavering**, **quavered**
to quaver is to tremble

quaver *NOUN* **quavers**
❶ a trembling sound ❷ a musical note equal to half a crotchet, written (♪)

quay (*say* kee) *NOUN* **quays**
a harbour wall or pier where ships can be tied up for loading and unloading

queasy *ADJECTIVE* **queasier**, **queasiest**
you feel queasy when you feel slightly sick

queen *NOUN* **queens**
❶ a woman who has been crowned as the ruler of a country ❷ a king's wife ❸ a female bee or ant that produces eggs ❹ a piece in chess, the most powerful on the board ❺ a playing card with a picture of a queen

queer *ADJECTIVE* **queerer**, **queerest**
❶ strange or odd ❷ (*old use*) ill or unwell • *I feel a bit queer.*

quench *VERB* **quenches**, **quenching**, **quenched**
❶ to quench your thirst is to drink until you are not thirsty any more ❷ to quench a fire is to put it out

query (*say* **kweer**-ee) *NOUN* **queries**
❶ a question ❷ a question mark

query *VERB* **queries**, **querying**, **queried**
to query something is to question whether it is true or correct

quest *NOUN* **quests**
a long search, especially for something precious or valuable
'Is this a proper quest we are on?' asked Tootles. 'A person could get killed!'–PETER PAN, J. M. Barrie

question *NOUN* **questions**
❶ something you ask • *I will try to answer your question.* ❷ a problem or subject for discussion • *The question is, where can we go on holiday?*
➤ **to be out of the question** is to be impossible or not even worth considering

question *VERB* **questions**, **questioning**, **questioned**
❶ to question someone is to ask them questions ❷ to question something is to be doubtful about it

questionable *ADJECTIVE*
causing doubt; not certainly true or correct

question mark *NOUN* **question marks**
the punctuation mark (?) put at the end of a question

questionnaire (*say* kwes-chon-**air**) *NOUN* **questionnaires**
a set of questions asked to get information for a survey

queue (*say* kew) *NOUN* **queues**
❶ a line of people or vehicles waiting for something ❷ (*in computing*) a list of tasks waiting to be dealt with, for example a list of documents waiting to be printed

queue (*say* kew) *VERB* **queues**, **queueing**, **queued**
people queue, or queue up, when they wait in a queue

quibble *VERB* **quibbles**, **quibbling**, **quibbled**
to quibble is to argue or complain about minor details

quibble *NOUN* **quibbles**
a quibble is a trivial complaint or objection

quiche (*say* keesh) *NOUN* **quiches**
an open tart with a savoury filling

quick *ADJECTIVE* **quicker**, **quickest**
❶ taking only a short time • *You were quick.* ❷ done in a short time • *She gave a quick answer.* ❸ able to learn or think quickly
➤ **quickly** *ADVERB*

quicken *VERB* **quickens**, **quickening**, **quickened**
❶ to quicken something is to make it quicker • *She quickened her pace.* ❷ to quicken is to become quicker

quicksand *NOUN* **quicksands**
quicksand is an area of loose wet sand that sucks in anything that falls into it

quick-witted *ADJECTIVE*
able to think quickly

quid *NOUN* **quid** (*informal*)
a pound (£1)

quiet *ADJECTIVE* **quieter**, **quietest**
❶ silent ❷ not loud • *He spoke in a quiet voice.* ❸ calm and peaceful • *They lead a quiet life.*
➤ **quietly** *ADVERB*

quiet *NOUN*
quiet is a time when it is calm and peaceful • *Let's have a bit of quiet now.*

quieten *VERB* **quietens**, **quietening**, **quietened**
❶ to quieten something or someone is to make them quiet ❷ to quieten is to become quiet

quill *NOUN* **quills**
❶ a bird's quills are its large feathers ❷ a pen made from a large feather ❸ a porcupine's quills are its long spines

quilt *NOUN* **quilts**
a thick soft cover for a bed

quince *NOUN*
a hard pear-shaped fruit used for making jam
They dined on mince, and slices of quince, Which they ate with a runcible spoon.—THE OWL AND THE PUSSYCAT, Edward Lear

quintet *NOUN* **quintets**
❶ a group of five musicians ❷ a piece of music for five musicians

quirk *NOUN* **quirks**
a peculiar way of behaving or working • *This old computer is full of quirks.*
➤ **quirky** *ADJECTIVE*

quit *VERB* **quits**, **quitting**, **quitted** *or* **quit**
❶ to quit something is to leave or abandon it ❷ (*informal*) to quit doing something is to stop it • *Quit teasing him!*

quite *ADVERB*
❶ rather or fairly • *He's quite a good swimmer.* ❷ completely or entirely • *I am quite all right.*

quiver *VERB* **quivers**, **quivering**, **quivered**
to quiver is to tremble
'Mr Stewart,' said I, in a voice that quivered like a fiddlestring, 'you are older than I am, and should know your manners.'—KIDNAPPED, Robert Louis Stevenson

quiver *NOUN* **quivers**
❶ a quiver is a tremble • *There was a quiver in her voice.* ❷ a quiver is also a container for arrows

quiz *NOUN* **quizzes**
a series of questions, especially as an entertainment or competition

quiz *VERB* **quizzes**, **quizzing**, **quizzed**
to quiz someone is to ask them a lot of questions

quota (*say* kwoh-ta) *NOUN* **quotas**
a fixed share or amount • *Each school has its quota of equipment.*

quotation *NOUN* **quotations**
❶ quotation is the action of repeating words that were first written or spoken by someone else ❷ a quotation is a set of words taken from a book or speech

quotation marks *PLURAL NOUN*
inverted commas, used to mark a quotation (*compare* **speech marks**)

quote *VERB* **quotes**, **quoting**, **quoted**
❶ to quote words is to use them in a quotation ❷ to quote someone is to quote words first used by them

Rr

rabbi (*say* rah-by) *NOUN* **rabbis**
a Jewish religious leader

rabbit *NOUN* **rabbits**
a furry animal with long ears that digs burrows

rabid (*say* rab-id) *ADJECTIVE*
❶ a rabid animal is affected with rabies
❷ you can say someone is rabid when they are fiercely enthusiastic about something

rabies (*say* ray-beez) *NOUN*
rabies is a fatal disease involving madness that affects dogs and cats and can be passed to humans

raccoon *NOUN* **raccoons**
a small North American meat-eating animal with grey-brown fur and a bushy, striped tail

race *NOUN* **races**
❶ a competition to be the first to reach a particular place or to do something ❷ a large group of people who have the same ancestors, and share certain physical features such as the colour of their skin and hair

race *VERB* **races, racing, raced**
❶ to race someone is to have a race against them • *I'll race you to the end of the road.*
❷ to race is to move very fast • *The other cyclists raced ahead.*
➤ **racer** *NOUN*

racecourse *NOUN* **racecourses**
a place where horse races are run

racial *ADJECTIVE*
to do with a person's race or with different races

racism (*say* ray-sizm) *NOUN*
racism is believing that one race of people is better than all the others and treating people badly and unfairly because they belong to a different race

racist *NOUN* **racists**
someone who treats other people badly and unfairly because they belong to a different race

racist *ADJECTIVE*
a racist attitude or remark is one that shows racism

rack *NOUN* **racks**
❶ a framework used as a shelf or container • *a plate rack* ❷ an ancient device for torturing people by stretching them

rack *VERB* **racks, racking, racked**
➤ **to rack your brains** is to think hard to remember something or solve a problem

racket *NOUN* **rackets**
❶ a bat with strings stretched across a frame, used in tennis and similar games ❷ a racket is also a loud noise or din • *Stop making that racket!* ❸ (*informal*) a dishonest or illegal business

radar (*say* ray-dar) *NOUN*
radar is a system that uses radio waves to show the position of ships or aircraft which cannot otherwise be seen
DID YOU KNOW? The word **radar** comes from the first letters of *radio detection and ranging.*

radiant *ADJECTIVE*
❶ radiating light or heat ❷ you can say someone is radiant when they look happy and beautiful
➤ **radiance** *NOUN* ➤ **radiantly** *ADVERB*

radiate *VERB* **radiates, radiating, radiated**
❶ to radiate heat, light or other energy is to send it out in rays ❷ to radiate is to spread out like the spokes of a wheel • *The city's streets radiate from the central square.*

radiation *NOUN*
❶ radiation is heat, light or other energy given out by something ❷ radiation is also energy or particles sent out by something radioactive

radiator *NOUN* **radiators**
❶ a device that gives out heat, especially a metal container through which steam or hot water flows ❷ a device that cools the engine of a motor vehicle

radical *ADJECTIVE*
❶ thorough and complete; going right to the roots of something • *The new head teacher made radical changes.* ❷ wanting to make changes or reforms • *He is a radical politician.*
➤ **radically** *ADVERB*

radical *NOUN* **radicals**
someone who is radical

radii *NOUN* (*plural of* **radius**)

radio *NOUN* **radios**
❶ radio is sending or receiving sound by means of electrical waves ❷ a radio is an apparatus for receiving broadcast sound programmes, or for receiving and sending messages

radioactive *ADJECTIVE*
radioactive substances have atoms that break up and send out radiation which produces electrical and chemical effects
➤ **radioactivity** *NOUN*

radish *NOUN* **radishes**
a small hard red vegetable with a hot taste, eaten raw in salads

radius *NOUN* **radii**
❶ a straight line from the centre of a circle to the circumference ❷ the length of this line

raffle *NOUN* **raffles**
a way of raising money by selling numbered tickets, some of which win prizes

raffle *VERB* **raffles, raffling, raffled**
to raffle something is to give it as a prize in a raffle

raft *NOUN* **rafts**
a floating platform of logs or barrels tied together

rafter *NOUN* **rafters**
each of the long sloping pieces of wood that hold up a roof

rag *NOUN* **rags**
❶ an old or torn piece of cloth ❷ to be dressed in rags is to be wearing very old, torn clothes

rage *NOUN* **rages**
great or violent anger
➤ **to be all the rage** (*informal*) is to be very fashionable or popular

rage *VERB* **rages, raging, raged**
❶ to rage is to be very angry ❷ to rage is also to be violent or noisy
The storm was raging outside. Rain lashed against the windows, the wind howled through the telegraph wires.—GRANNY NOTHING, Catherine MacPhail

ragged (*say* **rag**-id) *ADJECTIVE*
❶ torn or frayed • *a girl dressed in ragged clothes* ❷ not smooth; uneven • *They gave a ragged performance.*

raid *NOUN* **raids**
❶ a sudden attack ❷ an unexpected visit from police to search a place or arrest people

raid *VERB* **raids, raiding, raided**
to raid a place is to make a raid on it
➤ **raider** *NOUN*

rail *NOUN* **rails**
❶ a bar or rod that you can hang things on or that form part of a fence or banisters ❷ a long metal strip that is part of a railway track
➤ **by rail** on a train

railings *PLURAL NOUN*
a fence made of metal bars

railway *NOUN* **railways**
❶ the parallel metal strips that trains travel on ❷ a system of transport using rails

rain *NOUN*
rain is drops of water that fall from the sky

rain *VERB* **rains, raining, rained**
❶ to rain is to come down like rain • *After the explosion, fragments of glass rained on them from above.* ❷ to rain something is to send it down like rain • *They rained blows on him.*
➤ **it is raining** when rain is falling

rainbow *NOUN* **rainbows**
a curved band of colours that you can sometimes see in the sky when the sun shines through rain

raincoat *NOUN* **raincoats**
a waterproof coat

raindrop *NOUN* **raindrops**
a single drop of rain

rainfall *NOUN*
rainfall is the amount of rain that falls in a particular place or time

rainforest *NOUN* **rainforests**
a dense tropical forest in an area of very heavy rainfall

raise *VERB* **raises, raising, raised**
❶ to raise something is to move it to a higher place or to an upright position ❷ to raise an amount or number is to increase it • *Mum said she'd raise my pocket money soon.* ❸ to raise

money is to succeed in collecting it • *They raised £1,000 for Sports Relief.* ❹ to raise your voice is to speak loudly ❺ to raise a subject or idea is to mention it for people to think about ❻ to raise young children is to bring them up and educate them ❼ to raise animals is to breed them ❽ to raise a laugh or smile is to make people laugh or smile

raisin *NOUN* **raisins**
a dried grape

rake *NOUN* **rakes**
a gardening tool with a row of short spikes fixed to a long handle

rake *VERB* **rakes**, **raking**, **raked**
❶ to rake something is to move it or smooth it with a rake ❷ to rake, or rake around, is to search • *I raked around in my desk for the letter.*

rally *NOUN* **rallies**
❶ a large public meeting ❷ a competition to test skill in driving ❸ a series of strokes and return strokes of the ball in tennis or squash

rally *VERB* **rallies**, **rallying**, **rallied**
❶ to rally people is to bring them together for a united effort ❷ to rally, or rally round, is to come together to support someone ❸ to rally is to revive or recover after an illness or setback • *The team rallied when they realized they could win.*

RAM *(say* ram*) ABBREVIATION*
short for *random-access memory*, a type of computer memory with parts that can be located directly

ram *NOUN* **rams**
a male sheep

ram *VERB* **rams**, **ramming**, **rammed**
to ram something is to push one thing hard against another

Ramadan *(say* ram-a-**dan***) NOUN*
Ramadan is the ninth month of the Muslim year, when Muslims do not eat or drink during the day

ramble *NOUN* **rambles**
a long walk in the country

ramble *VERB* **rambles**, **rambling**, **rambled**
❶ to ramble is to go for a long walk in the country ❷ to ramble is also to say a lot without keeping to a subject
➤ **rambler** *NOUN*

ramp *NOUN* **ramps**
a slope joining two different levels

rampage *(say* ram-**payj***) VERB* **rampages**, **rampaging**, **rampaged**
to rampage is to rush about wildly or violently

rampage *NOUN*
➤ **to go on the rampage** is to rush about violently

ran *VERB (past tense of* **run***)*
• *I panicked and ran off.*

ranch *NOUN* **ranches**
a large cattle farm, especially in North America or Australia
➤ **rancher** a person who owns or runs a ranch

random *NOUN*
➤ **at random** by chance; without any purpose or plan

random *ADJECTIVE*
done or taken at random • *They took a random sample.*

rang *VERB (past tense of* **ring***)*
• *My mobile rang again.*

range *NOUN* **ranges**
❶ a collection of different things of the same type • *The shop sells a wide range of games and puzzles.* ❷ the limits of something, from the highest to the lowest • *Most of the children here are in the 8-11 age range.* ❸ a line of hills or mountains ❹ the distance that a gun can shoot, or an aircraft can fly, or a sound can be heard ❺ a place with targets for shooting practice ❻ a kitchen fireplace with ovens

range *VERB* **ranges**, **ranging**, **ranged**
❶ to range between two limits is to extend from one to the other • *Prices ranged from £1 to £50.* ❷ to range people or things is to arrange them in a line • *Crowds were ranged along the streets, hoping to see the King go by.* ❸ to range is to wander or move over a wide area • *Hens ranged all over the farm.*

ranger *NOUN* **rangers**
❶ someone who looks after a park or forest ❷ a mounted police officer in a remote area

a b c d e f g h i j k l m n o p q r s t u v w x y z

rank *NOUN* **ranks**
❶ a position in a series of people or things
• *He was promoted to the rank of captain.*
❷ a line of people or things

rank *VERB* **ranks**, **ranking**, **ranked**
to rank is to have a certain rank or place
• *She ranks among the greatest writers.*

ransack *VERB* **ransacks**, **ransacking**, **ransacked**
to ransack a place is to search it thoroughly, looking for something to steal, and leave it in a mess

ransom *NOUN* **ransoms**
money paid so that someone who has been kidnapped can be set free
➤ **to hold someone to ransom** is to keep them prisoner and demand a ransom

ransom *VERB* **ransoms**, **ransoming**, **ransomed**
to ransom someone who has been kidnapped is to free them by paying a ransom

rap *VERB* **raps**, **rapping**, **rapped**
to rap is to knock quickly and loudly

rap *NOUN* **raps**
❶ a rap is a rapping movement or sound
❷ rap is a kind of pop music in which you speak words rapidly in rhythm

rapid *ADJECTIVE*
moving or working at speed
➤ **rapidity** *NOUN* ➤ **rapidly** *ADVERB*

rapids *PLURAL NOUN*
part of a river where the water flows very fast

rapper *NOUN* **rappers**
someone who performs rap music

rare *ADJECTIVE* **rarer**, **rarest**
unusual; not often found or experienced
• *She died of a rare disease.*

rarely *ADVERB*
something happens rarely when it doesn't happen very often

rarity *NOUN* **rarities**
a rarity is a person or thing that is unusual

rascal *NOUN* **rascals**
a dishonest or mischievous person

rash *ADJECTIVE* **rasher**, **rashest**
you are rash when you do something quickly without thinking properly about it

By the time Hallowe'en arrived, Harry was regretting his rash promise to go to the Deathday Party.
—HARRY POTTER AND THE CHAMBER OF SECRETS, J. K. Rowling

rash *NOUN* **rashes**
❶ an outbreak of red spots or patches on the skin ❷ a number of unwelcome things happening about the same time • *A late winter storm caused a rash of accidents in the city.*

rasher *NOUN* **rashers**
a slice of bacon

raspberry *NOUN* **raspberries**
a small soft red fruit

Rastafarian (*say* ras-ta-**fair**-i-an) *NOUN* **Rastafarians**
a member of a religious group that started in Jamaica

rat *NOUN* **rats**
❶ an animal like a large mouse ❷ you can describe a nasty or treacherous person as a rat

rate *NOUN* **rates**
❶ how fast or how often something happens
• *The seedlings grow at a fast rate.* ❷ a charge or payment • *What is the rate for next-day delivery?*
➤ **at any rate** anyway • *I don't want to go, not yet at any rate.*

rate *VERB* **rates**, **rating**, **rated**
to rate something or someone is to regard them in a certain way or as having a certain value
• *The reviews rate the film very highly.* • *He is rated as one of the top players.*

rather *ADVERB*
❶ slightly; somewhat • *It was getting rather dark.* ❷ you would rather do one thing than another thing if you would prefer to do it
• *I think I'd rather do this later.* ❸ more truly or correctly • *He looked, or rather stared, in our direction.*

ratio (*say* **ray**-shi-oh) *NOUN* **ratios**
the relationship between two numbers; how many times one number goes into another
• *In a group of 2 girls and 10 boys, the ratio of girls to boys is 1 to 5.*

ration (*say* **rash**-on) *NOUN* **rations**
the amount of something one person is allowed to have

ration (*say* rash-on) *VERB* **rations, rationing, rationed**
to ration something is to give it out in fixed amounts because there is not a lot of it to share

rational (*say* rash-o-nal) *ADJECTIVE*
reasonable or sensible • *No rational person would do such a thing.*
➤ **rationally** *ADVERB*

rattle *VERB* **rattles, rattling, rattled**
❶ to rattle is to make a series of short sharp hard sounds ❷ to rattle something is to make it rattle ❸ (*informal*) to rattle someone is to make them nervous and confused

rattle *NOUN* **rattles**
❶ a rattling sound ❷ a baby's toy that rattles

rattlesnake *NOUN* **rattlesnakes**
a poisonous American snake that makes rattling sounds with its tail

rave *VERB* **raves, raving, raved**
❶ to be raving is to be talking wildly ❷ to rave about something is to talk very enthusiastically about it

raven *NOUN* **ravens**
a large black bird

ravenous (*say* rav-e-nus) *ADJECTIVE*
very hungry
➤ **ravenously** *ADVERB*

ravine (*say* ra-veen) *NOUN* **ravines**
a very deep narrow gorge

ravioli *NOUN*
ravioli is small squares of pasta filled with meat and vegetables and served with a sauce

raw *ADJECTIVE* **rawer, rawest**
❶ raw food is not cooked ❷ raw (for example) cotton or sugar is in its natural state before being processed • *What raw materials do you need?* ❸ you can say someone is raw when they don't have any experience • *a squad of raw recruits* ❹ with the skin removed • *The fox had a raw wound on its leg.* ❺ cold and damp • *There was a raw wind.*

ray *NOUN* **rays**
❶ a thin line of light, heat or other energy ❷ a large sea fish with a flat body and a long tail

razor *NOUN* **razors**
a device with a very sharp blade, used for shaving

reach *VERB* **reaches, reaching, reached**
❶ to reach a place is to go as far as it and arrive there ❷ to reach, or reach out, is to stretch out your hand to get or touch something

reach *NOUN* **reaches**
❶ the distance you can reach with your hand ❷ a distance that you can easily travel • *Mars is now within reach of human spacecraft.*

react *VERB* **reacts, reacting, reacted**
to react is to act in response to another person or thing

reaction *NOUN* **reactions**
an action or feeling caused by another person or thing

reactor *NOUN* **reactors**
an apparatus for producing nuclear power

read *VERB* **reads, reading, read**
❶ to read something written or printed is to look at it and understand it or say it aloud ❷ a gauge or instrument reads a certain amount when that is what it shows • *The thermometer reads 20°.*

readable *ADJECTIVE*
❶ a readable book is enjoyable to read ❷ readable writing is clear and easy to read

reader *NOUN* **readers**
❶ someone who reads ❷ a book that helps you learn to read

readily *ADVERB*
❶ willingly or eagerly • *She readily agreed to help.* ❷ quickly and without any difficulty • *All the ingredients you need are readily available.*

readiness *NOUN*
readiness is being ready for something

reading *NOUN* **readings**
❶ reading is the action of reading a book, magazine or newspaper ❷ a reading is an amount shown on a gauge or instrument

ready *ADJECTIVE* **readier, readiest**
❶ able or willing to do something or to be used at once; prepared ❷ quick • *He always has ready answers.*

➤ **at the ready** ready for action or ready to be used

ready-made *ADJECTIVE*
made already, and not made specially

real *ADJECTIVE*
❶ true or existing; not imaginary ❷ genuine; not a copy • *Are those pearls real?*

realism *NOUN*
realism is seeing or showing things as they really are

realist *NOUN* **realists**
someone who tries to see things as they really are

realistic *ADJECTIVE*
❶ true to life • *It is a very realistic painting.*
❷ seeing things as they really are • *She is realistic about her chances of winning.*
➤ **realistically** *ADVERB* you say realistically when you are talking about what you think can actually be achieved • *Realistically, I don't think we have much hope of winning.*

reality *NOUN* **realities**
❶ reality is what is real ❷ a reality is something that is real • *Cold and hunger are the realities of living on the street.*

realize (*also* **realise**) *VERB* **realizes, realizing, realized**
to realize something is to understand it or accept that it is true • *We began to realize that something was wrong.*
➤ **realization** *NOUN*

really *ADVERB*
truly; certainly; in fact • *Is the story really true?*
• *I really love your new hairstyle!*

realm (*say* relm) *NOUN* **realms**
❶ a kingdom ❷ an area of knowledge or activity

reap *VERB* **reaps, reaping, reaped**
❶ to reap corn is to cut it down and gather it in when it is ripe ❷ to reap a benefit is to gain it

reappear *VERB* **reappears, reappearing, reappeared**
to reappear is to appear again
➤ **reappearance** *NOUN*

rear *ADJECTIVE*
placed or found at the back • *They left the building by the rear exit.*

rear *NOUN* **rears**
the back part of something

rear *VERB* **rears, rearing, reared**
❶ to rear young children or animals is to bring them up or help them grow ❷ a horse or other animal rears, or rears up, when it rises up on its hind legs so that its front legs are in the air

rearrange *VERB* **rearranges, rearranging, rearranged**
to rearrange something is to arrange it differently
➤ **rearrangement** *NOUN*

reason *NOUN* **reasons**
❶ the reason for something is why it happens ❷ reason is thinking in a clear and logical way • *He wouldn't listen to reason.*

reason *VERB* **reasons, reasoning, reasoned**
❶ to reason is to think in a logical way ❷ to reason with someone is to try to persuade them of something

reasonable *ADJECTIVE*
❶ sensible or logical ❷ fair or moderate • *These are reasonable prices for what you get.*

reasonably *ADVERB*
❶ in a reasonable way; sensibly • *I didn't expect my parents to act reasonably.*
❷ fairly; somewhat
It had taken Mildred several weeks of falling off and crashing before she could ride the broomstick reasonably well.—THE WORST WITCH, Jill Murphy

reassure *VERB* **reassures, reassuring, reassured**
to reassure someone is to take away their doubts or fears
➤ **reassurance** *NOUN*

rebel (*say* ri-bel) *VERB* **rebels, rebelling, rebelled**
to rebel is to refuse to obey someone in authority, especially the government

rebel (*say* reb-el) *NOUN* **rebels**
someone who refuses to obey or fights against someone in authority

rebellion *NOUN* **rebellions**
❶ rebellion is when people refuse to obey or fight against someone in authority

❷ a rebellion is a fight against someone in authority, especially the government

rebellious *ADJECTIVE*
someone is rebellious when they refuse to obey authority or are likely to rebel

rebound *VERB* rebounds, rebounding, rebounded
to bounce back after hitting something

rebuild *VERB* rebuilds, rebuilding, rebuilt
to rebuild something is to build it again after it has been destroyed

recall *VERB* recalls, recalling, recalled
❶ to recall someone or something is to remember them ❷ to recall someone is to tell them to come back

recap *VERB* recaps, recapping, recapped
(*informal*)
to recap is to summarize what has been said

recapture *VERB* recaptures, recapturing, recaptured
to recapture something or someone is to capture them again, especially after they have escaped

recede *VERB* recedes, receding, receded
❶ to recede is to go back • *The floods have receded.* ❷ a person's hair is receding when they start to go bald at the front of their head

receipt (*say* ri-**seet**) *NOUN* receipts
❶ a receipt is a written statement saying that a payment has been received or goods have been delivered ❷ receipt is receiving something

receive *VERB* receives, receiving, received
❶ to receive something is to get it when it is given or sent to you • *Did you receive my email?* ❷ to receive an injury is to experience or suffer it ❸ to receive visitors is to greet them formally

receiver *NOUN* receivers
❶ someone who receives something ❷ a part of a radio or satellite that receives signals ❸ the part of a telephone that you hold to your ear

recent *ADJECTIVE*
made or happening a short time ago

recently *ADVERB*
something happened recently when it happened only a short time ago

receptacle *NOUN* receptacles
something for holding what is put into it; a container

reception *NOUN* receptions
❶ the sort of welcome that someone gets • *We were given a friendly reception.* ❷ a formal party to receive guests • *a wedding reception* ❸ a place in a hotel or office where visitors report or check in ❹ the quality of the signals your radio or television set receives • *We don't get good reception here.*

receptionist *NOUN* receptionists
someone whose job is to receive and welcome visitors to a hotel or office

recess *NOUN* recesses
❶ an alcove ❷ a time when work or business is stopped for a while

recession *NOUN* recessions
a reduction in trade or in the wealth of a country

recipe (*say* ress-i-pee) *NOUN* recipes
a list of ingredients and instructions for preparing or cooking food

recital (*say* ri-sy-tal) *NOUN* recitals
a performance of music or poetry by a small number of people

recite *VERB* recites, reciting, recited
to recite something such as a poem is to say it aloud

reckless *ADJECTIVE*
someone is reckless when they do things without thinking or caring about what might happen
➤ recklessly *ADVERB* ➤ recklessness *NOUN*

reckon *VERB* reckons, reckoning, reckoned
❶ to reckon something is to calculate or count it ❷ to reckon something is to think it or have an opinion about it • *I reckon it's about to rain.*

reclaim *VERB* reclaims, reclaiming, reclaimed
❶ to reclaim land is to make it suitable for farming or building on again by clearing

a b c d e f g h i j k l m n o p q r s t u v w x y z

or draining it ❷ to reclaim something is to get it back, especially after losing it • *I reclaimed my umbrella from the lost property office.*

recline *VERB* **reclines, reclining, reclined**
to lean or lie back

recognition *NOUN*
recognizing someone or something • *When he saw me, a smile of recognition appeared on his face.*

recognize (*also* **recognise**) *VERB* **recognizes, recognizing, recognized**
❶ to recognize someone or something is to know who they are because you have seen them before • *I thought I recognized your face.* ❷ to recognize a fault or mistake is to admit to it
➤ **recognizable** *ADJECTIVE*

recoil *VERB* **recoils, recoiling, recoiled**
to recoil is to move backwards suddenly • *He recoiled in horror.*

recollect *VERB* **recollects, recollecting, recollected**
to recollect something is to remember it

recollection *NOUN* **recollections**
❶ recollection is being able to remember something • *I have no recollection of seeing her before.* ❷ a recollection is something you remember

recommend *VERB* **recommends, recommending, recommended**
❶ to recommend something is to suggest it because you think it is good or suitable • *I recommend the strawberry ice cream.* ❷ to recommend an action is to advise someone to do it • *We recommend that you wear strong shoes on the walk.*
➤ **recommendation** *NOUN*

reconcile *VERB* **reconciles, reconciling, reconciled**
❶ to be reconciled with someone is to become friendly with them again after quarrelling or fighting with them ❷ you are reconciled to something when you are persuaded to accept or put up with it • *He became reconciled to the fact that he would never see her again.*
➤ **reconciliation** *NOUN*

reconstruction *NOUN* **reconstructions**
❶ reconstruction is building something up again ❷ a reconstruction is acting out an event that took place in the past • *They did a reconstruction of the bank robbery.*

record (*say* rek-ord) *NOUN* **records**
❶ a vinyl disc with recorded sound on it ❷ the best performance in a sport or the most remarkable event of its kind • *She broke the record for swimming 100 metres.* ❸ a set of facts or information about something that you write down and keep • *Keep a record of all the birds you see in the garden.*

record (*say* ri-**kord**) *VERB* **records, recording, recorded**
❶ to record music or sound or a television programme is to store it on a disk or computer ❷ to record things that have happened is to put them down in writing
➤ **recordings** *PLURAL NOUN*

recorder *NOUN* **recorders**
❶ a machine for recording sounds and pictures, usually with a microphone and camera ❷ a wooden musical instrument that you play by blowing into one end and covering holes with your fingers ❸ someone who records something

record player *NOUN* **record players**
a machine that plays vinyl records

recount *VERB* **recount, recounting, recounted**
to tell someone about something true that has happened • *We recounted our adventures.*

recover *VERB* **recovers, recovering, recovered**
❶ to recover is to get better after being ill ❷ to recover something is to get it back after losing it

recovery *NOUN*
❶ you make a recovery when you get better after being ill ❷ the recovery of something is getting it back after it was lost

recreation *NOUN* **recreations**
a game, hobby or other enjoyable pastime you do in your spare time
➤ **recreational** *ADJECTIVE*

A
B
C
D
E
F
G
H
I
J
K
L
M
N
O
P
Q
R
S
T
U
V
W
X
Y
Z

recruit *NOUN* **recruits**
someone who has just joined the armed forces or a business or club

recruit *VERB* **recruits**, **recruiting**, **recruited**
to recruit someone is to get them to join something you belong to

rectangle *NOUN* **rectangles**
a shape with four straight sides and four right angles
➤ **rectangular** *ADJECTIVE*

rectify *VERB* **rectifies**, **rectifying**, **rectified**
to rectify something is to correct it or put it right • *I will rectify this error immediately.*

recuperate *VERB* **recuperates**, **recuperating**, **recuperated**
to recuperate is to get better after you have been ill

recur *VERB* **recurs**, **recurring**, **recurred**
something recurs when it happens again
➤ **recurrence** *NOUN*

recycle *VERB* **recycles**, **recycling**, **recycled**
to recycle waste material is to treat it so that it can be used again • *Waste paper can be recycled to make cardboard.*

red *ADJECTIVE* **redder**, **reddest**
❶ of the colour of blood ❷ red hair is orange-brown in colour

red *NOUN* **reds**
a red colour
➤ **to see red** is to become suddenly angry

redden *VERB* **reddens**, **reddening**, **reddened**
to redden is to become red • *He reddened with embarrassment.*

reddish *ADJECTIVE*
fairly red

redeem *VERB* **redeems**, **redeeming**, **redeemed**
❶ to redeem something is to get it back by paying for it or handing over a voucher ❷ to redeem yourself is to do something good to make up for an earlier mistake ❸ to redeem someone is to save them from evil, as in some religions

redemption *NOUN*
redemption is redeeming or saving someone

red-handed *ADJECTIVE*
➤ **to catch someone red-handed** is to catch them while they are actually committing a crime or doing something wrong

redhead *NOUN* **redheads**
a person with reddish-brown hair

red herring *NOUN* **red herrings**
something that takes attention away from the real point or answer; a false clue

reduce *VERB* **reduces**, **reducing**, **reduced**
❶ to reduce something is to make it smaller or less ❷ to be reduced to something is to be forced to do it • *He was reduced to asking for more money.*

reduction *NOUN* **reductions**
❶ there is a reduction in something when it becomes smaller or less ❷ the amount by which something is reduced • *They gave us a reduction of £5.*

redundant *ADJECTIVE*
❶ to be redundant is to be no longer needed ❷ someone is made redundant when they lose their job because it is no longer needed
➤ **redundancy** *NOUN*

reed *NOUN* **reeds**
❶ a plant that grows in or near water ❷ a thin strip that vibrates to make the sound in some wind instruments, such as a clarinet, saxophone or oboe

reef *NOUN* **reefs**
a line of rocks or sand near the surface of the sea

reef knot *NOUN* **reef knots**
a symmetrical double knot for tying two cords together

reek *VERB* **reeks**, **reeking**, **reeked**
to reek is to have a strong unpleasant smell

reel *NOUN* **reels**
❶ a round device on which cotton or thread is wound ❷ a lively Scottish dance

reel *VERB* **reels**, **reeling**, **reeled**
to stagger • *He reeled back in shock.*
➤ **to reel something off** is to say a lot very quickly

refer *VERB* **refers**, **referring**, **referred**
❶ to refer to someone or something is to mention them or speak about them ❷ to refer

a
b
c
d
e
f
g
h
i
j
k
l
m
n
o
p
q
r
s
t
u
v
w
x
y
z

to (for example) a dictionary is to look at it so that you can find something out ❸ to refer a question or problem to someone else is to give it to them to deal with

referee *NOUN* **referees**
someone who makes sure that people keep to the rules of a game

referee *VERB* **referees, refereeing, refereed**
to referee a game is to act as referee in it

reference *NOUN* **references**
❶ a mention of something ❷ a place in a book or file where information can be found ❸ a description of the work someone has done and how well they have done it, used especially when someone is applying for a job
➤ **in** *or* **with reference to something** *or* **someone** concerning them or about them

referendum (*say* ref-er-en-dum) *NOUN* **referendums** *or* **referenda**
a vote on a particular question by all the people in a country

refill *VERB* **refills, refilling, refilled**
to refill something is to fill it again

refill *NOUN* **refills**
a container used to replace something that has been used up • *My pen needs a refill.*

refine *VERB* **refines, refining, refined**
to refine something is to purify or improve it

refined *ADJECTIVE*
❶ refined (for example) sugar or oil has been made pure by taking other substances out of it ❷ someone is refined when they have good manners and are well educated

refinement *NOUN* **refinements**
❶ refinement is the process of refining something ❷ a refinement is something special that improves a thing

refinery *NOUN* **refineries**
a factory for refining a product, such as oil

reflect *VERB* **reflects, reflecting, reflected**
❶ something reflects light or heat or sound when it sends it back from a surface ❷ a mirror or other shiny surface reflects something when it forms an image of it ❸ you reflect on something when you think seriously about it

reflection *NOUN* **reflections**
the image you can see in a mirror or other shiny surface

reflective *ADJECTIVE*
❶ sending back light • *The bike has a reflective rear lamp.* ❷ suggesting or showing serious thought • *The music has a reflective quality.*

reflex (*say* ree-fleks) *NOUN* **reflexes**
a movement or action that you do without any conscious thought

reflex angle *NOUN* **reflex angles**
an angle of between 180 and 360 degrees

reform *VERB* **reforms, reforming, reformed**
❶ to reform a person or thing is to improve them by getting rid of their faults ❷ someone reforms when they improve their behaviour

reform *NOUN* **reforms**
❶ reform is changing something to improve it ❷ a reform is a change made for this reason
➤ **reformation** *NOUN*

reformer *NOUN* **reformers**
someone who makes reforms

refrain *VERB* **refrains, refraining, refrained**
to refrain from something is to keep yourself from doing it • *Please refrain from talking.*

refrain *NOUN* **refrains**
the refrain is the chorus of a song

refresh *VERB* **refreshes, refreshing, refreshed**
❶ to refresh someone who is tired is to make them feel fresh and strong again ❷ to refresh an internet page is to make the most recent information appear on it

refreshments *PLURAL NOUN*
food and drink

refrigerate *VERB* **refrigerates, refrigerating, refrigerated**
to refrigerate something is to chill it so that it keeps in good condition
➤ **refrigeration** *NOUN*

refrigerator *NOUN* **refrigerators**
a cabinet in which you can store food at a low temperature to keep it fresh

refuel *VERB* **refuels, refuelling, refuelled**
to refuel a ship or aircraft is to supply it with more fuel

refuge *NOUN* **refuges**
a place where someone can go to be safe from danger

refugee (*say* ref-yoo-**jee**) *NOUN* **refugees**
someone who has had to leave their home or country because of war or persecution or disaster

refund (*say* ri-**fund**) *VERB* **refunds, refunding, refunded**
to refund money is to pay it back

refund (*say* **ree**-fund) *NOUN* **refunds**
money that is paid back to you

refusal *NOUN* **refusals**
refusal, or a refusal, is when someone refuses something

refuse (*say* ri-**fewz**) *VERB* **refuses, refusing, refused**
to refuse something, or to do something, is to say that you will not accept it or do it
• *They refuse to help.*

refuse (*say* **ref**-yooss) *NOUN*
rubbish or waste material

regain *VERB* **regains, regaining, regained**
to regain something is to get it back

regard *VERB* **regards, regarding, regarded**
❶ to regard someone or something as something is to think of them in a certain way • *I regard her as a friend.* ❷ to regard someone or something is also to look at them closely

regard *NOUN*
regard is consideration or respect • *They acted without regard for our safety.*
➤ **with regard to something** about it; in connection with it

regarding *PREPOSITION*
on the subject of; about • *There are rules regarding use of the library.*

regardless *ADJECTIVE*
paying no attention to something • *Buy it, regardless of the cost.*

regards *PLURAL NOUN*
kind wishes you send in a message • *Give your parents my regards.*

regatta (*say* ri-**gat**-a) *NOUN* **regattas**
a meeting for boat or yacht races

reggae (*say* **reg**-ay) *NOUN*
a style of music with a strong beat, originally from Jamaica

regiment *NOUN* **regiments**
an army unit consisting of two or more battalions
➤ **regimental** *ADJECTIVE*

region *NOUN* **regions**
❶ a part of a country ❷ a part of the world
• *These plants only grow in tropical regions.*
➤ **regional** *ADJECTIVE* belonging to a particular region

register *NOUN* **registers**
❶ an official list of names or information, especially of people present each day at a school ❷ the range of a voice or musical instrument

register *VERB* **registers, registering, registered**
❶ to register something or someone is to put their name on an official list ❷ a gauge or instrument registers a certain amount when that is what it shows • *The thermometer registered 25°.* ❸ to register a letter or parcel is to have it officially recorded for sending with special care

registration *NOUN*
registration is making an official record of something

regret *NOUN* **regrets**
you feel regret when you feel sorry or sad about something

regret *VERB* **regrets, regretting, regretted**
to regret something is to feel sorry or sad about it

regretful *ADJECTIVE*
feeling sorry or sad about something
➤ **regretfully** *ADVERB*

regrettable *ADJECTIVE*
you say something is regrettable when you wish it hadn't happened

regular *ADJECTIVE*
❶ always happening at certain times
• *The pups have regular feeding times.*
❷ even or symmetrical • *a regular row*

of teeth **❸** a regular size is normal or average • *Do you want a regular or large popcorn?* **❹** a regular soldier belongs to a country's permanent army
➤ **regularity** NOUN ➤ **regularly** ADVERB

regulate VERB **regulates**, **regulating**, **regulated**
to regulate something is to adjust or control it

regulation NOUN **regulations**
❶ a regulation is a rule or law **❷** regulation is the adjusting or controlling of something

rehearsal NOUN **rehearsals**
a rehearsal is when you practise something before performing it

rehearse VERB **rehearses**, **rehearsing**, **rehearsed**
to rehearse (for example) a play or piece of music is to practise it before you perform it

rehome VERB **rehomes**, **rehoming**, **rehomed**
to rehome an animal is to find a new home for it as a pet

reign VERB **reigns**, **reigning**, **reigned**
❶ to reign is to be king or queen **❷** something reigns when it is the most noticeable or important thing • *Silence reigned for a while.*

reign NOUN **reigns**
the time when someone is king or queen

rein NOUN **reins**
a strap used by a rider to guide a horse

reindeer NOUN **reindeer**
a kind of deer that lives in Arctic regions

reinforce VERB **reinforces**, **reinforcing**, **reinforced**
to reinforce something is to strengthen it

reinforcement NOUN **reinforcements**
a thing that strengthens something
➤ **reinforcements** extra troops or equipment sent to strengthen a military force

reject (*say* ri-**jekt**) VERB **rejects**, **rejecting**, **rejected**
❶ to reject something or someone is to refuse to accept them • *They have rejected my offer of help.* **❷** to reject something is to get rid of it • *Faulty parts are rejected at the factory.*
➤ **rejection** NOUN

reject (*say* **ree**-jekt) NOUN **rejects**
a thing that is got rid of, especially because it is faulty or poorly made

rejoice VERB **rejoices**, **rejoicing**, **rejoiced**
to rejoice is to be very happy or pleased

relate VERB **relates**, **relating**, **related**
❶ things relate to each other when there is a connection between them **❷** to relate one thing with another is to compare them **❸** to relate a story is to tell it

related ADJECTIVE
❶ two people are related when they belong to the same family **❷** two things are related when they are connected or linked in some way

relation NOUN **relations**
❶ a relation is someone who is related to you **❷** relation is the way that one thing is connected or compared with another

relationship NOUN **relationships**
❶ the way people or things are connected with each other **❷** the way people get on with one another • *There is a good relationship between the teachers and the children.* **❸** a friendship or romantic involvement between two people

relative NOUN **relatives**
your relatives are the people who are related to you

relative ADJECTIVE
❶ connected or compared with something **❷** compared with the average • *They live in relative comfort.*

relatively ADVERB
compared with other people or things; more or less • *Books are relatively cheap.*

relative pronoun NOUN
relative pronouns
one of the words *who*, *what*, *which* or *that*, placed in front of a clause to connect it with an earlier clause. In the sentence *We saw the author who had written the book*, the relative pronoun is *who*.

relax VERB **relaxes**, **relaxing**, **relaxed**
❶ to relax is to become less anxious or worried **❷** to relax is also to rest or stop working **❸** to relax a part of you is make it less stiff or tense • *Try to relax your arm.*
➤ **relaxation** NOUN

relay *VERB* **relays, relaying, relayed**
to relay a message is to pass it on
relay *NOUN* **relays**
❶ a race between two teams in which each member of the team runs part of the distance ❷ a fresh group taking the place of another • *The firefighters worked in relays.*

release *VERB* **releases, releasing, released**
❶ to release something or someone is to set them free or unfasten them ❷ to release a film or record is to make it available to the public
release *NOUN* **releases**
❶ release is being released ❷ a release is something released, especially a new film or piece of recorded music ❸ a release is a device that unfastens something • *The seat belt has a quick release.*

relegate (*say* rel-i-gayt) *VERB* **relegates, relegating, relegated**
❶ a sports team is relegated when it goes down into a lower division of a league ❷ to relegate something is to put it into a lower group or position than before
➤ **relegation** *NOUN*

relent *VERB* **relents, relenting, relented**
to relent is to be less angry or severe than you were going to be

relentless *ADJECTIVE*
❶ never stopping or letting up • *Their criticism was relentless.* ❷ showing no pity • *They faced a relentless enemy.*
➤ **relentlessly** *ADVERB*

relevant (*say* rel-i-vant) *ADJECTIVE*
connected with what you are discussing or dealing with
➤ **relevance** *NOUN*

reliable *ADJECTIVE*
able to be trusted or depended on
➤ **reliability** *NOUN*
➤ **reliably** *ADVERB* you are reliably informed about something when you are told it by someone you trust

reliant *ADJECTIVE*
you are reliant on someone or something when you rely on them and cannot do without them
➤ **reliance** *NOUN*

relic *NOUN* **relics**
something that has survived from an ancient time

relief *NOUN* **reliefs**
❶ a good feeling you get because something unpleasant has stopped or is not going to happen • *It was such a relief when we reached dry land.* ❷ relief is the ending or lessening of pain or suffering ❸ aid given to people in need • *The charity is involved in famine relief.* ❹ a relief is also a person or thing that takes over or helps with a job ❺ relief is also a method of making a map or design that stands out from a flat surface • *The model shows hills and valleys in relief.*

relieve *VERB* **relieves, relieving, relieved**
to relieve pain or suffering is to end or lessen it
➤ **to relieve someone of something** is to take it from them

relieved *ADJECTIVE*
feeling good because something unpleasant has stopped or is not going to happen

religion *NOUN* **religions**
what people believe about God or gods, and how they worship

religious *ADJECTIVE*
❶ to do with religion ❷ someone is religious when they they believe in a religion and follow it carefully

religiously *ADVERB*
to do something religiously is to do it with great attention or care • *He wrote up his diary religiously every night.*

relish *VERB* **relishes, relishing, relished**
to relish something is to enjoy it very much
'A little nonsense now and then, is relished by the wisest men,' Mr Wonka said.—CHARLIE AND THE GREAT GLASS ELEVATOR, Roald Dahl
relish *NOUN* **relishes**
❶ great enjoyment • *The dogs ate the leftovers with relish.* ❷ a spicy sauce or pickle to add flavour to food

reluctant *ADJECTIVE*
you are reluctant to do something when you do not want to do it
➤ **reluctance** *NOUN* ➤ **reluctantly** *ADVERB*

a b c d e f g h i j k l m n o p q r s t u v w x y z

rely *VERB* relies, relying, relied
➤ **to rely on someone** *or* **something**
is to trust them or need them to help or
support you

remain *VERB* remains, remaining,
remained
❶ to remain is to continue in the same place
or condition • *It will remain cloudy all day.*
❷ to remain is also to be left over • *A lot of
food remained after the party.*

remainder *NOUN* remainders
❶ something left over ❷ (*mathematics*) the
amount that is left over when you divide one
number into another

remains *PLURAL NOUN*
❶ something left over ❷ ruins or relics
❸ a dead body

remark *VERB* remarks, remarking,
remarked
to remark on something is to say something
that you have thought or noticed

remark *NOUN* remarks
something you say

remarkable *ADJECTIVE*
so unusual or impressive that you notice or
remember it
➤ **remarkably** *ADVERB*

remedy *NOUN* remedies
a cure for an illness or problem

remedy *VERB* remedies, remedying,
remedied
to put something right

remember *VERB* remembers,
remembering, remembered
❶ to remember something is to keep it in
your mind, or bring it into your mind when
you need to ❷ to remember someone is to be
thinking about them

remembrance *NOUN*
you do something in remembrance of someone
or something when you do it as a way of
remembering them

remind *VERB* reminds, reminding,
reminded
to remind someone is to help or make them
remember something • *The girl in that painting
reminds me of you.*

reminder *NOUN* reminders
a reminder of a person or thing is something
that makes you think about or remember
them

reminisce (*say* rem-in-**iss**) *VERB* reminisces,
reminiscing, reminisced
to think or talk about things you remember
➤ **reminiscent** *ADJECTIVE* to be reminiscent
of something is to remind you of it
➤ **reminiscences** *PLURAL NOUN* a person's
memories of their past life

remnant *NOUN* remnants
a small piece of something left over

remorse *NOUN*
remorse is deep regret for something wrong
you have done

remorseful *ADJECTIVE*
feeling remorse
➤ **remorsefully** *ADVERB*

remorseless *ADJECTIVE*
relentless; not stopping or ending
➤ **remorselessly** *ADVERB*

remote *ADJECTIVE* remoter, remotest
❶ far away • *He lived on a remote island.*
❷ unlikely or slight • *Their chances of winning
were remote.* ❸ able to be connected to or
operated from far away • *Scientists can study
the seabed using remote cameras.*
➤ **remotely** *ADVERB* something is not (for
example) remotely funny when it is not even
slightly funny
➤ **remoteness** *NOUN*

remote control *NOUN* remote controls
❶ remote control is controlling something
from a distance, usually by means of radio or
electricity ❷ a remote control is a device for
doing this

removal *NOUN* removals
removing or moving something

remove *VERB* removes, removing,
removed
to remove something is to take it away or take
it off

render *VERB* renders, rendering,
rendered
❶ to render someone (for example) speechless
or unconscious is to put them in that condition

• *The shock rendered her speechless.*
❷ to render help or a service is to provide it

rendezvous (*say* ron-day-voo) *NOUN* rendezvous
❶ a meeting with someone ❷ a meeting place
Exactly one hour later, Pronto arrived in a hired van at the agreed rendezvous.–PURE DEAD MAGIC, Debi Gliori

renew *VERB* renews, renewing, renewed
to renew something is to make it as it was before or replace it with something new
➤ **renewal** *NOUN*

renewable *ADJECTIVE*
able to be renewed or replaced; never completely used up

renown *NOUN*
fame • *Dickens is an author of great renown.*
➤ **renowned** *ADJECTIVE* famous • *The city is renowned for its food.*

rent *NOUN* rents
a regular payment for the use of something, especially a house or flat

rent *VERB* rents, renting, rented
to rent something is to pay money for the use of it

repair *VERB* repairs, repairing, repaired
to repair something is to mend it

repair *NOUN* repairs
❶ repair is mending something • *The car is in for repair.* ❷ a repair is a mended place
• *You can hardly see the repair.*
➤ **to be in good repair** is to be in good condition

repay *VERB* repays, repaying, repaid
❶ to repay money is to pay it back ❷ to repay someone's kindness is to do something for them in return
➤ **repayment** *NOUN*

repeat *VERB* repeats, repeating, repeated
to repeat something is to say it or do it again

repeat *NOUN* repeats
something that is repeated, especially a television programme

repeatedly *ADVERB*
several times; again and again

repel *VERB* repels, repelling, repelled
❶ to repel someone or something is to drive or force them away or apart ❷ to repel someone is to make them disgusted
➤ **repellent** *ADJECTIVE* disgusting

repent *VERB* repents, repenting, repented
to repent is to be sorry for what you have done
➤ **repentance** *NOUN* ➤ **repentant** *ADJECTIVE*

repetition *NOUN* repetitions
❶ repeating or doing something again
❷ something repeated

repetitive *ADJECTIVE*
something is repetitive when it is repeated too much and so becomes boring

replace *VERB* replaces, replacing, replaced
❶ to replace something is to put it back in its place ❷ to replace someone or something is to take their place ❸ to replace something is to put a new thing in the place of it • *We will have to replace the old engine with a new one.*

replacement *NOUN* replacements
❶ replacement is when something or someone is replaced for another ❷ a replacement is something used or given in place of another

replay *NOUN* replays
❶ a football match played for a second time after the first match has ended in a draw
❷ the playing or showing again of a recording

replay *VERB* replays, replaying, replayed
to replay a tape is to play it again

replica (*say* rep-li-ka) *NOUN* replicas
an exact copy

reply *NOUN* replies
something you say or write to deal with what someone else has asked or said

reply *VERB* replies, replying, replied
to reply is to give a reply

report *VERB* reports, reporting, reported
❶ to report something is to describe something that has happened or something you have studied ❷ to report someone is to complain about them to those in charge of them
❸ to report to someone is to tell them you have arrived or are available

a
b
c
d
e
f
g
h
i
j
k
l
m
n
o
p
q
r
s
t
u
v
w
x
y
z

report NOUN **reports**
❶ a description or account of something
❷ a regular statement of how someone has worked or behaved, especially at school
❸ an explosive sound • *We heard the report of a gun.*

reported speech NOUN
reported speech is when you report someone's words in a changed form, as in *He said that he would come* (reporting that someone has said the words 'I will come')

reporter NOUN **reporters**
someone whose job is to collect news for a newspaper or for radio or television

represent VERB **represents**, **representing**, **represented**
❶ to represent something or someone is to be a picture or model or symbol of them
❷ to represent something is also to be a typical example of it ❸ to represent someone is to support them by speaking or acting on their behalf

representation NOUN **representations**
a representation of a thing is something that shows or describes it

representative NOUN
a person or thing that represents others

representative ADJECTIVE
typical of a group

repress VERB **represses**, **repressing**, **repressed**
to repress something or someone is to control or restrain them by force
➤ **repression** NOUN ➤ **repressive** ADJECTIVE

reprieve (*say* ri-**preev**) NOUN **reprieves**
someone is given a reprieve when their punishment is postponed or cancelled, especially the death penalty

reprieve VERB **reprieves**, **reprieving**, **reprieved**
to reprieve someone is to cancel or postpone their punishment

reprimand VERB **reprimands**, **reprimanding**, **reprimanded**
to reprimand someone is to scold them or tell them off

reprimand NOUN **reprimands**
a telling-off

reprisal (*say* ri-**pry**-zal) NOUN **reprisals**
an act of revenge

reproach VERB **reproaches**, **reproaching**, **reproached**
to reproach someone is to blame them for something and show you are disappointed with them

reproach NOUN
reproach is blame or criticism • *His behaviour was beyond reproach.*

reproduce VERB **reproduces**, **reproducing**, **reproduced**
❶ to reproduce something is to make it be heard or seen again • *She tried to reproduce her mother's recipe.* ❷ to reproduce something is also to copy it • *The photo can be easily reproduced.* ❸ animals and people reproduce when they produce offspring

reproduction NOUN **reproductions**
❶ reproduction is the process of producing offspring ❷ a reproduction is a copy of something
➤ **reproductive** ADJECTIVE to do with producing offspring

reptile NOUN **reptiles**
a cold-blooded animal with dry scaly skin, such as a snake or lizard
➤ **reptilian** ADJECTIVE
DID YOU KNOW? The word **reptile** comes from a Latin word meaning 'to crawl'.

republic NOUN **republics**
a country ruled by a president and government that are chosen by the people

republican NOUN **republicans**
someone who supports the idea of a republic

repulsion NOUN
❶ repulsion is a feeling of disgust ❷ repulsion is also repelling something

repulsive ADJECTIVE
disgusting

reputation NOUN **reputations**
what most people think about a person or thing • *He has a reputation for being honest.*

request VERB **requests**, **requesting**, **requested**
to request something is to ask politely or formally for it

request *NOUN* **requests**
❶ the action of asking for something
❷ what someone asks for

require *VERB* **requires, requiring, required**
❶ to require something is to need or want it
❷ you are required to do something when you have to do it • *Pedestrians are required to walk on the pavements.*

requirement *NOUN* **requirements**
a requirement is something that is needed

reread *VERB* **rereads, rereading, reread**
to reread something is to read it again

rescue *VERB* **rescues, rescuing, rescued**
to rescue someone is to save them from danger or capture
➤ **rescuer** *NOUN*

rescue *NOUN* **rescues**
when someone is rescued

research *NOUN* **researches**
research is careful study or investigation to learn more about a subject
➤ **researcher** *NOUN*

resemblance *NOUN* **resemblances**
there is a resemblance between two or more things when they are similar

resemble *VERB* **resembles, resembling, resembled**
to resemble someone or something is to look or sound like them

resent *VERB* **resents, resenting, resented**
to resent something is to feel hurt or angry about it

resentful *ADJECTIVE*
hurt and angry about something
➤ **resentfully** *ADVERB*

resentment *NOUN*
to feel resentment is to feel hurt and angry about something

reservation *NOUN* **reservations**
❶ arranging for (for example) a restaurant table or seat on a train to be kept for you
❷ an area of land kept for a special purpose
❸ you have reservations about something when you feel doubtful or uneasy about it
• *I had reservations about accepting the invitation.*

reserve *VERB* **reserves, reserving, reserved**
to reserve something is to keep it or order it for a particular person or for a special use

reserve *NOUN* **reserves**
❶ a person kept ready to be used if necessary, especially an extra player in a sports team
❷ an area of land kept for a special purpose
• *This island is a nature reserve.*

reserved *ADJECTIVE*
❶ kept for someone • *These seats are reserved.*
❷ someone is reserved when they are shy or unwilling to show their feelings

reservoir (*say* rez-er-vwar) *NOUN* **reservoirs**
a place where water is stored, especially an artificial lake

reside *VERB* **resides, residing, resided**
to reside in a place is to live there

residence *NOUN* **residences**
a place where someone lives

resident *NOUN* **residents**
someone who lives in a particular place

resign *VERB* **resigns, resigning, resigned**
to give up your job or position
➤ **to resign yourself to something** is to accept a difficulty without complaining or arguing

resignation *NOUN* **resignations**
❶ resignation is accepting a difficulty without complaining ❷ a resignation is a letter saying you are resigning a job or position

resilient *ADJECTIVE*
able to recover quickly from something

resin (*say* rez-in) *NOUN* **resins**
resin is a sticky substance that comes from plants or is made artificially

resist *VERB* **resists, resisting, resisted**
to resist someone or something is to oppose them or try to stop them

resistance *NOUN*
resistance is fighting back or taking action against someone or something • *The pirates were met with armed resistance.*
➤ **resistant** *ADJECTIVE* to be resistant to something is not to be affected or damaged by it

a
b
c
d
e
f
g
h
i
j
k
l
m
n
o
p
q
r
s
t
u
v
w
x
y
z

resolute (say **rez**-o-loot) *ADJECTIVE*
determined or firm
➤ **resolutely** *ADVERB*

resolution *NOUN* **resolutions**
❶ resolution is being determined or firm
❷ a resolution is something you have decided to do ❸ the resolution of a story is the last part where we find out how the story comes to an end and how some of the difficulties faced by the characters are sorted out

resolve *VERB* **resolves, resolving, resolved**
❶ to resolve to do something is to decide to do it ❷ to resolve doubts or disagreements is to deal successfully with them

resort *NOUN* **resorts**
a place where people go for a holiday, especially by the sea
➤ **the last resort** the only thing you can do when everything else has failed

resort *VERB* **resorts, resorting, resorted**
to resort to something is to make use of it, especially when everything else has failed
• *In the end they resorted to threats.*

resound *VERB* **resounds, resounding, resounded**
to resound is to fill a place with sound or to echo

resource *NOUN* **resources**
resources are things that you have and are able to use • *The land is rich in natural resources.*

respect *NOUN* **respects**
❶ respect is admiration for someone's good qualities or achievements ❷ respect is also consideration or concern • *Have respect for people's feelings.* ❸ a respect is a detail or aspect • *In some respects, he is like his sister.*

respect *VERB* **respects, respecting, respected**
to respect someone is to have respect for them

respectable *ADJECTIVE*
❶ a respectable person has good manners and character ❷ something respectable is of a good size or standard
➤ **respectability** *NOUN*
➤ **respectably** *ADVERB*

respectful *ADJECTIVE*
showing respect; polite
➤ **respectfully** *ADVERB*

respecting *PREPOSITION*
concerning; to do with

respective *ADJECTIVE*
belonging to each one of several • *We went to our respective rooms.*

respectively *ADVERB*
in the same order as the people or things already mentioned • *My brother and I play the guitar and drums respectively.*

respiration *NOUN*
respiration is breathing
➤ **respiratory** *ADJECTIVE* to do with breathing

respirator *NOUN* **respirators**
a mask or machine for helping with people's breathing

respond *VERB* **responds, responding, responded**
to respond to someone or something is to reply or react to them

response *NOUN* **responses**
your response is how you reply or react to something

responsibility *NOUN* **responsibilities**
❶ responsibility is being responsible for something ❷ a responsibility is something for which you are responsible

responsible *ADJECTIVE*
❶ looking after something and likely to take the blame if anything goes wrong ❷ able to be trusted ❸ important and needing trust
• *She has a responsible job.* ❹ to be responsible for something is to be the cause of it
• *Faulty wiring was responsible for the fire.*
➤ **responsibly** *ADVERB*

rest *NOUN* **rests**
❶ a time when you can sleep or relax
• *Have a good rest over the weekend.*
❷ a support for something • *a chair with arm rests*
➤ **the rest** the part that is left; the others

rest *VERB* **rests, resting, rested**
❶ to rest is to sleep or relax ❷ to rest on or against something is to lean on it • *The ladder is resting against the wall.* ❸ to rest something is to lean or support it somewhere • *Rest the ladder on the roof.*

restaurant *NOUN* **restaurants**
a place where you can buy a meal and eat it

restful *ADJECTIVE*
giving a feeling of rest

restless *ADJECTIVE*
you are restless when you can't relax or keep still
➤ **restlessly** *ADVERB* ➤ **restlessness** *NOUN*

restore *VERB* **restores, restoring, restored**
to restore something is to put it back as it was or make it new again
➤ **restoration** *NOUN* ➤ **restorative** *ADJECTIVE*

restrain *VERB* **restrains, restraining, restrained**
to restrain someone or something is to hold them or keep them tightly controlled

restraint *NOUN*
self-control • *Show a little restraint.*

restrict *VERB* **restricts, restricting, restricted**
to restrict someone or something is to keep them within certain limits or stop them from acting freely
➤ **restriction** *NOUN* ➤ **restrictive** *ADJECTIVE*

result *NOUN* **results**
❶ a thing that happens because something else has happened ❷ the score or situation at the end of a game or competition or race ❸ the answer to a sum or problem ❹ the information you get from a computer search

result *VERB* **results, resulting, resulted**
to result is to happen as a result
➤ **to result in something** is to have it as a result • *The game resulted in a draw.*

resume *VERB* **resumes, resuming, resumed**
to resume, or to resume something, is to start again after stopping

resuscitate (*say* ri-**suss**-it-ate) *VERB* **resuscitates, resuscitating, resuscitated**
to resuscitate someone is to revive them after they have been unconscious

retail *NOUN*
retail is the business of selling goods to the public
➤ **retailer** *NOUN*

retain *VERB* **retains, retaining, retained**
❶ to retain something is to keep it • *Retain your tickets for inspection.* ❷ to retain something is to hold it in place

retina (*say* ret-i-na) *NOUN* **retinas**
a layer at the back of your eyeball that is sensitive to light

retire *VERB* **retires, retiring, retired**
❶ someone retires when they give up regular work at a certain age ❷ to retire is also to retreat or withdraw, or to go to bed
The last sound Peter heard before he was quite alone were the mermaids retiring one by one to their bedchambers under the sea.—PETER PAN, J. M. Barrie
➤ **retirement** *NOUN* the time when someone gives up regular work

retiring *ADJECTIVE*
a retiring person is shy and avoids company

retort *VERB* **retorts, retorting, retorted**
to retort is to reply quickly or angrily
'Swallows can't read, silly,' said Peter. 'Silly yourself,' retorted Phyllis; 'how do you know?'—THE RAILWAY CHILDREN, Edith Nesbit

retort *NOUN* **retorts**
a quick or angry reply

retrace *VERB* **retraces, retracing, retraced**
to retrace your steps is to go back the way you came

retreat *VERB* **retreats, retreating, retreated**
to go back when you are attacked or defeated

retrieve *VERB* **retrieves, retrieving, retrieved**
to retrieve something is to get it back or find it again
➤ **retrievable** *ADJECTIVE* ➤ **retrieval** *NOUN*

retriever *NOUN* **retrievers**
a dog that can find and bring back birds and animals that have been shot

return *VERB* **returns, returning, returned**
❶ to return is to come or go back to a place ❷ to return something is to give it or send it back

return *NOUN* **returns**
❶ when you come back to a place ❷ something that is given or sent back ❸ profit • *He gets a*

good return on his savings. ❹ a return ticket
• *Do you want a single or return?*

return ticket *NOUN* **return tickets**
a ticket for a journey to a place and back again

reunion *NOUN* **reunions**
a meeting of people who have not met for
some time

rev *VERB* **revs**, **revving**, **revved** (*informal*)
to rev an engine is to make it run quickly

rev *NOUN* **revs** (*informal*)
a revolution of an engine

Rev. *ABBREVIATION*
short for *Reverend* in titles, for example *Rev.*
Lee of Nibbleswicke.

reveal *VERB* **reveals**, **revealing**, **revealed**
to reveal something is to show it or make it
known

revelation *NOUN* **revelations**
a surprising fact that is made known

revenge *NOUN*
revenge is harming someone because they have
done harm to you • *The story tells how the evil
queen plots her revenge.*

revenue (*say* rev-e-nyoo) *NOUN* **revenues**
revenue is money that a business or organization
receives

revere (*say* ri-**veer**) *VERB* **reveres**, **revering**,
revered
to revere someone or something is to respect
them deeply or religiously

reverence *NOUN*
reverence is great respect or awe, especially
towards God or holy things
➤ **reverent** *ADJECTIVE*

Reverend *NOUN*
the title of a member of the clergy • *This is the
Reverend John Smith.*

reverse *NOUN*
the opposite way or side
➤ **in reverse** going in the opposite direction

reverse *VERB* **reverses**, **reversing**, **reversed**
❶ to reverse something is to turn it round
❷ to reverse is to go backwards in a vehicle
❸ to reverse a decision is to cancel it
➤ **reversal** *NOUN*

reversible *ADJECTIVE*
❶ a reversible change or decision can be easily
changed back ❷ reversible clothing can be
worn with either side on the outside

review *NOUN* **reviews**
❶ a published description and opinion of a
book or film or play, or a piece of music
❷ an inspection or survey of something

review *VERB* **reviews**, **reviewing**,
reviewed
❶ to review a book or play or film, or
a piece of music, is to write a review
of it ❷ to review something is to inspect
or survey it
➤ **reviewer** *NOUN*

revise *VERB* **revises**, **revising**, **revised**
❶ before you do an examination, you revise
when you go over work that you have already
done ❷ to revise something is to correct or
change it

revision *NOUN* **revisions**
❶ a revision is a change or correction
❷ revision is learning work before you do an
examination

revival *NOUN* **revivals**
a revival is when something becomes popular
again

revive *VERB* **revives**, **reviving**, **revived**
❶ to revive something is to start using it
again ❷ to revive someone is to make them
conscious again after fainting

revolt *VERB* **revolts**, **revolting**, **revolted**
❶ to revolt is to rebel ❷ something revolts you
when it disgusts or horrifies you

revolt *NOUN* **revolts**
a rebellion

revolting *ADJECTIVE*
something is revolting when it is very
unpleasant or disgusting • *What a revolting
smell!*

revolution *NOUN* **revolutions**
❶ a rebellion that overthrows the government
❷ a complete change ❸ one turn of a wheel
or engine

revolutionary *ADJECTIVE*
❶ to do with a revolution ❷ completely new or
original

revolutionize (*also* **revolutionise**) *VERB*
revolutionizes, **revolutionizing**, **revolutionized**
to revolutionize something is to change it
completely • *Einstein's ideas revolutionized
science.*

revolve *VERB* **revolves**, **revolving**, **revolved**
something revolves when it goes round in
a circle
*In the middle of the floor was a giant telescope,
which revolved slowly, keeping watch on the sky.*
—COMET IN MOOMINLAND, Tove Jansson

revolver *NOUN* **revolvers**
a pistol that has a revolving store for bullets
so that it can be fired several times without
having to be loaded again

reward *NOUN* **rewards**
something given to a person in return for
something they have done

reward *VERB* **rewards**, **rewarding**, **rewarded**
to reward someone is to give them a reward

rewarding *ADJECTIVE*
pleasing or satisfying

rewind *VERB* **rewinds**, **rewinding**, **rewound**
to rewind a video or recording is to wind it back
to the beginning

rewrite *VERB* **rewrites**, **rewriting**, **rewrote**,
rewritten
to rewrite something is to write it again or
differently

rheumatism (*say* roo-ma-tizm) *NOUN*
rheumatism is an illness that causes pain and
stiffness in a person's joints and muscles
➤ **rheumatic** *ADJECTIVE*

rhino *NOUN* **rhinos** (*informal*)
a rhinoceros

rhinoceros (*say* ry-**noss**-er-os) *NOUN*
rhinoceroses *or* **rhinoceros**
a large heavy mammal with a horn or two
horns on its nose and thick folded skin
DID YOU KNOW? The word **rhinoceros** comes from
Greek words meaning 'nose horn'.

rhododendron (*say* roh-do-**den**-dron)
NOUN **rhododendrons**
an evergreen shrub with large flowers

rhombus *NOUN* **rhombuses**
a shape with four equal sides and no right
angles, like a diamond on a playing card

rhubarb *NOUN*
rhubarb is a plant with pink or green stalks
used as food

rhyme *NOUN* **rhymes**
❶ similar sounds in the endings of words, as
in *bat* and *mat*, *batter* and *matter* ❷ a short
rhyming poem
rhyme *VERB* **rhymes**, **rhyming**, **rhymed**
❶ a poem rhymes when it has rhymes at the
ends of its lines ❷ one word rhymes with
another word when it forms a rhyme with it
• *Bat rhymes with hat.*

rhythm *NOUN* **rhythms**
a regular pattern of beats, sounds or
movements in music and poetry
➤ **rhythmic**, **rhythmical** *ADJECTIVE*
something is rhythmic or rhythmical when it
has a rhythm
➤ **rhythmically** *ADVERB*

rib *NOUN* **ribs**
your ribs are the curved bones above your waist

ribbon *NOUN* **ribbons**
a strip of nylon, silk or other material

rice *NOUN*
rice is white seeds from a cereal plant, used
as food

rich *ADJECTIVE* **richer**, **richest**
❶ someone is rich when they have a lot of
money or property ❷ costly or luxurious • *The
dresses were made of rich silks and velvets.*
❸ rich food contains a lot of fat, butter
or eggs ❹ a rich colour or sound is deep
and strong
➤ **richness** *NOUN*

riches *PLURAL NOUN*
wealth

richly *ADVERB*
thoroughly, completely • *The team's success is
richly deserved.*

rickety *ADJECTIVE*
a rickety (for example) bridge or chair is
unsteady and likely to break or fall down

ricochet (*say* **rik**-o-shay) *VERB* **ricochets**,
ricocheting, **ricocheted**
to bounce off something • *The bullets
ricocheted off the wall.*

a
b
c
d
e
f
g
h
i
j
k
l
m
n
o
p
q
r
s
t
u
v
w
x
y
z

rid VERB rids, ridding, rid
to rid a person or place of something unwanted is to free them from it • *He rid the town of rats.*
➤ **to get rid of something** *or* **someone** is to cause them to go away • *I wish I could get rid of these spots.*

riddance NOUN
➤ **good riddance** used to show that you are glad that something or someone has gone

riddle NOUN riddles
a puzzling question, especially as a joke

ride VERB rides, riding, rode, ridden
❶ to ride a horse or bicycle is to sit on it and be carried along on it ❷ to ride is to travel in a vehicle

ride NOUN rides
a journey on a horse or bicycle, or in a vehicle

rider NOUN riders
someone who rides a horse

ridge NOUN ridges
a long narrow part higher than the rest of something • *a mountain ridge*

ridicule VERB ridicules, ridiculing, ridiculed
to ridicule someone or something is to make fun of them

ridiculous ADJECTIVE
extremely silly or absurd
➤ **ridiculously** ADVERB

rifle NOUN rifles
a long gun. You hold it against your shoulder to fire it.

rift NOUN rifts
❶ a crack or split ❷ a disagreement or a break in a friendship

rig VERB rigs, rigging, rigged
❶ to rig a ship is to fit it with rigging, sails and other equipment ❷ to rig an election or competition is to control the result dishonestly
➤ **to rig something up** is to make it quickly

rigging NOUN
rigging is the ropes that support a ship's masts and sails

right ADJECTIVE
❶ on or towards the east if you think of yourself as facing north ❷ correct • *Is this sum right?* ❸ fair or honest • *It's not right to cheat.* ❹ conservative; not in favour of political reforms

right ADVERB
❶ on or towards the right • *Turn right.*
❷ completely • *Turn right round.* ❸ exactly • *She stood right in the middle.* ❹ straight; directly • *Go right ahead.*
➤ **right away** immediately

right NOUN rights
❶ the right side ❷ what is fair or just; something that people ought to be allowed • *They fought for their rights.*

right VERB rights, righting, righted
❶ to right something is to make it upright • *They learned how to right their canoe.*
❷ to right something is also to put it right • *The fault might right itself.*

right angle NOUN right angles
an angle of 90 degrees, like angles in a rectangle

righteous ADJECTIVE
morally right or good; doing the right thing
➤ **righteously** ADVERB
➤ **righteousness** NOUN

rightful ADJECTIVE
deserved or proper • *The bike was returned to its rightful owner.*
➤ **rightfully** ADVERB

right-hand ADJECTIVE
on the right side of something

right-handed ADJECTIVE
using the right hand more than the left hand

rightly ADVERB
correctly or fairly

rightness NOUN
the rightness of (for example) a decision is the fact that it is correct or fair

rigid (*say* rij-id) ADJECTIVE
❶ firm or stiff ❷ strict or harsh • *The rules are rigid.*
➤ **rigidity** NOUN
➤ **rigidly** ADVERB to rigidly keep to a rule is to strictly keep to it

rigorous *ADJECTIVE*
very strict and thorough • *hours of rigorous training*
➤ **rigorously** *ADVERB*

rim *NOUN* **rims**
the outer edge of a cup or wheel or other round object

rind *NOUN* **rinds**
the tough skin on bacon, cheese or fruit

ring *NOUN* **rings**
❶ a thin circular piece of metal you wear on a finger ❷ something in the shape of a circle • *We put a ring of shells around the sandcastle.* ❸ the place where a boxing match or other contest is held ❹ the space where a circus performs ❺ a ring is also a ringing sound
➤ **to give someone a ring** (*informal*) is to telephone them

ring *VERB* **rings, ringing, ringed**
to ring something is to surround it with a ring • *The islands are ringed by coral reefs.*

ring *VERB* **rings, ringing, rang, rung**
❶ to ring a bell is to make it sound ❷ a bell rings when it makes a clear musical sound ❸ to ring someone is to telephone them • *I'll ring you later tonight.*

ringleader *NOUN* **ringleaders**
someone who leads other people in rebellion or mischief or crime

ringlet *NOUN* **ringlets**
a long curled piece of hair

ring road *NOUN* **ring roads**
a road that goes right round a town

ringtone *NOUN* **ringtones**
the sound a mobile phone makes when it receives a call

rink *NOUN* **rinks**
a place made for skating

rinse *VERB* **rinses, rinsing, rinsed**
to rinse something is to wash it in clean water without soap

rinse *NOUN* **rinses**
a wash in clean water without soap

riot *NOUN* **riots**
wild or violent behaviour by a crowd of people in a public place

riot *VERB* **riots, rioting, rioted**
people riot when they run wild and behave violently in a public place

riotous *ADJECTIVE*
wild or unruly

rip *VERB* **rips, ripping, ripped**
to rip something is to tear it roughly

rip *NOUN* **rips**
a torn place

ripe *ADJECTIVE* **riper, ripest**
ready to be harvested or eaten
➤ **ripeness** *NOUN*

ripen *VERB* **ripens, ripening, ripened**
❶ to ripen something is to make it ripe
❷ to ripen is to become ripe

ripple *NOUN* **ripples**
a small wave on the surface of water

ripple *VERB* **ripples, rippling, rippled**
water ripples when it forms small waves on the surface

rise *VERB* **rises, rising, rose, risen**
❶ to rise is to go upwards • *Smoke was rising from the fire.* • *The sun rises in the east.*
❷ to rise is also to get larger or more
• *Prices rose this year.* ❸ a person rises when they get up from sleeping or sitting
• *They all rose as she came in.* ❹ people rise, or rise up, when they rebel • *The army rose against the government.*

rise *NOUN* **rises**
❶ an increase, especially in wages
❷ an upward slope
➤ **to give rise to something** is to cause it

risk *VERB* **risks, risking, risked**
to risk something is to take a chance of damaging or losing it • *They risked their lives during the rescue.*

risk *NOUN* **risks**
a chance that something bad will happen
• *There's a risk that the river might flood.*

risky *ADJECTIVE* **riskier, riskiest**
dangerous or involving risk

risotto *NOUN*
risotto is an Italian dish of rice cooked with vegetables and often with meat

rite *NOUN* **rites**
a ceremony or ritual

a b c d e f g h i j k l m n o p q r s t u v w x y z

ritual *NOUN* **rituals**
a regular ceremony or series of actions

rival *NOUN* **rivals**
a rival is someone who competes with another person or tries to do the same thing

rival *VERB* **rivals, rivalling, rivalled**
to rival someone or something is to be as good as they are • *Nothing can rival the taste of home-made ice cream.*

rivalry *NOUN* **rivalries**
a rivalry is when two people compete against each other

river *NOUN* **rivers**
a large natural stream of water flowing along a channel

rivet *NOUN* **rivets**
a strong metal pin for holding pieces of metal together

rivet *VERB* **rivets, riveting, riveted**
❶ to rivet something is to fasten it with rivets ❷ to rivet someone is to hold them still • *She stood riveted to the spot.* ❸ to be riveted by something is to be fascinated by it • *The children were riveted by his story.*
➤ **riveting** *ADJECTIVE* fascinating

road *NOUN* **roads**
a level way with a hard surface made for traffic to go along

roadside *NOUN* **roadsides**
the side of a road

roadway *NOUN* **roadways**
the middle part of the road, used by traffic

roam *VERB* **roams, roaming, roamed**
to roam is to wander
For many months, close to starvation, I roamed the hills and glens of the Highlands, hunting and scavenging for my food like some wild beast.—THE LAST WOLF, Michael Morpurgo

roar *NOUN* **roars**
a loud deep sound of the kind that a lion makes

roar *VERB* **roars, roaring, roared**
to roar is to make a loud deep sound

roast *VERB* **roasts, roasting, roasted**
❶ to roast food is to cook it in an oven or over a fire ❷ you say you are roasting when you are very hot

rob *VERB* **robs, robbing, robbed**
to rob someone or a place is to steal something from them • *He was robbed on his way to the bank.* • *Next they robbed a jewellery shop.*

robber *NOUN* **robbers**
someone who steals something

robbery *NOUN* **robberies**
a robbery is when something is stolen

robe *NOUN* **robes**
a long loose piece of clothing

robin *NOUN* **robins**
a small brown bird with a red breast

robot *NOUN* **robots**
a machine that imitates the movements of a person or does the work of a person
DID YOU KNOW? The word **robot** comes from a Czech word meaning 'forced labour'.

robust *ADJECTIVE*
tough and strong
➤ **robustness** *NOUN*

rock *NOUN* **rocks**
❶ a rock is a large stone ❷ rock is a large mass of stone ❸ rock is also a hard sweet usually shaped like a stick ❹ rock music

rock *VERB* **rocks, rocking, rocked**
❶ to rock is to move gently backwards and forwards or from side to side ❷ to rock something is to make it do this

rocker *NOUN* **rockers**
❶ a rocking chair ❷ a curved support for a chair or cradle

rockery *NOUN* **rockeries**
part of a garden where people grow flowers between rocks

rocket *NOUN* **rockets**
❶ a firework that shoots high into the air ❷ a pointed tube-shaped vehicle pushed into the air by hot gases, especially as a spacecraft or weapon

rocking chair *NOUN* **rocking chairs**
a chair which can be rocked by the person sitting in it

rock music *NOUN*
rock music is popular music with a heavy beat

rocky *ADJECTIVE* **rockier, rockiest**
❶ a rocky place is full of rocks ❷ unsteady or shaky

rod *NOUN* **rods**
❶ a long thin stick or bar ❷ a rod with a line attached for fishing

rode *VERB* (*past tense of* **ride**)
• *The knight rode away on his horse.*

rodent *NOUN* **rodents**
an animal that has large front teeth for gnawing things, such as a rat, mouse or squirrel
DID YOU KNOW? The word **rodent** comes from a Latin word that means 'gnawing'.

rodeo (*say* roh-**day**-oh *or* roh-di-oh) *NOUN* **rodeos**
a display or contest of cowboys' skill in riding and in controlling cattle

rogue *NOUN* **rogues**
a dishonest or mischievous person

role *NOUN* **roles**
❶ the part that an actor plays in a play, film or story ❷ the purpose something has
• *Computers have a role in teaching.*

roll *VERB* **rolls, rolling, rolled**
❶ to roll is to move along by turning over and over, like a ball or wheel ❷ to roll something is to make it do this ❸ to roll something, or roll something up, is to form it into the shape of a cylinder or ball ❹ to roll something soft, such as dough, is to flatten it by moving a round heavy object over it ❺ a ship rolls when it sways from side to side ❻ drums roll when they make a long rumbling sound

roll *NOUN* **rolls**
❶ a cylinder made by rolling something up ❷ a small loaf of bread shaped like a bun ❸ a list of names ❹ the rumbling sound of drums

roller *NOUN* **rollers**
❶ a cylinder-shaped object, especially one used for flattening things ❷ a long swelling wave in the sea

roller coaster *NOUN* **roller coasters**
a fairground ride where carriages run on a track with a series of tight turns and steep slopes

roller skate *NOUN* **roller skates**
roller skates are boots with two pairs of wheels fitted underneath, so that you can move smoothly over the ground
➤ **roller skating** *NOUN*

rolling pin *NOUN* **rolling pins**
a heavy cylinder you roll over pastry dough to flatten it

ROM (*say* rom) *ABBREVIATION*
short for *read-only memory*, a type of computer memory with information that can be accessed but not changed by the user

Roman *NOUN* **Romans**
a person who lived in ancient Rome
Roman *ADJECTIVE*
to do with ancient Rome • *the Roman empire*

Roman Catholic *NOUN* **Roman Catholics**
a member of the Church with the Pope in Rome at its head

romance *NOUN* **romances**
❶ romance is experiences and feelings connected with love ❷ a romance is a love affair or a love story

Roman numerals *PLURAL NOUN*
letters that represent numbers, as used by the ancient Romans (*compare* **Arabic numerals**): I = 1, V = 5, X = 10, L = 50, C = 100, D = 500 and M = 1,000

romantic *ADJECTIVE*
❶ to do with love or romance ❷ to do with emotions or imagination
➤ **romantically** *ADVERB*

romp *VERB* **romps, romping, romped**
to romp is to play in a lively way
romp *NOUN* **romps**
a spell of lively play

roof *NOUN* **roofs**
❶ the part that covers the top of a building or vehicle ❷ the ceiling of a cave ❸ the upper part of your mouth

rook *NOUN* **rooks**
❶ a black bird that looks like a crow ❷ a piece in chess, also called a *castle*

a
b
c
d
e
f
g
h
i
j
k
l
m
n
o
p
q
r
s
t
u
v
w
x
y
z

A
B
C
D
E
F
G
H
I
J
K
L
M
N
O
P
Q
R
S
T
U
V
W
X
Y
Z

room *NOUN* **rooms**
❶ a room is a part of a building with its own walls and ceiling ❷ room is space for someone or something • *Is there room for me?*

roomful *NOUN* **roomfuls**
the amount or number a room will hold

roomy *ADJECTIVE* **roomier, roomiest**
somewhere is roomy when there is plenty of room or space inside

roost *NOUN* **roosts**
the place where a bird rests

root *NOUN* **roots**
❶ the part of a plant that grows under the ground ❷ a source or basis of something • *People say that money is the root of all evil.* ❸ a number in relation to the number it produces when multiplied by itself • *9 is the square root of 81.*
➤ **to take root** is to grow roots or to become established • *The custom never took root in other countries.*

root *VERB* **roots, rooting, rooted**
❶ to root is to take root in the ground ❷ to root someone is to fix them firmly • *Fear rooted him to the spot.*
➤ **to root something out** is to find it and get rid of it

rope *NOUN* **ropes**
a strong thick cord made of strands twisted together
➤ **to show someone the ropes** is to show them how to do a job

rose *VERB* (*past tense of* **rise**)
• *Clouds of smoke rose from the building.*

rose *NOUN* **roses**
a scented flower with a long thorny stem

rosette *NOUN* **rosettes**
a large circular badge made of ribbons

rosy *ADJECTIVE* **rosier, rosiest**
❶ pink ❷ hopeful or cheerful • *The future looks rosy.*

rot *VERB* **rots, rotting, rotted**
to rot is to go soft or bad so that it is useless • *This wood has rotted.*

rot *NOUN*
❶ rot is decay ❷ (*informal*) rot is also nonsense • *Don't talk such rot.*

rota *NOUN* **rotas**
a list of people who have to do tasks

rotate *VERB* **rotates, rotating, rotated**
❶ to rotate is to go round like a wheel ❷ to rotate is to take turns at something • *The job of doing the washing-up rotates.*
➤ **rotation** *NOUN*

rotor *NOUN* **rotors**
the part of a machine that goes round, especially the large horizontal propeller of a helicopter

rotten *ADJECTIVE*
❶ rotted or decayed • *There was rotten fruit on the ground.* ❷ (*informal*) nasty or very bad • *We had rotten weather.*
➤ **rottenness** *NOUN*

Rottweiler *NOUN* **Rottweilers**
a large dog with short black and tan hair, often kept as a guard dog

rough *ADJECTIVE* **rougher, roughest**
❶ not smooth; uneven ❷ violent; not gentle • *Ice hockey is a rough game.* ❸ not exact; done quickly • *It's only a rough guess.*
➤ **roughness** *NOUN*

roughage *NOUN*
roughage is fibre in food, which helps you to digest it

roughen *VERB* **roughens, roughening, roughened**
to roughen something is to make it rough

roughly *ADVERB*
❶ approximately; not exactly • *There were roughly a hundred people there.* ❷ in a rough way; not gently • *She pushed him roughly out of the way.*

round *ADJECTIVE* **rounder, roundest**
❶ shaped like a circle or ball or cylinder ❷ full or complete • *We bought a round dozen.* ❸ a round trip is one that returns to the start

round *ADVERB*
❶ in a circle or curve; by a longer route • *Go round to the back of the house.* ❷ in every direction or to every person

• *Hand the cakes round.* ❸ in a new direction
• *Turn your chair round.* ❹ to someone's house or place of work • *Come round at lunchtime.*

round PREPOSITION
❶ on all sides of • *We'll put a fence round the field.* ❷ in a curve or circle about
• *The earth moves round the sun.* ❸ to every part of • *Show them round the house.*

round NOUN **rounds**
❶ each stage in a competition • *The winners go on to the next round.* ❷ a series of visits or calls made by a doctor, delivery person, or other person ❸ a whole slice of bread, or a sandwich made from two whole slices of bread ❹ a shot or series of shots from a gun; a piece of ammunition ❺ a song in which people sing the same words but start at different times

round VERB **rounds**, **rounding**, **rounded**
to round a place is to travel round it • *A large car rounded the corner.*
➤ **to round a number down** is to decrease it to the nearest lower number • *123.4 may be rounded down to 123.*
➤ **to round a number up** is to increase it to the nearest higher number • *123.7 may be rounded up to 124.*
➤ **to round something off** is to finish it
➤ **to round up people or things** is to gather them together

roundabout NOUN **roundabouts**
❶ a road junction at which traffic has to pass round a circular island
❷ a merry-go-round

roundabout ADJECTIVE
not using the shortest or most direct way
• *We went by a roundabout route.*

rounded ADJECTIVE
round in shape

rounders NOUN
rounders is a game in which players try to hit a ball and run round a circuit

roundly ADVERB
thoroughly or severely • *We were roundly told off for being late.*

rouse VERB **rouses**, **rousing**, **roused**
to rouse someone is to wake them up or make them excited • *A voice in my ear roused me from a deep sleep.*

rout (*say* rowt) VERB **routs**, **routing**, **routed**
to rout an enemy is to defeat them and chase them away

rout (*say* rowt) NOUN **routs**
a disorderly retreat after being defeated in a battle

route (*say* root) NOUN **routes**
the way you have to go to get to a place

routine (*say* roo-**teen**) NOUN **routines**
a regular or fixed way of doing things

rove VERB **roves**, **roving**, **roved**
to roam or wander
The Trunchbull's dangerous glittering eyes roved around the classroom.—MATILDA, Roald Dahl

rover NOUN **rovers**
❶ someone who roves; a wanderer
❷ a vehicle for driving over rough ground used in space missions • *NASA has designed a new Mars rover.*

row (*rhymes with* go) NOUN **rows**
a row is a line of people or things • *Our seats were in the front row.*

row (*rhymes with* go) VERB **rows**, **rowing**, **rowed**
to row a boat is to use oars to make it move
➤ **rower** NOUN

row (*rhymes with* cow) NOUN **rows**
❶ a great noise or disturbance • *Who's making that row?* ❷ a quarrel or noisy argument

row (*rhymes with* cow) VERB **rows**, **rowing**, **rowed**
people row when they have a noisy argument

rowdy ADJECTIVE **rowdier**, **rowdiest**
noisy and disorderly
➤ **rowdily** ADVERB ➤ **rowdiness** NOUN

rowing boat NOUN **rowing boats**
a small boat that you move forward by using oars

royal ADJECTIVE
to do with a king or queen

royalty NOUN
❶ royalty is being royal ❷ royalty is also a royal person or royal people • *We will be in the presence of royalty.*

rub VERB **rubs**, **rubbing**, **rubbed**
❶ to rub something is to move your hand or a cloth over it while pressing firmly

• *She rubbed her sore ankle.* • *Try rubbing the table with a cloth.* ❷ to rub things together is to move them back and forth while pressing against each other • *Flies often rub their front legs together.*

➤ **to rub something off** or **out** is to make it disappear by rubbing it

rub NOUN rubs

a rub is when you rub something • *He gave his hair a quick rub with a towel.*

rubber NOUN rubbers

❶ rubber is a strong elastic substance used for making tyres, balls, hoses and other things ❷ a rubber is a piece of rubber or soft plastic for rubbing out pencil marks

➤ **rubbery** ADJECTIVE

rubbish NOUN

❶ rubbish is things that are not wanted or needed ❷ rubbish is also nonsense

rubble NOUN

rubble is broken pieces of brick or stone

ruby NOUN rubies

a precious stone that is red in colour

The stone was a ruby, rough-hewn from the rock and the size of a hen's egg. It was worth a kingdom when cut and set.—THE SLEEPER AND THE SPINDLE, Neil Gaiman

rucksack NOUN rucksacks

a bag with shoulder straps that you carry on your back

rudder NOUN rudders

a flat hinged device at the back of a ship or aircraft, used for steering it

ruddy ADJECTIVE ruddier, ruddiest

red and healthy-looking • *He had a ruddy face.*

rude ADJECTIVE ruder, rudest

❶ not polite; not showing respect for other people • *It was rude of them to push in front of me.* ❷ indecent or improper • *a rude joke* ❸ roughly made • *We made a rude shelter for the night.*

➤ **rudely** ADVERB ➤ **rudeness** NOUN

ruffian NOUN ruffians

a violent brutal person

ruffle VERB ruffles, ruffling, ruffled

❶ to ruffle something is to disturb its smoothness • *The bird ruffled its feathers.*

❷ to ruffle someone is to annoy them or upset them

rug NOUN rugs

❶ a thick piece of material that partly covers a floor ❷ a thick blanket

rugby, rugby football NOUN

rugby is a kind of football game using an oval ball that players may kick or carry

DID YOU KNOW? The game of **rugby** is named after Rugby School in Warwickshire, where it was first played.

rugged (*say* rug-id) ADJECTIVE

something rugged has a rough or uneven surface or outline • *His face was lined and rugged.* • *This part of Wales has a rugged coastline.*

ruin VERB ruins, ruining, ruined

to ruin something is to spoil it or destroy it completely

ruin NOUN ruins

❶ a ruin is a building that has been so badly damaged that it has almost all fallen down ❷ ruin is when something is ruined or destroyed

➤ **to be in ruins** is to be destroyed • *My plans were in ruins.*

rule NOUN rules

❶ a rule is something that people have to obey ❷ rule is ruling or governing • *The country used to be under French rule.*

➤ **as a rule** usually; normally

rule VERB rules, ruling, ruled

❶ to rule people is to govern them; to rule is to be a ruler ❷ to rule something is to make a decision • *The referee ruled that it was a foul.* ❸ to rule a line is to draw a straight line with a ruler or other straight edge

ruler NOUN rulers

❶ someone who governs a country ❷ a strip of wood, plastic or metal with straight edges, used for measuring and drawing straight lines

ruling NOUN rulings

a judgement or decision • *I will give my ruling tomorrow.*

rum NOUN rums

rum is a strong alcoholic drink made from sugar cane

rumble *VERB* **rumbles, rumbling, rumbled**
to rumble is to make a deep heavy sound like thunder • *His stomach was rumbling.*

rumble *NOUN* **rumbles**
a long deep heavy sound • *There was a rumble of thunder in the distance.*

rummage *VERB* **rummages, rummaging, rummaged**
to turn things over or move them about while looking for something
Anthea was rummaging in the corner-drawers of her mind for a disagreeable answer.—THE PHOENIX AND THE CARPET, Edith Nesbit

rummy *NOUN*
rummy is a card game in which players try to form sets or sequences of cards

rumour *NOUN* **rumours**
something that a lot of people are saying, although it may not be true

rump *NOUN* **rumps**
the back part of an animal, above its hind legs

rumpus *NOUN* **rumpuses**
a noisy uproar
'Such a rumpus everywhere!' continued the Otter. 'All the world seems out on the river to-day.'—THE WIND IN THE WILLOWS, Kenneth Grahame

run *VERB* **runs, running, ran, run**
❶ to run is to move with quick steps and with both feet off the ground for a time ❷ to run is also to move or go or travel • *Tears ran down his cheeks.* ❸ a tap or your nose runs when liquid flows from it ❹ an engine or machine runs when it is working or functioning • *The engine was running smoothly.* ❺ to run something is to manage it or organize it • *She runs a corner shop.* ❻ to run someone somewhere is to give them a lift there
➤ **to run a risk** is to take a chance
➤ **to run away** is to leave a place quickly or secretly
➤ **to run into someone** is to meet them unexpectedly
➤ **to run out of something** is to have used up a supply of it
➤ **to run someone over** is to knock them down with a car or bicycle

run *NOUN* **runs**
❶ a spell of running • *Let's go for a run.*
❷ a point scored in cricket or baseball ❸ a series of damaged stitches in a pair of tights or other piece of clothing ❹ a continuous series of events • *They've had a run of good luck.* ❺ a place with a fence round it for keeping animals
➤ **to be on the run** is to be running away, especially from the police

runaway *NOUN* **runaways**
someone who has run away from home

rune *NOUN* **runes**
a rune is a letter from an ancient Norse alphabet
Runes were old letters originally used for cutting or scratching on wood, stone, or metal, and so were thin and angular.—THE HOBBIT, J. R. R. Tolkien

rung *VERB* (*past participle of* **ring**)
• *Has your friend rung yet?*

rung *NOUN* **rungs**
each of the short crossbars on a ladder

runner *NOUN* **runners**
❶ a person or animal that runs in a race ❷ the part of a sledge that slides along the ground

runner bean *NOUN* **runner beans**
a kind of climbing bean

runner-up *NOUN* **runners-up**
someone who comes second in a race or competition

runny *ADJECTIVE* **runnier, runniest**
flowing or moving like liquid

runt *NOUN* **runts**
the smallest piglet or other animal in a litter
Mr Arable studied Wilbur carefully. 'Yes, he's a wonderful pig,' he said. 'It's hard to believe that he was the runt of the litter.'—CHARLOTTE'S WEB, E. B. White

runway *NOUN* **runways**
a long strip with a hard surface for aircraft to take off and land

rural *ADJECTIVE*
to do with the countryside; in the country

rush *VERB* **rushes, rushing, rushed**
❶ to rush is to hurry ❷ to rush someone is to attack or capture them by surprise

a b c d e f g h i j k l m n o p q r s t u v w x y z

A
B
C
D
E
F
G
H
I
J
K
L
M
N
O
P
Q
R
S
T
U
V
W
X
Y
Z

rush NOUN
❶ a rush is a hurry • *I can't stop—I'm in a rush.* ❷ rushes are plants with thin stems that grow in wet or marshy places

rusk NOUN **rusks**
a kind of hard dry biscuit for babies to chew

Russian ADJECTIVE
to do with Russia or its people
Russian NOUN
❶ the main language of Russia ❷ (**Russians**) a person from Russia

rust NOUN
rust is a red or brown substance formed on metal that is exposed to air and dampness
rust VERB **rusts**, **rusting**, **rusted**
metal rusts when it develops rust

rustic ADJECTIVE
to do with the countryside

rustle VERB **rustles**, **rustling**, **rustled**
❶ to rustle is to make a gentle sound like dry leaves being blown by the wind ❷ to rustle horses or cattle is to steal them
➤ **to rustle something up** (*informal*) is to collect it or provide it quickly

rusty ADJECTIVE **rustier**, **rustiest**
❶ coated with rust ❷ not as good as it used to be because you have not had enough practice • *My French is a bit rusty.*

rut NOUN **ruts**
a deep groove made by wheels in soft ground
➤ **to be in a rut** is to have a dull life with no changes

ruthless ADJECTIVE
someone is ruthless when they are determined to get what they want and do not care if they hurt other people
➤ **ruthlessly** ADVERB ➤ **ruthlessness** NOUN

rye NOUN
rye is a cereal used to make bread and biscuits

Ss

sabbath NOUN **sabbaths**
the sabbath is the weekly day for rest and prayer, Saturday for Jewish people, Sunday for Christians

sabotage (*say* sab-o-tahzh) NOUN
sabotage is deliberately damaging machinery or equipment
sabotage VERB **sabotages**, **sabotaging**, **sabotaged**
to sabotage machinery or equipment is to damage it deliberately

sabre NOUN **sabres**
a type of sword with a curved blade

sabre-toothed cat NOUN **sabre-toothed cats**
a prehistoric animal like a large cat with two long curved canine teeth

sac NOUN **sacs**
any bag-like part of an animal or plant

saccharin (*say* sak-a-rin) NOUN
saccharin is a very sweet substance used as a substitute for sugar

sachet (*say* sash-ay) NOUN **sachets**
a small sealed packet of something such as shampoo or sugar

sack NOUN **sacks**
a large bag made of strong material
➤ **to get the sack** (*informal*) is to be dismissed from a job
sack VERB **sacks**, **sacking**, **sacked**
❶ (*informal*) to sack someone is to dismiss them from their job ❷ to sack a place is to plunder and destroy it in war

sacred ADJECTIVE
to do with God or a god; holy

sacrifice NOUN **sacrifices**
❶ giving up a thing that you value so that something good may happen • *If you want to save some money, you might have to make a few sacrifices.* ❷ killing an animal or person as an offering to a god
➤ **sacrificial** ADJECTIVE offered as a sacrifice

sacrifice *VERB* **sacrifices**, **sacrificing**, **sacrificed**
❶ to sacrifice something is to give it up so that something good may happen ❷ to sacrifice an animal or person is to kill them as an offering to a god

sad *ADJECTIVE* **sadder**, **saddest**
unhappy; showing sorrow or causing it
➤ **sadly** *ADVERB* ➤ **sadness** *NOUN*

sadden *VERB* **saddens**, **saddening**, **saddened**
something saddens you when it makes you sad or unhappy

saddle *NOUN* **saddles**
❶ a seat that you put on the back of a horse or other animal so that you can ride it ❷ the seat of a bicycle

saddle *VERB* **saddles**, **saddling**, **saddled**
to saddle an animal is to put a saddle on its back
➤ **to be saddled with something** is to have it as a burden or problem

safari (*say* sa-far-ee) *NOUN* **safaris**
an expedition to see or hunt wild animals

safari park *NOUN* **safari parks**
a large park where wild animals can roam around freely and visitors can watch them from their cars

safe *ADJECTIVE* **safer**, **safest**
❶ free from danger; protected ❷ not causing danger • *Drive at a safe speed.*

safe *NOUN* **safes**
a strong cupboard or box in which valuable things can be locked away safely

safeguard *NOUN* **safeguards**
something that protects you against danger

safeguard *VERB* **safeguard**, **safeguards**, **safeguarded**
to safeguard something is to protect it from danger

safely *ADVERB*
to do something safely is to do it without risk or danger • *The plane landed safely.*

safety *NOUN*
safety is being safe; protection • *We listened to a talk on road safety.*

safety belt *NOUN* **safety belts**
a belt to hold someone securely in a seat

safety pin *NOUN* **safety pins**
a curved pin made with a clip that closes to cover the point

sag *VERB* **sags**, **sagging**, **sagged**
something sags when it sinks slightly in the middle because something heavy is pressing on it

saga *NOUN* **sagas**
a long story with many adventures

said *VERB* (*past tense and past participle of* **say**)
• '*Look out,*' said Jamie. • *I didn't hear what she had said.*

sail *NOUN* **sails**
❶ a large piece of strong cloth attached to a mast to make a boat move ❷ a short voyage • *We went for a sail around the island.* ❸ an arm of a windmill
➤ **to set sail** is to start on a voyage in a ship

sail *VERB* **sails**, **sailing**, **sailed**
❶ to sail somewhere is to travel there in a ship ❷ a ship or boat sails when it starts out on a voyage • *What time does the ferry sail?* ❸ to sail a ship or boat is to control it

sailor *NOUN* **sailors**
❶ a member of a ship's crew ❷ someone who sails

saint *NOUN* **saints**
a holy or very good person
➤ **saintly** *ADJECTIVE*

sake *NOUN*
➤ **for the sake of something** in order to do it or get it • *He'll do anything for the sake of money.*
➤ **for someone's sake** in order to help them or please them • *She went to great trouble for his sake.*

salad *NOUN* **salads**
a mixture of vegetables eaten cold and often raw

salami *NOUN* **salamis**
salami is a kind of strong spicy sausage

salary *NOUN* **salaries**
a regular wage, usually paid every month

a
b
c
d
e
f
g
h
i
j
k
l
m
n
o
p
q
r
s
t
u
v
w
x
y
z

sale *NOUN* **sales**
❶ the selling of something ❷ a time when a shop sells things at reduced prices
➤ **for sale** *or* **on sale** able to be bought

salesman, **saleswoman** *NOUN* **salesmen**, **saleswomen**
a person whose job is to sell things

salesperson *NOUN* **salespeople**
a person whose job is to sell things

saline *ADJECTIVE*
containing salt

saliva (*say* sa-**ly**-va) *NOUN*
saliva is the natural liquid in your mouth

sally *VERB* **sallies**, **sallying**, **sallied**
➤ **to sally forth** *or* **sally out** is to rush forward or rush ahead

salmon *NOUN* **salmon**
a large fish with pink flesh, used for food

salon *NOUN* **salons**
a room or shop where a hairdresser or a beauty specialist works

saloon *NOUN* **saloons**
❶ a motor car with a hard roof ❷ a bar in a public house

salt *NOUN*
salt is the white substance that gives sea water its taste and is used for flavouring food
➤ **salty** *ADJECTIVE*

salt *VERB* **salts**, **salting**, **salted**
to salt food is to use salt to flavour or preserve it

saltire *NOUN* **saltires**
a diagonal cross used as a symbol on a flag

salute *VERB* **salutes**, **saluting**, **saluted**
to salute is to raise your hand to your forehead as a sign of respect or greeting

salute *NOUN* **salutes**
❶ the act of saluting ❷ when guns are fired as a sign of respect on an official occasion

salvage *VERB* **salvages**, **salvaging**, **salvaged**
to salvage something is to save or rescue it after a shipwreck or other disaster • *We managed to salvage our tent from the flood.*

salvation *NOUN*
salvation is saving someone or something

same *ADJECTIVE*
not different; exactly equal or alike • *We are the same age.* • *Look, these two leaves are exactly the same.*

samosa *NOUN* **samosas**
a small case of crisp pastry filled with a mixture of spicy meat or vegetables, originally from South Asia

sample *NOUN* **samples**
a small amount that shows what something is like

sample *VERB* **samples**, **sampling**, **sampled**
❶ to sample something is to take a sample of it • *Scientists sampled the lake water.* ❷ to sample something is also to try part of it • *She sampled the cake.*

samurai *NOUN* **samurai**
a warrior in ancient Japan

sanctuary *NOUN* **sanctuaries**
❶ a safe place, especially for someone who is being chased or attacked ❷ a place where wildlife is protected • *We visited a bird sanctuary.*

sand *NOUN*
sand is the tiny grains of rock that you find on beaches and in deserts

sand *VERB* **sands**, **sanding**, **sanded**
to sand a surface is to smooth or polish it with sandpaper or rough material

sandal *NOUN* **sandals**
a lightweight shoe with straps that go round your foot

sandbag *NOUN* **sandbags**
sandbags are bags filled with sand, used to build defences against flood water or bullets

sandcastle *NOUN* **sandcastles**
a model of a castle built out of wet sand on a beach

sandpaper *NOUN*
sandpaper is strong paper coated with hard grains, rubbed on rough surfaces to make them smooth

sands *PLURAL NOUN*
a beach or sandy area

sandstone *NOUN*
sandstone is rock made of compressed sand

sandwich *NOUN* **sandwiches**
slices of bread with meat, cheese or some other filling between them
DID YOU KNOW? The word **sandwich** is named after the Earl of *Sandwich*, who is said to have invented it so that he could eat at the same time as playing cards.

sandy *ADJECTIVE* **sandier, sandiest**
❶ made of sand; covered with sand
❷ sandy hair is yellow-red

sane *ADJECTIVE* **saner, sanest**
having a healthy mind, not mentally ill

sang *VERB* (*past tense of* **sing**)
• *We sang all our favourite songs.*

sanitary *ADJECTIVE*
free from germs and dirt; hygienic

sanitation *NOUN*
sanitation is arrangements for drainage and the disposal of sewage

sanity *NOUN*
sanity is being sane

sank *VERB* (*past tense of* **sink**)
• *My heart sank when I heard the news.*

sap *NOUN*
sap is the juice inside a tree or plant

sap *VERB* **saps, sapping, sapped**
to sap someone's strength or energy is to use it up or weaken it gradually • *The heat had sapped all my energy.*

sapling *NOUN* **saplings**
a young tree

sapphire *NOUN* **sapphires**
a bright blue jewel

sarcastic *ADJECTIVE*
you are being sarcastic when you mock someone or something by saying the opposite of what you mean • *Do you really like the colour, or are you being sarcastic?*
➤ **sarcasm** *NOUN* ➤ **sarcastically** *ADVERB*

sarcophagus *NOUN* **sarcophagi**
an ancient stone coffin decorated with carvings
DID YOU KNOW? The word **sarcophagus** means literally 'flesh-eating', because it was thought that the stone caused the body in the coffin to decay.

sardine *NOUN* **sardines**
a small sea fish, usually sold packed tightly in tins

sari (*say* sah-ree) *NOUN* **saris**
a long length of cloth worn as a dress, traditionally by South Asian women and girls

sash *NOUN* **sashes**
a strip of cloth worn round the waist or over one shoulder

sat *VERB* (*past tense and past participle of* **sit**)
• *We sat at our desks.* • *The class had already sat down.*

satchel *NOUN* **satchels**
a bag you wear over your shoulder or on your back, especially for carrying school books

satellite *NOUN* **satellites**
❶ a spacecraft sent into space to move in an orbit round a planet, in order to send and receive information ❷ a moon that moves in orbit round a planet

satellite dish *NOUN* **satellite dishes**
a dish-shaped aerial for receiving signals sent by satellite

satin *NOUN*
satin is a silky material that is shiny on one side

satisfaction *NOUN*
❶ satisfaction is the feeling of being satisfied
❷ satisfaction is also giving someone what they need or want

satisfactory *ADJECTIVE*
good enough; acceptable • *He tried to think of a satisfactory excuse.*
➤ **satisfactorily** *ADVERB*

satisfy *VERB* **satisfies, satisfying, satisfied**
❶ to satisfy someone is to give them what they need or want ❷ to be satisfied is to be sure of something • *I am satisfied that you have done your best.*

satnav *NOUN*
a system for finding out how to get to a place using information from satellites

satsuma *NOUN* **satsumas**
a kind of tangerine with a loose skin

a
b
c
d
e
f
g
h
i
j
k
l
m
n
o
p
q
r
s
t
u
v
w
x
y
z

saturate VERB **saturates**, **saturating**, **saturated**
❶ to be saturated is to be soaking wet
• *My clothes are saturated with rain.*
❷ to saturate a place is to make it take in as much as possible or too much of something
• *The town is saturated with tourists in the summer.*
➤ **saturation** NOUN

Saturday NOUN **Saturdays**
the seventh day of the week
DID YOU KNOW? **Saturday** is named after the Roman god *Saturn*.

Saturn NOUN
the sixth planet from the sun in our solar system
DID YOU KNOW? The planet **Saturn** is named after the Roman god of agriculture.

sauce NOUN **sauces**
a sauce is a thick liquid served with food to add flavour

saucepan NOUN **saucepans**
a metal cooking pan with a long handle

saucer NOUN **saucers**
a small curved plate for a cup to stand on

saucy ADJECTIVE **saucier**, **sauciest**
rude or cheeky

sauna (*say* **saw**-na *or* **sow**-na) NOUN **saunas**
a room filled with steam where people sit and sweat a lot, used as a kind of bath

saunter VERB **saunters**, **sauntering**, **sauntered**
to walk about in a leisurely way

sausage NOUN **sausages**
a tube of edible skin or plastic stuffed with minced meat and other ingredients

sausage roll NOUN **sausage rolls**
a small short roll of pastry filled with meat

savage ADJECTIVE
wild and fierce; cruel
➤ **savagely** ADVERB

savage VERB **savages**, **savaging**, **savaged**
an animal savages someone when it attacks them and bites or scratches them fiercely

savannah (*say* sa-**van**-a) NOUN **savannahs**
a grassy plain in a hot country, with few trees

save VERB **saves**, **saving**, **saved**
❶ to save someone or something is to free them from danger or harm ❷ to save something, especially money, is to keep it so that it can be used later ❸ to save computer data is to instruct the computer to keep it on its hard disk ❹ in football, to save a ball is to stop it going into your goal
➤ **saver** NOUN

savings PLURAL NOUN
your savings are the money that you have saved

saviour NOUN **saviours**
a person who saves someone

savoury ADJECTIVE
savoury food is tasty but not sweet

saw VERB (*past tense of* **see**)
• *I saw them both yesterday.*

saw NOUN **saws**
a tool with sharp teeth for cutting wood or other hard materials

saw VERB **saws**, **sawing**, **sawed**, **sawn** *or* **sawed**
to saw something is to cut it with a saw

sawdust NOUN
sawdust is powder that comes from wood when it is cut with a saw

saxophone NOUN **saxophones**
a wind instrument with a tube that curves upward and a reed in the mouthpiece
DID YOU KNOW? The **saxophone** is named after Adolphe *Sax*, a Belgian instrument-maker.

say VERB **says**, **saying**, **said**
to say something is to make words with your voice

say NOUN
➤ **to have a say** *or* **have your say** is to be able to speak or give your opinion

saying NOUN **sayings**
a well-known phrase or proverb

scab NOUN **scabs**
a hard crust that forms over a cut or graze while it is healing

scabbard NOUN **scabbards**
a cover for a sword or dagger

scaffold NOUN **scaffolds** (*historical*)
a platform on which criminals used to be executed

scaffolding *NOUN*
scaffolding is a structure of poles and planks for workers to stand on when building or repairing a house

scald *VERB* **scalds, scalding, scalded**
❶ to scald your skin is to burn it with very hot liquid or steam ❷ to scald something is to clean it with boiling water

scale *NOUN* **scales**
❶ a series of units or marks for measuring something • *We use the Celsius temperature scale.* ❷ the relationship between the size of something on a map or model and the actual size of the thing in the real world • *The scale of this map is one centimetre to the kilometre.* ❸ a series of musical notes going up or down in a fixed pattern ❹ the relative size or importance of something • *This film director loves to work on a grand scale.* ❺ one of the thin overlapping parts on the outside of fish, snakes and other animals ❻ scale is the coating that forms on the inside of kettles and pans

scale *VERB* **scales, scaling, scaled**
to scale something is to climb up it • *Mountain goats can scale rocky cliff faces with ease.*

scales *PLURAL NOUN*
a device for weighing things

scalp *NOUN* **scalps**
the skin on the top of your head

scaly *ADJECTIVE* **scalier, scaliest**
scaly skin is covered in scales

scamper *VERB* **scampers, scampering, scampered**
to run quickly with short steps
My earliest memories are a confusion of hilly fields and dark, damp stables, and rats that scampered along the beams above my head.—WAR HORSE, Michael Morpurgo

scampi *PLURAL NOUN*
scampi are large prawns

scan *VERB* **scans, scanning, scanned**
❶ to scan something is to look at every part of it ❷ to scan a piece of writing is to look over it quickly ❸ to scan an area, or a part of the body, is to sweep a radar or electronic beam over it in order to find

something ❹ poetry scans when it has a fixed rhythm

scan *NOUN* **scans**
a search or examination using a scanner

scandal *NOUN* **scandals**
❶ a scandal is a shameful or disgraceful action ❷ scandal is gossip that damages someone's reputation
➤ **scandalous** *ADJECTIVE*

Scandinavian *ADJECTIVE*
to do with Scandinavia (Norway, Sweden and Denmark, and sometimes Finland and Iceland)

scanner *NOUN* **scanners**
❶ a machine used to examine part of the body, using an electronic beam ❷ a machine that converts print and pictures into data that can be read by a computer

scanty *ADJECTIVE* **scantier, scantiest**
hardly big enough; small
➤ **scantily** *ADVERB*

scapegoat *NOUN* **scapegoats**
someone who gets all the blame for something that other people have done

scar *NOUN* **scars**
a mark left on your skin by a cut or burn after it has healed

scar *VERB* **scars, scarring, scarred**
an injury scars you when it leaves a permanent mark on your skin

scarab *NOUN* **scarab**
an ancient Egyptian symbol in the shape of a beetle

scarce *ADJECTIVE* **scarcer, scarcest**
not enough to supply people • *Wheat was scarce because of the bad harvest.*
➤ **to make yourself scarce** (*informal*) is to go away or keep out of the way

scarcely *ADVERB*
hardly; only just • *The pup was scarcely two days old.*

scarcity *NOUN*
there is a scarcity of something when there is not enough of it

scare *VERB* **scares, scaring, scared**
to scare someone is to frighten them

a
b
c
d
e
f
g
h
i
j
k
l
m
n
o
p
q
r
s
t
u
v
w
x
y
z

scare NOUN scares
a scare is a fright • *You gave me quite a scare.*

scarecrow NOUN scarecrows
a figure of a person dressed in old clothes, that farmers put in a field to frighten birds away from crops

scarf NOUN scarves
a strip of material that you wear round your neck or head

scarlet ADJECTIVE
bright red

scary ADJECTIVE scarier, scariest (*informal*)
frightening • *We told each other scary ghost stories.*
➤ **scarily** ADVERB ➤ **scariness** NOUN

scatter VERB scatters, scattering, scattered
❶ to scatter things is to throw them in all directions ❷ to scatter is to move quickly in all directions • *The crowd scattered when the police arrived.*

scavenge VERB scavenges, scavenging, scavenged
an animal or bird scavenges when it eats dead animals that have been killed by another animal
➤ **scavenger** NOUN

scene NOUN scenes
❶ the place where something happens • *Here is the scene of the crime.* ❷ a part of a play or film ❸ a view someone sees ❹ an angry or noisy outburst • *They made a scene about the money.*

scenery NOUN
❶ scenery is the natural features of an area • *We were admiring the scenery.* ❷ scenery is also things put on a stage to make it look like a place

scent (*say* sent) NOUN scents
❶ a pleasant smell or perfume ❷ an animal's smell, that other animals can follow
➤ **scented** ADJECTIVE

scent VERB scents, scenting, scented
to scent something is to discover it by its scent

sceptic (*say* skep-tik) NOUN sceptics
someone who does not believe things easily or readily

sceptical (*say* skep-tik-al) ADJECTIVE
you are sceptical when you do not believe things easily or readily

sceptre (*say* sep-ter) NOUN sceptres
a ceremonial staff carried by a king, queen or pharaoh

schedule (*say* shed-yool) NOUN schedules
a timetable of things that have to be done
➤ **to be on schedule** is to be on time; not late

scheme NOUN schemes
a plan of what to do

scheme VERB schemes, scheming, schemed
to scheme is to make secret plans

scholar NOUN scholars
❶ someone who studies a subject thoroughly ❷ someone who has been given a scholarship

scholarly ADJECTIVE
showing knowledge and learning

scholarship NOUN scholarships
❶ a scholarship is a grant of money given to someone for their education ❷ scholarship is knowledge and learning

school NOUN schools
❶ a place where children go to be taught ❷ the children who go there • *The whole school was invited to the show.* ❸ a school is also a group of whales or fish

schoolchild NOUN schoolchildren
a child who goes to school

schoolteacher NOUN schoolteachers
a teacher at a school

schooner (*say* skoo-ner) NOUN schooners
a sailing ship with two or more masts

science NOUN
science is the study of objects and happenings in the world that can be observed and tested
DID YOU KNOW? The word **science** comes from a Latin word meaning 'knowledge'.

science fiction NOUN
science fiction is stories about imaginary worlds, especially in space and in the future

scientific ADJECTIVE
❶ to do with science ❷ studying things carefully and logically

scientist *NOUN* **scientists**
someone who studies science or is an expert in science

sci-fi (*say* sy-fy) *NOUN* (*informal*)
science fiction

scissors *PLURAL NOUN*
a cutting device made of two movable blades joined together
SPELLING ALERT! There is a silent **c** in **scissors**. Think of the **c** in **c**utting to help you remember!

scoff *VERB* **scoffs, scoffing, scoffed**
to scoff at someone or something is to make fun of them

scold *VERB* **scolds, scolding, scolded**
to scold someone is to tell them off harshly

scone (*say* skon *or* skohn) *NOUN* **scones**
a small plain cake, usually eaten with butter and jam

scoop *NOUN* **scoops**
❶ a deep spoon for serving soft food such as ice cream or mashed potato ❷ a deep shovel ❸ (*informal*) an important piece of news that only one newspaper prints

scoop *VERB* **scoops, scooping, scooped**
to scoop something, or to scoop it out, is to take it out with a scoop or the palm of your hand

scooter *NOUN* **scooters**
❶ a simple type of bicycle on which you stand on a narrow platform and move forward by pushing one foot against the ground ❷ a kind of motorcycle with small wheels

scope *NOUN*
❶ opportunity or possibility for something • *There is scope for improvement.* ❷ the range or extent of something • *The new syllabus covers a wider scope of topics.*

scorch *VERB* **scorches, scorching, scorched**
to scorch something is to make it go brown by slightly burning it

scorching *ADJECTIVE*
very hot

score *NOUN* **scores**
❶ the number of points or goals made in a game • *What's the score?* ❷ (*old use*) a score is twenty • *He reached the age of four-score (= 80) years.*

score *VERB* **scores, scoring, scored**
❶ to score a goal or point in a game is to get it ❷ to score is to keep a count of the score in a game • *I thought you were scoring.* ❸ to score a surface is to scratch it
➤ **scorer** *NOUN*

scorn *NOUN*
scorn is treating a person or thing with contempt

scorn *VERB* **scorns, scorning, scorned**
to scorn someone or something is to have contempt for them

scornful *ADJECTIVE*
to be scornful is to be full of contempt and show no respect
➤ **scornfully** *ADVERB*

scorpion *NOUN* **scorpions**
an animal related to the spider, with pincers and a poisonous sting in its curved tail

Scot *NOUN* **Scots**
a person from Scotland

Scotch terrier *NOUN* **Scotch terriers**
a small terrier with rough hair

Scots *NOUN*
a language spoken in lowland Scotland
DID YOU KNOW? The words **glamour** and **warlock** come from Scots.

Scottish *ADJECTIVE*
to do with Scotland or its people

scoundrel *NOUN* **scoundrels**
a wicked or dishonest person

scour *VERB* **scours, scouring, scoured**
❶ to scour (for example) a pan or bath is to rub it hard with something rough until it is clean and bright ❷ to scour an area is to search it thoroughly

scout *NOUN* **scouts**
someone sent out ahead of a group in order to collect information

scowl *VERB* **scowls, scowling, scowled**
to scowl is to look bad-tempered

scowl *NOUN* **scowls**
an angry look

scramble *VERB* **scrambles, scrambling, scrambled**
❶ to scramble is to move quickly and clumsily • *We scrambled over the rocks to safety.*

a b c d e f g h i j k l m n o p q r s t u v w x y z

2 to scramble eggs is to cook them by mixing them and heating them in a pan **3** to scramble for something is to struggle to do it or get it

scramble NOUN **scrambles**
1 a climb or walk over rough ground
2 a struggle to get something • *There was a scramble for the best seats.* **3** a motorcycle race across rough country

scrap NOUN **scraps**
1 a scrap is a small piece of something
2 scrap is rubbish, especially unwanted metal
3 (*informal*) a fight

scrap VERB **scraps, scrapping, scrapped**
1 to scrap something is to get rid of it when you do not want it • *We decided to scrap the idea.* **2** (*informal*) to scrap is to fight or quarrel

scrape VERB **scrapes, scraping, scraped**
1 to scrape something is to rub it with something rough, hard or sharp **2** to scrape past or through is to only just get past or succeed • *She scraped through her exams.*
3 to scrape something together is to collect it with difficulty • *They scraped together enough money for a holiday.*

scrape NOUN **scrapes**
1 a scraping movement or sound **2** a mark made by scraping something **3** (*informal*) an awkward situation • *He's always getting into scrapes.*

scrappy ADJECTIVE **scrappier, scrappiest**
done carelessly or untidily

scratch VERB **scratches, scratching, scratched**
1 to scratch a surface is to damage it by rubbing something sharp over it **2** you scratch your skin when you rub it with your fingers because it itches

scratch NOUN **scratches**
1 a mark or cut made by scratching **2** the action of scratching • *I need to have a scratch.*
➤ **to start from scratch** is to begin at the very beginning
➤ **to be up to scratch** is to be up to the proper standard

scrawl NOUN **scrawls**
untidy writing • *Can you read my scrawl?*

scrawl VERB **scrawls, scrawling, scrawled**
to scrawl something is to write it in a hurried or careless way

scream NOUN **screams**
1 a loud high-pitched cry of pain or fear or anger **2** (*informal*) you can say something is a scream when it is very amusing

scream VERB **screams, screaming, screamed**
to scream is to make a loud high-pitched cry
Things happened to me that will probably make you scream when you read about them. That can't be helped.—THE WITCHES, Roald Dahl

screech NOUN **screeches**
a harsh high-pitched sound • *There was a screech of tyres as the car sped off.*

screech VERB **screeches, screeching, screeched**
to screech is to make a harsh high-pitched sound • *A flock of seagulls rose screeching into the air.*

screen NOUN **screens**
1 a surface on which films or television programmes or computer data are shown **2** a movable panel used to hide or protect something **3** a windscreen

screen VERB **screens, screening, screened**
1 to screen a film or television programme is to show it **2** to screen something is to hide it or protect it with a screen **3** to screen people is to test them to find out if they have a disease

screenplay NOUN **screenplays**
the script for a film or television drama

screenshot NOUN **screenshots**
an image of the display on the screen of a computer or mobile phone

screw NOUN **screws**
1 a metal pin with a spiral ridge round it, which holds things by being twisted into them **2** a propeller

screw VERB **screws, screwing, screwed**
1 to screw something is to fix it with screws **2** to screw something in or on is to fit it by turning it • *Screw the lid on to the jar.*
• *I screwed in the light bulb.*
➤ **to screw something up** is to twist or squeeze it into a tight ball

screwdriver *NOUN* **screwdrivers**
a tool for putting in or taking out screws

scribble *VERB* **scribbles**, **scribbling**, **scribbled**
to write untidily or carelessly, or to make meaningless marks

script *NOUN* **scripts**
❶ the words of a play, film or broadcast
❷ handwriting ❸ something you write, especially the answers you write to exam questions

scripture *NOUN* **scriptures**
a sacred book, especially the Bible

scriptwriter *NOUN* **scriptwriters**
someone who writes the script for a play, film or broadcast

scroll *NOUN* **scrolls**
a roll of paper or parchment with writing on it

scroll *VERB* **scrolls**, **scrolling**, **scrolled**
you scroll up or down on a computer screen when you move the text up or down on the screen to see what comes before or after

scrounge *VERB* **scrounges**, **scrounging**, **scrounged** (*informal*)
to scrounge something is to get it without paying for it • *He scrounged a meal from us.*
➤ **scrounger** *NOUN*

scrub *VERB* **scrubs**, **scrubbing**, **scrubbed**
to scrub something is to rub it with a hard brush

scrub *NOUN*
❶ a scrub is the action of scrubbing
• *You'll need to give your face a good scrub.*
❷ scrub is also low trees and bushes, or land covered with them

scruffy *ADJECTIVE* **scruffier**, **scruffiest**
shabby and untidy • *a scruffy pair of jeans*
➤ **scruffiness** *NOUN*

scrum, **scrummage** *NOUN* **scrums**, **scrummages** (*rugby*)
a group of players from each side who push against each other and try to win the ball with their feet

scrumptious *ADJECTIVE* (*informal*)
delicious
➤ **scrumptiousness** *NOUN*

scrutinize (*also* **scrutinise**) *VERB* **scrutinizes**, **scrutinizing**, **scrutinized**
to scrutinize something is to examine it or look at it closely

scrutiny *NOUN*
scrutiny is examining or looking at something closely

scuba diving *NOUN*
scuba diving is swimming underwater, breathing air from a supply carried on your back
DID YOU KNOW? The word **scuba** comes from the first letters of *self-contained underwater breathing apparatus.*

scuffle *NOUN* **scuffles**
a confused struggle or fight

scuffle *VERB* **scuffles**, **scuffling**, **scuffled**
people scuffle when they fight in a confused way

sculptor *NOUN* **sculptors**
someone who makes sculptures

sculpture *NOUN* **sculptures**
❶ a sculpture is something carved or shaped out of a hard material such as stone, clay or metal ❷ sculpture is the art or work of a sculptor

scum *NOUN*
scum is froth or dirt on the top of a liquid

scurry *VERB* **scurries**, **scurrying**, **scurried**
to scurry is to run or hurry with short steps
• *A large black beetle scurried across the floor.*

scurvy *NOUN*
a severe lack of vitamin C, caused by not eating enough fruit and vegetables

scuttle *NOUN* **scuttles**
a container for coal, kept by a fireplace

scuttle *VERB* **scuttles**, **scuttling**, **scuttled**
❶ to scuttle a ship is to sink it deliberately by making holes in the side or bottom ❷ to scuttle is also to run with short quick steps
*'Oh! Oh! Oh!' said Mrs Crabbity, and she turned and scuttled into her cottage like a small frightened spider.—*UNDER THE MOON, Vivian French

scythe (*say* syth) *NOUN* **scythes**
a tool with a long curved blade for cutting grass or corn

a b c d e f g h i j k l m n o p q r s t u v w x y z

sea *NOUN* **seas**
❶ the salt water that covers most of the earth's surface ❷ a large lake or area of water, such as the Mediterranean Sea
❸ a large area of something • *Across the table we saw a sea of faces.*
➤ **at sea** ❶ on the sea ❷ unable to understand something or cope with it • *He's completely at sea in his new job.*

seabed *NOUN*
the seabed is the bottom of the sea

sea cow *NOUN* **sea cows**
another name for **manatee**

seafaring *ADJECTIVE, NOUN*
travelling or working on the sea
➤ **seafarer** *NOUN*

seafood *NOUN*
seafood is fish or shellfish from the sea eaten as food

seagull *NOUN* **seagulls**
a sea bird with long wings

seahorse *NOUN* **seahorses**
a small fish that swims upright, with a head rather like a horse's head

seal *NOUN* **seals**
❶ a sea mammal with thick fur that breeds on land ❷ something designed to close an opening and stop air or liquid getting in or out ❸ a design pressed into a soft substance such as wax or lead

seal *VERB* **seals, sealing, sealed**
to seal something is to close it by sticking two parts together • *He sealed the envelope.*

sea level *NOUN*
sea level is the level of the sea halfway between high and low tide • *The mountain rises 1,000 metres above sea level.*

sea lion *NOUN* **sea lions**
a large kind of seal. The male has a kind of mane.

seam *NOUN* **seams**
❶ the line where two edges of cloth join together ❷ a layer of coal in the ground

seaman, **seawoman** *NOUN* **seamen, seawomen**
a sailor

seaplane *NOUN* **seaplanes**
an aeroplane that can land on water and take off from water

seaport *NOUN* **seaports**
a port on the coast

search *VERB* **searches, searching, searched**
❶ to search for something or someone is to look very carefully for them ❷ to search a person or place is to look very carefully for something they may have

search *NOUN* **searches**
❶ a very careful look for someone or something ❷ when you look for information in a computer database or on the internet • *Let's do a search for 'Roald Dahl'.*

search engine *NOUN* **search engines**
a computer program that helps you find information on the internet

searching *ADJECTIVE*
a searching question or look is a thorough one that is trying to find out the truth about something

searchlight *NOUN* **searchlights**
a light with a strong beam that can be turned in any direction

search party *NOUN* **search parties**
a group of people organized to look for someone or something

seashore *NOUN*
the seashore is the land close to the sea

seasick *ADJECTIVE*
someone is seasick when they are sick because of the movement of a ship
➤ **seasickness** *NOUN*

seaside *NOUN*
the seaside is a place by the sea where people go on holiday

season *NOUN* **seasons**
❶ one of the four main parts of the year: spring, summer, autumn and winter ❷ the time of year when a sport or other activity happens • *When does the football season start?*

season *VERB* **seasons, seasoning, seasoned**
to season food is to put salt, pepper or other strong-tasting things on it to flavour it

seasonal *ADJECTIVE*
happening only at certain times of the year
• *Fruit-picking is seasonal work.*

seasoning *NOUN* **seasonings**
seasoning is something strong-tasting like salt
and pepper, used to season food

season ticket *NOUN* **season tickets**
a ticket that you can use as often as you like for
a certain period

seat *NOUN* **seats**
❶ a piece of furniture for sitting on ❷ a place
in parliament or on a council or a board of
a business ❸ the place where something is
located • *London is the seat of government.*

seat *VERB* **seats**, **seating**, **seated**
a place seats a certain number of people when
it has that many seats for them • *The theatre
seats 3,000.*

seat belt *NOUN* **seat belts**
a strap to hold a person securely in the seat of
a vehicle or aircraft

seaward *ADVERB*
towards the sea

seaweed *NOUN* **seaweeds**
seaweed is plants that grow in the sea

secluded *ADJECTIVE*
a secluded place is away from large numbers
of people; quiet and hidden • *They found a
secluded beach for their picnic.*

seclusion *NOUN*
seclusion is being private or hidden • *She lived
in seclusion in the countryside.*

second *ADJECTIVE, NOUN*
the next after the first
➤ **to have second thoughts** is to wonder
whether your decision was really right

second *NOUN* **seconds**
❶ a very short period of time, one-sixtieth of
a minute ❷ a person or thing that is second
❸ seconds are products that are not of the
best quality

second *VERB* **seconds**, **seconding**,
seconded
❶ to second a proposal or motion is to
support it formally ❷ to second a fighter is to
be the person who helps and supports them in
a fight

secondary *ADJECTIVE*
coming second; not original or essential • *This is
of secondary importance.*

secondary school *NOUN*
secondary schools
a school for children who are about 11 years
old and older

second-hand *ADJECTIVE, ADVERB*
❶ bought or used after someone else has used
it • *I bought a second-hand bike.* • *Did you buy
it second-hand?* ❷ that sells used goods
• *a second-hand bookshop*

secondly *ADVERB*
as the second thing • *Secondly, I'd like to thank
my parents.*

secrecy *NOUN*
secrecy is being secret

secret *ADJECTIVE*
❶ that must not be told or shown to other
people ❷ that is not known by everyone

secret *NOUN* **secrets**
something that is secret
➤ **to do something in secret** is to do it
secretly

secret agent *NOUN* **secret agents**
a spy working for a country

secretary (*say* sek-re-tree) *NOUN*
secretaries
❶ someone whose job is to organize letters
and emails, answer the telephone and
make business arrangements for a person
or organization ❷ the chief assistant of a
government minister

secrete (*say* si-kreet) *VERB* **secretes**,
secreting, **secreted**
❶ to secrete something is to hide it carefully
❷ to secrete a substance in the body is to
release it • *Saliva is secreted in the mouth.*

secretive (*say* seek-rit-iv) *ADJECTIVE*
liking or trying to keep things secret
➤ **secretively** *ADVERB* ➤ **secretiveness** *NOUN*

secretly *ADVERB*
you secretly do something when you do it
without telling other people
*Jilly had always secretly thought how marvellous it
would be to have a dragon as a pet.–DRAGON RIDE,
Helen Cresswell*

a
b
c
d
e
f
g
h
i
j
k
l
m
n
o
p
q
r
s
t
u
v
w
x
y
z

secret service NOUN
a country's secret service is the government department in charge of spies and espionage

sect NOUN sects
a group of people who have special or unusual religious opinions or beliefs

section NOUN sections
a part of something • *Our school library has a large history section.* • *The tail section of the plane broke off.*

sector NOUN sectors
❶ a part of an area or activity ❷ a part of a circle made by drawing two straight lines from the centre to the circumference

secure ADJECTIVE
❶ firm and safe • *Is that ladder secure?*
❷ not likely to be lost • *I need a secure job.*
❸ made safe or protected from attack • *Check that all the doors and windows are secure.*
➤ **securely** ADVERB

secure VERB secures, securing, secured
❶ to secure something is to make it safe or firmly fixed ❷ to secure something is also to get hold of it • *She secured two tickets for the show.*

security NOUN
❶ security is being secure or safe ❷ security is also measures taken to prevent theft, spying or terrorism

sedate (*say* si-**dayt**) ADJECTIVE
calm and dignified
➤ **sedately** ADVERB

sediment NOUN
sediment is solid matter that settles at the bottom of a liquid

sedimentary (*say* sed-i-**men**-tree) ADJECTIVE
sedimentary rock is formed from layers of sand, stones or mud that have settled on the bottom of a lake or river

see VERB sees, seeing, saw, seen
❶ to see something or someone is to use your eyes to notice them or be aware of them
❷ to see someone is to meet or visit them • *See me after class.* ❸ to see something is to understand it • *I see what you mean.*
❹ to see someone as something is to imagine them being it • *Can you see yourself as a teacher?* ❺ to see that something happens is to make sure of it • *See that the windows are shut.* ❻ to see someone somewhere is to escort or lead them • *I'll see you to the door.*
➤ **to see through something** is not to be deceived by it
➤ **to see to something** is to deal with it

seed NOUN seeds
a tiny part of a plant that can grow in the ground to make a new plant

seedling NOUN seedlings
a very young plant

seek VERB seeks, seeking, sought
❶ to seek a person or thing is to try to find them ❷ to seek something is to try to achieve it • *She is seeking fame.*

seem VERB seems, seeming, seemed
to seem to be something or to have some quality is to appear that way or give that impression • *They seem happy in their new house.*

seemingly ADVERB
appearing to be • *The creature was seemingly fast asleep.*

seen VERB (*past participle of* see)
• *Have you seen the film yet?*

seep VERB seeps, seeping, seeped
a liquid or gas seeps when it flows slowly through or into or out of something
• *Water was seeping into the cellar.*

see-saw NOUN see-saws
a plank balanced in the middle, which goes up and down as people sitting on each end take turns to push up from the ground
DID YOU KNOW? The word **see-saw** comes from an old rhyme that people used when sawing wood.

seethe VERB seethes, seething, seethed
❶ a liquid seethes when it boils or bubbles
❷ you are seething when you are very angry or excited

segment NOUN segments
a part that is cut off or can be separated from the rest of something • *He ate a few segments of an orange.*

segregate (*say* seg-ri-gayt) *VERB*
segregates, segregating, segregated
to segregate people of different races or
religions is to keep them apart and make
them live separately
➤ segregation *NOUN*

seismograph *NOUN* seismographs
a device for detecting the strength of
earthquakes

seize (*say* seez) *VERB* seizes, seizing, seized
to seize someone or something is to take hold
of them suddenly or firmly
➤ to seize up is to become jammed or stuck

seizure *NOUN* seizures
a seizure is a sudden attack of an illness that
may include violent movement or loss of
consciousness, for example because of epilepsy
or a heart attack

seldom *ADVERB*
not often • *I seldom cry.*

select *VERB* selects, selecting, selected
to select a person or thing is to choose them
carefully

select *ADJECTIVE*
small and carefully chosen • *a select team of
top players*

selection *NOUN* selections
❶ selection is choosing people or things
carefully ❷ a selection is a number of things
that have been carefully chosen • *The book
contains a selection of poems.*

self *NOUN* selves
the type of person you are; your individual
nature • *You'll soon be feeling your old self
again.*

self-centred *ADJECTIVE*
a self-centred person is selfish and thinks too
much about themself
➤ self-centredness *NOUN*

self-confident *ADJECTIVE*
confident in what you can do
➤ self-confidence *NOUN*

self-conscious *ADJECTIVE*
embarrassed or shy because you know people
are watching you
➤ self-consciousness *NOUN*

self-control *NOUN*
self-control is the ability to control your own
behaviour or feelings

self-defence *NOUN*
❶ you act in self-defence when you do
something defending yourself against attack
❷ self-defence is also skill in defending yourself
if someone attacks you

selfie *NOUN* selfies
a photograph that you take of yourself, usually
on a mobile phone camera

selfish *ADJECTIVE*
having or doing what you want without
thinking of other people
➤ selfishly *ADVERB* ➤ selfishness *NOUN*

selfless *ADJECTIVE*
thinking of other people rather than yourself;
not selfish

self-raising flour *NOUN*
self-raising flour is flour that makes cakes and
pastry rise during cooking

self-respect *NOUN*
self-respect is the feeling that you are behaving
and thinking in the proper way

self-righteous *ADJECTIVE*
a self-righteous person is smug because they
are sure that they are a good person
➤ self-righteousness *NOUN*

self-service *ADJECTIVE*
a self-service shop or restaurant is one
where customers help themselves to things
and pay at the checkout for what they have
taken

self-sufficient *ADJECTIVE*
able to provide what you need without help
from others
➤ self-sufficiency *NOUN*

selkie *NOUN* selkies
(in Scottish stories) a mythological creature
which is half woman and half seal

sell *VERB* sells, selling, sold
to sell goods or services is to offer them in
exchange for money
➤ to sell out is to sell all your stock of
something

semaphore *NOUN*
a system of signalling in which people hold flags in various positions to indicate letters or numbers

semi– *PREFIX*
meaning 'half', as in *semicircle*

semibreve (*say* sem-i-breev) *NOUN* **semibreves**
the longest musical note normally used, written (◦)

semicircle *NOUN* **semicircles**
half a circle
➤ **semicircular** *ADJECTIVE*

semicolon *NOUN* **semicolons**
a punctuation mark (;), marking a more definite break in a sentence than a comma does

semi-detached *ADJECTIVE*
a semi-detached house is one that is joined to another house on one side

semi-final *NOUN* **semi-finals**
a match played to decide who will take part in the final
➤ **semi-finalist** *NOUN*

semitone *NOUN* **semitones**
half a tone in music

semolina *NOUN*
semolina is a milk pudding made with grains of wheat

senate (*say* sen-at) *NOUN*
❶ the governing council in ancient Rome
❷ the higher-ranking section of the parliament in France, the USA and some other countries

senator *NOUN* **senators**
a member of a senate

send *VERB* **sends**, **sending**, **sent**
❶ to send something somewhere is to arrange for it to be taken there ❷ to send someone somewhere is to tell them to go there
➤ **to send someone up** (*informal*) is to make fun of them

senior *ADJECTIVE*
❶ older than someone else ❷ higher in rank
• *He is a senior officer in the navy.*

senior *NOUN* **seniors**
someone is your senior when they are older or higher in rank than you are

senior citizen *NOUN* **senior citizens**
an older person, especially a pensioner

sensation *NOUN* **sensations**
❶ a feeling • *We had a sensation of warmth.*
❷ a very exciting event or the excitement caused by it • *The news caused a great sensation.*

sensational *ADJECTIVE*
causing great excitement or shock

sense *NOUN* **senses**
❶ the ability to see, hear, smell, touch or taste things ❷ the ability to feel or appreciate something • *She has a good sense of humour.* ❸ the power to think or make good judgements • *He hasn't got the sense to come in out of the rain.*
❹ meaning • *The word 'set' has many senses.*
➤ **to make sense** is to have a meaning you can understand

sense *VERB* **senses**, **sensing**, **sensed**
❶ to sense something is to feel it or be aware of it • *I sensed that she did not like me.*
❷ to sense something is also to detect it
• *This device senses radioactivity.*

senseless *ADJECTIVE*
❶ stupid; not sensible ❷ unconscious

sensible *ADJECTIVE*
wise; having or showing common sense
➤ **sensibly** *ADVERB*

sensitive *ADJECTIVE*
❶ affected by the sun or chemicals or something else physical • *I have sensitive skin.*
❷ easily offended or upset • *He is very sensitive about his age.* ❸ aware of other people's feelings
➤ **sensitively** *ADVERB*

sensitivity *NOUN* **sensitivities**
❶ sensitivity is being sensitive ❷ a sensitivity is something you are sensitive about

sensor *NOUN* **sensors**
a device or instrument for detecting something physical such as heat or light

sent *VERB* (*past tense and past participle of* **send**)
• *I sent the letter yesterday.* • *I would have sent you home if I'd known you were ill.*

sentence *NOUN* **sentences**
❶ a group of words that express a complete thought and form a statement or question or command ❷ the punishment given to a convicted person in a law court

sentence *VERB* **sentences**, **sentencing**, **sentenced**
to sentence someone is to give them a sentence in a law court • *They were sentenced to two years in prison.*

sentiment *NOUN* **sentiments**
❶ a sentiment is a feeling or opinion
❷ sentiment is a show of feeling or emotion

sentimental *ADJECTIVE*
showing or making you feel emotion, especially too much sad emotion • *That love story is too sentimental.*
➤ **sentimentality** *NOUN*
➤ **sentimentally** *ADVERB*

sentinel *NOUN* **sentinels**
a sentry
Jo was dismissed, but chose to march up and down the hall like a sentinel, having some fear that the prisoner might bolt.—LITTLE WOMEN, Louisa M. Alcott

sentry *NOUN* **sentries**
a soldier guarding something

separable *ADJECTIVE*
able to be separated from each other

separate (*say* sep-er-at) *ADJECTIVE*
❶ not joined to anything; on its own
• *I packed each present in a separate box.*
❷ not together; not with each other
• *They lead separate lives.*

separate (*say* sep-er-ayt) *VERB* **separates**, **separating**, **separated**
❶ to separate things or people is to take them away from others ❷ to separate is to become separate or move away from each other
❸ two people separate when they stop living together as a couple

separately *ADVERB*
people do something separately when they do it on their own, not together • *They arrived together but left separately.*

separation *NOUN*
separation is when people or things move apart or are taken away from each other

September *NOUN*
the ninth month of the year
DID YOU KNOW? **September** is based on the Latin word *septem* meaning 'seven', because it was the seventh month in the Roman calendar.

septic *ADJECTIVE*
a wound goes septic when it becomes infected with harmful bacteria

sequel (*say* see-kwel) *NOUN* **sequels**
❶ a book or film that continues the story of an earlier one ❷ something that results from an earlier event

sequence (*say* see-kwenss) *NOUN* **sequences**
❶ a series of things ❷ the order in which things should follow each other • *Arrange the playing cards in sequence, the highest first.*

sequin (*say* see-kwin) *NOUN* **sequins**
sequins are tiny bright discs sewn on clothes to decorate them

serene *ADJECTIVE*
calm and peaceful
➤ **serenely** *ADVERB* ➤ **serenity** *NOUN*

sergeant (*say* sar-jent) *NOUN* **sergeants**
a soldier or police officer who is in charge of others

sergeant major *NOUN* **sergeant majors**
a soldier who is one rank higher than a sergeant

serial *NOUN* **serials**
a story that is presented in separate parts over a period, for example week by week
SPELLING ALERT! You read or listen to a **serial**, but a **cereal** is something you eat for breakfast.

series *NOUN* **series**
❶ a number of things following each other or connected with each other ❷ a set of television or radio programmes with the same title

serious *ADJECTIVE*
❶ not funny; important • *We need a serious talk.* ❷ thoughtful or solemn • *His face was serious.* ❸ very bad • *They've had a serious accident.*
➤ **seriously** *ADVERB* ➤ **seriousness** *NOUN*

sermon *NOUN* **sermons**
a talk given by a preacher

serpent *NOUN* **serpents**
a snake

servant *NOUN* **servants**
a person whose job is to work in someone else's house

serve *VERB* **serves**, **serving**, **served**
❶ to serve people in a shop is to help them find the things they want to buy ❷ to serve food or drink is to give it to people at a meal ❸ to serve a person or organization is to work for them ❹ to serve is to be suitable for a purpose • *This tree stump will serve as a table.* ❺ (*tennis*) to serve is to start play by hitting the ball to your opponent
➤ **it serves you right** you deserve it
➤ **server** *NOUN*

serve *NOUN* **serves**
the action of serving in tennis

service *NOUN* **services**
❶ service is working for someone or something ❷ a service is something that helps people or supplies what they want • *There is a good bus service into town.* ❸ a service is also a religious ceremony in a church ❹ a service, or dinner service, is a set of crockery ❺ a vehicle or machine has a service when someone spends time repairing and maintaining it ❻ (*tennis*) a service is a serve
➤ **the services** the armed forces of a country

service *VERB* **services**, **servicing**, **serviced**
to service a vehicle or machine is to repair and maintain it

serviceable *ADJECTIVE*
suitable for everyday use or wear
'Those dresses are good, sensible, serviceable dresses, without any frills.'—ANNE OF GREEN GABLES, L. M. Montgomery

service station *NOUN* **service stations**
a place beside the road where you can buy petrol

serviette *NOUN* **serviettes**
a piece of cloth or paper for use at meals

sesame *NOUN*
a tropical plant, the seeds of which can be eaten or used to make an edible oil

session *NOUN* **sessions**
❶ a time spent doing one thing • *They were in the middle of a recording session.* ❷ a meeting or series of meetings • *The King will open the next session of Parliament.*

set *VERB* **sets**, **setting**, **set**
This word has many meanings, depending on the words that go with it:
❶ to set something somewhere is to put or place it there • *Set the vase on the table.*
❷ to set a device is to make it ready to work • *Have you set the alarm?* ❸ to set is to become solid or hard • *The jelly has set now.*
❹ the sun sets when it goes down towards the horizon ❺ to set someone doing something is to start them doing it • *The news set me thinking.* ❻ to set someone a task or problem is to give it to them to do or solve • *Has the teacher set your homework?*
➤ **to set about something** is to start doing it
➤ **to set off** *or* **set out** is to begin a journey
➤ **to set something out** is to display it or make it known • *She set out her reasons for leaving.*
➤ **to set something up** is to place it in position or get it started • *We want to set up a playgroup.*

set *NOUN* **sets**
❶ a group of people or things that belong together ❷ a radio or television receiver ❸ (*mathematics*) a collection of things that you treat as a group because they have something in common, such as being odd numbers ❹ a series of games in a tennis match ❺ the scenery on a stage

set square *NOUN* **set squares**
a device in the shape of a triangle, used for drawing parallel lines and to draw angles

sett *NOUN* **setts**
the underground burrow of a badger

settee *NOUN* **settees**
a sofa

setting *NOUN* **settings**
❶ the setting of a story is the place and time in which it happens ❷ the land and buildings around something • *The house stood in a rural setting.* ❸ a set of cutlery or crockery for one person

settle *VERB* **settles**, **settling**, **settled**
❶ to settle a problem, difficulty or argument is to solve it or decide about it ❷ to settle, or settle down, is to become relaxed or make

yourself comfortable • *He settled down in the armchair.* ❸ to settle somewhere is to go and live there • *The family settled in Canada.* ❹ something light such as dust or snow settles when it comes to rest on something • *The dust was settling on the books.* • *A bird flew down and settled on the fence.* ❺ to settle a bill or debt is to pay it

settlement *NOUN* settlements
❶ a settlement is a group of people or houses in a new area ❷ a settlement is also an agreement to end an argument

settler *NOUN* settlers
a person who moves with a group of others to live in a new country or area

seven *NOUN* sevens
the number 7

seventeen *NOUN* seventeens
the number 17
➤ seventeenth *ADJECTIVE, NOUN*

seventh *ADJECTIVE, NOUN*
the next after the sixth
➤ seventhly *ADVERB* in the seventh place; as the seventh one

seventy *NOUN* seventies
the number 70
➤ seventieth *ADJECTIVE, NOUN*

sever *VERB* severs, severing, severed
to sever something is to cut or break it off

several *DETERMINER, PRONOUN*
more than two but not many • *We have several paintings by this artist.* • *The painting is one of several in the gallery.*

severe *ADJECTIVE* severer, severest
❶ strict or harsh; not gentle or kind
'It's my opinion that you never think at all,' the Rose said, in a rather severe tone.—ALICE THROUGH THE LOOKING-GLASS, Lewis Carroll
❷ very bad or serious • *a severe head injury*
➤ severely *ADVERB*

severity *NOUN*
the severity of something is its extreme seriousness

sew *(say* so*) VERB* sews, sewing, sewed, sewn *or* sewed
❶ to sew cloth or other soft material is to use a needle and thread to join it or form it

into clothing ❷ to sew is to work with a needle and thread or with a sewing machine

sewage *(say* soo-ij*) NOUN*
sewage is waste matter carried away in drains

sewer *(say* soo-er*) NOUN* sewers
an underground drain that carries away sewage

sewing machine *NOUN* sewing machines
a machine for sewing things

sex *NOUN* sexes
❶ a sex is each of the two groups, male or female, that people and animals belong to ❷ sex is the instinct that causes members of the two sexes to be attracted to one another ❸ to have sex is to take part in sexual activity with another person, especially sexual intercourse
➤ sexual *ADJECTIVE*

sextet *NOUN* sextets
❶ a group of six musicians ❷ a piece of music for six musicians

shabby *ADJECTIVE* shabbier, shabbiest
❶ very old and worn
The stranger was wearing an extremely shabby set of wizard's robes which had been darned in several places.—HARRY POTTER AND THE PRISONER OF AZKABAN, J. K. Rowling
❷ mean or unfair • *What a shabby trick!*
➤ shabbiness *NOUN*

shack *NOUN* shacks
a roughly built hut

shade *NOUN* shades
❶ shade is an area sheltered from bright sunlight • *We sat down in the shade.* ❷ a shade is a colour, or how light or dark a colour is ❸ a shade is also a device that decreases or shuts out bright light ❹ a shade of something is a slight difference or amount • *He is a shade taller than his brother.*

shade *VERB* shades, shading, shaded
❶ to shade something or someone is to shelter them from bright light ❷ to shade a drawing is to make parts of it darker than the rest

shadow *NOUN* shadows
❶ a dark shape that falls on a surface when something is between it and the light ❷ an area that is dark because the light is blocked • *The stranger's face was in shadow.*

shadow *VERB* **shadows, shadowing, shadowed**
1 to shadow someone is to follow them secretly
2 to shadow something is to cast a shadow on it

shadowy *ADJECTIVE*
1 a shadowy place is dark and full of shadows
2 difficult to see or distinguish • *A shadowy figure appeared on the screen.*

shady *ADJECTIVE* **shadier, shadiest**
1 giving shade • *We sat under a shady tree.*
2 situated in the shade • *Find a shady spot.*
3 dishonest or suspect • *It was a shady deal.*

shaft *NOUN* **shafts**
1 a long thin rod or straight part of something
2 a deep narrow hole in a mine or building
• *They found an old mine shaft.* • *a lift shaft*
3 a beam of light

shaggy *ADJECTIVE* **shaggier, shaggiest**
having long untidy hair
➤ **shagginess** *NOUN*

shake *VERB* **shakes, shaking, shook, shaken**
1 to shake something is to move it quickly up and down or from side to side • *Have you shaken the bottle?* 2 to shake is to move in this way 3 to shake someone is to shock or upset them • *The news shook her.* 4 to shake is to tremble • *His voice was shaking.*
➤ **to shake hands** is to clasp someone's right hand as a greeting or as a sign that you agree

shake *NOUN* **shakes**
a quick movement up and down or from side to side • *Give the bottle a shake.*

shaky *ADJECTIVE* **shakier, shakiest**
shaking or likely to fall down
➤ **shakily** *ADVERB* ➤ **shakiness** *NOUN*

shall *VERB* (*past tense*) **should**
used with *I* and *we* to refer to the future
• *We shall arrive tomorrow.* • *We told them we should arrive the next day.*

shallow *ADJECTIVE* **shallower, shallowest**
not deep • *The stream is quite shallow here.*
• *We were playing in the shallow end of the pool.*

sham *NOUN* **shams**
a person or thing that is not genuine or what they claim to be

shamble *VERB* **shambles, shambling, shambled**
to walk in an awkward way, dragging your feet along the ground

shambles *NOUN*
you say something is a shambles when it is in great disorder or in a mess

shame *NOUN*
1 shame is a feeling of great sorrow or guilt because you have done something wrong
2 you say something is a shame when it is something that you regret or are sorry about
• *What a shame you won't be able to come.*

shame *VERB* **shames, shaming, shamed**
to shame someone is to make them feel ashamed

shameful *ADJECTIVE*
causing shame; disgraceful
➤ **shamefully** *ADVERB*

shameless *ADJECTIVE*
feeling or showing no shame
➤ **shamelessly** *ADVERB*

shampoo *NOUN* **shampoos**
shampoo is liquid soap for washing things, especially your hair

shampoo *VERB* **shampoos, shampooing, shampooed**
to shampoo something is to wash it with shampoo

DID YOU KNOW? The word **shampoo** comes from a Hindi word meaning 'press!'.

shamrock *NOUN*
shamrock is a small plant rather like clover, with leaves divided in three

shan't
short for *shall not* • *I shan't be much longer.*

shanty *NOUN* **shanties**
1 a sailor's traditional song 2 a roughly built hut

shape *NOUN* **shapes**
1 the outline of something or the way it looks
2 something that has a definite or regular form, such as a square, circle or triangle
3 the condition that something is in
• *The garden isn't in very good shape.*
➤ **to be out of shape** is to no longer have the normal shape • *The front wheel was twisted out of shape.*

➤ **to take shape** is to start to develop properly

shape *VERB* **shapes, shaping, shaped**
to shape something is to give it a shape
➤ **to shape up** is to develop well

shapeless *ADJECTIVE*
having no definite shape
With these words the Witch fell down in a brown, melted, shapeless mass and began to spread over the clean boards of the kitchen floor.—THE WIZARD OF OZ, L. Frank Baum

shapely *ADJECTIVE* **shapelier, shapeliest**
having an attractive shape

shapeshifter *NOUN* **shapeshifters**
a creature in stories that can change the form of its body

share *NOUN* **shares**
❶ one of the parts into which something is divided between several people or things ❷ part of a company's money, lent by someone who is then given part of the profits in return

share *VERB* **shares, sharing, shared**
❶ to share something, or share it out, is to divide it between several people or things ❷ to share something is to use it when someone else is also using it • *She shared a room with me.*

shark *NOUN* **sharks**
a large sea fish with sharp teeth

sharp *ADJECTIVE* **sharper, sharpest**
❶ a sharp object has an edge or point that can cut or make holes • *This is a sharp knife.* ❷ quick to learn or notice things • *She has sharp eyes.* • *It was sharp of you to spot that mistake.* ❸ sudden or severe • *We came to a sharp bend in the road.* • *I felt a sharp pain in my side.* ❹ slightly sour • *The apples taste sharp.* ❺ above the proper musical pitch
➤ **sharpness** *NOUN*

sharp *ADVERB*
❶ with a sudden change of direction • *Now turn sharp right.* ❷ punctually; exactly • *Be there at six o'clock sharp.*

sharp *NOUN* **sharps** (*music*)
the note that is a semitone higher than the natural note; the sign (♯) that indicates this

sharpen *VERB* **sharpens, sharpening, sharpened**
to sharpen something is to make it sharp or pointed
➤ **sharpener** *NOUN*

sharply *ADVERB*
to say something sharply is to say it in a critical or severe way

shatter *VERB* **shatters, shattering, shattered**
❶ to shatter is to break suddenly into lots of tiny pieces ❷ to shatter something is to break it in this way ❸ to shatter hopes or dreams is to show they are unreal ❹ someone is shattered when they are very upset by something • *We were shattered by the news.*

shave *VERB* **shaves, shaving, shaved**
❶ someone shaves when they scrape hair from their skin with a razor ❷ to shave something is to cut or scrape a thin slice off it
➤ **shaver** *NOUN*

shave *NOUN* **shaves**
the act of shaving the face • *Dad was having a shave.*
➤ **a close shave** (*informal*) a narrow escape

shawl *NOUN* **shawls**
a large piece of material for covering the shoulders or wrapping a baby

she *PRONOUN*
a female person or animal: used as the subject of a verb

sheaf *NOUN* **sheaves**
❶ a bundle of papers ❷ a bundle of corn stalks tied together after reaping

shear *VERB* **shears, shearing, sheared, shorn** or **sheared**
to shear a sheep is to cut the wool from it
➤ **shearer** *NOUN*
➤ **to shear off** is to break off

shears *PLURAL NOUN*
a tool like a very large pair of scissors for trimming grass and bushes or for shearing sheep

sheath *NOUN* **sheaths**
❶ a cover for the blade of a sword or dagger ❷ a cover that fits something closely

a
b
c
d
e
f
g
h
i
j
k
l
m
n
o
p
q
r
s
t
u
v
w
x
y
z

sheathe *VERB* **sheathes**, **sheathing**, **sheathed**
❶ to sheathe a sword is to put it into its sheath ❷ to sheathe something is to put a protective covering on it

shed *NOUN* **sheds**
a simply made building used for storing things or sheltering animals, or as a workshop

shed *VERB* **sheds**, **shedding**, **shed**
to shed something is to let it fall or flow
• *The trees had shed their leaves.* • *He was badly hurt and shedding blood.*

she'd
short for *she had* or *she would*

sheen *NOUN*
a soft shine on a surface

sheep *NOUN* **sheep**
a grass-eating animal kept by farmers for its wool and meat
PLURAL ALERT! The word **sheep** does not change in the plural: *a herd of black-faced sheep.*

sheepdog *NOUN* **sheepdogs**
a dog trained to guard and control sheep

sheepish *ADJECTIVE*
someone looks sheepish when they look shy or embarrassed
➤ **sheepishly** *ADVERB*

sheer *ADJECTIVE* **sheerer**, **sheerest**
❶ complete or total • *This is sheer madness!*
❷ extremely steep; vertical • *a sheer drop of fifty metres* ❸ sheer material is so thin that you can see through it
SPELLING ALERT! You can climb a **sheer** cliff, but you **shear** a sheep.

sheet *NOUN* **sheets**
❶ a large piece of lightweight material put on a bed ❷ a whole flat piece of paper, glass or metal • *You will need two sheets of newspaper.* ❸ a wide area of water, snow, ice or flame

sheikh (*say* shayk) *NOUN* **sheikhs**
the leader of an Arab people or community

shelf *NOUN* **shelves**
❶ a flat piece of hard material fitted to a wall or in a piece of furniture so that you can put things on it ❷ a flat level surface that sticks out from a cliff or under the sea

shell *NOUN* **shells**
❶ the hard outer covering round a nut or egg, or round an animal such as a snail or tortoise ❷ a metal case filled with explosive, fired from a large gun ❸ the walls or framework of a building or ship

shell *VERB* **shells**, **shelling**, **shelled**
❶ to shell something is to take it out of its shell ❷ to shell a building or ship or town is to fire explosive shells at it

she'll
short for *she will* • *She'll know what to do.*

shellfish *NOUN* **shellfish**
a sea animal that has a shell

shelter *NOUN* **shelters**
❶ a shelter is a place that protects people from danger or from the weather ❷ shelter is being protected from danger or from the weather
• *We found shelter from the rain.*

shelter *VERB* **shelters**, **sheltering**, **sheltered**
❶ to shelter somewhere is to stay there because you are protected from danger or from the weather • *We sheltered under the trees.*
❷ to shelter something or someone is to protect or cover them • *The hill shelters the house from the wind.*

shelve *VERB* **shelves**, **shelving**, **shelved**
❶ to shelve something is to put it on a shelf or shelves ❷ to shelve an idea or piece of work is to reject or postpone it

shepherd *NOUN* **shepherds**
someone whose job is to look after sheep

shepherd's pie *NOUN* **shepherd's pies**
a baked dish of minced meat covered with mashed potato

sherbet *NOUN* **sherbets**
a fizzy sweet powder or drink
DID YOU KNOW? The word **sherbet** comes from an Arabic word meaning 'a drink'.

sheriff *NOUN* **sheriffs**
the chief law officer of a county in various countries

sherry *NOUN* **sherries**
a kind of strong wine

she's
short for *she is* or *she has* • *She's my sister.*
• *She's been abroad.*

shield *NOUN* **shields**
① a large piece of metal or wood a person carries to protect their body in fighting
② a design or trophy in the shape of a shield
③ a protection from harm • *The heat shield protects the spacecraft as it enters the atmosphere.*

shield *VERB* **shields**, **shielding**, **shielded**
to shield someone or something is to protect them • *I was shielded from the wind.* • *She shielded her eyes from the sun.*

shift *NOUN* **shifts**
① a change of position or condition
② a group of workers who start work as another group finishes; the time when they work • *He's on the night shift this month.*
③ a lightweight dress that hangs loosely

shift *VERB* **shifts**, **shifting**, **shifted**
① to shift something is to move it ② to shift is to change position

shilling *NOUN* **shillings**
an old British coin that was worth a twentieth of a pound (now 5 pence)

shimmer *VERB* **shimmers**, **shimmering**, **shimmered**
to shine with a quivering light • *The sea shimmered in the midday sun.*

shin *NOUN* **shins**
the front of your leg between your knee and your ankle

shine *VERB* **shines**, **shining**, **shone** *or* (*in sense 3*) **shined**
① to shine is to give out or reflect bright light • *The sun shone all day.* ② to shine a torch or light somewhere is to point the light in that direction ③ to shine something is to polish it • *Have you shined your shoes?* ④ to shine is to do well or be excellent • *He does not shine in maths.*

shine *NOUN*
① shine is brightness ② a shine is an act of polishing • *Give your shoes a good shine.*

shingle *NOUN*
shingle is pebbles on a beach

shiny *ADJECTIVE* **shinier**, **shiniest**
bright or glossy

ship *NOUN* **ships**
a large boat, especially one that goes to sea

ship *VERB* **ships**, **shipping**, **shipped**
to ship something is to send it on a ship

shipping *NOUN*
① shipping is all the ships of a country
② shipping is also the business of carrying goods by ship

shipwreck *NOUN* **shipwrecks**
① when a ship is wrecked in a storm or accident at sea ② the remains of a wrecked ship
➤ **shipwrecked** *ADJECTIVE*

shipyard *NOUN* **shipyards**
a dockyard

shire *NOUN* **shires**
a county

shirk *VERB* **shirks**, **shirking**, **shirked**
you shirk a task or duty when you avoid doing it

shirt *NOUN* **shirts**
a piece of clothing you wear on the top half of the body, with a collar and sleeves
➤ **to be in your shirtsleeves** is to be wearing a shirt but not a jacket over it

shiver *VERB* **shivers**, **shivering**, **shivered**
you shiver when you tremble with cold or fear
➤ **shivery** *ADJECTIVE*

shiver *NOUN* **shivers**
an act of shivering • *I felt a shiver down my spine.*

shoal *NOUN* **shoals**
a large number of fish swimming together

shock *NOUN* **shocks**
① a shock is a sudden unpleasant surprise
② a shock is also a violent knock or jolt
③ shock is weakness caused by severe pain or injury ④ a shock, or electric shock, is a painful effect caused by a strong electric current passing through your body ⑤ a shock of hair is a bushy mass of hair
He was a man of fifty, with a shock of grizzled hair, ... bushy eyebrows, and the finest forehead that I ever saw.—MOONFLEET, J. Meade Faulkner

shock *VERB* **shocks**, **shocking**, **shocked**
① to shock someone is to give them a shock
② to shock someone is also to make them feel disgusted or appalled • *We were shocked to discover he had been lying all along.*

a
b
c
d
e
f
g
h
i
j
k
l
m
n
o
p
q
r
s
t
u
v
w
x
y
z

shocking ADJECTIVE
❶ horrifying or disgusting ❷ very bad
• *The weather's been shocking today.*

shoddy ADJECTIVE shoddier, shoddiest
of poor quality • *This is shoddy work.*

shoe NOUN shoes
❶ a strong covering you wear on your foot
❷ a horseshoe

shoelace NOUN shoelaces
a cord for fastening a shoe

shoestring NOUN
➤ to do something on a shoestring is to do
it with only a small amount of money

shone VERB (*past tense and past participle*
of shine)
• *Jamie shone his torch down the tunnel.*
• *The sun has shone all day.*

shook VERB (*past tense of* shake)
• *He shook with fear.*

shoot VERB shoots, shooting, shot
❶ to shoot a gun or other weapon is to fire it
❷ to shoot a person or animal is to fire a
gun at them ❸ to shoot somewhere is to
move very fast • *Two police cars shot past.*
❹ in football and hockey, to shoot is to kick
or hit a ball at the goal ❺ to shoot a film or
scene is to film or photograph it • *The film was
shot in New Zealand.*

shoot NOUN shoots
a young branch or new growth of a plant

shooting star NOUN shooting stars
a meteor

shop NOUN shops
❶ a building where people buy things
❷ a workshop

shop VERB shops, shopping, shopped
to shop is to go and buy things at shops

shopkeeper NOUN shopkeepers
someone who owns or looks after a shop

shoplifter NOUN shoplifters
someone who steals from shops
➤ shoplifting NOUN

shopper NOUN shoppers
someone who goes shopping

shopping NOUN
❶ shopping is buying things at shops
• *I like shopping.* ❷ shopping is also things
that you have bought in shops • *Let me help
you carry your shopping.*

shore NOUN shores
❶ the seashore ❷ the land along the edge of
a lake

shorn VERB (*past participle of* shear)
• *The farmer had shorn the sheep.*

short ADJECTIVE shorter, shortest
❶ not long; not lasting long • *Our cat has short
ginger hair.* • *I went for a short walk.* ❷ not tall
• *The cook was both short and stout.*
❸ not sufficient; scarce • *Food is short.*
❹ bad-tempered • *He was rather short with me.*
❺ short pastry is rich and crumbly, and
contains a lot of fat
➤ for short as a shorter form of something
• *Joanna is called Jo for short.*
➤ short for something a shorter form of
something • *Jo is short for Joanna.*
➤ to be short of something is to not have
enough of it • *We seem to be short of chairs.*
➤ shortness NOUN

short ADVERB
❶ before reaching the point aimed at
• *My ball fell just short of the hole.* ❷ suddenly
• *The horse stopped short.*

shortage NOUN shortages
there is a shortage when there is not enough of
something

shortbread NOUN
shortbread is a rich sweet biscuit made with
butter

shortcake NOUN shortcakes
❶ shortbread ❷ a light cake usually served
with fruit

short circuit NOUN short circuits
a fault in an electrical circuit in which
current flows along a shorter route than the
normal one

shortcoming NOUN shortcomings
a fault or failure • *He has many shortcomings.*

short cut NOUN short cuts
a route or method that is quicker than the
usual one

shorten *VERB* **shortens**, **shortening**, **shortened**
❶ to shorten something is to make it shorter
❷ to shorten is to become shorter

shorthand *NOUN*
shorthand is a set of special signs for writing words down as quickly as people say them

short–handed *ADJECTIVE*
to be short-handed is to not have enough people to help you

shortly *ADVERB*
❶ soon • *I'll be there shortly.* **❷** briefly or sharply • *'Go away,' she said shortly.*

shorts *PLURAL NOUN*
trousers with legs that stop at or above the knee

short–sighted *ADJECTIVE*
❶ unable to see things clearly when they are further away **❷** not thinking enough about what may happen in the future

shot *VERB* (*past tense and past participle of* **shoot**)
• *He shot me a furious look.* • *The rocket had shot upwards.*

shot *NOUN* **shots**
❶ a shot is the firing of a gun or other weapon
❷ shot is lead pellets fired from small guns
❸ a good or bad shot is a person judged by their skill in shooting • *She is a great shot.*
❹ a shot is a stroke in a game with a ball, such as tennis or snooker **❺** in photography, a shot is a photograph or filmed sequence
❻ a shot is a heavy metal ball thrown in athletic contests **❼** a shot at something is an attempt to do it • *Have a shot at this puzzle.*

shotgun *NOUN* **shotguns**
a gun for firing small lead pellets over a short distance

shot–put, **shot–putting** *NOUN*
a sport in which athletes throw a very heavy round ball as far as possible

should *VERB*
This word is used to express
❶ what someone ought to do • *You should have told me.* **❷** what someone expects
• *They should be here soon.* **❸** what might happen • *If you should happen to see him, tell him to come.*

shoulder *NOUN* **shoulders**
the part of your body between your neck and your arm

shoulder *VERB* **shoulders**, **shouldering**, **shouldered**
❶ to shoulder something is to put it or rest it on your shoulder or shoulders **❷** to shoulder blame or responsibility is to accept it

shoulder blade *NOUN* **shoulder blades**
each of the two large flat bones at the top of your back

shout *VERB* **shouts**, **shouting**, **shouted**
to shout is to speak or call very loudly

shout *NOUN* **shouts**
a loud cry or call

shove (*say* shuv) *VERB* **shoves**, **shoving**, **shoved**
to shove something is to push it hard
➤ **to shove off** (*informal*) is to go away

shovel (*say* shuv-el) *NOUN* **shovels**
a tool like a spade with the sides turned up, for lifting and moving coal, earth, sand, snow and other things

shovel *VERB* **shovels**, **shovelling**, **shovelled**
to shovel (for example) earth or snow is to move it or clear it with a shovel

show *VERB* **shows**, **showing**, **showed**, **shown**
❶ to show something is to let people see it
• *She showed me her new bike.* **❷** to show something to someone is to explain it to them
• *Can you show me how to do it?* **❸** to show someone somewhere is to guide or lead them there • *I'll show you to your seat.* **❹** to show is to be visible • *That stain won't show.*
➤ **to show off** is to try to impress people
➤ **to show something off** is to be proud of letting people see it

show *NOUN* **shows**
❶ an entertainment • *She loves TV game shows.*
❷ a display or exhibition • *Have you been to the flower show?*

show business *NOUN*
show business is the entertainment business; the theatre, films, radio and television

shower *NOUN* **showers**
❶ a brief fall of rain or snow • *It's only a shower.*
❷ a lot of small things coming or falling like rain • *They were met by a shower of stones.*

a
b
c
d
e
f
g
h
i
j
k
l
m
n
o
p
q
r
s
t
u
v
w
x
y
z

③ a device or cabinet for spraying water to wash the body; a wash in this

shower VERB showers, showering, showered

① to shower is to fall like rain **②** to shower someone with things is to give a lot of them • *He showered her with presents.* **③** to shower is to wash under a shower

showery ADJECTIVE
raining occasionally

showjumping NOUN
showjumping is a competition in which riders make their horses jump over fences and other obstacles
➤ **showjumper** NOUN

showman, show-woman NOUN
showmen, show-women
① a person whose job is to present shows and events **②** someone who is good at entertaining people

show-off NOUN show-offs
someone who is trying to impress other people

showy ADJECTIVE showier, showiest
likely to attract attention; bright or highly decorated
➤ **showily** ADVERB ➤ **showiness** NOUN

shrank VERB (*past tense of* shrink)
• *My jumper shrank in the wash.*

shrapnel NOUN
shrapnel is pieces of metal scattered from an exploding shell

shred NOUN shreds
① a tiny strip or piece torn or cut off something • *His cloak had been ripped to shreds.* **②** a very small amount of something • *There's not a shred of evidence for what you say.*

shred VERB shreds, shredding, shredded
to shred something is to tear or cut it into tiny strips or pieces

shrew NOUN shrews
a small animal rather like a mouse

shrewd ADJECTIVE shrewder, shrewdest
having common sense and showing good judgement
➤ **shrewdly** ADVERB ➤ **shrewdness** NOUN

shriek NOUN shrieks
a shrill cry or scream

shriek VERB shrieks, shrieking, shrieked
to shriek is to give a shrill cry or scream

shrill ADJECTIVE
a shrill sound is very high and loud • *the shrill blast of a whistle*
➤ **shrilly** ADVERB ➤ **shrillness** NOUN

shrimp NOUN shrimps
a small shellfish

shrine NOUN shrines
an altar or chapel or other sacred place

shrink VERB shrinks, shrinking, shrank, shrunk
① to shrink is to become smaller • *My dress has shrunk.* **②** to shrink something is to make it smaller, usually by washing it • *Their jeans have been shrunk.* **③** to shrink from something is to avoid it because you are afraid or embarrassed • *He shrank from meeting strangers.*

shrivel VERB shrivels, shrivelling, shrivelled
to shrivel or shrivel up is to become wrinkled and dry

shroud NOUN shrouds
a sheet in which a dead body is wrapped

shroud VERB shrouds, shrouding, shrouded
① to shroud a dead body is to wrap it in a shroud **②** to shroud something is to cover or conceal it • *The mountain was shrouded in mist.*

Shrove Tuesday NOUN
the day before Ash Wednesday, when people eat pancakes

shrub NOUN shrubs
a bush or small tree

shrubbery NOUN shrubberies
an area where shrubs are grown

shrug VERB shrugs, shrugging, shrugged
you shrug when you raise your shoulders slightly as a sign that you do not care or do not know

shrug NOUN shrugs
the act of shrugging

shrunk *VERB* (*past participle of* **shrink**)
• *My jumper has shrunk in the wash.*

shrunken *ADJECTIVE*
smaller than it used to be because it has shrunk

shudder *VERB* **shudders**, **shuddering**, **shuddered**
you shudder when you shake because you are cold or afraid

shudder *NOUN* **shudders**
the act of shuddering

shuffle *VERB* **shuffles**, **shuffling**, **shuffled**
❶ to shuffle is to drag your feet along the ground as you walk ❷ to shuffle playing cards is to mix them by sliding them over each other several times

shuffle *NOUN* **shuffles**
the act of shuffling • *Give the cards a quick shuffle.*

shunt *VERB* **shunts**, **shunting**, **shunted**
to shunt a railway train or wagons is to move them from one track to another

shut *VERB* **shuts**, **shutting**, **shut**
❶ to shut a door or window, or a lid or cover, is to move it so that it blocks up an opening ❷ to shut is to become closed • *The door shut suddenly.*
➤ **to shut down** is to stop work or business
➤ **to shut up** (*informal*) is to stop talking

shut *ADJECTIVE*
closed • *Keep your eyes shut.*

shutter *NOUN* **shutters**
❶ a panel or screen that can be closed over a window ❷ the device in a camera that opens and closes to let light fall on the film

shuttle *NOUN* **shuttles**
❶ a train or bus or aircraft that makes frequent short journeys between two places ❷ a space shuttle ❸ the part of a loom that carries the thread from side to side

shuttlecock *NOUN* **shuttlecocks**
a small rounded piece of cork or plastic with a ring of feathers fixed to it, that you use in the game of badminton

shy *ADJECTIVE* **shyer**, **shyest**
timid and afraid to meet or talk to other people
➤ **shyly** *ADVERB* ➤ **shyness** *NOUN*

sibling *NOUN* **siblings**
your siblings are your brothers and sisters
• *I have three siblings: two sisters and one brother.*

sick *ADJECTIVE* **sicker**, **sickest**
❶ ill or unwell • *He looks after sick animals.*
❷ you feel sick when you feel that you are going to vomit; you are sick when you vomit
➤ **to be sick of something** *or* **someone** is to be tired of them or fed up with them

sicken *VERB* **sickens**, **sickening**, **sickened**
❶ to sicken someone is to disgust them
❷ to sicken is to start feeling ill

sickly *ADJECTIVE* **sicklier**, **sickliest**
❶ often ill; unhealthy • *a sickly child*
❷ making people feel sick • *There was a sickly smell.*
➤ **sickliness** *NOUN*

sickness *NOUN* **sicknesses**
an illness or disease

side *NOUN* **sides**
❶ a flat surface, especially one that joins the top and bottom of something ❷ a line that forms the edge of a shape • *A triangle has three sides.* ❸ the outer part of something that is not the front or the back
• *The instructions are on the side of the box.*
❹ a position or space to the left or right of something • *There's a window on either side of the door.* ❺ your sides are the parts of your body from your armpits to your hips
• *I've got a pain down my right side.*
❻ a group of people playing, arguing or fighting against another group • *They are on our side.*

side *VERB* **sides**, **siding**, **sided**
to side with someone is to support them in a quarrel or argument

sideboard *NOUN* **sideboards**
a long heavy piece of furniture with drawers and cupboards and a flat top

sideburns *PLURAL NOUN*
sideburns are strips of hair growing on each side of someone's face in front of their ears
'What did this Snatcher look like?' 'Big bloke with sideburns … and a glass eye,' replied Jim.—HERE BE MONSTERS, Alan Snow

a b c d e f g h i j k l m n o p q r s t u v w x y z

sidecar *NOUN* **sidecars**
a small compartment for a passenger, fixed to the side of a motorcycle

sideline *NOUN* **sidelines**
something that you do in addition to your normal work or activity

sideshow *NOUN* **sideshows**
a small entertainment forming part of a large show, especially at a fair

sideways *ADVERB, ADJECTIVE*
❶ to or from the side • *Crabs walk sideways.* • *She gave me a sideways glance.* ❷ with one side facing forward • *We sat sideways in the bus.*

siding *NOUN* **sidings**
a short railway line leading off the main line

sidle *VERB* **sidles**, **sidling**, **sidled**
to move sideways
Enormous crabs were sidling in and out between the shells, telling each other how strange it was that the water had disappeared.—COMET IN MOOMINLAND, Tove Jansson

siege (*say* seej) *NOUN* **sieges**
when an army surrounds a place until the people inside surrender

sieve (*say* siv) *NOUN* **sieves**
a device made of mesh or perforated metal or plastic, used to separate harder or larger parts from liquid

sift *VERB* **sifts**, **sifting**, **sifted**
❶ to sift a fine or powdery substance is to pass it through a sieve ❷ to sift facts or information is to examine or select them

sigh *NOUN* **sighs**
a sound you make by breathing out heavily when you are sad, tired or relieved

sigh *VERB* **sighs**, **sighing**, **sighed**
to sigh is to make a sigh

sight *NOUN* **sights**
❶ sight is the ability to see • *Owls have very good sight.* ❷ a sight is something that you see • *The mountains there are a wonderful sight.* ❸ the sights of a place are the interesting places worth seeing there • *a tour of the sights of Paris* ❹ you can describe something silly or ridiculous to look at as a sight • *What a sight you are!*
➤ **to be in sight** is to be able to be seen

➤ **to be out of sight** is to be no longer able to be seen

sight *VERB* **sights**, **sighting**, **sighted**
to sight something is to see it or observe it
SPELLING ALERT! **Sight** is different from **site**, which refers to a place: *The camping site was nowhere in sight.*

sightseeing *NOUN*
sightseeing is going round looking at interesting places
➤ **sightseer** *NOUN*

sign *NOUN* **signs**
❶ a mark or symbol that stands for something • *a minus sign* ❷ a board or notice that tells or shows people something ❸ something that shows that a thing exists • *There are signs of rust.* ❹ an action or signal giving information or a command • *She made a sign to them to be quiet.*

sign *VERB* **signs**, **signing**, **signed**
❶ you sign your name when you write your signature on something ❷ to sign is to make a sign or signal • *He signed to them to follow him.* ❸ to sign someone is to give them a contract for a job, especially in a professional sport • *They have signed three new players.*

signal *NOUN* **signals**
❶ a device or gesture or sound or light that gives information or a message ❷ a series of radio waves sent out or received

signal *VERB* **signals**, **signalling**, **signalled**
to signal to someone is to give them a signal
➤ **signaller** *NOUN*

signal box *NOUN* **signal boxes**
a building from which railway signals and points are controlled

signalman, **signalwoman** *NOUN*
signalmen, **signalwomen**
a person who controls railway signals

signature *NOUN* **signatures**
your name written by yourself

significance *NOUN*
the significance of something is its meaning or importance

significant *ADJECTIVE*
something is significant when it has a meaning or importance
➤ **significantly** *ADVERB*

signify *VERB* **signifies, signifying, signified**
to signify something is to mean it or indicate it

signing, sign language *NOUN*
signing is a way of communicating by using movements of your hands instead of sounds, used by people who are deaf

signpost *NOUN* **signposts**
a sign at a road junction showing the names and distances of the places that each road leads to

Sikh (*say* seek) *NOUN* **Sikhs**
someone who believes in **Sikhism**, which is a religion of South Asia that has one God

silence *NOUN* **silences**
silence is when no sound can be heard

silence *VERB* **silences, silencing, silenced**
to silence someone or something is to make them silent

silent *ADJECTIVE*
without any sound; not speaking
➤ **silently** *ADVERB*

silhouette (*say* sil-oo-et) *NOUN* **silhouettes**
a dark outline of something seen against a light background

silicon *NOUN*
silicon is a substance found in many rocks and used in making microchips

silk *NOUN*
❶ silk is a fine soft thread produced by silkworms for making their cocoons ❷ silk is also smooth shiny cloth made from this thread
➤ **silken** *ADJECTIVE*

silkworm *NOUN* **silkworms**
a kind of caterpillar that covers itself with a cocoon of fine threads when it is ready to turn into a moth

silky *ADJECTIVE* **silkier, silkiest**
silky hair or fur is soft, smooth and shiny like silk
➤ **silkiness** *NOUN*

sill *NOUN* **sills**
a strip of stone or wood or metal underneath a window or door

silly *ADJECTIVE* **sillier, silliest**
foolish
➤ **silliness** *NOUN*

DID YOU KNOW? There is no adverb *sillily*, because it would be too difficult to say!

silver *NOUN*
❶ silver is a shiny white precious metal ❷ silver is also coins made of this metal or a metal that looks like it ❸ silver is also a grey-white colour

silver wedding *NOUN* **silver weddings**
the 25th anniversary of a wedding

silvery *ADJECTIVE*
❶ shiny and silver in colour ❷ a silvery sound is gentle and clear • *a silvery laugh*

similar *ADJECTIVE*
one thing is similar to another when it is like it in some ways but not exactly the same
➤ **similarly** *ADVERB*

similarity *NOUN* **similarities**
❶ the similarity between two things is the fact that they are similar ❷ a similarity between two things is a way in which they are similar

simile (*say* sim-i-lee) *NOUN* **similes**
a kind of expression in which you describe something by comparing it with something else, for example *cold as ice* or *as smooth as silk*

simmer *VERB* **simmers, simmering, simmered**
food simmers when it boils very gently over a low heat
➤ **to simmer down** is to become calm after being anxious or angry

simple *ADJECTIVE* **simpler, simplest**
❶ easy • *That's a simple question to answer.* ❷ not complicated • *It was a simple plan, but it worked.* ❸ plain • *She was wearing a simple dress.* ❹ not having much sense or intelligence
➤ **simplicity** *NOUN*

simplify *VERB* **simplifies, simplifying, simplified**
to simplify something is to make it simple or easy to understand

a b c d e f g h i j k l m n o p q r s t u v w x y z

simply *ADVERB*
❶ in a simple way • *Explain it simply.*
❷ completely • *It's simply marvellous.*
❸ only or merely • *It's simply a question of time.*

simulate *VERB* **simulates, simulating, simulated**
❶ to simulate something is to reproduce the conditions for it • *The machine simulates a space flight.* ❷ to simulate a feeling or state is to pretend to have it • *I tried to simulate interest.*
➤ **simulation** *NOUN* ➤ **simulator** *NOUN*

simultaneous (*say* sim-ul-**tay**-ni-us) *ADJECTIVE*
two things are simultaneous when they happen at the same time
➤ **simultaneously** *ADVERB*

sin *NOUN* **sins**
a wicked act that breaks a religious or moral law

sin *VERB* **sins, sinning, sinned**
to sin is to commit a sin
➤ **sinner** *NOUN*

since *CONJUNCTION*
❶ from the time when • *A lot has happened since I last saw you.* ❷ because • *Since we missed our bus, we had to walk home.*

since *PREPOSITION*
from a certain time • *The weather has been cold since Christmas.*

since *ADVERB*
between then and now • *He has not been seen since.*

sincere *ADJECTIVE* **sincerer, sincerest**
you are being sincere when you mean what you say and express your true feelings • *I gave them my sincere good wishes.*
➤ **sincerely** *ADVERB* ➤ **sincerity** *NOUN*

sinew *NOUN* **sinews**
strong tissue that joins a muscle to a bone

sinful *ADJECTIVE*
wicked; guilty of sin
➤ **sinfulness** *NOUN*

sing *VERB* **sings, singing, sang, sung**
❶ to sing is to make musical sounds with your voice ❷ birds and insects sing when they make musical sounds

singe (*say* sinj) *VERB* **singes, singeing, singed**
to singe something is to burn it slightly

singer *NOUN* **singers**
someone who sings

single *ADJECTIVE*
❶ only one; not double ❷ designed for one person • *The bedroom had two single beds.* ❸ not married ❹ for a journey in one direction only

single *NOUN* **singles**
❶ a single ticket ❷ a recording with one song or short piece of music on it ❸ you play singles in tennis when you play against only one other person

single *VERB* **singles, singling, singled**
➤ **to single someone out** is to pick them from other people

single file *NOUN*
➤ **in single file** in a line, one behind the other

single-handed *ADJECTIVE*
by your own efforts; without any help

single-minded *ADJECTIVE*
thinking only about one thing you are determined to achieve

single parent *NOUN* **single parents**
a person who is bringing up a child or children without a partner

single ticket *NOUN* **single tickets**
a ticket for a journey you make to a place but not back again

singly *ADVERB*
one at a time or one by one • *You can buy the cards singly or in a pack of ten.*

singular *NOUN* **singulars**
the form of a word meaning only one person or thing, such as *child* and *mouse*

singular *ADJECTIVE*
❶ in the singular; meaning only one • *'Mouse' is a singular noun.* ❷ extraordinary • *Emmeline Pankhurst was a woman of singular courage.*

sinister *ADJECTIVE*
looking or seeming evil or harmful • *The jailer gave a sinister laugh.*
DID YOU KNOW? The word **sinister** comes from the Latin word for 'left', because the Romans thought the left side was unlucky.

sink *VERB* **sinks**, **sinking**, **sank**, **sunk**
❶ to sink is to go under water • *The ship sank in a storm.* ❷ to sink something is to make it go under water • *They fired on the ship and sank it.* ❸ to sink, or to sink down, is to go or fall down to the ground • *He sank to his knees.*
➤ **to sink in** is to be gradually understood

sink *NOUN* **sinks**
a fixed basin with taps to supply water

sinus (*say* sy-nus) *NOUN* **sinuses**
your sinuses are the hollows in the bones of your skull, connected with your nose • *My sinuses are blocked.*

sip *VERB* **sips**, **sipping**, **sipped**
to sip a drink is to drink it slowly in small mouthfuls

sip *NOUN* **sips**
a sip is a small mouthful to drink • *She took a sip of the magic potion.*

siphon *NOUN* **siphons**
a bent tube used for transferring liquid from one container to another at a lower level

siphon *VERB* **siphons**, **siphoning**, **siphoned**
to siphon liquid is to transfer it with a siphon

sir *NOUN*
a word sometimes used when speaking politely to a man, instead of his name • *Can I help you, sir?*
➤ **Sir** the title given to a knight • *Sir Paul McCartney*

sire *NOUN* **sires** (*old use*)
a word formerly used when speaking to a king
The tailor smiled and bowed his head. 'O honoured sire,' he softly said, 'This marvellous magic cloth has got Amazing ways to keep you hot.'—RHYME STEW, Roald Dahl

siren *NOUN* **sirens**
a device that makes a loud hooting or screaming sound, usually as a warning signal

sister *NOUN* **sisters**
❶ your sister is a woman or girl who has the same parents as you ❷ a senior nurse in a hospital

sister-in-law *NOUN* **sisters-in-law**
a person's sister-in-law is the sister of their husband or wife, or the wife of their brother or sister

sit *VERB* **sits**, **sitting**, **sat**
❶ to sit is to rest on your bottom, as you do when you are on a chair ❷ to sit someone, or to sit someone down, is to put them in a sitting position ❸ to sit an examination or test is to do it • *We sit our end-of-year exam this afternoon.* ❹ to sit somewhere is to be situated or positioned there • *The house sits on top of a hill.* ❺ to sit for someone is to act as a babysitter

site *NOUN* **sites**
❶ the place where something has been built or will be built • *They're clearing the site for the new stadium.* ❷ a place where something happened • *This is the site of a famous battle.*

site *VERB* **sites**, **siting**, **sited**
to site something somewhere is to locate or build it there

sit-in *NOUN* **sit-ins**
a protest in which a lot of people sit down in a place and refuse to move

sitting room *NOUN* **sitting rooms**
a room with comfortable chairs for sitting in

situated *ADJECTIVE*
to be situated in a particular place or position is to be placed there • *The town is situated close to the sea.*

situation *NOUN* **situations**
❶ a place or position; where something is ❷ all the things that are happening to someone at a particular time; the way things are • *We found ourselves in a very tricky situation.*

six *NOUN* **sixes**
the number 6

sixpence *NOUN* **sixpences**
an old British coin that was worth half a shilling

sixteen *NOUN* **sixteens**
the number 16
➤ **sixteenth** *ADJECTIVE, NOUN*

sixth *ADJECTIVE, NOUN*
the next after the fifth
➤ **sixthly** *ADVERB* in the sixth place; as the sixth one

sixty *NOUN* **sixties**
the number 60
➤ **sixtieth** *ADJECTIVE, NOUN*

a
b
c
d
e
f
g
h
i
j
k
l
m
n
o
p
q
r
s
t
u
v
w
x
y
z

size *NOUN* sizes
❶ how big a person or thing is
❷ the measurement something is made in
• *I wear a size four shoe.*

size *VERB* sizes, sizing, sized
➤ **to size something** *or* **someone up**
(*informal*) is to form an opinion about them

sizeable *ADJECTIVE*
fairly large

sizzle *VERB* sizzles, sizzling, sizzled
to make a crackling and hissing sound • *The bacon sizzled in the pan.*

skate *NOUN* skates
❶ an ice skate or roller skate ❷ a skate is also a large, flat edible sea fish

skate *VERB* skates, skating, skated
to skate is to move around on skates
➤ **skater** *NOUN*

skateboard *NOUN* skateboards
a small board with wheels, used for standing and riding on
➤ **skateboarder** *NOUN*
➤ **skateboarding** *NOUN*

skeletal *ADJECTIVE*
❶ to do with a skeleton ❷ bony and thin, like a skeleton • *a face with skeletal features*

skeleton *NOUN* skeletons
❶ the framework of bones in a person's or animal's body ❷ the framework or shell of a new building ❸ a small toboggan for one person that you ride lying down and head first

sketch *NOUN* sketches
❶ a quick or rough drawing ❷ a short amusing play

sketch *VERB* sketches, sketching, sketched
to sketch something or someone is to make a sketch of them

sketchy *ADJECTIVE* sketchier, sketchiest
roughly drawn or described, without any detail • *Reports of what happened are still sketchy.*

skewer *NOUN* skewers
a long wooden or metal or plastic pin that you push through meat to hold it together while it is being cooked

ski (*say* skee) *NOUN* skis
a long flat strip of wood or metal or plastic, fastened to each foot for moving quickly over snow

ski *VERB* skis, skiing, skied *or* ski'd
to ski is to travel on snow wearing skis
➤ **skier** *NOUN*

skid *VERB* skids, skidding, skidded
to skid is to slide accidentally, especially in a vehicle

skid *NOUN* skids
a skidding movement • *The car went into a skid on the icy road.*

skilful *ADJECTIVE*
having or showing a lot of skill
➤ **skilfully** *ADVERB*

skill *NOUN* skills
❶ to do something with skill is to do it well
❷ a type of work or ability that you learn through training and practice • *I've been practising my cooking skills.*
➤ **skilled** *ADJECTIVE*

skim *VERB* skims, skimming, skimmed
❶ to skim is to move quickly over a surface
❷ to skim something is to remove it from the surface of a liquid, especially to take the cream off milk

skimmed *ADJECTIVE*
skimmed milk has had the cream removed

skimp *VERB* skimps, skimping, skimped
to use or provide less than is needed for something

skimpy *ADJECTIVE* skimpier, skimpiest
skimpy clothes do not cover much of your body

skin *NOUN* skins
❶ the outer covering of a person's or animal's body ❷ the outer covering of a fruit or vegetable ❸ a thin firm layer that has formed on the surface of a liquid

skin *VERB* skins, skinning, skinned
to skin something is to take the skin off it

skinny *ADJECTIVE* skinnier, skinniest
very thin

skip *VERB* skips, skipping, skipped
❶ to skip is to jump or move along by hopping from one foot to the other ❷ to skip is also to jump with a skipping rope ❸ to skip something

is to miss it out or ignore it • *You can skip the last chapter.*

skip *NOUN* **skips**
❶ a skipping movement ❷ a large metal container for taking away builders' rubbish

skipper *NOUN* **skippers**
the captain of a ship or team

skipping rope *NOUN* **skipping ropes**
a length of rope, usually with a handle at each end, that you swing over your head and under your feet as you jump

skirt *NOUN* **skirts**
a piece of clothing that hangs down from the waist

skirt *VERB* **skirts**, **skirting**, **skirted**
to skirt something is to go round the edge of it

skirting, **skirting board** *NOUN* **skirtings**, **skirting boards**
a narrow board round the wall of a room, close to the floor

skit *NOUN* **skits**
a play or sketch or poem that makes fun of something by imitating it

skittish *ADJECTIVE*
lively and excitable

skittle *NOUN* **skittles**
a piece of wood or plastic shaped like a bottle, that you try to knock down with a ball in a game of **skittles**

skull *NOUN* **skulls**
the framework of bones in your head which contains your brain
➤ **skull and crossbones** an emblem, especially on a pirate's flag, showing a skull with two bones crossed beneath it

skunk *NOUN* **skunks**
a black and white furry animal from North America that can make an unpleasant smell

sky *NOUN* **skies**
the space above the earth, where you can see the sun, moon and stars

skydive *NOUN* **skydives**
a skydive is when someone jumps from an aircraft and performs acrobatics in the air before landing with a parachute
➤ **skydiving** *NOUN*

skylark *NOUN* **skylarks**
a small brown bird that sings as it hovers high in the air

skylight *NOUN* **skylights**
a window in a roof

skyscraper *NOUN* **skyscrapers**
a very tall building

slab *NOUN* **slabs**
a thick flat piece of something

slack *ADJECTIVE* **slacker**, **slackest**
❶ loose; not pulled tight • *The rope was slack.*
❷ lazy; not busy or working hard
➤ **slackly** *ADVERB* ➤ **slackness** *NOUN*

slacken *VERB* **slackens**, **slackening**, **slackened**
❶ to slacken something is to loosen it
❷ to slacken is to become slower or less busy
• *Her pace gradually slackened.*

slacks *PLURAL NOUN*
loose-fitting casual trousers

slain *VERB* (*past participle of* **slay**)
• *George had slain the dragon.*

slalom *NOUN* **slaloms**
a ski race down a winding course with sharp turns

slam *VERB* **slams**, **slamming**, **slammed**
❶ to slam (for example) a door is to shut it hard or loudly ❷ to slam something is to hit it with great force • *He slammed the ball into the net.*

slang *NOUN*
slang is a kind of colourful language used in less formal writing and speaking

slant *VERB* **slants**, **slanting**, **slanted**
❶ to slant is to slope or lean ❷ to slant news or information is to present it from a particular point of view

slant *NOUN* **slants**
❶ a sloping or leaning position • *The caravan floor was at a slant.* ❷ a way of presenting news or information from a particular point of view

slap *VERB* **slaps**, **slapping**, **slapped**
❶ to slap someone is to hit them with the palm of your hand ❷ to slap something somewhere is to put it there forcefully or carelessly
• *We slapped paint on the walls.*

a
b
c
d
e
f
g
h
i
j
k
l
m
n
o
p
q
r
s
t
u
v
w
x
y
z

slap *NOUN* **slaps**
to give someone a slap is to slap them

slapstick *NOUN*
slapstick is noisy lively comedy, with people hitting each other, throwing things and falling over

slash *VERB* **slashes, slashing, slashed**
❶ to slash something is to make large cuts in it ❷ to slash prices or costs is to reduce them a lot

slash *NOUN* **slashes**
❶ a large cut ❷ a sloping line (/) used to separate words or letters

slat *NOUN* **slats**
a thin strip of wood or plastic, usually arranged to overlap with others, for example in a blind or screen

slate *NOUN* **slates**
❶ slate is a kind of grey rock that is easily split into flat plates ❷ slates are flat pieces of this rock used to cover a roof

slaughter (*say* slor-ter) *VERB* **slaughters, slaughtering, slaughtered**
❶ to slaughter an animal is to kill it for food ❷ to slaughter people or animals is to kill a lot of them

slaughter *NOUN*
slaughter is the killing of a lot of people or animals

slave *NOUN* **slaves**
a person who is owned by someone else and has to work for them without being paid

slave *VERB* **slaves, slaving, slaved**
to slave over something is to work very hard

slavery *NOUN*
slavery is being a slave or the system of having slaves

slay *VERB* **slays, slaying, slew, slain** (*old use*)
to slay someone is to kill them
'Who hath dared to wound thee?' cried the Giant;
'tell me, that I may take my big sword and slay
him.'—THE SELFISH GIANT, Oscar Wilde

sled *NOUN* **sleds** (*North American*)
a sledge

sledge *NOUN* **sledges**
a vehicle for travelling over snow, with strips of metal or wood instead of wheels

sledgehammer *NOUN* **sledgehammers**
a very large heavy hammer

sleek *ADJECTIVE* **sleeker, sleekest**
smooth and shiny • *Afghan hounds have long sleek hair.*

sleep *NOUN*
❶ sleep is the condition in which your eyes are closed, your body is relaxed and your mind is unconscious • *You need some sleep.* ❷ a sleep is a time when you are sleeping • *Did you have a good sleep?*

sleep *VERB* **sleeps, sleeping, slept**
to sleep is to have a sleep

sleeper *NOUN* **sleepers**
❶ someone who is asleep ❷ each of the wooden or concrete beams on which a railway line rests ❸ a railway carriage equipped for sleeping in

sleeping bag *NOUN* **sleeping bags**
a warm padded bag for sleeping in, especially when you are camping

sleepless *ADJECTIVE*
unable to sleep; without sleep • *We've had a sleepless night.*

sleepover *NOUN* **sleepovers**
a night that you spend at a friend's house

sleepwalker *NOUN* **sleepwalkers**
someone who walks around while they are asleep
➤ **sleepwalking** *NOUN*

sleepy *ADJECTIVE* **sleepier, sleepiest**
feeling tired and wanting to go to sleep
➤ **sleepily** *ADVERB* ➤ **sleepiness** *NOUN*

sleet *NOUN*
sleet is a mixture of rain with snow or hail

sleeve *NOUN* **sleeves**
the part of a piece of clothing that covers your arm

sleeveless *ADJECTIVE*
a sleeveless (for example) jumper or dress is one without sleeves

sleigh (*say* slay) *NOUN* **sleighs**
a large sledge pulled by horses

slender *ADJECTIVE* **slenderer, slenderest**
❶ slim or thin ❷ slight or small • *Their chances of winning are slender.*

slept *VERB* (*past tense and past participle of* **sleep**)
• *I slept until ten o'clock.* • *The baby has slept all night.*

sleuth (*say* slooth) *NOUN* **sleuths** (*informal*)
a detective
In detective stories, when the sleuth revisits the scene of the crime, he nearly always finds a clue that has been overlooked by the ordinary police.
—THE LONDON EYE MYSTERY, Siobhan Dowd

slew *VERB* (*past tense of* **slay**)
• *George slew the dragon.*

slice *NOUN* **slices**
a thin flat piece cut off something

slice *VERB* **slices**, **slicing**, **sliced**
to slice something is to cut it into slices

slick *ADJECTIVE* **slicker**, **slickest**
done quickly and in a clever way, without obvious effort

slick *NOUN* **slicks**
a large patch of oil floating on water

slide *VERB* **slides**, **sliding**, **slid**
❶ to slide is to move smoothly over a flat or polished or slippery surface • *She loved sliding down the banister.* ❷ to slide somewhere is to move there quickly or secretly • *The thief slid behind a bush.*

slide *NOUN* **slides**
❶ a sliding movement ❷ a structure for children to play on, with a smooth slope for sliding down ❸ a type of photograph that lets light through and that can be shown on a screen ❹ a small glass plate on which you can examine things under a microscope ❺ a fastener for keeping your hair tidy

slight *ADJECTIVE* **slighter**, **slightest**
very small; not serious or important

slightly *ADVERB*
in a slight way; not seriously • *They were slightly hurt.*

slim *ADJECTIVE* **slimmer**, **slimmest**
❶ thin and graceful ❷ small; hardly enough
• *We have a slim chance of winning.*

slim *VERB* **slims**, **slimming**, **slimmed**
to slim is to try to make yourself thinner, especially by dieting

slime *NOUN*
slime is unpleasant wet slippery stuff
• *There was slime on the pond.*

slimy *ADJECTIVE* **slimier**, **slimiest**
covered in slime, or like slime

sling *VERB* **slings**, **slinging**, **slung**
❶ to sling something somewhere is to throw it there roughly or carelessly • *You can sling your wet clothes into the washing machine.* ❷ to sling something is also to hang it up or support it so that it hangs loosely • *He had slung the bag round his neck.*

sling *NOUN* **slings**
❶ a piece of cloth tied round your neck to support an injured arm ❷ a device for throwing stones

slink *VERB* **slinks**, **slinking**, **slunk**
to slink somewhere is to move there slowly and quietly because you feel guilty or don't want to be noticed • *He slunk off to bed.*

slip *VERB* **slips**, **slipping**, **slipped**
❶ to slip is to slide without meaning to or to fall over ❷ to slip somewhere is to move there quickly and quietly • *He slipped out of the house before anyone was awake.* ❸ to slip something somewhere is to put it there quickly without being seen • *She slipped the letter into her pocket.* ❹ to slip something is to escape from it • *The dog slipped its leash.*
➤ **to slip up** is to make a mistake

slip *NOUN* **slips**
❶ an accidental slide or fall • *One slip and you could fall into the river.* ❷ a small mistake ❸ a small piece of paper ❹ a piece of underwear like a thin dress or skirt
➤ **to give someone the slip** is to escape from them or avoid them

slipper *NOUN* **slippers**
a soft comfortable shoe for wearing indoors

slippery *ADJECTIVE*
smooth or wet so that it is difficult to stand on or hold

slipshod *ADJECTIVE*
a slipshod piece of work is careless or badly done
DID YOU KNOW? The word **slipshod** originally meant wearing slippers or badly fitting shoes.

a
b
c
d
e
f
g
h
i
j
k
l
m
n
o
p
q
r
s
t
u
v
w
x
y
z

slit *NOUN* slits
a long narrow cut or opening

slit *VERB* slits, slitting, slit
to slit something is to make a slit in it

slither *VERB* slithers, slithering, slithered
to slip or slide along, often unsteadily
• *The snake slithered away.* • *We were slithering around on the ice.*

sliver (*say* sli-ver) *NOUN* slivers
a thin strip of wood, glass or other material

slog *VERB* slogs, slogging, slogged
❶ to slog something is to hit it hard or wildly ❷ to slog is to work hard • *I'm slogging away at my essay.* ❸ to slog is also to walk with effort • *We slogged through the snow.*

slog *NOUN*
a piece of hard work or effort • *Climbing up that hill was a real slog.*

slogan *NOUN* slogans
a short catchy phrase used to advertise something or to sum up an idea

slop *VERB* slops, slopping, slopped
❶ to slop liquid is to spill it over the edge of its container ❷ liquid slops when it spills in this way

slope *VERB* slopes, sloping, sloped
to slope is to go gradually downwards or upwards or to have one end higher than the other

slope *NOUN* slopes
❶ a sloping surface ❷ the amount by which a surface slopes • *The hill has a slope of 30°.* ❸ the side of a mountain

sloppy *ADJECTIVE* sloppier, sloppiest
❶ liquid and spilling easily ❷ careless or badly done • *Their work is sloppy.* ❸ (*informal*) too sentimental or romantic • *What a sloppy story.*
➤ **sloppily** *ADVERB* ➤ **sloppiness** *NOUN*

slops *PLURAL NOUN*
liquid waste matter

slosh *VERB* sloshes, sloshing, sloshed (*informal*)
you slosh liquid, or it sloshes, when it gets splashed in a messy or careless way

slot *NOUN* slots
a narrow opening to put things in

sloth (*rhymes with* both) *NOUN* sloths
❶ sloth is laziness ❷ a sloth is a long-haired South American animal that lives in trees and moves very slowly

slouch *VERB* slouches, slouching, slouched
to move or stand or sit in a lazy way, especially with your head and shoulders bent forwards

slovenly (*say* sluv-en-lee) *ADJECTIVE*
careless or untidy • *a man wearing a slovenly suit*

slow *ADJECTIVE* slower, slowest
❶ not quick; taking more time than usual ❷ a clock or watch is slow when it shows a time earlier than the correct time

slow *ADVERB*
at a slow rate; slowly • *Go slow.*
➤ **slowness** *NOUN*

slow *VERB* slows, slowing, slowed
❶ to slow, or to slow down, is to go slower ❷ to slow something, or to slow it down, is to make it go slower

slowcoach *NOUN* slowcoaches (*informal*)
someone who moves or works slowly

slowly *ADVERB*
at a slow rate or speed

sludge *NOUN*
sludge is thick sticky mud

slug *NOUN* slugs
❶ a small slimy animal like a snail without its shell ❷ a pellet for firing from a gun

slum *NOUN* slums
an area of dirty and crowded houses in a city

slumber *NOUN* (*old use*)
slumber is peaceful sleep

slumber *VERB* slumbers, slumbering, slumbered
to slumber is to sleep peacefully

slump *VERB* slumps, slumping, slumped
to slump is to fall heavily or suddenly

slump *NOUN* slumps
a slump is a sudden fall in prices or trade

slung *VERB* (*past tense and past participle of* sling)
• *She slung the sack over her shoulder.* • *He had slung his clothes on the floor.*

slunk VERB (*past tense and past participle of* slink)
• *She slunk out the door.* • *The thieves had slunk off.*

slur NOUN slurs
something that harms a person's reputation; an insult

slush NOUN
slush is snow that is melting on the ground
➤ **slushy** ADJECTIVE

sly ADJECTIVE slyer, slyest
cunning or mischievous
➤ **slyly** ADVERB ➤ **slyness** NOUN

smack VERB smacks, smacking, smacked
to smack someone is to slap them with your hand

smack NOUN smacks
a slap with your hand

small ADJECTIVE smaller, smallest
not large; less than the normal size

smallpox NOUN
smallpox is a serious contagious illness that causes a fever and produces spots that leave scars on the skin

smart ADJECTIVE smarter, smartest
❶ neat and well dressed ❷ clever and quick-thinking ❸ fast • *We'll need to walk at a smart pace.*
➤ **smartness** NOUN

smart VERB smarts, smarting, smarted
to smart is to feel a stinging pain

smarten VERB smartens, smartening, smartened
❶ to smarten something or someone is to make them smarter • *You need to smarten yourself up a bit.* ❷ to smarten is to become smarter

smartly ADVERB
❶ to be smartly dressed is to have nice clothes on ❷ to move smartly is to do so quickly

smartphone NOUN smartphones
a mobile phone that has internet access and can run small computer applications

smash VERB smashes, smashing, smashed
❶ to smash is to break into pieces noisily and violently; to smash something is to break it in this way ❷ to smash into something is to hit it with great force • *The lorry left the road and smashed into a wall.* ❸ (*informal*) to smash something or someone is to destroy them or defeat them completely

smash NOUN smashes
❶ the act or sound of smashing ❷ a collision between vehicles

smashing ADJECTIVE (*informal*)
excellent

smear VERB smears, smearing, smeared
to smear something dirty or greasy is to rub it thickly over a surface

smear NOUN smears
a dirty or greasy mark made by smearing

smell VERB smells, smelling, smelt or smelled
❶ you smell something when you use your nose to sense it ❷ to smell is to give out a smell • *The cheese smells funny.*

smell NOUN smells
❶ a smell is something you can smell, especially something unpleasant ❷ smell is the ability to smell things • *I have a good sense of smell.*

smelly ADJECTIVE smellier, smelliest
having an unpleasant smell

smelt VERB smelts, smelting, smelted
to smelt ore is to melt it in order to get metal from it

smile NOUN smiles
an expression on your face that shows you are pleased or amused, with your lips stretched and turning upwards at the ends

smile VERB smiles, smiling, smiled
to smile is to give a smile

smilodon NOUN smilodons
another name for **sabre-toothed cat**

smite VERB smites, smiting, smote, smitten (*old use*)
to strike someone with a hard blow

smith NOUN smiths
someone who makes things out of metal

smithereens PLURAL NOUN
something is smashed or blown to smithereens when it is broken into lots of tiny fragments

a
b
c
d
e
f
g
h
i
j
k
l
m
n
o
p
q
r
s
t
u
v
w
x
y
z

smock *NOUN* **smocks**
a long loose top

smog *NOUN*
smog is a mixture of smoke and fog

smoke *NOUN*
smoke is the grey or blue mixture of gas and particles that rises from a fire

smoke *VERB* **smokes**, **smoking**, **smoked**
❶ something smokes when it gives out smoke • *The fire is smoking.* ❷ someone smokes when they breathe in the smoke from a lit cigarette or pipe

smokeless *ADJECTIVE*
smokeless fuel burns without giving off much smoke

smoky *ADJECTIVE* **smokier**, **smokiest**
a smoky room is full of smoke
➤ **smokiness** *NOUN*

smooth *ADJECTIVE* **smoother**, **smoothest**
❶ having an even surface without any marks or roughness ❷ a smooth liquid or substance has no lumps in it ❸ moving without bumps or jolts • *We had a smooth ride.* ❹ not harsh; flowing easily • *She spoke in a smooth voice.*
➤ **smoothness** *NOUN*

smooth *VERB* **smooths**, **smoothing**, **smoothed**
to smooth something is to make it smooth and flat

smoothie *NOUN* **smoothies**
a thick smooth drink made from crushed fruit

smoothly *ADVERB*
❶ something flows smoothly when it does so easily and evenly ❷ an event goes smoothly when it happens without any problems

smote *VERB* (*past tense of* **smite**)

smother *VERB* **smothers**, **smothering**, **smothered**
❶ to smother someone is to cover their face so that they can't breathe ❷ to smother something is to cover it thickly • *The cake was smothered in chocolate icing.* ❸ to smother a fire is to put it out by covering it

smoulder *VERB* **smoulders**, **smouldering**, **smouldered**
to burn slowly without a flame

smudge *NOUN* **smudges**
a dirty or messy mark made by rubbing something

smudge *VERB* **smudges**, **smudging**, **smudged**
to smudge paint or ink is to touch it while it is still wet and make it messy

smug *ADJECTIVE* **smugger**, **smuggest**
too pleased with yourself
➤ **smugly** *ADVERB* ➤ **smugness** *NOUN*

smuggle *VERB* **smuggles**, **smuggling**, **smuggled**
to smuggle something is to bring it into a country secretly and illegally
➤ **smuggler** *NOUN*

snack *NOUN* **snacks**
a quick light meal

snag *NOUN* **snags**
an unexpected difficulty or obstacle

snag *VERB* **snags**, **snagging**, **snagged**
to snag something you are wearing is to catch it on something sharp

snail *NOUN* **snails**
a small animal with a soft body and a hard spiral shell
SPOT THE DIFFERENCE! Snails have shells, but **slugs** do not.

snake *NOUN* **snakes**
a reptile with a long narrow body and no legs

snap *VERB* **snaps**, **snapping**, **snapped**
❶ something snaps when it breaks suddenly with a sharp noise ❷ an animal snaps when it bites suddenly or quickly • *The dog snapped at me.* ❸ to snap something is to say it quickly and angrily • *There's no need to snap.* ❹ to snap your fingers is to make a sharp snapping sound with them ❺ to snap something or someone is to take a quick photograph of them

snap *NOUN* **snaps**
❶ a snap is the act or sound of snapping ❷ a snap is also an informal photograph taken quickly ❸ snap is a card game in which players shout 'Snap!' when they spot two cards of the same value

snappy *ADJECTIVE* **snappier**, **snappiest**
quick and lively

snapshot NOUN **snapshots**
an informal photograph taken quickly

snare NOUN **snares**
a trap for catching animals

snare VERB **snares, snaring, snared**
to snare an animal is to catch it in a snare

snarl VERB **snarls, snarling, snarled**
an animal snarls when it growls angrily

snarl NOUN **snarls**
a snarling sound

snatch VERB **snatches, snatching, snatched**
to snatch something is to grab it quickly
• *He snatched the bag from me.*

snatch NOUN **snatches**
❶ a short piece of conversation or music
❷ (*informal*) a robbery or theft

sneak VERB **sneaks, sneaking, sneaked** or
(*North American*) **snuck**
❶ to sneak somewhere is to move there quietly
and secretly ❷ (*informal*) to sneak on someone
is to tell tales about them

sneak NOUN **sneaks** (*informal*)
a person who tells tales

sneakers PLURAL NOUN (*North American*)
trainers

sneaky ADJECTIVE **sneakier, sneakiest**
dishonest or deceitful
➤ **sneakily** ADVERB

sneer VERB **sneers, sneering, sneered**
to speak or behave in a scornful way

sneeze VERB **sneezes, sneezing, sneezed**
you sneeze when you push air through your
nose suddenly and uncontrollably • *She was
sneezing a lot because of her cold.*

sneeze NOUN **sneezes**
the action or sound of sneezing

sniff VERB **sniffs, sniffing, sniffed**
❶ to sniff is to make a noise by drawing air in
through your nose ❷ to sniff something is to
smell it with a sniff

sniff NOUN **sniffs**
the action or sound of sniffing or smelling
something

sniffle VERB **sniffles, sniffling, sniffled**
to keep sniffing because you have a cold or
are crying

snigger VERB **sniggers, sniggering,
sniggered**
to snigger is to give a quiet sly laugh

snigger NOUN **sniggers**
a quiet sly laugh

snip VERB **snips, snipping, snipped**
to snip something is to cut a small piece or
pieces off it

snip NOUN **snips**
an act of snipping something

sniper NOUN **snipers**
someone who shoots at people from a
hiding place

snippet NOUN **snippets**
a short piece of news or information

snivel VERB **snivels, snivelling, snivelled**
to snivel is to cry or complain in a
whining way

snob NOUN **snobs**
someone who despises people who have not
got wealth or power or particular tastes or
interests
➤ **snobbery** NOUN

snobbish ADJECTIVE
thinking or behaving like a snob
➤ **snobbishness** NOUN

snooker NOUN
a game played with long sticks (called *cues*) and
22 balls on a cloth-covered table

snoop VERB **snoops, snooping, snooped**
to pry or try to find out about someone else's
business

snooze NOUN **snoozes** (*informal*)
a short sleep or nap • *Grandad was having a
quiet snooze on the sofa.*

snooze VERB **snoozes, snoozing, snoozed**
to snooze is to have a short sleep or nap

snore VERB **snores, snoring, snored**
to breathe noisily while you are sleeping

snorkel NOUN **snorkels**
a tube with one end above the water, worn by
an underwater swimmer to get air

snort VERB **snorts, snorting, snorted**
to snort is to make a loud noise by forcing air
out through your nose

a
b
c
d
e
f
g
h
i
j
k
l
m
n
o
p
q
r
s
t
u
v
w
x
y
z

snort NOUN **snorts**
a snorting noise

snout NOUN **snouts**
an animal's snout is the front part sticking out from its head, with its nose and mouth

snow NOUN
snow is frozen drops of water falling from the sky as small white flakes

snow VERB **snows, snowing, snowed**
➤ **it is snowing** when snow is falling

snowball NOUN **snowballs**
snow pressed into the shape of a ball for throwing

snowboard NOUN **snowboards**
a board like a short broad ski, used for riding downhill on snow
➤ **snowboarder** NOUN
➤ **snowboarding** NOUN

snowdrop NOUN **snowdrops**
a small white flower that blooms in early spring

snowflake NOUN **snowflakes**
a flake of snow

snow leopard NOUN **snow leopards**
a large wild cat with pale fur patterned with dark spots, which lives in high mountains in Asia

snowman NOUN **snowmen**
a shape like a person that is made of snow

snowplough NOUN **snowploughs**
a vehicle or device for clearing snow from a road or railway track

snowshoe NOUN **snowshoes**
snowshoes are broad frames with a mesh, that you can attach to your feet so that you can walk over deep snow without sinking in

snowstorm NOUN **snowstorms**
a storm with snow falling

snowy ADJECTIVE **snowier, snowiest**
❶ with snow falling • *We're expecting snowy weather.* ❷ covered with snow • *a snowy winter landscape* ❸ white like snow • *a head of snowy hair*
➤ **snowiness** NOUN

snub VERB **snubs, snubbing, snubbed**
to snub someone is to treat them in a scornful or unfriendly way

snub-nosed ADJECTIVE
having a short turned-up nose

snuck VERB (*North American*) (*past tense of* **sneak**)

snuff NOUN
snuff is powdered tobacco that is taken into the nose by sniffing

snug ADJECTIVE **snugger, snuggest**
warm and cosy • *We found a snug corner by the fire.*
➤ **snugly** ADVERB

snuggle VERB **snuggles, snuggling, snuggled**
to curl up in a warm comfortable place • *She snuggled down in bed.*

snuggly ADJECTIVE **snugglier, snuggliest**
warm and comfortable; cosy • *a snuggly pair of slippers*

so ADVERB
❶ in this way; to such an extent • *Why are you so cross?* ❷ very • *Cricket is so boring.* ❸ also • *I was wrong but so were you.*
➤ **and so on** and other similar things • *They took food, water, spare clothing and so on.*
➤ **or so** or about that number • *We need about fifty or so.*
➤ **so as to** in order to
➤ **so far** up to now
➤ **so what?** (*informal*) what does that matter?

so CONJUNCTION
for that reason • *They threw me out, so I came here.*

soak VERB **soaks, soaking, soaked**
to soak someone or something is to make them very wet or leave them in water
➤ **to soak something up** is to take in a liquid in the way that a sponge does

so-and-so NOUN **so-and-sos** (*informal*)
❶ a person whose name you don't know or can't remember • *Old so-and-so told me.* ❷ an unpleasant person • *He's a real so-and-so.*

soap NOUN **soaps**
❶ soap is a substance you use with water for washing and cleaning things ❷ (*informal*) a soap is a soap opera
➤ **soapy** ADJECTIVE

soap opera *NOUN* **soap operas**
a television serial about the day-to-day life of a group of imaginary people

soar *VERB* **soars, soaring, soared**
❶ to soar is to rise or fly high in the air • *The Mars rocket soared into space.* ❷ to soar is also to increase a lot • *The temperature continues to soar.*

sob *VERB* **sobs, sobbing, sobbed**
to sob is to cry with gasping noises

sob *NOUN* **sobs**
a sound of sobbing

sober *ADJECTIVE*
❶ not drunk ❷ calm and serious • *She had a sober expression.* ❸ not bright or showy • *The room was painted in sober colours.*
➤ **soberly** *ADVERB*

so-called *ADJECTIVE*
named in what may be the wrong way • *Even the so-called experts couldn't solve the problem.*

soccer *NOUN*
soccer is a game played by two teams which try to kick an inflated ball into their opponents' goal

sociable (*say* **soh**-sha-bul) *ADJECTIVE*
sociable people are friendly and like to be with other people

social (*say* **soh**-shal) *ADJECTIVE*
❶ to do with people meeting one another in their spare time • *Let's join a social club.* ❷ living in groups, not alone • *Bees are social insects.* ❸ to do with society or a community • *They were writing a social history of the area.*
➤ **socially** *ADVERB*

social distancing *NOUN*
a way of slowing the spread of an infectious disease, that involves people keeping a safe distance away from other people

social media *NOUN*
websites where people post personal messages and photographs to share with friends

society *NOUN* **societies**
❶ a society is a community of people; society is people living together in a group or nation ❷ a society is also a group of

people organized for a particular purpose • *He's joined a dramatic society.* ❸ society is also company or companionship • *We enjoy your society.*

sociology (*say* soh-see-**ol**-o-jee) *NOUN*
sociology is the study of how people behave in different societies
➤ **sociologist** *NOUN*

sock *NOUN* **socks**
a soft piece of clothing that covers your foot and the lower half of your leg
➤ **to pull your socks up** (*informal*) is to try to do better

sock *VERB* **socks, socking, socked** (*informal*)
to sock someone is to hit or punch them hard • *He socked me on the jaw.*

socket *NOUN* **sockets**
a device or hole that something fits into, especially the place where an electric plug or bulb is put to make a connection

soda *NOUN*
❶ soda is a substance made from sodium, such as baking soda ❷ soda is also soda water

soda water *NOUN*
soda water is fizzy water used in drinks

sodium (*say* **soh**-di-um) *NOUN*
sodium is a soft silver-white metal

sofa *NOUN* **sofas**
a long soft seat with sides and a back
DID YOU KNOW? The word **sofa** comes from an Arabic word *suffa*, which has the same meaning.

soft *ADJECTIVE* **softer, softest**
❶ not hard or firm; easily pressed or cut into a new shape ❷ smooth; not rough or stiff ❸ gentle; not loud • *He spoke in a soft voice.*
➤ **softness** *NOUN*

soft drink *NOUN* **soft drinks**
a drink that does not contain alcohol

soften *VERB* **softens, softening, softened**
❶ to soften something is to make it softer ❷ to soften is to become softer

softly *ADVERB*
❶ in a gentle way • *She closed the door softly behind her.* ❷ to speak softly is to speak quietly

software NOUN
programs and data which are not part of the machinery (the *hardware*) of a computer

soggy ADJECTIVE soggier, soggiest
very wet and heavy • *The ground was soggy underfoot.*
➤ **sogginess** NOUN

soil NOUN
soil is the loose earth that plants grow in
The soil began to fly out furiously behind Mr Fox as he started to dig for dear life with his front feet.
—FANTASTIC MR FOX, Roald Dahl

soil VERB soils, soiling, soiled
to soil something is to make it dirty • *I don't want to soil my new trainers.*

solar ADJECTIVE
to do with the sun or powered by the sun's energy

solar panel NOUN solar panels
a panel that absorbs the sun's rays in order to generate heat or electricity

solar system NOUN
the solar system is the sun and the planets that revolve round it

sold VERB (*past tense and past participle of* sell)
• *He sold his bike.* • *Shops have sold thousands of copies of the book.*

solder NOUN
solder is a soft alloy that is melted to join pieces of metal together

solder VERB solders, soldering, soldered
to solder two pieces of metal is to join them together with solder

soldier NOUN soldiers
a member of an army

sole NOUN soles
❶ the sole is the bottom part of a shoe or foot
❷ a sole is also a flat edible sea fish

sole ADJECTIVE
single or only • *It was the sole topic of conversation.*
➤ **solely** ADVERB

solemn ADJECTIVE
serious and dignified
The children could hardly look into the Lion's royal, solemn eyes, for he was both good and terrible

at the same time.—THE LION, THE WITCH AND THE WARDROBE, C. S. Lewis
➤ **solemnly** ADVERB ➤ **solemnity** NOUN

solicitor NOUN solicitors
a lawyer who advises clients and prepares legal documents

solid ADJECTIVE
❶ keeping its shape; not a liquid or gas
❷ not hollow; with no space inside • *These bars are made of solid steel.* ❸ firm or strongly made • *The house is built on solid foundations.*
❹ strong and reliable • *They gave solid support.*
➤ **solidity** NOUN

solid NOUN solids
❶ a solid thing ❷ a three-dimensional shape, such as a cube, sphere or cone

solidify VERB solidifies, solidifying, solidified
❶ to solidify is to change from a liquid into a solid ❷ to solidify something is to make it solid

solidly ADVERB
❶ something is solidly built when it is firmly and strongly built ❷ to rain solidly is to rain continuously

solitary ADJECTIVE
❶ alone; on your own • *He lived a solitary life.*
❷ single • *This is a solitary example.*

solitude NOUN
solitude is being on your own

solo NOUN solos
something sung or performed by one person alone

soloist NOUN soloists
someone who plays or sings a solo

solstice NOUN solstices
either of the two times in the year when the sun is at its furthest point north or south of the equator. The **summer solstice** is about 21 June, and the **winter solstice** is about 22 December, in the northern hemisphere.

soluble ADJECTIVE
❶ a soluble substance is able to be dissolved
❷ a soluble problem or puzzle is able to be solved

solution *NOUN* solutions
❶ the answer to a problem or puzzle ❷ a liquid with something dissolved in it

solve *VERB* solves, solving, solved
to solve a problem or puzzle is to find an answer to it

solvent *NOUN* solvents
a liquid in which other substances can be dissolved

solvent *ADJECTIVE*
to be solvent is to have enough money to pay your debts

sombre *ADJECTIVE*
❶ sombre colours are dark or dull ❷ a sombre mood or expression is gloomy or sad • *We set off next morning in a sombre mood.*

some *DETERMINER*
❶ a few or a little • *I've brought some sandwiches.* ❷ a certain amount of • *Would you like some cake?* ❸ an unknown person or thing • *There was some problem with the buses today.*

some *PRONOUN*
a certain or unknown number or amount • *Some of the books are damaged.* • *I only watched some of the film.*

somebody *PRONOUN*
someone; some person

somehow *ADVERB*
in some way • *We must finish the work somehow.*

someone *PRONOUN*
some person

somersault (*say* sum-er-solt) *NOUN* somersaults
a movement in which you turn head over heels and land on your feet

something *PRONOUN*
a certain or unknown thing

sometime *ADVERB*
at some time • *I saw her sometime last year.*

sometimes *ADVERB*
at some times but not always • *We sometimes walk to school.*

somewhat *ADVERB*
to some extent; rather • *He was somewhat annoyed.*

somewhere *ADVERB*
in or to some place

son *NOUN* sons
a person's male child

sonar *NOUN*
sonar is a system using the echo from sound waves to locate objects underwater
DID YOU KNOW? The word **sonar** comes from the first letters of *sound navigation and ranging.*

song *NOUN* songs
❶ a song is a tune with words for singing ❷ a bird's song is the musical sounds it makes ❸ song is singing • *She was so happy she burst into song.*

songbird *NOUN* songbirds
a bird that sings sweetly

sonic *ADJECTIVE*
to do with sound or sound waves

sonnet *NOUN* sonnets
a kind of poem with 14 lines

soon *ADVERB* sooner, soonest
❶ in a short time from now ❷ not long after something • *She became ill but was soon better.* ❸ early or quickly • *You spoke too soon.*
➤ **as soon** as willingly • *I'd just as soon stay at home.*
➤ **sooner or later** at some time in the future

soot *NOUN*
soot is the black powder left by smoke in a chimney or on a building
➤ **sooty** *ADJECTIVE*

soothe *VERB* soothes, soothing, soothed
❶ to soothe someone is to make them calm ❷ to soothe a pain or ache is to ease it

sophisticated (*say* sof-iss-ti-kay-tid) *ADJECTIVE*
❶ someone is sophisticated when they are used to a fashionable or cultured life and have experienced a lot of different things ❷ something is sophisticated when it is complicated and highly developed • *The phone comes with a sophisticated camera.*
➤ **sophistication** *NOUN*

sopping *ADJECTIVE*
very wet; soaked

a
b
c
d
e
f
g
h
i
j
k
l
m
n
o
p
q
r
s
t
u
v
w
x
y
z

soppy ADJECTIVE **soppier**, **soppiest** (*informal*)
sentimental or silly

soprano (*say* so-**prah**-noh) NOUN
sopranos
a woman or a boy with a high singing voice

sorcerer NOUN **sorcerers**
someone who can do magic

sorceress NOUN **sorceresses**
a woman who can do magic

sorcery NOUN
magic or witchcraft

sore ADJECTIVE **sorer**, **sorest**
❶ painful or smarting • *I've got a sore throat.*
❷ (*informal*) annoyed or upset
➤ **soreness** NOUN

sore NOUN **sores**
a red and painful place on your skin

sorely ADVERB
seriously; very • *I was sorely tempted to run away.*

sorrow NOUN **sorrows**
sorrow is sadness or regret
➤ **sorrowful** ADJECTIVE feeling sorrow
➤ **sorrowfully** ADVERB

sorry ADJECTIVE **sorrier**, **sorriest**
❶ you are sorry that you did something when you regret doing it or want to apologize
• *I'm sorry I forgot to send you a birthday card.*
❷ you feel sorry for someone when you feel pity for them or are sad that something bad has happened to them • *I'm sorry you've been ill.*

sort NOUN **sorts**
❶ a group of things or people that are similar; a kind • *What sort of fruit do you like?*
❷ (*computing*) putting data in a particular order • *Can you run an alphabetical sort on these names?*

sort VERB **sorts**, **sorting**, **sorted**
to sort things is to arrange them in groups or kinds
➤ **to sort something out** is to organize it or arrange it

SOS NOUN
an SOS is an urgent appeal for help from someone whose life is in danger

sought VERB (*past tense and past participle of* **seek**)
• *We sought a place to hide.* • *Police had sought the criminal everywhere.*

soul NOUN **souls**
a person's invisible spirit that some people believe goes on living after the body has died

sound NOUN **sounds**
❶ sound is vibrations in the air that you can detect with your ear ❷ a sound is something that you can hear ❸ a sound is also a narrow passage of water

sound VERB **sounds**, **sounding**, **sounded**
❶ to sound is to make a sound • *An alarm sounded in the distance.* ❷ to sound something is to make a sound with it
• *The lookout sounded his horn.* ❸ to sound a certain way is to give that impression when heard • *You sound in a good mood.*
❹ to sound a river or sea is to test the depth of it
➤ **to sound someone out** is to try to find out what they think or feel about something

sound ADJECTIVE **sounder**, **soundest**
❶ not damaged or harmed; in good condition • *The lost puppy turned up safe and sound.* ❷ reasonable or correct
• *a piece of sound advice* ❸ reliable or secure • *The castle was built on sound foundations.* ❹ thorough or deep • *She has a sound knowledge of French.* • *I am a sound sleeper.*
➤ **soundness** NOUN

soundly ADVERB
❶ you sleep soundly when you sleep deeply
❷ to be soundly beaten is to be completely or thoroughly beaten

soundtrack NOUN **soundtracks**
the sound or music that goes with a film or television programme

soup NOUN **soups**
a liquid food made from vegetables or meat

sour ADJECTIVE **sourer**, **sourest**
❶ having a sharp taste like vinegar or lemons
❷ unpleasant or bad-tempered
➤ **sourly** ADVERB ➤ **sourness** NOUN

A B C D E F G H I J K L M N O P Q R S T U V W X Y Z

source *NOUN* **sources**
❶ the place where something comes from
❷ the place where a river starts

south *NOUN*
❶ the direction to the right of a person facing east ❷ the part of a country or city that is in this direction

south *ADJECTIVE, ADVERB*
❶ towards the south or in the south • *The city lies south of the river.* ❷ coming from the south • *A south wind was blowing.*

south-east *NOUN, ADJECTIVE, ADVERB*
midway between south and east

southerly (*say* su*th*-er-lee) *ADJECTIVE*
a southerly wind is one that blows from the south

southern (*say* su*th*-ern) *ADJECTIVE*
from or to do with the south

southerner (*say* su*th*-er-ner) *NOUN*
southerners
someone who lives in the south of a country

southward, **southwards** *ADJECTIVE, ADVERB*
towards the south

south-west *NOUN, ADJECTIVE, ADVERB*
midway between south and west

souvenir (*say* soo-ven-**eer**) *NOUN* **souvenirs**
something that you buy or keep to remind you of a person, place or event
DID YOU KNOW? The word **souvenir** comes from a French word meaning 'to remember'.

sovereign (*say* **sov**-rin) *NOUN* **sovereigns**
❶ a king or a queen ❷ an old British gold coin that was worth £1

sow (*rhymes with* **go**) *VERB* **sows**, **sowing**, **sowed**, **sown** *or* **sowed**
to sow seeds is to put them into the ground so that they will grow into plants

sow (*rhymes with* **cow**) *NOUN* **sows**
a sow is a female pig

soya bean *NOUN* **soya beans**
a kind of bean from which edible oil and flour are made

soy sauce *NOUN*
a sauce made with fermented soya beans, used in Asian cooking

space *NOUN* **spaces**
❶ space is the whole area outside the earth, where the stars and planets are • *Yuri Gagarin was the first human to travel in space.* ❷ space is also an area or volume • *Is there enough space for another passenger?* ❸ a space is an empty area or gap • *There is a space at the back of the cupboard.* • *Leave a space for your name and address.* ❹ a space is also a period of time • *They moved house twice in the space of a year.*

space *VERB* **spaces**, **spacing**, **spaced**
to space things, or space things out, is to arrange them with gaps or periods of time between them

spacecraft *NOUN* **spacecraft**
a vehicle for travelling in outer space

spaceship *NOUN* **spaceships**
a spacecraft

space shuttle *NOUN* **space shuttles**
a spacecraft that can travel into space and return to earth

space station *NOUN* **space stations**
a satellite which orbits the earth and is used as a base by scientists and astronauts

spacewalk *NOUN* **spacewalks**
a walk that an astronaut takes outside a spacecraft

spacious *ADJECTIVE*
large and roomy • *a spacious kitchen*
➤ **spaciously** *ADVERB*
➤ **spaciousness** *NOUN*

spade *NOUN* **spades**
❶ a tool with a long handle and a wide blade for digging ❷ a playing card with black shapes like upside-down hearts on it

spaghetti (*say* spa-**get**-ee) *NOUN*
spaghetti is pasta made in long thin strips
SPELLING ALERT! There is a silent *h* and a double *t* in **spaghetti**. Think of the phrase *hot spaghetti at tea time* to help you remember!

spam *NOUN*
spam is unwanted email that is sent to a large number of people

span *NOUN* **spans**
❶ the length from one end of something to the other ❷ the distance between the tips of

a
b
c
d
e
f
g
h
i
j
k
l
m
n
o
p
q
r
s
t
u
v
w
x
y
z

your thumb and little finger when your hand is spread out ❸ a part of a bridge between two supports ❹ a period of time

span *VERB* **spans, spanning, spanned**
to span something is to reach from one side or end of it to the other • *A wooden bridge spanned the river.*

spaniel *NOUN* **spaniels**
a breed of dog with long ears and silky fur

Spanish *ADJECTIVE*
to do with Spain or its people

Spanish *NOUN*
the main language of Spain, Mexico and some other countries
DID YOU KNOW? The words **alligator, canyon** and **tornado** come from Spanish.

spanner *NOUN* **spanners**
a tool for tightening or loosening a nut

spar *NOUN* **spars**
a strong pole used for a mast or boom on a ship

spar *VERB* **spars, sparring, sparred**
to spar is to practise boxing • *He was my sparring partner.*

spare *VERB* **spares, sparing, spared**
❶ to spare something is to afford it or be able to give it to someone • *Can you spare a moment?* ❷ to spare someone is to avoid harming them or making them suffer something unpleasant ❸ to spare something is to use it or treat it economically • *No expense will be spared.*

spare *ADJECTIVE*
❶ not used but kept ready in case it is needed; extra • *Where's the spare wheel?* • *What do you do in your spare time?* ❷ thin or lean

spare *NOUN* **spares**
a spare thing or part • *The local garage sells spares.*

sparing *ADJECTIVE*
careful or economical, especially with money

spark *NOUN* **sparks**
❶ a tiny flash of electricity ❷ a tiny glowing piece of something hot

spark *VERB* **sparks, sparking, sparked**
to spark is to give off sparks

sparkle *VERB* **sparkles, sparkling, sparkled**
to shine with a lot of tiny flashes of bright light • *The sea sparkled in the sunlight.*

sparkler *NOUN* **sparklers**
a firework that sparkles

sparrow *NOUN* **sparrows**
a small brown bird

sparse *ADJECTIVE* **sparser, sparsest**
small in number or amount; thinly scattered • *Vegetation on the island is sparse.*
➤ **sparsely** *ADVERB* ➤ **sparseness** *NOUN*

spat *VERB* (*past tense and past participle of* **spit**)
• *She angrily spat out her reply.* • *The cat had spat out a ball of fur.*

spatter *VERB* **spatters, spattering, spattered**
to spatter something is to splash it or scatter it in small drops or pieces • *The lorry spattered mud all over the pavement.*

spawn *NOUN*
spawn is the eggs of frogs, fish and other water animals

spawn *VERB* **spawns, spawning, spawned**
frogs, fish and other water animals spawn when they lay their eggs

speak *VERB* **speaks, speaking, spoke, spoken**
❶ to speak is to say something • *I spoke to them this morning.* ❷ to speak a language is to be able to talk in it • *Do you speak German?*
➤ **to speak up** is to say something more clearly or loudly

speaker *NOUN* **speakers**
❶ a person who is speaking or making a speech ❷ the part of (for example) a radio or computer that the sound comes out of

spear *NOUN* **spears**
a long pole with a sharp point, used as a weapon

spear *VERB* **spears, spearing, speared**
to spear something is to pierce it with a spear or something pointed

special *ADJECTIVE*
❶ different from other people or things; unusual ❷ meant for a particular person or purpose • *You'll need special training.*

specialist *NOUN* **specialists**
an expert in a particular subject

speciality *NOUN* **specialities**
❶ something that someone specializes in
Dr Dandiffer is an ethnobotanist. His speciality is the medicinal use of tropical plants.—TIME STOPS FOR NO MOUSE, Michael Hoeye
❷ a special product, especially a food

specialize (*also* **specialise**) *VERB*
specializes, specializing, specialized
to specialize is to give particular attention to one subject or thing • *The gallery specializes in modern art.*
➤ **specialization** *NOUN*

specially *ADVERB*
for a special purpose • *I came specially to see you.*

species (*say* spee-shiz) *NOUN* **species**
a group of animals or plants that have similar features and can breed with each other

specific *ADJECTIVE*
❶ definite or precise ❷ to do with a particular thing • *The money was given for a specific purpose.*

specifically *ADVERB*
❶ in a special way or for a special purpose • *The car is designed specifically for disabled people.* ❷ clearly and precisely • *I specifically said we had to go.*

specification *NOUN* **specifications**
a detailed list or description of something

specify *VERB* **specifies, specifying, specified**
to specify a person or thing is to name or mention them precisely • *The recipe specified brown sugar, not white.*

specimen *NOUN* **specimens**
❶ a small amount or sample of something ❷ an example of one kind of plant, animal or thing • *We saw a fine specimen of an oak.*

speck *NOUN* **specks**
❶ a tiny piece of something ❷ a tiny mark or spot

speckled *ADJECTIVE*
covered with small spots

spectacle *NOUN* **spectacles**
❶ an exciting sight or display ❷ a ridiculous sight

spectacles *PLURAL NOUN*
a pair of lenses in a frame, worn over your eyes to help improve your eyesight

spectacular *ADJECTIVE*
exciting and impressive to see • *The special effects in the film are spectacular.*

spectator *NOUN* **spectators**
a person who watches a game or show

spectre (*say* spek-ter) *NOUN* **spectres**
a ghost
'Ghost of the Future,' he exclaimed, 'I fear you more than any spectre I have seen.'—A CHRISTMAS CAROL, Charles Dickens

spectrum *NOUN* **spectra**
❶ the band of colours like those in a rainbow ❷ a range of things or ideas • *She has a broad spectrum of interests.*

speech *NOUN* **speeches**
❶ speech is the ability to speak or a person's way of speaking ❷ a speech is a talk given to a group of people

speechless *ADJECTIVE*
unable to speak, especially because you are surprised, frightened or angry
Mr and Mrs Bucket stood hugging each other, speechless with fright.—CHARLIE AND THE GREAT GLASS ELEVATOR, Roald Dahl

speech marks *PLURAL NOUN*
inverted commas, used to show that someone is speaking (*compare* **quotation marks**)

speed *NOUN* **speeds**
❶ the speed of something is the rate at which it moves or happens ❷ speed is being quick or fast

speed *VERB* **speeds, speeding, sped** *or* **speeded**
to speed is to go very fast or too fast • *Drivers can be fined for speeding.*
➤ **to speed up** is to become quicker

speedboat *NOUN* **speedboats**
a fast motor boat

speedometer (*say* spee-**dom**-it-er) *NOUN* **speedometers**
a device in a vehicle that shows its speed

speedy *ADJECTIVE* **speedier, speediest**
quick or fast • *We need a speedy reply.*
➤ **speedily** *ADVERB*

spell *VERB* **spells, spelling, spelt** *or* **spelled**
to spell a word is to give its letters in the right order
'Esio trot is simply tortoise spelled backwards,' Mr Hoppy said.—ESIO TROT, Roald Dahl

spell *NOUN* **spells**
❶ a spell is a period of time • *a spell of unusually dry weather* ❷ a spell is also a set of words that is supposed to have magic power
They walked three times around the lake, trying all the way to think of a simple spell that would subdue a dragon.—HARRY POTTER AND THE GOBLET OF FIRE, J. K. Rowling

spellcheck *VERB* **spellchecks, spellchecking, spellchecked**
to check the spelling of a word or document using a computer program

spellcheck *NOUN* **spellchecks**
a spellcheck is when you check your spelling using a computer program

spellchecker *NOUN* **spellcheckers**
a computer program you use to check your writing to see if your spelling is correct

spelling *NOUN* **spellings**
❶ the way in which letters are put together to form words ❷ how well someone can spell • *Her spelling is improving.*

spelling bee *NOUN* **spelling bees**
a spelling competition

spend *VERB* **spends, spending, spent**
❶ to spend money is to use it to pay for things ❷ to spend time is to pass it doing something • *He spent the weekend painting his bedroom.* ❸ to spend energy or effort is to use it up • *She spends all her spare energy on gardening.*

sphere *NOUN* **spheres**
❶ a perfectly round solid shape; a globe or ball ❷ an area of activity or interest
➤ **spherical** *ADJECTIVE*

spice *NOUN* **spices**
a strong-tasting substance used to flavour food, often made from the dried parts of plants

spicy *ADJECTIVE* **spicier, spiciest**
spicy food tastes strongly of spices

spider *NOUN* **spiders**
a small animal with eight legs that spins webs to catch insects on which it feeds
SPOT THE DIFFERENCE! Spiders have eight legs whereas **insects** have six legs.

spied *VERB* (*past tense and past participle of* **spy**)
• *They spied a ship on the horizon.* • *I think they have spied us.*

spike *NOUN* **spikes**
a pointed piece of metal; a sharp point

spiky *ADJECTIVE* **spikier, spikiest**
something is spiky when it is full of spikes or sharp points • *Holly trees have spiky leaves.*
➤ **spikiness** *NOUN*

spill *VERB* **spills, spilling, spilt** *or* **spilled**
❶ to spill something is to let it fall out of a container by accident • *Careful or you'll spill your juice.* ❷ to spill is to fall out of a container • *The coins came spilling out.*

spill *NOUN* **spills**
when something gets spilt • *There's been an oil spill at sea.*

spin *VERB* **spins, spinning, spun**
❶ to spin is to turn round and round quickly ❷ to spin something is to make it spin ❸ to spin is also to make pieces of wool or cotton into thread by twisting them ❹ to spin a web or cocoon is to make it out of threads
A young spider knows how to spin a web without any instructions from anybody.—CHARLOTTE'S WEB, E. B. White

spin *NOUN* **spins**
❶ a spinning movement ❷ a short outing in a car

spinach *NOUN*
spinach is a vegetable with dark green leaves

spinal *ADJECTIVE*
a spinal injury is one affecting a person's spine

spindle *NOUN* **spindles**
❶ a thin rod on which you wind thread
❷ a pin or bar that turns round, or on which something turns round

spindly *ADJECTIVE* **spindlier, spindliest**
long or tall and thin • *The baby giraffe stood on its spindly legs.*

spine *NOUN* **spines**
❶ the line of bones down the middle of your back ❷ a sharp point on an animal or plant • *This cactus has sharp spines.* ❸ the back part of a book where the pages are joined together

spine-chilling *ADJECTIVE*
frightening and exciting • *We heard a spine-chilling ghost story.*

spinneret *NOUN* **spinnerets**
the part of a spider's body that produces thread for its web
The spider stood on its head, pointed its spinnerets in the air, and let loose a cloud of fine silk.
—CHARLOTTE'S WEB, E. B. White

spinning wheel *NOUN* **spinning wheels**
a machine for spinning thread out of wool or cotton

spin-off *NOUN* **spin-offs**
something extra produced while you are making something else

spinster *NOUN* **spinsters** (*old use*)
an insulting word for a woman who has not married

spiral *ADJECTIVE*
going round and round a central point, getting further from it with each turn

spiral *NOUN* **spirals**
something with a spiral shape

spire *NOUN* **spires**
a tall pointed part on top of a church tower

spirit *NOUN* **spirits**
❶ a person's spirit is their soul or their deepest thoughts and feelings ❷ a spirit is a ghost or other supernatural being ❸ spirit is courage or liveliness ❹ a person's spirits are their mood or the way they feel • *She was in good spirits after the exam.* ❺ a spirit is also a strong alcoholic drink

spiritual *ADJECTIVE*
❶ to do with the human soul and with a person's deepest thoughts and feelings
❷ to do with religious beliefs
➤ **spiritually** *ADVERB*

spit *VERB* **spits, spitting, spat**
❶ to spit is to send drops of liquid forcibly out of your mouth • *He spat into the basin.*
❷ (*informal*) to spit is to rain lightly • *It's only spitting.*

spit *NOUN* **spits**
❶ spit is saliva that has been spat out
❷ a spit is a long thin metal spike to hold meat while it is roasted ❸ a spit is also a narrow strip of land sticking out into the sea

spite *NOUN*
spite is a desire to hurt or annoy someone
➤ **in spite of something** although something has happened or is happening • *They went out in spite of the rain.*

spiteful *ADJECTIVE*
behaving unkindly in order to hurt or annoy someone
➤ **spitefully** *ADVERB*

spittle *NOUN*
saliva, especially when it is spat out

splash *VERB* **splashes, splashing, splashed**
❶ to splash liquid is to make it fly about, as you do when you jump into water ❷ to splash is to fly about in drops • *The water splashed all over me.* ❸ to splash someone or something is to make them wet by sending drops of liquid towards them • *The bus splashed us as it went past.*

splash *NOUN* **splashes**
the action or sound of splashing

splendid *ADJECTIVE*
magnificent; very fine
➤ **splendidly** *ADVERB*

splendiferous *ADJECTIVE* (*informal*)
splendid and wonderful • *We had a splendiferous time!*

splendour *NOUN*
splendour is magnificent and grand display or appearance • *The pharaoh's tomb was decorated with regal splendour.*

splint NOUN **splints**
a straight piece of wood or metal that is tied to a broken arm or leg to hold it firm

splinter NOUN **splinters**
a small sharp piece of wood or glass broken off a larger piece

splinter VERB **splinters**, **splintering**, **splintered**
to splinter is to break into splinters

split VERB **splits**, **splitting**, **split**
❶ to split is to break into parts ❷ to split something is to divide it into parts
➤ **to split up** ❶ is to divide into parts ❷ is to separate after being together for some time

split NOUN **splits**
a crack or tear in something, where it has split
➤ **the splits** a movement in gymnastics with your legs stretched widely in opposite directions

splodge NOUN **splodges** (informal)
a patch or smear of something soft or runny
• Don't leave splodges of paint on the carpet!

splutter VERB **splutters**, **spluttering**, **spluttered**
❶ to splutter is to make a quick series of spitting or coughing sounds • The smoke from the bonfire made him splutter. ❷ to splutter is also to speak quickly and unclearly

spoil VERB **spoils**, **spoiling**, **spoilt** or **spoiled**
❶ to spoil something is to damage it and so make it less good or useful • The rain spoilt our holiday. ❷ to spoil someone is to make them selfish by always letting them have what they want

spoils PLURAL NOUN
valuable things taken by invaders in war

spoilsport NOUN **spoilsports**
someone who spoils other people's fun

spoke VERB (past tense of **speak**)
• Suddenly a voice spoke.

spoke NOUN **spokes**
each of the rods or bars that go from the centre of a wheel to the rim

spoken VERB (past participle of **speak**)
• Nobody had spoken yet.

spokesman, **spokeswoman** NOUN **spokesmen**, **spokeswomen**
a person who speaks on behalf of other people

spokesperson NOUN **spokespersons**
a person who speaks on behalf of a group of people

sponge NOUN **sponges**
❶ a lump of soft material containing lots of tiny holes, used for washing ❷ a sea creature from which this kind of material is made ❸ a soft lightweight cake or pudding

sponge VERB **sponges**, **sponging**, **sponged**
❶ to sponge something is to wash it with a sponge ❷ (informal) to sponge is to get money from people without doing anything for them • He was always sponging off his friends.

spongy ADJECTIVE **spongier**, **spongiest**
soft and absorbent like a sponge
➤ **sponginess** NOUN

sponsor VERB **sponsors**, **sponsoring**, **sponsored**
❶ to sponsor someone is to promise to give them money if they do something difficult and give the money to charity ❷ to sponsor something or someone is to provide money to support them

sponsor NOUN **sponsors**
someone who provides money to support a person or thing, or who supports someone who sets out to do something for charity
➤ **sponsorship** NOUN

spontaneous (say spon-**tay**-ni-us) ADJECTIVE
something spontaneous happens or is done without being planned
The assembled company—including young Eddie Dickens—burst into spontaneous applause. —AWFUL END, Philip Ardagh
➤ **spontaneously** ADVERB
➤ **spontaneity** NOUN

spooky ADJECTIVE **spookier**, **spookiest** (informal)
strange and quite frightening; haunted by ghosts • a dark and spooky graveyard
➤ **spookily** ADVERB

spool NOUN **spools**
a rod or reel for winding on something such as thread or film or tape

spoon NOUN **spoons**
a piece of metal or wood or plastic consisting of a small bowl with a handle, used for lifting food to your mouth or for stirring or measuring

spoon VERB spoons, spooning, spooned
to spoon something is to lift it or take it with a spoon

spoonful NOUN spoonfuls
as much as a spoon will hold

sport NOUN sports
❶ a sport is a game that exercises your body, especially a game you play out of doors • *What sports do you play?* ❷ sport is games of this sort • *Are you keen on sport?* ❸ (informal) a sport is someone who plays or behaves fairly and unselfishly • *Come on, be a sport.*

sporting ADJECTIVE
❶ connected with sport; interested in sport ❷ behaving fairly and unselfishly

sports car NOUN sports cars
an open low-built fast car

sportsman, **sportswoman** NOUN sportsmen, sportswomen
a person who takes part in sport

sportsmanship NOUN
sportsmanship is behaving fairly and generously in sport and in other ways

sportswear NOUN
clothing that you wear to play sports

spot NOUN spots
❶ a small round mark ❷ a pimple on your skin ❸ a small amount of something • *We're having a spot of bother.* ❹ a place • *I found a quiet spot to sit and read.*
➤ **on the spot** immediately; there and then • *We can repair your bike on the spot.*

spot VERB spots, spotting, spotted
❶ to spot someone or something is to notice them or see them • *He spotted an old friend in the crowd.* ❷ to be spotted is to be marked with spots

spotless ADJECTIVE
perfectly clean

spotlight NOUN spotlights
a strong light with a beam that shines on a small area

spotter NOUN spotters
someone who goes to watch or study things that interest them for a hobby • *They are keen trainspotters.*

spotty ADJECTIVE spottier, spottiest
marked with spots
➤ **spottiness** NOUN

spout NOUN spouts
❶ a pipe or opening from which liquid can pour ❷ a jet of liquid

spout VERB spouts, spouting, spouted
❶ to spout is to come out in a jet of liquid ❷ (informal) to spout is also to speak for a long time

sprain VERB sprains, spraining, sprained
you sprain your ankle or wrist when you injure it by twisting it

sprain NOUN sprains
an injury by spraining

sprang VERB (past tense of spring)
• *Suddenly the lid sprang open.*

sprawl VERB sprawls, sprawling, sprawled
❶ you sprawl when you sit or lie with your arms and legs spread out ❷ to be sprawled is to be spread out loosely or untidily • *There were newspapers sprawled all over the floor.*

spray VERB sprays, spraying, sprayed
❶ to spray liquid is to scatter it in tiny drops over something ❷ to spray something is to cover it with liquid in this way

spray NOUN sprays
❶ tiny drops of liquid sprayed on something ❷ a device for spraying liquid ❸ a small bunch of flowers

spread VERB spreads, spreading, spread
❶ to spread something is to lay or stretch it out to its full size • *The bird spread its wings and flew away.* ❷ to spread something over a surface is to make it cover the surface • *He spread a thick layer of jam on his toast.* ❸ to spread news or information is to make it widely known ❹ news or information spreads when it becomes widely known • *The story spread quickly round the village.*

spread NOUN spreads
❶ something you can spread on bread ❷ the breadth or extent of something ❸ (informal) a large meal

sprightly ADJECTIVE sprightlier, sprightliest
lively and energetic

a b c d e f g h i j k l m n o p q r s t u v w x y z

A B C D E F G H I J K L M N O P Q R S T U V W X Y Z

spring *NOUN* **springs**
❶ spring is the season of the year when most plants start to grow, between winter and summer ❷ a spring is a coil of wire that goes back to its original shape when you bend it or squeeze it and let it go ❸ a spring is also a sudden upward movement ❹ a spring is also a place where water rises out of the ground and becomes a stream

spring *VERB* **springs, springing, sprang, sprung**
❶ to spring is to move quickly or suddenly • *He sprang to his feet.* ❷ to spring, or spring up, is to develop or come from something • *This squabble has sprung from a misunderstanding.* ❸ to spring something on someone is to surprise them with it

springboard *NOUN* **springboards**
a springy board from which people jump or dive

spring-clean *VERB* **spring-cleans, spring-cleaning, spring-cleaned**
to spring-clean a house is to clean it thoroughly, usually in spring

springy *ADJECTIVE* **springier, springiest**
something springy will spring back to its original position when you bend or squeeze it and then let it go • *a patch of springy heather*
➤ **springiness** *NOUN*

sprinkle *VERB* **sprinkles, sprinkling, sprinkled**
to sprinkle liquid or powder is to make tiny drops or pieces of it fall on something
➤ **sprinkler** *NOUN*

sprint *VERB* **sprints, sprinting, sprinted**
to sprint is to run very fast for a short distance
➤ **sprinter** *NOUN*

sprint *NOUN* **sprints**
a short fast race

sprite *NOUN* **sprites**
a sprite is a fairy or elf

sprout *VERB* **sprouts, sprouting, sprouted**
❶ a plant sprouts when it starts to produce leaves or shoots ❷ to grow or start appearing
When Artemis smiled, as he did now, one almost expected vampire fangs to sprout from his gums.
—ARTEMIS FOWL, Eoin Colfer

sprout *NOUN* **sprouts**
a Brussels sprout

spruce *NOUN* **spruces**
a spruce is a kind of fir tree

spruce *ADJECTIVE* **sprucer, sprucest**
neat and smart • *Jeff looked spruce in a shirt and tie.*

sprung *VERB* (*past participle of* **spring**)
• *A friendship had sprung up between the two.*

spud *NOUN* **spuds** (*informal*)
a potato

spun *VERB* (*past tense and past participle of* **spin**)
• *He spun round.* • *She sold all the wool she had spun.*

spur *NOUN* **spurs**
❶ a sharp device that a rider wears on the heel of their boot to urge a horse to go faster ❷ a ridge that sticks out from a mountain
➤ **on the spur of the moment** on an impulse; without planning

spur *VERB* **spurs, spurring, spurred**
to spur someone, or to spur someone on, is to encourage them

spurt *VERB* **spurts, spurting, spurted**
a liquid spurts when it gushes out or up
• *Blood was spurting from the cut.*

spurt *NOUN* **spurts**
❶ a jet of liquid ❷ a sudden increase in speed
• *He put on a spurt and caught us up.*

spy *NOUN* **spies**
someone who works secretly to find out things about another country or person

spy *VERB* **spies, spying, spied**
❶ to spy is to be a spy or to watch secretly
• *Have you two been spying on me?*
❷ to spy someone or something is to see them or notice them • *We spied a ship on the horizon.*

spyglass *NOUN* **spyglasses**
a small telescope

squabble *VERB* **squabbles, squabbling, squabbled**
people squabble when they quarrel about something unimportant

squabble *NOUN* **squabbles**
a quarrel or argument

squad *NOUN* **squads**
a small group of people working or being trained together

squadron *NOUN* **squadrons**
part of an army, navy or air force

squalid *ADJECTIVE*
dirty and unpleasant • *He lived in a squalid little flat.*
➤ **squalor** *NOUN*

squall *NOUN* **squalls**
❶ a sudden storm or strong wind ❷ a baby's loud cry
➤ **squally** *ADJECTIVE*

squander *VERB* **squanders**, **squandering**, **squandered**
to squander money or time is to waste it

square *NOUN* **squares**
❶ a shape with four equal sides and four right angles ❷ in a town, an area surrounded by buildings ❸ the result of multiplying a number by itself • *9 is the square of 3.*

square *ADJECTIVE*
❶ shaped like a square ❷ forming a right angle or having right angles ❸ used for units of measurement that give an area, such as a square metre and a square foot. For example, a square metre is the size of a square with each side one metre long. ❹ equal or even • *The teams are all square with six points each.* • *If you pay for lunch, we'll be square.*

square *VERB* **squares**, **squaring**, **squared**
❶ to square something is to make it have square edges and corners ❷ to square a number is to multiply it by itself • *3 squared is 9.* ❸ to square with something is to match it or agree with it • *His story doesn't square with yours.*

squarely *ADVERB*
directly or exactly • *The ball hit him squarely in the mouth.*

square root *NOUN* **square roots**
the number that gives a particular number if it is multiplied by itself • *3 is the square root of 9.*

squash *VERB* **squashes**, **squashing**, **squashed**
❶ to squash something is to squeeze it so that it loses its shape ❷ to squash a person or thing into something is to force them into it

when there is not much space • *We squashed ourselves into the minibus.*

squash *NOUN* **squashes**
❶ a squash is when people or things are pressed together because there is not enough space • *There was a tremendous squash outside the stadium.* ❷ squash is a fruit-flavoured drink ❸ squash is also a game played with rackets and a small ball in a special indoor court

squat *VERB* **squats**, **squatting**, **squatted**
❶ to squat is to sit back on your heels ❷ to squat in an unoccupied house is to live there without permission
➤ **squatter** *NOUN*

squat *ADJECTIVE* **squatter**, **squattest**
short and fat

squawk *VERB* **squawks**, **squawking**, **squawked**
to squawk is to make a loud harsh cry

squawk *NOUN* **squawks**
a loud harsh cry

squeak *VERB* **squeaks**, **squeaking**, **squeaked**
to make a short high-pitched sound or cry

squeak *NOUN* **squeaks**
a short high-pitched sound or cry

squeaky *ADJECTIVE* **squeakier**, **squeakiest**
something is squeaky when it makes squeaks • *a squeaky floorboard*

squeal *VERB* **squeals**, **squealing**, **squealed**
to squeal is to make a long shrill sound

squeal *NOUN* **squeals**
a long shrill sound

squeeze *VERB* **squeezes**, **squeezing**, **squeezed**
❶ to squeeze something is to press it from opposite sides, especially so that you get liquid out of it ❷ to squeeze somewhere is to force a way into or through a place or gap • *We squeezed into the car.*

squeeze *NOUN* **squeezes**
❶ the action of squeezing ❷ a tight fit • *We all got on the bus, but it was a bit of a squeeze.* ❸ a time when money is difficult to get or borrow

squelch *VERB* **squelches**, **squelching**, **squelched**
to squelch is to make a sound like someone treading in thick mud

a b c d e f g h i j k l m n o p q r s t u v w x y z

squelch *NOUN* **squelches**
a squelching sound

squid *NOUN* **squid** or **squids**
a sea animal with eight short arms and two long tentacles
SPOT THE DIFFERENCE! Both **octopuses** and **squid** have eight arms, but squid have an extra pair of tentacles.

squidgy *ADJECTIVE* **squidgier**, **squidgiest** (*informal*)
soft and slightly wet or moist • *a slice of squidgy chocolate cake*
➤ **squidginess** *NOUN*

squiggle *NOUN* **squiggles**
a short curly or wavy line
➤ **squiggly** *ADJECTIVE*

squint *VERB* **squints**, **squinting**, **squinted**
❶ to squint at something is to peer at it or look at it with half-shut eyes ❷ to squint is to have eyes that look in different directions

squint *NOUN* **squints**
a fault in someone's eyesight that makes them squint

squire *NOUN* **squires**
❶ in the Middle Ages, a young nobleman who served a knight ❷ a landowner of a large country estate

squirm *VERB* **squirms**, **squirming**, **squirmed**
to wriggle about, especially when you feel awkward or embarrassed

squirrel *NOUN* **squirrels**
a small animal with grey or red fur and a bushy tail, that lives in trees and eats nuts

squirt *VERB* **squirts**, **squirting**, **squirted**
to squirt something is to send it out in a strong jet of liquid; to squirt is to come out like this • *The orange juice squirted in his eye.*

squish *VERB* **squishes**, **squishing**, **squished** (*informal*)
to squish something is to squash it • *Try not to squish the sandwiches!*
➤ **squishy** *ADJECTIVE*

St *ABBREVIATION*
short for *saint* or *street*

stab *VERB* **stabs**, **stabbing**, **stabbed**
to stab someone is to pierce or wound them with something sharp • *She stabbed him with a knife.*

stab *NOUN* **stabs**
❶ the action of stabbing ❷ a sudden sharp pain

stabilizer (*also* **stabiliser**) *NOUN* **stabilizers**
a device for keeping a vehicle or ship steady

stability *NOUN*
stability is being stable or firm

stabilize (*also* **stabilise**) *VERB* **stabilizes**, **stabilizing**, **stabilized**
❶ to stabilize something is to make it stable ❷ to stabilize is to become stable

stable *ADJECTIVE* **stabler**, **stablest**
steady or firmly fixed • *Be careful! That ladder is not stable.*
➤ **stably** *ADVERB*

stable *NOUN* **stables**
a stable is a building where horses are kept

stack *NOUN* **stacks**
❶ a neat pile of things ❷ a haystack ❸ a large amount of something • *I've got a stack of work to do.* ❹ a single small chimney

stack *VERB* **stacks**, **stacking**, **stacked**
to stack things is to pile them up neatly

stadium *NOUN* **stadiums**
a sports ground surrounded by seats for spectators

staff *NOUN* **staffs**
❶ the people who work in an office or shop ❷ the teachers in a school or college ❸ a thick stick for walking with ❹ a set of five lines on which music is written

stag *NOUN* **stags**
a male deer

stage *NOUN* **stages**
❶ a platform for performances in a theatre or hall ❷ the point that you have reached in a process or journey • *We've reached the final stage of the competition.*

stage *VERB* **stages**, **staging**, **staged**
❶ to stage a performance is to present it on a stage ❷ to stage an event is to organize it • *They decided to stage a protest.*

stagecoach *NOUN* **stagecoaches**
a horse-drawn coach of a kind that used to travel regularly along the same route

stagger *VERB* **staggers, staggering, staggered**
❶ to stagger is to walk unsteadily ❷ to stagger someone is to amaze or shock them • *I was staggered at the price.* ❸ to stagger events is to arrange them so that they do not all happen at the same time
➤ **staggering** *ADJECTIVE*

stagnant *ADJECTIVE*
stagnant water is not flowing or fresh

stain *NOUN* **stains**
❶ a dirty mark that is difficult to remove
The next morning, however, when they came down to breakfast, they found the terrible stain of blood once again on the floor.—THE CANTERVILLE GHOST, Oscar Wilde
❷ something bad in someone's character or past record

stain *VERB* **stains, staining, stained**
❶ to stain something is to make a stain on it • *The juice has stained my dress.* ❷ to stain material or wood is to colour it

stainless *ADJECTIVE*
without stains

stainless steel *NOUN*
stainless steel is steel that does not rust easily

stair *NOUN* **stairs**
each of a series of steps that take you from one floor to another in a building

staircase *NOUN* **staircases**
a set of stairs

stake *NOUN* **stakes**
❶ a thick pointed stick to be driven into the ground ❷ the thick post to which people used to be tied for execution by being burnt alive ❸ an amount of money you bet on something
➤ **to be at stake** is to be at risk of being lost

stake *VERB* **stakes, staking, staked**
to stake money is to use it on a bet
➤ **to stake a claim** is to claim something or get a right to it

stalactite *NOUN* **stalactites**
a stony spike hanging like an icicle from the roof of a cave

stalagmite *NOUN* **stalagmites**
a stony spike standing like a pillar on the floor of a cave

stale *ADJECTIVE* **staler, stalest**
no longer fresh • *This bread has gone stale.* • *The air in here smells stale.*

stalk *NOUN* **stalks**
the main part of a plant, from which the leaves and flowers grow

stalk *VERB* **stalks, stalking, stalked**
❶ to stalk a person or animal is to follow or hunt them stealthily ❷ to stalk is to walk in a proud or stiff way

stall *NOUN* **stalls**
❶ a table or stand where things are sold, usually in the open air • *We're running an ice cream stall at the summer fair.* ❷ a place for one animal in a stable or shed

stall *VERB* **stalls, stalling, stalled**
❶ a vehicle stalls when the engine stops suddenly ❷ to stall is to delay or hold things up to give yourself more time • *I could tell he was stalling for time.*

stallion *NOUN* **stallions**
a male horse

stalls *PLURAL NOUN*
the seats on the ground floor of a theatre or cinema

stamen (*say* **stay-men**) *NOUN* **stamens**
the part of a flower that produces pollen

stamina (*say* **stam-in-a**) *NOUN*
stamina is the strength and energy you need to keep doing something for a long time • *Do you have the stamina to run a marathon?*

stammer *VERB* **stammers, stammering, stammered**
to stammer is to keep repeating the sounds at the beginning of words

stammer *NOUN* **stammers**
a tendency to stammer

stamp *NOUN* **stamps**
❶ a small piece of gummed paper with a special design on it; a postage stamp ❷ when you bang your foot on the ground ❸ a small block with raised letters for printing words or marks on something; the words or marks made with this

a b c d e f g h i j k l m n o p q r **s** t u v w x y z

stamp *VERB* **stamps**, **stamping**, **stamped**
① to stamp is to bang your foot heavily on the ground **②** to stamp an envelope or parcel is to put a postage stamp on it **③** to stamp something is also to put marks on it with a stamp • *The librarian stamped my books.*

stampede *NOUN* **stampedes**
a sudden rush of animals or people

stampede *VERB* **stampedes**, **stampeding**, **stampeded**
animals or people stampede when they rush in a stampede

stand *VERB* **stands**, **standing**, **stood**
① to stand is to be on your feet without moving • *She stood at the back of the hall.*
② to stand something somewhere is to put it upright there • *Stand the vase on the table.*
③ something stands somewhere when that is where it is • *The castle stood on the top of a hill.* **④** something stands when it stays unchanged • *My offer still stands.* **⑤** to stand a difficulty or hardship is to be able to bear it • *I can't stand the heat.*
➤ **it stands to reason** it is reasonable or obvious
➤ **to stand by** is to be ready for action
➤ **to stand for something** **①** is to tolerate it or put up with it • *She won't stand for any arguments.* **②** is to mean something • *'Dr' stands for 'Doctor'.*
➤ **to stand in for someone** is to take their place
➤ **to stand out** is to be clear or obvious
➤ **to stand up for someone** is to support them or defend them

stand *NOUN* **stands**
① something made for putting things on • *Use a music stand.* **②** a stall where things are sold or displayed **③** a building at a sports ground, that is open at the front with rows of seats for spectators **④** when someone resists an attack or defends their opinion • *She was determined to make a stand for her rights.*

standard *NOUN* **standards**
① how good something is • *They reached a high standard of work.* **②** a thing used to measure or judge something else • *The metre is the standard for length.*
③ a special flag, especially one used by an army

standard *ADJECTIVE*
of the usual or ordinary kind

standardize (*also* **standardise**)
VERB **standardizes**, **standardizing**, **standardized**
to standardize something is to make it a standard size or type

standby *NOUN* **standbys**
something or someone kept to be used if they are needed

stand-offish *ADJECTIVE*
cold and formal; not friendly
'Lately,' Count Olaf said, 'I have been very nervous about my performances … and I'm afraid I may have acted a bit standoffish.'–THE BAD BEGINNING, Lemony Snicket

standstill *NOUN*
a complete stop • *The blizzard brought traffic to a standstill.*

stank *VERB* (*past tense of* **stink**)
• *The shed stank of damp wood.*

stanza *NOUN* **stanzas**
a group of lines in a poem

staple *NOUN* **staples**
① a tiny piece of metal used to fasten pieces of paper together **②** a U-shaped nail
➤ **stapler** *NOUN*
a machine for putting staples in paper

staple *VERB* **staples**, **stapling**, **stapled**
to staple pieces of paper is to fasten them together with a staple

staple *ADJECTIVE*
main or normal • *Rice is their staple food.*

star *NOUN* **stars**
① a large mass of burning gas that you see as a bright speck of light in the sky at night
② one of the main performers in a film or show; a famous entertainer **③** a shape with five or six points

star *VERB* **stars**, **starring**, **starred**
① to star in a film or show is to be one of the main performers **②** a film or show stars someone when it has them as a main performer

starboard *NOUN*
starboard is the right-hand side of a ship or aircraft when you are facing forward

starch NOUN starches
❶ starch is a white carbohydrate in bread, potatoes and other food ❷ starch is also a form of this substance used to stiffen clothes

stare VERB stares, staring, stared
to look continuously at someone or something without moving your eyes

stare NOUN stares
a long fixed look • *I gave him a hard stare.*

starfish NOUN starfish *or* starfishes
a sea animal shaped like a star with five points

starling NOUN starlings
a noisy black or brown speckled bird

starry ADJECTIVE
a starry sky or night is full of stars

start VERB starts, starting, started
❶ to start something is to take the first steps in doing it ❷ to start, or start out, is to begin a journey ❸ to start is also to make a sudden movement of surprise • *They all started at the noise outside.*

start NOUN starts
❶ the act of starting; the point or place where something starts ❷ an advantage that someone starts with • *We gave the rest of the team 10 minutes' start.* ❸ a sudden movement of surprise • *It gave me quite a start when the hooter sounded.*

starter NOUN starters
❶ someone who starts a race ❷ a device for starting the engine of a vehicle

startle VERB startles, startling, startled
to startle a person or animal is to surprise or alarm them

starve VERB starves, starving, starved
❶ someone starves when they suffer or die because they do not have enough food ❷ to starve someone is to make them suffer or die in this way • *The prisoners had been starved to death.* ❸ to starve someone of something they need is to deprive them of it • *They adopt pets who have been starved of love.* ❹ (*informal*) to be starving is to be very hungry
➤ **starvation** NOUN

state NOUN states
❶ the quality of a person or thing or their circumstances; the way they are ❷ a nation ❸ a division of a country ❹ you can refer to a government and its officials as the state
➤ **to be in a state** (*informal*) is to be upset

state VERB states, stating, stated
to state something is to say it clearly or formally

stately ADJECTIVE statelier, stateliest
grand and dignified
➤ **stateliness** NOUN

stately home NOUN stately homes
a large and splendid house that a noble family has owned for many years

statement NOUN statements
❶ words that state something ❷ a formal account of something that happened • *A witness has given a statement to the police.* ❸ a report made by a bank about the money in a person's account

state school NOUN state schools
a school which gets its money from the government and does not charge fees

statesman, stateswoman NOUN statesmen, stateswomen
a person who is important or skilled in governing a state

static ADJECTIVE
not moving or changing

static electricity NOUN
static electricity is electricity which is present in something but does not flow as a current

station NOUN stations
❶ a set of buildings where people get on or off trains or buses ❷ a building for police, firefighters or other workers ❸ a place from which radio or television broadcasts are made

station VERB stations, stationing, stationed
to station a person somewhere is to place them there for a particular purpose • *Sean was stationed at the door to welcome guests.*

stationary ADJECTIVE
not moving; still • *The bus hit a stationary vehicle.*
SPELLING ALERT! A vehicle can be **stationary**, but you write on **stationery**. Think of the **er** in *paper* to help you remember!

stationery NOUN
stationery is paper, envelopes and other things used for writing

a
b
c
d
e
f
g
h
i
j
k
l
m
n
o
p
q
r
s
t
u
v
w
x
y
z

statistic NOUN **statistics**
a piece of information expressed as a number
• *These statistics show that the population has doubled.*

statistics NOUN
statistics is the study of information that is expressed as numbers

statue NOUN **statues**
a model made of stone or metal to look like a person or animal

status NOUN **statuses**
❶ a person's status is their position or rank in relation to other people • *What is your status in the company?* ❷ status is high rank or prestige

staunch ADJECTIVE
firm and loyal • *They are the team's most staunch supporters.*

stave NOUN **staves**
a stave is a set of five lines on which music is written

stave VERB **staves, staving, staved**
➤ **to stave something off** is to keep something unwelcome away or delay it
• *I ate a banana to stave off my hunger.*

stay VERB **stays, staying, stayed**
❶ to stay somewhere is to continue to be there or to remain there ❷ to stay somewhere or with someone is to spend time as a visitor
• *We stayed in a little hotel near the sea.*

stay NOUN **stays**
a period of time spent somewhere • *We didn't have time for a long stay.*

steady ADJECTIVE **steadier, steadiest**
❶ not shaking or moving; firm ❷ regular or constant; not changing much • *They kept up a steady pace.*
➤ **steadily** ADVERB

steady VERB **steadies, steadying, steadied**
to steady something is to make it steady

steak NOUN **steaks**
a thick slice of meat or fish

steal VERB **steals, stealing, stole, stolen**
❶ to steal something is to take and keep it when it does not belong to you ❷ to steal somewhere is to move there stealthily • *He stole out of the room.*

stealthy ADJECTIVE **stealthier, stealthiest**
moving or doing something secretly and quietly so that you are not noticed
➤ **stealth** NOUN ➤ **stealthily** ADVERB

steam NOUN
steam is the gas or vapour that comes from boiling water
➤ **to run out of steam** (*informal*) is to have no energy left

steam VERB **steams, steaming, steamed**
❶ to steam is to give out steam ❷ to steam somewhere is to move using the power of steam • *The boat steamed down the river.*
❸ to steam food is to cook it with steam
➤ **to steam up** is to be covered with mist or condensation • *The windows have steamed up.*

steam engine NOUN **steam engines**
an engine driven by steam

steamer NOUN **steamers**
a steamship

steamship NOUN **steamships**
a ship driven by steam

steamy ADJECTIVE **steamier, steamiest**
a steamy room is full of steam
➤ **steaminess** NOUN

steed NOUN **steeds** (*old use*)
a horse

steel NOUN
steel is a strong metal made from iron and carbon

steel VERB **steels, steeling, steeled**
➤ **to steel yourself** is to find courage to do something difficult

steel band NOUN **steel bands**
a style of band that originated in Trinidad, playing instruments usually made from oil drums

steely ADJECTIVE **steelier, steeliest**
tough or hard, like steel • *She had a steely look in her eyes.*

steep ADJECTIVE **steeper, steepest**
rising or sloping sharply
➤ **steeply** ADVERB ➤ **steepness** NOUN

steeple NOUN **steeples**
a church tower with a spire

steeplejack *NOUN* **steeplejacks**
a person who climbs tall steeples or chimneys to do repairs

steer *VERB* **steers, steering, steered**
to steer a vehicle is to make it go in the direction you want

steer *NOUN* **steers**
a steer is a young bull kept for its beef

steering wheel *NOUN* **steering wheels**
a wheel for steering a vehicle

stegosaur *NOUN* **stegosaurs**
a dinosaur with a double row of bony plates along its back

stem *NOUN* **stems**
❶ the main central part of a plant or tree; a stalk ❷ (*grammar*) the main part of a word, to which different endings are attached. For example, *call* is the stem of the words *caller*, *called*, *calls* and *calling*.

stem *VERB* **stems, stemming, stemmed**
to stem from something is to start there or come from it • *The problem stems from lack of money.*

stench *NOUN* **stenches**
a very unpleasant smell

stencil *NOUN* **stencils**
a piece of card or metal or plastic with pieces cut out of it, used to produce a picture or design

step *NOUN* **steps**
❶ a movement you make with your foot when you are walking, running or dancing ❷ the sound of a person putting down their foot when walking ❸ each of the level surfaces on a stair or ladder ❹ each of a series of actions

step *VERB* **steps, stepping, stepped**
to step is to tread or walk
➤ **to step something up** is to increase it

stepchild *NOUN* **stepchildren**
a child that someone's husband or wife has from an earlier marriage. A boy is a **stepson** and a girl is a **stepdaughter**.

stepfather *NOUN* **stepfathers**
a man who is married to, or is the partner of, your mother or father but is not your own father

stepladder *NOUN* **stepladders**
a folding ladder with flat treads

stepmother *NOUN* **stepmothers**
a woman who is married to, or is the partner of, your father or mother but is not your own mother

stepping stone *NOUN* **stepping stones**
stepping stones are a line of stones put in a river or stream to help people walk across

stereo *ADJECTIVE*
stereo sound comes from two different directions to give a natural effect

stereo *NOUN*
stereo sound or recording

sterile *ADJECTIVE*
❶ clean and free from germs ❷ not able to have children or reproduce
➤ **sterility** *NOUN*

sterilize (*also* **sterilise**) *VERB* **sterilizes, sterilizing, sterilized**
❶ to sterilize something is to make it free from germs ❷ to sterilize a person or animal is to make them unable to bear young
➤ **sterilization** *NOUN*

sterling *NOUN*
sterling is British money; pounds and pence • *The price is given in both sterling and euros.*

stern *ADJECTIVE* **sterner, sternest**
strict and severe • *Miss Phipps wore her usual stern expression.*
➤ **sternly** *ADVERB* ➤ **sternness** *NOUN*

stern *NOUN* **sterns**
the stern is the back part of a ship

stethoscope (*say* steth-o-skohp) *NOUN* **stethoscopes**
a device used by doctors for listening to a patient's heartbeat or breathing

stew *VERB* **stews, stewing, stewed**
to stew food is to cook it slowly in liquid

stew *NOUN* **stews**
a dish of meat and vegetables cooked slowly in liquid

steward *NOUN* **stewards**
❶ a person whose job is to look after the passengers on a ship or aircraft ❷ an official who looks after the arrangements at a public event

stick *NOUN* **sticks**
❶ a long thin piece of wood ❷ a walking stick ❸ the long thin piece of wood used to hit the

a b c d e f g h i j k l m n o p q r s t u v w x y z

ball in hockey or other ball games ❹ a long thin piece of something • *some crunchy carrot sticks*

stick VERB **sticks, sticking, stuck**
❶ to stick something sharp into a thing is to push it in roughly • *He stuck a pin in the map on the wall.* ❷ to stick things together is to fasten or join them ❸ something sticks when it becomes fixed or jammed • *The drawer keeps sticking.* ❹ (*informal*) you can't stick something when you can't bear it • *I can't stick the noise any longer.*
➤ **to stick out** is to come out from a surface or be noticeable
➤ **to stick up for someone** (*informal*) is to support or defend them

sticker NOUN **stickers**
a label or sign for sticking on something

stick insect NOUN **stick insects**
an insect with a long thin body that looks like a twig

sticky ADJECTIVE **stickier, stickiest**
❶ able or likely to stick to things ❷ (*informal*) unpleasant or nasty • *He came to a sticky end.*
➤ **stickily** ADVERB ➤ **stickiness** NOUN

stiff ADJECTIVE **stiffer, stiffest**
❶ not able to bend or turn or change its shape easily • *This door handle is stiff.*
• *Add water to make a stiff dough.*
❷ not able to move or bend your body easily • *I woke up feeling stiff all over.*
❸ difficult or tough • *They faced some stiff competition.* ❹ strong or severe • *A stiff breeze was blowing.* ❺ not relaxed or natural
• *The acting is quite stiff and wooden.*
➤ **stiffly** ADVERB ➤ **stiffness** NOUN

stiffen VERB **stiffens, stiffening, stiffened**
❶ to stiffen something is to make it stiff
❷ to stiffen is to become stiff

stifle VERB **stifles, stifling, stifled**
❶ to be stifled is to find it difficult or impossible to breathe ❷ to stifle a noise or yawn is to stop it happening
John clapped his hands on the ill-fated pirate's mouth to stifle the dying groan.—THE ADVENTURES OF PETER PAN, J. M. Barrie

stile NOUN **stiles**
an arrangement of steps or bars for people to climb over a fence

still ADJECTIVE **stiller, stillest**
❶ not moving ❷ silent • *In the night, the streets are still.* ❸ not fizzy
➤ **stillness** NOUN

still ADVERB
❶ up to this or that time • *He was still there.*
❷ even; yet; in a greater amount • *They wanted still more food.* ❸ however • *They lost. Still, they have another game.*

still VERB **stills, stilling, stilled**
to still something is to make it still

stilts PLURAL NOUN
❶ a pair of poles on which you can walk high above the ground ❷ supports for a house built over water

stimulate VERB **stimulates, stimulating, stimulated**
❶ to stimulate someone is to make them excited or interested ❷ to stimulate something is to encourage it to develop • *His new book stimulated an interest in wildlife.*
➤ **stimulation** NOUN

stimulus NOUN **stimuli**
something that encourages a thing to develop or produces a reaction

sting NOUN **stings**
❶ the part of an insect or plant that can cause pain or a wound ❷ a painful area or wound caused by an insect or plant

sting VERB **stings, stinging, stung**
❶ an insect or plant stings you when it wounds or hurts you with a sting • *She was stung by a wasp.* ❷ part of your body stings when you feel a sharp or throbbing pain there • *My back is stinging from sunburn.*

stingray NOUN **stingrays**
a large sea fish with a flat diamond-shaped body and a tail with a poisonous sting

stingy (*say* stin-jee) ADJECTIVE **stingier, stingiest** (*informal*)
mean; not generous
➤ **stinginess** NOUN

stink NOUN **stinks**
❶ an unpleasant smell ❷ (*informal*) an unpleasant fuss or complaint

stink VERB **stinks, stinking, stank** *or* **stunk, stunk**
to stink is to have an unpleasant smell • *That cheese stinks!*

stir VERB **stirs, stirring, stirred**
❶ to stir something liquid or soft is to move it round and round, especially with a spoon
❷ to stir is to move slightly or start to move after sleeping or being still • *She didn't stir all afternoon.*
➤ **to stir something up** is to excite or arouse it • *They are always stirring up trouble.*

stir NOUN **stirs**
❶ an act of stirring • *Give it a stir.* ❷ a fuss or disturbance • *The news caused a stir.*

stirrup NOUN **stirrups**
a metal loop that hangs down on each side of a horse's saddle to support the rider's foot

stitch NOUN **stitches**
❶ a loop of thread made in sewing or knitting
❷ a sudden pain in your side caused by running

stoat NOUN **stoats**
an animal rather like a weasel, also called an *ermine*

stock NOUN **stocks**
❶ a stock of things is an amount of them kept ready to be sold or used ❷ stock is a collection of farm animals, also called *livestock*
❸ a person's stock is the line of their ancestors
❹ stock is a liquid used in cooking, made from the juices you get by stewing meat, fish or vegetables ❺ stock is also a garden flower with a sweet smell

stock VERB **stocks, stocking, stocked**
❶ a shop stocks goods when it keeps a supply of them to sell ❷ to stock a place is to provide it with a stock of things
• *The explorers stocked their base camp with tinned food.*
➤ **to stock up** is to buy a large supply of something

stockade NOUN **stockades**
a fence made of large stakes

stocking NOUN **stockings**
a piece of clothing that covers the whole of someone's leg and foot

stockpile NOUN **stockpiles**
a large stock of things kept in reserve

stocks PLURAL NOUN (*historical*)
a wooden framework with holes for people's legs and arms, in which criminals were locked as a punishment

stocky ADJECTIVE **stockier, stockiest**
short and solidly built
The wagon was drawn by two stocky black horses, both well groomed out and immaculate in well-oiled harness.—WAR HORSE, Michael Morpurgo

stodgy ADJECTIVE **stodgier, stodgiest**
❶ thick and heavy; not easy to digest
• *The pudding's very stodgy.* ❷ dull and boring
• *I found the book a bit stodgy.*
➤ **stodginess** NOUN

stoke VERB **stokes, stoking, stoked**
to stoke a furnace or fire is to add fuel to it

stole VERB (*past tense of* **steal**)
• *They stole a famous painting.*

stole NOUN **stoles**
a wide piece of material worn round the shoulders by women

stolen VERB (*past participle of* **steal**)
• *Someone has stolen my packed lunch.*

stomach NOUN **stomachs**
❶ the part of your body where food starts to be digested ❷ the front part of your body that contains your stomach; your abdomen

stomach VERB **stomachs, stomaching, stomached**
to stomach something is to tolerate it or put up with it • *I can't stomach their awful jokes.*

stomp VERB **stomps, stomping, stomped**
to stomp is to step or tread heavily and noisily
• *Debra stomped angrily up the stairs.*

stone NOUN **stones** or **stone**
❶ stone is the hard solid mineral of which rocks are made ❷ a stone is a piece of this mineral
❸ a stone is also a jewel ❹ a stone is also the hard seed in the middle of some fruits, such as a cherry, plum or peach ❺ a stone is also a unit of weight equal to 14 pounds or about 6.35 kilograms • *She weighs 6 stone.*

stone VERB **stones, stoning, stoned**
❶ to stone someone is to throw stones at them
❷ to stone fruit is to take the stones out of it

stone-cold ADJECTIVE
extremely cold

stony ADJECTIVE **stonier, stoniest**
❶ stony ground is full of stones ❷ hard like stone ❸ unfriendly or hostile • *Our question was met by a stony silence.*

A B C D E F G H I J K L M N O P Q R S T U V W X Y Z

stood VERB (*past tense and past participle of* **stand**)
• *A man stood up to speak.* • *We should have stood up to those bullies.*

stool NOUN **stools**
a small seat without a back

stoop VERB **stoops, stooping, stooped**
❶ to stoop is to bend your body forwards and downwards ❷ to stoop to doing something is to lower your standards of behaviour • *I didn't think he'd stoop to cheating.*

stop VERB **stops, stopping, stopped**
❶ to stop something is to finish doing it, or make it finish ❷ to stop is to be no longer moving or working or to come to an end ❸ to stop something is to prevent it happening or continuing • *Please go out and stop that noise.* ❹ to stop a hole or gap, or stop it up, is to fill it ❺ to stop at a place is to stay there briefly

stop NOUN **stops**
❶ when something stops or ends • *She brought her bike to a stop.* ❷ a place where a bus or train stops regularly

stoppage NOUN **stoppages**
❶ an interruption in the work of a business or factory ❷ a blockage in something

stopper NOUN **stoppers**
something that fits into the top of a bottle or jar to close it

stopwatch NOUN **stopwatches**
a watch that you can start or stop, used for timing races

storage NOUN
storage is the storing of things

store VERB **stores, storing, stored**
❶ to store things is to keep them until they are needed ❷ to store information is to save it in a computer's memory

store NOUN **stores**
❶ a place where things are stored ❷ things kept for future use ❸ a shop, especially a large one
➤ **to be in store** is to be waiting to happen soon • *There is a treat in store for you.*

storey NOUN **storeys**
one whole floor or level of a building

stork NOUN **storks**
a large bird with long legs and a long beak

storm NOUN **storms**
❶ a period of bad weather with strong winds, rain or snow, and often thunder and lightning ❷ a violent attack or outburst • *There was a storm of protest.*
➤ **a storm in a teacup** is a big fuss over something unimportant

storm VERB **storms, storming, stormed**
❶ to storm is to move or shout angrily • *He stormed out of the room.* ❷ soldiers or police storm a place when they attack it suddenly • *They stormed the castle.*

stormy ADJECTIVE **stormier, stormiest**
❶ likely to end in a storm • *The weather is stormy today.* ❷ loud and angry • *We had a stormy meeting.*

story NOUN **stories**
❶ an account of real or imaginary events • *a story about a haunted house* ❷ (*informal*) a lie • *Stop telling stories!*

stout ADJECTIVE **stouter, stoutest**
❶ rather fat ❷ thick and strong • *She carried a stout stick.* ❸ brave • *The defenders put up a stout resistance.*
➤ **stoutly** ADVERB ➤ **stoutness** NOUN

stove NOUN **stoves**
a device that produces heat for warming a room or for cooking • *We brought a camping stove for boiling water.*

stow VERB **stows, stowing, stowed**
to stow something is to pack it or store it away • *Mia stowed the map carefully in her pocket.*
➤ **to stow away** is to hide on a ship or aircraft so that you can travel without paying

stowaway NOUN **stowaways**
someone who stows away on a ship or aircraft

straddle VERB **straddles, straddling, straddled**
❶ to straddle something is to sit or stand with your legs either side of it ❷ to straddle something is also to be built across it • *A long bridge straddles the river.*

straggle VERB **straggles, straggling, straggled**
❶ to straggle is to walk too slowly and not keep up with the rest of a group ❷ to straggle is also

to grow or move in an untidy way • *Brambles straggled across the path.*

➤ **straggler** *NOUN* someone who does not keep up with the rest of a group

➤ **straggly** *ADJECTIVE* straggly hair grows or hangs untidily

straight *ADJECTIVE* **straighter, straightest**
❶ going continuously in one direction; not curving or bending ❷ level • *Is this picture straight?* ❸ tidy; in proper order ❹ honest or frank • *Give me a straight answer.*

straight *ADVERB*
❶ in a straight line • *Go straight on, then turn left.* ❷ at once; directly • *I came straight here.*

straightaway *ADVERB*
immediately; at once

straighten *VERB* **straightens, straightening, straightened**
❶ to straighten something is to make it straight ❷ to straighten is to become straight

straightforward *ADJECTIVE*
❶ easy to understand or do; not complicated ❷ honest or frank

strain *VERB* **strains, straining, strained**
❶ to strain something is to stretch it or push it or pull it hard or too hard ❷ to strain a muscle is to damage it by using it too much ❸ to strain is to make a great effort to do something ❹ to strain liquid is to put it through a sieve to take out any lumps or other things in it

strain *NOUN* **strains**
❶ the strain on something is when it is stretched or pulled too hard • *The rope broke under the strain.* ❷ a strain is an injury caused by straining ❸ strain is the effect on someone of too much work or worry

strainer *NOUN* **strainers**
a device for straining liquids

strait *NOUN* **straits**
a narrow stretch of water connecting two seas

straits *PLURAL NOUN*
➤ **to be in dire straits** is to have severe difficulties

strand *NOUN* **strands**
❶ each of the threads or wires twisted together to make a rope or cable ❷ a lock of hair

stranded *ADJECTIVE*
❶ left on sand or rocks in shallow water • *We could see a stranded ship.* ❷ left in a difficult or lonely position • *They were stranded in the desert.*

strange *ADJECTIVE* **stranger, strangest**
❶ unusual or surprising ❷ not known or experienced before
➤ **strangely** *ADVERB* ➤ **strangeness** *NOUN*

stranger *NOUN* **strangers**
❶ a person you do not know ❷ a person who is in a place they do not know

strangle *VERB* **strangles, strangling, strangled**
to strangle someone is to kill them by pressing their throat and so prevent them breathing
➤ **strangulation** *NOUN*

strap *NOUN* **straps**
a flat strip of leather or cloth or plastic for fastening things together or holding them in place

strap *VERB* **straps, strapping, strapped**
to strap something is to fasten it with a strap or straps

strategy *NOUN* **strategies**
❶ a strategy is a plan to achieve or win something ❷ strategy is planning a war or military campaign
➤ **strategic** *ADJECTIVE*

stratum (*say* strah-tum) *NOUN* **strata**
a layer or level • *You can see several strata of rock in the cliffs.*

straw *NOUN* **straws**
❶ straw is dry cut stalks of corn ❷ a straw is a narrow tube that you can drink through

strawberry *NOUN* **strawberries**
a small red juicy fruit, with its seeds on the outside

stray *VERB* **strays, straying, strayed**
to wander or become lost

stray *ADJECTIVE*
❶ wandering around lost • *We found a stray cat.* ❷ out of place; separated from all the others • *a stray hair or two*

stray *NOUN* **strays**
a stray dog or cat

streak NOUN **streaks**
❶ a long thin line or mark ❷ a streak of something is a trace or sign of it • *He has a cruel streak.*

streak VERB **streaks, streaking, streaked**
❶ to streak something is to mark it with streaks ❷ to streak somewhere is to move there very quickly

streaky ADJECTIVE **streakier, streakiest**
marked with streaks
➤ **streakiness** NOUN

stream NOUN **streams**
❶ a narrow river or brook ❷ liquid flowing in one direction • *a stream of molten lava* ❸ a number of things moving in the same direction, such as traffic ❹ a continuous flow of video or other data from the internet

stream VERB **streams, streaming, streamed**
❶ to stream is to move in a strong or fast flow • *People streamed into the stadium.* ❷ to stream is also to produce a flow of liquid • *Blood was streaming from the wound.* ❸ to stream video or other data is to send or receive it in a continuous flow

streamer NOUN **streamers**
a long strip of paper or ribbon

streamline VERB **streamlines, streamlining, streamlined**
❶ to streamline a vehicle or object is to give it a smooth shape that helps it to move easily through air or water ❷ to streamline an activity or operation is to make it work more efficiently

street NOUN **streets**
a road with houses beside it in a city or town

strength NOUN **strengths**
❶ strength is how strong a person or thing is • *The Hulk has superhuman strength.* ❷ a person's strengths are the things they are good at • *My real strengths are drawing and painting.*
SPELLING ALERT! The word **strength** has a letter **g** in it, just like the adjective **strong**.

strengthen VERB **strengthens, strengthening, strengthened**
❶ to strengthen something or someone is to make them stronger ❷ to strengthen is to become stronger

strenuous ADJECTIVE
needing or using great effort and determination
➤ **strenuously** ADVERB

stress NOUN **stresses**
❶ a stress is a force or pressure that pulls or pushes or twists something ❷ stress is the effect on someone of too much work or worry or pressure ❸ stress is also emphasis, especially the extra force with which you pronounce part of a word or phrase

stress VERB **stresses, stressing, stressed**
❶ to stress part of a word or phrase is to pronounce it with extra emphasis ❷ to stress a point or idea is to emphasize it ❸ to stress someone is to make them suffer stress

stretch VERB **stretches, stretching, stretched**
❶ to stretch something is to pull it so that it becomes longer or wider ❷ something stretches when it becomes longer or wider when it is pulled ❸ you stretch, or stretch out, when you reach out with your arms or extend your arms and legs fully ❹ to stretch somewhere is to extend or continue there • *The wall stretches all the way round the park.*
➤ **stretchy** ADJECTIVE

stretch NOUN **stretches**
❶ the action of stretching something • *I got up and had a good stretch.* ❷ a continuous period of time or area of land or water

stretcher NOUN **stretchers**
a framework like a light folding bed with handles at each end, for carrying a sick or injured person

strew VERB **strews, strewing, strewed, strewn** or **strewed**
to strew things is to scatter them over a surface • *Flowers were strewn over the path.*

stricken ADJECTIVE
overcome or strongly affected by a feeling or illness

strict ADJECTIVE **stricter, strictest**
❶ demanding that people obey rules and behave well • *The teachers are all fairly strict.* ❷ complete or exact • *He's not really a hero in the strict sense of the word.*
➤ **strictness** NOUN

strictly to stroke

strictly ADVERB
❶ something is (for example) strictly forbidden when it is completely forbidden ❷ you say something is not strictly true when it is not exactly true

stride VERB strides, striding, strode, stridden
to walk with long steps
Sir Daniel strode forth into the village street, and, by the red glow of a torch, inspected his new troops. —THE BLACK ARROW, Robert Louis Stevenson

stride NOUN strides
a long step you take when walking or running
➤ **to take something in your stride** is to cope with it easily

strife NOUN
strife is fighting or quarrelling

strike VERB strikes, striking, struck
❶ to strike something or someone is to hit them ❷ to strike people or a place is to attack them suddenly • *A major hurricane struck the island.* ❸ to strike a match is to light it by rubbing it against something rough ❹ a clock strikes a number when it rings chimes at that hour • *The clock struck twelve at midnight.* ❺ workers strike when they stop working as a protest against their pay or conditions ❻ to strike oil or gold is to find it by drilling or mining ❼ to strike someone in some way is to make them think that way • *It struck me as odd that the house was silent.*
➤ **to strike up** is to begin playing or singing

strike NOUN strikes
❶ a hit ❷ when workers refuse to work, as a way of making a protest ❸ a find of oil or gold underground

striker NOUN strikers
❶ a worker who is on strike ❷ in football, an attacking player who tries to score goals

striking ADJECTIVE
something is striking when it is so interesting or attractive that you cannot help noticing it
The most striking pup of all was one who had a perfect horse-shoe of spots on his back—and had therefore been named 'Lucky'. —THE HUNDRED AND ONE DALMATIANS, Dodie Smith

string NOUN strings
❶ string is thin rope or cord for tying things; a string is a piece of thin rope ❷ in music, a string is a piece of stretched wire or nylon

used in an instrument to make sounds ❸ a string of things is a line or series of them • *There was a string of buses along the High Street.*

string VERB strings, stringing, strung
❶ to string something is to hang it on a string ❷ to string pearls or beads is to thread them on a string ❸ to string beans is to remove the tough fibre from them ❹ to string a racket or musical instrument is to put strings on it
➤ **to string something out** is to spread or stretch it out

stringed ADJECTIVE
in music, stringed instruments are ones that have strings, especially members of the violin family

strings PLURAL NOUN
the stringed instruments in an orchestra

stringy ADJECTIVE stringier, stringiest
❶ long and thin like string ❷ stringy meat contains tough fibres
➤ **stringiness** NOUN

strip NOUN strips
❶ a strip is a long narrow piece of something • *Cut a strip of cardboard.* ❷ a strip is also a special outfit worn by a sports team • *What colour is the new football strip?*

strip VERB strips, stripping, stripped
❶ to strip something is to take a covering off it ❷ to strip someone of something is to take it away from them • *He was stripped of his Olympic medal.*

stripe NOUN stripes
❶ a long narrow band of colour ❷ something worn on the sleeve of a uniform to show the rank of the person wearing it

striped, stripy ADJECTIVE
something is striped or stripy if it has stripes

strive VERB strives, striving, strove, striven
to strive to do something is to try hard to do it

strode VERB (past tense of stride)
• *He strode confidently into the room.*

stroke NOUN strokes
❶ a hit or movement made by swinging your arm ❷ one of the styles you can use to swim • *I'm learning back stroke.* ❸ a line

495

drawn by a pen or brush ❹ a sudden illness that often causes someone to be paralysed

stroke VERB **strokes, stroking, stroked**
to stroke something is to move your hand gently along it • *Does your cat like being stroked?*

stroll VERB **strolls, strolling, strolled**
to walk slowly

stroll NOUN **strolls**
a short leisurely walk

strong ADJECTIVE **stronger, strongest**
❶ having great power, energy or effect
❷ not easily broken or damaged • *The gate was held by a strong chain.* ❸ having a lot of flavour or smell • *Do you like your tea strong?*
❹ having a particular number or size • *The game had a crowd 20,000 strong.*

strong ADVERB
➤ **to be going strong** is to be making good progress

stronghold NOUN **strongholds**
a fortress or other place that is well defended

strongly ADVERB
❶ in a strong way; with strength • *They fought back strongly.* ❷ very much • *The room smelt strongly of perfume.*

strove VERB (*past tense of* **strive**)
• *She strove to improve her singing.*

struck VERB (*past tense and past participle of* **strike**)
• *The clock struck three.* • *The storm had struck by nightfall.*

structure NOUN **structures**
❶ a structure is something that has been built or put together ❷ a thing's structure is the way that it is built or made
➤ **structural** ADJECTIVE
➤ **structurally** ADVERB

struggle VERB **struggles, struggling, struggled**
❶ to struggle is to move your body about violently while you are fighting or trying to get free ❷ to struggle to do something is to make strong efforts to do it

struggle NOUN **struggles**
❶ fighting or trying to get free ❷ a great effort

strum VERB **strums, strumming, strummed**
to strum a guitar is to sound it by running your finger across its strings

strung VERB (*past tense and past participle of* **string**)
• *The archer strung his bow.* • *His sister had strung along with him.*

strut VERB **struts, strutting, strutted**
to walk proudly or stiffly
All the dukes and lords and famous men would arrive in their big cars ... and Mr Hazell would strut about like a peacock welcoming them.—DANNY THE CHAMPION OF THE WORLD, Roald Dahl

strut NOUN **struts**
❶ a strutting walk ❷ a bar of wood or metal that strengthens a framework

stub VERB **stubs, stubbing, stubbed**
❶ you stub your toe when you knock it against something hard ❷ to stub, or to stub out, a cigarette or cigar is to put it out by pressing it against something hard

stub NOUN **stubs**
a short piece of something left after the rest has been used up or worn down

stubble NOUN
❶ stubble is the short stalks of corn left in the ground after a harvest ❷ stubble is also the short stiff hairs growing on a person's chin when they have not shaved

stubborn ADJECTIVE
not willing to change your ideas or ways; obstinate
➤ **stubbornly** ADVERB ➤ **stubbornness** NOUN

stuck VERB (*past tense and past participle of* **stick**)
• *Dylan stuck his hands in his pockets.*
• *Have you stuck a stamp on the envelope?*

stuck ADJECTIVE
unable to move or make progress • *Is anyone else stuck?*

stuck-up ADJECTIVE (*informal*)
unpleasantly proud or snobbish

stud NOUN **studs**
a small metal button or knob fixed into something

student NOUN students
someone who studies, especially at a college or university

studio NOUN studios
❶ a place where radio or television broadcasts are made ❷ a place where cinema or television films are made ❸ the room where an artist or photographer works

studious ADJECTIVE
a studious person likes to spend time studying
➤ **studiously** ADVERB ➤ **studiousness** NOUN

study VERB studies, studying, studied
❶ to study is to spend time learning about something ❷ to study something is to look at it carefully

study NOUN studies
❶ study is the process of studying ❷ a study is a room used for studying or writing

stuff NOUN
❶ stuff is a substance or material • *What's this stuff at the bottom of the glass?* ❷ stuff is also a group of things or a person's possessions • *Will you move your stuff off the table?*

stuff VERB stuffs, stuffing, stuffed
❶ to stuff something is to fill it tightly, especially with stuffing • *She stuffed the turkey.* ❷ to stuff one thing inside another is to push it in carelessly • *He stuffed the paper into his pocket.*

stuffing NOUN stuffings
❶ stuffing is material used to fill the inside of something ❷ stuffing is also a savoury mixture you put into meat or vegetables before cooking them

stuffy ADJECTIVE stuffier, stuffiest
❶ a stuffy room is badly ventilated, without enough fresh air ❷ formal and boring • *the stuffy world of politics*
➤ **stuffiness** NOUN

stumble VERB stumbles, stumbling, stumbled
❶ to stumble is to lose your balance or fall over something ❷ to stumble when you are speaking is to make mistakes or hesitate

stump NOUN stumps
❶ the bottom of a tree trunk left in the ground when the tree has fallen or been cut down

❷ each of the three upright sticks of a wicket in cricket

stump VERB stumps, stumping, stumped
something stumps you when it is too difficult for you • *The last question stumped everyone.*

stun VERB stuns, stunning, stunned
❶ to stun someone is to knock them unconscious ❷ something stuns you when it shocks or confuses you • *They were stunned by the news.*

stung VERB (past tense and past participle of **sting**)
• *Tears stung Alisha's eyes.* • *He jumped as if he'd been stung by a bee.*

stunk VERB (past tense and past participle of **stink**)
• *The room stunk of smoke.* • *The mouldy cheese had stunk for days in the fridge.*

stunt NOUN stunts
❶ something daring or dangerous done in a film or as part of a performance ❷ something unusual done to attract publicity or attention

stupefy VERB stupefies, stupefying, stupefied
to stupefy someone is to make them unable to think or feel properly

stupendous ADJECTIVE
amazing; tremendous • *Suddenly Trish let out a stupendous sneeze!*

stupid ADJECTIVE stupider, stupidest
without reason or common sense; not clever or thoughtful
➤ **stupidity** NOUN ➤ **stupidly** ADVERB

sturdy ADJECTIVE sturdier, sturdiest
strong and solid
➤ **sturdiness** NOUN

stutter VERB stutters, stuttering, stuttered
to stutter is to keep repeating the sounds at the beginning of words

stutter NOUN stutters
a tendency to stutter • *He has a slight stutter.*

sty NOUN sties
a pigsty

stye (also **sty**) NOUN styes or sties
a sore swelling on your eyelid

a
b
c
d
e
f
g
h
i
j
k
l
m
n
o
p
q
r
s
t
u
v
w
x
y
z

style *NOUN* **styles**
❶ a style is the way that something is done, made, said or written ❷ style is being smart and elegant ❸ a style is also a part of the pistil in a flower

style *VERB* **styles, styling, styled**
to style something is to give it a special style

stylish *ADJECTIVE*
fashionable and smart
➤ **stylishly** *ADVERB*

sub *NOUN* **subs** (*informal*)
❶ a submarine ❷ a subscription ❸ a substitute, especially in sports

sub– *PREFIX*
meaning 'below', as in *submarine* and *subway*
DID YOU KNOW? The prefix **sub-** comes from a Latin word *sub* meaning 'under'.

subcontinent *NOUN* **subcontinents**
a large area of land that forms part of a continent • *the Indian subcontinent*

subdivide *VERB* **subdivides, subdividing, subdivided**
to subdivide something that has already been divided is to divide it again into smaller parts

subdue *VERB* **subdues, subduing, subdued**
❶ to subdue someone is to overcome them or bring them under control ❷ to subdue a person or animal is to make them quieter or gentler

subject (*say* sub-jikt) *NOUN* **subjects**
❶ the person or thing that is being talked or written about ❷ something that is studied ❸ (*grammar*) the person or thing that is doing the action stated by the verb in a sentence, for example *dog* in the sentence *the dog chewed a bone* ❹ someone who must obey the laws of a particular ruler or government

subject (*say* sub-jikt) *ADJECTIVE*
➤ **subject to something** depending on it or likely to be affected by it • *The area is subject to storms.*

subject (*say* sub-jekt) *VERB* **subjects, subjecting, subjected**
to subject someone to something is to make them experience or suffer it • *They subjected him to a string of questions.*

subjective *ADJECTIVE*
influenced by your own beliefs or ideas • *His account of what happened is rather subjective.*

submarine *NOUN* **submarines**
a type of ship that can travel under water

submerge *VERB* **submerges, submerging, submerged**
❶ to submerge is to go under water
❷ to submerge something or someone is to put them under water

submission *NOUN* **submissions**
❶ submission is submitting to someone
❷ a submission is something that you submit or offer to someone

submissive *ADJECTIVE*
willing to obey

submit *VERB* **submits, submitting, submitted**
❶ to submit to someone is to give in to them or agree to obey them ❷ to submit something to someone is to hand it in or offer it to be considered • *I submitted an entry to the competition.*

subordinate (*say* sub-or-din-at) *ADJECTIVE*
less important, or lower in rank

subordinate *NOUN* **subordinates**
someone who is subordinate to someone else

subordinate (*say* sub-or-din-ayt) *VERB* **subordinates, subordinating, subordinated**
to subordinate something is to treat it as less important than something else
➤ **subordination** *NOUN*

subscribe *VERB* **subscribes, subscribing, subscribed**
to subscribe to something is to pay money to receive it regularly or to be a member of a club or society
➤ **subscriber** *NOUN*

subscription *NOUN* **subscriptions**
money you pay to subscribe to something

subsequent *ADJECTIVE*
coming later or after something else
• *Subsequent events proved that she was right.*
➤ **subsequently** *ADVERB*

subside *VERB* **subsides, subsiding, subsided**
❶ to subside is to sink • *The house has subsided over the years.* ❷ to subside is also to become quiet or normal • *The noise subsided after midnight.*

subsidy *NOUN* **subsidies**
money paid to keep prices low or to support an industry or activity

substance *NOUN* **substances**
❶ something that you can touch or see; what something is made of ❷ the essential part of something

substantial *ADJECTIVE*
❶ large or important ❷ strong and solid

substitute *VERB* **substitutes**, **substituting**, **substituted**
to substitute one thing or person for another is to use the first one instead of the second • *In this recipe you can substitute oil for butter.*
➤ **substitution** *NOUN*

substitute *NOUN* **substitutes**
a person or thing that is used instead of another

subtle (*say* **sut**-el) *ADJECTIVE* **subtler**, **subtlest**
❶ slight and delicate • *a subtle flavour*
❷ ingenious but not obvious • *Your jokes are too subtle for me.*
➤ **subtly** *ADVERB* ➤ **subtlety** *NOUN*

subtract *VERB* **subtracts**, **subtracting**, **subtracted**
to subtract one amount from another is to take it away • *If you subtract 2 from 7, you get 5.*
➤ **subtraction** *NOUN*

suburb *NOUN* **suburbs**
an area of houses on the edge of a city or large town
➤ **suburban** *ADJECTIVE*

subway *NOUN* **subways**
an underground passage for pedestrians

succeed *VERB* **succeeds**, **succeeding**, **succeeded**
❶ to succeed is to do or get what you wanted or intended ❷ to succeed someone is to be the next person to do what they did, especially to be king or queen

success *NOUN* **successes**
❶ success is doing or getting what you wanted or intended ❷ a success is a person or thing that does well • *The plan was a complete success.*

successful *ADJECTIVE*
having success
➤ **successfully** *ADVERB*

succession *NOUN* **successions**
❶ a series of people or things ❷ the right to be the next person to do something, especially becoming king or queen

successive *ADJECTIVE*
following one after another
➤ **successively** *ADVERB*

successor *NOUN* **successors**
a person or thing that comes after another
• *My old teacher handed over to her successor.*

such *ADJECTIVE*
❶ of the same kind • *Cakes and sweets and all such food is delicious.* ❷ so great or so much
• *That was such fun!*

such-and-such *ADJECTIVE*
one in particular but you are not saying which
• *He promises to come at such-and-such a time but is always late.*

suck *VERB* **sucks**, **sucking**, **sucked**
❶ to suck liquid or air is to take it in through your mouth • *The kittens sucked milk from a bottle.* ❷ to suck something is to move it around inside your mouth • *She was sucking a sweet.* ❸ to suck something is also to draw it in or absorb it • *The boat was sucked into the whirlpool.* • *He sucked in his cheeks.*

suck *NOUN* **sucks**
the action of sucking

suction *NOUN*
suction is producing a vacuum so that liquid or air is drawn in

sudden *ADJECTIVE*
happening or done quickly and unexpectedly
➤ **suddenness** *NOUN*

suddenly *ADVERB*
quickly and unexpectedly

sudoku (*say* soo-**doh**-koo) *NOUN* **sudokus**
a puzzle in which you put numbers in a grid, trying not to repeat a number in any row or column

suds *PLURAL NOUN*
froth on soapy water

a b c d e f g h i j k l m n o p q r s t u v w x y z

sue VERB sues, suing, sued
to sue someone is to start a claim in a law court to get money from them

suede (say swayd) NOUN
suede is leather with one side soft and velvety

suet NOUN
suet is hard fat from cattle and sheep, used in cooking

suffer VERB suffers, suffering, suffered
❶ to suffer is to feel pain or misery ❷ to suffer something unpleasant is to have to put up with it

suffering NOUN sufferings
suffering is pain or misery

sufficient ADJECTIVE
enough • *Have we sufficient food?*
➤ **sufficiently** ADVERB to a sufficient degree • *I got my breath back sufficiently to speak.*

suffix NOUN suffixes
a word or syllable joined to the end of a word to change or add to its meaning, as in child*ish*, forget*ful*, lione*ss* and rust*y*

suffocate VERB suffocates, suffocating, suffocated
❶ to suffocate is to suffer or die because you cannot breathe ❷ to suffocate someone is to make it impossible or difficult for them to breathe
➤ **suffocation** NOUN

suffragette NOUN suffragettes
(*historical*)
a woman who campaigned for the right of women to be able to vote
'I think it's wonderful that you're a suffragette, Mrs Roberts. I shall be one myself when I'm older,' I said.—OPAL PLUMSTEAD, Jacqueline Wilson

sugar NOUN
a sweet food obtained from the juices of various plants, such as sugar beet or sugar cane

sugary ADJECTIVE
sugary food or drink has a lot of sugar in it

suggest VERB suggests, suggesting, suggested
❶ to suggest something is to offer it as an idea or possibility ❷ to suggest something is also to give an idea or hint of something • *Your smile suggests that you agree with me.*

suggestion NOUN suggestions
something that you mention to someone as an idea or possibility

suicide NOUN suicides
suicide is killing yourself deliberately

suit NOUN suits
❶ a matching set of jacket and trousers or jacket and skirt, that are meant to be worn together ❷ a set of clothing for a particular activity • *He wore a diving suit.* ❸ each of the four sets in a pack of playing cards: spades, hearts, diamonds and clubs ❹ a case in a law court

suit VERB suits, suiting, suited
❶ to suit someone or something is to be suitable or convenient for them ❷ a piece of clothing or hairstyle suits you when it looks good on you

suitable ADJECTIVE
satisfactory or right for a particular person, purpose or occasion
➤ **suitability** NOUN ➤ **suitably** ADVERB

suitcase NOUN suitcases
a container with a lid and a handle, for carrying clothes and other things on journeys

suite (say sweet) NOUN suites
❶ a set of rooms in a hotel ❷ a set of matching furniture ❸ a set of short pieces of music

suitor NOUN suitors
a person's suitor is someone who wants to marry them

sulk VERB sulks, sulking, sulked
to be silent and bad-tempered because you are not pleased

sulky ADJECTIVE sulkier, sulkiest
sulking or inclined to sulk
➤ **sulkily** ADVERB ➤ **sulkiness** NOUN

sullen ADJECTIVE
sulking and gloomy
➤ **sullenly** ADVERB ➤ **sullenness** NOUN

sulphur NOUN
sulphur is a yellow chemical used in industry and medicine

sultan NOUN **sultans**
the ruler of certain Muslim countries

sultana NOUN **sultanas**
a raisin without seeds

sum NOUN **sums**
❶ a total, or the amount you get when you add numbers together ❷ a problem in arithmetic ❸ an amount of money

sum VERB **sums, summing, summed**
➤ **to sum up** is to give a summary at the end of a discussion or talk

summarize (also **summarise**) VERB
summarizes, summarizing, summarized
to summarize something is to give a short statement of its main points • *Can you summarize the plot in one sentence?*

summary NOUN **summaries**
a short statement of the main points of something said or written

summer NOUN **summers**
the warm season between spring and autumn

summit NOUN **summits**
❶ the top of a mountain or hill ❷ a meeting between the leaders of powerful countries

summon VERB **summons, summoning, summoned**
to summon someone is to order them to come or appear
➤ **to summon something up** is to find it in yourself • *She summoned up the courage to speak.*

summons NOUN **summonses**
a command to someone to appear in a law court

sun NOUN
❶ the star round which the earth travels, and from which it gets warmth and light ❷ a star elsewhere in the universe ❸ warmth and light from the sun • *Let's sit outside in the sun.*

sun VERB **suns, sunning, sunned**
to sun yourself is to warm yourself in the sun
➤ A related adjective is **solar**.

sunbathe VERB **sunbathes, sunbathing, sunbathed**
to sit or lie in the sun to get a suntan

sunburn NOUN
sunburn is the redness of the skin someone gets if they are in the sun for too long
➤ **sunburned** (also **sunburnt**) ADJECTIVE

sundae (*say* sun-day) NOUN **sundaes**
a mixture of ice cream with fruit, nuts and cream

Sunday NOUN **Sundays**
the first day of the week
DID YOU KNOW? **Sunday** is an Old English name meaning 'day of the sun'.

sundial NOUN **sundials**
a device that shows the time by a shadow made by the sun

sunflower NOUN **sunflowers**
a tall flower with a large round yellow head

sung VERB (*past participle of* **sing**)
• *I've never sung this song before.*

sunglasses PLURAL NOUN
dark glasses you wear to protect your eyes from strong sunlight

sunk VERB (*past participle of* **sink**)
• *The boat had sunk in a storm.* • *I hoped the lesson had sunk in.*

sunlight NOUN
sunlight is light from the sun
➤ **sunlit** ADJECTIVE

sunny ADJECTIVE **sunnier, sunniest**
❶ having a lot of sunshine • *It's a sunny day.*
❷ full of sunshine • *What a sunny room.*

sunrise NOUN **sunrises**
sunrise is the time when the sun first appears; dawn • *They left at sunrise.*

sunset NOUN **sunsets**
sunset is the time when the sun sets

sunshade NOUN **sunshades**
a parasol or other device to protect people from the sun

sunshine NOUN
sunshine is warmth and light that come from the sun

sunspot NOUN **sunspots**
a dark patch on the sun's surface

sunstroke NOUN
sunstroke is an illness caused by being in the sun for too long

a
b
c
d
e
f
g
h
i
j
k
l
m
n
o
p
q
r
s
t
u
v
w
x
y
z

suntan *NOUN* **suntans**
a brown colour of the skin caused by the sun
➤ **suntanned** *ADJECTIVE*

super *ADJECTIVE* (*informal*)
excellent or very good

super– *PREFIX*
meaning 'over' or 'beyond', as in *superhuman*

superb *ADJECTIVE*
magnificent or excellent
➤ **superbly** *ADVERB*

superficial *ADJECTIVE*
❶ on the surface • *It's only a superficial cut.*
❷ not deep or thorough • *His knowledge of French is fairly superficial.*
➤ **superficially** *ADVERB*

superfluous (*say* soo-**per**-floo-us) *ADJECTIVE*
not necessary; no longer needed

superglue *NOUN*
a type of very strong glue that sets quickly

superhero *NOUN* **superheroes**
a fictional character with superhuman powers • *Who's your favourite superhero: Superman or Wonder Woman?*
SPELLING ALERT! Remember to put an e in the plural: *a team of superheroes.*

superhuman *ADJECTIVE*
more than a human being is normally capable of • *He believed he had superhuman powers.*

superintendent *NOUN* **superintendents**
❶ someone who is in charge ❷ a police officer above the rank of inspector

superior *ADJECTIVE*
❶ higher or better than another person or thing • *This robot's brain is vastly superior to ours.* ❷ greater in strength or number • *They were driven back by a superior enemy force.* ❸ showing that you think you are better than other people • *The voice spoke in a clipped and superior tone.*

superior *NOUN* **superiors**
someone of higher rank or position than another person

superiority *NOUN*
❶ superiority is being better than something else ❷ superiority is also behaviour that shows you think you are better than other people

superlative (*say* soo-**per**-la-tiv) *ADJECTIVE*
of the highest quality

superlative *NOUN* **superlatives**
the form of an adjective or adverb that expresses 'most' • *The superlative of 'big' is 'biggest', and the superlative of 'bad' is 'worst'.*

supermarket *NOUN* **supermarkets**
a large self-service shop that sells food and other goods

supernatural *ADJECTIVE*
not belonging to the natural world or having a natural explanation

superpower *NOUN* **superpowers**
a power or ability that humans do not normally have
'Superpowers?' I folded my arms and sneered. 'What, so now you can fly and shoot lightning from your fingertips?'—MY BROTHER IS A SUPERHERO, David Solomons

supersonic *ADJECTIVE*
faster than the speed of sound

superstition *NOUN* **superstitions**
a belief or action that is not based on reason or evidence • *It is a superstition that 13 is an unlucky number.*
➤ **superstitious** *ADJECTIVE*

supervise *VERB* **supervises**, **supervising**, **supervised**
to supervise someone or something is to be in charge of them
➤ **supervision** *NOUN* ➤ **supervisor** *NOUN*

supper *NOUN* **suppers**
a meal or snack eaten in the evening

supple *ADJECTIVE* **suppler**, **supplest**
able to bend easily; flexible, not stiff
➤ **suppleness** *NOUN*

supplement *NOUN* **supplements**
❶ something added as an extra ❷ an extra section added to a book or newspaper
➤ **supplementary** *ADJECTIVE*

supplier *NOUN* **suppliers**
someone who gives or sells something to people who need it • *a supplier of school meals*

supply *VERB* **supplies**, **supplying**, **supplied**
❶ to supply something is to give or sell it to people who need it ❷ to supply someone is to give them what they need

supply NOUN **supplies**
❶ a supply of something is an amount of it kept ready to be used when needed • *We keep a supply of paper in the cupboard.*
❷ supplies are food, medicines or equipment needed by (for example) an army or an expedition • *The truck was carrying medical supplies.*

support VERB **supports**, **supporting**, **supported**
❶ to support something is to hold it so that it does not fall down ❷ to support someone or something is to give them help or encouragement ❸ to support a sports team is to like them and want them to do well • *Which football team do you support?*

support NOUN **supports**
❶ support is the action of supporting • *You can rely on my support.* ❷ a support is a person or thing that supports

supporter NOUN **supporters**
someone who gives support, especially to a sports team

suppose VERB **supposes**, **supposing**, **supposed**
to suppose something is to think that it is likely or true
➤ **to be supposed to do something** is to have to do it as an order or duty

supposedly ADVERB
so people believe or think • *They are supposedly millionaires.*

suppress VERB **suppresses**, **suppressing**, **suppressed**
to suppress something is to keep it hidden or stop it happening • *He managed to suppress a smile.*
➤ **suppression** NOUN

supremacy NOUN
supremacy is having more power or a higher position than anyone else

supreme ADJECTIVE
highest or greatest; most important
➤ **supremely** ADVERB

sure ADJECTIVE **surer**, **surest**
❶ confident about something; having no doubts • *Are you sure you locked the door?*
❷ very likely to happen or do something

• *Don't worry, we're sure to win.* ❸ completely true or known • *One thing is sure: that is not a human footprint.* ❹ reliable • *Daffodils are a sure sign that spring has arrived.*
➤ **to make sure of something** is to find out that it is true or right

sure ADVERB (*informal*) certainly; of course
• *Sure, I'll come with you.*

surely ADVERB
❶ certainly or definitely
'They are evil sailors,' said Jip, 'and their ship is very swift. They are surely the pirates of Barbary.'—THE STORY OF DOCTOR DOLITTLE, Hugh Lofting
❷ it must be true; I feel sure • *Surely you must be mistaken.*

surf NOUN
surf is the white foam of waves breaking on rocks or the seashore

surf VERB **surfs**, **surfing**, **surfed**
❶ to surf is to go surfing ❷ to surf the internet is to browse through it

surface NOUN **surfaces**
❶ the outside of something ❷ each of the sides of something, especially the top part

surface VERB **surfaces**, **surfacing**, **surfaced**
❶ to surface is to come up to the surface from under water • *The submarine slowly surfaced.* ❷ to surface a road or path is to give it a hard covering layer

surfboard NOUN **surfboards**
a board used in surfing

surfing NOUN
surfing is the sport of balancing yourself on a board that is carried towards the seashore by the waves
➤ **surfer** NOUN

surge VERB **surges**, **surging**, **surged**
to move forwards or upwards like waves
• *The crowd surged forward to get a better view.*

surge NOUN **surges**
a sudden rush forward or upward

surgeon NOUN **surgeons**
a doctor who deals with disease or injury by cutting or repairing the affected parts of the body

a
b
c
d
e
f
g
h
i
j
k
l
m
n
o
p
q
r
s
t
u
v
w
x
y
z

surgery NOUN **surgeries**
❶ a surgery is a building or room where a doctor or dentist sees patients ❷ surgery is also the work of a surgeon

surgical ADJECTIVE
to do with a surgeon or surgery
➤ **surgically** ADVERB

surname NOUN **surnames**
your last name, which you share with other members of your family

surpass VERB **surpasses**, **surpassing**, **surpassed**
to surpass someone is to do better or be better than them

surplus NOUN **surpluses**
an amount left over after you have spent or used what you need

surprise NOUN **surprises**
❶ a surprise is something that you did not expect ❷ surprise is the feeling you have when something unexpected happens

surprise VERB **surprises**, **surprising**, **surprised**
❶ to surprise someone is to be a surprise to them ❷ to surprise someone is also to catch or attack them unexpectedly

surrender VERB **surrenders**, **surrendering**, **surrendered**
❶ to surrender to someone is to stop fighting and admit that you have been beaten ❷ to surrender something to someone is to give it over to them

surrender NOUN
when someone surrenders • *The crew held up their hands in surrender.*

surround VERB **surrounds**, **surrounding**, **surrounded**
to surround someone or something is to be or come all round them • *A tall hedge surrounded the garden.*

surroundings PLURAL NOUN
the things or conditions around a person or place

survey (*say* ser-vay) NOUN **surveys**
❶ a general look at a topic or activity ❷ a detailed inspection or examination of a building or area

survey (*say* ser-vay) VERB **surveys**, **surveying**, **surveyed**
to survey something is to inspect it or make a survey of it

surveyor NOUN **surveyors**
someone whose job is to make close inspections of buildings and land

survival NOUN
survival is staying alive

survive VERB **survives**, **surviving**, **survived**
❶ to survive is to stay alive • *Cacti can survive in very dry climates.* ❷ to survive an accident or disaster is to remain alive in spite of it • *Only one passenger survived the crash.* ❸ to survive someone is to continue living after they have died

survivor NOUN **survivors**
someone who survives, especially after an accident or disaster

sushi (*say* soo-shee) NOUN
a Japanese dish of balls of cooked rice with raw seafood or vegetables

suspect (*say* su-spekt) VERB **suspects**, **suspecting**, **suspected**
❶ to suspect something is to think that it is likely or possible ❷ to suspect someone is to think that they have done something wrong or are not to be trusted

suspect (*say* sus-pekt) NOUN **suspects**
someone who is thought to have done something wrong

suspend VERB **suspends**, **suspending**, **suspended**
❶ to suspend something that is happening is to stop it for a time ❷ to suspend someone is to take away their job or position for a time • *He was suspended from the team for bad behaviour.* ❸ to suspend something is to hang it up

suspense NOUN
suspense is an anxious or uncertain feeling you have while you are waiting for something to happen or for news about something • *Don't keep us in suspense—who won?*

suspension NOUN **suspensions**
❶ suspension is suspending something or someone ❷ a vehicle's suspension is the set of

springs and other devices that make the ride more comfortable

suspension bridge *NOUN* **suspension bridges**
a bridge supported by cables

suspicion *NOUN* **suspicions**
❶ suspicion is feeling that someone has done something wrong or cannot be trusted
❷ a suspicion is a slight or uncertain feeling about something or someone

suspicious *ADJECTIVE*
❶ making you suspect someone or something
• *That email address looks suspicious.*
❷ suspecting someone or something
• *I'm suspicious about what happened.*
➤ **suspiciously** *ADVERB*

sustain *VERB* **sustains, sustaining, sustained**
❶ to sustain something is to keep it going
• *It's difficult to sustain such an effort.*
❷ to sustain someone is to give them energy or strength • *We'd packed sandwiches to sustain us on our walk.* ❸ to sustain an injury is to be injured

sustainable *ADJECTIVE*
❶ using methods and natural products in a way that does not harm the environment
❷ able to be continued for a long time

swagger *VERB* **swaggers, swaggering, swaggered**
to walk or behave in a conceited way
Mr. Toad, arrayed in goggles, cap, gaiters, and enormous overcoat, came swaggering down the steps.—THE WIND IN THE WILLOWS, Kenneth Grahame

Swahili *NOUN*
a language spoken by many people in East Africa
DID YOU KNOW? The words **jumbo** and **safari** come from Swahili.

swallow *VERB* **swallows, swallowing, swallowed**
to swallow something is to make it go down your throat
Alice swallowed one of the cakes, and was delighted to find that she began shrinking directly.—ALICE'S ADVENTURES IN WONDERLAND, Lewis Carroll
➤ **to swallow something up** is to cover or hide it

swallow *NOUN* **swallows**
a swallow is a small bird with a forked tail and pointed wings

swam *VERB* (*past tense of* **swim**)
• *She swam to the other end of the pool.*

swamp *VERB* **swamps, swamping, swamped**
❶ to swamp something is to flood it
❷ to be swamped is to be overwhelmed with a large number of things • *They have been swamped with complaints.*

swamp *NOUN* **swamps**
a marsh

swan *NOUN* **swans**
a large white water bird with a long neck and powerful wings

swank *VERB* **swanks, swanking, swanked** (*informal*)
to swagger or boast

swap *VERB* **swaps, swapping, swapped** (*informal*)
to swap something is to exchange one thing for another • *After the game they swapped jerseys.*

swap *NOUN* **swaps**
❶ an act of swapping • *Let's do a swap.*
❷ something you swap for something else

swarm *NOUN* **swarms**
a large number of insects flying or moving about together

swarm *VERB* **swarms, swarming, swarmed**
❶ bees or other insects swarm when they move in a swarm ❷ to be swarming is to be crowded with people • *The town is swarming with tourists in summer.*

swastika (*say* **swos**-ti-ka) *NOUN* **swastikas**
a sign formed by a cross with its ends bent at right angles, used as a symbol by the Nazis in Germany

swat (*say* swot) *VERB* **swats, swatting, swatted**
to swat a fly or other insect is to hit or crush it

sway *VERB* **sways, swaying, swayed**
to move gently from side to side

swear *VERB* **swears, swearing, swore, sworn**
❶ to swear is to make a solemn promise
• *She swore to tell the truth.* ❷ to swear

someone to secrecy is to make them promise not to tell anyone **❸** to swear is also to use very rude or offensive words
> **to swear by something** is to have a lot of confidence in it

swear word NOUN **swear words**
a word that is very rude or offensive, used especially by someone who is very angry

sweat (*say* swet) VERB **sweats**, **sweating**, **sweated**
you sweat when you give off moisture through the pores of your skin, especially when you are hot or doing exercise

sweat (*say* swet) NOUN
sweat is moisture that you give off when you sweat

sweater (*say* swet-er) NOUN **sweaters**
a jersey or pullover

sweatshirt NOUN **sweatshirts**
a thick cotton jersey

sweaty ADJECTIVE **sweatier**, **sweatiest**
covered or damp with sweat
> **sweatiness** NOUN

swede NOUN **swedes**
a large kind of turnip with purple skin and yellow flesh

sweep VERB **sweeps**, **sweeping**, **swept**
❶ to sweep a room or floor is to clean or clear it with a broom or brush • *He swept the floor.* **❷** to sweep something away is to move or change it quickly • *The flood has swept away the bridge.* **❸** to sweep somewhere is to go there swiftly or proudly • *She swept out of the room.*

sweep NOUN **sweeps**
❶ a sweeping action or movement • *Give this room a sweep.* **❷** a chimney sweep

sweeper NOUN **sweepers**
❶ a machine for sweeping floors **❷** (*football*) a defensive player at the back

sweet ADJECTIVE **sweeter**, **sweetest**
❶ tasting of sugar or honey **❷** very pleasant • *The sweet smell of roses filled the air.* **❸** charming or delightful • *What a sweet little kitten.*
> **sweetly** ADVERB > **sweetness** NOUN

sweet NOUN **sweets**
❶ a small shaped piece of sweet food made of sugar or chocolate **❷** a pudding; the sweet course in a meal

sweetcorn NOUN
sweetcorn is the juicy yellow seeds of maize

sweeten VERB **sweetens**, **sweetening**, **sweetened**
to sweeten something is to make it sweet

sweetheart NOUN **sweethearts**
a person you love very much

sweet pea NOUN **sweet peas**
a climbing plant with sweet-smelling flowers

sweet potato NOUN **sweet potatoes**
a root vegetable with a reddish skin and sweet pulpy flesh

swell VERB **swells**, **swelling**, **swelled**, **swollen** *or* **swelled**
to get bigger or louder

swell NOUN **swells**
the rise and fall of the sea's surface

swelling NOUN **swellings**
a swollen place on your body

swelter VERB **swelters**, **sweltering**, **sweltered**
to be uncomfortably hot

swept VERB (*past tense and past participle of* **sweep**)
• *She swept past him into the kitchen.* • *After he had swept the floor, he washed the dishes.*

swerve VERB **swerves**, **swerving**, **swerved**
to move suddenly to one side • *The car swerved to avoid the cyclist.*

swerve NOUN **swerves**
a swerving movement

swift ADJECTIVE **swifter**, **swiftest**
quick; moving quickly and easily
> **swiftly** ADVERB > **swiftness** NOUN

swift NOUN **swifts**
a small bird rather like a swallow

swig NOUN **swigs** (*informal*)
a swig is a large mouthful of a drink
The BFG shook the bottle vigorously. The pale green stuff fizzed and bubbled. He removed the cork and took a tremendous gurgling swig.—THE BFG, Roald Dahl

swill VERB **swills, swilling, swilled**
to swill something is to rinse or flush it

swill NOUN
swill is a sloppy mixture of waste food given to pigs

swim VERB **swims, swimming, swam, swum**
❶ to swim is to move yourself through the water or to be in the water for pleasure
❷ to swim a stretch of water is to cross it by swimming • *She is training to swim the Channel.* ❸ to be swimming in liquid or with liquid is to be covered in it or full of it • *Their eyes were swimming with tears.*
❹ your head swims when you feel dizzy

swim NOUN **swims**
a spell of swimming • *Let's go for a swim.*

swimmer NOUN **swimmers**
someone who swims • *Are you a good swimmer?*

swimming baths PLURAL NOUN
a public swimming pool

swimming costume NOUN **swimming costumes**
a piece of clothing worn for swimming

swimming pool NOUN **swimming pools**
a specially built pool with water for people to swim in

swimsuit NOUN **swimsuits**
a one-piece swimming costume

swindle VERB **swindles, swindling, swindled**
to swindle someone is to get money or goods from them dishonestly
➤ **swindler** NOUN

swindle NOUN **swindles**
a trick to swindle someone

swine NOUN **swine** or **swines**
❶ (old use) a pig ❷ (informal) an unpleasant person or a difficult thing

swing VERB **swings, swinging, swung**
❶ to swing is to move to and fro or in a curve
❷ to swing something is to turn it quickly or suddenly • *He swung the car round to avoid the bus.*

swing NOUN **swings**
❶ a swinging movement • *He took a swing at the ball.* ❷ a seat hung on chains or ropes so that it can move backwards and forwards

➤ **to be in full swing** is to be full of activity or working fully

swipe VERB **swipes, swiping, swiped**
❶ to swipe someone or something is to give them a hard hit ❷ (informal) to swipe something is to steal it ❸ to swipe a credit or identity card is to pass it through a special electronic device that reads the details on it

swipe NOUN **swipes**
a hard hit

swirl VERB **swirls, swirling, swirled**
❶ to swirl is to move around quickly in circles
The door opened and fat white flakes of snow swirled in, to faint away into water as they met the heat of the parlour.—CLOCKWORK, Philip Pullman
❷ to swirl something is to make it do this

swirl NOUN **swirls**
a swirling movement

swish VERB **swishes, swishing, swished**
to make a hissing or rustling sound

swish NOUN **swishes**
a swishing sound

Swiss roll NOUN **Swiss rolls**
a thin sponge cake spread with jam or cream and rolled up

switch NOUN **switches**
❶ a device that you press or turn to start or stop something working, especially by electricity ❷ a sudden change • *There has been a last-minute switch of plan.*

switch VERB **switches, switching, switched**
❶ to switch a device on or off is to use a switch to make it work or stop working
❷ to switch something is to change it suddenly

swivel VERB **swivels, swivelling, swivelled**
to turn round or from side to side
The snowcat ran swiftly but softly through the forest, his black-tipped ears swivelling from side to side as he ran.—THE WIZARDS OF ONCE, Cressida Cowell

swollen VERB (past participle of **swell**)
• *The rains had swollen the river.*

swollen *ADJECTIVE*
something that has swelled a lot is swollen
• *One eye was bruised and swollen.*

swoon *VERB* swoons, swooning, swooned
(*old use*)
to faint from fear or weakness

swoop *VERB* swoops, swooping, swooped
❶ to swoop is to dive or come down suddenly
The post owls arrived, swooping down through rain-flecked windows, scattering everyone with droplets of water.—HARRY POTTER AND THE HALF-BLOOD PRINCE, J. K. Rowling
❷ to swoop is also to make a sudden attack or raid

swoop *NOUN* swoops
a sudden dive or attack

swop *VERB* swops, swopping, swopped
(*informal*)
to swap

sword (*say* sord) *NOUN* swords
a weapon with a long pointed blade fixed in a handle

swore *VERB* (*past tense of* swear)
• *He swore to tell the truth.*

sworn *VERB* (*past participle of* swear)
• *She has sworn to tell the truth.*

swot *VERB* swots, swotting, swotted
(*informal*)
to study hard

swot *NOUN* swots (*informal*)
someone who swots

swum *VERB* (*past participle of* swim)
• *She had swum the Channel in record time.*

swung *VERB* (*past tense and past participle of* swing)
• *He sat up and swung his legs out of the bed.*
• *The gate had swung open in the wind.*

sycamore *NOUN* sycamores
a tall tree with winged seeds

syllable *NOUN* syllables
a word or part of a word that has one separate sound when you say it. For example, *ant* has one syllable and *el-e-phant* has three syllables.
➤ **syllabic** *ADJECTIVE*

syllabus (*say* sil-a-bus) *NOUN* syllabuses
a list of things to be studied by a class or for an examination

symbol *NOUN* symbols
❶ a mark or sign with a special meaning
❷ a thing that stands for something
• *The crescent is a symbol of Islam.*

symbolic, symbolical *ADJECTIVE*
acting as a symbol of something
➤ **symbolically** *ADVERB*

symbolism *NOUN*
symbolism is the use of symbols to stand for something

symbolize (*also* **symbolise**) *VERB*
symbolizes, symbolizing, symbolized
to symbolize something is to be a symbol of it
• *Owls are said to symbolize wisdom.*

symmetrical (*say* sim-et-rik-al) *ADJECTIVE*
able to be divided into two halves which are exactly the same but the opposite way round
• *Wheels and butterflies are symmetrical.*
➤ **symmetrically** *ADVERB*

symmetry *NOUN*
something has symmetry when it can be divided into two halves which are exactly the same but the opposite way round

sympathetic *ADJECTIVE*
feeling sympathy or understanding for someone
➤ **sympathetically** *ADVERB*

sympathize (*also* **sympathise**) *VERB*
sympathizes, sympathizing, sympathized
to sympathize with someone is to show or feel sympathy for them

sympathy *NOUN* sympathies
❶ sympathy is the sharing or understanding of other people's feelings or opinions
❷ sympathy is also the feeling of being sorry for someone's unhappiness or suffering

symphony *NOUN* symphonies
a long piece of music for an orchestra
➤ **symphonic** *ADJECTIVE*

symptom *NOUN* symptoms
something wrong with you that is a sign that you have an illness • *Red spots are a symptom of measles.*
➤ **symptomatic** *ADJECTIVE*

synagogue (*say* sin-a-gog) *NOUN* **synagogues**
a building where Jewish people meet to worship

synchronize (*say* sink-ro-nyz) (*also* **synchronise**) *VERB* **synchronizes**, **synchronizing**, **synchronized**
❶ to synchronize things is to make them happen at the same time ❷ to synchronize watches or clocks is to set them to show the same time
➤ **synchronization** *NOUN*

synonym (*say* sin-o-nim) *NOUN* **synonyms**
a word that means the same or nearly the same as another word. For example, *big* and *large* are synonyms, and *unhappy* is a synonym of *sad.*
➤ **synonymous** *ADJECTIVE*

synthesis *NOUN* **syntheses**
synthesis is when different things or parts are combined into a whole thing or system

synthesizer (*also* **synthesiser**) *NOUN* **synthesizers**
an electronic musical instrument that can make many different sounds

synthetic *ADJECTIVE*
artificially made; not natural
➤ **synthetically** *ADVERB*

syringe *NOUN* **syringes**
a device for sucking in a liquid and squirting it out

syrup *NOUN* **syrups**
a thick sweet liquid
➤ **syrupy** *ADJECTIVE*

system *NOUN* **systems**
❶ a set of parts or things or ideas that work together • *the digestive system* • *the solar system* ❷ a well-organized way of doing something • *We have a new system for taking books out of the library.*

systematic *ADJECTIVE*
using a system; careful and well planned
➤ **systematically** *ADVERB*

Tt

tab *NOUN* **tabs**
❶ a small strip or flap that sticks out ❷ an additional document or page that can be opened on a computer screen

tabby *NOUN* **tabbies**
a grey or brown cat with dark streaks in its fur
DID YOU KNOW? The word **tabby** originally meant a kind of striped cloth produced in an area of Baghdad called *al-Attabiyya.*

table *NOUN* **tables**
❶ a piece of furniture with a flat top supported on legs ❷ a list of facts or numbers arranged in rows and columns ❸ a list of the results of multiplying a number by other numbers • *Do you know your multiplication tables?*

tablecloth *NOUN* **tablecloths**
a cloth for covering a table

tablespoon *NOUN* **tablespoons**
a large spoon used for serving food

tablespoonful *NOUN* **tablespoonfuls**
as much as a tablespoon will hold

tablet *NOUN* **tablets**
❶ a pill ❷ a flat piece of stone or wood with words carved or written on it ❸ a small flat portable computer

table tennis *NOUN*
table tennis is a game played on a table divided in the middle by a net, over which you hit a small ball with bats

tack *NOUN* **tacks**
❶ a tack is a short nail with a flat top ❷ tack is also equipment for horses, such as harnesses and saddles

tack *VERB* **tacks**, **tacking**, **tacked**
❶ to tack something is to nail it with tacks ❷ to tack material is to sew it together quickly with long stitches ❸ to tack is to sail a zigzag course to get full benefit from the wind

tackle *VERB* **tackles, tackling, tackled**
❶ to tackle a task is to start doing it
❷ in football or hockey, to tackle a player is to try to get the ball from them or (in rugby) to bring them to the ground

tackle *NOUN* **tackles**
❶ tackle is equipment, especially for fishing
❷ a tackle is when you tackle someone in football or rugby or hockey

tacky *ADJECTIVE* **tackier, tackiest**
❶ sticky or not quite dry • *The paint is still tacky.* ❷ (*informal*) cheaply made and showing poor taste
➤ **tackiness** *NOUN*

tact *NOUN*
tact is skill in not offending or upsetting people

tactful *ADJECTIVE*
careful not to offend or upset people by saying something unkind
➤ **tactfully** *ADVERB*

tactics *PLURAL NOUN*
someone's tactics are the methods they use to achieve or win something
➤ **tactical** *ADJECTIVE*

tactless *ADJECTIVE*
likely to offend or upset people; having no tact
➤ **tactlessly** *ADVERB*

tadpole *NOUN* **tadpoles**
a young frog or toad at a stage when it has an oval head and a long tail and lives in water

taekwondo (*say* ty-kwon-**doh**) *NOUN*
a Korean martial art involving punching and kicking.

tag *NOUN* **tags**
❶ a label tied or stuck to something ❷ the metal or plastic part at the end of a shoelace
❸ tag is a game in which one person chases the others

tag *VERB* **tags, tagging, tagged**
❶ to tag something is to fix a tag or label on it
❷ to tag a person is to add a link to a photo on social media to identify the person shown in the photo • *Is it OK if I tag you in that photo?*
➤ **to tag along** is to go along with other people

tail *NOUN* **tails**
❶ the part that sticks out from the rear end of the body of an animal or bird ❷ the part at the end or rear of something, such as an aeroplane or comet ❸ the side of a coin opposite the head

tail *VERB* **tails, tailing, tailed**
to tail someone is to follow them without them seeing you
➤ **to tail off** is to become less and less or smaller and smaller

tailback *NOUN* **tailbacks**
a long line of traffic stretching back from an obstruction

tailless *ADJECTIVE*
not having a tail

tailor *NOUN* **tailors**
someone whose job is to make clothes

take *VERB* **takes, taking, took, taken**
This word has many meanings, depending on the words that go with it. ❶ to take something or someone is to get hold of them or bring them into your possession • *He took a cake from the plate.* • *Who do you think took the money?* • *They took many prisoners.* ❷ to take someone or something somewhere is to carry or drive or convey them there • *Shall I take you to the station?* • *Take this parcel to the post.* ❸ to take something useful or pleasant is to make use of it • *Do you take sugar?* • *You must take a holiday this year.* • *Do take a seat.* ❹ to take someone or something is to need them for a purpose • *It will take two people to lift the table.* ❺ to take a piece of information is to make a note of it • *Take their names and addresses.* ❻ to take a class for a subject is to teach it to them • *Who takes you for maths?* ❼ to take one number from another is to subtract it • *Take two from ten and you get eight.* ❽ to take an examination is to do it • *I'm taking my piano exam today.* ❾ to take a joke is to accept it well ❿ to take a photograph or picture is to produce it with a camera
➤ **to take off** is to leave the ground at the beginning of a flight
➤ **to take part in something** is to share in doing it
➤ **to take place** is to happen

➤ **to take someone in** is to fool or deceive them
➤ **to take something over** is to take control of it
➤ **to take something up** is to start doing it
• *I've taken up swimming.*

takeaway NOUN takeaways
❶ a place that sells cooked food for customers to take away ❷ a meal from a takeaway

takings PLURAL NOUN
money that has been received, especially by a shopkeeper

talcum powder NOUN
talcum powder is a sweet-smelling powder put on the skin to dry it or make it smell pleasant

tale NOUN tales
a story

talent NOUN talents
a natural ability or skill to do something well
• *You have a real talent for music.*

talented ADJECTIVE
someone is talented when they have the ability or skill to do something well

talk VERB talks, talking, talked
to talk is to speak or have a conversation
➤ **talker** NOUN

talk NOUN talks
❶ a conversation or discussion ❷ a lecture
• *She gave a talk about her latest book.*

talkative ADJECTIVE
someone is talkative when they talk a lot

tall ADJECTIVE taller, tallest
❶ higher than the average • *They sat under a tall tree.* ❷ measured from the bottom to the top • *The bookcase is two metres tall.*
➤ **a tall story** is a story that is hard to believe

tally VERB tallies, tallying, tallied
one thing tallies with another when they match or agree • *Do your figures tally with mine?* • *Their answers don't tally.*

Talmud NOUN
a collection of writings on Jewish religious law

talon NOUN talons
a strong claw, especially on a bird of prey

tambourine NOUN tambourines
a round musical instrument like a small drum with metal discs fixed around the edge so that it jingles when you shake it or hit it

tame ADJECTIVE tamer, tamest
❶ a tame animal is one that is gentle and not afraid of people ❷ something is tame when it is dull or uninteresting
➤ **tamely** ADVERB ➤ **tameness** NOUN

tame VERB tames, taming, tamed
to tame a wild animal is to make it used to being with people
➤ **tamer** NOUN

tamper VERB tampers, tampering, tampered
➤ **to tamper with something** is to interfere with it or change it so that it will not work properly

tan NOUN tans
❶ a tan is a suntan ❷ tan is a yellow-brown colour

tan VERB tans, tanning, tanned
❶ to tan your skin is to make it darker with a suntan ❷ to tan the skin of a dead animal is to make it into leather

tandem NOUN tandems
a bicycle for two riders, one behind the other

tang NOUN
a strong flavour or smell

tangerine (*say* tan-jer-**een**) NOUN tangerines
a kind of small orange
DID YOU KNOW? The word **tangerine** is named after *Tangier* in Morocco, where the fruit originally came from.

tangle VERB tangles, tangling, tangled
❶ you tangle something, or it tangles, when it becomes twisted or muddled • *My fishing line has tangled.* ❷ something is tangled up when it is twisted together in an untidy mess • *These computer cables are all tangled up.*

tangle NOUN tangles
a twisted or muddled mass of (for example) hair or wire

tank NOUN tanks
❶ a large container for a liquid or gas
❷ a heavy armoured vehicle used in war

tankard *NOUN* **tankards**
a large heavy mug for drinking from

tanker *NOUN* **tankers**
❶ a large ship for carrying oil ❷ a large lorry for carrying a liquid

tanner *NOUN* **tanners**
someone who tans animal skins to make leather

tantalize (*also* **tantalise**) *VERB* **tantalizes**, **tantalizing**, **tantalized**
to tantalize someone is to torment them by showing them something good that they cannot have
DID YOU KNOW? The word **tantalize** comes from *Tantalus* in Greek mythology, whose punishment was to stand near water and fruit which were always out of his reach.

tantrum *NOUN* **tantrums**
an outburst of bad temper

tap *NOUN* **taps**
❶ a device for letting out liquid or gas in a controlled flow ❷ a quick light hit, or the sound it makes • *I gave him a tap on the shoulder.* ❸ tap is tap-dancing

tap *VERB* **taps**, **tapping**, **tapped**
❶ to tap someone or something is to give them a tap or gentle hit • *I tried tapping on the window.* ❷ to tap a source of information or supplies is to make use of it ❸ to tap a telephone is to fix a device to it so that you can hear someone's conversation

tap-dancing *NOUN*
tap-dancing is dancing in hard shoes that make sharp tapping sounds on the floor

tape *NOUN* **tapes**
❶ tape is soft material such as cloth or paper or plastic in a thin strip ❷ tape is also a strip of plastic with a magnetic coating used to record sound

tape *VERB* **tapes**, **taping**, **taped**
❶ to tape something is to fasten it by sticking it or tying it with tape ❷ to tape music or sound is to record it on tape or digitally

tape measure *NOUN* **tape measures**
a long strip marked in centimetres or inches for measuring things

taper *VERB* **tapers**, **tapering**, **tapered**
something tapers when it gets narrower towards one end

taper *NOUN* **tapers**
a piece of string thinly coated with wax, for lighting things

tapestry (*say* **tap**-i-stree) *NOUN* **tapestries**
a piece of strong cloth with pictures or patterns woven or embroidered on it

tapeworm *NOUN* **tapeworms**
a long flat worm that can live as a parasite in the intestines of people and animals

tapir *NOUN* **tapirs**
a large pig-like animal with a long flexible snout, found in rainforests

tar *NOUN*
tar is a thick black sticky liquid made from coal or wood and used in making roads

tar *VERB* **tars**, **tarring**, **tarred**
to tar something is to cover it with tar

tarantula (*say* ta-**ran**-tew-la) *NOUN* **tarantulas**
a large hairy poisonous spider found in tropical countries

target *NOUN* **targets**
something that you aim at and try to hit or reach

target *VERB* **targets**, **targeting**, **targeted**
to target something or someone is to aim at them

tarmac *NOUN*
❶ (*trademark*) tarmac is a mixture of tar and broken stone, used for making a hard surface on roads and paths and open areas. Tarmac is short for *tarmacadam*. ❷ the tarmac is an area covered with tarmac, especially on an airfield • *The plane was standing on the tarmac, waiting to take off.*

tarnish *VERB* **tarnishes**, **tarnishing**, **tarnished**
❶ metal tarnishes when it becomes stained and less shiny ❷ to tarnish something is to spoil it • *The scandal tarnished his reputation.*

tarpaulin *NOUN* **tarpaulins**
a large sheet of waterproof canvas

tart *NOUN* **tarts**
a tart is a pie containing fruit, jam, custard or treacle
In the very middle of the court was a table, with a large dish of tarts upon it: they looked so good, that it made Alice quite hungry to look at them.—ALICE'S ADVENTURES IN WONDERLAND, Lewis Carroll

tart *ADJECTIVE* **tarter, tartest**
sour-tasting • *The apples are tart.*

tartan *NOUN* **tartans**
a woollen cloth with a pattern of squares and stripes in different colours, especially as worn in the Scottish Highlands

task *NOUN* **tasks**
a piece of work that needs to be done
➤ **to take someone to task** is to tell them off for doing something wrong

task force *NOUN* **task forces**
a group of people, especially soldiers, given a special task to do

tassel *NOUN* **tassels**
a bundle of threads tied together at the top and used to decorate something

taste *VERB* **tastes, tasting, tasted**
❶ to taste food or drink is to eat or drink a small amount to see what it is like ❷ food or drink tastes a certain way when it has a particular flavour • *The milk tastes sour.*

taste *NOUN* **tastes**
❶ the taste of something is the flavour it has when you taste it • *The milk has a strange taste.* ❷ taste is the ability to taste things ❸ your tastes are the things you like or prefer • *What are your tastes in music?* ❹ you show taste when you are able to choose things that are of good quality or go together well • *The way she dresses shows good taste.* ❺ a taste is a tiny amount of food • *Can I have a taste of your pudding?*

tasteful *ADJECTIVE*
something that is tasteful is well chosen or of good quality • *The decorations were very tasteful.*
➤ **tastefully** *ADVERB*

tasteless *ADJECTIVE*
❶ tasteless food has no flavour ❷ a tasteless joke is unpleasant or vulgar
➤ **tastelessly** *ADVERB*

tasty *ADJECTIVE* **tastier, tastiest**
tasty food has a strong pleasant taste
➤ **tastiness** *NOUN*

tattered *ADJECTIVE*
tattered clothing is badly torn and ragged

tatters *PLURAL NOUN*
➤ **in tatters** badly torn

tattoo *NOUN* **tattoos**
❶ a picture or pattern made on someone's skin with a needle and dye ❷ a drumming sound • *He beat a tattoo on the table with his fingers.* ❸ an outdoor entertainment including military music and marching

tattoo *VERB* **tattoos, tattooing, tattooed**
someone is tattooed when they have a tattoo on their skin

tatty *ADJECTIVE* **tattier, tattiest**
shabby and worn
The Viking Hotel was beginning to look a bit tatty. What it really needed was a good coat of paint.—VIKING AT SCHOOL, Jeremy Strong

taught *VERB* (*past tense and past participle of* **teach**)
• *My dad taught me to play guitar.*
• *I remembered what I had been taught.*

taunt *VERB* **taunts, taunting, taunted**
to taunt someone is to jeer at them or insult them

taunt *NOUN* **taunts**
an insulting or mocking remark

taut *ADJECTIVE* **tauter, tautest**
stretched tightly
➤ **tautly** *ADVERB* ➤ **tautness** *NOUN*

tavern *NOUN* **taverns** (*old use*)
an inn or pub

tawny *ADJECTIVE* **tawnier, tawniest**
brown-yellow

tax *NOUN* **taxes**
an amount of money that people and businesses have to pay to the government for public use

tax *VERB* **taxes, taxing, taxed**
❶ to tax someone is to charge them a tax ❷ to tax goods or someone's income is to put a tax on them
➤ **taxation** *NOUN*

taxi *NOUN* **taxis**
a car with a driver which you can hire for journeys, with a meter for recording the distance

taxi *VERB* **taxis**, **taxiing**, **taxied**
an aircraft taxis when it moves slowly along the ground before taking off or after landing

taxpayer *NOUN* **taxpayers**
someone who pays taxes

tea *NOUN* **teas**
❶ tea is a drink made by pouring hot water on the dried leaves of an evergreen shrub ❷ tea is also the dried leaves of this shrub ❸ tea is also a meal eaten in the late afternoon or early evening

teabag *NOUN* **teabags**
a small bag of tea for making tea in a cup

teacake *NOUN* **teacakes**
a kind of bun, usually toasted and eaten with butter

teach *VERB* **teaches**, **teaching**, **taught**
❶ to teach someone is to show them how to do something or give them knowledge about something ❷ to teach a subject is to give lessons in it • *She taught us history last year.*

teacher *NOUN* **teachers**
someone who teaches people at a school or college

tea cloth, **tea towel** *NOUN* **tea cloths**, **tea towels**
a cloth you use for drying washed dishes and cutlery

teacup *NOUN* **teacups**
a cup for drinking tea

teak *NOUN*
teak is a hard strong wood from Asia

tea leaf *NOUN* **tea leaves**
tea leaves are the dried leaves used to make tea

team *NOUN* **teams**
❶ a set of players who form one side in a game or sport ❷ a group of people who work together

teapot *NOUN* **teapots**
a pot with a handle and spout, for making and pouring out tea

tear (*say* tair) *VERB* **tears**, **tearing**, **tore**, **torn**
❶ to tear something is to make a split in it or to pull it apart ❷ to tear something is also to pull or remove it with force • *He tore the poster off the wall.* ❸ to tear is to become torn • *This paper tears easily.* ❹ (*informal*) to run along very quickly • *They tore off down the street.*

tear (*say* tair) *NOUN* **tears**
a hole or split made by tearing something

tear (*say* teer) *NOUN* **tears**
a drop of water that comes from your eye when you cry

tearful *ADJECTIVE*
❶ a tearful person cries easily ❷ a tearful voice or action is done when you are crying
Signora Strega-Borgia bid the children a tearful farewell and set off to complete her degree in advanced witchcraft.—PURE DEAD MAGIC, Debi Gliori
➤ **tearfully** *ADVERB* ➤ **tearfulness** *NOUN*

tease *VERB* **teases**, **teasing**, **teased**
to tease someone is to make fun of them and say things to make them annoyed

teaspoon *NOUN* **teaspoons**
a small spoon for stirring tea

teaspoonful *NOUN* **teaspoonfuls**
as much as a teaspoon will hold • *Add two teaspoonfuls of sugar.*

teat *NOUN* **teats**
❶ a nipple through which a baby drinks milk ❷ the cap of a baby's feeding bottle

technical *ADJECTIVE*
❶ to do with technology or the way things work ❷ using the words that only people who know a lot about a subject will understand • *This book is full of technical words.*

technicality *NOUN* **technicalities**
a small detail of the law or a process

technically *ADVERB*
❶ something is technically possible when the technology exists to do it ❷ something is technically allowed when it is allowed according to a set of rules

technician *NOUN* **technicians**
someone whose job is to look after scientific equipment and do practical work in a laboratory

technique (*say* tek-**neek**) *NOUN* **techniques**
a particular method of doing something skilfully

technology *NOUN* **technologies**
technology is the study of machinery and the way things work
➤ **technological** *ADJECTIVE*

teddy bear *NOUN* **teddy bears**
a soft furry toy bear

tedious (*say* tee-di-us) *ADJECTIVE*
slow or long; boring • *It was a long and tedious journey.*
➤ **tediously** *ADVERB* ➤ **tediousness** *NOUN*

tedium *NOUN*
tedium is a dull or boring time or experience

teem *VERB* **teems**, **teeming**, **teemed**
❶ to teem with something is to be full of it • *The river was teeming with fish.* ❷ to teem, or teem down, is to rain very hard

teenage *ADJECTIVE*
❶ in your teens • *a group of teenage girls*
❷ to do with teenagers • *teenage fashion*

teenager *NOUN* **teenagers**
a person in their teens

teens *PLURAL NOUN*
the time of your life between the ages of 13 and 19 • *She took up football in her teens.*

tee-shirt *NOUN* **tee-shirts**
another spelling of **T-shirt**

teeth *NOUN* (*plural of* **tooth**)

telecommunications *NOUN*
telecommunications is sending news and information over long distances by telephone, internet, television and radio

telegram *NOUN* **telegrams**
a message sent by telegraph

telegraph *NOUN* **telegraphs**
telegraph is a way of sending messages by using electric current along wires or by radio

telepathy (*say* til-ep-a-thee) *NOUN*
telepathy is communication of thoughts from one person's mind to another without speaking, writing or gestures
➤ **telepathic** *ADJECTIVE*

telephone *NOUN* **telephones**
a device using electric wires or radio to enable someone to speak to another person who is some distance away

telephone *VERB* **telephones**, **telephoning**, **telephoned**
to telephone someone is to speak to them by telephone
 DID YOU KNOW? The word **telephone** comes from Greek words meaning 'far-off sound'.

teleport *VERB* **teleports**, **teleporting**, **teleported**
in science fiction, to be teleported is to be transported instantly through space and time • *The crew were teleported on to the surface of the planet.*
➤ **teleportation** *NOUN*

telescope *NOUN* **telescopes**
a tube with lenses at each end, through which you can see distant objects more clearly because they look closer and larger
Now the Wicked Witch of the West had but one eye, yet that was as powerful as a telescope, and could see everywhere.—THE WONDERFUL WIZARD OF OZ, L. Frank Baum

telescopic *ADJECTIVE*
to do with telescopes

televise *VERB* **televises**, **televising**, **televised**
to televise an event is to film it and put it on television

television *NOUN* **televisions**
❶ television is a system using radio waves to reproduce pictures on a screen ❷ a television, or a television set, is a device for receiving these pictures

tell *VERB* **tells**, **telling**, **told**
❶ to tell something to someone is to give them information by speaking to them ❷ to tell someone to do something is to order them to do it ❸ to tell is to reveal a secret • *Promise you won't tell.* ❹ to tell something is to recognize it • *Can you tell the difference between butter and margarine?*
➤ **all told** in all, altogether • *There are six cousins, all told.*
➤ **to tell someone off** is to scold them
➤ **to tell tales** is to report someone else's bad behaviour

tell-tale to tense

tell-tale *NOUN* **tell-tales**
someone who tells tales

tell-tale *ADJECTIVE*
revealing something that is supposed to be
secret • *He had a tell-tale spot of jam on
his chin.*

telly *NOUN* **tellies** (*informal*)
❶ telly is television ❷ a telly is a television
set

temper *NOUN* **tempers**
❶ a person's mood • *He is in a good temper.*
❷ an angry mood • *She was in a temper.*
➤ **to lose your temper** is to become very
angry

temperament *NOUN* **temperament**
the temperament of a person or animal is the
way they usually behave

temperate *ADJECTIVE*
a temperate climate is neither extremely hot
nor extremely cold

temperature *NOUN* **temperatures**
❶ the temperature of something is how
hot or cold it is ❷ an unusually high body
temperature • *She's feverish and has a
temperature.*

tempest *NOUN* **tempests** (*old use*)
a violent storm

tempestuous *ADJECTIVE*
very violent and stormy
➤ **tempestuousness** *NOUN*

temple *NOUN* **temples**
❶ a place of worship in some religions, for
example Hinduism and Buddhism ❷ your
temples are on the side of your head between
your forehead and your ear

tempo *NOUN* **tempos**
the tempo of a piece of music is its speed or
rhythm

temporary *ADJECTIVE*
only lasting or used for a short time • *They
were using a temporary classroom.*
➤ **temporarily** *ADVERB*

tempt *VERB* **tempts**, **tempting**, **tempted**
to tempt someone is to try to make them do
something wrong or foolish

temptation *NOUN* **temptations**
temptation, or a temptation, is when someone
is being tempted

tempting *ADJECTIVE*
something is tempting when it is hard to resist

ten *NOUN* **tens**
the number 10
➤ A related adjective is **decimal**.

tenant *NOUN* **tenants**
someone who rents a house or building or
a piece of land from a landlord
➤ **tenancy** *NOUN*

tend *VERB* **tends**, **tending**, **tended**
❶ something tends to happen when it is
likely to happen or is what usually happens
• *This room tends to get very stuffy.* ❷ to tend
something or someone is to look after them
• *You need to tend the young plants carefully.*

tendency *NOUN* **tendencies**
the way a person or thing is likely to behave
• *She has a tendency to be lazy.*

tender *ADJECTIVE* **tenderer**, **tenderest**
❶ not tough or hard; easy to chew ❷ delicate
or sensitive • *Orchids are tender plants.*
❸ gentle or loving • *She gave me a tender
smile.*
➤ **tenderly** *ADVERB* ➤ **tenderness** *NOUN*

tender *VERB* **tenders**, **tendering**, **tendered**
to tender something is to give it or offer it

tendon *NOUN* **tendons**
a piece of strong tissue in the body that joins
a muscle to a bone

tendril *NOUN* **tendrils**
the part of a climbing plant that twists round
something to support itself

tennis *NOUN*
tennis is a game played with rackets and a ball
on a court with a net across the middle

tenor *NOUN* **tenors**
a singer with a high male voice

tense *ADJECTIVE* **tenser**, **tensest**
❶ tightly stretched • *All his muscles were
tense.* ❷ to be tense is to be nervous and not
able to relax ❸ a tense situation makes people
feel nervous and unable to relax
➤ **tensely** *ADVERB*

516

tense *NOUN* **tenses**
a tense is a form of a verb that shows when something happens. The past tense of come is *came*, the present tense is *come* and the future tense is *will come*.

tension *NOUN* **tensions**
❶ tension is a feeling of anxiety or nervousness about something about to happen ❷ tension is also how tightly stretched a rope or wire is

tent *NOUN* **tents**
a shelter made of canvas or cloth supported by upright poles

tentacle *NOUN* **tentacles**
a long bending part of the body of an octopus and some other animals

tenth *ADJECTIVE, NOUN*
the next after the ninth
➤ **tenthly** *ADVERB* in the tenth place; as the tenth one

tepee (*say* **tee-pee**) *NOUN* **tepees**
a traditional Native American tent, made from skins or canvas on a frame of poles

tepid *ADJECTIVE*
tepid liquid is only slightly warm; lukewarm

teriyaki *NOUN*
a Japanese dish of grilled fish or meat flavoured with soy sauce

term *NOUN* **terms**
❶ the time when a school or college is open for teaching ❷ a definite period • *He was sentenced to a term of imprisonment.* ❸ a word or expression with a special meaning • *I don't understand these technical terms.* ❹ the terms of an agreement are the conditions offered or agreed • *They won't agree to our terms.*
➤ **to be on good** *or* **bad terms** is to be friendly or unfriendly with someone

term *VERB* **terms, terming, termed**
to term something is to give it a special name • *This type of poem is termed a limerick.*

terminal *NOUN* **terminals**
❶ a building where passengers arrive or depart • *an airport terminal* ❷ a place where a wire is connected to a battery or electric circuit ❸ a computer keyboard and screen used for sending data to or from the main computer

terminal *ADJECTIVE*
a terminal illness is one that cannot be cured and that the person will die from

terminate *VERB* **terminates, terminating, terminated**
you terminate something, or it terminates, when it ends or stops • *This train terminates here.*
➤ **termination** *NOUN*

terminus *NOUN* **termini**
the station at the end of a railway or bus route

termite *NOUN* **termites**
a small insect that eats wood and lives in large groups

terrace *NOUN* **terraces**
❶ a row of houses joined together ❷ a level area on a slope or hillside ❸ a paved area beside a house

terracotta *NOUN*
a hard reddish-brown clay used to make pots and sculptures

terrapin *NOUN* **terrapins**
a kind of small turtle that lives in water

terrible *ADJECTIVE*
awful; very bad

terribly *ADVERB*
awfully; badly • *I'm terribly sorry I kept you waiting.* • *He was missing his parents terribly.*

terrier *NOUN* **terriers**
a kind of strong lively small dog

terrific *ADJECTIVE* (*informal*)
❶ very good or excellent • *That's a terrific idea!* ❷ very great • *The space rocket flew at a terrific speed.*
➤ **terrifically** *ADVERB* very; greatly

terrify *VERB* **terrifies, terrifying, terrified**
to terrify a person or animal is to make them very frightened

territory *NOUN* **territories**
an area of land, especially an area that belongs to a country or person
➤ **territorial** *ADJECTIVE*

terror *NOUN* **terrors**
terror is great fear

a
b
c
d
e
f
g
h
i
j
k
l
m
n
o
p
q
r
s
t
u
v
w
x
y
z

terrorism NOUN
terrorism is when people use violence, such as setting off bombs, to try to force a government to do what they want
➤ **terrorist** NOUN

terrorize (*also* **terrorise**) VERB **terrorizes, terrorizing, terrorized**
to terrorize someone is to terrify them with threats

test NOUN **tests**
❶ a short set of questions to check someone's knowledge, especially in school ❷ a series of questions or experiments to get information about someone or something • *They gave her a test to see if she had diabetes.* ❸ (*informal*) a test match in cricket or rugby

test VERB **tests, testing, tested**
❶ to test someone is to give them a test
❷ to test something is to use it so that you can find out whether it works properly or find out more about it

testament NOUN **testaments**
❶ a written statement ❷ each of the two main parts of the Bible, the **Old Testament** and the **New Testament**

testify VERB **testifies, testifying, testified**
to testify is to give evidence or swear that something is true

testimony NOUN **testimonies**
evidence; what someone testifies

test match NOUN **test matches**
a cricket or rugby match between teams from different countries

test tube NOUN **test tubes**
a tube of thin glass closed at one end, used for experiments in chemistry

testy ADJECTIVE **testier, testiest**
irritable or slightly bad-tempered
➤ **testily** ADVERB

tether VERB **tethers, tethering, tethered**
to tether an animal is to tie it up so that it cannot move far

tether NOUN **tethers**
a rope for tying an animal
➤ **to be at the end of your tether** is to be unable to stand something any more

tetrahedron NOUN **tetrahedrons**
a solid shape that has four triangular sides

text NOUN **texts**
❶ the words of something printed or written
❷ a written message sent using a mobile phone

text VERB **texts, texting, texted**
you text someone when you send them a text on a mobile phone
➤ **texting** NOUN

textbook NOUN **textbooks**
a book that teaches you about a subject

textiles PLURAL NOUN
kinds of cloth; fabrics

texture NOUN **textures**
the way that the surface of something feels when you touch it • *Silk has a smooth texture.*

than CONJUNCTION
compared with another person or thing • *His sister is taller than him.* • *His sister is taller than he is.*

thank VERB **thanks, thanking, thanked**
to thank someone is to tell them you are grateful for something they have given you or done for you
➤ **thank you** words that you say when you thank someone

thankful ADJECTIVE
feeling glad that someone has done something for you
➤ **thankfulness** NOUN

thankfully ADVERB
you say thankfully when you are pleased and relieved about something • *Thankfully, no one was hurt.*

thankless ADJECTIVE
a thankless job or task is one that is not very enjoyable and that you are not likely to get any thanks for

thanks PLURAL NOUN
❶ words that thank someone • *Please give her my thanks.* ❷ (*informal*) a short way of saying 'Thank you' • *That's fantastic—thanks!*
➤ **thanks to someone** or **something** because of them • *We won the match thanks to great teamwork.*

that *DETERMINER*
the one there • *Whose is that book?*

that *CONJUNCTION*
used to introduce a fact or statement or result
• *I hope that you are well.* • *Do you know that it is one o'clock?* • *The puzzle was so hard that no one could solve it.*

that *PRONOUN*
❶ the one there • *Whose book is that?* ❷ which or who • *This is the book that I wanted.* • *Are you the person that I saw the other day?*

thatch *NOUN*
thatch is straw or reeds used to make a roof

thatch *VERB* **thatches**, **thatching**, **thatched**
to thatch a roof is to make it with straw or reeds

thaw *VERB* **thaws**, **thawing**, **thawed**
something thaws when it melts and is no longer frozen • *The snow was beginning to thaw.*

the *DETERMINER* (*called the* **definite article**)
a particular one; that or those

theatre *NOUN* **theatres**
❶ a building where people go to see plays or shows ❷ a special room where surgical operations are done

theatrical *ADJECTIVE*
to do with plays or acting
➤ **theatrically** *ADVERB* in an exaggerated or dramatic way • *Danny sighed theatrically.*

thee *PRONOUN* (*old use*)
you, referring to one person and used as the object of a verb • *I will allow thee one favour.*

theft *NOUN* **thefts**
theft is stealing

their *DETERMINER*
belonging to them • *This is their house.*

theirs *PRONOUN*
belonging to them • *This house is theirs.*

them *PRONOUN*
a word used for *they* when it is the object of a verb, or when it comes after a preposition • *I saw them yesterday.* • *I'll speak to them later.*

theme *NOUN* **themes**
❶ a main idea or subject of (for example) a book or speech ❷ a short tune or melody

theme park *NOUN* **theme parks**
an amusement park with rides and activities connected with a special subject or theme

themselves *PLURAL NOUN*
them and nobody else, used to refer back to the subject of a verb • *They have hurt themselves.*
➤ **by themselves** on their own; alone • *They did the work all by themselves.*

then *ADVERB*
❶ at that time • *I lived in London then.* ❷ after that; next • *Then they came home.* ❸ in that case; therefore • *If you are going, then I can stay.*

theology *NOUN*
theology is the study of God and religion

theoretical *ADJECTIVE*
based on theory and not on practice or experience

theory *NOUN* **theories**
❶ a theory is an idea or set of ideas suggested to explain something ❷ the theory of a subject is the ideas and principles behind it, rather than the practice
➤ **in theory** according to what should happen

therapy *NOUN* **therapies**
a way of treating a physical or mental illness, especially without using surgery or medicine
➤ **therapist** *NOUN*

there *ADVERB*
❶ in or to that place • *We're going there tomorrow.* ❷ a word that you say to call attention to someone or something or to refer to them • *There's a spider in the bath.* • *There has been a mistake.*
SPELLING ALERT! **There** is different from **their**, which means 'belonging to them': '*Where is their house?*' '*It's over there.*'

thereabouts *ADVERB*
near there • *They live in York or thereabouts.*

therefore *ADVERB*
for that reason; and so

thermal *ADJECTIVE*
to do with heat; using heat

thermometer NOUN thermometers
a device for measuring temperature

Thermos NOUN Thermoses (*trademark*)
a kind of vacuum flask

thermostat NOUN thermostats
a device that automatically controls the temperature of a room or piece of equipment

thesaurus NOUN thesauri or thesauruses
a kind of dictionary in which words with similar meanings are listed in groups together, instead of one long list in alphabetical order
DID YOU KNOW? The word **thesaurus** comes from a Greek word meaning 'treasure-house'.

these DETERMINER, PRONOUN
the people or things here • *Whose are these shoes?* • *These are the ones I want.*

they PRONOUN
❶ the people or things that someone is talking about ❷ people in general • *They say it's a very good film.* ❸ he or she; a person • *If anyone arrives late, they will have to wait outside.*

they'd
short for *they had* or *they would*

they'll
short for *they will* • *They'll be here soon.*

they're
short for *they are* • *They're leaving now.*

they've
short for *they have* • *They've already left.*

thick ADJECTIVE thicker, thickest
❶ measuring a lot from one side to the other • *He cut himself a thick slice of cake.*
❷ measured from one side to the other
• *The wall is ten centimetres thick.* ❸ dense or closely packed together • *The town was in thick fog.* ❹ not very runny • *a dollop of thick cream* ❺ (*informal*) stupid

thicken VERB thickens, thickening, thickened
you thicken something, or it thickens, when it becomes thicker • *As he stirred the sauce, it started to thicken.*

thicket NOUN thickets
a group of trees and shrubs growing close together

thickly ADVERB
❶ to be thickly cut is to be cut in thick pieces ❷ to be thickly covered in something is to be covered in a deep layer of it

thickness NOUN thicknesses
the thickness of something is how thick it is

thief NOUN thieves
someone who steals things

thigh NOUN thighs
the part of your leg above your knee

thimble NOUN thimbles
a metal or plastic cover that you put on the end of your finger to protect it when you are sewing

thin ADJECTIVE thinner, thinnest
❶ measuring a small amount from one side to the other ❷ not fat ❸ not dense or closely packed together ❹ runny or watery
➤ **thinness** NOUN

thin VERB thins, thinning, thinned
❶ to thin something, or thin something out, is to make it less thick or less crowded
❷ to thin, or thin out, is to become less dense or less crowded • *The crowds had thinned by late afternoon.*

thine ADJECTIVE (*old use*)
yours (referring to one person) • *All I have is thine.*

thing NOUN things
❶ a thing is any object that can be touched or seen or thought about ❷ your things are your belongings or possessions • *You can leave your things in a locker.*

think VERB thinks, thinking, thought
❶ to think is to use your mind ❷ to think something is to have it as an idea or opinion
• *I think that's a good idea.* ❸ to be thinking of doing something is to be planning to do it

thinly ADVERB
❶ to be thinly cut is to be cut in thin pieces ❷ to be thinly covered in something is to be covered in a thin layer of it

third ADJECTIVE, NOUN
the next after the second
➤ **thirdly** ADVERB as the third thing

third NOUN **thirds**
each of three equal parts into which something can be divided

Third World NOUN
an old-fashioned way to describe developing countries of Asia, Africa, and South and Central America

thirst NOUN
thirst is the feeling that you need to drink

thirsty ADJECTIVE **thirstier, thirstiest**
when you are thirsty, you feel that you need to drink
➤ **thirstily** ADVERB

thirteen NOUN **thirteens**
the number 13
➤ **thirteenth** ADJECTIVE, NOUN

thirty NOUN **thirties**
the number 30
➤ **thirtieth** ADJECTIVE, NOUN

this DETERMINER, PRONOUN
the one here • *Take this pen.* • *This is the one.*

thistle NOUN **thistles**
a wild plant with prickly leaves and purple or white or yellow flowers

thorax NOUN **thoraces** or **thoraxes**
❶ the part of your body between your neck and your abdomen ❷ the part of an insect's body between the head and abdomen, to which the legs and wings are joined

thorn NOUN **thorns**
a small pointed growth on the stem of roses and other plants

thorny ADJECTIVE **thornier, thorniest**
❶ full of thorns; prickly ❷ a thorny problem is a difficult one that causes argument or disagreement

thorough ADJECTIVE
❶ done properly and carefully • *This is a thorough piece of work.* ❷ absolute or complete • *Everything was in a thorough mess.*
➤ **thoroughness** NOUN

thoroughly ADVERB
❶ to do something thoroughly is to do it properly and carefully ❷ to be thoroughly (for example) exhausted or bored is to be completely exhausted or bored

those DETERMINER, PRONOUN
the ones there • *Where are those cards?* • *Those are the ones I want.*

thou PRONOUN (*old use*)
you (referring to one person) • *Thou shalt get thy reward.*

though CONJUNCTION
in spite of the fact that; even if • *It is not true, though he says it is.*

though ADVERB
however; all the same • *She's right, though.*

thought NOUN **thoughts**
❶ a thought is something that you think; an idea or opinion ❷ thought is thinking • *I can see you've put a lot of thought into this.*

thought VERB (*past tense and past participle of* **think**)
• *I thought you liked pizza.* • *Have you thought about where you want to go?*

thoughtful ADJECTIVE
❶ involving a lot of thinking • *Sherlock fell into a thoughtful silence.* ❷ a thoughtful person always thinks of other people and what they would like • *It was thoughtful of you to ask.*
➤ **thoughtfully** ADVERB
➤ **thoughtfulness** NOUN

thoughtless ADJECTIVE
not thinking of other people and what they would like; reckless
➤ **thoughtlessly** ADVERB
➤ **thoughtlessness** NOUN

thousand NOUN **thousands**
the number 1,000
➤ **thousandth** ADJECTIVE, NOUN

thrash VERB **thrashes, thrashing, thrashed**
❶ to thrash someone is to keep hitting them hard with a stick or whip ❷ to thrash a person or team is to defeat them completely in a game or sport ❸ to thrash, or thrash about, is to fling your arms and legs about wildly

thread NOUN **threads**
❶ a long piece of cotton, wool, nylon or other material used for sewing or weaving ❷ a long thin piece of something ❸ the spiral ridge round a screw or bolt

thread VERB **threads, threading, threaded**
❶ to thread a needle is to put a thread through its eye ❷ to thread a long and

a
b
c
d
e
f
g
h
i
j
k
l
m
n
o
p
q
r
s
t
u
v
w
x
y
z

thin material is to put it through or round something ❸ to thread a piece of string is to put beads on it

threadbare *ADJECTIVE*
clothes are threadbare when they are worn thin with threads showing

threat *NOUN* **threats**
❶ a warning that you will punish or harm someone if they do not do what you want ❷ a danger

threaten *VERB* **threatens**, **threatening**, **threatened**
❶ to threaten someone is to warn them that you will punish or harm them if they do not do what you want ❷ to threaten is to be a danger to someone or something • *The clouds threatened a storm.*

three *NOUN* **threes**
the number 3

three–dimensional, **3–D** *ADJECTIVE*
having three dimensions: length, width and height or depth

thresh *VERB* **threshes**, **threshing**, **threshed**
to thresh corn is to beat it so that you separate the grain from the husks

threshold *NOUN* **thresholds**
❶ a slab of stone or board under the doorway of a building; the entrance ❷ the beginning of something important • *We are on the threshold of a great discovery.*

threw *VERB* (*past tense of* **throw**)
• *Grandad threw the ball to me.*

thrift *NOUN*
thrift is being careful with money and not wasting it

thrifty *ADJECTIVE* **thriftier**, **thriftiest**
careful with money and not wasting it
➤ **thriftiness** *NOUN*

thrill *NOUN* **thrills**
❶ a sudden feeling of excitement ❷ something that gives you this feeling

thrill *VERB* **thrills**, **thrilling**, **thrilled**
something thrills you when it gives you a sudden feeling of excitement

thriller *NOUN* **thrillers**
an exciting story or film, usually about crime or spying

thrilling *ADJECTIVE*
very exciting

thrive *VERB* **thrives**, **thriving**, **thrived** *or* **throve**, **thrived** *or* **thriven**
to prosper or grow strongly

throat *NOUN* **throats**
❶ the front of your neck ❷ the tube in your neck that takes food and air into your body

throb *VERB* **throbs**, **throbbing**, **throbbed**
to beat or vibrate with a strong rhythm
My injured leg throbbed terribly as the wagon rocked from side to side on its slow journey away from the battle front.—WAR HORSE, Michael Morpurgo

throb *NOUN* **throbs**
a throbbing sound or feeling

throne *NOUN* **thrones**
❶ a special chair for a king or queen ❷ the position of being king or queen • *The prince is heir to the throne.*

throng *NOUN* **throngs**
a large crowd of people

throttle *VERB* **throttles**, **throttling**, **throttled**
to throttle someone is to squeeze their throat and strangle them

throttle *NOUN* **throttles**
a device to control the flow of fuel to an engine

through *ADVERB, PREPOSITION*
❶ from one end or side to the other • *We had to crawl through the tunnel.* • *Push the needle through.* ❷ because of; by means of • *Your playing will get better through practice.*
❸ (*informal*) finished • *Are you through with the hairdryer?*

through *ADJECTIVE*
❶ travelling all the way to a place • *a through train to Dover* ❷ a through road is open to traffic at both ends
SPELLING ALERT! Through is different from **threw**, which is the past tense of *throw*: *Who threw that ball through the window?*

throughout *PREPOSITION, ADVERB*
all the way through

throve to ticklish

throve VERB (*past tense of* thrive)
• *The kittens throve in their new home.*

throw VERB throws, throwing, threw, thrown
❶ to throw something or someone is to send them through the air ❷ to throw something somewhere is to put it there carelessly • *He came in and threw his coat on the chair.* ❸ to throw a part of your body is to move it quickly • *She threw her head back and laughed.* ❹ to throw someone into a certain state is to put them in that state • *We were thrown into confusion.*
➤ **to throw something away** is to get rid of it

throw NOUN throws
a throwing action or movement • *That was a good throw.*

thrush NOUN thrushes
a bird that has a white front with brown spots

thrust VERB thrusts, thrusting, thrust
to thrust something somewhere is to push it there with a lot of force • *Leo thrust his hands into his pockets.*

thud NOUN thuds
the dull sound of something heavy falling
thud VERB thuds, thudding, thudded
to fall with a thud

thumb NOUN thumbs
the short thick finger at the side of each hand
➤ **to be under someone's thumb** is to be controlled or ruled by them

thump VERB thumps, thumping, thumped
❶ to thump someone or something is to hit them heavily ❷ to thump is to make a dull heavy sound
thump NOUN thumps
an act or sound of thumping

thunder NOUN
thunder is the loud rumbling noise that you hear with lightning during a storm
thunder VERB thunders, thundering, thundered
❶ to thunder is to make the noise of thunder ❷ someone thunders when they speak with a loud booming voice

thunderous ADJECTIVE
extremely loud • *The curtain came down to thunderous applause.*

thunderstorm NOUN thunderstorms
a storm with thunder and lightning

Thursday NOUN Thursdays
the fifth day of the week
DID YOU KNOW? Thursday is an Old English name meaning 'day of thunder' and is named after the Norse god *Thor.*

thus ADVERB
❶ in this way
'Thus was Wonka-Vite invented!' said Mr Wonka. 'And thus was it made safe for all to use!'—CHARLIE AND THE GREAT GLASS ELEVATOR, Roald Dahl
❷ therefore • *It was night-time and thus hard to see.*

thy ADJECTIVE (old use)
your (referring to one person) • *Thou shalt get thy reward.*

tick NOUN ticks
❶ a small mark, usually (✓), made next to something when checking it as a sign that it is correct or has been done ❷ each of the regular clicking sounds that a clock or watch makes ❸ (informal) a moment • *I won't be a tick.*

tick VERB ticks, ticking, ticked
❶ to tick something is to mark it with a tick • *She ticked the correct answers.* ❷ a clock or watch ticks when it makes regular clicking sounds
➤ **to tick someone off** (informal) is to scold them or tell them off

ticket NOUN tickets
a piece of paper or card that allows you to do something such as see a show or travel on a bus or train

tickle VERB tickles, tickling, tickled
❶ to tickle someone is to keep touching their skin lightly so that they get a tingling feeling that can make them laugh and wriggle ❷ to tickle is to have a tickling or itching feeling • *My throat is tickling.* ❸ to tickle someone is also to please or amuse them

ticklish ADJECTIVE
❶ someone is ticklish when they are likely to laugh or wriggle if they are tickled ❷ awkward or difficult • *This is a ticklish situation.*

523

tidal ADJECTIVE
to do with tides or affected by tides

tidal wave NOUN **tidal waves**
a huge sea wave moving with the tide

tiddler NOUN **tiddlers** (informal)
a very small fish

tiddlywink NOUN **tiddlywinks**
a small counter that you flip into a cup with another counter in the game of **tiddlywinks**

tide NOUN **tides**
the regular rising or falling of the sea, which usually happens twice a day

tide VERB **tides, tiding, tided**
➤ **to tide someone over** is to give them what they need, especially money, for the time being

tidy ADJECTIVE **tidier, tidiest**
① a tidy place is neat and orderly, with things in the right place • *Her bedroom was surprisingly tidy.* ② a tidy person keeps things neat and in the right place ③ (informal) fairly large • *That's a tidy sum of money.*
➤ **tidily** ADVERB ➤ **tidiness** NOUN

tidy VERB **tidies, tidying, tidied**
to tidy a place is to make it neat by putting things away in the right place

tie VERB **ties, tying, tied**
① to tie something is to fasten it with string, rope or ribbon ② to tie a knot or bow is to make one in a strip of material such as a ribbon ③ two players or teams tie when they finish a game or competition with an equal score or position

tie NOUN **ties**
① a thin strip of material tied round the collar of a shirt with a knot at the front ② the result of a game or competition in which two players or teams have the same position or score ③ one of the matches in a competition

tie-break, tie-breaker NOUN **tie-breaks, tie-breakers**
an extra game, or part of a game, played when the result so far is a tie

tiger NOUN **tigers**
a large wild animal of the cat family, with yellow and black stripes

tight ADJECTIVE **tighter, tightest**
① fitting very closely or firmly fastened • *These shoes are a bit tight.* ② fully stretched • *Is this string tight enough?* ③ (informal) mean or stingy • *They're a bit tight with their money.*
➤ **tightly** ADVERB ➤ **tightness** NOUN

tight ADVERB
① firmly • *Hold on tight.* ② fully stretched • *Now pull the string tight.*

tighten VERB **tightens, tightening, tightened**
① to tighten something is to make it tighter • *These screws need to be tightened.* ② to tighten is to become tighter

tightrope NOUN **tightropes**
a tightly stretched rope above the ground, for acrobats to perform on

tights PLURAL NOUN
a piece of clothing that fits tightly over the lower parts of the body including the legs and feet

tigress NOUN **tigresses**
a female tiger

tile NOUN **tiles**
a thin piece of baked clay or other hard material used in rows to cover roofs, walls or floors
➤ **tiled** ADJECTIVE covered with tiles

till PREPOSITION, CONJUNCTION
until

till NOUN **tills**
a drawer or box for money in a shop; a cash register

till VERB **tills, tilling, tilled**
to till soil or land is to plough it ready for planting

tiller NOUN **tillers**
a handle used to turn a boat's rudder

tilt VERB **tilts, tilting, tilted**
① to tilt is to slope or lean ② to tilt something is to tip it or make it slope

tilt NOUN **tilts**
a sloping position

timber NOUN **timbers**
① timber is wood used for building or making things ② a timber is a beam of wood

time *NOUN* **times**
❶ time is a measure of the continued existence of everything in years, months, days and other units ❷ you ask the time when you want to know what point in the day it is, as shown on a watch or clock • *What's the time?* ❸ a time is a particular moment or period of things existing or happening • *Come back another time.* • *The film is set in Victorian times.* ❹ a time is also an occasion • *This is the first time I've been here.* ❺ a time is also a period that is suitable or available for something • *Is there time for something to eat?* ❻ time is the rhythm and speed of a piece of music
➤ **at times** *or* **from time to time** sometimes or occasionally
➤ **in time** *or* **on time** soon or early enough; not late • *Make sure you get to the station in time.* • *The train left on time.*

time *VERB* **times, timing, timed**
❶ to time something is to measure how long it takes ❷ to time an event or activity is to arrange the time when it will happen • *You timed your arrival perfectly.*

timer *NOUN* **timers**
a device for timing things

times *VERB*
multiplied by • *5 times 3 is 15 (5 × 3 = 15).*

timetable *NOUN* **timetables**
a list of the times when things happen, such as buses and trains leaving and arriving, and when school lessons take place

timid *ADJECTIVE*
nervous and easily frightened
➤ **timidly** *ADVERB* ➤ **timidity** *NOUN*

timing *NOUN*
timing is choosing the right time to do something • *Arriving at lunchtime was good timing.*

timpani (*say* timp-a-nee) *PLURAL NOUN*
kettledrums

tin *NOUN* **tins**
❶ tin is a soft white metal ❷ a tin is a metal container for preserving food

tin *VERB* **tins, tinning, tinned**
to tin food is to preserve it in tins

tingle *VERB* **tingles, tingling, tingled**
part of your body tingles when you have a

slight stinging or tickling feeling there • *The cold water made my skin tingle.*

tingle *NOUN* **tingles**
a tingling feeling

tinker *VERB* **tinkers, tinkering, tinkered**
to tinker with something is to try to mend or improve it, often without really knowing how to • *He loves tinkering with old clocks.*

tinker *NOUN* **tinkers** (*historical*)
someone who travelled around mending pots and pans

tinkle *VERB* **tinkles, tinkling, tinkled**
something tinkles when it makes a gentle ringing sound

tinkle *NOUN* **tinkles**
a tinkling sound

tinsel *NOUN*
tinsel is strips of glittering material used for decoration

tint *NOUN* **tints**
a shade of a colour, especially a pale one

tint *VERB* **tints, tinting, tinted**
to tint something is to colour it slightly

tiny *ADJECTIVE* **tinier, tiniest**
very small • *The chicks were tiny when they first hatched.*

tip *NOUN* **tips**
❶ the part at the very end of something • *Can you touch the tips of your toes?* ❷ a small amount of money given to thank someone who has helped you ❸ a quick piece of advice or useful information • *The website gives tips on how to write great stories.* ❹ a place where rubbish is left ❺ a very untidy place • *This room is a tip!*

tip *VERB* **tips, tipping, tipped**
❶ to tip something is to turn it upside down or tilt it • *She tipped the water out of the bucket.* • *He tipped his head back and laughed.* ❷ to tip rubbish is to leave it somewhere ❸ to be tipped with something is to have it at the tip • *The wizard's wand was tipped with silver.* ❹ to tip someone is to give them a tip to thank them for helping you ❺ to tip someone is also to name them as likely to win or succeed

tiptoe *VERB* **tiptoes, tiptoeing, tiptoed**
to walk on your toes very quietly or carefully

The children ... awoke almost before the night had drained away from the sleeping house and tiptoed through the hall in their stockinged feet.—BEDKNOBS AND BROOMSTICKS, Mary Norton

tiptoe NOUN
➤ **on tiptoe** walking or standing on your toes

tire VERB tires, tiring, tired
❶ to tire someone is to make them tired
❷ to tire is to become tired

tired ADJECTIVE
feeling that you need to sleep or rest
➤ **to be tired of something** is to have had enough of it
➤ **tiredness** NOUN

tireless ADJECTIVE
having a lot of energy; not tiring easily
➤ **tirelessly** ADVERB

tiresome ADJECTIVE
annoying

Grown-ups never understand anything by themselves, and it is tiresome for children to be always and forever explaining things to them.—THE LITTLE PRINCE, Antoine de Saint-Exupéry

tissue NOUN tissues
❶ tissue, or tissue paper, is thin soft paper ❷ a tissue is a piece of this ❸ tissue is also the substance of which an animal or plant is made

tit NOUN tits
a kind of small bird with a musical song, such as a *blue tit*
➤ **tit for tat** something equal given in return

titbit NOUN titbits
a small piece of something

title NOUN titles
❶ the name of something such as a book, film, painting or piece of music ❷ a word that shows a person's position or profession, such as *Sir, Lady, Dr* or *Mrs* ❸ a legal right to something, especially land or property

titter VERB titters, tittering, tittered
to giggle or laugh in a silly way

to PREPOSITION
❶ towards • *They set off to London.* ❷ as far as; so as to reach • *I am soaked to the skin.*

❸ compared with; rather than • *She prefers cats to dogs.*

to ADVERB
to the usual or closed position • *Push the door to.*
➤ **to and fro** backwards and forwards

toad NOUN toads
an animal like a large frog, that lives on land

toadstool NOUN toadstools
a fungus that looks like a mushroom and is often poisonous

toast VERB toasts, toasting, toasted
❶ to toast food is to cook it by heating it under a grill or in front of a fire ❷ to toast someone or something is to have a drink in their honour

toast NOUN toasts
❶ toast is toasted bread ❷ a toast is when people are asked to toast someone or something with a drink • *Let's drink a toast to the bride and groom.*

toaster NOUN toasters
an electrical device for toasting bread

tobacco NOUN
tobacco is the dried leaves of certain plants prepared for smoking in cigarettes, cigars or pipes

tobacconist NOUN tobacconists
a shopkeeper who sells cigarettes, cigars and tobacco

toboggan NOUN toboggans
a small sledge for sliding downhill
➤ **tobogganing** NOUN

today NOUN
this day • *Today is Monday.*

today ADVERB
❶ on this day • *We have gym today.*
❷ nowadays • *Dodos are extinct today.*

toddler NOUN toddlers
a young child who is just learning to walk

toe NOUN toes
❶ each of the five separate parts at the end of each foot ❷ the part of a shoe or sock that covers your toes

toffee *NOUN* **toffees**
❶ toffee is a sticky sweet made from butter and sugar ❷ a toffee is a piece of this

toga *NOUN* **togas**
a long loose piece of clothing worn by men in ancient Rome

together *ADVERB*
with another person or thing; with each other • *They went to school together.* • *Now glue the two parts together.*

toil *VERB* **toils, toiling, toiled**
❶ to toil is to work hard ❷ to toil is also to move slowly and with difficulty • *We toiled up the hill, dragging the sledge behind us.*

toilet *NOUN* **toilets**
❶ a large bowl with a seat that you use for getting rid of waste from your body ❷ a room with a toilet in it

toilet paper *NOUN*
toilet paper is paper for cleaning yourself after you have used a toilet

token *NOUN* **tokens**
❶ a card or voucher that you can exchange for goods in a shop ❷ a piece of metal or plastic you use instead of money to pay for something ❸ a sign or signal of something • *These flowers are a small token of my gratitude.*

told *VERB* (*past tense and past participle of* **tell**)
• *I told the truth.* • *I've already told you the answer.*

tolerable *ADJECTIVE*
able to be tolerated; bearable
➤ **tolerably** *ADVERB* to do something tolerably well is to do it fairly well

tolerant *ADJECTIVE*
accepting or putting up with other people's behaviour and opinions when you do not agree with them
➤ **tolerance** *NOUN* ➤ **tolerantly** *ADVERB*

tolerate *VERB* **tolerates, tolerating, tolerated**
to tolerate something is to allow it or put up with it although you do not approve of it

toll *NOUN* **tolls**
❶ a payment charged for using a bridge or road ❷ an amount of loss or damage • *The death toll in the earthquake is rising.*

toll *VERB* **tolls, tolling, tolled**
to toll a bell is to ring it slowly

tom, tomcat *NOUN* **toms, tomcats**
a male cat

tomato *NOUN* **tomatoes**
a soft round red fruit with seeds inside it, eaten as a vegetable
SPELLING ALERT! Remember to put an e in the plural: *a tin of chopped tomatoes.*

tomb (*say* toom) *NOUN* **tombs**
a place where a dead body is buried; a grave

tomboy *NOUN* **tomboys** (*old use*)
a girl who enjoys rough noisy games and activities

tombstone *NOUN* **tombstones**
a memorial stone set up over a grave

tomorrow *NOUN, ADVERB*
the day after today

tom-tom *NOUN* **tom-toms**
a type of drum that you beat with the palms of your hands

ton *NOUN* **tons**
❶ a unit of weight equal to 2,240 pounds or about 1,016 kilograms ❷ (*informal*) a large amount • *There's tons of room.*

tone *NOUN* **tones**
❶ a sound in music or speech ❷ each of the five larger intervals between two notes in a musical scale ❸ a shade of a colour ❹ the quality or character of something

tone *VERB* **tones, toning, toned**
➤ **to tone something down** is to make it softer or quieter
➤ **to tone in** is to blend or fit in well, especially in colour

tongs *PLURAL NOUN*
a tool with two arms joined at one end, used to pick things up or hold them

tongue *NOUN* **tongues**
❶ the long soft part that moves about inside your mouth ❷ a language • *He spoke in his native tongue.* ❸ the flap of material under the

laces of a shoe ❹ the part inside a bell that makes it ring

tongue-tied ADJECTIVE
to be tongue-tied is to feel too shy or embarrassed to speak

tongue-twister NOUN tongue-twisters
a sentence or phrase that is very difficult to say, for example *Red lorry, yellow lorry*

tonic NOUN tonics
something that makes a person healthier or stronger

tonight ADVERB, NOUN
this evening or night

tonne NOUN tonnes
a metric ton, a unit of weight equal to 1,000 kilograms

tonsillitis NOUN
tonsillitis is a disease that makes your tonsils extremely sore

tonsils PLURAL NOUN
your tonsils are two small masses of soft flesh inside your throat

too ADVERB
❶ also • *My sister has freckles too.* ❷ more than is wanted or allowed or wise • *Don't add too much water.*

took VERB (past tense of take)
• *I took no notice of what he said.*

tool NOUN tools
a device that you use to help you do a particular job, such as a hammer or saw

toolbar NOUN toolbars
a row of symbols on a computer screen that show the different things that you can do with a particular program

tooth NOUN teeth
❶ each of the hard white bony parts that grow in your gums, used for biting and chewing ❷ each in a row of sharp points on a saw or comb
➤ **toothed** ADJECTIVE
➤ A related adjective is **dental**.

toothache NOUN
toothache is a pain in one of your teeth

toothbrush NOUN toothbrushes
a small brush on a long handle, for brushing your teeth

toothpaste NOUN toothpastes
toothpaste is a creamy paste for cleaning your teeth

top NOUN tops
❶ the top is the highest part of something • *They climbed to the very top of the hill.* ❷ the upper surface of something • *Put it on the desk top.* ❸ the covering or stopper of a jar or bottle ❹ a piece of clothing you wear on the upper part of your body • *Is that a new top you're wearing?* ❺ a top is also a toy that you turn to make it spin on its point

top ADJECTIVE
highest or most important • *They were travelling at top speed.*

top VERB tops, topping, topped
❶ to top something is to put a top on it • *The cake was topped with lemon icing.* ❷ to be at the top of something • *She always tops the class in maths.*
➤ **to top something up** is to fill it to the top when it is already partly full

top hat NOUN top hats
a tall stiff black or grey hat worn with formal clothes

topic NOUN topics
a subject that you are writing or talking or learning about

topical ADJECTIVE
to do with things that are happening or in the news now • *a topical TV documentary*
➤ **topicality** NOUN

topmost ADJECTIVE
highest • *I wasn't tall enough to reach the topmost shelf.*

topping NOUN toppings
food that is put on the top of (for example) a cake or pizza

topple VERB topples, toppling, toppled
❶ to topple, or topple over, is to fall over ❷ to topple something is to make it fall over ❸ to topple someone in power is to overthrow them

top secret ADJECTIVE
extremely secret

topsy-turvy ADVERB, ADJECTIVE
upside down; muddled

torch NOUN **torches**
❶ a small electric lamp that you hold in your hand ❷ a stick with burning material on the end, used as a light

tore VERB (*past tense of* **tear**)
• *She tore open the parcel.*

torment VERB **torments**, **tormenting**, **tormented**
❶ to torment someone is to make them suffer or feel pain ❷ to torment someone is also to keep annoying them deliberately
➤ **tormentor** NOUN

torment NOUN **torments**
torment is great suffering

torn VERB (*past participle of* **tear**)
• *The old house had been torn down.*

tornado (*say* tor-**nay**-doh) NOUN **tornadoes**
a violent storm or whirlwind
DID YOU KNOW? The word **tornado** comes from a Spanish word meaning 'thunder'.

torpedo NOUN **torpedoes**
a long tube-shaped missile sent under water to destroy ships and submarines

torpedo VERB **torpedoes**, **torpedoing**, **torpedoed**
to torpedo a ship is to attack it with a torpedo

torrent NOUN **torrents**
a very strong stream or fall of water
The wind howled, the rain came down in torrents, and the waves got so high, they splashed right over the boat.—THE STORY OF DOCTOR DOLITTLE, Hugh Lofting

torrential ADJECTIVE
falling in torrents • *torrential rain*

torso NOUN **torsos**
the main part of the human body, not including the head, arms or legs

tortilla NOUN **tortillas**
a Mexican flat round bread made from either wheat or maize flour

tortoise (*say* **tor**-tus) NOUN **tortoises**
a slow-moving animal with a shell over its body

torture VERB **tortures**, **torturing**, **tortured**
to torture someone is to make them feel great pain, especially so that they will give information

torture NOUN **tortures**
torture is something done to torture a person
➤ **torturer** NOUN

Tory NOUN **Tories**
a Conservative

toss VERB **tosses**, **tossing**, **tossed**
❶ to toss something is to throw it into the air ❷ to toss a coin is to throw it in the air and see which side it lands on, as a way of deciding something ❸ to toss is to move about restlessly in bed • *She was tossing and turning all night.*

total NOUN **totals**
the amount you get by adding everything together

total ADJECTIVE
❶ complete; including everything • *What is the total amount?* ❷ complete • *There was total darkness outside.*
➤ **totally** ADVERB

total VERB **totals**, **totalling**, **totalled**
❶ to total something is to add it up ❷ to total an amount is to reach it as a total • *Sales totalled over £50,000 this month.*

totem pole NOUN **totem poles**
a pole carved or painted by Native American people with the symbols (totems) of their peoples or families

totter VERB **totters**, **tottering**, **tottered**
to walk unsteadily or wobble

toucan NOUN **toucans**
a tropical bird with a large, brightly coloured beak

touch VERB **touches**, **touching**, **touched**
❶ you touch something when you feel it lightly with your hand or fingers ❷ to touch something is to come into contact with it or hit it gently ❸ to be touching something is to be next to it so that there is no space in between ❹ to touch something is also to interfere or meddle with it • *Don't touch*

A
B
C
D
E
F
G
H
I
J
K
L
M
N
O
P
Q
R
S
T
U
V
W
X
Y
Z

anything in this room. ❺ to touch an amount is to just reach it • *His temperature touched 100 degrees.* ❻ to touch someone is to affect their emotions • *We were touched by his sad story.*

➤ **to touch down** is to land in an aircraft or spacecraft

➤ **to touch something up** is to improve it by making small changes or additions

touch *NOUN* **touches**
❶ a touch is an act of touching • *You can find any train timetable you want at the touch of a button.* ❷ touch is the ability to feel things by touching them ❸ a touch is also a small thing that greatly improves something • *We're just putting the finishing touches to it.* ❹ touch is also communication with someone • *We have lost touch with them.* ❺ touch is also the part of a football or rugby pitch outside the playing area • *He kicked the ball into touch.*

touchscreen *NOUN*
a screen on a computer or mobile phone which you can touch to open and run programs

touchy *ADJECTIVE* **touchier, touchiest**
someone who is touchy is easily or quickly offended
➤ **touchiness** *NOUN*

tough *ADJECTIVE* **tougher, toughest**
❶ strong; hard to break or damage • *You'll need tough shoes for the climb.* ❷ tough food is hard to chew ❸ rough or violent • *The police were dealing with tough criminals.* ❹ firm or severe • *Don't be too tough on her.* ❺ difficult • *It was a tough decision.*
➤ **toughly** *ADVERB* ➤ **toughness** *NOUN*

toughen *VERB* **toughens, toughening, toughened**
to toughen someone or something, or toughen them up, is to make them tougher

tour *NOUN* **tours**
a journey in which you visit several places • *a tour of the Highlands*

tourism *NOUN*
tourism is travelling or being on holiday abroad

tourist *NOUN* **tourists**
someone who is travelling or on holiday abroad

tournament *NOUN* **tournaments**
a competition in which there is a series of games or contests

tow (*rhymes with* **go**) *VERB* **tows, towing, towed**
to tow a vehicle or boat is to pull it behind you in another vehicle • *They towed our car to a garage.*

tow *NOUN*
an act of towing

toward, towards *PREPOSITION*
❶ in the direction of • *We carried on walking towards the village.* ❷ in relation to • *He has always behaved fairly towards me.* ❸ as a contribution to • *I'll put the money towards a new bicycle.*

towel *NOUN* **towels**
a piece of soft cloth that you use for drying yourself

towelling *NOUN*
towelling is material that towels are made of

tower *NOUN* **towers**
a tall narrow building or part of a building
tower *VERB* **towers, towering, towered**
to tower above or over things is to be taller than them • *The skyscrapers towered above the city.*

tower block *NOUN* **tower blocks**
a tall building containing offices or flats

town *NOUN* **towns**
a place with many houses, shops, schools, offices and other buildings

town hall *NOUN* **town halls**
a building with offices for the local council and usually a hall for public events

toxic *ADJECTIVE*
poisonous • *The planet has a toxic atmosphere.*
➤ **toxicity** *NOUN*

toy *NOUN* **toys**
something to play with

toy *VERB* **toys, toying, toyed**
to toy with an idea is to think about it casually or idly

toyshop *NOUN* **toyshops**
a shop that sells toys

trace *NOUN* **traces**
❶ a mark or sign left by a person or thing • *He vanished without a trace.* ❷ a very small amount of something • *They found traces of blood on the carpet.*

trace *VERB* **traces**, **tracing**, **traced**
❶ to trace someone or something is to find them after a search • *Police are trying to trace one of the witnesses.* ❷ to trace a picture or map is to copy it by drawing over it on thin paper you can see through

traceable *ADJECTIVE*
able to be traced or found

track *NOUN* **tracks**
❶ a path made by people or animals ❷ tracks are marks left by a person or thing ❸ a set of rails for trains or trams to run on ❹ a road or area of ground prepared for racing ❺ a metal belt used instead of wheels on a heavy vehicle such as a tank or tractor
➤ **to keep track of something** *or* **someone** is to know where they are or what they are doing

track *VERB* **tracks**, **tracking**, **tracked**
❶ to track a person or animal is to follow them by following the signs they leave ❷ to track something is to follow or observe it as it moves

tracksuit *NOUN* **tracksuits**
a warm loose suit of a kind worn by athletes for jogging and warming up

tract *NOUN* **tracts**
❶ an area of land ❷ a part of your body along which something passes • *your digestive tract* ❸ a short pamphlet or essay, especially about religion

traction *NOUN*
❶ traction is the ability of a vehicle to grip the ground • *The car's wheels lost traction in the mud.* ❷ traction is also a medical treatment in which an injured arm or leg is pulled gently for a long time by means of weights and pulleys

tractor *NOUN* **tractors**
a motor vehicle with large rear wheels, used for pulling farm machinery or heavy loads

trade *NOUN* **trades**
❶ trade is the business of buying or selling

or exchanging things ❷ a trade is a job or occupation, especially a skilled craft

trade *VERB* **trades**, **trading**, **traded**
to trade is to buy or sell or exchange things
➤ **to trade something in** is to give it towards the cost of something new • *He traded in his motorcycle for a car.*

trademark *NOUN* **trademarks**
a symbol or name that only one manufacturer is allowed to use

trader *NOUN* **traders**
someone who buys and sells things in trade

tradesman *NOUN* **tradesmen**
a person employed in a trade, especially one that involves a skill such as plumbing or carpentry

trade union *NOUN* **trade unions**
an organization of workers in a particular industry, set up to help improve pay and work conditions

tradition *NOUN* **traditions**
❶ tradition is the passing down of customs and beliefs from one generation to the next ❷ a tradition is a custom or belief passed on in this way

traditional *ADJECTIVE*
❶ passed down from one generation to the next • *a book of traditional folk tales* ❷ following older ideas rather than modern ones • *We go to a very traditional school.*
➤ **traditionally** *ADVERB*

traffic *NOUN*
❶ traffic is vehicles, ships or aircraft moving along a route ❷ traffic is also trade, especially in something illegal or wrong

traffic *VERB* **traffics**, **trafficking**, **trafficked**
to traffic in something is to trade in it illegally

traffic lights *PLURAL NOUN*
a set of coloured lights used to control traffic at road junctions and other hazards

traffic warden *NOUN* **traffic wardens**
an official whose job is to make sure that vehicles are parked legally

tragedy *NOUN* **tragedies**
❶ a play with unhappy events or a sad ending ❷ a very sad event

a
b
c
d
e
f
g
h
i
j
k
l
m
n
o
p
q
r
s
t
u
v
w
x
y
z

A
B
C
D
E
F
G
H
I
J
K
L
M
N
O
P
Q
R
S
T
U
V
W
X
Y
Z

tragic *ADJECTIVE*
❶ very sad or distressing ❷ to do with tragedy
➤ **tragically** *ADVERB*

trail *NOUN* **trails**
❶ a path or track through the countryside or a forest ❷ the scent and marks left behind by an animal as it moves ❸ marks left behind by something that has passed

trail *VERB* **trails, trailing, trailed**
❶ to trail an animal is to follow the scent or marks it has left behind ❷ you trail something, or it trails, when it drags along the ground behind you ❸ to trail behind someone is to follow them more slowly or at a distance
• *A few walkers trailed behind the others.*
❹ to trail is also to hang down or float loosely
• *She wore a long trailing scarf.*

trailer *NOUN* **trailers**
❶ a truck or other container that is pulled along by a car or lorry ❷ a short film advertising a film or television programme that will soon be shown

train *NOUN* **trains**
❶ a group of railway coaches or trucks joined together and pulled by an engine ❷ a number of people or animals moving along together, especially in a desert • *a camel train* ❸ a series of things • *The train of events began in London.* ❹ a long part of a dress that trails on the ground

train *VERB* **trains, training, trained**
❶ to train someone is to give them skill or practice in something ❷ to train is to learn how to do a job • *He's training to be a doctor.* ❸ to train is also to practise for a sporting event • *She was training for the race.* ❹ to train a plant is to make it grow in a particular direction • *Roses can be trained up walls.* ❺ to train a gun is to aim it at a target
• *He trained his rifle on the bridge.*

trainer *NOUN* **trainers**
❶ a person who trains people or animals
❷ a soft shoe with a rubber sole, worn for running and sport

traitor *NOUN* **traitors**
someone who betrays their country or friends

tram *NOUN* **trams**
a passenger vehicle that runs along rails set in the road

tramp *NOUN* **tramps**
❶ a person without a home or job who walks from place to place ❷ a long walk ❸ the sound of heavy footsteps

tramp *VERB* **tramps, tramping, tramped**
❶ to tramp is to walk with heavy footsteps
❷ to tramp is also to walk for a long distance

trample *VERB* **tramples, trampling, trampled**
to trample something, or to trample on it, is to crush it by treading heavily on it

trampoline (*say* **tramp**-o-leen) *NOUN* **trampolines**
a large piece of canvas joined to a frame by springs, used by gymnasts for jumping on

trance *NOUN* **trances**
a dreamy or unconscious condition like sleep

tranquil *ADJECTIVE*
quiet and peaceful
➤ **tranquillity** *NOUN*

tranquillizer (*also* **tranquilliser**) *NOUN* **tranquillizers**
a drug used to make a person or animal calm and relaxed

trans- *PREFIX*
meaning 'across', as in *transatlantic*

transatlantic *ADJECTIVE*
across the Atlantic Ocean or on the other side of it

transfer (*say* trans-**fer**) *VERB* **transfers, transferring, transferred**
❶ to transfer someone or something is to move them from one place to another
❷ to transfer something is to give it or pass it on to someone else

transfer (*say* **trans**-fer) *NOUN* **transfers**
❶ the process of moving a person or thing from one place to another ❷ a piece of paper with a picture or design that can be transferred to another surface by soaking or heating the paper

transferable *ADJECTIVE*
a ticket is transferable when it can be used by someone other than the person who bought it

transform *VERB* **transforms, transforming, transformed**
to transform a person or thing is to change their form or appearance to something quite different • *The caterpillar is transformed into a butterfly.*
➤ **transformation** *NOUN*

transformer *NOUN* **transformers**
a device used to change the voltage of an electric current

transfusion *NOUN* **transfusions**
putting blood taken from one person into another person's body

transistor *NOUN* **transistors**
❶ a tiny electronic device that controls a flow of electricity ❷ a portable radio that uses transistors to strengthen the signal it receives

transition *NOUN* **transitions**
a change from one thing to another

transitive *ADJECTIVE*
a verb is transitive when it is used with a direct object, for example *ate* in *they ate breakfast* (but not in *they ate early*)

translate *VERB* **translates, translating, translated**
to translate something said or written in one language is to say or write it in another language
➤ **translation** *NOUN* ➤ **translator** *NOUN*

translucent *ADJECTIVE*
something is translucent when it allows light to shine through, without being fully transparent
➤ **translucence** *NOUN*

transmission *NOUN* **transmissions**
❶ transmission is transmitting something ❷ a transmission is a radio or television broadcast

transmit *VERB* **transmits, transmitting, transmitted**
❶ to transmit a broadcast or signal is to send it out ❷ to transmit something is to send it or pass it from one person or place to another

transmitter *NOUN* **transmitters**
a device for transmitting radio signals

transparency *NOUN* **transparencies**
❶ transparency is being transparent ❷ a transparency is a type of transparent photograph that you can project on a screen

transparent *ADJECTIVE*
something is transparent when you can see through it

transpire *VERB* **transpires, transpiring, transpired**
❶ to transpire is to become known • *It transpired that she had known nothing about it.* ❷ to transpire is also to happen • *This is what transpired.* ❸ plants and animals transpire when they emit moisture through their leaves or skin

transplant *VERB* **transplants, transplanting, transplanted**
❶ to transplant a body organ is to remove it from one person and put it in another ❷ to transplant a plant is to move it from one place to another
➤ **transplantation** *NOUN*

transplant *NOUN* **transplants**
❶ when a body organ is removed from one person and put in another • *a heart transplant* ❷ something that is transplanted

transport (*say* trans-**port**) *VERB* **transports, transporting, transported**
to transport people or things is to take them from one place to another
➤ **transportation** *NOUN*

transport (*say* **trans**-port) *NOUN*
❶ transport is the process of transporting people or things ❷ transport is also vehicles used to do this

transporter *NOUN* **transporters**
a heavy vehicle for transporting large objects, such as cars

trap *NOUN* **traps**
❶ a device for catching and holding animals ❷ a plan or trick to capture, detect or cheat someone ❸ a two-wheeled carriage pulled by a horse ❹ a bend in a pipe, filled with liquid to prevent air or gas escaping

trap *VERB* **traps, trapping, trapped**
❶ to trap a person or animal is to catch them in a trap ❷ to trap someone is to capture, detect or cheat them ❸ to be trapped is to

a
b
c
d
e
f
g
h
i
j
k
l
m
n
o
p
q
r
s
t
u
v
w
x
y
z

A B C D E F G H I J K L M N O P Q R S **T** U V W X Y Z

be stuck in a dangerous situation you can't escape from • *They were trapped in the burning building.*

trapdoor *NOUN* **trapdoors**
a door in a floor or ceiling or roof

trapeze *NOUN* **trapezes**
a bar hanging from two ropes, used as a swing by acrobats

trapezium *NOUN* **trapeziums**
a four-sided figure that has only two parallel sides, which are of different length

trapezoid *NOUN* **trapezoids**
a four-sided figure with no two sides parallel

trash *NOUN*
trash is rubbish or nonsense

travel *VERB* **travels, travelling, travelled**
to travel is to go from one place to another

travel *NOUN*
travel is going on journeys • *Do you enjoy foreign travel?*

travel agent *NOUN* **travel agents**
a person or business whose job is to arrange travel and holidays for people

traveller *NOUN* **travellers**
❶ someone who is travelling or who often travels ❷ a person who lives in a vehicle and does not settle in one place

trawler *NOUN* **trawlers**
a fishing boat that pulls a large net behind it

tray *NOUN* **trays**
a flat piece of wood or metal or plastic, used for carrying food, cups, plates and other household things

treacherous *ADJECTIVE*
❶ betraying someone; not loyal ❷ dangerous
The snow was deep and treacherous, with a thick, shiny crust of ice on top.—ODD AND THE FROST GIANTS, Neil Gaiman
➤ **treacherously** *ADVERB*

treachery *NOUN*
treachery is doing something that betrays someone

treacle *NOUN*
treacle is a thick sweet sticky liquid made from purified sugar

tread *VERB* **treads, treading, trod, trodden**
to tread on something is to walk on it or put your foot on it

tread *NOUN* **treads**
❶ the sound someone makes when they walk • *We heard the tread of footsteps upstairs.*
❷ the part of a staircase or ladder that you put your foot on ❸ the part of a tyre that touches the ground

treason *NOUN*
treason is betraying your country

treasure *NOUN* **treasures**
❶ treasure is a collection of valuable things like jewels or money ❷ a treasure is a precious thing

treasure *VERB* **treasures, treasuring, treasured**
to treasure something is to think that it is very precious

treasure hunt *NOUN* **treasure hunts**
a game in which people try to find a hidden object

treasurer *NOUN* **treasurers**
an official who is in charge of the money of an organization or club

treasury *NOUN* **treasuries**
a place where treasure is stored
➤ **the Treasury** the government department in charge of a country's income

treat *VERB* **treats, treating, treated**
❶ to treat someone or something in a certain way is to behave towards them in that way • *She treats her friends very kindly.* ❷ to treat a person or animal is to give them medical care • *He was treated for sunstroke.* ❸ to treat someone is to pay for their food or drink or entertainment • *I'll treat you to an ice cream.*

treat *NOUN* **treats**
❶ something special that gives someone pleasure ❷ the act of treating someone by paying for them • *This is my treat.*

treatment *NOUN* **treatments**
❶ your treatment of someone is the way you treat them ❷ treatment is medical care

treaty *NOUN* **treaties**
a formal agreement between two or more countries

treble *ADJECTIVE*
three times as much or three times as many

treble *NOUN* **trebles**
❶ treble the amount of something is three times as much or as many ❷ a treble is a child with a high singing voice

treble *VERB* **trebles**, **trebling**, **trebled**
❶ to treble something is to make it three times as big ❷ to treble is to become three times as big

tree *NOUN* **trees**
a tall plant with leaves, branches and a thick wooden stem called a *trunk*

tree house *NOUN* **tree houses**
a small hut built in the branches of a tree for playing in

trek *VERB* **treks**, **trekking**, **trekked**
to make a long walk or journey

trek *NOUN* **treks**
a long walk or journey

trellis *NOUN* **trellises**
a framework of crossing wooden or metal bars, used to support climbing plants

tremble *VERB* **trembles**, **trembling**, **trembled**
to shake gently, especially because you are afraid

tremble *NOUN* **trembles**
a trembling movement or sound

tremendous *ADJECTIVE*
❶ very large or very great
Then, without warning, there was a tremendous SPLASH! right at Measle's side and Measle received a great wave of water directly in his face.—MEASLE: THE MONSTER OF MUCUS!, Ian Ogilvy
❷ excellent • *That's a tremendous idea!*
➤ **tremendously** *ADVERB*

tremor *NOUN* **tremors**
❶ a shaking or trembling ❷ a small earthquake

trench *NOUN* **trenches**
a long hole or ditch dug in the ground

trend *NOUN* **trends**
the general direction in which something is going or developing

trendy *ADJECTIVE* **trendier**, **trendiest**
(*informal*)
fashionable; trying to be up to date
➤ **trendiness** *NOUN*

trespass *VERB* **trespasses**, **trespassing**, **trespassed**
to trespass is to go on someone's land or property without their permission • *The sign said 'No Trespassing'.*
➤ **trespasser** *NOUN*

trestle *NOUN* **trestles**
each of a set of supports on which you place a board to make a table

T-rex *NOUN* **T-rexes**
short for **tyrannosaurus rex**

trial *NOUN* **trials**
❶ trying or testing something to see how well it works ❷ the process of hearing all the evidence about a crime in a law court in order to find out whether someone is guilty of it
➤ **on trial** being tried out, or being tried in a law court

triangle *NOUN* **triangles**
❶ a flat shape with three straight sides and three angles ❷ a percussion instrument made from a metal rod bent into a triangle

triangular *ADJECTIVE*
in the shape of a triangle

triathlon (*say* try-ath-lon) *NOUN* **triathlons**
a sports competition in which athletes take part in three different events, usually swimming, cycling and running
➤ **triathlete** *NOUN*

tribe *NOUN* **tribes**
a group of families living together, ruled by a leader or chief
➤ **tribal** *ADJECTIVE*

tribesman, **tribeswoman** *NOUN* **tribesmen**, **tribeswomen**
a person who belongs to a particular tribe

tributary *NOUN* **tributaries**
a river or stream that flows into a larger river or a lake

a b c d e f g h i j k l m n o p q r s t u v w x y z

tribute NOUN **tributes**
❶ something said or done as a mark of respect or admiration for someone ❷ money that people in one country used to have to pay a powerful ruler in another country

triceratops NOUN **triceratops**
a dinosaur with three horns on its head and snout, and a bony frill above its neck

trick NOUN **tricks**
❶ something done to deceive or fool someone ❷ a skilful act that creates an illusion to entertain people • *My brother likes doing magic tricks.*

trick VERB **tricks, tricking, tricked**
to trick someone is to deceive or fool them
➤ **trickery** NOUN

trickle VERB **trickles, trickling, trickled**
liquid trickles when it flows slowly in small quantities

trickle NOUN **trickles**
a slow gradual flow

trickster NOUN **tricksters**
someone who plays tricks on people

tricky ADJECTIVE **trickier, trickiest**
❶ difficult or awkward • *There were a couple of tricky questions in the quiz.* ❷ cunning or deceitful
➤ **trickiness** NOUN

tricycle NOUN **tricycles**
a vehicle like a bicycle with three wheels

trident NOUN **tridents**
a spear with three prongs • *a statue of Neptune holding a trident*

tried VERB (*past tense and past participle of* **try**)
• *He tried to cover up his laugh with a cough.*
• *I have tried to be patient with you.*

trifle NOUN **trifles**
❶ a pudding made of sponge cake covered with custard, fruit and cream ❷ a very small amount of something ❸ something that has little importance or value

trifle VERB **trifles, trifling, trifled**
to trifle with someone or something is to treat them without seriousness or respect

trifling ADJECTIVE
very small or unimportant

trigger NOUN **triggers**
a lever that is pulled to fire a gun

trigger VERB **triggers, triggering, triggered**
to trigger something, or trigger it off, is to start it happening

trillion NOUN **trillions**
a million million (1,000,000,000,000)

trilobite (*say* tril-o-byt) NOUN **trilobites**
a type of fossil with a body divided into three parts

trilogy NOUN **trilogies**
a group of three books or films about the same characters

trim ADJECTIVE **trimmer, trimmest**
neat and tidy

trim VERB **trims, trimming, trimmed**
❶ you trim something when you cut the edges or unwanted parts from it ❷ to trim clothing is to decorate its edges • *The gown was trimmed with fur.* ❸ in a boat, to trim the sails is to arrange them to suit the wind

trim NOUN
an act of trimming • *My hair needs a quick trim.*

trio NOUN **trios**
❶ three people or things ❷ a group of three musicians ❸ a piece of music for three musicians

trip VERB **trips, tripping, tripped**
❶ to trip, or trip over, is to catch your foot on something and fall or stumble ❷ to trip someone, or trip them up, is to make them fall or stumble ❸ to trip, or trip along, is to move with quick gentle steps

trip NOUN **trips**
❶ a short journey or outing ❷ the action of tripping or stumbling

tripe NOUN
❶ tripe is part of the stomach of an ox used as food ❷ (*informal*) tripe is also nonsense

triple ADJECTIVE
❶ three times as much or three times as many ❷ consisting of three parts or involving three people or groups

triple *VERB* **triples, tripling, tripled**
to triple something is to make it three times as big

triplet *NOUN* **triplets**
each of three children or animals born at the same time to the same mother

tripod (*say* **try**-pod) *NOUN* **tripods**
a stand with three legs, for supporting a camera or other instrument

triumph *NOUN* **triumphs**
❶ a triumph is a great success or victory
❷ triumph is a feeling of victory or success
• *They returned home in triumph.*

triumph *VERB* **triumphs, triumphing, triumphed**
to triumph is to win or succeed

triumphant *ADJECTIVE*
enjoying a victory or celebrating one
'He has done it!' Uncle Aquila was announcing in a kind of triumphant grumble. 'He has done it, by Jupiter!'—THE EAGLE OF THE NINTH, Rosemary Sutcliff
➤ **triumphantly** *ADVERB*

trivial *ADJECTIVE*
not important or valuable
➤ **trivially** *ADVERB* ➤ **triviality** *NOUN*

trod *VERB* (*past tense of* **tread**)
• *Laura trod in something slippery.*

trodden *VERB* (*past participle of* **tread**)
• *Many other people had trodden this path.*

troll *NOUN* **trolls**
a creature in Scandinavian mythology, either a dwarf or a giant

trolley *NOUN* **trolleys**
❶ a basket on wheels, used in supermarkets
❷ a small table on wheels, used for serving food and drink

trombone *NOUN* **trombones**
a large brass musical instrument with a sliding tube

troop *NOUN* **troops**
an organized group of people, especially soldiers

troop *VERB* **troops, trooping, trooped**
people troop when they move along in large numbers

troops *PLURAL NOUN*
soldiers

trophy *NOUN* **trophies**
a cup or other prize you get for winning a competition

tropic *NOUN* **tropics**
a line of latitude about 23.5° north of the equator (**Tropic of Cancer**) or about 23.5° south of the equator (**Tropic of Capricorn**)
➤ **the tropics** the hot regions between these two latitudes

tropical *ADJECTIVE*
a tropical (for example) plant, bird or rainforest is one found in the tropics

trot *VERB* **trots, trotting, trotted**
❶ a horse trots when it runs gently without cantering or galloping ❷ a person trots when they run gently with short steps

trot *NOUN* **trots**
a trotting run
➤ **on the trot** (*informal*) one after another

trouble *NOUN* **troubles**
trouble is something that causes worry or difficulty
➤ **to be in trouble** is to be likely to get punished because of something you have done
➤ **to take trouble** is to take great care in doing something

trouble *VERB* **troubles, troubling, troubled**
❶ to trouble someone is to cause them worry or difficulty ❷ to trouble someone is also to bother or disturb them • *Sorry to trouble you, but can you spare a minute?* ❸ to trouble to do something is to make an effort to do it • *Nobody troubled to ask us what we wanted.*

troublesome *ADJECTIVE*
causing trouble or worry

trough (*say* trof) *NOUN* **troughs**
❶ a long narrow box for animals to eat or drink from ❷ an area of low pressure between two areas of high pressure

troupe (*say* troop) *NOUN* **troupes**
a group of touring actors or other performers

a
b
c
d
e
f
g
h
i
j
k
l
m
n
o
p
q
r
s
t
u
v
w
x
y
z

trousers *PLURAL NOUN*
a piece of clothing worn over the lower half of your body, with two parts to cover your legs

trout *NOUN* trout
a freshwater fish

trowel *NOUN* trowels
❶ a tool for digging small holes or lifting plants ❷ a tool with a flat blade for spreading cement or mortar

truant *NOUN* truants
a pupil who stays away from school without permission
➤ **to play truant** is to stay away from school without permission
➤ **truancy** *NOUN*

truce *NOUN* truces
an agreement to stop fighting for a while

truck *NOUN* trucks
❶ a lorry ❷ an open railway wagon for carrying goods ❸ a cart

trudge *VERB* trudges, trudging, trudged
to walk slowly and heavily

true *ADJECTIVE* truer, truest
❶ real or correct; telling what actually exists or happened • *This is a true story.* ❷ genuine or proper • *He was the true heir.* ❸ loyal and faithful • *You are a true friend.*
➤ **to come true** is to actually happen • *I hope your dreams come true.*

truly *ADVERB*
❶ truthfully ❷ sincerely or genuinely • *I am truly sorry.* ❸ absolutely or completely • *a truly awful experience*

trump *NOUN* trumps
a playing card of a suit that ranks above the others for one game or round of play

trump *VERB* trumps, trumping, trumped
to trump a card is to beat it by playing a trump

trumpet *NOUN* trumpets
a brass musical instrument with a narrow tube that widens at the end
➤ **trumpeter** *NOUN*

trumpet *VERB* trumpets, trumpeting, trumpeted
❶ an elephant trumpets when it makes a loud

sound ❷ to trumpet something is to announce it loudly

truncheon *NOUN* truncheons
a short thick stick carried as a weapon by a police officer

trundle *VERB* trundles, trundling, trundled
to move along heavily, especially on wheels
• *A lorry trundled across the bridge.*

trunk *NOUN* trunks
❶ the main stem of a tree ❷ an elephant's long flexible nose ❸ a large box with a hinged lid, for carrying or storing clothes and other things ❹ the human body except for the head, legs and arms

trunks *PLURAL NOUN*
shorts worn for swimming, boxing and other activities

trust *VERB* trusts, trusting, trusted
❶ to trust someone or something is to believe that they are good or truthful or reliable ❷ to trust that something is so is to hope it
• *I trust that you are well.*

trust *NOUN*
❶ trust is the feeling that a person or thing can be trusted ❷ trust is also responsibility or being trusted • *We left our dog in the trust of our next-door neighbour.*

trustworthy *ADJECTIVE*
able to be trusted; reliable
➤ **trustworthiness** *NOUN*

trusty *ADJECTIVE* trustier, trustiest
trustworthy or reliable • *a trusty companion*

truth *NOUN* truths
❶ truth is the quality of being true; the facts about something ❷ a truth is something that is true

truthful *ADJECTIVE*
❶ telling the truth • *Pinocchio tries to be always truthful.* ❷ true • *This is a truthful account of what happened.*
➤ **truthfully** *ADVERB* ➤ **truthfulness** *NOUN*

try *VERB* tries, trying, tried
❶ to try to do something is to make an effort to do it or to see if you can do it • *Please try to keep still.* ❷ to try something is to use it to see if it works or to taste it to see if you like it
• *Would you like to try a spoonful?* ❸ to try

someone in a law court is to find out whether they are guilty of a crime, by hearing all the evidence about it ❹ to try someone, or try their patience, is also to annoy them over a long time

➤ **to try something on** is to put on clothes to see if they fit or look good

➤ **to try something out** is to use it to see if it works

try *NOUN* **tries**
❶ a go at trying something; an attempt • *You can have one last try.* ❷ (*rugby*) putting the ball down on the ground behind your opponents' goal to score points

T-shirt *NOUN* **T-shirts**
a shirt or vest with short sleeves

tsunami (*say* soo-**nah**-mee) *NOUN* **tsunami** *or* **tsunamis**
a huge sea wave caused by an earthquake

tub *NOUN* **tubs**
a round container for liquids or soft stuff such as ice cream

tuba (*say* tew-ba) *NOUN* **tubas**
a large brass musical instrument that makes a deep sound

tube *NOUN* **tubes**
❶ a tube is a long thin hollow piece of material such as metal, plastic, rubber or glass ❷ a tube is also a long hollow container for something soft such as toothpaste ❸ the tube is the underground railway in London • *She goes to work by tube.*

tuber *NOUN* **tubers**
a thick rounded plant root or stem that produces buds

tubing *NOUN*
tubing is a length or piece of tube

tubular *ADJECTIVE*
shaped like a tube

tuck *VERB* **tucks, tucking, tucked**
to tuck something somewhere is to push a loose edge of it there so that it is tidy or hidden • *Now tuck in the flap of the envelope.* • *She tucked her hair under her cap.*

➤ **to tuck in** (*informal*) is to eat heartily

➤ **to tuck someone up** is to put the bedclothes snugly round them

tuck *NOUN* **tucks**
a tuck is a flat fold stitched in a piece of clothing

tuck shop *NOUN* **tuck shops**
a shop that sells snacks to children

Tuesday *NOUN* **Tuesdays**
the third day of the week
DID YOU KNOW? **Tuesday** is named after *Tiw*, the Anglo-Saxon god of war.

tuft *NOUN* **tufts**
a bunch of soft or fluffy things such as threads, grass, hair or feathers, held or growing together

tug *VERB* **tugs, tugging, tugged**
to tug something is to pull it hard

tug *NOUN* **tugs**
❶ a hard or sudden pull ❷ a small powerful boat used for towing ships

tug-of-war *NOUN* **tugs-of-war**
a contest between two teams pulling a rope from opposite ends

tulip *NOUN* **tulips**
a large bright cup-shaped flower that grows on a tall stem from a bulb

tumble *VERB* **tumbles, tumbling, tumbled**
❶ to tumble is to fall over or fall down clumsily ❷ to tumble to something is to suddenly realize it or be aware of it

tumble *NOUN* **tumbles**
a clumsy fall

tumble dryer *NOUN* **tumble dryers**
a machine that dries washing in a rotating drum with heated air passing through

tumbler *NOUN* **tumblers**
❶ a drinking glass with no stem or handle ❷ an acrobat

tummy *NOUN* **tummies** (*informal*)
your stomach

tumour (*say* tew-mer) *NOUN* **tumours**
an abnormal growth on or in someone's body

tumult (*say* tew-mult) *NOUN*
an uproar or state of great confusion

a
b
c
d
e
f
g
h
i
j
k
l
m
n
o
p
q
r
s
t
u
v
w
x
y
z

tumultuous *ADJECTIVE*
noisy and excited
The teams walked onto the pitch to tumultuous applause.—HARRY POTTER AND THE CHAMBER OF SECRETS, J. K. Rowling

tuna (*say* tew-na) *NOUN* **tuna** *or* **tunas**
a large sea fish, often used for food

tundra *NOUN*
tundra is a large area of flat land in cold regions (especially northern Canada and Siberia) with no trees and with soil that is frozen for most of the year

tune *NOUN* **tunes**
a short piece of music; a pleasant series of musical notes
➤ **to be in tune** is to be at the correct musical pitch

tune *VERB* **tunes, tuning, tuned**
❶ to tune a musical instrument is to adjust it to be in tune ❷ to tune a radio or television is to adjust it to receive a particular broadcasting station ❸ to tune an engine is to adjust it so that it works smoothly

tuneful *ADJECTIVE*
having a pleasant tune
➤ **tunefulness** *NOUN*

tunic (*say* tew-nik) *NOUN* **tunics**
❶ a jacket that is part of some uniforms ❷ a loose piece of clothing with no sleeves

tunnel *NOUN* **tunnels**
a passage made underground or through a hill

tunnel *VERB* **tunnels, tunnelling, tunnelled**
to tunnel is to make a tunnel

turban *NOUN* **turbans**
a covering for the head, made by wrapping a long strip of cloth round it, worn especially by Sikh, Hindu or Muslim men

turbine *NOUN* **turbines**
a machine or motor that is driven by a flow of water or gas or wind

turbulent *ADJECTIVE*
moving violently; heaving • *The seas in March can be turbulent.*
➤ **turbulence** *NOUN*

turf *NOUN* **turfs** *or* **turves**
❶ turf is short grass with the soil it is growing in ❷ a turf is a piece of grass and soil cut out of the ground

turkey *NOUN* **turkeys**
a large bird with a bald head kept on farms for its meat

Turkish delight *NOUN*
Turkish delight is a sweet consisting of lumps of flavoured jelly covered in powdered sugar.

turmeric *NOUN*
a bright yellow spice used in Asian cooking

turmoil *NOUN*
turmoil is a great disturbance or confusion

turn *VERB* **turns, turning, turned**
❶ to turn is to move round or move to a new direction; to turn something is to make it move in this way ❷ to turn (for example) pale is to change appearance and become pale ❸ to turn into something is to change into it • *The frog turned into a prince.* ❹ to turn something into something else is to change it • *You can turn milk into cheese.* ❺ to turn a device on or off is to use a switch to make it work or stop working ❻ to turn (for example) a radio or television up or down is to make it louder or quieter
➤ **to turn out** is to happen a certain way • *The weather's turned out fine.*
➤ **to turn something down** is to refuse it
➤ **to turn up** is to appear or arrive suddenly or unexpectedly

turn *NOUN* **turns**
❶ the action of turning; a turning movement • *Give the key three turns.*
❷ a place where a road bends; a junction • *Take the next turn on the left.* ❸ a task or duty that people do one after the other • *It's your turn to wash up.* ❹ a short performance in a show ❺ (*informal*) an attack of illness; a nervous shock • *It gave me a nasty turn.*
➤ **a good turn** is a favour you do for someone
➤ **in turn** first one and then the other; following one after another

turncoat *NOUN* turncoats
someone who changes sides or changes what they believe

turnip *NOUN* turnips
a plant with a large round white root used as a vegetable

turnstile *NOUN* turnstiles
a revolving gate that lets one person through at a time

turntable *NOUN* turntables
a revolving platform or support, especially the part of a record player that you put the record on

turpentine (*say* ter-pen-tyn) *NOUN*
turpentine is a kind of oil used to make paint thinner and to clean paintbrushes

turquoise (*say* ter-kwoiz) *NOUN*
❶ a sky-blue or green-blue colour ❷ a blue stone used to make jewellery

turret *NOUN* turrets
❶ a small tower in a castle ❷ a revolving structure containing a gun

turtle *NOUN* turtles
a sea animal that looks like a tortoise
➤ **to turn turtle** is to capsize

tusk *NOUN* tusks
one of a pair of long pointed teeth that stick out of the mouth of an elephant or walrus or boar

tussle *NOUN* tussles
a hard struggle or fight
tussle *VERB* tussles, tussling, tussled
to struggle or fight over something

tutor *NOUN* tutors
a teacher who teaches one person or a small group at a time

TV (*say* tee-vee) *NOUN* TVs
television, or a television set • *What's on TV tonight?* • *Who switched off the TV?*

twang *NOUN* twangs
the ringing sound made by a plucked string or cord • *the twang of a guitar*
twang *VERB* twangs, twanging, twanged
a string or cord twangs when it makes a ringing sound

tweak *VERB* tweaks, tweaking, tweaked
❶ to tweak something is to twist it or pull it sharply ❷ to tweak an engine or system is to make slight adjustments to it
tweak *NOUN* tweaks
a tweaking movement

tweed *NOUN*
tweed is a thick rough woollen cloth

tweet *NOUN* tweets
❶ a tweet is the high-pitched sound made by a young bird ❷ a tweet is also a message posted on the social network X
tweet *VERB* tweet, tweeting, tweeted
❶ a young bird tweets when it makes a high-pitched sound ❷ to tweet is to post a message on the social network X

tweezers *PLURAL NOUN*
a small tool for gripping or picking up small things like stamps and hairs

twelve *NOUN* twelves
the number 12
➤ **twelfth** *ADJECTIVE, NOUN*

twenty *NOUN* twenties
the number 20
➤ **twentieth** *ADJECTIVE, NOUN*

twice *ADVERB*
❶ two times; on two occasions ❷ double the amount

twiddle *VERB* twiddles, twiddling, twiddled
to twiddle something is to turn it round or over and over in an idle way • *He was twiddling a knob on the radio.*
twiddle *NOUN* twiddles
a twiddling movement

twig *NOUN* twigs
a short thin branch or shoot
twig *VERB* twigs, twigging, twigged (*informal*)
to twig something is to realize what it means • *I suddenly twigged what she was talking about.*

twilight *NOUN*
twilight is the time of dim light just after sunset

a
b
c
d
e
f
g
h
i
j
k
l
m
n
o
p
q
r
s
t
u
v
w
x
y
z

A
B
C
D
E
F
G
H
I
J
K
L
M
N
O
P
Q
R
S
T
U
V
W
X
Y
Z

twin *NOUN* **twins**
❶ each of two children or animals born at the same time from one mother ❷ each of two things that are exactly alike

twin *VERB* **twins**, **twinning**, **twinned**
one city or town is twinned with one in another country when they have an arrangement involving exchange visits and other cultural events that they do together

twine *NOUN*
twine is strong thin string

twinge *NOUN* **twinges**
a sudden pain or unpleasant feeling

twinkle *VERB* **twinkles**, **twinkling**, **twinkled**
to sparkle or shine with flashes of bright light

twinkle *NOUN* **twinkles**
a twinkling light

twirl *VERB* **twirls**, **twirling**, **twirled**
to twirl is to turn round and round quickly; to twirl something is to make it do this
• *Inspector Cox kept twirling the ends of his moustache.*

twirl *NOUN* **twirls**
a twirling movement

twist *VERB* **twists**, **twisting**, **twisted**
❶ to twist something is to turn its ends in opposite directions ❷ to twist is to turn round or from side to side • *The road twisted through the hills.* ❸ to twist something is to bend it out of its proper shape • *The front wheel of your bike is twisted.* • *I think I've twisted my ankle.*

twist *NOUN* **twists**
a twisting movement or action

twitch *VERB* **twitches**, **twitching**, **twitched**
to twitch is to jerk or move suddenly and quickly; to twitch something is to make it do this

twitch *NOUN* **twitches**
a twitching movement

twitter *VERB* **twitters**, **twittering**, **twittered**
birds twitter when they make quick chirping sounds

two *NOUN* **twos**
the number 2

two-dimensional, **2-D** *ADJECTIVE*
having two dimensions: length and width; flat

two-faced *ADJECTIVE*
dishonest or deceitful

tying *VERB* (*present participle of* **tie**)
• *Tom is tying his shoelaces.*

type *NOUN* **types**
❶ a type is a group or class of similar people or things • *T-rex is a type of dinosaur.* • *a new type of breakfast cereal* ❷ type is letters and figures designed for use in printing

type *VERB* **types**, **typing**, **typed**
to type something is to write it using the keys on a keyboard or touchscreen

typhoon *NOUN* **typhoons**
a violent windy storm

typical *ADJECTIVE*
❶ having the usual qualities or features of a particular type of person or thing • *They live in a typical suburban house.* ❷ as you would expect from a particular person or thing
• *That's just typical of my luck!*
➤ **typically** *ADVERB*

typist *NOUN* **typists**
a person who types, especially as their job

tyrannosaurus rex *NOUN*
a large meat-eating dinosaur with powerful jaws and small claw-like front legs

tyranny (*say* **ti**-ra-nee) *NOUN* **tyrannies**
tyranny is a cruel or unjust way of ruling people
➤ **tyrannical** *ADJECTIVE*

tyrant (*say* **ty**-rant) *NOUN* **tyrants**
someone who rules people cruelly or unjustly

tyre *NOUN* **tyres**
a covering of rubber fitted round the rim of a wheel to make it grip the road and run smoothly

Uu

udder *NOUN* **udders**
the bag-like part of a cow, goat or ewe, from which milk is taken

UFO *NOUN* **UFOs**
short for *unidentified flying object*, for example an unknown spacecraft

ugly *ADJECTIVE* **uglier, ugliest**
❶ not beautiful; unpleasant to look at
Nine fearsome, ugly, half-naked, fifty-feet-long brutes lay sprawled over the ground in various grotesque attitudes of sleep.—THE BFG, Roald Dahl
❷ threatening or dangerous • *The crowd was in an ugly mood.*
➤ **ugliness** *NOUN*
DID YOU KNOW? The word **ugly** comes from an Old Norse (Viking) word meaning 'to dread'.

ukulele (*say* yoo-ku-**lay**-lee) *NOUN*
ukuleles
a small four-stringed guitar, originally from Hawaii
DID YOU KNOW? The word **ukulele** comes from a Hawaiian word meaning 'jumping flea'.

ulcer *NOUN* **ulcers**
a sore on the inside or outside of your body

ultimate *ADJECTIVE*
furthest in a series of things; final
➤ **ultimately** *ADVERB* finally or eventually

ultra– *PREFIX*
meaning 'beyond', as in *ultraviolet*

ultraviolet *ADJECTIVE*
ultraviolet light is light beyond the violet end of the spectrum, that causes your skin to tan

umbrella *NOUN* **umbrellas**
a mushroom-shaped piece of cloth stretched over a folding frame, which you open to protect yourself from rain
DID YOU KNOW? The word **umbrella** comes from an Italian word meaning 'a little shade'.

umpire *NOUN* **umpires**
someone who makes sure that people keep to the rules in cricket, tennis and some other games

un– *PREFIX*
meaning 'not', as in *uncommon*, or added to verbs to make the action of the verb opposite to normal, as in *undo*

unable *ADJECTIVE*
not able • *She was unable to hear.*

unaided *ADJECTIVE*
without any help

unanimous (*say* yoo-**nan**-i-mus) *ADJECTIVE*
a unanimous decision or vote is one where everyone agrees
➤ **unanimously** *ADVERB*

unarmed *ADJECTIVE*
without weapons • *unarmed combat*

unattractive *ADJECTIVE*
not attractive; ugly
➤ **unattractiveness** *NOUN*

unavoidable *ADJECTIVE*
not able to be avoided; bound to happen
➤ **unavoidably** *ADVERB*

unaware *ADJECTIVE*
not knowing about something • *The guests were completely unaware of the danger.*

unawares *ADVERB*
unexpectedly; without someone knowing • *His question caught me unawares.*

unbearable *ADJECTIVE*
something is unbearable when it is so painful or unpleasant that you cannot bear or endure it
➤ **unbearably** *ADVERB*

unbelievable *ADJECTIVE*
❶ difficult to believe ❷ amazing
➤ **unbelievably** *ADVERB*

unborn *ADJECTIVE*
not yet born

uncalled for *ADJECTIVE*
not justified or necessary • *Your rudeness is uncalled for.*

a b c d e f g h i j k l m n o p q r s t u v w x y z

uncanny *ADJECTIVE*
strange and mysterious • *There was an uncanny silence.*
➤ **uncannily** *ADVERB*

uncertain *ADJECTIVE*
❶ not certain • *He is uncertain about what to do.* ❷ not reliable • *The weather is uncertain at the moment.*
➤ **uncertainly** *ADVERB* ➤ **uncertainty** *NOUN*

uncle *NOUN* **uncles**
❶ the brother of your father or mother
❷ the husband or male partner of your aunt or uncle

unclean *ADJECTIVE*
not clean; dirty

unclear *ADJECTIVE*
not clear; not easy to see or understand
➤ **unclearly** *ADVERB*

uncomfortable *ADJECTIVE*
not comfortable
➤ **uncomfortably** *ADVERB*

uncommon *ADJECTIVE*
not common; unusual

unconscious *ADJECTIVE*
❶ not awake or knowing what is happening around you because you have fainted or been knocked out ❷ not aware of something • *I was still unconscious of the danger.*
➤ **unconsciously** *ADVERB*
➤ **unconsciousness** *NOUN*

uncontrollable *ADJECTIVE*
unable to be controlled
➤ **uncontrollably** *ADVERB*

uncountable *ADJECTIVE*
unable to be counted; too many to count

uncouth (*say* un-kooth) *ADJECTIVE*
rude and rough in manner

uncover *VERB* **uncovers, uncovering, uncovered**
❶ to uncover something is to take the cover or top off it ❷ to uncover a secret or something unknown is to discover it

undecided *ADJECTIVE*
you are undecided about something when you have not made up your mind about it

undeniable *ADJECTIVE*
impossible to deny; certainly true
➤ **undeniably** *ADVERB*

under *PREPOSITION*
❶ lower than; below • *the cupboard under the stairs* ❷ less than • *You have to be under 13 to take part.* ❸ ruled or controlled by • *The islands were once under Viking rule.* ❹ in the process of; undergoing • *The road is under repair.* ❺ using; moving by means of • *The robot moves under its own power.*

under *ADVERB*
in or to a lower place • *Slowly the submarine went under.*

underarm *ADJECTIVE, ADVERB*
with the arm kept below shoulder level and moving forward and upwards

undercarriage *NOUN* **undercarriages**
an aircraft's undercarriage is its landing wheels and the parts that support them

underclothes *PLURAL NOUN*
underwear

undercooked *ADJECTIVE*
food is undercooked when it has not been cooked for long enough

underdog *NOUN* **underdogs**
the person or team in a contest that is expected to lose

underdone *ADJECTIVE*
not properly done or cooked

underfoot *ADVERB*
❶ on the ground where you are walking • *It was slippery underfoot.* ❷ under someone's feet • *People were trampled underfoot in the panic.*

undergo *VERB* **undergoes, undergoing, underwent, undergone**
to undergo something is to experience it or go through it • *The city has undergone many changes over the years.*

underground *ADJECTIVE, ADVERB*
❶ under the ground ❷ done or working in secret

underground *NOUN* **undergrounds**
a railway that runs through tunnels under the ground

undergrowth *NOUN*
undergrowth is bushes and other plants growing closely under tall trees

underhand *ADJECTIVE*
secret and deceitful

underlie *VERB* **underlies, underlying, underlay, underlain**
to underlie something is to be the cause or basis of it • *Hard work underlies the team's success this season.*

underline *VERB* **underlines, underlining, underlined**
❶ to underline something you have written is to draw a line under it ❷ to underline a fact is to emphasize it or show it clearly • *This accident underlines the need to be careful.*

undermine *VERB* **undermines, undermining, undermined**
❶ to undermine someone's efforts or plans is to weaken them gradually ❷ to undermine something is to make a hollow or tunnel beneath it

underneath *PREPOSITION, ADVERB*
below or beneath

underpants *PLURAL NOUN*
a piece of men's underwear

underpass *NOUN* **underpasses**
a place where one road or path goes under another

understand *VERB* **understands, understanding, understood**
❶ to understand something is to know what it means or how it works ❷ to understand something is also to have heard about it • *I understand you've not been well.* ❸ to understand someone is to know what they are like and why they behave the way they do

understandable *ADJECTIVE*
❶ able to be understood ❷ reasonable or normal • *It is understandable to feel that way.*
➤ **understandably** *ADVERB*

understanding *NOUN*
❶ understanding is the power to understand or think; intelligence ❷ an understanding is when people have an agreement ❸ understanding is also sympathy or tolerance

understanding *ADJECTIVE*
sympathetic and helpful • *He was very understanding when I was ill.*

understudy *NOUN* **understudies**
an actor who learns a part in a play so that they can play the part if the usual actor isn't able to perform

undertake *VERB* **undertakes, undertaking, undertook, undertaken**
to undertake something is to agree or promise to do it

undertaker *NOUN* **undertakers**
someone whose job is to arrange funerals

undertaking *NOUN* **undertakings**
something that someone agrees to do

underwater *ADJECTIVE*
placed or used or done below the surface of water

underwear *NOUN*
underwear is clothes you wear next to your skin, under other clothes

underworld *NOUN*
❶ in mythology, the underworld is the place for the spirits of the dead • *Cerberus, a monstrous three-headed dog, guarded the entrance to the underworld.* ❷ the underworld is also people who are regularly involved in crime

undesirable *ADJECTIVE*
not wanted or liked

undeveloped *ADJECTIVE*
not yet developed

undo *VERB* **undoes, undoing, undid, undone**
❶ to undo something is to unfasten or unwrap it • *Can you undo this knot?* ❷ to undo something already done is to cancel the effect of it • *He has undone all our careful work.* ❸ when you undo a change you have made on a computer, you change it back

undoubted *ADJECTIVE*
definite or certain
➤ **undoubtedly** *ADVERB*

undress *VERB* **undresses, undressing, undressed**
❶ to undress is to take your clothes off
❷ to undress someone is to take their clothes off

unearth *VERB* **unearths, unearthing, unearthed**
❶ to unearth something is to dig it up
❷ to unearth something is also to find it after searching for it

unearthly *ADJECTIVE*
supernatural; strange and frightening

uneasy *ADJECTIVE* **uneasier, uneasiest**
anxious or worried • *I had the uneasy feeling that someone was watching.* • *The silence made us all uneasy.*
➤ **uneasily** *ADVERB* ➤ **uneasiness** *NOUN*

unemployed *ADJECTIVE*
to be unemployed is to be without a job
➤ **unemployment** *NOUN*

uneven *ADJECTIVE*
❶ not level, flat or regular • *The path was uneven.* ❷ not of the same quality throughout • *It was an uneven performance.*
➤ **unevenly** *ADVERB* ➤ **unevenness** *NOUN*

unexpected *ADJECTIVE*
not expected; surprising
➤ **unexpectedly** *ADVERB*

unfair *ADJECTIVE*
not fair; unjust
➤ **unfairly** *ADVERB* ➤ **unfairness** *NOUN*

unfaithful *ADJECTIVE*
not faithful or loyal
➤ **unfaithfully** *ADVERB*
➤ **unfaithfulness** *NOUN*

unfamiliar *ADJECTIVE*
not familiar

unfasten *VERB* **unfastens, unfastening, unfastened**
to unfasten something is to open it when it has been fastened

unfavourable *ADJECTIVE*
not favourable or helpful
➤ **unfavourably** *ADVERB*

unfinished *ADJECTIVE*
not finished

unfit *ADJECTIVE*
❶ someone is unfit when they are not fit or fully healthy ❷ to be unfit for something is to be not suitable • *The path was unfit for walking without boots.*

unfold *VERB* **unfolds, unfolding, unfolded**
❶ to unfold something is to open it or spread it out • *Carefully, she unfolded the letter.*
❷ to unfold a story or plan is to make it known gradually ❸ a story unfolds when it becomes known gradually

unforeseen *ADJECTIVE*
something unforeseen happens without being expected
Bill scratched his head. 'This is an unforeseen predicament,' he said.—THE MAGIC PUDDING, Norman Lindsay

unforgettable *ADJECTIVE*
impossible to forget

unforgivable *ADJECTIVE*
not able to be forgiven

unfortunate *ADJECTIVE*
❶ unlucky ❷ you say something is unfortunate when you wish it hadn't happened • *It was a very unfortunate thing to say.*

unfortunately *ADVERB*
you say unfortunately when you are sad about something • *Unfortunately, I have to leave early.*

unfriendly *ADJECTIVE*
not friendly
➤ **unfriendliness** *NOUN*

ungrateful *ADJECTIVE*
not grateful
➤ **ungratefully** *ADVERB*

unhappy *ADJECTIVE* **unhappier, unhappiest**
❶ not happy or pleased ❷ you say something is unhappy when you wish it hadn't happened; regrettable • *It was an unhappy choice of words.*
➤ **unhappily** *ADVERB* ➤ **unhappiness** *NOUN*

unharmed *ADJECTIVE*
not injured or harmed • *The animals escaped the fire unharmed.*

unhealthy ADJECTIVE **unhealthier, unhealthiest**
❶ not in good health ❷ not good for you
• *an unhealthy diet of fast food*
➤ **unhealthily** ADVERB
➤ **unhealthiness** NOUN

unheard-of ADJECTIVE
never known or done before; extraordinary

unhelpful ADJECTIVE
not giving any help • *The instructions were unhelpful.*
➤ **unhelpfully** ADVERB

unicorn (*say* yoo-ni-korn) NOUN **unicorns**
an imaginary animal in stories, like a horse with a long straight horn growing out of the front of its head

uniform NOUN **uniforms**
the special clothes worn by members of an army or school or organization
uniform ADJECTIVE
always the same; not changing

uniformed ADJECTIVE
wearing a uniform

unify VERB **unifies, unifying, unified**
❶ to unify groups or countries is to bring them together to create a single group or country ❷ to unify is to join together into one whole

unimportant ADJECTIVE
not important
➤ **unimportance** NOUN

uninhabited ADJECTIVE
a place is uninhabited when there is nobody living there

unintentional ADJECTIVE
not done deliberately
➤ **unintentionally** ADVERB

uninterested ADJECTIVE
not interested

uninteresting ADJECTIVE
not interesting

union NOUN **unions**
❶ the joining of things together; a united thing ❷ a trade union

Union Jack NOUN **Union Jacks**
the flag of the United Kingdom

unique (*say* yoo-**neek**) ADJECTIVE
something is unique when it is the only one of its kind • *Everyone's fingerprints are unique.* • *This jewel is unique.*
➤ **uniquely** ADVERB ➤ **uniqueness** NOUN

unisex ADJECTIVE
designed to be suitable for everyone, not specifically men or women

unison (*say* yoo-ni-son) NOUN
➤ **in unison** said or done by people together at the same time

unit NOUN **units**
❶ an amount used in measuring or counting, such as a centimetre or a pound ❷ a single person or thing ❸ a group of people or things that belong together

unite VERB **unites, uniting, united**
❶ to unite several people or things is to form them into one thing or group ❷ people or things unite when they join together

unity NOUN **unities**
❶ unity is being united or having agreement ❷ a unity is a complete thing

universal ADJECTIVE
including everyone and everything
➤ **universally** ADVERB to be universally accepted is to be accepted by everyone

universe NOUN
the universe is everything that exists, including the earth and living things and all the stars and planets

university NOUN **universities**
a place where people go to study for degrees after they have left school

unjust ADJECTIVE
not fair or just
➤ **unjustly** ADVERB

unkempt ADJECTIVE
untidy or dishevelled • *a troll with shaggy unkempt, hair*

unkind ADJECTIVE **unkinder, unkindest**
cruel and not kind
➤ **unkindly** ADVERB ➤ **unkindness** NOUN

a
b
c
d
e
f
g
h
i
j
k
l
m
n
o
p
q
r
s
t
u
v
w
x
y
z

unknown *ADJECTIVE*
not known

unleaded *ADJECTIVE*
unleaded petrol does not contain lead

unless *CONJUNCTION*
except when; if not • *We cannot go unless we are invited.*

unlike *PREPOSITION*
not like • *Unlike me, she enjoys sport.*

unlike *ADJECTIVE*
not alike; different • *The two children are very unlike.*

unlikely *ADJECTIVE* **unlikelier, unlikeliest**
not likely to happen or be true

unload *VERB* **unloads, unloading, unloaded**
to unload a container or vehicle is to take off the things it carried

unlock *VERB* **unlocks, unlocking, unlocked**
to unlock a door or container is to open it with a key

unlucky *ADJECTIVE* **unluckier, unluckiest**
not lucky
➤ **unluckily** *ADVERB* as the result of bad luck

unmarried *ADJECTIVE*
not married; single

unmistakable *ADJECTIVE*
not likely to be mistaken for something or someone else; clear and definite
➤ **unmistakably** *ADVERB*

unnatural *ADJECTIVE*
not natural or normal
➤ **unnaturally** *ADVERB*

unnecessary *ADJECTIVE*
not needed
➤ **unnecessarily** *ADVERB*

unoccupied *ADJECTIVE*
a house is unoccupied when it is empty, with no one living there

unpack *VERB* **unpacks, unpacking, unpacked**
to unpack a suitcase or bag is to take out the things in it

unpleasant *ADJECTIVE*
not pleasant
➤ **unpleasantly** *ADVERB*
➤ **unpleasantness** *NOUN*

unplug *VERB* **unplugs, unplugging, unplugged**
❶ to unplug an electrical device is to disconnect it by taking its plug out of the socket ❷ (*informal*) to unplug is to stop using your smartphone or computer, or using social media, for a while

unpopular *ADJECTIVE*
not liked or enjoyed by people
➤ **unpopularity** *NOUN*

unravel *VERB* **unravels, unravelling, unravelled**
❶ to unravel something is to unwind it or take the knots from it ❷ to unravel a problem or mystery is to investigate it and solve it

unreal *ADJECTIVE*
not real; existing only in the imagination

unreasonable *ADJECTIVE*
not reasonable or fair

unrest *NOUN*
unrest is a discontented feeling among a group of people, or the trouble caused by it

unroll *VERB* **unrolls, unrolling, unrolled**
to unroll something is to open it when it has been rolled up

unruly (*say* un-**roo**-lee) *ADJECTIVE*
badly behaved and difficult to control
➤ **unruliness** *NOUN*

unsafe *ADJECTIVE*
not safe; dangerous

unsatisfactory *ADJECTIVE*
not satisfactory; unacceptable • *The repair work was unsatisfactory.*
➤ **unsatisfactorily** *ADVERB*

unscrew *VERB* **unscrews, unscrewing, unscrewed**
to unscrew something is to undo it by turning it or by removing screws

unseemly *ADJECTIVE*
not proper or suitable; indecent

unseen to unworthy

unseen *ADJECTIVE*
not seen or noticed • *He managed to slip out of the room unseen.*

unselfish *ADJECTIVE*
not selfish; not thinking only about yourself
➤ **unselfishly** *ADVERB*
➤ **unselfishness** *NOUN*

unsightly *ADJECTIVE*
not pleasant to look at; ugly
➤ **unsightliness**

unsteady *ADJECTIVE* **unsteadier, unsteadiest**
shaking or wobbling or likely to fall
➤ **unsteadily** *ADVERB*
➤ **unsteadiness** *NOUN*

unsuccessful *ADJECTIVE*
not successful
➤ **unsuccessfully** *ADVERB*

unsuitable *ADJECTIVE*
not suitable
➤ **unsuitably** *ADVERB*

unsure *ADJECTIVE*
not sure; uncertain • *I was unsure of what to say.*

unthinkable *ADJECTIVE*
too bad or unlikely to be worth thinking about

untidy *ADJECTIVE* **untidier, untidiest**
messy and not tidy
➤ **untidily** *ADVERB* ➤ **untidiness** *NOUN*

untie *VERB* **unties, untying, untied**
to untie something is to undo it when it has been tied

until *PREPOSITION, CONJUNCTION*
up to a particular time or event • *The shop is open until 8 o'clock.* • *We'll stay until your bus arrives.*

untimely *ADJECTIVE*
happening too soon or at an unsuitable time
➤ **untimeliness** *NOUN*

unto *PREPOSITION* (*old use*)
to

untold *ADJECTIVE*
too great to be counted or measured • *The hurricane caused untold damage.*

untoward *ADJECTIVE*
inconvenient or unfortunate • *I hope nothing untoward happens.*

untrue *ADJECTIVE*
not true

untrustworthy *ADJECTIVE*
not able to be trusted; unreliable
➤ **untrustworthiness** *NOUN*

untruthful *ADJECTIVE*
not telling the truth
➤ **untruthfully** *ADVERB*

unused (*say* un-**yoozd**) *ADJECTIVE*
not yet used
➤ **unused to something** (*say* un-**yoost**) not familiar with something • *The creature was unused to daylight.*

unusual *ADJECTIVE*
different from what is usual or normal; strange or rare
The crew was unusual in that it consisted of a mixture of sailors and rats, working as equal partners together.—HERE BE MONSTERS, Alan Snow
➤ **unusually** *ADVERB*

unwanted *ADJECTIVE*
not wanted

unwell *ADJECTIVE*
not well; ill

unwilling *ADJECTIVE*
you are unwilling to do something when you don't want to do it
➤ **unwillingly** *ADVERB* ➤ **unwillingness** *NOUN*

unwind (*rhymes with* **find**) *VERB* **unwinds, unwinding, unwound**
❶ to unwind something is to unroll it
❷ to unwind is to become unrolled
❸ (*informal*) to unwind is also to relax after you have been working hard

unwise *ADJECTIVE*
foolish • *It would be unwise to go alone.*

unworthy *ADJECTIVE* **unworthier, unworthiest**
not deserving something; not good enough for something
➤ **unworthiness** *NOUN*

a b c d e f g h i j k l m n o p q r s t u v w x y z

unwrap VERB unwraps, unwrapping, unwrapped
to unwrap something is to take it out of its wrapping

unzip VERB unzips, unzipping, unzipped
to unzip something is to undo it when it is zipped up

up ADVERB
❶ in or to a standing or upright position • *You can stand up now.* ❷ in or to a high or higher place or level • *Lift the lid up slowly.* • *Can you turn the volume up?* ❸ completely • *They've used up all the milk.* ❹ out of bed • *It's time to get up.* ❺ finished • *Your time is up.* ❻ (informal) happening • *Something is up.*
➤ **ups and downs** changes of luck, sometimes good and sometimes bad
➤ **to be up to something** is to be doing something mysterious or suspicious • *What are they up to?*
➤ **up to date** ❶ modern or fashionable ❷ having the latest information • *Keep me up to date with what happens.*

up PREPOSITION
in or to a higher position on something • *We raced up the stairs excitedly.*

upbringing NOUN upbringings
your upbringing is the way you have been brought up

update VERB updates, updating, updated
to update something is to bring it up to date

update NOUN updates
❶ the version of something that has the most recent information • *We were waiting for a news update.* ❷ the most recent improvement to a computer program

upgrade VERB upgrades, upgrading, upgraded
to upgrade a machine is to improve it by installing new parts in it

upheaval NOUN upheavals
a sudden violent change or disturbance

uphill ADJECTIVE, ADVERB
❶ sloping upwards; going up a slope • *The path led us uphill.* ❷ difficult • *They faced an uphill struggle.*

uphold VERB upholds, upholding, upheld
to uphold a decision or belief is to support it or agree with it

upholstery NOUN
upholstery is covers and padding for furniture

upkeep NOUN
the upkeep of something is the cost of looking after it and keeping it in good condition

uplands PLURAL NOUN
the highest part of a country or region

upload VERB uploads, uploading, uploaded
to upload data is to transfer it from a local computer or phone to the internet

upon PREPOSITION
on

upper ADJECTIVE
higher in position or rank

upper case NOUN
upper case is capital letters

upper class NOUN upper classes
the highest class in society, especially the aristocracy
➤ **upper-class** ADJECTIVE

upright ADJECTIVE
❶ standing straight up; vertical ❷ honest
upright NOUN uprights
an upright post or support

uprising NOUN uprisings
a rebellion or revolt against the government

uproar NOUN
uproar is a loud or angry noise or disturbance • *The room was in uproar.*

upset (say up-set) ADJECTIVE
unhappy or anxious about something
upset (say up-set) VERB upsets, upsetting, upset
❶ to upset someone is to make them unhappy or anxious ❷ to upset something is to knock it over and spill its contents
upset (say up-set) NOUN upsets
❶ a slight illness • *He's got a stomach upset.* ❷ an unexpected result or setback

• *Losing the game on Saturday was a real upset.*

upshot *NOUN*
what happens in the end • *The upshot was that we had to stay behind.*

upside down *ADJECTIVE, ADVERB*
❶ with the upper part underneath instead of on top; the wrong way up
'We're UPSIDE DOWN!' gasped Mr Twit. 'We must be upside down. We are standing on the ceiling looking down at the floor!'—THE TWITS, Roald Dahl
❷ in disorder or confusion • *Their lives had been turned upside down.*

upstairs *ADVERB, ADJECTIVE*
to or on a higher floor in a house or other building

upstart *NOUN* upstarts
someone who quickly reaches a position of power and behaves in an arrogant way

upstream *ADJECTIVE, ADVERB*
in the direction opposite to the flow of a river or stream

uptake *NOUN*
➤ **to be quick on the uptake** is to be quick to understand
➤ **to be slow on the uptake** is to be slow to understand

uptight *ADJECTIVE* (*informal*)
upset or nervous about something

up-to-date *ADJECTIVE*
❶ modern or fashionable ❷ having the latest information • *The website gives up-to-date advice.*
SPELLING ALERT! Note that you spell **up-to-date** without hyphens when it comes after a noun: *Is this information up to date?*

upward *ADJECTIVE, ADVERB*
going towards what is higher
➤ **upwards** *ADVERB*

Uranus *NOUN*
the seventh planet from the sun in our solar system
DID YOU KNOW? The planet **Uranus** is named after the Greek god of the sky.

urban *ADJECTIVE*
to do with a town or city

urchin *NOUN* urchins
a young child who looks poorly dressed and not cared for

Urdu *NOUN*
a language spoken in northern India and Pakistan
DID YOU KNOW? The words **khaki** and **pyjamas** come from Urdu.

urge *VERB* urges, urging, urged
❶ to urge someone to do something is to try to persuade them to do it ❷ to urge people or animals is to drive them forward

urge *NOUN* urges
a sudden strong desire or wish • *an uncontrollable urge to giggle*

urgent *ADJECTIVE*
needing to be done or dealt with immediately
➤ **urgency** *NOUN* ➤ **urgently** *ADVERB*

urinate *VERB* urinates, urinating, urinated
to pass urine

urine (*say* yoor-in) *NOUN*
urine is the waste liquid that collects in your bladder and is passed out of your body

urn *NOUN* urns
❶ a large metal container with a tap, in which water is heated ❷ a kind of large vase for holding the ashes of a person who has been cremated

US, USA *ABBREVIATION*
short for *United States (of America)*

us *PRONOUN*
a word used for *we*, usually when it is the object of a sentence, or when it comes after a preposition • *I think they saw us.* • *They are waving to us.*

usable *ADJECTIVE*
able to be used • *Is this password still usable?*

usage (*say* yoo-sij) *NOUN* usages
the way that something is used, especially the way that words and language are used

USB *NOUN*
short for *universal serial bus*, a method for connecting external devices, such as cameras or mobile phones, to a computer

USB stick *NOUN* **USB sticks**
a type of memory stick that uses a USB connection

use (*say* yooz) *VERB* **uses**, **using**, **used**
to use something is to perform an action or job with it • *Are you using my pen?*
➤ **used to** did in the past • *We used to live in Belfast.*
➤ **to be** *or* **get used to something** is to be or become familiar with it through routine • *I'm used to getting up early.*
➤ **to use something up** is to use all of it, so that none is left

use (*say* yooss) *NOUN* **uses**
❶ the action of using something or being used ❷ the purpose or value of something • *Can you find a use for this box?* • *This money is no use to us.*

used (*say* yoozd) *ADJECTIVE*
not new; second-hand • *They sell used bicycles and scooters.*

useful *ADJECTIVE*
able to be used a lot, or able to do something that needs to be done • *Dictionaries are useful for checking the meaning of words.*
➤ **usefully** *ADVERB* ➤ **usefulness** *NOUN*

useless *ADJECTIVE*
❶ not having any use ❷ (*informal*) not very good at something • *I'm useless at drawing.*
➤ **uselessly** *ADVERB* ➤ **uselessness** *NOUN*

user *NOUN* **users**
someone who uses something

user-friendly *ADJECTIVE*
designed to be easy to use • *The dictionary app is very user-friendly.*

usher *NOUN* **ushers**
someone who shows people to their seats in a cinema or theatre

usher *VERB* **ushers**, **ushering**, **ushered**
to usher someone is to lead them in or out of a place • *We were ushered into the back of the room.*

usherette *NOUN* **usherettes**
a woman who shows people to their seats in a cinema or theatre

usual *ADJECTIVE*
as happens often or all the time; expected • *He sat in his usual chair by the fire.* • *She was late as usual.*

usually *ADVERB*
something usually happens when it happens on most occasions or normally

usurp (*say* yoo-zerp) *VERB* **usurps**, **usurping**, **usurped**
to usurp power or a position is to take it by force from someone else

utensil (*say* yoo-ten-sil) *NOUN* **utensils**
a tool or device, especially one you use in the house

utilize (*also* **utilise**) *VERB* **utilizes**, **utilizing**, **utilized**
to utilize something is to make use of it

utmost *ADJECTIVE*
greatest • *Guard this letter with the utmost care.*

utter *VERB* **utters**, **uttering**, **uttered**
to utter something is to say it clearly, or to make a sound with your mouth • *Carefully, she uttered the words of the magic spell.*

utter *ADJECTIVE*
complete or absolute
Sheltered under a clump of Scots pine, the beasts gazed up at the moonlit sky in a state of utter contentment.—PURE DEAD WICKED, Debi Gliori

utterance *NOUN* **utterances**
an utterance is something that someone says

utterly *ADVERB*
completely or thoroughly • *The whole day was utterly ruined!*

U-turn *NOUN* **U-turns**
❶ a turn a vehicle makes when it is driven round in one movement to face the opposite direction ❷ a complete change of ideas or opinions

vacancy *NOUN* **vacancies**
a job, or a room in a guest house, that is available and not taken

vacant *ADJECTIVE*
❶ empty; not filled or occupied • *There were no vacant seats.* ❷ not showing any expression • *He gave a vacant stare.*
➤ **vacantly** *ADVERB*

vacate *VERB* **vacates, vacating, vacated**
to vacate a place is to leave it empty

vacation (*say* vay-**kay**-shon) *NOUN* **vacations**
a holiday, especially between the terms at a university

vaccinate (*say* **vak**-si-nayt) *VERB* **vaccinates, vaccinating, vaccinated**
to vaccinate someone is to protect them from an illness by injecting them with a vaccine
➤ **vaccination** *NOUN*

vaccine (*say* **vak**-seen) *NOUN* **vaccines**
a type of medicine injected into people to protect them from illness
DID YOU KNOW? The word **vaccine** comes from the Latin word *vacca* meaning 'cow', because the first vaccine was taken from cows.

vacuum *NOUN* **vacuums**
a completely empty space; a space without any air in it

vacuum *VERB* **vacuums, vacuuming, vacuumed**
to clean something using a vacuum cleaner

vacuum cleaner *NOUN* **vacuum cleaners**
an electrical device that sucks up dust and dirt from the floor

vacuum flask *NOUN* **vacuum flasks**
a container with double walls that have a vacuum between them, for keeping liquids hot or cold

vagina (*say* va-**jy**-na) *NOUN* **vaginas**
the passage in a woman's body that leads from the outside of her body to her womb

vague *ADJECTIVE* **vaguer, vaguest**
not definite or clear • *I only have a vague memory of his face.*
➤ **vaguely** *ADVERB* ➤ **vagueness** *NOUN*

vain *ADJECTIVE* **vainer, vainest**
❶ too proud of yourself, especially of how you look ❷ unsuccessful or useless • *They made vain attempts to save him.*
➤ **in vain** with no result; without success • *I tried in vain to call for help.*
➤ **vainly** *ADVERB*

valentine *NOUN* **valentines**
❶ a card sent on St Valentine's Day (14 February) to someone you love ❷ the person you send a valentine to

valiant *ADJECTIVE*
brave or courageous
➤ **valiantly** *ADVERB*

valid *ADJECTIVE*
able to be used or accepted; legal • *Your passport is not valid.*
➤ **validity** *NOUN*

valley *NOUN* **valleys**
an area of low land between hills

valour *NOUN*
valour is bravery, especially in a battle

valuable *ADJECTIVE*
❶ worth a lot of money ❷ very useful or important • *She gave me valuable advice.*

valuables *PLURAL NOUN*
things that are worth a lot of money

value *NOUN* **values**
❶ the amount of money that something could be sold for ❷ how useful or important something is

value *VERB* **values, valuing, valued**
❶ to value something is to think that it is important or worth having • *I value her friendship.* ❷ to value something is also to work out how much it could be sold for

valueless *ADJECTIVE*
having no value

a
b
c
d
e
f
g
h
i
j
k
l
m
n
o
p
q
r
s
t
u
v
w
x
y
z

valve *NOUN* **valves**
a device used to control the flow of gas or liquid

vampire *NOUN* **vampires**
in stories, a creature that sucks people's blood

van *NOUN* **vans**
❶ a small lorry with a covered area for goods at the back ❷ a railway carriage used for goods or for the train's guard

vandal *NOUN* **vandals**
someone who deliberately breaks or damages things, especially buildings
➤ **vandalism** *NOUN*
DID YOU KNOW? The word **vandal** is based on the *Vandals*, a Germanic people who invaded the Roman Empire in the 5th century.

vane *NOUN* **vanes**
❶ a pointer that shows which way the wind is blowing ❷ the blade or surface of a propeller, sail of a windmill or other device that moves through air or water

vanilla *NOUN*
vanilla is a flavouring made from the pods of a tropical plant

vanish *VERB* **vanishes, vanishing, vanished**
to disappear completely • *The magician vanished in a puff of smoke.*

vanity *NOUN*
vanity is being too proud of yourself, especially of how you look

vanquish *VERB* **vanquishes, vanquishing, vanquished**
to vanquish someone is to win a victory over them

vaporize (*also* **vaporise**) *VERB* **vaporizes, vaporizing, vaporized**
to turn into vapour

vapour *NOUN* **vapours**
a visible gas, such as mist or steam, which some liquids and solids can be turned into by heat

variable *ADJECTIVE*
able or likely to change

variable *NOUN* **variables**
a variable is something that varies or can vary

variation *NOUN* **variations**
❶ a variation in something is a change in it • *There have been slight variations in temperature.* ❷ variation is the process of changing something ❸ a variation is a different form of something

varied *ADJECTIVE*
of various kinds; full of variety • *She has varied interests.*

variety *NOUN* **varieties**
❶ a variety is a number of different kinds of the same thing • *There was a variety of cakes to choose from.* ❷ a variety is a particular kind of something • *There are many varieties of butterfly.* ❸ variety is a situation where things are not always the same • *Their lives are full of variety.* ❹ variety is also a form of entertainment made up of short performances of singing, dancing and comedy

various *ADJECTIVE*
❶ of different kinds • *We talked about various things.* ❷ several • *There are various species of cactus.*
➤ **variously** *ADVERB*

varnish *NOUN* **varnishes**
a liquid that dries to form a hard shiny surface on wood or other surfaces

varnish *VERB* **varnishes, varnishing, varnished**
to varnish wood or another surface is to put varnish on it

vary *VERB* **varies, varying, varied**
❶ to vary is to keep changing • *The weather varies a lot here.* ❷ things vary when they are different from each other • *The T-shirts are the same, although the colours vary.* ❸ to vary something is to make changes to it

vase (*say* vahz) *NOUN* **vases**
a jar used for holding flowers or as an ornament

vast *ADJECTIVE*
very large or wide • *the vast expanse of outer space*
➤ **vastly** *ADVERB* ➤ **vastness** *NOUN*

VAT *ABBREVIATION*
short for *value-added tax*, a tax on things you buy

vat *NOUN* vats
a very large container for holding liquid

vault *VERB* vaults, vaulting, vaulted
you vault something, or vault over it, when you jump over it, using your hands to support you or with the help of a pole

vault *NOUN* vaults
❶ a jump done by vaulting ❷ an arched roof ❸ an underground room for storing money and valuables

veal *NOUN*
veal is the meat from a calf

Veda *PLURAL NOUN*
the ancient writings of the Hindu religion

veer *VERB* veers, veering, veered
to swerve or change direction suddenly
• *The road suddenly veered to the left.*

vegan (*say* **vee**-gan) *NOUN* vegans
someone who does not use or eat any products made from animals or animal products

vegan *ADJECTIVE*
vegan food or products are not made from animals or animal products

vegetable *NOUN* vegetables
a plant that can be used as food

vegetarian (*say* vej-i-**tair**-i-an) *NOUN* vegetarians
someone who does not eat meat

vegetarian *ADJECTIVE*
vegetarian food does not contain meat

vegetate *VERB* vegetates, vegetating, vegetated
to lead a dull life doing nothing interesting

vegetation *NOUN*
vegetation is plants that are growing

veggie *ADJECTIVE* (*informal*)
vegetarian • *a veggie burger and chips*

vehicle *NOUN* vehicles
a means of carrying people or things, especially on land. Cars, buses, trains and lorries are vehicles.

veil *NOUN* veils
a piece of thin material used to cover a person's face or head

veil *VERB* veils, veiling, veiled
❶ to veil something is to cover it with a veil ❷ to veil something such as a hint or a threat is to suggest it without being clear about it

vein *NOUN* veins
❶ your veins are the tubes in your body that carry blood towards your heart ❷ a line or streak on a leaf or rock or insect's wing ❸ a long deposit of a mineral in the middle of rock

velociraptor *NOUN* velociraptors
a small fast-moving dinosaur with large claws on its back legs

velocity (*say* vil-**os**-i-tee) *NOUN* velocities
velocity is speed in a particular direction

velodrome *NOUN* velodromes
a sports stadium with a steeply banked track for cycle racing

velvet *NOUN*
velvet is a soft material with short furry fibres on one side
➤ **velvety** *ADJECTIVE* soft, like velvet

vendetta *NOUN* vendettas
a long-lasting quarrel or feud

vending machine *NOUN* vending machines
a machine that you can buy food, drinks or other things from

vendor *NOUN* vendors
someone who is selling something

venerable *ADJECTIVE*
worthy of respect or honour because of being so old

vengeance *NOUN*
vengeance is harming or punishing someone because they have done harm to you
➤ **with a vengeance** very strongly or effectively

vengeful *ADJECTIVE*
a vengeful person wants to punish someone who has harmed them
➤ **vengefulness** *NOUN*

a
b
c
d
e
f
g
h
i
j
k
l
m
n
o
p
q
r
s
t
u
v
w
x
y
z

venison *NOUN*
venison is the meat from a deer

Venn diagram *NOUN* **Venn diagrams**
(*mathematics*)
a diagram using circles to show how sets of
things relate to one another

venom *NOUN*
❶ venom is the poison of snakes ❷ venom is
also a feeling of bitter hatred for someone

venomous *ADJECTIVE*
❶ poisonous ❷ full of bitter hatred
'Those creatures, my dear ignorant boy,
are the most brutal, vindictive, venomous,
murderous beasts in the entire universe!'
—CHARLIE AND THE GREAT GLASS ELEVATOR,
Roald Dahl

vent *NOUN* **vents**
an opening in something, especially to let out
smoke or gas
➤ **to give vent to something** is to express
your feelings openly • *He gave vent to*
his anger.

ventilate *VERB* **ventilates**, **ventilating**,
ventilated
to ventilate a place is to let fresh air come into
it and move around it
➤ **ventilation** *NOUN*

ventilator *NOUN* **ventilators**
❶ a device that brings in and moves air around
a place ❷ a machine that helps someone
to breathe

ventriloquist (*say* ven-**tril**-o-kwist) *NOUN*
ventriloquists
an entertainer who speaks without moving
their lips, making it appear that a dummy
is speaking
➤ **ventriloquism** *NOUN*

venture *NOUN* **ventures**
something new that you decide to do that is
risky or daring

venture *VERB* **ventures**, **venturing**,
ventured
to venture somewhere is to go there even
though you know it might be dangerous or
difficult

venue *NOUN* **venues**
a place where an event is held

Venus *NOUN*
the second planet from the sun in our solar
system
DID YOU KNOW? The planet **Venus** is named after
the Roman goddess of love and beauty.

veranda (*say* ver-**an**-da) *NOUN* **verandas**
an open terrace with a roof along the outside
of a house

verb *NOUN* **verbs**
a verb is a word that shows what someone
or something is doing, such as *be, go, make,*
stop or *think*

verbal *ADJECTIVE*
spoken rather than written • *We had a verbal*
agreement.
➤ **verbally** *ADVERB*

verdant *ADJECTIVE*
green and lush with vegetation • *an island*
covered in verdant jungle

verdict *NOUN* **verdicts**
the decision reached by a judge or jury about
whether someone is guilty of a crime

verge *NOUN* **verges**
a strip of grass beside a road or path

verge *VERB* **verges**, **verging**, **verged**
➤ **to verge on** *or* **be on the verge of**
something is to be very near to something
• *Her reply verged on rudeness.* • *He was on the*
verge of tears.

verify *VERB* **verifies**, **verifying**, **verified**
to verify something is to find or show whether
it is true or correct

vermin *PLURAL NOUN*
vermin are animals or insects that damage
crops or food or carry disease, such as rats
and fleas

verruca (*say* ver-**oo**-ka) *NOUN* **verrucas**
a kind of wart on the sole of your foot

versatile (*say* **ver**-sa-tyl) *ADJECTIVE*
able to do or be used for many different
things
➤ **versatility** *NOUN*

verse *NOUN* **verses**
❶ verse is writing in the form of poetry
❷ a verse is a group of lines in a poem
or song

version *NOUN* **versions**
❶ someone's account of something that has happened • *We only know his version of the story.* ❷ a different form of a thing • *The book is coming out in a paperback version.*

versus *PREPOSITION*
against or competing with, especially in sport • *The final will be Brazil versus Germany.*

vertebra (*say* ver-ti-bra) *NOUN* **vertebrae**
each of the bones that form your backbone

vertebrate (*say* ver-ti-brit) *NOUN* **vertebrates**
an animal with a backbone

vertex *NOUN* **vertices**
the highest point of a hill, or of a cone or triangle

vertical *ADJECTIVE*
going directly upwards, at right angles to something level or horizontal
➤ **vertically** *ADVERB*

vertigo *NOUN*
vertigo is feeling dizzy because you are high up

very *ADVERB*
to a great amount; extremely • *It is very frosty this morning.*

very *ADJECTIVE*
❶ exact or actual • *That's the very thing I need!* ❷ extreme • *They had reached the very end of their journey.*

Vesak (*say* ves-ak) *NOUN*
Vesak is an important festival of Buddhism, held in April to May

vessel *NOUN* **vessels**
❶ a boat or ship ❷ a container for liquids ❸ a tube inside an animal or plant, carrying blood or some other liquid

vest *NOUN* **vests**
a piece of underwear you wear on the top half of your body

vestment *NOUN* **vestments**
a piece of outer clothing worn by the clergy or choir at a church service

vestry *NOUN* **vestries**
a room in a church where the vestments are kept and the clergy and choir prepare for a service

vet *NOUN* **vets**
a person trained to treat sick animals

veteran *NOUN* **veterans**
❶ a person with long experience of something ❷ a soldier who has returned from a war

veterinary (*say* vet-rin-ree) *ADJECTIVE*
to do with the medical treatment of animals

veto (*say* vee-toh) *NOUN* **vetoes**
❶ a refusal to let something happen ❷ the right to stop something from happening

veto *VERB* **vetoes, vetoing, vetoed**
to veto something is to refuse to let it happen

vex *VERB* **vexes, vexing, vexed**
to vex someone is to annoy them or cause them worry
➤ **vexation** *NOUN*

via (*say* vy-a) *PREPOSITION*
going through; stopping at • *This train goes from Edinburgh to London via York.*

viaduct (*say* vy-a-dukt) *NOUN* **viaducts**
a long bridge with many arches, carrying a road or railway over low ground

vibrate *VERB* **vibrates, vibrating, vibrated**
to move quickly from side to side and with small movements • *Sound waves make your eardrum vibrate.*
➤ **vibration** *NOUN*

vicar *NOUN* **vicars**
a member of the clergy who is in charge of a parish

vicarage *NOUN* **vicarages**
the house of a vicar

vice *NOUN* **vices**
❶ a vice is a bad or evil habit ❷ vice is evil or wickedness ❸ a vice is also a tool for holding something tightly in place while you work on it

vice-president *NOUN* **vice-presidents**
a deputy to a president

vice versa (*say* vys-ver-sa) *ADVERB*
vice versa means the other way round. For example, *you can read the dictionary from A to Z, or vice versa,* means 'you can read the dictionary from A to Z, or from Z to A'.

a b c d e f g h i j k l m n o p q r s t u **v** w x y z

vicinity *NOUN* **vicinities**
the area near or surrounding a particular place
• *Are there any parks in the vicinity?*

vicious (*say* **vish**-us) *ADJECTIVE*
❶ cruel and aggressive • *a vicious temper*
❷ severe or violent • *a vicious attack of flu*
➤ **viciously** *ADVERB* ➤ **viciousness** *NOUN*

victim *NOUN* **victims**
someone who is killed or injured as a result of
an accident, disaster or crime • *the victim of a
gruesome murder*

victimize (*also* **victimise**) *VERB* **victimizes,
victimizing, victimized**
to victimize someone is to pick them out and
treat them unfairly

victor *NOUN* **victors**
the winner of a battle or contest

Victorian *ADJECTIVE*
belonging to the time when Queen Victoria
reigned (1837-1901)
Victorian *NOUN* **Victorians**
a person who lived during Queen Victoria's
reign

victorious *ADJECTIVE*
someone is victorious when they win a battle or
contest or game

victory *NOUN* **victories**
victory is winning a battle or contest or game

video (*say* **vid**-i-oh) *NOUN* **videos**
❶ video is the recording of moving pictures
and sound ❷ a video is also a television
programme or film recorded on a camera or
mobile phone
video *VERB* **videos, videoing, videoed**
to video something is to record it on a video
camera or mobile phone

view *NOUN* **views**
❶ what you can see from one place • *There's a
fine view from the top of the hill.* ❷ someone's
opinion • *What are your views on climate
change?*
➤ **in view of something** because of it
➤ **on view** shown for people to see
view *VERB* **views, viewing, viewed**
❶ to view something is to look at it carefully
• *The stranger viewed us warily.* ❷ to view

something or someone in a certain way is to
think about them in that way

viewer *NOUN* **viewers**
someone who watches something, especially a
television programme

viewpoint *NOUN* **viewpoints**
your viewpoint is your opinion about
something

vigil (*say* **vi**-jil) *NOUN* **vigils**
a period spent awake during the night to keep
watch or pray
*'Sir Bendu,' he said, 'I ran away from the chapel
where I was to spend my vigil on the eve of the
ceremony that would make me a knight.'*—THE LETTER
FOR THE KING, Tonke Dragt

vigilant (*say* **vij**-i-lant) *ADJECTIVE*
someone is vigilant when they are watching
carefully for something
➤ **vigilance** *NOUN* ➤ **vigilantly** *ADVERB*

vigorous *ADJECTIVE*
full of strength and energy • *a vigorous
handshake*
➤ **vigorously** *ADVERB*

vigour *NOUN*
vigour is strength and energy

Viking *NOUN* **Vikings**
a Scandinavian explorer, pirate or trader in the
8th to 10th centuries
Viking *ADJECTIVE*
to do with the Vikings • *a Viking longship*

vile *ADJECTIVE* **viler, vilest**
disgusting or bad • *What a vile smell.*

villa *NOUN* **villas**
a house, especially a large one in its own
grounds, or one used for holidays abroad

village *NOUN* **villages**
a group of houses and other buildings in the
country, smaller than a town

villager *NOUN* **villagers**
someone who lives in a village

villain *NOUN* **villains**
a wicked person or criminal
➤ **villainy** *NOUN* wickedness

vine *NOUN* **vines**
a plant on which grapes grow

vinegar *NOUN*
vinegar is a sour liquid used to flavour food

vineyard (*say* vin-yard) *NOUN* **vineyards**
an area of land where vines are grown to produce grapes for making wine

vintage *NOUN* **vintages**
❶ all the grapes that are harvested in one season, or the wine made from them
❷ something's vintage is the period from which it comes

vintage *ADJECTIVE*
from a period in the past • *vintage clothes*

vinyl (*say* vy-nil) *NOUN*
vinyl is a kind of plastic

viola (*say* vee-oh-la) *NOUN* **violas**
a stringed instrument rather like a violin but slightly larger and with a lower pitch

violate *VERB* **violates**, **violating**, **violated**
❶ to violate a rule or law is to break it
❷ to violate a person or place is to treat them without respect
➤ **violation** *NOUN*

violence *NOUN*
❶ violence is when someone uses force to hurt or kill people ❷ violence is also force that damages things • *We weren't prepared for the violence of the storm.*

violent *ADJECTIVE*
❶ to be violent is to use force to hurt people
❷ something such as a storm or an emotion is violent when it is strong and forceful
Towards evening a violent storm of rain came on, and the wind was so high that all the windows and doors in the old house shook and rattled.
—THE CANTERVILLE GHOST, Oscar Wilde
➤ **violently** *ADVERB*

violet *NOUN* **violets**
❶ a blue-purple colour ❷ a small plant that usually has purple flowers

violin *NOUN* **violins**
a musical instrument with four strings, played with a bow
➤ **violinist** *NOUN*

VIP *NOUN* **VIPs**
a very important person • *Several VIPs will be invited to the event.*

viper *NOUN* **vipers**
a small poisonous snake

viral (*say* vy-ral) *ADJECTIVE*
❶ caused by a virus or to do with a virus
• *She is recovering from a viral infection.*
❷ spreading very quickly and widely on the internet or social media • *Within hours, the video went viral.*

virtual *ADJECTIVE*
❶ amounting to the real thing in effect
• *His red face was a virtual admission of guilt.*
❷ using virtual reality • *Click here to go on a virtual tour of the gallery.*

virtually *ADVERB*
in effect; nearly • *She virtually admitted it.*

virtual reality *NOUN*
virtual reality is an image or environment created by a computer that imitates the real world and that you can be part of

virtue *NOUN* **virtues**
❶ a virtue is a good quality in a person's character • *Honesty is a virtue.* ❷ virtue is moral goodness

virtuous *ADJECTIVE*
a virtuous person behaves in a very good way
➤ **virtuously** *ADVERB*

virus (*say* vy-rus) *NOUN* **viruses**
❶ a microscopic creature that can cause disease ❷ a disease caused by a virus
• *The doctor said I had a virus.* ❸ a hidden set of instructions in a computer program that is designed to destroy data

visa *NOUN* **visas**
an official mark put on someone's passport by officials of a foreign country to show that the holder of the passport has permission to enter that country

visibility *NOUN*
visibility is how far you can see clearly
• *Visibility is down to 20 metres.*

visible *ADJECTIVE*
able to be seen • *The ship was visible on the horizon.*
➤ **visibly** *ADVERB*

vision *NOUN* **visions**
❶ vision is the ability to see ❷ a vision is something that you see or imagine, especially

a b c d e f g h i j k l m n o p q r s t u v w x y z

in a dream ❸ vision is also imagination and understanding • *They need a leader with vision.*

visit *VERB* **visits, visiting, visited**
❶ to go see a person or place ❷ to stay somewhere for a while

visit *NOUN* **visits**
❶ going to see a person or place ❷ a short stay somewhere

visitor *NOUN* **visitors**
someone who is visiting or staying at a place

visor (*say* **vy-zer**) *NOUN* **visors**
the clear part of a helmet that closes over the face

visual *ADJECTIVE*
to do with seeing; used for seeing
➤ **visually** *ADVERB*

visualize (*also* **visualise**) *VERB* **visualizes, visualizing, visualized**
to visualize something is to form an image of it in your mind • *I tried to visualize what life would be like on Mars.*

vital *ADJECTIVE*
❶ extremely important; essential • *It is vital that we get there on time.* ❷ connected with life; needed in order to live
➤ **vitally** *ADVERB* something is vitally important when it is extremely important

vitality *NOUN*
vitality is liveliness or energy

vitamin *NOUN* **vitamins**
each of several substances which are present in some foods and which you need to stay healthy

vivid *ADJECTIVE*
bright and clear • *The colours are very vivid.* • *She gave a vivid description of the storm.*
➤ **vividly** *ADVERB* to remember something vividly is to remember it very clearly
➤ **vividness** *NOUN*

vivisection *NOUN*
vivisection is doing experiments on live animals as part of scientific research

vixen *NOUN* **vixens**
a female fox

vlog *NOUN* **vlogs**
a series of videos that someone regularly posts on the internet about their own life or activities
➤ **vlogging** *NOUN*

vlogger *NOUN* **vloggers**
a person who regularly makes videos about their own life or activities and posts them on the internet

vocabulary *NOUN* **vocabularies**
❶ the vocabulary of a language is all the words used in it ❷ a person's vocabulary is the words that they know and use

vocal *ADJECTIVE*
to do with the voice; using your voice
➤ **vocally** *ADVERB*

vocalist *NOUN* **vocalists**
a singer in a band

vocation *NOUN* **vocations**
a job or activity that you feel strongly you want to do
➤ **vocational** *ADJECTIVE*

vodka *NOUN* **vodkas**
vodka is a strong alcoholic drink, originally from Russia

voice *NOUN* **voices**
❶ the sound you make when you speak or sing ❷ the ability to speak or sing • *She has lost her voice.*

voice *VERB* **voices, voicing, voiced**
to voice something is to say it clearly and strongly • *He voiced the objections to the plan.*

voicemail *NOUN*
a system that lets you leave spoken messages for someone on their phone

void *NOUN* **voids**
a void is an empty space or hole

volcano *NOUN* **volcanoes**
a mountain with a hole at the top, formed by molten lava which has burst through the earth's crust
➤ **volcanic** *ADJECTIVE*
DID YOU KNOW? The word **volcano** comes from *Vulcan*, the name of the Roman god of fire.

volcanology *NOUN*
volcanology is the study of volcanoes and volcanic eruptions
➤ **volcanologist** *NOUN*

A B C D E F G H I J K L M N O P Q R S T U V W X Y Z

vole *NOUN* **voles**
a small animal rather like a rat

volley *NOUN* **volleys**
❶ a number of bullets or shells fired at the same time ❷ in ball games, hitting or kicking the ball back before it touches the ground

volleyball *NOUN*
volleyball is a game in which two teams hit a large ball to and fro over a net with their hands

volt *NOUN* **volts**
a unit for measuring the force of an electric current
DID YOU KNOW? The **volt** is named after an Italian scientist called Alessandro Volta, who invented the electric battery.

voltage *NOUN* **voltages**
voltage is electric force measured in volts

volume *NOUN* **volumes**
❶ the amount of space filled by something ❷ the strength or power of sound • *Turn down the volume!* ❸ an amount • *The volume of work has increased.* ❹ a book, especially one of a set

voluntary *ADJECTIVE*
done or doing something because you want to, not for pay
➤ **voluntarily** *ADVERB*

volunteer *VERB* **volunteers, volunteering, volunteered**
❶ to volunteer is to offer to do something that you do not have to do ❷ to volunteer (for example) information or time is to provide it willingly without being asked for it • *Several people generously volunteered their time.*

volunteer *NOUN* **volunteers**
someone who volunteers to do something

vomit *VERB* **vomits, vomiting, vomited**
to bring food back from the stomach through your mouth

vortex *NOUN* **vortices**
a whirling spiral of air or water; a whirlpool or whirlwind • *The ship was being dragged into the vortex.*

vote *VERB* **votes, voting, voted**
❶ to vote for someone or something is to show which you prefer by putting up your hand or making a mark on a piece of paper ❷ to vote to do something is to say that you want to do it • *I vote we go away this weekend.*

vote *NOUN* **votes**
❶ a way of choosing someone or something by getting people to put up their hand or make a mark on a piece of paper ❷ a choice you make by voting ❸ the right to vote

voter *NOUN* **voters**
someone who votes, especially in an election

vouch *VERB* **vouches, vouching, vouched**
➤ **to vouch for something** is to say that it is true or genuine

voucher *NOUN* **vouchers**
a piece of paper showing that you are allowed to pay less for something or that you can get something in exchange

vow *VERB* **vows, vowing, vowed**
to make a solemn promise to do something
vow *NOUN* **vows**
a solemn promise

vowel *NOUN* **vowels**
any of the letters a, e, i, o, u and sometimes y

voyage *NOUN* **voyages**
a long journey by ship or in a spacecraft
➤ **voyager** *NOUN*

VR *ABBREVIATION*
short for *virtual reality*, an image or environment created by a computer that imitates the real world and that you can be part of

vulgar *ADJECTIVE*
rude; without good manners
➤ **vulgarity** *NOUN*

vulgar fraction *NOUN* **vulgar fractions**
a fraction shown by numbers above and below a line, such as ½ and ⅞ (*compare* **decimal fraction**)

vulnerable *ADJECTIVE*
able to be harmed or attacked easily

vulpine *ADJECTIVE*
to do with foxes, or like a fox

vulture *NOUN* **vultures**
a large bird that eats dead animals

a
b
c
d
e
f
g
h
i
j
k
l
m
n
o
p
q
r
s
t
u
v
w
x
y
z

Ww

wad *NOUN* **wads**
a pad or bundle of soft material or pieces of paper

waddle *VERB* **waddles, waddling, waddled**
to walk with short steps, rocking from side to side, like a duck
Aunt Sponge, fat and pulpy as a jellyfish, came waddling up behind her sister to see what was going on.—JAMES AND THE GIANT PEACH, Roald Dahl

waddle *NOUN* **waddles**
a waddling walk

wade *VERB* **wades, wading, waded**
to wade through water or mud is to walk through it

wafer *NOUN* **wafers**
a thin kind of biscuit, often eaten with ice cream

waffle *NOUN* **waffles**
❶ a waffle is a crisp square pancake with a pattern of squares on it ❷ waffle is talking for a long time without saying anything important or interesting

waffle *VERB* **waffles, waffling, waffled**
to waffle is to talk or write waffle

wag *VERB* **wags, wagging, wagged**
❶ a dog wags its tail when it moves it quickly from side to side because it is happy or excited ❷ you wag your finger when you move it up and down or from side to side

wag *NOUN* **wags**
a wagging movement

wage, wages *NOUN*
the money paid to someone for the job they do

wage *VERB* **wages, waging, waged**
to wage a war or campaign is to fight it

wager (*say* way-jer) *NOUN* **wagers**
a bet

wager *VERB* **wagers, wagering, wagered**
to wager someone is to make a bet with them

waggle *VERB* **waggles, waggling, waggled**
to waggle something is to move it quickly to and fro

wagon *NOUN* **wagons**
❶ a cart with four wheels, pulled by a horse or ox ❷ an open railway truck

wagtail *NOUN* **wagtails**
a small bird with a long tail that it moves up and down when it is standing still

wail *VERB* **wails, wailing, wailed**
to make a long sad cry

wail *NOUN* **wails**
a sound of wailing

waist *NOUN* **waists**
the narrow part in the middle of your body

waistcoat *NOUN* **waistcoats**
a close-fitting jacket without sleeves, worn over a shirt and under a jacket

wait *VERB* **waits, waiting, waited**
❶ to wait, or to wait for something, is to stay somewhere until something happens • *We can wait here until nightfall.* ❷ to wait for someone is to stay somewhere until they arrive • *I'll wait for you at the front door.* ❸ to wait is also to be a waiter or waitress

wait *NOUN* **waits**
a time spent waiting • *We had a long wait for the bus.*
SPELLING ALERT! You **wait** in a queue, but you use scales to check your **weight**.

waiter *NOUN* **waiters**
a man who serves people with food in a restaurant or hotel

waiting room *NOUN* **waiting rooms**
a room provided for people who are waiting for something

waitress *NOUN* **waitresses**
a woman who serves people with food in a restaurant or hotel

waive *VERB* **waives, waiving, waived**
to waive a right or privilege is to say you do not need it • *She waived her right to a free ticket.*

wake *VERB* **wakes, waking, woke, woken**
❶ you wake, or wake up, when you stop sleeping ❷ to wake someone, or wake them up, is to

make them stop sleeping • *Try not to wake the baby.*

wake *NOUN* **wakes**
❶ the trail left on the water by a ship or boat
❷ what is left when something is gone, or when something unusual has happened
• *The storm left a lot of damage in its wake.*

waken *VERB* **wakens, wakening, wakened**
to waken someone is to wake them

walk *VERB* **walks, walking, walked**
to move along on your feet at an ordinary speed

walk *NOUN* **walks**
❶ a journey on foot ❷ the way that someone walks • *We set off at a brisk walk.* ❸ a path or route for walking • *There are some lovely walks near here.*

walkabout *NOUN* **walkabouts**
an informal stroll among a crowd by an important visitor

walker *NOUN* **walkers**
someone who goes for a walk, especially a long one

walkie-talkie *NOUN* **walkie-talkies**
a small portable radio transmitter and receiver

walking stick *NOUN* **walking sticks**
a stick a person carries or uses as a support while walking

wall *NOUN* **walls**
❶ a structure built of brick or stone and forming one of the sides of a building or room, or going round a garden or other space
❷ the outer surface of something, such as the stomach

wall *VERB* **walls, walling, walled**
to wall something, or wall it in, is to surround or enclose it with a wall

wallaby (*say* **wol**-a-bee) *NOUN* **wallabies**
a kind of small kangaroo

wallet *NOUN* **wallets**
a small flat folding case for holding banknotes, credit cards and small documents

wallop *VERB* **wallops, walloping, walloped**
(*informal*)
to wallop someone is to hit or beat them

wallow *VERB* **wallows, wallowing, wallowed**
❶ to wallow is to roll about in water or mud
❷ to wallow in something is to get great pleasure from it • *They are wallowing in luxury.*

wallpaper *NOUN* **wallpapers**
wallpaper is paper used to cover the walls of rooms

walnut *NOUN* **walnuts**
a kind of nut with a wrinkled surface

walrus *NOUN* **walruses**
a large Arctic sea animal that looks like a large seal and has two long tusks

waltz *NOUN* **waltzes**
a dance with three beats to a bar

waltz *VERB* **waltzes, waltzing, waltzed**
to waltz is to dance a waltz

wand *NOUN* **wands**
a short thin rod used by a magician, wizard or fairy

wander *VERB* **wanders, wandering, wandered**
❶ to wander is to go about without trying to reach a particular place ❷ to wander, or wander off, is to stray or get lost • *Don't let the sheep wander.*
➤ **wanderer** *NOUN*

wane *VERB* **wanes, waning, waned**
❶ the moon wanes when its bright area gets gradually smaller (the opposite is **wax**)
❷ to wane is to become less or smaller or less strong • *The popularity of the show was waning.*

wangle *VERB* **wangles, wangling, wangled**
(*informal*)
to wangle something is to get it or arrange it by trickery or clever planning • *I'll see if I can wangle you a ticket to the match.*

want *VERB* **wants, wanting, wanted**
❶ to want something is to feel that you would like to have it or do it ❷ to want something is also to need it • *Your hair wants cutting.*

want *NOUN* **wants**
❶ a want is a wish to have something
❷ want of something is a lack of it • *They died for want of water.*

a
b
c
d
e
f
g
h
i
j
k
l
m
n
o
p
q
r
s
t
u
v
w
x
y
z

wanted ADJECTIVE
someone is wanted when they are being looked for by the police as a suspected criminal
• *He was a wanted man.*

war NOUN wars
❶ war is fighting between nations or armies; a war is a period of fighting ❷ a war is also a serious struggle or effort against something bad such as crime or disease

warble VERB warbles, warbling, warbled
to sing gently, the way some birds do

warble NOUN warbles
a warbling sound

ward NOUN wards
❶ a long room with beds for patients in a hospital ❷ a child looked after by a guardian

ward VERB wards, warding, warded
➤ **to ward something off** is to keep it away
• *He put his arms up to ward off the blows.*

warden NOUN wardens
❶ an official in charge of a hostel or college, or who supervises something ❷ a traffic warden

warder NOUN warders
an official in charge of prisoners in a prison

wardrobe NOUN wardrobes
❶ a cupboard to hang your clothes in
'This must be a simply enormous wardrobe!' thought Lucy, going still further in and pushing the soft folds of the coats aside to make room for her.—THE LION, THE WITCH AND THE WARDROBE, C. S. Lewis
❷ a stock of clothes or costumes

warehouse NOUN warehouses
a large building where goods are stored

wares PLURAL NOUN
goods offered for sale

warfare NOUN
warfare is fighting or waging war

warhead NOUN warheads
the explosive head of a missile

warlike ADJECTIVE
warlike people are fond of fighting or are likely to start a war

warlock (say wor-lok) NOUN warlocks
a man who practises witchcraft; a sorcerer
Before the horror-struck eyes of his guests, the warlock cast aside his wand, and seized a silver dagger.—THE TALES OF BEEDLE THE BARD, J. K. Rowling
DID YOU KNOW? Warlock was originally a Scottish word and was made popular in the nineteenth century by the author Sir Walter Scott.

warlord NOUN warlords
a powerful military leader in a region

warm ADJECTIVE warmer, warmest
❶ fairly hot; not cold or cool ❷ warm clothes are thick and keep you warm ❸ a warm person is enthusiastic or friendly • *They gave us a warm welcome.* ❹ (*informal*) close to the right answer, or to something hidden • *You're getting warm now.*

warm VERB warms, warming, warmed
❶ to warm something is to make it warm
• *I felt the sun warming my face.* ❷ to warm, or warm up, is to become warm
➤ **to warm up** is to do gentle exercises to prepare yourself before playing sport

warmly ADVERB
❶ you are warmly dressed when you are dressed in warm clothes ❷ to warmly welcome or greet someone is to do it in a very friendly way

warmth NOUN
❶ warmth is being warm or keeping warm
• *The cattle huddled together for warmth.*
❷ warmth is also being friendly and enthusiastic • *She was touched by the warmth of their welcome.*

warn VERB warns, warning, warned
to warn someone is to tell them about a danger or difficulty that might affect them

warning NOUN warnings
something said or written to warn someone

warp (say worp) VERB warps, warping, warped
❶ to warp, or be warped, is to become bent or twisted out of shape because of dampness or heat ❷ to warp someone's ideas or judgement is to distort them
• *Jealousy warped his mind.*

warrant NOUN **warrants**
a document that gives the police the right to arrest someone or search a place

warrant VERB **warrants**, **warranting**, **warranted**
to warrant something is to justify or deserve it • *Nothing warrants such rudeness.*

warren NOUN **warrens**
a piece of ground where there are many rabbit burrows

warrior NOUN **warriors**
someone who fights in battles; a soldier

warship NOUN **warships**
a ship designed for use in war

wart NOUN **warts**
a small hard lump on your skin

warthog NOUN **warthogs**
an African wild pig with curved tusks

wary ADJECTIVE **warier**, **wariest**
cautious and careful • *I gave the tiger a wary glance.*
➤ **warily** ADVERB ➤ **wariness** NOUN

was VERB (1st and 3rd person singular past tense of **be**)
• *I was born here.* • *She was a famous artist.*

wash VERB **washes**, **washing**, **washed**
❶ to wash something is to clean it with water ❷ you wash when you clean yourself with water ❸ to wash is to flow over or against something • *Waves washed over the beach.* ❹ to be washed somewhere is to be carried along by the force of moving water • *The boxes were washed overboard.* ❺ (*informal*) an explanation or excuse won't wash when it is not acceptable or believable • *That story just won't wash.*
➤ **to wash up** is to wash the dishes and cutlery after a meal

wash NOUN **washes**
❶ the action of washing ❷ the disturbed water behind a moving ship ❸ a thin coating of colour or paint

washable ADJECTIVE
able to be washed without being damaged

washbasin NOUN **washbasins**
a small basin with taps, holding water for washing your hands and face

washer NOUN **washers**
❶ a small ring of metal or rubber placed between two surfaces, especially under a bolt or screw, to fit them tightly together ❷ a washing machine

washing NOUN
washing is clothes that need to be washed or have been washed

washing machine NOUN **washing machines**
a machine for washing clothes

washing-up NOUN
washing-up is washing the dishes and cutlery after a meal

wash-out NOUN **wash-outs** (*informal*)
a complete failure

wasn't
short for *was not* • *It wasn't your fault.*

wasp NOUN **wasps**
a stinging insect with black and yellow stripes across its body

wastage NOUN
wastage is losing something by waste

waste VERB **wastes**, **wasting**, **wasted**
❶ to waste something is to use more of it than you need to, or to use it without getting much value from it ❷ to waste something is also to fail to use it • *You are wasting a good opportunity.*
➤ **to waste away** is to become thinner and weaker

waste ADJECTIVE
❶ left over or thrown away because it is not wanted • *What shall we do with all this waste paper?* ❷ not used or usable • *We came to an area of waste land.*

waste NOUN **wastes**
❶ a waste is wasting something or not using it well • *It's a waste of time.* ❷ waste is things that are not wanted or used ❸ a waste is also an area of desert or frozen land • *We flew over the wastes of Alaska.*

wasteful ADJECTIVE
wasting things or not using them well • *It's very wasteful to use so much packaging.*
➤ **wastefully** ADVERB ➤ **wastefulness** NOUN

watch *VERB* **watches, watching, watched**
❶ to watch someone or something is to look at them for some time ❷ to watch, or watch out, is to be on guard or ready for something to happen • *Watch for the light to change.* ❸ to watch something is also to take care of it • *His job is to watch the sheep.*

watch *NOUN* **watches**
❶ a device like a small clock, usually worn on a person's wrist ❷ a period of being on guard or on duty

watchdog *NOUN* **watchdogs**
a dog kept to guard buildings

watchful *ADJECTIVE*
alert and watching carefully
➤ **watchfulness** *NOUN*

watchman *NOUN* **watchmen**
someone whose job is to guard a building at night

water *NOUN* **waters**
❶ water is a transparent colourless liquid that is a compound of hydrogen and oxygen ❷ an area of water such as a sea or lake • *The steps go down to the water's edge.*

water *VERB* **waters, watering, watered**
❶ to water a plant is to sprinkle water over it • *Have you watered the flowers?* ❷ to water an animal is to give it water to drink ❸ your eyes or mouth water when they produce tears or saliva • *The smell of baking makes my mouth water.*
➤ **to water something down** is to dilute it or make it weaker

watercolour *NOUN* **watercolours**
❶ a paint that can be mixed with water ❷ a painting done with this kind of paint

watercress *NOUN*
a kind of cress that grows in water

water cycle *NOUN*
the process by which water falls to the ground as rain and snow, runs into rivers and lakes, flows into the sea, evaporates into the air and forms clouds, and then falls to the ground again

waterfall *NOUN* **waterfalls**
a place where a river or stream flows over a cliff or large rock

watering can *NOUN* **watering cans**
a container with a long spout, for watering plants

waterlogged *ADJECTIVE*
waterlogged ground is so wet it cannot soak up any more water

watermark *NOUN* **watermarks**
❶ a mark showing the level of water ❷ a faint design in some types of paper, which you can see if you hold it up to the light

watermelon *NOUN* **watermelons**
a melon with juicy red flesh and a hard green rind

waterproof *ADJECTIVE*
able to keep water out • *a waterproof jacket*

waterskiing *NOUN*
the sport of skimming over the surface of water on flat boards (**waterskis**) while being towed by a motor boat

water slide *NOUN* **water slides**
a slide into a swimming pool with running water and twists and turns

watertight *ADJECTIVE*
❶ made so that water cannot get into it ❷ a watertight excuse or plan is carefully prepared so that it has no mistakes or weaknesses

waterway *NOUN* **waterways**
a river or canal that ships can travel on

waterworks *NOUN*
a place with pumping machinery for supplying water to a district

watery *ADJECTIVE*
❶ like water ❷ full of water • *You have watery eyes.*

watt *NOUN* **watts**
a unit of electric power
DID YOU KNOW? The **watt** is named after Scottish engineer, James Watt (1736–1819), who invented a type of steam engine.

wave *VERB* **waves, waving, waved**
❶ to wave is to move your hand from side to side, usually to say hello or goodbye ❷ you wave something, or it waves, when it moves from side to side or up and down

wave to wear

• *Flags were waving in the wind.* ❸ to wave hair is to make it curl

wave *NOUN* **waves**
❶ a moving ridge on the surface of water, especially on the sea ❷ a curling piece of hair ❸ (*science*) one of the to-and-fro movements in which sound and light and electricity travel ❹ the action of waving your hand • *He gave us a little wave.* ❺ a sudden build-up of something strong • *She felt a wave of anger.*

wavelength *NOUN* **wavelengths**
the size of a sound wave or electric wave

waver *VERB* **wavers, wavering, wavered**
❶ to waver is to be unsteady or uncertain • *They wavered between two choices.*
❷ to waver is also to move unsteadily

wavy *ADJECTIVE* **wavier, waviest**
full of waves or curves

wax *NOUN* **waxes**
wax is a soft substance that melts easily, used for making candles, crayons and polish
➤ **waxy** *ADJECTIVE*

wax *VERB* **waxes, waxing, waxed**
❶ to wax something is to cover it with wax
❷ the moon waxes when its bright area gets gradually larger (the opposite is **wane**)

waxwork *NOUN* **waxworks**
a model made of wax, especially a full-size model of a person

way *NOUN* **ways**
❶ how something is done; a method or manner
❷ the way to a place is how you get there
❸ a road or path leading from one place to another ❹ a distance • *Is it a long way?*
❺ a respect • *It's a good idea in some ways.*
❻ a condition or state • *Things are in a bad way.*
➤ **to get your own way** is to make people let you have what you want
➤ **in the way** blocking something or stopping something from progressing
➤ **no way** (*informal*) that is impossible; that is not true

WC *ABBREVIATION*
short for *water closet*, meaning a toilet

we *PRONOUN*
a word used by someone to mean 'I and someone else' or 'I and others'

weak *ADJECTIVE* **weaker, weakest**
❶ without much strength or energy
❷ easy to break, bend or defeat ❸ poor at doing something
➤ **weakly** *ADVERB*

weaken *VERB* **weakens, weakening, weakened**
❶ to weaken something is to make it weaker
❷ to weaken is to become weaker

weakling *NOUN* **weaklings**
a weak person or animal

weakness *NOUN* **weaknesses**
❶ weakness is being weak ❷ a weakness a person has is one of their faults or something they don't do well ❸ a weakness is also something you cannot help liking • *Chocolate is my weakness.*

wealth *NOUN*
❶ wealth is a lot of money or property
❷ a wealth of something is a lot of it
• *The book has a wealth of illustrations.*

wealthy *ADJECTIVE* **wealthier, wealthiest**
someone is wealthy when they have a lot of money or property

weapon *NOUN* **weapons**
something used to harm or kill people in a battle or fight

wear *VERB* **wears, wearing, wore, worn**
❶ to wear something is to be dressed in it
❷ to wear something is to damage it by rubbing or using it; to wear is to become damaged like this • *The carpet has worn thin.*
❸ to last • *This cloth wears well.*
➤ **to wear off** is to become less strong or intense
➤ **to wear out** is to become weak or useless
➤ **to wear someone out** is to make them very tired
➤ **wearer** *NOUN*

wear *NOUN*
❶ wear is clothes of a particular type
• *a range of casual wear* ❷ wear is gradual damage done by rubbing or using something

567

weary *ADJECTIVE* **wearier, weariest**
very tired
➤ **wearily** *ADVERB* ➤ **weariness** *NOUN*

weasel *NOUN* **weasels**
a small fierce animal with a slender body

weather *NOUN*
weather is the rain, snow, wind, sunshine and temperature at a particular time or place
➤ **to be under the weather** is to feel ill or depressed

weather *VERB* **weathers, weathering, weathered**
❶ to weather is to become worn because of being exposed to the weather ❷ to weather something is to make it suffer the effects of the weather • *The wind and rain have weathered the cliffs.* ❸ you weather a difficulty when you come through it successfully • *They weathered the storm.*

weathercock *NOUN* **weathercocks**
a pointer, often shaped like a cockerel, that turns in the wind and shows which way the wind is blowing

weave *VERB* **weaves, weaving, wove, woven**
❶ to weave material or baskets is to make them by crossing threads or strips over and under each other ❷ (*past tense also* **weaved**) to weave is to twist and turn • *He weaved skilfully through the traffic.*
➤ **weaver** *NOUN*

web *NOUN* **webs**
❶ a net of thin sticky threads that spiders spin to catch insects ❷ a complicated system • *They were caught up in a web of lies.* ❸ the Web is part of the internet • *I downloaded it from the Web.*

webbed *ADJECTIVE*
webbed feet have toes joined by pieces of skin, as ducks' feet do

webcam *NOUN* **webcams**
a camera that films things that are happening and broadcasts them live over the internet

website *NOUN* **websites**
a place on the internet where you can get information

wed *VERB* **weds, wedding, wedded** *or* **wed**
to wed someone is to marry them

we'd
short for *we had* or *we should* or *we would*

wedding *NOUN* **weddings**
the ceremony that takes place when two people get married

wedge *NOUN* **wedges**
❶ a piece of wood or metal or plastic that is thick at one end and thin at the other, pushed between things to force them apart or to hold them tight ❷ something shaped like a wedge • *a wedge of cheese*

wedge *VERB* **wedges, wedging, wedged**
to wedge something is to hold it in place, especially with a wedge

Wednesday *NOUN* **Wednesdays**
the fourth day of the week
DID YOU KNOW? Wednesday is named after the Norse god *Odin* or *Woden*.

wee *ADJECTIVE* **weer, weest** (*Scottish*)
❶ small • *These shoes are too wee for me.*
❷ younger • *I have a wee brother and a big sister.*

weed *NOUN* **weeds**
a wild plant that grows where it is not wanted

weed *VERB* **weeds, weeding, weeded**
to weed the ground is to remove weeds from it

weedy *ADJECTIVE* **weedier, weediest**
❶ full of weeds ❷ thin and weak

week *NOUN* **weeks**
❶ a period of seven days, especially from Sunday to the following Saturday ❷ the part of the week that doesn't include the weekend

weekday *NOUN* **weekdays**
any day except Saturday and Sunday

weekend *NOUN* **weekends**
Saturday and Sunday

weekly *ADJECTIVE, ADVERB*
every week • *She writes a weekly blog.*
• *She updates her blog weekly.*

weep *VERB* **weeps, weeping, wept**
to cry or shed tears

weeping willow NOUN **weeping willows**
a kind of willow tree that has drooping branches

weigh VERB **weighs, weighing, weighed**
❶ to weigh something is to find out how heavy it is ❷ to weigh a certain amount is to have that as its weight • *How much do you weigh?*
➤ **to weigh someone down** is to make them unhappy or trouble them
➤ **to weigh something down** is to hold it down with something heavy
➤ **to weigh something up** is to think about it carefully before deciding what to do

weight NOUN **weights**
❶ weight is the measure of how heavy someone or something is • *When did you last check your weight?* ❷ a weight is also a heavy object, used to hold things down

weightless ADJECTIVE
astronauts in spacecraft are weightless when they float around because there is no gravity
➤ **weightlessness** NOUN

weightlifting NOUN
weightlifting is the sport or exercise of lifting heavy weights

weighty ADJECTIVE **weightier, weightiest**
❶ heavy ❷ important • *These are weighty matters.*

weir (*say* weer) NOUN **weirs**
a small dam across a river or canal to control the flow of water

weird (*say* weerd) ADJECTIVE **weirder, weirdest**
very strange or unnatural • *There was something weird about the silence.*
➤ **weirdly** ADVERB ➤ **weirdness** NOUN

welcome NOUN **welcomes**
a kind or friendly greeting or reception

welcome ADJECTIVE
❶ that you are glad to get or see • *This is a welcome surprise.* ❷ allowed or free to do or take something • *You are welcome to use my bicycle.*

welcome VERB **welcomes, welcoming, welcomed**
to welcome someone or something is to show that you are pleased when they arrive

weld VERB **welds, welding, welded**
to weld pieces of metal or plastic together is to join them by using heat or pressure
➤ **welder** NOUN

welfare NOUN
welfare is people's health, happiness and comfort

welfare state NOUN
a system of paying for health care and other social services from public funds

well NOUN **wells**
a deep hole dug or drilled to get water or oil out of the ground

well ADVERB **better, best**
❶ in a good or successful way • *She can play the guitar quite well now.* ❷ thoroughly • *Wash your hands well.* ❸ actually; probably • *It may well be our last chance.*
➤ **as well** also
➤ **to be well off** is to be fairly rich or fortunate

well ADJECTIVE
❶ in good health • *I could see he was not well.* ❷ good or satisfactory • *All is well.*

we'll
short for *we shall* or *we will*

well-being NOUN
well-being is health or happiness

wellies PLURAL NOUN (*informal*)
wellington boots

wellington boots, wellingtons PLURAL NOUN
knee-length rubber or plastic waterproof boots
DID YOU KNOW? Wellington boots are named after the Duke of Wellington, a British statesman and soldier who defeated Napoleon at the Battle of Waterloo.

well-known ADJECTIVE
known to many people

well-mannered ADJECTIVE
having good manners

Welsh ADJECTIVE
to do with Wales or its people
Welsh NOUN
a language spoken in Wales

a b c d e f g h i j k l m n o p q r s t u v w x y z

went VERB (past tense of **go**)
• I went out to the cinema.

wept VERB (past tense and past participle of **weep**)
• She wept bitterly when she left. • I could have wept with pride.

were VERB (plural and 2nd person singular past tense of **be**)
• The streets were empty. • You were fast asleep.

we're
short for we are • We're nearly there.

werewolf NOUN **werewolves**
in stories, a werewolf is a person who changes into a wolf when there is a full moon

west NOUN
❶ the direction where the sun sets
❷ the part of a country or city that is in this direction

west ADJECTIVE, ADVERB
❶ towards the west or in the west
• The village lies west of the mountains.
❷ coming from the west • There was a west wind blowing.

westerly ADJECTIVE
a westerly wind is one that blows from the west

western ADJECTIVE
from or to do with the west

western NOUN **westerns**
a film or story about the people of western America in the 19th century and early 20th century

West Indian ADJECTIVE
to do with any of the islands of the West Indies

westward, westwards ADJECTIVE, ADVERB
towards the west

wet ADJECTIVE **wetter, wettest**
❶ covered or soaked in water or other liquid
❷ not yet set or dry • Watch out for wet paint.
❸ rainy • It's been wet here all day.
➤ **wetness** NOUN

wet VERB **wets, wetting, wet** or **wetted**
to wet something is to make it wet

wet blanket NOUN **wet blankets**
(informal)
someone who is gloomy and who prevents other people from enjoying themselves

wet suit NOUN **wet suits**
a rubber suit that clings to the skin, worn by divers and windsurfers to keep them warm and dry

we've
short for we have • We've met before.

whack VERB **whacks, whacking, whacked**
to whack someone or something is to hit them hard

whack NOUN **whacks**
a hard hit or blow

whale NOUN **whales**
a very large sea mammal which breathes through a blowhole on its head

whaling NOUN
whaling is hunting and killing whales
• an international ban on whaling

wharf (say worf) NOUN **wharves** or **wharfs**
a quay where ships are loaded or unloaded

what DETERMINER
❶ used to ask the amount or kind of something • What kind of bike have you got?
❷ used to say how strange or great a person or thing is • What a fool you are!

what PRONOUN
❶ what thing or things • What did you say?
❷ the thing that • This is what you must do.

whatever PRONOUN
❶ anything or everything • Do whatever you like. ❷ no matter what • I'll be there whatever happens.

whatever DETERMINER
of any kind or amount • Get whatever help you can.

wheat NOUN
wheat is a cereal plant from which flour is made

wheel NOUN **wheels**
❶ a round device that turns on an axle passing through its centre. Wheels are used to move vehicles or work machinery. ❷ a horizontal revolving disc on which clay is made into a pot

wheel *VERB* wheels, wheeling, wheeled
❶ to wheel a bicycle or cart is to push it along on its wheels ❷ to wheel is to move in a curve or circle • *The line of soldiers wheeled to the right.*

wheelbarrow *NOUN* wheelbarrows
a small cart with one wheel at the front and two handles at the back

wheelchair *NOUN* wheelchairs
a chair on wheels for a person who cannot walk

wheeze *VERB* wheezes, wheezing, wheezed
to make a whistling or gasping noise as you breathe

whelk *NOUN* whelks
a shellfish that looks like a snail

when *ADVERB*
at what time • *When can you come to tea?*
when *CONJUNCTION*
❶ at the time that • *The bird flew away when I moved.* ❷ because; considering that • *Why do you smoke when you know it is dangerous?*

whenever *CONJUNCTION*
at any time; every time • *Whenever I see him, he's smiling.*

where *ADVERB, CONJUNCTION*
❶ in or to what place • *Where have you put the glue?* ❷ in or to that place • *Leave it where it is.*

whereabouts *ADVERB*
roughly where; in what area • *Whereabouts is Timbuktu?*
whereabouts *NOUN*
the place where something is • *Have you any idea of her whereabouts?*

whereas *CONJUNCTION*
but on the other hand • *Some people like liquorice, whereas others hate it.*

whereupon *CONJUNCTION*
after that; and then

wherever *ADVERB, CONJUNCTION*
in or to whatever place; no matter where

whether *CONJUNCTION*
used to introduce more than one possibility • *I don't know whether they are here or not.*

whey *NOUN*
whey is the watery liquid left when milk forms curds

which *DETERMINER*
what particular • *Which way did he go?*
which *PRONOUN*
❶ what person or thing • *Which is your desk?* ❷ the person or thing just mentioned • *Here's my book, which you asked me to bring.*

whichever *PRONOUN, DETERMINER*
that or those which; any which • *Take whichever you like.* • *Choose whichever cake you prefer.*

whiff *NOUN* whiffs
a slight smell of something • *He caught a whiff of perfume as she walked past him.*

while *CONJUNCTION*
❶ during the time that; as long as • *She was singing while she worked.* ❷ but; although • *She has fair hair, while her brother has dark hair.*
while *NOUN*
a period of time • *We have waited all this while.*
while *VERB* whiles, whiling, whiled
➤ **to while away time** is to pass it doing something leisurely • *We whiled away the time telling ghost stories.*

whilst *CONJUNCTION*
while

whim *NOUN* whims
a sudden desire to do or have something

whimper *VERB* whimpers, whimpering, whimpered
to cry with a low trembling sound
whimper *NOUN* whimpers
a sound of whimpering

whine *VERB* whines, whining, whined
❶ to whine is to make a long high piercing sound ❷ to whine is also to complain in an annoying way
whine *NOUN* whines
a whining sound

whinny *VERB* whinnies, whinnying, whinnied
a horse whinnies when it neighs gently

a
b
c
d
e
f
g
h
i
j
k
l
m
n
o
p
q
r
s
t
u
v
w
x
y
z

whip *NOUN* **whips**
a cord or strip of leather fixed to a handle and used for hitting people or animals

whip *VERB* **whips, whipping, whipped**
❶ to whip a person or animal is to beat them with a whip ❷ to whip cream is to beat it until it becomes thick and frothy
➤ **to whip something out** (*informal*) is to take it out quickly or suddenly • *She whipped out a pen and began to take notes.*
➤ **to whip something up** is to stir up people's feelings • *They tried to whip up more support.*

whir (*also* **whirr**) *VERB* **whirs** *or* **whirrs, whirring, whirred**
to make a continuous buzzing sound
The light startled the creatures, and one of them took to the air, its wings whirring heavily through the dust.—CORALINE, Neil Gaiman

whir *NOUN* **whirs** *or* **whirrs**
a continuous buzzing sound

whirl *VERB* **whirls, whirling, whirled**
you whirl something round, or it whirls, when it turns or spins very quickly

whirl *NOUN* **whirls**
when something turns or spins very quickly

whirlpool *NOUN* **whirlpools**
a strong current of water going round in a circle and pulling things towards it

whirlwind *NOUN* **whirlwinds**
a very strong wind that whirls around or blows in a spiral

whisk *VERB* **whisks, whisking, whisked**
❶ to whisk cream or eggs is to beat them until they are thick or frothy ❷ to whisk something somewhere is to move it there very quickly
• *A waiter whisked away my plate.*

whisk *NOUN* **whisks**
❶ a device for whisking eggs or cream ❷ a whisking movement

whisker *NOUN* **whiskers**
❶ whiskers are the long stiff hairs on the face of a cat or other animal ❷ you can refer to the hair growing on a person's face as their whiskers

whisky *NOUN* **whiskies**
a kind of very strong alcoholic drink

whisper *VERB* **whispers, whispering, whispered**
to speak very softly or secretly

whisper *NOUN* **whispers**
a very soft voice or sound

whist *NOUN*
whist is a card game usually for four people

whistle *VERB* **whistles, whistling, whistled**
❶ you whistle when you make a shrill or musical sound by blowing through your lips ❷ something whistles when it makes a shrill sound • *The wind whistled through the forest.*

whistle *NOUN* **whistles**
❶ a whistling sound ❷ a device that makes a shrill sound when you blow into it

white *ADJECTIVE* **whiter, whitest**
❶ of the very lightest colour, like snow or milk ❷ having light-coloured skin ❸ white coffee is coffee with milk

white *NOUN* **whites**
❶ a white colour ❷ the substance round the yolk of an egg, which turns white when it is cooked

whiteboard *NOUN* **whiteboards**
a board with a white surface for writing on with special pens

white-hot *ADJECTIVE*
something is white-hot when it is extremely hot, or so hot that heated metal looks white

whiten *VERB* **whitens, whitening, whitened**
❶ to whiten something is to make it white ❷ to whiten is to become white

whitish *ADJECTIVE*
something is whitish when it is fairly white in colour

Whitsun *NOUN*
Whitsun is Whit Sunday, or the period around it

whizz *VERB* **whizzes, whizzing, whizzed**
❶ to whizz is to move very quickly
Blue and yellow smoke shot out from every part of the machine. Wheels whizzed. Levers clicked.—PROFESSOR BRANESTAWM STORIES, Norman Hunter

② to whizz is also to sound like something rushing through the air

who PRONOUN
① which person or people • *Who said that?*
② the person or people spoken about
• *These are the people who live here.*

whoever PRONOUN
any person who • *Whoever comes is welcome.*

whole ADJECTIVE
① all of something • *Could you eat a whole pizza?* **②** not broken or damaged • *The egg was still whole and unhatched.*

whole NOUN **wholes**
a complete thing; all the parts of something • *I read the whole of the book in one weekend.*
➤ **on the whole** considering everything; mainly

wholemeal ADJECTIVE
wholemeal flour or bread is made from the whole grain of wheat

whole number NOUN **whole numbers**
a number without a fraction

wholesale ADJECTIVE, ADVERB
① wholesale goods are sold in large quantities to shops that then sell them again to customers **②** on a large scale; including everybody or everything • *There has been wholesale destruction.*

wholesome ADJECTIVE
healthy and good for you • *We all need wholesome food.*

wholly ADVERB
completely or entirely

whom PRONOUN
a word used for *who* when it is the object of a verb or comes after a preposition, for example *the boy whom I saw* or *the girl to whom I spoke*

whoop NOUN **whoops**
a loud excited cry
The little man gave a great whoop of joy and threw his bowl of mashed caterpillars right out of the tree-house window.—CHARLIE AND THE CHOCOLATE FACTORY, Roald Dahl

whoop VERB **whoops, whooping, whooped**
to whoop is to give a loud excited cry

whoopee EXCLAMATION
a word you say when you are feeling very happy

whooping cough (*say* **hoop**-ing-kof) NOUN
whooping cough is an infectious illness that causes spasms of coughing and gasping for breath

whoosh VERB **whooshes, whooshing, whooshed**
to whoosh is to move quickly with a rushing sound • *A bat whooshed past in the night air.*

whoosh NOUN **whooshes**
a sudden movement with a rushing sound • *There was a whoosh of wings as the dragon took flight.*

who's
short for *who is* or *who has* • *Who's that?* • *Who's been invited?*

whose DETERMINER, PRONOUN
① belonging to what person • *Whose bike is that?* • *Whose is this?* **②** of which; of whom • *the girl whose party we went to*
SPELLING ALERT! **Whose** is different from **who's**, which means 'who is' or 'who has': *Who's coming to the party? Who's done their homework?*

why ADVERB
for what reason or purpose

wick NOUN **wicks**
① the string that goes through the middle of a candle and is lit to give a flame **②** the strip of material that you light in a lamp or heater that uses oil

wicked ADJECTIVE **wickeder, wickedest**
① very bad or cruel; doing things that are wrong **②** mischievous • *He gave a wicked smile.* **③** (*informal*) very fine or good • *That's a wicked goal!*
➤ **wickedly** ADVERB ➤ **wickedness** NOUN

wicker, wickerwork NOUN
wicker or wickerwork is reeds or canes woven together to make baskets and furniture

wicket NOUN **wickets**
① in cricket, each set of three stumps with two bails on top of them **②** the part of a cricket ground between or near the wickets

a
b
c
d
e
f
g
h
i
j
k
l
m
n
o
p
q
r
s
t
u
v
w
x
y
z

wicketkeeper *NOUN* **wicketkeepers**
the fielder in cricket who stands behind the batter's wicket

wide *ADJECTIVE* **wider, widest**
❶ measuring a lot from one side to the other • *a wide expanse of moorland* ❷ from one side to the other • *The room is 4 metres wide.* ❸ covering a large range • *She has a wide knowledge of music.*

wide *ADVERB* **wider, widest**
❶ you are wide awake when you are completely or fully awake ❷ to open or spread something wide is to open or spread it as far as possible ❸ far from the target • *The shot went wide.* ❹ over a large area • *They travelled far and wide.*

widely *ADVERB*
among many people • *They are widely admired.*

widen *VERB* **widens, widening, widened**
❶ to widen something is to make it wider ❷ to widen is to become wider

widespread *ADJECTIVE*
existing or found in many places; common

widow *NOUN* **widows**
a woman whose husband or wife has died

widower *NOUN* **widowers**
a man whose wife or husband has died

width *NOUN* **widths**
the width of something is how much it measures from one side to the other

wield (*say* weeld) *VERB* **wields, wielding, wielded**
to wield a weapon or tool is to hold it and use it • *a picture of a knight wielding a sword*

wife *NOUN* **wives**
the woman that a person is married to

wifi (*say* wy-fy) *NOUN*
wifi is a wireless connection to the internet • *Does your phone have wifi?*

wig *NOUN* **wigs**
a covering of false hair worn on the head

wiggle *VERB* **wiggles, wiggling, wiggled**
to wiggle something is to move it from side to side

wiggle *NOUN* **wiggles**
a wiggling movement

wild *ADJECTIVE* **wilder, wildest**
❶ wild animals and plants live or grow in their natural state and are not looked after by people ❷ wild land is in its natural state and has not been changed by people • *We need to conserve the wild parts of the planet.* ❸ not controlled; very angry or excited • *The crowd went wild.* ❹ very foolish or unreasonable • *She has some wild ideas.*
➤ **wildness** *NOUN*

wild *NOUN* **wilds**
❶ animals live in the wild when they live in their natural environment ❷ the wilds are areas of a country far from towns and cities, where there are few people

wildebeest (*say* wil-de-beest) *NOUN* **wildebeest**
another name for **gnu**

wilderness *NOUN* **wildernesses**
an area of wild country; a desert

wildlife *NOUN*
wildlife is wild animals in their natural setting

wildly *ADVERB*
in a way that is not controlled • *My heart was beating wildly.*

wilful *ADJECTIVE*
❶ someone is wilful when they are determined to do exactly what they want ❷ something is wilful when it is done deliberately • *a wilful act of destruction*
➤ **wilfully** *ADVERB* ➤ **wilfulness** *NOUN*

will *VERB* (*past tense* **would**)
used to refer to the future • *I will be there at 12 o'clock.*

will *NOUN* **wills**
❶ will is the power to use your mind to decide and control what you do ❷ someone's will is what they choose or want • *He was forced to sign against his will.* ❸ someone's will to do something is their determination to do it • *She has a strong will to win.* ❹ a will is a legal document saying what is to be done with someone's possessions after they die

willing ADJECTIVE
ready and happy to do what is wanted • *Are you willing to help?*
➤ **willingly** ADVERB ➤ **willingness** NOUN

willow NOUN willows
a tree with thin flexible branches, often growing near water

wilt VERB wilts, wilting, wilted
a plant wilts when it loses freshness and droops

wily ADJECTIVE wilier, wiliest
crafty or cunning
➤ **wiliness** NOUN

wimp NOUN wimps (*informal*)
a feeble or timid person
➤ **wimpy** ADJECTIVE

win VERB wins, winning, won
❶ to win a contest or game or battle is to do better than your opponents ❷ to win something is to get it by using effort or in a competition • *She won second prize.*

win NOUN wins
a success or victory

wince VERB winces, wincing, winced
to wince is to make a slight movement because you are in pain or embarrassed

winch NOUN winches
a device for lifting or pulling things, using a rope or cable that goes round a wheel or drum

winch VERB winches, winching, winched
to winch something is to lift it or pull it with a winch

wind (*rhymes with* **tinned**) NOUN winds
❶ wind, or a wind, is a current of air ❷ wind is gas in the stomach or intestines that makes you uncomfortable ❸ wind is also breath used for a purpose, such as running ❹ in an orchestra, the wind is the wind instruments

wind (*rhymes with* **find**) VERB winds, winding, wound
❶ a road, path or river winds when it twists and turns • *The river winds down the valley.* ❷ to wind something is to wrap or twist it round something else • *She wound her scarf round her neck.*

❸ to wind a watch or clock is to tighten its spring so that it works
➤ **to wind up somewhere** is to end up there • *We wound up where we had started.*

windfall NOUN windfalls
❶ a fruit blown down from a tree ❷ a piece of unexpected good luck, especially a sum of money

wind farm NOUN wind farms
an area with a group of windmills or wind turbines for collecting energy

wind instrument NOUN wind instruments
a musical instrument played by blowing, such as a flute or clarinet

windmill NOUN windmills
a mill with four long arms called *sails* which are turned by the wind

window NOUN windows
❶ an opening in a wall or roof to let in light and air, usually filled with glass ❷ the glass in a window opening ❸ an area on a computer screen used by a particular program
DID YOU KNOW? The word **window** comes from Old Norse (Viking) words meaning 'wind eye'.

windpipe NOUN windpipes
the tube through which air reaches your lungs

windscreen NOUN windscreens
the window at the front of a motor vehicle

windsurfing NOUN
windsurfing is surfing on a board with a sail fixed to it
➤ **windsurfer** NOUN

wind turbine NOUN wind turbines
an upright machine with large vanes that rotate in the wind to generate electricity

windward ADJECTIVE
facing the wind, especially on a ship

windy ADJECTIVE windier, windiest
with a lot of wind • *It's a windy day today.*

wine NOUN wines
❶ an alcoholic drink made from grapes or other plants ❷ a dark red colour

wing *NOUN* **wings**
❶ a bird's or insect's wings are the parts it uses for flying ❷ an aircraft's wings are the long flat parts that stick out from its sides and support it in the air ❸ a part of a building that extends from the main part ❹ each side of a theatre stage, out of sight of the audience ❺ the part of a motor vehicle's body above a wheel ❻ each of the players in football and other ball games, whose place is at the side of the field ❼ a section of a political party, having particular views
➤ **on the wing** flying
➤ **to take wing** is to fly away

wing *VERB* **wings, winging, winged**
❶ a bird wings its way when it flies a long way ❷ to wing someone is to wound them in the side

winged *ADJECTIVE*
winged insects or other creatures have wings • *Pegasus was a mythical winged horse.*

wingless *ADJECTIVE*
wingless insects have no wings

wingspan *NOUN* **wingspans**
the distance across the wings of a bird or aeroplane

wink *VERB* **winks, winking, winked**
❶ you wink when you close and open one of your eyes quickly ❷ a light winks when it flickers or twinkles
It looked like Aladdin's cave. Necklaces and bracelets hung winking from the roof of the shelter.–STIG OF THE DUMP, Clive King

wink *NOUN* **winks**
❶ when you close and open one of your eyes quickly ❷ a short period of sleep • *I didn't sleep a wink.*

winkle *NOUN* **winkles**
a shellfish that is used for food

winkle *VERB* **winkles, winkling, winkled**
➤ **to winkle something out** is to find it with a lot of effort

winner *NOUN* **winners**
❶ a person who wins something ❷ (*informal*) something very successful • *Her new book is a winner.*

winnings *PLURAL NOUN*
the money someone wins in a game or by betting

winter *NOUN* **winters**
the coldest season of the year, between autumn and spring

wintry *ADJECTIVE* **wintrier, wintriest**
❶ wintry weather is cold, like winter ❷ a wintry smile is cold and unfriendly

wipe *VERB* **wipes, wiping, wiped**
to wipe something is to rub it gently to dry it or clean it
➤ **to wipe something out** is to destroy it or cancel it

wipe *NOUN* **wipes**
the action of wiping • *I'll just give the table a quick wipe.*

wiper *NOUN* **wipers**
a device for wiping something, especially on a vehicle's windscreen

wire *NOUN* **wires**
a thin length of metal used to carry electric current or for making fences

wire *VERB* **wires, wiring, wired**
to wire something, or wire it up, is to connect it with wires to carry electricity

wireless *ADJECTIVE*
something that is wireless can send and receive signals without using wires • *a set of wireless headphones*

wireless *NOUN* **wirelesses** (*old use*)
a radio set

wiring *NOUN*
wiring is the system of wires carrying electricity in a building or in a device

wiry *ADJECTIVE* **wirier, wiriest**
❶ a wiry person is lean and strong ❷ wiry hair is tough and stiff

wisdom *NOUN*
❶ wisdom is being wise ❷ wisdom is also wise sayings or writings

wisdom tooth *NOUN* **wisdom teeth**
a molar tooth that may grow at the back of your jaw much later than the other teeth

wise *ADJECTIVE* **wiser, wisest**
knowing or understanding many things and so able to make sensible decisions
➤ **wisely** *ADVERB* sensibly • *He wisely decided to tell the truth.*

A B C D E F G H I J K L M N O P Q R S T U V W X Y Z

wish *VERB* **wishes, wishing, wished**
❶ to wish something, or wish to do something, is to think or say that you would like it
❷ to wish someone something is to say that you hope they will get it • *They wished us luck.*

wish *NOUN* **wishes**
❶ something you want ❷ when you wish for something • *Make a wish.* • *We send you our best wishes.*

wishbone *NOUN* **wishbones**
a forked bone from the breast of a chicken or other bird

wisp *NOUN* **wisps**
a thin piece or line of something light or fluffy, such as hair or smoke

wistful *ADJECTIVE*
thinking sadly about something you can no longer have
Pollyanna laughed again, but she sighed, too; and in the gathering twilight her face looked thin and wistful.—POLLYANNA, Eleanor H. Porter
➤ **wistfully** *ADVERB*

wit *NOUN* **wits**
❶ wit is intelligence ❷ wit is also a clever kind of humour ❸ a wit is a witty person
➤ **to keep your wits about you** is to stay alert

witch *NOUN* **witches**
a woman who is believed to use magic

witchcraft *NOUN*
witchcraft is using magic, especially to make bad things happen

with *PREPOSITION*
There are many meanings, of which the most important are ❶ having • *a crocodile with powerful jaws* ❷ in the company of or accompanied by • *You can bring a friend with you.* ❸ using • *Stir the mixture with a wooden spoon.* ❹ against • *They always argue with each other.* ❺ because of • *He went purple with rage.* ❻ towards or concerning • *Be careful with that hot plate.*

withdraw *VERB* **withdraws, withdrawing, withdrew, withdrawn**
❶ to withdraw something is to take it away or take it back • *She withdrew her offer.*
❷ to withdraw is to retreat or drop out of something • *The troops have withdrawn from the frontier.* • *His injury meant he had to withdraw from the race.*

withdrawal *NOUN* **withdrawals**
❶ withdrawal is when someone withdraws something or withdraws from a place
❷ a withdrawal is an amount of money someone takes out of their bank account

wither *VERB* **withers, withering, withered**
a plant withers when it shrivels or wilts

withhold *VERB* **withholds, withholding, withheld**
to withhold something is to refuse to give it to someone • *He has withheld his permission.*

within *PREPOSITION, ADVERB*
inside; not beyond something • *We were still within sight of land.* • *Noises were coming from within.*

without *PREPOSITION*
❶ not together with • *Don't go without me!*
❷ not having or using; free from • *This cake is made without flour.*

withstand *VERB* **withstands, withstanding, withstood**
to withstand something is to resist it or put up with it successfully • *The bridge is designed to withstand high winds.*

witness *NOUN* **witnesses**
❶ a person who sees something happen and can describe it • *There were no witnesses to the accident.* ❷ a person who gives evidence in a law court

witness *VERB* **witnesses, witnessing, witnessed**
to witness an event is to see it happening
It seemed that all the other Minpins from the big tree had turned up as well to witness the great victory over the dreaded Gruncher.—BILLY AND THE MINPINS, Roald Dahl

witty *ADJECTIVE* **wittier, wittiest**
clever and amusing
➤ **wittily** *ADVERB*

wizard *NOUN* **wizards**
❶ a man or boy who has magic powers

a
b
c
d
e
f
g
h
i
j
k
l
m
n
o
p
q
r
s
t
u
v
w
x
y
z

'You knew?' said Harry. 'You knew I'm a—a wizard?' —HARRY POTTER AND THE PHILOSOPHER'S STONE, J. K. Rowling

❷ a person who is very good at something
• *She's a wizard with computers.*

DID YOU KNOW? The word **wizard** comes from an old meaning of *wise* and originally meant 'a wise person'.

wizardry *NOUN*
❶ the practice of using magic powers • *a book of magic spells and wizardry* ❷ great skill at doing something

wizened *ADJECTIVE*
shrivelled or wrinkled with age • *a face like a wizened apple*

woad *NOUN*
a type of body paint used by the ancient Celts

wobble *VERB* **wobbles**, **wobbling**, **wobbled**
to wobble is to move unsteadily from side to side

wobble *NOUN* **wobbles**
a wobbling movement
➤ **wobbly** *ADJECTIVE*

woe *NOUN* **woes**
❶ someone's woes are their troubles and misfortunes ❷ woe is great sorrow

woeful *ADJECTIVE*
❶ a woeful person is very sad ❷ you can say something is woeful when it is very bad or serious • *His answer shows a woeful lack of knowledge.*
➤ **woefully** *ADVERB*

wok *NOUN* **woks**
a deep round-bottomed frying pan used in Chinese cookery

woke *VERB* (*past tense of* **wake**)
• *Hana woke with a start.*

woken *VERB* (*past participle of* **wake**)
• *Jack had woken early.*

wolf *NOUN* **wolves**
a wild animal like a large fierce dog

wolf *VERB* **wolfs**, **wolfing**, **wolfed**
to wolf down food is to eat it greedily
• *I was so hungry, I wolfed down a whole pizza.*

woman *NOUN* **women**
a grown-up female human being

womb (*say* woom) *NOUN* **wombs**
the part of a female's body where babies develop before they are born

wombat *NOUN* **wombats**
an Australian animal like a small bear with short legs

won *VERB* (*past tense and past participle of* **win**)
• *We won the game easily.* • *He looks as if he has just won the lottery.*

wonder *VERB* **wonders**, **wondering**, **wondered**
❶ to wonder about something is to be trying to decide about it • *I wonder what we should do next.* ❷ to wonder at something is to feel surprise and admiration about it

wonder *NOUN* **wonders**
❶ wonder is a feeling of surprise and admiration ❷ a wonder is something that makes you feel surprised and admiring
➤ **no wonder** it is not surprising

wonderful *ADJECTIVE*
marvellous or excellent • *What a wonderful day for a picnic!*
➤ **wonderfully** *ADVERB*

won't
short for *will not* • *We won't forget.*

wood *NOUN* **woods**
❶ wood is the substance that trees are made of ❷ a wood is a lot of trees growing together

wooded *ADJECTIVE*
a wooded area is covered with growing trees

wooden *ADJECTIVE*
❶ made of wood ❷ stiff or awkward • *His movements were wooden.*

woodland *NOUN* **woodlands**
land covered with trees

woodlouse *NOUN* **woodlice**
a small crawling creature with seven pairs of legs, living in rotten wood or damp soil. It rolls itself into a ball if it is alarmed.

woodpecker NOUN woodpeckers
a bird that taps tree trunks with its beak to find insects

woodwind NOUN
in an orchestra, the woodwind is the wind instruments that are usually made of wood or plastic, such as the clarinet and oboe

woodwork NOUN
❶ woodwork is making things with wood ❷ woodwork is also things made out of wood

woodworm NOUN woodworm or woodworms
the larva of a beetle that bores into wood

woody ADJECTIVE woodier, woodiest
❶ like wood or made of wood ❷ full of trees

woof NOUN woofs
the barking sound made by a dog

wool NOUN
❶ wool is the thick soft hair of sheep or goats ❷ wool is also thread or cloth made from this hair

woollen ADJECTIVE
made of wool

woollens PLURAL NOUN
clothes made of wool

woolly ADJECTIVE woollier, woolliest
❶ covered with wool ❷ made of wool or like wool ❸ vague and not clear • *He has woolly ideas.*
➤ **woolliness** NOUN

word NOUN words
❶ a set of sounds or letters that has a meaning and is written with a space before and after it ❷ a brief talk with someone • *Can I have a word with you?* ❸ your word is when you promise to do something • *The knight solemnly swore to keep his word.* ❹ a command or signal to do something • *Run when I give the word.* ❺ a message or piece of news • *We sent word that we had arrived safely.*

word VERB words, wording, worded
to word something is to express it in words

word class NOUN word classes
each of the groups (also called *parts of speech*) into which words can be divided in grammar: noun, adjective, verb, pronoun, adverb, preposition, conjunction, determiner, exclamation

wording NOUN
the wording of something is the words used to say it

wordy ADJECTIVE wordier, wordiest
using too many words • *He gave a very wordy speech.*
➤ **wordiness** NOUN

wore VERB (*past tense of* **wear**)
• *She wore her new dress to the party.*

work VERB works, working, worked
❶ to work is to spend time doing something that needs effort or energy ❷ to work is also to have a job or be employed • *She works in a bank.* ❸ something works when it operates correctly or successfully • *Is the lift working?* ❹ to work something is to make it act or operate • *Can you work the lift?* ❺ to work (for example) loose is to become gradually loose • *The screw had worked loose.*
➤ **to work out** is to succeed or reach the right answer
➤ **to work something out** is to find the answer to it

work NOUN works
❶ work is something that you have to do that needs effort or energy • *Digging is hard work.* ❷ a person's work is their job • *What work do you do?* ❸ at school, your work is something you write or produce • *Please get on with your work quietly.* ❹ a work is a piece of writing or music or painting • *The book has all the works of Shakespeare.*
➤ **to be at work** is to be working

worker NOUN workers
❶ someone who works ❷ a bee or ant that does the work in a hive or colony but does not produce eggs

workforce NOUN workforces
the number of people who work for a business or factory

a b c d e f g h i j k l m n o p q r s t u v **w** x y z

working class NOUN working classes
people who do paid manual or industrial work
➤ working-class ADJECTIVE

workman NOUN workmen
a man who does manual work

workmanship NOUN
workmanship is skill in making something

workout NOUN workouts
a session of physical exercise or training

works NOUN
a factory or industrial site

works PLURAL NOUN
the moving parts of a machine

worksheet NOUN worksheets
a sheet of paper with a set of questions about a subject for students

workshop NOUN workshops
a place where things are made or mended

world NOUN worlds
❶ the world is the earth with all its countries and peoples ❷ a world is a planet • *The film is about creatures from another world.* ❸ everything to do with a particular subject or activity • *He knows a lot about the world of sport.*

worldly ADJECTIVE worldlier, worldliest
❶ to do with life on earth ❷ only interested in money and possessions

world war NOUN world wars
a war involving many countries all over the world

worldwide ADJECTIVE, ADVERB
over the whole world

worm NOUN worms
a small thin wriggling animal without legs, especially an earthworm

worm VERB worms, worming, wormed
to worm your way somewhere is to get there by wriggling or crawling
➤ to worm something out of someone is to get them to tell you something secret

worn VERB (past participle of wear)
• *Have you ever worn high heels?*

worn ADJECTIVE
damaged because it has been rubbed or used so much • *The carpet was worn in patches.*
➤ to be worn out is to be very tired

worried ADJECTIVE
anxious or troubled about something • *Sherlock had a worried look on his face.*
➤ worriedly ADVERB

worry VERB worries, worrying, worried
❶ to worry is to feel anxious or troubled about something • *Don't worry—everything will be fine!* ❷ to worry someone is to make them feel anxious or troubled about something • *What is it that's worrying you?* ❸ an animal worries its prey when it holds it in its teeth and shakes it

worry NOUN worries
❶ worry is worrying or being anxious • *There was a look of worry on her face.* ❷ a worry is something that makes you anxious

worse ADJECTIVE, ADVERB
more bad or more badly; less good or less well • *The pain is getting worse.* • *The team did worse than expected.*

worsen VERB worsens, worsening, worsened
❶ to worsen is to become worse ❷ to worsen something is to make it worse

worship VERB worships, worshipping, worshipped
to worship God or a god is to give them praise or respect
➤ worshipper NOUN

worship NOUN
worship is worshipping; religious ceremonies or services

worst ADJECTIVE, ADVERB
most bad or most badly; least good or least well • *This is our worst result so far.* • *I was the worst dressed person there.*

worth ADJECTIVE
❶ having a certain value • *This stamp is worth £100.* ❷ deserving something; good or important enough for something • *That book is worth reading.*

worth NOUN
a thing's worth is its value or usefulness

worthless ADJECTIVE
having no value; useless

worthwhile *ADJECTIVE*
important or good enough to be worth doing

worthy *ADJECTIVE* **worthier**, **worthiest**
deserving respect or support • *The sale is for a worthy cause.*
➤ **worthily** *ADVERB* ➤ **worthiness** *NOUN*

would *VERB* (*past tense of* **will**)
❶ • *We said we would help if we could.* ❷ used in polite questions or requests • *Would you like some tea?*

wouldn't
short for *would not* • *I wouldn't do that.*

wound (*say* wownd) *VERB* (*past tense and past participle of* **wind**)
• *The path wound through the woods.* • *She had wound a plaster round her finger.*

wound (*say* woond) *NOUN* **wounds**
an injury done to a part of a person's or animal's body, especially one in which the skin is cut

wound (*say* woond) *VERB* **wounds**, **wounding**, **wounded**
❶ to wound a person or animal is to give them a wound ❷ to wound someone is to hurt their feelings

wove *VERB* (*past tense of* **weave**)
• *They wove in and out of the parked cars.*

woven *VERB* (*past participle of* **weave**)
• *The wizard had woven his magic.*

wow *EXCLAMATION*
a word you say when you are amazed by something • *Wow! That's amazing!*

wrap *VERB* **wraps**, **wrapping**, **wrapped**
to wrap something is to put paper or some other covering round it

wrap *NOUN* **wraps**
a shawl or cloak worn to keep you warm

wrapper *NOUN* **wrappers**
a piece of paper or plastic that something is wrapped in

wrapping *NOUN* **wrappings**
wrapping is material used to wrap something, especially a present

wrath (*rhymes with* **cloth**) *NOUN* (*old use*)
anger
➤ **wrathful** *ADJECTIVE* angry

wreak (*say* reek) *VERB* **wreaks**, **wreaking**, **wreaked**
➤ **to wreak havoc** is to cause great destruction or disorder
➤ **to wreak revenge** is to inflict a terrible revenge

wreath (*say* reeth) *NOUN* **wreaths**
flowers and leaves and branches bound together to make a circle

wreathe (*say* reeth) *VERB* **wreathes**, **wreathing**, **wreathed**
to be wreathed in something is to be covered in it or decorated with it • *Her face was wreathed in smiles.*

wreck *VERB* **wrecks**, **wrecking**, **wrecked**
to wreck something is to damage or ruin it so badly that it cannot be used again

wreck *NOUN* **wrecks**
a badly damaged ship or car

wreckage *NOUN*
wreckage is the pieces of something that has been wrecked

wren *NOUN* **wrens**
a very small brown bird

wrench *VERB* **wrenches**, **wrenching**, **wrenched**
to wrench something is to pull or twist it suddenly or violently
At the Faun's cave a terrible surprise awaited them. The door had been wrenched off its hinges and everything lay smashed on the floor.—THE LION, THE WITCH AND THE WARDROBE, C. S. Lewis

wrench *NOUN* **wrenches**
❶ a wrenching movement ❷ a tool for gripping and turning bolts or nuts

wrestle *VERB* **wrestles**, **wrestling**, **wrestled**
❶ to wrestle with someone is to fight them by grasping them and trying to throw them to the ground ❷ to wrestle with a problem or difficulty is to struggle to solve it
➤ **wrestler** *NOUN* ➤ **wrestling** *NOUN*

wretch *NOUN* **wretches**
someone who is unhappy, poor or disliked

a
b
c
d
e
f
g
h
i
j
k
l
m
n
o
p
q
r
s
t
u
v
w
x
y
z

wretched (*say* rech-id) *ADJECTIVE*
❶ poor and unhappy • *a wretched beggar*
❷ not satisfactory or pleasant • *This wretched car won't start.*

wriggle *VERB* **wriggles**, **wriggling**, **wriggled**
to twist and turn your body

wriggle *NOUN* **wriggles**
a wriggling movement
➤ **wriggly** *ADJECTIVE*

wring *VERB* **wrings**, **wringing**, **wrung**
❶ to wring something wet, or to wring it out, is to squeeze or twist it to get the water out of it ❷ to wring something is to squeeze it violently • *I'll wring your neck!*
➤ **wringing wet** very wet; soaked

wrinkle *NOUN* **wrinkles**
❶ wrinkles are the small lines and creases that appear in your skin as you get older
❷ a small crease or line on the surface of something

wrinkle *VERB* **wrinkles**, **wrinkling**, **wrinkled**
something wrinkles when wrinkles appear in or on it
➤ **wrinkled** *ADJECTIVE*

wrist *NOUN* **wrists**
the joint that connects your hand to your arm

wristwatch *NOUN* **wristwatches**
a watch that you wear on your wrist

write *VERB* **writes**, **writing**, **wrote**, **written**
❶ to write words or signs is to put them on paper or some other surface so that people can read them ❷ to write a story or play or a piece of music is to be the author or composer of it ❸ to write to someone is to send them a letter
➤ **to write something off** is to think it is lost or useless

writer *NOUN* **writers**
a person who writes; an author

writhe (*say* ryth) *VERB* **writhes**, **writhing**, **writhed**
to twist your body about because you are in pain or discomfort

writing *NOUN* **writings**
❶ writing is something you write
❷ your writing is the way you write

wrong *ADJECTIVE*
❶ not fair or morally right • *It is wrong to cheat.* ❷ incorrect • *Your answer is wrong.*
❸ not working properly • *There's something wrong with the engine.*
➤ **wrongly** *ADVERB*

wrong *ADVERB*
wrongly • *You guessed wrong.*

wrong *NOUN* **wrongs**
something that is wrong
➤ **to be in the wrong** is to have done or said something wrong

wrong *VERB* **wrongs**, **wronging**, **wronged**
to wrong someone is to do wrong to them

wrongful *ADJECTIVE*
not correct; mistaken • *a case of wrongful imprisonment*
➤ **wrongfully** *ADVERB*

wrote *VERB* (*past tense of* **write**)
• *He wrote his name down.*

wrung *VERB* (*past tense and past participle of* **wring**)
• *She wrung her hands.* • *He had wrung the paper into a ball.*

wry *ADJECTIVE* **wryer**, **wryest**
slightly mocking or sarcastic • *He gave a wry smile.*
➤ **wryly** *ADVERB*

Xmas *NOUN* (*informal*)
Christmas

X-ray *NOUN* **X-rays**
a photograph of the inside of something, especially a part of the body, made by a kind of radiation that can pass through something solid

X-ray *VERB* **X-rays, X-raying, X-rayed**
to X-ray something is to make an X-ray of it

xylophone (*say* zy-lo-fohn) *NOUN* **xylophones**
a musical instrument made of wooden bars of different lengths, that you hit with small hammers
DID YOU KNOW? The word **xylophone** comes from Greek words meaning 'wood sound'.

yacht (*say* yot) *NOUN* **yachts**
a sailing boat used for racing or cruising
DID YOU KNOW? The word **yacht** comes from a Dutch word meaning 'hunting or pirate ship'.

yachtsman, yachtswoman *NOUN*
yachtsmen, yachtswomen
a person who sails in a yacht

yam *NOUN* **yams**
a tropical vegetable that grows underground

yank *VERB* **yanks, yanking, yanked**
to yank something is to pull it strongly and suddenly

yap *VERB* **yaps, yapping, yapped**
a small dog yaps when it makes a shrill barking sound

yap *NOUN* **yaps**
a shrill barking sound

yard *NOUN* **yards**
❶ a yard is a measure of length, 36 inches or about 91 centimetres ❷ a yard is also a piece of ground beside a building, or one used for a special purpose • *an old railway yard*

yarn *NOUN* **yarns**
❶ yarn is thread spun by twisting fibres together ❷ (*informal*) a yarn is a tale or story

yawn *VERB* **yawns, yawning, yawned**
❶ you yawn when you open your mouth wide and breathe in deeply because you are tired or bored ❷ to yawn is also to form a wide opening • *The chasm yawned in front of them.*

yawn *NOUN* **yawns**
an act of yawning

ye *PRONOUN* (*old use*)
you (referring to more than one person)

year *NOUN* **years**
the time that the earth takes to go right round the sun, about 365 ¼ days or twelve months
➤ A related adjective is **annual**.

a
b
c
d
e
f
g
h
i
j
k
l
m
n
o
p
q
r
s
t
u
v
w
x
y
z

yearly *ADJECTIVE, ADVERB*
every year

yearn *VERB* **yearns**, **yearning**, **yearned**
to yearn for something is to long for it

yeast *NOUN*
yeast is a substance used in baking bread and in making beer and wine

yell *NOUN* **yells**
a loud cry or shout

yell *VERB* **yells**, **yelling**, **yelled**
to cry or shout loudly

yellow *NOUN* **yellows**
the colour of ripe lemons and buttercups

yellow *ADJECTIVE* **yellower**, **yellowest**
❶ yellow in colour ❷ (*informal*) cowardly

yelp *VERB* **yelps**, **yelping**, **yelped**
to make a shrill bark or cry, as a dog does when it is hurt

yelp *NOUN* **yelps**
a yelping sound

yes *EXCLAMATION*
a word you say when you agree with someone or something • *Yes, I'd love to come.*

yesterday *NOUN, ADVERB*
the day before today

yet *ADVERB*
❶ up to now; by this time • *Has the postman called yet?* ❷ eventually; still • *I'll get even with him yet.* ❸ in addition; even • *She became yet more excited.*

yet *CONJUNCTION*
nevertheless • *It is strange, yet it is true.*

yeti (*say* yet-ee) *NOUN* **yetis**
a legendary creature like a huge hairy ape or bear that is thought to live in the Himalayas

yew *NOUN* **yews**
an evergreen tree with red berries and dark leaves like needles

yield *VERB* **yields**, **yielding**, **yielded**
❶ to yield is to surrender or give in • *He yielded to persuasion.* ❷ to yield a crop or profit is to produce it • *These trees yield good apples.*

yield *NOUN* **yields**
an amount produced by something • *What is the yield of wheat per acre?*

yippee *EXCLAMATION*
a word you say when you are feeling very happy

yodel *VERB* **yodels**, **yodelling**, **yodelled**
to sing or shout with your voice going rapidly from low to high notes

yoga *NOUN*
yoga is a Hindu system of exercise, meditation and self-control

yoghurt (*say* yog-ert) *NOUN* **yoghurts**
yoghurt is milk made thick by the addition of bacteria, giving it a sharp taste

yoke *NOUN* **yokes**
a curved piece of wood put across the necks of animals pulling a cart

yoke *VERB* **yokes**, **yoking**, **yoked**
to yoke animals is to harness them or link them by means of a yoke

yolk (*rhymes with* **coke**) *NOUN* **yolks**
the yellow part of an egg

Yom Kippur *NOUN*
the Day of Atonement, an important Jewish religious festival

yonder *ADVERB, ADJECTIVE* (*old use*)
over there

Yorkshire pudding *NOUN* **Yorkshire puddings**
a pudding made of batter and usually eaten with roast beef

you *PRONOUN*
❶ the person or people someone is speaking to • *Who are you?* ❷ people; anyone • *You can never be too sure.*

you'd
short for *you had* or *you would*

you'll
short for *you will* • *You'll like this book.*

young *ADJECTIVE* **younger**, **youngest**
having lived or existed only a short time; not old

young *PLURAL NOUN*
an animal's or bird's young are its babies

youngster *NOUN* **youngsters**
a young person or child

your *DETERMINER*
belonging to you • *Is this your pencil?*
SPELLING ALERT! **Your** is different from **you're**, which means 'you are': *You're almost there!*

you're
short for *you are* • *You're my best friend.*

yours *PRONOUN*
belonging to you • *Is this book yours?*
➤ **Yours faithfully, Yours sincerely, Yours truly** ways of ending a letter before you sign it

yourself *PRONOUN* **yourselves**
you (referring to one person) and nobody else, used to refer back to the subject of a verb
• *Have you hurt yourself?*
➤ **by yourself** *or* **yourselves** on your own
• *Did you do the work all by yourself?*

youth *NOUN* **youths**
❶ youth is being young, or the time when you are young • *She had been a gymnast in her youth.* ❷ a youth is a young man ❸ youth also means young people • *Today's youth have grown up with computers.*

youth club *NOUN* **youth clubs**
a club providing leisure activities for young people

youthful *ADJECTIVE*
someone is youthful when they are young or seem to be young
➤ **youthfulness** *NOUN*

youth hostel *NOUN* **youth hostels**
a hostel where young people can stay cheaply when they are on holiday

you've
short for *you have* • *You've told me that before.*

yo-yo *NOUN* **yo-yos**
a round wooden or plastic toy that moves up and down on a string which you hold

yuck *EXCLAMATION*
a word you say when you feel disgusted • *Yuck! That tastes revolting!*

yummy *ADJECTIVE* **yummier, yummiest** (*informal*)
delicious
➤ **yumminess** *NOUN*

Zz

zap *VERB* **zaps, zapping, zapped** (*informal*)
❶ to zap something or someone is to attack or destroy them with a ray or special power • *An evil wizard can zap you with a flick of his wand.* ❷ to zap is to move very quickly • *Suddenly an idea zapped into my head.*

zeal *NOUN*
zeal is keenness, especially in doing what you believe to be right

zealous (*say* zel-us) *ADJECTIVE*
very enthusiastic
➤ **zealously** *ADVERB*

zebra *NOUN* **zebras**
an African animal like a horse with black and white stripes

zebra crossing *NOUN* **zebra crossings**
part of a road marked with broad white stripes for pedestrians to cross

zenith *NOUN*
❶ the part of the sky directly above you
The south wind began to blow and the June sunset reddened the sky to the zenith.—WATERSHIP DOWN, Richard Adams
❷ the highest point of something

zero *NOUN* **zeros**
nought; the figure 0

zest *NOUN*
zest is great enjoyment or enthusiasm

zigzag *NOUN* **zigzags**
a line or route full of sharp turns from one side to the other

zigzag *VERB* **zigzags, zigzagging, zigzagged**
to move in a series of sharp turns from one side to the other
The tunnel veered to the left, zigzagged violently, and came to an end on a ledge overlooking a great void.—THE WEIRDSTONE OF BRISINGAMEN, Alan Garner

a
b
c
d
e
f
g
h
i
j
k
l
m
n
o
p
q
r
s
t
u
v
w
x
y
z

zinc *NOUN*
zinc is a white metal

zip *NOUN* **zips**
❶ a zip is a device with two rows of small teeth that fit together, used to join two pieces of material ❷ a zip is also a sharp sound like a bullet going through the air ❸ (*informal*) zip is liveliness or energy

zip *VERB* **zips, zipping, zipped**
❶ to zip something, or zip it up, is to fasten it with a zip ❷ to zip, or zip along, is to move quickly with a sharp sound

zodiac (*say* zoh-di-ak) *NOUN*
an area of the sky divided into twelve equal parts, called **signs of the zodiac**, each named after a constellation

zombie *NOUN* **zombies**
❶ in stories, a zombie is a dead person who turns into a creature that feeds on human brains ❷ (*informal*) someone who seems to be doing things without thinking, often because they are very tired • *I'm feeling a bit like a zombie this morning!*

zone *NOUN* **zones**
a district or area set aside for a particular use
• *This is a pedestrian zone.*

zoo *NOUN* **zoos**
a place where wild animals are kept so that people can look at them or study them

zoology (*say* zoo-ol-o-jee *or* zoh-ol-o-jee) *NOUN*
zoology is the study of animals
➤ **zoological** *ADJECTIVE* ➤ **zoologist** *NOUN*

zoom *VERB* **zooms, zooming, zoomed**
❶ to move or travel very quickly
• *Superman zoomed across the sky with his cape flying behind him.* ❷ to make a computer image or page of text bigger on the screen
➤ **to zoom in** *or* **zoom out** is to adjust the focus of a camera so that objects appear either closer or further away

zoom lens *NOUN* **zoom lenses**
a camera lens that can focus on things that are far away and make them appear closer

Writing letters and emails

A formal letter or email

15 Market Street
Hilltown
Town
LF22 7ST

The Editor
Highfield Publishers
77 Broad Street
London W1

30th May 2024

Dear Sir or Madam

I am writing to enquire whether you would be interested in publishing a book I have written. The book is about the life of my grandfather, Henry Robinson, who was an explorer in the Arctic and Antarctic in the 1920s. It is based on the diary he kept on his journeys, and could be illustrated with photographs from his collection.

If you are interested in this proposal I can send you the manuscript. Thank you for your consideration.

Yours faithfully

James Robinson

James Robinson

When you write to an organization or a person you do not know, keep your letter or email short and to the point. !

your address

the address you are writing to

the date

In an email you do not need to include this information.

If you know the person's name, write 'Dear Mr . . . ', 'Miss', 'Ms', or 'Mrs'. If you do not know their name, write 'Dear Sir' or 'Madam'.

If you have written the person's name at the top of the letter, sign off 'Yours sincerely'. If you have written 'Sir' or 'Madam', sign off 'Yours faithfully'.

Print your name below your signature.

An informal letter or email

35 Main Street
Hightown
LQ22 7HH

28th February 2024

Dear Auntie Susy

Thank you so much for my lovely birthday present—the jumper is so cosy and I love the colour.

I had a great day—mum took me and some friends to the cinema and then we came back here for tea and birthday cake. We all stayed up really late too. Now I'm back at school. I'm in the swimming team so I have to get up early to practise a lot. I'm getting really fast though so it's worth it!

Hope to see you soon,

Lots of love

Sarah

When you write to a friend or relation, the language is very informal, as if you are speaking directly to the other person.

your address

the date

You can leave out 'Dear . . . ' and write 'Hi . . . ' if you wish.

In an email you do not need to include this information. !

There is no need to write the address of the person you are writing to.

You can sign off in many ways, such as 'love from'.

An email

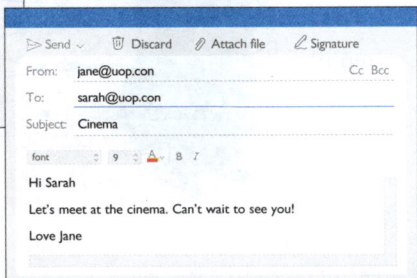

> Send ⌄   🗑 Discard   📎 Attach file   ✏ Signature

From: jane@uop.con   Cc Bcc

To: sarah@uop.con

Subject: Cinema

font   9   A B I

Hi Sarah

Let's meet at the cinema. Can't wait to see you!

Love Jane

587

The human body

The body

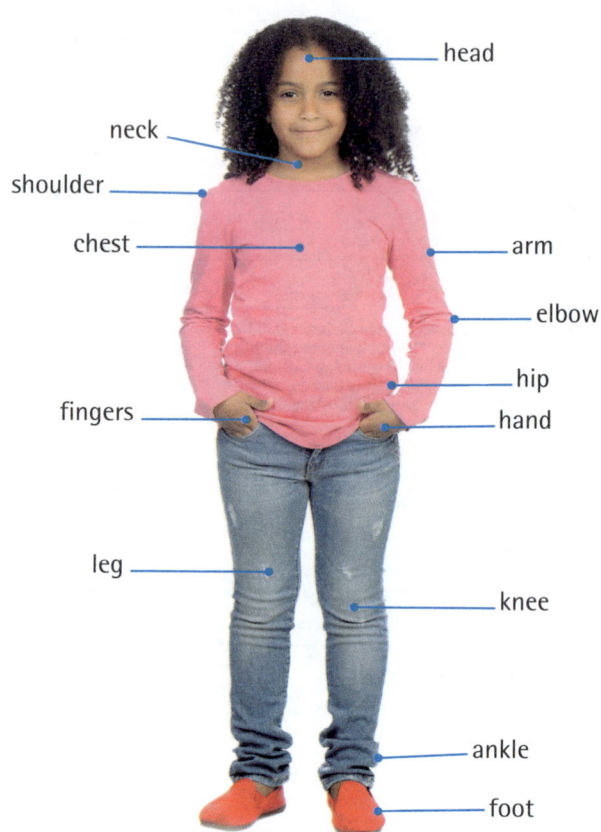

head

neck

shoulder

chest

arm

elbow

hip

fingers

hand

leg

knee

ankle

foot

The face

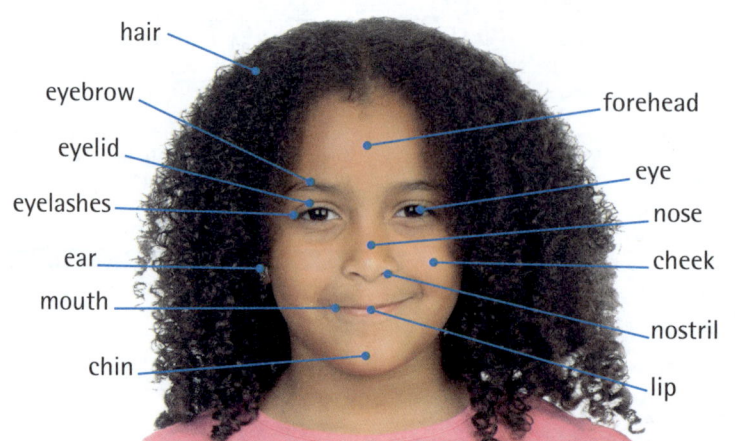

hair

eyebrow

eyelid

eyelashes

ear

mouth

chin

forehead

eye

nose

cheek

nostril

lip

The 5 senses

- **touch**
- **sight**
- **hearing**
- **taste**
- **smell**

The skeleton

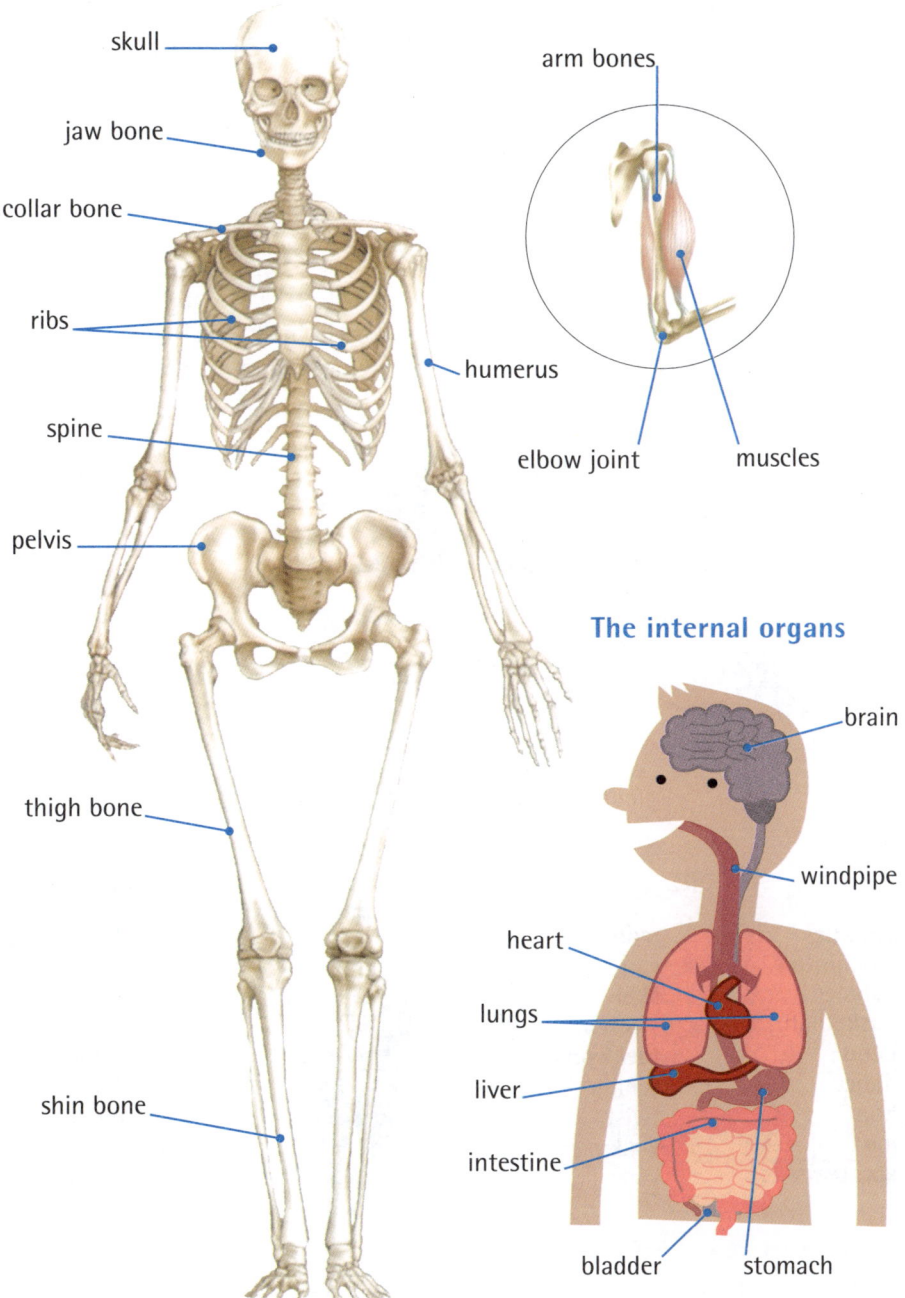

skull

jaw bone

collar bone

ribs

spine

pelvis

thigh bone

shin bone

arm bones

humerus

elbow joint

muscles

The internal organs

brain

windpipe

heart

lungs

liver

intestine

bladder

stomach

Healthy living, food and cooking

Keeping healthy

clean	drink	hygiene	safety
dentist	eat	medicine	sleep
diet	exercise	relax	wash
doctor	food	rest	water

Healthy eating

fatty and sweet foods
(eat very little)

protein foods
(eat some)

fruit and vegetables
(eat at every meal)

carbohydrate foods
(eat at every meal)

Types of food

cereals
dairy
eggs
fish
fruit
meat
vegetables

Nutrients

carbohydrates
fats
minerals
proteins
vitamins

Exercise

athletics	march
badminton	run
balance	skip
basketball	stretch
bend	taekwondo
dance	tennis
hop	twist
jog	walk
karate	yoga

running

People who take part in sport

athlete
coach
competitor
Olympian
Paralympian
player
sports person

Things you can use for cooking

bowl
chopping board
chopsticks
cooker
dish
fork
frying pan
gas
grill
knife
oven
plate
saucepan
sieve
spoon
whisk
wok

chopping
board

cutlery

whisk

wooden spoon

sieve

wok

chopsticks

Ways you can prepare food

beat	peel
blend	roll
chop	sieve
combine	slice
crush	spread
drain	sprinkle
grate	stir
knead	strain
measure	weigh
mix	whisk

Ways you can cook food

bake	poach
barbecue	roast
boil	simmer
cook	steam
fry	stew
grill	toast

591

Volcanoes

• A volcano that often erupts is an **active** volcano.

• A scientist who studies volcanoes is a **volcanologist**.

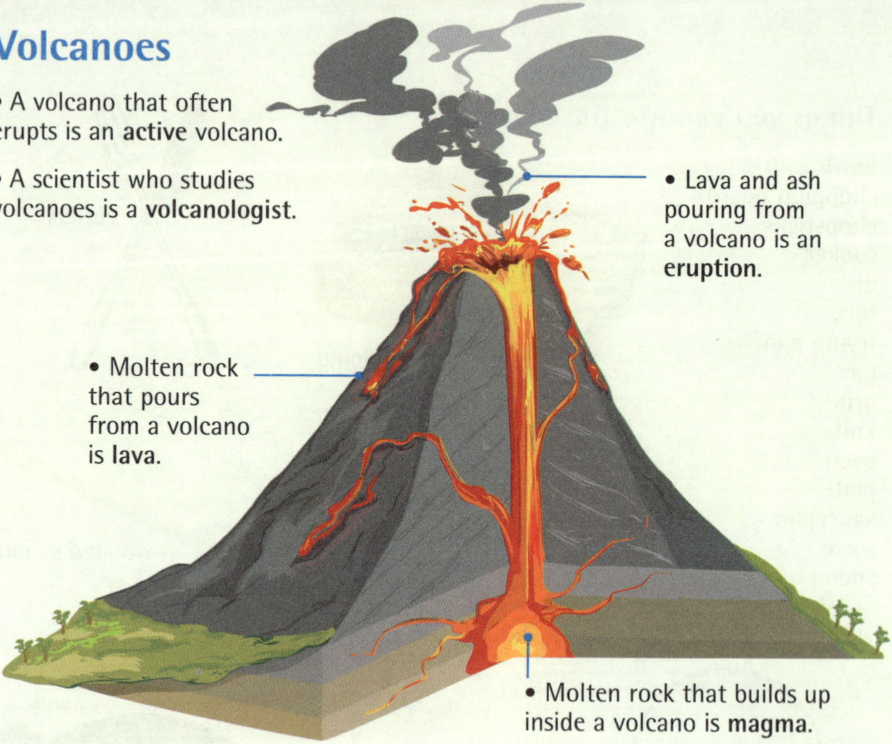

• Lava and ash pouring from a volcano is an **eruption**.

• Molten rock that pours from a volcano is **lava**.

• Molten rock that builds up inside a volcano is **magma**.

Pirates

Things you might find on a pirate ship

barrels
kegs
cabin
crow's nest
deck
hammock
lantern
mast

pirate flag
rigging
sail
treasure chest
wheel

People you might find on a pirate ship

cabin boy or girl
captain
captives
cook
crew
first mate
lookout
stowaway

• A pirate flag is a **Jolly Roger** or **skull and cross bones**.

• A pirate ship might sail on the **high seas**.

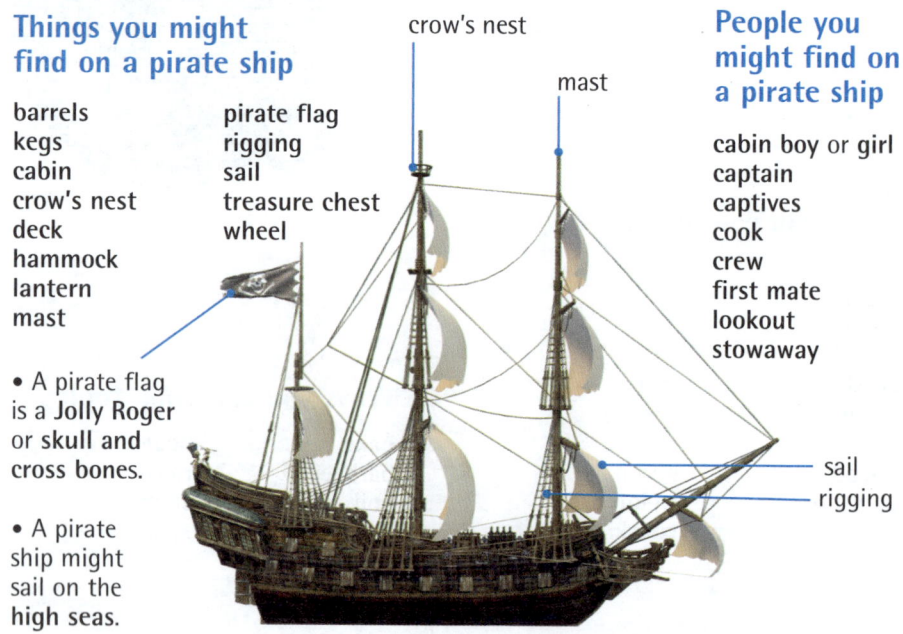

crow's nest

mast

sail

rigging

592

Transport

By air

helicopter
plane

plane

helicopter

By land

bicycle
bus
car
coach
motorcycle
scooter
skateboard
taxi
train
truck
van

truck

train

taxi

By water

barge
boat
canoe
ferry
hovercraft
liner
ship
speedboat
tanker
yacht

ship

Computing

Equipment

computer
keyboard
laptop
mobile phone
modem
monitor
mouse
screen
tablet
telephone
television
touchscreen
video
webcam

Using computers

bar chart
bold
calculate
coding
copy
cut and paste
database
document
file
find and replace
folder
formula
italics
menu
move
order
record
sort
spellcheck
spreadsheet
sum

Using the internet

address
AI
app
attachment
blog
chat
cloud
download
email
key word
online safety
screen break
search
social media
surf
tag
tweet
upload
vlog
VR
website
wifi

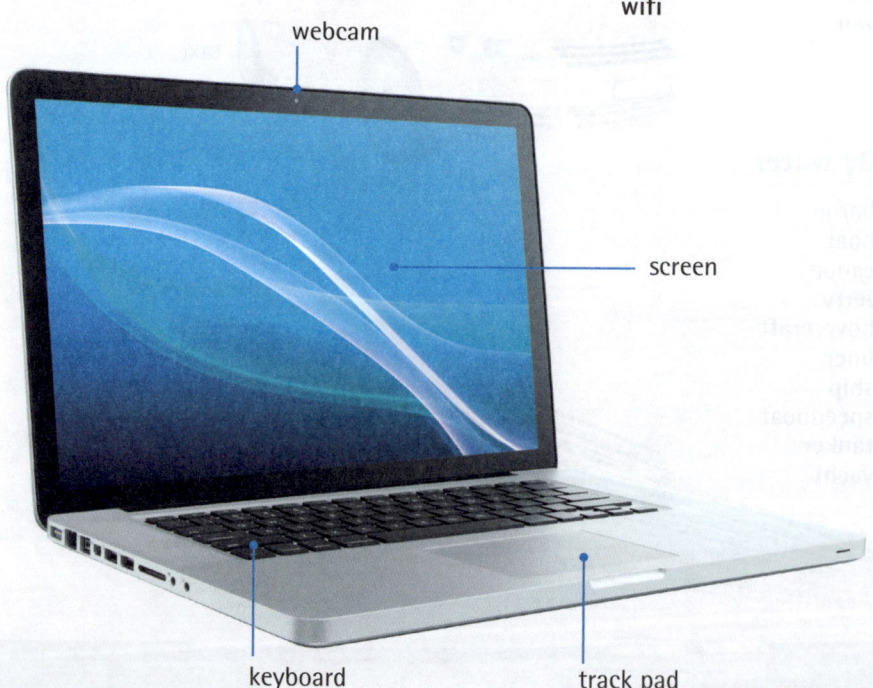

webcam

screen

keyboard

track pad

Word origins

The word **algebra** comes from an Arabic word meaning 'putting broken parts together'.

The word **tabby** originally meant a kind of striped cloth produced in an area of Baghdad called al-Attabiyya.

The word **robot** comes from a Czech word meaning 'forced labour'.

The word **yacht** comes from a Dutch word meaning 'hunting or pirate ship'.

An old word for a **giraffe** is *camelopard*, which means 'camel leopard'.

The word **dandelion** comes from French words meaning 'lion's tooth', because of its jagged leaves.

The word **porcupine** comes from old French words meaning 'prickly pig'.

The word **daisy** comes from Old English words meaning 'day's eye', because the petals open in the morning and close at night.

The words **galore** and **slogan** come from Gaelic.

The words **delicatessen** and **waltz** come from German.

The word **geography** comes from Greek words meaning 'earth writing'.

The word **ukulele** comes from a Hawaiian word meaning 'jumping flea'.

The word **shampoo** comes from a Hindi word meaning 'press'!

Useful idioms and phrases

to be in hot water or **deep water** is to be in trouble or difficulty

to bury the hatchet is to agree to stop quarrelling or fighting

to stick up for someone is to support or defend them

something is on the cards when it is likely to happen

to head someone off is to get in front of them in order to turn them aside

a machine **breaks down** when it stops working properly

to see to something is to deal with it

to run the gauntlet is to face a lot of criticism or risks

to pipe down is to be quiet

to bring someone round is to make them conscious again after they have fainted

to muck about is to behave stupidly or idly

to pull someone's leg is to tease them

to hit it off with someone is to get on well with them when you meet them

something dawns on you when you begin to realize it

to brush something up is to improve your knowledge of it

to close down is to stop doing business

to be carried away is to become very excited

to see to something is to deal with it

to hang around is to wait around doing nothing

596

Grammar

Word classes:

Verb

A **verb** names an action.
• *The bird flew away.*

Adjective

An **adjective** gives more information about a noun. It normally goes before the noun.
• *The little green bird flew away.*

Noun

A **noun** names a person or thing.
• *The bird pecked the apple.*

A **common noun** is a noun that refers to people or things in general.

A **proper noun** is a noun that identifies a particular person, place or thing. Proper nouns begin with capital letters.

A **concrete noun** is a noun that refers to people or places that exist physically and can be seen, touched, smelled, heard or tasted.

An **abstract noun** is a noun that refers to ideas, qualities and conditions —things that cannot be seen or touched.

Collective nouns refer to groups of people or things.

Pronoun

A **pronoun** can be used instead of a noun. Using a pronoun avoids using the noun again and again.
• *The bird pecked the apple and ate it.*

Possessive pronouns tell you who or what owns a noun.
• *The bird pecked his apple.*

Relative pronouns introduce more information about the noun.
• *the bird who sat on a branch*

Conjunction

A **conjunction** links words or groups of words.
• *A cat climbed the tree* as *the little bird pecked the apple* and *ate it noisily.*
• *The cat paused* because *he didn't want to scare it away.*

A **coordinating conjunction** joins words or groups of words which are of the same importance in the sentence, e.g. **and**.

A **subordinating conjunction** joins words or groups of words which add extra meaning but which are not as important as the rest of the sentence.

Adverb

An **adverb** gives more information about a verb, an adjective or another adverb. It can go either before or after the verb. It tells you how, when, where and how often something happens.
• *Later, the bird* eagerly *pecked the apple* twice *and ate it* noisily*.

Preposition

A **preposition** shows how things are related. It can describe the position of something, the time when something happens, or the way something is done. It can link nouns and pronouns in a sentence.
• *The cat crept* up *to the tree. The cat tried to pounce* on *the bird but crashed* into *the tree.*

Determiner

A **determiner** goes in front of a noun and its adjectives to help to tell you which person or thing the sentence is about or how many or how much of them there are.

Auxiliary verb

Auxiliary, or helping **verbs**, are used with main verbs to show when something has happened. The auxiliary verbs are **be, do** and **have**.
• *I* am *eating the nuts.*

Modal verb

Modal verbs are auxiliary verbs which are used to express possibility or wanting, as well as the future.
• *I* should *share these apples.*

Spelling

Here are some useful rules:

To make a noun plural

Normally just add **–s**:
skirts   ties   pianos   stars

But watch out for some words ending in **–o** that need **–es**:
echoes, heroes, potatoes, tomatoes, volcanoes, etc.

To words ending in **–ch, –s, –sh, –x** or **–z**, add **–es**:
dress → dresses   box → boxes   stitch → stitches

To words ending in **–f** and **–fe**, change to **–ves**:
scarf → scarves   life → lives   half → halves

But watch out for these exceptions:
beliefs, proofs, roofs, etc.

To words ending in a consonant followed by **–y**, change the **y** to **i** and add **–es**:
copy → copies   cry → cries   party → parties

Adding –ing and –ed to verbs

Normally just add **–ing** or **–ed**:
load → loading → loaded   open → opening → opened
stay → staying → stayed

For short words ending in **–e** usually leave off the **e**:
race → racing → raced   blame → blaming → blamed

For many short words that end with one consonant, double the last consonant:
slam → slamming → slammed   tip → tipping → tipped

For longer words ending with one consonant and having the stress on the last syllable, double the last consonant:
compel → compelling → compelled   prefer → preferring → preferred

For words ending in **–y** after a consonant, change the **y** to an **i** before adding **–ed**:
try → trying → tried

For words ending in **–ie**, change the **ie** to **y** before adding **–ing**:
lie → lying → lied   tie → tying → tied

Watch out for these exceptions:
lay → laid   pay → paid   say → said

Spelling

Adding –er and –est to adjectives

Normally just add **–er** and **–est**, unless the word already ends in **–e**:
cold → colder → coldest   wide → wider → widest

For many short words that end with one consonant, change to a double consonant:
wet → wetter → wettest   dim → dimmer → dimmest

If the word has two syllables and ends in **–y**, change the **y** to an **i**:
dirty → dirtier → dirtiest   happy → happier → happiest

Adding –ly

Adding **–ly** to an adjective makes it into an adverb:
slowly, badly, awkwardly

If the word ends in **–ll** just add **–y**:
full → fully

For words ending in **–y** and with more than one syllable, leave off the **–y** and add **–ily**:
happy → happily   hungry → hungrily

For words ending in **–le**, leave off the **e**:
idle → idly   simple → simply

For adjectives ending in **–ic**, usually add **–ally**:
basic → basically   drastic → drastically

But watch out for other special ones:
public → publicly

Punctuation

Punctuation marks

Full stop .

A **full stop** comes at the end of a sentence. It shows that a sentence is complete and finished.
• *I like swimming.*

Capital letters A B C

Capital letters are used at the beginning of sentences.
• *The bird likes to eat seeds.*

Capital letters are used for proper nouns, or names of things, people, places and titles.

Always use a capital letter when you use **I** to talk about yourself.

Question mark ?

A **question mark** comes at the end of a sentence which is asking a question.
• *Where are you?*

Exclamation mark !

An **exclamation mark** comes at the end of an exclamation. It shows that the sentence is about something urgent or surprising, or shows anger.
• *It's a goal!*

An exclamation also comes at the end of a command. A command is a sentence which gives an order or instruction.
• *Run!*

Comma ,

A **comma** can be used to separate things in a list.
• *I like to eat apples, seeds, grapes and nuts.*

A comma can be used to show a break in a sentence. A comma can separate different parts of a sentence and shows you where you should pause when you are reading.
• *I like swimming, but I love ice skating!*

A comma can make the meaning of a sentence clear and change what you are trying to say.
• *Let's eat Grandma!*
• *Let's eat, Grandma!*

Colon :

A **colon** can be used to introduce a list.
• *I love the following foods: apples, seeds, grapes and nuts.*

A colon can be used to introduce examples or explanations. The part of the sentence after the colon gives a little more information about what comes before it.
• *The boy eats lots of snacks: he needs lots of energy for swimming.*

You don't need a capital letter for the word that comes after a colon, unless it is a proper noun.

Semicolon ;

A **semicolon** can be used in lists. A semicolon can separate longer phrases in a list that has been introduced by a colon, or which is more complicated than a simple list of words.
• *The children need to bring with them: an extra jumper if the weather is cold; a cup, a plate and a bowl; a knife, a fork and a spoon.*

A semicolon can be used to show a break in a sentence. A semicolon can show that a break is longer, or more important than a break made by a comma.
• *The film was brilliant; I had a great time.*

Dash —

A **dash** can show a break in a sentence that is longer, or more important, than a break made by a comma.
• *The fire spread quickly and the trees were engulfed—I was scared.*

Brackets ( ) or [ ]
Commas , Dashes —

Brackets, **commas** or **dashes** can all be used to separate a word or phrase that has been added to a sentence as an explanation or an afterthought. The word or phrase inside the brackets, commas or dashes is called a **parenthesis**.
• *The moon (which orbits the earth) shines in the sky at night.*

Ellipsis ...

Ellipsis is used to show that a word has been missed out or a sentence is not finished.
• *Don't tell me . . .*

Hyphen —

A **hyphen** is used to join two or more words.
• *chock-full*   • *fair-haired*

A hyphen is used to avoid confusion over meaning.
• *a mouse eating ogre*
• *a mouse-eating ogre*

Inverted commas ' ' or " "

Inverted commas or speech marks show when a person is speaking.
• *'I'm beginning to understand,' he said.*

The punctuation at the end of spoken words always comes inside the final set of inverted commas.
• *'I can't hold on!' Alex cried.*

Apostrophe '

An **apostrophe** can be used to show that letters are missed out of a word (a contraction).
• *I'm sure I didn't pick up the pen.*

An apostrophe can show ownership or possession. This means that something belongs to someone or something.
• *the boy's pen*
• *James's hat*
• *the witnesses' statement*
• *the girls' bags*
• *children's books*

Bullet points •

Bullet points are used to organize a list in order to make it clear.
Plans for the summer holiday:
• *finish reading my book*
• *mend my bike*
• *put up my posters.*